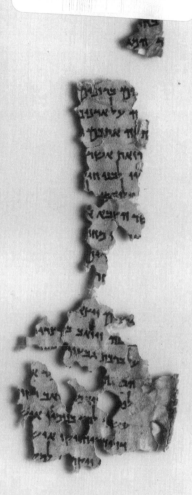

**Hermeneia
—A Critical
and Historical
Commentary
on the Bible**

1 Chronicles

A Commentary

by Ralph W. Klein

Edited by
Thomas Krüger

**Fortress
Press**   Minneapolis

**1 Chronicles
A Commentary**

Copyright © 2006 Augsburg Fortress

Images on endpapers: Photo © Israel Antiquities
Authority. Used by permission.

Cover and interior design by Kenneth Hiebert
Typesetting and page composition by
The HK Scriptorium

Genealogical charts discussed in the commentary
are available under the Genealogies tab on the
Fortress Press web page for this book:
www.fortresspress.com/1chronicles

Library of Congress Cataloging-in-Publication Data

Klein, Ralph W.
  1 Chronicles : a commentary / Ralph W. Klein ;
Thomas Krüger, editor.
    p. cm. — (Hermeneia—a critical and historical
commentary on the Bible)
  Includes bibliographical references and indexes.
  ISBN 0-8006-6085-4 (alk. paper)
  1. Bible. O.T. Chronicles, 1st—Commentaries. I.
Title: One Chronicles. II. Title: First Chronicles. III.
Krüger, Thomas, 1959- IV. Title. V. Series.

  BS1345.53.K54 2006
  222'.6307—dc22

                    2005036157

The paper used in this publication meets the minimum requirements of American National Standard
for Information Sciences—Permanence of paper for
Printed Library Materials, ANSI Z329.48–1984.

Manufactured in the U.S.A.

  10 09 08 07 06   1 2 3 4 5 6 7 8 9 10

■ To Marilyn

The Author

Ralph W. Klein is Christ Seminary-Seminex Professor
of Old Testament at the Lutheran School of Theology
at Chicago. His books include *Textual Criticism of the Old
Testament* (1974), *Israel in Exile* (1979), *1 Samuel* (WBC,
1983), and *Ezekiel: The Prophet and His Message* (1988).
He is editor of *Currents in Theology and Mission* and an
associate editor of *Catholic Biblical Quarterly*.

Endpapers

In the photo in the front of the book, the fragmentary
texts are from 4QSam^a, dated to the first century B.C.E.
The two fragments on the left are from 2 Sam 2:29–3:8;
the fragments on the right are from 2 Samuel 2:5-16
and 2:25-27. First Chronicles 3:1–4 is based on 2 Samuel
3:2-5. The fragmentary texts in the back of book are also
from 4QSam^a. The fragments on the left are from
2 Samuel 21:8-9, 12, 23:21-22, and 24:16-20; the fragments on the right are from 2 Samuel 22:24-26 and
2 Samuel 22:30–23:6. First Chronicles 21:15-21 is based
on 2 Samuel 24:16-20. Variant readings in such Qumran
manuscripts and renewed study of the Septuagint have
shown that the Chronicler often used a text of Samuel
different from the standard Masoretic Text.

Contents
1 Chronicles

■ **Commentary**

■ **Indexes**

The name *Hermeneia,* Greek ἑρμηνεία, has been chosen as the title of the commentary series to which this volume belongs. The word *Hermeneia* has a rich background in the history of biblical interpretation as a term used in the ancient Greek-speaking world for the detailed, systematic exposition of a scriptural work. It is hoped that the series, like its name, will carry forward this old and venerable tradition. A second, entirely practical reason for selecting the name lies in the desire to avoid a long descriptive title and its inevitable acronym, or worse, an unpronounceable abbreviation.

The series is designed to be a critical and historical commentary to the Bible without arbitrary limits in size or scope. It will utilize the full range of philological and historical tools, including textual criticism (often slighted in modern commentaries), the methods of the history of tradition (including genre and prosodic analysis), and the history of religion.

Hermeneia is designed for the serious student of the Bible. It will make full use of ancient Semitic and classical languages; at the same time, English translations of all comparative materials—Greek, Latin, Canaanite, or Akkadian—will be supplied alongside the citation of the source in its original language. Insofar as possible, the aim is to provide the student or scholar with full critical discussion of each problem of interpretation and with the primary data upon which the discussion is based.

Hermeneia is designed to be international and interconfessional in the selection of authors; its editorial boards were formed with this end in view. Occasionally the series will offer translations of distinguished commentaries which originally appeared in languages other than English. Published volumes of the series will be revised continually, and eventually, new commentaries will replace older works in order to preserve the currency of the series. Commentaries are also being assigned for important literary works in the categories of apocryphal and pseudepigraphical works relating to the Old and New Testaments, including some of Essene or Gnostic authorship.

The editors of *Hermeneia* impose no systematic-theological perspective upon the series (directly, or indirectly by selection of authors). It is expected that authors will struggle to lay bare the ancient meaning of a biblical work or pericope. In this way the text's human relevance should become transparent, as is always the case in competent historical discourse. However, the series eschews for itself homiletical translation of the Bible.

The editors are heavily indebted to Fortress Press for its energy and courage in taking up an expensive, long-term project, the rewards of which will accrue chiefly to the field of biblical scholarship.

The editor responsible for this volume is Thomas Krüger of the University of Zurich.

Peter Machinist　　　　*Helmut Koester*
For the Old Testament　　For the New Testament
Editorial Board　　　　　Editorial Board

A little more than twenty-six years ago I received a letter from Frank Cross inviting me to write the Hermeneia commentary on Chronicles. My doctoral dissertation at Harvard had dealt with the text-critical implications of 1 Esdras, a translation of 2 Chronicles 35–36, Ezra 1–10, and Nehemiah 8 from the canon, in addition to narrative materials in 1 Esdras, and I had written a *Forschungsbericht* on Ezra and Nehemiah for the G. Ernest Wright memorial volume, *Magnalia Dei* (1976). Still that letter came as a great surprise and with significant affirmation. I knew much about the Chronicler, but still had (have) much to learn. In the last quarter century the landscape of Chronicles research has shifted a great deal.

I organized the Chronicles-Ezra-Nehemiah Section of the Society of Biblical Literature, which remains a vibrant and ever-growing cadre of scholars who have offered me much encouragement and frequent new insights. During the early 1980s I did the usual kinds of preparatory work for writing a commentary, including the articles on Chronicles and Ezra-Nehemiah for the *Anchor Bible Dictionary*. Especially stimulating to my development have been graduate seminars at the Lutheran School of Theology at Chicago and the Divinity School of the University of Chicago. About the time I was ready to write, I became dean at the Lutheran School of Theology at Chicago, a term that lasted from 1988 to 1999. I kept up on the literature during this period, but undertaking a major writing project was out of the question. My life after the deanship has been preoccupied by writing this commentary, a work that has been significantly improved, I would hope, by the delay.

Of necessity this commentary deals at length with the genealogies in 1 Chronicles. Readers wishing to see "the big picture" of genealogical relationships may review the comprehensive charts available online at the Fortress Press website under the Genealogies tab: www.fortresspress.com/1chronicles.

Libraries and librarians are a scholar's lifeblood, and I have been immeasurably helped by the resources and the places to write offered by the Jesuit-Krauss-McCormick Library at my home institution, by the library of the Albright Institute and the École Biblique et Archéologique in Jerusalem, by the University Library and by Tyndale House in Cambridge, England, and by the library of Philipps Universität in Marburg, where the first volume in this project was brought to an end and the second was given a great beginning.

It is hard to know where to stop in naming people who welcomed us or who advanced this project through their own fresh insights and/or hospitality, but I need to mention at least Peter R. Ackroyd, Klaus Peter Adam, Leslie C. Allen, Roddy L. Braun, Frank Moore Cross, Katharine J. Dell, Raymond B. Dillard, John Emerton, Tamara Eskenazi, Erhard S. Gerstenberger, Seymour Gitin, Robert Gordon, M. Patrick Graham, Sara Japhet, Jörg Jeremias, Isaac Kalimi, Magnar Kartveit, Rainer Kessler, Gary N. Knoppers, Jack Lundbom, Steven L. McKenzie, Mark Throntveit, Peter Welten, Thomas Willi, H. G. M. Williamson, and John Wright. My deepest apologies to the many others whom I leave out for lack of space or for failing memory. Thomas Krüger of the University of Zurich edited the manuscript with skill and great empathy. Primus Vannutelli left to all of us a synopsis of Samuel/Kings and Chronicles without equal.

Since 1983 I have been on the faculty of the Lutheran School of Theology at Chicago, and it has been generous in granting leave time to facilitate my scholarship. Hearty thanks to President James Kenneth Echols, Dean Kathleen D. (Kadi) Billman, and the Board of the seminary. Financial assistance for recent leaves came from the Alexander von Humboldt Stiftung in Germany and Thrivent Financial for Lutherans in the United States.

This project could not have come this far without the support and encouragement of my wife, Marilyn, who, while I was solving text-critical problems or untangling genealogies, was pursuing her own calling as a volunteer at the Victoria Augusta Hospital and the Peace Center for the Blind in Jerusalem, as a caregiver for a three-year-old, wheelchair-bound boy in Marburg, and as the person who held open the door to the full panoply of life. Marilyn is a networker par excellence, and most of the people I met during our stays abroad resulted from her contacts. Most recently Marburg provided an ideal setting for writing, and for both of us to visit sites in Germany and Austria from which our ancestors had emigrated in the nineteenth century. To her this volume is dedicated with profound respect and with deepest gratitude and love.

I often regale my students with an anecdote about Hermann Gunkel, who, after a lifetime of work on the Psalter, wrote: "When I am at the end, I am just beginning." "This beginning" in Chronicles is indebted to all who have cared enough about the Chronicler over the centuries to read his work carefully and critically and sympathetically—and to leave behind a written record of their reading.

Ralph W. Klein
Lutheran School of Theology at Chicago
August 31, 2004

Reference Codes

1. Abbreviations

AASF	Annales Academiae scientiarum fennicae
AB	Anchor Bible
ABD	*Anchor Bible Dictionary*, ed. D. N. Freedman (6 vols.; New York: Doubleday, 1992)
ABS	Archaeology and Biblical Studies
ADPV	Abhandlungen des Deutschen Palästinavereins
AJBI	*Annual of the Japanese Biblical Institute*
AJSL	*American Journal of Semitic Languages and Literature*
Akk.	Akkadian
ANES	*Ancient Near Eastern Studies*
ANET	*Ancient Near Eastern Texts Relating to the Old Testament*, ed. James B. Pritchard (3d ed.; Princeton: Princeton Univ. Press, 1969)
AOAT	Alter Orient und Altes Testament
AOS	American Oriental Series
Arab.	Arabic version
ASE	*Annali di storia dell' exegesi*
AtAbh	Alttestamentliche Abhandlungen
ATD	Das Alte Testament Deutsch
AUSS	*Andrews University Seminary Studies*
b.	Babylonian Talmud
B. Batra	*Baba Batra*
Ber.	*Berakot*
BA	*Biblical Archaeologist*
BARev	*Biblical Archaeology Review*
BASOR	*Bulletin of the American Schools of Oriental Research*
BBB	Bonner biblische Beiträge
BBET	Beiträge zur biblischen Exegese und Theologie
BDB	F. Brown, S. R. Driver, and C. A. Briggs, *Hebrew and English Lexicon of the Old Testament* (Oxford: Clarendon Press, 1907)
BEATAJ	Beiträge des Erforschung des Alten Testaments und des antiken Judentums
BEThL	Bibliotheca ephemeridum theologicarum lovaniensium
BHK	*Biblia hebraica*, ed. R. Kittel (3d ed.; Stuttgart: Württembergische Bibelanstalt, 1937)
BHS	*Biblia hebraica Stuttgartensia*, ed. K. Elliger and W. Rudolph (5th ed.; Stuttgart: Deutsche Bibelgesellschaft, 1997)
Bib	*Biblica*
BJS	Brown Judaic Studies
BKAT	Biblischer Kommentar, Altes Testament
BN	*Biblische Notizen*
BR	*Biblical Research*
BRev	*Bible Review*
BT	*Bible Translator*
BWANT	Beiträge zur Wissenschaft vom Alten Testament
BZ	*Biblische Zeitschrift*
BZAW	Beihefte zur Zeitschrift für die alttestamentliche Wissenschaft
CAT	Commentaire de l'Ancien Testament
CBC	Cambridge Bible Commentary
CBQ	*Catholic Biblical Quarterly*
ConBOT	Coniectanea biblica: Old Testament Series
COS	*Context of Scripture*, ed. W. W. Hallo (3 vols.; Leiden: Brill, 1997–2002)
CR:BS	*Currents in Research: Biblical Studies*
CurTM	*Currents in Theology and Mission*
DDD	*Dictionary of Deities and Demons in the Bible* (ed. Karel van der Toorn, Bob Becking, and Pieter W. van der Horst; 2d ed.; Grand Rapids: Eerdmans, 1999)
EA	Tell el-Amarna tablets
EAEHL	*Encyclopaedia of Archaeological Excavations in the Holy Land* (ed. Ephraim Stern; 2d ed.; Jerusalem: Israel Exploration Society, 1993)
EHS	Europäische Hochschulschriften
ErFor	Erträge der Forschung
ErIsr	*Eretz Israel*
ExpT	*Expository Times*
FAT	Forschungen zum Alten Testament
FOTL	Forms of the Old Testament Literature
FRLANT	Forschungen zur Religion und Literatur des Alten und Neuen Testaments
FS	Festschrift
GKC	Wilhelm Gesenius, *Hebrew Grammar*, ed. E. Kautzsch, trans. A. E. Cowley (2d ed.; Oxford: Oxford Univ. Press, 1910)

HALOT	*Hebrew and Aramaic Lexicon of the Old Testament*, ed. Ludwig Koehler, Walter Baumgartner, Johann Jakob Stamm, and Benedikt Hartmann; trans. and ed. M. E. J. Richardson et al. (5 vols.; Leiden: Brill, 1994–1999)	*KAI*	H. Donner and W. Röllig, *Kanaanäische und aramäische Inschriften* (2d ed.; 3 vols.; Wiesbaden: Harrassowitz, 1966–1969)
HAR	*Hebrew Annual Review*	KAT	Kommentar zum Alten Testament
HAT	Handbuch zum Alten Testament	*KJV*	*King James Version*
Heb.	Hebrew	*LASBF*	*Liber annuus Studii biblici franciscani*
Hen	*Henoch*	lit.	literally
HKAT	Handkommentar zum Alten Testament	*LS*	*Louvain Studies*
HS	*Hebrew Studies*	LUÅ	Lunds universitets årsskrift
HSAT	Die heilige Schrift des Alten Testaments, ed. Feldmann	LXX	Septuagint
HSAT	*Die Heilige Schrift des Alten Testaments*, ed. E. Kautzsch and A. Bertholet (4th ed.; 2 vols.; Tübingen: Mohr [Siebeck], 1922–1923)	*m.*	Mishnah tractate
		ʿArak.	*ʿArakin*
		masc.	masculine
		MGWJ	*Monatschrift für Geschichte und Wissenschaft des Judentums*
		MR	map reference
		MS(S)	manuscript(s)
HSM	Harvard Semitic Monographs	MT	Masoretic text
HTR	*Harvard Theological Review*	*NAB*	*New American Bible*
HUCA	*Hebrew Union College Annual*	NAC	New American Commentary
ICC	International Critical Commentary	NCB	New Century Bible
		NEB	*New English Bible*
IDB	*Interpreter's Dictionary of the Bible*, ed. G. A. Buttrick (4 vols.; Nashville: Abingdon, 1962)	NEchtB	Neue Echter Bibel
		NIV	*New International Version*
		NJPS	*New Jewish Publication Society Version*
IEJ	*Israel Exploration Journal*		
Int	*Interpretation*	*NRSV*	*New Revised Standard Version*
JANESCU	*Journal of the Ancient Near Eastern Society of Columbia University*	n.s.	new series
		NT	New Testament
JAOS	*Journal of the American Oriental Society*	OBO	Orbis biblicus et orientalis
		ÖBS	Österreichische biblische Studien
JB	*Jerusalem Bible*	OG	Old Greek
JBL	*Journal of Biblical Literature*	OL	Old Latin
JBQ	*Jewish Bible Quarterly*	OLA	Orientalia lovaniensia analecta
JBR	*Journal of Bible and Religion*	*Or*	*Orientalia*
JBS	*Jerusalem Biblical Studies*	OT	Old Testament
JHS	*Journal of Hebrew Scriptures*	*OTE*	*Old Testament Essays*
JNES	*Journal of Near Eastern Studies*	OTL	Old Testament Library
JNSL	*Journal of Northwest Semitic Languages*	OTS	Oudtestamentische Studiën
		PEFQS	*Palestine Exploration Fund Quarterly Statement*
JPOS	*Journal of the Palestine Oriental Society*		
		PEQ	*Palestine Exploration Quarterly*
JPSV	*Jewish Publication Society Version*	*PJ*	*Palästina Jahrbuch*
JQR	*Jewish Quarterly Review*	pl.	plural
JSem	*Journal of Semitics*	Q	Qere
JSJ	*Journal for the Study of Judaism*	*RB*	*Revue biblique*
JSOT	*Journal for the Study of the Old Testament*	*RE*	*Realencyklopädie für protestantische Theologie und Kirche*
JSOTSup	Journal for the Study of the Old Testament Supplement Series	*REB*	*Revised English Bible*
		ResQ	*Restoration Quarterly*
JSP	*Journal for the Study of the Pseudepigrapha*	*RSR*	*Recherches de science religieuse*
		RSV	*Revised Standard Version*
JSS	*Journal of Semitic Studies*	S	superscription (in Psalms)
JTS	*Journal of Theological Studies*	SBLDS	Society of Biblical Literature Dissertation Series
Jub.	*Jubilees*		
K	Ketib	SBLMS	SBL Monograph Series

SBLSCS	SBL Septuagint and Cognate Studies	ZAW	*Zeitschrift für die alttestamentliche Wissenschaft*
SBT	Studies in Biblical Theology	ZDPV	*Zeitschrift des deutschen Palästina-Vereins*
SEÅ	*Svensk exegetisk årsbok*		
Sem	*Semitica*		
SémBib	*Sémiotique et bible*		
sg.	singular		
SJOT	*Scandinavian Journal of the Old Testament*		
SKKAT	Stuttgarter kleiner Kommentar, Altes Testament		
SOTSMS	Society for Old Testament Study Monograph Series		
SP	Samaritan Pentateuch		
STDJ	Studies on the Texts of the Desert of Judah		
SUNVAO	Skrifter utgitt av Det Norske Videnskaps-Akademi i Oslo		
Sup	Supplement		
Syr	Syriac version		
TA	*Tel Aviv*		
TDOT	*Theological Dictionary of the Old Testament,* ed. G. J. Botterweck et al., trans. D. E. Green et al. (Grand Rapids: Eerdmans, 1974–)		
TEV	*Today's English Version*		
Tg	Targum		
ThLZ	*Theologische Literaturzeitung*		
ThZ	*Theologische Zeitschrift*		
TJ	*Trinity Journal*		
T. Jud.	*Testament of Judah*		
TLOT	*Theological Lexicon of the Old Testament,* ed. E. Jenni and C. Westermann, trans. Mark E. Biddle (3 vols.; Peabody, Mass.: Hendrickson, 1997)		
TOTC	Tyndale Old Testament Commentaries		
TynBul	*Tyndale Bulletin*		
UF	*Ugarit-Forschungen*		
Vg	Vulgate		
VT	*Vetus Testamentum*		
VTSup	Vetus Testamentum Supplements		
WBC	Word Biblical Commentary		
WMANT	Wissenschaftliche Monographien zum Alten und Neuen Testament		
WO	*Die Welt des Orients*		
WUNT	Wissenschaftliche Untersuchungen zum Neuen Testament		
YNER	Yale Near Eastern Researches		
ZAH	*Zeitschrift für Althebräistik*		

2. Commentaries, Short Titles

Commentaries[1]

Ackroyd, Peter R. *I and II Chronicles, Ezra, Nehemiah.* Torch Bible Commentaries. London: SCM, 1973.

Allen, Leslie C. "The First and Second Books of Chronicles." Pages 297–659 in vol. 3 of *The New Interpreter's Bible.* Edited by L. E. Keck. Nashville: Abingdon, 1999.

Barnes, William Emery. *The Books of Chronicles.* Cambridge Bible for Schools and Colleges 13. Cambridge: Cambridge Univ. Press, 1899.

Becker, Joachim. *1 Chronik.* NEchtB. Würzburg: Echter Verlag, 1986.

——. *2 Chronik.* NEchtB. Würzburg: Echter Verlag, 1988.

Benzinger, Immanuel. *Die Bücher der Chronik erklärt.* Kurzer Hand-Commentar zum Alten Testament 20. Tübingen: Mohr (Siebeck), 1901.

Bertheau, Ernst. *Die Bücher der Chronik erklärt.* 2d ed. Kurzgefasstes exegetisches Handbuch zum Alten Testament 15. Leipzig: Hirzel, 1873.

Braun, Roddy L. *1 Chronicles.* WBC 14. Waco: Word, 1986.

Bückers, Hermann, CSSR. *Die Bücher der Chronik oder Paralipomenon.* Die Heilige Schrift für das Leben Erklärt 4/1. Freiburg: Herder, 1952.

Cazelles, H., P. S. S. *Les Livres des Chroniques.* 2d ed. La Sainte Bible. Paris: Cerf, 1961.

Coggins, R. J. *The First and Second Books of the Chronicles.* CBC. Cambridge: Cambridge Univ. Press, 1976.

Curtis, Edward Lewis, and Albert Alonzo Madsen. *A Critical and Exegetical Commentary on the Books of Chronicles.* ICC. New York: Scribner's, 1910.

Dentan, Robert C. *The First and Second Book of the Kings; The First and Second Book of the Chronicles.* Laymen's Bible Commentary 7. Richmond: John Knox, 1964.

De Vries, Simon J. *1 and 2 Chronicles.* FOTL 11. Grand Rapids: Eerdmans, 1989.

Dillard, Raymond B. *2 Chronicles.* WBC 15. Waco: Word, 1987.

---

1   In the following commentary, these commentaries will be referred to by the last name of the author and the page number. While Johnstone and Myers give different names to their two volumes, these volumes will be referred to by the numbers 1 and 2 followed by the page number. Elmslie's two commentaries are referred to by shortened forms of their titles. The short commentary of Rothstein (1923) is cited as Rothstein. His longer commentary (1927) is referred to as Rothstein-Hänel.

Eisemann, Moshe. *Divrei Hayamim. I Chronicles. A New Translation with a Commentary Anthologized from Talmudic, Midrashic and Rabbinic Sources.*[2] Brooklyn: Mesorah, 1987.

Ellison, H. L. "I and II Chronicles." Pages 369–94 in *New Bible Commentary*. Edited by Donald Guthrie et al. 3d ed. Grand Rapids: Eerdmans, 1970.

Elmslie, W. A. L. *The Books of Chronicles.* 2d ed. Cambridge Bible for Schools and Colleges. Cambridge: Cambridge Univ. Press, 1916.

————. "The First and Second Books of Chronicles." Pages 339–548 in vol. 3 of *The Interpreter's Bible*. Edited by George A. Buttrick. Nashville: Abingdon, 1954.

Fritsch, Charles T. "Commentary on First and Second Books of the Chronicles." Pages 208–19 in *The Interpreter's One-Volume Commentary on the Bible*. Edited by C. M. Laymon. Nashville: Abingdon, 1971.

Galling, Kurt. *Die Bücher der Chronik, Esra, Nehemia.* ATD 12. Göttingen: Vandenhoeck & Ruprecht, 1954.

Goettsberger, Johann. *Die Bücher der Chronik oder Paralipomenon.* HSAT 4/1. Bonn: Peter Hanstein, 1939.

Harvey-Jellie, W. R. *Chronicles.* Century Bible. London: T. C. & E. C. Jack, 1906.

Herbert, A. S. "I and II Chronicles." Pages 357–69 in *Peake's Commentary on the Bible*. Edited by Matthew Black and H. H. Rowley. London: Nelson, 1962.

Japhet, Sara. *I and II Chronicles: A Commentary.* OTL. Louisville: Westminster John Knox, 1993.

Jarick, John. *1 Chronicles.* Readings: A New Biblical Commentary. Sheffield: Sheffield Academic Press, 2000.

Johnstone, William. *1 and 2 Chronicles,* vol. 1: *1 Chronicles 1–2 Chronicles 9: Israel's Place Among the Nations;* vol. 2: *2 Chronicles 10–36: Guilt and Atonement.* JSOTSup 253. Sheffield: Sheffield Academic Press, 1998.

Keil, Carl Friedrich. *The Books of the Chronicles.* Translated by Andrew Harper. Biblical Commentary on the Old Testament 35. Edinburgh: T. & T. Clark, 1872. English translation of *Biblischer Commentar über die nachexilischen Geschichtsbücher: Chronik, Esra, Nehemia und Esther.* Biblischer Commentar über das Alte Testament 5. Leipzig: Dörffling und Franke, 1870.

Kittel, Rudolf. *The Books of Chronicles.* Translated by B. W. Bacon. Sacred Books of the Old Testament 20. Leipzig: Hinrichs, 1895.

————. *Die Bücher der Chronik.* HKAT 6/1. Göttingen: Vandenhoeck & Ruprecht, 1902.

Knoppers, Gary N. *I Chronicles 1–9.* AB 12A. New York: Doubleday, 2004.

————. *I Chronicles 10–29.* AB 12B. New York: Doubleday, 2004.

Laffey, Alice L. "1 and 2 Chronicles." Pages 110–15 in *The Women's Bible Commentary*. Edited by C. A. Newsom and S. H. Ringe. Louisville: Westminster John Knox, 1992.

Langton, Stephen. *Commentary on the Book of Chronicles.* Edited by Avrom Saltman. Ramat Gan: Bar-Ilan Univ. Press, 1978.[3]

Mangan, Celine, O. P. *1-2 Chronicles, Ezra, Nehemiah.* Old Testament Message 13. Wilmington, DE: Glazier, 1982.

McConville, J. G. *I & II Chronicles.* Daily Study Bible Series. Philadelphia: Westminster, 1984.

McKenzie, Steven L. *1 & 2 Chronicles.* Abingdon Old Testament Commentaries. Nashville: Abingdon, 2004.

Meyer, Ivo. *Gedeutete Vergangenheit: Die Bücher der Könige–Die Bücher der Chronik.* SKKAT 7. Stuttgart: Katholisches Bibelwerk, 1976.

Michaeli, F. *Les livres des Chroniques, d'Esdras et de Néhémie.* CAT 16. Neuchâtel: Delachaux et Niestlé, 1967.

Myers, Jacob M. *I Chronicles.* AB 12. Garden City, NY: Doubleday, 1965.

————. *II Chronicles.* AB 13. Garden City, NY: Doubleday, 1965.

Neteler, B. *Die Bücher der Chronik.* Münster: Theissing, 1899.

North, Robert, S.J. "The Chronicler: 1-2 Chronicles, Ezra, Nehemiah." Pages 362–98 in *The New Jerome Biblical Commentary*. Edited by Raymond E. Brown, Joseph A. Fitzmyer, and Roland E. Murphy. Englewood Cliffs, NJ: Prentice-Hall, 1990.

Osty, E., and J. Trinquet. *La Bible: Premier et deuxième livre des Chroniques.* Paris: Rencontre, 1970.

Öttli, Samuel, and Johannes Meinhold. *Die geschichtlichen Hagiographen (Chronika, Esra, Nehemiah, Ruth, Esther).* Kurzgefasster Kommentar zu den Heiligen Schriften Alten und Neuen Testaments 8. Nördlingen: Beck, 1889.

Rehm, Martin. *Die Bücher der Chronik.* 2d ed. Echter Bibel. Würzburg: Echter Verlag, 1954.

Rothstein, Johann Wilhelm. *Die Bücher der Chronik.* Pages 562–677 in vol. 2 of *HSAT*. 4th ed. Translated by E. Kautzsch. Edited by A. Bertholet. Tübingen: Mohr (Siebeck), 1923.

Rothstein, Johann Wilhelm, and Johannes Hänel. *Das Erste Buch der Chronik Übersetzt und Erklärt.* Kommentar zum Alten Testament 18/2. Leipzig: Deichertsche Verlagsbuchhandlung, 1927.

2   These sources include what is known elsewhere as Pseudo-Rashi and is called Mefaresh in this commentary. It will be cited as Pseudo-Rashi.

3   Langton lived from 1158 to 1228.

Rudolph, Wilhelm. *Chronikbücher*. HAT 21. Tübingen: Mohr (Siebeck), 1955.

Schlögl, P. N. *Die Bücher der Chronik Übersetzt und Erklärt*. Kurzgefasster wissenschaftlicher Kommentar zu den Heiligen Schriften des Alten Testaments I/3/2. Vienna: Mayer, 1911.

Selman, Martin J. *1 Chronicles*. TOTC 10a. Downers Grove, IL: InterVarsity Press, 1994.

——. *2 Chronicles*. TOTC 10b. Downers Grove, IL: InterVarsity Press, 1994.

Slotki, Israel Wolf. *Chronicles: Hebrew Text and English Translation*. Soncino Books of the Bible. New York: Soncino, 1952.

Sutcliffe, L. "I and II Paralipomenon (Chronicles)." Pages 351–74 in *A Catholic Commentary on the Holy Scripture*. Edited by Bernard Orchard et al. London: Nelson, 1953.

Thompson, J. A. *1, 2 Chronicles*. NAC 9. Nashville: Broadman, 1994.

Tuell, Steven S. *First and Second Chronicles*. Interpretation. Louisville: Westminster John Knox, 2001.

van den Born, A. *Kronieken*. De Boeken van Het O.T. 5/1. Roermond en Maaseik: Romen & Zonen, 1960.

Wilcock, M. *The Message of Chronicles*. Bible Speaks Today. Downers Grove, IL: InterVarsity Press, 1987.

Willi, Thomas. *Chronik*. BKAT XXIV/1. Neukirchen-Vluyn: Neukirchener Verlag, 1991.

Williamson, H. G. M. *1 and 2 Chronicles*. NCB. Grand Rapids: Eerdmans, 1982.

Zöcker, Otto. *The Book of the Chronicles*. Translated by James G. Murphy. Lange's Commentary. New York: Scribner's, 1877.

Short Titles[4]

Aharoni, *Land of the Bible*
    Aharoni, Yohanan. *The Land of the Bible: A Historical Geography*. Revised and enlarged ed. Translated by A. F. Rainey. Philadelphia: Westminster, 1979.

Albright, "List"
    Albright, William Foxwell. "The List of Levitic Cities." Pages 49–73 in *Louis Ginzberg Jubilee Volume*, vol. 1: *English Section*. New York: American Academy for Jewish Research, 1945.

Allen, *Greek Chronicles*
    Allen, Leslie C. *The Greek Chronicles: The Relationship of the Septuagint of I and II Chronicles to the Masoretic Text*, part 1: *The Translator's Craft*; part 2: *Textual Criticism*. VTSup 25, 27. Leiden: Brill, 1974.

Auld, *Kings Without Privilege*
    Auld, A. Graeme. *Kings Without Privilege: David and Moses in the Story of the Bible's Kings*. Edinburgh: T. & T. Clark, 1994.

Bartlett, *Edom and the Edomites*
    Bartlett, John R. *Edom and the Edomites*. JSOTSup 77. Sheffield: JSOT Press, 1989.

Boling, *Judges*
    Boling, Robert G. *Judges*. AB 6A; Garden City, NY: Doubleday, 1975.

Braun, "Chronicles, Ezra, and Nehemiah"
    Braun, Roddy L. "Chronicles, Ezra, and Nehemiah: Theology and Literary History." Pages 52–64 in *Studies in the Historical Books of the Old Testament*. Edited by J. A. Emerton. VTSup 30. Leiden: Brill, 1979.

Braun, "Solomon"
    _____. "Solomon, the Chosen Temple Builder: The Significance of 1 Chronicles 22, 28, and 29 for the Theology of Chronicles," *JBL* 95 (1976) 581–90.

Braun, "Solomonic Apologetic"
    _____. "Solomonic Apologetic in Chronicles," *JBL* 92 (1973) 503–16.

Cross, *Canaanite Myth*
    Cross, Frank Moore. *Canaanite Myth and Hebrew Epic*. Cambridge: Harvard Univ. Press, 1973.

Cross, "Reconstruction"
    _____. "A Reconstruction of the Judean Restoration," *JBL* 94 (1975) 4–18.

Danby, *Mishnah*
    Danby, Herbert. *The Mishnah*. Oxford: Oxford Univ. Press, 1933.

Demsky, "Clans of Ephrath"
    Demsky, Aaron. "The Clans of Ephrath: Their Territory and History," *TA* 13–14 (1986–1987) 46–59.

Dennerlein, *Bedeutung Jerusalems*
    Dennerlein, Norbert. *Die Bedeutung Jerusalems in den Chronikbüchern*. BEATAJ 46; Frankfurt am Main: Lang, 1999.

de Vaux, *Ancient Israel*
    de Vaux, Roland. *Ancient Israel: Its Life and Institutions*. Translated by John McHugh. London: Darton, Longman & Todd, 1961.

de Vaux, *Early History*
    _____. *The Early History of Israel*. Translated by David Smith. Philadelphia: Westminster, 1978.

Dörfuss, *Mose*
    Dörfuss, Ernst Michael. *Mose in den Chronikbüchern: Garant theokratischer Zukunftserwartung*. BZAW 219. Berlin: de Gruyter, 1994.

Driver, *Notes*
    Driver, S. R. *Notes on the Hebrew Text and the Topography of the Books of Samuel*. 2d ed. Oxford: Clarendon, 1913.

Dyck, *Theocratic Ideology*
    Dyck, Jonathan E. *The Theocratic Ideology of the Chronicler*. Biblical Interpretation Series. Leiden: Brill, 1998.

Edelman, "Deuteronomist's David"
    Edelman, Diana. "The Deuteronomist's David and the Chronicler's David: Competing or Contrasting Ideologies?" Pages 67–83 in *The Future of the Deuteronomistic History*. Edited by T. Römer. BEThL 147. Leuven: Leuven Univ. Press, 2000.

Edelman, "Edom"
    _____. "Edom: A Historical Geography." Pages 1–11 in *You Shall Not Abhor an Edomite For He Is Your Brother: Edom and Seir in History and Tradition*. Edited by D. V. Edelman. ABS 3. Atlanta: Scholars Press, 1995.

Ehrlich, *Randglossen*
    Ehrlich, Arnold B. *Randglossen zur Hebräischen Bibel*. 7 vols. 1914. Reprinted Hildesheim: Olms, 1968.

---

4   Books and articles listed here are referred to in two or more chapters of the commentary. Other books and articles are cited fully on the first appearance in the commentary, but referred to subsequently in the same chapter by short titles.

Elliger, "Dreissig Helden Davids"
Elliger, Karl. "Die dreissig Helden Davids," *PJ* 31 (1935) 29–75.

Endres, Millar, and Burns, *Parallels*
Endres, John C., S.J., William R. Millar, and John Barclay Burns, eds. *Chronicles and Its Synoptic Parallels in Samuel, Kings, and Related Biblical Texts*. Wilmington, DE: Glazier, 1998.

Eskenazi, "Literary Approach"
Eskenazi, Tamara. "A Literary Approach to Chronicles' Ark Narrative (1 Chronicles 13–16)." Pages 258–74 in *Fortunate the Eyes That See*. FS D. N. Freedman. Edited by A. B. Beck, A. H. Bartelt, Paul R. Raabe, and C. A. Franke. Grand Rapids: Eerdmans, 1995.

Fincke, *Samuel Scroll*
Fincke, Andrew. *The Samuel Scroll from Qumran: 4QSamᵃ Restored and Compared to the Septuagint and 4QSamᶜ*. STDJ 43. Leiden: Brill, 2001.

Fishbane, *Biblical Interpretation*
Fishbane, Michael. *Biblical Interpretation in Ancient Israel*. Oxford: Clarendon, 1985.

Gabriel, *Friede*
Gabriel, Ingeborg. *Friede über Israel: Eine Untersuchung zur Friedenstheologie in Chronik I 10–II 36*. ÖBS 10. Klosterneuburg: ÖKB, 1990.

Galil, *Chronology*
Galil, Gershon. *The Chronology of the Kings of Israel & Judah*. Studies in the History and Culture of the Ancient Near East 9. Leiden: Brill, 1996.

Gordon, *Syriac*
Gordon, Robert P., in collaboration with P. B. Dirksen. *The Old Testament in Syriac According to the Peshiṭta Version*, part IV, fascicle 2: *Chronicles*. Leiden: Brill, 1998.

Graham, *Utilization*
Graham, M. Patrick. *The Utilization of 1 and 2 Chronicles in the Reconstruction of Israelite History in the Nineteenth Century*. SBLDS 116. Atlanta: Scholars Press, 1990.

Graham, Hoglund, and McKenzie, *Chronicler as Historian*
Graham, M. Patrick, Kenneth G. Hoglund, and Steven L. McKenzie. *The Chronicler as Historian*. JSOTSup 238. Sheffield: Sheffield Academic Press, 1997.

Graham and McKenzie, *Chronicler as Author*
Graham, M. Patrick, and Steven L. McKenzie, eds. *The Chronicler as Author*. JSOTSup 263. Sheffield: Sheffield Academic Press, 1999.

Graham, McKenzie, and Knoppers, *Chronicler as Theologian*
Graham, M. P., S. L. McKenzie, and G. N. Knoppers, eds. *The Chronicler as Theologian: Essays in Honor of Ralph W. Klein*. JSOTSup 371. Sheffield: Sheffield Academic Press, 2003.

Gunneweg, *Esra*
Gunneweg, A. H. J. *Esra*. KAT 19/1. Gütersloh: Mohn, 1985.

Halpern, *David's Secret Demons*
Halpern, Baruch. *David's Secret Demons: Messiah, Murderer, Traitor, King*. Grand Rapids: Eerdmans, 2001.

Herbert, *Reconstructing*
Herbert, Edward D. *Reconstructing Biblical Dead Sea Scrolls: A New Method Applied to the Reconstruction of 4QSamᵃ*. STDJ 22. Leiden: Brill, 1997.

Im, *Davidbild*
Im, Tae-Soo. *Das Davidbild in den Chronikbüchern: David as Idealbild des theokratischen Messianismus für den Chronisten*. EHS 23/263. Frankfurt am Main: Peter Lang, 1985.

Ishida, *Studies*
Ishida, Tomoo, ed. *Studies in the Period of David and Solomon and Other Essays*. Winona Lake, IN: Eisenbrauns, 1982.

Japhet, "Conquest and Settlement"
Japhet, Sara. "Conquest and Settlement in Chronicles," *JBL* 98 (1979) 205–18.

Japhet, *Ideology*
_____. *The Ideology of the Book of Chronicles and Its Place in Biblical Thought*. Translated by Anna Barber. BEATAJ 9. Frankfurt am Main: Peter Lang, 1989.

Japhet, "Interchanges"
_____. "Interchanges of Verbal Roots in Parallel Texts in Chronicles," *HS* 28 (1987) 9–50.

Japhet, "Relationship"
_____. "The Relationship between Chronicles and Ezra-Nehemiah." Pages 298–313 in *Congress Volume, Leuven 1989*. VTSup 43. Edited by J. A. Emerton; Leiden: Brill, 1991.

Japhet, "Supposed Common Authorship"
_____. "The Supposed Common Authorship of Chronicles and Ezra-Nehemiah, Investigated Anew," *VT* 18 (1968) 330–71.

Johnson, *Purpose*
Johnson, Marshall D. *The Purpose of the Biblical Genealogies: With Special Reference to the Setting of the Genealogies of Jesus*. 2d ed. Cambridge: Cambridge Univ. Press, 1988.

Kalimi, "Abfassungszeit"
Kalimi, Isaac. "Die Abfassungszeit der Chronik—Forschungstand und Perspektiven," *ZAW* 105 (1993) 223–33.

Kalimi, "Date of Chronicles"
_____. "The Date of Chronicles: The Biblical Text, the Elephantine Papyri and the El-Ibrahimia's Aramaic Grave Inscription." Pages 347–71 in *God's Word for Our World*, vol. 1: *Biblical Studies in Honour of Simon John De Vries*. Edited by J. Harold Ellens, D. L. Ellens, Isaac Kalimi, and Rolf P. Knierim. JSOTSup 388. London: T & T Clark, 2004.

Kalimi, *Geschichtsschreibung*
_____. *Zur Geschichtsschreibung des Chronisten: Literarisch-historiographische Abweichungen der Chronik von ihren Paralleltexten in den Samuel- und Königsbüchern*. BZAW 226. Berlin: de Gruyter, 1995.

Kalimi, "History of Interpretation"
_____. "History of Interpretation: The Book of Chronicles in Jewish Tradition from Daniel to Spinoza," *RB* 105 (1998) 5–41.

Kalimi, "Jerusalem"
_____. "Jerusalem—The Divine City: The Representation of Jerusalem in Chronicles Compared with Earlier and Later Jewish Compositions." Pages 189–204 in Graham, McKenzie, and Knoppers, *Chronicler as Theologian*.

Kalimi, "Paranomasia"
_____. "Paronomasia in the Book of Chronicles," *JSOT* 67 (1995) 27–41.

Kallai, *Historical Geography*
Kallai, Zecharia. *Historical Geography of the Bible*. Jerusalem: Magnes, 1986.

Kartveit, *Motive und Schichten*
Kartveit, Magnar. *Motive und Schichten der Landtheologie in I Chronik 1–9*. ConBOT 28. Stockholm: Almquist & Wiksell, 1989.

Kegler and Augustin, *Deutsche Synopse*
  Kegler, J., and M. Augustin, eds. *Deutsche Synopse zum
  Chronistischen Geschictswerk*. 2d ed. BEATAJ 33. Frankfurt am
  Main: Peter Lang, 1993.

Kelly, *Retribution and Eschatology*
  Kelly, Brian E. *Retribution and Eschatology in Chronicles*. JSOTSup
  211. Sheffield: Sheffield Academic Press, 1996.

Klein, *1 Samuel*
  Klein, Ralph W. *1 Samuel*. WBC 10. Waco: Word, 1983.

Klein, "Ezra & Nehemiah"
  _____. "The Books of Ezra & Nehemiah." Pages 661–851 in
  The New Interpreter's Bible. Vol. 3. Edited by L. E. Keck.
  Nashville: Abingdon, 1999.

Klein, "How Many in a Thousand?"
  _____. "How Many in a Thousand?" Pages 270–82 in Graham,
  Hoglund, and McKenzie, *Chronicler as Historian*.

Klein, "Narrative Texts"
_____. "Narrative Texts: Chronicles, Ezra, and Nehemiah." Pages
  385–401 in *The Blackwell Companion to the Bible*. Edited by Leo
  G. Perdue. Oxford: Blackwell, 2001.

Kleinig, *Lord's Song*
  Kleinig, John W. *The Lord's Song: The Basis, Function and
  Significance of Choral Music in Chronicles*. JSOTSup 156.
  Sheffield: JSOT Press, 1993.

Kleinig, "Recent Research"
  _____. "Recent Research in Chronicles," *CR:BS* 2 (1994) 43–76.

Knauf, *Ismael*
  Knauf, Ernst Axel. *Ismael: Untersuchungen zur Geschichte Palästinas
  und Nordarabiens im 1 Jahrtausend v. Chr.* ADPV. Wiesbaden:
  Harrassowitz, 1985.

Knoppers, "Hierodules"
  Knoppers, Gary N. "Hierodules, Priests, or Janitors? The Levites
  in Chronicles and the History of the Israelite Priesthood," *JBL*
  118 (1999) 49–72.

Knoppers, "Images of David"
  _____. "Images of David in Early Judaism: David as Repentant
  Sinner in Chronicles," *Bib* 76 (1995) 449–70.

Knoppers, "Intermarriage"
  _____. "Intermarriage, Social Complexity, and Ethnic Diversity
  in the Genealogy of Judah," *JBL* 120 (2001): 15–30.

Knoppers, "Sources"
  _____. "Sources, Revisions, and Editions: The Lists of
  Jerusalem's Residents in MT and LXX Nehemiah 11 and
  I Chronicles 9," *Textus* 20 (2000) 141–68.

Knoppers and Harvey, "Omitted and Remaining Matters"
  Knoppers, Gary N., and Paul B. Harvey Jr. "Omitted and
  Remaining Matters: On the Names Given to the Book of
  Chronicles in Antiquity," *JBL* 121 (2002) 227–43.

Kratz, *Komposition*
  Kratz, Reinhard G. *Die Komposition der erzählenden Bücher des
  Alten Testaments*. Untitaschenbücher für Wissenschaft.
  Göttingen: Vandenhoeck & Ruprecht, 2000.

Kropat, *Syntax*
  Kropat, Arno. *Die Syntax des Autors der Chronik verglichen mit der
  seiner Quellen: Ein Beitrag zur historischen Syntax des Hebräischen*.
  BZAW 16. Giessen: Töpelmann, 1909.

Kutscher, *Language*
  Kutscher, E. Y. *The Language and Linguistic Background of the
  Isaiah Scroll (1QIsaᵃ)*. STDJ 6. Leiden: Brill, 1974.

Laban and Ben Zvi, "Observations"
  Laban, Antje, and Ehud Ben Zvi. "Observations on Women in
  the Genealogies of 1 Chronicles 1–9," *Bib* 84 (2003) 457–78.

Lemke, "Synoptic Studies"
  Lemke, Werner E. "Synoptic Studies in the Chronicler's
  History." Th.D. diss. Harvard Divinity School, 1964.

Lemke, "Synoptic Problem"
  _____. "The Synoptic Problem in the Chronicler's History,"
  HTR 58 (1965) 349–63.

Levin, "Understanding Biblical Genealogies"
  Levin, Yigal. "Understanding Biblical Genealogies," *CR:BS* 9
  (2001) 11–46.

Levin, "Chronological Aspects"
  _____. "Chronological Aspects of the Chronicler's
  Genealogies." Paper read at the SBL Annual Meeting, Toronto,
  2002, 1–28.

Lipschits and Blenkinsopp, *Judah and the Judeans*
  Lipschits, Oded, and Joseph Blenkinsopp, eds., *Judah and the
  Judeans in the Neo-Babylonian Period*. Winona Lake, IN:
  Eisenbrauns, 2003.

Mason, *Preaching the Tradition*
  Mason, Rex. *Preaching the Tradition: Homily and Hermeneutics after
  the Exile. Based on the 'Addresses' in Chronicles, the 'Speeches' in the
  Books of Ezra and Nehemiah and the Postexilic Prophetic Books*.
  Cambridge: Cambridge Univ. Press, 1990.

Mazar, "Cities"
  Mazar, Benjamin. "The Cities of the Priests and of the Levites."
  Pages 193–205 in *Congress Volume: Oxford 1959*. VTSup 7.
  Leiden: Brill, 1960.

McCarter, *I Samuel*
  McCarter, P. Kyle, Jr. *I Samuel*. AB 8. Garden City, NY:
  Doubleday, 1980.

McCarter, *II Samuel*
  _____. *II Samuel*. AB 9. Garden City, NY: Doubleday, 1984.

McIvor, *Targum*
  McIvor, J. Stanley. *The Targum of Chronicles*. Aramaic Bible 19.
  Collegeville, MN: Liturgical Press, 1994.

McKenzie, *Chronicler's Use*
  McKenzie, Steven L. *The Chronicler's Use of the Deuteronomistic
  History*. HSM 33. Atlanta: Scholars Press, 1984.

Mettinger, *Solomonic State Officials*
  Mettinger, Tryggve N. D. *Solomonic State Officials: A Study of the
  Civil Government of the Israelite Monarchy*. ConBOT 5; Lund:
  Gleerup, 1971.

Milgrom, *Leviticus 1–16*
  Milgrom, Jacob. *Leviticus 1–16*. AB 3. New York: Doubleday,
  1991.

Milgrom, *Leviticus 17–22*
  _____. *Leviticus 17–22*. AB 3A. New York: Doubleday, 2000.

Milgrom, *Leviticus 23–27*
  _____. *Leviticus 23–27*. AB 3B. New York: Doubleday, 2001.

Mosis, *Untersuchungen*
  Mosis, Rudolf. *Untersuchungen zur Theologie des chronistischen
  Geschichtswerks*. Freiburger theologische Studien 92. Freiburg:
  Herder, 1973.

Noth, *Chronicler's History*
  Noth, Martin. *The Chronicler's History*. Translated by H. G. M. Williamson. JSOTSup 50. Sheffield: JSOT Press, 1987 (German original: 1943).

Noth, *Deuteronomistic History*
  _____. *The Deuteronomistic History*. JSOTSup 15. Sheffield: JSOT Press, 1981 (German original: 1943).

Noth, *Josua*
  _____. *Josua*. HAT 7. Tübingen: Mohr (Siebeck), 1953.

Noth, "Liste"
  _____. "Eine siedlungsgeographische Liste in 1 Chr. 2 und 4," *ZDPV* 55 (1932) 97–124.

Noth, *Personennamen*
  _____. *Die israelitischen Personennamen im Rahmen der gemein-semitischen Namengebung*. BWANT 3/10. Stuttgart: Kohlhammer, 1928.

Oeming, *Wahre Israel*
  Oeming, Manfred. *Das wahre Israel: Die "genealogische Vorhalle" 1 Chronik 1–9*. BWANT 128. Stuttgart: Kohlhammer, 1990.

Olmo Lete and Sanmartín, *Ugaritic Language*
  Olmo Lete, Gregorio, and Joaquín Sanmartín. *A Dictionary of the Ugaritic Language in the Alphabetic Tradition*. Handbuch der Orientalistik 67. 2d ed. Leiden: Brill, 2004.

Osborne, "Genealogies"
  Osborne, William L. "The Genealogies of 1 Chronicles 1–9." Ph.D. diss. Dropsie University, 1979.

Peltonen, "Jigsaw"
  Peltonen, Kai. "A Jigsaw Without a Model? The Date of Chronicles." Pages 225–71 in *Did Moses Speak Attic? Jewish History and Historiography in the Hellenistic Period*. Edited by Lester L. Grabbe. JSOTSup 37. Sheffield: Sheffield Academic Press, 2001.

Peltonen, *History Debated*
  _____. *History Debated: The Historical Reliability of Chronicles in Pre-Critical and Critical Research*. Publications of the Finnish Exegetical Society 64. 2 vols. Göttingen: Vandenhoeck & Ruprecht, 1996.

Petersen, *Late Israelite Prophecy*
  Petersen, David L. *Late Israelite Prophecy: Studies in Deutero-Prophetic Literature and in Chronicles*. SBLMS 23. Missoula, MT: Scholars Press, 1977.

Pisano, *Additions or Omissions*
  Pisano, S. *Additions or Omissions in the Books of Samuel: The Significant Pluses and Minuses in the Massoretic, LXX and Qumran Texts*. OBO 57. Leiden: Brill, 1984.

Pitard, *Ancient Damascus*
  Pitard, Wayne T. *Ancient Damascus: A Historical Study of the Syrian City-State from Earliest Times until Its Fall to the Assyrians in 732 B.C.E.* Winona Lake, IN: Eisenbrauns, 1987.

Pohlmann, "Korrespondenzen und Divergenzen"
  Pohlmann, K.-F. "Zur Frage von Korrespondenzen und Divergenzen zwischen den Chronikbüchern und dem Esra/Nehemia-Buch." Pages 314–30 in *Congress Volume: Leuven 1989*. Edited by J. A. Emerton. VTSup 43. Leiden: Brill, 1991.

Polzin, *Late Biblical Hebrew*
  Polzin, Robert. *Late Biblical Hebrew: Toward an Historical Typology of Biblical Hebrew Prose*. HSM 12. Missoula, MT: Scholars Press, 1976.

von Rad, *Geschichtsbild*
  Rad, Gerhard von. *Das Geschichtsbild des Chronistischen Werkes*. BWANT 54. Stuttgart: Kohlhammer, 1930.

Riley, *King and Cultus*
  Riley, William. *King and Cultus in Chronicles: Worship and the Reinterpretation of History*. JSOTSup 160. Sheffield: JSOT Press, 1993.

Rooke, "Kingship as Priesthood"
  Rooke, Deborah W. "Kingship as Priesthood: The Relationship between the High Priesthood and the Monarchy." Pages 187–208 in *King and Messiah in Israel and the Ancient Near East*. Edited by J. Day. JSOTSup 270. Sheffield: Sheffield Academic Press, 1999.

Rudolph, *Esra und Nehemia*
  Rudolph, Wilhelm. *Esra und Nehemia*. HAT 20. Tübingen: Mohr (Siebeck), 1949.

Schniedewind, *Word of God*
  Schniedewind, William M. *The Word of God in Transition: From Prophet to Exegete in the Second Temple Period*. JSOTSup 197. Sheffield: Sheffield Academic Press, 1995.

Seow, *David's Dance*
  Seow, C. L. *Myth, Drama, and the Politics of David's Dance*. HSM 44. Atlanta: Scholars Press, 1989.

Shaver, Judson R. *Torah and the Chronicler's History Work*. BJS 196. Atlanta: Scholars Press, 1989.

Steins, *Chronik*
  Steins, Georg. *Die Chronik als kanonisches Abschlussphänomen: Studien zur Entstehung und Theologie von 1/2 Chronik*. BBB 93. Weinheim: Beltz Athenäum, 1995.

Strübind, *Tradition als Interpretation*
  Strübind, Kim. *Tradition als Interpretation in der Chronik: König Josaphat als Paradigma chronistischer Hermeneutik und Theologie*. BZAW 201. Berlin: de Gruyter, 1991.

D. Talshir, "Reinvestigation"
  Talshir, David. "A Reinvestigation of the Linguistic Relationship Between Chronicles and Ezra-Nehemiah," *VT* 38 (1988) 165–93.

Z. Talshir, *From Origin to Translation*
  Talshir, Zipora. *1 Esdras: From Origin to Translation*. SBLSCS 47. Atlanta: Scholars Press, 1999.

Z. Talshir, *Text Critical Commentary*
  _____. *I Esdras: A Text Critical Commentary*. SBLSCS 50. Atlanta: Society of Biblical Literature, 2001.

Throntveit, *When Kings Speak*
  Throntveit, Mark A. *When Kings Speak: Royal Speech and Royal Prayer in Chronicles*. SBLDS 93. Atlanta: Scholars Press, 1987.

Torrey, *Ezra Studies*
  Torrey, Charles Cutler. *Ezra Studies*. 1910. Reprinted New York: KTAV, 1970.

Ulrich, *Qumran Text*
  Ulrich, Eugene Charles, Jr. *The Qumran Text of Samuel and Josephus*. HSM 19. Missoula, MT: Scholars Press, 1978.

Vannutelli, *Libri Synoptici*
  Vannutelli, Primus. *Libri Synoptici Veteris Testamenti*. Rome: Pontifical Biblical Institute, 1931.

Weippert, "Geographische System"
  Weippert, Helga. "Das geographische System der Stämme Israels," *VT* 23 (1973) 76–89.

Welch, *Postexilic Judaism*
  Welch, Adam C. *Postexilic Judaism*. Edinburgh: Blackwood, 1935.

Welch, *Work*
_____. *The Work of the Chronicler: Its Purpose and Its Date.*
London: Oxford Univ. Press, 1939.

Wellhausen, *Prolegomena*
Wellhausen, Julius. *Prolegomena to the History of Ancient Israel:
With a Reprint of the Article Israel from the Encyclopaedia
Britannica.* With a preface by W. Robertson Smith. 1957.
Cleveland: Meridian, 1961.

Welten, *Geschichte und Geschichtsdarstellung*
Welten, Peter. *Geschichte und Geschichtsdarstellung in den
Chronikbüchern.* WMANT 42. Neukirchen-Vluyn: Neukirchener
Verlag, 1973.

Wenham, *Genesis 1–15*
Wenham, Gordon J. *Genesis 1–15.* WBC 1. Waco: Word, 1987.

Wenham, *Genesis 16–50*
_____. *Genesis 16–50.* WBC 2. Waco: Word, 1994.

Willi, *Chronik als Auslegung*
Willi, Thomas. *Die Chronik als Auslegung: Untersuchungen zur liter-
arischen Gestaltung der historischen Überlieferung Israels.* FRLANT
106. Göttingen: Vandenhoeck & Ruprecht, 1972.

Willi, *Juda–Jehud–Israel*
_____. *Juda–Jehud–Israel: Studien zum Selbstverständnis des
Judentums in persischer Zeit.* FAT 12. Tübingen: Mohr (Siebeck),
1995.

Willi, "Late Persian Judaism"
_____. "Late Persian Judaism and Its Conception of an Integral
Israel According to Chronicles: Some Observation on Form and
Function of the Genealogy of Judah in 1 Chronicles 2.3–4.23."
Pages 146–162 in *Second Temple Studies,* vol. 2: *Temple and
Community in the Persian Period.* Edited by T. C. Eskenazi and K.
H. Richards. JSOTSup 175. Sheffield: JSOT Press, 1994.

Williamson, "Dynastic Oracle"
Williamson, H. G. M. "The Dynastic Oracle in the Books of
Chronicles." Pages 305–18 in vol. 3 of *Essays on the Bible and the
Ancient World: FS I. L. Seeligmann.* Edited by Alexander Rofé and
Yair Zakovitch. 3 vols. Jerusalem: Rubinstein, 1985.

Williamson, "Eschatology"
_____. "Eschatology in Chronicles," *TynBul* 28 (1977) 115–54.

Williamson, *Ezra, Nehemiah*
_____. *Ezra, Nehemiah.* WBC 16. Waco: Word, 1985.

Williamson, *Israel*
_____. *Israel in the Books of Chronicles.* Cambridge: Cambridge
Univ. Press, 1977.

Williamson, "Origins"
_____. "The Origins of the Twenty-four Priestly Courses: A
Study of I Chronicles XXIII-XXVII." Pages 251–68 in *Studies in
the Historical Books of the Old Testament.* Ed. J. Emerton. VTSup
30. Leiden: Brill, 1979.

Williamson, "Sources"
_____. "Sources and Redaction in the Chronicler's Genealogy
of Judah," *JBL* 98 (1979) 351–59.

Wilson, *Genealogy and History*
Wilson, Robert R. *Genealogy and History in the Biblical World.*
YNER 7. New Haven: Yale Univ. Press, 1977.

Wilson, "Interpreting"
_____. "Between 'Azel' and 'Azel': Interpreting the Biblical
Genealogies," *BA* 42 (1979) 11–22.

Wright, "From Center"
Wright, John W. "From Center to Periphery: 1 Chronicles 23–27
and the Interpretation of Chronicles in the Nineteenth
Century." Pages 20–42 in *Priests, Prophets and Scribes: Essays on
the Formation and Heritage of Second Temple Judaism in Honour of
Joseph Blenkinsopp.* Edited by Eugene Ulrich, John W. Wright,
Robert P. Carroll, and Philip R. Davies. JSOTSup 149. Sheffield:
Sheffield Academic Press, 1992.

Wright, "Guarding the Gates"
_____. "Guarding the Gates: 1 Chronicles 26.1-19 and the Roles
of the Gatekeepers in Chronicles," *JSOT* 48 (1990) 69–81.

Wright, "Legacy of David"
_____. "The Legacy of David in Chronicles: The Narrative
Function of 1 Chronicles 23–27," *JBL* 110 (1991) 229–42.

Zevit, *Religions of Israel*
Zevit, Ziony. *The Religions of Ancient Israel: A Synthesis of
Parallactic Approaches.* London: Continuum, 2001.

Name

In the Hebrew Bible, Chronicles[1] is called ספר דברי הימים "The Book of the Events[2] of the Days," reflecting rabbinic tradition. This title indicates one understanding of Chronicles, namely, that the book[3] deals with past events.[4] These words without an additional modifier are not found in the text of Chronicles itself[5] but may be related to lost works cited in Kings, such as ספר דברי הימים למלכי ישראל "The Book of the Events of the Days of the Kings of Israel" or ספר דברי הימים למלכי יהודה "The Book of the Events of the Days of the Kings of Judah."[6] These source citations are renamed "The Book of the Kings of Judah and Israel," or "The Book of the Kings of Israel and Judah," in Chronicles.[7] The reference to the kings of Israel and Judah may have been dropped from "The Book of the Events of the Days" in the title of Chronicles since it would not apply to 1 Chronicles 1–9.

The Septuagint's name for Chronicles is $\Pi\alpha\rho\alpha$-$\lambda\epsilon\iota\pi o\mu\acute{\epsilon}\nu\omega\nu$[8] A' and B'. The title *Paraleipomena*, "Things Omitted" or "Things Left Behind," indicates a second understanding of the book's purpose, to record events left out by earlier histories, such as Samuel and Kings.[9] In Codex Alexandrinus the title is slightly longer: "The Things Omitted regarding the Kings of Judah" (cf. some manuscripts of the Peshitta[10]). This is a third understanding of the purpose of Chronicles, which reflects the fact that Chronicles primarily focuses its narrative on Judah and only includes the history of the Northern Kingdom when it affects Judah. In a way the name *Paraleipomena* is inappropriate, since Chronicles not only includes "things that have been omitted" but it also "takes over" or "includes" a large amount of material from Samuel-Kings.

In his preface to his translation of Samuel-Kings (the "prologus galeatus"), Jerome called the book "*Paralipomenon One and Two*" and noted that it touched on historical events omitted in the books of Kings and explained innumerable questions pertinent to the Gospel.[11] In the same work Jerome also called it a "Chronicle [*Chronicon* = $\chi\rho o\nu\iota\kappa\acute{o}\nu$] of All Divine History," a fourth understanding of the purpose of Chronicles. Jerome identified it with a genre of historiography of his time, which gave a summary of past history arranged according to a chronological outline.[12] Chronicles begins with Adam, the first human according to Genesis, and continues until the fall of Jerusalem in 586 BCE. Unlike the *chronica* of Eusebius and Jerome himself, which synchronized sacred and secular history, the biblical "Chronicon" tells only the story of the relationship between God and God's people. In the Vulgate translation the book is called *Liber I and II Paralipomenon*.

---

1   For a comprehensive discussion of the history of the names ascribed to Chronicles, see Knoppers and Harvey, "Omitted and Remaining Matters," 227–43.

2   Lit. "Words."

3   In Jewish tradition 1 and 2 Chronicles were considered one book with the *masorah finalis* appearing only at the end of what we call 2 Chronicles. A marginal note at 1 Chr 27:25, חצי הספר בפסוקים "half of the book in verses," indicates the midpoint of this one book. The division of the book into two by LXX eventually found its way into Hebrew Bibles, but that is not attested before 1448 (Rudolph, III).

4   Knoppers and Harvey, "Omitted and Remaining Matters," 230.

5   The only places where this phrase occurs in the biblical text itself are at Neh 12:23 and Esth 2:23.

6   E.g., in 1 Kgs 14:19 and 29, respectively.

7   See the section on Sources below.

8   The title is genitive plural. Apparently one is to translate "[The book of] the Things Omitted."

9   This name is also used in the Ethiopic translation.

Werner H. Schmidt, *Old Testament Introduction* (New York: Crossroad, 1984) 160, points to a second possible understanding of this name. Since Chronicles was largely parallel to Samuel-Kings, he conjectures that Chronicles might at first have been left out of the Greek translation and only later included in it. Cf. Strübind, *Tradition als Interpretation*, 10, who suggests that the books of Chronicles were first left out of the canon (!) and only later included in it.

10   "The book of Chronicles, namely, the book remembering the days of the kings of Judah." See the apparatus in Gordon, *Syriac*, 1.

11   *Prologus in libro Regum* and *Epist.* 53.8, as cited in Knoppers and Harvey, "Omitted and Remaining Matters," 227, 232. Jerome, *Prologus in libro Regum* in *Biblia sacra iuxta vulgatam versionem* (ed. B. Fischer et al.; 3d ed.; Stuttgart: Deutsche Bibelgesellschaft, 1984) 365.

12   Knoppers and Harvey, "Omitted and Remaining Matters," 237.

In his translation of the historical books, published in 1524, Martin Luther showed his indebtedness to Jerome's preface to his translation of Samuel and Kings by giving Chronicles the title *Die Chronika*.[13] In 1535 Miles Coverdale, one of the early translators of the Bible into English, followed Luther's lead and gave this book the name Chronicles for the first time in English.

Canonicity and Place in the Canon

The canonicity of Chronicles was apparently never disputed in antiquity. According to the Babylonian Talmud (*B. Batra* 14b), the order of books in the last part of the Ketubim is Daniel, Esther, Ezra (= Ezra-Nehemiah), Chronicles.[14] This location may also be reflected in Matt 23:35//Luke 11:51.[15] Kalimi suggests that the talmudic sages may have wanted to contrast the climax of the Hebrew canon (reporting the return to Zion and Jerusalem) with the Christian canon of the OT, which put Malachi's prophecy (3:23-24 [4:5-6]) about the coming of Elijah the prophet as the preparation for the birth of Jesus at the climax of its canon. Roger Beckwith suggests Chronicles was put at the end of the Bible because it recapitulates the whole biblical story.[16] In

Codex Leningradensis and the Aleppo Codex,[17] however, Chronicles is the *first* book in the Writings. This location may represent chronological calculations, since Chronicles begins with Adam, the first human being, and the canon then closes with Daniel in the exile and Ezra and Nehemiah from the postexilic period.[18] McIvor, on the other hand, suggests that Chronicles was put before Psalms in these manuscripts since Chronicles, in which David plays such a major role, was considered an appropriate introduction to the Psalter, which was attributed to Davidic authorship.[19] In the Septuagint the *Paraleipomena* appear after the four books of Reigns (= Samuel-Kings) and before 1 Esdras (*Εσδρας Α´*) and the Greek translation of Ezra-Nehemiah (*Εσδρας Β´*).

Language

Older studies of the language of Chronicles provided lists of characteristic words that were common in Chronicles, with the occurrences of these terms in Ezra and Nehemiah also included in the listing,[20] or they alleged significant Aramaic influence on the language of Chronicles.[21] S. R. Driver, for example, provided a list of forty-six words, syntactical usages, and prepositions

---

13   *Das erste Buch der Chronika; das andere Buch der Chronika.* Cf. Rudolph, III. Knoppers and Harvey, "Omitted and Remaining Matters," 242. In modern German Bibles Chronicles is called *Das erste Buch der Chronik* and *Das zweite Buch der Chronik.*

14   See Isaac Kalimi, "History of Interpretation," 23–25.

15   This passage refers to martyrs from Abel to Zechariah son of Barachiah. The first of these martyrs is a reference to the murder of Abel in Gen 4:8-16; the second, apparently, a reference to 2 Chr 24:20-21, although the patronymic "son of Barachiah" in Matthew belongs to the later prophet Zechariah (Zech 1:1) rather than to Zechariah the son of the priest Jehoiada. Thus these martyrs appear in the first and last books of the Bible, Genesis and Chronicles. Cf. Roger Beckwith, *The Old Testament Canon of the New Testament Church* (Grand Rapids: Eerdmans, 1985) 115, 123, 127, and 220. Julio C. Trebolle Barrera, "Origins of a Tripartitie Old Testament Canon," in *The Canon Debate* (ed. L. M. McDonald and J. A. Sanders; Peabody, MA: Hendrickson, 2002) 131, however, thinks that Matthew refers to Zechariah the son of Baris who died in the first Jewish revolt, or that the passage simply points to the last murder in the

Bible, without implying that Chronicles is the last book in the Bible.

16   Beckwith, *Old Testament Canon*, 158.

17   Curtis and Madsen, 2, note that this is the order followed in general also by Spanish codices.

18   See Steins, *Chronik*, 511. While Steins makes an important point that Chronicles harmonizes earlier traditions by writing a new work rather than making glosses to other works, I am not persuaded by his hypothesis that Chronicles was written to close the canon, not least because of the very late date this requires for the composition of the book.

19   McIvor, *Targum*, 13.

20   S. R. Driver, *An Introduction to the Literature of the Old Testament* (9th ed.; Edinburgh: T. & T. Clark, 1913) 535–40; Curtis and Madsen, 27–36. The latter also make a harsh judgment about the language of the Chronicler, 27, speaking of his "slovenly and careless composition."

21   Arno Kropat, *Die Syntax des Autors der Chronik* (BZAW 16; Giessen: Töpelmann, 1909); cf. Curtis and Madsen, 27.

that characterized the author's style, and that list was expanded to one hundred thirty-six by Curtis and Madsen.[22] These lists remain valuable indices of the author's vocabulary and style, but their relevance to the question of the unity of Chronicles and Ezra-Nehemiah is vigorously contested. The strong Aramaic influence on the language of Chronicles detected by Kropat had convinced him that Aramaic was the chief commercial and literary language of the time when Chronicles was written.[23] Robert Polzin's Harvard dissertation effectively reversed this last judgment and found only three of nineteen grammatical/syntactical features of Chronicles to be the result of direct Aramaic influence.[24] Even in the vocabulary of Chronicles, Polzin found that only fourteen of sixty-four words identified as Late Biblical Hebrew showed clear Aramaic influence.[25] Polzin also presented a careful description of "Late Biblical Hebrew," which he divided into two main categories: (a) the language of Chronicles, Ezra, and the non-Nehemiah Memoir parts of Nehemiah,[26] which is relatively free of archaisms; and (b) the language of the Nehemiah Memoir,[27] Esther, and the Hebrew parts of Daniel, which is replete with deliberate archaisms.[28]

In 1968 Sara Japhet noted that earlier scholars had not only concluded that Chronicles and Ezra-Nehemiah belonged to the same linguistic stratum, but they also believed that the language of these books bore the personal stamp of one author.[29] As these scholars highlighted the similarity of the language in these books, they tended to overlook or neglect the differences between them. Japhet's article then presented cases of linguistic opposition, divergent use of specific technical terms, and divergent styles in the books of Chronicles on the one hand and Ezra-Nehemiah on the other. She concluded: "Our investigation of the differences between the two books . . . has proven that the books could not have been written or compiled by the same author."[30] She added that study of other features of the books would support these conclusions.

The findings of this seminal study, which was the first blow in what would lead to a widespread rejection of the notion that the Chronicler's History included Chronicles, Ezra, and Nehemiah, have now been called into question. David Talshir observed that there is no necessary linguistic opposition between the two books and the affinity between them is extremely high.[31] Talshir noted that all of Japhet's examples of the full and short imperfect consecutive forms in the first person from Ezra-Nehemiah[32] occur only in the Nehemiah Memoir, which everyone admits is of separate authorship. After a complete review of the evidence, Talshir concluded that there is complete symmetry between Chronicles and Ezra-Nehemiah in all forms of the imperfect consecutive. Some of the differences in first person forms between Chronicles and Ezra-Nehemiah detected by Japhet are only orthographic and should be attributed to different copyists of the text instead of different authors.[33] Japhet also had noticed a difference in theophoric names, with Ezra-Nehemiah uniformly spelling these names with a final -yâ while Chronicles

---

22 They remark (p. 27): "The following list contains the more marked peculiarities of the Chronicler's writings, including new words and phrases, old ones with a new or unusual sense, and syntactical usages peculiar to him, and also all of these found frequently in other late books as well as occasionally in earlier writings, but which are particular favourites with the Chronicler, hence characteristic of his style."

23 As summarized in Polzin, *Late Biblical Hebrew*, 14.

24 Ibid., 69. This is in tension with pp. 61–69, where he lists six features under this category, and 159, where he mentions that five words meet this criterion. Apparently he concluded that only three of these features had been *directly* influenced by Aramaic usage.

25 Ibid., 123–50, 160.

26 Identified by him as Neh 7:6—12:26.

27 Identified by him as Neh 1:1-7:5 and 12:27—13:21.

28 Polzin, *Late Biblical Hebrew*, 159. Cf. Japhet, "Relationship," 303.

29 "Supposed Common Authorship," 330–71. She mentions L. Zunz, "Dibre-Hayamim oder die Bücher der Chronik," in *Die Gottesdienstlichen Vorträge der Juden, historisch Entwickelt* (Berlin: Asher, 1832) 13–36; and F. C. Movers, *Kritische Untersuchungen über die biblische Chronik* (Bonn: Habicht, 1834).

30 Japhet, "Supposed Common Authorship," 371.

31 D. Talshir, "Reinvestigation," 165–93.

32 Chronicles regularly uses the full imperfect consecutive form in the first person and the short imperfect consecutive form in the second and third persons. Japhet, "Supposed Common Authorship," 334–36, argued that the author of Ezra-Nehemiah used the full and short forms haphazardly in all three persons.

33 So already Cross, "Reconstruction," 14.

prefers *-yāhū*, but it also uses the shorter form *-yâ*. Ezra-Nehemiah, however, is dealing with postexilic history, where the short form of names was normal, while Chronicles tries to use the classical long form when dealing with preexilic history.

Talshir also criticizes Japhet's arguments about technical terms.[34] Chronicles uses קדשׁ in the *hitpael* more than טהר in the *hitpael*, but קדשׁ as a verb is not used at all in Ezra-Nehemiah and טהר only once (Ezra 6:20).[35] Hence there is almost nothing for comparison in Ezra-Nehemiah. In the terms for high priest, Chronicles prefers כהן הראשׁ over הכהן הגדול, but הכהן הגדול does not appear at all in Ezra-Nehemiah (outside the Nehemiah Memoir) and הכהן הראשׁ does appear in Ezra 7:5. Talshir also sees no opposition between מחלקת (a division of the cultic personnel) and משׁמרת (a word connoting the fulfillment of a certain cultic role or the appointment to such a role). Word pairs, consequently, do not constitute proof for different authors.[36] The rest of Talshir's article attempts to show similarity in syntax (nine items; pp. 179–81), idioms and other expressions (thirty-two items; pp. 182–85), and vocabulary (twenty-one items; pp. 185–88) between Chronicles and Ezra-Nehemiah. While admitting that lack of linguistic opposition is not proof of identical authorship, Talshir believes that the theory of single authorship would seem to deserve serious consideration in the future (p. 193). Talshir's findings do much more to undercut Japhet's criticisms of the unity of Chronicles-Ezra-Nehemiah, in my judgment, than to establish or prove unity of authorship. I will return to the question of the supposed unity of Chronicles-Ezra-Nehemiah below.

H. G. M. Williamson addressed the question of similarities in style between Chronicles and Ezra-Nehemiah in his doctoral dissertation.[37] Williamson identified criteria for determining unity of authorship on the basis of the lists in Driver and Curtis and Madsen. These criteria are: (1) A substantial number of words or stylistic peculiarities must be identified before common authorship can be supported. (2) These peculiarities must be identified from both Chronicles and Ezra-Nehemiah. On the basis of this criterion, Williamson excludes forty-seven entries from the lists. (3) Any distribution of these peculiarities outside Chronicles and Ezra-Nehemiah suggests we are dealing with features of Late Biblical Hebrew and not with common authorship. On the basis of this criterion, Williamson excludes another twenty-seven entries from the list. (4) The words or expressions in question should be expressed in other literature of this same period in a different way. (5) Words that meet the above criteria should be checked to see if they are used with the same meaning in Chronicles and in Ezra-Nehemiah. Williamson finds that thirty-two of the words are inconclusive to the debate about unity[38] and that twenty-eight point to diversity of authorship.[39] That leaves six words that suggest unity of authorship, and the best of these in his judgment is עד ל־ before a substantive[40] and the expression שׂמחה גדולה "great joy." Williamson attempted to put the burden of the linguistic argument about the unity of Chronicles and Ezra-Nehemiah on those who support this hypothesis (contrast Talshir above).

Polzin identified the following grammatical and/or syntactic features of the language of Chronicles:[41]

A. Features not attributable to Aramaic influence
1. Radically reduced use of את with pronominal suffix to express the direct object. Instead the Chronicler primarily uses object suffixes on verbs.
2. Increased use of את before nouns in the nominative case (את emphatic; 1 Chr 2:9; 16:39).

---

34 "Reinvestigation," 176–79.

35 Japhet, "Supposed Common Authorship," 342, refers also to Neh 12:30 and 13:22, but both are from the Nehemiah Memoir.

36 "Reinvestigation," 177. He dismisses the rest of the examples offered by Japhet because they do not show lexical opposition, but only reveal linguistic characteristics of the respective books. This criticism would also apply to the twenty-eight cases that Williamson discussed that supposedly show diversity of authorship (see below).

37 Williamson, *Israel*, 39–59. Williamson brackets out the Nehemiah Memoir in this comparison.

38 Ibid., 45–52.

39 Ibid., 52–58.

40 Cf. also D. Talshir, "Reinvestigation," 184; Polzin, *Late Biblical Hebrew*, 69.

41 *Late Biblical Hebrew*, 28–69. The examples cited in parentheses are illustrative, not exhaustive.

3. Expression of possession by prospective pronominal suffix with a following noun (1 Chr 7:9), or לְ plus a noun (2 Chr 31:18), or שֶׁל plus a noun.[42]

4. Collectives are construed as plurals almost without exception (1 Chr 13:4; 29:9).

5. The Chronicler exhibits a preference for plural forms of words and phrases that the earlier language uses in the singular (1 Chr 5:24; 12:30).

6. The infinitive absolute in immediate connection with a finite verb of the same stem is almost completely lacking (except for 1 Chr 4:10 and 2 Chr 28:19); the infinitive absolute used as a command is not found at all.

7. Less frequent use of בְּ and כְּ with the infinitive construct, and when one of these prepositions is used, it is often without some form of the verb הָיָה.

8. Repetition of a singular word for emphasis (1 Chr 28:14, 15).

9. The Chronicler shows a merging of the third feminine plural suffix with the third masculine plural suffix (1 Chr 23:22; 28:15).

10. The first person singular imperfect with final ה (lengthened imperfect or cohortative) is found only once in Chronicles (1 Chr 22:5).

11. The verb form וַיְהִי greatly recedes in usage.[43]

12. With cardinal numbers, the Chronicler prefers to place the substantive before the numeral and almost always puts the substantive in the plural (2 Chr 3:15; 4:6).

13. The Chronicler shows an increased use of the infinitive construct with לְ.

B. Features caused by Aramaic influence[44]

1. The Chronicler often mentions the material that is being weighed followed by its weight or measure (1 Chr 22:14); older Hebrew has an appositional order: the weight or measure is followed by the material weighed or measured (2 Kgs 5:23).

2. *Lāmed* is used very often as the sign of the accusative (1 Chr 5:26).

3. With the preposition מִן, the final *nûn* is often not assimilated before a noun without an article.[45]

4. The Chronicler uses the emphatic *lāmed* before the last element of a list (1 Chr 28:1; 29:6).

5. רַבִּים used attributively is placed twice in Chronicles before the substantive (1 Chr 28:5).[46]

6. Use of עַד־לְ before a substantive (1 Chr 4:39).

Polzin shows that items A.2-9 and 11-13 and B.1-2 are also true of the language of Ezra. Chronicles and Ezra have three additional linguistic features in common:[47]

1. Reduced occurrence of the periphrastic conjugation (הָיָה plus the active participle).

2. Reduced use of נָא, the particle of entreaty.

3. Neither Chronicles nor Ezra uses the word מַדּוּעַ.

Because of these fifteen features in common between the language of Chronicles and Ezra, Polzin speaks of "an extremely strong case for similarity in authorship of Chr and Ezr."[48]

Mark A. Throntveit admits that Polzin has shown that Chronicles, Ezra, and Nehemiah belong to the same literary stratum.[49] But on the basis of Williamson's criteria for determining common authorship,[50] he concludes that only two of the fifteen points of comparison Polzin makes between Chronicles and Ezra can be used to show identity of authorship. These are the lack of the infinitive absolute to articulate a command (A.6) and the reduced use of the periphrastic conjugation. The first of these, of course, is an argument from silence. Throntveit suggests changing Polzin's conclusion to "an extremely strong case for similarity in *language.*"

---

42 Polzin, *Late Biblical Hebrew,* 39, cites only Song 3:7: מטתו שלשלמה "the litter of Solomon." I do not believe this usage appears in Chronicles, but see 1 Chr 5:20 and 27:27 for שׁ used as a relative pronoun.

43 Ibid., 56–58.

44 Polzin, ibid., 61–69, seems to attribute only numbers 1, 2, and 3 from the following list to *direct* Aramaic influence. Number 5 is attested in Syriac, a dialect of Aramaic.

45 Fifty-one of the ninety-eight occurrences of this phenomenon in the OT are in Chronicles.

46 Polzin, *Late Biblical Hebrew,* 68, apparently construes Neh 9:28 as part of Chronicles, or at least of the Chronicler's History.

47 Ibid., 71.

48 Ibid.

49 Mark A. Throntveit, "Linguistic Analysis and the Question of Authorship in Chronicles, Ezra, and Nehemiah," *VT* 32 (1982) 215.

50 *Israel,* 39–40.

The result of this discussion about the language of Chronicles is that it is inconclusive in deciding whether Chronicles and Ezra-Nehemiah are one work or two.[51] But there is a general consensus that in syntax, grammar, and vocabulary the books of Chronicles are fully a part of Late Biblical Hebrew. Willi[52] and Welten[53] have concluded that Ezra-Nehemiah and Chronicles are two works by the same author. If so, his later work (Chronicles) seems much less troubled by issues like intermarriage. While I consider this conclusion doubtful, both they and I agree that Chronicles is to be interpreted as a literary work in its own right and not part of a longer work consisting of Chronicles-Ezra-Nehemiah.

Extent of the Chronicler's Work

Since the time of Zunz and Movers in the early nineteenth century (see n. 29 above) and until quite recently, the overwhelming majority of scholars have believed that the Chronicler's History consisted of 1 and 2 Chronicles, Ezra, and Nehemiah.[54] Within this consensus, of course, there were many scholars who held large parts of Chronicles to be secondary (see the discussion of Unity below), and also many who believed that the Nehemiah Memoir and/or other parts of Ezra-Nehemiah were also secondary. Four kinds of evidence lay behind this consensus. (1) The linguistic identity of Chronicles-Ezra-Nehemiah; but as noted in the previous section, this argument has proved to be inconclusive one way or the other; (2) the overlap between 2 Chr 36:22-23 and Ezra 1:1-3a; (3) the witness of 1 Esdras; and (4) agreement of the books in theology, purpose, and perspective. I shall review the last three arguments in the following paragraphs.

1. *The overlap between 2 Chr 36:22-23 and Ezra 1:1-3a.* These passages are nearly identical, with Chronicles breaking off abruptly after the words "and let him come up." Ezra 1:3 continues: "to Jerusalem, which is in Judah, and let him build the house of Yahweh the God of Israel. He is the God who is in Jerusalem." This overlap implies that the story told in 1 and 2 Chronicles is continued in Ezra-Nehemiah. More important for our discussion, however, is whether this overlap indicates that at one time these books were part of a unified Chronicler's History that included Chronicles-Ezra-Nehemiah, as maintained in articles by Menahem Haran.[55] Haran argued that Chronicles and Ezra-Nehemiah were separated because they were too long for one scroll and that these overlapping verses served as catch lines to indicate to the reader where the narrative continued. He adduced parallels to this procedure from Mesopotamia and the Greco-Roman world. While this conclusion is possible, it is not necessary, and the overlap could be understood in a more neutral sense, namely, that the history of Judah/Israel continues in Ezra-Nehemiah, without requiring unity of authorship between the works. Japhet proposes that the Chronicler wished to end the work with a pointer to the future and therefore borrowed this passage that pointed forward to the time of Ezra and Nehemiah.[56] Williamson, 419, considers these verses secondary in Chronicles.

2. *The content of 1 Esdras.* This work, preserved only in Greek and daughter translations, is a valuable resource for the textual criticism of 2 Chronicles 35–36, as noted under Textual Criticism below. But its content has also been used to support the idea that Chronicles, Ezra, and at least part of Nehemiah were once a unity.[57] 1 Esdras is a somewhat paraphrastic translation of 2 Chronicles 35–36; Ezra 1–10; and Neh 8:1-13a. Almost all scholars admit that the text of the book is fragmentary, at least at the end, since it breaks off in the middle of a sentence.[58] Is it also fragmentary at the beginning, since the narra-

---

51 This is conceded by Gunneweg, *Esra*, 26, in his own defense of Chronicles-Ezra-Nehemiah as one work.

52 *Chronik als Auslegung*, 180.

53 *Geschichte und Geschichtsdarstellung*, 199.

54 A notable exception was Welch, *Postexilic Judaism*, 186; idem, *Work*, 1. See also Elmslie, "Chronicles," 345, 547. This reverses the position Elmslie had taken in *Books of Chronicles*, xvi–xvii. In his first commentary Elmslie dated Chronicles to the first half of the 3d century; in his second commentary he dated it to the latter half of the 5th century or a little later.

55 Menahem Haran, "Book-Size and the Device of

Catch-Lines in the biblical Canon," *JJS* 36 (1985) 1–11; idem, "Explaining the Identical Lines at the End of Chronicles and the Beginning of Ezra," *BRev* 2 (1986) 18–20.

56 "Relationship," 309–10.

57 See esp. K.-F. Pohlmann, *Studien zum dritten Esra: Ein Beitrag zur Frage nach dem ursprünglichen Schluss des chronistischen Geschichtswerks* (FRLANT 104; Göttingen: Vandenhoeck & Ruprecht, 1970).

58 This opinion, however, has been challenged by Arie van der Kooij, "On the Ending of the Book of 1 Esdras," in *VII Congress of the International*

tive commences midcourse in the reign of Josiah, the account of whose reign actually begins in 2 Chr 34:1-33 in Chronicles? Did the translation known as 1 Esdras once include (most of) the rest of 1 and 2 Chronicles? If so, and if Ezra 10 is followed directly by Nehemiah 8, the account of Ezra's reading of the law, does 1 Esdras represent a fragment of the translation of Chronicles-Ezra-Nehemiah before the Nehemiah Memoir had been added to it?

Two issues tend to undercut this interpretation. An addition in 1 Esdr 1:21-22 (23-24), following the book's translation of 2 Chr 35:19, warmly praises Josiah and perhaps hints that the author began his book only with the reign of Josiah.[59] The second verse of this addition[60] seems to allude to 2 Kgs 23:15-20, the fulfillment of the prophecy about Josiah in 1 Kgs 13:1-3, with this consequence according to Zipora Talshir: "Josiah's actions were foretold long ago, in the early days, in the book that told the history of the sinners against the Lord (the sins of Jeroboam); and God's word had come true in Josiah's day."[61] The author of Chronicles thought that Josiah himself was responsible for his actions, not some ancient prophecy, and the contrast described in 1 Esdr 1:22 (24) between the piety of Josiah and his subjects also contrasts with 2 Chr 34:33.[62] The Chronicler also would not have delayed the consequence of the sinners' deeds to some later time, such as the time of Josiah, but these sins would have demanded an immediate impact on Judah's fate. Clearly 1 Esdr 1:22 (24) was not written by the Chronicler.[63] While v. 22 (24) refers to the sins of others, it does not connect these sins to the reign of

Manasseh, as one might have expected from the account of 2 Kings. An addition in Chronicles LXX at this same point is a translation of 2 Kgs 23:24-27, a passage not included in Chronicles MT. This addition explains the continued anger of Yahweh during the time of Josiah as something provoked by the sins of Manasseh. Reflection on 1 Esdr 1:21-22 (23-24) led Williamson, like Z. Talshir, to conclude that 1 Esdras never included anything before the reign of Josiah,[64] although one might guess that 1 Esdras once started with the beginning of Josiah's reign in 2 Chronicles 34.[65]

Much more crucial to the whole argument is the probability that 1 Esdr 9:37 is a translation of Neh 7:72 (73), and 1 Esdr 9:38 is a translation of Neh 8:1a.[66] Neh 7:72b (73b) is usually construed as the introduction to Ezra's reading of the law in Nehemiah 8, while 7:72a (73a) is taken as the conclusion of the list of returnees in 7:5b-72a (5b-73a). The verses preceding the list of returnees, 7:1-5a, are from the Nehemiah Memoir and report Nehemiah's observations about the insufficient population of Jerusalem. Williamson concludes that the list of returnees was included in the Nehemiah Memoir and that 7:72a (73a) forms a transition to the continuation of this document in Nehemiah 11, where lots are cast to bring ten percent of the people to Jerusalem.[67] The presence of a translation for 7:72a in 1 Esdras indicates that the translator knew the present shape of Nehemiah 7 and 8 and that therefore one cannot conclude that he knew a text of Ezra-Nehemiah to which the Nehemiah Memoir had not yet been added. Z. Talshir, who accepts the original unity of Chronicles-Ezra-

---

Organization for Septuagint and Cognate Studies: Leuven, 1989 (SBLSCS 31; Atlanta: Scholars Press, 1991) 37–49.

59 Z. Talshir, *From Origin to Translation*, 15–21. Talshir believes that this addition was first made in a Hebrew text of Chronicles and was not added by the translator himself. Arie van der Kooij, "Zur Frage des Anfangs des 1. Esrabuches," *ZAW* 103 (1991) 239–52, argues that 1:21-22 (23-24) has parallels in 2 Kgs 22:11-20 and 2 Chr 34:19-28 and that therefore 2 Chronicles 34 could not have been included in 1 Esdras.

60 "In ancient times the events of his reign have been recorded—concerning those who sinned and acted wickedly toward the Lord beyond any other people or kingdom, and how they grieved the Lord deeply, so that the words of the Lord fell upon Israel" *(NRSV)*.

61 Z. Talshir, *From Origin to Translation*, 17.

62 Z. Talshir, *Text Critical Commentary*, 38.

63 See also Tamara Eskenazi, "The Chronicler and the Composition of 1 Esdras," *CBQ* 48 (1986) 39–61.

64 *Israel*, 20.

65 Van der Kooij, "Zur Frage," argues that the present beginning of the book was also the original beginning.

66 See the comparison of the Greek of 1 Esdras with a Hebrew retroversion and the text of Neh 7:72 MT in Z. Talshir, *Text Critical Commentary*, 484.

67 *Ezra, Nehemiah*, 267–69.

Nehemiah, at least agrees with Williamson that one cannot conclude from 1 Esdras that Nehemiah 8 once followed directly after Ezra 10.[68] She believes that 1 Esdras omitted the story of Nehemiah in order to structure the history of the restoration around the figures of Zerubbabel and Ezra. Williamson and Z. Talshir have disproved that the text of 1 Esdras presupposes a Chronicler's History that still lacked the Nehemiah Memoir, and they have made it unlikely that 1 Esdras ever included any history before Josiah. For Williamson this takes 1 Esdras out of the proofs for an original history consisting of Chronicles-Ezra-Nehemiah;[69] for Z. Talshir it does not.

3. *Agreement in theology, purpose, and perspective between Chronicles and Ezra-Nehemiah?*[70] While no one would deny similarity in language and a focus on the cult in the two books, as well as a time of composition in the postexilic period, Japhet, Williamson, and Braun have pointed to theological or ideological distinctions between the two books that make common authorship unlikely. The principal pieces of evidence are the following:

a. *Attitude toward mixed marriages.* Ezra-Nehemiah is extremely critical of those who have intermarried. Ezra 9 refers to intermarriage with the peoples of the land (vv. 1-2), whose abhorrent practices are like those of the Hittites, Perizzites, Jebusites, Ammonites, Moabites, Egyptians, and Amorites.[71] The "peoples of the land"

are those who are not considered to be full members of the community, perhaps referring to those who had not been in exile and those who had not been fully accepted into the Golah community for other reasons.[72] The accusation of abhorrent practices might include the worship of other gods, sexual immorality, or following a detestable diet.[73] As a result of the criticism of intermarriage, more than one hundred men divorced their wives and sent their children away (Ezra 10:18-44). The problem of mixed marriages came up again during the tenure of Nehemiah, this time involving marriages with women of Ashdod, many of whose children spoke the language of Ashdod but not the language of Judah (Neh 13:23).[74] Nehemiah violently confronted those who had intermarried and forced them to take an oath not to give their daughters to the Ashdodite sons or take their daughters for their own sons (13:24-25). In 13:26 Nehemiah refers to Solomon's sin on account of such women. Chronicles nowhere condemns mixed marriages and in fact does not include the indictment against Solomon's many marriages with foreign women in 1 Kings 11. Even more remarkably, the Chronicler reports a number of other marriages of Israelites with foreigners without ever issuing a word of rebuke: 1 Chr 2:3, Judah marries a Canaanite Bath-shua; 2:17, David's sister Abigail bore a son to Jether the Ishmaelite; 2:34-35, the Judahite Sheshan gave his daughter to his Egyptian slave; 3:2,

---

68 *From Origin to Translation,* 34, 57.

69 H. G. M. Williamson, "The Problem with First Esdras," in *After the Exile: Essays in Honour of Rex Mason* (ed. J. Barton and D. J. Reimer; Macon, GA: Mercer Univ. Press, 1996) 201–16, repeats and expands his previous arguments, specifically claiming that the inclusion of Ezra 2 in 1 Esdras demonstrates that the book was based on the canonical form of Ezra and Nehemiah.

70 This section is based on J. D. Newsome, "Toward a New Understanding of the Chronicler and His Purposes," *JBL* 94 (1975) 201–17; Williamson, *Israel,* 60–70; idem, "Did the Author of Chronicles also Write the Books of Ezra and Nehemiah?" *BRev* 3 (1987) 56–59; Braun, "Chronicles, Ezra, and Nehemiah"; Tamara Eskenazi, *In an Age of Prose* (SBLMS 36; Atlanta: Scholars Press, 1988) 14–36; Japhet, "Relationship"; De Vries, 8–10. For the opposite position see Pohlmann, "Konvergenzen und Divergenzen." One of his stronger points is the series of references back from festivals to ever earlier figures that cuts across Chronicles and

Nehemiah: 2 Chr 30:26, Hezekiah's Passover and the time of Solomon; 2 Chr 35:18, Josiah's Passover and the time of Samuel; and Neh 8:17, the Feast of Booths and the time of Joshua. Of course, the author of 2 Chronicles could also have constructed the references in 2 Chronicles 30 and 35 on the basis of his knowledge of Nehemiah 8. Pohlmann finds anti-Levitical tendencies in Ezra and pro-Levitical tendencies in Nehemiah, and he believes that these two works were brought together by a Levite-friendly redaction that also expanded the role of the Levites in Chronicles at the same time.

71 I follow the translation of *JPS* (cf. *NIV*). According to *NRSV,* these intermarriages were with the Hittites and other foreigners in the list of pre-Israelite inhabitants.

72 See Klein, "Ezra & Nehemiah," 733.

73 See Bezalel Porten, *Archives from Elephantine* (Berkeley: Univ. of California Press, 1968) 249.

74 I believe the mention of Ammon and Moab in this verse is secondary. See Klein, "Ezra & Nehemiah," 848. The references from Nehemiah are all from

David himself was married to Maacah the daughter of Talmai king of Geshur; 4:17, the Judahite Mered married Bithiah daughter of Pharaoh; 4:22, some of the descendants of Shelah married into Moab; 7:14, Manasseh had an Aramean concubine; 8:8, the Benjaminite Shaharaim had sons in the country of Moab, presumably through a Moabite wife; 2 Chr 2:13 (14), Huram sends Huram-abi, the son of a Danite woman and a Tyrian father to work on the temple; 2 Chr 8:11, Solomon was married to Pharaoh's daughter; and 2 Chr 12:13, Rehoboam's mother was Naamah the Ammonite (she was the wife of Solomon).[75] The hostile attitude toward intermarriage in Ezra-Nehemiah contrasts strikingly with the nondefensive attitude in Chronicles toward such marriages. Ezra-Nehemiah seems to be dealing with a controversial contemporary issue; Chronicles is reporting events that happened more than five centuries earlier, but seems unperturbed by the intermarriages of that time.

b. *The early history of Israel.* Chronicles focuses on the patriarch Jacob, whom it always refers to by the name Israel.[76] The name Israel is substituted for "Abraham" in 1 Chr 16:13a in the Chronicler's quotation of Ps 105:6. In the genealogy at the beginning of the book, the beginning of the people as the elect of God seems to occur not with Abraham but with Israel (1 Chr 2:1-2; chaps. 2–8 give details of the descendants of the sons of Israel). In the *Vorlage* of Chronicles at 1 Kgs 3:8, the people are referred to as an entity that cannot be numbered or counted, using an expression that describes the descendants of Ishmael in Gen 16:10. When the Kings passage is incorporated in Chronicles (2 Chr 1:9), the people are said to be "as numerous as the dust of the earth." The latter expression is used of Jacob/Israel in Gen 28:14. In Chronicles the exodus tends to be downplayed or de-emphasized. In Solomon's prayer at the dedication of the temple in the Chronicler's *Vorlage,* the king refers to the exodus in 1 Kgs 8:21 and 53. In 1 Kgs 8:21 the king mentions the covenant Yahweh made with

the ancestors when he brought them out of the land of Egypt. That becomes the covenant Yahweh made with the Israelites in 2 Chr 6:11. The Chronicler does not include 1 Kgs 8:53, but in 2 Chr 6:41-42 he includes quotations from Ps 132:8-10 and 132:1, which contain a dynastic promise to David and report David's efforts on behalf of the ark. The high role of Jacob/Israel does not occur in Ezra. Nehemiah bases his appeal to Yahweh on the basis of the exodus (Neh 1:10), and the confession in Nehemiah 9 refers to the election of Abraham (vv. 7-8), and the exodus and related events, including the conquest, are central to vv. 9-25.

c. *The fall of the northern kingdom.* Chronicles does not include the fall of the northern kingdom from 2 Kings 17 and presupposes that the north is inhabited by genuine Israelites after the Assyrian conquest (2 Chr 30:5-11, 18, 25). The only reference to the exile of northern tribes mentions only the two and one-half Transjordanian tribes in 1 Chr 5:26 at the time of Tiglath-pileser. In Ezra, on the other hand, we find references to the resettlement of the land in the time of Esarhaddon (v. 2) and the time of Osnappar (v. 10; apparently a reference to Ashurbanipal). Zerubbabel sharply rejects the offer of the northerners connected to Esarhaddon to participate in the temple project (v. 3). The Chronicler, on the other hand, has a genuinely positive attitude toward the north. Six Judean kings have military and religious activities in the north: 2 Chr 15:8, Asa; 19:4, Jehoshaphat; 30:10-11, Hezekiah; 34:6, 21 (contrast 2 Kgs 22:13); 2 Chr 21:4, Jehoram; 2 Chronicles 28, Ahaz. After the division of the kingdom, priests and Levites from the north side with Rehoboam in Jerusalem, joined by representatives of all the tribes (11:16). Asa and Hezekiah make covenants with the people of the north (15:9-15; 31). Northerners released Judean captives, whom they described as their kin (28:8, 11). Monies for Josiah came from Ephraim, Manasseh, and the remnant of Israel (34:9).[77]

---

the Nehemiah Memoir and therefore are to be distinguished from the other parts of the Ezra-Nehemiah book.

75 The only exception is the marriage alliance Jehoshaphat made with the house of Ahab (2 Chr 18:1; 19:2; 22:3), but the issue here is more on the alliance Jehoshaphat made. Such alliances are often criticized by the Chronicler. Therefore, Pohlmann's

citing of this example ("Korrespondenzen und Divergenzen," 318) carries little force.

76 There are two exceptions, in 1 Chr 16:13, 17, where the Chronicler is quoting from the Psalter (Ps 105:6, 10).

77 See Roddy L. Braun, "A Reconsideration of the Chronicler's Attitude Toward the North," *JBL* 96 (1977) 59–62.

d. *Immediate retribution.* Chronicles is noted for its doctrine of retribution (see also below), in which a king, for example, is rewarded or punished for good deeds or errors within his own lifetime. There is virtually no trace of this doctrine in Ezra-Nehemiah, except in Ezra 9 (vv. 8, 9, and 15) and Nehemiah 9 (vv. 31, 33, and 36), which refer to God's righteousness in inflicting punishment, punishment understood as servitude, and talk of a remnant.[78] Gunneweg tries to downplay this difference by stating that while Chronicles uses retribution to support the fall of the northern kingdom and Judah, that justification was no longer necessary to repeat in the postexilic community.[79] In his opinion Chronicles had used retribution to explain the fall of Jerusalem, but in Ezra-Nehemiah retribution functions only as a warning.[80] Japhet has noted, however, that retribution in Chronicles is not simply a response to the fall of Jerusalem, but that each and every event in Israel's history has to be explained in terms of the Chronicler's belief system, and that the Chronicler feels compelled to explain good as well as evil.[81]

e. *The Nethinim and the sons of Solomon's servants.* These groups are mentioned throughout Ezra-Nehemiah, but they are absent from Chronicles except for an incidental mention of the Nethinim in 1 Chr 9:2, which is borrowed from Neh 11:3. The Chronicler considered the gatekeepers (1 Chr 9:17-18) and the singers (2 Chr 5:12) Levites, while they have not attained this status in Ezra-Nehemiah (Ezra 7:24; Neh 11:19; 13:10).[82]

f. *Israel.* In Chronicles Israel is described as made up of the twelve tribes, and the Chronicler uses the term "remnant" to refer to those in the north, or in both kingdoms, after the fall of Samaria (cf. 2 Chr 30:6; 34:9, 21).[83] Ezra on the other hand distinguishes sharply between the "holy seed" and the other peoples of the lands (Ezra 9:2; cf. 3:3; 4:1-5), and "Israel" consists of Judah and Benjamin, the postexilic community.[84] In criticism of this point in general and von Rad in particular, Pohlmann calls attention to Ezra 6:21, where the Passover is eaten in Israel by the people of Israel who had returned from exile, and also by everyone who had joined them and separated themselves from the pollutions of the peoples of the land. He argues that the Golah community in Ezra is seen as "the true Israel," but also as a kind of core ("Kernisrael") to which others can join.[85]

g. *Greater emphasis on the Davidic monarchy in Chronicles.*[86] Chronicles is dominated by David and the covenant Yahweh made with him,[87] while David plays a minor role in Ezra-Nehemiah and no mention is made of the covenant with him.[88] Abijah's sermon in 2 Chronicles 13 stresses the eternal character of the Davidic rule (cf. 1 Chr 12:39-40; 17:13-14; 22:9-10; and 28:6-7). Ezra-Nehemiah, on the other hand, insists on the importance of the Sinai covenant and the promise to Israel's ancestors, and makes no reference to the Davidic ancestry of Zerubbabel (cf. 1 Chr 3:19; Hag 2:23). Scholars are divided on whether there is a messianic hope in Chronicles; there is surely not one in Ezra-Nehemiah.

These substantive differences in theology, purpose, and perspective have convinced me that Chronicles and Ezra-Nehemiah are separate works, each of which needs to be interpreted in its own right.[89]

---

78   See Braun, "Chronicles, Ezra, and Nehemiah," 55.
79   *Esra*, 26.
80   A future falling away from God would lead to the destruction of the ransomed remnant as well (Ezra 9:14). Cf. also Pohlmann, "Konvergenzen und Divergenzen," 318.
81   *Ideology*, 154–55, and see in general her discussion of guiding principles for divine action and retribution, 150–76.
82   See Japhet, "Supposed Common Authorship," 351–54. Nehemiah 11 is later than Ezra 2//Nehemiah 7 since the singers are included among the Levites (Neh 11:15-17), although the gatekeepers have not yet attained Levitical status in this document (v. 19).
83   See Williamson, *Israel*, 125–26.
84   Von Rad, *Geschichtsbild*, 24.
85   "Konvergenzen und Divergenzen," 322–23.
86   See Sara Japhet, "Sheshbazzar and Zerubbabel against the Background of the Historical and Religious Tendencies of Ezra-Nehemiah," *ZAW* 94 (1982) 68–80.
87   1 Chr 17:1-15; 2 Chr 7:18; 13:5; 21:7; 23:3.
88   In Ezra 3:10 and Neh 12:24 reference is made to David's liturgical instructions.
89   Japhet, "Relationship," 306, concludes: "It is true that some of these points [similar to those rehearsed above] are debated among scholars, and in certain cases different views on the scope of the books under consideration, and their supposed sources, may influence a scholar's stand; still, the overwhelming accumulation and variety of issues suffice to show how different the two theological voices are."

Unity

In the commentary on 1 Chronicles in this volume I have ascribed very few passages to a second hand, a trend already evident in the commentaries by Williamson, 12–15,[90] De Vries, 13,[91] Japhet, 7, and Johnstone, 1:22.[92] This contrasts with the majority of commentators in the twentieth century and with a number of recent European monographs as well.[93] My approach is based in part on the general trend in much current scholarship, particularly in North America, to focus on the final form of the text[94] in a synchronic fashion. It also results from my belief that the reasons given for considering passages secondary are often weak and ambivalent or flow from circular reasoning. For example, in *Chronicler's History,* Noth argued that the Chronicler did not put much emphasis on the Levites only after he had deleted most of the passages from 1 Chronicles that emphasize the Levites. Noth also deleted most of the genealogical information in chaps. 2–8 because of his opinion that the Chronicler only included the material corresponding to Numbers 26 (and Genesis 46) in his genealogy of the twelve tribes. While the Chronicler's reliance on Genesis 46 and Numbers 26 is undeniable, this need not have prevented him from including tribal genealogical information available from other sources. My reticence to identify

secondary passages can be contrasted with the alternate conclusions outlined in the following paragraphs.

The commentary on 1 Chronicles by Rothstein and Hänel identified a number of redactions in Chronicles. The oldest redaction, Ch[P], was completed soon after 432 BCE, and reflected the fact that the Chronicler still used P as a separate literary entity. The person responsible for this redaction used the *Vorlage* of Samuel-Kings[95] and also the canonical Samuel-Kings. The redaction that Rothstein and Hänel called Ch[R] was written about 400 BCE and relied on the completed version of the Hexateuch and the canonical version of Samuel-Kings. Rothstein and Hänel also referred to an earlier redaction of 1 Chr 15:1–16:3, which they called Ch[G] and dated to the time of Ezra. Between Ch[P] (432 BCE) and Ch[R] (400 BCE), they found a redaction Ch[M] in chaps. 15 and 22–27. In their opinion there were numerous isolated additions after Ch[R].

In *Postexilic Judaism* and *Work of the Chronicler,* Adam C. Welch posited two editions of Chronicles. The first author, who worked during the exile, about the time of Ezekiel, based his work on the pentateuchal source D. This author may never have been in exile. Welch considered 1 Chronicles 1–9 as a later addition, as was any passage that shows influence from the Priestly source.[96] The reviser, who was active shortly after the exile, based his

---

90 Williamson ascribes a few passages in chaps. 15–16 (15:4, 11, 14; 16:6); 23:13b-14, 25-32; 24:1-19, 20-32; 25:7-31; 26:4-8, 12-18; 27:1-34, and a few isolated other passages to a pro-priestly redactor, who worked about a generation after the Chronicler himself. See Williamson, "Origins."

91 De Vries provides a list of thirteen minor glosses and the following substantive expansions: 1 Chr 2:34-41, 42-50aβ, 52-55; 6:35-38 (50-53); 15:23-24; 23:24b-32; 24:1-19, 20-31; 25:7-31; 26:4-8, 12-18; 27:1-34; 2 Chr 24:5b-6; 29:25; 34:6-9, 11-16.

92 See already Myers, 1:lxiii.

93 See now Kratz, *Komposition,* 14–53. He ascribes only 1 Chr 2:1-2, 3a, 4-5, 9-15, from the first eleven chapters of 1 Chronicles to the original composition and finds large parts of the rest of the two books to be secondary additions as well (see chart on pp. 52–53). He finds the genealogy of Judah/David a "passable beginning" to the history of the kingdom that begins in 1 Chronicles 11. Since he notes, however, that all Israel" gathered before David (11:1), he includes 2:1-2 (the list of the twelve sons of

Israel) in the original draft (p. 27). With such radical surgery, one only reconstructs and interprets a document of one's own making, having little to do with the accomplishment of the Chronicler himself. As this commentary will show, both the genealogies in 1 Chronicles 1–9 and the report of the death of Saul in 1 Chronicles 10 are indispensable for understanding the Chronicler's purpose.

94 I understand "final form" to include revisions made via the principles of textual criticism.

95 Throughout this commentary I will be referring to the text of Samuel-Kings used by the Chronicler as his *Vorlage* (the manuscript of Samuel-Kings that lay before him). Rothstein and Hänel in this case are using this term to refer to an earlier historical account that was used by the author of Samuel-Kings in composing his work.

96 Note that this is directly opposite to the hypothesis of Rothstein and Hänel.

revisions on P and focused on questions about temple, personnel, and cult.

Martin Noth, who held to a single Chronicler as the author of the book, considered the following passages in 1 Chronicles[97] secondary: 12:1-23;[98] 12:24-41; 15:4-10, 16-24; 16:5-38,[99] 41-42; 22:17-19;[100] 23:3—27:34.[101] From the genealogies in 1 Chronicles 1–9 Noth retained *only* 1:1—2:5; 2:9-15;[102] 4:24; 5:3; 6:1-4, 34-48 (16-19, 49-53); 7:1, 12-13,[103] 14-19 (in part); 7:20, 30; 8:1. His criterion for originality in chaps. 2–8 was that the Chronicler originally included only such genealogical material as is found in Numbers 26 (paralleled in part in Genesis 46). He judged 1 Chr 9:1-34, the inhabitants of Jerusalem, secondary since Jerusalem is captured only later in the narrative. On the list of Gibeonites in 8:29-32//9:35-38, he remarked that the Chronicler had no reason to include this material. He admits that part of the genealogy of Saul in 8:33-40//9:39-44 might have been included, but decides that the genealogy is traced down much too far and, besides, 7:12 shows that the Chronicler would only include the genealogy of Benjamin from Numbers 26.[104]

In his commentary in 1954 Kurt Galling identified two Chroniclers who had similar outlooks but differed in their attitude toward their sources. The first Chronicler, ChrG, was anti-Samaritan and did his work around 300 BCE. The second Chronicler, about 200 BCE, included the Nehemiah Memoir in the Chronicler's History and interwove the careers of Ezra and Nehemiah. This second Chronicler added the lists of priests and Levites in chaps. 23–27 and many other passages.[105]

Frank Moore Cross identified three stages in the redaction of Chronicles: Chr[1] includes a genealogical introduction, much of 1 Chronicles 10–2 Chronicles 34, and the *Vorlage* of 1 Esdr 1:1—2:15; 5:1-62 (2 Chronicles 35–36; Ezra 1:1—3:13).[106] This stage of the work was designed to support the restoration of the kingdom under Zerubbabel during the late sixth century; Chr[2] includes a short version of the genealogical lore in 1 Chronicles 1–9 plus 1 Chronicles 10–2 Chronicles 34 and the *Vorlage* of 1 Esdras (2 Chronicles 35–36; Ezra 1–10; and Nehemiah 8), and it was written after Ezra's mission in 458 BCE;[107] and Chr[3] is the final form of the Chronicler's History, encompassing all of 1 and 2 Chronicles and Hebrew Ezra-Nehemiah, and was dated by

---

97 Noth, *Chronicler's History,* 36, found few additions in 2 Chronicles: 2 Chr 5:11bβ, and the mention of the singers in 5:12a and 13a, and perhaps in 8:14-15. He also found small additions in 23:18 and 35:15. The list of additions in Rudolph, 1–5, is remarkably similar to Noth for 1 Chronicles, but he finds significantly more secondary passages in 2 Chronicles. Willi, *Chronik als Auslegung,* 194–204, largely follows Noth and Rudolph in identifying secondary passages in 1 Chronicles, but he finds many more secondary cultically oriented passages in 2 Chronicles. While he denies these passages came from a single "second Chronicler," he notes that many of them deal with cultic organization and were probably made at the turn from the 3d to the 2d century BCE.

98 This passage was added later than 1 Chr 12:24-41.

99 The psalm materials in vv. 7-36 were a more recent element within this addition.

100 Noth, *Chronicler's History,* 149, n. 2, was uncertain about 1 Chr 22:14-16.

101 Noth also believed the words "priests and Levites" in 1 Chr 23:2 were part of this expansion.

102 1 Chr 2:16-17 were an addition based on 2 Sam 2:18 and 17:25.

103 Noth, *Chronicler's History,* 37, conjecturally reconstructed this text and then used the reconstruction as a template to determine which parts of the rest

of the genealogies were original. See the discussion in the commentary.

104 Mosis, *Untersuchungen,* 44, follows Noth on 1 Chr 23:(2b)—27:34 and also identifies some secondary passages in 1 Chronicles 22, 28, and 29.

105 For a critique of this position see Welten, *Geschichte und Geschichtsdarstellungen,* 189–91. Many of the "topoi" studied by Welten in 2 Chronicles had been assigned to the second Chronicler by Galling. On 1 Chronicles Galling assigned to the second Chronicler passages that Noth also considered secondary, but Galling assigned them to one revision while Noth interpreted them as independent additions at various times.

106 "Reconstruction," 11–14. Cf. Newsome, "Toward a New Understanding," 201–17; and Petersen, *Late Israelite Prophecy,* 57–60. In *From Epic to Canon,* 165–69, Cross slightly revised his hypothesis to include some of the genealogical introduction in all three editions. This revised position is described in my summary.

107 Cross believes that this recension included the story of the three pages (1 Esdr 3:1—5:6), but that this story was later suppressed by the redactor responsible for Chr[3]. A number of recent studies, however, have indicated that 1 Esdras is a literary work in its own right and was built around the story of the

Cross to about 400 BCE or shortly thereafter. Cross deals with large units and does not deal with redactional issues in individual passages. The ending for his Chr[1] is determined by his very early date for the Chronicler, and his identification of the passages in Chr[2] is the result of his decision that 1 Esdras is a fragment of the original arrangement of the Chronicler's History that from the start included (parts of) Ezra, with Nehemiah following immediately after Ezra 10.[108]

Date

Kai Peltonen[109] and Isaac Kalimi[110] have published recent articles on the date of the books of Chronicles, and the following discussion is dependent on their research. Decisions about the unity or lack of unity of Chronicles with Ezra-Nehemiah are crucial in this discussion, as are the questions about secondary passages in Chronicles itself.[111] During the time I have been working on Chronicles, scholars have proposed a wide array of dates for the composition of this work, from 520–515 BCE to the Maccabean era (ca. 160 BCE), thus ranging over three and a half centuries.[112] The narrative sections of Chronicles tell the story of the death of Saul, Israel's first king, and the subsequent history of the united and Judean monarchies, until the exile in 586 BCE. The last

events reported in Chronicles are the seventy-year sabbath rest of the land (2 Chr 36:21)[113] and the decree of Cyrus permitting Jews to return home from Mesopotamia and rebuild the temple in 539 BCE (36:22-23).[114] There is unanimous agreement among recent scholars, therefore, that this is a postexilic work, but the evidence for a more specific date within that period is thin and ambiguous. The author of Chronicles mentions no historical events after the genealogical reference to Zerubbabel (except for his descendants in 1 Chr 3:20-24),[115] and which religious, social, economic, or political conditions he is addressing with this massive book must be inferred indirectly from the issues emphasized in the book.

The description of David in the apocryphal book of Sirach (usually dated 200–180 BCE) seems to presuppose the Chronicler's depiction of David: "He [David] placed singers before the altar, to make sweet melody with their voices. He gave beauty to the festivals, and arranged their times throughout the year" (47:9-10). Eupolemos, a Jewish historian who flourished about 150 BCE in Judea, seems to have known Chronicles in a Greek translation.[116] These witnesses set a terminus ante quem in the early second century BCE.

The earliest date in the current discussion, the late sixth century, is associated with Braun, xxix, Cross

---

three pages. See Steven L. McKenzie, "The Chronicler as Redactor," in Graham and McKenzie, *Chronicler as Author*, 72–78; Z. Talshir, *From Origin to Translation*, 3–109; and Williamson, "Problem with 1 Esdras."

108 Cross's Chr[1] is dependent in part on an article by David Noel Freedman, "The Chronicler's Purpose," *CBQ* 23 (1961) 436–42.

109 Peltonen, "Jigsaw," 225–71. Peltonen also reviews the proposals of Joel Weinberg and Rainer Albertz, who attempted to connect the emphases in Chronicles to specific chronological settings (late 5th century and between 330 and 250 BCE, respectively). But they offer no more evidence in addition to that surveyed below, and their re-creation of the issues allegedly addressed by the Chronicler is equally unsure.

110 Kalimi, "Abfassungszeit," 223–33. See also idem, "Könnte die aramäische Grabinschrift aus Ägypten als Indikation für die Datierung der Chronikbücher fungieren"? *ZAW* 110 (1998) 79–82. This inscription of Akabiah the son of Elioenai dates to the early 3d century. Akkub the son of Elioenai is mentioned in 1 Chr 3:24, but his brother Anani is mentioned in

an Elephantine papyrus from the late 5th century.

111 These questions concern especially the genealogies and lists in 1 Chronicles 1–9; 12:1-23 (22); 23–27, and parts of chaps. 15–16. See the discussion of Unity above. If the genealogy of the descendants of Jehoiachin is part of the original edition, a date no earlier than ca. 400 BCE is possible.

112 Somewhat earlier, Welch, *Work*, 156, even made the time of the Chronicler contemporary with the programs of Ezekiel in the first half of the 6th century.

113 The exile in fact lasted only from 586 to 538, or forty-eight years.

114 Zerubbabel, a leader in the early postexilic community, is mentioned in 1 Chr 3:19.

115 This makes Chronicles distinctly different from Ezra-Nehemiah, which records the work of Ezra and Nehemiah in the 5th century. Some, who date Ezra to Artaxerxes II, would extend that date into the 4th century.

116 See Kalimi, "History of Interpretation," 14–17; and Ehud Ben Zvi, "The Authority of 1-2 Chronicles in the Late Second Temple Period," *JSP* 3 (1988) 72–73, and nn. 73–74, p. 84. The relevance of Sirach and Eupolemus has been recently challenged

(Chr[1]),[117] Dillard, xix, Freedman (515 BCE),[118] McKenzie,[119] Newsome (525–515 BCE),[120] Petersen,[121] Throntveit (527–527 BCE),[122] and Willoughby.[123] Advocates of a third-century date include Noth (300–200 BCE),[124] Pfeiffer (250 BCE or a little earlier),[125] Smend,[126] Strübind,[127] Torrey (250 BCE or a little later),[128] and Welten (300–250 BCE),[129] and a second-century date is supported by Spinoza[130] and Steins.[131] Driver (shortly after 333 BCE)[132] and Wellhausen[133] dated the book after the fall of Persia, and Willi placed it either toward the end of the Persian Empire or at the beginning of the Hellenistic period.[134] The date of 400 or a little later is chosen by Albright,[135] Myers, Rudolph, X (first decades of 4th century BCE), and Rothstein-Hänel.[136] Perhaps a majority of scholars, including myself, argue for a fourth-century date: Allen, 301 (first half of 4th century), Curtis and Madsen, 6 (close of the 4th century, ca. 300 BCE), De Vries, 16, Japhet, 23–28, Kleinig,[137] Oeming,[138] and Williamson, 16.

The following evidence in Chronicles itself is usually brought into the discussion:

• The genealogy of the sons of Jehoiachin (1 Chr 3:17-24). The MT extends the genealogy after Zerubbabel, who flourished about 520 and may have been born about 575, for six generations, but the LXX extends his descendants to a full eleven generations. If one calculates twenty years to a generation,[139] the MT would imply a date in the late fifth century at the earliest; the LXX would extend

by Steins, *Chronik*, 491–93. McKenzie, 15, claims that Chronicles is also cited or alluded to in 1 Maccabees (90 BCE), Daniel (ca. 165 BCE), and certain of the Dead Sea Scrolls (ca. 200 BCE).

117 Cross, "Reconstruction," 4–18. The second and third editions identified by Cross were composed in 450 and 400 or a little later.

118 Freedman, "Chronicler's Purpose."

119 McKenzie, *Chronicler's Use*, 25–26.

120 Newsome, "Toward a New Understanding."

121 Petersen, *Late Israelite Prophecy*, 58.

122 Throntveit, *When Kings Speak*, 97–107.

123 B. E. Willoughby, "I and II Chronicles, Ezra, Nehemiah," in *The Books of the Bible* (ed. B. W. Anderson; New York: Scribner's, 1989) 1:155–59.

124 *Chronicler's History*, 73, 83–87. Noth thought that Chronicles was written in reaction to the schism with the Samaritans, although the decisive break with that community is now dated much later, to the last years of the 2d century BCE. See Frank Moore Cross, "Aspects of Samaritan and Jewish History in Late Persian and Hellenistic Times," *HTR* 59 (1966) 201–11.

125 Robert H. Pfeiffer, *Introduction to the Old Testament* (New York: Harper, 1948) 811–12.

126 Rudolph Smend, *Die Entstehung des Alten Testaments* (3d ed.; Theologische Wissenschaft 1; Stuttgart: Kohlhammer, 1984) 228.

127 Strübind, *Tradition als Interpretation*, 23–25, 200.

128 *Ezra Studies*, 30, 35.

129 Welten, *Geschichte und Geschichtsdarstellung*, 199–200.

130 He dated it after the restoration of the temple by Judah the Maccabee; hence after 166 BCE. Spinoza thought that some pseudepigraphical books were better than Chronicles. See Kalimi, "History of Interpretation," 39.

131 Steins, *Chronik*, 491–99. Steins mentions an article

by Ulrich Kellermann, "Anmerkungen zum Verständnis der Tora in den chronistischen Schriften," *BN* 42 (1988) 49–92, which identifies striking agreements between the picture of cultic irregularities and cultic reforms in 1-2 Chronicles on the one hand and 1-2 Maccabees on the other. The only substantive difference between Chronicles and the later period is in the abolition of circumcision in 1 and 2 Maccabees. Kellermann himself dates Chronicles to the early 3d century. Steins argues that the Chronicler did not just anticipate the threat that became reality in the 2d century, but he was reacting to the challenges of the Maccabean period itself.

132 *Introduction*, 518.

133 *Prolegomena*, 171.

134 See Kalimi, "Abfassungszeit," 227. Galling dated the first edition of Chronicles to 300 and the second to 200.

135 William Foxwell Albright, "The Date and Personality of the Chronicler," *JBL* 40 (1921) 119–21.

136 Rothstein-Hänel, lxix, date the original composition to 432 BCE, with the final form achieved by ca. 400.

137 Kleinig, *Lord's Song*, 22.

138 Oeming, *Das wahre Israel*, 44–47.

139 The number twenty is only a very approximate round number and perhaps should be considerably higher. Kalimi, "Abfassungszeit," 230, lists proposals ranging from twenty to thirty years per generation. Kalimi himself chooses twenty-three or twenty-four, and dates the end of the genealogy to 382–376 BCE. The date of Zerubbabel's birth is only an educated guess.

the date to the early third century (see textual notes 33-37 to chap. 3 and the commentary to 1 Chronicles 3).[140] Supporters of a sixth-century date argue that this genealogy was not part of the original edition of Chronicles.

- The reference to Persian coins, ten thousand darics, in 29:7. This coin was first minted by Darius I (522–486 BCE). This coin is backdated by the Chronicler to the reign of David, and it is felt that some time would have had to pass since its first appearance for the author to commit such an anachronism. Hence a date late in the fifth century for Chronicles would seem to be the earliest possible moment.[141]

- The connection between Tadmor and Hamath-zobah in 2 Chr 8:3-4 seems to reflect the Persian provincial administration and would put the Chronicler in the Persian period (539–333 BCE).[142]

- The Chronicler writes that the laments spoken about Josiah can be found in "the Lamentations" (הקינות; 2 Chr 35:25). Japhet, 27, mentions that Lamentations had an influence on Chronicles and suggests (p. 1043) that the reference to lamentations in 2 Chr 35:25 points to the biblical book by the same name. But the biblical book is usually known by its first word, איכה. The word קינה does not appear in Lamentations, but is used of the book in later rabbinic tradition.

- The seer Hanani seems to quote Zech 4:10 in his address to Asa (2 Chr 16:9). Zechariah flourished in the last quarter of the sixth century, and sufficient time would again need to pass for his work to be cited as an authoritative source.[143]

- Two passages in Chronicles have been borrowed from Ezra-Nehemiah: 1 Chr 9:2-17 (from Neh 11:3-19) and 2 Chr 36:22-23 (from Ezra 1:1-3a).[144] If Ezra-Nehemiah is dated to about 400 BCE, Chronicles would be somewhat later. While I believe that the first of these passages at least is a part of the original book of Chronicles, that is by no means a unanimous position, and the originality of 2 Chr 36:22-23 is also much debated. Japhet, 26–27, notes in general that the development of cultic institutions and personnel in Chronicles seems to be later than Ezra-Nehemiah. The singers in Chronicles are considered Levites, but that is not yet the case in Ezra 2:41//Neh 7:44. The gatekeepers are Levites in 1 Chr 9:18, but this is not yet the case in Ezra 2:42//Neh 7:45, nor even in Neh 11:19. Nehemiah 8 reports Ezra reading the book of the law of Moses as if it were a novel event, but Chronicles implies that this same book has always been at hand (De Vries, 17). The organization of the twenty-four priestly courses in 1 Chronicles 24 would again suggest a date (considerably) later than Ezra-Nehemiah, but the originality of this chapter in Chronicles itself is hotly debated.[145]

- If the war machines mentioned in 2 Chr 26:15 are catapults, it might suggest a Hellenistic date for Chronicles, since catapults were first used about 400 BCE in Syracuse, but the Persians may have had a device for hurling large stones almost a century earlier than that.[146]

- Linguistic evidence discussed earlier in this introduction supports a postexilic date for Chronicles, since the language of Chronicles is part of Late

---

140 A papyrus from Elephantine in 407 BCE was sent to Bagohi, the governor of Yehud, Jehohanan the high priest, and Ostanes the brother of Anani, asking for permission to rebuild their destroyed temple in Egypt. Is this Anani the same as the last person named in 1 Chr 3:24?

141 Mosis, *Untersuchungen*, 105–6, and Throntveit, *When Kings Speak*, 97–107, believe that this reference is part of a secondary addition to Chronicles.

142 See Williamson, 229–30.

143 Cf. also Zech 1:2-4 and 2 Chr 30:6-7, and Zech 8:10 and 2 Chr 15:5-6. McKenzie, 18, refers to allusions to Malachi in 2 Chr 30:6-9 and the influence of Lamentations on 2 Chronicles 30.

144 Allen, 300, believes that Ezra 9–10 is also reflected in 2 Chr 24:26. The conspirators who killed Joash

according to the latter verse are made sons of Ammonite and Moabite women due to an association with names in Ezra 10:22-23, 27, 33, 43. See also M. P. Graham, "A Connection Proposed Between II Chr 24, 26 and Ezra 9-10," *ZAW* 97 (1985) 256–58.

145 Cf. also the organization into twenty-four of the Levites, singers, and gatekeepers in chaps. 23, 25, 26, though the originality of these chapters is also contested.

146 See esp. Welten, *Geschichte und Geschichtsdarstellung*, 98–114, for the argument based on the late invention of the catapult, and Williamson, 337–38, for the earlier evidence for the Persians hurling stones.

Biblical Hebrew.[147] But the present state of typological linguistic investigation does not allow a more specific identification of time within the postexilic period. The lack of evidence for Greek influence or terminology might suggest a date before the time of Alexander.[148] The introduction to Daniel 2–6, composed some time before the Maccabean period, presupposes knowledge of 2 Chr 36:6b-7, not included in 2 Kgs 24:1. Daniel (1:1-2) refers to the vessels of the house of God that were taken by the Babylonians during the reign of Jehoiakim.[149] As noted above, the Wisdom of Jesus the Son of Sirach (= Ecclesiasticus), in 47:8-10, at the beginning of the second century BCE, hails David as the one who established singers and musical groups in the Jerusalem temple.[150]

Other, external evidence is equally ambiguous. If the author of Chronicles was Ezra, as affirmed by the Talmud and supported in the twentieth century by W. F. Albright,[151] a more precise date might be achieved. But the date of Ezra himself is uncertain (did he come to Jerusalem in 458 or 398?), and my discussion of the extent of the Chronicler's history has argued that Chronicles and Ezra-Nehemiah are quite separate works, and that Chronicles is likely written later than Ezra-Nehemiah. The author of Chronicles also knew the Pentateuch[152] and the Deuteronomistic History in their more or less final form. The final form of the Deuteronomistic History is no earlier than 550, and the textual differences between the text of Samuel-Kings used by the Chronicler and the MT (see the discussion of Textual Criticism below) suggests that some time had passed since that mid-sixth-century date.[153] The date of the composition of the Pentateuch is also highly contested, with a common opinion placing that date at about 400.

The working hypothesis that I follow is that Chronicles was composed in the first half of the fourth century BCE, before the end of the Persian period and the arrival of Alexander the Great.

Author and Place

The author of Chronicles is anonymous,[154] and his identity can only be clarified by his interests: the Davidic

---

147 See esp. Polzin, *Late Biblical Hebrew*, 12-15, 27-84.
148 Cf. Peter R. Ackroyd, *The Age of the Chronicler* (Auckland: Commercial, 1970) 7–8. As Peltonen, "Jigsaw," 238, admits, the degree of Persian impact on Chronicles is also quite meager. Japhet, 26, notes the small number of Persian words: גנזך (1 Chr 28:11), פרבר (26:18), and אדרכן (29:7). She suggests that this might place the date of authorship just after the Persian period and before major Hellenistic influence, i.e., in the last part of the 4th century. Gary N. Knoppers, "Classical Historiography and the Chronicler's History: A Re-examination," *JBL* 122 (2003) 627–50, believes that a number of features of the Chronicler's use of genealogies can best be explained by analogy to Greek historiography. He also points out that Greek influence was present in Palestine long before the arrival of Alexander the Great.
149 See Kalimi, "History of Interpretation," 9–10. For other citations of Chronicles in late Second Temple period literature, see Ben Zvi, "Authority of 1-2 Chronicles," 59–88. Both authors note the relative inattention to Chronicles in Jewish sources. See the disparaging rabbinic references in Ben Zvi, 85, n. 86.
150 Cf. 1 Chr 15:16-21; 16:4-42; 25:1-31. See Kalimi, "History of Interpretation," 12, and Ben Zvi,

"Authority of 1-2 Chronicles," who claims, however, that this was a widespread tradition concerning David and therefore the dependence in this case is not conclusive.
151 Albright, "Date and Personality," 104–24.
152 See Schniedewind, *Word of God*, 133, n. 11; 194, n. 16. In both notes Schniedewind criticizes Judson R. Shaver, *Torah and the Chronicler's History Work* (BJS 196; Atlanta: Scholars Press, 1989), who had argued that the Chronicler's law book was not the Pentateuch in its present form.
153 McKenzie, *Chronicler's Use*, 189–210, proposed that the first edition of Chronicles only used the first edition of the Deuteronomistic History (= Dtr[1], purportedly composed in preexilic times). But see the discussion and criticism of this theory under Textual Criticism.
154 *b. B. Batra* 15a ascribed authorship to Ezra. Japhet, "Relationship," 298, points out that the medieval exegete David Kimḥi ascribed a minor role to Ezra in composing Chronicles.

dynasty and especially its support of the temple in Jerusalem, its clergy, and its cult. His emphasis on the Levites has sometimes been taken as an indication of his own Levitical identity, although that only seems to me only a possibility rather than a probability. But his deep knowledge of the temple, its ritual, and its clergy does suggest he was numbered among the temple personnel. He was certainly a resident of the postexilic province of Yehud and probably of Jerusalem itself. While the Chronicler was no doubt part of a larger movement of thought, there is no reason to think that the book was composed by a "corporate personality" or school rather than an individual.[155]

Nature of the Work

Form criticism in biblical studies has often fared better with shorter genres, such as laments, miracle stories, prophetic oracles, or proverbs than with larger compositions, such as the Pentateuch or the New Testament Gospels. Attempts to define these larger works build largely on deductions made from the texts themselves, from comparison with biblical works or known extra-biblical documents.

In trying to understand the nature of the writing in 1 and 2 Chronicles a number of hypotheses have been put forth.[156] Wellhausen considered Chronicles "midrash," a Jewish type of exegesis operating with far different presuppositions than modern critical exegesis. For Wellhausen, whose views here may be tinged with an anti-Judaic spirit, the free way in which the Chronicler reinterpreted and reworked his sources destroyed the credibility of the work as a historical source for the pre-exilic period.

Thomas Willi, who is writing a major commentary on Chronicles in the Biblischer Kommentar series, classifies Chronicles as "interpretation" or "exegesis"; that is, it is an interpretation of significant parts of the Deuteronomistic History, which he believed was considered canonical at the time of the Chronicler. Kalimi raises seven criticisms of this point of view: (1) The books of Samuel and Kings were not considered canonical or at least not as immutable by the Chronicler; (2) the exegetical methods used by the rabbinic sages in their interpretation of the Pentateuch were not known by the Chronicler and attempts to find them in Chronicles are anachronistic; (3) the Chronicler's main purpose was not exegesis—the Chronicler often included texts from Samuel-Kings without comment even though they bristled with difficulties, and about half of the material in the book of Chronicles comes from no biblical source; (4) there are hundreds of literary, stylistic, and linguistic differences between Chronicles and its *Vorlage* that do not fall under the category of commentary; (5) the Chronicler omitted many texts from Samuel and Kings and rearranged others—the genre "commentary" does not explain this; (6) most of the changes in Chronicles stem from his usage of earlier works, in which he saw difficulties or contradictions with other biblical passages, or he attempted to provide evaluations of his sources; and (7) the category of commentary totally negates the value of Chronicles as a source for the preexilic period. Although much information in Chronicles is historically unreliable, the Chronicler also included texts with indispensable historical information.[157]

Kalimi dismisses those who consider the Chronicler as a theologian although one might argue whether theologians necessarily write in the genre of contemporary

---

155 Japhet, "Relationship," 312.

156 I am especially indebted for the following discussion to Isaac Kalimi, "Was the Chronicler a Historian?" in *The Chronicler as Historian: Essays in Honor of Ralph W. Klein* (ed. M. Patrick Graham, Steven L. McKenzie, and Gary N. Knoppers; London: T & T Clark, 2003) 73–89. See also Kenneth G. Hoglund, "The Chronicler as Historian: A Comparativist Perspective," in *Chronicler as Historian*, 19–29. See also Tomotoshi Sugimoto, "The Chronicler's Techniques in Quoting Samuel-Kings," *AJBI* 16 (1990) 30–70.

157 Perhaps Chronicles could also be compared with the genre called "rewritten Bible," known from

Qumran and in the works of Josephus. Such works retell some portion of the Bible while interpreting it through paraphrase, elaboration, allusion to other texts, expansion, conflation, rearrangement, and other techniques. In this case, of course, the "rewritten Bible" also became part of the Bible itself. For a study of this genre and its characteristics, which identifies Chronicles as an early forerunner of the rewritten Bible, see Philip S. Alexander, "Retelling the Old Testament," in *It Is Written: Scripture Citing Scripture. Essays in Honour of Barnabas Lindars, SSFI* (ed. D. A. Carson and H. G. M. Williamson; Cambridge: Cambridge Univ. Press, 1988) 99–121.

systematic theologians or whether the Yahwist or Second Isaiah were not also theologians. The trouble with the classification of the Chronicler as theologian or his work as theological is that it does not clarify a great deal about how the Chronicler went about his task. The theological emphases underlined by Ackroyd in his brief commentary and in numerous other publications indicate quite clearly the importance of theology in the agenda of the Chronicler and therefore make Kalimi's criticism of this label an overstatement at the least.[158]

Kalimi insists, finally, that the Chronicler is a historian: "The author deals with the past; he collects material from the earlier books and perhaps additional sources; he selects from the sources, evaluates, and interprets them; he makes connections between the sources; and above all, his work as a whole is imprinted with a unique 'philosophy of history.'"[159] The difference of course is that this evaluation of his earlier sources is only done implicitly. As a narrator of past events, according to Kalimi, he deserves the title historian, although what he writes is sacred rather than secular history. He articulates his view in the guise of speeches and prayers by leading figures. Kalimi considers the Chronicler a creative artist, who selects material suitable to his purposes from earlier sources and presents his account in a fresh style, in a new literary mode. The Chronicler is a different kind of historian than the Deuteronomistic Historian or nearly contemporary Greek historians, and dramatically different from post-Enlightenment historians as well. Every generation has its own kind of historian.[160]

Kenneth G. Hoglund (see note 156) attempts to explain some of the ways in which the Chronicler differs from the Deuteronomist by comparing him to ancient Greek works of historiography. He compares the opening nine chapters of genealogy to the style of Acusilaus of Argo (early 5th century BCE), but one might suppose that the Chronicler and his audience were directly familiar with the sociological function of genealogies and so came independently to using them in a literary work.[161] Hoglund compares the role of the prophets in Chronicles to the "wise counselors" in Greek histories, but there is a much more direct source for this function of the prophets in the roles of prophets in the Deuteronomistic History or in the traditions of the so-called writing prophets. One of the most interesting parallels between Chronicles and Greek histories proposed by Hoglund is the use of large numbers to render military accounts credible, but while this is a possible source for this stylistic feature, it is hardly the only one conceivable. Hoglund finds a parallel to Greek histories in the way the Chronicler cites sources, but as we will see below, almost all of these citations are merely renaming of sources cited already in the Deuteronomistic History. The Chronicler and the Greek historians use speeches composed by the author, but that technique was employed already in the Deuteronomistic History. Hoglund also notes that both the Chronicler and the Greek historians borrowed earlier narratives without attribution. Every historian, without doubt, is indebted to the cultural influences of his or her day, and the Chronicler's method of writing history reflects consciously and unconsciously literary and cultural conventions of the time, but I do not find the parallels with Greek histories distinctive enough to conclude that the Chronicler was actually acquainted with any of these histories.[162] Comparative study of Greek and Hebrew historiography is still at an early stage but has already yielded some results.

John Van Seters makes the following observation about Israelite historiography: "It was the product of a

---

158 See Ackroyd's *Exile and Restoration* (OTL; Philadelphia: Westminster, 1968); idem, *The Chronicler in His Age* (JSOTSup 101; Sheffield: JSOT Press, 1991); and Graham, McKenzie, and Knoppers, *Chronicler as Historian*.

159 "Was the Chronicler a Historian?" 83.

160 In discussing the possible historicity of Manasseh's imprisonment in Babylon, W. F. Stinespring, "Eschatology in Chronicles," *JBL* 80 (1961) 218, wrote: "The question is irrelevant. The Chronicler was an eschatologist, not a historian, and he was telling the eschatological truth that in the new king-

dom God will be in strict control, and things will come out even."

161 See Yigal Levin, "Who Was the Chronicler's Audience? A Hint from His Genealogies," *JBL* 122 (2003) 229–45.

162 On the usefulness of comparisons with Greek historiography, see also John Van Seters, *In Search of History* (New Haven: Yale Univ. Press, 1983), esp. 8–54.

complex literary history, the work of authors dependent upon written models and sources who combined genres of great variety and structured the whole with conscious compositional techniques."[163] Van Seters calls Chronicles revisionist historiography that functions as legitimation for the contemporary Jerusalem community and its institutions.[164] I would prefer to call Chronicles a work of historiography and of theology. While the primary biblical parallel is the book of Kings, Chronicles also departs from that model and its theology especially in his incorporation of genealogies and other lists and in his efforts to legitimate the Jerusalem temple, its clergy, and its rituals. In his recent commentary, 34, Steven L. McKenzie calls Chronicles "a theological rewriting of Bible history for instructional purposes."

Regardless of how we assess the genre of the work as a whole, the Chronicler used many smaller genres that can be more easily classified. These include narratives, speeches and prayers, lists, and genealogies.[165] The speeches and prayers incorporated by and presumably composed by the Chronicler are listed in the following paragraphs.

Speeches and Prayers[166]

1. *By kings.* Royal speeches appear with the following kings: David, 1 Chr 13:2-3; 15:2, 12-13; 22:6-16; 22:17-19; 28:2-10; 28:20-21; 29:1-5, 20 (all without *Vorlage* in the Deuteronomistic History); Abijah, 2 Chr 13:4-12; Asa, 2 Chr 14:7; Jehoshaphat, 2 Chr 19:6-7, 9-11; 20:20; Hezekiah, 2 Chr 29:5-11, 31; 30:6-9; 32:7-8; Josiah, 2 Chr 35:3-6. Rex Mason has classified 1 Chr 13:2-3 as an "overture"; 2 Chr 13:4-12 and 30:6-9 as "calls to repentance"; 2 Chr 20:20 and 35:3-6 as "exhortations"; all the rest are seen as "encouragements for a task." Throntveit

has pointed out the structural role of 2 Chr 13:4-12 and 30:6-9 as an *inclusio* at the beginning of the divided monarchy (Abijah) and the resumption of the united monarchy under Hezekiah. He also notes that another *inclusio* involves the speeches dealing with the ark in 1 Chr 13:2-3 (David) and 2 Chr 35:3-6 (Josiah). These speeches are spoken only by kings whom the Chronicler views favorably, or in the pious portion of the king's reign if the Chronicler has both positive and critical things to say about that king.

There are also six royal prayers: David, 1 Chr 17:16-24//2 Sam 7:18-29; 1 Chr 29:10-19; Solomon, 2 Chr 6:12-40//1 Kgs 8:22-53; Asa, 2 Chr 14:10 (11); Jehoshaphat, 20:5-12; Hezekiah, 30:18-19. Hence two of the prayers are taken over from the Deuteronomistic History with some modification and four others are attributable to the Chronicler's hand. The prayers in 1 Chronicles 17 and 29 provide a frame around David's preparations for the building of the temple, while the prayers of Asa and Jehoshaphat are prayers before a battle, with some ties to 2 Chr 6:34-35//1 Kgs 8:44-45. Hezekiah's intercessory prayer also shows a connection with 2 Chr 6:20.

2. *Speeches by prophets.* The Chronicler incorporated with some changes five prophetic speeches from the Deuteronomistic History: Nathan, 1 Chr 17:1-15// 2 Sam 7:1-17; Gad, 1 Chr 21:9-12, 18// 2 Sam 24:11-13, 18; Shemaiah, 2 Chr 11:2-4//1 Kgs 12:22-24; Micaiah, 2 Chr 18:12-27//1 Kgs 22:13-28; and Huldah, 2 Chr 34:22-28//2 Kgs 22:14-20. In addition, he included speeches for the following prophets that lack a *Vorlage:* Shemaiah the prophet, 2 Chr 12:5-8;[167] Azariah (who has

---

163 Ibid., 51.

164 "The Chronicler's Account of Solomon's Temple-Building: A Continuity Theme," in Graham, Hoglund, and McKenzie, *Chronicler as Historian,* 300.

165 See esp. the commentary of De Vries, who concentrates on form-critical questions, and Kegler and Augustin, *Deutsche Synopse,* 22–63.

166 For study of the Chronicler's speeches see Mark A. Throntveit, "The Chronicler's Speeches and Historical Reconstruction," in Graham, Hoglund, and McKenzie, *Chronicler as Historian,* 225–45; idem, *When Kings Speak;* Otto Plöger, "Reden und Gebete im deuteronomistischen und chronistischen

Geschichtswerk," in *Aus der Spätzeit des Alten Testaments: Studien* (Göttingen: Vandenhoeck & Ruprecht, 1971) 50–66; Mason, *Preaching the Tradition;* and Ehud Ben Zvi, "When the Foreign Monarch Speaks," in Graham and McKenzie, *Chronicler as Author,* 209–28. See also McKenzie, 31–32. For an early interpretation of these speeches see Samuel R. Driver, "The Speeches in Chronicles," *The Expositor,* 5th Series, 1 and 2 (1895) 241–56 and 286–308.

167 He uses the messenger formula (2 Chr 12:5), and reports that the word of Yahweh came to him (2 Chr 12:7).

the Spirit of God),[168] 15:1-7; Hanani the seer (הראה), 16:7-9; Jehu ben Hanani the seer (החזה), 19:2-3; Eliezer who acted as a prophet (התנבא), 20:37; a letter from Elijah the prophet, employing the messenger formula, 21:12-15; Zechariah, 24:20-22; the man of God, 25:7-9; an anonymous prophet, 25:15-16; Oded the prophet, 28:9-11. The figure Shemiah gave one speech that was taken over from the Deuteronomistic History and one that was added by the Chronicler. A Jehu ben Hanani was also active in the Northern Kingdom (1 Kgs 16:1, 7) about fifty years earlier than his namesake in Chronicles. Elijah is known from the book of Kings as a prophet to the Northern Kingdom and was taken to heaven before the reign of Jehoram. The ten prophetic speeches that are without a *Vorlage* all support the doctrine of retribution that is central to the Chronicler's message, and they all appear in the period of the divided monarchy (from Rehoboam to Ahaz). They promise blessing and reward to those who seek God and judgment and disaster to those who do not. They also issue calls for repentance and warnings[169] before judgment is imposed.

3. *Speeches by clergy.* There are only three of these in Chronicles,[170] all without *Vorlage* in the Deuteronomistic History: Jahaziel the Levite,[171] 2 Chr 20:14-17; Azariah the priest, 26:17-18; and Azariah the high priest, 31:10. Jahaziel offers an oracle of salvation in response to a national lament; Azariah and his priestly colleagues criticize Uzziah for taking over their prerogative with regard to incense; and Azariah pronounces a blessing on all who support the temple.

4. *Speeches by others.* These include: an address by Amasai, an army officer, 1 Chr 12:19 (18); Huram's letter to Solomon, 2 Chr 2:10-15 (11-16); the speech of the Queen of Sheba, 2 Chr 9:5-8//1 Kgs 10:6-9; an address by Ephraimite leaders supporting Oded's prophecy, 2 Chr 28:12-13; Sennacherib's speech, 2 Chr 32:10-15// 2 Kings 18, but with much revision; a speech by Neco, the Egyptian king, criticizing Josiah, 2 Chr 35:21; and a decree by Cyrus the Persian king relating to the rebuilding of the temple and the return of the Jewish exiles, 2 Chr 36:23//Ezra 1:1-3.

All of the speeches and prayers in Chronicles that are not taken from the *Vorlage* in Samuel-Kings or Ezra are to be assigned to the Chronicler himself.

Genealogies

Genealogies form a major part of Chronicles, especially in the so-called genealogical vestibule (1 Chronicles 1–9) and in the lists of clergy (chaps. 23–26) and have been the object of significant research in recent decades.[172] Much of this research has focused on

---

168 The Spirit of God is connected also with Amasai (see Speeches by Others below), Jahaziel (listed with the Speeches by Clergy below), and Zechariah (see later in this paragraph). Neco says that God, who was with him, commanded (אמר) him to hurry (see Speeches by Others below). William M. Schniedewind, "Prophets and Prophecy in the Books of Chronicles," in Graham, Hoglund, and McKenzie, *Chronicler as Historian*, 222, suggests that these inspired messengers are the forerunners of the inspired text interpreters of Second Temple Judaism and that the Chronicler saw himself as such an inspired messenger who exhorts the people. The inspired messengers spoke primarily to the people, while those designated as prophets spoke to the king.

169 For example, the anonymous prophet and the man of God in 2 Chr 25:7-9, 15-16; Zechariah in 2 Chr 24:20-22.

170 I have classified Zechariah's speech in 2 Chr 24:20-22 as prophetic; it could also be included among the priestly speeches.

171 This is the only speech delivered by a Levite in the book of Chronicles. This fact alone would call into

question the genre called "Levitical sermon" by Gerhard von Rad, "The Levitical Sermon in I & II Chronicles," in *The Problem of the Hexateuch and Other Essays* (New York: McGraw-Hill, 1966) 267–80. Von Rad included in this category: 1 Chr 28:2-10; 2 Chr 15:2-7; 16:7-9; 19:6ff.; 20:15-17, 20; 25:7ff.; 29:5-11; 30:6-9; 32:7-8a. In addition to the speech by the Levite Jehaziel, six of these speeches are delivered by kings and three by prophets. Von Rad identified three parts in these sermons: a quotation of an ancient source, its application to a situation in the past, and an exhortation to faith and action. More recent scholars hold that these speeches are neither Levitical nor are they sermons, though von Rad believed that these sermons reflected standard Levitical practices. See D. Mathias, "'Levitische Predigt' und Deuteronomismus," *ZAW* 96 (1984) 23–49; Braun, xxiv–xxv; Mason, *Preaching the Tradition*, 257–59. Japhet, "Relationship," 307, points out that this literary category is completely absent from Ezra-Nehemiah.

172 Other major biblical collections of genealogical material are at Exod 6:14-27 and Num 26:5-65. For discussion of recent advances in understanding

genealogies preserved in ancient Near Eastern texts (primarily linear) and on sociological investigations of oral linear and segmented genealogies in modern tribal societies in Africa in order to understand better the nature and function of the biblical genealogies.

Genealogies are of two types: segmented (branched family tree) and linear.[173] Segmented genealogies reflect a person's status, rights, and obligations and are expressed as kinship ties. Social equals are expressed as brothers, sisters, or cousins. Social inferiors are expressed as children, and social superiors as parents or grandparents. These genealogies reflect social reality rather than necessarily biological reality. Linear genealogies relate an individual or group to an individual or group in the past and are used to support claims to power or property. Linear genealogies may be descending (moving down the generations from parent to child) or ascending (moving up the generations from child to parent).

Segmented and linear genealogies have two things in common: depth and fluidity. Segmented genealogies ordinarily do not go back more than five generations, but linear genealogies may extend as many as nineteen generations though they rarely reach that far. Telescoping (loss of generations) can appear, particularly in linear genealogies. Oral genealogies show fluidity and they change when relationships change.[174] Without such change the genealogies lose their usefulness. Fluidity can be seen in biblical genealogies by comparing the genealogy of the tribe of Manasseh in Num 26:29-33 and Josh 17:1-3 with Manasseh's genealogy in 1 Chr 7:14-19. Four different genealogies of Benjamin are given in Gen 46:21; Num 26:38-40; 1 Chr 7:6-12; and 8:1-40. The conflicts among the four versions of the descendants of Esau are to be explained on functional grounds (Gen 36:9-14; 15-19; 40-43; 1 Chr 1:36-35).[175] This fluidity is characteristic of ancient and modern genealogies. Genealogical conflict (fluidity) may be a mark of authenticity, and all versions of a genealogy may be accurate in light of their function. Robert R. Wilson warns, however, that not every genealogical change indicates a corresponding political or geographical change.[176]

---

genealogies, see Roddy L. Braun, "1 Chronicles 1–9 and the Reconstruction of the History of Israel: Thoughts on the Use of Genealogical Data in Chronicles in the Reconstruction of the History of Israel," in Graham, Hogland, and McKenzie, *Chronicler as Historian*, 92–105; J. J. Finkelstein, "The Genealogy of the Hammurapi Dynasty," *JCS* 20 (1966) 95–118; Marshall D. Johnson, *The Purpose of the Biblical Genealogies: With Special Reference to the Setting of the Genealogies of Jesus* (2d ed.; Cambridge: Cambridge Univ. Press, 1988). Kartveit, *Motive und Schichten, passim;* Yigal Levin, "Understanding Biblical Genealogies," *CR:BS* 9 (2001) 11–46; idem, "Who Was the Chronicler's Audience? A Hint from His Genealogies," *JBL* 122 (2003) 229–45; Abraham Malamat, "King Lists of the Old Babylonian Period and Biblical Genealogies," *JAOS* 88 (1968) 163–73; idem, "Tribal Societies: Biblical Genealogies and African Lineage Systems," *Archives Européennes de Sociologie* 14 (1973) 126–36; Oeming, *Wahre Israel, passim;* William L. Osborne, "The Genealogies of 1 Chronicles 1–9" (Ph.D. diss., Dropsie University, 1979); Gary A. Rendsburg, "The Internal Consistency and Historical Reliability of the Biblical Genealogies," *VT* 40 (1990) 185–206; Joel P. Weinberg, "Das Wesen und die funktionelle Bestimmung der Listen in I Chr 1–9," *ZAW* 93 (1981) 91–114; Thomas Willi, "Late Persian Judaism and Its Conception of an Integral Israel according

to Chronicles," in *Second Temple Studies,* vol. 2: *Temple and Community in the Persian Period* (ed. T. C. Eskenazi and K. H. Richards; JSOTSup 175; Sheffield: Sheffield Academic Press, 1994) 146–62; and Robert R. Wilson, "The Old Testament Genealogies in Recent Research," *JBL* 94 (1975) 169–89; idem, *Genealogy and History in the Biblical World* (New Haven: Yale Univ. Press, 1977); idem, "Between 'Azel' and 'Azel': Interpreting the Biblical Genealogies," *BA* 42 (1979) 11–22. My discussion is particularly indebted to Levin and Wilson.

173 Osborne, "Genealogies," 318, and Braun, 2, have outlined the four formulas through which kinship is expressed: (1) The sons of PN[1]: PN[2]; (2) PN[1] became the father of PN[2] or PN[1] gave birth to PN[2]; (3) PN[1], son of PN[2], always in ascending order; (4) PN[1], his son PN[2], always in descending order.

174 There may be a change in kinship relationship or names may be added or deleted. See Braun, 4.

175 Wilson, "Interpreting," 20. The first represents social relationships among Edomite groups, the second political relationships among these groups, and the third geographical relationships. The passage in Chronicles lists the seven sons of Eliphaz found in Gen 36:11-12 and omits all comments about genealogical relationships.

176 "Old Testament Genealogies," 186. Braun, "1 Chronicles 1–9," notes that genre confusion is also possible and claims that the author of 1 Chr

When the oral genealogies are reduced to writing, their fluidity dramatically decreases.

Genealogies function within three spheres: the domestic sphere, the politico-jural sphere, and the religious sphere. In the domestic sphere the genealogies express interpersonal relationships or biological ties and often indicate status, standing in the community, ecomonic and geographical relations or rights and obligations. They define social rights and obligations and are usually segmented. Members of a clan residing in a community may identify themselves as descendants of an eponymous ancestor who was the founder or builder of the town. He is often called the "father" of the town. Genealogies in the politico-jural sphere may be segmented or linear and reflect the amount of political power that various people or groups possess. Genealogies justify holding a particular office, such as king or chief. When societies are organized according to kinship lines, legal and political relationships are stated in genealogical terms. Segmented genealogies do not usually have political functions in monarchical societies. Genealogies in the religious sphere may be segmented or linear and show the importance of people within the religious hierarchy or their membership in a religious society. These genealogies may also be used as part of an ancestor cult. A genealogy will always have a domestic, political, or religious function. Study of the Safaitic inscriptions from the last centuries BCE and first centuries CE show that historical notes are often included in the genealogies, as also in the OT.[177]

Genealogies may be applied to different situations. The genealogies in 1 Chronicles 1, for example, include almost all the genealogies from Genesis, where they served a variety of functions.[178] In Chronicles these genealogies locate Israel among the nations and show its relationship to them; they also define the territory that belonged to Israel in the past and may belong to it again in the future. Marshall Johnson provides a helpful list of nine functions of genealogies within the OT;[179] and Braun, 3, indicates that many of these are interpenetrating and overlapping.

The tribal genealogies in 1 Chronicles 2–8 exhibit disparities in length, form, and detail among the different tribal lists. They consist of core tribal material, taken from or similar to the material in the Pentateuch, geographical indications of the tribe's territory, and miscellaneous names and historical notes.[180] The complex genealogy of Judah is one hundred verses long and seems to be arranged chiastically, whereas Simon is only twenty verses long and consists of core information based on Num 26:12-14, the tribe's towns and dwelling places, and various anecdotes or historical notes. Reuben and Gad have lists of tribal chiefs down to the Assyrian captivity,[181] with stories and references to tribal territories and they also have references to a census. Transjordanian Manasseh has a territorial description and lists of tribal leaders but no real genealogical data. Issachar mentions a military census in the days of David. The genealogy of Benjamin in 1 Chr 7:6-12 refers to a military census. Zebulun and probably Dan are missing from the list, perhaps because of textual error (see the commentary). Naphtali reflects only the core data from Gen 46:24. Manasseh and Ephraim are primarily segmented and full of geographical and historical information, although there is a long linear genealogy within Ephraim. Asher also refers to a military census. The order of these tribes within chaps. 2–8 will be discussed in the commentary.

Yigal Levin has made a strong case for Israel remaining a tribal society, with genealogies as a living reality, long after the establishment of the monarchy.[182] He believes that the genealogies especially of Judah, Benjamin, Levi, Ephraim, Manasseh, and Asher were adapted from the living oral traditions of these tribes.[183]

7:20-29 understood Num 26:6 to be linear when it is actually segmented.

177 Johnson, *Purpose,* 61.

178 The genealogy of Adam in Genesis 5 bridged the gap from creation to the time of the flood. The genealogical materials dealing with Edom in Genesis 36 fill out the history of Esau, Jacob's brother, from the time of the patriarchs until their descendants meet one another during the monarchical period.

179 Johnson, *Purpose,* 77–82.

180 Johnson, *Purpose,* 55–56.

181 A tribal census is mentioned during the reign of Jotham. The Chronicler does not mention the exile of the other tribes composing the northern kingdom.

182 "Understanding Biblical Genealogies," 32; idem, "Chronicler's Audience," 242; contra Japhet, *Ideology,* 300–302.

183 "Chronicler's Audience," 242–43.

The Chronicler's audience therefore would readily accept the use of genealogies, whereas to us these materials often strike us as esoteric.

Chronicles and History

One of the most controversial aspects of the study of Chronicles since Wilhelm de Wette has been the question of the historical value of the Chronicler's account of the preexilic period. Two dissertations have explored this question at length.[184] There were two nineteenth-century challenges to the credibility of Chronicles as a source for reconstructing the history of the preexilic period: (1) the use of historical criticism by de Wette[185] and others, which emphasized the differences between the picture of preexilic history in Chronicles and Samuel-Kings; and (2) the hypothesis of an exilic or postexilic date for P, which was brought to its classic expression by Julius Wellhausen.[186]

Prior to de Wette, Chronicles was regarded as a reliable source for the preexilic history of Israel. De Wette rejected Chronicles for reconstruction of the preexilic period and denied that the Chronicler had been able to use noncanonical, lost sources. The history in Samuel-Kings was older and more original than that in Chronicles. The Chronicler had drastically altered the account in Samuel-Kings in a careless and even ignorant manner; his own biases were in favor of the Levites and the Judean cult. The Chronicler in fact favored Judah and hated Israel. Chronicles therefore had no value as a historical source. De Wette's position was supported by Wilhelm Gesenius[187] and C. P. W. Gramberg.[188] Many nineteenth-century scholars concluded on the basis of their research that Chronicles was dominated by theological biases and filled with inaccurate information. Those who replied to this challenge tried to vindicate the historical testimony of Chronicles and feared that the challenge to the historicity of Chronicles was at the same time a challenge to the Christian faith and the authority of Scripture. They attempted to show that adequate and accurate sources lay behind the narrative. F. K. Movers, for example, argued that the author of Chronicles used as sources the canonical books of Samuel-Kings and the royal annals of the two kingdoms. The latter, after undergoing two editions, were known as the "Midrash on the Book of Kings." He concluded that these two sources were in essential agreement. Movers talked about the didactic and parenetic character of Chronicles, but was not willing to relativize its historical value.[189] C. F. Keil, a proponent of confessional orthodoxy, denied that the Chronicler used Samuel-Kings but proposed that he was dependent instead on a source called "The Book of the Kings of Israel and Judah."[190] Other scholars, such as J. G. Dahler, tried to harmonize the accounts of Samuel-Kings and Chronicles and thought Chronicles was completely historical.[191] In his *History of Israel*,[192] Heinrich Ewald represented a mediating position, a compromise between the positions of de Wette and Keil.[193]

In the mid-nineteenth century a number of scholars argued that the source document P in the Pentateuch dated from exilic or postexilic times, replacing the for-

184 Graham, *Utilization*, and Peltonen, *History Debated*. Peltonen's survey begins in the precritical period and continues until the present day. The following summary is dependent on the findings of Graham and Peltonen. See also Sara Japhet, "The Historical Reliability of Chronicles: The History of the Problem and Its Place in Biblical Research," *JSOT* 3 (1985) 83–107; and Braun, "1 Chronicles 1–9."

185 W. M. L. de Wette, *Kritischer Versuch über die Glaubwürdigkeit der Bücher der Chronik mit Hinsicht auf die Geschichte der Mosaischen Bücher und Gesetzgebung* (vol. 1 of *Beiträge zur Einleitung in das Alte Testament* (Halle: Schimmelpfennig, 1806).

186 Wellhausen, *Prolegomena*, 10–13 and *passim*.

187 *Geschichte der hebräischen Sprache und Schrift* (Leipzig: Vogel, 1815).

188 Carl Peter Wilhelm Gramberg, *Die Chronik nach ihrem geschichtlichen Charakter und ihrer Glaubwürdigkeit neu geprüft* (Halle: Eduard Anton, 1823).

189 Franz Karl Movers, *Kritische Untersuchungen über die biblische Chronik* (Bonn: T. Habicht, 1834).

190 *Apologetischer Versuch über die Bücher der Chronik and über die Integrität des Buches Esra* (Berlin: Ludwig Oehmigke, 1833). See also his commentary.

191 *De librorum Paralipomenon auctoritate atque fide historica disputat* (Leipzig: Johannis Henrici Heitz, 1819).

192 *History of Israel* (4th ed.; 8 vols.; London: Longman Green, 1878–1886); original: *Geschichte des Volkes Israel bis Christus* (7 vols.; Göttingen: Vandenhoeck & Ruprecht, 1843–1852).

193 Ernst Bertheau, who was a student of Ewald, published the first historical-critical commentary on Chronicles in 1854. He felt it was possible to find in Chronicles a wealth of reliable historical information about ancient Israel.

mer idea that P was one of the earliest sources, and this was accompanied by a rejection of the historical accuracy of P.[194] When the similarities between P and Chronicles were noted, it was also concluded that Chronicles did not offer a reliable witness to Israel's preexilic history. Wellhausen believed that Chronicles was composed three hundred years after Samuel-Kings, and that the additional materials in Chronicles were in accord with P and presupposed the completed Pentateuch. He traced the alterations and additions of Chronicles to the same fountainhead—the judaizing of the past, a rewriting of history so that it became congruent with the Priestly Code.[195] The only historical value of Chronicles was thought to stem from an analysis of its theological agenda, which would help reconstruct the beliefs and institutions for the postexilic Jewish community. Wellhausen thus emphatically rejected the mediating position of his teacher Ewald. Attempts by Archibald H. Sayce[196] and others to bolster the credibility of Chronicles and its sources by an appeal to archaeology were met with sharp criticism by S. R. Driver.[197] The most prominent advocate in the twentieth century for the historicity of Chronicles on the basis of

archaeology was William Foxwell Albright. In his judgment archaeology had confirmed numerous details in the genealogies, the Davidic origin of the guilds of temple singers, data relating to military campaigns and building projects, and the report of Jehoshaphat's judicial reform.[198] Albright's position was followed by John Bright in writing his history of Israel.[199] A diametrically opposite position was taken by Robert North.[200]

C. C. Torrey believed that Chronicles was nothing but religious fiction and that as a historian the Chronicler is completely untrustworthy. The source citations in Chronicles were only literary adornments to give the work authority. It needs to be added, however, that Torrey's primary focus was on the book of Ezra.[201] Gerhard von Rad conceded that the Chronicler wrote history according to his own biases and the religious circumstances of his day, but von Rad was primarily interested in the theological view of history in Chronicles.[202] While most scholars followed Wellhausen in saying that the Chronicler based himself on the Priestly source, von Rad believed that the Chronicler used the completed Pentateuch, and there was more evidence for him being influenced by Deuteronomic rather than Priestly theol-

---

194 Eduard Reuss, Wilhelm Vatke, K. H. Graf, Abraham Kuenen, John William Colenso, and Julius Wellhausen.

195 Wellhausen, *Prolegomena*, 223.

196 See *The "Higher Criticism" and the Verdict of the Monuments* (London: SPCK, 1894); idem, "Archaeology v. Old Testament Criticism," *The Contemporary Review* 68 (1895) 477–84; idem, *The Early History of the Hebrews* (New York: Macmillan, 1897); idem, *Monument Facts and Higher Critical Fancies* (3d ed.; New York: Revell, 1904).

197 "Hebrew Authority," in *Authority and Archaeology* (ed. D. G. Hogarth; New York: Charles Scribner's Sons, 1899) 1–152. Peltonen, *History Debated*, 2:479, remarks: "Sayce and those who accepted his position were guilty of neglecting the methodological questions concerning the applicability of archaeology to the study of the literary remains of ancient Israel, of underestimating the problems raised by 'higher criticism,' and of playing down or even completely obscuring the new questions evoked by archaeology."

198 See "The Judicial Reform of Jehoshaphat," in *Alexander Marx Jubilee Volume* (New York: Jewish Theological Seminary of America, 1950) 61–82; idem, *Archaeology and the Religion of Israel* (4th ed.; Baltimore: Johns Hopkins Univ. Press, 1956)

125–29; idem, "A Votive Stele Erected by Ben Hadad I of Damascus to the God Melcarth," *BASOR* 87 (1942) 23–29. Albright reaffirmed this position at many points throughout his writings. In "The Date and Personality of the Chronicler," *JBL* 40 (1921) 105, however, Albright had concluded that the Chronicler "shows a total lack of historical sense in dealing with the preëxilic age."

199 John Bright, *A History of Israel* (3d ed.; Philadelphia: Westminster, 1981) 229–30 and n. 3. Cf. also the commentary by Myers, and H. Neil Richardson, "The Historical Reliability of Chronicles," *JBR* 26 (1958) 9-12.

200 "Does Archaeology Prove Chronicles Sources?" in *A Light unto My Path: Old Testament Studies in Honor of Jacob M. Myers* (Philadelphia: Temple Univ. Press, 1973) 375–401.

201 *The Composition and Historical Value of Ezra-Nehemiah* (BZAW 2; Giessen: Töpelmann, 1896). See also his collected essays, *Ezra Studies* (1910; repr. New York: KTAV, 1970).

202 See *Geschichtsbild, passim.*

ogy. The Chronicler's Levitical ark theology, in von Rad's opinion, was in considerable tension with the Aaronic tabernacle theology of P.

In 1943 Martin Noth dated the Chronicler to Ptolemaic times and believed that what determined the outlook and theology of Chronicles was its critical attitude toward the Samaritan cult community.[203] Because he considered most of the genealogies and lists to be secondary, Noth did not believe the Chronicler had a primary interest in promoting Levitical claims. In citing sources, the Chronicler was merely imitating his *Vorlage* in the Deuteronomistic History and hence these citations had no historical value. Noth admitted that on at least two occasions Chronicles contained information that must have come from preexilic sources: 2 Chr 32:30, the report of Hezekiah's water tunnel, and 35:20-24, the last battle and death of Josiah. Note the reference to Carchemish in v. 20, where Neco was going to try to prop up the remnant of the Assyrian Empire as a buffer against the Babylonians. Noth also placed historical value in the reports of fortification projects[204] and some of his war accounts.[205] Noth devoted more space in his monograph to the form of the Chronicler's work, its traditio-historical nature, and its theological ideas than to its use as a historical source.[206]

Peter Welten also found only a few notices from preexilic times in Chronicles.[207] But Welten concluded that the so-called topoi dealing with fortresses and buildings,[208] makeup of the army,[209] and war reports[210] were creations of the Chronicler and reflected the circumstances of his own time and place. They were fictitious except for the few passages identified by Noth as coming from sources. In 2 Chronicles 10–36, to which Welten's study was restricted, old material in addition to Samuel-Kings plays a subordinate role. The net result of Noth's and Welten's work is that they consider Chronicles as essentially useless in reconstructing Israel's preexilic history.[211]

Some of the most controversial questions about preexilic history are in 2 Chronicles, and so I will need to address this issue again in the second volume of this commentary. The issues regarding history in 1 Chronicles are themselves less controverted.

Some more recent commentators (e.g., Williamson, Johnstone, Japhet) have recognized that in the genealogies of 1 Chronicles 2–8 there is much authentic information about the various tribes of Israel, though this information is fragmentary, sometimes broken, of unequal extent for the tribes, and often almost impossible to date to a given century. Passages like 1 Chronicles 9 and 11 are in part borrowed from or dependent on earlier passages such as Neh 11:1-19 and 2 Samuel 23.

It is also recognized today that the Chronicler sometimes rearranged the order of his material for theological or ideological reasons. David's first action, after his coronation in Chronicles, is an attempt to bring the ark to Jerusalem (1 Chr 13:1-14//2 Sam 6:1-3, 5-11), and this account is followed by notices about Hiram's support (1 Chr 14:1-2//2 Sam 5:11-12), David's wives and children (1 Chr 14:3-7//2 Sam 5:13-16), and his wars with the Philistines (1 Chr 14:8-16//2 Sam 5:17-25). The Chronicler's literary purposes, not different information about history, led to this shifting of events.

The listing of the various ranks of clergy in chaps. 23–26, regardless of whether these chapters are original or secondary to the book, represents authentic but postexilic data. Almost all scholars would recognize that crediting David with these appointments is anachronistic. The enormous numbers dealing with David's donations for the temple are recognized as hyperbole,[212] and the report of the extensive temple preparations done by David is also seen as part of the Chronicler's theological emphasis rather than historical fact. The list of twelve supervisors over the king's property in 27:25-31 and the seven advisors to David in 27:32-34 may be authentic material from the time of David.[213] Perhaps the materi-

---

203 *Chronicler's History*, 69-73, 97-106.

204 2 Chr 11:5b-10aα, 26:9; 26:15a; and 33:14a.

205 2 Chr 13:3-20; 14:8-14; 26:6-8a; 27:5; and 28:18. In the first two cases the Chronicler had extensively rewritten his source materials.

206 Peltonen, *History Debated*, 2:652.

207 *Geschichte und Geschichtsdarstellung*. He considered historical 2 Chr 11:5b, 6a-10aβ, 26:6a and 10; 32:30a. He also found notions from preexilic times in 2 Chr 11:22-23 and 21:1-4.

208 2 Chr 11:5-12; 14:5-6; 17:12-13; 26:9-10; 27:3-4; 32:5-6a; 33:14. Cf. 1 Chr 11:8-9 and 2 Chr 8:1-6.

209 2 Chr 14:7; 17:14-19; 26:11-15; 2 Chr 25:5; 1 Chr 27:1-15.

210 2 Chr 13:3-20; 14:8-14; 20:1-30; 26:6-8; 27:5-6.

211 Cf. Peltonen, *History Debated*, 2:662.

212 See Klein, "How Many in a Thousand?" 270-82.

213 For 1 Chr 27:16-22 see the commentary.

als in chap. 12, not paralleled in the Deuteronomistic History, have some authentic historical information, but the large numbers, indicating that the most distant tribes were the most loyal to David, seems clearly to have arisen as part of the Chronicler's message. The identification of Gibeon as the place where the tabernacle was located until the time of Solomon is probably related to the Chronicler's attempt to explain why Solomon went to worship at the Gibeonite high place, not to historical fact. Other items from 1 Chronicles with potential implications for reconstructing the history of Israel will be examined in the commentary itself.

Textual Criticism

Two aspects of the discipline of textual criticism have importance for a commentator on Chronicles.[214] The first is the establishment of the best text of 1 and 2 Chronicles itself, based on the ancient versions, especially the LXX, and, rarely, conjectural emendation of the text. The text of no book of the Bible is preserved perfectly, and all books must be corrected. In general, the MT of Chronicles is fairly well preserved,[215] surely in a way much superior to the books of Samuel, but my translations for every chapter are annotated with multiple textual notes that attempt to apply standard text-critical principles to the Hebrew text of Chronicles. But a second aspect of textual criticism is of equal or even greater importance in Chronicles since it has become clear that the *Vorlage* used by the Chronicler, especially in the books of Samuel,[216] was often different from the MT. Hence before one ascribes a change noted in Chronicles to the Chronicler, one needs to determine as far as possible whether a reading now in Chronicles may

once have been in the Samuel textual tradition, as witnessed by LXX, LXX[L], Qumran manuscripts, Josephus, or other witnesses.[217] If the reading of Chronicles different from the MT of Samuel and Kings is found in one of the alternate Samuel textual traditions, it is obviously not a change made by the Chronicler. Present resources and methodologies, of course, do not allow us to reconstruct perfectly the *Vorlage* of the Chronicler, that is, the text of Samuel and Kings that lay before the Chronicler. Commentators on the books of Samuel and Kings, in turn, often have to evaluate the readings in Chronicles as they study the textual history of Samuel and Kings.[218]

Witnesses to the Text
Dead Sea Scrolls

Only two small fragments of the books of Chronicles (4Q118) were discovered among the Dead Sea Scrolls, containing portions of the text of 2 Chr 28:27–29:3.[219] The fragments have been dated for paleographic reasons to 50–25 BCE. The first fragment has only one complete word in it, which does not correspond to any reading in Chronicles MT or LXX. The second fragment has three minor variants: בן אחז for בני in 28:17; איבה for אביה in 29:1; and והוא for הוא in 29:3. They will be discussed in the translations to those passages in the second volume of this commentary. Because of the brevity of these fragments, they contribute little to the understanding of the text of Chronicles.

Septuagint

While I will refer to the Greek translation of Chronicles in the commentary as LXX or Chronicles LXX, this work is called Παραλειπομένων in Greek

---

214 On the present state of OT textual criticism see Emanuel Tov, *Textual Criticism of the Hebrew Bible* (2d ed.; Minneapolis: Fortress Press, 2001).

215 Curtis and Madsen, 36; Rudolph, IV. On the spelling of the numerous names in Chronicles, there is much uncertainty both in MT and in the versions.

216 I restrict the discussion primarily to Samuel since Kings does not serve as a *Vorlage* in 1 Chronicles except for a couple verses in 1 Chronicles 29. I plan to address the text-critical relationship of the Kings *Vorlage* in the second volume of this commentary. McKenzie, *Chronicler's Use*, 155, concluded that observations about the Chronicler's *Vorlage* in

Samuel do not apply to his *Vorlage* in Kings.

217 In 1 Chr 8:33-34 and 9:39-40, without *Vorlage* in the Deuteronomistic History, the Chronicler retains the older forms of the names Esh-baal and Meri(b)-baal, a son and a grandson of Saul, whose names when they do appear in Samuel MT are spelled polemically as Ish-bosheth (2 Sam 2:8) and Mephibosheth (2 Sam 4:4–21:7).

218 See, e.g., Driver, *Notes*; McCarter, *I Samuel* and *II Samuel;* and Klein, *1 Samuel.*

219 Julio Trebolle Barrera, "4QChr," in Eugene Ulrich et al., *Qumran Cave 4: XI: Psalms to Chronicles* (DJD 16; Oxford: Clarendon, 2000) 295–97.

manuscripts and "Paraleipomena" in scholarly litera-ture.[220] As with most books in the OT, the LXX is the most significant of the ancient versions for the textual criticism of Chronicles. Leslie Allen has made a thor-ough study of this translation in his dissertation, and his findings will be followed in this introductory material.[221] Allen concluded that Chronicles LXX was translated in Egypt, probably in the second century BCE.[222] This deci-sion was made in explicit criticism of C. C. Torrey, who had earlier argued that the translator of Chronicles was Theodotion from the second century CE.[223] Allen consid-ered Chronicles LXX and the translation of Ezra and Nehemiah called *Esdras B′* as separate translations, and he recognized the vast difference between Chronicles LXX and those parts of Chronicles, 2 Chronicles 35–36, that are included in the Greek translation known as *1 Esdras (Esdras A′).*

Allen identified four groups of manuscripts among the forty-six manuscripts of Chronicles LXX that were available to him. These groups are:

L or Lucianic manuscripts: b and e_2. These manuscripts are sometimes matched by minuscules f j k, g i n y,[224] and 350, and sporadically by other manuscripts and the Armenian daughter translation. The Bohairic and Ethiopic have close affinity with L, and this group has links with Theodoret. L exhibits the usual characteristics

of the Lucianic recension[225] and gives the impression of being most carefully corrected to MT.[226] Manuscripts of the G group (see below) provide the type of text that underlies this recension.

R: MSS d p q t z. Sometimes allied to this group are MSS 44, 68, 74, 122, 125, 144, 236, 246, 314, 321, 346, 610, and MS j in 1 Chronicles. Also allied to this group from time to time are MSS f i m n y and c_2. L and R have been corrected independently to MT.

O or Hexaplaric manuscripts: AN aceghn Armenian, and the Syro-Hexaplaric recension. Cf. also from time to time MSS bf ijmoy, 46, 381, 728. This group attempts to improve the rugged style of the Greek and make correc-tions toward the MT.[227] This group is ultimately based on the text type known as G.

G: B and c_2, except for the last six chapters of 2 Chronicles, where c_2 is allied with R. At times MSS A N f g h i j and m join this group. O, L, and R are revi-sions of a Greek *Vorlage* most like G. The Old Latin depends on another revised text form, like L and R, but the basic text form seems again to be group G.[228]

Allen notes that the translator of Chronicles LXX sometimes borrowed vocabulary and cultic details from the LXX of the Pentateuch. He also concluded that Chronicles LXX is not to be identified with the *kaige* recension since it violates ten of the nineteen character-

---

220 The Vg, as noted above, calls these books *Para-lipomenon I and II.*

221 Allen, *Greek Chronicles.* Allen insists (1:26–31, 175–218) that Chronicles LXX and the translator's Hebrew *Vorlage* have absorbed contamination from parallel texts in Samuel-Kings. In this he follows in part Gillis Gerleman (*Studies in the Septuagint, II: Chronicles* [LUÅ 43/3; Lund: Gleerup, 1946]; idem, *Synoptic Studies in the Old Testament* [LUÅ 44/5; Lund: Gleerup, 1948]) and differs from Martin Rehm (*Textkritische Untersuchungen zu den Parallelstellen der Samuel-Königsbücher und der Chronik* [AtAbh 13/3; Münster: Aschendorff, 1937]) and James Donald Shenkel ("A Comparative Study of the Synoptic Parallels in I Paraleipomena and I-II Reigns," *HTR* 62 [1969] 63–85), who argued that the translator of Chronicles had used and thus revised the Greek text of Samuel and Kings in mak-ing his own translation.

222 *Greek Chronicles,* 1:23. See also Kalimi, *Geschichtsschreibung,* 12–13, n. 44. Gerleman, *Studies in the Septuagint,* 3–45, also argued for a 2d-century date.

223 Torrey's views can be found conveniently in his col-lected essays, *Ezra Studies,* 66–81. Cf. Curtis and Madsen, 38–40.

224 y is a member of this group until 1 Chr 11:4. At v. 5 it joins group O.

225 It adds names and replaces pronouns by names; sub-stitutes synonyms, indulges in neo-Atticisms. Cf. Allen, *Greek Chronicles,* 1:67.

226 Allen, *Greek Chronicles,* 1:73, identifies seventeen cases where Josephus cites a text of Chronicles LXX that must be called proto-Lucian.

227 Torrey had claimed that A and related MSS had the oldest form of the text. See Allen, *Greek Chronicles,* 1:87.

228 *Greek Chronicles,* 1:107. On p. 108 Allen lists verses where the OL throws valuable light on the his-tory of the Greek text. For the text of the OL of 2 Chronicles see R. Weber, *Les anciennes versions Latines du deuxième livre des Paralipomène* (Rome: Libreria Vaticana, 1945). OL readings are also sup-plied in the apparatus to the Cambridge Septuagint.

istics of that recension, complies with only four of those characteristics, and has a nodding acquaintance with four more. Therefore it has nothing in common with a systematic revision like *kaige*. Allen rejects Shenkel's proposal that the translator used an earlier recension of the LXX of Samuel and Kings in making his translation of Chronicles.[229] Allen is convinced instead that Chronicles LXX and the translator's Hebrew text have absorbed varying amounts of contamination from parallel texts in Samuel and Kings.[230] Behind the intensive Greek corruption and the idiosyncrasies of the translation lies a Hebrew text that may in very many cases be easily related to MT; or, rather, it is a valuable witness to the state of the text of Chronicles in second-century BCE Egypt.[231] The translation shows thirty-six alignments with the Qere and sixteen with the Ketib. Vowel letters were much less frequent in the *Vorlage* of the LXX than in MT.[232] The second volume of Allen's work is dedicated to identifying and analyzing Chronicles LXX's differences from Chronicles MT.

1 Esdras

1 Esdras is a Greek translation of 2 Chronicles 35–36, Ezra 1–10, and Nehemiah 8, and incorporates the story of the three pages (1 Esdr 3:1–5:6), which lacks a canonical parallel.[233] The translation is much less formally equivalent than Chronicles LXX, and Zipora Talshir has published two monographs that discuss the relationship of this translation to MT.[234] The document was known by Josephus and may go back as far as the second century BCE. This document will play a significant role in this commentary only in the textual criticism of 2 Chronicles 35–36 in the second volume.[235]

Syriac, Targum, and Other Witnesses

Study of the Syriac translation of Chronicles has been greatly enhanced by the splendid critical edition of R. P. Gordon.[236] Gordon collated twenty-nine manuscripts in preparing this edition and the text is based principally on MS *B. 21 Inferiore* of the Ambrosian Library in Milan (7th century CE). The text of the Peshitta was often harmonized with the parallel texts of Samuel-Kings, which considerably lessens its value for the textual critic.

The Targum rarely has importance for textual criticism in Chronicles, but its exegetical comments or interpretations are often quite enlightening.[237]

The Vulgate too is of secondary importance, but occasionally confirms variant readings discovered in the LXX or other versions.

Textual Characteristics of the Chronicler's Vorlage in Samuel

One of the early fruits of research on the Dead Sea Scrolls was the discovery that the text of Samuel (and perhaps Kings) used by the Chronicler was at times different from the MT and that this variant text of Samuel could be discovered through 4QSam[a,b, and c], Samuel LXX, and Samuel LXX[L].[238] 4QSam[a] is a manuscript from the first century BCE, 4QSam[b and c] are from the

---

229 *Greek Chronicles*, 2:182.

230 Ibid., 1:217.

231 Ibid., 2:168.

232 Ibid., 2:167.

233 The equivalent of Ezra 4:7-24 is placed after 1:11 and before the account of the three pages, and the equivalent of 2:1–4:5 is put after that account. From a literary perspective this apocryphal work is to be evaluated as a piece of literature in its own right and not as a fragment of a translation of the so-called Chronicler's History.

234 Z. Talshir, *From Origin to Translation;* idem, *Text Critical Commentary*. See also my own earlier study of this text, "Studies in the Greek Texts of the Chronicler" (Ph.D. diss., Harvard, 1966).

235 For the text of 1 Esdras see Robert Hanhart, *Esdrae liber I* (Septuaginta Vetus Testamentum Graecum 8/1; Göttingen: Vandenhoeck & Ruprecht, 1974).

236 Gordon, *Syriac*. See also Michael P. Weitzman, *The Syriac Version of the Old Testament: An Introduction* (Cambridge: Cambridge Univ. Press, 1999).

237 See McIvor, *Targum;* and R. Le Déaut and J. Robert, *Targum des Chroniques*, vol. 1: *Introduction et Traduction;* vol. 2: *Texte et Glossaire* (AnBib 51; Rome: Biblical Institute Press, 1971). The latter authors (1:27) date its final redaction to the 8th or 9th century CE. See also A. Sperber, *The Bible in Aramaic*, vol. IV.A: *The Hagiographa* (Leiden: Brill, 1968).

238 See the pioneering studies of Frank Moore Cross, "The History of the Biblical Text in the Light of Discoveries in the Judean Desert," *HTR* 57 (1964) 281–99; "The Contribution of the Qumran Discoveries to the Study of the Biblical Text," *IEJ* 16 (1966) 81–95; and "The Evolution of a Theory of Local Texts," *1972 Proceedings of the International Organization for Septuagint and Cognate Studies* (ed. R. A. Kraft; SBLSCS 2; Missoula, MT: Society of Biblical Literature, 1972) 108–26. See my earlier discussion of these insights in *Textual Criticism of the Old Testament* (Philadelphia: Fortress Press, 1974) 70–73. The Lucianic MSS in Samuel-Kings are b o $c_2 e_2$.

third century BCE, Samuel LXX was presumably translated from a Hebrew text in Egypt in the second century BCE, and behind Samuel LXX[L], the Lucianic text of Samuel, usually dated to the early fourth century CE,[239] one can recover a proto-Lucianic recension of Samuel made in the first century BCE, probably in Palestine. This proto-Lucianic revision was based on the Old Greek translation.

Unfortunately, the LXX of Samuel and Kings offers further complexities. In terminology used since the time of Henry St. John Thackeray, the Greek translation of Samuel and Kings (called "Reigns" or "Kingdoms") needs to be divided into five sections:

α   1 Samuel
ββ   2 Sam 1:1–9:13
βγ   2 Sam 10:1–1 Kgs 2:11
γγ   1 Kgs 2:12–21:43
γδ   1 Kings 22–2 Kings 25

In sections α, ββ, and γγ, the text contained in LXX[B], which is the text presented at the top of the page in the Cambridge Septuagint, is a copy of the Old Greek translation, made in Egypt in the second century BCE on the basis of a Hebrew text, that is related to, but an offshoot of, the text of Samuel preserved in Palestine. In sections βγ and γδ, however, the text contained in LXX[B] is part of the *kaige* recension, a revision of the Old Greek toward the proto-MT in the first century CE. The Old Greek in these sections is lost, but the proto-Lucianic recension can be partially recovered from LXX[L] and is retained in readings from the sixth column of Origen's Hexapla (usually identified as Theodotion). This means that we have a series of windows that offer indirect and direct access to the history of the pre-MT of Samuel in Palestine:

a. Chronicles, when it incorporates Samuel texts: first half of the fourth century BCE

b. 4QSam[b and c]: third century BCE (unfortunately, the fragments of these scrolls do not contain parts of the books of Samuel used by the Chronicler)

c. the Old Greek translation of LXX: second century BCE (sections α, ββ, γγ in Reigns), based on a manuscript that is a descendant of the Palestinian tradition[240]

d. 4QSam[a]: first century BCE

e. the proto-Lucianic recension of the LXX: first century BCE[241]

f. the *kaige* recension: first-century CE revision of the Old Greek toward the proto-MT

g. Josephus: end of the first century CE, who used a Greek Bible of the proto-Lucianic tradition in writing his narrative based on the books of Samuel in his *Jewish Antiquities* (see discussion of Ulrich below)

Dissertations at Harvard University by Werner Lemke,[242] Eugene Charles Ulrich Jr.,[243] and Steven L. McKenzie[244] explored aspects of this divergent text of Samuel and Kings that helps us understand more precisely the text of the *Vorlage* that lay before the Chronicler. Lemke protested against excessively tendentious interpretations of Chronicles that tried to explain ideologically every departure of Chronicles from the MT of Samuel and Kings. In 1 Chronicles 10–21 Lemke counted nearly one hundred instances in which the LXX of Samuel agreed with Chronicles against Samuel MT.[245] His insightful observations about the divergent text of the *Vorlage* at times downplays the significant ways that the Chronicler did in fact alter the text of his *Vorlage*.

Ulrich, now one of the chief editors of the Dead Sea Scrolls, was one of the first scholars to have full access to the text of 4QSam[a].[246] He combined a careful analysis of this text and the MT and LXX of Samuel with a judicious investigation of the text presupposed by Josephus

---

239 Lucian died in 311 or 312 CE.

240 Cross, "History of the Biblical Text," 295, believes this Hebrew text separated from the Old Palestinian textual tradition no later than the 4th century BCE.

241 Proto-Lucianic readings are occasionally supported by readings in OL.

242 "Synoptic Studies" (1964). Part of his findings were published in "Synoptic Problem" (1965).

243 *Qumran Text* (1978).

244 *Chronicler's Use* (1984).

245 "Synoptic Problem," 362, n. 41.

246 As of this writing, the full scholarly edition of 4QSam[a] has not been published. The readings are largely accessible through the works of Ulrich and McKenzie and the textual notes of McCarter, *I Samuel* and *II Samuel*. McCarter's textual notes are indispensable for understanding the textual history of Samuel and also for understanding the relationship of this text to Chronicles. For provisional access to the text of 4QSam[a] see now also Herbert, *Reconstructing;* and Fincke, *Samuel Scroll.*

in the *Antiquities* and was able to show in many cases that Josephus utilized a non-Masoretic form of Samuel now known from the LXX, LXX[L], or 4QSam[a]. He developed in detail the discovery by Adam Mez of the relationship between Josephus and the Lucianic, that is, proto-Lucianic, version of the LXX.

While McKenzie made very helpful observations on dozens of the non-Masoretic readings in Samuel, his principal aim in his dissertation was to use text-critical insights in support of redaction-critical research. He adopted the redactional theories of his advisor, Frank Cross, on the Deuteronomistic History and on Chronicles. Cross had proposed that there was a preexilic edition of the Deuteronomistic History,[247] written during the reign of Josiah, which he called Dtr[1]. The history was then revised in the exile into its final form, which he called Dtr[2].[248] Cross also had identified three stages in the redaction of Chronicles as well: Chr[1] (late 6th century BCE), Chr[2] (ca. 450), and Chr[3] (400 or a little later).[249] McKenzie argued that the author of Chr[1] used Dtr[1] as his *Vorlage* in Samuel-Kings. But the theories of Cross on the redactional history of Chronicles have not found wide acceptance, and McKenzie came to a series of redactional judgments that are unlikely, including the idea that the account of the exile and repentance of Manasseh in 2 Chr 33:10-13 originally stood in Dtr[1]. When passages he understands as Dtr[2] have parallels in Chronicles, he assigns these passages in Chronicles to (Cross's) Chr[2] or Chr[3]. McKenzie also argued, as mentioned above, that the Chronicler's Hebrew text of Kings was quite different in character from his text of Samuel.

The text of Samuel LXX, Kings LXX, and Chronicles LXX is conveniently available through the splendid editions of the Cambridge Septuagint.[250] Many of the variants in Chronicles LXX and other ancient versions are reported accurately in the apparatus to *BHS,* which was edited by Wilhelm Rudolph, the author of a German commentary on Chronicles that I cite frequently throughout my commentary. Rudolph's textual notes in his commentary offer important explanations for his suggestions in *BHS.* Unfortunately the textual apparatus to the books of Samuel in *BHS,* prepared by P. A. H. de Boer, is quite deficient, and many of the variants from Samuel MT recorded in the footnotes to my translation of Chronicles go completely unnoted in *BHS.* In the first textual footnote to the translation of those chapters in Chronicles that have a *Vorlage* in the books of Samuel—1 Chronicles 10, 11, 13–21—I list the numbers of the footnotes in each chapter containing readings in that chapter that presuppose a text of Samuel other than Samuel MT. Frequent references in the commentary itself underscore the significance of some of these non-MT readings for understanding the methodology of the Chronicler. Other textual notes, of course, address textual difficulties in Chronicles itself regardless of the reading in the *Vorlage* of the Deuteronomistic History.

Sources

Sources from Samuel, Kings, and Psalms

The primary source used by the Chronicler for 1 Chronicles 10–2 Chronicles 36 is the books of Samuel and Kings, but the copy of these books, the Chronicler's *Vorlage,* was not identical with the MT of these books (see the discussion of Textual Criticism above and the textual notes to the translation).[251]

In the nineteenth century and again in the late twentieth century, some scholars have proposed that Chronicles did not use Samuel and Kings, but that Chronicles and Samuel-Kings independently had access to a com-

247 Deuteronomy 1–4; Joshua; Judges; 1 and 2 Samuel; 1 and 2 Kings.

248 Frank Moore Cross, "The Themes of the Book of Kings and the Structure of the Deuteronomistic History," in *Canaanite Myth,* 274–89.

249 Cf. the discussion of this theory above under Unity.

250 *The Old Testament in Greek,* vol. 2: *The Later Historical Books,* part 1: *I and II Samuel;* part 2: *I and II Kings;* part 3: *I and II Chronicles* (ed. Alan England Brooke, Norman McLean, and Henry St. John Thackeray; London: Cambridge Univ. Press, 1927–1932). The Hebrew and Greek texts of Samuel-Kings are also printed in Vannutelli, *Libri Synoptici,* but he used the Holmes and Parsons edition of the early 19th century.

251 For a general review of the issue see Adrien-M. Brunet, O. P., "Le Chroniste et ses sources," *RB* 60 (1953) 481–508; *RB* 61 (1954) 349–86.

mon source now lost to us. C. F. Keil can stand for many conservative scholars in the nineteenth century who posited a common source behind Samuel-Kings and Chronicles as a defense against the attack on the historicity of Chronicles in the wake of the work of de Wette.[252] This source theory constituted an indispensable link between Keil's historical conservatism and his confessional presuppositions,[253] and ran the risk of arguing in a vicious circle: the historical reliability of Chronicles was justified by his use of reliable sources, and the reliability of his sources was justified by the reliability of Chronicles itself. Hence historical criticism was basically excluded.

More recently A. G. Auld has returned to the notion of a common source for Samuel-Kings and Chronicles with results dramatically different from the work of Keil.[254] This common source was for Auld a history of

the Judahite monarchy. Auld argued that where one history, Samuel-Kings or Chronicles, lacks an account, it was lacking in the common source. Hence the history of the northern kingdom, largely lacking in Chronicles, was also largely lacking in the common source and in the first draft of Samuel-Kings. This makes the history of the northern kingdom as reported in 1 Kings 12–2 Kings 17 a very late composition and of little historical value. But, as McKenzie asks about the source proposed by Auld, why would a history of the Judahite monarchy begin with Saul?[255] Does not 1 Chr 10:13-14 presuppose knowledge of at least 1 Samuel 18 and probably of 1 Samuel 13 and 15?[256] My commentary will show numerous places where the Chronicler alludes to or presupposes knowledge of passages in the books of Samuel that he did not include in his own narration of history.[257] To exclude them from the common source and from the

---

252 C. F. Keil, *Apologetischer Versuch über die Bücher der Chronik und über die Integrität des Buches Esra* (Berlin: Ludwig Oehmigke, 1833). See the thorough discussion of Kai Peltonen, "Function, Explanation and Literary Phenomena: Aspects of Source Criticism as Theory and Method in the History of Chronicles Research," in Graham and McKenzie, *Chronicler as Author*, 18–69, esp. 24–27. Keil's approach was anticipated earlier in the work of J. G. Eichhorn, who argued that the author of Chronicles knew the accounts of David and Solomon from 2 Samuel and 1 Kings, but did not use them as sources. Chronicles, in his view, used trustworthy, noncanonical source material, which had also been used by the author of Samuel and Kings. For de Wette see *Kritischer Versuch über die Glaubwürdigkeit der Bücher der Chronik mit Hinsicht auf die Geschichte der Mosaischen Bücher und Gesetzgebung* (Halle: Schimmelpfennig & Compagnie, 1806).

253 See Peltonen, "Source Criticism as Theory," 26. Aspects of this conservative attitude toward the Chronicler's sources and the idea that the Chronicler and Deuteronomistic Historian shared a common source show up in H. R. Macy, "The Sources of the Books of Chronicles: A Reassessment" (Ph.D. diss., Harvard, 1975) 117, 125, 127, 170, and passim.

254 See Auld, *Kings Without Privilege*; idem, "What Was the Main Source of the Books of Chronicles," in Graham and McKenzie, *Chronicler as Author*, 91–99. Cf. C. Y. S. Ho, "Conjectures and Refutations: Is 1 Samuel XXX 1-13 Really the Source of 1 Chronicles X 1-12?" *VT* 45 (1995) 82–106. Ho was a student of Auld. For my evaluation of his article see the commentary on 1 Chronicles 10.

255 Auld, "What Was the Main Source," in Graham and McKenzie, *Chronicler as Author*, 92, responds by calling the common source "The Book of Two Houses," dealing with Jerusalem's royal and divine houses.

256 Steven L. McKenzie, "The Chronicler as Redactor," in Graham and McKenzie, *Chronicler as Author*, 81. Auld, "What Was the Main Source," suggests that the Chronicler had on his desk only the Book of the Two Houses, but he knew of the additional stories about Saul that were included in the Former Prophets by ear or by repute, or he knew about Saul's resort to a consultation with a medium but only in a preliminary, nonelaborated form. He also tries to reply to McKenzie's other difficulties with his hypothesis, mentioned in the next note, with equally little success, in my judgment.

257 See also McKenzie, "Chronicler as Redactor," 82–85, who notes the mention of Michal in 1 Chr 15:29, which presupposes knowledge of the stories about Michal in 1 and 2 Samuel. In 1 Chr 20:5 the Chronicler changed 2 Sam 21:19 so that Elhanan killed not Goliath but Lahmi the brother of Goliath, but that change presupposes he knew the conflict between 2 Sam 21:19 and the story of David killing Goliath in 1 Samuel 17. The Chronicler refers to Ahab in 2 Chronicles 18, 21, and 22, but never introduces him, thus assuming that the reader would know about Ahab from 1 and 2 Kings. In 2 Chr 32:24 the Chronicler summarized Hezekiah's prayer and the accompanying sign from 2 Kgs 20:1-11. The verse in Chronicles is too short to have been the source from which the longer story developed.

earlier version of Samuel-Kings seems arbitrary to me. Rather, I believe that the Chronicler used the nearly final form of Samuel-Kings, although from a copy of the text of those books that is often variant from the MT of Samuel and Kings.[258]

The relationship between Chronicles and its source in Samuel-Kings and Psalms can be outlined as in table 1.[259] Passages printed in italics have a different order in Chronicles than they do in the *Vorlage*.

Table 1

1 Chronicles		1 Samuel	
10:1-12	death of Saul	31:1-13	
10:13-14	evaluation of Saul		
		2 Samuel	
		1:1—4:12	interregnum
11:1-3	anointing of David	5:1-3	
		5:4-5	chronology of David
11:4-9	David captures Jerusalem	5:6-10	
11:10	chiefs supporting David		
11:10-41a	*David's warriors*	*23:8-39*	
11:41b-47	more warriors		
12:1-22(21)	leaders who rallied to David at Ziklag		
12:23-40 (22-39)	soldiers who rallied to David at Hebron		
13:1-4	invitation to bring the ark to Jerusalem		
13:5-7	the ark's journey begins	6:1-3	
		6:4	note about Ahio
13:8-14	Uzzah killed for touching the ark	6:5-11	
14:1-2	*Hiram's support; David's kingdom established*	*5:11-12*	
14:3-7	*David's wives and children in Jerusalem*	*5:13-16*	
14:8-16	*Philistines defeated*	*5:17-25*	
15:1-3	preparations for moving the ark		
15:4-10	six Levite chiefs		
15:11-15	clergy ordered to carry ark		
15:16-24	installation of Levitical musicians		
		6:12a	house of Obed-Edom blessed
15:25—16:3	ark brought to Jerusalem	6:12b-19a	
16:4-7	David appoints Levites to thank and praise		

258 See also Zipora Talshir, "The Reign of Solomon in the Making: Pseudo-Connections between 3 Kingdoms and Chronicles," *VT* 50 (2000) 233–49, who shows the variations of Kings LXX and Chronicles from Kings MT are unrelated and offer no support for Auld's hypothesis about a common source behind Kings and Chronicles.

259 When no passage is listed in the Samuel-Kings column, we can assume an addition by the Chronicler. When no passage is listed in the Chronicles column, we have an omission by the Chronicler. This list is only an approximation, since on some occasions the Chronicler copies his source word for word while at other times he recasts his *Vorlage*, paraphrases it, omits parts of verses, and the like.

16:8-22	Israel's praise	**Ps 105:1-15**
16:23-33	international and cosmic praise	Ps 96:1b-13a
16:34-36	thanksgiving and petition	Ps 106:1b, 47-48
16:37-42	regular worship established	
16:43	David's blessing	**2 Sam 6:19b-20a**
		6:20b-23 David rebuked by Michal
17:1-15	oracle of Nathan	7:1-17
17:16-27	prayer of David	7:18-29
18:1-13	defeat of the Philistines	8:1-14
18:14-17	officers of David	8:15-18
		9:1-13 story of Mephibosheth
19:1-19	defeat of Ammonites and Arameans	10:1-19
20:1a	spring as time of war	11:1a
		11:1b-12:25 David and Bathsheba
20:1b	Joab attacked Rabbah of the Ammonites	12:26
		12:27-29 David summoned to Rabbah
20:2-3	David seized Ammonite crown and returned to Jerusalem	12:30-31
		13:1—20:6 crimes and rebellions[260]
		21:1-17 dismemberment of Saul's descendants; exploits of David's warriors
20:4-8	Elhanan killed Lahmi the brother of Goliath	21:18-22
		22:1-51 (= Ps 18:1-51 [S-50])
		23:1-7 last words of David
21:1-4a	David incited to take a census	24:1-4a
		24:4b-7 Joab's census
21:4b-15	report of census	24:8-16
21:16	angel with drawn sword	
21:17-25	purchase of threshing floor of Ornan; altar erected	24:17-25
21:18—22:1	tabernacle and altar of burnt offering at Gibeon	
22:2-5	David provides materials for temple	
22:6-16	David's private speech to Solomon	
22:17-19	leaders commanded to build temple	
23:1-2	Solomon made king by David	
23:3-32	families of Levites and their functions	
24:1-31	twenty-four priestly courses; more Levites	
25:1-31	Levitical singers	
26:1-32	Levitical gatekeepers; other Levites	
27:1-34	commanders of monthly divisions; tribal leaders; David's administrators	

---

260   These include the rape of Tamar and the murder of Amnon; the revolt and death of Absalom; negotiations for David's restoration to the throne; rebellion of Sheba; and a listing of the officers of David.

28:1-10	David's public speech to Solomon		
28:11-21	David's instructions for building the temple		
29:1-9	David's contributions to the temple		
29:10-22a	David's praise of God; sacrifices by assembly	**1 Kings**	
29:22b	anointing of Solomon and Zadok	Cf. 1:39	
29:23a	Solomon sat on the throne	1:46 (cf. 2:12)	
29:23b-25	Yahweh magnified Solomon		
29:26	summary of David's reign		
29:27	*length of David's reign*	*2:11*	
29:28	death of David	1:1—2:10	death of David[261]
29:29-30	sources: words of Samuel, Nathan, and Gad		

2 Chronicles[262]

1:1-13	Solomon granted wisdom at Gibeon	**1 Kings**	
		2:12-46	Solomon's rivals exiled or killed
		3:1-15	+ marriage to Pharaoh's daughter
		3:16-28	judgment of prostitutes
		4:1-20	Solomon's officials
		5:1-14	Magnificence; wisdom
		(4:21-34)	
1:14-17	*chariots and horses*	*10:26-29*	
1:18—2:15	Treaty with Huram	5:15-22 (5:1-8); *7:13-14;*[263] 5:23-26	
(16)		(9-12)	
2:16-17	census	5:27-32 forced labor	
(17-18)		(13-18)	
3:1-4a	Solomon begins to build the temple	6:1-3	
		6:4-20a	details of the temple
3:4b-5a	the nave	6:20b-22	
3:5b-9	gold decoration		
3:10-11	cherubim	6:23-24	
3:12-14	cherubim		
		6:25-38	cherubim and other furnishings
		7:1-12	Solomon's other buildings
3:15—4:5	Huram's work in temple	7:15-26	
		7:27-37	ten stands
4:6aα	ten basins	7:38-39a	
4:6aβ-9	lampstands, tables, etc.		

---

261 This pericope contains reports of the following incidents: an aged David is warmed by Abishag on his deathbed; the revolt of David's son Adonijah; the intervention of Bathsheba and Nathan on behalf of Solomon; the anointing of Solomon; the death of David.

262 This listing may need to be revised once the commentary on 2 Chronicles has been written. In some cases, such as 2 Chr 1:6b-13a//1 Kgs 3:5-15 and 2 Chr 24:1-27//2 Kgs 12:1-22, the synoptic passages show considerable difference from one another.

263 Hiram, the Tyrian craftsman, who worked on the temple.

4:10-22	the sea, pillars, etc.	7:39b-50	
5:1-11a	ark into temple	7:51—8:10a	
5:11b-13a	Levites		
5:13b-14	glory of Yahweh	8:10b-11	
6:1-40	Solomon's speech and prayer at dedication	8:12-53	
6:41-42	quotation from Psalms	**Ps 132:8-10, 1**	
7:1a	Solomon finishes prayer	**1 Kgs 8:54a**	
7:1b-3	fire from heaven		
		8:54b-61	Solomon blesses assembly
7:4-10	Sacrifices and dismissal of people	8:62-66	
7:11-22	Yahweh appears again to Solomon	9:1-9	
8:1-2	Huram gives cities to Solomon	9:10-13	Solomon gives cities to Hiram
		9:14-16	corvée; Gezer as dowry
8:3-16	further activities	9:17-25	
8:17-18	fleet at Ezion-geber	9:26-28	
9:1-25	Queen of Sheba, wisdom, wealth	10:1-26	
9:26	*extent of Solomon's rule*	*5:1*	
9:27-28	silver, cedar, horses	10:27-28a	
		10:28b—11:40	apostasy and enemies
9:29-31	death of Solomon	11:41-43	
10:1—11:4	Rehoboam becomes king	12:1-24	
11:5-23	Rehoboam's fortifications		
		12:25—14:20	Jeroboam I
12:1	Rehoboam abandoned Torah		
12:2	Shishak attack	14:25	
12:3-9a	new details about Shishak		
12:9b-11	Booty taken by Shishak	14:26-28	
12:12	Rehoboam humbled himself		
12:13-14	*Summary of reign*	*14:21-22a*	
		14:22b-24	Sins of Judah
12:15-16	Abijah becomes king	14:19-31	Abijam becomes king
13:1-2	war with Jeroboam	15:1-2, 6	
		15:3-5	Evaluation of Abijam
13:3-21	Abijah's sermon to the north		
13:22-23	death of Abijah; Asa king	15:7-10	+ synchronism
(13:22—14:1)			
14:1-2 (2-3)	evaluation of Asa	15:11-12	
14:3-14	war with Cushites		
(4-15)			
15:1-15	Azariah's sermon; covenant to seek Yahweh		
15:16-19	cultic measures; war	15:13-16	
16:1-6	alliance with Ben-hadad	15:17-22	
16:7-10	Hanani rebukes Asa		
16:11-14	regnal resumé	15:23-24a	
17:1	Jehoshaphat becomes king	15:24b	
		15:25—21:29[264]	

---

264 Reigns of Nadab, Baasha, Elah, Zimri, Omri, Ahab; Elijah cycle.

265 Reigns of Ahaziah and Joram; Elijah and Elisha stories.

266 Reigns of Zechariah, Shallum, Menahem, Pekahiah, Pekah.

32:1-23	battle against Sennacherib[267]	18:13–19:31	
32:24	Hezekiah's sickness	20:1a	
		20:1b-11	Hezekiah healed
32:25-30	further acts of Hezekiah		
32:31	visit by Babylonian officials	20:12-19	
32:32-33	regnal resumé	20:20-21	
33:1-10	reign of Manasseh	21:1-10	
		21:11-16	rebuke of Manasseh
33:11-17	captivity and repentance		
33:18-20	regnal resumé	21:17-18	
33:21-25	reign of Amon	21:19-26	
34:1-2	Josiah becomes king	22:1-2	
34:3-7	reform of Josiah		
34:8-33	book of law; Huldah; covenant	22:3–23:3	
		23:4-20	Josiah's reforms
35:1-19	Passover	23:21-23	
		23:24-27	judgment because of Manasseh
35:20-27	*death of Josiah*	*23:29, 30a, 28*	
36:1-4	Jehoahaz deposed; Jehoiakim becomes king	23:30b-35	
36:5-8	reign of Jehoiakim	23:36–24:7	
36:9-10	reign of Jehoiachin	24:8-17	
36:11-13a	reign of Zedekiah	24:18-20	
36:13b-17	rejection of God's messengers		
36:18-20	vessels taken; temple burned; exile		
		25:1-21	destruction of Jerusalem
36:21	Jeremiah's prophecy; sabbath for the land		
36:22-23	Yahweh stirs up spirit of Cyrus	Ezra 1:1-3a	

We will see in this commentary that the Chronicler assumes his readers' familiarity with events he omits from Samuel and Kings, that he omits things that do not fit with his purposes, that he rearranges items in retelling Israel's story, and that he even changes the evaluation of certain kings. Of course there are also hundreds of changes in detail, sometimes for theological or ideological reasons, but others apparently because of literary or linguistic sensitivities.[268]

Other Biblical Sources

In the genealogies in particular, one can find parallel information in the Pentateuch and the book of Joshua,

although the form of the genealogy in Chronicles often differs from that in the *Vorlage*.[269] In many cases the Chronicler himself may have recast the genealogy; at other times, he *may* have had an alternate version of the genealogy that just happened to overlap with canonical information. Noth and other scholars have used the distinction between genealogical information contained in the Bible and other genealogical information to separate between primary and secondary materials. Table 2 provides an approximate list of corresponding information to 1 Chronicles 1–9 in other biblical books.

---

267 The Chronicler has completely rewritten the long report in 2 Kings 18–19.

268 Kalimi, *Geschichtsschreibung, passim,* has compiled a comprehensive list of such literary changes.

269 In 1 Chr 1:1-4 the genealogy of the pre-flood patriarchs is merely a list of names without stating that Adam became the father of Seth, etc.

Table 2

1 Chronicles[270]		Other biblical books
1:1-4	Adam to Shem, Ham, and Japheth	Gen 5:1-32; 10:1
1:5-23	descendants of Shem, Ham, and Japheth	Gen 10:2-4, 6-9a, 13-18a, 22-29
1:24-27	Shem to Abraham	Gen 11:10-26; cf. 17:5
1:28-34	descendants of Ishmael and Isaac	Gen 25:12-16a, 2-4, 19; cf. 16:15; 21:2-3
1:35-54	descendants of Esau and Seir; kings and chiefs of Edom	Gen 36:4-5a, 11-12a, 20-28, 31-43
2:1-2	descendants of Israel	Gen 35:22b-26; cf. Exod 1:2-5
2:3-8	descendants of Judah	Genesis 38; 46:12; Num 26:19-22; Josh 7:1; 1 Kgs 5:11 (4:31)
2:10-12	from Ram to Jesse	Ruth 4:18-22; cf. 1 Sam 16:6-9; 2 Sam 2:18
2:13	David and his brothers	1 Sam 16:6-9; 17:13
2:16-17	Zeruiah and Abigail	2 Sam 17:25; 19:14
2:20	Hur-Uzi-Bezalel	Exod 31:2; 35:30; 38:22
2:49	Achsah the daughter of Caleb	Josh 15:16-17; Judg 1:12-23
3:1-4	descendants of David born at Hebron	2 Sam 3:2-5; 5:5, 14-16; cf. 13:1
3:5-9	children of David born at Jerusalem[271]	2 Sam 5:13-16
3:10-16	descendants of Solomon who served as kings	1 and 2 Kings
4:24	sons of Simeon	Num 26:12-14 (cf. also Gen 46:10; Exod 6:15)
4:28-33bα	places associated with Simeon	Josh 19:1-9
5:1	Reuben's incest	Gen 35:22
5:3	sons of Reuben	Exod 6:14; cf. Gen 46:9; Num 26:5-7
5:11	Gad	Gen 30:10-11
5:25-26	exile of Transjordanian tribes	Cf. 2 Kgs 15:19-20, 29; 17:6; 18:11
5:27-41 (6:1-15); cf. 1 Chr 6:35-38 (6:50-53)		Exod 6:16-24; Num 3:17, 19; 1 Sam 1:1; 8:2; Ezra 7:1-5; Neh 11:10-11; 1 Chr 9:10-11; 2 Esdr 1:1-3
6:39-66 (54-81)	the cities of the priests and Levites	Josh 21:1-40[272]
7:1	descendants of Issachar	Num 26:23-24 (cf. Gen 46:13)
7:6	descendants of Benjamin (cf. 1 Chr 8:1-2)	Gen 46:21; Num 26:38-41
7:13	descendants of Naphtali	Gen 46:24; Num 26:48-49
7:14-19	descendants of Manasseh	cf. Num 26:29-34 and Josh 17:1-3
7:20	descendants of Ephraim	Num 26:35-36
7:29	towns of Manasseh	Josh 17:11
7:30-40	descendants of Asher	Gen 46:17; cf. Num 26:44-46
8:1-2	descendants of Benjamin (cf. 1 Chr 7:6)	Gen 46:21;[273] Num 26:38-41
8:33-34//9:39-40	some ancestors and descendants of Saul[274]	1 Sam 9:1-2; 14:49-51; 31:2
9:2-17a	list of those who lived in the land and in Jerusalem	Neh 11:3-19

---

270 Chronicles did not include the genealogies of Cain (Gen 4:17-26), Terah (11:27-32), and Nahor (22:21-24).

271 Cf. also 1 Chr 14:3-7.

272 The Chronicler moves Josh 21:5-9 to a position after 21:19.

273 This includes in this case the text preserved in LXX.

274 See also under Other Presumed Nonbiblical Sources below.

The Chronicler also shows wide acquaintance with the legal and cultic materials in the Pentateuch and patterns some of his accounts of the temple building on the earlier account of the tabernacle. These matters are taken up in the commentary itself.

Source Citations Given in Chronicles

Chronicles also contains fourteen source citations that can be compared with parallel references in the book of Kings. Table 3 refers to the name of the sources themselves; other differences in these paragraphs will be treated in the commentary.

Table 3

Chronicles	Kings
1. David	
1 Chr 29:29 in the acts[275] of Samuel[276] the seer,[277] and in the acts of Nathan the prophet, and in the acts of Gad who saw visions[278]	
2. Solomon	
2 Chr 9:29 in the acts of Nathan the prophet, the prophecy of Ahijah the Shilonite, and in the visions of the seer Iddo, which he saw concerning Jeroboam the son of Nebat	1 Kgs 11:41 in the book of the acts of Solomon
3. Rehoboam	
2 Chr 12:15 in the acts of Shemaiah the prophet and Iddo who saw visions	1 Kgs 14:29 in the book of the chronicles[279] of the kings of Judah
4. Abijah/Abijam	
2 Chr 13:22 in the history[280] of the prophet Iddo	1 Kgs 15:7 in the book of the chronicles of the kings of Judah
5. Asa	
2 Chr 16:11 in the book of the kings of Judah and Israel	1 Kgs 15:23 in the book of the chronicles of the kings of Judah
6. Jehoshaphat	
2 Chr 20:34 in the acts of Jehu the son of Hanani, which are recorded in the book of the kings of Israel	1 Kgs 22:6 (45) in the book of the chronicles of the kings of Judah
7. Jehoram	
	2 Kgs 8:23 in the book of the chronicles of the kings of Judah

---

275 This word represents דברי in these source citations.

276 Samuel died, of course, before David ever became king. The Chronicler is here apparently acknowledging Samuel's role in recording the early days of David as reported in 1 Samuel. The Chronicler did not include any parts of the book of Samuel that came before the prophet's death.

277 הראה.

278 החזה. This could also be translated as "the seer," but I have chosen this alternate translation to distinguish this title from הראה.

279 This word represents דברי הימים in these source citations.

280 מדרש. Cf. 2 Chr 24:27.

8. Joash

2 Chr 24:27 in the history of the book of the kings[281]

2 Kgs 12:20 (19) in the book of the chronicles of the kings of Judah

9. Amaziah

2 Chr 25:26 in the book of the kings of Judah and Israel

2 Kgs 14:18 in the book of the chronicles of the kings of Judah

10. Uzziah/Azariah

2 Chr 26:22 Isaiah the prophet the son of Amoz wrote

2 Kgs 15:6 in the book of the chronicles of the kings of Judah

11. Jotham

2 Chr 27:7 in the book of the kings of Israel and Judah

2 Kgs 15:36 in the book of the chronicles of the kings of Judah

12. Ahaz

2 Chr 28:26 in the book of the kings of Judah and Israel

2 Kgs 16:19 in the book of the chronicles of the kings of Judah

13. Hezekiah

2 Chr 32:32 in the vision of Isaiah the prophet the son of Amoz, in the book of the kings of Judah and Israel

2 Kgs 20:20 in the book of the chronicles of the kings of Judah

14. Manasseh

2 Chr 33:18-19 in the acts of the kings of Israel . . . in the chronicles of his visionaries[282]

2 Kgs 21:17 in the book of the chronicles of the kings of Judah

15. Amon[283]

2 Kgs 21:25 in the book of the chronicles of the kings of Judah

16. Josiah

2 Chr 35:27 in the book of the kings of Israel and Judah

2 Kgs 23:28 in the book of the chronicles of the kings of Judah

17. Jehoiakim

2 Chr 36:8 in the book of the kings of Israel and Judah and Judah

2 Kgs 24:5 in the book of the chronicles of the kings of Judah

---

Kings lacks a source citation for David, and the source citation for Solomon in Chronicles is unique. The other fifteen source citations in Kings are all to the same document: "the book of the chronicles of the kings of Judah." Mordechai Cogan believes that this book, like its parallel for the northern kingdom,[284] surveyed and summarized the monarchic period, and was based on source materials, such as records of war, tribute pay-ments, royal projects, and so on. The books for the northern and southern kingdoms were both commonly known, in his opinion, and were held to be authoritative.[285] No source citation in Kings and Chronicles is given for Ahaziah, Athaliah, Jehoahaz, Jehoiachin, and Zedekiah. In addition, Chronicles MT lacks a source citation for Jehoram (#7) and Amon (#15). With the single exception of #16,[286] all of the

---

281 This item and item 10 are the only source refer-ences for the kings after Solomon that do not con-tain the name Israel.

282 חוזי. MT חוֹזָי "Hozai." LXX presupposes החוזים "the visionaries."

283 Benzinger, 129, suggests that the equivalent of 2

Kgs 21:25-26 was lost in Chronicles by haplography (homoioteleuton). Cf. *BHS*.

284 "The book of the chronicles of the kings of Israel."

285 Mordechai Cogan, *1 Kings* (AB 10; New York: Doubleday, 2001) 89–91.

286 And the addition of a source citation #1.

source citations in Chronicles appear at the same place within the narrative in Chronicles as in Kings, even when, as in ##5, 6, and 9, important parts of the king's reign are reported after the source citation.

Chronicles refers to one source by at least five different names: (1) the book of the kings of Israel and Judah (##11, 16, 17); (2) the book of the kings of Judah and Israel (##5, 9, 12, 13);[287] (3) the book of the kings of Israel (#6); (4) the acts of the kings of Israel (#14); and (5) the history of the book of the kings (#8). Despite the variation between "book," "acts," and "history," and the variations among the names of the nation itself,[288] I assume that the author is referring to the same document.

Note also that the Chronicler refers eight times to prophets or prophetic figures in these source citations: (1) Samuel, Nathan, and Gad (#1 David); (2) Nathan, Ahijah, and Iddo (#2 Solomon); (3) Shemaiah and Iddo (#3 Rehoboam); (4) Iddo (#4 Abijah); (5) Jehu (#6 Jehoshaphat); (6) Isaiah (#10 Uzziah); (7) Isaiah (#13 Hezekiah); and (8) his seers (#14 Manasseh). Jehu's words are said to be recorded in the book of the kings of Israel, and "the book of the kings of Judah and Israel" is in apposition to "the vision of Isaiah" in #13.[289] Thus the Chronicler relates the prophetic writings to the book of the kings mentioned in the previous paragraph. All of the prophetic source references occur with kings whom the Chronicler views favorably, at least for part of their reign.

What is the meaning of these prophetic references and the reference to a source called "the book of the kings"? Five proposals may be considered.

1. The Chronicler is following a literary convention based on the parallel source citations in the canonical book of Kings,[290] or, more radically, these citations are "mere show."[291] But if the Chronicler were only following a literary convention or merely arbitrarily claiming authority for his work, why would he not add source citations for the kings' reigns where these citations were missing in the book of Kings?

2. Both the Deuteronomistic Historian and the Chronicler had access to a compilation known as "the chronicles of the kings of Judah" or a similar title. That is, both the Deuteronomistic Historian and the Chronicler used the same source. The Deuteronomistic Historian chose not to use certain passages, while the Chronicler chose to include them.[292] This would explain how the Chronicler got the additional information he includes about various kings. But I have already noted above the unlikelihood that Samuel-Kings and Chronicles independently used a common source. This explanation does not really account for the prophetic references that show up in Chronicles, nor does it account for the fact that the Chronicler does not add this kind of citation for those reigns where it is omitted in Kings.

3. The Chronicler is referring to an elaborated version of the canonical book of Kings, perhaps called "the midrash on the book of kings" (2 Chr 24:27; cf. #8 above and 2 Chr 13:22).[293] Positing this hypothetical source, of course, does little to clarify the real origin of the Chronicler's additional information, but substitutes one unknown for another, and it also does not explain why the Chronicler claims to have used this source only at those places where the Deuteronomistic Historian also had inserted a source citation.

4. The Chronicler repeated *and* reworded the source citations found in the Deuteronomistic History, but understood them now as references to the Deuteronomistic History itself rather than to some other kind of

---

287　The first of these is written המלכים ליהודה, and the last three מלכי יהודה.

288　Williamson, 19, notes that "Judah" is never used alone in these titles, but "Israel" always appears before or after it, with the exception of 2 Chr 24:27, where no nation is mentioned. In 20:34 and 33:18 "Israel" by itself refers to the southern kingdom.

289　There is variety again, both in the references to the document (acts, chronicles, history, prophecy, visions, and the reference to the writing of Isaiah) and to the prophetic titles (prophet, seer, [the one] who saw visions, visionaries).

290　Noth, *Chronicler's History,* 53.

291　Torrey, *Ezra Studies*, 223. On p. 230 Torrey refers to the supposedly midrashic version of the book of Kings (see #3 below) as a "phantom 'source.'"

292　Anson F. Rainey, "The Chronicler and His Sources—Historical and Geographical," in Graham, Hoglund, and McKenzie, *Chronicler as Historian*, 43.

293　Driver, *Introduction*, 527–32; Curtis and Madsen, 23–24, and Rudolph, XI. Japhet, 21–22, affirms this position, but on p. 23 she admits uncertainty about what the source citations are referring to. Already F. C. Movers, *Kritische Untersuchungen über die biblische Chronik: Ein Beitrag zur Einleitung in das alte Testament* (Bonn: T. Habicht, 1834) posited such a source document.[294] Note that in his narrative about Solomon, the Chronicler does not use information from sources other than the account in 2 Kings.[295] This interpretation fits well with the (later) understanding of Samuel and Kings as part of the Former Prophets, but it does not fit so well with the many reigns in which Chronicles presents additional information.

5. By these source citations, the Chronicler was explaining his understanding of the tradition history of the book of Kings.[296] That is, the Chronicler believed that the prophets had recorded contemporary events[297] and that these prophetic works had been gathered together into a "book of the kings,"[298] probably for both the northern and the southern kingdom. The Chronicler also thought that the Deuteronomistic History was an epitome of that book of the kings. By repeating and rewording the source citations found in his *Vorlage,* the Chronicler was explaining why he considered that *Vorlage* to have prophetic authority—because it was based ultimately on prophetic accounts of contemporary events that had been gathered into a book of the kings. These source citations in this understanding do not clarify the origin of the additional material Chronicles reports for many reigns. The same can be said for interpretation #4 as well. I believe either this explanation or the previous one offers a plausible understanding for the use of these source citations in Chronicles.

As Japhet, 23, has noted, however, the question of the source citations, and the questions about the sources available to the Chronicler are quite separate issues in any case. Hence the Chronicler's use of sources and the value of these sources need to be evaluated independently of these source citation references.

Other Allusions to Sources

In addition to the source citations for kings' reigns, Chronicles contains a series of other allusions to sources:

1. 1 Chr 9:1 "the book of the kings of Israel." This same title is given as a source for the reign of Jehoshaphat in 2 Chr 20:34 above and is similar to a number of the other source citations. With this title at 1 Chr 9:1 the Chronicler seems to be referring to the source for some or all of the genealogies provided in chaps. 2–8. None of the five explanations for the royal source citations really helps here unless we assume that the hypothetical elaborated book of Kings (#3) also contained a genealogical preface. That preface, of course, is what seems unique about the book of Chronicles itself. There can be no question (see the next section) that the Chronicler indeed did have access to genealogical sources, but exactly how this "book of the kings of Israel" relates to the royal source citations is not clear.

2. 1 Chr 16:40 "all that is written in the law of Yahweh."[299] A reference to (a part of) the Pentateuch.

2. 1 Chr 23:27 "For according to the last words of David these were the number of the Levites from twenty years old and upward." In the commentary I assign this verse to a secondary hand. This reference ascribes Davidic authority to the change in age for the beginning of Levitical service described in 1 Chr 23:24. The Chronicler himself would probably have considered all the speeches of David from chaps. 22–29 as David's last words.

3. 1 Chr 24:6 "The scribe Shemaiah the son of Nethanel, from the Levites, wrote them [= the divisions of the sons of Aaron] down." This seems to refer to a source document that recorded the twenty-four priestly courses now attested in 1 Chr 24:7-19.

---

source. He felt that this source was a revision of the book of Kings in a postexilic spirit. Movers also believed that the Chronicler used the books of Samuel and Kings as a source. See Peltonen, "Function," 29–31. Among the four sources posited by I. Benzinger in his commentary were: (a) Samuel-Kings; (b) midrashic writings; (c) source material from a historical work of postexilic origin; and (d) defective and fragmentary lists. See Peltonen, "Function," 56–57.

294 Cf. Williamson, 18.

295 Cf. Noth, *Chronicler's History,* 53, though he adds on 157, n. 12, that one needs to consider a few allu-

sions to the Pentateuch in the Chronicler's account of Solomon.

296 Willi, *Chronik als Auslegung,* 231–41.

297 See esp. 2 Chr 26:22.

298 See esp. 2 Chr 20:34.

299 Cf. the references to the law in 1 Chr 22:12 and seventeen times in 2 Chronicles. In 2 Chr 23:18 and elsewhere this source is ascribed to Moses.

4. 1 Chr 27:24 "the book of the chronicles of King David." 1 Chr 27:23-24 was added by someone other than the Chronicler in an attempt to exonerate David for the census he took in 1 Chronicles 21. I believe that this source reference is an allusion to chap. 21.

5. 2 Chr 29:30 "the words of David and of the seer Asaph." This is probably an allusion to the Psalter.

6. 2 Chr 35:4 "the written directions of King David of Israel and the written directions of his son Solomon." The written directions of David refer to (parts of) 1 Chronicles 23–27; the written directions of Solomon seem to refer back to 2 Chr 8:14.

7. 2 Chr 35:25 "they [= the laments for Josiah] are recorded in the lamentations." The book of Lamentations in the Bible does not contain any references to Josiah, and its title in Hebrew, איכה, is different from the word laments (הקינות) here. The Chronicler thus refers to an otherwise unknown collection of laments.[300]

Other Presumed Nonbiblical Sources

The Chronicler had access to other oral or written sources for at least some of his information, even though he does not specify where this information comes from. I refer especially to the genealogical materials in 1 Chronicles 2–8, which he took from genealogical collections or even in some cases from living memory. For the tribe of Naphtali, he seems to have had only the information supplied by the Bible itself, but for the other tribes he had voluminous additional information. While many commentators have said the Chronicler used both biblical and extrabiblical genealogical information in constructing his genealogies for the tribes, information parallel to the biblical data may already have been recorded in his nonbiblical source. The genealogical information is diverse in genre and may have come from a wide variety of sources. That the Chronicler had much more information for some tribes than for others also strongly suggests that he was dependent on whatever genealogical sources were available and that he did not manufacture these data. Williamson, 46, has called attention to what appears to be information from a military census list in 1 Chr 5:23-24; 7:2, 4-5, 7, 9, 11, 40. Another document taken from a source is 1 Chr 27:25-34, the twelve supervisors over David's property and the list of seven advisors or associates of David.[301]

Noth, however, has argued that the Chronicler had nothing but the books of Samuel in their present form as his *Vorlage* for the history of David.[302] In general, most scholars contend that the availability of source documents to the Chronicler should be evaluated on a case-by-case basis. Noth contended that we can assume that the Chronicler made use of ancient sources only where allowance for the overall character of Chronicles has been made and where cogent arguments can be advanced in favor of such a claim.[303] Noth suspected that the Chronicler used only one source document besides the Deuteronomistic History for the period of the monarchy.[304] I will discuss source documents for 2 Chronicles in the introduction to that volume.[305]

Postexilic Sources

Finally, the Chronicler also used documents containing information from postexilic times and sometimes ascribed those to an earlier period, such as the time of David.

• 1 Chr 3:17-24, the descendants of Jeconiah (= Jehoiachin). Two of these names, Shealtiel and Zerubbabel, are known in other biblical materials.[306]

---

300 For a contrary opinion see Japhet, 1043, and the discussion of this passage under Date above.

301 For 1 Chr 27:16-22, see the commentary.

302 *Chronicler's History*, 56. But see the commentary on 1 Chr 11:41b-47 and (at least parts of) 1 Chronicles 12.

303 *Chronicler's History*, 53.

304 Ibid., 60.

305 Noth, ibid., 57–61, believed the following items in 2 Chronicles may have come from a source document: 11:5b-10aα (Rehoboam's fortresses); 13:3-20 (aspects of Abijah's war against Jeroboam); 14:8-14 (aspects of Asa's campaign against the Cushites);

26:6-8a (Uzziah's wars with the Philistines); 26:9 (Uzziah's building of fortifications in Jerusalem); 26:15 (Uzziah's catapults); 27:5 (Jotham's Ammonite campaign); 28:18 (cities captured by Philistines from Ahaz); 32:30 (Hezekiah's tunnel); 33:14a (Manasseh's building projects); 35:20-24 (some details of Josiah's last battle and death).

306 The identity of Zerubbabel's father is unclear. See the commentary on 1 Chr 3:19.

- 1 Chr 5:27-41 (6:1-15), the list of high priests. In the commentary I understand this as the "master list" of the high priests, from which other lists have been excerpted in 1 Chr 6:35-38 (50-53); Ezra 7:1-5; 2 Esdr 1:1-3; Neh 11:10-11; 1 Chr 9:10-11.
- 1 Chr 6:1-15 (16-30), the genealogy of the regular Levites.
- 1 Chr 6:16-34 (31-49), the linear pedigrees of the Levitical singers.

Williamson, 23, concluded his own study of the Chronicler's sources with these words: "Overall the Chronicler shows himself as the master, not the servant, of his sources." We can see in many cases exactly how he has accepted, rearranged, or reworded his biblical source in Samuel-Kings and the Psalter. One can propose that he used similar methods on his extrabiblical sources, but, lacking the original copies of those sources, it is hard to be more specific. It is difficult for me to understand how Williamson concludes on the same page that "he [the Chronicler] has handled his biblical sources more conservatively than others." That may be true, but how would one know, except that one would expect him to show respect toward what was surely by his time an authoritative text.

Central Themes

While a full statement on the Chronicler's theology must wait for the publication of the second volume in this commentary, a number of primary themes and emphases need to be mentioned already here.

Kingship

The Davidic kingship in Israel is identified in Chronicles with the kingdom of Yahweh (1 Chr 10:14; 17:1-15; 28:5; 29:23), and the kingship of the Northern Kingdom is considered illegitimate (2 Chr 13:8). The divine commitment to the Davidic dynasty decreases the attention given to the events of exodus and Sinai in the book.[307] The two kings of the united monarchy, David and Solomon, are presented in an idealized fashion, with a far greater emphasis on their public actions than on their private lives. The Chronicler omits David's controversial struggles with Saul, his adultery with Bathsheba, the murder of Uriah, and the revolt of Absalom. Nothing is said of the weakness of his final days, the vain efforts of Abishag to warm him, or his vengeful advice to Solomon in 1 Kings 1–2. It is an overstatement, however, to say that David is presented as perfect. His sins are noted in 1 Chr 15:13 (improper care for the ark) and in 21:1, 3, 8 (the census), and he was barred from building the temple because he was a shedder of blood (22:8) and a man of war (28:3).

The Chronicler offers a radically revised picture of Solomon as well. Solomon's rise to power did not come through the conniving of Nathan and Bathsheba, who took advantage of David's weakness during his final illness, nor is there any mention of the attempt by Solomon's brother Adonijah, supported by the king's sons and all his royal officials, to usurp the throne. Rather, David, presumably in full command of his powers, designates Solomon as king in fulfillment of the oracle of Nathan (17:15; 22:9-10), and he cites a divine oracle designating Solomon as the king chosen by Yahweh (28:6-7, 10). The people, including all the sons of King David, made Solomon king before the death of his father (29:22-25). Solomon's idolatry and apostasy, induced by his many foreign wives, is omitted completely (1 Kgs 10:28b–11:40).[308] Even his journey to sacrifice at the "high place" at Gibeon (1 Kgs 3:2-6) is cast in a different light since according to the Chronicler the tent of meeting/the tabernacle was located there (2 Chr 1:3-6).

The chief contribution of David was his preparation for the building of the temple and his establishment of several classes of lesser clergy; the chief contribution of Solomon was the erection of the temple itself. In several

---

307 In my judgment Japhet, 47, overstates this issue and concludes that for the Chronicler Israel has had a virtually undisturbed continuity in the land. As Williamson, 24, has pointed out, the Chronicler assumes knowledge of themes like exodus and Sinai. The Chronicler's notion of the land enjoying its Sabbaths during the exile also runs counter to Japhet's conclusion about a virtually unbroken existence in the land.

308 The Nehemiah Memoir, on the other hand, emphasizes these charges: "Did not King Solomon of Israel sin on account of such women? Among the many nations there was no king like him, and he was beloved by his God, and God made him king over Israel; nevertheless, foreign women made even him to sin" (Neh 13:26).

studies Braun has noted how the Chronicler treats David and Solomon in parallel and complementary ways (1 Chr 22:12 and 2 Chr 1:10; 1 Chr 29:12 and 2 Chr 1:11-12; 1 Chr 22:3-4 and 2 Chr 2:1-2; cf. also 2 Chr 7:10; 11:17; 35:4).[309]

Temple and Cult

The temple in Jerusalem and its worship life are central in Chronicles. Jerusalem even plays a role in the opening genealogies (1 Chr 3:4-5; 5:36, 41; 6:17 [6:10, 15, 32]; 8:28, 32; 9:3, 34, 38). The temple is mentioned in 5:36 (6:10), and the high priests and lists of Levites[310] are at the center of the genealogical unit that opens the book (5:27—6:66 [6:1-81]). David appointed Levites to the service of song at the tabernacle, and they continued this service in the temple after it had been built by Solomon (6:16-17 [31-32]). Among the postexilic inhabitants of Jerusalem are priests, Levites, gatekeepers, and singers (9:10-34). David's first action after his anointing (11:1-3) is the capture of Jerusalem (11:4-9). After we are told about all those who rallied to David at Hebron from all Israel (11:10—12:41 [40]), David assembled all Israel to bring the ark from Kiriath-jearim to Jerusalem (chap. 13). That effort was foiled because the Levites had not been asked to carry the ark (15:13), but the second attempt to bring the ark to Jerusalem was completely successful. David took the occasion to appoint Levites to invoke, thank, and praise, both at the ark in Jerusalem and at the tabernacle in Gibeon (chap. 16). The oracle of Nathan promises David a dynasty and authorizes his son to build the temple (17:1-15). David's wars in chaps. 18–20 provide the opportunity to acquire vast quantities of bronze, which Solomon used in the temple construction. After the nearly disastrous census in chap. 21, David acquired the site for the altar of burnt offering

and the temple itself (22:1). The speeches of David in chaps. 22, 28, and 29 endorse Solomon as temple builder and reveal David's own generous provision of raw materials for the temple. In the midst of these speeches, David appointed a number of Levites, including those charged to be officers and judges, gatekeepers, and singers (chaps. 23–26). From 2 Chr 1:18 (2:1) through 8:16 Solomon is involved with the building and dedication of the temple. Abijah criticizes the Northern Kingdom severely for having an alternate worship site and an alternate clergy and maintains that Yahweh is with those who maintain the temple in Jerusalem (13:8-12). Five later kings initiate cultic reforms (Asa, Jehoshaphat, Joash, Hezekiah, and Josiah), and faithfulness in maintaining proper worship becomes the criterion by which kings are judged. Hezekiah, the first king after the fall of the north, is a second Solomon, who cleanses the temple (29:12-36), celebrates a Passover to which he also invites northerners (chap. 30), and reorders the Levites and arranges for their support (31:12-19). When the king of the Chaldeans burned down the temple, this action was seen as fulfillment of the word of Jeremiah (36:19-20).

The Chronicler gives surprising little attention to the high priests, who are often thought to have displaced the king in importance in the postexilic period. The chief priest Azariah, however, does severely criticize Uzziah for cultic encroachment (2 Chr 26:16-21), and the Chronicler does provide a master list of the high priests (1 Chr 5:27-41 [6:1-15]). The high priest Jehoiada also deposed Athaliah and put Joash on the throne. After Jehoiada's death, Joash listened to advisors, initiated syncretistic practices, and gave orders to kill Zechariah, Jehoiada's son (2 Chr 24:15-22).

---

309   Braun, "Solomonic Apologetic" and "Solomon."

310   A full statement about the Levites will be given in vol. 2 of the commentary. See provisionally Kurt Möhlenbrink, "Die levitischen Überlieferungen des Alten Testaments," *ZAW* 52 (1934) 184–231; A. H. J. Gunneweg, *Leviten und Priester: Hauptlinien der Traditionsbildung und Geschichte des israelitisch-jüdischen Kultpersonals* (Göttingen: Vandenhoeck & Ruprecht, 1965); Merlin D. Rehm, "Priests and Levites," *ABD* 4:297–309; Paul D. Hanson, "1 Chronicles 15–16 and the Chronicler's Views on the Levites," in *"Sha'arei Talmon": Studies in the Bible, Qumran, and the Ancient Near East Presented to* Shemaryahu Talmon (Winona Lake, IN: Eisenbrauns, 1992) 69–77; Uwe Glessmer, "Leviten in spätnachexilischer Zeit: Darstellungsinteressen in den Chronikbüchern und bei Josephus," in *Gottes Ehre erzählen: Festschrift für Hans Seidel zum 65. Geburtstag* (Leipzig: Thomas Verlag, 1994) 127–51; Knoppers, "Hierodules"; and Joachim Schaper, *Priester und Leviten im achämenidischen Juda* (Tübingen: Mohr Siebeck, 2000).

Israel[311]

A number of earlier scholars felt that the advocacy for the Jerusalem temple and its worship was also a polemic against the Samaritan community.[312] That has changed in more recent times both because the Samaritan schism is now dated considerably after the time of the Chronicler,[313] and because a different, more inclusive attitude has been detected within Chronicles after scholars recognized that it is not part of a Chronicler's History that included Ezra and Nehemiah.

While the Northern Kingdom is considered politically and religiously illegitimate by the Chronicler, the residents of that territory are considered part of Israel. The genealogy of the tribes in chaps. 2–8 includes the northern tribes, all of whom are descendants of "Israel," the Chronicler's consistent way of designating the patriarch Jacob. While prominence is given to the tribes of Judah, Levi, and Benjamin in these genealogies, all of whom were members of the Chronicler's community, they only form a framework that includes the other tribes. All Israel was involved in the coronation of David (1 Chr 11:1//2 Sam 5:1) and of Solomon (1 Chr 29:20-22), and all of Israel's officials were present when David addressed Solomon (chap. 28). All Israel was involved in the conquest of Jerusalem (11:4-9)[314] and the transfer of the ark to that city (13:4; 15:3), and in the building and dedication of the temple (2 Chr 7:8//1 Kgs 8:55). When the northern tribes broke away from the south, they did not give up their position as children of Israel. Those from all the tribes of Israel who had decided to seek Yahweh came to Jerusalem to sacrifice to Yahweh (2 Chr 11:16). Even at the conclusion of his sermon that is sharply critical of the north, Abijah calls the northern-

ers "Israelites" (13:12). Great numbers of people from the north deserted to Asa because they perceived that Yahweh was with him (15:9). At the time of Ahaz, the north took captive two hundred thousand of their "brothers" (מֵאֲחֵיהֶם; 28:8; cf. vv. 11, 15) from the south. Admonished by the prophet Oded, the northerners repented and sent the captives back, with clothing and food, to Jericho (28:8-15). The Chronicler uses the term "remnant" for those left in the north (34:9) or those in both kingdoms (34:21) after the fall of Samaria. Hezekiah invited all Israel and Judah, including especially Ephraim and Manasseh, to his Passover (30:1, 11, 18, 21, 25-26; 31:1). Repentance included a recognition of the temple in Jerusalem. Josiah's reforms extended to the towns of Manasseh, Ephraim, and Naphtali (34:6, 9), and Hilkiah is told to inquire of Yahweh about those who are left in Israel and Judah (34:21). The unity of Israel, in the Chronicler's view, is based on the worship of Yahweh at his temple in Jerusalem. Japhet, 46, writes, "According to the Chronicler's portrayal, there are no Gentiles in the land of Israel; all its dwellers are 'Israel,' either through their affiliation with the tribes or as the attached 'sojourners.'"

Reward and Retribution

The doctrine of rewards and punishments takes on a special form in Chronicles.[315] While throughout the Bible it is expected that faithfulness is followed by reward or well-being, and unfaithfulness by punishment, in Chronicles these rewards/punishments are more immediate and individual, normally taking place within a person's lifetime. There is no accumulated sin or merit as in the book of Kings.[316] For Saul the consequences of

---

311 See Braun, "Reconsideration"; Williamson, *Israel*, 87–140.

312 Among many, Torrey, Noth, and Rudolph.

313 See Frank Moore Cross, "Aspects of Samaritan and Jewish History in Late Persian and Hellenistic Times," *HTR* 59 (1966) 202–11; James D. Purvis, *The Samaritan Pentateuch and the Origin of the Samaritan Sect* (HSM 2; Cambridge: Harvard Univ. Press, 1968); R. J. Coggins, *Samaritans and Jews: The Origins of Samaritanism Reconsidered* (Atlanta: John Knox Press, 1975). Cf. now also Ingrid Hjelm, *The Samaritans and Early Judaism: A Literary Analysis* (JSOTSup 303; Sheffield: Sheffield Academic Press, 2000).

314 The *Vorlage* at 2 Sam 5:6 has the king and his pri-

vate army conquering Jerusalem.

315 For a fresh study of this concept and a review of previous research, see Kelly, *Retribution and Eschatology.* Cf. Japhet, *Ideology,* 150–98.

316 Japhet, *Ideology,* 166–67, identifies five changes introduced by the Chronicler to his *Vorlage:* in the case of any transgression, an appropriate punishment is introduced by the Chronicler; whenever piety is displayed with no mention of recompense, the Chronicler adds a fitting reward; when any incident which might be a punishment remains unexplained, the Chronicler adds a suitable sin; whenever a possible reward is mentioned without the appropriate causes for it, the Chronicler provides the source of merit; if two occurrences, one a

his unfaithfulness were his death and the loss of his king-dom (1 Chr 10:13-14). In a speech constructed by the Chronicler, David outlines both the positive and nega-tive possibilities of behavior: "If you seek him, he will be found by you, but if you abandon him, he will cast you off forever" (28:9). But warnings are often issued by prophets between the sin and the resultant punishment, and God responds positively to those who repent.[317] In a passage not contained in the *Vorlage*, Yahweh announces to Solomon: "If my people who are called by my name humble themselves, pray, seek my face, and turn from their wicked ways, then I will hear from heaven, and will forgive their sin and heal their land" (2 Chr 7:14). Brian Kelly has argued that the Chronicler is less concerned to demonstrate strict relationships between acts and conse-quences than to emphasize Yahweh's benevolence and mercy toward the people (cf. 1 Chr 22:12; 29:18; 2 Chr 30:18). This is in criticism of Japhet, who believes that retribution takes place in relationship to a principle of absolute divine justice.[318] Kelly believes that Yahweh's covenant mercy (1 Chr 17:13) is the fundamental convic-tion against which the Chronicler's doctrine of retribu-tion must be assessed. For a number of kings Chronicles divides their life into a period of faithfulness followed by reward, and unfaithfulness followed by judgment: Asa (2 Chronicles 14–15 vs. chap. 16), Jehoram (21:1-7 vs. 21:8-20), Joash (23:11–24:14 vs. 24:15-27), Amaziah (25:1-13 vs. 25:14-28), Uzziah (26:1-15 vs. 26:16-23); or of unfaithfulness followed by judgment, and faithfulness followed by reward: Manasseh (33:1-11 vs. 33:12-20). Characteristic rewards in Chronicles are rest and quiet, building projects, military victories, a large family, wealth, international reputation, and respect from citizens. The verb צלח "to succeed" or "to prosper" expresses the reward for righteous actions.[319]

Attitude toward the Persians

The present book of Chronicles ends with words announcing that the decision of Cyrus to build the tem-ple of Jerusalem and to let the exiles return to the land is the fulfillment of the word of Jeremiah and the result of Yahweh's stirring up the spirit of Cyrus (2 Chr 36:22-33). While there is a question whether these words are original to Chronicles or only added from Ezra 1 to show the connection between the two works, it is remarkable that the Chronicler utters no critique of the Persians elsewhere and seems content with the implicit permission of the Persians for worship connected with the Jerusalem temple. For all of his focus on David and his descendants and the everlasting promise made by God to David, the Chronicler nowhere explicitly advo-cates the reestablishment of the Davidic monarchy, let alone a rebellion against the Persian Empire. He seems relatively content with life under Persian suzerainty, pro-vided that the worship at the temple in Jerusalem is able to continue without restraint. Ezra and Nehemiah express a similar attitude, although a plaintive note in Neh 9:37 complains that the rich yield of the land goes to kings whom God has set over them because of their sins, and as a result "we are in great distress."

Personal Piety

The focus on the worship of the temple and the rights of its clergy might suggest that the Chronicler had a very wooden idea of piety and the religious life. But we need to note how much the word "joy" is used in his his-tory[320] and how warmly he can speak of faith: "Believe in Yahweh your God, and you will be established; believe his prophets and you will succeed" (2 Chr 20:20). The cult must be performed with a whole heart,[321] and the cultic counterpart of that is the temple's music. Hezekiah prayed for northerners who had set their hearts to seek God even though they had not followed the sanctuary's rules on cleanliness (30:18-20). Humbling oneself is always viewed as appropriate action (7:14; 12:6-12; 30:6-11; 32:26; 33:12-14). Prayer too is effective (32:20, 24; cf. Manasseh at 33:13).

---

possible sin, the other an apparent punishment, are described independently, the Chronicler makes a causal connection between the two.

317   2 Chr 12:7; 15:2-7; 30:6-9, 18-19.
318   *Ideology*, 153, 164–65.
319   1 Chr 22:11, 13; 29:23; 2 Chr 7:11; 14:6; 20:20; 24:20; 26:5; 31:21; 32:30. Cf. 2 Chr 13:12.
320   1 Chr 12:39-41 (38-40). Note the emphasis there on

singleness of mind. Cf. also 1 Chr 15:25; 29:7, 17 (generous giving), 22; 2 Chr 7:8-10; 20:28; 23:16-18; 29:30; 30:21-26. In 2 Chr 31:4-10 the citizens of Judah bring their tithes and generous donations.
321   David orders Solomon to serve Yahweh with a whole heart and a willing spirit (1 Chr 28:9).

Future Hope?

While the Chronicler provides justification for the worshiping community as he knew it, there are also indications that he hoped for a different, better future. The genealogies in chaps. 2–8, for example, portray an ideal Israel, composed of all twelve tribes and spread out over a far wider territory than the postexilic province of Yehud. Oeming believes that the geographical notes in the opening genealogies are programmatic, outlining a land of Israel that is modeled in the past and still expected for the future.[322] Chronicles offers an implicit appeal to people in the north to support the temple and its worship in Jerusalem, and 1 Chr 9:3 notes that the new Jerusalem already includes people from Ephraim and Manasseh. During Hezekiah's reform, in 2 Chr 30:6-9, it is promised that repentance by those who are in the land will lead to the return of the exiles in Mesopotamia. This can also be taken as a call for the Chronicler's audience to turn to Yahweh with the expectation of a subsequent return to the land from the growing Diaspora. In the psalm placed in the mouth of the singers we read: "Save us, O God of our salvation, and gather us and deliver us from the nations" (1 Chr 16:35). Kelly concludes: "The Chronicler indicates how Israel may continue to possess its inheritance . . . and he holds out the possibility of a more extensive fulfilment."[323] Did the Chronicler expect a restoration of the Davidic monarchy? The covenant God made with David is viewed as everlasting (2 Chr 13:5; 21:7; 23:3). William Riley has concluded that the Davidic kingship was primarily cultic in its mission and only provisional: "The Davidic covenant persisted for the Chronicler and his audience in the task (which the people had from the days of David himself) to worship at the Temple and to provide for its needs and the needs of the cultus."[324] Williamson, 221, admits that Chronicles is not messianic, but believes it does see an abiding validity for the Davidic line, and that the building of the temple has confirmed, but not absorbed, this hope.[325] The genealogy of Davidic descendants after the exile, 1 Chr 3:17-24, probably extending down to the time of the Chronicler himself, may have been preserved by heirs of David who hoped for some kind of restoration of the monarchy. What is not clear is whether the Chronicler's inclusion of this genealogy means that he shared that hope.

---

322 Oeming, *Wahre Israel*, 209–10.
323 *Retribution and Eschatology*, 182.
324 Riley, *King and Cultus*, 201.
325 See also his "Eschatology in Chronicles," *TynBul* 28 (1977) 115–54; idem, "The Dynastic Oracle in the Books of Chronicles," in *Essays on the Bible and the Ancient World: FS I. L. Seeligmann* (ed. Alexander Rofé and Yair Zakovitch; 3 vols.; Jerusalem: Rubinstein, 1985) 3:305–18. For a nonmessianic understanding of Chronicles, see Donald F. Murray, "Dynasty, People, and the Future: The Message of Chronicles," *JSOT* 58 (1993) 71–92.

---

326 The reference to Yahweh handing over the kingdom
  to David (1 Chr 10:14) and the summary of David's
  reign in 29:26-30 bracket the beginning and ending
  of David's reign.

327 This section of the outline and of 2 Chronicles in
     general will be filled out in the second volume.

Commentary

Translation

1/ Adam, Seth, Enosh; 2/ Kenan, Mahalalel, Jared; 3/ Enoch, Methuselah, Lamech; 4/ Noah,[1] Shem, Ham, and Japheth.

5/ The descendants of Japheth: Gomer, Magog, Madai, Javan,[2] Tubal, Meshech, and Tiras. 6/ The descendants of Gomer: Ashkenaz, Riphath,[3] and Togarmah.[4] 7/ The descendants of Javan: Elishah, Tarshish,[5] Kittim, and Rodanim.[6] 8/ The[7] descendants of Ham: Cush, Egypt, Put,[8] and Canaan. 9/ The descendants of Cush: Seba, Havilah, Sabta,[9] Raamah,[10] and Sabteca. The descendants of Raamah: Sheba and Dedan. 10/ Cush became the father of Nimrod;[11] he was the first to be a mighty man[12] on the earth.[13] 11/ Egypt became the father of Ludim,[14] Anamim, Lehabim, Naphtuhim. 12/ Pathrusim, Casluhim, from whom the Philistines went forth, and the Caphtorim.[15] 13/ Canaan became the father of Sidon[16] his firstborn and Heth, 14/ and the Jebusites, the Amorites, the Girgashites, 15/ the Hivites, the Arkites, and the Sinites, 16/ the Arvadites, the Zemarites, and the Hamathites. 17/ The descendants of Shem: Elam, Asshur, Arpachshad,[17] Lud, and Aram. And the descendants of Aram:[18] Uz, Hul, Gether, and Mash.[19] 18/ Arpachshad became the father of[20] Shelah, and Shelah became the father of Eber. 19/ To Eber were born two sons: the name of the one was Peleg (for in his days the world was divided), and the name of his brother was Joktan. 20/ Joktan became the father of Almodad, Sheleph, Hazarmaveth, Jerah, 21/ Hadoram, Uzal, Diklah, 22/ Ebal,[21] Abimael, Sheba, 23/ Ophir,[22] Havilah, and Jobab. All these were the descendants of Joktan.

24/ Shem, Arpachshad, Shelah; 25/ Eber, Peleg, Reu; 26/ Serug, Nahor, Terah; 27/ Abram (that is,[23] Abraham).

28/ The descendants of Abraham: Isaac and Ishmael. 29/ These[24] are their generations:[25] the firstborn of Ishmael: Nebaioth;[26] and Kedar, Adbeel,[27] Mibsam, 30/ Mishma,[28] Dumah, Massa,[29] Hadad, Tema, 31/ Jetur, Naphish, and Kedemah. These are the descendants of Ishmael. 32/ The descendants of Keturah the concubine of Abraham: she bore[30] Zimran, Jokshan,[31] Medan, Midian, Ishbak, and Shuah. The descendants of Jokshan: Sheba[32] and Dedan.[33] 33/ The descendants of Midian: Ephah, Epher,[34] Hanoch, Abida, and Eldaah. All these are the descendants of Keturah.

34/ Abraham became the father of Isaac. The descendants of Isaac: Esau and Israel.[35] 35/ The descendants of Esau: Eliphaz, Reuel, Jeush,[36] Jalam, and Korah. 36/ The descendants of Eliphaz: Teman, Omar,[37] Zephi,[38] Gatam, Kenaz,[39] Timna, and Amalek.[40]

1 LXX reads "Noah, the sons of Noah," thus making clear that Shem, Ham, and Japheth are not *three generations* subsequent to Noah. This is probably an addition, but the words could also have been lost in MT by homoioteleuton. The latter opinion is favored by David Noel Freedman and David Miano, "Is the Shorter Reading Better? Haplography in the First Book of Chronicles," in *Emanuel: Studies in Hebrew Bible, Septuagint, and Dead Sea Scrolls in Honor of Emanuel Tov* (ed. Shalom M. Paul et al.; VTSup 94; Leiden: Brill, 2003) 688.

2 LXX adds a mistaken gloss "Elishah," which could be based on v. 7, where Elishah is listed as the first son of Javan rather than as his brother, but Allen, *Greek Chronicles,* 1:184, argues that this addition should be linked to Gen 10:2 LXX. On pp. 184–85 Allen shows frequent influence of Genesis LXX on Chronicles LXX, and a number of these contacts are reflected in the following notes. See also E. Podechard, "Le premier chapître des Paralipomènes," *RB* 13 (1916) 363–86.

3 וריפת with many Hebrew MSS, LXX, Vg, and Gen 10:3; Chronicles MT: ודיפת "Diphath." *Dālet* and *rêš* are easily confused in Hebrew script.

4 ותוגרמה (plene) vs. Gen 10:3: ותגרמה (defective).

5 ותרשיש with LXX, Vg, Gen 10:4; Chronicles MT: ותרשישה "Tarshishah." See the ending on the preceding name Elishah. Japhet, 57, points out that several names with a final *hê* in Chronicles have lost their locative function.

6 ורודנים. Many Hebrew MSS, Syr, and Gen 10:4 MT have a scribal error based on the *dālet/rêš* confusion: ודודנים "and Dodanim." Genesis LXX and SP agree with Chronicles MT.

7 בני; LXX, Syr, and Gen 10:6: ובני "And the sons of." Cf. vv. 5 and 17.

8 ופוט; cf. Gen 10:6 SP, LXX. Gen 10:6 MT: פוט.

9 וסבתא; Gen 10:7: וסבתה.

10 ורעמא, also three words later; Gen 10:7 (both times): ורעמה.

11 נמרוד and Gen 10:8 SP (plene) vs. Gen 10:8 MT: נמרד (defective).

12 גבור (plene) vs. Gen 10:8: גבר (defective). Chronicles LXX: γίγας κυνεγὸς "a giant, a hunter (or hound-leader)." Cf. Gen 10:9: גבר ציד "a mighty man of game."

13 LXX lacks vv. 11-16. Rudolph, 6–7, suggests that these verses were not yet in the *Vorlage* used by the translator. Allen, *Greek Chronicles,* 2:159, tentatively suggests that a nationalistically minded Jewish scribe deleted this passage dealing with Egypt and Canaan. In my judgment, this lacuna does not represent a more original text, but is the result of acci-

37/ The descendants of Reuel: Nahath, Zerah,[41] Shammah, and Mizzah. 38/ The descendants of Seir: Lotan, Shobal, Zibeon, Anah, Dishon,[42] Ezer, and Dishan. 39/ The descendants of Lotan: Hori, Homam,[43] and the sister of Lotan was Timna.[44] 40/ The descendants of Shobal: Alian,[45] Manahath, Ebal, Shephi,[46] and Onam.[47] The descendants of Zibeon: Aiah[48] and Anah. 41/ The descendant[49] of Anah: Dishon.[50] The descendants of Dishon:[51] Hamran,[52] Eshban, Ithran, and Cheran. 42/ The descendants of Ezer: Bilhan, Zaavan,[53] and Akan.[54] The descendants of Dishan:[55] Uz and Aran.

43/ These are the kings who ruled in the land of Edom before a king ruled for the Israelites:[56] Bela[57] the son of Beor, and the name of his city was Dinhabah. 44/ Bela died, and Jobab the son of Zerah from Bozrah ruled in his place. 45/ And Jobab died, and Husham[58] from the land of the Temanites ruled in his place. 46/ Husham[59] died, and Hadad the son of Bedad,[60] who defeated Midian in the plains of Moab, ruled in his place, and the name of his city was Avith.[61] 47/ Hadad died,[62]and Samlah from Masrekah ruled in his place. 48/ Samlah died, and Shaul from Rehoboth on the river ruled in his place. 49/ Shaul died, and Baal-hanan the son of Achbor ruled in his place. 50/ Baal-hanan[63] died, and Hadad[64] ruled in his place, and the name of his city was Pai,[65] and his wife's name was Mehetabel the daughter of Matred, daughter[66] of Me-zahab.[67] 51/ Hadad died, and the chiefs of Edom were: Chief Timna, Chief Aliah,[68] Chief Jetheth, 52/ Chief Oholibamah,[69] Chief Elah, Chief Pinon, 53/ Chief Kenaz, Chief Teman, Chief Mibzar,[70] 54/ Chief Magdiel, Chief Iram.[71] These are the chiefs of Edom.

2:1/ These are the[72] descendants of Israel: Reuben, Simeon, Levi, and Judah, Issachar, and Zebulun, 2/ Dan,[73] Joseph, and Benjamin, Naphtali, Gad, and Asher.

---

dental textual loss. See also Freedman and Miano, "Is the Shorter Reading Better?" 688.

14 לודיים K; Q and Gen 10:13, correctly, לודים.

15 *NRSV* makes "from whom the Philistines went forth" modify Caphtorim (cf. Amos 9:7). Japhet, 52, notes that this clause was already displaced in Genesis and therefore should not be changed in Chronicles.

16 צידן (plene) here and Gen 10:15 SP vs. Gen 10:15: צידן (defective).

17 LXX omits the rest of this verse and the following verses through the word "Arpachshad" in v. 24 because of homoioteleuton. See already Goettsberger, 30–31.

18 ובני ארם with one Hebrew MS, LXX[A, other MSS], Arab., and Gen 10:23; Chronicles MT lacks "and the descendants of Aram" by homoioteleuton.

19 ומש with a few Hebrew MSS, Syr, Arab., and Gen 10:23 MT (Genesis SP: ומשא); Chronicles MT ומשך "and Meshech." Cf. v. 5, where Meshech is correctly listed as a son of Japheth.

20 LXX[A and other MSS] add: "Cainan, and Cainan become the father of." The same addition is made in the LXX at Gen 10:24 and 11:12-13. Luke 3:35 also adds this additional generation, showing that its genealogy was constructed using LXX. Freedman and Miano, "Is the Shorter Reading Better?" 689, suggest haplography in MT here and in Gen 10:24 and 11:12-13.

21 עיבל; cf. Gen 10:28 SP. Some Hebrew MSS, LXX[minuscules], Syr, and Gen 10:28: עובל "Obal."

22 אופיר (plene) vs. Gen 10:29: אופר (defective).

23 LXX omits "Abram (that is,)" because of homoioarchton.

24 אלה; Gen 25:12, 13 ואלה. Chronicles abbreviates in this context.

25 תלדותם; Chronicles LXX תלדת (lacking "their"; hence: "These are the generations of the firstborn of Ishmael"). My translation designates Nebaioth as the firstborn of Ishmael. Gen 25:23: לתולדתם, but the Chronicler has recast his *Vorlage* here.

26 נביות (plene) vs. Gen 25:13 נבית (defective).

27 ואדבאל. LXX Ναβδαιηλ; cf. Gen 25:13 LXX.

28 משמע; Gen 25:14 ומשמע.

29 משא; Gen 25:14 ומשא.

30 ילדה. LXX reads: "and she bore to him," agreeing with Gen 25:2: ותלד לו. For the intentional omission of "to him" by the Chronicler, see the discussion of the originality of the genealogy of Keturah under Structure. "She bore" is absent from Syr.

31 Jokshan and the following four names lack את (the sign of the definite direct object), which is present in Gen 25:3.

32 Sheba and Dedan lack את, which is present in Gen 25:3.

33 *BHS* (cf. Johnstone, 1:33) restores: "and the sons of Dedan were Asshurim, Letushim, and Leummim" from Gen 25:3b with Vg, Arab. (cf. LXX[AN, other MSS]). Freedman and Miano, "Is the Shorter Reading Better?" 690, would also restore "Raguel and Nabdiel," found only in LXX. It seems more likely that this reading in the versions is a correction to Genesis. At Gen 25:3 *BHS* suggests, on the basis of 1 Chr 1:33, that the three names may be an addition to the text of Genesis!

34 ועפר and Gen 25:4 SP (plene) vs. Gen 25:4 MT: ועיפר (defective).

35 LXX[B] "Jacob and Esau" instead of "Esau and Israel." Note that Isaac is listed before Ishmael in v. 28. LXX[A, other MSS]: "Esau and Jacob."

36 ויעוש. So also Gen 36:5 Q, SP, versions; Gen 36:5 K: יעיש.

37 ואומר; Gen 36:11: אומר.

38 צפי. Many Hebrew MSS, LXX[minuscules], Syr, and Gen 36:11: צפו "Zepho." The latter reading was probably influenced by the following *wāw* conjunction.

39 קנז; Chronicles LXX, Syr, Tg, and Gen 36:11: וקנז.

40 For "Timna, and Amalek," LXX[B] reads: "and of Timna, Amalek." In Gen 36:12 Timna (the sister of Lotan; cf. Gen 36:22 and 1 Chr 1:39) is the concubine of Eliphaz, the firstborn of Esau, and they were the parents of Amalek. For "Timna, and Amalek," Chronicles LXX[AN, minuscules] and Arab. read: "Timna the concubine of Eliphaz bore to him Amalek," thus approximating Gen 36:22.

41 זרח; Gen 36:13: וזרח.

42 ודישן (defective) vs. Gen 36:21 ודישון (plene).

43 והומם; Gen 36:22: והימם "Hemam." The latter reading is also noted in Masorah Magna 21. Genesis LXX and Chronicles LXX Αιμαν. Allen, *Greek Chronicles*, 2:185, suggests that Chronicles LXX has been influenced by Genesis LXX. Willi, 14, argues that the form of the name with an internal *yôd* is more likely the original reading.

44 Intead of the last clause, LXX reads: Αιλαϑ και Ναμνα. Allen, *Greek Chronicles*, 2:84, argues that Αιλαϑ is from an original Α(α)ιϑαλ and is an abbreviation for "sister of L." The translator apparently read ונמנע instead of תמנע for the last word (Allen, *Greek Chronicles*, 2:123).

45 עלין. Some Hebrew MSS, LXX[L], and Gen 36:23 read עלון "Alvan." The latter corresponds to the Edomite form of the name (Willi, 14).

46 שפי; a few Hebrew MSS and Gen 36:23: שפו "Shepho." The final *wāw* may have been precipitated by the following conjunction.

47 ואונם; one Hebrew MS and LXX read ואונן "Onan."

48 איה; Gen 36:24: ואיה, but the conjunction is lacking there in a few Hebrew MSS, SP, and the versions.

49 בן with *Sebir;* MT: בני "sons of." While this correc-

tion makes for a more consistent text, it is possible that the Chronicler himself erred by mechanically writing "descendants" from the Genesis *Vorlage.* "Descendants" is correct in Gen 36:25, where the "descendants" of Anah are Dishon and Oholibamah the daughter of Anah.

50 דישון and Gen 36:25 SP (plene) vs. Gen 36:25 MT דשן (doubly defective). Both are vocalized "Dishon." Gen 36:25 adds: "and Oholibamah daughter of Anah." Freedman and Miano, "Is the Shorter Reading Better?" 690, suggest haplography in Chronicles.

51 דישון. This plene reading is attested also in Gen 36:26 SP and Syr; Gen 36:26 MT: דשן "Dishan" (based on defective orthography). *BHS* tentatively suggests emending the text of Genesis to agree with Chronicles. LXX[AL] adds: "and Elibamah the daughter of Anah," which is a correction to Gen 36:25.

52 חמרן. Many Hebrew MSS, LXX[AL, other MSS], and Gen 35:26: חמדן "Hemdan."

53 וזעון. Gen 36:27 SP: ווען "Zouan" (metathesis of *'ayin* and *wāw*). Cf. 1 Chr 1:42 LXX, which has been assimilated to the Genesis LXX reading.

54 ועקן with many Hebrew MSS, LXX[A, other MSS], Arab., and Gen 36:27; Chronicles MT: יעקן "Jaakan." The initial *wāw* was misread as a *yôd.*

55 דישן with Gen 36:28; Chronicles MT: דישון "Dishon." Dishan is the last-named son of Seir in v. 38. Note that Chronicles is plene and Genesis defective.

56 Instead of "the kings . . . Israelites," LXX reads "their kings." Allen, *Greek Chronicles,* 2:22–23, suggests that αὐτῶν is a mistake for Αιδωμ, one of the spellings of Edom. Hence LXX originally read: "the kings of Edom."

57 בלע; LXX בלק "Balak" (also in v. 34); Tg בלעם "Balaam" (also in v. 34).

58 חושם; LXX and Syr: חשם "Hashum" (also in v. 46). Compare the plene reading in MT with Gen 36:34: חשם "Husham" (defective).

59 חושם (plene) vs. Gen 36:35 חשם (defective).

60 בדד; LXX ברד "Barad."

61 עוית with Q, LXX[minuscules], Tg, Vg, and Gen 36:35; K עיות "Ayuth." LXX[B] (cf. Gen 36:35 LXX) has incorrectly attached the first three letters of v. 47 (וים) to the ending of this word: Γεϑϑαιμ.

62 LXX[B] lacks a translation at this point for vv. 47b, 48, and 49a ("and Samlah from Masrekah . . . Shaul died"), but then includes these words after v. 51a. The words were lost by homoioarchton (וימלך) and then reinserted at the wrong place.

63 בעל חנן. Some Hebrew MSS and LXX add בן עכבור "the son of Achbor," as in Gen 36:39. This patronymic, however, is lacking also in Gen 36:39 SP.

64 הדד; cf. Gen 36:39 SP. Some Hebrew MSS, Tg, and

Gen 36:39 MT: הדר "Hadar." LXX adds "the son of Barad" (cf. Gen 36:39 LXX and 1 Chr 1:46).

65 פעי. Many Hebrew MSS, LXX[L], Syr, Tg, Vg, and Gen 36:39: פעו "Pau." The final *wāw* arose by assimilation to the following conjunction.

66 בת; Syr, Arab. "son." Cf. Gen 36:39 LXX and Syr. Rudolph, 9, suggests on the basis of Deut 1:1 (Di-zahab) that Me-zahab is a place name and therefore emends בת to מן "from."

67 LXX omits "and his wife's name was Mehetabel the daughter of Matred, daughter of Me-zahab." Cf. Allen, *Greek Chronicles*, 2:159. Perhaps a copyist skipped from one καί to the next.

68 עליה K; Q, many Hebrew MSS, Tg, Vg, and Gen 36:40: עלוה "Alvah." Chronicles LXX: Γωλα = עולה; Syr: ענוא.

69 אהליבמה. LXX "Elibamas." Cf. Gen 36:41 LXX.

70 מבצר. LXX[L] "Bamael."

71 עירם; LXX "Zaphoein; cf. Gen 36:43 LXX.

72 LXX adds "names of the." It interprets 2:1-2 as the introduction to the following chapters instead of the conclusion to chap. 1.

73 *BHS* tentatively suggests moving this name after Benjamin. See the commentary.

1:1—2:2

Structure

The opening unit of Chronicles consists of genealogical information, drawn entirely from the book of Genesis and covering the period from Adam to the birth of the twelve sons of Israel (see the genealogical chart "Descendants from Adam"). It may be outlined as follows:

I. 1:1-4. A linear genealogy[1] from Adam to Shem, Ham, and Japheth, the sons of Noah, based on Gen 5:1-32.

II. 1:5-23. Segmented genealogy[2] of Japheth, Ham, and Shem and their descendants drawn from the Table of Nations[3] in Gen 10:1-29 and divided into three sections. These are the nations that emerged after the flood.

   A. 1:5-7. Descendants of Japheth (//Gen 10:2-4)

   B. 1:8-16. Descendants of Ham (//Gen 10:6-9a, 13-18a)

   C. 1:17-23. Descendants of Shem (//Gen 10:22-29)

III. 1:24-27. Linear genealogy from Shem through Abraham and his two sons, Isaac and Ishmael, based on Gen 11:10-26

IV. 1:28—2:2. Segmented genealogy of the descendants of Abraham's sons, drawn from Gen 25:1-4, 12-16, 19, and 36:4-5, 11-13, 20-43, and divided into the following sections:

   A. 1:28. Caption

   B. 1:29-31. Descendants of Ishmael

   C. 1:32-33. Descendants of Keturah

   D. 1:34—2:2. Descendants of Isaac's Sons: Esau and Israel

      1. 1:34-54. Descendants of Esau

         a. 1:34-37. Descendants of Esau himself

         b. 1:38-42. Descendants of Seir

         c. 1:43-51a. Kings of Edom

         d. 1:51b-54. Chiefs of Edom

      2. 2:1-2. Descendants of Israel

One can see that the author has alternated between linear (1:1-4, 24-27) and segmented (1:5-23; 1:28—2:2) genealogies, as did the material in Genesis on which he was dependent. His linear genealogies, however, are really only lists of names, lacking even the conjunction "and," except for the final name in v. 4. The reader needs to infer the genealogical connection known through Genesis. These lists contrast markedly therefore

---

1 A linear genealogy traces a single line from parent to child and often has the function of establishing legitimacy (e.g., of kings or high priests). The linear genealogies in vv. 1-4 and 24-27 also connote the passing of time.

2 A segmented or collateral genealogy branches out to include siblings. Such genealogies often define familial and/or intertribal relationships. For linear and segmented genealogies see A. Malamat, "King Lists of the Old Babylonian Period and Biblical Genealogies," *JAOS* 88 (1968) 168–73; idem, "Tribal Societies: Biblical Genealogies and African Lineage Systems," *European Journal of Sociology* 14 (1973) 126–36.

3 For an interpretation of this chapter see the commentaries on Genesis and B. Oded, "The Table of Nations (Genesis 10)—A Socio-cultural Approach," *ZAW* 98 (1986) 14–31.

with the form of the source chapters in Genesis 5 and 11, where each generation is generally listed as follows: "X lived a number of years and became the father of Y. X lived after the birth of Y for a number of years and had other sons and daughters. Thus all the days of X were so and so many years" (the last sentence is in Genesis 5 only). The thirteen names in the first linear genealogy (1 Chr 1:1-4) present a diachronic history and end with Noah, Shem, Ham, and Japheth. But these four men are not to be taken as brothers, or as a sequence of four generations, but as a father and his three sons, as in Gen 5:32 and Gen 10:1.[4] The conclusion of this first genealogy is signaled by the insertion of the conjunction "and" before the last name. The reference to the three sons of Noah leads over smoothly to the following segmented genealogy, which lists the many descendants of each son who present a synchronic picture of the makeup of the nations of the world. Shem, Ham, and Japheth are in the tenth generation *after* Adam, and Abram/Abraham is in the tenth generation *including* Shem. The Chronicler's decision to use only a list of names in his linear genealogies means that he omits all incidental or anecdotal data from the source chapters in Genesis, such as Seth's being in the likeness or image of Adam (Gen 5:3) or that Enoch walked with God and was no more because God took him (Gen 5:24).[5] While the linear genealogy in Gen 11:10-26 presents a diachronic picture that ends with three sons in the last generation, Abram, Nahor, and Hur, the Chronicler mentions only Abram since the other two brothers play no significant role in the rest of the story. At the end of this second linear genealogy, the Chronicler makes his first addition to the Genesis material by inserting a gloss, "that is, Abraham," reflecting the patriarch's change of name in Gen 17:5.

The first of the segmented genealogies (1 Chr 1:5-23) is based on the Table of Nations in Genesis 10, and the Chronicler here follows in general both its content—except for the omissions noted below—and its form. The order of the descendants of the sons of Noah, however, is reversed from v. 4: Japheth, Ham, and Shem instead of Shem, Ham, and Japheth (a chiasm). In this case the Chronicler follows the order in his *Vorlage* (Japheth, Gen 10:2-4; Ham, Gen 10:6-9a, 13-18a; and Shem, Gen 10:22-29), and the son, Shem, through whom Abraham and Israel itself are to be born is listed last, signaling his preferred status and facilitating the transition to the second linear genealogy (Shem to Abraham). Such an inverted order will be followed later with the descendants of Abraham, even when that is counter to the *Vorlage*. The Chronicler omits from Genesis 10 most of v. 1,[6] v. 5, vv. 9b-12, 18b-21,[7] and vv. 30-32. Thus he leaves out the תולדת formula, the reference to the flood in Gen 10:1, 32, the dispersal of the sons of Japheth, almost all of the anecdotal information about Nimrod, material about the dispersal of the people and boundaries of Canaan, the conclusion of the genealogy of Ham and the introduction to the genealogy of Shem, a note about the territory of Joktan, the conclusion to the genealogy of Shem, and the conclusion to the whole Table of Nations. There are seventy or seventy-one nations in the Chronicler's version of the Table of Nations: fourteen descendants of Japheth (seven sons and seven grandsons), thirty or thirty-one descendants of Ham (four sons, twenty-three or twenty-four grandsons, and four[8] great grandsons), and twenty-six descendants of Shem (five sons, four grandsons through Aram, and seventeen descendants of Arpachshad).[9]

The second of the segmented genealogies (1 Chr 1:28—2:2) is extraordinarily complex, but it is based on

---

4   The LXX made this clear by its addition, noted under textual note 1, but the MT is *lectio difficilior* and is to be preferred.

5   Cf. also Gen 5:29; 11:10 (the reference to the flood).

6   "And these are the generations of the sons of," and "sons were born to them after the flood."

7   The MT of 1 Chr 1:17 also omits Gen 10:23a, "and the sons of Aram were," but I have restored that reading for text-critical reasons. See textual note 18.

8   It is not clear whether the Philistines are to be counted among the sons or the grandsons.

9   Cf. Willi, 29, for references to "seventy nations" in rabbinic and pseudepigraphic literature. Rudolph, 7, and Willi, 29, argue that the number seventy should be achieved by omitting Nimrod. Johnstone, 1:28, counts Nimrod and therefore has a total of seventy-one. Curtis and Madsen, 77, note that some also have found seventy descendants of Abraham in this chapter: twelve descendants of Ishmael, thirteen descendants of Keturah, two descendants of Isaac, sixteen descendants of Esau, and twenty-seven of Seir. But I believe that the literary unit begun in chap. 1 continues through 2:2, which would add

the *Vorlage* contained in portions of Genesis 25, 35, and 36. The descendants of the three mothers of Abraham's children are mentioned in the order of Hagar (vv. 29-31; Ishmael and his twelve descendants), Keturah (vv. 32-33), and Sarah (1:34—2:2; Isaac and his descendants), although only Keturah of the three mothers is mentioned by name. The position of Ishmael before the sons of Keturah is in reverse order to that of the genealogies in Genesis (Keturah, 25:1-4; Ishmael, 25:12-16), just as the position of Esau before Israel is opposite that of the genealogies in Genesis (Israel, Gen 35:23-26a; Esau, Genesis 36). Keturah's position will be discussed further below when we consider whether parts of 1 Chronicles 1 are secondary. The Chronicler added 1:34 to materials taken from Genesis: "Abraham became the father of Isaac. The descendants of Isaac: Esau and Israel." The first sentence incorporates the only use of a *wāw* consecutive with an imperfect in this chapter, aside from the death notices of the kings of Edom, where it was taken over from the *Vorlage*.[10] The content is apparently based on Gen 25:19,[11] אברהם הוליד את יצחק (Abraham became the father of Isaac), although the Chronicler has changed the word order of the first two words and replaced the verb in the perfect tense with his *wāw* consecutive with the imperfect. The second sentence added by the Chronicler in v. 34, "The descendants of Isaac: Esau and Ishmael," follows the order of the sons of Isaac mentioned at Isaac's burial, Esau and Jacob (Gen 35:29), but "Jacob" has been replaced by "Israel," as throughout the work of the Chronicler, except for two references to Jacob in 1 Chr 16:13, 17, which have been taken over as part of the psalms included in this work. This order conveniently puts the sons of Israel last in contrast to the genealogical lists themselves in Genesis (Esau, chap. 36; Jacob, 35:23-26a). In many cases the genealogical line passes through the firstborn son, as does the inheritance of family property, but not always so. The line of Shem continues primarily through his third son, Arpachshad,

not Shem's oldest son, Elam. So also the elect line of Isaac passes through his second son, Israel, and not his eldest son, Esau.

In the genealogy of Ishmael (vv. 29-31), the Chronicler omits Gen 25:12 (the תלדת formula and the mention of Hagar) and recasts Gen 25:13a (see the commentary to 1 Chr 1:29). He also omitted Gen 25:16-18 (the conclusion to the genealogy, the age of Ishmael, and the geographical boundaries assigned to the Ishmaelites). For Keturah (vv. 32-33), the Chronicler omitted all but the last word of Gen 25:1 (Abraham's taking of Keturah as a wife), the signs of the definite direct object for five of her six sons from Gen 25:2, and Gen 25:5-6 (Abraham's gift of everything to Isaac and his expelling the children of his concubines [presumably the children of Hagar and Keturah] out of the promised land during his own lifetime). From Gen 25:6, however, the Chronicler took the word פילגש "concubine" and used it to replace the title אשה "wife" in his description of Keturah in v. 32 (Gen 25:1). The section on Keturah in Chronicles begins and ends with the words "the sons of Keturah" in vv. 32 and 33 (*inclusio*). The creation of this *inclusio* resulted in an awkward beginning of v. 32, where the phrase "the descendants of Keturah the concubine of Abraham" has to be construed as a *casus pendens*.[12] For the omission of "to him" from Gen 25:2, see the discussion below on the originality of the genealogy of Keturah.[13]

The Chronicler included the materials on Esau/Seir/Edom from Genesis 36 in the same order as in his *Vorlage*, although he omitted significant portions of that chapter, whose contents may be outlined as follows:

1. the descendants of Esau and his separation from Jacob (vv. 1-8//1 Chr 1:35)
2. the descendants of Esau the father of the Edomites (vv. 9-14//1 Chr 1:36-37)
3. the chiefs of the sons of Esau (vv. 15-19)
4. the sons of Seir the Horite (vv. 20-28//1 Chr 1:38-42)

---

twelve additional descendants. It is also not clear how Seir relates to the lineage of Esau.

10 All the previous verbs in vv. 10, 11, 12, 13, 18, 19, 20, and 32 are in the perfect.

11 Cf. Gen 25:12.

12 Japhet, 61, proposes that there has been a conflation of two parallel clauses: "the sons of Keturah" and "Keturah bore."

13 Instead of "Jokshan became the father of" from Gen 25:3, the Chronicler reads "and the sons of Jokshan were." This does not change the information provided by the genealogy.

5. the chiefs of the Horites (vv. 29-30)

6. the kings who ruled in Edom (vv. 31-39//1 Chr 1:43-51a)

7. the chiefs of Esau (vv. 40-43//1 Chr 1:51b-54).

The Chronicler's listing of Esau's sons in v. 35 and Esau's grandsons in vv. 36-37, while considerably recast in structure, follows the information in sections 1-2 of Genesis 36, but omits all references to the three wives of Esau (Adah, Basemath, and Oholibamah) and refers to Timna and Amalek as if they were the sixth and seventh sons of Esau's son Eliphaz and not, respectively, a concubine of Eliphaz and the child she and Eliphaz produced. Did the Chronicler omit these four women in order to remove the flaw of intermarriage with an outsider from the descendants of the family of Abraham? One might counter that he retained Keturah, the concubine of Abraham, but in the present genealogy she only bears children and not specifically for him, that is, Abraham. Or did the Chronicler omit the mention of wives because they seemed irrelevant to him? Despite the pressure Edom may have been exerting on the southern border of Judah at the time of the Chronicler, the author omitted the discussion of Edom's settlement pattern in Gen 36:6-8. The Chronicler also omitted sections 3 and 5 of Genesis 36, which list the chiefs of the sons of Esau (Gen 36:15-19)[14] and the chiefs of the Horites (Gen 36:29-30),[15] respectively. By adding the words "and Hadad died and they were" at the beginning of 1 Chr 1:51, in place of the words "and these are the names of," the Chronicler made the chiefs of Esau in section 7 clearly subsequent to the kings who ruled in Edom (sec-tion 6). In the Genesis *Vorlage* the chronological relationship between these two sections is unclear. In general, the Chronicler is extraordinarily faithful to the text of his *Vorlage* in sections 6 and 7 of Genesis 36. He did omit "and there ruled in Edom" from Gen 36:32, which may have seemed redundant; the patronym "son of Achbor" from Gen 36:39;[16] and the references to families, localities, and names from Gen 36:40 and to settlements in the land from Gen 36:43. The Chronicler's version of section 4 of Genesis 36 in 1 Chr 1:38-42 contains the same list of twenty-seven descendants of Seir with minor omissions of individual words,[17] the gentilic and the appositional phrase for Seir in Gen 36:20,[18] an anecdote about Anah in 36:24b,[19] and the mention of Oholibamah the daughter of Anah in 36:25b, who is identified as the wife of Esau in Gen 36:2 and 14.[20]

Against the chapter division in the Hebrew Bible, I consider 1 Chr 2:1-2 to be the continuation, indeed, the climax of chap. 1. The genealogy in 1 Chronicles 1 would make little theological sense if the very long section on Esau and Edom were its conclusion and climax.[21] Of course, given the present chapter division, 2:1-2 does double duty as the climax of chap. 1 and as the introduction to the detailed genealogies of the tribes in chaps. 2–8.

Some of the differences between Chronicles and Genesis in these genealogies represent variants that can be attributed to copyist's errors or a different stage in the use of orthography. All of these are noted under textual notes to the translation. These include:

---

14 These chiefs consist of Esau's son Eliphaz and his seven children (including Amalek, the child from his concubine). Gatam (v. 16) is listed as the sixth son rather than the fourth son as in v. 13, and the addition of Korah in v. 16 is unexplained. Since these verses basically repeat the information from vv. 10-12, their omission by the Chronicler is easy to understand.

15 These chiefs are the same as the seven sons of Seir in vv. 20-21.

16 But he retained its occurrence in Gen 36:38 in 1 Chr 1:49.

17 אלה "these" is omitted from Gen 36:20, 23, 24, 25, 26, 27.

18 "These are the sons of Seir the Horite, the inhabitants of the land."

19 "He is the Anah who found the springs in the wilderness, as he pastured the donkeys of his father Zibeon."

20 These references in Genesis, however, have misread the information in Gen 36:25 and identified the Anah mentioned in 36:20 with the Anah mentioned in v. 24. The result is that Oholibamah is construed as the daughter of Anah the son of Esau's son Zibeon (hence the great-granddaughter of Esau) instead of the daughter of Esau's son Anah (hence the granddaughter of Esau).

21 De Vries, 31, finds an *inclusio* between 1 Chr 2:1-2 and 9:1a and considers "the sons of Judah" in 2:3 too abrupt an introduction for the lengthy genealogical lists that follow.

a. Nine cases of interchange between *wāw* and *yôd* (textual notes 21, 37, 39, 44, 46, 47, 55, 66, 69).

b. Five cases of interchange between *dālet* and *rêš* (textual notes 3, 6, 53, 61, 65).

c. One case where Chronicles has added an additional final *hê* (textual note 5) and three cases where it has a final *ʾālep* instead of a final *hê* (textual notes 9 and 10 [twice]).

d. Fourteen cases of plene versus defective spelling. Plene writing in Chronicles (textual notes 4, 11, 12, 16, 22, 25, 26, 35, 51, 52, 56, 59, 60); plene writing in Genesis (textual note 43).

e. Two cases of metathesis of individual letters: 1 Chr 1:42//Gen 36:27 (textual note 54); 1 Chr 1:46//Gen 36:35 (textual note 62).

f. Nine cases where Chronicles lacks the conjunction that is present in Genesis (textual notes 7, 24, 28, 29, 34, 37, 38, 42, 49).[22]

Secondary Materials?

A number of scholars have considered all (Galling, 19[23]) or part of chap. 1 to be secondary. For example, Rudolph, 6–7, judged vv. 4b-23, 32-34a, and 43-54 to be later additions. One basis for deleting this material was the shorter nature of the LXX. The Vaticanus manuscript of the LXX lacks vv. 11-16 (see textual note 13) and vv. 17b-24a (see textual note 17) and places its translation for vv. 47b-49a after v 51a (see textual note 62). The last two readings can be accounted for by homoioteleuton and resultant correction.[24] No such mechanical reason for an omission can be identified in the first case, but a Hebrew text corresponding to the shorter text of LXX does not seem more original[25] and it is likely that these verses were left out accidentally as well.[26]

Rudolph also objected to the repetition in the genealogy of Shem since vv. 17-22 from Gen 10:22-25 overlap with and anticipate vv. 24-25 from Gen 11:10-18.[27] But since this overlap exists already in the *Vorlage*, it seems hypercritical to object to that overlap here. Rudolph also noted that the segmented genealogy in vv. 4b-23 conflicted with the linear genealogies in vv. 1-4 and 24-27 and argued for an analogy between the Chronicler's omission of the brothers of Abraham from Gen 11:26bβ and Rudolph's own proposal to omit the detailed genealogy of the brothers of Shem. All the materials taken from the Table of Nations, however, are important for outlining the contemporary world of which the Chronicler's Israel was a part.

Rudolph felt that the lists of kings and chiefs in the line of Esau performed no function and were therefore secondary, but that argument cuts both ways. If they were so meaningless, why would a secondary hand fill them in? If the supplementation were only for the sake of completeness, we might have suspected other things omitted from Genesis to be included as well. Willi has argued that the Chronicler's interest in Edom, despite the general hostility to this nation throughout biblical history,[28] might reflect a passage like Deut 23:8 (7): "You shall not abhor any of the Edomites, for they are your kin." The list of Edomite kings and chiefs, as changed in

---

22 Some of these variations are noted by Gillis Gerleman, *Synoptic Studies in the Old Testament* (Lund: Gleerup, 1948); and by Oeming, *Wahre Israel,* 76–77. Cf. also Henry L. Gilbert, "The Forms of the Names in 1 Chronicles 1–7 Compared with Those in Parallel Passages in the Old Testament," *AJSL* 13 (1897) 279–98.

23 See also now Kratz, *Komposition,* 27, 52.

24 Allen, *Greek Chronicles,* 2:134, 136.

25 Cf. Kartveit, *Motive und Schichten,* 20. Rudolph, 7, suggested that all of vv. 5-23 were not added at one time, but why would a person who added the sons of Ham omit the descendants of Egypt (vv. 11-12) and Canaan (vv. 13-16) if he had included these two names already in v. 8?

26 Perhaps vv. 11-16 were shortened after the homoioteleuton of vv. 17b-24a since the numerous descendants of Ham in these verses would dwarf the number of the remaining sons of Shem in the segmented genealogy: Elam, Asshur, and Arpachshad.

27 Shem, Arpachshad, Shelah, Eber, and Peleg appear in both sets of verses. Thereafter the genealogies diverge with the second genealogy following Peleg, and the first following Joktan, Peleg's brother.

28 E.g., Ezek 35:5. For other passages on Edom see Willi, 27 and 45.

Chronicles by the addition of v. 51a, shows that kingship arose in Edom before it did in Israel, and it also ended in Edom before it did in Israel. So the nation of Edom continues after kingship in the nation ended, just as Israel of the Chronicler's day continues after its kingship had ended. Hence the genealogy of Esau is not as functionless as Rudolph thought.[29] Next to the twelve tribes of Israel in chaps. 2–8, the descendants of Esau have the most prominent role in the genealogies and take up twenty of fifty-four verses in chap. 1.

Perhaps the most difficult question about a secondary addition involves Keturah in vv. 32-33. As Williamson, 43, has noted, the descendants of Keturah seem out of place in the present context. After the caption in v. 28, "the descendants of Abraham: Isaac and Ishmael," and the reference to "their" generations in the following verse, with Isaac and Ishmael as the antecedent of "their," we would not expect to find a genealogy for Keturah and her sons.[30] Williamson also notes the greater number of changes in regard to the *Vorlage* in these verses and he points out the order of Ishmael and Keturah from Genesis is reversed, but without any compelling theological reason to do so. Willi, 18–19, has observed, however, that Keturah's descendants are pointedly called the sons of Keturah twice in vv. 32-33, rather than the sons of Abraham as in v. 28, and v. 32 says they are the children *she* bore, leaving out, significantly, the phrase "to him," that is, to Abraham, contained in the *Vorlage*. If the sequence among the sons mentioned in v. 28 requires Ishmael to be first and Isaac second, the choice for the placement of Keturah would be either before Ishmael, so that there would be a listing in an ascending sequence of importance: Keturah, Ishmael, Isaac; or after Ishmael, that is, lower in rank than him, with the order we now have in the text: Ishmael, Keturah, and Isaac. The antecedent of "their" in v. 29 could be to all the sons: the sons of Ishmael, the sons of Keturah, and the sons of Isaac.[31] Hence, with other recent commentators,[32] I ascribe these verses also to the Chronicler himself.

Detailed Commentary

1:1-4. Linear Genealogy from Adam to Shem, Ham, and Japheth

■ **1** *Adam, Seth, and Enosh*: The Chronicler follows Gen 5:3-9 and does not include Cain and Abel nor the descendants of Cain listed in Gen 4:17-22 since none of these people or their descendants play a role in the

---

Adam—Seth—Enosh—Kenan—Mahalalel—Jared—Enoch—Methuselah—Lamech—Noah⌐Shem
⌊Ham
⌊Japheth

---

29 Kartveit, *Motive und Schichten*, 116, argued that the listing of Edom's territory was a subtle polemic against Edom's encroachment into Judah's southern territories at the end of the 4th century and an attempt to push them back to their former areas, but the locations are mostly unknown, which makes a polemic against Edom's encroachment unlikely. Also unconvincing is the proposal by Oeming, *Wahre Israel*, 87–88, that links this section to 1 Chr 18:12-13, where David defeats Edom and puts a governor there. Oeming goes on to propose that 1:43 should be translated: "These are the kings who ruled in the land of Edom before a king of the Israelites ruled (in the land of Edom)," which he correlates with chap. 18. In my judgment, however,

the translation is untenable. See the commentary on v. 43.

30 This was pointed out already by E. Podechard, "Le premier chapître des Paralipomènes," *RB* 13 (1916) 363-86, who retained the rest of the chapter for the Chronicler. The descendants of Seir in v. 37, however, are also not explicitly referred to in the caption to this section in v. 35: "the descendants of Esau."

31 Those who object that Keturah's sons are Abraham's children while Ishmael's and Isaac's children are Abraham's grandchildren are probably nit-picking. Cf. Oeming, *Wahre Israel*, 82.

32 Kartveit, *Motive und Schichten*, 21–22; Oeming, *Wahre Israel*, 82–83; and Willi, 22–27.

world after the flood. In a sense the election of Israel begins with Adam.[33] The Chronicler does not bother with explaining where Seth and Enosh found spouses, although *Jubilees* reports that both married their sisters (*Jub.* 4:11, 13).

■ **2** *Kenan, Mahalalel, Jared:* Cf. Gen 5:12-18.

■ **3** *Enoch, Methuselah, Lamech:* Cf. Gen 5:21-29.

■ **4** *Noah, Shem, Ham, and Japheth:* Cf. Gen 5:32 and 10:1.

The linear genealogy branches out into three strands in its last generation, preparing the way for the inclusion of the segmented genealogy from Genesis 10 in vv. 5-23.

A mosaic inscription in the synagogue floor excavated at En-gedi and dated to the fifth or sixth century CE may help us to understand the significance of this first linear genealogy. It reads as follows:[34]

Text

אדם שת אנוש קינן מהללאל ירד	.1
חנוך מתושלח למך נח שם חם ויפת	.2
טלה שור האומים סדטן ארי בתולה	.3
מאוזנים עקרב קישת גדי ודלי דגים	.4
ניסן אייר סיון תמון תמוז אב אילול	.5
תשרי מרחשון כסליו טבית שבט	.6
ואדר אברהם יצחק יוקעב שלום	.7
חנניה מישאיל ועזריה שלום על ישראל	.8
דכירין לטב יוסה ועזרון וחזיקיו בנוה דחלפי	.9
כל מן דיהיב פלגו בן גבר לחבריה הי אמר	.10
לשן ביש על הבריה לעממחמיה הי גניב	.11
זבותיה דחבריה הי מן דגלי רזה דקרתה	.12
לעממיה דין דעינוח משוטטן בלך ארעה	.13
והמי סתירתה הוא יתן אפוה בגברה	.14
ההו ובזרעיה ויעקור יתיה מן תחות שומיה	.15
יומרון כל עמה אמן ואמן סלה	.16

רבי יוסה בר הלפי חזקיו בר חלפי דכירין לטב	.17
דסני סגי חנון עבדו לשמה דרחמנה שלום	.18

Translation

1. Adam, Seth, Enosh, Kenan, Mahalalel, Jared,
2. Enoch, Methuselah, Lamech, Noah, Shem, Ham, and Japheth.

3. Aries, Taurus, Gemini, Cancer, Leo, Virgo,
4. Libra, Scorpio, Sagittarius, Capricorn, and Aquarius, Pisces.
5. Nisan, Iyar, Sivan, Tammuz, Av, Elul,
6. Tishrei, Marḥeshvan, Kislev, Tevet, Shevat,
7. and Adar. Abraham, Isaac, Jacob. Peace.
8. Ḥananiah, Mishael, and Azariah. Peace unto Israel.

9. May they be remembered for good: Yose and Ezron and Ḥizziqiyu the sons of Ḥilfi.
10. Anyone causing a controversy between a man and his friend, or whoever
11. slanders his friend before the Gentiles, or whoever steals
12. the property of his friend, or whoever reveals the secret of the town
13. to the Gentiles—he whose eyes range through the whole earth[35]
14. and who sees hidden things, he will set his face on that
15. man and on his seed and will uproot him from under the heavens.
16. And all the people said: Amen and Amen. Selah.[36]

33 Cf. Japhet, 56; idem, *Ideology*, 116–24. Japhet holds that the relation between the God and people of Israel exists a priori and is not the result of any historical process. This view, however, may make too much of the somewhat diminished emphasis on the exodus in the book. See the Conclusion below.

34 Text and translation from Lee I. Levine, "The Inscription in the ʿEn Gedi Synagogue," in *Ancient Synagogues Revealed* (Jerusalem: Israel Exploration Society) 140. The translation has been slightly modified in capitalization and punctuation. See also Ralph W. Klein, "The Faith and the World," *CurTM* 28 (2001) 335–40. Note the plene spellings of נוח and יפית in distinction to MT. Isaac Kalimi, "History of Interpretation: The Book of Chronicles in Jewish Tradition," *RB* 105 (1998) 31, attributes this orthographic difference to the fact that the mosaic maker was reciting from memory.

35 Cf. 2 Chr 16:9, "for the eyes of Yahweh survey the whole earth."

36 Cf. 1 Chr 16:36, "And all the people said, 'Amen, and praise Yahweh.'"

17. Rabbi Yose the son of Ḥilfi, Ḥiziqiyu the son of Ḥilfi, may they be remembered for good,
18. for they did a great deal in the name of the Merciful One. Peace.

The first eight lines of the inscription are in Hebrew and the final ten in Aramaic. The first two lines are a citation of 1 Chr 1:1-4, set off by a double line, followed by the names of the signs of the zodiac in lines 3-4,[37] the names for the months of the year in lines 5-7a, and two sets of Jewish pillars of the community in lines 7b-8: Abraham, Isaac, and Jacob; and the three companions of Daniel, Hananiah, Mishael, and Azariah. The Aramaic section begins with a blessing for three men, who may have donated this inscription, in line 9, and it continues with a curse against anyone who violates four values of the community in lines 10-16. The final lines, 17-18, repeat a blessing for two of the three men mentioned in line 9.

It is the Hebrew section that is pertinent to this commentary. It begins by listing thirteen antediluvian ancestors (as presented in 1 Chr 1:1-4) as pillars of the world (ll. 1-2), and the Hebrew section concludes by listing two sets of Jewish heroes (Abraham, Isaac, and Jacob; Hananiah, Mishael, and Azariah) who are pillars of the world from a Jewish perspective (ll. 7-8). A rabbinic tradition clarifies the reason for these two pairs of names: "Upon whom does the world rest? Upon three pillars. Some say (that they are) Abraham, Isaac, and Jacob; others say Hananiah, Mishael, and Azariah, and still others say the three sons of Korah."[38] The zodiac signs (ll. 3-4) and the months of the year (ll. 5-7a), representing the solar and lunar years, respectively, reflect the structure and order of the universe as a whole. Levine suggests that the ancestors of the world, the zodiac signs, the months of the year, and the biblical figures may function as witnesses to the community oath and adjure members to

stand fast in their vows. Willi, 50–51, adds that the citation from Chronicles demonstrates the antiquity and universal validity of the tradition of doctrine and prayer practiced in this synagogue. Both sets of specifically Jewish leaders are considered people of prayer.[39] This inscription, like 1 Chronicles 1 itself, shows that a relationship to the entire structure of the universe and participation in specifically Jewish practices and beliefs do not exclude one another, but belong integrally together. The twelve months with their twelve animals might symbolically represent the twelve tribes of Israel, and these months in any case are surrounded by the thirteen primeval heroes and the two sets of heroes from Jewish history. Similarly, at Beth Alpha the sacrifice of Isaac and temple and synagogue motifs are portrayed alongside the zodiac.[40] Israel's history, there and here, is coupled with the order of the cosmos.

1:5-23. Segmented Genealogy of Japheth, Ham, and Shem

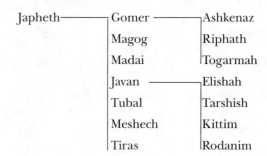

■ **5** *The descendants of Japheth:* Cf. Gen 10:2-5.[41] The listing here, as in Genesis, presents the nations as if they were all descended from an eponym, an ancestor with the same name. The territory of Japheth lies north and west of Israel. Japheth has seven sons and seven grandsons; three of the grandsons are descended from Gomer and four from Javan. While the full background informa-

---

37 In other contemporary Jewish synagogues—Husifa, Tiberias, Beth Alpha, and Naʿaran—both the design of the zodiac and the names of the zodiac signs appear.

38 *Midrash Tehillim* I, 15, cited in Levine, "Inscription in the ʿEn Gedi Synagogue," 142.

39 For Abraham, Isaac, and Jacob see *b. Ber.* 25b, and for the three friends of Daniel see Dan 3:28.

40 Ralph W. Klein, "The Faith and the World," *CurTM* 28 (2001) 335–340.

41 The Chronicler follows Genesis quite closely, even in the use of conjunctive *wāw* at the same places, including the somewhat surprising omission of the conjunction before Kittim in 1 Chr 1:7//Gen 10:4. For a study of the Japhethites see Édouard Lipiński, "Les Japhétites selon Gen 10,2-4 et 1 Chr 1,5-7," *ZAH* 3 (1990) 40–53, who dates the list of names to the end of the 7th or the beginning of the 6th century.

tion on each nation is more germane in a commentary on Genesis, to which the reader is referred (also for the possible sources and the sociological realities described therein), I note the following facts about each of these nations:[42]

Name/ Eponym	Identity/location
Gomer:	Ancestor of the Cimmerians, who are attested in the Assyrian Royal Annals, and located first in the Ukraine and then near Lake Van. They captured the Phrygian king Midas in 676 BCE and Gyges of Lydia at Sardis in 644 BCE.[43] Gomer, Magog, Tubal, Meshech, and Togarmah are all mentioned as dangerous, warring nations in Ezekiel 38–39.
Magog:	Identification uncertain. Some have suggested a derivation from Akkadian $mā(t)$ $gūgi$, "the land of Gyges?; others interpret "Ma" as a prefix meaning "place of." Hence: "the place of Gog." Josephus (Ant. 1.123) related Magog to the Scythians and Jerome to the Goths. For Gog of the land of Magog see the commentaries on Ezek 38:1-6; 39:6, where Magog is associated with Beth-togarmah in the far north.
Madai:	The Medes were located south of the Caspian Sea, in present-day Iran, and southeast of Lake Urmia. Cyrus the Persian conquered them and used their forces, combined with his own, to capture Babylon.
Javan:	This name corresponds to Ionia, an area of Greek settlement in southwest Asia Minor (Smyrna and Ephesus were two of its cities). Later Ionia included the Greek population on both sides of the Aegean Sea.
Tubal:	This country is called Tabal in the Assyrian inscriptions and is located in southeast Cappadocia, south of the Halys River. It is often linked in the Bible with Meshech (e.g., Ezek 27:13; 32:26; 38:2-3; 39:1; cf. Isa 66:19; and see Meshech below). The people living in this region were called Tibarenoi by Herodotus.
Meshech:	This name occurs only here, in Ps 120:5, and in Ezekiel where it is associated with Tubal (27:13; 32:26; 38:2-3; 39:1; cf. Isa 66:19 LXX).[44] Akkadian sources, as early as Tiglath-pileser I, mention a people $muškaya$ and a land $mušku$ in east Asia Minor.
Tiras:	This people is often identified with the Turša, who were among the Sea Peoples repulsed by Merneptah in 1232 BCE. Others connect them to the Etruscans. Josephus (Ant. 1.125) identified them with the Thracians.

The descendants of Gomer:

Ashkenaz:	According to Assyrian records, the Ishkuza appeared between the Black and Caspian Seas in the 8th and 7th centuries and drove out the Cimmerians. Herodotus says they are to be identified with the Scythians. Since the Middle Ages, this term has been used to designate Jews from northern and eastern Europe.
Riphath:	Josephus (Ant. 1.126) identified Riphath with Paphlagonia (bordering on the Black Sea), and a location in Asia Minor is likely because of Riphath's association with Ashkenaz and Togarmah (see the next entry).[45]
Togarmah:	Assyrian texts refer to *Til-garimmu* and to *Tegarama*, on the eastern border of Tubal, usually identified with the modern city of Gurun, north of Carchemish.[46]

---

42 For the data listed below and more on each of these names, see the appropriate entries in *ABD*.

43 See Askold I. Ivantchik, *Les Cimmerians au Proche-Orient* (OBO 127; Göttingen: Vandenhoeck & Ruprecht, 1993).

44 For its mistaken occurrence in 1 Chr 1:17 MT, see textual note 19.

45 Richard S. Hess, "Riphath," *ABD* 5:775.

46 David W. Baker, "Togarmah," *ABD* 6:594–95.

■ **7** *The descendants of Javan:*

Elishah:	The name *Alašiya* is widely attested in the 2d millennium as a name for the eastern end of Cyprus and later for the island as a whole. The word has a Sumerian etymology meaning "copper," which is also the etymological background of the name Cyprus itself.[47]
Tarshish:[48]	Jonah fled toward Tarshish in the west, and some would locate this site at Tartessus, a Phoenician colony in Spain. Others would locate it at Carthage (Ezek 27:12). Cf. also *tarsisi* in Akkadian sources, where its exact location is unclear. Tarshish is often associated with smelting or refining of metal.
Kittim:	These people are to be related to Kition, a town near modern Larnaca on the southern coast of Cyprus. In 1 Macc 1:1 Kittim (= Macedonia) is named as the birthplace of Alexander the Great and later, e.g., at Qumran, "Kittim" becomes a code word for the Romans.[49]
Rodanim:	These people hail from the island of Rhodes, off the southwest coast of Turkey.

■ **8** *The descendants of Ham:* Cf. Gen 10:6-17. The descendants of Ham are located south of the Mediterranean, in North Africa and the Arabian peninsula, and the territory of Ham also includes Palestine and Syria. In Pss 78:51; 105:23, 27; and 106:22, Ham stands for Egypt.[50]

Cush:[51]	Nubia, modern-day Sudan. Cushites are traditionally understood as Ethiopians in the LXX and in English versions.
Egypt:	Israel's well-known neighbor. Egypt and related words are frequently mentioned also in Chronicles (27 times).

```
Ham ──── Cush ──── Seba
                    Havilah
                    Sabta
                    Raamah ──┬ Sheba
                    Sabteca  └ Dedan
                    Nimrod
         Egypt ──── Ludim
                    Anamim
                    Lehabim
                    Napthuhim
                    Pathrusim
                    Casluhim ─────── Philistines
                    Caphtorim
         Put
         Canaan ─── Sidon
                    Heth
                    Jebusites
                    Amorites
                    Girgashites
                    Hivites
                    Arkites
                    Sinites
                    Arvadites
                    Zemarites
                    Hamathites
```

---

47 Lipiński, "Japhétites," 50–51, suggests that the transcription for *Alašiya* in Hebrew should be אלשיה, not אלישה, although the position of the *yôd* seems to be a very minor difference. He proposes instead that this is a reference to Ulysses.

48 For the remainder of this chapter, I cite other occurrences of the names when they appear elsewhere in the books of Chronicles. For Tarshish cf. 2 Chr 9:21; 20:36-37.

49 David W. Baker, "Kittim," *ABD* 4:93.

50 See Édouard Lipiński, "Les Chamites selon Gen 10,6-20 et 1 Chr 1,8-16," *ZAH* 5 (1992) 135–62. He reconstructs an original list that had seven descendants of Cush, seven of Egypt, and ten descendants of Canaan, or twenty-eight descendants in all. However that may be, the Chronicler clearly presupposed the list of Hamites as preserved in Genesis 10 MT. Lipiński dates the list to the 7th century.

51 Cf. 2 Chr 12:3; 14:8-12 (9-13); 16:8; 21:16.

Put: Some identify Put with Somalia (Egyp. *pun.t*) and the LXX sometimes, but not in this passage, translates it as Libya. Put is the only son of Ham who is not given further descendants.

Canaan:[52] The land on the eastern shore of the Mediterranean, including modern Lebanon, southern Syria, and most of Palestine west of the Jordan. Canaan was one of three Egyptian provinces in Syria-Palestine, which accounts for its association with Ham rather than with Shem, as one might expect from the language spoken by the Canaanites.

■ **9** *The descendants of Cush:* The names of the seven descendants of Cush are similar in formation with no use of plurals or gentilics.

Seba: Modern-day Abyssinia in northeast Africa, on the west coast of the Red Sea.[53]

Havilah: A land in southern Arabia, inhabited by Ishmaelites and Amalekites according to Gen 25:18 and 1 Sam 15:7. Havilah is the biblical form of the old tribal federation of *Ḥaulān* in southwest Arabia. Havilah also appears in the line of Shem, v. 23.

Sabta: Perhaps to be identified with Shabwat, the capital of Ḥaḍramaut (Hazarmaveth; cf. v. 20), at the eastern edge of the desert Ramlat as-Sabʾatayn.[54]

Raamah: An uncertain site, probably from southern Arabia.

Sabteca: A tribe or place in southern Arabia or Ethiopia.[55]

The descendants of Raamah:

Sheba:[56] A kingdom in southwest Arabia, referred to in native sources as Saba. It is the most important of the four south Arabian states of Sabaʾ Maʿin, Qatabān, and Ḥaḍramaut. See also v. 22, where Sheba is a son of Joktan and a grandson of Eber, who is a descendant of

Shem; and v. 32, where Sheba is a son of Jokshan and therefore grandson of Keturah (cf. also Dedan). The genealogies in Genesis 10 and 1 Chronicles 1 combine at times several genealogical lineages.

Dedan: Identified with Khuraybah, just north of the modern village of al-ʿUla in the Ḥijāz. Cf. also v. 32, where Dedan is identified as a son of Jokshan and therefore grandson of Keturah (cf. also Sheba).

■ **10** *Cush became the father of Nimrod; he was the first to be a mighty man on the earth:* Beginning in this verse, and continuing in vv. 11, 13, 18, and 20, the writer uses ילד in the *hiphil* ("became the father of") to describe the man's role in the human reproductive process. This usage comes from Genesis 10, where it is usually attributed to J (BDB, 408b, 2a). A legendary eponym from Mesopotamia, Nimrod has been identified as a god, a Mesopotamian hero such as Gilgamesh or Lugalbanda, or an historical personage such as Sargon of Agade or Tukulti-Ninurta I. In Gen 10:10-12, not included in Chronicles, he is associated with Babylon and especially Assyria. As a result, many scholars identify the Cush from whom Nimrod is descended as a reference to the Kassites.[57] Since the Chronicler omitted Gen 10:9-12, the Mesopotamian associations of Nimrod are not contained in Chronicles. It is not clear why the Chronicler retained this reference at all since most other anecdotal references are omitted.[58] Johnstone, 1:30, notes that Nimrod and Nebuchadnezzar (2 Chr 36:6-13) are the first and last "Babylonian" tyrants mentioned in Chronicles.

■ **11** *Egypt became the father of:* Only one of Egypt's seven descendants can be identified with any confidence and all employ the plural form of the gentilic (see also Kittim and Rodanim in v. 7). Singular gentilics appear in vv. 14-16. All of these forms are taken from Genesis.

Ludim: Unknown, but several biblical passages associate Lud with Egypt and other related countries (Isa 66:19; Jer 46:9; Ezek 27:10; 30:5).

52 Cf. 1 Chr 2:3; 16:18.
53 W. W. Müller, "Seba," *ABD* 5:1064.
54 W. W. Müller, "Sabtah," *ABD* 5:861–62. Cf. Lipiński, "Chamites," 145.
55 W. W. Müller, "Sabtecta," *ABD* 5:862–63. He also discusses the similarity of this name to Shebitku or Shabataka, the second ruler of the Twenty-fifth or Ethiopian Dynasty in Egypt. This identification is adopted by Lipiński, "Chamites," 146–47.
56 Cf. 2 Chr 9:1.
57 See E. A. Speiser, *Genesis* (AB 1; Garden City, NY: Doubleday, 1964) 66–67.
58 Cf. Oeming, *Wahre Israel,* 95–96.

Josephus (*Ant.* 1.144) associated these people with the Lydians. Cf. v. 17, where Lud is descended from Shem.

Anamim: Unidentified.

Lehabim: Unidentified. Some scholars would interpret this word לְהָבִים as an alternate spelling for לוּבִים (Libyans), who lived west of Egypt. Cf. 2 Chr 12:3 and 16:8.

Napuhim: Several locations within Egypt have been proposed, but none of them is certain.[59]

■ **12** *Pathrusim:* The Pathrusim appear only here and in the Table of Nations, but biblical references to Pathros[60] indicate that it is a subsection of Egypt. The area between Memphis and Aswan in Upper Egypt is known in Egyptian as *p'-t'-rs(y).*[61]

Casluhim: Unidentified.[62]

from whom the Philistines went forth: The Philistines (Egyp. *P-r-š-t-w*) came to Canaan from the Aegean basin. After their defeat by Ramesses III, they settled on the coast of Palestine, whose name derives from that of the Philistines. Because of passages like Jer 47:4 and Amos 9:7, which associate the Philistines with Caphtor, many scholars believe that this clause should modify the Caphtorim rather than the Casluhim.[63] While this association is probably historically correct, this reading was connected to Casluhim already in Gen 10:14, so there is no warrant for changing it in Chronicles. The Philistines appear a number of times in both books of Chronicles.[64]

Caphtorim:[65] The people of Crete.

■ **13** *Canaan became the father of:* The eleven sons of Canaan are listed as gentilics except for the first two, Sidon and Heth.[66]

Sidon[67] *his firstborn:* Sidon (MR 184329) is located on the Phoenician coast, forty kilometers north of Tyre. Cf. Gen 10:15 and 19. For "firstborn" see v. 29, where Nebaioth is identified as the firstborn of Ishmael.

Heth:[68] The Hittites were an Indo-European people who established an empire in Asia Minor in the mid-2d millennium BCE. After the destruction of their empire ca. 1200, Neo-Hittite states arose in the north and continued for the next five centuries. It is probably the Neo-Hittite people who are mentioned here and who are listed elsewhere as pre-Israelite inhabitants of the land. The Hittites and the next five names appear in the list of pre-Israelite inhabitants of the land in Deut 7:1. All but the Hivites from this list also appear in Gen 15:19-21, which also adds the Canaanites to the pre-Israelite inhabitants.

■ **14** *Jebusites:*[69] The gentilics of vv. 14-16 are singular in form, whereas in vv. 11-12 they were plural. These pre-Israelite inhabitants of Jerusalem are also included in the conventional lists of pre-Israelite inhabitants of the land.[70]

Amorites:[71] These Amorites, who are part of the pre-Israelite inhabitants of the land (see the previous entry) are to be distinguished from the West Semitic people known primarily from their names in Akkadian documents. Note that here their ancestry is traced not to Shem

---

59 David W. Baker, "Naphtuhim," *ABD* 4:1022.

60 Isa 11:1; Jer 44:1; 44:15; Ezek 29:14; 30:14.

61 David W. Baker, "Pathos," *ABD* 5:178.

62 Richard S. Hess, "Casluhim," *ABD* 1:877–78. Lipiński, "Chamites," 152–54, identifies them with a people known as the Colchidiens.

63 *NRSV* makes this change both here and in Genesis 10.

64 The first mention is with Saul (1 Chr 10:1) and the last with Ahaz (2 Chr 28:18).

65 Cf. Deut 2:23; Amos 9:7; Jer 47:4.

66 Japhet, 59 (referring to Pseudo-Rashi and Kimḥi), notes that there are twelve Canaanite nations, if

Canaan itself is included, possibly paralleling the twelve sons of Israel.

67 Cf. 1 Chr 22:4.

68 Cf. Uriah the Hittite in 1 Chr 11:41. The Hittites, Jebusites, and Amorites are connected to the history of Jerusalem in Ezek 16:45.

69 For Jebus and Jebusite(s) cf. 1 Chr 11:4-5; 21:15, 18, 28; 2 Chr 3:1; 8:7.

70 Num 13:29; Ezra 9:1; Neh 9:8.

71 Cf. 2 Chr 8:7.

but to Canaan and through him to Ham, reflecting their Palestinian location.

Girgashites: Another of the pre-Israelite inhabitants of the land,[72] this name or one similar to it has been found in the Ugaritic tablets (*grgš* or *bn grgš*).[73]

■ **15** *Hivites:*[74] Another of the pre-Israelite inhabitants of the land, the Hivites are often confused in biblical texts with the Horites. In the lists of pre-Israelite inhabitants of the land, they are usually mentioned before the Jebusites (e.g., Deut 7:1).

Arkites: Not attested outside this passage and the *Vorlage* in the Table of Nations. They should probably be associated with the Phoenician town of Irqata (Tell Arqa; MR 250436), about nineteen kilometers northeast of Tripoli.[75] The next four references are also to cities in Phoenicia or Syria.

■ **16** *Arvadites:* This city, modern Ruad (MR 229473), is on an island off the Phoenician coast. Two hundred soldiers from Arvad fought against Shalmaneser III at the battle of Qarqar in 853 BCE.

Zemarites: Akkadian documents refer to a city called Ṣimir, located somewhere between Arvad and Tripoli. Willi, 37, puts it 19 kilometers southeast of Ruad.

Hamathites:[76] Hamath is located in central Syria on the Orontes (MR 312503).

■ **17** *The descendants of Shem:* Cf. Gen 10:22-29. The descendants of Shem spread west from Mesopotamia.[77]

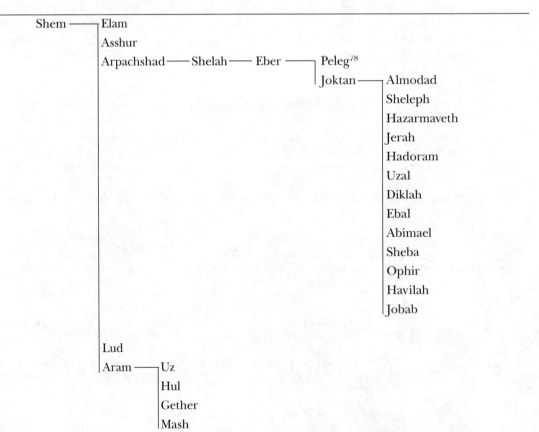

Elam:[79] Located east of Mesopotamia, from the Caspian Sea to the Persian Gulf, Elam is one of the least known among ancient Near Eastern states.

Asshur:[80] The city of Asshur was located on the Tigris River. In the 14th century it became the capital of a land that was for the first time called Assyria. In the 9th century Ashurnasirpal II moved the capital to Calah (Nimrud), and in the 8th century Sennacherib moved it to Nineveh. "Asshur" can also refer to Assyria itself.

Arpachshad: The first part of this name has been identified with Arrapḫa, a Hurrian name, to be located at modern Kirkuk. The second part of the name is related to *kaśdîm* (Chaldeans).[81] Although Arpachshad is the third son of his father, the line of Shem is continued through him for four more generations (cf. v. 24).

Lud: Possibly this refers to the Lydians (Josephus, *Ant.* 1.144), known in Assyrian as Luddu. Some would connect Lud to Lubdu, a people on the Upper Tigris (Wenham, *Genesis 1–15*, 230). Cf. also v. 11 above, where the Ludim are descendants of Egypt.

Aram: The name of an important Aramean nation, located in southern Syria, which existed between the 11th and 8th centuries BCE. Its capital was Damascus. Aram and the Arameans are mentioned frequently in Chronicles.

the descendants of Aram:

Uz: A country in northwest Arabia connected with either Aram (cf. Gen 22:21) or Edom (Gen 36:28; 1 Chr 1:42).

Hul: Unidentified.

Gether: Unidentified.

Mash: Probably unidentified, but see Mt. Masius (Tur Abdin) in northern Mesopotamia. Chronicles MT reads "Meshech."[82]

■ **18** *Arpachshad became the father of:* Although Arpachshad is the third son of his father, the line of Shem is continued through him for four more generations in the linear genealogy, beginning at v. 24.

Shelah: A personal name (cf v. 24).

Eber: This may refer to a geographic region ("beyond the river"), an ethnic group,[83] or a personal name (cf. v. 25).

■ **19** *Peleg:* The Akk. *palgu* means "canal," but a geographic name Phalga, known only from Hellenistic times, denotes the region where the Euphrates and Balikh rivers divide. Willi, 38, makes Peleg the ancestor of the northern Semites. Cf. v. 25. *(for in his days the world was divided):* An etymological etiology of the name Peleg (the verbal root פלג means "split," "divide"). Perhaps this is an allusion to the dispersion of peoples after the Tower

---

72 Gen 15:21; Deut 7:1; Josh 3:10; 24:11. See the singular in Neh 9:8.

73 David W. Baker, "Girgashite," *ABD* 2:1028. Cf. Olmo Lete and Sanmartín, *Ugaritic Language*, 308.

74 2 Chr 8:7.

75 Richard S. Hess, "Arkite," *ABD* 1:393–94.

76 1 Chr 18:3, 9; 2 Chr 8:4. Lebo-hamath is the northern border of the Davidic-Solomonic kingdom in 1 Chr 13:5 and 2 Chr 7:8.

77 For a reconstruction of the original form of this list, antedating both Genesis 10 and 1 Chronicles 1, see Édouard Lipiński, "Les Sémites selon Gen 10,21-30 et 1 Chr 1,17-23," *ZAH* 6 (1993) 193–215. He believes that the Table of Nations centers on Mt. Zaphon in North Syria, which Job 26:7 considered the pivot around which the world revolved.

78 For the continuation of Peleg's line see v. 25.

79 Cf. the Benjaminite Elam in 1 Chr 8:24 and the gatekeeper Elam in 1 Chr 26:3.

80 Cf. 1 Chr 5:6, 26; 2 Chr 28:16-21; 30:6; throughout chap. 32; 33:11.

81 Does the second element of the name explain why the (Neo-) Babylonians are not mentioned in the Table of Nations?

82 See textual note 19.

83 On the *'apîru* see J. Bottéro, *Le problème des Ḫabiru à la 4ᵉ rencontre assyriologique internationale* (Cahiers de la société asiatique 12; Paris: Impr. nationale, 1954); Moshe Greenberg, *The Hab/piru* (AOS 39: New Haven: American Oriental Society, 1955); Oswald Loretz, *Habiru-Hebräer* (BZAW 160; Berlin: de Gruyter, 1984); and Nadav Na'aman, "Ḫabiru and Hebrews: The Transfer of a Social Term to the Literary Sphere," *JNES* 45 (1986) 271–88. Na'aman understands the status of the uprooted people living on the edge of society in the books of Judges and Samuel as identical to the Ḫabiru of ancient Near Eastern texts.

of Babel incident in Genesis 11. Peleg's descendants resume in v. 25.

Joktan: The settlements of his thirteen descendants (vv. 20-22)[84] range from Mesha to Sephar, in the hill country of the east, that is, southwest Arabia. The relationship of this name (from the verbal root קטן meaning "to be small") to Jokshan (1 Chr 1:32), the son of Keturah, is not clear.[85] Both Joktan and Jokshan have sons named Sheba and Dedan.

■ **20** *Joktan became the father of:*

Almodad: A tribe or region in south Arabia. A note in Gen 10:30 puts all the names in this list in the region between Mesha and Sephar, the hill country of the east. Unfortunately neither of these latter sites can be located with any certainty.

Sheleph: Arab geographers refer to a Yemenite tribe bearing the name of as-Salif or as-Sulaf. A Sabean inscription places this tribe at the stronghold Māwiyat, present-day Ḥusn al-Ghurāb.[86]

Hazarmaveth: A name of a tribe and a name of the country, Ḥaḍramaut, inhabited by it. This name refers to a deep valley about 170 kilometers away from the south Arabian coast, east of Yemen. Together with Saba', Maʿīn, and Qatabān it is one of the four great pre-Islamic Arab states.[87]

Jerah: A tribe or region in south Arabia.

■ **21** *Hadoram:*[88] A tribe or region in south Arabia. It may be identified with the Yemenite *Dauram*, on the upper part of the Wadi Ḍahr, about

16 kilometers northwest of Ṣanʿā'. The identification proposed by Willi, 38, with the name of certain bedouin tribes is impossible because the correct form of that name is Ahl al-Ḥadara, not Ahl al-Hadara.[89]

Uzal: A tribe or region in south Arabia. The frequent identification of Uzal with Ṣanʿā', the capital of Yemen, has to be given up.[90]

Diklah: A tribe or region in south Arabia, possibly referring etymologically to the date palm (*HALOT*, 1:229).

■ **22** *Ebal:* The corresponding name in Gen 10:28 is Obal. Wenham, *Genesis 1–15*, 231, proposes an identification with ʿUbāl, a site between Ḥodeida and Ṣanʿā', or a Yemenite tribe Banū ʿUbal (*HALOT*, 794).

Abimael: An unidentified Arabian region or tribe.

Sheba:[91] The kingdom of Sheba in southwest Arabia is referred to in native sources as Saba. Sheba is also known as a descendant of Ham, through Cush and Raamah, and the brother of Dedan (v. 9 above), and as a descendant of Abraham and Keturah, through Jokshan, and the brother of Dedan (v. 32 below).

■ **23** *Ophir:*[92] Unknown tribe or region in south Arabia. Other passages in Chronicles associate the region with gold.

Havilah: Cf. on v. 9 above, where Havilah is a descendant of Ham through Cush.

Jobab: A Sabaean tribe with a similar name (*yhybb*) was one of three tribal federations of Sumʿay in the central highland of Yemen.

1:24-27. Linear Genealogy of Shem

Shem—Arpachshad—Shelah—Eber—Peleg—Reu—Serug—Nahor—Terah—Abram⌐Isaac
                                                                      └Ishmael

---

84 Does this presuppose some kind of tribal federation?

85 Richard S. Hess, "Joktan," *ABD* 3:935.

86 W. W. Müller, "Sheleph," *ABD* 5:1192–93.

87 W. W. Müller, "Hazarmaveth," *ABD* 3:85–86.

88 In 1 Chr 18:10 and 2 Chr 10:18 there are individuals named Hadoram, not connected to this people.

89 W. W. Müller, "Hadoram," *ABD* 3:16.

90 W. W. Müller, "Uzal," *ABD* 6:775.

91 Cf. 21 Chr 9:1.

92 1 Chr 29:4; 2 Chr 8:18; 9:10.

■ **24** *Shem,*[93] *Arpachshad, Shelah:* Cf. Gen 11:10-12. The previous names have sketched out the entire world of nations, but now the genealogy turns to the ancestral line that will lead to Israel and to other nations descending from Abraham.[94] Israel is to be understood within these two sets of nations. As with the linear genealogy in vv. 1-4, the Chronicler presents this genealogy as a simple list of names.

■ **25** *Eber, Peleg, Reu:* Cf. Gen 11:14-18. For Eber see v. 18. While Joktan was given thirteen sons in the segmented genealogy in vv. 20-22, his brother Peleg had none there (v. 19). The main line of Shem that leads to Israel passes through him, however, and so the genealogy proceeds through his son Reu.

Reu: Unlike other figures, Reu cannot be associated with any geographic area in northern Mesopotamia.

■ **26** *Serug, Nahor, Terah:* Cf. Gen 11:20-24.

Serug: The root of this word appears in several Mesopotamian place names. No sure identification is possible.

Nahor: A site Naḫur is listed in the Mari texts and is thought to be located near Harran on the Upper Balikh River.

Terah: This name is often associated with *Til ša turāḫi,* found in Neo-Assyrian texts and located near Harran on the Balikh River.

■ **27** *Abram (that is, Abraham):* Abraham is in the tenth generation of the line of Shem. The Chronicler took the name Abram from Gen 11:26, but then interpreted it with the parenthetical remark, or gloss, that points to the change of Abram's name in Gen 17:5. The analogous name change of Jacob to Israel is not reported in 1 Chronicles 1 since the patriarch is always called Israel, except for 1 Chr 16:13, 17. These are the first words in the chapter not taken directly from a genealogy in Genesis. This type of name interpretation appears in the references to "Esau (that is,

Edom)" in Gen 36:1, 8, which the Chronicler did not include in this chapter. While the goal of this whole chapter is the list of the sons of Israel in 1 Chr 2:1-2, it is significant, as Oeming, 79, has observed, that the name Abraham (Abram) occurs five times in this chapter (twice in this verse, vv. 28, 32, 34). The Chronicler omitted the rest of the subsequent genealogical information in Gen 11:26, namely, Abram's brothers Nahor and Haran, and vv. 27-32, the detailed information about the sons of Terah, their wives, and Lot.

1:28-54. Segmented Genealogy of the Descendants of Abraham's Sons

1:28. Caption

■ **28** *The descendants of Abraham: Isaac and Ishmael:* The Chronicler drafted this verse, since it is not in the genealogies of Genesis, but the information behind it is contained in Gen 25:8, the account of the death of Abraham, and Gen 25:9, the account of Abraham's burial by Isaac and Ishmael (who are listed in that order). The stories in Genesis 16–17 could also serve as the source of this information. The Chronicler introduces the descendants of Isaac with the same "the descendants of X" formula in v. 34, only after enumerating the descendants of Ishmael (vv. 29-31) and Keturah (vv. 32-33).

1:29-31. Descendants of Ishmael

■ **29** *These are their generations:* The Chronicler has rephrased this clause from Gen 25:12-13, where we read: "And these are the generations (תלדת) of Ishmael . . . according to their generations" (לתולדתם). The antecedent of "their" in 1 Chr 1:29 is either Isaac and Ishmael in v. 28, or, since the sons of Keturah will also be reported in vv. 32-33, it may anticipate all three sets of sons. The Chronicler uses the expression "generations" a number of times,[95] but this is the only time that he includes one of its uses from the genealogies in

93   Tg calls Shem here, but not in vv. 4 and 17, "Shem the great," which is usually taken as a reference to Melchizedek, who is equated with Shem in some targumim to Gen 14:18. By identifying Melchizedek with Shem, Melchizedek was brought inside the Jewish fold and hence there was no priesthood outside

Judaism. Cf. McIvor, *Targum,* 41, n. 61.

94   Johnstone, 1:32, compares the double introduction of Shem in vv. 17 and 24 with the double resumption of Benjamin in chap. 8 and 9:35-44.

95   1 Chr 5:7; 7:2, 4, 9; 8:28; 9:9, 34; 26:31.

Genesis.[96] The descendants of Ishmael are located south and east of Palestine.

```
Abraham ─┬─ Isaac
         └─ Ishmael ──────── Nebaioth
                             Kedar
                             Adbeel
                             Mibsam
                             Mishma
                             Dumah
                             Massa
                             Hadad
                             Tema
                             Jetur
                             Naphish
                             Kedemah
```

Nebaioth his firstborn: This tribe is mentioned in Assyrian inscriptions from the time of Ashurbanipal and was probably located in the region around Ḥâ'il.[97] Nebaioth and Kedar are mentioned together in Isa 60:7. For "firstborn" see also Sidon, v. 13.

Kedar: This tribe was the most powerful of a group of north Arabian tribes and is attested frequently in Assyrian and Neo-Babylonian sources.[98]

Adbeel: Cf. the tribal and personal name Idiba'ilu mentioned in the inscriptions of Tiglath-pileser III (*ANET*, 283).

Mibsam: מבשם is derived from the word for "balm"

(בֹּשֶׂם), and this tribe may have been involved in the spice trade. [99]

■ **30** *Mishma:* Knauf concludes from this passage, Gen 25:19, and 1 Chr 4:25 that Mibsam and Mishma were two Ishmaelite clans that lived in the Negeb during the exilic and/or post-exilic periods.[100]

Dumah: An oasis in north central Saudi Arabia, on the Wadi Sirhan. It lies on the trade routes from Arabia to Amman and Damascus. It is first referred to in the inscriptions of Sennacherib and later those of Esarhaddon.

Massa: The Massaeans paid tribute to Tiglath-pileser III in 734 BCE after he had conquered Gaza. In the mid-7th century they raided a caravan of the Nebaioth. Massa may be the same as the site Mesha, marking the northern border of the sons of Jokshan in Gen 10:30, a verse omitted by the Chronicler.[101]

Hadad: This name is to be distinguished from the name Hadad in 1 Chr 1:46, 47, 50, 51 since it begins with a *ḥêt* rather than a *hê*. Hadad does not appear in Assyrian inscriptions.

Tema: Taymâ' is one of the major caravan cities of north Arabia, where three trade routes merge. Cf. Job 2:11 and 6:19. It is mentioned in Mesopotamian inscriptions from Sennacherib through Nabonidus.

■ **31** *Jetur:* Cf. 1 Chr 5:19, where the Hagrites, Jetur, Naphish, and Nodab are listed as enemies of Reuben, Gad, and the half-tribe of Manasseh, all presumably originating from the east.

---

96 In Genesis it appears in 2:4; 5:1, followed by a genealogy; 6:9, followed by the flood story; 10:1, followed by the genealogy of the Table of Nations (cf. v. 32); 11:10, followed by the genealogy of Shem; 11:27, followed by the genealogy of Terah; 25:12, followed by the genealogy of Ishmael (cf. v. 13); 25:19, followed by the genealogy of Isaac; 36:1, 9, followed by the genealogy of Esau; and 37:2, followed by the Joseph story. All of the genealogies introduced by תלדות in Genesis are included in 1 Chronicles 1. In addition to the omission of the sons of Cain in Gen 4:17-22, already discussed, the Chronicler omits the offspring of Lot's daughters in

Gen 19:37-38; the sons of Nahor in Gen 22:20-24, and the descendants of Dedan and Midian in Gen 25:3-4.

97 Ernst Axel Knauf, "Nebaioth," *ABD* 4:1053.
98 Ernst Axel Knauf, "Kedar," *ABD* 4:9–10.
99 See Ernst Axel Knauf, "Mibsam," *ABD* 4:805. For the reference to Mibsam and Mishma in 1 Chr 4:25, see the commentary.
100 For a revocalization of Mishma and a suggested connection to a known Arabic tribe see Ernst Axel Knauf, "Mishma," *ABD* 4:871.
101 Ernst Axel Knauf, "Massa," *ABD* 4:600.

Naphish:	Cf. 1 Chr 5:19. A chief of this tribe in northern Transjordan is mentioned in a letter to Ashurbanipal.[102]
Kedemah:	Knauf interprets this last name as a personification of the peoples of the east, and proposes that it was added to the list in order to reach the number twelve.[103]

C. 1:32-33. Descendants of Keturah

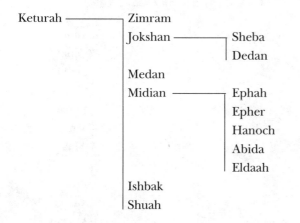

■ **32** *The descendants of Keturah the concubine of Abraham: she bore:* Cf. Gen 25:1-4, where she is identified as Abraham's wife. The third line of descent from Abraham has six sons and seven grandsons. As mentioned under Structure, the Chronicler omits from Gen 25:2 the words "to him," thus de-emphasizing Abraham's relationship to these descendants. Other concubines named in the genealogies are Maacah (1 Chr 2:48-49), an Aramean concubine (7:14), and David's generic concubines (3:9).[104] I. Eph'al points out that the common denominator of the sons of Keturah is their connection with international trade.[105]

Zimran:	Unidentified.
Jokshan:	Unidentified.
Medan:	Medan may be a tribe or a settlement in Wâdi Mudân, south of Midian.[106]
Midian:	Midian is the eponymous ancestor of the Midianites. Mendenhall argues that the Midianites emerged as a political entity east of the Gulf of Aqaba in the 13th century.[107]
Ishbak:	Ishbak is mentioned in an inscription of Shalmaneser III (*māt Iašbuqi; ANET,* 278) and is located in northern Syria.
Shuah:	Shuah is identified with Akk. *Sūḫu,* a country on the middle Euphrates. Cf. Bildad the Shuhite in Job 2:11.
the descendants of Jokshan: Sheba and Dedan:	In Gen 10:7//1 Chr 1:9 Sheba and Dedan are listed as the sons of the Hamite Raamah, and in Gen 10:28// 1 Chr 1:22 Sheba is an Arabian tribe that descended from the Shemite Joktan. The Chronicler used the expression "the descendants of Jokshan" instead of "Jokshan became the father of," which is found in the *Vorlage* at Gen 25:3.
Sheba:	Cf. v. 9, where Sheba is identified as a descendant of Ham.
Dedan:	This name is identified with the ruins of Khuraybah, north of the modern village of al-'Ula in the Ḥijāz. Cf. v. 9, where Dedan is identified as a descendant of Ham through Raamah.[108]

■ **33** *The descendants of Midian:*

Ephah:	The five following names comprise the clans, tribes, or people inhabiting Midian. Ephah may have been the leading tribe in this country. It is mentioned as a city and a people in

102 Ernst Axel Knauf, "Naphish," *ABD* 4:1020.

103 Ernst Axel Knauf, "Kedemah," *ABD* 4:10.

104 See Laban and Ben-Zvi, "Observations," 467–68. They also note, 478, that numerous references to women in the genealogies indicate that ideologically constructed gender expectations have been transgressed in the past with good results.

105 "'The Sons of Keturah' and 'The Sons of Ishmael,'" in *Bible and Jewish History Dedicated to the Memory of J. Liver* (ed. B. Uffenheimer; Tel Aviv: Tel Aviv Univ. Press, 1971) 161–68. See also idem, *The Ancient Araba* (Jerusalem: Magnes, 1982) 233.

106 Knauf, "Medan," *ABD* 4:656.

107 George E. Mendenhall, "Midian," *ABD* 4:815–18.

108 The Chronicler omitted the continuation of Gen 25:3 at this point: "The sons of Dedan were Asshurim, Letushim, and Leummim." See textual note 33.

the annals of Tiglath-pileser III and of Sargon II, respectively.

Epher: Knauf cites three areas or towns in northwest Arabia that may have preserved the name of this tribe.[109]

Hanoch: The Hebrew form of this name (חֲנוֹךְ) can also be rendered in English as Enoch. This Hanoch may be related to the city Cain named after his son Enoch (Gen 4:17).

Abida: This name may be identified with the town of al-Bad', 25 kilometers east of the Gulf of Aqaba and 120 kilometers south of al-Aqaba in northwest Arabia.[110]

Eldaah: Unidentified.

1:34—2:2. Descendants of Isaac's Sons: Esau and Israel

■ **34** *Abraham became the father of Isaac. The descendants of Isaac: Esau and Israel:* Abraham's siring of Isaac is carefully underscored, as in Gen 35:19. For the next generations we read only of "the descendants of Isaac" (v. 34), the "descendants of Esau (v. 35), and "the descendants of Israel" (2:1). This familiar genealogy of Jacob/Israel, known from Genesis, is also the first mention of Israel in the book. Israel in itself and in its relation to others is the subject of the entire work. The use of "Israel" for "Jacob" as the name of the third patriarch prevails throughout the work, except for 1 Chr 16:13, 17. The change of "Jacob" into "Israel" is first made in Gen 32:28 and 35:10.

1: 35-54. Descendants of Esau

■ **35** *The descendants of Esau:*[111] The Chronicler's interest is primarily in the descendants of Esau (five sons and eleven grandsons) and not the nation of Edom that was traced back to Esau. Consequently he left out a number of the references to Edom: "Esau, that is, Edom" from Gen 36:1, 8, 19; "Esau the father of Edom" from 36:9, 43; "in the land of Edom" from 36:16, 17, 21, 32. The only references to Edom he retains deal with the kings (1 Chr 1:43) and the chiefs (1:51, 54) of Edom, respectively.

1:35-37. Descendants of Esau Himself

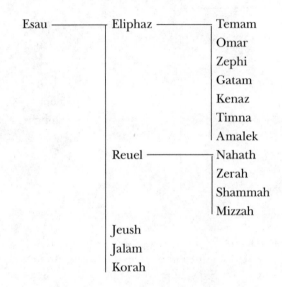

Eliphaz, Reuel, Jeush, Jalam, and Korah: In Gen 36:4-5 Adah is named as the mother of Eliphaz, Basemath as the mother of Reuel, and Oholibamah as the mother of Jeush, Jalam, and Korah, but the names of these wives of Esau are omitted by the Chronicler. The name Reuel

109 Ernst Axel Knauf, "Epher," *ABD* 2:534–35.

110 Mark J. Fritz, "Abida," *ABD* 1:14.

111 I will not identify all of the sons of Esau and Seir since this would be more appropriate to a commentary on Genesis or to a history of Edom, and many of them are unknown. See Bartlett, *Edom and the Edomites,* 86–90, who concludes, 88, with regard to Gen 36:20-28//1 Chr 1:38-42: "In short, Seir's sons and grandsons seem to be associated with the clans of the Negev on the southern fringes of Judah, and thus to the region west of the Wadi 'Araba with which the place name Seir itself may be connected." On the sons of Esau in Gen 36:1-14 (cf. 1 Chr 1:35-37), he concludes, 90, that there is little to indicate the writer was drawing on genuinely Edomite material and much to suggest that he was preparing a list of names appropriate to the much later Edom that he knew. See also E. A. Knauf, "Alter und Herkunft der edomitischen Königsliste Gen 36.31-39," *ZAW* 97 (1985) 245–53; Piotr Bienkowski, "The Edomites: Archaeological Evidence from Transjordan," in *You Shall Not Abhor an Edomite for He Is Your Brother* (ed. D. V. Edelman; ABS 3; Atlanta: Scholars Press, 1995) 41–92; and B. Dicou, *Edom, Israel's Brother and Antagonist: The Role of Edom in Biblical Prophecy and Story* (JSOTSup 169; Sheffield: JSOT Press, 1994); Walter Kornfeld, "Die Edomiterlisten (Gn 36; 1 C 1) im Lichte des altarabischen Namensmateriales," in *Mélanges bibliques et orientaux en l'honneur de M. Mathias Delcor* (ed. A. Caquot, S. Légasse, and M. Tardieu; AOAT 215; Neukirchen-Vluyn: Neukirchener Verlag, 1985) 231–36.

appears elsewhere as the Midianite father-in-law of Moses (Exod 2:18).

■ **36** *The descendants of Eliphaz: Teman, Omar, Zephi, Gatam, Kenaz, Timna, and Amalek:* The only other Eliphaz known in the Bible is one of Job's friends, who on each of his six occurrences is called the Temanite.[112] Hence it is not surprising to find Teman listed as the eldest son of Eliphaz here. Teman, as we will see in v. 45, is a region in Edom, and the genealogical link in this verse connects Esau to that region. The reference to Eliphaz calls to mind Job himself, who was from the land of Uz (1:1). The LXX of Job 42:17 locates Uz south of Palestine, between the Negeb and the Sinai peninsula. Uz was originally situated in northwest Arabia between Dedan and Edom.[113] In 1 Chr 1:42//Gen 36:28 Uz is made a grandson of Seir. The Chronicler treats Timna and Amalek as the sixth and seventh children[114] of Eliphaz and the grandchildren of Esau, whereas in Gen 36:12 Timna was the female concubine of Eliphaz, and they together were the parents of Amalek (see textual note 41). No clear rationale for this change is evident.[115] Timna is considered a grandchild of Esau, while in 1 Chr 1:39 *and* Gen 36:22 she is tied genealogically to Seir as his daughter and the sister of Lotan. The presence of Timna in both the lineage of Esau and the lineage of Seir shows a clear tie between the two ancestors.[116] The association of Esau with Amalek, who inhabited the Negeb and who often opposed Israel,[117] supplements our knowledge of Esau's geographical location. Bartlett concludes his discussion of Gen 36:12: "The Amalekites are here given a somewhat lower status, and the editor may be quietly making the point that Israel's arch-enemy Edom is known by the company it keeps."[118]

■ **37** *The descendants of Reuel: Nahath, Zerah, Shammah, and*

Mizzah: Very little is known of these descendants of Esau, who are also listed as clans in Gen 36:17. Is Zerah, here identified as a grandson of Esau, the same as Zerah, the descendant of Judah in 1 Chr 2:4, 6? Note also that there is a Zerah among the sons of Simeon (4:24).

1:38-42. Descendants of Seir

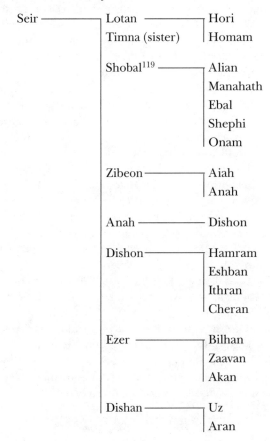

112 Job 2:11; 4:1; 15:1; 22:1; 42:7, 9.
113 Ernst Axel Knauf, "Uz," *ABD* 6:770–71.
114 Perhaps both are even considered sons, instead of a daughter and a son.
115 I noted above, in the commentary on v. 35, the omission of the names of Esau's wives. Japhet, 63, considers three possibilities for this change: (a) a different understanding of the ethnic context; (b) a stylistic distillation; or (c) a textual corruption. Wilson, "Interpreting Biblical Genealogies," 20, notes that the Chronicler lists the seven names in the order in which they appear in Gen 36:11-12 and omits all genealogical relationships between the

persons named. He surmises that the Chronicler expected the reader to be able to supply the missing information.
116 Bartlett, *Edom and the Edomites*, 87.
117 E.g., Exod 17:8-16; 1 Sam 14:48; 15:1-32; 2 Sam 1:8, 13.
118 *Edom and the Edomites,* 89. Is the Chronicler softening that critique by getting rid of Timna's status as a concubine and including Timna and Amalek as full-born children of Eliphaz?
119 Cf. 1 Chr 2:50, 52, where Shobal is part of Caleb; and 4:1, 2, where it is part of Judah.

■ 38 *The descendants of Seir: Lotan, Shobal, Zibeon, Anah, Dishon, Ezer, and Dishan:* No genealogical bridge is constructed from Seir to any ancestor, including Esau, although Bartlett holds that Esau's primary genealogical connection is with Seir rather than with Edom.[120] Seir is originally the name for a geographical feature, the precipice leading from the Transjordanian plateau down to the Wadi al-ʿArabah, but it eventually became a synonym for Edom.[121] Seir is generally taken to mean "hairy," suggesting a forested region. Edelman proposes, however, that the name might mean "goaty" (and derived from the same root) or "whirled away" or "made bare" (from *sʿr* II), referring to a mountainous region that was windswept or barren.[122] She places Seir in the eastern Negeb highlands. The Chronicler omitted Gen 36:9, 21, and 43b, which connect Esau, Seir, and Edom. In 36:20 Seir is called a Horite, and in 36:30 we are told that clans of the Horites inhabited the land of Seir. Bartlett notes that a number of the descendants of Seir are associated with the clans of the Negeb on the southern fringes of Judah.[123] Lotan may be a variant of the name Lot, and he is associated with the Dead Sea area and, through the sons of his daughters, with the Moabites and Ammonites (Gen 19:30-38). In addition to its relationship with Seir, Shobal is among the Calebite families in 1 Chr 2:50-52.

■ 39 *and the sister of Lotan was Timna:* Timna is usually identified with the concubine of Eliphaz (Gen 36:12; in 1 Chr 1:36 this Timna is understood as a child of Eliphaz). Timna also refers to the territory inhabited by an Edomite clan, located at the southern end of the

Arabah, about 30 kilometers north of the Gulf of Aqaba (cf. also 1 Chr 1:51).[124]

■ 40 *The descendants of Shobal: Alian, Manahath, Ebal, Shephi, and Onam:* Bartlett suggests a connection between Manahath and the Calebite Menuhoth (1 Chr 2:52), and between Onam and a Jerahmeelite with the same name (2:26).

■ 41 *The son of Anah: Dishon. The descendants of Dishon: Hamran, Eshban, Ithran, and Cheran:* In his genealogical charts, Myers, 2:234, mistakenly makes this Dishon the son of Anah who is a descendant of Zibeon (Gen 36:2; 1 Chr 1:38) and therefore the great grandson of Seir, whereas this Dishon should be identified as the son of Anah the son of Seir (1 Chr 1:38). This Dishon therefore is the grandson of Seir. Each son of Seir, according to my understanding of the genealogy, has a child or children in a second generation. In Myers's reading Seir's sons Anah and Dishon do not have children, and Zibeon's genealogy alone extends for three additional generations after him.[125] Bartlett links Ithran to Jether (2:32), the Ithrites (2:53), and the town Jattir (Josh 21:14).[126]

■ 42 *The descendants of Ezer: Bilhan, Zaavan, and Akan:* Bartlett associates Akan with Jaakan (1 Chr 1:42) and the "descendants of Jaakan," who are situated between the wilderness of Sinai and Ezion-geber in Num 33:31 and Deut 10:6.

The descendants of Dishan: Uz and Aran: Aran may be related to the Jerahmeelite Oren (1 Chr 2:25).[127]

---

120 *Edom and the Edomites,* 87. He bases this on the dependence of Gen 36:9-14 on Gen 36:20-28. See also his earlier study, "The Land of Seir and the Brotherhood of Edom," *JTS,* n.s. 20 (1969) 1–20.

121 See Ernst Axel Knauf, *Midian: Untersuchungen zur Geschichte Palästina und Nordarabiens am Ende des 2. Jahrtausends v. Chr.* (ADPV; Wiesbaden: Harrassowitz, 1988) 50–60; idem, "Seir," *ABD* 5:1072–73.

122 Edelman, "Edom," 7. Esau, of course, also had a "hairy" reputation (Gen 25:25; 27:11, 23).

123 *Edom and the Edomites,* 88.

124 Manfred Görg, "Der biblische Name des Kupferminengebiets von Timna," *BN* 65 (1992) 5–8, proposed an Egyptian name for this area *ʿtk,* found in the Papyrus Harris and in 1 Sam 30:30 בעתך.

125 A similar mistake was made by the editor of Gen 36:14, who ties Esau's wife Oholibamah, the daugh-

ter of Anah, to the Anah of 36:24 who found the springs in the wilderness and who is the grandson of Seir through Zibeon. Oholibamah is in fact the daughter of the Anah of 36:20 and 25, who is the son of Seir. Instead of Oholibamah being the granddaughter of Dishon, as in 36:25, she becomes his great-granddaughter in 36:14, and in 36:2, which is dependent on v. 14.

126 *Edom and the Edomites,* 88.

127 Ibid.

1:43-51a. Kings of Edom

■ **43** *These are the kings who ruled in the land of Edom before a king ruled for the sons of Israel:* This citation from Gen 36:31 indicates that the following eight kings, who were unrelated to one another and hence not dynastic, and who hailed from a variety of cities, ruled before David (or Saul?[128]) came to power in Israel.[129] Hadad, at the time of Solomon, was from the royal house of Edom (1 Kgs 11:14-15), presupposing the principle of a hereditary monarchy. According to Exod 15:15, Edom was ruled by אלופים (chiefs). This king list, with its nondynastic succession, would seem to fit typologically between these two types of government. For the absolute date of this king list, however, see the summary following the commentary on v. 50.

Table 4 shows the information supplied for each king.

Table 4. Kings of Edom

Name	Father's Name	Capital/Hometown
B. Bela	Beor	Dinhabah
A. Jobab	Zerah	Bozrah
A. Husham		Land of the Temanites
B. Hadad	Bedad	Avith
A. Samlah		Masrekah
A. Shaul		Rehoboth on the river
C. Baal-hanan	Achbor	
B. Hadad		Pai

Four of these kings, prefixed with an "A" in table 4, are said to be "from" a given city, while the three kings, prefixed with a "B" in the table, are followed by "and the name of his city was X." No city is given for Baal-hanan, prefixed with a "C." Bartlett believes the list was put together from sources A, B, and C. Many scholars believe that some of these kings may have reigned at the same time and that the succession described in the Hebrew text is artificial. As will be seen, we actually know very little about the people mentioned in this list.

Bela the son of Beor, and the name of his city was Dinhabah: Bartlett notes that Bela the son of Beor has been compared with, and even identified with, Balaam the son of Beor, mentioned in the OT,[130] and identified as a prophet in the inscription discovered at Tell Deir ʿAllā.[131] This seems like an extraordinarily unlikely confusion, however, and offers no explanation for the loss of the final *mêm* nor for the fact that Bela is identified as a king of Edom and Balaam as a prophet hired by Balak the son of Zippor king of Moab.[132] Eusebius and Jerome located Dinhabah at Dannaia, 13 kilometers north of Areopolis (Er-Rabba), or at Danaba, north of the Arnon. Both of these sites are in Moab.[133]

■ **44** *Bela died, and Jobab the son of Zerah from Bozrah ruled in his place:* Each king's death in this list is recorded, and it is followed by a succession formula in vv. 44, 45, 46, 47, 48, 49, and 50. The death notice of Hadad in v. 51 is not found in the *Vorlage* at Gen 36:40 (see the commentary on v. 51). Jobab is the only king from list A to be

---

128 Cf. ibid., 95, citing a translation "before a king ruled in Israel," based on LXX[L]. LXX[A], which he also cites in this context, actually favors David: "before a king ruled in Jerusalem." On the whole pericope see his earlier study, "The Edomite King-List of Genesis xxxvi.31-39 and I Chron. I.43-50," *JTS*, n.s. 16 (1965) 301–14.

129 Becker, 1:16 (cf. already Curtis and Madsen, 77), construed the sentence to mean that these kings of Edom ruled before a king of Israel ruled there in Edom. But for that one would expect מלך בני ישראל ("king of the sons of Israel"), not מלך לבני ישראל ("king for the sons of Israel"). Two Hebrew MSS and LXX in Gen 36:31 read מלך בישראל ("king in Israel"), seemingly confirming the usual understanding of this verse.

130 Num 22:5; 24:3, 15; 31:8; Deut 23:4; Josh 13:22; 24:9; Mic 6:5.

131 *Edom and the Edomites,* 96.

132 While various homelands are cited for Balaam (Pethor [Num 22:5]; Aram [23:7]; the land of Amaw [22:5]; or Midian [31:8]), he is never considered an Edomite. Edward Lipiński, *The Aramaeans: Their Ancient History, Culture, Religion* (OLA 100; Leuven: Peeters, 2000) 358–62, accepts the equation of Bela with Balaam and argues that the two kings in list B named Hadad are also Aramean, with the conclusion that the B section of the king list was originally Aramean rather than Edomite. Similarly, A. Lemaire, "Hadad l'Édomite ou Hadad l'Araméen?" *BN* 43 (1988) 14–18; idem, "Balaʿam/Belaʿ fils de Beʿôr," *ZAW* 102 (1990) 180–87.

133 The geographical information in these verses unless otherwise noted is from Bartlett, *Edom and the Edomites,* 45–54.

provided with a father's name. Is his father Zerah the same person as the son of Reuel and grandson of Esau mentioned in v. 37 (Gen 36:13; cf. Gen 36:17, a verse not included by the Chronicler)? Bozrah was the most important city in Edom (Amos 1:12) and is usually located at Buseira (MR 208016), some 35 kilometers southeast of the Dead Sea. It became the central city of political Edom in the eighth and seventh centuries (Isa 34:6; 63:1; Jer 49:13, 22, 27; Amos 1:11-12).[134]

■ **45** *Husham from the land of the Temanites:* Teman designated a region of Edom and became a poetic synonym for Edom itself.[135] In Jer 49:20 Teman is named as a synonym of Edom (cf. Hab 3:3; Obad 9).

■ **46** *Hadad the son of Bedad, who defeated Midian in the plains of Moab . . . and the name of his city was Avith:* Knauf suggests that *Ghuwaith,* etymologically the same as Avith, was the clan or tribe to which Hadad belonged and that Avith was its place of encampment.[136] The location of Avith is unknown. No details of Hadad's battle with the Midianites are known, and this reference seems insufficient to question Hadad's relationship to Edom (*pace* Bartlett, 97). This is the only historical incident recorded for the kings listed in vv. 43-51a.

■ **47** *Samlah from Masrekah:* Masrekah may be identified with Jebel Mushrāq, about halfway betwen Maʿān and Aqaba.[137]

■ **48** *Shaul from Rehoboth on the river:* The name Shaul is spelled the same way in Hebrew as David's predecessor Saul. While "the river" in Hebrew often refers to the Euphrates, this seems highly unlikely as a location for the hometown of a king of Edom (contra *NRSV*). Zwickel has suggested Râs er-Riḥâb (MR 208038), overlooking Wadi al-Ḥasâ from the south, as a site for Rehoboth.[138] This site is in the northwest corner of Edom.

■ **49** *Baal-hanan the son of Achbor:* Neither the king's name[139] nor the name of his father leads to any further insights.[140] He is the only king in the list for whom no place name is ascribed.

■ **50** *Hadad ruled in his place, and the name of his city was Pai:* During the reign of Solomon, Hadad of the Edomite royal house revolted against Solomon. He stayed for a time in Egypt and married a daughter of Pharaoh (1 Kgs 11:14-22). It is unclear whether this Hadad from the era of Solomon has any relationship to Hadad from the city of Pai or to Hadad the son of Bedad in v. 46.[141] Wenham links Pai to Wadi Fai at the south end of the Dead Sea, but many scholars consider the location of Pai (or Pau in Gen 36:39) to be unknown. The LXX rendering would link it to Peor in Moab.[142]

his wife's name was Mehetabel, the daughter of Matred, the daughter of Me-zahab: This is the only time the wife of any of these Edomite kings is mentioned, and here we are

---

134 See Edelman, "Edom," 1.

135 Ernst Axel Knauf, "Teman," *ABD* 6:347–48, places Teman in the northern part of Edom on the basis of Amos 1:12; Bartlett, *Edom and the Edomites,* 40, 89, places it in the southern part of Edom. Knauf argues, unconvincingly in my judgment, that the Temanite in this verse refers to Taima in north Arabia. Edelman, "Edom," 10, places Teman in the northern portion of the Edomite plateau in the region surrounding Bozrah (cf. Amos 1:12; Ezek 25:13).

136 Ernst Axel Knauf, "Avith," *ABD* 1:530.

137 Ernst Axel Knauf, "Samlah," *ABD* 4:600, believes the place is unidentified.

138 See W. Zwickel, "Rehobot-Nahar," *BN* 29 (1985) 28–34. Burton MacDonald, "The Wadi el-Ḥasā Survey, 1979, and Previous Archaeological Work in Southern Jordan," *BASOR* 245 (1982) 35–52, found Iron Age pottery at the site. Ernest Axel Knauf, "Rehoboth," *ABD* 5:664, takes "Rehoboth" as a designation of a landscape, not a town. Knauf, "Supplementa Ismaelitica," *BN* 38/39 (1987) 44–49, notes that Zwickel's site is situated on a wadi, not a river, and therefore finds his identification highly unlikely.

139 Cf. David's commissioner for olives and sycamores in 1 Chr 27:28.

140 Other Achbors are mentioned in 2 Kgs 22:12, 24; Jer 26:22; 36:12.

141 For a full discussion see Bartlett, *Edom and the Edomites,* 107–13.

142 *Genesis 15–50,* 340. Num 23:28; 25:18; 31:16; Josh 22:17. Johnstone, 1:35, observes that we are now thirteen generations removed from Abraham (Abraham, Isaac, Esau, Esau's sons and grandsons, and eight generations of kings), and that David was in the fourteenth generation after Abraham (1 Chr 2:1, 4-5, 9-15). After this last king, Edom then moves to tribal chiefs and kingship passes to Israel. Edom's kings are from many families; Israel's all from the house of David. Under Jehoram, a king of Judah, the Edomites resumed kingship (2 Chr 21:8).

given also the names of the queen's mother and perhaps grandmother[143] (form critically, a pedigree). Me-zahab (= "gold water") may, however, be the name of Matred's town rather than her mother's name. See 2 Kgs 15:10, where Shallum the son of Jabesh refers to Shallum who hails from Jabesh.[144] Di-zahab in Deut 1:1 is also a town with the word "gold" in it. While "Matred" might be interpreted as a male name and therefore the *son* of Me-zahab (see textual note 67), the attestation for that alternate interpretation in Chronicles is weak.

Summary: Of the seven place names associated with these kings of Edom, only one is known for sure (Bozrah) and a second regional name (Teman) is probable. Only one of these kings, Jobab the son of Zerah, is connected, even tenuously, to the genealogy of Esau. With such weak evidence it is little wonder that scholars can date this list anywhere from the eleventh to the fifth century. Zwickel (see the reference in n. 136) dates it to the end of the second millennium BCE, Bartlett holds that the core of the list is no earlier than the eighth century and that it was edited by a Deuteronomistic hand in the seventh century,[145] Knauf dates it to the end of the sixth or the beginning of the fifth century,[146] and Lemaire believes that it is a list of Aramean kings from the eleventh century.[147] This uncertainty, of course, has little bearing on the interpretation of Chronicles, since the author found this list of Edomite kings in his *Vorlage* of Genesis and took it at face value.

■ **51a** *Hadad died, and the chiefs of Edom were:* This replaces the text of Gen 36:40: "These are the names of the chiefs of Esau."[148] While the chronological relationship between the "kings" and the "chiefs" in Genesis is indeterminate, the reading in Chronicles makes the eleven chiefs (אלופים) clearly subsequent to the list of Edomite kings. The Chronicler may have wanted to draw

a parallel between Edom and Israel in that both were in his day in a post-monarchical period. The Chronicler's omission of Gen 36:43bβ, "according to their settlements in the land that they held," turns the regional chiefs into national leaders. Wenham suggests that the names of the chiefs may originally have referred to administrative districts of Edom since some of the names are place names.[149] The closest parallel use of the word "chiefs" is in Exod 15:15,[150] where we read of the "chiefs of Edom," the "leaders [אילי, lit. 'rams'] of Moab," and the inhabitants (ישבי, possibly "rulers") of Canaan. The poet who composed this verse in Exodus apparently used three synonymous expressions to designate the political leaders of these countries, and no ranking of them over against one another seems plausible.[151]

1:51b-54. Chiefs of Edom

■ **51b** *Chief Timna:* This chief (cf. Gen 36:40) is apparently not the concubine of Eliphaz the son of Esau, who was the sister of Lotan the son of Seir (Gen 36:12, 22//1 Chr 1:36,[152] 39).

■ **52** *Chief Oholibamah:* Oholibamah is mentioned six times in Genesis 36 as the wife of Esau.[153] None of these passages is included in Chronicles. Presumably the chief here and in the parallel passage in Gen 36:41 is a man.

Chief Pinon: This may be a topographic name, possibly to be identified with the mining colony at Khirbet Fênān (MR 197004) in the Wadi ʿAraba, 32 kilometers south of the Dead Sea.[154]

■ **53** *Chief Kenaz, Chief Teman:* Chiefs by these names also appear among the chiefs of the sons of Esau in Gen 36:15, a passage omitted by the Chronicler. They are also both sons of Eliphaz in 1 Chr 1:36//Gen 36:11. Kenaz is the eponymous ancestor of the Kenizzites (Num 32:12; Josh 14:6, 14; 15:7; Judg 1:13; 3:9, 11).

---

143 So Laban and Ben Zvi, "Observations," 463.
144 Cf. Ernst Axel Knauf, "Mezahab," *ABD* 4:804, who mistakenly locates this passage in 1 Kings.
145 *Edom and the Edomites*, 101.
146 "Alter und Herkunft der edomitischen Königsliste Gen. 36, 31-39," *ZAW* 97 (1985) 245-53.
147 See the references to Lemaire and Lipiński in n. 130 above.
148 The equation of Esau and Edom is also made in Gen 36:43 at the end of the list of chiefs where they are called "chiefs of Edom," as in the last words of 1 Chronicles 1.

149 *Genesis 16–50*, 340.
150 Cf. Zech 9:7; 12:5-6.
151 Contra Willi, 45. Cf. also Frank M. Cross Jr. and David Noel Freedman, "The Song of Miriam," *JNES* 14 (1948) 248–49.
152 See the commentary on 1 Chr 1:36, where Timna is considered a son of Eliphaz.
153 Vv. 2, 5, 14, 18 (twice), 25.
154 Ulrich Hübner, "Pinon," *ABD* 5:373. Cf. Punon in Num 33:42-43.

Chief Mibzar: The name means "fortified city" or "fortification" and may be identified with Mabsara/Mabsar in the vicinity of Petra.[155]

■ **54** *Chief Magdiel:* Wenham connects this to the village Majadil, 6 kilometers northeast of Tafileh.[156]

2. 2:1-2. Descendants of Israel

```
Israel ──────┬── Reuben
             ├── Simeon
             ├── Levi
             ├── Judah
             ├── Issachar
             ├── Zebulun
             ├── Dan
             ├── Joseph
             ├── Benjamin
             ├── Naphtali
             ├── Gad
             └── Asher
```

■ **2:1-2** *These are the descendants of Israel:* This list of the descendants of Israel is very similar to Gen 35:22b-26a (cf. Exod 1:2-5), which begins with the sons of Leah (Reuben, Simeon, Levi, Judah, Issachar, and Zebulun), continues with the sons of Rachel (Joseph and Benjamin), and concludes with the sons of the handmaids: Rachel's handmaid Bilhah (Dan and Naphtali) and Leah's handmaid Zilpah (Gad and Asher).[157] Dan is the exception to this order of the tribes, appearing after Zebulun, the last Leah tribe, and before Joseph, the first Rachel tribe; there is no other precedent for this position of Dan before the sons of Rachel. Rudolph, 8–9, and many commentators correct the text, without versional support, and move Dan to a position after Benjamin. Others have noted that Dan is in the seventh position,

always an important location in a genealogy, and suggest that Dan may have been put in this position since he is the first son attributable legally to Rachel, through her handmaid. Rachel states this son of her handmaid will be born "upon my [Rachel's] knees" (Gen 30:3), and she herself gave the boy his name (Gen 30:6).[158] Certainty on this issue is impossible. The use of the conjunction "and" divides the twelve sons into four groups: Reuben, Simeon, Levi, and Judah; Issachar and Zebulun; Dan, Joseph, and Benjamin; Naphtali, Gad, and Asher.

Conclusion

The author of 1 Chronicles 1 drew his information from the present book of Genesis and presumably could assume that readers would know the story told in that book. Oeming notes that chap. 1 serves almost as a funnel leading to Israel's central position within the total human family.[159] The segmented genealogies themselves relate Israel to other peoples, but the order of the genealogical listing is significant. After treating Japheth and Ham, the sons of Noah, the genealogy turns to the descendants of Shem, from whom Abraham and Israel came. Among the descendants of Abraham, the genealogy treats the descendants of Ishmael and Keturah before turning to the descendants of Isaac, and among the descendants of Isaac it gives extensive treatment to Esau before coming at last to the descendants of Israel. This strongly implies Israel's election without actually mentioning it. But it also implies that Israel is to understand itself within the circle of all the nations,[160] at whose center Israel stands. In any case the climax of this opening unit is with Israel and his descendants, not with Abraham. The linear genealogy from Adam to Shem, Ham, and Japheth in vv. 1-4 leads to the segmented

---

155 Ulrich Hübner, "Mibzar," *ABD* 4:806.

156 *Genesis 16–50,* 341.

157 Unlike other such lists, however, the mothers are not named (cf. Gen 29:31–30:24; 35:16-20, 23-26). Cf. also Zecharia Kallai, "The Twelve-Tribe Systems of Israel," *VT* 47 (1997) 53–90, who puts both of these texts in his category 1b. He also ascribes to this category Gen 46:8-25, which Braun, 30, holds to be the model for 1 Chr 2:1-2. See Kallai, "A Note on the Twelve-Tribe Systems of Israel," *VT* 49 (1999) 125-27. See also Weippert, "Geographische System," 76, n. 3, who follows Noth in putting these

verses in the so-called genealogical system in which she also includes 1 Chr 27:16-22.

158 Keil, 57–58. Cf. J. M. Sasson, "A Genealogical 'Convention' in Biblical Chronography?" *ZAW* 90 (1978) 171–85; Willi, 46.

159 *Wahre Israel,* 90.

160 The Chronicler gives special attention to Edom and Seir. As Gary N. Knoppers, "Shem, Ham and Japheth: The Universal and the Particular in the Genealogy of Nations," in Graham, McKenzie, and Knoppers, *Chronicler as Theologian,* 25, 31, points out, the genealogies of Judah and Simeon develop

genealogy of the descendants of Noah in vv. 5-23, and the linear genealogy in vv. 24-27 from Shem to Abraham leads to the segmented genealogy of the descendants of Abraham in 1 Chr 1:28–2:2, climaxing with the descendants of Israel itself in the last two verses. Thus this genealogy covers the time from the first human Adam to the twelve sons of Israel, ancestors of the twelve tribes of Israel. This is a history of all days, a universal history, beginning with Adam and extending to Israel. As noted in the introduction, Jerome (*Prologus galeatus*) called it a "chronicle of the entire divine history." Oeming notes the extent of the Chronicler's world suggested by the nations in this chapter, from southern Russia in the north to Ethiopia in the south, and from Spain in the west to India in the east.[161]

The chapter implies the diversity *and* the unity of the world and it suggests that Israel understood its role within the family of nations and as a witness to all humanity. Edom's kingship began before Israel's and ended also before Israel's kingship, and the end of its kingship does not mean the end of Edom—any more than the end of kingship in Israel would signify its demise. The next eight chapters will spell out what Israel

is, in its tribal structure (chaps. 2–8) and in its present configuration (chap. 9). I believe that the Chronicler here suggests that the small community within the Persian province of Yehud could lay claim to the legacy of all Israel. These coming genealogical chapters may also hint at an eschatological hope and dream that remnants of those tribes will again rally around the temple in Jerusalem.

Just as the inscription on the synagogue floor at Engedi balances the thirteen antediluvian ancestors with two sets of specifically Jewish heroes and relates these pillars of the faith to the order and structure of the world as represented by the zodiac and the calendar, so the first unit in Chronicles may relate Israel to the panoply of the nations of the world. Israel and the world belong together. One may detect here testimony to the greatness of Israel's God, who governs this whole world and guides the funneling process down to Israel—even though there is no mention of God at all in this opening unit.

---

many of the ties hinted in the 1 Chr 1:29-33 (the descendants of Ishmael and Keturah) and 1:35-54 (the descendants of Esau and Seir).

161   *Wahre Israel,* 97.

2

Translation

3/ The descendants of Judah: Er, Onan, and Shelah. Three sons were born[1] to him from Bath-shua,[2] a Canaanite woman, but Er the firstborn of Judah was evil in the eyes of Yahweh[3] and he put him to death.[4]
4/ Tamar, his daughter-in-law, bore for him Perez and Zerah. All the sons of Judah were five. 5/ The sons of Perez: Hezron and Hamul.[5] 6/ The sons of Zerah: Zimri,[6] Ethan, Heman, Calcol, and Darda,[7] five in all. 7/ The sons of Zimri: Carmi; and the sons of Carmi:[8] Achar,[9] the troubler of Israel, who acted unfaithfully with regard to things put under the ban. 8/ The sons[10] of Ethan: Azariah.

9/ The sons of Hezron who were born to him: Jerahmeel, Ram, and Chelubai.[11]

10/ Ram became the father of Amminadab, and Amminadab became the father of Nahshon, the prince of the sons[12] of Judah. 11/ And Nahshon became the father of Salma,[13] and Salma became the father of Boaz. 12/ Boaz became the father of Obed, and Obed became the father of Jesse. 13/ Jesse[14] became the father of Eliab his firstborn, Abinadab[15] the second, Shimea[16] the third, 14/ Nethanel the fourth, Raddai the fifth, 15/ Ozem the sixth, David the seventh.[17] 16/ Their sisters: Zeruiah and Abigail. The sons of Zeruiah: Abshai,[18] Joab, and Asahel, three. 17/ Abigail gave birth to Amasa, and the father of Amasa was Jether the Ishmaelite.[19]

18/ Caleb the son of Hezron became the father of Jerioth,[20] with Azubah his wife.[21] These were her sons: Jesher, Shobab, and Ardon. 19/ Azubah died and Caleb took Ephrath for himself, and she bore to him Hur. 20/ Hur became the father of Uri, and Uri became the father of Bezalel. 21/ Later Hezron had sexual relations[22] with the daughter of Machir the father of Gilead. When he took her, he was sixty years old, and she bore to him Segub. 22/ Segub became the father of Jair, who had twenty-three cities in the land of Gilead. 23/ Geshur and Aram seized from them Havvoth-jair together with Kenath and its villages, sixty cities. All these are the sons[23] of Machir the father of Gilead.[24] 24/ After the death of Hezron, Caleb had sexual relations with[25] Ephrath,[26] (and the wife of Hezron was Abijah,)[27] and she bore to him Ashhur the father of Tekoa.

25/ The descendants of Jerahmeel, the firstborn of Hezron: Ram his firstborn, Bunah,[28] Oren, Ozem, and Ahijah.[29] 26/ Jerahmeel had another wife, and her name was Atarah. She was the mother of Onam. 27/ The sons of Ram, the firstborn of Jerahmeel: Maaz, Jamin,[30] and Eker. 28/ The sons of Onam: Shammai and Jada. And the sons of Shammai: Nadab and Abishur. 29/ And the name of the wife of Abishur was Abihail,[31] and she bore to him Ahban and Molid. 30/ The sons

1 נולד. The verb is *niphal* 3d masc. sg. perfect, although the subject is in the plural. One Hebrew MS puts the verb in the plural, but the singular verb form appears five times in Chronicles (1 Chr 2:3, 9; 3:1, 4; 26:6), each time with a plural subject. Cf. GKC §145. Willi, 84, ascribes a catchword function to this verb form and notes that the root ילד appears 51 times in the 100 verses of this genealogy.

2 מבת־שוע. Cf. Gen 38:2: "Judah saw the daughter of a Canaanite man and his [LXX "her"] name was Shua." Gen 38:12 and the text here are ambiguous and could be translated either "the daughter of Shua" or "Bath-shua," but the appositional phrase suggests the reading I have chosen. Cf. also the wife of David who has the same name in 1 Chr 3:5.

3 This is the first of more than five hundred occurrences of the Tetragrammaton in Chronicles, and it is the divine name used more than all the other names combined. I have chosen to use this spelling rather than LORD, as in most English versions, or YHWH, as in many scholarly works (the latter abbreviation, of course, cannot be pronounced). In Judaism this divine name is not pronounced.

4 *BHS* suggests an insertion on the basis of Gen 38:10 that MT has lost by homoioteleuton: "And also Onan his second son was evil in the eyes of Yahweh, and he put him to death" (cf. Tg: "Er and Onan were doing what was evil before the Lord and he killed them"). This view is now supported by Freedman and Miano, "Is the Shorter Reading Better?" 691.

5 LXX, Syr, and Gen 46:12 SP: וחמואל "Hamuel."

6 זמרי; Josh 7:1 זבדי "Zabdi"; Chronicles LXX[B] Ζαμβρεὶ. There is a similar spelling difference between King Zimri in MT (1 Kgs 16:9) and LXX Ζαμβρι.

7 ודרדע with many Hebrew MSS LXX[cursive MSS], Syr, Tg, Arab., and 1 Kgs 5:11 (4:32); MT: ודרע "and Dara," which has lost a *dālet* after an initial *dālet* and a *rêš*.

8 ובני זמרי כרמי ובני כרמי with *BHS* on the basis of Josh 7:1, 18; Chronicles MT reads only ובני כרמי "And the sons of Carmi." The rest of the original reading was lost by haplography due to homoioarchton. Curtis and Madsen, 85, note that in genealogies the plural "sons of" can be used when only one descendant follows, as with the sons of Zimri here. See 1 Chr 2:8, 30, 31, 42.

9 עכר. A few Hebrew MSS read עכן "Achan," an assimilation to Josh 7:1. Since Joshua LXX reads Αχαρ, the Chronicler may have found his spelling in the *Vorlage* of Joshua. Yair Zakovitch, "A Study of Precise and Partial Derivations in Biblical Etymology," *JSOT* 15 (1980) 36–38, argues that the change was made by the Chronicler and then borrowed by Joshua LXX.

of Nadab: Seled and Appaim,[32] and Seled died childless. 31/ The son[33] of Appaim: Ishi. The son of Ishi: Sheshan. The son of Sheshan: Ahli. 32/ The sons of Jada, the brother of Shammai: Jether and Jonathan, and Jether died childless. 33/ The sons of Jonathan: Peleth and Zaza. These were the sons of Jerahmeel.

34/ Sheshan had no sons, only daughters; but Sheshan had an Egyptian slave whose name was Jarha. 35/ So Sheshan gave his daughter to Jarha his slave as a wife, and she bore to him Attai. 36/ And Attai became the father of Nathan, and Nathan became the father of Zabad. 37/ Zabad became the father of Ephlal, and Ephlal became the father of Obed.[34] 38/ Obed became the father of Jehu, and Jehu became the father of Azariah.
39/ Azariah became the father of Helez, and Helez became the father of Eleasah.
40/ Eleasah became the father of Sismai, and Sismai became the father of Shallum.
41/ Shallum became the father of Jekamiah, and Jekamiah became the father of Elishama.

42/ The sons[35] of Caleb the brother of Jerahmeel: Mesha[36] his firstborn. He was the father of Ziph.[37] The sons of Mesha: Mareshah[38] the father of Hebron. 43/ The sons of Hebron: Korah, Tappuah, Rekem, and Shema. 44/ Shema became the father of Raham, the father of Jorkeam,[39] and Rekem became the father of Shammai. 45/ The son of Shammai: Maon; and Maon was the father of Beth-zur. 46/ Ephah the concubine of Caleb bore Haran, Moza, and Gazez,[40] and Haran became the father of Jahdai.[41]
47/ The sons of Jahdai:[42] Regem, Jotham, Geshan, Pelet, Ephah, and Shaaph.
48/[43] Maacah, Caleb's concubine, bore[44] Sheber and Tirhanah. 49/ She also bore[45] Shaaph the father of Madmannah, Sheva the father of Machbenah, and X[46] the father of Gibea; and the daughter of Caleb was Achsah. 50/ These were the sons of Caleb.[47]

The sons[48] of Hur the firstborn of Ephrathah: Shobal the father of Kiriath-jearim. 51/ Salma the father of Bethlehem, and Hareph the father of Beth-gader.
52/ Shobal father of Kiriath-jearim had sons: Reaiah,[49] half of the Manahathites.[50] 53/ The families of Kiriath-jearim: the Ithrites, the Puthites, the Shumathites, and the Mishraites; from these came the Zorathites[51] and the Eshtaolites. 54/ The sons of Salma:[52] Bethlehem and[53] the Netophathites, Atroth-beth-joab, and half of the Manahathites, the Zorites. 55/ The families of the Siphrites[54] settled[55] at Jabez: the Tirathites, the Shimeathites, and the Sucathites. These are the Kinites,[56] who came from Hammath, father of Beth-rechab.

10 *Sebir* changes to the singular. Myers, 1:9, raises the possibility that a name in addition to Azariah has dropped out. But see what was said about "sons of" in n. 8.

11 וְאַת כְּלוּבִי. LXX: "Caleb [LXX^B Χαβελ, LXX^A Χαλεβ] and Aram." For the spelling Chelubai, see the commentary (cf. vv. 18, 42). "Aram" (אֲרָם) results from a miswritten dittograph of the first word in the following verse (וְרָם).

12 בְּנֵי. LXX presupposes בֵּית "house."

13 שַׂלְמָא on both occurrences in this verse; LXX and Ruth 4:21: שַׂלְמוֹן "Salmon"; Ruth 4:20: שַׂלְמָה "Salmah."

14 וְאִישַׁי. Normally Jesse is spelled יִשַׁי, and this seems to be the spelling in LXX, as well as in MT of the previous verse.

15 וַאֲבִינָדָב; LXX וַאֲמִינָדָב "Amminadab," under the influence of v. 10.

16 וּשְׁמָעָא; cf. 2 Sam 21:21 Q. Following 1 Sam 16:9 and 17:13, Syr reads וְשַׁמָּה "Shammah." 2 Sam 21:21 K: שִׁמְעִי "Shimei."

17 דָוִיד חַשִּׁבְעִי. Syr, Arab.: "Elihu the seventh and David the eighth." This variant reading is a harmonization with 1 Sam 16:10-11 and 17:12, according to which Jesse had eight sons. For Elihu see the commentary to 1 Chr 27:18.

18 אַבְשָׁי; Syr, Tg, Vg, Arab. read אֲבִישַׁי "Abishai." Cf. LXX. The vocalization of MT is used throughout Chronicles and in 2 Sam 10:10; the rest of the occurrences in 1 and 2 Samuel read "Abishai."

19 יֶתֶר הַיִּשְׁמְעֵאלִי. Cf. 2 Sam 17:25 LXX^A. One Chronicles Hebrew MS, LXX^L, Tg, and 2 Sam 17:25 MT: יִתְרָא הַיִּשְׂרְאֵלִי "Ithra the Israelite" (apologetic harmonization). הַיִּשְׁמְעֵאלִי is lacking in one Chronicles Hebrew MS and Syr. Tg expands this verse and reads in part: "Jether, the Israelite; they called him Jether, the Ishmaelite," and so conflates the two readings.

20 Wellhausen, *De gentibus et familiis Judaeis quae 1. Chr.2.4. enumerantur* (Ph.D. diss.; Göttingen: Officina Academica Dieterishiana, 1870) 33, changed וְאֵת יְרִיעוֹת to בַּת יְרִיעוֹת "[Caleb the son of Hezron became the father of sons, with Azubah his wife] the daughter of Jerioth." See the next note and the commentary.

21 אֶת עֲזוּבָה אִשְׁתוֹ אֵת, following the conjecture in *BHS*; cf. Syr, Tg, Arab. Japhet, 67, reads מֵעֲזוּבָה אֵת instead of MT אֶת עֲזוּבָה אִשָּׁה וְאֵת, which results in a similar translation. MT can be translated: "[Caleb the son of Hezron became the father of Azubah,] a woman, and [Jerioth]" or "[Caleb the son of Hezron became a father through Azubah] a wife and through [Jerioth]." See the commentary.

22 בא חזרון אל. But the literal sense of "go to" could also indicate that the party represented by the male part, here Hezron (the Hezronites?), moved to the territory of the female partner, here Machir-Gilead. Cf. v. 24.

23 בני; LXX לבני "belong to the sons of."

24 The whole verse is lacking in Syr by homoioteleuton.

25 בא כלב with LXX, Vg (cf. BHS). Lit. "Caleb went in to." MT בכלב "in Caleb-[Ephrathah]." No such town is known.

26 The final hê on Ephrath is the hê directive. Contrast 1 Chr 4:4.

27 ואשת חזרון אביה. BHS proposes אשת חזרון אביהו "[Ephrathah] the wife of Hezron his father." Cf. Wellhausen, Gentibus et familiis, 13–14. But there is no versional support for this and it makes Caleb marry his father's wife (though presumably not his mother). Williamson, 53–54, has proposed that the words "and the wife of Hezron was Abijah" are a misplaced gloss on v. 21, where no name is given for the daughter of Machir, the sexual partner of Hezron.

28 ובונה; a few Hebrew MSS: ובנה. Cf. LXX, Syr: και Βααννα.

29 ואחיה, with Tg, Vg; MT lacks the conjunction. LXX αχιοου "his brother." Syr "their sister." Rudolph, 16, מאחיה (haplography of mêm) "from Ahijah" (= spouse of Jerahmeel).

30 רימין; Syr ויבין "Jabin."

31 אביהיל; many Hebrew MSS, Syr, Tg, Arab.: אביחיל (cf. LXX). Rudolph, 16; and Allen, Greek Chronicles, 2:115, retain MT. Cf. Noth, Personennamen, 39–40.

32 אפים; LXXᴮ "Ephraim" (אפרים), also in the next verse.

33 ובן with Sebir and Vg; MT ובני "sons." See n. 8.

34 עובד; Syr יובב "Jobab," also for the first word in the next verse.

35 ובני. Myers, 1:11, emends to ובן "son." See n. 8.

36 מישע; LXX מרשה "Mareshah," which also lacks "Mesha" in the second half of the verse (as does MT). RSV followed LXX on both names and also deleted "the father of" before Hebron. Hence: "Mareshah his firstborn, who was the father of Ziph. The sons of Mareshah: Hebron."

37 BHS adds: "And his second son was Mareshah the father of Hebron." The editor claims the reading was lost by homoioteleuton (BHS) or, more correctly, homoioarchton (Rudolph, 18). The rest of the verse then reads: "and the sons of Mareshah the father of Hebron." Rudolph, 18, deletes "the sons of Hebron" at the beginning of v. 43 as a dittography (actually only Hebron is repeated). Other solutions are recorded by Japhet, 86. Her choice, which is also mine, is reported in the next note.

38 ובני מישע מרשה "Mesha" is a conjectural addition. MT ובני מרשה "The sons of Mareshah," but Mareshah has not yet been introduced.

39 ירקעם; BHS notes a proposed change to יקדעם "Jokdeam" (cf. Josh 15:56), but Rudolph, 18, recommends against this change.

40 גזו; a few Hebrew MSS: גזן "Gazen."

41 יהדי; cf. BHS; Rudolph, 18. MT גזז "Gazez." MT makes Gazez both the son and the grandson of Caleb and leaves Jahdai in v. 47 unconnected to the genealogy of Judah. A Ram, of course, is both the son of Hezron and the grandson of Hezron (through his father Jerahmeel) in vv. 25 and 27. See the commentary.

42 יְהְדַי; a few Hebrew MSS: יַהְדִי "Jahdi."

43 Syr omits vv. 48-49.

44 ילדה את (3d fem. sg.); MT ילד (3d masc. sg.).

45 ותלד; BHS (cf. Curtis and Madsen, 99) suggests ויולד "and [Shaaph the father of Madmannah] became the father of [Sheva]" but this requires a further change, moving v. 49a to the end of v. 47. I have taken the subject of the sentence to be Maacah from v. 18, which suggests that את should be inserted before Shaaph. Japhet, 87, also considers this and an alternative reconstruction, in which Shaaph is interpreted as another of Caleb's concubines, with the name of her son, who was the father of Madmannah, and her designation as concubine being lost: "Shaaph bore [x] the father of Madmannah." Tg is similar. See the commentary.

46 The absence of the conjunction before Sheva suggests the loss of Gibea's father's name. If one follows Rudoph and Curtis and Madsen in the previous note, Sheva is the father of both Machbenah and Gibea. See the commentary.

47 "These were the sons of Caleb" is the conclusion to the previous paragraph and not the beginning of a new section as the verse division might suggest. Cf. v. 33b: "These were the sons of Jerahmeel."

48 בני with LXX, Vg; MT בן "son."

49 BHS proposes ראיה; cf. 1 Chr 4:2. MT הראה "the seer." Demsky, "Clans of Ephrath," 46–59, understands the reading in MT as an alternate form of the gentilic. Cf. הימנה "the Imnite" in Num 26:44 and GKC §125d, n. 1.

50 BHS proposes המנחתי; cf. v. 54. MT המנחות "the Menuhoth" (confusion of wāw/yôd and metathesis of last two letters). The article may also be an alternate form of the gentilic, as in the previous note.

51 הצרעתי here and in 1 Chr 4:2; v. 54: הצרעי "Zorites."

52 שלמא; BHS adds אבי "father of" before "Bethlehem" and suggests this word was lost by haplography. Cf. v. 51, where Salma is called the father of Bethlehem, and vv. 50, 52, where Shobal is called the father of Kiriath-jearim. See the commentary.

84

53 *BHS* suggests deleting "and" as a result of the emendation in the previous note. Rudolph, 22, in addition raised the alternate possibility of a lacuna after Bethlehem.

54 סְפָרִים with *BHS*. Willi, 69, construes it as a reference to people who came from Kiriath-sepher; MT סֹפְרִים "scribes."

55 יֹשְׁבוּ K; Q יֹשְׁבֵי (*qal* participle) "who settled."

56 הַקִּינִים. The spelling with an internal *ḥîreq* is anomalous since everywhere else in the OT the internal vowel is a *ṣērê*, but this is the only place where the plural form of the word occurs. Consonantally, of course, there is no difference between this word and other occurrences of the word "Kenite."

2:3-55

Structure

The genealogy of the tribe of Judah extends from 1 Chr 2:3 through 4:23 and may be outlined as follows (see the genealogical chart "Descendants of Judah").[1]

I. 2:3-8. Genealogy from the patriarch Judah himself, including the three children born to him by Bath-shua (Er, Onan, and Shelah) and the two children born to him by Tamar (Perez and Zerah). Verse 5 records two sons born to Perez, and vv. 6-8 record five sons of Zerah, two grandsons, and a great-grandson. For the descendants of Shelah see section III.

II. 2:9–4:20. Descendants of Hezron

  A. 2:9. Three sons of Hezron: Jerahmeel, Ram, and Chelubai.

  B. 2:10-17. Descendants of Ram. This section begins with a linear genealogy of Ram leading to Jesse in the tenth generation after Judah (vv. 10-12). Next comes a segmented genealogy, consisting of the seven sons of Jesse (vv. 13-15) and his two daughters, Zeruiah and Abigail, the first of whom has three sons and the second of whom has one son (vv. 16-17).

  C. 2:18-24. Various genealogical notices

    1. 2:18. Jerioth, the daughter of Caleb and Azubah, and her three sons

    2. 2:19-20. Hur, the son of Caleb and Ephrath, and Hur's son and grandson

    3. 2:21-23. Segub the son and Jair the grandson, who are descended from Hezron and the daughter of Machir. Jair had twenty-three cities in Gilead, but Geshur and Aram seized a total of sixty cities from them

    4. 2:24. After the death of Hezron, Caleb and Ephrathah had a child Ashhur, who was the father of Tekoa (cf. 4:5-8)

  D. 2:25-33. Segmented genealogy of the descendants of Jerahmeel, the firstborn of Hezron

  E. 2:34-41. A linear genealogy extending from Sheshan, who is in the seventh generation of a genealogy beginning with Jerahmeel (vv. 25-33), and extending for another fourteen additional generations, ending with Elishama

  F. 2:42-50aα. A segmented genealogy of the descendants of Caleb and an unidentified woman, and of Caleb and two concubines, Ephah and Maacah. Altogether Caleb had eight sons and one daughter, and the descendants of three of his sons are followed through several generations.

  G. 2:50aβ-55. A segmented genealogy of Hur the firstborn of Caleb and Ephrathah (cf. v. 19), and of two of his sons, Shobal (cf. 4:2) and Salma. The descendants of their third son, Hareph (v. 51) are given in 4:3-4.

  H. 3:1-24. Genealogy of the descendants of David that can be divided into segmented (vv. 1-9, 15-24) and linear (vv. 10-14) sections

    1. 3:1-4. Children of David who were born in Hebron

    2. 3:5-9. Children of David who were born in Jerusalem

---

1 While it will be necessary to refer to chaps. 3 and 4 briefly in these opening remarks, the principal discussion of them will be deferred to subsequent chapters in this commentary. For a review of past interpretations of this chapter, see Gary N. Knoppers, "'Great among His Brothers,' but Who Is He?" *JHS* 3 (2001) 1–27. One of the oldest of these is G. Richter, "Untersuchungen zu den Geschlechtsregistern der Chronik," *ZAW* 34 (1914) 107–41, with concentration on Judah on pp. 107–24.

3. 3:10-16. Descendants of Solomon who served as kings of Judah

4. 3:17-24. Descendants of Jeconiah for seven generations

I. 4:1-20. Genealogical fragments

1. 4:1. Linear genealogy that reviews the basic outline of the genealogy in chap. 2

2. 4:2-4. Segmented genealogy of the sons of Hur, the son of Caleb and Ephrathah, consisting of the descendants of Reaiah the son of Shobal and of Hareph the brother of Shobal and Salma (cf. section II.G)

3. 4:5-8. Segmented genealogy from Ashhur, the son of Caleb and Ephrathah, that traces his descendants through his two wives, Helah and Naarah (cf. 2:24 in section II.C.4)

4. 4:9-10. Etiological account of Jabez, a name that was used for a city in 2:55

5. 4:11-12. Genealogy from Chelub, who is probably to be identified with Caleb

6. 4:13-15. Segmented genealogy of the sons of Kenaz that traces the lines of Othniel, Seraiah, and Caleb the son of Jephunneh

7. 4:16-20. Genealogies from Jehallelel, Ezrah, and Shimon

III. 4:21-23. Genealogy from Shelah the son of Judah (cf. section I and 2:3)

The Chronicler begins his genealogy of the tribes of Israel with Judah (2:3–4:23) and ends it with Benjamin (8:1-40; cf. 7:6-12; 9:35-44), the two principal tribes that made up the province of Yehud.[2] These two genealogies now form a bracket around the other tribal genealogies. In the middle of the genealogies of the Israelite tribes, the Chronicler places the genealogy from Levi, 5:27–6:66 (6:1-81), to whose descendants he will give major attention in his work. Judah's position at the head of the tribal genealogies may be explained by 5:2: "Judah became preeminent among his brothers [cf. Gen 49:8] and a ruler came from him." The word ruler (נגיד) refers

to David and his descendants, who are at the center of the genealogy from Judah (1 Chr 3:1-24).[3] The genealogy from Judah is the longest of the genealogies, with one hundred verses; that from Levi is next with eighty-one verses; and that from Benjamin is the third longest with fifty-seven verses. In 28:4 Yahweh's choice of David is related to his choice of Judah to be leader (נגיד). Judah's importance is also recognized in the Priestly writings in the Pentateuch. The tribe of Judah is located on the east side of the tent of meeting, and it is the first tribe to set out on any march (Num 2:1-9). Nahshon of the tribe of Judah presented his dedication offering on the first day (Num 7:12; cf. vv. 13-83). The genealogy from Judah is therefore in the first position despite the fact that in 1 Chronicles 1 the favored branch of the family is listed after the nonfavored branch.

The rationale behind the ordering of the tribes after Judah is not completely clear. Japhet detects a counterclockwise movement, beginning with Simeon (4:24-43) to Judah's south and continuing with the Transjordanian tribes from south to north: Reuben (5:1-10), Gad (5:11-17, [18-22 deals with the two and one half tribes as a group]), and the half-tribe of Manasseh (5:23-26). Next comes the long section on Levi (5:27–6:66 [6:1-81]), followed by the northern tribes on the west side of the Jordan: Issachar (7:1-5), [Zebulun, Dan (7:12?)],[4] Naphtali (7:13), and then the tribes in Israel's midsection: Manasseh (7:14-19), Ephraim (7:20-29), and Benjamin (8:1-40).[5] Strictly speaking, Naphtali should come before Issachar, and the locations of the second genealogy from Benjamin (7:6-11) and Asher (7:30-40) are unexplained in this scenario. This may be related to the fact that materials for Issachar, Benjamin (7:6-11), and Asher are taken from a military census list, but that still leaves several loose ends. The clearest thing about the ordering of the tribes is that Judah and Benjamin are at the beginning and end and Levi is in the middle.

The genealogy from Judah itself is by no means easy to unravel, as the outline above demonstrates. As the

---

2   The Chronicler notes that Benjamin stayed with Judah after the division of the monarchy (2 Chr 11:1, 3, 10, 12, 23; 14:8; 15:2, 8-9; 17:17; 25:5; 31:1; 34:9, 32).

3   Reuben's displacement from the first position is attributed to his sexual crime with Bilhah the concubine of his father (1 Chr 5:2; cf. Gen 36:22 and

Gen 49:4). In 1 Chr 5:2 Judah's preeminence is affirmed despite the fact that the birthright belonged to Joseph (see the commentary on 5:2).

4   Zebulun and possibly Dan are not attested in the present state of the text. For discussion see the commentary on chap. 7.

5   Japhet, *Ideology*, 352–55. Cf. Williamson, 46–47.

textual notes make evident, a number of verses also require significant, sometimes conjectural, emendation. These uncertain details, however, do not affect the overall understanding a great deal. More significantly, a genealogical notice about Hezron the father of Caleb (2:21-23) interrupts the genealogy from Caleb (2:18-20), and the genealogies from Jerahmeel (2:25-33 and 2:34-41) also interrupt the second part of the genealogy from Caleb (that begins with 2:24). After the genealogy from Caleb resumes (2:42-50aα and 50aβ-55), it is interrupted by the genealogy from David (3:1-24, linking back to Ram in 2:10-17, where it had been interrupted) and then the genealogy from Caleb is continued in 4:1-8. The genealogies in 4:9-20 are chaotic and fragmentary. It is often impossible to connect these short genealogies directly with Judah or with one another. Occasionally textual criticism can solve some of the riddles (see the textual notes), but text-critical methods alone can by no means resolve all of the problems.

H. G. M. Williamson detected a chiastic arrangement in the genealogy from Judah that provides partial explanation for the structure of chaps. 2–4.[6] With slight revisions, it may be diagrammed as follows:

I. Judah's sons via Bath-shua (beginning with "The descendants of Judah" in v. 3): Er, Onan, and Shelah (2:3)

II. Genealogy of Judah's sons via Tamar: Perez and Zerah (2:4-8)

III. Genealogy of Judah's descendants through the sons of Hezron son of Perez: Jerahmeel, Ram, and Chelubai/Caleb (2:9-4:7)

  A. Genealogy from Ram (2:10-17)

  B. Genealogy from Caleb (2:18-24)[7]

    C. Genealogy from Jerahmeel (2:25-33)

    C'. More genealogy from Jerahmeel (2:34-41)

  B'. More genealogy from Caleb (2:42-55)

  A'. More genealogy from Ram (in the descendants of David; 3:1-24)

II'. More descendants of Perez through the line of Caleb (beginning with "The descendants of Judah," 4:1-20; cf. 2:3)

 I'. Genealogy from Shelah, the only surviving son of Judah and Bath-shua (4:21-23)

Section II' (4:1-20) is perhaps the weakest part of this chiasm since in 4:2-8 it consists of materials separated from their original source in 2:50b-52 by the intrusion of 2:53-55 and the descendants of David in 3:1-24, and it also consists of heterogeneous materials in 4:9-20 that can only loosely be connected to the genealogy from Judah.

In his commentary on Chronicles, Thomas Willi, 100, calls attention to the many geographical notices in these genealogies that are almost always related to a formula in which a given person is identified as the "father" of a town, city, or region,[8] and he detects in these references a key to the structuring of chaps. 2–4. Willi notes that the geographical notices in the first genealogy from Caleb (2:42-50aα) refer to territory south of Hebron, where the families of Caleb resided before the exile. In the second section of the genealogy from Caleb (2:50aβ-55), the Calebites have moved north, with an epicenter at Bethlehem, perhaps reflecting pressure by the Edomites in the south, who were under pressure in turn from the Nabateans. The details will be discussed in the commentary below, but note as a case in point that the Siphrites, located at Kiriath-sepher, identified with Khirbet er-Rabud some 18 kilometers southwest of Hebron, have moved to Jabez, which must be in the vicinity of Jerusalem (2:55). Willi, 109, also proposes that the importance of chap. 3 is not limited to its information about David and the royal line, but David him-

---

6   "Sources," 351–59.

7   Verses 21-23 are an intrusive fragment dealing with descendants of Hezron himself.

8   2:21, 23, Machir the father of Gilead; 2:24 and 4:5, Ashhur the father of Tekoa; 2:42, Mesha the father of Ziph and Maresha the father of Hebron; 2:44, Raham the father of Jorkeam; 2:45, Maon the father of Beth-zur; 2:49, Shaaph the father of Madmannah, Sheva the father of Machbenah, and X the father of Gibea; 2:50, 52, Shobal the father of Kiriath-jearim; 2:51, Salma the father of Bethlehem and Hareph the father of Beth-gader; 2:55, Hammath the father of Beth-rechab; 4:3, Hareph the father of Beth-gader and X the father of Etam; 4:4, Penuel the father of Gedor, Ezer the father of Hushah, and Hur the father of Bethlehem; 4:11, Mehir the father of Eshton; 4:12, Tehinnah the father of Ir-nahash; 4:14, Joab the father of Ge-harashim; 4:17, Ishbah the father of Eshtemoa; 4:18, Jered the father of Gedor, Heber the father of Soco, and Jekuthiel the father of Zanoah; 4:19, Naham the father of Keilah; 4:21, Er the father of Lecah and Laadah the father of Mareshah. Cf. also the history of research on this term in Oeming, *Wahre Israel*, 127–29.

self had children both in Hebron (3:1-4) and later in Jerusalem (3:5-9) and that his descendants still lived, or lived again, in Jerusalem (3:10-24) in spite of the exile, which is recorded in vv. 16-18. Postexilic Davidic figures appear in v. 19 and presumably in the following verses. Chapter 4 then completes the genealogy from Judah and identifies sixteen cities that are traced back to a specific father or founder.

Where did the Chronicler get the information contained in chap. 2?[9] All of the genealogical information in section I, vv. 3-8, is derived from other biblical texts (Genesis 38; 46:12; Num 26:19-22; Josh 7:1; 1 Kgs 5:11 [4:31]), with the exception of Azariah the son of Etham in v. 8.[10] The genealogy from Ram to Jesse in vv. 10-12 is related to and probably taken from the genealogy appended to the book of Ruth (4:18-22).[11] The data about David and his three oldest brothers in v. 13 are known from the Deuteronomistic History (1 Sam 16:6-9; 17:13; cf. 2 Sam 21:21//1 Chr 20:7), and the data about Zeruiah and Abigail (vv. 16-17) are traceable to biblical data and inferences drawn from them (2 Sam 17:25; 19:14; details in the commentary). Note, however, that the Chronicler attributes only seven sons to Jesse instead of eight, and it is here alone in the Bible that Zeruiah and Abigail are identified as sisters of David. We do not know how the Chronicler learned the names of David's other three brothers. Verse 20 is based on Exod 31:2, 35:30, and

38:22. After v. 20 we no longer have biblical parallels to the genealogy from Judah until we come to Achsah the daughter of Caleb in v. 49 (cf. Josh 15:16-17; Judg 1:12-13) and to the descendants of David in 1 Chr 3:1-19.

For the rest of 1 Chr 2:3–4:23, I conclude that the Chronicler had access to other genealogical materials, of an oral or written sort, or that the Chronicler composed certain verses himself. The arrangement of the whole genealogy from Judah in any case, whether following the structures detected by Williamson or Willi or even following other guidelines, are attributable to the Chronicler. The specific verses attributable to the Chronicler's own editorial activity with some probability are:

■ **2:9** Before the time of the Chronicler, Jerahmeel and Caleb were not considered to be brothers nor is there evidence that they had been included within the genealogy from Judah (see commentary on v. 9 as well). Jerahmeel and Caleb are identified as brothers and sons of Hezron in 2:25-33 and 2:42-50aα respectively, and this could have been found in a source (so Williamson), or added by the Chronicler, as I prefer.[12] The Chronicler could have known about Ram's descent from Hezron by consulting Ruth 4:19.

■ **2:18-24** While much of the information in these verses may predate the Chronicler, he is the one who placed this material at this point in the chapter, and the Chronicler is probably the one who joined these diverse materi-

---

9 Williamson, "Sources," 352–56, identified four types of sources: (a) biblical materials; (b) 2:25-33 and 42-50a, segmented genealogies of Jerahmeel and Caleb; (c) 2:18-19, 24, 50b-52; 4:2-7; and (d) an assortment of miscellaneous fragments: 2:21-23, 34-41; 4:8-23. Williamson believes that the establishment of Jerahmeel and Caleb as brothers and as sons of Hezron was found by the Chronicler in the second source. That may be building too much on the parallel opening and closing formulas to 2:25-33 and 2:42-50a since these could have been added by the Chronicler. I believe that the Chronicler himself was responsible for making this genealogical link via v. 9. Williamson, 357, himself argues strenuously and convincingly for assigning v. 9 to the Chronicler. Japhet, 69, finds one major source behind 2:25-33; 2:42-50a; and 2:50b-55 plus 4:2-4. Each of the sections begins and ends with similar formulas. She believes that the rest of the material without biblical parallels is partly taken from sources and is partly editorial. The Chronicler is taken as the author of

the whole composition.

10 For Achar see the commentary. Willi, "Late Persian Judaism," 152, notes that the starting point for the genealogy of Judah is in Genesis 38, not in Numbers 26 or Genesis 46 as in most of the other tribal genealogies.

11 See the discussion in Kartveit, *Motive und Schichten*, 60. Others think that Chronicles was the source of the genealogy in Ruth: Rudolph, 16; C. McCarthy, "The Davidic Genealogy in the Book of Ruth," *Proceedings of the Irish Biblical Association* 9 (1985) 53–62; and Noth, *Chronicler's History*, 151, n. 27, who points out that Chronicles includes the names of David's brothers.

12 So also Willi, 78; idem, "Late Persian Judaism," 158–60. Willi attributes vv. 25aα and 50aα to the same hand that formulated 2:9.

als into a unit. In any case v. 20, which identifies Hur the son of Caleb with Hur the grandfather of Bezalel, one of the builders of the tabernacle, is surely the contribution of the Chronicler. Verses 21-23, which list descendants of Hezron the father of Caleb in the midst of the genealogy from Caleb and report an unusual link between Judah and Gilead, no doubt stem from older tradition even if it is impossible to date this information to a specific century. The Chronicler probably included these three verses to show the absence of the Hezronites from the Bethlehem or northern Judean area, which made possible the settlement of the Calebite sons of Hur in that region (vv. 50aβ-55).[13] The Chronicler no doubt found in his sources the notice about Hezron's death in v. 24 and the dating of Caleb and Ephrath's children before and after that event in vv. 18-19 on the one hand and v. 24 on the other. Following Williamson,[14] I consider the parenthetical comment identifying the wife of Hezron as Abijah (v. 24) to be a later, misplaced gloss, intended to be inserted after Hezron in v. 21. Otherwise there is no reason to doubt that the information in these three verses goes back to Calebite oral or written sources.

The remaining information that came from sources is:

■ **2:25-33,** the segmented genealogy from Jerahmeel. Note the similar opening and closing formulas that mark off this unit from the surrounding context. Compare the similarly formulated paragraph dealing with Caleb below (2:42-50aα).

■ **2:34-41,** the linear genealogy from Sheshan to Elishama, covering fifteen generations. Since Elishama plays no other role in Chronicles, there is no reason to think the Chronicler would have invented this genealogy. Note also the mixed ancestry of Elishama (Sheshan's daughter married Jarha an Egyptian slave), which the Chronicler included without any criticism but is unlikely to have composed from scratch. There is also a conflict between 2:31, where Sheshan is the father of a son named Ahlai, and 2:34 where Sheshan is said to have

had no sons. Such a conflict suggests an independent origin for this and the previous unit.

■ **2:42-50aα,** an older genealogy of the Calebites, when they still lived in an area surrounding Hebron (see the commentary for details). Note again the similar opening and concluding formulas, as in 2:25-33. These two genealogies are likely from the same source, although it is not possible to determine with any certainty whether the identification of Jerahmeel and Caleb as brothers and sons of Hezron, which is not known elsewhere in the Bible, was found in the source or added by the Chronicler.

■ **2:50aβ-55,** a genealogy from Hur the firstborn of Caleb and Ephrathah. I believe this refers to the status of these Calebites in postexilic times, at the time of the Chronicler (so Willi, 99), when they lived in an area farther to the north, with its center at Bethlehem (see the commentary for details). It is hard to determine whether the Calebites themselves formulated the material in this way or whether it was first recorded by the Chronicler, but I incline to the former position because of the obscurity of the data and the absence of any vocabulary specifically attributable to the Chronicler.

■ For the materials in chaps. 3–4 see the discussion under Structure for both chapters.

There is no compelling reason to deny any of this material to the first edition of the Chronicler's work, as was done by many scholars in the nineteenth and twentieth centuries. Julius Wellhausen wrote his doctoral dissertation on chaps. 2 and 4 and attributed only 2:9 (without the word "Ram") and two genealogies reflecting preexilic times (2:25-33, the genealogy from Jerahmeel, and 2:42-50, the older materials on Caleb) to the Chronicler. All the rest, including all of the genealogical materials dealing with Judah in chaps. 3–4, he considered secondary, although he did not deny that older information might be contained in these segments.[15]

In a work first published in 1943, Martin Noth attributed only 1 Chr 2:3-5 and 9-15 to the Chronicler and considered all the rest of 2:16—4:23 to come from sec-

---

13   So Willi, 93–94.
14   "Sources," 354–55.
15   Cf. Oeming, *Wahre Israel,* 108, where a summary of the complicated literary criticism of Rothstein is also provided. Wellhausen's position is summarized in *Prolegomena,* 216–18. Cf. Willi, 73–74.

ondary hands.[16] In an earlier article,[17] Noth focused primarily on the "X father of Y" passages (see note 8 above) and concluded that this unique usage[18] established parts of chaps. 2 (vv. 24, 42-50aα, 50bβ-52, 54-55) and 4 as an older document that could be dated not long after the death of Solomon.[19] He noted that the cities listed did not correspond to the postexilic boundaries of Yehud. The need for such an early date disappears if vv. 50bβ-55 are separated from Noth's hypothetical "X father of Y" document and dated to the time of the Chronicler (see above).

Wilhelm Rudolph, 10–13, attributed only 2:3-9, 25-33, 10-17, and 42-50aα to the Chronicler and in that order,[20] which was expanded in several stages by 2:18-19, 21-23, 24, 34-41, 50aβ-55,[21] with 3:1—4:23 forming an even later expansion, and finally by the movement of 2:18-19 (expanded by v. 20) and 2:24[22] to their present locations. The expansions, in Rudolph's view, are not free inventions but rest on sources. I have already stated my alternate interpretation of vv. 18-24. Rudolph dismissed the genealogy in vv. 34-41 since it is a second genealogy from Jerahmeel. Note, however, that it is linear and not segmented. While these genealogies have two different tradition histories, there is no reason to exclude the second genealogy from Jerahmeel from the Chronicler's original version. The genealogy from Caleb (2:50aβ-55) is rejected by Rudolph on similar grounds and because it represents postexilic conditions, rather than the pre-exilic tradition in the earlier genealogy from Caleb. Willi's proposed northern migration of the Calebites

and their settlement in the vicinity of Bethlehem sufficiently explains why the second genealogy is preserved in the text.

Finally, Magnar Kartveit[23] has subjected these chapters to a vigorous literary-critical analysis, but the result is his ascribing only 2:3-8, 9b* (mentioning only Ram,[24] without Jerahmeel and Caleb), 10-17, 21-24, and 4:5-7 to the Chronicler and the identification of seven glosses, and six post-Chronistic redactions. He does not detect any ancient sources, but only the recording of postexilic relationships between cities inside and outside the province of Judah and the attempt to establish rights to the land. Willi, 77, suggests that Kartveit has used on Chronicles a method that would be more appropriate for an older text that had developed over a long period of time, but Willi argues convincingly that the Chronicler put these chapters together at one time as an author.

Detailed Commentary

2:3-8. Genealogy from the Patriarch Judah Himself

■ **3** *The descendants of Judah: Er, Onan, and Shelah:* The Chronicler could have found this information in the narrative about Judah that begins in Gen 38:1-5 or in the genealogy from Judah at Gen 46:12 (cf. Num 26:19-21). Three sons in the genealogy from Judah are also listed for Hezron (2:9), Ram (2:27), Neariah (3:23), Helah (4:7), Eshton (4:12), Caleb son of Jephunneh (4:15, as reconstructed), Jether (4:17), and Jether by his Judahite wife (4:18; the text is very uncertain).

---

16 *Überlieferungsgeschichtliche Studien* (2d ed.; Tübingen: Niemeyer, 1957), 119-120. See Noth, *Chronicler's History*, 38–39. Similarly, Kratz, *Komposition*, 26, 52, ascribes only 1 Chr 2:1-2, 3a, 4-5, 9-15 to the original work of the Chronicler. In fact, these are the only verses he retains from the first ten chapters.

17 Martin Noth, "Eine siedlungsgeographische Liste in 1. Chr 2 und 4," *ZDPV* 55 (1932) 97–124. Noth also concluded that Hur came from a marriage of Hezron with Ephrath, which depended in part on his acceptance of three emendations made by Wellhausen to 1 Chr 2:24. This is contradicted, of course, by v. 19.

18 Actually there are other references in the Bible, such as 1 Chr 7:31 and Gen 4:19-22.

19 Noth, "Liste," 119. It consisted of (a) the descen-

dants of Shelah, 4:21-23; (b) the descendants of Hezron and Ephrathah, 2:50aβ-52; 4:2; 2:54-55; 4:3-4, 16-19; 4:4b; (c) the descendants of Caleb and Ephrathah, 2:24; 4:5-12; and (d) other descendants of Caleb 2:42-50aα.

20 Rudolph thought the order was determined by the order of the names in 2:9.

21 Rudolph saw vv. 21-23 as a supplement to v. 9, vv. 34-41 as a supplement to vv. 25-33, and vv. 18-19 plus vv. 50aβ-55 as a supplement to vv. 42-50aα.

22 This verse had been added in connection with 4:5-8.

23 *Motive und Schichten*, 36–61, 120–25.

24 In ibid., 57, Kartveit writes that only Hur is certain for this stage in v. 9. He clearly intended to write "Ram."

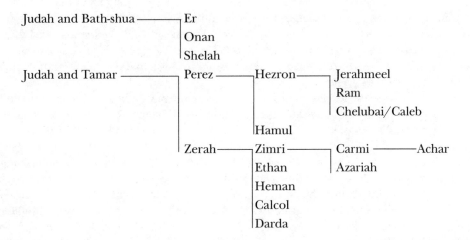

```
Judah and Bath-shua ———— Er
                           Onan
                           Shelah

Judah and Tamar ———————— Perez ——— Hezron ——— Jerahmeel
                                                 Ram
                                                 Chelubai/Caleb
                                    Hamul
                          Zerah ——— Zimri ——— Carmi ———— Achar
                                    Ethan      Azariah
                                    Heman
                                    Calcol
                                    Darda
```

Three sons were born to him from Bath-shua, a Canaanite woman: The name of this woman might also be translated "the daughter of Shua," which is the way the name has to be construed in Gen 38:2. The Chronicler makes no criticism of this liaison, as the author of Ezra and Nehemiah surely would have.[25] Japhet, 74, notes that "one of the goals of these genealogies is the inclusion, rather than exclusion, of the non-Israelite elements in the people of Israel."[26] Hence the Chronicler's identification of her as a Canaanite is not surprising. There are five additional references to intermarriage with foreigners in the genealogy of Judah—all recorded *without* criticism: Jether the Ishmaelite was married to Abigail the sister of David, and she gave birth to Amasa (2:17); an unnamed daughter of Sheshan, a descendant of Jerahmeel, was married to Jarha, an Egyptian slave (2:34-35);

David himself was married to Maacah the daughter of Talmai king of Geshur, and she was the mother of Absalom (3:2); Mered, a Judahite whose genealogical connection to Judah is not clear, married Bithiah the daughter of Pharaoh (4:17);[27] and some of the descendants of Shelah married into Moab (4:22).[28] As the next verse will show, the Chronicler is not adverse to criticizing members of the Judean genealogy when that is appropriate. The reference to the numerical sum of "three" is to be compared with the same number in v. 16 and with the number five in vv. 4 and 6.

Er the firstborn of Judah was evil in the eyes of Yahweh and he put him to death: The Chronicler names no specific sin which Er committed, as also Gen 38:6 does not, but does make his sin a capital crime.[29] This is the first example in Chronicles of the relationship of sin and

25 Oeming, *Wahre Israel,* 121–23, argues against the Chronicler being open to marriage with outsiders. Tg calls her "the trading woman." "Canaan" does have this meaning elsewhere (Job 40:30 [41:6]; Hos 12:8 [7]; Zeph 1:11, lit. "people of Canaan"). Tg seems to be protecting Judah from the charge of marrying a woman from one of the forbidden foreign nations.

26 So also Willi, *Chronik als Auslegung,* 190–94; contra Oeming, *Wahre Israel,* 121.

27 This is the second reference to intermarriage with an Egyptian. In one case the Egyptian spouse was male and in this case female.

28 Or perhaps they ruled there or worked there. See the commentary on this verse. While the Chronicler

omitted the indictment of Solomon's wives from 1 Kings 11, he included, without judgment, Solomon's moving his wife who was the daughter of Pharaoh from the city of David to his palace (2 Chr 8:11//1 Kgs 9:24). The Chronicler, however, did omit 1 Kgs 3:1; 7:8; and 9:16. On intermarriage in this chapter see Knoppers, "Intermarriage," 15–30.

29 Cf. also Gen 46:12; Num 26:19. Note the pun between עֵר "Er" and רַע "evil." Cf. Achar in v. 7 and Jabez in 1 Chr 4:9.

punishment (retribution). The genealogy of Judah also contains criticism for Achar in v. 7. In any case, Er lost any advantage of being the firstborn through his sinful action (cf. Reuben in 5:1). This is the first reference to the divine name Yahweh—in fact to the Deity at all[30]—in Chronicles. The Chronicler omitted the loveless act by which Onan spilled his seed on the ground and thus did not carry through his levirate obligations, leading again to divine punishment (Gen 38:8-10).[31]

■ 4 *Tamar, his daughter-in-law, bore for him Perez and Zerah:*[32] This information was available to the Chronicler in the colorful story of Gen 38:11-30 (cf. Gen 46:12; Num 26:20). The ethnic identity of Tamar is not given in the Bible, and some postcanonical works identify her as an Aramean (*Jub.* 41:1-2; *T. Jud.* 10:1). Judah praises Tamar for her actions in conceiving a child through him, but he had acted without overt intention and did not sleep with her again (Gen 38:26). Neither his nor her actions are criticized in Chronicles; perhaps their success in producing the next generation in the descendants of Judah was thought to outweigh the condemnations of a man sleeping with his daughter-in-law in Lev 18:12; 20:12.

■ 5 *The sons of Perez: Hezron and Hamul:* These two sons of Perez are mentioned in Gen 46:12 and Num 26:20-21, and Hezron is also mentioned in Ruth 4:18-19.[33] Hezron's other association with Judah in earlier tradition is as an otherwise unknown city by this name on Judah's southern border between Kadesh-barnea (MR 096006) and Addar (also unknown; Josh 15:3). The line of Hezron is continued in v. 9, but outside of the generic

"Hamulites" in Num 26:21, nothing further is known about Hamul or his descendants.

■ 6 *The sons of Zerah: Zimri, Ethan, Heman, Calcol, and Darda:* Zimri is apparently a misreading of Zabdi in Josh 7:1, perhaps on the basis of a variant reading now attested in Joshua.[34] In addition to the orthographic reasons for this change, Rod R. Hutton suggests that the Chronicler was trying to link this person to the singing of cultic music (cf. Ethan and Heman below).[35] Compare the verb זמר "to play an instrument" or "sing" (*HALOT* 1:273) and the noun מזמור a technical term for a psalm (*HALOT,* 566). In Joshua, Achan is the son of Carmi son of Zabdi son of Zerah, of the tribe of Judah. The other four names of the sons of Zerah are taken from 1 Kgs 5:11 (4:31): "He [Solomon] was wiser . . . than Ethan the Ezrahite, and Heman, Calcol, and Darda, children of Mahol."[36] "Ezrahite" (האזרחי) closely resembles "Zerahite" (הזרחי)[37] in Hebrew, and LXX[B] and related manuscripts in Kings spell the word with an initial *zēta* in Greek. Ethan is identified as a son of Zerah also in the Tg to Kings. The Chronicler understood all four as Zerahites despite the fact that the last three are called children of Mahol in Kings and are possibly Canaanites.[38] Heman and Ethan are called Ezrahites[39] in the superscriptions to Psalms 88 and 89, respectively, although presumably they were considered in these superscriptions to be from the tribe of Levi[40] instead of Judah. Perhaps both tribes numbered them among their ancestors. Heman the son of Joel and Ethan the son of Kushaiah are identified as singers at the time of David in 1 Chr 15:17, 19, but they were Levites there and not descen-

---

30   The first reference to "God of Israel" comes in 1 Chr 4:10.

31   Oeming, *Wahre Israel,* 121. Rudolph in *BHS* suggests a sentence was lost by textual error (see textual note 4).

32   A Zerah is also a descendant of Esau via Reuel (1 Chr 1:37) and the father of an Edomite king.

33   Cf. also Jashobeam son of Zabdiel, a descendant of Perez in the time of David (1 Chr 27:2-3), and the postexilic descendants of Perez (Neh 11:4-6 and 1 Chr 9:4-6).

34   Note Josh 7:1 LXX[B] in textual note 6, which shows evidence of both a *mêm* and a *rêš*, as in the Hebrew name Zimri.

35   *ABD* 6:1094–95.

36   Perhaps this name refers to liturgical dance (Pss

149:3; 150:4). Myers, 1:13, observes: "The Chronicler's interest in Zerah's list lies in its connection with the musical guilds."

37   Num 26:13, 20; Josh 7:17; 1 Chr 27:11, 13.

38   Cf. W. F. Albright, *Archaeology and the Religion of Israel* (4th ed.; Baltimore: Johns Hopkins Univ. Press, 1956), 127. Tg adds the following comment to these five: "All of them officials upon whom the spirit of prophecy rested."

39   In both cases the Greek translates "the Israelite."

40   They were apparently considered temple singers and contemporaries of David in these psalms.

dants of Judah. Curtis and Madsen, 85, suggest that the Ethan and Heman of Israel's early traditions have each evolved into two sets of persons in the Chronicler's genealogies. Since they were considered proverbially wise men already at the time of Solomon, the author apparently felt no tension in making them grandchildren of Judah. The only other Zerahites in the OT are Sibbecai the Hushathite and Marai the Netophathite (27:11, 13).

■ **7** *The sons of Zimri: Carmi; and the sons of Carmi: Achar, the troubler of Israel:* The source for the name Carmi was Josh 7:1, 18, although I should note that my text is a conjectural reconstruction precisely on the basis of that passage (see textual note 8). Instead of Achar, the Hebrew text of Josh 7:1, 18, 19, 20, 24 reads Achan, but the LXX in all five cases reads Αχαρ (Achar). Achan is very likely the original reading, with Achar arising in the text history of Joshua by assimilation to the word עכר ("to trouble") in Josh 7:24-26, where the incident is located in the Valley of Achor.[41] Achan is also accused of troubling (עכרתנו) Israel. The Chronicler continues that exegetical tradition by giving Achar the epithet "troubler," formed from the same Hebrew verb.[42] Is the failure of Achar from the line of Zerah a hint of why Perez, whose right of firstborn was gained in an unusual birth (Gen 38:27-30), was the favored line and the ancestor of David?

who acted unfaithfully: The source of the verb מעל is in Josh 7:1, but the first use of this verb in Chronicles antic-ipates one of the major vocables used for sinfulness in the books of Chronicles.[43]

■ **8** *The sons of Ethan: Azariah:* Most commentators say that the identity of Azariah is unknown, and one might wonder why the Chronicler would create a son for a figure Ethan, "borrowed" from another context. I suspect the similarity between the Hebrew word "Ezrahite" אזרחי and "Azariah" עזריה will prove to be the source of the Chronicler's addition.[44]

2:9—4:10. Descendants of Hezron
2:9. Three Sons of Hezron: Jerahmeel, Ram, and Chelubai

■ **9** *The sons of Hezron who were born to him: Jerahmeel, Ram, and Chelubai:* Before the time of Chronicles, the only references to the Jerahmeelites are in 1 Sam 27:10, where David misled Achish king of Gath by telling him that he had been making raids against the Negeb of Judah, the Negeb of the Jerahmeelites, and the Negeb of the Kenites, when he had actually been attacking the Geshurites, the Girzites, and the Amalekites, and in 1 Sam 30:29, where the towns of the Jerahmeelites were among those receiving the booty from David's raids. Hence the Jerahmeelites were associated geographically with Judah already in the David traditions and they are now included via their eponymous ancestor Jerahmeel within that tribe's genealogy as well.[45] Jerahmeel is listed as Hezron's firstborn in v. 25. The mention of the towns

---

41 Ludwig Koehler, "Hebräische Etymologien," *JBL* 59 (1940) 38–39, proposed that Achan was a secondary change that introduced a euphemism for Achar, which he parsed as "unfortunate man."

42 See R. S. Hess, "Achan and Achor: Names and Wordplay in Joshua 7," *HAR* 14 (1994) 94–96.

43 Cf. Oeming, *Wahre Israel*, 124–26. The verb is used at key points in Israel's history, always in material added by the Chronicler: 1 Chr 5:25 (infidelity led to the exile of the two and one-half Transjordanian tribes); 9:1 (Judah was taken into exile because of infidelity); 10:13 (twice; Saul's unfaithfulness led to his death and the loss of the kingship); 2 Chr 12:2 (infidelity during the reign of Rehoboam led to the invasion of Shishak); 26:16, 18 (unfaithfulness in Uzziah's inappropriate approach to the incense altar was the cause of his leprosy); 28:19 (twice; the infidelity of Ahaz led to the victory of the Philistines), 22 (further unfaithfulness of Ahaz); 29:6 (Hezekiah confesses the unfaithfulness of the ances-tors, leading to the need for reform), 19 (a reference to the unfaithfulness of Ahaz); 30:7 (another reference to the unfaithfulness of the ancestors); 33:19 (a summary statement on Manasseh's unfaithfulness in the first part of his life before his imprisonment and repentance); and 36:14 (twice; the infidelity of Zedekiah, the priests, and the people led to the destruction of Jerusalem and the temple). The verb is also used in Ezra 9:24; 10:2, 6, 10 (twice); Neh 1:8; 13:27.

44 Less likely in my judgment is Japhet's reference (76) to Azariah the son of Nathan in 1 Kgs 4:5.

45 Gershon Galil, "The Jerahmeelites and the Negeb of Judah," *JANESCU* 28 (2001) 38, 42, locates the region of the Jerahmeelites between Arad and Beersheba. He also argues that the Jerahmeelites are not to be considered "non-Israelite" in their origin.

of the Jerahmeelites in 1 Sam 30:29 would seem to belie the common understanding of them as nomadic.

The genealogical connection between Perez, Hezron, and Ram (1 Chr 2:5, 9) is also attested in the genealogy at the end of the book of Ruth (Ruth 4:18-19).[46] Whereas the other two names in this verse, Jerahmeel and Chelubai, are fitted out with complex segmented tribal genealogies later in the chapter, Ram is included only as part of the linear genealogy leading from Judah-Perez-Hezron to Ram and then on to David (see vv. 10-17) and David's descendants (3:1-24).

I take Chelubai as an alternate spelling of Caleb. Caleb the son of Jephunneh was one of the twelve spies or scouts, representing the tribe of Judah, at least according to P (Num 13:6; 34:19). The spies were sent by Moses to reconnoiter the land, and Caleb alone (Num 13:30 J; cf. Deut 1:36) or he and Joshua (Num 14:6, 30, 38; 26:65 P) were rewarded because of their fidelity in bringing back a good report on the land and believing that Yahweh would give them the land. They were the only two from the exodus generation itself who were able to enter the land.[47] Caleb is also identified as a Kenizzite in the Hexateuch (Num 32:12; Josh 14:6[48]), and he was given the city of Hebron or Kiriath-arba, within Judah, when the land was apportioned (Josh 14:13-14; 15:13;[49] 21:12; 1 Chr 6:41 [56; the city itself was a Levitical city, but its environs belonged to Caleb]; cf. Num 34:19).[50] Caleb's nephew Othniel, the son of Caleb's younger brother Kenaz, captured the city of Debir or Kiriath-sepher, and Caleb gave him his daughter Achsah as a reward (Josh 15:15-19//Judg 1:11-15).

The Chronicler refers to Caleb the son of Jephunneh in 1 Chr 4:15, where he is listed right after the sons of Kenaz (4:13-14), but no explicit connections are made to the genealogy of Judah for either the sons of Kenaz or Caleb the son of Jephunneh although they are clearly considered Judahite. Despite Caleb the son of Jephunneh's relationship to the Kenizzites and his association with Judah in passages like Josh 14:6 and 15:13,[51] no one before the Chronicler had traced his genealogical line all the way back to Judah the son of Jacob.

In writing 1 Chr 2:9, the Chronicler linked Jerahmeel and Chelubai/Caleb genealogically to Judah and made them brothers of Ram by construing all three as sons of Hezron, but he thereby created a tension with those passages that make Caleb the son of Jephunneh.[52] This genealogical addition in v. 9, however, allowed the Chronicler to use the two genealogies of Jerahmeel available to him in 2:25-33 and 34-41, as well as the genealogies of Caleb in 2:42-50aα and 2:50aβ-55. The spelling Chelubai is unique in the Bible, although a Chelub appears in 4:11 (see the commentary on this verse), but the name Caleb is surely intended here, as indicated by v. 18, where Caleb is the son of Hezron, and by v. 42, where Caleb is identified as the brother of Jerahmeel. The LXX reads "Caleb" instead of Chelubai in this verse as well (see textual note 11). The Chronicler gives the Calebites descended from Hezron a direct tie to the genealogy of Judah, while he does not provide such a direct genealogical connection to the other Calebite traditions related to Caleb the brother of Shucah (4:11-12) and Caleb the son of Jephunneh (4:15; cf. 6:41 [56]). It is

46 Regardless of whether Ruth 4:18-22 was original in that book or added secondarily, it seems clear that this was borrowed from Ruth into Chronicles, where the Chronicler expands it by adding the eight siblings of David and also his descendants in chap. 3. Note that the genealogy in 1 Chr 2:10-17 does not begin with Perez or end with David, as the genealogy in Ruth does (Willi, 89).

47 Cf. Sir 46:1-10.

48 In this verse he appears before Joshua, with the whole tribe of Judah. Othniel son of Kenaz is identified as Caleb's younger brother in Judg 3:9. Cf. Josh 15:17; Judg 1:13; 3:11.

49 This verse actually effects a compromise between Josh 14:13-14, where Hebron is given to Caleb, and 15:54, where Hebron is among the towns of Judah,

by designating Hebron as Caleb's portion *within* Judah. Cf. Rudolph, 21. In 15:13-14 Caleb conquered Hebron/Kiriath-arba by driving out the three sons of Anak.

50 Part of Judah was known as the Negeb of Caleb (1 Sam 30:14). Nabal, the first husband of Abigail, one of David's wives, was a Calebite (1 Sam 25:3), living in Carmel (MR 162092), about 8 miles southeast of Hebron (MR 160103).

51 Contact between David from the tribe of Judah and the Calebites is also reported in 1 Sam 25:3 and 30:14.

52 For the chronological problems involving Caleb and Bezalel in 1 Chr 2:20, and for discussion of Achsah his daughter in 2:49, see the commentary on those verses.

likely that the Calebites were not originally Israelites or at least were only gradually integrated into the tribal genealogies. In Gen 36:9-11 (cf. Gen 36:15, 42; 1 Chr 1:36, 53), Kenaz, otherwise known as Caleb's younger brother, is identified as a descendant of Eliphaz the son of Edom. The Kenizzites, descendants from this eponymous ancestor, are listed in Gen 15:19 as one of the pre-Israelite inhabitants of the land. In this genealogy in chaps. 2–4, the Kenizzites become Judahite (1 Chr 4:13-14).

The reason for the order of the three sons of Hezron in this verse is not clear, especially since it does not correspond to the order of their descendants in the rest of this chapter. According to v. 25, however, Jerahmeel was the firstborn of Hezron. Willi, 86, believes that Ram as the only genuine Judean tribe was put in the middle, with the two secondarily Judean tribes put alongside him. One could also argue that Ram, the ancestor of David, is put up as high as possible in the genealogy, although the first position was excluded by v. 25.

2:10-17. Descendants of Ram

[Judah—Perez—Hezron][53]—Ram—Amminadab—Nahshon—Salma—Boaz—Obed—Jesse[—David]

■ **10** *Amminadab became the father of Nahshon, the prince of the sons of Judah:* As noted under the previous verse, the genealogy from Perez to David has been borrowed from Ruth 4:18-22.[54] In the book of Ruth, Boaz is in the seventh position beginning with Perez, and David is in the tenth position. Both positions often indicate a privileged status within genealogies. Nahshon the son of Amminadab was chosen from the tribe of Judah to assist Moses and Aaron in taking the census of the people in the wilderness period (Num 1:7; cf. 2:3; 7:12, 17; 10:14).[55] In Num 1:16 he and the other assistants are called leaders or "princes" (נשיא) of their ancestral tribes, which supports the Chronicler's addition of Nahshon's title נשיא in this verse.[56] Nahshon himself is called the prince of the people of Judah in Num 2:3.[57] The symbolic features of this genealogy (seventh and tenth position) seem to be the guiding principles since clearly there are more than eleven generations in the purported eight hundred year plus years between Judah and David, and more than five generations in the three

hundred plus years between Nahshon and David.[58] Hence there has been considerable telescoping in this genealogy.

■ **11** *And Nahshon became the father of Salma:* Salma was the founder of Bethlehem according to tradition (vv. 50 and 54).

```
Jesse ──── Eliab
           Abinadab
           Shimea
           Nethanel
           Raddai
           Ozem
           David
           Zeruiah ──────────────── Abshai
                                     Joab
                                     Asahel
           Abigail and Jether the Ishmaelite ──── Amasa
```

---

53 1 Chr 2:3-5, 9.

54 The sequence Boaz/Ruth-Obed-Jesse-David also occurs in Ruth 4:17, just before the genealogy proper. For Salma in v. 11 see the commentary at 1 Chr 2:51, 54. De Vries, 38, speaks of the *hôlîd* style in vv. 10-13, 18a, 20, 36-41, 44, 46b, referring to the use of the *hiphil* perfect of ילד in these verses.

55 According to Exod 6:23, Aaron married Elisheba, who was the daughter of Amminadab and the sister of Nahshon, but the text does not explicitly state that this Amminadab was from the tribe of Judah.

56 Cf. Gary A. Rendsburg, "The Internal Consistency and Historical Reliability of the Biblical Genealogies," *VT* 40 (1990) 185–204.

57 Nahshon's sister Elizabeth was Aaron's wife (Exod 6:23). See also Num 1:7; 7:12; and 10:14. Cf. Johnstone, 1:46.

58 J. M. Sasson, "Genealogical 'Convention' in Biblical Chronography," *ZAW* 90 (1978) 171–72, notes how significant individuals are placed in the seventh, or sometimes even fifth, position in a genealogy.

■ **13** *Jesse became the father of Eliab, his firstborn, Abinadab, the second, Shimea, the third:* These three sons are known from the books of Samuel: Eliab (1 Sam 16:6; 17:13, 28);[59] Abinadab (1 Sam 16:8; 17:13); and Shimea שמעא (in 1 Sam 16:9 and 17:13 his name is spelled שמה "Shammah," in 2 Sam 13:3, 32 it is spelled שמעה "Shimeah,"[60] and in 2 Sam 21:21[61] K it is spelled שמעי "Shimei" and Q שמעה "Shimeah").

■ **14** *Nethanel the fourth, Raddai the fifth:* These brothers of David are not listed earlier in the Bible, and the name Raddai appears only here in the Bible. See also the next verse.

■ **15** *Ozem the sixth, David the seventh:* Ozem is not mentioned earlier in the Bible as a brother of David (cf. 1 Chr 2:25, where a person by this name is a son of Jerahmeel). It is likely that the Chronicler had access to an alternate list of all of David's brothers since he identifies David as the seventh son whereas in 1 Samuel he is the eighth son (1 Sam 16:10-11; 17:12).[62] Isaac Kalimi has pointed out that Josephus (*Ant.* 6.161–163) and the painter of the fresco of Samuel's anointing of David in the synagogue at Dura-Europos (3d century CE), follow the number of sons given by the Chronicler.[63] Seven sons are also attributed to Elioenai, the last parent in the Davidic line (1 Chr 3:24). David is also in the seventh generation after Ram.

■ **16** *Their sisters: Zeruiah and Abigail:* This is the first and only time these women are explicitly identified as sisters of David in the Bible.[64] Here they also serve as heads of families. Abigail is identified as the sister of Zeruiah in 2 Sam 17:25, where her husband is called Ithra the Israelite in MT. יתרא "Ithra" is an alternate spelling for the name יתר "Jether" (cf. 1 Chr 2:17), and in fact the LXX in Samuel reads Ιοθορ = יתר consonantally. LXX[A] in 2 Sam 17:25 calls her husband "the Ishmaelite,"[65] as in 1 Chr 2:17. In 2 Sam 17:25 Abigail is said to be the daughter of Nahash.[66] If the Lucianic and some other Greek manuscripts in 2 Sam 17:25, which make her the daughter of Jesse, represent old readings in that verse, the Chronicler came to this information about the parentage of Zeruiah and Abigail from an alternate text form of 2 Sam 17:25.[67] The Chronicler may also have made these women sisters of David because David calls Amasa, the son of Abigail, "my bone and flesh" in 2 Sam 19:14 (13).

Abshai, Joab, and Asahel: These three men are often identified as sons of Zeruiah[68] in 1 and especially 2 Samuel, but we might expect Joab to be listed before Abshai (cf. 2 Sam 2:18). The spelling אבשי (Abshai) is regular in Chronicles, but in Samuel his name is always spelled אבישי (Abishai), except for 2 Sam 10:10, where אבשי occurs.[69]

---

59 According to 2 Chr 11:18, Eliab's daughter Abihail was the mother of Mahalath, one of Rehoboam's wives. *KJV* made her one of Rehoboam's wives.

60 His son in these verses is named Jonadab.

61 In the parallel passage from Chronicles (1 Chr 20:7) it is spelled שמאה "Shimeah." In both books his son is called Jonathan.

62 The Peshitta harmonizes by making Elihu (cf. 1 Chr 27:18 MT, but LXX Eliab) the seventh and David the eighth son.

63 Isaac Kalimi, "A Transmission of Tradition: The Number of Jesse's Sons," *ThZ* 57 (2001) 1–9. Kalimi also finds this preference in rabbinic literature and some medieval Christian art and attributes it to the special role that the number seven played in the religious view of their generations. Kalimi isolates an even earlier tradition in Samuel according to which Jesse had only four sons (1 Sam 16:6-9, 11-13; 17:13-14).

64 This would make David and Joab uncle and nephew, respectively. Japhet, 71, calls them first cousins. Other sisters in the genealogy of Judah are Tamar, the only woman mentioned from David's children (1 Chr 3:9), Shelomith (3:10), Hazzelelponi (4:3), and the Judahite wife who is the sister of Naham (4:19).

65 LXX[M] reads "the Jezreelite."

66 McCarter, *II Samuel*, 392, believes that "Nahash" arose as a textual error under the influence of "son of Nahash" in 2 Sam 17:27. Others take Nahash as Abigail's mother's name or the name of an earlier husband of Jesse's wife. If this latter interpretation is correct, Abigail would only be a half-sister to David. If the author of Samuel did not think Abigail was a daughter of Jesse, the identification of Nahash is less crucial.

67 But McCarter, *II Samuel*, 392, takes this reading in 2 Sam 17:25 as a secondary correction.

68 The name of Zeruiah's husband is unknown, but according to 2 Sam 2:32 his grave was at Bethlehem.

69 But LXX has "Abishai."

2:18-24. Various Genealogical Notices

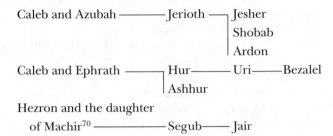

■ **18** *Caleb the son of Hezron became the father of Jerioth, with Azubah his wife:* Willi, 91, finds significance in the etymologies of Caleb's wife Azubah[71] and his daughter Jerioth. He interprets Azuba as "deserted,"[72] a reference to the steppe, and he interprets the daughter's name as "tent curtains,"[73] implying a seminomadic existence for them.

These were her sons: Jesher, Shobab, and Ardon: Nothing is known of these three sons of Jerioth (cf. Japhet, 79; Braun, 39), although Shobab is also the name of one of David's sons (1 Chr 3:5; 14:4; 2 Sam 5:14).

■ **19** *Azubah died and Caleb took Ephrath for himself, and she bore to him Hur:* If Willi's interpretation of the names Azubah and Jerioth from the previous verse is correct, the "death" of Azubah and Caleb's "marriage" to Ephrath would mark a shift in Caleb's territory. Ephrath

(or Ephrathah, 1 Chr 4:4) is a clan which had its center in or near Bethlehem and extended as far north as Kiriath-jearim (MR 159135; 1 Chr 2:50, 52, 53; cf. Ps 132:6) and as far south as Tekoa (MR 170115; 1 Chr 2:24; 4:5).[74]

■ **20** *Hur became the father of Uri, and Uri became the father of Bezalel:* For this genealogy the Chronicler is dependent on Exod 31:2, 35:30, 38:22, where Bezalel, one of the craftsmen appointed by God to work on the tabernacle (cf. the bronze altar at which Solomon inquires at the beginning of his reign in 2 Chr 1:5),[75] is given the same father and grandfather as here and is linked to the tribe of Judah. It is doubtful that the Hur mentioned in those Exodus passages is to be identified with Hur the son of Caleb. Caleb and Bezalel would be contemporaries in the wilderness wanderings even though Caleb is Bezalel's great-grandfather. It is likely that this is the Chronicler's attempt to tie the sanctuary genealogically to the tribe of Judah, through Caleb, just as he tied the monarchy to the ancestors in that period in vv. 10-17. Thus he forges another link between kingship and temple. A Hur is also the companion of Moses and Aaron in the battle against the Amalekites (Exod 17:10, 12; cf. Exod 24:14), though neither his tribe nor his descendants are identified there.

■ **21** *Later Hezron had sexual relations[76] with the daughter of Machir the father of Gilead:* The next three verses explain

---

70   Machir is identified as the father of Gilead in v. 24.

71   Other wives in this genealogy of Judah include Ephrathah and Abijah (2:24), Atarah (2:26), Abihail (2:29), the daughter of Sheshan (2:35), the seven wives of David mentioned by name (3:1-5), Helah and Naarah (4:5), and the Judahite wife (4:19). See also the concubines listed at 2:46.

72   Johnstone, 1:48: "desolate one"; cf. Isa 6:12. Tg says she was called Azubah because she was barren and despised.

73   Tg builds on this word by adding that Azubah spun goats' hair upon the goats' bodies, without shearing them, for the curtains of the tabernacle.

74   Rachel died on the way to Ephrath (Gen 35:19; 48:7; cf. Ps 132:6). Japhet, 78, believes that this verse represents the Chronicler's restructuring of the genealogy of Judah. According to her understanding, Ephrath was first married to Hezron and only after his death did she marry Caleb. Jerahmeel and Caleb came from Hezron's first wife and Hur from Ephrath. In 1 Chr 2:50 and 4:4 Hur is called

the firstborn of Ephrath, and this is understood by her to mean the first child born to her during her marriage with Hezron. The Chronicler replaced Hur with Ram among the sons of Hezron and made Hur the son of Caleb and Ephrath. In this reconstruction v. 24 reads: "After the death of Hezron, Caleb went to (had sexual relations with) Ephrath the wife of Hezron his father, and she bore to him Ashhur the father of Tekoa."

75   Johnstone, 1:49, gives details about his responsibilities.

76   Tg: "seduced." McIvor, *Targum*, 50, asks whether this might be an anti-Christian tendency in Tg since Hezron figures in the genealogies of Jesus in Matt 1:3 and Luke 3:33.

how the family of Hezron, which once was settled in Judah, perhaps around Bethlehem, migrated toward Gilead, leaving a vacuum around Bethlehem, which the Calebites filled according to 1 Chr 2:50aβ-55. This move of Hezron to Gilead[77] is portrayed under the metaphor of marriage or sexual relations, but the verse could be translated literally and express the moving of the clan of Hezron: "Hezron went to the daughter[78] of Machir." Machir is the son of Manasseh (Gen 50:23), and his geographic location is expressed in the term "father of Gilead." The source for the Chronicler's information is Num 32:39-42,[79] which reports that the descendants of Machir went to Gilead, captured it, dispossessed the Amorites who were there, and settled there (cf. Josh 17:1).

When he took her, he was sixty years old, and she bore to him Segub: Segub (שׂוּב) is unknown, but Braun, 40, identifies him conjecturally with Argob (ארגב), a region connected elsewhere with Gilead and Jair. Segub's son Jair (v. 22), a son of Manasseh, according to Num 32:41 (Deut 3:14), captured villages in Gilead and renamed them Havvoth-jair (cf. v. 23),[80] thus linking these villages to an eponymous ancestor. Jair is made the grandson of Hezron in v. 22, and his villages are said to number twenty-three in the same verse. A judge called Jair the Gileadite had thirty towns in this region (Judg 10:3-4), but it is unclear how this number of towns relates to the number twenty-three in v. 22. Nobah, otherwise unknown and not mentioned in Chronicles, captured Kenath (MR 302341; see the reference to this place in the next verse) and its villages in the same context (Num 32:42; Judg 8:11).

Whether the Chronicler had any information linking Hezron to this area or, as seems likely, was merely using this excerpt from Numbers to lay claim to portions of Gilead for Judah cannot be determined.

When he took her, he was sixty years old: This notice foreshadows the death of Hezron in v. 24.

■ **23** *Geshur and Aram seized from them Havvoth-jair together with Kenath and its villages, sixty cities:* The antecedent of "them" could be some combination of Hezron, the daughter of Machir, Segub, and Jair, or the inhabitants of Gilead in general. This no doubt reflects a historical memory of a loss of Israelite territory to the kingdom of Geshur, located in the environs of Bethsaida, and undefined Aramean forces.[81] David married the daughter of the king of Geshur (2 Sam 3:3; 1 Chr 3:2), and Absalom fled there after he had killed Amnon (2 Sam 13:37). He later referred to it as "Geshur in Aram" (2 Sam 15:8). The number sixty seems designed to include all cities belonging to Havvoth-jair and Kenath. Kenath is east of Argob in Bashan. In Num 32:42 Nobah went and captured Kenath and its villages and renamed it Nobah after himself.

■ **24** *After the death of Hezron, Caleb had sexual relations with Ephrath:* The "death" of Hezron could refer to his departure from the northern half of Judah, and Caleb's sexual relationship with Ephrath expresses metaphorically a move of Calebites into this territory. Note that the Hebrew says literally "Caleb went to Ephrath." Cf. v. 21.

---

77   Deut 3:4, 14; 1 Kgs 4:13.
78   Daughters in the genealogy of Judah are also recorded for Sheshan (2:34-35), Achsah the daughter of Caleb (2:49), Maacah daughter of Talmai king of Geshur (3:2), Bath-shua the daughter of Ammiel (3:5), and Bithiah the daughter of the Pharaoh (4:18).
79   Cf. Num 26:29; Josh 17:1; Deut 3:13-15.
80   The villages of Jair are in Gilead according to Judg 10:3 and 1 Kgs 4:13, but in Bashan according to Josh 13:30. There are thirty villages according to Judg 10:4 and sixty according to Josh 13:30.
81   Benjamin Mazar, "Geshur and Maacah," *JBL* 80 (1961) 16–28; idem, "The Aramean Empire and Its Relations with Israel," *BA* 25 (1962) 98–120, dated this event to the time of Ben-hadad I, who attacked

Israel when he had received a bribe from Asa. Mazar's basis for this date was a change in the Aramean confederacy that led to Geshur's loss of national identity (cf. 1 Kgs 20:23-24; 22:3). J. Maxwell Miller, "Geshur and Aram," *JNES* 28 (1969) 60–61, argued that the Israelite king in 1 Kings 20 and 22 was really Jehoahaz and that the loss of Gilead did not take place until the time of Jehu or Jehoahaz. Wayne Pitard, *Ancient Damascus*, 151, suggests that this incident *may* be reflected in the attack of Hazael during the reign of Jehu (2 Kgs 10:32-33) or Jehoahaz (13:25).

(and the wife[82] of Hezron was Abijah): Following William-son, 53–54, I understand this to be a misplaced gloss on "the daughter of Machir" in v. 21. While Abijah is usu-ally the name of a man, Abijah is the name of Hezekiah's *mother* in 2 Chr 29:1.

Ashhur the father of Tekoa: The product of Caleb's rela-tionship with Ephrath is the founding or occupation of Tekoa (MR 170115).[83]

2:25-33. Descendants of Jerahmeel

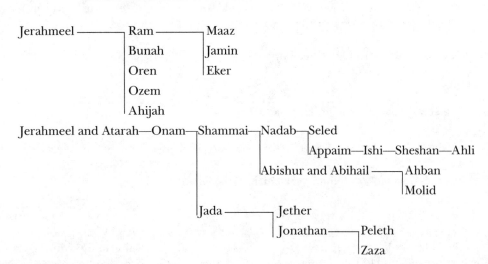

■ **25-33** It is more efficient to discuss the first genealogy of Jerahmeel as a unit rather than by individual verses.[84] In distinction from the genealogies of Caleb in 2:42-55, none of the names can be identified definitively with a place, although Rudolph saw a resemblance between Atarah (v. 26) and Atroth-beth-joab in 2:54,[85] and between Molid (v. 29) and the town of Moladah (Josh 15:26; MR 142074), some 6 or 7 miles northeast of Beer-sheba (MR 134072).[86] The name Abishur (v.29) could be construed as "the father of Shur," and Shur is located south of Palestine and east of Egypt.[87] This lack of place

names might imply a seminomadic lifestyle, but I noted above the reference to towns of the Jerahmeelites in 1 Sam 30:29. In any case, preexilic traditions put Jerah-meel in the far south. Rudolph, 19, detected a similarity of some names in the descendants of Jerahmeel to the descendants of Esau/Edom in the previous chapter: אֹרֶן Oren in v. 25 and אֲרָן Aran in 1:42; אוֹנָם Onam in v. 26 and in 1:40; שַׁמַּי Shammai in v. 28 (cf. the Calebite Sham-mai at 2:44-45) and שַׁמָּה Shammah in 1:37. While Jerah-meel seems to be separate from Judah in pre-Davidic times, two of the theophoric names are formed with the

---

82 See textual note 26. Laban and Ben Zvi, "Observa-tions," 459, construe Abijah as the wife of Hezron and the mother of Ashhur.

83 Curtis and Madsen, 92, claim that Hur in v. 19 and Ashhur in v. 24 are identical. Descendants of Caleb are "fathers" of Ziph, Hebron, Jorkeam, and Beth-zur in 2:42-45.

84 Almost all the observations made here were already seen by Rudolph, 19; cf. now also Willi, 96–97.

85 Some translate it "crowns of the house of Joab," possibly referring to Bethlehem (MR 169123) and

Netophath (MR 170119). Others would locate it near Tekoa (MR 170115). Demsky, "Clans of Ephrath," 53, puts it within a triangle formed by these three cities. See Susan E. McGary, *ABD* 1:522.

86 Galil, "Jerahmeelites," 34, calls attention to a possi-ble reference to Arad of the Jerahmeelites in the inscription of Shishak at Karnak, and proposes that the names *Fltm*, *Yrhm*, and *Ann* there may be identi-fied with Peleth, Jerahmeel, and Onam in this genealogy.

87 Gen 16:7; 20:1; 25:18; Exod 15:22; 1 Sam 15:7; 27:8.

name Yahweh: Ahijah in v. 25 and Jonathan in v. 33, indicating a possible religious connection to Judah. As we have seen above, marriages often connote tribal migration or expansion. Eight names are associated with Jerahmeel's first marriage (vv. 25, 27), but sixteen with his second marriage with "another wife,"[88] whose name was Atarah (vv. 26, 28-33). Two of these individuals are said to have died childless, Seled, v. 30, and Jether, v. 32, indicating that these clans or families became extinct. A further expansion may be seen in the marriage of Abishur, the great-grandson of Jerahmeel, to Abihail in

v. 29. While only Ram, the first son in Jerahmeel's first marriage,[89] is given descendants for one generation, the descendants of Onam, the only son of the second marriage, are followed for at least three generations through his son Jada, and in the case of Shammai for six generations (Shammai–Nadab–Appaim–Ishi–Sheshan–Ahli). This depth of the genealogy and the greater number of names in this second "marriage" probably indicate the stronger part of the tribe.

2:34-41. From Sheshan to Elishama

daughter of Sheshan and Jarha—Attai—Nathan—Zabad—Ephlal—Obed—Jehu—Azariah—Helez

Eleasah—Sismai[90]—Shallum—Jekamiah—Elishama

■ **34** *Sheshan had no sons, only daughters:* This verse begins a linear genealogy related to Sheshan, a descendant of Jerahmeel, first mentioned in v. 31. This genealogy is designed to legitimate Elishama (v. 41), who is fourteen generations after Sheshan, in the fifteenth generation.[91] Only the Davidic (3:1-24), priestly (5:27-44 [6:1-15]), and Saulide linear genealogies are longer (8:29-40 and 9:35-44). Sheshan himself is the tenth member in a genealogy going back to Judah: Judah–Perez–Hezron–Jerahmeel–Onam–Shammai–Nadab–Appaim–Ishi–Sheshan. The remark that Sheshan had no sons conflicts with v. 31,

where Sheshan had a son named Ahli. Curtis and Madsen, 94, proposed that Ahli was a woman, while the rabbis concluded that Ahli had died during the lifetime of his father and therefore Sheshan was considered not to have had a son.[92] Since the genealogies in vv. 25-33 and 34-41 come from different social settings and have different purposes, harmonization is not necessary. David, like Sheshan, is in the tenth generation after Judah so that Elishama, who comes fourteen generations after Sheshan, would be dated roughly three hundred or more years later, toward the end of the monarchy.

---

88   Galil, "Jerahmeelites," 35, suggests that the appellation "another wife" means that the descendants of Onam did not fundamentally belong to the Jerahmeelites, but were appended to this family.

89   One might consider whether this Ram should be identified with his "uncle" Ram the son of Hezron in 2:9-17, with an implication of a shift in Ram's social status, but since his sons are different in the two genealogies (Maaz, Jamin, and Eker vs. Amminadab), it may only be the case of two independent individuals with the same name. Cf. also Ram in Job 32:3, who seems to be a third individual. Demsky, "Clans of Ephrath," 50, does suggest that the Ram in v. 27 is the same as the one mentioned in vv. 9-10, and that this clan has been absorbed by Jerahmeel. Note that the name of Salma (v. 11), a

descendant of Ram, shows up among the descendants of Hur (son of Caleb and Ephrath) in vv. 51 and 54.

90   Myers, 1:15, notes that this name appears as a Phoenician deity in an Aramaic incantation text from Arslan Tash.

91   See the thorough and insightful study of Sara Japhet, "The Israelite Legal and Social Reality as Reflected in Chronicles: A Case Study," in *Sha'arei Talmon: Studies in the Bible, Qumran, and the Ancient Near East* (ed. Michael Fishbane and Emmanuel Tov; Winona Lake, IN: Eisenbrauns, 1992) 79–91.

92   According to Eisemann, 30, Pseudo-Rashi derived the name Ahli (אחלי) from חלה ("to be sick") and so accounted for his early death.

■ **35** *Sheshan gave his daughter to Jarha his slave as a wife:* Because Sheshan lacked male heirs, he might have instituted a procedure like that followed in the case of the five daughters of Zelophehad (Num 27:1-11; Josh 17:3-6). These women, who had no brothers, successfully requested permission from Moses to inherit the property of their father, who had died, in order to preserve his name. In a subsequent ruling, it was decided that the daughters of Zelophehad must marry within their tribe lest their inheritance pass to the other tribe into which they had married (Num 36:1-12). Judging by the precedent of the daughters of Zelophehad, Sheshan's name and property would have passed to his son-in-law. Since his Egyptian slave was clearly not part of the tribe of Judah, property would have been lost for Judah.[93] The slave laws in Lev 25:39-54, however, differentiate between an Israelite master (vv. 39-46) and a non-Israelite one (vv. 47-54), and within the former set of laws about an Israelite master, between a master with an Israelite slave (vv. 39-43) and with a non-Israelite slave (vv. 44-46). For an Israelite slave of an Israelite master, the slave's children would be his own and bear his name, while for a foreign slave of an Israelite master, the children born would belong to the master. This explains the rationale behind Sheshan's action: the marriage with a non-Israelite slave would keep the property within Israel.[94] As Milgrom points out, if the slave were an Israelite, he would be set free, at the latest, in the Jubilee Year, and the children would belong to the slave, not to the master.[95] Japhet also points out that the text shows no disapproval of such a mixed marriage, in sharp distinction to Deut 7:3-4; 1 Kgs 11:1-13; Ezra 9–10; Neh 10:30 (31); and 13:23-27.[96]

she bore to him Attai: Japhet proposes that the antecedent to "him" is Sheshan, in accordance with the law in Leviticus just discussed. I believe her point about Attai and subsequent generations being considered descendants of Sheshan would still be valid even if the antecedent of "him" would be Jarha, which seems likely to me in the structure of the sentence. Physically she might bear children for Jarha, but according to the inheritance laws they would belong to Sheshan. The pronoun is ambiguous.

■ **36-40** The rest of the names in vv. 36-40 do not yield much additional information, although at least two of them—Jehu and Azariah—are Yahwistic (cf. Jekamiah in the next verse).

■ **41** *Shallum became the father of Jekamiah, and Jekamiah became the father of Elishama:* Among the bullae published by Nahman Avigad and dating to the time just before the Babylonian destruction of Jerusalem are three impressions of a single seal inscribed "Belonging to Jekamiah the son of Meshullam."[97] Shallum and Meshullam are interchangeable (cf. 1 Chr 9:17 and Neh 12:25). There is no way of telling, of course, whether these names are the same individuals as in the genealogy. Elishama is the person for whom this genealogy was constructed and preserved. The genealogy makes clear that he is a full member of the community, since he can trace his genealogy all the way back to Judah, and the Egyptian slave in his ancestry is fourteen/fifteen generations in the past. His genealogy far exceeds that of a person descended from Edom or Egypt, who could only be admitted to the community in the third generation (Deut 23:8-9). In fact, it far exceeds the ten generations needed for a descendant of Ammon or Moab to be admitted to the assembly of Yahweh (Deut 23:3). The

---

93   While there are several cases where an Israelite man marries a slave as a (secondary) wife, this is the only case in the Bible where an Israelite woman marries a male slave. Japhet shows that the name Jarha might plausibly be considered to have an Egyptian etymology.

94   Apparently because it would be inappropriate for a free woman to marry a slave, Tg has Sheshan emancipate Jarha before he gives him his daughter in marriage.

95   Jacob Milgrom, *Leviticus 23–27* (AB 3b; New York: Doubleday, 2000) 2231.

96   Cf. the marriage of Mered with the daughter of the Egyptian pharaoh in 1 Chr 4:18 and the four other marriages with foreigners discussed in the commentary on v. 3.

97   Nahman Avigad, *Corpus of West Semitic Stamp Seals* (rev. Benjamin Sass; Jerusalem: Israel Academy of Sciences and Humanities, 1997) 206, n. 526 a-c. A Jekamiah is also the fifth son of the captive king Jeconiah (Jehoiachin) in 1 Chr 3:18. An Elijah son of Jekamiah appears on a seal, dated ca. 700 BCE. See Carl Graesser Jr., "The Seal of Elijah," *BASOR* 220 (1975) 63–66.

rabbis identified him as the grandfather of Ishmael the son of Nethaniah, who killed Gedaliah (2 Kgs 25:25; Jer 41:1) while G. Richter identified him with the scribe of Jehoiakim (Jer 36:12, 20-21).[98] Willi, 99, observes that

however old the segmented part of the genealogy of Jerahmeel in 2:25-33 is, the linear genealogy ending with Elishama comes close to the time period of the Chronicler.

2:42-50aα. Descendants of Caleb

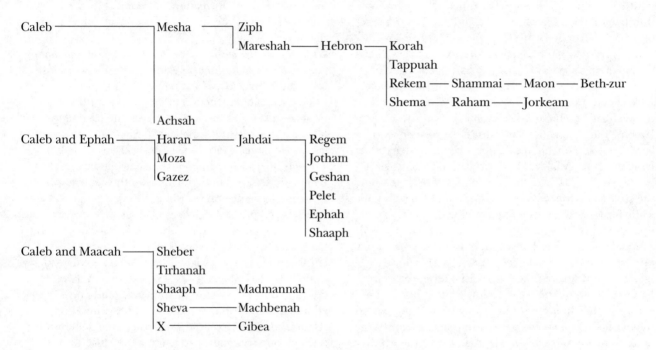

Many of the names in this genealogy and the one following it can be identified as place names and some of

these can be specifically located on a map. These names are presented in table 5:[99]

98 G. Richter, "Untersuchungen zu den Geschlechtsregistern der Chronik," *ZAW* 36 (1914) 123–24. Rudolph, 19, who considers this part of the genealogy secondary, dates Elishama to the time of the redactor who added this section. Cf. Japhet, "Israelite Legal and Social Reality," 81, n. 12. Since the father of Elishama is not given in either 2 Kgs 25:25 or Jeremiah 36, no certainty can be achieved.

99 In addition to names, whether of individuals, families, or places, that are attested only here and otherwise unknown, I note: Korah (v. 43), a family name in Edom (1:35); Shammai (v. 44), an Edomite name

(1:37) and a Jerahmeelite name (2:28); and Ephah (vv. 46-47), a descendant of Midian (1:33). Elsewhere the Calebites were closely identified with Judah and occupied Hebron (Josh 14:13; 15:13; Judg 1:20). See Myers, 1:15.

Table 5

v. 42 Ziph[100]	MR 162098	Josh 15:55
Mareshah	140111	Josh 15:44; Mic 1:15
Hebron	160103	Josh 15:54
v. 43 Tappuah[101]	154105	Josh 15:53 Beth-tappuah
Shema		Josh 15:26. Location unknown, but listed next to Moladah (MR 142074) in Joshua.
v. 44 Jorkeam		Otherwise unknown, but Jokdeam (see textual note 39) is mentioned in Josh 15:56[102] next to Zanoah (MR 150125).
v. 45 Maon	162090	Josh 15:55; 1 Sam 25:2
Beth-zur[103]	159110	Josh 15:58; cf. 2 Chr 11:7 and Neh 3:16. The border for the postexilic area called Yehud ran between Beth-zur and Hebron (MR 160103).
v. 48 Maacah		A place name in 1 Chr 11:43; 27:16. Common name of women and families; also refers to settlements. Cf. Jezaniah the Maacathite (Jer 40:8).
v. 49 Madmannah	143084[104]	Josh 15:31, listed between Ziklag and Sansannah. It is among twenty-nine towns in the extreme south, toward the boundary of Edom

	(Josh 15:21-32). This may be in the area known in the days of David as the Negeb of Caleb in 1 Sam 30:14.
Gibea גבעא	Unknown. A גבעה is mentioned in Josh 15:57 in the same general region with Ziph and Maon.

Of the seven cities for whom map references are given above, the territory covered extends from Mareshah (MR 140111) in the northwest to Beth-zur (MR 159110) in the northeast, and to Ziph (162098) and Maon (162090) in the southeast, and to Madmannah (MR 143084) in the southwest. The cities in this list can be plotted on the map of Judean provinces (Josh 15:21-62),[105] where they appear in the following districts: (1) Madmannah, Shema (see Moladah); (2) Jokdeam (see Zanoah); (4) Mareshah; (6) Hebron, (Beth-)Tappuah; (7) Gibea (see Ziph and Maon), Maon, Ziph; and (8) Beth-zur. I do not mean to propose any relationships between these lists, but only to show graphically that all of these cities are in the southern part of Judah, with none coming from the northern or northeastern regions labeled by Aharoni as ##9, 10, 11, 12. Hebron, Madmannah, and Maon are even outside the southern boundary of the province of Yehud from the Chronicler's time.[106] This geographical situation has led most commentators to consider this the older of the two Calebite genealogies and to date it to preexilic times. Hebron (MR 160103) seems to be the main center around which the other sites cluster.

■ **42** *Mareshah the father of Hebron:* Hebron is the "grandson" of Caleb according to this verse, which expresses

---

100 Beth-zur (v. 45), Hebron, Ziph, and Maresha (v. 42) are listed among Rehoboam's fortresses in 2 Chr 11:7-10.

101 Identified here with Beth-tappuah. There also is an unidentified site Tappuah mentioned in Josh 15:34.

102 It may be associated with Ziph and Maon, which are mentioned in Josh 15:55.

103 Johnstone, 1:52, locates it north of Hebron. Curtis and Madsen, 96: 4 miles north of Hebron.

104 Harold Brodsky, "Madmannah," *ABD* 4:463, argues for a location at Khirbet Tatrīt, considerably south-

west of Hebron (MR 160103). Willi, 103, gives the correct MR for Khirbet Tatrīt, but mistakenly locates it northeast of Bethlehem (MR 169123).

105 Aharoni, *Land of the Bible*, 346.

106 Ziph and Mareshah seem to be near the southern border, and Beth-zur is one of the southern border points.

genealogically Caleb's possession of Hebron in earlier biblical sources. Ran Zadok argues that Mareshah would not have had enough significance until the Persian period to be considered the father of Hebron. In preexilic sources it always lags significantly behind the neighboring city of Lachish in importance.[107]

■ **43** *The sons of Hebron: Korah:* Johanan, the son of Kareah (Jer 40:8), is probably a descendant of Korah, the first clan listed under Hebron.[108] J. Maxwell Miller, partially on the basis of vv. 42-43, has also argued that the Korahites, to whom eleven psalms are attributed (42–49; 84, 85, 87, and 88), entered Palestine from the direction of Edom (cf. Gen 36:5, 14, 16, 18, where Korah is a descendant of Esau and Oholibamah) and settled among the Calebites in the vicinity of Hebron.[109] He notes that "sons of Korah" (בני קרח) are mentioned in an inscription found in a room associated with the sanctuary at Arad.[110]

■ **46, 48** *Ephah the concubine of Caleb* and *Maacah, Caleb's concubine:* Significant tribal history may lie behind the mention of these two concubines and their descendants (migration, merger, or expansion?), but the unknown character of almost all their descendants blocks our further understanding.[111] These are the only two women explicitly called concubines in Judah's genealogy, except for the generic reference to David's concubines in 1 Chr 3:9.[112] The name Ephah, the concubine of Caleb, also appears as the name of a descendant of Jahdai in v. 47.[113] Interestingly, both of the concubines are given names whereas the mother of the children listed in vv. 42-45 is not even mentioned.

Haran became the father of Jahdai: Jahdai is based on a conjectural emendation of the text (see textual note 41), and this change has the advantage of connecting Jahdai in v. 47 directly to the genealogy of Judah. If one were to retain the MT (Haran became the father of Gazez), Gazez is both the son of Caleb and Ephah and their grandson (through Haran), showing that Gazez traced its origins back to Caleb in two different ways. Since Gazez is unknown elsewhere, it is difficult to choose between these options, but I prefer the emendation because it makes the next verse more coherent.

■ **47** *The sons of Jahdai: Regem, Jotham, Geshan, Pelet, Ephah, and Shaaph:* If the connection to the genealogy discussed in the previous verse is correct, one notes that Ephah appears here three generations later in the genealogy than in v. 46. A town Beth-pelet is mentioned in the Judahite province list (Josh 15:27) and as a city where Judahites settled in the postexilic period (Neh 11:26). Pelet may be connected with this town as may one of David's heroes, Helez the Paltite, in 2 Sam 23:26.[114]

■ **49** *She also bore Shaaph the father of Madmannah, Sheva the father of Machbenah, and X the father of Gibea:* Again the interpreter is faced with a dilemma caused by textual corruption and/or genealogical fluidity (see textual notes 45 and 46). In my translation Maacah the concubine of Caleb bears three additional sons, each of whom is the "father" of a geographical entity. If one follows Rudolph's reconstruction (see textual note 45), Shaaph the descendant of Jahdai (v. 47) is the "father" of

---

107 Ran Zadok, "On the Reliability of the Genealogical and Prosopographical Lists of the Israelites in the Old Testament," *TA* 25 (1998) 244.

108 Demsky, "Clans of Ephrath," 56.

109 "The Korahites of Southern Judah," *CBQ* 32 (1970) 58–68.

110 See Yohanan Aharoni, *Arad Inscriptions* (Jerusalem: Israel Exploration Society, 1981) 80–82. Aharoni conjectures that the ostracon on which this and other names were found is a list of contributors to the Arad sanctuary.

111 For Maacah see 1 Chr 3:2; 19:7; Gen 22:24; Josh 13:13. Johnstone, 1:52, raises the possibility that Tirhanah (v. 48) was a woman, the mother of Shaaph and Sheva.

112 Others that we might count as concubines are Tamar (1 Chr 2:4), the daughter of Machir with whom Hezron had sexual relations (2:21), and Ephrathah, the partner of Caleb (2:24). Other references to concubines occur in 1:32 (Keturah) and 7:14 (the Aramean concubine of Manasseh).

113 In Gen 25:4//1 Chr 1:33 and Isa 60:6 Ephah is a Midianite name. Does this indicate a Calebite link to Midianite territory?

114 See S. Talmon, "The Town Lists of Simeon," *IEJ* 15 (1965) 235–41. Talmon notes, however, that this man is called Helez the Pelonite in 1 Chr 11:27.

Madmannah, and Shaaph's son Sheva is the "father" of Machbenah and Gibea.

and the daughter of Caleb was Achsah: This information was available to the Chronicler from Josh 15:16-19 and Judg 1:12-15. These passages tell us that Caleb the son of Jephunneh gave his daughter Achsah as a wife to his nephew Othniel, the son of Kenaz (cf. 1 Chr 4:13), to reward him for capturing Kiriath-sepher. Thus Achsah forms a link between Caleb the conqueror of Hebron (MR 160103) and the Kenizzite[115] settlement in Kiriath-sepher (= Debir; MR 151093). The Chronicler here associates her with Caleb the son of Hezron and the brother of Jerahmeel, and not with Caleb the son of Jephunneh whose nephew was Othniel. It is unclear in Chronicles which wife of Caleb was intended to be the mother of Achsah. Achsah's name was presumably included for the sake of completeness.

■ **50aα** *These were the sons of Caleb.* This is the conclusion to the preceding genealogy of the Calebites. If one were to follow the verse division in the Hebrew Bible, it could lead to a reading, "These were the sons of Caleb the son of Hur the firstborn of Ephrathah," which would make Caleb the son, not the father, of Hur (cf. 2:19).[116]

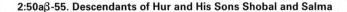

2:50aβ-55. Descendants of Hur and His Sons Shobal and Salma

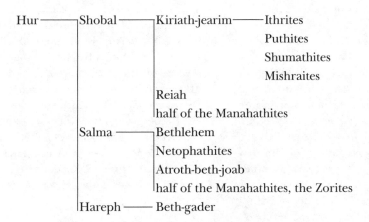

■ **50** *The sons of Hur the firstborn of Ephrathah:* The genealogy in 2:50aβ-55 continues the line of Hur from vv. 19-20, but this genealogy will be interrupted by the listing of David's descendants in chap. 3 and then will be continued in 4:2[117] and ends with 4:4: "These are the sons of Hur the firstborn of Ephrathah, the father of Bethlehem." Hur's descent from Caleb and Ephrath is recorded in v. 19. The spelling of Ephrathah with a final *hê* in this verse is an alternate or by-form of Ephrath in v. 19 and is not to be confused with the *hê* directive on the end of the name Ephrath in v. 24. Ephrathah is associated with Bethlehem in Mic 5:1 (2). This reference to Ephrathah and the reference to Salma the father of Bethlehem in the next verse and v. 54 create a transition

115 Cf. Num 32:12; Josh 14:6, 13; Judg 1:13.
116 Demsky, "Clans of Ephrath," 50, retains the MT reading בן חור (see textual note 47) and considers "Ben Hur" as the oldest son of Caleb-Ephrath.
117 On 1 Chr 4:1, which brings readers back to where they were at the end of chap. 2, see the commentary.

to the genealogy of that great Bethlehemite David in 3:1-24 (Japhet, 73). Willi, 99, believes this section of the genealogy presupposes the location of the Calebites at the time of the Chronicler and is north of that presupposed in 2:42-50aα. The sites that can be located with some surety range from Kiriath-jearim (MR 159135) in the northwest, to Manahath (MR 167128) in the northeast, to Beth-zur (MR 159110) in the southeast, and to Mareshah (MR 140118) in the southwest. The genealogy in 2:42-50aα ranges from MR 84-111, south to north, while the present genealogy ranges from MR 110-135, south to north.

Shobal the father of Kiriath-jearim: Shobal, son of Hur, was the founder or leader of Kiriath-jearim (MR 159135),[118] located 9 miles west of Jerusalem. It is the center from which people migrated out[119] in the rest of Shobal's genealogy, which is continued in vv. 52-53 and 4:2.[120]

■ **51** *Salma the father of Bethlehem, and Hareph the father of Beth-gader:* Salma, the second son of Hur, was the founder or leader of Bethlehem (MR 169123). His name also appeared among the descendants of Ram in v. 11, and he is the father of Boaz, who with his son, grandson, and great grandson (Obed, Jesse, and David) all hailed from Bethlehem (vv. 12-15; cf. Ruth 4:20-21). Salma's inclusion among the descendants of Hur may indicate that the clan of Ram was eventually absorbed by the descendants of his brother Caleb.[121] Hareph,[122] the third son of Hur, was the founder or leader of Beth-gader, which a number of scholars[123] have identified with Gedor (MR 158115), 9 miles southwest of Bethle-

hem. Penuel, a descendant of Hareph, is identified as a "father" of Gedor in 1 Chr 4:4 and Jered is its "father" in 4:18. The genealogy of Hareph is continued in 4:3-4 if the emendation to v. 3 that I have made there is accepted (textual note 5 in chap. 4).

■ **52** *Shobal the father of Kiriath-jearim had sons: Reiah, half of the Manahathites:* The sons of Shobal the father of Kiriath-jearim represent a relationship, and perhaps a migration, to other localities. The genealogy of Reiah the son of Shobal is continued at 4:2. The town Manahath is located at el-Mâlḥa (MR 167128),[124] north and a little west of Bethlehem and southeast of Kiriath-jearim.[125] There is also evidence for a Benjaminite presence there (8:6). With the father-son relationship between Shobal the descendant of Hur and Manahath, compare the Edomite list at 1:38, 40, where Shobal appears as the father of Manahath and among the descendants of Seir, whose clans are identified as Horite in Gen 36:20. Apparently these Horites (החרי) associated with Judah through the similar-sounding Hur (חור).

■ **53** *the Ithrites, the Puthites, the Shumathites, and the Mishraites; from these came the Zorathites and the Eshtaolites:* Demsky associated the Ithrites with a hypothetical בית יתר Bether, which he locates west and slightly north of Bethlehem.[126] He proposes a metathesis of *rêš* and *'ayin* in המשרעי (Mishraites) and associates them with שערים Shaaraim (cf. Josh 15:36; 1 Sam 17:52; 1 Chr 4:31), which he locates 2.5 miles southeast of Beth-shemesh at

---

118 Cf. Josh 15:60, where it is listed among the cities of Judah.

119 Cf. the map in Demsky, "Clans of Ephrath," 55. The migratory interpretation, of course, is not sure, but at least the genealogy shows a relationship among these various sites.

120 Shobal is also listed as a descendant of Seir (1 Chr 1:38) and the father of Manahath (Gen 36:20, 33//1 Chr 1:40).

121 A Ram is also listed as the firstborn of Jerahmeel in v. 25, and three of his sons are listed in v. 27. See the commentary on those verses.

122 Hareph (חרף) is closely related consonantally to the gentilic of Shepatiah the Hariphite (החריפי K; החרופי Q and *NRSV* "Haruphite"). He was one of the warriors who joined David at Hebron (1 Chr

12:6 [5]). The family of Hariph occurs in the list of those who returned from the exile (Neh 7:24), and the name appears among the signers of the "firm agreement" in Neh 10:20 (19). Demsky, "Clans of Ephrath," 51, surmises that Hareph was the ancestor of the Hariphite family that returned from exile.

123 See the bibliography in Demsky, "Clans of Ephrath," 51.

124 It is in the upper part of the Rephaim Valley, modern el-Mālḥa. Cf. Josh 15:59a LXX (Μανοχώ) and 1 Chr 2:54.

125 Cf. the Bethlehem district of Josh 15:59a LXX.

126 "Clans of Ephrath," 52. Cf. Josh 15:59a LXX[B] Θεϑὴρ and LXX[A and other MSS] Βαιϑὴρ. Ithrites appear among David's military heroes (1 Chr 11:40//2 Sam 23:38), where, following Elliger, their

Khirbet Se'ira. Zorah is at Ṣar'ah (MR 148131), just north of Beth-shemesh (MR 147128), and Eshtaol (MR 151132) is located northeast of Zorah.[127] Zorah and Esh-taol are listed among the cities of Judah in Josh 15:33, but they were Danite cities according to Judg 13:2, 25.[128] Both this genealogy and the province list of Judah in Josh 15:20-62 are later than Dan's migration to the north. If we put together the information in vv. 52-53, the genealogy suggests that clans related to Shobal migrated at some point from Kiriath-jearim to Mana-hath, Bether, and Shaaraim, and some families migrated to Zorah[129] and Eshtaol.

■ **54** *The sons of Salma: Bethlehem and the Netophathites, Atroth-beth-joab, and half of the Manahathites, the Zorites:* Continuing the genealogy of v. 51, where Salma is referred to as the "father" of Bethlehem, the genealogy now lists five geographical entities as Salma's descen-dants. Netophah is located at Khirbet Bad Falûḥ (MR 171119), 3 miles southeast of Bethlehem.[130] If Atroth-beth-Joab is the hometown of Joab, David's general, it should probably be located near Tekoa (170115; cf. 2 Sam 14:1-2).[131] Putting together the information in vv. 51 and 54, the genealogy implies that part of the clan of Salma migrated north from Bethlehem to Manahath,

where there were also representatives of Shobal, and part of the clan migrated south from Bethlehem to Netophah and Atroth-beth-joab. Some clans moved on from Manahath to Zorah (cf. v. 53).[132]

■ **55** *The families of the Siphrites settled at Jabez: the Tirathites, the Shimeathites, and the Sucathites:* C. Knights has proposed that this difficult verse describes the migration of three otherwise unknown Kenite families, the Tirathites, the Shimeathites, and the Sucathites, from the lands of Hammath, the founder or leader of a town Beth-rechab, to Kiriath-sepher,[133] whose inhabi-tants are here called Siphrites, and the subsequent fur-ther migration of the families to an unknown site called Jabez.[134] Somewhere along the line the Kenites gained recognition as descendants of Caleb through Hur.[135] In Gen 15:19 the Kenites are named as one of the pre-Israelite inhabitants of the land. Positive relations between the Kenites and Israelites are known as early as the Song of Deborah (Judg 5:24-27; cf. 4:17-21), where Jael the wife of Heber the Kenite killed Sisera, a Canaan-ite army commander, who was fighting against Israel.[136] The MT has "scribes" instead of Siphrites, but it seems unlikely that scribes would be located only at one place and at an unknown place at that.[137]

---

city is often identified as Jattir (MR 151084), but that seems much too far south for this context. See, however, Baruch Halpern, "The Rise of Abimelek Ben-Jerubbaal," *HAR* 2 (1978) 79–100.

127 The antecedent of "from these" is unclear. Does it refer to the Mishraites or to all four gentilics?

128 Cf. Josh 19:41. Zorah was one of the cities that was settled on Israel's return from exile (Neh 11:29).

129 In 2 Chr 11:10 Zorah is one of Rehoboam's fortresses.

130 Levites lived there in postexilic times (1 Chr 9:16), as did singers (Neh 12:28), and people from Netophah were among those who returned from exile (Ezra 2:21-22//Neh 7:26). Two of David's mighty men, Maharai and Heleb/Heled/Heldai, who also were supervisors of the royal service, came from this city (1 Chr 11:30//2 Sam 23:28-29; cf. 1 Chr 27:13, 15).

131 In 1 Kgs 2:34 his house is located near the wilder-ness.

132 The spelling difference between הצרעי in v. 54 and הצרעתי in v. 53 and 4:2 is not explained. *HALOT* 3:1057, lists both of them as gentilics of צָרְעָה .

133 The city, also known as Debir, is located at Khirbet er-Rabūd (MR 151093). Kurt Galling, "Zur

Lokalisierung von Debir," *ZDPV* 70 (1954) 139, thought that Kiriath-sepher should be understood etymologically as "Book City." Since leather made from sheep or goat skins was the primary writing material in Palestine, it gained this name because of its production of leather.

134 An anecdote about a person named Jabez appears in 1 Chr 4:9-10. See C. H. Knights, "Kenites = Rech-abites? 1 Chronicles ii 55 reconsidered," *VT* 43 (1993) 10–18.

135 Isaac Kalimi, "Three Assumptions about the Ken-ites," *ZAW* 100 (1988) 391, notes that there is no biblical mention of the Kenites after the time of David, and the Kenites may have been assimilated into the tribe of Judah during the monarchy.

136 Saul mentions the kindness of the Kenites to the Israelites when they came out of Egypt (1 Sam 15:6). In Judg 1:16 and 4:11, the father-in-law of Moses is called a Kenite.

137 Samuel Klein, "Die Schreiberfamilien: 1 Chronik 2:55," *MGWJ* 70 (1926) 410–16, used this passage in an attempt to prove there were scribes in the preex-ilic period.

These are the Kenites who came from Hammath, father of Beth-rechab: Knights argues that this verse does not support the idea that the Rechabites were Kenites even though this passage has frequently been used to argue for a primitive connection between these two groups. In fact, this passage does not refer to the Rechabites at all. Beth-rechab is a place name, of which Hammath is its "father" or founder, and not a name for (a guild of) Rechabites.[138] The site of Beth-rechab is unknown, but may be related to Beth-marcaboth (Josh 19:5; 1 Chr 4:31) in the Beer-sheba area.[139] Hammath[140] is a personal name, as is expected with the "X father of Y" formula. The genealogy of the sons of Hur continues in 4:2. The insertion of chap. 3 and the addition of 4:1 are both the work of the Chronicler (Japhet, 73).[141]

Conclusion

The Chronicler begins his genealogies of the twelve tribes with the genealogy of Judah, the most important tribe of the postexilic community. His chiastic arrangement of this genealogy puts the most important Judahite, David, at the center of this genealogy. The Judahite ancestors of David are recorded in this chapter, and his descendants are recorded in chap. 3. The Chronicler's use of these materials may have been limited in part by those genealogies that were available to him, but some of his motivation or message can be inferred from a careful study of this genealogy. Willi may well be right that the Chronicler was noting a movement of the Calebites-Judahites from the area around Hebron to the area around Bethlehem and Jerusalem, just as the kingship of David itself started in Hebron and ended up in Jerusalem. The Chronicler's openness to outsiders can be seen in that he included six instances in which a Judahite had married a foreigner, but none of these liaisons is judged or condemned. While there are limitations on the understanding of this passage because of the fragmentary state of parts of the genealogy, the careful reader can also partially discern the function of some of these genealogies before they were included in the Chronicler's work.[142]

---

138 The Rechabite leader in Jer 35:2-19 and 2 Kgs 10:15-17, 23 is Jehonadab (or Jondabab), the son of Rechab. Rechab is probably a personal name in these accounts and not a reference to the city of Rechab (1 Chr 4:12) or Beth-rechab (2:55). For an understanding of the Rechabites as a guild of smiths, see Frank S. Frick, "Rechab," *ABD* 5:630–32; idem, "The Rechabites Reconsidered," *JBL* 90 (1971) 279–87.

139 In both passages there is a reference to Hazar-susah or Hazar-susim, which is located just west of Beer-sheba at Khirbet Abu Suseim.

140 Shemaryahu Talmon, "1 Chron. 2:55," *IEJ* 10 (1969) 174–80, argued that Hammath was a noun meaning "family" and translated "These are the Kenites who come from the family-in-law of the house of Rechab" (cf. *NEB:* "These were the Kenites who were connected by marriage with the ancestor of the Rechabites"). This noun is otherwise unattested in Hebrew, and Knights, "Kenites = Rechabites?" 14, has noted that בא followed by the preposition "from" always has a spatial or geographical meaning. Talmon, 178, identified Jehonadab as the father of the house of Rechab, which has been ruled out by Knights's disassociation of the Kenites with the Rechabites.

141 Williamson, 59, however, dates 1 Chr 4:1 earlier than Chronicles and notes that this verse has a different line of descent from Judah. He also argues that a list beginning "the sons of X" in Chronicles is never followed with a list of names from father to son, but only by a list of brothers. But if the Chronicler is summing up where the genealogy had been before the interruption of chap. 3, he may have broken from his usual genealogical style. See also 3:16.

142 Gerrie Snyman, "A Possible World of Text Production for the Genealogy in 1 Chronicles 2.3–4.23," in Graham, McKenzie, and Knoppers, *Chronicler as Theologian,* 32–60, finds in the genealogy of Judah a calculated effort to include people who had not been part of the preexilic tribe of Judah. The people in this territory were administered by a ruling elite with ties to the Persian imperial government. Membership in the community was linked via this genealogy to the pre-deportation history of the territory.

3

Translation 3:1-24

3:1—4:23 Descendants of David; Genealogical Fragments

1/ These were the sons of David who were born to him in Hebron: the firstborn Amnon, by Ahinoam the Jezreelite; the second[1] Daniel,[2] by Abigail the Carmelite;[3] 2/ the third Absalom[4] the son of Maacah, daughter of Talmai king of Geshur; the fourth Adonijah the son of Haggith; 3/ the fifth Shephatiah, by Abital;[5] the sixth Ithream, by his wife[6] Eglah. 4/ Six were born to him[7] in Hebron, and he reigned there for seven years and six months.[8] And he reigned thirty-three years in Jerusalem.[9] 5/ And these were born[10] to him in Jerusalem: Shimea,[11] Shobab, Nathan, and Solomon, four by Bathshua[12] the daughter of Ammiel.[13] 6/ Then Ibhar, Elishama,[14] Eliphelet, 7/ Nogah, Nepheg, Japhia, 8/ Elishama, Eliada,[15] and Eliphelet, nine.[16] 9/ All these were David's sons, besides the sons of the concubines; and Tamar was their sister.

10/ The son[17] of Solomon: Rehoboam, Abijah his son, Asa his son, Jehoshaphat his son, 11/ Joram his son, Ahaziah his son, Joash his son, 12/ Amaziah his son, Azariah[18] his son, Jotham his son, 13/ Ahaz his son, Hezekiah his son, Manasseh his son, 14/ Amon his son, Josiah his son; 15/ and the sons of Josiah: Johanan[19] the firstborn, the second Jehoiakim, the third Zedekiah, the fourth Shallum. 16/ The descendants of Jehoiakim: Jeconiah his son, Zedekiah his son; 17/ and the sons[20] of Jeconiah, the captive:[21] Shealtiel his son,[22] 18/ and Malchiram, Pedaiah, Shenazzar, Jekamiah, Hoshama,[23] and Nedabiah. 19/ The sons of Pedaiah:[24] Zerubbabel and Shimei;[25] and the sons[26] of Zerubbabel:[27] Meshullam and Hananiah, and Shelomith was their sister; 20/ and Hashubah,[28] Ohel,[29] Berechiah, Hasadiah, and Jushab-hesed,[30] five.[31] 21/ The sons[32] of Hananiah: Pelatiah and Jeshaiah, the sons of[33] Rephaiah, the sons of[34] Arnan, the sons of[35] Obadiah, the sons of[36] Shecaniah.[37] 22/ The sons[38] of Shecaniah: Shemaiah. And the sons of Shemaiah:[39] Hattush, Igal,[40] Bariah, Neariah, and Shaphat, six. 23/ The sons[41] of Neariah: Elioenai, Hizkiah, and Azrikam, three. 24/ The sons of Elioenai: Hodaviah,[42] Eliashib, Pelaiah, Akkub, Johanan, Delaiah, and Anani, seven.

1 השני, with LXX, Syr, Tg. MT lacks the article by haplography. Cf. 2 Sam 3:3: ומשנהו "his second." In readings discussed in textual notes 3, 5, 7, and 9, Chronicles presupposes a text of Samuel other than Samuel MT.

2 דניאל. Chronicles LXX[ANrell] Δαλουια, following 2 Sam 3:3 LXX; Chronicles Syr. klb, following 2 Sam 3:3 MT כלאב (the first three letters of the next word are לאב). For Chronicles MT see Josephus, *Ant.* 7.21. The text of 4QSam[a] reads דלויע according to Herbert, *Reconstructing*, 104, but there is some uncertainty about each of the letters. Ulrich, *Qumran Text*, 81, reads דלויה, which McCarter, *II Samuel 7*, 101, adopts as the original reading for 2 Sam 3:3.

3 הכרמלית. Cf. 2 Sam 3:3 4QSam[a] (which actually preserves only the definite article), LXX, OL (which also call Abigail the Carmelite and do not mention Nabal); 2 Sam 3:3 MT: אשת נבל הכרמלי "the wife of Nabal the Carmelite" (cf. 2 Sam 2:2).

4 אבשלום with many Hebrew MSS and versions; MT adds a preposition *lāmed*, perhaps under the influence of Abigail, which is written with this preposition in the previous verse. Braun, 48, proposes that the *lāmed* is used "loosely." Chronicles LXX and Syr presuppose אבישלום "Abishalom," following Samuel LXX.

5 לאביטל; cf. 2 Sam 3:4 LXX. 2 Sam 3:4 MT בן אביטל "the son of Abital."

6 אשתו; LXX[L], Syr, following 2 Sam 3:5, "the wife of David."

7 לו. 2 Sam 3:5 MT, LXX[BAMN]: לדוד. Both readings are combined in Samuel LXX[L], demonstrating that the reading in Chronicles is probably based on an alternate text of Samuel.

8 LXX[Bhc₂] lack "and he reigned there for seven years and six months."

9 2 Sam 5:5 LXX puts the words "in Jerusalem" at the end of the clause as in Chronicles; Samuel MT puts them at the beginning of the clause.

10 נולדו. Rudolph, 24, interprets MT (cf. 1 Chr 20:8) as a combination of נולדו (*niphal* 3d masc. pl. perfect, with two Hebrew MSS) and ילדו (*pual/qal* passive 3d masc. pl. imperfect). Cf. 2 Sam 5:14 הילדים, a plural noun and 1 Chr 14:4 הילודים, a *qal* passive participle.

11 שמעא. Syr, following 1 Chr 14:4 and 2 Sam 5:14, שמוע "Shammua."

12 לבת־שוע. One Hebrew MS and Vg (cf. LXX): לבת־שבע "Bathsheba." Syr omits "four by Bathshua," a harmonization with 2 Sam 5:14.

13 עמיאל. 2 Sam 11:3 אליעם "Eliam." The two elements of the name have been reversed.

14 ואלישמע. 1 Chr 14:5 and 2 Sam 5:15 ואלישוע "Elishua"; cf. two Hebrew MSS of 1 Chr 3:6. Nonetheless, the MT reading, though secondary in

anticipation of Elishama in v. 8, should be retained as the earliest attestable reading in this verse, contra *NIV*.

15 ואלידע. 1 Chr 14:7 ובעלידע "Beeliada"; cf. 2 Sam 5:15 LXX.

16 תשעה; *BHS* proposes an emendation: שבעה "seven," based on its deletion of Eliphelet and Nogah from vv. 6-7.

17 ובן. A few Hebrew MSS, LXX, Syr: ובני "sons."

18 עזרע; many Hebrew MSS עזריהו. LXX[L], Syr, Arab. presuppose עזיה "Uzziah," a correction to the corresponding spelling in Kings. Syr, Tg: "his son Azariah, that is, Uzziah." See the discussion under Structure.

19 יוהנן; LXX[Nbnye]2, Arab.: Jehoahaz." See the commentary.

20 ובני; *Sebir:* ובן "and the son." Cf. Syr. Braun, 49, notes that the singular "son" is followed by more than one son in vv. 20, 21, 23, that the plural "sons" is followed by many sons in vv. 17, 19, 22b, 24, and that the plural "sons" is followed by a single son in v. 22.

21 האסר. The article is lacking in MT by haplography after יכניה. LXX and Vg construe this word as a personal name and Syr joins it to the following name. Assir does appear elsewhere as a proper noun (Exod 6:24; 1 Chr 6:7, 8, 22 [22, 23, 37]).

22 בנו; *BHS* proposes בכרו "his firstborn." Omitted by LXX[ab*] and Vg. Williamson, 57, would follow the *BHS* proposal or omit the word. See the commentary for an explanation of the MT reading.

23 הושמע. Syr lost the initial *hê* by haplography.

24 פדיה; LXX שאלתיאל "Shealtiel." Cf. Hag 1:1; Ezra 3:2; Matt 1:12; Luke 3:27. Syr "Nedabiah." LXX[bdfjpqtzc]2 correct the original LXX to MT. See the commentary.

25 Omitted by LXX[Bdpc]2.

26 ובני, with *Sebir* and some Hebrew MSS, LXX, Syr, Arab.; MT ובן "and the son."

27 זרבבל. *BHS* suggests a possible addition בבבל "in Babylon," which was lost by homoioteleuton. See the commentary.

28 *BHS* notes a proposed addition at the beginning of the verse: ואחרי שובו "and after his return," and suggests deleting the initial *wāw* on Hashubah. See the commentary.

29 ואהל. Syr יהואיל ויהו. Cf. LXX[m] οιηλ.

30 ויושב חסד with LXX; conjunction lacking in MT. LXX[Aal] presuppose ישוב החסד, parsing the verbal part of the name as *qal* instead of *hophal*.

31 חמש; one would expect חמשה.

32 ובני with *Sebir* and a few Hebrew MSS, LXX, Syr, Tg, Arab.; MT ובן "The son."

33 בני. One Hebrew MS, LXX, Vg: בנו "his son." Rudolph, 28, and *BHS* propose reading only ו "and." See the commentary for this note and the following three notes.

34 בני. LXX, Vg: בנו "his son." Rudolph, 28, and *BHS* read only ו "and."

35 בני. LXX, Vg: בנו "his son." Rudolph, 28, and *BHS* read only ו "and."

36 בני. LXX, Vg: בנו "his son." Rudolph, 28, and *BHS* read only ו "and."

37 LXX adds "his son."

38 ובני. *Sebir* and LXX, Vg, Syr: ובן "son."

39 Rudolph, 28, and *BHS* delete "And the sons of Shemaiah."

40 ויגאל; LXX "Joel."

41 ובני with *Sebir* and some Hebrew MSS, LXX, Tg; MT ובן "The son."

42 הודיוהו Q, Tg; cf. LXX. K הדיוהו (omission of *mater lectionis*; metathesis of *yôd* and *wāw*).

3:1-24

Structure

This chapter contains a genealogy of the descendants of David, beginning with David's own children, continuing with his descendants after Solomon who were the kings of Judah, and finishing with the descendants of Jehoia-chin, the second last king of Judah, for eight more generations (see the genealogical chart "Descendants of David").[1] Only the last section, section 4, is without a comprehensive biblical parallel.[2] This whole chapter forms part II.H in the genealogy of Judah running from 2:3 through 4:23 (see Structure in the commentary on chap. 2).

---

1   For social scientific observations on the early parts of this genealogy, see James W. Flanagan, "Succession and Genealogy in the Davidic Dynasty," in *The Quest for the Kingdom of God* (FS G. E. Mendenhall; ed. H. B. Huffmon, F. A. Spina, and A. R. W. Green; Winona Lake, IN: Eisenbrauns, 1983) 35–55.

2   Shealtiel is mentioned in the Bible from the first generation after Shecaniah, Zerubbabel from the second, and possibly Hattush from the sixth. See the commentary.

1. 3:1-4. Children of David who were born in Hebron (//2 Sam 3:2-5; 5:5)
2. 3:5-9. Children of David who were born in Jerusalem (//2 Sam 5:13-16 and 1 Chr 14:3-7)
3. 3:10-16. Descendants of Solomon who served as kings of Judah
4. 3:17-24. Descendants of Jeconiah for seven generations

The names in section 1 appear here only as a list whereas in 2 Samuel the list is integrated into the narrative. In 2 Sam 3:1 the list is introduced as follows: "There was a long war between the house of Saul and the house of David; David grew stronger and stronger, while the house of Saul became weaker and weaker."[3] It is readily understandable why the Chronicler omitted this verse since in 1 Chronicles 10–11 he describes a seamless transition from the reign of Saul to David, with no mention of the rival kingship set up by Ishbosheth. In the Chronicler's telling, the whole house of Saul came to an end on the battlefield at Gilboa. The exact nature of the list in section 1 itself is somewhat unclear since each of the six wives mentioned bears one child,[4] and three of these six sons play an important role in the discussion of the succession to David in 2 Samuel and 1 Kings: Absalom in 2 Samuel 13–19, until his death by the hand of Joab (cf. also 2 Sam 20:6); Amnon in 2 Samuel 13, until he was killed by the servants of Absalom in v. 29; and Adonijah in 1 Kings 1–2, where he attempted to get himself anointed king while David was on his deathbed. Thanks to the planning of Nathan and Bathsheba, Solomon became king during David's lifetime and Adonijah was executed by Benaiah on orders from Solomon in 1 Kgs 2:25. None of these three stories was included by the Chronicler, and these three men are not even mentioned in his work outside this passage. The list seems originally to be a list of the firstborn of each of six of David's wives during his reign in Hebron rather than the total number of children born there as stated in vv. 1 and 4. Detailed differences between vv. 1-4 and its *Vorlage* will be discussed in the commentary.

The unique feature of section 2, the children of David who were born in Jerusalem, is that its substance is also included in 1 Chr 14:3-7 at a spot corresponding to its position in the narrative of 2 Samuel 5. While Rudolph, 11, 26, used this duplication as one of his reasons for denying 1 Chronicles 3 to the Chronicler, the different use of this list of the descendants born in Jerusalem in its two contexts justifies the duplication. This list differs in genre from section 1, where a mother was named for each child, since only Bath-shua is mentioned among the mothers of David's children, and then only here in v. 5 and not either in the *Vorlage* from 2 Sam 5:14 or in its use at 1 Chr 14:3-7. While 2 Sam 5:13 is included at 1 Chr 14:3, it is omitted here in chap. 3, although there are two allusions to it in 1 Chr 3:9 ("concubines," his daughter Tamar), which was composed by the Chronicler. Verse 9 serves as a summary conclusion to this section in Chronicles. Note how "All these were David's sons" in v. 9 forms an *inclusio* with "These were the sons of David" in v. 1.

Section 3 provides a genealogical list of the descendants of Solomon who served as king in Jerusalem. Athaliah is omitted, perhaps because of the evil character of her reign (see 2 Chr 22:10—23:21), but also surely because she was not a descendant of David since she was the granddaughter of Omri and the daughter of Ahab (2 Chr 21:6; 22:2). For two of these royal names, the Chronicler employs the spelling of the name given in the book of Kings or Jeremiah rather than in his own narrative.[5] Azariah (v. 12) is the king known in the narrative of Chronicles as Uzziah (2 Chronicles 26; cf. 2 Chr 27:2), but known primarily though not exclusively as Azariah in Kings (2 Kings 15; cf. 14:21).[6] The king called Jeconiah (יכניה) in this genealogy (vv. 16-17) is called Jehoiachin (יהויכין) in both the narrative of Chronicles (2 Chr 36:8-9) and in the narrative of Kings (2 Kgs 24:6,

---

3   After the listing of David's wives and their sons, presumably indicating the growth of David's strength, the paragraph continues with an account of Abner's growing strength in the rival reign of Ishbosheth (2 Sam 3:6).

4   Abigail and Ahinoam were married to David before his reign began in Hebron, though we are not told if they had children before David's days in Hebron.

5   But he does use the name Abijah for the successor of Rehoboam in v. 10 (as in 2 Chr 12:16; 13:1, 22, 23) rather than Abijam (as in 1 Kgs 14:31; 15:1, 7 [twice], 8).

6   The name Uzziah appears in 2 Kgs 15:30, 32, 34. See the correction to Uzziah in some Chronicles versions (textual note 18).

8, 12, 15; 25:27//Jer 52:31). The form Jeconiah does appear in Esth 2:6; Jer 24:1; 27:20; 28:4; and 29:2.[7] These spelling variations suggest either that the Chronicler constructed this list on the basis of the Kings' narrative (Williamson, 56), or, more likely in my judgment, that he was using an independent list of the names of the kings from a source that was available to him. The form of the genealogy changes in vv. 15-16 since three sons of Josiah succeeded him on the throne whereas there was only one son who served as king in the place of his father in each of the previous cases. The differences in vv. 15-16 from the narrative in both Kings and Chronicles confirm the conclusion that the Chronicler was drawing on an independent list of kings. For discussion of the complications or unclarities in this genealogy see the commentary.

The descendants of Jeconiah, section 4, are known to us in the Bible only through these verses, except for Shealtiel, Zerubbabel, and perhaps Shecaniah and Hattush.[8] There are textual uncertainties in each verse[9] and an important conflict between the information about Zerubbabel's father in v. 19 and data available about Zerubbabel elsewhere in the Bible. The source used by the Chronicler in these verses is otherwise unknown to us.

How do these four sections function in Chronicles? I referred earlier to the chiasm detected by Williamson in the genealogy of Judah, in which the sons of Ram in 2:10-17, ending with the listing of David and his siblings in vv. 13-17, are matched in the chiasm by chap. 3, the descendants of David. By placing Judah at the head of the tribes, Benjamin at the end, and the Levites in the middle, the Chronicler has given special prominence to the tribe of Judah, and it makes a good deal of sense for him to provide genealogical detail on the most promi-

nent family within that tribe, namely the ancestors and the descendants of David the first king.[10] The chiastic arrangement of Ram in 2:10-17 and this chapter give emphasis to both the ancestry and the descendants of David. Throughout the narrative sections of Chronicles, beginning with 10:14, David and his descendants will be the leading characters in every generation. We can only conjecture as to why the list of descendants after the exile was preserved. Some, like Zerubbabel or even Shelomith, could have used this genealogy to show their status as heirs of David, and other individuals or groups may have taken pride in this ancestry. Perhaps it gave legitimacy to some individual or group, much as the genealogy of Saul functioned in its prebiblical context to give the pedigree of a military group (see the commentary on 8:40). Some may even have hoped for a restoration of the Davidic kingship, though we find no expectation that could be termed messianic in this listing in Chronicles itself.[11]

Willi, 108, has called attention to the minimal use of explicitly royal vocabulary in chap. 3. Remarkably, the only use of the word "king" in this chapter refers to Talmai, the king of Geshur (v. 2). The only use of the verb "to reign" refers to David in v. 4. This has led him to stress another implicit emphasis of this chapter: the nearly uninterrupted inhabitation of Jerusalem as exemplified by the family of David. Sections 1 and 2 show the movement from Hebron to Jerusalem, stressed in vv. 4-5, just as the Calebites in 2:50aβ-55 moved from the Hebron region to the northern part of Judah. The descendants of Solomon dwelled in Jerusalem for the next four centuries. While there had been a brief hiatus due to the exile (note the reference to the captivity of Jeconiah in v. 17), the subsequent list of Jeconiah's descendants shows that the Davidic, and therefore also

---

7   Coniah (כניהו), a third spelling of this name, occurs in Jer 22:24, 28; 37:1.

8   For Shealtiel and Pedaiah in vv. 17-19 and for Shecaniah and Hattush in vv. 21-22, see the commentary. Shelomith (v. 19) and Anani (v. 24) are probably attested extrabiblically as the commentary below will point out.

9   In the reconstruction below, there are eight generations after Jeconiah to the end of the genealogy. Japhet, 94, sets the possible range from seven to fourteen generations after Jeconiah.

10   David and his line are given prominence because of

the predominant character of Judah among the tribes.

11   Contra J. W. Rothstein, *Die Genealogie des Königs Jojachin und seiner Nachkommen (1 Chron. 3, 17-24) in geschichtlicher Beleuchtung: Eine kritische Studie zur jüdaischen Geschichte und Literatur* (Berlin: Ruther & Reichard, 1902). Johnson, *Purpose*, 139–256 discusses the messianic interpretation of the Davidic genealogies in the NT (Matt 1:1-17 and Luke 3:23-38). For extensive bibliography on this question, see Gary N. Knoppers, "The Davidic Genealogy: Some

the Judahite and Israelite, inhabiting of Jerusalem continued until the Chronicler's day. One of the functions of 4:1-23 according to this interpretation is to show descendants of Caleb or Judah living throughout individual regions of the territory of the tribe (Willi, 120). While chap. 3 does interrupt the genealogy of Caleb, the section of the genealogy of Judah after the interruption of chap. 3 forms part of a new composition, put together by the Chronicler from various sources (see the discussion in chap. 4).

Finally, this genealogy may be evaluated for its chronological implications, for its own date and for the date of Chronicles, but with the caution that the exact number of generations contained in this genealogy is uncertain (see especially the commentary on v. 21). If Shealtiel (v. 17) was born after Jeconiah was taken captive and there were five sons of Jeconiah by 592 BCE, we can date the birth of Pedaiah (v. 18), the third son born to Jeconiah in captivity to about 595 BCE. Allowing twenty years between one descendant's birth and that of his son (Josiah was fourteen when his first son was born and Jehoiakim eighteen),[12] we can then propose the following birthdates: Zerubbabel (v. 19) 575; Hananiah (v. 19) 555; Shecaniah (v. 21) 535; Shemaiah (v. 22) 515; Neariah (v. 22) 495; Elioenai (v. 23) 475; and Anani (v. 24) 455, making him forty-eight years old in 407 BCE (when his name seems to appear in one of the Elephantine papyri).[13] If this genealogy is original in Chronicles, it precludes a date for authorship before the late fifth century. See also the discussion of Date in the Introduction.

Detailed Commentary

3:1-4. Children of David Who Were Born in Hebron
3:1-4[14]

David and Ahinoam	——————	Amnon
David and Abigail	——————	Daniel
David and Maacah	——————	Absalom
David and Haggith	——————	Adonijah
David and Abital	——————	Shephatiah
David and Eglah	——————	Ithream

■ **1** *These were the sons of David who were born to him in Hebron:* The corresponding text in the *Vorlage* at 2 Sam 3:2 reads: "And sons were born to David at Hebron." The Chronicler uses the *niphal* third masculine singular perfect for the word "born," as in 1 Chr 2:3, 9 and 3:4, instead of the *niphal* imperfect with *wāw* consecutive third masculine plural.[15] Note that the first four verses focus on Hebron (MR 160103) while the rest of the chapter refers to Jerusalem (MR 172131).

the firstborn Amnon by Ahinoam the Jezreelite: David's marriage to Ahinoam is reported in 1 Sam 25:43.[16] Ahinoam and Abigail were taken captive when the Amalekites raided Ziklag but were later rescued by David (1 Sam 30:5, 18). David took Ahinoam and Abigail to Hebron when he went there to be anointed by Judah (2 Sam 2:2-4). For Amnon's rape of his half-sister Tamar and his subsequent death, see 2 Samuel 13.

the second Daniel, by Abigail the Carmelite: The text of the *Vorlage* in 2 Sam 3:3 MT reads: "And his second

---

Contextual Considerations from the Ancient Mediterranean World," *Transeuphratène* 21 (2001) 37, n. 10.

12 The number twenty is admittedly arbitrary, and in three cases (Hananiah, Shecaniah, and Neariah) the line was not continued through the oldest son. Hence the chronology might extend for a few more decades beyond the figures suggested in my calculations.

13 Jacob M. Myers, "The Kerygma of the Chronicler," *Int* 20 (1966) 260, assigns twenty-five years to a generation, which places the birth of Anani at 405 BCE, obviously too late if this is the person named in the Elephantine papyri.

14 2 Sam 3:3-5 adds the conjunction "and" before "third," "fourth," "fifth," and "sixth." It spells

"Amnon" אמנון (plene) instead of אמנן (defectively). It also adds the conjunction before "his second" in v. 3, whereas 3:1 reads "the second."

15 Q: 4QSam^a ויולד *niphal* 3d masc. sg. imperfect with *wāw* consecutive. K is *pual* (*qal* passive?) 3d masc. pl. imperfect with *wāw* consecutive.

16 Note that Ahinoam was also the name of Saul's wife (1 Sam 14:50).

Chileab by Abigail the wife of Nabal the Carmelite." Abigail's own Judahite tribal ancestry is attested by the Chronicler since he calls Abigail herself, and not Nabal, "the Carmelite,"[17] but the Chronicler does omit the fact that she was the (former) wife of Nabal.[18] If this omission is meant to suppress the questionable status of Abigail, it is important to note that this change is already known in the textual history of Samuel (cf. textual note 3). No biographical detail in narrative contexts is provided for Chileab (Samuel) or Daniel (Chronicles) by either book. Many scholars assume he died at an early age since he seems not to be among the competitors to be David's successor.[19] The LXX of 2 Sam 3:3 reads $\Delta\alpha\lambda ov\iota\alpha$,[20] which can be transliterated into Hebrew as דלאה and so serve as a transitional term between "Chileab" and "Daniel" (Curtis and Madsen, 100). A better transliteration, however, would be דלויה, which McCarter adopts as the original reading in Samuel.[21] Ordinal numerals for children also occur for the sons of Josiah in 1 Chr 3:15 (cf. the sons of Jesse in 2:13-15).

■ **2** *The third Absalom the son of Maacah, daughter of Talmai king of Geshur:* Note that Maacah, a foreign wife, is mentioned without criticism by the Chronicler, as has been true with other foreign marriages in the genealogy of Judah.[22] This was probably a political marriage by David, laying claim to an area that may have been under the control of Ishbaal the son of Saul.[23]

the fourth Adonijah the son of Haggith: Adonijah's attempt to seize the throne and his subsequent execution by order of Solomon is reported in 1 Kings 1–2. Nothing is known about Haggith except that she is Adonijah's mother.

■ **3** *The fifth Shephatiah, by Abital:* In 2 Sam 3:4 Shephatiah is called "the son of Abital" בן אביטל instead of the expression used here, לאביטל, but this synonymous variant is already attested by the LXX in Samuel and therefore is not to be attributed to the Chronicler (see textual note 5).

the sixth Ithream, by his wife Eglah: In 1 Chr 3:3 Eglah is called "his wife," whereas 2 Sam 3:5 calls her "the wife of David." No significance is to be given to this change and the Lucianic family of MSS in Chronicles changes the text back to agree with Samuel MT.

■ **4** *Six were born to him in Hebron:* The Chronicler changes the *qal* passive[24] imperfect from 2 Sam 3:5 to the *niphal* perfect. His addition of the number "six" corresponds to his frequent inclusion of totals for the number of children in this chapter,[25] but it also corresponds to the mention of "six" sons in 2 Sam 3:2 LXX[L]. If this latter reading was the source of the Chronicler's addition in this verse, it would be another case where he was dependent on a non-MT reading in Samuel.

and he reigned there for seven years and six months. And he reigned thirty-three years in Jerusalem: This text is not

---

17　This gentilic refers to Carmel (MR 162092), a town about 8 miles southeast of Hebron (MR 160103; for Carmel see Josh 15:12; 1 Sam 25:2; 27:3; 30:5; 2 Sam 2:2; and 3:3, all but the first referring either to Nabal or Abigail).

18　Cf. 1 Sam 27:3, 30:5; 2 Sam 2:2. In each case *NRSV* translates אשת as "widow." Tg puns on the letters of Chileab (כל = all and אב = father), adding after Daniel: "that is, Chileab, who resembled his own father in every way." This resemblance between Daniel/Chileab and David was apparently meant to allay the suspicion that he had been conceived when Abigail was still married to Nabal. Cf. McIvor, *Targum,* 55, n. 4.

19　Halpern, *David's Secret Demons,* 365, n. 12, notes that rabbinic tradition concluded that Chileab was fathered by Nabal and was only born after Abigail married David. This explained for them why he was not part of the struggle for succession.

20　This reading is also attested by the majority of LXX MSS in Chronicles, which have probably been cor-

rected to the text of Samuel, although Chronicles LXX[B] presupposes "Daniel" by its reading $\Delta\alpha\mu\nu\iota\eta\lambda$.

21　*II Samuel,* 101. דלויה became דלאב under the influence of the following word (ולאבינגל), and a *dālet/kāp* switch led to Chileab. But the development from either Dalouiah or Chileab into Daniel is unexplained.

22　Judah and Bath-shua; Jether the Ishmaelite and Abigail the sister of David; a daughter of Sheshan, a descendant of Jerahmeel and Jarha an Egyptian slave; the Judahite Mered and Bithiah daughter of Pharaoh; and some descendants of Shelah who married into Moab.

23　J. D. Levenson and B. Halpern, "The Political Import of David's Marriages," *JBL* 99 (1980) 507–18.

24　*HALOT* 2:412. Interpreted by BDB, 408, as *pual.*

25　"Four" in v. 5; "nine" in v. 8; "five" in v. 20; "six" in v. 22; "three" in v. 23; "seven" in v. 24.

contained in 2 Sam 3:5, but a very similar text is contained in 2 Sam 5:5, which served here as the Chronicler's source: "In Hebron he reigned over Judah seven years and six months, and in Jerusalem he ruled thirty-three years over Israel and Judah."[26] The Chronicler omitted "over Judah" from the first clause and "over Israel and Judah" from the second since David's reign already in Hebron was over all Israel (1 Chr 11:1-3).[27] The LXX of 2 Sam 5:5, like 1 Chr 3:4, puts the words "in Jerusalem" at the end of the clause. Jerusalem was captured by David (1 Chr 11:4-9//2 Sam 5:6-10), which had originally been possessed by the Jebusites, who were not replaced until the time of David (cf. Josh 15:63). This is the first mention of Jerusalem in Chronicles. Altogether the word appears 151 times in the books of Chronicles, about 23 percent of its mentions in the whole OT.[28]

3:5-9. Children of David Who Were Born in Jerusalem

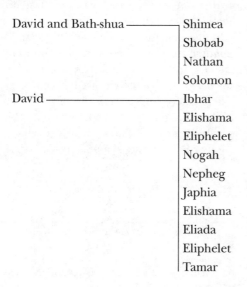

David and Bath-shua — Shimea
Shobab
Nathan
Solomon
David — Ibhar
Elishama
Eliphelet
Nogah
Nepheg
Japhia
Elishama
Eliada
Eliphelet
Tamar

■ **5** *And these were born to him in Jerusalem:* This reading corresponds approximately to 2 Sam 5:14 and the Chronicler's own version of this clause at 1 Chr 14:4, with the customary substitution of the *niphal* perfect verb form[29] and the omission of the word "names." *Shimea, Shobab, Nathan, and Solomon, four by Bath-shua the daughter of Ammiel:* The four names are the same as those in the Samuel *Vorlage* as well as the Chronicler's own text in 1 Chr 14:4.[30] The surprise is that the Chronicler now makes all four of them children of Bath-shua, his spelling of the name of David's well-known wife Bathsheba. This spelling creates a parallel with the first wife of Judah in 1 Chr 2:3-4.[31] The inclusion of this name implies that Solomon is the fourth child of David and Bath-shua, whereas 2 Sam 12:24-25, not included in Chronicles, makes clear that Solomon is the first child of David and Bathsheba, after the death of their son conceived in adultery. The difficulty would be removed if "four" were identified as a later gloss made by someone who added the total number of children here and at the end of the verse ("nine"), as frequently elsewhere in this chapter, without noticing the factual difficulty these additional numbers created.[32] Without the number four, one might translate "Shimea, Shobab, and Nathan, and Solomon by Bath-shua." Isaac Kalimi, however, has pointed out that the list of names is constructed according to the "three-four" principle, meaning that the fourth name, Solomon, is in the most important position.[33] As with the choice of David, the three oldest brothers are disqualified and the youngest chosen. Solomon also was born in the proper place, Jerusalem. Solomon and all the subsequent kings, yes, even all the descendants of David and Solomon down to Anani, were born and lived there, except for Jeconiah, who was exiled to Babylon, and his sons and grandsons, who

---

26 Cf. also 1 Chr 29:27//1 Kgs 2:11.

27 He also did not include David's age of 30 at his accession from 2 Sam 5:4.

28 The statistics are from Kalimi, "Jerusalem," 202.

29 See textual note 10, however, and the mixed vocalization in MT.

30 On the spelling variation Shimea/Shammua see textual note 11.

31 This parallel makes it unlikely that Bath-shua is to be translated "the daughter of Shua," as Braun, 29, suggests in his note to 1 Chr 2:3.

32 Willi, 111, observes that the Masoretes put a small *zāqēp* over the number "four," apparently in an attempt to separate it from Bath-shua.

33 Isaac Kalimi, "The View of Jerusalem in the Ethnographical Introduction of Chronicles (1 Chr 1–9)," *Bib* 83 (2002) 557. Kalimi errs, of course, in claiming that the Chronicler invented the list of four sons, since they are taken from 2 Sam 5:14.

were born in Babylon. Of the nineteen sons of David mentioned in vv. 1-8, Solomon occupies at number ten the exact center position, with nine before him and nine after him. In 2 Sam 11:3 the two parts of the name of Bathsheba's father are given in reverse order: "Eliam" אליעם for "Ammiel" עמיאל, but presumably referring to the same individual.[34] If Eliam the son of Ahithophel the Gilonite, one of David's warriors (2 Sam 23:34), is her father, it raises questions about why this Ahithophel chose to be the counselor of Absalom (2 Sam 15:12–17:23) rather than being the counselor of his grand-daughter's husband. Citing the name of a married woman's father, whether Eliam or Ammiel, implies the high standing of the man (McCarter, *II Samuel*, 285).

■ **6-7** *Eliphelet and Nogah:* Rudolph, 24, deleted both names as dittographic, with this Eliphelet anticipating the second Eliphelet in v. 8, and Nogah being a miswritten duplicate of Nepheg in v. 7. The two names are present in 1 Chr 14:5-6, but missing in 2 Sam 5:15. Deleting these names, however, requires the additional change of "nine" at the end of the verse to "seven." It seems better to explain the shorter list of names in 2 Sam 5:15 by haplography.[35] While it may seem strange to have two sons by the same name Eliphelet, they may well have come from different mothers, or an earlier Eliphelet died and a later brother was named after him.[36] Retaining these names as original in Chronicles also keeps Solomon in the middle position (see above) with nine brothers before him and nine brothers after him.

■ **8** *Eliada:* This name corresponds to the name in 2 Sam 5:16 MT, but is different from the Chronicler's own parallel version of this text in 1 Chr 14:7, where we find "Beeliada." Such "baal" names were acceptable in early Israel,[37] but were considered offensive later on and so corrected both in this verse and in 2 Sam 5:16.[38]

■ **9** *All these were David's sons, besides the sons of the concubines, and Tamar was their sister:* This verse is present at this point neither in the Chronicler's *Vorlage* at 2 Sam 5:14-16 nor his own parallel text at 1 Chr 14:3-7. It indicates that all of David's children named so far were born of women recognized as David's wives and presumably of higher status than those born of concubines. Concubines were mentioned among the women David took in Jerusalem in 2 Sam 5:13,[39] and this may have suggested to the Chronicler the addition of "sons of the concubines" in 1 Chr 3:9. The additional and unnamed "sons and daughters" in 2 Sam 5:13 and 1 Chr 14:3 permitted the Chronicler to include a reference to Tamar, a name known to him from 2 Samuel 13, where she is identified as the sister of Absalom. This created another parallel listing of women connected to both Judah and David, in addition to Bath-shua: the Tamar connected to Judah was Judah's daughter-in-law, the mother of his children Perez and Zerah (1 Chr 2:4), while the Tamar connected to David was his daughter. All the children of David mentioned in the Deuteronomistic History are included in 1 Chr 3:1-9—plus Eliphelet and Nogah, or twenty children in all. As is frequently the case in these genealogies, women are listed at the end of a person's children.

---

34   Cf. "Jeconiah" יכניה and "Jehoiachin" יהויכין. Halpern, *David's Secret Demons*, 349–50, n. 7, denies that Ammiel and Eliam are the same person and asks whether the Chronicler was making Bathsheba the sister of Machir the son of Ammiel, with whom Mephibosheth had stayed before he was taken into David's household in Jerusalem.

35   McCarter, *II Samuel*, 148, notes that space considerations indicate that these names were present in 4QSam[a], and they are present in a number of Samuel LXX MSS (d e f l m p q s t w z). See also Willi, 70.

36   In 1 Chronicles 14 there is also a very slight spelling variation between the names: אלפלט (v. 5) and אליפלט (v. 7).

37   Note the name of Saul's son Ishbaal, which is also

spelled Ishbosheth (in which the word "shame" is substituted for "Baal"). Cf. also Jerubbaal and Jerubbosheth. The later judgment on such names is reflected in Hos 2:19 (17): "I will remove the names of the baals from her mouth."

38   The earlier reading in Samuel LXX[B] is Βααλειμαϑ, and Samuel LXX[L] has Βααλειδαϑ.

39   On the omission of "concubines" in 1 Chr 14:3 see the commentary on that verse.

3:10-16. Descendants of Solomon Who Served as Kings of Judah
3:10-14

Solomon—Rehoboam—Abijah—Asa—Jehoshaphat—Joram—Ahaziah—Joash—Amaziah—Azariah—Jotham

Ahaz—Hezekiah—Manasseh—Amon—Josiah

■ **10** *Abijah his son:* The Chronicler here uses the spelling of the name of Solomon's grandson found in his own narrative rather than "Abijam," which is used in the Kings' narrative (1 Kgs 14:31;[40] 15:1, 7 [twice], 8). Contrast his spelling practice with Azariah and Jeconiah noted above under Structure. Willi, 112, notes that there is no reference to any of the people in this section as kings, but only as prominent citizens and inhabitants of Jerusalem.

3:15-18

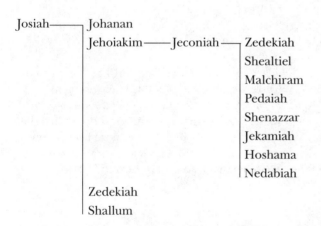

■ **15** *And the sons of Josiah: Johanan the firstborn, the second Jehoiakim, the third Zedekiah, the fourth Shallum:* The order of the successors of Josiah on the throne were (1) his son Jehoahaz (2 Chr 36:1), also known as Shallum (Jer 22:11); (2) his son Jehoiakim (2 Chr 36:4), also known as Eliakim;[41] (3) Jehoiakim's son Jehoiachin (2 Chr 36:8), called Jeconiah in vv. 16-17[42] and Coniah elsewhere;[43] and finally (4) Josiah's son Zedekiah (2 Chr 36:10), also known as Mattaniah.[44] The birth order of Josiah's sons was: Jehoiakim, born in 634;[45] Jehoahaz, born in 632;[46] and Zedekiah, born in 619.[47] Hence the order of Josiah's sons in this verse corresponds neither to their chronological ages (since Shallum should precede Zedekiah), nor to the sequence of their reigns (since Shallum should precede Jehoiakim) despite the fact that they are called the firstborn, second, third, and fourth. Even the age of Josiah, born in 648,[48] is somewhat of a problem. Josiah would have been only fourteen when Jehoiakim was born, and Johanan would have been born even earlier, though with kings having more than one wife the birth date need not be much earlier. Rudolph, 27, and Willi, 113, propose that Johanan never attained the throne because of his early death, even perhaps before the death of his father Josiah, and he was consequently ignored in other biblical writings outside of Chronicles.

---

40 Note that a few Hebrew MSS, LXX, Syr, Tg read Abijah here as well.
41 2 Kgs 23:34//2 Chr 36:4.
42 Esth 2:7; Jer 24:1; 27:20; 28:4; 29:2.
43 Jer 22:24, 28; 37:1.
44 2 Kgs 24:17.
45 2 Kgs 23:36. Jehoiakim would have been eighteen when his son Jehoiachin was born (24:8).
46 2 Kgs 23:31. Jehoahaz and Zedekiah had the same mother, Hamutal.
47 Cf. 2 Kgs 24:18. Rudolph, 28, speculates that Zedekiah was actually born somewhere between

634 and 632 and so was thrity-four to thirty-six years old when he ascended the throne. Hence the order of the four sons is their birth order: Johanan the firstborn, Jehoiakim 634, Zedekiah between 634 and 632, and Shallum/Jehoahaz 632. Cf. also Williamson, 56, and Japhet, 98.

48 2 Kgs 22:1.

Rudolph, 26–27, Willi, 113, and Japhet, 98, dismiss the variant reading of "Jehoahaz" for Johanan in some LXX manuscripts (see textual note 19), since accepting it would imply that Jehoahaz was older than Jehoiakim, would create one individual under two different names in the verse (Jehoahaz and Shallum), and would make Jer 22:10-12 incomprehensible since this passage states that Shallum succeeded his father Josiah.[49]

This may be as far as we can go, but it may be worthwhile reconsidering the variant reading "Jehoahaz" recorded in some LXX manuscripts. If "Jehoahaz" and "Shallum" were ancient variants in the first position, as sons of Josiah, then the present text might be a conflation, with Johanan[50] replacing Jehoahaz in the first position and Shallum being moved to the end of the verse. In this conjectural reconstruction, we would have had originally a sequence of Josiah's sons—Jehoahaz/Shallum—Jehoiakim—Zedekiah—corresponding to their sequence on the throne, not to their birth order.

■ **16** *The descendants of Jehoiakim: Jeconiah his son, Zedekiah his son:* Following the genre employed in vv. 10-14 (X, Y his son, Z his son), the logical, and I believe correct, way to understand this verse is that Jeconiah was the son of Jehoiakim, and Zedekiah—not be confused with the king Zedekiah in v. 15[51]—was the son of Jeconiah. This Zedekiah would probably have been born to Jeconiah before the exile,[52] and Jeconiah's sons mentioned in v. 17 would have been born after Jeconiah's captivity had begun, as v. 17 also states: "the sons of Jeconiah the captive." Jeconiah would be relatively young as a father by our standards (eighteen or younger), but Josiah himself according to the biblical chronology was about fourteen when he became the father of Eliakim/Jehoiakim. The majority of commentators understand Jeconiah and

Zedekiah in this verse as brothers, the sons of Jehoiakim (Rudolph, 28; Myers, 1:20; Williamson, 57; Japhet, 98). "His son" after Zedekiah would be understood either as "the son of Jehoiakim" or "the successor of Jehoiachin."[53] In my judgment a careful form-critical analysis of v. 16 designates that Zedekiah is the son of Jehoiachin and not his brother or the person who followed him as king. But where did the Chronicler get this information? The texts of Kings and Chronicles at the accession of Zedekiah give a mixed and confusing witness about this king's relationship to Josiah and Jehoiachin:

■ 2 Chr 36:10 MT: King Zedekiah was Jehoiachin's brother (אחיו), and both were the sons of Jehoiakim (this agrees with the majority interpretation of 1 Chr 3:16).

■ 2 Chr 36:10 LXX and 2 Kgs 24:17 LXX[L]: King Zedekiah was the son of Josiah and therefore Jehoiachin's uncle (ἀδελφὸν τοῦ πατρὸς αὐτοῦ = אחי אביו). The same relationship is presupposed in 2 Kgs 24:17 MT, but with a different Hebrew word for uncle: (דדו)[54] This is probably the correct historical interpretation. Cf. also 1 Chr 3:15.

■ 2 Kgs 24:17 LXX: King Zedekiah was the son of Jehoiachin (υἱὸν αὐτοῦ).[55]

Most scholars emend אחיו in 2 Chr 36:10 MT on the basis of Chronicles LXX to אח אביו. The reading in 2 Kgs 24:17 LXX could be interpreted either as an attempt to harmonize with a genealogical notice like the one now preserved in 1 Chr 3:16, or, more likely in my judgment, the genealogy in 3:16 is a calculation based on the variant textual tradition preserved by 2 Kgs 24:17 LXX.

---

49 For Willi the Chronicler's inclusion of Johanan shows that he had information in addition to that which is in the book of Kings and that he was more interested in any case in these people as inhabitants of Jerusalem than in their service as kings.

50 יוחנן "Johanan" would then be a miswriting of יואחז "Jehoahaz" (2 Chr 36:2, 4), as *BHK* proposed. It may be, of course, that this variant in a few LXX MSS is nothing else than a correction to the information in Kings, but if so, it is a very awkward and inaccurate correction.

51 The latter's name, in v. 15, is spelled צדקיהו, and the Zedekiah of v. 16 is spelled צדקיה.

52 Note that 2 Kgs 24:15 mentions the king's wives (plural) were taken into exile with Jehoiachin, and Jer 22:28 refers to the exiling of Coniah (= Jehoiachin) and his children (seed).

53 This would mean, at least for Japhet, 98, that Zedekiah the son of Josiah in v. 15 is not a reference to the Zedekiah who became king.

54 1 Esdr 1:44, which corresponds to 2 Chr 36:10, omits any relationship between Zedekiah and others.

55 My interpretation of 1 Chr 3:16 also makes Zedekiah the son of Jehoiachin, but this Zedekiah is not the king.

3:17-24. Descendants of Jeconiah for Seven Generations

3:17-22a

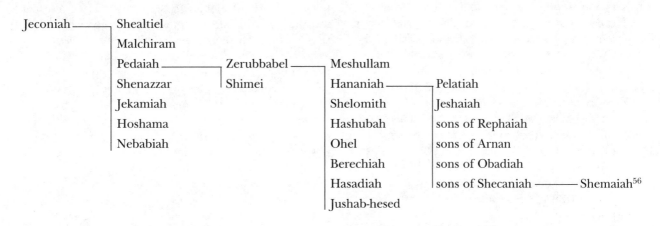

■ **17-18** *and the sons of Jeconiah, the captive: Shealtiel his son, and Malchiram, Pedaiah, Shenazzar, Jekamiah, Hoshama, and Nedabiah.*[57] Japhet, 99, who does not accept the addition of the definite article to אסר ("the captive"; see textual note 21), interprets this word as a name Assir and makes Shealtiel and the people mentioned in v. 18 sons of Assir.[58]

The seven sons born to Jeconiah in captivity include Shealtiel (v. 17), who is specifically called Jeconiah's son, but the six men mentioned in v. 18 are also Jeconiah's sons and hence Shealtiel's brothers. Willi, 116, argues that "his son" after Shealtiel shows that the text had reached the same genealogical plane as in v. 16, where Zedekiah is the son of Jeconiah in his Jerusalem days. Shealtiel is his son in captivity, as well as all those mentioned in v. 18. Jeconiah's seven sons[59] remind the reader of the seven sons of Jesse (of whom the seventh was David) and of the seven sons of Elioenai (v. 24; of whom the last was Anani). One of the so-called Weidner

texts, dated to 592, speaks of five sons of Jehoiachin for whom rations were provided.[60] Braun, 52, notes that the sixth and seventh sons may have been born subsequently—after all, Jehoiachin was only twenty-three in 592. Although Jehoiachin was eighteen in 597, five sons could have been born to him before 592, especially if he had his children by more than one wife (2 Kgs 24:15 mentions that the king's wives [plural] were taken captive). In having children in exile, Jeconiah and later Zerubbabel, intentionally or not, were fulfilling the command to have sons and daughters in exile, to multiply there and not decrease (Jer 29:6; Willi, 117).

In a monograph devoted to this chapter, Rothstein came to a number of conclusions that form a coherent if unlikely picture.[61] He decided that Shealtiel (pp. 11–12) and Malchiram (p. 16)[62] were born in exile, before Jehoiachin was released from prison in 561, but that they were executed by Nebuchadrezzar in connection with the revolutionary stirrings in Judah in 594–593

56 To be continued at v. 22b.

57 Syr introduces "his son" after every name, giving a continuous line of descent from Jeconiah. In v. 19 Syr incorrectly omits Pedaiah, and Zerubbabel and Shimei are made the sons of the preceding Nedabiah.

58 Cf. LXX and Vg, perhaps influenced by the name

of the son (or grandson) of Korah in Exod 6:24; 1 Chr 6:7, 8, 22 (22, 23, 37).

59 This listing ignores Zedekiah the son of Jeconiah in v. 16

60 *ANET*, 308. Cf. John M. Berridge, "Jehoiachin," *ABD* 3:661–63.

61 *Genealogie.*

(pp. 24–25). Pedaiah and the other sons of Jehoiachin were born after Jeconiah's release. In his view Shenazzar is actually the Babylonian name for Pedaiah (p. 27), which reappears as Sheshbazzar in Ezra 1:8. Zerubbabel's Babylonian name ("seed of Babylon") shows that he was born just before Pedaiah left Babylon (p. 65), while Shimei ("Yahweh has heard") was born after Pedaiah's return to Palestine (p. 67). Zerubbabel, in Rothstein's reckoning, was only nineteen years old in 520 (p. 73).

A number of scholars in addition to Rothstein have identified Shenazzar and Sheshbazzar, the leader of the Jewish community after the return from exile (Ezra 1:8, 11; 5:14, 16; cf. 1 Esdr 2:12, 15; 6:18, 20). Since the divine names contained in the two names are Sin (the moon god) and Shamash (the sun god), respectively, however, Shenazzar and Sheshbazzar should be seen as two distinct persons.[63]

■ **19** *The sons of Pedaiah: Zerubbabel and Shimei:* According to Ezra 3:2, 8; 5:2; Neh 12:1; Hag 1:1, 12, 14; 2:2, and 23 (cf. Matt 1:12 and Luke 3:27), Zerubbabel is the son of Shealtiel (v. 17), not the son of Pedaiah. Rothstein concluded that Zerubbabel was the son of Pedaiah, who was considered the firstborn of Jeconiah, after the previous execution of Shealtiel and Malchiram.[64] The identification of Zerubbabel's s father as Shealtiel resulted from someone who understandably considered Shealtiel as the firstborn, the one through whom the Davidic line continued. Myers, 1:21,[65] suggested that Shealtiel died early and Pedaiah became the head of the family or, following Keil, 81–82, or Rudolph, 29, that Pedaiah had married the widow of Shealtiel and sired Zerubbabel in a levirate marriage.[66] Albright once proposed that there were two Zerubbabels who were cousins, one the son of Shealtiel and the other the son of Pedaiah.[67] In a commentary on Hag 1:2, Ibn Ezra suggested that Zerubbabel was the son of Shealtiel but was brought up by Pedaiah (Japhet, 101). The hypothesis that Zerubbabel was the child of a levirate marriage is the most plausible proposal, but perhaps we should admit that the Bible identifies two people as Zerubbabel's father and that there is no certain way to resolve this conflict.

and the sons of Zerubbabel: Meshullam and Hananiah, and Shelomith was their sister: Nahman Avigad raised the possibility that Shelomith was the woman named on a bulla dated to the late sixth century and reading, "Shelomith maidservant of Elnathan the governor."[68] Shelomith could either be a secondary wife of the governor (cf. Gen 21:10) or a high-ranking functionary.[69] Willi, 117, notes that the mention of the sister Shelomith in this verse brings the first group of Zerubbabel's children to an end (cf. 1 Chr 3:9; 7:24, 30, where a daughter is mentioned at the end of a genealogical section), and he believes these three children were born before Zerubbabel's return from exile. Hence the children mentioned in the next verse were born after the return. Rudolph, 28–29, came to a similar conclusion and even added "in Babylon" to this verse and "after his return" to v. 20 (see textual notes 27 and 28). In Willi's view, Zerubbabel's

62   He parsed Malchiram ("my king is exalted") as a double entendre referring both to the exaltation of Yahweh and to Jehoiachin's submission before Nebuchadrezzar.

63   See P. R. Berger, "Zu den Namen ששבצר and שנאצר (Esr. 1:8, 11; 5:14, 16 bzw. 1 Chr. 3:18)," *ZAW* 83 (1971) 98–100; and Tamara C. Eskenazi, "Sheshbazzar," *ABD* 5:1208; contra Myers, 1:18; Curtis and Madsen, 103. Cross, *From Epic to Canon,* 179, n. 21, defends the equation of Shenazzar and Sheshbazzar on the basis of LXX[A] in 1 Esdras.

64   *Genealogie,* 52.

65   Cf. Curtis and Madsen, 101.

66   See also Karl-Martin Beyse, *Serubbabel und die Königserwartungen der Propheten Haggai und Sacharja* (Arbeiten zur Theologie 48; Stuttgart: Calwer, 1972)

28–30.

67   William Foxwell Albright, "The Date and Personality of the Chronicler," *JBL* 40 (1921) 108–9.

68   Elnathan also appears on another bulla from the late 6th century: "belonging to Elnathan the governor." See E. M. Meyers, "The Shelomith Seal and the Judean Restoration: Some Additional Considerations," *ErIsr* 18 (1985) 33–38; H. G. M. Williamson, "The Governors of Judah under the Persians," *TynBul* 39 (1988) 59–82; A. Lemaire, "Zorobabel et la Judée à la lumière de l'épigraphie (fin du VIe s. av. J.-C.)," *RB* 103 (1996) 48–57; P. Bordreuil et al., "Deux ostraca paléo-hébreux de la Collection Sh. Moussaïeff," *Sem* 46 (1996) 74–76.

69   *Bullae and Seals from a Post-Exilic Judean Archive* (Qedem 4; Jerusalem: Institute of Archaeology,

having children in two places echoes David's siring children in both Hebron and Jerusalem. Several scholars have seen special significance in the etymological meanings of these names, in that they praise the good news of the return from exile: Meshullam = "Recompensed" (Curtis and Madsen, 102) or "Restored" (Braun, 54), Hananiah = "Yahweh is gracious," and Shelomith = "peace."

■ **20** *and Hashubah, Ohel, Berechiah, Hasadiah, and Jushab-hesed, five:* Following Willi's proposal mentioned in the previous verse, these five names may be children born after Zerubbabel's return from exile. Myers, 1:18, interprets similarly and translates the *wāw* conjunction at the beginning of this verse by "Then." Since the children of Zerubbabel's son Hananiah are mentioned in v. 21, Rothstein, 29, conjecturally restored the name of Zerubbabel's son Meshullam at the beginning of v. 20: "The sons of Meshullam." Rudolph, 29, and Japhet, 101, however, note that elsewhere in this list sons are traced in each generation through one individual. The names in this verse too have been thought to refer to the momentous events of the return: Hashubah = "Consideration,"[70] Ohel = "Tent [of Yahweh?]," Berechiah = "Yahweh has blessed," Hasadiah = "Yahweh has shown loyalty," Jushab Hesed = "Let covenant loyalty be restored."[71] The total number of the sons is recorded here and in vv. 22, 23, and 24. The number "five" makes sense only if the names in this verse are considered distinct from the children of Zerubbabel listed in v. 20.

■ **21** *The sons of Hananiah: Pelatiah and Jeshaiah, the sons of Rephaiah, the sons of Arnan, the sons of Obadiah, and the sons of Shecaniah.*

■ **22** *The sons of Shecaniah: Shemaiah:* I have retained the MT, with some hesitancy, except that I have changed "The son of Hananiah" to "The sons of Hananiah" (see textual note 32). The difficulty with this form of the text is that it lists two sons, Pelatiah and Jeshaiah, and then provides no individual names for the groups called the sons of Rephaiah, Arnan, and Obadiah[72] (for Shecaniah see the next verse). Every interpretation of this verse must remain tentative. One explanation offered for "sons of," which I support, is that Rephaiah, Arnan, and Obadiah were founders of distinguished *families* at the time of the writer for whom no individuals are named.[73] Rothstein, 43, and Rudolph, 28, conjecturally changed the last four "the sons of" in the verse to the conjunction "and" (textual notes 33–36). While this seems arbitrary, it does put all six names in v. 21 in the same generation, as seems to be the case in MT. Another possibility is to follow the LXX and to change the four occurrences of בני (the sons of) to בנו (his son), and also add a fifth בנו after Shecaniah, following LXX alone (see textual notes 33–37 and Japhet, 93),[74] which would make this verse into a sequence of six generations after Hananiah, with Pelatiah alone being the son of Hananiah:[75] Pelatiah–Jeshaiah–Rephaiah–Arnan–Obadiah–Shecaniah.[76] Keil, 84, considered the materials from "the sons of Rephaiah" to the end of the chapter to be a genealogical fragment whose connection to Zerubbabel is unascertainable.

Hebrew University, 1976), p. 11, #14. Cf. S. Talmon, "Ezra and Nehemiah," *IDBSup* 325; and Carol L. Meyers and Eric M. Meyers, *Haggai, Zechariah 1–8* (AB 25B; Garden City, NY: Doubleday, 1987) 12–13. If MT is preferred over LXX, the descendants of this Shelomith may have accompanied Ezra on his trip to Palestine (Ezra 8:10). See Tamara C. Eskenazi, "Out from the Shadows: Biblical Women in the Postexilic Era," *JSOT* 54 (1992) 38–39.

70   Or if חשבה is considered a shortened form of read חשביה (Hashabiah) "Yahweh has shown consideration." The vocalizarion in MT as a *qal* passive fem. sg. participle is unusual. *BHS* records a proposal חֲשֻׁבָה = Noth, *Personennamen,* 189.

71   The verb is parsed as *hophal*. If *qal* is read (see textual note 29): "Let covenant loyalty return."

72   De Vries, 42, takes these as regular introductions to a name list, but argues that the lists are left vacant because no data are available; similarly, Allen, 330, who understands these names as four additional generations.

73   Curtis and Madsen, 102, citing Bertheau. See now Willi, 119.

74   There are no other cases where the expression "his son" precedes the word it modifies. Williamson, 58, suggests that the versions may have tried to correct a difficult verse by drawing on the analogy of vv. 10-13.

75   In which case the MT could be retained for the first two words: "The son of Hananiah:"

76   Alternately, according to Japhet, all the names could be from one generation with "his son" in each

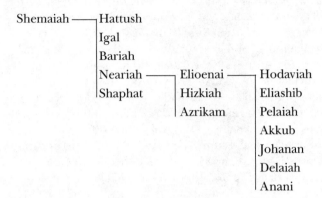

Shemaiah —— Hattush
Igal
Bariah
Neariah —— Elioenai —— Hodaviah
Shaphat   Hizkiah   Eliashib
             Azrikam   Pelaiah
                           Akkub
                           Johanan
                           Delaiah
                           Anani

■ **22** *The sons of Shecaniah: Shemaiah. And the sons of Shemaiah: Hattush, Igal, Bariah, Neariah, and Shaphat, six:* The central interpretive problem in this verse is the number "six."[77] Since there are only five sons in the generation beginning with Hattush, Rothstein, 94, Rudolph, 28, Williamson, 58, and Allen, 330, deleted "And the sons of Shemaiah." If, however, the first "The sons of" in the verse is understood in the sense of "The descendants of," then Shemaiah in his own generation and his five sons would make a total of six descendants. One apparent advantage of the alternate interpretation that deletes "the sons of Shemaiah" is that it makes

Hattush the son of Shecaniah and suggests that he was the person of the same name and parentage mentioned in Ezra 8:2-3 as the head of a household accompanying Ezra on his return to Jerusalem. But in addition to depending on this conjectural deletion, there are textual difficulties in any case with Ezra 8:2-3,[78] and Hattush is a relatively common name used for four individuals in the OT (Neh 3:10; 10:5 [4]; 12:2). Japhet, 102, notes that Hattush is only said to be "from the sons of" Shecaniah in Ezra 8:2, and his exact parentage is given in this verse, that is, his father was Shemaiah and his grandfather Shecaniah. She suggests either that a name has fallen out or that the number of sons is wrong and should be five.[79]

■ **24** *The sons of Elioenai: Hodaviah, Eliashib, Pelaiah, Akkub, Johanan, Delaiah, and Anani, seven:* An Aqabiah son of Elioenai is attested in an early Ptolemaic inscription from Alexandria, dating to the beginning of the third century BCE, but Kalimi doubts whether these two individuals can be identified.[80] The most interesting name in this list is Anani, who, as Braun, 54, suggests, might be identified with an Anani mentioned with the high priest Johanan and his own brother Ostanes/Avastana (a Persian name) in one of the Elephantine papyri that has been dated to 407 BCE (*ANET*, 492; *COS* 3:128). That brother Ostanes, of course, does not appear in v. 24. Willi, 120, calls attention to the interpretation of

case referring to Hananiah. She cites v. 16 as an analogy, but in my view this verse too is to be interpreted as describing a father, son, and grandson, not a father and two sons. Willi, 118, notes twelve generations after Zerubbabel in LXX. The longer genealogy in LXX would make the terminus a quo for the date of this genealogy and for the Chronicler ca. 300 BCE. The terminus a quo in our understanding of this chapter is about a century earlier. See the discussion of date above at the end of the Structure section.

77 The name Igal is similar to the name גאליהו עבד המלך found on a 7th-century seal. See William J. Fulco, "A Seal from Umm el Qanāfid," *Or* 48 (1979) 107–8.

78 One must ignore the verse division and change מבני שכניה "from the sons of Shecaniah," which would imply a wider family, to בן שכניה "the son of Shecaniah."

79 Japhet, 102, concludes from the mention of three Babylonian names in vv. 17-24 (Shenazzar, Zerubba-

bel, and Hattush) and the fact that Hattush's father was in Babylon, according to Ezra 8:2-3, that the provenance of the list is Babylonian. Hence all or some of Zerubbabel's children stayed in or returned to Babylon. But if the list is preserved in Babylon, how did the Chronicler get it? As noted above, the sons of Zerubbabel in v. 20 and the sons of Hananiah in v. 21 were probably born in Palestine. If Japhet were right, Willi's proposal to understand the list as describing the continuing inhabitation of Jerusalem would not work.

80 I. Kalimi, "Könnte die aramäische Grabinschrift aus Ägypten als Indikation für die Datierung der Chronikbücher fungieren?" *ZAW* 110 (1998) 79–81. The similarity between Akkub the son of Elioenia and Akabiah the son of Elioenai could be merely an accident, or, if Akabiah is a descendant of Akkub, it could be evidence for the use of papponomy in that family.

the name Anani in the Tg,[81] which associates this person with the king, the anointed, because of the consonantal resemblance of Anani (עֲנָנִי) with the word "clouds of" in Dan 7:13 (עֲנָנֵי). Anani, the last name among the descendants of David, is also the seventh son of Elioenai, just as David was the seventh son of Jesse (1 Chr 2:15).

Conclusion

The Chronicler has interrupted the genealogy of Hur to give a genealogy of David and his descendants. The names from David to Zedekiah, the kings of the united monarchy and of the kingdom of Judah until the exile, will be the principal characters in the narrative beginning in 1 Chronicles 10 and continuing until 2 Chronicles 36. To include these Davidides, the core members of the tribe of Judah, makes perfect sense. The Chronicler's continuation of the line into the postexilic period would be justified by its mention of Zerubbabel, the leader in the early years of the return; by the reference to Shelomith, if indeed she did marry the governor Elnathan; by Hattush, if indeed he was a Davidide who returned with Ezra; and by the last Davidide known to the Chronicler, Anani, who may have held a position of leadership according to the Elephantine papyri. The Chronicler presumably did not have later genealogical records for the house of David. Willi may well be right that the family of David also illustrates the nearly unbroken inhabitation of Jerusalem, except for the exile of Jeconiah and his immediate sons. Jeconiah's grandson Zerubbabel returned to Jerusalem in any case and the whole land in the meantime had been enjoying its Sabbaths in an empty land (2 Chr 36:21).[82]

In the eight generations after Jeconiah the captive, the genealogy is primarily segmented, with the line passing on more often than not through a son other than the firstborn: Pedaiah is the fourth oldest son; Hananiah is the second oldest; the sons of Shecaniah are the sixth oldest; and Neriah is the fourth oldest. Only Zerubbabel, Shemaiah, and Elioenai were both the firstborn and the ones through whom the line continued. Sterility may account for some of this change, but one suspects that social status played a role in determining how the line would continue, especially when the line moved past the second oldest son.

The segmented form of the genealogy makes it unlikely that the principal reason for preservation of the genealogy was the hope for a restoration of the Davidic throne, although Zerubbabel's Davidic lineage surely played a role in the office held by him, and it may have been the reason that the governor Elnathan married Shelomith. But it is hard to see either in this genealogy or in the Chronicler's narrative itself a messianic hope or even a longing for the restoration of Davidic kingship.[83]

---

81 "Anani—he is the king Messiah who will be revealed."

82 The land of course was not really empty. See the commentary on 2 Chr 36:21.

83 For further discussion and for caution about the lack of future hope placed in the line of David, see H. G. M. Williamson, "Eschatology in Chronicles," *TynBul* 28 (1977) 115–54. Williamson notes that with the completion of the Davidic-Solomonic period the dynasty has been eternally established. Solomon's prayer at the dedication of the temple emphasizes the royalist interpretation of the promise to David and the fact that the promise is not exhausted with the completion of the temple. Hence the promise to David has eternal validity. He concludes, 154: "It is by no means absurd to maintain that the Chronicler would have inherited and passed on a continuing tradition of hope centred on the Davidic family."

1/ The sons of Judah: Perez, Hezron, Caleb,[1] Hur, and Shobal.

2/ Reaiah the son of[2] Shobal became the father of Jahath, and Jahath became the father of Ahumai and Lahad. These were the families of the Zorathites. 3/ These are the sons of Hareph, the father of Beth-gader: X[3] the father[4] of Etam,[5] Jezreel, Ishma, and Idbash; and the name of their sister was Hazzelel-poni,[6] 4/ and Penuel was the father of Gedor, and Ezer was the father of Hushah. These are the sons of Hur the firstborn of Ephrathah, the father of[7] Bethlehem.

5/ Ashhur the father of Tekoa had two wives, Helah and Naarah; 6/ Naarah bore to him Ahuzzam, Hepher, Temeni, and Haahashtari. These were the sons of Naarah. 7/ The sons of Helah: Zereth, Zohar,[8] Ethnan, and Koz.[9] 8/ Koz became the father of Anub and Zobebah,[10] and the families of Aharhel son of Harum.[11]

9/ Jabez was honored more than his brothers; and his mother named him Jabez, saying, "Because I bore him in pain." 10/ Jabez called on the God of Israel, saying, "Oh that[12] you would thoroughly bless me and enlarge my territory, and let your hand be with me, and act without regard to the evil [inherent in my birth and name] so as not to cause me pain."[13] God brought to pass that which he had requested.

11/ Chelub[14] the brother[15] of Shuhah[16] became the father of Mehir, who was the father of Eshton. 12/ Eshton became the father of Beth-rapha, Paseah, and Tehinnah[17] the father of Ir-nahash.[18] These are the men of Rechab.[19]

13/ The sons of Kenaz: Othniel and Seraiah; and the sons of Othniel: Hathath and Meonothai.[20] 14/ And Meonothai became the father of Ophrah; and Seraiah became the father of Joab the father of Ge-harashim, so named because they were artisans. 15/ The sons of Caleb the son of Jephunneh:[21] Ir and Elah,[22] and Naam; these were the sons of Kenaz.[23, 24]

16/ The sons of[25] Jehallelel: Ziph, Ziphah, Tiria, and Asarel. 17/ The sons[26] of Ezrah: Jether, Mered, Epher, and Jalon, and Jether became the father of[27] Miriam, Shammai, and Ishbah the father of Eshtemoa. 18/ And his Judahite[28] wife bore Jered father of Gedor, Heber father of Soco, and Jekuthiel father of Zanoah. And[29] these are the sons of Bithiah, the daughter of Pharaoh, whom Mered took as his wife: X.[30] 19/ The sons of his Judahite wife,[31] the sister of Naham, the father[32] of Keilah:[33] the Garmite and Eshtemoa[34] the Maacathite. 20/ The sons of Shimon: Amnon, Rinnah, Ben-hanan, and Tilon.[35] The

1 וכלב, as conjectured by Wellhausen; Curtis and Madsen, 104; *BHS;* Japhet, 104; et al.; MT וכרמי "Carmi." This last reading, adopted by Williamson, 59, and Willi, 67, may have arisen under the influence of names Hezron and Carmi in 5:3. See also the commentary. A spelling of כלבי or כלובי (see 2:9) may have facilitated the change from Caleb to Carmi.

2 וראיה בן. LXX incorrectly divides the sentence: ". . . and Reaiah his son. And Shobal became the father. . . ."

3 The name of the father of Etam is missing. See textual note 5.

4 אבי. LXX "sons."

5 ואלה בני חרף אבי בית גדר . . . אבי עיטם. A conjectural replacement for MT ואלה אבי עיטם "And these are the father of Etam (?)." Cf. Rothstein, 51; Noth, "Liste," 103; Rudolph, 30; Myers, 1:23; Japhet, 107. In 2:51 Hareph is called the father of Beth-gader, and he is the only son of Hur whose descendants were not given there. Syr reads: "And these are the sons of Amminadab the father of Ahizarel ['ḥyzr'l]." Curtis and Madsen, 105; ואלה בני חור אבי עיטם "And these are the sons of Hur the father of Etam." Similarly Demsky, "Clans of Ephrath," 53.

6 ושם אחותם הצללפוני. Rudolph, 30, emends: (שמה) הצב לפני שם אחותה "(her name) was placed before the name of her sister," and considers it a marginal notation to the name Helah in v. 5 since the names of the sisters in vv. 6-7 are put in the reverse order.

7 אבי. Rudolph, 30, arbitrarily substitutes היא "that is." Cf. Gen 35:19. He argues that "the father of Bethlehem" does not harmonize with 1 Chr 2:19, 24 (where the children of Hur are named), or 2:51 (where Salma is called the father of Bethlehem). See the commentary.

8 וצהר Q, LXX; cf. Gen 46:10; Exod 6:15. K, Vg, Tg: יצחר "Izhar."

9 וקוץ with Tg; "and Koz" was lost by haplography in MT and the other versions. Would the original reading be preserved in Tg alone, or is this version harmonizing, in this case correctly?

10 והצבבה. *BHK* and Curtis and Madsen, 107–8, read ויעבץ "Jabez" in anticipation of v. 9.

11 בן חרום. Rudolph, 30, deletes these words since Koz is the father of the families of Aharhel. Willi, 70, calls the text corrupt. See the commentary.

12 Cf. GKC §§151e; 167a.

13 According to Rudolph, 30, עָצְבִּי is a doubly abnormal spelling for עָצְבֵנִי. Cf. GKC §§61a (unusual *dāgēš*); 115c (suffix as accusative).

14 וכלוב; LXX, Syr, Vg: καὶ Χαλεβ "Caleb." See the commentary.

sons of Ishi: Zoreth, and the son of[36] Zoeth was X.[37]

21/ The sons of Shelah son of Judah: Er father of Lecah, Laadah father of Mareshah, and the families of the guild of linen[38] workers at Beth-ashbea; 22/ and Jokim,[39] and the men of Cozeba, and Joash, and Saraph, who had married[40] into Moab but returned[41] to Lehem[42] (now the records are ancient[43]).[44] 23/ These were the potters and[45] the inhabitants of Netaim and Gederah; they lived there with the king in his service.[46]

15 אחי. Some Hebrew MSS: אבי "father." This is apparently an independent variant from LXX, for which see the next note.

16 Instead of Chelub the brother of Shuhah, LXX reads "Caleb the father of Achsah." While LXX may be right in its interpretation of Chelub as Caleb (see the commentary), it shows harmonistic tendencies when it makes the Caleb of this verse into the father of Achsah. On Achsah see 2:49.

17 תחנה; LXX Θαμνα "Timnah."

18 עיר נחש; LXX adds "the brother of Εσελων the Kenizzite." LXX thus makes this descendant of Chelub/Caleb into a Kenizzite, just as Caleb is considered a Kenizzite in our reconstructed text of v. 15 and in other OT passages as well. Allen, *Greek Chronicles,* 2:142–43, argues that the Greek represents two misplaced glosses on v. 15. The first was an attempt to make Jephunneh the brother of Hezron, and the second was an attempt to make Caleb a Kenizzite.

19 רכב with LXX; MT רכה "Recah." Cf. 2:55; Curtis and Madsen, 108; and Rudolph, 32. Tg translates: "these are the men of the Great Synagogue." C. H. Knights, "The Text of 1 Chronicles IV 12: A Reappraisal," *VT* 37 (1987) 375–77, argues that the translator of the Tg must also have read בכר and then connected that with a rabbinic tradition that the Rechabites sat in the Sanhedrin.

20 ומעונתי with LXX[L], Vg; lost in MT and versions by haplography. Note *sons* of Othniel would seem to require more than the one name Hathath.

21 Syr lists six sons of Caleb, including Elah and Naam. For the text see the apparatus in *BHK* and *BHS*.

22 עיר ואלה with LXX, Vg; MT עירו אלה (wrong word division).

23 אלה בני קנז. This is a conjectural transposing of the first two words and is adopted by Rothstein, 58; Curtis and Madsen, 110; Williamson, 60; Braun, 55–56; and Japhet, 111. MT ובני אלה וקנז, "and the sons of Elah and Kenaz," though this makes little sense after the preceding three nouns. *Sebir* reads ובן for ובני, and a few Hebrew MSS, LXX, Tg, Vg lack "and" before Kenaz; hence: "The son of Elah was Kenaz." Willi, 71, believes a name has dropped out before "Kenaz"; hence: "The sons of Elah were X and Kenaz." No certainty can be reached, but also very little is at stake for the interpreter.

24 Rudolph, 32, inserts: "And the sons of X: Jehallelel and Ezrah," names which he believes were lost by homoioarchton. Even this conjecture does nothing to link these figures to the overall genealogical structure of Judah.

25 ובני; LXX ובנו "and his son," with Kenaz being the antecedent of "his."

26 וּבְנֵי with *Sebir*, many Hebrew MSS, LXX, Vg; MT וּבֵן "son."

27 וַיֵּלֶד יֶתֶר with LXX; MT וַתַּהַר "And she conceived." וַיֵּלֶד was lost by haplography after the previous וְיָלוֹן "Jalon" and then יֶתֶר was changed to וַתַּהַר because of the following אֵת. Cf. Rudolph, 32; Braun, 55. Willi, 135, replaces וַיֵּלֶד with וְיָלוֹן. Curtis and Madsen, 111), and Japhet, 114, move the clause from the next verse, "And these are the sons of Bithiah, the daughter of Pharaoh, whom Mered took as his wife," to a position after "and Jalon" and add "and bore" after "she conceived." Cf. *NRSV*. *NIV* retains MT for the most part, but makes the changes discussed in textual notes 26 and 29, and then replaces "and she conceived" in v. 17 with "one of Mered's wives gave birth to."

28 וְאִשְׁתּוֹ הַיְהֻדִיָּה; Rudolph, 34, reads: וַלְמֶרֶד שְׁתֵּי נָשִׁים אִשָּׁה מִצְרִיָּה וְאִשָּׁה יְהוּדִיָּה וְאִשְׁתּוֹ הַמִּצְרִיָּה "Mered had two wives, an Egyptian wife and a Judahite wife. And his Egyptian wife." Cf. Richter, "Zu den Geschlechtsregistern 1 Chronik 2–9," *ZAW* 49 (1931) 266; Noth, "Liste," 107; Galling, 23. Willi, 71, retains MT. Knoppers, "Genealogy of Judah," 21, n. 33, offers a fresh alternative. He considers וְאִשְׁתּוֹ הַיְהֻדִיָּה "His Judahite wife" to be a misplaced doublet of an original אִשְׁתּוֹ הַיְהוּדִיָּה at the beginning of v. 19 (see textual note 31). This triggered a displacement in the order of v. 18, which originally began with v. 18b: "These are the sons of Bithiah the daughter of Pharaoh whom Mered took. She bore Jered . . . Zanoah." V. 19 would continue as in my translation.

29 וְאֵלֶּה; deleted by Rudolph, 34.

30 Willi, 68, 71, proposes that the names of the sons of Bithiah have been accidentally omitted.

31 אִשְׁתּוֹ הַיְהוּדִיָּה, with LXX^AN min Ἰουδαίας* LXX^B Ἰδουίας; MT אֵשֶׁת הוֹדִיָּה "the wife of Hodiah." Cf. Japhet, 115, and *NRSV*.

32 *NRSV* translates this word as "fathers" and thus makes the sons of the wife of Hodiah fathers of Keilah the Garmite and Eshtemoa the Maacathite.

33 Rudolph, 34, adds at this point on the basis of a

plus in LXX after "Naham" וְשִׁימוֹן אֲבִי דְּלָיָה אֲבִי . . . "Delaiah the father of . . . , and Shimon, the father of Ioman. And the sons of Naham, the father of Keilah: [a missing name]. . . ." But Willi, 71, has shown that there is a double rendering in LXX of "Naham the father of Keilah" in this verse and of "Shimon Amnon" in the next verse.

34 וְאֶשְׁתְּמֹעַ; Rudolph, 34, reads יִשְׁעִי "Ishi." Note that Eshtemoa already occurs in v. 17.

35 וְתִילוֹן, with Q, LXX, Vg, Tg; K (cf. LXX^L) וְתוֹלוֹן "Tolon."

36 וּבֶן; LXX וּבְנֵי "sons of."

37 At least one name was lost. Cf. Rudolph, 36. Various LXX MSS supply additional names at this point.

38 הַבָּאִים. Cf. Curtis and Madsen, 28, #9. The word occurs five times in Chronicles. Cf. Esth 1:6; 8:15; Ezek 27:16.

39 וְיוֹקִים; LXX וִיהוֹיָקִים, "Jehoiakim."

40 Rudolph, 36, "amtiert" (held office), following meaning 1 rather than 2 of the root בעל (*HALOT* 1:142).

41 וַיָּשֻׁבוּ (*qal* imperfect 3d masc. pl. with *wāw* consecutive from שׁוּב; cf. *HALOT* 2:446; and Rudolph, 36). MT וְיֹשְׁבֵי (anomalous). LXX = וַיָּשִׁב (Allen, *Greek Chronicles*, 2:107).

42 לֶחֶם or בֵּית לֶחֶם, "Bethlehem." For "but returned in Lehem" *KJV* has "Jashubilehem." Cf. BDB, 1000.

43 עֲתִיקִים. Cf. M. Dijkstra, "A Note on I Chr IV 22-23," *VT* 25 (1975) 671–74, who suggests a translation "remote" or "obscure." Rudolph, 36: "weggerückt" = "moved away."

44 Rudolph, 36, suggests that an omission has occurred, since he finds it impossible to consider the people in v. 22aβ potters.

45 וְיֹשְׁבֵי; the conjunction is lacking in LXX, Vg: "who were the inhabitants." The *wāw* can also have explicative force: "namely."

46 בִּמְלַאכְתּוֹ; considered a gloss by Rudolph, 36, to prevent the misunderstanding that they actually lived in the king's residence. Cf. the commentary.

4:1-23

Structure

In 4:1-23 the Chronicler completes the genealogy of Judah that was begun in 2:3. The genealogy of Hur, the son of Caleb and Ephrathah, was interrupted by the genealogy of the descendants of David in chap. 3. Part II′ of the genealogy of Judah is vv. 1-20 and part III is vv. 21-23 (see the discussion of Structure in chap. 2). It is difficult to achieve a totally coherent reading of this portion of the genealogy, in part because the text seems to have suffered severely from mistakes in copying, in part because the author seems to have utilized fragmentary sources that even he may not fully have understood, and in part because the overall design and intention of this section are not clear. I begin with the following outline of part II′:

A. 4:1. Linear genealogy reviewing the basic outline of the genealogy in chap. 2. As in 1:1-4 and 24-27, this genealogy consists only of a list of names and the reader has to link them with genealogical terms, such as A became the father of B, and B became the father of C.

B. 4:2-4. Segmented genealogy of the sons of Hur, the son of Caleb and Ephrathah (v. 4), consisting of the descendants of Reaiah, the great-grandson, through Shobal and Hur, of Caleb and Ephrathah (v. 2), and a genealogy, at least as I have reconstructed the text (see textual note 5), of Hareph, the grandson, through Hur, of Caleb and Ephrathah, and the brother of Shobal and Salma (2:50-51). The genealogy of Shobal was begun in 2:52-53 and continued in the genealogy of his son Reaiah in 4:2, while the genealogy of Salma was given in 2:54-55. In the genealogy of Hareph, we find the first of sixteen references in the chapter to someone being the "father" of a city (see the discussion of this phenomenon in the commentary to chap. 2, n. 8).

C. 4:5-8. Segmented genealogy of Ashhur, the son of Caleb and Ephrathah (2:24), tracing his descendants through his two wives, Helah and Naarah.

D. 4:9-10. Etiological account of a person named Jabez. This name was used for a city in 2:55.

E. 4:11-12. Genealogy of Chelub, who is probably to be identified with Caleb (see the commentary).

F. 4:13-15. Segmented genealogy of the sons of Kenaz (vv. 13 and 15, as reconstructed) tracing the lines of Othniel, Seraiah, and Caleb the son of Jephunneh.

G. 4:16-20. Genealogies of Jehallelel (v. 16), Ezrah (vv. 17-19), and Shimon (v. 20). The genealogical relationship of these three individuals to Judah is not stated, and no consensus on the structure of the genealogy of Ezrah has been achieved. These seem to be fragmentary genealogical notices that the Chronicler has included near the end of his discussion of Judah.

III. 4:21-23. Genealogy of Shelah, the third son of Judah through his wife Bath-shua (2:3). While the intervening verses have dealt with the descendants of Perez (2:4-5 and 2:9—4:19) and Zerah (2:4, 6-8), Judah's children through Tamar, the Chronicler concludes his genealogy of Judah by providing a genealogy for the one son born to Judah and Bath-shua who had descendants. The references to Shelah form an *inclusio* for the whole genealogy of Judah.

Design and Intention

This relatively complicated outline does not adequately indicate the many uncertainties about genealogical and geographical details faced by readers of this chapter. A rationale for the arrangement of the chapter may be found in the fact that after the introduction and recapitulation in v. 1, the Chronicler deals with the genealogy of Caleb's great-grandson Reaiah and his grandson Hareph in vv. 2-4, with the genealogy of Caleb's son Ashhur in vv. 5-8, with the genealogy of Caleb himself in vv. 11-12, and with the genealogy of Caleb's ancestral relationship to the Kenizzites in vv. 13-15, before including miscellaneous genealogical details in vv. 16-20 and returning to the beginning of the genealogy of Judah in vv. 21-23. The exact rationale for placing vv. 9-10, the etiology about Jabez, at its present location escapes us.

The overall intention of the Chronicler in chaps. 2–4 is clear: he gives the genealogy of Judah here first, the genealogy of Benjamin last in chaps. 8–9, and the genealogy of Levi in the middle, because these are the three tribes that make up the Jewish community of his time. In addition to the reason he gives for the demotion of the tribe of Reuben in 5:1-2, it is easily understandable why Judah would be given the first position, namely, because this tribe and its territory were central to an understanding of the postexilic community and because from this tribe came the dynasty of David, whose kings are the main characters in the narratives that follow and whose dynastic promise is embraced by the Chronicler in 1 Chronicles 17 and elsewhere. The genealogy of David, therefore, is surrounded by a multitude of genealogical details about Judah. Judah has preeminence, even in its genealogy, but it is also only one part of the twelve tribes of Israel.

In his recent monograph (*Judah–Jehud–Israel*) and in the first fascicles of his commentary in the Biblischer Kommentar series, Thomas Willi has called attention to the geographical details of chaps. 2–4 as being central to their meanings. In chap. 2 he saw movement within the tribe from the southern regions around Hebron to the more northern regions around Bethlehem and Jerusalem, and he noted David's move from Hebron to Jerusalem in chap. 3 and the ongoing occupation of Jerusalem by his descendants throughout the monarchical period and indeed up to the time of the Chronicler himself. Willi, 121, deemphasizes the connection of the genealogies of chap. 4 with those of chaps. 2–3, and finds the overall intention in this chapter the answer to the question: How does it go with the cities outside Hebron and Jerusalem, in terms of settlement? He calls attention to the sixteen references to "X the father of Y city."[1] There are five references to these "fathers" in section 2 (vv. 2-4), one in section 3 (vv. 5-8), two in section 5 (vv. 11-12), one in section 6 (vv. 13-15), five in section 7 (vv. 16-20), and two in part III (vv. 21-23). Section 7, which seems so obscure to us, may have been important to the Chronicler because it supplied so much geographical detail. The cities referred to in twelve of these formulas can be located on the map with some certainty.[2] Another four cities mentioned in the genealogies, but not included in the formulas, can also be identified.[3] While I appreciate and accept Willi's interpretation, it should not diminish the fact that the central purpose of this chapter is to continue the emphasis on the preeminence of Judah. The cities and towns mentioned are primarily in the western part of the province of Yehud, and several are outside that province itself: Anub, Eshtemoa, Maon, Soco, Zanoah, and Ziph.[4] If this geography were *the* intention of the Chronicler in this chapter, one might have expected notices that would more clearly correspond to the Judah of postexilic times.

The date of these disparate materials is uncertain. Few would accept Noth's dating to an early time in the divided monarchy[5] since there is no clear administrative purpose to this list and it does not seem to conform to what we know from elsewhere about the administration of the kingdom. Rudolph, 14, dated it to postexilic

times, while Japhet, 106, felt that it reflects preexilic conditions. She noted Late Biblical Hebrew in the word בֵּן in v. 21 and the phrase בעלו למואב in v. 22, to which could be added the possibly Persian word הָאֲחַשְׁתָּרִי in v. 6. That cities are listed that go beyond the borders of the postexilic province of Yehud suggests to me that the Chronicler has included preexilic materials, and that would fit the reference to the king in v. 23, which hardly refers to the Persian king.

Detailed Commentary

4:1. Linear Genealogy Reviewing the Basic Outline of the Genealogy in Chapter 2

Perez—Hezron—Caleb—Hur—Shobal

■ **1** *The sons of Judah: Perez, Hezron, Caleb, Hur, and Shobal:* If it is correct to restore the word "Caleb" (see textual note 1), this linear genealogy reviews the basic core of the genealogy of Judah from chap. 2: Perez (2:4); Hezron (2:5); Caleb (2:9 Chelubai); Hur (2:19); and Shobal (2:50). Shobal is the father of Reaiah, with whose descendants v. 2 continues. Hence the Chronicler reminds the reader where the discussion was before the inclusion of the list of Davidic descendants in chap. 3. I believe that this verse was written by the Chronicler himself, and its style as a list of names that needs to be interpreted as a linear genealogy conforms to what we have already seen at 1:1-4, 24-27.[6] If "Carmi," the reading in the MT, is retained, an awkward genealogy results that

---

1 4:3, Hareph the father of Beth-gader and X the father of Etam; 4:4, Penuel the father of Gedor, Ezer the father of Hushah, and Hur the father of Bethlehem; 4:5, Ashhur the father of Tekoa; 4:11, Mehir the father of Eshton; 4:12, Tehinnah the father of Ir-nahash; 4:14, Joab the father of Geharashim; 4:17, Ishbah the father of Eshtemoa; 4:18, Jered father of Gedor, Heber father of Soco, and Jekuthiel father of Zanoah; 4:19, Naham the father of Keilah; 4:21, Er father of Lecah and Laadah father of Mareshah. Willi counts only fifteen since he does not follow the same reconstruction employed here for v. 3 (see textual note 5).

2 Beth-Gader, Etam, Gedor, Hushah, Bethlehem, Tekoa, Eshtemoa, Soco, Zanoah, Keilah, Mareshah.

3 Zorah, Anub, Maon, and Ziph.

4 In chap. 2 the cities of Hebron, Maon, and Tappuah were also outside the boundaries of Yehud.

5 "Liste," 116–17.

6 Williamson, "Sources," 356, believes this verse was in the source that came to the Chronicler, because it does not have the same descent from Judah that the Chronicler had and because the expression "the sons of X" is always used to introduce a group of brothers, not a linear genealogy. The first objection is met by my reconstructing Caleb as part of the text and the second by my understanding of 1 Chr 3:16, where "the sons of Jeconiah" is followed by a linear genealogy.

requires the arbitrary insertion of three additional names and the repositioning of Carmi if it is not to contradict the data in chap. 2.[7] The very minor role played by Zerah in chap. 2 and his complete absence from chap. 4 also make the following reconstruction unlikely (additional names are in brackets).

Judah——Perez——Hezron——[Caleb]—Hur——Shobal
      [Zerah]—[Zimri]——Carmi

Willi, 122, who retains Carmi in v. 1, attempts to transcend the genealogical difficulties by interpreting this verse as a thematic presentation of the earlier southern and later northern settlement patterns he detected in chap. 2. He builds on the etymologies of Hezron and Carmi (courtyard dweller and vineyard person) and suggests they represent the old Judah in the Hebron area, whereas Hur and Shobal represent the newer settlements in the north. He also believes that the order of names in v. 1 is inverted in the subsequent verses in a chiastic pattern. This works fairly well for Shobal, whose son Reaiah's genealogy in v. 2 includes Zorah in the northern half of Judah, and also for Hur, to whom he assigns the materials in vv. 3-4. His ascription of vv. 5-12 to Hezron and Carmi, however, does not seem apt since the only geographic connection is Tekoa and the genealogical materials themselves are from Ashhur, who is the younger son of Caleb and hence without immediate relationship to Hezron, while Carmi seems to appear here only because the theory requires it. Willi, 123, notes that the materials in vv. 13-20 deal primarily with the south, in the regions around Debir (MR 151103) and Hebron (MR 160103), but he also finds references to more northerly cities such as Gedor (MR 158115), Soco,

Zanoah,[8] and Keilah (MR 150113). This dual geography leads him to associate these verses with the etymology of the first name in v. 1, Perez, which means "break through," "spread out," or the like. While I believe that Willi is correct in noting the important geographical emphases in this chapter, he also tends, in my judgment, to overplay his hand.

4:2-4. Segmented Genealogy of the Sons of Hur

Shobal ——— Reaiah ——— Jahath——┬ Ahumai
                                            └ Lahad

■ **2** *Reaiah the son of Shobal became the father of Jahath, and Jahath became the father of Ahumai and Lahad. These were the families of the Zorathites:* Reaiah is also mentioned in the segmented genealogy of Shobal in 2:52.[9] The Zorathites, who are viewed as Reaiah's descendants in 4:2, are linked to families associated with Kiriath-jearim, of whom Shobal himself is "father," in 2:52-53.[10] Older biblical traditions connect Zorah (MR 148131) with Dan (Josh 19:41; Judg 13:2), and its and Eshtaol's (MR 151132) connection with Judah was forged through the families of Kiriath-jearim (MR 159125) in 1 Chr 2:53.[11] Such fluidity is expected in genealogies. Jahath, Ahumai and Lahad are attested only here.

---

7   Hezron is the father of Jerahmeel, Ram, and Chelubai in 2:9, not Carmi. And Caleb, not Carmi, is the father of Hur in 2:19. For the reconstructed position of Carmi in 2:7, see textual note 8 to chap. 2 and the commentary on 2:7. See also the graphic presentation of the genealogy in Demsky, "Clans of Ephrath," 53 (cf. p. 49), which does retain Carmi. He, however, considers Hur, Shobal, Salma, and Hareph as brothers and believes the connection of them with Hezron was made either through Ram or Caleb.

8   With both Soco and Zanoah, there are two cities

identified with these names, and in each case I prefer the southern location: Soco MR 150090 and Zanoah MR 155095.

9   See textual note 48 in chap. 2

10   Williamson, 59, believes that this variant led to the disruption of 4:2 from 2:52.

11   Zorah is listed among the towns of Judah in Josh 15:33. Zorah was the site of one of Rehoboam's fortresses in 2 Chr 11:10, as were other towns mentioned in this chapter: Bethlehem, Etam, Tekoa, Soco, Mareshah, and Ziph. Zorah was inhabited in postexilic times (Neh 11:29).

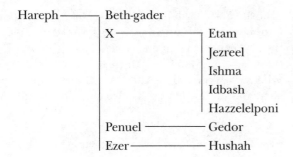

Hareph———Beth-gader
X———┬— Etam
     ├ Jezreel
     ├ Ishma
     ├ Idbash
     └ Hazzelelponi
Penuel ——————— Gedor
Ezer ———————— Hushah

■ **3** *These are the sons of Hareph, the father of Beth-gader: X the father of Etam, Jezreel, Ishma, and Idbash; and the name of their sister was Hazzelelponi:* This conjectural reconstruction of this verse as the descendants of Hareph the son of Hur takes account of the fact that descendants had already been given for Hur's other two sons, Shobal and Salma, in 2:52-54.[12] Some kind of connection to Hur in any case is assured by v. 4b: "These are the sons of Hur." Hareph was identified as the father of Beth-gader in 2:51, and the person represented by X is presumably a son of Hareph and the "father" of Etam (MR 167121),[13] located about 2 miles southwest of Bethlehem (MR 169123). I have interpreted Jezreel, Ishma, Idbash, and Hazzelelponi as descendants of X the father of Etam; they could also be his siblings. Jezreel should probably be understood as a Judahite town,[14] which was populated/founded by the same group that populated Etam, or it can be understood as a sibling of X or even as an ethnic group like the unknown Ishma and Idbash. The name Hazzelelponi has not been satisfactorily explained. Names of women/sisters usually appear at the end of a list of descendants (1:39; 3:9, 19; 7:30),[15] but there is no basis for improving the spelling of her name (see textual note 6) or moving her to another position in the genealogy.

■ **4** *and Penuel was the father of Gedor, and Ezer was the father of Hushah:* The conjunctions before Penuel and Ezer suggest that they were siblings of "X," with the listing of X's descendants ending with Hazzelelponi. Gedor (MR 158115),[16] southwest of Etam and 6.5 miles north of Hebron (MR 160103), and Hushah (MR 162124), northwest of Etam and 5 miles west of Bethlehem (MR 169123),[17] were "fathered" by Penuel and Ezer, respectively.

These are the sons of Hur the firstborn of Ephrathah, the father of Bethlehem: Hur's birth data here are congruent with 2:19, but Hur's fathering of Bethlehem is in tension with 2:54, where the same role is assigned to his son Salma. Bethlehem's "father" has moved up one generation in the genealogy, to Hur. In any case this tension does not justify the emending of the text to get rid of the father/son relationship between Hur and Bethlehem, as proposed by Rudolph (see textual note 7). This summary statement on Hur brings to an end a section of the genealogy that began in 2:50aβ.

4:5-8. Segmented Genealogy from Ashhur

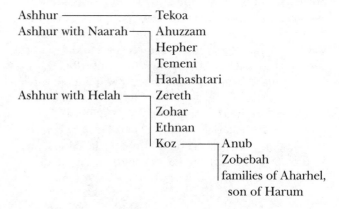

Ashhur ——————— Tekoa
Ashhur with Naarah—┬ Ahuzzam
                   ├ Hepher
                   ├ Temeni
                   └ Haahashtari
Ashhur with Helah ─┬ Zereth
                   ├ Zohar
                   ├ Ethnan
                   └ Koz ─┬ Anub
                          ├ Zobebah
                          └ families of Aharhel, son of Harum

---

12   Demsky, "Clans of Ephrath," 49–53, interprets vv. 3-4 as direct sons of Hur with no connection to Hareph.

13   Etam is mentioned in a list of eleven Judean towns preserved only in the LXX at Josh 15:59a, but lost in MT.

14   Cf. Josh 15:56, where it is paired with Jokdeam and Zanoah, and 1 Sam 25:43 and 27:3, according to which David married Ahinoam of Jezreel. J. D. Levenson and B. Halpern, "The Political Import of David's Marriages," *JBL* 99 (1980) 507–18, identify this with the northern Jezreel (MR 181218).

15   The last part of her name, פוני, may be a partially miswritten dittography of Penuel פנואל in v. 4 (Japhet, 107), but the remaining part of the name is still unexplained.

16   Presumably the same as Beth-gader. Willi, 124, notes it is 11 kilometers west of Tekoa. See also Sarah Ben-Arieh, "A Late Bronze Age Tome from Tell Jedur," *ErIsr* 15 (1981) 115–28.

17   It is frequently identified with Ḥūsân. Hushites are mentioned in connection with David in 2 Sam 21:18; 23:27//1 Chr 11:29; 1 Chr 20:4; 27:11.

■ **5** *Ashhur the father of Tekoa had two wives, Helah and Naarah:* Just as there is an apparent linguistic relationship between the names Ashhur (אשחור)[18] and his older brother Hur (חור; 2:19, 24), so Ashhur and Hur are the fathers of neighboring towns, Tekoa (MR 170115) and Bethlehem (MR 169123). Nothing is known about Ashhur's two wives, and their children are presented in the following verses in chiastic order.

■ **6** *Naarah bore to him Ahuzzam, Hepher, Temeni, and Haahashtari:* The king of Hepher is mentioned just after the king of Tappuah (MR 172168) in Josh 12:17, and all the land of Hepher is linked to Socoh[19] in the third Solomonic district 1 Kgs 4:10. Willi, 124, notes that a Hepher is the grandfather of the daughters of Zelophehad from Manassite Gilead (Num 26:32-33; 27:1; Josh 17:2-3). If this Hepher is the same person, it would represent a connection between Judah and Gilead, as in 1 Chr 2:21-22. Adam Zertal, however, has identified Hepher with Tell el-Muhaffar (MR 170205) just northwest of Dothan (MR 172202), which would place it in western Manasseh.[20] If this identification is correct, it is the only certain geographical information that can be gained from this verse. The great distance between Hepher and Tekoa calls for considerable caution. Temeni could be translated as "the southerner"[21] or it may be a gentilic name related to Timnah. Haahastari may have a Persian etymology.[22] If so, this would be a relatively late item in this genealogy.[23] Willi, 125, uses this evidence to deny that this genealogy reflects pre-state or even monarchical times.

■ **7** *The sons of Helah: Zereth, Zohar, Ethnan, and Koz:* Zohar is the name of one of Simeon's sons (Gen 46:10) and is the father's name of Ephron the Hittite, who lived near Hebron (Gen 23:8; 25:9). Japhet, 108, and Willi, 125, connect Ethnan (אתנן) to Ithnan (יתנן) mentioned in Josh 15:23 as a settlement in the southernmost part of Judah. If I have correctly reconstructed Koz in this verse (see textual note 9), giving Helah four sons just like Naarah, Oeming's observation that Ashhur has seven sons, like Jesse and Elioenai, becomes moot, since he had eight.[24]

■ **8** *Koz became the father of Anub and Zobebah, and the families of Aharhel son of Harum:* Anub ענוב may be identified with Anab (ענב MR 145091),[25] northeast of Beer-sheba (MR 134072). It appears in the list of Judean towns at Josh 15:50. Zobebah is unknown.[26] Something seems to be amiss with the text at the end of this verse since Koz cannot be the father of (the families of) Aharhel if Harum is.[27]

---

18 W. Sütterlin, "Thekoa," *PJ* 17 (1921) 42, n. 1, suggested a relationship between this name and Beit Saḥur, a town east of Bethlehem and on the road to Tekoa. If this is correct, his fathering of Tekoa makes perfect sense.

19 This is a site in Sharon, mentioned only here in the Bible, but also attested in Egyptian documents. See Mordecai Cogan, *I Kings* (AB 10; New York: Doubleday, 2000) 206. There are also two sites named Socoh in the southern part of Judah (Josh 15:35, 48).

20 *ABD* 3:138–39. This identification is endorsed by Cogan, *I Kings*, 206–7. Zelophehad's daughter Hoglah is connected to Beth-hoglah in the vicinity of Yaṣid (MR 176189).

21 Demsky, "Clans of Ephrath," 54, relates this either to Timnah in the Shephelah (MR 141132), where Amos from Tekoa carried on his occupation as a tender of sycamore figs (Amos 7:14) or to the southern Timnah (Josh 15:57) located near Maon and Ziph (Josh 15:55; MR 163090 and 162098, respectively). Judah's encounter with Tamar occurred while he was traveling toward Timnah (Gen 38:12).

22 Willi, 125; Rudolph, 14. See *HALOT* 1:37, which associates the word with the Persian word ḫšaça, meaning rule or dominion. Cf. Esth 8:10, 14. Myers, 1:28, considers this derivation very doubtful and cites C. C. Torrey, "Medes and Persians," *JAOS* 66 (1946) 7–8, who sees in this word the name Cyaxeres.

23 Because of this lateness, Williamson, 59, considers it secondary to the original compilation of the genealogy.

24 *Wahre Israel*, 105.

25 Cf. Josh 11:21, where in the account of Joshua's campaign it is associated with Debir (MR 151093) and Hebron (MR 160103).

26 Demsky, "Clans of Ephrath," 55, suggests that it may be related to Zobah (2 Sam 23:36; MR 162132) on the northern border of Judah, but this seems far removed from the other locations in vv. 5-8.

27 Demsky, "Clans of Ephrath," 55–56, takes Harum as a by-form of Ram, most of whose family was adopted into Jerahmeel. He also suggests that Aharhel is a dissimilated eponym, with a prefixed 'ālep, of the population of Halhul (MR 160109). Both points seem doubtful.

4:9-10. Etiological Account of Jabez

■ **9** *Jabez was honored more than his brothers; and his mother named him Jabez, saying, "Because I bore him in pain":* The only other mother who names her child in the genealogies is Maacah (1 Chr 7:16); here the father is not even mentioned. This etiological anecdote is unconnected genealogically to Judah, although a town Jabez with Kenite/Judahite population is mentioned in 2:55.[28] The two clauses in this verse—"Jabez was honored more than his brothers" and "Because I bore him in pain"[29]—comprise the conditions that are to be explained etiologically. The connection between Jabez's mother's pain and his name is not really philologically based, but is a popular etymology.[30] Note that the second and third letter of the Hebrew root are reversed: Jabez יעבץ and "in pain" בעצב. The problem seems to be understood this way: How can it be that someone named Jabez יעבץ, perhaps understood as the equivalent of Jazeb יעצב, meaning "he causes pain," is so respected ("honored more than his brothers") and presumably prosperous in the community? Why would someone with a name like that be more honored than his brothers? One's name is usually one's destiny: *nomen est omen.* Or, as the next verse will ask, is it? There also may be a conscious allusion to Gen 3:16: "to the woman he said, 'I will greatly increase your pangs in childbearing; in pain (בעצב) you shall bring forth children.'"[31]

■ **10** *Jabez called on the God of Israel, saying:* Jabez's action runs parallel to that of his mother and was the antidote to it: "she called (or named) her son, saying, . . . and he called (on the God of Israel) saying, . . ." His prayer was meant to counteract the threatening character of his name. This is the first reference to the divine title "God of Israel" in Chronicles.[32] In the midst of this extensive genealogy of one tribe, Judah, the Chronicler gives an all-Israel perspective through this prayer. As Willi notes, 126, the families and clans of Judah are not so much Jewish colonists but representatives and placeholders of a greater, eschatologically understood Israel. Perhaps this message was sufficient to justify the inclusion of this anecdote, even if it is really not connected genealogically to the context.

"Oh that you would thoroughly bless me and enlarge my territory, and let your hand be with me, and act without regard to the evil [inherent in my birth and name] so as not to cause me pain": The translation "thoroughly bless" is an attempt to show the force of the use of the infinitive absolute with a finite verb. Jabez asks for divine blessing in three forms. First, he wanted the expansion of his territory, a particularly appropriate petition within a genealogy so focused on geography and also appropriate for the relatively confined space of postexilic Yehud. Second, he requested the presence of God's hand, which would be the opposite of having God's hand against him. Think of the promise in Isa 66:14: "And it shall be known that the hand of Yahweh is with his servants, and his indignation is against his enemies." God's hand *with* Jabez would be the opposite of his hand *against* him.[33] Third, Jabez asked for liberation from the dire consequences of his birth and name, so that he would not suffer pain, as his mother had at his birth and as his name threatened him every moment of his life. He desired

---

28 If 1 Chr 4:2 followed 2:55 in a source document, this may have seemed an appropriate point to place this story, at the conclusion of the genealogies of Hur and Ashhur. The juxtaposition of 2:54 and 2:55 suggests that Jabez was occupied by descendants of Hur through the line of Salma. Did this anecdote once follow 2:55, but was moved when the Davidic descendants were inserted in chap. 3? Or has there been some kind of loss between 4:8 and 4:9 that would have given Jabez a direct genealogical connection to Judah?

29 One might also translate "in hard work" or "in painful struggle."

30 Cf. the popular etymological etiologies for the names Moab and Ammon (Gen 19:36-38), the names of Jacob's children in Genesis 29–30, and of Peleg in 1 Chr 1:19.

31 Cf. also Gen 35:18: בן־אוני ("son of sorrow") is the etiology given for Benjamin, whose mother died in childbirth.

32 It also appears in the genealogies at 1 Chr 5:26. The "God of Israel" or "Yahweh the God of Israel" appears 33 times in Chronicles. Japhet, *Ideology,* 20, notes that this epithet testifies to a direct bond between God and the people. By his very essence, Yahweh is the God of Israel.

33 For the peril of having the divine hand in opposition, see Isa 1:25; 5:25; Ezek 13:9.

that his name would not be his fate.[34] R. Christopher Heard has published a quite different understanding of 1 Chr 4:9-10.[35] He takes the suffix on עצבי ("cause me pain") as subjective and revocalizes מרעה as the word for "pastureland." The last half of v. 10 would then read: "Let your hand be with me, and make pastureland (available) without my causing grief (or: without my having to struggle for the additional land)." He also proposes that the brothers whom Jabez outranks in honor are the Simeonites (4:39-43) and the Reubenites, Gadites, and Manassites in 5:10, 18-22 who violently conquered Hagrite territory. Asking God for territory is the more honored path toward land acquisition. The Chronicler therefore seeks a nonviolent, nonvictimizing means of land acquisition. While the proposed theological message is very attractive, the necessity to add the word "available" and the somewhat forced interpretation of עצבי as referring to nonviolence make this proposal somewhat unlikely. Instead I think the author is stressing that God brought to pass that which Jabez had requested: in reporting God's answer to the prayer of Jabez, the Chronicler explains the high honor and apparent prosperity[36] Jabez enjoyed in spite of his name and because of his piety and prayer. This might be seen as the first reference to the doctrine of retribution in the book, a doctrine that plays such a central role in the narratives of Chronicles.[37]

4:11-12. Genealogy of Chelub

Unnamed parents ── ┌ Chelub ── Mehir ── Eshton ── ┌ Beth-rapha
                     └ Shuhah   │ Paseah
                                                       └ Tehinnah Ir-nahash

■ **11** *Chelub the brother of Shuhah became the father of Mehir, who was the father of Eshton:* Chelub's parents are not named, so it is not possible to fit him into the genealogy of Judah with certainty. Rudolph, 32, identifies him as a completely new individual, Chelub, whose name means something like "basket." I prefer to see Chelub as a by-form of Caleb (cf. Chelubai in 1 Chr 2:9). In this case the Chronicler may have believed he was including another fragmentary tradition about Caleb that helped to round out the picture of Judah. Perhaps because of his own uncertainty, the Chronicler did not make the identification with Caleb explicit. Unfortunately none of the other names in this verse can be identified, although I assume that Eshton is a place name. Japhet, 111, analyzed Shuhah שׁוּחָה as a metathesized variant for Hushah חוּשָׁה (cf. v. 4).[38]

■ **12** *Eshton became the father of Beth-rapha, Paseah, and Tehinnah the father of Ir-nahash:* The people of the unidentified town of Eshton founded three other cities and there was further migration from Tehinnah to a town called Ir-nahash. Neither of these last two towns is identified.[39] One of the descendants of Benjamin is called "Rapha" in 8:2, but Beth-rapha might more likely be connected to the Valley of Rephaim southwest of

---

34 While the final clause is very compressed, there is no justification for inserting the word ישועתי after the verb, as Rudolph, 30, proposed: "so that you will effect my good fortune, without harm and without causing me woe." On the basis of an Arabic etymology, D. Winton Thomas, "Translating Hebrew 'ĀSĀH," *BT* 17 (1966) 190–93, suggested a meaning "turn." Hence: "[you, God,] turn yourself from evil." Japhet, 110, points out that each of the four lines of the prayer rhymes because they end with the suffix of the first common singular.

35 R. Christopher Heard, "Echoes of Genesis in 1 Chronicles 4:9-10: An Intertextual and Contextual Reading of Jabez's Prayer," *JHS* 4 (2002) 1–28. Available at http://purl.org/jhs.

36 His territory had in fact been expanded.

37 A best-selling book in the United States, Bruce Wilkinson, *The Prayer of Jabez* (Sisters, OR: Multnomah, 2000), has interpreted the prayer of Jabez for very individualistic and materialistic purposes. See the critique by Rodney Clapp and John Wright, "God as Santa," *Christian Century* 119 (2002) 29–31.

38 See also BDB, 1001.

39 Williamson, 60, parses Ir-nahash as "city of the

Jerusalem (11:15; 14:9). The "sons of Paseah" are mentioned among the Nethinim (temple servants) in the list of those who returned from exile Ezra 2:49//Neh 7:51, but the word "Paseah" is probably to be understood there as the name of a person, since the list uses "men of" to refer to citizens of a city but "sons of" to refer to descendants of a person. In any case the location of the town Paseah is unknown.

These are the men of Rechab: "Men of" (cf. the previous comment) suggests that Rechab is a town, probably to be identified with Beth-rechab in 1 Chr 2:55.[40] This final clause seems to identify all of the people in vv. 11 and 12, or at least all the people in v. 12, as the men of Beth-rechab.[41] There seems to be no reason to identify them with the Rechabites, who were an ascetic group that carried out the commands of their ancestor Jonadab the son of Rechab not to raise crops, tend vineyards, or drink wine, and who did not build houses but lived in tents. The Rechabites were so-called because they traced their origins to a man named Rechab.[42]

4:13-15. Segmented Genealogy of the Sons of Kenaz

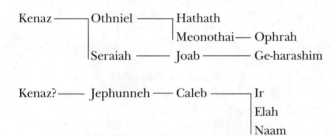

13 *The sons of Kenaz: Othniel and Seraiah; and the sons of Othniel: Hathath and Meonothai:* Othniel was the nephew of Caleb the son of Jephunneh (see the discussion of their relationship in the commentary on 2:9 and 49), and Othniel is consistently referred to as the son of Kenaz (Josh 15:17; Judg 1:13; 3:9, 11). Kenaz is the younger brother of Caleb. Kenaz is related genealogically in the Bible to both Edom, where he is identified as the son of Eliphaz, the firstborn of Esau and Adah (see 1 Chr 1:36//Gen 36:11), and to Judah. The association with Judah, however, is not worked out in genealogical detail, that is, we are not told the missing genealogical links between Judah and Kenaz. Caleb the son of Jephunneh is called a Kenizzite in Num 32:12 (cf. Josh 14:6, 14),[43] and he is associated with the tribe of Judah in Num 13:6. Kenaz is thought to be the eponymous ancestor of the Kenizzites (referred to only in Gen 15:19 among the pre-Israelite inhabitants of the land). Seraiah and Hathath are unknown, but Meonothai[44] is usually related to Maon (MR 162090), about 8 miles southeast of Hebron (MR 160103).[45] Since Caleb the son of Jephunneh was given Hebron by Joshua, according to tradition (Josh 14:13), the close relationship of these men and their cities is to be expected. Othniel is associated with the city of Kiriath-sepher (MR 151093), southwest of Hebron and northwest of Maon in Josh 15:16-17 (see the commentary on 1 Chr 2:9 and 55).

14 *And Meonothai became the father of Ophrah:* While there are sites called Ophrah in Benjamin (Josh 18:23)

---

craftsman," which may account for the position of the following verses, which mention the Valley of Craftsmen in v. 14, linen workers in v. 21, and potters in v. 23. Others have proposed "Snake city," "city of copper," or "city of smiths." Jo Ann H. Seely, "Irnahash," *ABD* 3:462, listed three possible locations: Deir Nakhkhas (MR 142113), favored by Abel; Khirbet en-Nahas (MR 191010), south of the Dead Sea, favored by Glueck; somewhere in the area of Tekoa, favored by Aharoni. See also *HALOT* 2:691; Frank S. Frick, "Rechab," *ABD* 5:630–32.

40 See the commentary there for its possible identification with Beth-marcaboth, west of Beer-sheba.

41 Cf. "these are the men of Kenaz" at the end of v. 15.

42 See Jehonadab the son of Rechab in 2 Kgs 10:15-17,

23, and Jer 35:2-19; and the article by C. H. Knights, "Kenites = Rechabites? 1 Chronicles ii 55 reconsidered," *VT* 43 (1993) 10–18.

43 Some scholars have associated the Kenizzites with the Horites on the basis of names in Gen 36:20-30. See H. L. Ginsberg and B. Maisler, "Semitised Hurians in Syria and Palestine," *JPOS* 14 (1934) 258–59, but this has been deemed unconvincing by de Vaux, *Early History,* 137.

44 *HALOT* 2:611. "Maon" means "dwelling" or "related." The form is feminine plural with a gentilic ending *-ay.*

45 In Josh 15:55 Maon is associated with Carmel (MR 162092), just to the north of Maon, and with Ziph (MR 162098), north of Carmel.

and Manasseh (Judg 6:11), there may have been such a town in southern Judah too, since the name apparently refers to the nature of the soil.[46]

Joab the father of Ge-harashim, so named because they were artisans: Joab, otherwise unknown, is the founder or colonizer of a town called Ge-harashim (lit. "the valley of the craftsmen").[47] Lod (MR 140151) and Ono (MR 137159) are located in the "valley of craftsmen" in postexilic times (Neh 11:35),[48] but these cities are much farther to the north and west than other Kenizzite references (about 30 miles northwest of Jerusalem).[49] Glueck located the Valley of the Craftsmen mentioned in this verse in an area southeast of the Dead Sea, along with Ir-nahash, mentioned in v. 12.[50]

■ **15** *The sons of Caleb the son of Jephunneh: Ir and Elah and Naam.* Caleb is identified three times as a Kenizzite in earlier writings (Num 32:12; Josh 14:6, 14), and that seems to be presupposed by the conclusion to this verse, which refers to the preceding entries as "the sons of Kenaz." The Chronicler, however, does not draw a specific genealogical link from Caleb to Kenaz, nor does he resolve the question of how Caleb the son of Hezron (1 Chr 2:9) and Caleb the son of Jephunneh relate to each other, let alone how they relate to Chelub in 4:11. Japhet, 113, believes that the Chronicler ascribed a full Judean affiliation to the main Calebite tribe through Hezron, as he did with the Jerahmeelites, but that Caleb the son of Jephunneh and his brother Othniel represent an earlier stage in the history of tradition. Unfortunately, the three names considered "sons" of Caleb do not offer much help. Are they meant to be cities or people? Ir is the common word for "city," and Naam is totally unknown. Elah could be located in the Valley of Elah, where David fought Goliath (1 Sam 17:2, 19; 21:19), probably the Wadi es-Sant, about 15 miles west

southwest of Bethlehem, but Elah means "terebinth," and an unknown village may have adopted that name.[51] Note also the Edomite chieftain with the name Elah (Gen 36:41//1 Chr 1:36).

4:16-20. Genealogies from Jehallelel, Ezrah, and Shimon

Jehallelel ——┬ Ziph
             │ Ziphah
             │ Tiria
             │ Asarel

■ **16** *The sons of Jehallelel: Ziph, Ziphah, Tiria, and Asarel:* The section of this genealogy in vv. 16-20 is very difficult. How, for example, does Jehallel relate to any of the preceding descendants of Judah? Noth related Jehallelel and Ezra to Hazzelelponi and Ezer in vv. 3-4, thus linking them to Hur or Hareph, but has had few followers.[52] The context of course demands that he must be descended from Judah and perhaps implies that he is even related to Caleb (see also Ezrah below). Ziph (MR 162098) is located southeast of Hebron (MR 160103), north of Carmel (MR 162092) and Maon (MR 162090; see v. 13),[53] and Ziphah may be a dittograph of it, but note that there are two Ziphs in the town lists of Judah, at Josh 15:24 and 55. Ziphah's location is unknown in any case. According to 1 Chr 2:42, Mesha, the firstborn of Caleb, was the "father" of Ziph. Ziph is one of four cities that appear on the *lmlk* jar handles[54] and was the site of one of Rehoboam's fortresses (2 Chr 11:8). Albright compared Tiria to a tribe "Tayaru" found on an

---

46   Aharoni, *Land of the Bible*, 109; *HALOT* 2:862–63 (reddish-white color of the dust).

47   I. Mendelsohn, "Guilds in Ancient Palestine," *BASOR* 80 (1940) 19, suggested that Joab was president of the craftsmen's guild and chief magistrate of the place inhabited by craftsmen.

48   See M. Har-El, "The Valley of the Craftsmen (Ge' Haharasim)," *PEQ* 109 (1977) 75–86.

49   The Chronicler attributes the founding of Lod and Ono to Elpaal a Benjaminite in 1 Chr 8:12. The book of Nehemiah assumes these cities are outside the postexilic province of Yehud (Neh 6:2).

50   Nelson Glueck, "Kenites and Kennizzites," *PEQ* 72 (1940) 22–24.

51   Contrary to Willi, 131, it does seem erroneous *(abwegig)* to associate Elah with Elath (אילה) on the Gulf of Aqaba.

52   Noth, "Liste," 105.

53   Hence it is outside the province of Yehud. Cf. 1 Sam 23:14.

54   H. Darrell Lance, "Stamps, Royal Jar Handle," *ABD* 6:184-185.

Egyptian stele from the time of Seti I.[55] The location for it and Asarel[56] remain unknown.

■ **17-20** The textual problems in these verses are severe. A literal translation of MT shows the difficulties: "The son of Ezrah: Jether, Mered, Epher, and Jalon, and she conceived Miriam, Shammai, and Ishbah the father of Eshtemoa. 18/ And his Judahite wife bore Jered father of Gedor, Heber father of Soco, and Jekuthiel father of Zanoah. And these are the sons of Bithiah, the daughter of Pharaoh, whom Mered took as his wife. 19/ The sons of the wife of Hodiah, the sister of Naham, the father of Keilah: the Garmites and Eshtemoa the Maacathite." Who is "she" in v. 17 and why does she only conceive and not bear? Who is the antecedent of "his" in v. 18? Why are both the Judahite wife in v. 18 and the wife of Hodiah in v. 19 nameless? And why are Hodiah's sons ascribed to his wife and not to both parents? Note that there are ten textual notes in my translation of these verses (textual notes 26–35), with the reconstruction discussed in note 27 anything but certain. I find myself in general agreement with Willi rather than Japhet on the interpretation of these verses, while Rudolph goes another and quite adventuresome way altogether. The following graphics show the disparate genealogies each of these scholars has created.[57]

4:17-19 Japhet[58]

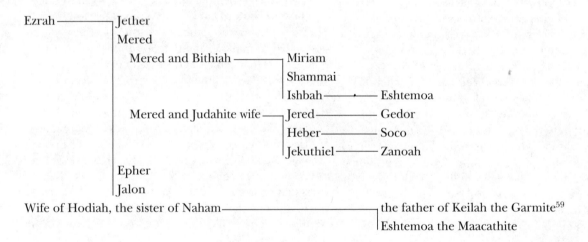

---

55 William F. Albright, "The Smaller Beth-Shan Stele of Sethos I (1309–1290 B.C.)," *BASOR* 125 (1952) 30. He also compared Asarel with Asriel in Manasseh (Num 26:31; Josh 17:2; 1 Chr 7:14) and linked Epher in 1 Chr 4:17 to the Apiru mentioned on the stele. Other ties between Judah and Manasseh appear in 2:21-23.

56 אשראל. Cf. אשראלה "Asarelah" among the sons of Asaph in 1 Chr 25:2.

57 For Rudolph I have included v. 16 in the graphic presentation since his differences emerge already there.

58 Japhet moves v. 18b to a position after v. 17a (cf. textual note 27), reads the first word of v. 17 as "sons" instead of "son" (cf. textual note 26), and adds ותלד after ותהר in v. 17a (cf. textual note 27). She retains the MT at the start of v. 19 (cf. textual note 31).

59 Or "Garmite" may be a second son of "X," making three sons altogether.

4:17-19 Willi[60]

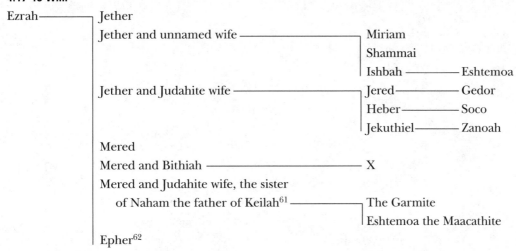

```
Ezrah ─────┬─ Jether
           │  Jether and unnamed wife ──────────────────┬─ Miriam
           │                                            │  Shammai
           │                                            │  Ishbah ───────── Eshtemoa
           │  Jether and Judahite wife ─────────────────┬─ Jered ───────── Gedor
           │                                            │  Heber ───────── Soco
           │                                            │  Jekuthiel ──────── Zanoah
           │  Mered
           │  Mered and Bithiah ────────────────────────── X
           │  Mered and Judahite wife, the sister
           │     of Naham the father of Keilah[61] ──────┬─ The Garmite
           │                                            │  Eshtemoa the Maacathite
           │  Epher[62]
```

4:20 Japhet and Willi

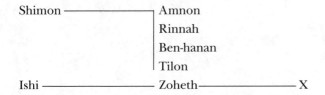

```
Shimon ──────────────┬─ Amnon
                     │  Rinnah
                     │  Ben-hanan
                     │  Tilon
Ishi ─────────────────── Zoheth ──────────────── X
```

60 Willi follows a text like my translation except as indicated under n. 60 below.

61 Willi, 135, also considers and finally rejects an alternate translation for the last part of the verse beginning with Naham: "Naham the father of Keilah the Garmite and the Maacathite Eshtemoa." In this case the sons of neither of Mered's wives are mentioned in the text.

62 Willi, 135, replaces Jalon (וילון) with ויולד "he became the father of." Cf. textual note 27.

Rudolph[63]

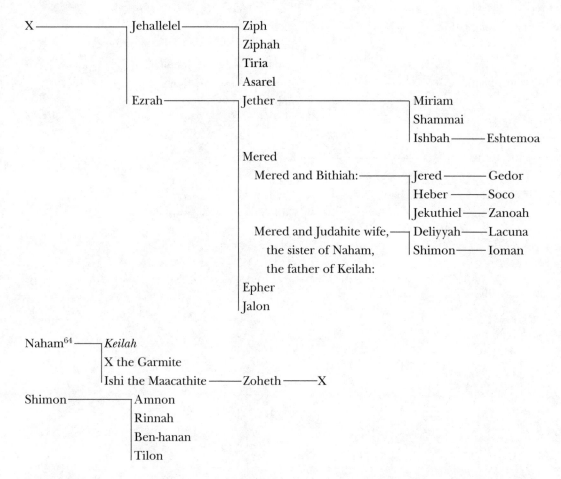

```
X ————————————┬— Jehallelel ————————┬— Ziph
              │                      │  Ziphah
              │                      │  Tiria
              │                      └  Asarel
              │
              └— Ezrah ——————————————┬— Jether ——————————————┬— Miriam
                                     │                       │  Shammai
                                     │                       └  Ishbah ——————— Eshtemoa
                                     │
                                     │  Mered
                                     │     Mered and Bithiah: ——————┬— Jered ——————— Gedor
                                     │                              │  Heber ——————— Soco
                                     │                              └  Jekuthiel ———— Zanoah
                                     │
                                     │     Mered and Judahite wife, —┬— Deliyyah ———— Lacuna
                                     │        the sister of Naham,   └  Shimon ——————— Ioman
                                     │        the father of Keilah:
                                     │
                                     │  Epher
                                     └  Jalon
```

```
Naham[64] ————┬— Keilah
              │  X the Garmite
              └  Ishi the Maacathite ——— Zoheth ——— X

Shimon ———————┬— Amnon
              │  Rinnah
              │  Ben-hanan
              └  Tilon
```

Each of the (non-Rudolph) reconstructions has difficulties, but some kind of conjecture is necessary to overcome the great difficulties in MT. In Japhet's reconstruction there is no convincing explanation of how v. 18b got displaced to its present position. In Willi's reconstruction the replacement of an original "and Jether became the father of" by "Jalon and she conceived" is equally difficult, especially for the "Jether"/ "she conceived" switch. The choice between "the wife of Hodiah" and "his [Mered's] Judahite wife" depends on how much credence one puts on the LXX evidence. On the basis of my own translation, which is close to that of Willi, I will now interpret this genealogy, discussing the significant alternatives in Japhet's interpretation where appropriate.

---

63 Rudolph makes an addition at the start of v. 16 (textual note 24), a second addition in v. 18 (textual note 28), and a third in v. 20 (textual note 33). He also makes the same changes that I do in textual notes 26 and 31, and the same change Willi made in textual note 27. He also replaces Eshtemoa with Ishi in v. 19 (textual note 34).

64 He was the brother of Mered's Judahite wife.

■ **17** *The sons of Ezrah: Jether, Mered, Epher, and Jalon:*
None of these names is known, but Jether's and Mered's
descendants will be traced in the following verses. In
Japhet's reconstruction only Mered had descendants,
and Willi does not include Jalon. Ezrah is not connected
explicitly to the genealogy of Judah except by being
placed in this context.

*and Jether became the father of Miriam, Shammai, and Ish-
bah father of Eshtemoa:* Eshtemoa (MR 156089) is well outside the province of Yehud, about 8.5 miles southwest of
Hebron (MR 160103).[65] It also appears in v. 19, where
Eshtemoa the Maacathite is listed among the sons of
Mered, Jether's brother. The only other Miriam in the
Bible is the well-known sister of Moses. It seems to be
the name of a man here.[66] The name Shammai appears
in 2:28 and 44-45 in other genealogical relationships, but
these are no doubt different people with the same common name. Instead of Jether as ancestor, Japhet's reconstruction places Mered and Bithiah as parents here, thus
making Pharaoh's daughter the mother of Miriam!

■ **18** *And his Judahite wife bore Jered father of Gedor, Heber
father of Soco, and Jekuthiel father of Zanoah:* The three
sons of Jether in the previous verse are presumably
purely Calebite in their heritage, but the sons mentioned
here are a mixture of Calebite and Judahite lineages
(Willi, 133).[67] While the three sons of Jether and his
Judahite wife[68] are otherwise unknown, the three towns

"fathered" by them are all well known: Gedor, about 6.5
miles north of Hebron (MR 158115; cf. v. 4 above, where
Penuel is listed as its father, and 2:51, where Hareph is
identified as father of Beth-gader, which may be an alternate name for Gedor); Soco (MR 150090),[69] about 10
miles southwest of Hebron and 3 miles west of Eshtemoa
(MR 156089);[70] and Zanoah is either located at Khirbet
Zanu (MR 150125; Josh 15:34), a little over 2 miles
southeast of Beth-shemesh (MR 147128) in the northern
Shephelah;[71] or, more likely, this is a reference to a town
by the same name in the southern hill country of Judah
(Josh 15:56), possibly to be located at Khirbet Beit Amra
(MR 155095).[72]

*And these are the sons of Bithiah, the daughter of Pharaoh,
whom Mered took as his wife: X:* In this reconstruction I
assume that the names of the children of Mered and
Bithiah have been accidentally omitted, whereas in
Japhet's reconstruction the children of Mered and
Bithiah were Miriam, Shammai, and Ishbah (see v. 17).
This is the sixth occasion in the genealogy of Judah
where an Israelite marries a foreign woman.[73] One
might wonder about the likelihood of an insignificant
Judean like Mered marrying a daughter of Pharaoh. In
addition, both parts of the name Bithiah seem Semitic,
the second theophoric part Yahwistic, rather than Egyptian.[74] Since the reputed marriage of Solomon to a
daughter of Pharaoh has been greeted by modern schol-

---

65 Cf. Josh 15:50; 21:14; 1 Sam 30:28. Braun, 59, puts
    it 20 miles south of Hebron!
66 The Tg, however, identifies her with Ephrath.
    Laban and Ben Zvi, "Observations," 463, believe
    that she is "most likely" a daughter.
67 If Knoppers's reconstruction is followed (cf. textual
    note 28), Gedor, Heber, and Jekuthiel are the sons
    of Mered and Bithiah, and there is no need to iden-
    tify a lacuna at the end of this verse.
68 In Japhet's reconstruction the parents are Jether's
    brother Mered and his Judahite wife.
69 Josh 15:48.
70 Braun, 59, notes that Rudolph, 35, and Myers, 1:29,
    argue for a southern location, while Noth and van
    Selms favor a northern site in the Shephelah (Josh
    15:35; 2 Chr 28:18; MR 147121). Japhet, 115, says
    Socoh is either a town in the vicinity of Zanoah or a
    town near Eshtemoa. Zanoah is in the Shephelah.
71 Cf. Josh 15:34. This city was reoccupied by those
    returning from exile (Neh 11:30), and its inhabi-

tants participated in the rebuilding of the wall of
Jerusalem (Neh 3:13).
72 See the discussion in Wade R. Kotter, "Zanoah,"
    ABD 6:1039.
73 Tg adds: "She [Bithiah] became a proselyte, and
    Mered, who was Caleb, married her, for he had
    opposed the advice of the spies." The rabbis identi-
    fied Mered with Caleb since he rejected (מרד) the
    counsel of the other spies, and they identified
    Bithiah with the daughter of Pharaoh who pulled
    Moses out of the Nile (Exod 2:7). See McIvor, *Tar-
    gum*, 60. Tg, therefore, treats this mixed marriage in
    a quite different way. Bithiah becomes a proselyte
    before Mered marries her.
74 H. C. Lo, "Bithiah," *ABD* 1:750.

ars with astonishment, even skepticism (1 Kgs 3:1; 7:8; 9:16; 11:1),[75] how much more doubtful does this marriage of an Israelite commoner to Pharaoh's daughter seem.

Richard Steiner has supported the plausibility of this marriage. He calls attention to the resemblance between the name Bithiah, at least in the Babylonian and Alexandrian reading traditions,[76] to Bint(i)-'Anat (the Daughter of Anat), the Semitic name of the daughter and later wife of Ramesses II, and the lack of such names formed by "daughter" or "son" and a divine name among native Israelites. He hypothesizes that the name was later changed, during the woman's lifetime or later, from "Daughter of Anat" to "Daughter of Yahweh" or Bithiah. He hypothesizes further that she may have been a granddaughter or great-granddaughter of Ramesses III, at which time Egypt had lost considerable power and prestige and could no longer afford to be choosy when marrying off a daughter. Despite the strength of his case, there are three troublesome points about this proposal in my judgment: evidence that the genealogy of Judah, or even this part of it, came from the twelfth or eleventh century is very weak; a name change from a Canaanite to an Israelite name is demanded (although the Hadoram/Jehoram analogy in 1 Chr 18:10; 2 Sam 8:10 is useful); and finally, Bithiah's husband Mered is elevated by Steiner, arbitrarily in my judgment, to a Judahite prince or elder.[77]

Whatever the historical truth may be,[78] the union of Mered and Bithiah is another in a long list of mixed marriages included without critique in this genealogy: Judah with a Canaanite woman (1 Chr 2:3); the Ishmaelite Jether (2:17); Jarha the Egyptian slave (2:34); the Canaanite Bath-shua as the mother of the Shelanites (2:3; 4:21-23), and the marriage, or at least relationship, of three Shelanite men/families to Moab (4:22). Genealogically the notice of this marriage also shows a close relationship between families of Judah and families from Egypt at some period.

■ **19** *The sons of his Judahite wife, the sister of Naham, the father of Keilah:* It is strange that the name of Mered's Judahite wife is not preserved, but that of her brother is.[79] Naham founded Keilah (MR 150113), located about 7 miles east of Mareshah (MR 140111) and 8 miles northwest of Hebron in the southwest section of Yehud. Representatives from this city worked on the wall of Jerusalem at the time of Nehemiah (Neh 3:17-18).[80]

the Garmite and Eshtemoa the Maacathite: Mered's Judahite wife had two descendants. The word "Garmite" is unknown. Eshtemoa was joined to the genealogy of Judah in two different ways since it is linked genealogically to Ishbah, the grandson, through Jether, of Ezrah (v. 17), and here to Mered, the brother of Jether. The epithet Maacathite—related to Maacah—suggests another tie between Judah and northeast Transjordan (cf. 1 Chr 2:48 and 3:2).

■ **20** *The sons of Shimon: Amnon, Rinnah, Ben-hanan, and Tilon. The sons of Ishi: Zoheth, and the son of Zoheth was: X:* It is not clear how Shimon and Ishi fit into the genealogy, and there is apparently a lacuna where the name of the son of Zoheth should be. None of the names in this verse is known.

---

75 None of these passages occurs in Chronicles, but the Chronicler does refer to this marriage in 2 Chr 8:11//1 Kgs 9:24. See Abraham Malamat, "Aspects of the Foreign Policies of David and Solomon," *JNES* 22 (1963) 8–17; idem, "A Political Look at the Kingdom of David and Solomon and Its Relations with Egypt," in Ishida, *Studies*, 198–200; and D. B. Redford, *Egypt, Canaan, and Israel in Ancient Times* (Princeton: Princeton Univ. Press, 1992) 310–11. Rudolph, 35, finds here an intentional comparison with Solomon, which seems unlikely to me.

76 LXX^A *Βεθθια*.

77 See Richard C. Steiner, "*Bittĕ-Yâ*, daughter of Pharaoh (1 Chr 4,18), and *Bint(i)-'Anat,* daughter of Ramesses II," *Bib 79* (1998) 394–408.

78 Knoppers, "Intermarriage," 21, observes that this

marriage acknowledges traditional Egyptian interests in southern Judah. In other words, the "marriage" reflects tribal relationships and not necessarily an actual marriage between a man and a woman.

79 H. C. Lo, "Naham," *ABD* 4:995, identifies Naham as the sister-in-law of Hodiah. In the MT these sons come from the nameless wife of Hodiah (see textual note 31).

80 Cf. also Josh 15:44 and 1 Sam 23:1.

4:21-23. Genealogy from Shelah

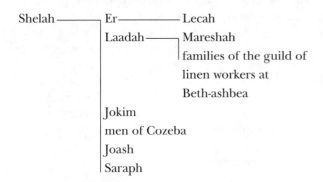

Shelah —— Er —————— Lecah
Laadah —— Mareshah
families of the guild of
linen workers at
Beth-ashbea
Jokim
men of Cozeba
Joash
Saraph

■ **21** *The sons of Shelah son of Judah: Er father of Lecah, Laadah father of Mareshah, and the families of the guild of linen workers at Beth-ashbea:* With this verse the Chronicler returns to 1 Chr 2:3 and Shelah the third son of Judah and Bath-shua. Shelah's role as parent in Genesis 38 is unclear since we are only told that his father delayed to give him to Tamar. Ironically here he fathers a child named Er, which he was supposed to do with Tamar according to the principles of levirate marriage. Er is both the firstborn of Judah and his grandson, through Shelah, showing again fluidity in the Judahite genealogy.[81] There is no indication here that Tamar was the mother of this child. Lecah[82] and Laadah are unknown. Mareshah (MR 140111), about 15 miles south-west of Beth-zur (159119), is a well-known town in the Shephelah, where Rehoboam placed one of his fortresses (2 Chr 11:8). In 1 Chr 2:42 Mareshah is listed as the grandson of Caleb and the "father" of Hebron. The reference to the guild of the linen[83] workers provides information on vocations much like the artisans in the Valley of the Craftsmen (v. 14) and the potters (v. 23). Unfortunately, the town of Beth-ashbea is unknown, but we would assume that both it and Lecah were in the vicinity of Mareshah.[84]

■ **22** *and Jokim, and the men of Cozeba, and Joash, and Saraph, who had married into Moab but returned to Lehem:* Jokim is a shortened form of Jehoiakim (see textual note 39). The men of Cozeba, Joash, and Saraph had either intermarried (בעלו) with women from Moab (cf. *NRSV, JPSV*),[85] ruled there (cf. *NIV*),[86] or worked there.[87] In any case, these men had later returned to Lehem or Bethlehem. If the interpretation of the name Lehem as Bethlehem is correct, their journey echoes that of Naomi from the book of Ruth. If these men had intermarried with Moab, note again that this mixed marriage is not criticized. Even their working there without critique is striking. Since Moab disappeared from history in the sixth century and only reemerged to play a role in Maccabean times, we seem to be dealing with a preexilic tradition.[88] The town Cozeba is often compared with Chezib, where Shelah's mother bore him (Gen 38:5) or Achzib (possibly

---

81 Japhet, 116, calls attention to the fact that Ram was the son of Hezron in 1 Chr 2:9 and his grandson through Jerahmeel in 2:25. I interpret the latter reference to mean that the Ramites were eventually absorbed into Jerahmeel. Japhet also notes that Dishon is the son and grandson of Seir (Gen 36:21, 25//1 Chr 1:38, 41). There may be a reference to a Shelanite in 1 Chr 9:5//Neh 11:5 (see the commentary).

82 E. Meyer turned Lecah into Lachish. Cf. Aharoni, *Land of the Bible,* 247.

83 בוץ; cf. 1 Chr 15:27 (//2 Sam 6:14); 2 Chr 2:13; 3:14; 5:12; Esth 1:6; 8:15; Ezek 27:16. The more common and older word in the OT is שש. Avi Hurvitz, "The Usage of שש and בוץ in the Bible and Its Implication for the Date of P," *HTR* 60 (1967) 117–21, notes that בוץ did not penetrate into Biblical Hebrew until the 6th century. He also notes that בוץ is common in Aramaic and Akkadian, whereas שש is Egyptian in origin.

84 Japhet, 117, suggests that Beth-ashbea may refer to the ethnic affiliation of the linen workers.

85 LXX translates with κατοικεω = "settled." Tg identifies Joash with Mahlon and Saraph with Chilion, the spouses of Ruth and Orpah from the book of Ruth, and adds: "who took wives from the daughters of Moab."

86 As David did according to 2 Sam 8:2. For this interpretation one would expect the verb to be followed by *bêt,* not *lāmed,* but for the translation "marry" one would expect a direct object, not a prepositional phrase.

87 See M. Dijkstra, "A Note on 1 Chr IV 22-23," *VT* 25 (1975) 671–74, who took בעל as a phonetic variant of פעל.

88 But note Pahath-moab, who is known as the ancestor of one of the clans that returned from the Babylonian exile in Ezra 2:6; 8:4; 10:30; Neh 3:11; 7:11; 10:14. Allen, 331, dates the incident in this verse to the time of the united monarchy.

MR 145116; cf. Josh 15:44 [which also mentions Keilah and Mareshah]; Mic 1:14), both of which have the same three radicals.[89]

(now the records are ancient): This comment, possibly by the Chronicler himself, points to the general antiquity of this information. I share this judgment, for while a few items noted above (the Persian name, the word used for linen) seem late, much of the rest would seem to be pre-exilic. The remark about the records being ancient may reflect puzzlement over the fact that Shelah disappears out of the history of Judah only to reappear in postexilic references such as 1 Chr 9:5 and Neh 11:5.

■ **23** *These were the potters and the inhabitants of Netaim and Gederah:* The potters are the final guild mentioned in this chapter (see vv. 14, 21) and refer to the following towns of Netaim and Gederah.[90] The towns Netaim and Gederah mean something like "plantings" or "(animal) pen" and so cannot be located with certainty topographically,[91] although a Gederah does appear in the second administrative district of Judah (Josh 15:36).

they lived there with the king in his service: "There" probably refers to Lehem = Bethlehem and hence only the families of Cozeba, Joash, and Saraph were involved in making pottery, not all the Shelanites. The final phrase does not mean that they were living in the residence/palace of the king, but that they prepared pottery for him, full or part-time. "King" surely refers to one of the Davidic kings, not the great king of Persia. In the early years of the twentieth century, R. A. Stewart Macalister interpreted chaps. 2 and 4 as a genealogy of pottery families and interpreted the four names that appear on the pottery handles that have been found by archaeologists as people rather than places. He arranged them in the order of Memshat (which he believed was miswritten as Mareshah in the Bible), Ziph, Hebron, and Sochoh,

assigning the first two to the years 817–798 and the last two to 734–719. A few years later, however, he dated the genealogies and the stamped jar handles to postexilic times. While Macalister's articles abound with speculations and arbitrary emendations, Peter Welten concluded that he was probably right in his notion that potters who were not exclusively in royal service would occasionally fill orders from the king for storage vessels and mark them with the royal stamps to separate them from their regular production.[92]

Conclusion

The twenty-three verses that continue the genealogy of Judah form an *inclusio* with the beginning of that genealogy because of its ending with the sons of Shelah (vv. 21-23). The earlier (2:3-55) and later (4:1-23) parts of the genealogy of Judah form an envelope around the genealogy of David and his descendants, who are the centerpiece of the tribe of Judah in chap. 3.

Willi may be right that the Chronicler is concerned in this chapter to report the status of the settlement of Judahite cities aside from Hebron and Jerusalem, particularly as he refers to individuals W or X who was the "father" of city Y or Z. The reference to the God of Israel in the prayer of Jabez (vv. 9-10) sounds an all-Israel signal right in the midst of this extensive genealogy of only one tribe.

The fragmentary and uncertain information in this chapter, whether because of textual error or the nature of the genealogies that the Chronicler was able to assemble, prevents pushing on to any more certain message in 4:1-23.

---

89 Curtis and Madsen, 113. A. Demsky, "The Houses of Achzib: A Critical Note on Micah 1:14b," *IEJ* 16 (1966) 215, proposes that the Judean town of Achzib was the site of a royal industrial plant.

90 See Siegfried Mittmann, "'Königliches *bat*' und '*ṭēṭ*-Symbol': Mit einem Beitrag zu Micha 1,14b und 1 Chronik 4,21-23," *ZDPV* 107 (1991) 61.

91 But see Rudolph, 37. W. F. Albright, "The Administrative Divisions of Israel and Judah," *JPOS* 4 (1925) 17–54, identified Netaim with Khirbet en-Nuweiti, south of the Wadi Elah.

92 Peter Welten, *Die Königs-Stempel* (ADPV; Wiesbaden:

Harrassowitz, 1969) 128–30. See R. A. Stewart Macalister, "The Craftsmen's Guild of the Tribe of Judah," *PEFQS* (1905) 243–53, 328–42; idem, "Some Further Observations on the 'Craftsmen's Guild' of Judah," *PEFQS* (1908) 71–75; idem, *The Excavation of Gezer 1902–1905 and 1907–1909* (London: 1912) 2:210. Macalister also published a preliminary note on his findings in "The Royal Potters: 1 Chr 4:23," *ExpT* 16 (1904/1905) 379–80.

4

Translation

24/ The sons of Simeon: Nemuel,[1] Jamin, Jarib,[2] Zerah,[3] Shaul; 25/ Shallum was his son, Mibsam his son, Mishma his son, 26/[4] Hammuel his son,[5] Zaccur his son, Shimei his son. 27/ Shimei had sixteen sons and three[6] daughters; but his brothers did not have many sons, nor did all their families[7] multiply like the Judahites.

28/ They lived in Beer-sheba, Shema,[8] Moladah, Hazar-shual, 29/ Bilhah,[9] Ezem, Tolad,[10] 30/ Bethuel,[11] Hormah, Ziklag, 31/ Beth-marcaboth, Hazar-susim,[12] Beth-biri,[13] and Shaaraim.[14] These were their cities until David became king.[15] 32/ And their villages were Etam, Ain, Rimmon,[16] Tochen,[17] and Ashan, five cities, 33/ along with all their villages that were round about these towns as far as Baal.[18] These[19] were their settlements. And they kept a genealogical record for themselves:[20] 34/ Meshobab, Jamlech, Joshah son of Amaziah, 35/ Joel, Jehu[21] son of Joshibiah son of Seraiah son of Asiel, 36/ Elioenai, Jaakobah, Jeshohaiah, Asaiah, Adiel, Jesimiel,[22] Benaiah, 37/ Ziza son of Shiphi son of Allon son of Jedaiah son of Shimri son of Shemaiah[23]—38/ these are the ones who entered by names [into the genealogical record][24] as princes in their clans, and their ancestral houses increased greatly.

39/ They journeyed to the entrance of Gerar,[25] to the east of the valley, to seek pasture for their flocks, 40/ where they found fertile, good pasture, and the land was spacious, quiet, and peaceful; those who lived there formerly were from[26] Ham. 41/ They, registered by name, came in the days of Hezekiah king[27] of Judah, and attacked their tents and the Meunim[28] who were found there, and put them under the ban until this day,[29] and settled in their place, because there was pasture there for their flocks. 42/ And some of them,[30] five hundred men of the Simeonites, went to Mount Seir, and their leaders were Pelatiah, Neariah, Rephaiah, and Uzziel, sons of Ishi; 43/ they destroyed the remnant of the Amalekites that had escaped, and they have lived there to this day.

1 נמואל; Gen 46:10; Exod 6:15: ימואל "Jemuel."
2 יריב; Syr Gen 46:10; Exod 6:15; Num 26:12: יכין "Jachin." See the commentary.
3 זרח; Syr Gen 46:10; Exod 6:15: צחר "Zohar."
4 LXX; MT adds ובני משמע "the sons of Mishma." See the commentary. Rudolph, 38, retains MT and interprets the three persons in this verse as brothers.
5 LXX^ANrell add "Zabbud." Cf. Ezra 8:14 K. This is a miswritten dittography of the following name Zaccur.
6 LXX; MT "six," under the influence of the preceding "sixteen." A strong case could also be made for the originality of the number "six." Willi, 68, 71, adopts LXX in his translation, but then gives Shimei twenty-two children in his commentary (p. 143).
7 משפחתם, with two Hebrew MSS, LXX; MT משפחתם, "their family."
8 ושמע with LXX; lacking in MT. Cf. Josh 15:26; 19:2 (ושבע, "Sheba," under the influence of Beer-sheba; LXX^B Shema); Neh 11:26 (ישוע, "Jeshua"). Cf. LXX^L, which puts Shema after Moladah.
9 ובבלהה; Josh 19:3 ובלה "and Balah"; Josh 15:29 בעלה "Baalah."
10 ובתולד; Syr, Arab.: ואלתולד. Cf. Josh 15:30; 19:4
11 ובבתואל; cf. Josh 19:4 ובתול "Bethul." Chronicles Syr. (wb)nsl; cf. Josh 15:30 וכסיל "Chesil"; LXX "Bethel."
12 סוסים; Josh 19:5 סוסה "susah."
13 ובבית בראי; Josh 19:6 ובית לבאות "Beth-lebaoth"; 15:32 לבאות "Lebaoth."
14 ובשערים; Josh 15:32 ושלחים "Shilhim"; Josh 19:6 ושרוחן "Sharuhen."
15 מלך; a few Hebrew MSS, LXX, Syr, Vg: מלך "(until) king (David)."
16 A few Hebrew MSS, LXX, Syr make Rimmon explicitly a separate city by adding a conjunction. Cf. Josh 15:32 "Ain and Rimmon." In Neh 11:29 En-rimmon is one city.
17 ותכן; Josh 15:42; 19:7 ועתר "Ether," which may be a variant for Tochen. Joshua LXX, however, adds θαλχα = Tochen.
18 בעל; LXX בעלת באר "Baalat." Josh 19:8 בעלת באר "Baalath-beer."
19 זאת מושבתם. Note the disagreement in number between the demonstrative pronoun and the predicate noun. See the commentary, where I interpret this as a remnant of זאת נחלת "This was the inheritance" from Josh 19:8.
20 והתיחשם להם; Josh 19:8 למשפחתם "according to their families."
21 ויהוא; LXX והוא "and he."
22 וישימאל; two Hebrew MSS, LXX^Aal: וישמאל "and Ishmael." LXX^B lacks "Adiel, Jesimiel."
23 שמעיה; LXX שמעון "Simeon." Cf. v. 24.

24   The words supplied in brackets refer back to the introduction of this list in v. 33. Rudolph, 40, suggests הָאֵלֶּה "those designated by name," or הָרֹאשִׁים "those who were stressed." But see the commentary.

25   גרר, with LXX Γεραρα; LXX[min] Βηθγαδωρ. MT גדר "Gedor." *Dālet* and *rêš* are easily confused in Hebrew script. Gedor (cf. 1 Chr 4:3, 18) would require a migration of Simeon to the north, into Judahite territory. Rudolph, 41, identifies this site with Geder in the Negeb (cf. Josh 12:13).

26   מן; LXX מבני "from the sons of."

27   The Hebrew would also permit a translation: "They, registered by name in the days of Hezekiah, came. . . ." Cf. Curtis and Madsen, 116–17. The analogy with v. 38, however, led to the translation above.

28   Q מעונים; K מעינים "Meinim." Syr, Arab.: "springs." Tg presupposes מְעוֹנִים "dwellings." *BHS* chooses the last reading and adds a 3d masc. pl. suffix ("their"). See the commentary.

29   עד היום הזה. *BHS* suggests moving this phrase after "place."

30   ומהם. J. R. Porter, "Anticipation of Subject and Object in Biblical Hebrew," *JTS*, n.s. 14 (1963) 373, concludes that the people designated by the suffix are not the same as those designated by the following noun phrase. The reference is to a section of the Simeonites, who in turn belonged to a wider group. *JPSV:* "And some of them, five hundred of the Simeonites."

Structure

The second of the tribal genealogies is that of Simeon (see the genealogical chart "Descendants of Simeon"). The tribe of Simeon, which is often associated with the tribe of Judah, also in Chronicles,[1] follows therefore in an appropriate sequence after Judah. The genealogy of Simeon is relatively short and its materials may be outlined in the following way:[2]

I. 4:24-27. The names of the sons of Simeon, concluding with a comparison with the Judahites

II. 4:28-33bα. Places associated with the tribe of Simeon

III. 4:33bβ-43. Princes of Simeon and places to which the tribe migrated

    A. 4:33bβ-38. Thirteen princes of Simeon, concluding with a notice of their population increase

    B. 4:39-41. Expansion to the west

    C. 4:42-43. Expansion to the east

In section I v. 24 is clearly dependent on Num 26:12-14, with some resemblance also to the genealogies of Simeon in Gen 46:10 and Exod 6:15. Verses 25-27 provide a linear genealogy of Shaul, the youngest son of Simeon, for six more generations, ending with Shimei who, unlike other Simeonites, had many descendants. The source of this genealogical information about Shaul is unknown.

The localities in section II, vv. 28-33bα, correspond fairly closely to Josh 19:1-9, the tribal territory of Simeon, with some spelling differences and other small divergences, but the Chronicler has also redacted this material to fit his own purposes.[3] The names in vv. 28-31 closely follow the cities listed in Josh 19:2-4: Beer-sheba, Sheba, Moladah, Hazar-shual, Balah, Ezem, Eltolad, Bethul, Hormah, Ziklag, Beth-marcaboth, Hazar-susah, Beth-lebaoth, and Sharuhen. The differences between the two lists have been discussed in textual notes 8–14, or they will be discussed in the commentary. The names

1   1 Chr 2:1; 4:24, 42; 6:50 (65), Levitical cities, with the order Judah–Simeon–Benjamin; 12:25-27 (24-26), David's warriors with the order Judah–Simeon–Levi; 27:16-18, a list of David's officers, with the order Reuben–Simeon–Levi–Judah; 2 Chr 15:9, Asa gathers many out of Judah, Benjamin, Ephraim, Manasseh, and Simeon; 34:6, Josiah's reform in Judah and Jerusalem, as well as in the cities of Manasseh, Ephraim, Simeon, and Naphtali.

2   Rudolph, 39, attributes only vv. 24-27 to the Chronicler, with vv. 28-33 added later from Josh 19:2-8,

and vv. 34-43 added even later. He considers the following clauses to be glosses: "These were their cities until David became king" (v. 31), and "They, registered by name, came in the days of Hezekiah king of Judah" (v. 41).

3   The only other passages from Joshua 13–21 used by the Chronicler in 1 Chronicles 1–9 are 1 Chr 6:39-66 (54-81)//Josh 21:1-42, the list of Levitical cities, and Josh 17:11-13, the cities of Ephraim (1 Chr 7:28). Towns of Simeon are also mentioned in the account of Josiah (2 Chr 34:6). As far as the sites can be identified, they are in a rectangle marked by

in vv. 32-33 run parallel to the towns in Josh 19:7-8: Ain, Rimmon, Ether, Ashan, Baalath-beer, and Ramah of the Negeb. Again, the differences have been discussed in textual notes 16–18 or they will be discussed in the commentary. Parallel geographic information appears in a section of the province list in Josh 15:20-32, which forms the first district of that administrative document,[4] and in Neh 11:25-29, which mentions a number of these Simeonite settlements as places where some of the people of Judah lived, but does not attribute them to Simeon.[5] Simeon's traditional location was in and around Beersheba, and that city is the only one of the twenty places mentioned in vv. 28-33 that can be identified with absolute confidence. The source document from which the Chronicler drew made clear that Simeon's territory

had been incorporated in greater Judah (Josh 19:1, 9; cf. Judg 1:3), and the Chronicler also drew his explicit comparison of Simeon with Judah from Josh 19:9 (v. 27; see the commentary). The book of Joshua provides no boundary list for the tribe of Simeon itself.

Section III, vv. 33bβ-43, is material known only through Chronicles. It begins with a list of thirteen leaders or princes of Simeon.[6] For ten of these leaders we are given only their names, for one we are also given the man's father, for another we are given his father, grandfather, and great-grandfather, and for a third man his line is traced back to the sixth generation, that is, to the man's great-great-great-grandfather. The expansion to the west, vv. 39-41, dated to the time of Hezekiah in v. 41, resembles the attack on the city of Dan in the

map references on the north from 093097 to 143097, and on the south from 093072 to 143072. See the commentary for discussion of individual cities.

4   Willi, 143. Albrecht Alt, "Judas Gaue unter Josia," *PJ* 21 (1925) 100–116, dated this document to the time of Josiah and believed that the Simeonite lists were extracted from it. Y. Aharoni, "The Negeb of Judah," *IEJ* 8 (1958) 26–38, considers the list of Simeonite cities in Josh 19:1-8 to be the oldest, followed by Joshua 15. Both are earlier than 1 Chr 4:28-33, which is more accurate due to its infrequent copying. See also Aharoni, *Land of the Bible,* 260–62 and 352, where he dates Josh 15:21-62 to the time of Uzziah. Zecharia Kallai-Kleinmann, "The Town Lists of Judah, Simeon, Benjamin, and Dan," *VT* 8 (1958) 134–60; idem, *Historical Geography,* 349–61, concludes that Josh 15:21-62 is from the time of Jehoshaphat, but has been supplemented by vv. 45-47 (mentioning Edron, Ashdod, and Gaza) in the time of Hezekiah. He finds traces of David's census in the two Simeonite lists = 19:2-8 and 1 Chr 4:24-43. In his view 1 Chronicles 4 is earlier than Josh 19:2-8, and Joshua 19 antedates the 9th century, reflecting the closing days of David's life or the beginning of Solomon's reign (p. 355). Mathias Augustin, "The Role of Simeon in the Book of Chronicles," in *Proceedings of the Tenth World Congress of Jewish Studies* (1990) 139–40, writes: "We have a basic document in Josh 15 and an additional list in Josh 19:1-9 from the time of Josiah." He believes the latter list serves a special purpose: the political claim of a pan-Israelite empire. Josh 19:1-9 was composed out of Josh 15:26b-32. The reference to David in 1 Chr 4:31b is only a literary remark to give this text the ring of

antiquity. Frank Moore Cross and G. Ernest Wright, "The Boundary and Province Lists of the Kingdom of Judah," *JBL* 75 (1956) 214, note that Alt and Noth considered Josh 15:26-32 primary over Josh 19:2-7. The Simeonite list in their (Alt-Noth) view is an artificial construction created from the second part of the Judahite province list. In the judgment of Cross and Wright, 226, Josh 15:21-62 represents a revised edition of the Judahite province list, brought up to date in the court of Jehoshaphat during the second quarter of the 9th century BCE. Josh 15:26-32 and 19:2-8 are dependent on an earlier Simeonite list, while 1 Chronicles 4 depends on Joshua 19. Shemaryahu Talmon, "The Town Lists of Simeon," *IEJ* 15 (1965) 235–41, sees the nucleus of these lists in one document that was the basis for all three Simeonite town lists and that reflects, as mentioned in 1 Chr 4:31, circumstances from the time of David. It is thus in David's days that the territory of Simeon began to be reckoned among the possessions of Judah. Nadav Na'aman, "The Inheritance of the Sons of Simeon," *ZDPV* 96 (1980) 136–52, esp. 143, also believes that the Simeonite lists are old and that the Simeonite cities have later been incorporated into the Judahite administrative document in Joshua 15.

5   Moladah, Hazar-shual, Beer-sheba, Ziklag, and Enrimmon. The sites listed in these verses were under Edomite or Arabic hegemony at the time of Nehemiah.

6   Williamson, 62, believes that this list of names in vv. 34-38 was already combined with the historical anecdotes in vv. 39-43 in the Chronicler's source. Augustin, "Role of Simeon," 140, concludes that this list of names gives no hint of knowledge of preexilic times.

book of Judges: the land in both cases is "broad of hands" (Judg 18:10 and 1 Chr 4:40), and the people attacked are quiet and unsuspecting (Judg 18:7, 27, and 1 Chr 4:40). The expansion to the east, vv. 42-43, describes a movement of five hundred men toward Mount Seir, led by four otherwise unknown persons, and an attack on the Amalekites. With both expansions of the Simeonite territory we are told that the resultant conditions persist "until this day" (vv. 41, 43).[7]

Little is known of the history of Simeon and the Simeonites. The story of their and Levi's violence toward the people of Shechem resulted in Jacob's rebuke (Gen 34:25-31) and his curse (Gen 49:5-7) of Simeon and Levi, though neither of these passages is mentioned in Chronicles. Many scholars assume that these stories reflect the defeat or decline of Simeon in its original setting in central Palestine, with the remnants of this tribe attaching themselves to the tribe of Judah, especially in its southern regions. Simeon does not appear in the blessing of Moses in Deuteronomy 33.[8]

Detailed Commentary

4:24-27. Names of the Sons of Simeon

```
Simeon ─┬─ Nemuel
        │  Jamin
        │  Jarib
        │  Zerah
        └─ Shaul─Shallum─Mibsam─Mishma─Hammuel─Zaccur─Shimei ─┬─ sixteen sons
                                                                └─ three daughters
```

■ **24** *Nemuel, Jamin, Jarib, Zerah, Shaul:* The Chronicler drew the names of these five sons of Simeon from earlier biblical passages, none of which agrees exactly with this verse:

Gen 46:10	Exod 6:15	Num 26:12-14	1 Chr 4:24
Jemuel	Jemuel	Nemuel[9]	Nemuel
Jamin	Jamin	Jamin	Jamin
Ohad	Ohad		
Jachin	Jachin	Jachin	Jarib
Zohar	Zohar	Zerah	Zerah
Shaul	Shaul	Shaul	Shaul

Genesis 46 and Exodus 6 are in total agreement with one another, but v. 24 in Chronicles resembles most closely Numbers 26. The only difference between the latter two lists is in the third name, Jarib, for which the other three lists have Jachin. Numbers and Chronicles read Nemuel and Zerah over against Jemuel and Zohar in the Genesis and Exodus lists.[10] Numbers and Chronicles lack the name Ohad and the notice that Shaul was the son of a Canaanite woman.[11] While all the names except Nemuel appear elsewhere in the Bible, the other occurrences of these names designate different people and do not advance our understanding of the Simeonite

---

7   The inclusion of historical notes in genealogies has been clarified by study of the Safaitic inscriptions (cf. 1 Chr 5:10; 7:21-22). These crude inscriptions were found in an area southeast of Damascus and date to the 1st centuries BCE and CE. They include references to tribal battles, the pasturing of cattle, and the loss of a watering place for camels. Johnson

notes that the heads of ancestral houses in the biblical genealogies are often military commanders and that military census lists were themselves organized in genealogical form. See Willi, 145; Johnson, *Purpose,* 61–64.

8   Simeon may be hinted at in the words, "Yahweh, give heed (שׁמע) to Judah" (Deut 33:7).

traditions. In addition to Saul, the first Israelite king (whose name is spelled the same as Shaul in Hebrew), there is a Shaul who is an Edomite king (1 Chr 1:48-49//Gen 36:37-38) and a Korahite Levite (1 Chr 6:9 [24]).

■ **25** *Shallum was his son, Mibsam his son, Mishma his son:* Rothstein, 76, and Rudolph, 38, understand the three men in this verse as brothers rather than as representatives of three generations. While Shallum is an exceedingly common name,[12] Mibsam and Mishma appear elsewhere only in the genealogy of Ishmael, where they are back to back and in the same order (Gen 25:13-14//1 Chr 1:29-30). The etymology of Mibsam is from the root בשׂם (Arabic *bašām*), meaning "balm," and may show the tribe's involvement with the spice trade.[13] Mishma[14] is from the root שׁמע, as is the name Simeon itself.[15] See also Shimei (vv. 26-27) and Shemaiah (v. 37). Remnants of Simeonite clans may have become groups within Ishmaelite groups that settled in the Negeb in exilic and postexilic times, or, more likely, given the etymology of Mibsam, Ishmaelite families may have been taken into the genealogy of Simeon.[16] Willi, 142, following Knauf, believes that the Chronicler, in his efforts to create a list of Simeonites, drew on settlement relationships after the Idumean migration.

■ **26** *Hammuel his son, Zaccur his son, Shimei his son:* Without coming to a conclusion, Japhet, 121, discusses whether the names in vv. 25-26 should be read as a linear genealogy, as in my translation and interpretation, or whether the names in one or both verses should be

considered as brothers. The omission of the initial "the sons of Mishma" in the LXX (see textual note 4) decides the question decisively in favor of the linear genealogy, which I think likely in any case because of the "X his son, Y his son" formula.[17] The linear genealogy puts Shimei in the seventh generation after Simeon. The longer the genealogy the better it is able to bridge the gap between the patriarchal and the settlement periods. A scribe may have added "the sons of Mishma" to this verse in MT in an attempt to create brothers for Shimei,[18] which he may have thought to be required by the comparison between Shimei's and his brothers' descendants in v. 27. The linear genealogy shows the importance of Shimei, which fits well with the listing of his many descendants in the next verse.

■ **27** *Shimei had sixteen sons and three daughters:* Shimei's prolific engendering of children makes him an exception to the rule among the Simeonites since his brother Simeonites in general did not have many children (see v. 27b). The genealogy in the next clause draws a contrast between the declining tribe of Simeon and the growing tribe of Judah, which in the Chronicler's day was the main tribe in Israel.

his brothers did not have many sons, nor did all their families multiply like the Judahites: The Chronicler's comparison of Simeon and Judah, no doubt dependent on Josh 19:9,[19] recognizes the marginalized situation of Simeon. Willi, 143, finds here a possible echo of Gen 49:7.[20]

---

9   In each case this passage in Numbers lists the person's name and his clan (Nemuel and the clan of the Nemuelites, etc.) and it also supplies a total number for the tribe of Simeon (22,200).

10   Zerah (זרח) differs from Zohar (זחר) consonantally only in the metathesis of the last two letters.

11   It is doubtful in my judgment that this reflects a more favorable treatment of Simeon rather than Judah in these genealogies (*pace* Johnstone, 1:66). Osborne, "Genealogies," 248, n. 1, proposes that Shaul's having a Canaanite mother may account for him being listed last among Simeon's sons.

12   E. R. Achtemeier identifies fourteen different individuals with this name in *IDB* 4:304. Kartveit, *Motive und Schichten,* 61, finds the antecedent of "his" unclear and suspects a loss of text before this verse.

13   See Ernst Axel Knauf, "Mibsam," *ABD* 4:805.

14   Ernst Axel Knauf, "Mishma," *ABD* 4:871, suggests that it means "those who have joined (the tribe of) Šama'il."

15   At his birth Leah said, "Yahweh has heard (שׁמע) that I am hated" (Gen 29:33).

16   Williamson, 62.

17   Cf. the commentary on 1 Chr 3:16.

18   Willi, 143, identifies a number of Levites and Judahites with the name Shimei.

19   "Because the portion of the tribe of Judah was too large for them, the tribe of Simeon obtained an inheritance within their inheritance."

20   "Cursed be their [Simeon and Levi] anger, for it is fierce, and their wrath, for it is cruel! I will divide them in Jacob, and scatter them in Israel." (Willi writes "Gen 45:7b," but surely he means chap. 49.)

4:28-33bα. Places Associated with Simeon

■ **28** *They lived in Beer-sheba, Shema, Moladah, Hazar-shual:* In Josh 19:1-9 the word "inheritance" (נחלה) occurs seven times, but it does not reappear in this context in Chronicles.[21] Kartveit argues that these cities were not necessarily part of the province called Yehud, but that people who traced their lineage to Simeon lived in them during the postexilic period.[22] Beer-sheba is frequently identified today with Tell es-Seba‘ (MR 134072).[23] Since there is some question about each of the other cities, a location of Simeon in the general vicinity of Beer-sheba is the only geographic assignment that can be made with certainty. Shema is unknown (but note the root שמע, the root of "Simeon"),[24] while Moladah[25] is placed by Aharoni at Khirbet el-Waṭen (MR 142074), 5.5 miles east-north-east of Beer-sheba.[26] The precise location of Hazar-shual is unknown. It is placed in the southernmost district of Judah in Josh 15:28 and is also one of the settlements south of Jerusalem occupied by exiles returning from Babylon (Neh 11:27).

■ **29** *Bilhah, Ezem, Tolad:* None of these towns is known with any certainty, though the names Ezem[27] and Tolad[28] have turned up on inscriptions from Tell esh-Sheri‘ah (MR 119088) and Beer-sheba, respectively, and Ezem and Tolad are probably to be sought near the site where

they are mentioned in the inscriptions. The location of Bilhah is unknown.

■ **30** *Bethuel, Hormah, Ziklag:* The location of Hormah is contested; the name means something like "destruction" and could be assigned to many sites. The following locations have been suggested: Tell el-Milḥ (MR 152069), 7 miles northeast of Beer-sheba;[29] Tell esh-Sheri‘ah (MR 119088), 12 miles northwest of Beer-sheba; and Tell Masos (Aharoni and Boling;[30] MR 146069) and Tel Ira (Aharoni;[31] MR 148071), both southeast of Beer-sheba.[32] Nadav Na’aman argued that Hormah's location need not be sought in the vicinity of Arad, called attention to its position right before Ziklag in Josh 15:30; 19:4; and 1 Chr 4:30, and tentatively suggested it be located at Tell el-Ḥuwēlife, where there are Late Bronze II and Iron II remains (MR 137087).[33] Judah and Simeon together are credited with conquering a city called Zephath, devoting it to destruction, and renaming it Hormah (Judg 1:17). For Talmon this justifies the ascription of Hormah to Simeon in the premonarchic period.[34] Ziklag is now commonly identified as Tell esh-Sheri‘ah (MR 119088), but Volkmar Fritz has proposed that Tell es-Seba‘ (MR 134072)[35] is the actual site. Bethuel is unknown (cf. Bethul in Josh 19:4 and textual note 11). Kallai proposes that Achish the king of Gath, in giving David Ziklag, did not give him a Philistine city, but rather a Simeonite city.

---

21 The Chronicler uses this noun only in 1 Chr 16:18//Ps 105:11; 2 Chr 6:27//1 Kgs 8:36; and 10:16//1 Kgs 12:16. See also the discussion at v. 33.

22 *Motive und Schichten,* 133.

23 Na’aman, "Inheritance," 149–51, locates Beer-sheba a few miles to the west at Bīr es-Seba‘.

24 Na’aman, "Inheritance," 146, locates it at Tell es-Seba‘ and locates Beer-sheba a few miles to the west. See the previous note.

25 Eleven of the thirteen names are prefaced with the locative particle בְּ, which is lacking only for Moladah and Hazar-shual. Kartveit, *Motive und Schichten,* 128, concludes from this that these two cities are secondary.

26 *Land of the Bible,* 261. Both the Hebrew and Arabic names deal with childbearing.

27 E. D. Oren and E. Netzer, "Tel Sera‘ (Tell esh-Shari‘a)," *IEJ* 24 (1974) 264–66. See also Jeffrey R. Zorn, "Ezem," *ABD* 2:722.

28 Y. Aharoni, *Beer-sheba I* (Tel Aviv: Tel Aviv Univ., Institute of Archaeology, 1973) 71–73.

29 Y. Aharoni, "Arad: Its Inscription and Temple," *BA* 31 (1968) 2–32.

30 Aharoni, *Land of the Bible,* 71–73; Boling, *Judges,* 327. Na’aman, "Inheritance," 141–42, reports that this is the most common identification. He notes this site was abandoned from the 10th century until the mid-7th century.

31 Yohanan Aharoni, "Nothing Early and Nothing Late," *BA* 39 (1976) 55–76. See esp. 71–73.

32 See Jeffries M. Hamilton, "Hormah," *ABD* 3:288–89. Cf. Num 14:45; 21:3; Deut 1:44; Josh 12:14; 15:30; 19:4; Judg 1:17; 1 Sam 30:30.

33 Na’aman, "Inheritance." Na’aman observes that no Late Bronze Age remains have been found in excavations at either Tell Masos or Tell el-Milḥ.

34 "Town Lists of Simeon," 238.

35 Most scholars identify this site with Beer-sheba. See Volkmar Fritz, "Where Is David's Ziklag?" *BARev* 19 (1993) 58–61, 76. Na’aman, "Inheritance," 149–51, locates Beer-sheba at Bīr es-Seba‘, largely on the lack of the remains for a sanctuary at Tell es-Seba‘.

The inhabitants of the city were Israelite, but the city was under the rule of Achish.[36]

■ **31** *Beth-marcaboth, Hazar-susim, Beth-biri, and Shaaraim:* The older name for Beth-marcaboth ("the house of the chariots," "chariot depot") may be Madmannah (Josh 15:31),[37] perhaps identifiable with Khirbet Umm ed-Deimneh. Iron Age pottery has been discovered at the nearby Khirbet Tatrit (MR 143084), about 12 miles northeast of Beer-sheba.[38] Hazar-susim means something like "village of horses" or "horse depot" and is usually identified with Hazar-susah ("mare village"; Josh 19:5). In the parallel passage from Josh 15:31 we find the name "Sansannah" in a similar sequence of cities. This site is to be identified with Khirbet esh-Shamsaniyat (MR 140083), about 10 miles northeast of Beer-sheba, or Sbalat Abu Susein (MR 103074), about 20 miles west of Beer-sheba.[39] For Shaaraim Josh 15:32 has Shilhim and Josh 19:6 has Sharuhen. The latter city has been located at Tell el-Far'ah south (MR 100076), 20 miles west of Beer-sheba, or at Tell el-'Ajjûl (MR 093097), another 5 miles farther to the west and about 13 miles north of Tell el-Far'ah;[40] the locations of Shaaraim and Shilhim are unknown. Kallai holds that the towns Sharuhen, Shilhim, and Shaaraim are not to be identified with one another, but the changing names represent fluidity in the genealogy, indicating different time periods.[41] The variation between Beth-biri and Beth-lebaoth (Josh 19:6)

is unexplained. Neither site can be identified. These last two variations may represent different stages in the development of these genealogies or they may result from textual mistakes.

These were their cities until David became king: The Chronicler alleges that an administrative change was made at the time of David and assigns the cities mentioned in vv. 28-31 to that time. This remark may be based on 1 Sam 27:6, which states that after Achish gave David Ziklag, "Ziklag has belonged to the kings of Judah to this day." In Josh 19:6 the cities listed in vv. 2-6 are deemed "thirteen cities [*NRSV:* towns] with their villages."[42] Several cities were no longer Simeonite even before David's reign (perhaps Ziklag, Hormah, Ashan, Athach; 1 Sam 27:6; 30:26-30).[43]

■ **32** *And their villages were Etam, Ain, Rimmon, Tochen, and Ashan, five cities:* The Chronicler used the expression "their[44] villages," which in Josh 19:6 referred to settlements around the previous thirteen cities, to introduce the next five place names, but he creates a tension by including the apposition "cities," which is what these locales were called in Josh 19:7.[45] Etam and Tochen are not in the corresponding text at Josh 19:7; Etam is an addition and Tochen apparently a scribal variant. There is an Etam that is located 2-3 miles south of Bethlehem and therefore presumably outside the territory of Simeon (Khirbet el-Khôkh, MR 166121); perhaps

---

36 *Historical Geography,* 355.

37 The only other occurrence of Madmannah is in 1 Chr 2:49, where it belongs to the Calebites.

38 Jeffrey R. Zorn, "Beth-Marcaboth," *ABD* 1:690. Na'aman, "Inheritance," 145, locates Madmannah at Khirbet Tatrit. Na'aman also notes that Madmannah and Sansannah do not appear in the town lists of Simeon, and that Madmannah is known as Calebite in 1 Chr 2:49. Beth-pelet of Josh 15:27 also belonged to the Calebites (2:47). He concludes that the Bible distinguishes clearly between Simeonite and Calebite towns.

39 Jeffrey R. Zorn, "Hazar-susah," *ABD* 3:84–85.

40 Rüdiger Liwak, "Sharuhen," *ABD* 5:1163–64. Na'aman, "Inheritance," 148, emphatically denies that Tell el-'Ajjûl was within the borders of Judah.

41 *Historical Geography,* 354.

42 There are actually fourteen cities listed in Josh 19:4-6, though the second, Sheba, may have arisen by dittography. See Richard D. Nelson, *Joshua* (OTL; Louisville: Westminster John Knox, 1997) 217, but

see also textual note 8 to this chapter.

43 Despite this chronological notice and the references to Hezekiah (v. 41) and "to this day" in vv. 41, 43, Oeming, *Wahre Israel,* 132–33, does not believe the Chronicler had access to reports of real political or military actions, but he believes the Chronicler was only composing "theological history."

44 The masculine gender of this pronoun refers back to the Simeonites. In Josh 19:6 "their" is feminine plural and therefore refers to the villages surrounding the thirteen cities.

45 In Joshua they are called "four cities," since Etam was not included in that listing.

another southern city had the same name. The name Etam means something like "where the birds of prey are" (*HALOT* 2:817) and so might have been used at more than one place.[46] Tochen תכן here and Ether עתר (Josh 19:7)[47] may be variants on Athach עתך (1 Sam 30:30),[48] which is in a list of cities where there were "elders of Judah," and to which David sent spoil from Ziklag (1 Sam 30:26-30). Ain and Rimmon are listed as separate cities here and in Josh 19:7, but written as En-rimmon in Neh 11:29. The site is probably Khirbet Khuweilfeh (MR 137087).[49] Ashan (cf. Bor-ashan in 1 Sam 30:30) may be Tell Beit Mirsim (MR 141096),[50] about 6 miles north of En-rimmon, 12 miles southwest of Hebron, and 8 miles southeast of Lachish.[51]

■ **33bα** *along with all their villages that were round about these towns as far as Baal. These were their settlements:* The wording through the word "Baal" is a citation from Josh 19:8. The name of the city of Baal in Joshua is actually Baalath-beer, which is followed by another city, Ramah of the Negeb, with which it is apparently identified.[52] Significantly, the Chronicler makes no mention of the "inheritance of the tribe of Simeon" from Josh 19:8-9. His picture of Israel does not include, or at least surely does not emphasize, the fact that Israel was once outside the land, and that Israel entered the land and distrib-

uted it among the tribes. His picture of the twelve tribes and their distribution on the land fits in more with the structure of the way the world is. In the words of Japhet, 122, Israel in Chronicles has lived "in the land from time immemorial."[53] Hence this verse refers to "their settlements" or "dwelling places," not "their inheritance."[54] The absence of the word "inheritance" may only result, however, from the fact that Simeon has been assimilated within Judah. There may be an eschatological hint in this verse as well—this is the way that things someday will be again.[55]

4:33bβ-43. Princes of Simeon and Places to Which the Tribe Migrated

4:33bβ-38. Thirteen Princes of Simeon

■ **33bβ** *And they kept a genealogical record for themselves:* I have chosen to ignore the verse division in the Hebrew Bible and to begin the new paragraph with these final two Hebrew words in v. 33 (= 33bβ; cf. *NEB, JPSV, REB*). Some commentators, building on the traditional verse division, note that the following list of names has no introduction (e.g., Japhet, 123). A literal translation of these words would be: "And their enrollment by genealogy for themselves."[56]

---

46   Cf. the rock of Etam (Judg 15:8, 11); 1 Chr 4:3 (textual note 5); 2 Chr 11:6.

47   Cross and Wright, "Boundary and Province Lists," 214, note that Ether and Ashan of Josh 19:7 have been misplaced in Josh 15:42 to the Libnah-Mareshah province of Judah (province IV in the Shephelah). Cf. textual note 17.

48   Or it could also be a variant of Jattir יתר in 1 Sam 30:27. Hormah and Bor-ashan are also sites where elders of Judah lived, although Hormah and Ashan are called Simeonite here.

49   "Rimmon" seems to be preserved in the nearby Khirbet Umm er-Rammamin. Na'aman, "Inheritance," 143, makes this the location of Hormah. Na'aman, "Inheritance," 147, refrains from making specific identifications for these sites, but suggests that they should be located between Tell Halif on the south and Tell Beit Mirsim on the north.

50   Kallai, *Historical Geography*, 357.

51   Aharoni, *Land of the Bible*, 262. Other suggestions are in Kartveit, *Motive und Schichten*, 131–32.

52   Kallai, *Historical Geography*, 359, notes that Josh 19:8 LXX[B] reads "Baalath until you come [reading

באך instead of באר] to Ramath-negeb." According to 1 Sam 30:27, David sent presents to Ramoth of the Negeb and other cities, a number of them once known as Simeonite. Na'aman, "Inheritance," 146, proposes that Baalath might be identified with Tell Masos, and Ramath-negeb with Tell Ira.

53   See also Sara Japhet, "Conquest and Settlement in Chronicles," *JBL* 98 (1979) 205–18.

54   Note that the word translated "these" is actually "this" (fem. sg.), which the Chronicler took from Josh 19:8, where it introduced a clause, "This was the inheritance. . . ." Cf. textual note 19.

55   Augustin, "Role of Simeon," 141, who generally denies the historical reliability of these materials, comes to a similar conclusion: "With the endeavors of expansion of this group [the tribe of Simeon] the Chronicler is mediating the hope that one day this territory mentioned in 1 Chr 4:28-33 can not only be regained for the Jerusalem and Judaean community, but in analogy to the reports of conquest expanded to the west and the south."

56   The root of the verb is שׂחי. Cf. 1 Chr 5:1, 7, 17; 7:5, 7, 9, 10; 9:1, 22; 2 Chr 12:15; 31:16-19. Outside

■ **34-37** The most interesting thing about the list of the following thirteen names in these verses is that they are not stereotypical and that they are presented in four different formats: ten names are without a father's name, one (Amaziah) has a patronymic, one (Asiel) has three generations of ancestors, and one (Shemaiah) has five generations of ancestors. There seems to be no reason, therefore, to argue that the Chronicler himself invented this list. Are the thirteen princes to be connected to the thirteen cities mentioned in Josh 19:6?[57]

The Princes
Meshobab
Jamlech
Amaziah—Joshah
Joel
Asiel—Seraiah—Joshibiah—Jehu
Elioenai
Jaakobah
Jeshohaiah
Asaiah
Adiel
Jesimiel
Benaiah
Shemaiah—Shimri—Jedaiah—Allon—Shiphi—Ziza

■ **37** *Ziza son of Shiphi son of Allon son of Jedaiah son of Shimri son of Shemaiah:* What is tantalizing about the linear genealogy of Ziza, recorded in ascending order, is the possibility that Shemaiah שמעיה is to be identified with Shimei שמעי from v. 27.[58] If Shimei in the Chronicler's mind lived in the premonarchic period, Ziza would be one hundred or more years later. This would not reach all the way to Hezekiah, v. 41, but other intervening generations may have been lost. At the least, this genealogy indicates that many years had passed between v. 27 and the events recounted in vv. 38-43.

■ **38** *These are the ones who entered [into the genealogical record] by names as princes in their clans:* Despite the awk-

wardness or elliptical character of this clause (cf. v. 33bβ), there seems to be no reason to adopt any of the emendations discussed in textual note 24. If textual corruption is present, there is no solution so far proposed that improves the reading. The content of this clause seems to be echoed by the statement "these were the ones written by names" in v. 41,[59] and it brings the list of names in vv. 34-37 to a satisfactory conclusion. The Chronicler in any case had access to a list of Simeonite "princes." According to Niehr the word נשׂיא, "prince," in P has four principal functions:[60] the leader of a whole tribe (Num 1:4, 16), the chief of a clan (3:24), a military leader (1:16, the "princes" were heads of thousands and hundreds; 10:4), and in general the title of a respected or exalted person (Gen 23:6; 34:2). Any of the last three of these functions—separately or together—would fit the functions of these Simeonite princes.[61] Niehr himself interprets the references to princes in 1 Chr 4:38 and 7:40 as heads of families.

and their ancestral houses increased greatly: This use of the verb פרץ (increased) is illustrated by the way the Israelites multiplied and increased (lit. "spread") during their oppression in Egypt (Exod 1:12). The verb could refer to the breaking out of the child from the womb or the spreading out of the increased population (cf. Hos 4:10).

4:39-41. Expansion to the West

■ **39** *They journeyed to the entrance of Gerar to the east of the valley to seek pasture for their flocks:* A population increase among the Simeonites—despite the notice in v. 27 that their families did not multiply like the Judahites—necessitated that some families move west for better grazing, toward ("to the entrance of") Gerar (Tell Abū Hureireh, MR 112087),[62] one of the largest tells in the western Negeb, about 4 miles west and a little south of Ziklag.[63] If Ziklag represents the western edge of the Simeonite territory, Gerar is outside that territory.[64] Kartveit points

---

Chronicles it is used only in Ezra 2:62//Neh 7:64; Ezra 8:1, 3; Neh 7:5.

57   So Johnstone, 1:68.

58   This possibility is raised by Japhet, 124. Willi, 146, considers it possible but not provable.

59   Japhet, 124, believes that the writing of the names may allude to some kind of census.

60   H. Niehr, נשׂא *nāśî*'," *TDOT* 10:44–53, esp. 50.

61   "Tribal leader" would fit 1 Chr 2:10 and 5:6.

62   See Y. Aharoni, "The Land of Gerar," *IEJ* 6 (1956) 26–32.

63   Assuming its location at Tell esh-Sheriʻah, but see the discussion at v. 30.

64   Kallai, *Historical Geography*, 356.

out that this move is parallel to and verbally patterned after the story of Isaac's migration in Genesis 26.[65] Isaac went to Gerar because of famine in the land (Gen 26:1, 17), and increased population required the Simeonites to migrate there to seek more pasture ground. In Genesis the land was called Rehobot (רחבות, Gen 26:22); here it is "spacious," literally "broad of hands" (רחבת ידים, v. 40). The "valley" (גיא) in this verse might be compared to the "valley (נחל) of Gerar in Gen 26:17. Abraham and Lot had also discovered that the land could not support both of them (Gen 13:6), but the migration of Lot was peaceful, while here the migration of Simeon led to a battle.[66]

■ **40** *the land was spacious, quiet, and peaceful:* We have already noted above (under Structure) that the word "quiet" calls to mind the conditions at Laish when it was attacked by the Danites (Judg 18:7, 27). The peaceful or relaxed situation here (שלוה) recalls the situation of Hazor in an oracle of Jeremiah (49:31): "a nation at ease (שליו), that lives secure . . . that has no gates or bars, that lives alone."

those who lived there formerly were from Ham: According to the Table of Nations (1 Chr 1:8, 12//Gen 10:6, 14), Canaanites and Philistines were descendants of Ham. The genealogist or the Chronicler may have been thinking of Abimelech the Philistine who lived at Gerar (Gen 26:1).

■ **41** *They, registered by name, came in the days of Hezekiah king of Judah:* "Those registered by name," that is, those whose names were written down, repeats the substance of v. 38a[67] and refers to the thirteen princes who were listed in vv. 34-37. The phrase "in the days of Hezekiah" could modify when these names were recorded or, more likely in my judgment, when the attack itself took place.[68] I believe that this chronological link may be reli-able, since we know that Hezekiah campaigned against the Philistines as far as Gaza (MR 099101), northwest of Gerar (MR 112087; 2 Kgs 18:8, an account not included in Chronicles). Hezekiah's attack was correlated with his rebellion against the king of Assyria (2 Kgs 18:7), which led to Sennacherib's famous invasion in 701 BCE. It is impossible to tell whether the Simeonite raid was part of that national effort or independent of it. Oeming, how-ever, doubts whether this is a reliable historical record and feels that Hezekiah is being rewarded by the Chroni-cler for his cultic reforms (2 Chronicles 29–32) by being given territorial expansion.[69] It should be noted, how-ever, that the victory here is credited to the Simeonites, not to Hezekiah. Augustin situates this notice in Persian-Hellenistic times.[70] Willi, 153, finds here "more than an archival notice." He takes Hezekiah as a representative of Yahweh's kingdom, which has now passed from Judah to the Babylonians and thence to the Persians. Thanks to the Simeonites, in his view, the region of the northern Negeb and the coastal plain was no longer oriented toward Egypt and the south, but toward the sphere of the empire *(Weltreich),* which was finally bestowed by the God of Jerusalem and had in Jerusalem's cult its spiri-tual center. Finally, Lindsay finds here evidence for Hezekiah's efforts to prepare for the Assyrian invasion by reinforcing the Negeb by clearing out Edomite set-tlers. One group of Simeonites struck westward toward Philistia and settled the area around Gerar, while another group went eastwards and displaced the settlers of Mount Seir.[71]

attacked their tents and the Meunim, who were found there: The attack on their tents is parallel to Asa's attack on the אהלי מקנה ("tents of livestock," i.e., the tents of those who had livestock) in 2 Chr 14:14 (15).[72] Much more uncertain is who is meant by the Meunim. Borger and

65 *Motive und Schichten,* 134.

66 Aharoni, *Land of the Bible,* 218, dates this incident to the conquest or settlement period. But the genealo-gist had already reached the era of David in v. 31.

67 Japhet, 125, finds here evidence for a possible con-flation of two texts.

68 Cf. Braun, 67; Willi, 151. Willi notes that the offi-cials of Hezekiah were also credited with recording the proverbs of Solomon (Prov 25:1). Na'aman, "Inheritance," 152, takes this as evidence that the Simeonites retained their tribal organization into the 8th century.

69 *Wahre Israel,* 133.

70 "Role of Simeon," 140. Kartveit, *Motive und Schichten,* 134, does not know what historical cir-cumstances lie behind this account, but considers it an edifying midrash on the old history, which intends to clarify the land rights in this region.

71 John Lindsay, "Edomite Westward Expansion: The Biblical Evidence," *ANES* 36 (1999) 48–89.

72 This makes the emendation of Ehrlich, *Randglossen,* 7:329, to אהלי חם "the tents of Ham" unnecessary.

Tadmor identified them with an Arabian tribe Mu'-nayya, located between Palestine and Egypt, and attested in an inscription of Tiglath-pileser III,[73] though Knauf has called this derivation into question because of the considerably different vocalization of the Hebrew word.[74] One might wonder whether such vowel differences should play a major role in view of the late addition of the vowel points in Hebrew and the uncertainty between Meunites (K) and Meinites (Q) in the text itself. Knauf himself identifies the Meunim as the Minaeans, people associated with the south Arabian city-state of 400 BCE and later, whose outposts are attested at Gaza and Petra. Knauf takes the reference to the "valley" in v. 39 as a designation of the Wadi Mûsâ at the entrance of Petra and interprets the whole incident as reflecting conflicts from the time of the Chronicler.[75] Welten believes that when the Chronicler was writing on his own, without a *Vorlage*, he used "Seir" to refer to the heartland of Edom and "Meunim" to designate the Idumeans contemporary to the time of the Chronicler who were encroaching on Israelite settlements.[76] Rudolph, 42, following the Tg, interprets the word מעוניהם as (their) "habitations." Willi, 152, suggests that the Chronicler presupposes three stages in the ownership of this territory: first by the descendants of Ham, then by the Meunim, and finally by the Simeonites.

and put them under the ban until this day: While putting a people under the ban, that is, destroying them militarily, is a technical term from the holy war traditions, this does not justify dismissing the whole narrative in vv. 41-43 as mere "war reports with a positive outcome" and a continuation of the conquest tradition.[77] The notice "until this day" could refer to the era of the Chronicler, or to the era when this information was reported in the Chronicler's source. The only other use of this term in nonsynoptic materials occurs in 1 Chr 5:26, where the exile of the half-tribe of Manasseh continues until the Chronicler's own day. Descendants of Simeon, therefore, may have been living in this area at the time of the Chronicler. It is not impossible, of course, that the Chronicler would also see an eschatological dimension in this passage, meaning that this territory would/should someday be restored to Simeon and to Israel.

4:42-43. Expansion to the East

■ **42** *And some of them, five hundred men of the Simeonites:* The number of men in the eastern raid is comparable to the size of the warriors associated with David (1 Sam 22:2, about four hundred; 1 Sam 23:13, about six hundred) and therefore seems large. Perhaps the number included women and children.

went to Mount Seir: This suggests an expansion into Edomite territory in the southern part of the Negeb, though the exact area is not given (cf. 2 Chr 20:10, 22-23).[78]

Pelatiah, Neariah, Rephaiah, and Uzziel, sons of Ishi: These four leaders, otherwise unknown, were from the sons of Ishi. An Ishi is mentioned among the sons of Judah in 1 Chr 4:20, where his own ancestry is unclear. The names Pelatiah,[79] Neariah, and Rephaiah all appear

73   R. Borger and H. Tadmor, "Zwei Beiträge zur alttes-tamentlichen Wissenschaft aufgrund der Inschriften Tiglatpilesers III," *ZAW* 94 (1982) 250–51. The Borger-Tadmor identification is accepted by N. Na'aman, "Pastoral Nomads in the Southeastern Periphery of the Kingdom of Judah in the 9th-8th Centuries BCE," *Zion* 52 (1987) 261–76; and Japhet, 124–25. Japhet observes that the isolated character of these people, noted above in the comparison with Judges 18, means that we should not expect strong political ties.

74   Heb. *mĕ'ûnîm* vs. **ma'ănîm*. See Ernst Axel Knauf, "Mu'näer und Mëuniter," *WO* 16 (1985) 115.

75   In his opinion the reference to Hezekiah is only a cross-reference to the battle of Uzziah with the Meunim in 2 Chr 26:7-8.

76   *Geschichte und Geschichtsdarstellung*, 145.

77   So Oeming, *Wahre Israel*, 133.

78   Bartlett, *Edom and the Edomites*, 44, notes that Mt. Seir in this and a number of other passages could refer to a location west of the Wadi 'Araba. Japhet, 126, and Aharoni, *Land of the Bible*, 40, 388, identify Mt. Seir with Edomite territory east of the Jordan.

79   The root letters of this word פלט are the same as הפלטה "that had escaped" later in this verse.

among the descendants of David in chap. 3 (3:21-22). This suggests the postexilic provenance of these names and perhaps of this tradition itself.

■ **43** *they destroyed the remnant of the Amalekites that had escaped:* The Chronicler associates the Amalekites with Edom since Amalek is a grandson of Esau through Eliphaz (1 Chr 1:35-36//Gen 36:10-12). The "remnant of the Amalekites"—Amalek and the Amalekites are only mentioned here and in 1 Chr 18:11 in Chronicles—might refer to those who survived the attacks of Saul (1 Sam 14:48; 15:2-3), David (2 Sam 8:12), or others. The Simeonites' warlike character in this verse is very much in line with early biblical traditions about the Simeonites in Gen 34:25-31 and 49:5-7.

and they have lived there to this day: The Chronicler's source (see v. 41) knew of Simeonite settlers in former Edomite/Amalekite territory.[80]

Conclusion

The Chronicler presents genealogical and other information on Simeon directly after Judah. This may reflect Simeon's second position in the birth order, but surely also the territorial and other connections between Simeon and Judah with which the Chronicler was familiar (see n. 1 above). His resources for Simeon, however, are much more limited than they were for Judah. He presents a list of five Simeonites taken from Num 26:12-14; a linear genealogy, otherwise unknown, of Shaul, the youngest son of Simeon; a list of places where the Simeonites lived (reworked from Josh 19:1-8); a list of thirteen Simeonite princes; and two accounts of Simeonite growth and expansion, both west and east. The place names in this chapter, insofar as they are known, are beyond the boundaries of Yehud. Their presence here may indicate that some settlers who claimed Simeonite lineage lived in these sites in the Chronicler's age and/or that the expansion, connected in one case with Hezekiah, one of the most stellar kings according to the Chronicler, might portend future geographic and population growth by the community. The comparison between the rapid growth of the Judahites and the slow growth of the Simeonites in v. 27 may be a concession to the fact that the Judahites were a thriving group at the time of the Chronicler whereas the tribal heritage of Simeon had virtually disappeared.

---

80   Oeming, *Wahre Israel,* 133, finds an anti-Edomite polemic here and in the accounts of two wars against the Edomites in 2 Chr 20:10-23 and 25:11-14. He points out (p. 134) that archaeologists have found no trace of Judahite tribes in Edom, but only the reverse. It must be noted, however, that the connection between artifacts and specific peoples is very hard to prove. Augustin, "Role of Simeon," 141, believes a segment of the Nabateans is represented here by the name Amalekites.

5

Translation

1/ The sons of Reuben the firstborn of Israel.
(He was the firstborn, but because he
defiled[1] the bed of his father his birthright[2]
was given[3] to the sons of Joseph[4] the son of
Israel, but not so that he[5] is enrolled in the
genealogy according to the birthright. 2/ It is
true that Judah was preeminent among his
brothers and a ruler came from him, but the
birthright[6] belonged to Joseph.)

3/ The sons of Reuben the firstborn of Israel:
Hanoch, Pallu, Hezron, and Carmi. 4/ The
sons of Joel:[7] Shemaiah[8] his son, Gog[9] his
son, Shimei his son, 5/ Micah his son, Reaiah
his son, Baal[10] his son, 6/ Beerah his son,
whom Tillegath[11]-pilneser, king of Assyria,
took into exile. He was a prince of the
Reubenites. 7/ And his relatives,[12] according
to their clans[13] when the genealogy of their
generations was constructed: Jeiel,[14] the
chief, and Zechariah, 8/ and Bela son of
Azaz, son of Shema,[15] son of Joel—who settled in Aroer, as far as Nebo and Baal-meon.
9/ And they[16] also settled in the east by the
edge of the desert that reaches to the
Euphrates River, because their cattle had
multiplied in the land of Gilead. 10/ And in
the days of Saul they made war with the
Hagrites,[17] who fell by their hand;[18] and they
lived in their tents throughout[19] the entire
region east of Gilead.

11/ The sons of Gad lived beside them[20] in the
land of Bashan as far as Salecah: 12/ Joel
the chief, and Shapham[21] the second, Janai,
and Shaphat[22] in Bashan. 13/ Their kindred
according to their fathers' houses: Michael,
Meshullam, Sheba, Jorai, Jacan, Zia, and
Eber,[23] seven.[24] 14/ These were the sons of[25]
Abihail son of Huri, son of Jaroah,[26] son of
Gilead, son of Michael, son of Jeshishai, son
of Jahdo, son of Buz.[27] 15/ Ahi son of Abdiel,
son of Guni, was chief in their fathers'
house, 16/ and they lived in Gilead,[28] in
Jabesh[29] and in its towns, and in all the pasturelands of Sharon up[30] to its limits. 17/ All
these were enrolled in their genealogies in
the days of Jotham[31] king of Judah and in
the days of Jeroboam[32] king of Israel. 18/
Reuben, Gad,[33] and the half-tribe of Manasseh had mighty men, people carrying
shield and sword and drawing the bow,
skilled in warfare, forty-four thousand
seven hundred sixty, ready to go to battle.
19/ They made war on the Hagrites, Jetur,
Naphish, and Nodab; 20/ and they were
given help[34] against them, and the Hagrites
and all who were with them[35] were given
into their hands, for they cried to God in the
battle, and he granted their entreaty
because they trusted in him. 21/ They took
captive[36] their livestock: fifty[37] thousand
camels, two hundred fifty thousand sheep,

1 LXX ἐν τῷ ἀναβῆναι "ascended," a harmonization
with Gen 48:15; 49:4. P. J. Williams, "The LXX of
1 Chronicles 5:1-2 as an Exposition of Genesis
48–49," *TynBul* 49 (1998) 369–71, shows that the
LXX variants in textual notes 1, 2, 3, 4, and 6
depend on the translator's meditation on "blessing"
and the "right of the firstborn" described in Genesis 48–49.

2 בכרתו; LXX εὐλογίαν αὐτοῦ ברכתו "his blessing."
LXX presupposes the same metathesis in v. 2 (note
6 below), but MT is preferable.

3 נתנה *niphal*; LXX נתן "he [i.e., his father] gave." Cf.
Gen 48:22.

4 לבני יוסף; LXX לבנו יוסף "to his son Joseph." Syr,
Arab.: ליוסף אחיו "to Joseph his brother." In Gen
48:13-19 Israel blesses Joseph (cf. 49:22-26) and also
Ephraim and Manasseh.

5 Here, implicitly, Joseph. Cf. Japhet, 129.

6 והבכרה; LXX ברכתו "his blessing."

7 בני יואל; cf. LXX[L] בנו יואל "Joel his son"; and Syr,
Arab.: בני כרמי "and the sons of Carmi." These are
attempts to make a genealogical connection to the
previous verse. Johnstone, 1:73, adopts LXX[L]. See
the commentary.

8 LXX adds "and Benaiah" (ובניה), a miswritten dittography of the following בנו "his son."

9 גוג; LXX גוג; Syr, Arab.: ודואג "and Doeg."

10 בעל; LXX[B] יואל "Joel." Syr בלע is a metathesis of
MT.

11 תלגת; many Hebrew MSS, LXX[Aal], Syr, Tg: תגלת
"Tiglath." There are no less than four spellings of
this name in its six OT occurrences (see the commentary).

12 ואחיו; Rudolph, 44, ואחר "later." See the commentary.

13 למשפחתיהם with LXX[L], Syr, Tg, Arab.; MT, LXX:
למשפחתיו "according to his clans." Rudolph, 44,
relates the antecedent of "his" to the Reubenites in
v. 6b.

14 יעיאל; LXX יואל "Joel."

15 שמע; LXX[L], Syr: שמעי "Shimei."

16 While the verb is 3d masc. sg., the subject is the collective "Reubenites" in v. 6. Braun, 69, 71: "He
dwelt as far as the beginning of the wilderness
which reaches to the Euphrates River."

17 הַהַגְרִיים = הַהַגְרִאים. GKC §93x. Cf. 2 Chr 17:11
ערביאים. LXX τοὺς παροίκους = הגרים "the sojourners."

18 Japhet, 129, "into."

19 וישבו באהליהם על; LXX κατοικοῦντες ἐν σκηναῖς
= יושבי באהלים עד "living in tents until."

20 *BHS* proposes to insert "in the land of Gilead and."

21 ושפם; LXX[L], Vg: ושפן "Shaphan." LXX[B] ושבט
"Shabat."

22 ושפט; LXX[ANrell] "Ahibuz." Rudolph, 46, reads הַשֹּׁפֵט

155

and two thousand donkeys, as well as one hundred thousand people. 22/ Many fell slain, for the war was from God. And they lived in their territory until the exile.

23/ The sons of the half-tribe of Manasseh lived in the land, from Bashan[38] to Baal-hermon, Senir, and Mount Hermon.[39] They were numerous. 24/ These were the heads of their fathers' houses: Epher,[40] Ishi, Eliel, Azriel, Jeremiah, Hodaviah, and Jahdiel, mighty warriors, famous men, heads of fathers' houses. 25/ They acted unfaithfully toward the God of their fathers, and prostituted themselves to the gods of the peoples of the land, whom God had destroyed before them. 26/ So he stirred up the spirit of Pul the king of Assyria, even[41] the spirit of[42] Tillegath-pilneser the king of Assyria, and he[43] carried them into exile, namely,[44] the Reubenites, the Gadites, and the half-tribe of Manasseh, and he brought them to Halah, Habor,[45] and[46] the river of Gozan,[47] until this day.

"the judge," with Tg and LXX (ὁ γραμματεύς). Braun, 69, ויעני שפט "while Janai judged in Bashan."

23 ועבר; a few Hebrew MSS and LXX ועבד "Obed" representing the *dālet/rêš* confusion.

24 LXX "eight."

25 אלה בני. Japhet, 129, deletes these words. See the commentary.

26 ירוח. One Hebrew MS ירוע; LXX presupposes יחדו. Cf. Allen, *Greek Chronicles*, 2:64.

27 בוז. The reading in LXX[ANrell] αχιβους presupposes a metathesis with the first word in the next verse אחיבוז :אחי. Allen, *Greek Chronicles*, 1:27–28, suggests that the reading in LXX[B], Ζαβουχαμ, is a corrupted version of MT: בוז followed by אחי. LXX[L] attests only βουζ, thus lacking a translation for אחי, as does Syr.

28 Omitted in Syr.

29 ביבש. This conjecture goes back to Barnes in the Cambridge Bible and has been adopted by Rudolph, 46, *BHS*. MT בבשן "in Bashan." Cf. vv. 11-12. Japhet, 129, retains both Gilead and Bashan and adds "in Golan." See the commentary.

30 עד with LXX, Vg. MT על.

31 יותם; LXX[by] "Joash"; LXX[e2] "Joab."

32 LXX[L] adds "[the son] of Joash."

33 וגד with LXX[BL], Syr, Tg, Vg; MT וגדי "and Gadite," perhaps under the influence of the following word that ends in a *yôd*.

34 ויעזרו; LXX[L] "and they cried out" (ויזעקו).

35 וכל אהליהם. LXX τὰ σκηνώματα = וכל שעמהם "their tents."

36 וישבו; Rothstein, 102, and Rudolph, 48, וישלו "They plundered."

37 LXX "five."

38 בארץ מבשן; Syr, Arab. (cf. *BHS*): בארץ הבשן "in the land of Bashan." Japhet, 129, adds a third possibility: "in the land X from Bashan."

39 LXX adds "and in Lebanon."

40 עפר; MT ועפר "and Epher." Delete conjunction with the versions.

41 Or "namely." For this use of the conjunction see Deut 9:8, 22. Moshe Anbar, "Poul roi d'Assyrie et Tilgath-Pilnéser roi d'Assyrie," *BN* 48 (1989) 7, suggests that a later scribe inserted the word רוח ("the spirit of") before Tillegath-pilneser.

42 ואת רוח. I take the conjunction as explicative (cf. BDB, 252, 1.b.c), but MT may have conflated two synonymous variants: "the spirit of Pul the king of Assyria" and "the spirit of Tillegath-pilneser the king of Assyria." Syr lacks the first of these names, though this may be due to homoioarchton. The following two verb forms are in the singular. It is highly unlikely that the Chronicler intended two kings of Assyria (contra Curtis and Madsen, 125). Cf. 2 Kgs 15:19, 29. See the commentary.

156

43 Rudolph, 50, believes that the antecedent is probably God.

44 לראובני. Cf. BDB, 514 f (d). Polzin, *Late Biblical
Hebrew*, 67, calls this usage "lamedh emphatic."

45 וחבור, with LXX, Syr, Arab.; cf. 2 Kgs 17:6; 18:11.
MT adds והרא "Hara" by dittography.

46 MT; omitted by Syr. *BHS* suggests deleting the conjunction.

47 Syr adds וערי מדי "and in the cities of the Medes"
from 2 Kgs 17:6; 18:11, but lacks "until this day."
Rudolph, 50, proposes that "the cities of the

Medes" may lie hidden in עד היום הזה "until this day," or that
"the cities of the Medes" was dropped out by homoioarchton.
Cf. Willi, 160. 2 Kgs 17:6 LXX[L] καὶ Ορη Μήδων ἑὼς τῆς
ἡμέρας ταύτης "and the mountains of the Medes until this
day." Kings MT understands only Habor as a river, designated
"the river of Gozan"; Kings LXX understands both the Habor
and the Halah as the rivers of Gozan. Chronicles apparently
understands Habor, Halah, and Hara as cities and the river of
Gozan as a separate entity.

5:1-26

Structure

After providing an expansive genealogy for the preeminent tribe Judah (1 Chr 2:3–4:23) and a much
shorter genealogy for the closely related tribe of Simeon,
whose territory was eventually absorbed into Judah
(4:24-43), the Chronicler next turns to genealogical
materials on Reuben, Gad, and the (eastern) half of
Manasseh in Transjordan. He proceeds in a south-to-
north direction for these Transjordanian tribes before
continuing with the tribe of Levi and then moving to the
Cisjordan tribes. This chapter may be outlined as follows:

I. 5:1-10. Tribe of Reuben
  A. 5:1-2. Right of the firstborn in relationship to
  Reuben, Joseph, and Judah
  B. 5:3-8a. Descendants of Reuben
  C. 5:8b-10. Areas of Reubenite settlement, both orig-
  inally and as a result of a military engagement
  against the Hagrites after their cattle increased
II. 5:11-17. Tribe of Gad
  A. 5:11. Area of the Gadite settlement
  B. 5:12-15. Descendants of Gad
  C. 5:16-17. Further specification of the Gadite settle-
  ment and a notice about their genealogical
  enrollment

III. 5:18-22. Successful military engagement of Reuben,
Gad, and the half-tribe of Manasseh against the
Hagrites, Jetur, Naphish, and Nodab. This attack led
to the capture of a huge number of animals and an
equally huge number of human prisoners. The two
and one-half tribes occupied the captured land until
the exile.
IV. 5:23-24. Half-tribe of Manasseh
  A. 5:23. Area of this half-tribe's settlement
  B. 5:24. Descendants of Manasseh
V. 5:25-26. Unfaithfulness of (Reuben, Gad, and)[1] the
half-tribe of Manasseh and their resultant exile to
Assyria

Reuben is structured similarly to Simeon, but with
some variations.[2] There is also a structural similarity
between the genealogies of Reuben and Gad. The first
set of verse numbers in the following list refers to
Reuben and the second to Gad: main list, 4-6, 12; attention to kinsmen, 7-8a, 13-15; notes about tribal pasture,
9-10, 16. Gad and Manasseh do not open with a presentation of the tribe's families, as with Reuben, Judah,
Simeon, and almost all of the tribes in chap. 7.
Given that there was persistent tension between the
Cisjordanian and Transjordanian tribes and the fact that
the Transjordanian tribes had been exiled about four
centuries before the Chronicler, it is not surprising that
our author would not have abundant materials on any of

---

1 The unfaithfulness seems at first to be that of Manasseh alone (v. 25), but the consequences, in military defeat, involve the two and one-half tribes in
v. 26.

2 See Oeming, *Wahre Israel*, 135–36. Williamson, 63,
thinks these two genealogies may have come from
same source.

these tribes. His twenty-six verses for the two and one-half tribes are to be compared with the one hundred verses for Judah alone. In addition, since Reuben, at least, ceased to function as a consolidated tribe no later than the eleventh century,[3] and since these two and one-half tribes were part of the Northern Kingdom rather than Judah and were not always or consistently under Israelite control, the paucity of genealogical information and/or its fragmentary condition is even less surprising.

Here as elsewhere in 1 Chronicles 1–9 there are many unknown names, but there are also great uncertainties about the structure of the genealogies themselves and about the links between various names and other genealogical material that will be discussed, though not necessarily resolved, in the commentary. Here is a list of the most burning problems (cf. also textual note 27): (1) Why does the Chronicler not use any of the genealogical material available to him from the Bible itself for Gad and the half-tribe of Manasseh? (2) How are the sons of Joel (vv. 4-6) related genealogically to Reuben and his four sons mentioned in v. 3? (3) Is Joel in v. 4 to be identified with Joel in v. 8? (4) What is the antecedent of "who" in v. 8 or of "they" in v. 9? (5) Verse 14 introduces "the sons of Abihail," but instead of providing a list of these sons, the text traces the ancestry of Abihail himself for seven generations. (6) How do the seven heads of father's houses in v. 24 relate to the patriarch Manasseh? These problems may have arisen because of the fragmentary and inaccurate materials available to the Chronicler or to the vicissitudes of subsequent textual transmission. Despite all of these complications and uncertainties about the genealogical detail, these lists of names are not stereotypical, thus implying that the Chronicler got them from some kind of archival source, regardless of how inadequate we might judge the source or sources to be.

After reviewing and criticizing the literary-critical proposals of Noth, Rudolph, and Kartveit, Ulrike Schorn presents her own proposal in her book on the Reubenite traditions.[4] She assigns vv. 1-17 to the original draft of the Chronicler, with vv. 18-22 and vv. 25-26 and vv. 23-24 identified as supplements by an editor fully in line with the Chronicler's theological perspective. She notes that the statement in the original draft that the Hagrites "fell by their hand" (v. 10) is modified in v. 20 by a statement that the Hagrites "were given into their hands" by God (see the commentary). The vague expansion of Reuben into the tents of the Hagrites in v. 10 is modified in vv. 21-22 by the acquisition of an enormous amount of booty and the notice that the two and one-half Transjordanian tribes settled in their territory. Verses 25-26 continue the theme of vv. 18-22 by naming the unfaithfulness of the two and one-half tribes and their exile at the hand of Tiglath-pileser, already adumbrated in v. 6. Like a number of other scholars, she is also concerned with the position of vv. 23-24 that introduces the half-tribe of Manasseh since that half-tribe had already been part of the military campaign described in vv. 18-22,[5] and since these verses preempt the genealogy of the (whole) tribe of Manasseh in 7:14-19. In her view the secondary verses (vv. 18-26) were added by someone fully in accord with the Chronicler's thinking, so that one could also consider that the tensions between vv. 1-17, on the one hand, and vv. 18-22 + 25-26 and vv. 23-24, on the other hand, could also result from the Chronicler's own redaction of the genealogical materials that were available to him. In any case, there is a strong theological continuity between her *Grundschicht* in vv. 1-17 and the allegedly secondary materials.

Peter J. Williams has identified material that he classifies as the "warrior formula" in v. 18. It consists of the tribe or group from which the warriors came, the arms of the warriors, their number, and the readiness of the soldiers for war. Such warrior formulas are found at sev-

---

3   Frank Moore Cross, "Reuben, First-Born of Jacob," *ZAW* 100 (Sup, 1988) 48, n. 6. Cross admits that scattered elements tracing their lineage to Reuben may have survived. See the commentary on v. 8.

4   Ulrike Schorn, *Ruben und das System der Zwölf Stämme Israels* (BZAW 248; Berlin: de Gruyter, 1997) 268–73.

5   If vv. 23-24 were placed before vv. 18-22, the victories of the two and one-half tribes in vv. 18-22

would be put back-to-back with vv. 25-26. The latter verses describe the unfaithfulness of the tribes and their exile. The Chronicler may have wanted to put chronological distance between these two events.

eral other places in Chronicles.[6] Williams uses this typical formula of the Chronicler to argue that the materials in vv. 18-26 came from the Chronicler himself. He also calls attention to terminology characteristic of the Chronicler in these verses.

Two kinds of material in this chapter confront the modern reader with serious methodological issues. First, these materials refer to three synchronisms: a battle in the time of Saul (11th century; v. 10), a census in the time of Jotham king of Judah and Jeroboam II king of Israel (mid-8th century; v. 17), and the exiling of the two and one-half tribes by Tillegath-pilneser (= Tiglath-pileser III) (ca. 734; vv. 6, 26; cf. v. 22). What is the historical accuracy of these dates and the military or other events associated with them? Second, a number of statements about the settlement patterns of these tribes correlate imperfectly with geographical data otherwise associated with them. Are the divergences between this material and the evidence recorded elsewhere in the Bible to be attributed to the Chronicler's interpretation of that biblical data, or were there also nonbiblical sources dealing with the settlement of these tribes available to him? In both of these cases, I believe the Chronicler did have access to data probably coming from preexilic times.[7]

Despite the difficulties with which this chapter bristles, I believe that the Chronicler included all of these materials as part of his overall genealogical introduction to his work. (Little would be lost if vv. 18-26 were attributed with Schorn to an editor fully in sympathy with the Chronicler's theology.) Despite many criticisms about the Transjordanian tribes in earlier biblical materials and their exclusion from Ezekiel's picture of the renewed land in chap. 47, for the Chronicler these two and one-half tribes—and perhaps their land—were part of Israel in the past and possibly would be so again. But the Chronicler also saw theological justification for the exiling of these tribes that had led to judgment lasting until his own day (vv. 25-26).

Detailed Commentary

5:1-10. Tribe of Reuben

■ **1** *He [Reuben] was the firstborn, but because he defiled the bed of his father his birthright was given to the sons of Joseph the son of Israel:* The OT is unanimous in making Reuben biologically the firstborn of the sons of Jacob/Israel (Gen 29:22; 35:23; 46:8; 49:3; Num 1:10; 26:5). Cross has explored some of the traditions preserved in the Bible that date from a period when Reuben was much more prominent than the tribe is in the final form of the biblical text.[8] Whatever the sociological or political reasons for Reuben's decline, the tribe's diminishment is explained theologically here as judgment for his incestuous sexual relationship with the concubine of his father (Gen 35:22). In his deathbed blessing of his sons (Gen 49:3-4), Jacob mentions this incident and declares: "You [Reuben] shall no longer excel."[9] The Chronicler uses this tradition to explain, belatedly, why Judah and not Reuben is the first in the tribal genealogies, and to make an explicit point made nowhere else in the Bible that the right of the firstborn passed from Reuben to the sons of Joseph.[10] This second point builds on another tradition in Genesis: Jacob blessed the children of Joseph, Ephraim and Manasseh, and made them equal members among the tribes with the first and second tribes, Reuben and Simeon (Gen 48:5; cf. 48:15-16, 20). Since the firstborn son normally got a double portion of the

6   Peter J. Williams, "Israel Outside the Land: The Transjordanian Tribes in 1 Chronicles 5," in *Windows into Old Testament History* (ed. V. P. Long, D. W. Baker, and G. J. Wenham; Grand Rapids: Eerdmans, 2002) 147–60. Other examples of this formula occur at 1 Chr 12:9, 25 (8, 24); 2 Chr 14:7a, b; 17:17, 18; 25:5.

7   For detailed support of this position see ibid.

8   Cross, "Reuben." Matthias Augustin, "Neue territorialgeschichtliche Aspekte zu 1 Chronik 1–9 am Beispiel der Rubeniten," in *Nachdenken über Israel, Bibel und Theologie. FS für Klaus-Dietrich Schunck zu seinem 65. Geburtstag* (ed. H. M. Niemann et al.;

BEATAJ 37; Frankfurt am Main: Peter Lang, 1994) 308, questions not only the historicity of the Reubenite materials in chap. 5, but "with full justification" also argues that the tribes of Reuben and Simeon never existed but were only "theological conceptions."

9   Oeming, *Wahre Israel*, 137, suggests that both Reuben and Bilhah should have been executed according to Lev 20:11. The latter law, of course, deals explicitly with a wife rather than with a concubine, but in any case this is more an issue for interpreters of Genesis rather than Chronicles.

10   See Willi, "Late Persian Judaism," 154–55.

inheritance (Deut 21:17; 2 Kgs 2:9), that double portion was given to the two sons of Joseph. The honored position of Ephraim and Manasseh, the core of the Northern Kingdom, shows the Chronicler's open attitude toward the north and how far he was from making a polemic against the Samaritans a central motif in his message.[11] The Chronicler ignores the contention between Joseph and Jacob about whether Manasseh the older son or Ephraim the younger son would receive the greater blessing, which Jacob had resolved by crossing his hands to give Ephraim a blessing with his right hand (Gen 48:17-20). But he retains the idea that both sons of Joseph were blessed.

but not so that he is enrolled in the genealogy according to his birthright: This translation assumes that Joseph is the subject of this clause.[12] Japhet argues that Reuben is enrolled first in 1 Chr 2:1, but observes that the stone of stumbling in the ordering of the genealogies has always been the lengthy unit beginning with Judah in 2:3. Dirksen concludes that Reuben is the subject of the clause and provides an innovative translation of this verse: "His birthright was given to the sons of Joseph, and not to those who were registered for the birthright."[13] Dirksen appeals to an infrequently used meaning of the Hebrew root יחשׁ and the use of metonymy, but the same point comes across with a more conventional translation if Reuben is understood collectively here (cf. below on vv. 8-9): "so that he [Reuben] is not enrolled in the genealogy according to the birthright." The choice between this translation and the one provided in my translation of the chapter is not clear. Neither Reuben as the oldest son nor Joseph whose sons received the double portion normally given to the firstborn occupies the first genealogical position in 2:3–9:1. Judah is preeminent among his brothers, although he was not the firstborn or the holder of the birthright.

■ **2** *It is true that Judah was preeminent among his brothers and a ruler came from him:* The Chronicler has already shown that preeminence in putting the genealogy of

Judah in the first position (2:3–4:23) and in recounting the ancestors and descendants of the "ruler"[14] David (2:10-17; 3:1-24) within that genealogy. But just as he reworked the materials of Genesis 48–49 to make his points about Reuben and Joseph, so he could appeal to the same source for his word about Judah and David. In his poetic blessing, Jacob said: "Judah, your brothers shall praise you" and "your father's sons shall bow down to you" (Gen 49:8); and again, "The scepter shall not depart from Judah, nor the ruler's staff from between his feet" (49:10). In that same chapter the high status of Joseph (49:22-26) exists alongside the high status of Judah, just as here. In the first two verses of this chapter the Chronicler has provided negative and positive reasons for the high rank of Judah. Negatively, his position was made possible by the diminution of Reuben; positively, the role of Judah is underscored by the line of David descended from him.

but the birthright belonged to Joseph: This clause repeats the point made at the end of v. 1. There are three players in this delicately balanced presentation: Reuben, who was physically the first child born to the patriarch Jacob/Israel; Judah, the principal tribe at the time of the Chronicler and the one whose exalted status is signified both by the kings who came from its midst and its first position in the genealogical lists from 1 Chr 2:3–8:40; and Joseph, who in the Chronicler's unique view now had the right of the firstborn. Rudolph, 42, reverses this clear intention of the text by proposing to insert the words ולא לו after the word "birthright" in v. 2, which could be rendered "but the birthright belonged to him [Judah] and not to Joseph."

Genealogy from Reuben

Reuben ──	Hanoch
	Pallu
	Hezron
	Carmi

11 Cf. 1 Chr 9:3: "Some of the people of Judah, Benjamin, Ephraim, and Manasseh lived in Jerusalem"; 2 Chr 30:10: So the couriers went from city to city through the country of Ephraim and Manasseh . . . but they laughed them to scorn"; 31:1: "All Israel . . . pulled down the high places and the altars throughout all Judah and Benjamin, and in Ephraim and Manasseh. Cf. Williamson, *Israel*, 89–95.

12 Cf. Japhet, 129, 133; Curtis and Madsen, 119; and *NEB*.

13 Piet B. Dirksen, "1 Chronicles 5:1-2," *JNSL* 25 (1999) 17–23.

14 The *lāmed* on the word לנגיד "ruler" is emphatic.

■ **3** *The sons of Reuben the firstborn of Israel: Hanoch, Pallu, Hezron, and Carmi:* The text repeats "the sons of Reuben the firstborn of Israel" from v. 1 in order to move to the genealogy proper. Literally, the Hebrew text puts the names in pairs "Hanoch and Pallu, Hezron and Carmi," and this list of names and the use of the conjunction conforms exactly to Exod 6:14, with close parallels in Gen 46:9 and Num 26:5-7.[15] The Chronicler does not include the further descendants of Reuben given in Num 26:8-11, namely, Dathan and Abiram, who, with Nemuel, were sons of Eliab the son of Pallu and whose rebellion is recorded both in these verses and in Numbers 16.[16] While their rebellion could also have been used to explain the decline of Reuben, the Chronicler found adequate explanation for this phenomenon in the text of Genesis.

Joel—Shemaiah—Gog—Shimei—Micah—Reaiah—Baal—Beerah

■ **4-6** *The sons of Joel: Shemaiah his son, Gog his son, Shimei his son, Micah his son, Reaiah his son, Baal his son, Beerah his son:*[17] Two things are unusual about the introductory words, "The sons of Joel." First, such a form often, but not always,[18] introduces a group of brothers, whereas I, guided by the repeated "his son," take the following names to be a linear descending genealogy tracing Beerah to the seventh earlier generation, where we find his ancestor Joel. This linear genealogy suggests the passing of much time from the era of the patriarch to the exile referred to in v. 6. None of these eight individuals is known elsewhere (except perhaps for Joel in v. 8). The presence of "Baal" among the descendants of Beerah might suggest some antiquity to this verse and perhaps a northern provenance.[19] Much more troubling, however, is that the Chronicler, at least in the present form of the text, draws no connection between Joel and Reuben himself or Reuben's four sons mentioned in v. 3. A similar gap appears between the sons of Gad and the patriarch himself in v. 12, and between the sons of the half-tribe of Manasseh and the patriarch in v. 24. The Chronicler affirms at the end of v. 6 that Beerah and his ancestors were in fact Reubenites (see the next reading). Cogan has pointed out that Joel and Jeiel (cf. v. 7) are two sons of Nebo who divorced their foreign wives at the time of Ezra (10:43). They represent Transjordanians who had returned with the Judahites from exile.[20] Perhaps these descendants of Reuben living in Transjordan had been exiled by Nebuchadnezzar and then returned to Yehud.

whom Tillegath-pilneser, king of Assyria, took into exile: The great Assyrian king, Tiglath-pileser III (*Tukultī-apil-Ešarra* ["my trust is in the firstborn of the shrine Esarra") ruled from 745 to 727, captured the city of Gaza in 734, and defeated the coalition of Rezin king of Damascus and Pekah of northern Israel in 732, as a result of which he created three major Assyrian provinces in the Northern Kingdom. The cities attacked by Tiglath-pileser according to the biblical account are much farther north, but include parts of Gilead (see the end of v. 9).[21] He is mentioned six times in the Bible with two different spellings of the first element in his

---

15   It remains possible that the Chronicler knew these four sons of Reuben from some nonbiblical source. If the latter were the case, it might help to explain the failure to include the names of Gad's children, who may not have been mentioned in that nonbiblical source. Allen, 337, mistakenly takes the names of Reuben's sons as a linear genealogy.

16   Cf. also On the son of Peleth in Num 16:1.

17   Tg adds: "who was Beerah the prophet." This is apparently a reference to Hos 1:1, where the prophet Hosea is called the son of Beeri.

18   Cf. 1 Chr 3:16.

19   Williamson, 64.

20   See Mordechai Cogan, "The Men of Nebo—Repatriated Reubenites," *IEJ* 29 (1979) 37–39. Cf. the sons of Pahath-moab ("Governor of Moab"; Ezra 2:6//Neh 7:21) and the men of Nebo (Ezra 2:29//Neh 7:33).

21   2 Kgs 15:29 mentions his capture of Ijon (MR 205308), Abel-beth-maacah (MR 204296), Janoah (MR 173265), Kedesh (MR 199279), Hazor (MR 203269), and the territory of Naphtali.

name and four different spellings of the second element in his name: תלגת פלנסר here and in 2 Chr 28:20; תלגת פלנאסר in 1 Chr 5:26; תגלת פלאסר in 2 Kgs 15:29 and 16:10 and תגלת פלסר in 2 Kgs 16:7.[22] Both Chronicles' spellings have metathasized the second and third letters in the first element in his name,[23] apparently for euphonic reasons.[24] Tiglath-pileser's exiling of the two and one-half Transjordanian tribes is recorded in v. 26 (cf. also v. 22).

He was a prince of the Reubenites: That Beerah was a tribal leader or prince (נשׂיא) suggests the reason why his genealogy was remembered back to the seventh generation, that is, to Joel (vv. 4-6). This fact presupposes that long after the tribe had disappeared as a consolidated force, individual families still claimed a genealogical heritage within it.[25] "Reubenites," while singular in Hebrew, is understood collectively. Tracing Beerah back for seven generations would give a sense of completeness to his genealogy, but of course would not be anywhere near enough generations historically to reach back to the patriarchal period.

■ **7-8** *Jeiel, the chief, and Zechariah, and Bela son of Azaz, son of Shema, son of Joel:* According to the Chronicler, Bela had three "brothers" or "relatives"[26]—Jeiel, Zechariah, and Bela—who are known to us only from these verses. The ascending genealogy of Bela can be depicted in two different ways:

Joel—Shema—Azaz—Bela

or by combining the information of this verse with the information in vv. 4-5:

Joel—Shemaiah/Shema ┬ Gog—Shimei—Micah—Reaiah—Baal—Beerah
　　　　　　　　　　 └ Azaz—Bela

The first genealogy simply traces his ancestry back to his great-grandfather Joel, who is apparently not to be identified with the Joel in v. 4. The second genealogy, however, assumes that Bela's great-grandfather is to be identified with Joel the ancestor of Beerah. Joel's son is spelled differently in the two verses, שמעיה in v. 4 and שמע in v. 8, lacking the divine name in the second spelling. The second reconstruction presupposes that a number of generations have been accidentally lost between Bela and Shema in a process called telescoping, or that Bela was several generations older than Beerah.[27]

who settled in Aroer, as far as Nebo and Baal-meon: The antecedent of "who" is ambiguous, referring either to Bela and the families related to him (Japhet, 135), or to the collectively understood "Reubenite" from v. 6 (Rudolph, 45-46; Allen, 337). Aroer (MR 228097), just north of the Arnon River, which flows into the middle

---

22　For an explanation and justification for this scheme of transliteration into Hebrew, see A. R. Millard, "Assyrian Royal Names in Biblical Hebrew," *JSS* 21 (1976) 7. Millard ascribes the metathesis of letters in Chronicles and the intrusion of a *nûn* in 1 Chr 5:6, 26 and 2 Chr 28:20 to inner-Hebrew variants.

23　Cf. אלמגים "almug wood" in 1 Kgs 10:11, which became אלגומים "algum wood" in 2 Chr 9:10. Willi, *Chronik als Auslegung*, 87, discusses this metathesis.

24　Oeming, *Wahre Israel*, 141, suggests that the usual spelling of "Pileser" would sound like פלא שׂר "wonder prince" and that תגלת would be related to "lead into exile." He suggests that the Chronicler relativized his name by making these changes. The Masoretic vocalization, however, suggests no such possible confusion on "Pileser," and why the Chron-

icler would want to dissociate this king from exile escapes me.

25　See the discussion of postexilic Reubenites in Ezra 10:43 in the commentary on vv. 7-8 below.

26　Rudolph, 45, considers "chief" to be equivalent to "firstborn," but then wonders why the firstborn Jeiel is not the "prince" and why he is listed after his brother Beerah. To avoid these difficulties he arbitrarily changes "his brother" (v. 7) to "later." See textual note 12.

27　So Rudolph, 45.

of the Dead Sea from the east, was a city built by Gad (Num 32:34) and formed the border between Reuben and Gad (Josh 13:16, 25).[28] Nebo (MR 220131) and Baal-meon (Khirbet Maʿin; MR 219120), both of which are Reubenite according to Num 32:38, form the northern border of Reuben's territory. In the Mesha stela the king of Moab claims to control these three cities, and they are considered to be Moabite in Jeremiah 48 (vv. 1, 6, 19, 22, and 23[29]). Mesha claims that he took Nebo from Israel at the command of Kemosh.[30] According to the traditions about Bela, Reubenites had prospered and controlled three important Transjordanian cities that were in Moab's hands by the mid-ninth century. By the second half of the eighth century, Beerah and his contemporaries were taken into exile. According to the Mesha inscription all three of these cities were occupied by Israel for a long time, but were captured by Mesha, who built them as Moabite localities.[31] Reubenite or Israelite presence in the territory of Moab is claimed in these verses in the eighth as well as in the eleventh century (see v. 10). Oeming observes that this genealogy and the Mesha inscription contain Israelite and Moabite claims that overlap both temporally and geographically. Since only one can be historical, he settles for the Mesha inscription, considering the Reubenite genealogy only as a theological conception without historical worth.[32] But in his mid-ninth-century inscription Mesha explicitly states that this territory was captured by Omri and only recaptured by Moab in the time of Omri's "son," by which he probably refers to Jehoram, Omri's grandson.[33] It is surely not impossible that before, during, and after Omri's control of these cities there were people there who claimed Reubenite lineage. If Baala the Baal-meonite from the Samaria Ostracon no. 27 refers to a person from the same Transjordanian town, Baal-meon may have been again in Israelite hands in the mid-eighth century, thus confirming the general accuracy of our text. By 600 BCE the city was again in Moabite control (Jer 48:23).[34]

■ **9** *And they also settled in the east by the edge of the desert that reaches to the Euphrates River:* Verses 9-10 describe an undefined expansion of the Reubenites[35] to the east. We are not told the extent of that expansion, since the reference to the Euphrates modifies the desert rather than Reubenite territory.

because their cattle had multiplied in the land of Gilead: Both the Reubenites and the Gadites were renowned for herding cattle in the Bible (Num 32:1; cf. Judg 5:16). Larger herds, probably to be correlated with a larger human population, required larger grazing land. In a number of passages Reuben and Gad are given the same or overlapping territory (Num 32:29, 33; Deut 3:12, 16), indicating that the weaker tribe Reuben was eventually absorbed by Gad. This joint territory included Gilead, jointly given to the Gadites and Reubenites (Num 32:29). The most common description of Gilead is the region from the Arnon in the south (halfway along the eastern shore of the Dead Sea) to Bashan in the north (east of the Sea of Galilee).[36]

■ **10** *And in the days of Saul they made war with the Hagrites:* Such a war is not attested in other biblical passages, nor is it clear how the Reubenites related to the

---

28   Cf. Deut 2:26; 3:12: Josh 12:2. Aroer was also one of the cities to which David sent presents (1 Sam 30:28).

29   I assume that Beth-meon and Baal-meon refer to the same place.

30   *COS* 2:137–38.

31   Ibid.

32   *Wahre Israel,* 139–41. See also Matthias Augustin, "Neue territorialgeschichtliche Überlegungen am Beispiel rubenitischer Texte in 1 Chronik 1–9," in *"Dort ziehen Schiffe dahin . . . "* (ed. M. Augustin and K.-D. Schunck; BEATAJ 28; Bern: Peter Lang, 1992) 27–30.

33   See Klaas A. D. Smelik, *Writings from Ancient Israel* (Edinburgh: T. & T. Clark, 1991) 48. The northern half of Transjordan was contested between Aram and Israel. Ahab's attack on Ramoth-gilead in

1 Kings 22 indicates that it was then under Aramean control. Hazael attacked throughout the territory (2 Kgs 10:32-33; 13:3), but there were also Israelite revivals under Jehoahaz (13:5) and especially under Jeroboam II (14:25, 28).

34   This assumes that Beth-meon is the same city as Baal-meon.

35   I understand the subject of the verb collectively (see textual note 16). So also Japhet, 135. Note the suffix "their" on the word "cattle" (מקניהם) and the use of a plural verb "made" (עשׂו) in v. 10.

36   Joel C. Slayton, "Bashan," *ABD* 1:623–24; M. Otto-son, "Gilead," *ABD* 2:1020–22.

authority of King Saul himself in this battle. This is the first reference to Saul in Chronicles (see 1 Chr 8:29-40 and 9:35-44 for his genealogy, and the account of his death in chap. 10). The Hagrites are listed with other Transjordanian enemies of Israel in Ps 83:7 (6): "The tents of Edom and the Ishmaelites, Moab and the Hagrites." Knauf believes that 1 Chr 5:10 reflects tribal conflicts at the time of the Chronicler,[37] and Eph'al concludes that the mention of Jetur, Naphish, and Nodab with the Hagrites in v. 19 can come from a tradition no earlier than the eighth century.[38] But there is a Hagrite already among David's officers (1 Chr 11:38//2 Sam 23:36),[39] and one of the officials of David, Jaziz the Hagrite, was over the flocks (1 Chr 27:30). The relationship of the Hagrites to Hagar, the concubine of Abraham, is unclear.[40] Japhet, 135, affirms the connection of the Hagrites to Hagar, but it would seem more likely to trace Hagar's descendants through Ishmael. In any case, the Hagrites are not to be associated with the later Agraioi or Agraei mentioned by the Greek and Latin geographers.[41] An account of a conflict of the two and one-half Transjordanian tribes with the Hagrites appears in vv. 18-22.

5:11-17. Tribe of Gad

■ **11** *The sons of Gad lived beside them in the land of Bashan as far as Salecah:* Gad is the son of Jacob/Israel and his concubine Zilpah, Leah's maid (Gen 30:10-11), though his mother is not mentioned here. The Chronicler lists the territory of the Gadites first, before mentioning indi-

vidual Gadites. This puts it in a chiastic arrangement with the individual Reubenites and territorial notes on the Reubenites in vv. 3-10. The Chronicler places the Gadites "beside" the Reubenites and describes their territory in Bashan, reaching as far as Salecah. This corrects the impression given by some passages, noted above, that the Reubenites and Gadites occupied the same territory. The association of the Reubenites, Gadites, and the half-tribe of Manasseh with Bashan is already given in Num 32:33: "Moses gave to them—to the Gadites and to the Reubenites and to the half-tribe of Manasseh son of Joseph—the kingdom of King Sihon of the Amorites and the kingdom of King Og of Bashan." "Salecah" is routinely mentioned in descriptions of Bashan and the territory taken from Sihon king of the Amorites and Og king of Bashan (Deut 3:10; Josh 12:5; 13:11), but its location is unknown.[42] Normally, Bashan extends from the Mount Hermon area in the north to about the Yarmuk River in the south. In Joshua "all Bashan" is given to the half-tribe of Manasseh, as well as the northern half of Gilead (Josh 13:29-31).[43] The oldest reliable source on Gad in the OT (Num 32:33) lists four cities that formed the original core of Gad: Dibon (MR 224104), Ataroth (MR 213109), Aroer (228097), and Atroph-shophan (location unknown), all north of the Arnon and south of the tribe of Reuben. Gad was later forced out of this position and resettled farther to the north, as in this verse.[44] King Mesha, in the ninth-century stela named after him, calls himself the Dibonite, implying that he was born at Dibon and that it was under Moabite control at his time. The Mesha stela also

37   Knauf, *Ismael*, 49–52. This is also the opinion of John Van Seters, *Abraham in History and Tradition* (New Haven: Yale Univ. Press, 1975) 62.

38   Israel Eph'al, *The Ancient Arabs: Nomads on the Borders of the Fertile Crescent 9th–5th Centuries B.C.* (Jerusalem: Magnes, 1982) 239.

39   Mibhar son of Hagri. See the discussion in McCarter, *II Samuel*, 493–94; and this commentary on 11:38. In Hebrew "son of Hagri" (בן הגרי in 11:38 is closer to "Bani the Gadite" (בני הגדי; 2 Sam 23:36) than one might guess from the English translations.

40   David F. Graf, "Hagrites," *ABD* 3:24.

41   In agreement with Graf, ibid.; contra Braun, 76. The Agraioi are probably the inhabitants of Hofuf-Thaj located in the al-Hasa oases in northwest Arabia, on the Persian Gulf.

42   Salecah (סלכה) is sometimes identified with Ṣalchad (MR 311212; cf. Aharoni, *Land of the Bible*, 441), some 40 miles east of Ramoth-gilead. The names sound somewhat similar in English, but two of the four letters are actually different. Cf. Kartveit, *Motive und Schichten*, 138. Rudolph, 47, puts it near Edrei (Der'ā, MR 253224) on the southern coast of the Sea of Galilee.

43   Cf. Num 32:39-40 and Deut 3:13-15.

44   Cf. Deut 3:12 (half the hill country of Gilead), 16; 4:43 (Ramoth-gilead; MR 244210); 29:7-8.

states that "the men of Gad lived in the land of Ataroth from ancient times."[45] "Ancient times" implies at least several generations, perhaps going back to the time of Saul and David (cf. 1 Sam 13:7). Since Mesha claims to have conquered Medeba (MR 225124), north and east of Ataroth, Moab may have been content to leave Ataroth untouched as it moved northward along the King's Highway. As noted above under Structure, the Chronicler does not include any of Gad's descendants listed in Gen 46:16 and Num 26:15-17.

■ **12-13** *Joel the chief, and Shapham the second, Janai, and Shaphat in Bashan:* Nothing is known about these four tribal chiefs,[46] who are probably to be considered brothers. Some commentators reduce the number to three by interpreting "Shaphat" as a participle "who judged" modifying Janai (see textual note 22).[47] Verse 13 goes on to list seven kindred, by their fathers' houses,[48] and concluding with the number "seven." Unfortunately, these names are also unknown, as are the connecting genealogical links between any of the eleven names in vv. 12-16 and the patriarch Gad. Their residence in Gilead (v. 16) and in Jabesh (v. 16; MR 214201) legitimates their assignment to the tribe of Gad.

■ **14-15** *These were the sons of Abihail son of Huri, son of Jaroah, son of Gilead, son of Michael, son of Jeshishai, son of Jahdo, son of Buz. Ahi son of Abdiel, son of Guni, was chief in their fathers' house:* This verse is one of the most problematical sections in all the genealogies. After "These were the sons of Abihail," one would expect a list of brothers, or, as we have seen on a few occasions a linear genealogy: X his son; Y his son; Z his son, etc. Instead we find a pedigree of Abihail stretching back in time for seven generations:[49] Buz–Jahdo–Jehishai–Michael–Gilead–Jaroah–Huri–Abihail, and then a pedigree of Ahi, the chief, going back another two generations: Guni–Abdiel–Ahi.

There are several ways out of this dilemma, all of them plausible but some more conjectural than others.

1. The families who traced their origin to Abihail have been lost, as has the name of the individual whose pedigree is given in v. 14. One would reconstruct the sentence to read: "These were the sons of Abihail: A, B, C, etc. X son of Abdiel . . . son of Guni, was chief in their fathers' house." See the suggestion of Japhet, 137.

2. Japhet, 137, herself claims that "Ahi" at the beginning of v. 15 is missing from LXX and should be deleted. She suggests also deleting "These were/are the sons of" from the beginning of v. 14. This results in a list of eleven Gadite fathers' houses in vv. 12-13 and a chief Abihail in vv. 14-15, who traced his genealogy back for nine additional generations. I believe that she has misread the LXX evidence (see textual note 27), and her deletion of אלה בני seems arbitrary.

3. My translation (cf. *TEV, NAB, NIV,* and *NEB*) takes "These were the sons of Abihail" as a conclusion to the previous v. 13 or the previous two verses (vv. 12-13), rather than as an introduction of another list of names. A pedigree is then given for Abihail. This makes Abihail the "father" of all the names in v. 13, or in vv. 12-13, and also a descendant of Buz. Ahi is then identified as a chief in the Gadite fathers' house. A slight difficulty would be the relationship between Joel, who is called "the chief" in v. 12, and Ahi, who is called "chief" in v. 15.

Japhet, 137, raises the possibility that Guni גוני in v. 15 might be related to Shuni שוני, the third of seven sons traditionally ascribed to Gad (Gen 46:16; Num 26:15). Otherwise, none of the sons of Gad known from elsewhere in the Bible is included here.

■ **16** *and they lived in Gilead, in Jabesh and in its towns, and in all the pasturelands of Sharon up to its limits:* We have already seen that Gad is assigned to Gilead (see the com-

---

45   *COS* 2:137.
46   Japhet, 136, notes that the word "chief" is more common in chaps. 23–26 than in chaps. 1–9. Cf. 23:8, 11, 16, etc., with 5:7; 9:17.
47   Japhet, 136, points out that the title "judge" is never used in any of the tribal genealogies. Rudolph, 47, interprets "chief" and "second" not as a reference to their birth order but as titles: "chief" and "deputy."
48   Note the different spellings in vv. 13 בית אבותיהם

and 15 בית אבותם, which Braun, 76, takes as evidence that these are gleanings from separate sources.
49   De Vries, 57. He defines "pedigree" as a list in which a descendant traces his direct lineage to a remote ancestor, naming all the males in the line of descent (p. 433). Cf. 6:18-32 (33-47); 9:16.

mentary on v. 9), but there are also passages that ascribe Gad to the territory called Bashan, as in the MT of this verse (see textual note 29). The possessive pronoun "its" used with towns is feminine, while both Gilead and Bashan are masculine and are regions rather than individual cities. This problem is resolved if we accept the conjectural reading Jabesh (Tell el-Maqlûb; MR 214201), southwest of Ramoth-gilead (MR 244210), since cities in Hebrew are feminine. Japhet's proposal, 137, to add "in the Golan" after "in Gilead and in Bashan" is plausible because of the frequent reference to "Golan in Bashan" (possibly Saḥm el-Jōlân; MR 238243; Deut 4:43; Josh 20:8; Josh 21:27//1 Chr 6:56 [71]), but seems to be too far north for Gad, since it is about 22 miles northwest of Ramoth-gilead. The "pasturelands of Sharon" is an equally difficult reading. Such pasturelands were probably open to all members of the community and are mentioned in priestly contexts and in the list of Levitical cities. The problem lies with "Sharon," which cannot refer to the plain of Sharon along the Mediterranean coast, and the reference to the men of Sharon in line 13 of the Mesha stela would surely be a site considerably farther south. Another possible location for these pasturelands is *Sārūna* in an inscription of Amenhotep II (Šarūna of EA 241:4), although this replaces one unknown with another.[50] Braun, 76, makes an interesting proposal to replace Sharon שרון with Sirion שרין, an alternate name for Mount Hermon.[51]

■ **17** *All these were enrolled in their genealogies in the days of Jotham king of Judah and in the days of Jeroboam king of Israel:* In many modern chronological reconstructions, this synchronism presents no problems.[52] Galil, for example, dates Jeroboam II to 790–750/749 and Jotham to 758/757–742/741.[53] Hence the two kings overlap for seven or eight years. Jeroboam is credited with restoring the borders of Israel from Lebo-hamath to the Sea of the Arabah (2 Kgs 14:25), which makes his taking of a Transjordanian census plausible. It seems unlikely to most scholars, however, that both northern and southern kings would have engaged in a common census of Transjordanian lands since these lands were never controlled by Judah[54] and only intermittently by Israel. Hence Jeroboam is the one who would be expected to take a census of Gad since it belonged to the Northern Kingdom.[55] It is also possible to understand this verse as a mere chronological reference point—the census is dated to the time when both Jeroboam II and Jotham were on the throne—without explicitly indicating who took the census.

---

50 See Harry W. Weeks, "Sharon," *ABD* 5:1161–63.

51 Hermon, Sirion, Senir, Gilead, Bashan, Salecah, and Edrei are all found in Deut 3:9-10. Cf. Ps 29:6.

52 For Wellhausen, *Prolegomena*, 213, however, this was a prime example of the Chronicler's nonhistorical character: "Jotham and Jeroboam . . . make so impossible a synchronism that the partisans of Chronicles will have it that none is intended." Wellhausen was basing himself on 2 Kgs 15:32, where Jotham became king in the second year of Pekah, i.e., during the reign of the sixth king after Jeroboam. Jotham's service as co-regent during his father's illness, however, makes the Chronicler's synchronism possible.

53 Galil, *Chronology*, 147. Jotham was co-regent with his father Uzziah, who in fact outlived him. Uzziah is dated by Galil to 788/787–736/735. In the reconstruction of Edwin R. Thiele, *A Chronology of the Hebrew Kings* (Grand Rapids: Zondervan, 1977) 75, which proposes many new co-regencies in order to uphold the dates of the MT, this synchronism does

not work. Thiele dates Jeroboam to 793–753 and Jotham to 750–732. He does not discuss the current passage. William Hamilton Barnes, *Studies in the Chronology of the Divided Monarchy of Israel* (HSM 48; Atlanta: Scholars Press, 1991) 153, dates Jeroboam II to 784–744 and Jotham to 751–736. The standard German chronology by Joachim Begrich, *Die Chronologie der Könige von Israel und Juda* (Beiträge zur historischen Theologie 3; Tübingen: Mohr [Siebeck], 1929) 155, dates Jeroboam II to 787/786–747/746 and Jotham as co-regent from 758/757 to 747/746 and then as king until 743/742. Cf. also Japhet, 138; Rudolph, 48–49.

54 We do read of a war between Jotham and the Ammonites in 2 Chr 27:5 that would show Jotham's activity in Transjordan.

55 Myers, 1:37–38, suggested that the Chronicler added the reference to Jotham to accord with his scheme of making the Davidic dynasty the backbone of his work.

5:18-22. Successful Military Engagement of Reuben, Gad, and the Half-Tribe of Manasseh

■ **18** *Reuben, Gad, and the half-tribe of Manasseh had mighty men, people carrying shield and sword and drawing the bow, skilled in warfare, forty-four thousand seven hundred sixty, ready to go to battle:* Verses 18-22 and 25-26 are theological compositions of the Chronicler written to illustrate the positive and negative consequences of faith and infidelity, respectively. This unit expands on the earlier battle of the Reubenites with the Hagrites, and again there is no evidence of involvement by the central government authority. בני חיל "mighty men" or "valiant warriors" is used a number of times in Chronicles (26:7, 9, 39, 23; 2 Chr 26:17; 28:6) and only twice elsewhere (Deut 3:18; Judg 18:2). The word pair "shield and sword" is used elsewhere only at Ps 76:4 (3). The Chronicler mentions this type of shield (מגן) eleven times, but he also refers to the larger shield צנה in 1 Chr 12:25 (24); 2 Chr 9:15; and 14:7. The word "sword" is used nineteen times in Chronicles. This is one of nine references to the bow or bows in Chronicles.[56] In the genealogy of Benjamin, the sons of Ulam are said to be "mighty warriors, drawing the bow" (1 Chr 8:40). Instead of drawing the bow, we might translate "bending the bow," that is, by firmly planting the foot in the middle of the bow (*HALOT* 1:231). For "ready for battle" see 7:11; 12:34, 37; 2 Chr 25:5; 26:11. One of the more interesting parallels to this passage occurs in Cant 3:7-8: "Around it [the litter of Solomon] are sixty mighty men of the mighty men of Israel, all equipped with swords and expert in war, each with his

sword at his thigh because of alarms by night." Canticles uses the *pual* passive participle of למד for the word "expert" or "trained," whereas Chronicles uses the *qal* passive participle of the same root. The total numbers for the troops of the two and one-half tribes—44,760—are no doubt larger than these tribes could have mustered at any time historically,[57] though they are actually smaller than figures given elsewhere: Numbers 1: Reuben 46,500 (v. 21); Gad 46,550 (v. 25); the whole tribe of Manasseh 32,200 (v. 35); total for the three tribes: 125,250; Numbers 26: Reuben 43,700 (v. 7); Gad 40,500 (v. 18); the whole tribe of Manasseh 52,700 (v. 34); total for the three tribes: 136,900; 1 Chronicles 12: Reubenites, Gadites, and half-tribe of Manasseh 120,000 (v. 37; see the commentary).[58] In the genealogies themselves, Issachar is credited with 145,000 troops (1 Chr 7:1-4), Benjamin with 59,434 (7:6-11), and Asher with 26,000 (7:40).

■ **19** *They made war on the Hagrites, Jetur, Naphish, and Nodab:* The war of the Reubenites with the Hagrites in the days of Saul was referred to briefly in v. 10, but the account in vv. 18-22 involves the two and one-half Transjordanian tribes acting together[59] and is undated. The enemy is now expanded beyond the Hagrites to include Jetur, Naphish, and Nodab. Jetur and Naphish are known elsewhere only from the genealogy of Ishmael (Gen 25:15[60]//1 Chr 1:31). Since Eph'al dates the genealogy of Ishmael no earlier than the eighth century, this would seem to be the earliest possible date for this battle as well—if it ever took place. Actually, Eph'al believes that the Chronicler added these two names so

---

56   1 Chr 5:18; 8:40; 10:3; 12:2 (twice); 2 Chr 14:7 (8); 17:17; 18:33; 26:14. See also the "spear" רמח in 1 Chr 12:25 (24) and חנית in 12:35 (34).

57   I believe that the numbers throughout Chronicles are to be translated literally as "thousands" and not as "military units" or the like. See Klein, "How Many in a Thousand?" Later in this paragraph astronomically high numbers are used to emphasize divine participation in the victory.

58   Williamson, 46, proposes that the Chronicler supplied the total number based on the separate figures in his source.

59   Cf. 1 Chr 12:28-29 (37-38). Japhet, 138, notes that the Chronicler in this way is heir to earlier biblical traditions, such as Numbers 32 and Josh 1:12-15, where the Reubenites and Gadites agree to cross

over the Jordan to help with the conquest of Cisjordan before taking possession of their own land.

60   Eph'al, *Ancient Arabs,* 61, 67, 100–101, 239, dates the list in Genesis no earlier than the 8th century. On p. 67 he states that the "Hagrites" (Hagarites in his spelling) appear only in the period of the judges (for which Ps 83:7[6] provides evidence) and the early monarchy. See the listing of the passages dealing with the Hagrites at v. 10.

167

that the date of Ishmael's genealogy is irrelevant for dating this battle. Knauf identifies "Nodab" with Adbeel (Gen 25:13), a tribe that is attested in 734/733 when Tiglath-pileser entrusted it to control the Egyptian border.[61] It is not mentioned elsewhere in the Bible.

■ **20** *and they were given help against them, and the Hagrites and all who were with them were given into their hand:* Japhet, 139, notes the large amount of Late Biblical Hebrew and specific Chronistic terminology in vv. 18-22. Features of Late Biblical Hebrew include: the infinitive absolute replacing a finite verb נעתור v. 19; omission of the pronoun governing a relative clause; conjunction of sentences by כי; results precede causes, and the use of simple tenses and nominal clauses (cf. Curtis and Madsen, 125). Specific Chronistic vocabulary is: "help" or "become strong, prevail" עזר;[62] "trust." The two passive verbs in the citation from v. 20a strongly imply that the help that was given to the two and one-half tribes came from God, and that the Hagrites and their associates (without repetition of the names Jetur, Naphish, and Nodab) were handed over to the Israelite tribes by God himself. This may be a theological correction to v. 10, where we are told that the Hagrites fell by their [the Reubenites] hand.

for they cried to God in the battle, and he granted their entreaty because they trusted in him: No real fighting takes place in this holy war. The tribes cried out in prayer to God and were helped. Similar cries of prayer bring victory for Jehoshaphat in 2 Chr 18:31[63] (cf. 20:9; 32:20-21). Oeming remarks that this illustrates the principle that whoever cries to God and trusts in God will have suc-

cess.[64] The only other uses of the verb עתר (grant an entreaty) in Chronicles are in the Chronicler's special account of Manasseh's repentance (2 Chr 33:13, 19). Aside from 32:10, where Chronicles quotes Sennacherib as saying, "On what are you trusting, that you undergo the siege of Jerusalem?"[65] this is the only use of the verb בטח "trust" in the whole work of the Chronicler. The usual words for such a faith posture are שען in the *niphal*, usually translated "rely on" (13:18; 14:11; 16:7-8) or אמן in the *hiphil*, usually translated "believe" (20:20).

■ **21** *They took captive their livestock: fifty thousand camels, two hundred fifty thousand sheep, and two thousand donkeys, as well as one hundred thousand people:* The word "livestock" מקניהם echoes the abundant "cattle" מקניהם of the Reubenites in v. 9. The numbers, of course, are wildly beyond belief, adding further evidence that the details in this section are not historical but designed to contrast what happens when people trust and what happens when they act faithlessly (cf. v. 25). Some of the other numbers of sheep in the book of Chronicles, extraordinarily large in their own right, pale in comparison with the booty taken in this battle: 120,000 sheep sacrificed by Solomon at the dedication of the temple (2 Chr 7:5); 7,000 sheep captured during the reign of Asa (15:11); the Arabs brought 7,700 rams to Jehoshaphat (17:11); 3,000 sheep were sacrificed by Hezekiah (29:33); and 17,000 sheep were contributed to the assembly by Hezekiah and the officials (30:24).[66] The human captives, described as נפש אדם (translated as "people"), may imply female, virginal captives, judging by the use of this term in Num 31:35, 40, 46.[67]

---

61 Ernst Axel Knauf, "Nodab," *ABD* 4:1134. Knauf derives both Nodab and Abdiel from *Nadab'il ("God has called up, excited"). The LXX's transliterations of Abdeel and Nodab indicate that the two names were regarded as identical.

62 In addition to many uses in the *qal*, the verb is used in the *niphal*, as here, only in 2 Chr 26:15; Ps 28:7; and Dan 11:34.

63 See the parallel in 1 Kgs 22:32, where Jehoshaphat merely shouts when he is discovered. In Chronicles that shout becomes a prayer that is then answered.

64 *Wahre Israel*, 141.

65 In the *Vorlage* (2 Kgs 18:19//Isa 36:4) a similar question is asked by the Rabshakeh.

66 The booty taken from Midian during the wilderness period is similarly unrealistic: 675,000 sheep, 72,000

oxen, 61,000 donkeys, and 32,000 persons, defined here as women who had not known a man by sleeping with him (Num 31:32-35).

67 Other uses of this expression are in priestly contexts at Lev 24:17; Num 9:6-7; 19:11, 13; Ezek 27:13.

■ **22** *Many fell slain, for the war was from God:* This statement makes explicit what was implicit throughout these verses: that this victory was solely due to God's intervention and came as a response to the faithful attitude and actions of the two and one-half tribes. Here many fall slain because the war was from God; in v. 10, by way of contrast, many fell because of the hand of the Reubenites. Japhet, 139, points out the absence of any centralized initiative or control in this war, which surely would have been impossible during the monarchical period. The artificial character of these verses, their lack of historical realism, and the explicit theological agenda are in striking contrast to the rest of the chapter.

And they lived in their territory until the exile: This seems to harmonize the idea that the Reubenites lived in the tents of the Hagrites throughout the region east of Gilead (v. 10) and the idea that Tiglath-pileser exiled the Reubenite Beerah in v. 6. The fact and the cause of the exile will be described in vv. 25-26.

5:23-24. Half-Tribe of Manasseh

■ **23** *The sons of the half-tribe of Manasseh lived in the land, from Bashan to Baal-hermon, Senir, and Mount Hermon:* As noted above, under Structure, the description of the half-tribe of Manasseh would be expected before vv. 18-22, where a military campaign of the two and one-half tribes is described. In 7:14-19 we have an account of the whole tribe of Manasseh and not just its western half as many translations suggest.[68] In Schorn's view this description of east Manasseh provides a detail that was felt to be missing in the *Grundschicht*. Williamson, 66–67, feels that the material in vv. 23-24 comes from a military census list and would be more at home in the genealogy of Manasseh at 7:14-19, where it is missing.[69] For the half-tribe of Manasseh, as with Gad, there are no children cited from the lists of the descendants of Manasseh in Gen 46:20 LXX,[70] Num 26:29-34, or Josh 17:2. Instead, the Chronicler provides in this verse a description of Manasseh's territory (cf. 1 Chr 5:8b-10 for Reuben and v. 11 for Gad). The Chronicler will continue his discussion of this tribe in 7:14-19. For the Chronicler the area associated with this half-tribe was once part of "the land."[71] Mount Hermon marks the northernmost point of land taken from Og king of Bashan (Deut 3:8; cf. Josh 11:17; 12:7), which we learn is called Sirion by the Sidonians and Senir by the Amorites (Deut 3:9; cf. Ezek 27:5). In Cant 4:8 Senir and Hermon are two separate mountains. Normally, Bashan extends from the Mount Hermon area in the north to about the Yarmuk River in the south (cf. Deut 3:10). Baal-hermon appears elsewhere only in Judg 3:3 as Mount Baal-hermon. Franklyn proposes that Baal-hermon is one of the three peaks on Hermon, with the two others being Senir and Mount Hermon itself.[72] Rudolph, 49, proposed an identification of Baal-hermon with Baneas, later known as Caesarea Philippi.

■ **24** *Epher, Ishi, Eliel, Azriel, Jeremiah, Hodaviah, and Jahdiel, mighty warriors, famous men, heads of fathers' houses:* None of these persons is known from elsewhere, and we are not told their relationship to the genealogy of the patriarch Manasseh or to any localities. "Heads of fathers' houses" is used in 7:1, 6 for military commanders. The same expression "mighty warriors, famous men, (heads) of fathers' houses," is used to describe the Ephraimite warriors who joined David at Hebron (12:31). For "mighty warriors," compare "mighty men" in v. 18.

---

68   Schorn, *Ruben*, 272.

69   This census list in genealogical form also shows up in the genealogy of Issachar (1 Chr 7:1-5), Benjamin (7:6-12), and Asher (7:30-40, esp. v. 40).

70   LXX adds to MT: "And there were sons born to Manasseh, which the Syrian concubine bore to him, Machir. And Machir became the father of Gilead. And the sons of Ephraim the brother of Manasseh: Sutalaam and Taam. And the sons of Sutalaam: Edom."

71   Kartveit, *Motive und Schichten*, 145, notes that the Chronicler also refers to Transjordan as "the land"

in 1 Chr 19:3, against his *Vorlage* at 2 Sam 10:3.

72   Paul Nimrah Franklyn, "Baal-Hermon," *ABD* 1:552.

5:25-26. Unfaithfulness of (Reuben, Gad, and) the half-tribe of Manasseh

■ **25** *They acted unfaithfully toward the God of their fathers, and prostituted themselves to the gods of the peoples of the land:* The Chronicler in the final two verses of the chapter presents the negative alternative in the theory of retribution—following the positive presentation of this notion in vv. 18-22—drawing on materials from 2 Kings that describe the exile alluded to in v. 22. The exile of the two and one-half Transjordanian tribes (v. 26) is seen as retribution for their infidelity,[73] in this case seen specifically in their breach of the First Commandment. The verb מעל (act unfaithfully) is a characteristic judgment of the Chronicler (see the list of passages at 2:7).[74] This is the first reference to the God of the fathers/ancestors in Chronicles, which appears altogether twenty-seven times in the book.[75] The "God of their/your ancestors" is used in conscious contrast here to "the gods of the peoples of the land." Compare the similar contrast in 2 Chr 32:19: "They spoke of the God of Jerusalem as if he were like the gods of the peoples of the earth." The verb "prostituted" זנה (qal) is only used elsewhere in Chronicles in the *hiphil* to describe the falling away during the reign of Jehoram (2 Chr 21:11, 13).[76]

whom God had destroyed before them: The comparison between Israel's behavior and the behavior of the nations whom God had destroyed appears also in 2 Chr 33:9. For guilt and retribution see 1 Chr 21:8 and 2 Chr 26:16-21.[77] This explicit reference to the conquest of the land contradicts Japhet's assertion that in Chronicles Israel had lived in the land from time immemorial.

■ **26** *So he stirred up the spirit of Pul the king of Assyria, even the spirit of Tillegath-pilneser the king of Assyria:* The Chronicler would have known of these two names for the king of Assyria, respectively, from 2 Kgs 15:19 and 29. Pul is a hypocoristicon by which Tiglath-pileser III is known in some cuneiform sources and in the Ptolemaic Canon. It is not his throne name as king of Babylon.[78] God's stirring up the spirit of the Assyrian king to bring about the exile of the two and one-half Transjordanian tribes is balanced at the end of the books of Chronicles by Yahweh's stirring up the spirit of Cyrus, king of the Persians, to send the Jewish exiles home and to authorize the rebuilding of the temple (2 Chr 36:22-23//Ezra 1:1-4). Yahweh also stirs up the spirit of the Philistines and of the Arabs against Jehoram (2 Chr 21:16).[79] In 2 Kgs 16:7 Tiglath-pileser came at the request of Ahaz.

he carried them into exile, namely, the Reubenites, the Gadites, and the half-tribe of Manasseh: The antecedent of "he" could be either Yahweh (so Rudolph, 50) or Tillegath-pilneser. In v. 6 it was the Assyrian king himself who exiled Beerah. Exile is also mentioned in v. 22. The Chronicler apparently dates the exiling of these tribes to the campaign of Tiglath-pileser III against Pekah in 732. The Deuteronomistic Historian records that the Assyrian king "captured Ijon, Abel-beth-maacah, Janoah, Kedesh, Hazor, Gilead, and Galilee, all the land of Naphtali; and he carried the people captive to [unspecified locations in] Assyria" (2 Kgs 15:29). All of these Israelite sites, except for Gilead, are in Cisjordan, while

---

73   A first reading of v. 25 after vv. 23-24 implies the sin was that of Manasseh, but as one learns in the next verse the consequence involved Reuben, Gad, and the half-tribe of Manasseh so that the pronoun "they" in v. 25 probably anticipates the same group of tribes.

74   Cf. 2 Chr 36:14: "All the leading priests and the people also were exceedingly unfaithful (מעל), following all the abominations of the nations; and they polluted the house of the LORD that he had consecrated in Jerusalem."

75   1 Chr 12:18 (17); 29:20; 2 Chr 7:22; 11:16; 13:12, 18; 14:3 (4); 15:12; 19:4; 20:6, 33; 24:18, 24; 28:6, 9, 25; 29:5; 30:7, 19, 22; 33:12; 34:32, 33; 36:15.

76   The verb זנה is used in Judges to indicate Israel's apostasy (2:17; 8:27, 33).

77   Japhet, *Ideology*, 191–93, lists the wars in Chronicles that are described according to the principle of reward and punishment.

78   Mordechai Cogan and Hayim Tadmor, *II Kings* (AB 11; Garden City, NY: Doubleday, 1988) 171–72.

79   Cf. Jer 51:11, where Yahweh stirs up the spirit of the kings of the Medes to destroy Babylon. See also Hag 1:14, where Yahweh stirs up the spirit of Zerubbabel and Joshua.

this verse in Chronicles refers only to the Transjordanian tribes.

and he brought them to Halah, Habor, and the river of Gozan, until this day: The Chronicler has anachronistically brought together information from the account of Tiglath-pileser's attack on the northern regions of Israel in 732 (2 Kgs 15:29) and the account of the cities to which the king of Assyria exiled the Israelites from Samaria in 721 (17:6; 18:11).[80] A variety of locations has been proposed for Halah, including Halahhu, an Assyrian town northeast of Nineveh; Halahhu, on the west bank of the Tigris River, near the Lower Zab River, 70 miles south of Nineveh; and Calah/Nimrud, 18 miles south of Nineveh.[81] Habor is a tributary of the Euphrates, joining it about 60 miles north of Mari, and there is also a district known by the same name. It is known in Akkadian as *ḫabûr* and in modern times as *al-Khābūr*.[82] Gozan, later Gausanitis, is modern Tell Halaf on the Turkish/Syrian border. By the time of the Chronicler there had been no return from this exile—and perhaps he expected none;[83] in any case he added, from 2 Kgs 17:23, 34, 41, that their exile lasted "until this day."[84] The northern and western parts of the Northern Kingdom, on the other hand, had undergone no significant change, and the majority of the inhabitants remained there, awaiting the return of their colleagues (2 Chr 30:6-9).[85]

Conclusion

The genealogies of the two and one-half Transjordanian tribes continue the Chronicler's "all Israel" theme and

even add an implicit claim to this territory. Reuben's position as the third tribe in the genealogies is explained with reference to his sexual misconduct, a clear expression of retribution theology. Judah's preeminence is related to its Davidic legacy (cf. chap. 3) while the right of the firstborn given to Joseph demonstrates the Chronicler's openness to the north and its two most prominent tribes, Ephraim and Manasseh.

The genealogies available to the Chronicler for these tribes were short and fragmentary with several open links. Historical allusions in these genealogies are difficult to evaluate but include a war at the time of Saul (v. 10), a census at the time of Jotham and Jeroboam II (v. 17), and a victory of the three and one-half tribes against the Hagrites until their exile from the land (vv. 18-22). Tillegath-pilneser's role in that exile is noted on two occasions (vv. 6 and 26).

The Chronicler uses the occasion of these genealogies to give a positive and a negative example of retribution theology. The Reubenites, Gadites, and Manassites trusted God and cried to him at the time of battle and so were given divine help that led to a great victory, with many captives (both animal and human) and a fearsome number of casualties among the enemy (vv. 18-22). These same tribes, however, acted unfaithfully toward the God of their fathers and prostituted themselves to the gods of the people of the land, and this led to Tillegath-pilneser's carrying them into exile (vv. 25-26).

---

80   Both of these passages also include "the cities of the Medes" as places of exile. Obad 20 mentions Halah as one of the places of exile.

81   See Henry O. Thompson, "Halah," *ABD* 3:25. Cogan and Tadmor, *II Kings*, 197, locate it at the Assyrian town northeast of Nineveh.

82   Gary A. Herion, "Habor," *ABD* 3:10.

83   Cf. Num 34:11-12 (P) and Ezekiel's map of the

promised land in 47:13—48:29, which does not include Transjordan.

84   In Kings the reference is to the time of the writer of 2 Kings 17 or his source, but in Chronicles it would be to the time when the Chronicler lived and worked.

85   See Japhet, *Ideology,* 364–73.

6

Translation

5:27 (6:1)/ The sons of Levi: Gershon, Kohath, and Merari. 28 (6:2)/ And the sons of Kohath: Amram, Izhar, Hebron, and Uzziel.
29 (6:3)/ And the children of Amram: Aaron, Moses, Miriam. And the sons of Aaron: Nadab, Abihu, Eleazar, and Ithamar.
30 (6:4)/ Eleazar became the father of Phineas, Phinehas became the father of Abishua, 31 (6:5)/ Abishua became the father of Bukki, Bukki became the father of Uzzi, 32 (6:6)/ Uzzi became the father of Zerahiah, Zerahiah became the father of Meraioth, 33 (6:7)/ Meraioth became the father of Amariah, Amariah became the father of Ahitub, 34 (6:8)/ Ahitub became the father of Zadok, Zadok became the father of Ahimaaz, 35 (6:9)/ Ahimaaz became the father of Azariah (it was he[1] who served as priest in the temple that Solomon built in Jerusalem),[2] Azariah became the father of Johanan,
36 (6:10)/ Johanan became the father of Azariah, 37 (6:11)/ Azariah became the father of Amariah, Amariah became the father of Ahitub, 38 (6:12)/ Ahitub became the father of Zadok, Zadok became the father of Shallum, 39 (6:13)/ Shallum became the father of Hilkiah, Hilkiah became the father of Azariah,
40 (6:14)/ Azariah became the father of Seraiah, Seraiah became the father of Jehozadak, 41 (6:15)/ Jehozadak went into exile[3] when Yahweh exiled Judah and Jerusalem by the hand of Nebuchadnezzar.

6:1 (16)/ The sons of Levi: Gershom,[4] Kohath, and Merari. 2 (17)/ These are the names of the sons of Gershom: Libni and Shimei.
3 (18)/ The sons of Kohath: Amram, Izhar, Hebron, and Uzziel. 4 (19)/ The sons of Merari: Mahli and Mushi. These are the families of the Levites according to their fathers:
5 (20)/ Of Gershom: Libni his son, Jahath his son, Zimmah his son, 6 (21)/ Joah[5] his son, Iddo his son, Zerah his son, Jeatherai his son. 7 (22)/ The sons of Kohath: Amminadab[6] his son, Korah his son, Assir his son, 8 (23)/ Elkanah his son,[7] Ebiasaph[8] his son, Assir[9] his son,[10] 9 (24)/ Tahath his son, Uriel his son, Uzziah his son, and Shaul his son.
10 (25)/ The sons of Elkanah: Amasai and his brother Mahath,[11] 11 (26)/ Elkanah his son,[12] Zuphai[13] his son, Nahath[14] his son, 12 (27)/ Eliab[15] his son, Jeroham[16] his son, Elkanah his son, Samuel his son.[17]
13 (28)/ The sons of Samuel: Joel[18] his first-born, the second Abijah.[19] 14 (29)/ The sons of Merari: Mahli his son,[20] Libni his son, Shimei his son, Uzzah his son,
15 (30)/ Shimea his son, Haggiah his son, and Asaiah his son.

16 (31)/ These are the people whom David

1 One Hebrew MS, LXX[L], Syr, Arab. add עזריה "Azariah." This gloss may have been precipitated by the secondary location of this parenthesis in v. 36. See the next note.

2 This parenthesis has been moved here from its original position after Azariah at the end of v. 36a. Cf. Curtis and Madsen, 128–29; and many others.

3 בגולה (cf. Jer 48:1; Amos 1:15) or בגלות (cf. Jer. 40:1) with Tg; cf. Syr, Arab. The word is lacking in MT and LXX because of haplography with the following בהגלות. Rothstein, 109, following Ehrlich, changed הלך "went" to הוליד "became the father of" and added the name "Joshua." See Neh 12:10, 11.

4 גרשם; Syr gršwn "Gershon." Cf. Exod 6:16; Num 3:17.

5 יואח; LXX "Joab."

6 עמינדב; LXX[ANabgye₂] "Izhar" (יצהר). Cf. vv. 3, 23 (18, 38) and Exod 6:18, 21. This reading is adopted by Rudolph, 54; BHS; and Curtis and Madsen, 131. See the commentary.

7 בנו; omitted by LXX[Bal].

8 ואביסף; the importance of the conjunction is discussed in the commentary. Some Hebrew MSS, LXX[min]: ואביאסף. Cf. also this name in v. 22 (37).

9 בנו ואסיר "his son, Assir"; BHS בניו אסיר "his sons Assir."

10 בנו; lacking in Syr.

11 ואחיו מחת; MT ואחימות "and Ahimoth." Rudolph, 54 (cf. BHS) considers אחיו as a gloss added because Mahath is identified here as the brother of Amasai, but as the son of Amasai in v. 20 (35). Cf. also 2 Chr 29:19.

12 בנו K, LXX, Tg; Q בני "the sons of." MT mistakenly adds a second אלקנה "Elkanah." It is lacking in a few Hebrew MSS, LXX, Syr.

13 צופי with LXX; MT צופי "Zophai." Syr ṣwp "Zuph"; cf. v. 20 Q and 1 Sam 1:1b. 1 Sam 1:1a צופים.

14 ונחת; BHK suggests emending to ותוח "Toah" (v. 19 [34] or 1 Sam 1:1 LXX) or ותחו "Tohu" (1 Sam 1:1).

15 אליאב; v. 19 (34) אליאל "Eliel." 1 Sam 1:1 אליהו "Elihu."

16 For an explanation of the spelling variants in LXX see Allen, Greek Chronicles, 2:162.

17 שמואל בנו, with LXX[byc₂e₂]; lacking in MT and LXX because of homoioteleuton. This reading is necessary for the sense of the passage, but it is unclear whether the Lucianic MSS retain the original reading or have made an appropriate correction to a faulty text.

18 יואל with LXX[L], Syr, Arab.; cf. 1 Sam 8:2. Lacking in MT and LXX because of homoioteleuton. See also 1 Chr 6:18 (33).

19 והשני אביה, with LXX[L], Syr, Arab. When "Joel" was lost by homoioteleuton after "Samuel" (see the previous note), the following ordinal number in MT

appointed over the song in the house of Yahweh, after the ark had come to rest. 17 (32)/ They were also the ones ministering in song before the tabernacle of the tent of meeting until Solomon built the house of Yahweh in Jerusalem; and they carried out their service according to their custom. 18 (33)/ These are the men who served; and their sons were: Of the sons of the Kohathites:[21] Heman, the singer, the son of Joel, son of Samuel, 19 (34)/ son of Elkanah, son of Jeroham,[22] son of Eliel, son of Toah,[23] 20 (35)/ son of Zuph,[24] son of Elkanah, son of Mahath, son of Amasai, 21 (36)/ son of Elkanah, son of Joel, son of Azariah, son of Zephaniah, 22 (37)/ son of Tahath, son of Assir, son of Ebiasaph,[25] son of Korah, 23 (38)/ son of Izhar, son of Kohath, son of Levi, son of Israel; 24 (39)/ and his[26] brother Asaph, who stood on his right, namely, Asaph son of Berechiah, son of Shimea, 25 (40)/ son of Michael, son of Baaseiah,[27] son of Malchijah, 26 (41)/ son of Ethni, son of Zerah, son of Adaiah, 27 (42)/ son of Ethan, son of Zimmah, son of Shimei, 28 (43)/ son of Jahath,[28] son of Gershom, son of Levi. 29 (44)/ On the left were their brothers[29] from the sons[30] of Merari: Ethan son of Kishi,[31] son of Abdi, son of Malluch, 30 (45)/ son of Hashabiah, son of Amaziah, son of Hilkiah, 31 (46)/ son of Amzi, son of Bani, son of Shemer, 32 (47)/ son of Mahli, son of Mushi, son of Merari, son of Levi; 33 (48)/ and their kindred the Levites were being dedicated for all the service of the tabernacle of the house of God.

34 (49)/ But Aaron and his sons made offerings on the altar of burnt offering and on the incense altar, performing all the work of the most holy place, to make atonement for Israel according to everything which Moses the servant of God commanded. 35 (50)/ These are the sons of Aaron: Eleazar his son, Phinehas his son, Abishua his son, 36 (51)/ Bukki his son, Uzzi his son, Zerahiah his son, 37 (52)/ Meraioth his son, Amaziah his son, Ahitub his son, 38 (53)/ Zadok his son, Ahimaaz his son.

39 (54)/ These are their dwelling places according to their encampments within their borders: to the sons of Aaron of the Kohathite family[32]—for the lot fell to them[33]— 40 (55)/ to them they gave Hebron in the land of Judah and its pasturelands surrounding it, 41 (56)/ but the fields of the city and its villages they gave to Caleb the son of Jephunneh. 42 (57)/ To the sons of Aaron they gave the city[34] of refuge: Hebron with its pasturelands,[35] Libnah with its pasturelands, Jattir[36] with its pasturelands,[37] Eshtemoa with its pasturelands,

20 בנו, with Syr; lacking in MT and LXX.

21 הקהתי; LXX, Syr, Vg: קהת "Kohath."

22 For an explanation of the spelling variants in LXX see Allen, *Greek Chronicles*, 2:162.

23 תוח; LXX[AN] תהו "Tohu." Cf. v. 11 (26) and 1 Sam 1:1.

24 צוף with many Hebrew MSS, Q; cf. v. 11 (26). K ציף "Ziph."

25 אביסף; LXX[AN] presupposes אביאסף. Cf. v. 8 (23).

26 The antecedent is Heman in v. 18 (33).

27 בעשיה; a few Hebrew MSS, LXX[BL], Syr: מעשיה "Maaseiah."

28 Rothstein, 118; Williamson, 73–74; and Japhet, 145, propose switching the order of Shimei and Jahath. *BHS* adds בן שמעי "the son of Shimei" after "Jahath." Cf. v. 2 (17). Kurt Möhlenbrink, "Die levitischen Überlieferungen des Alten Testaments," *ZAW* (1934) 202, deletes "the son of Jahath." See the commentary.

29 אֲחֵיהֶם; LXX, Syr, Arab., Tg: אֲחִיהֶם "their brother." Hence: "from the sons of their brother Merari," if the change advocated in the next note is adopted.

30 ומבני with Rothstein, 118, and Rudolph, 56, on analogy with v. 18 (33); MT ובני "and the sons of."

31 קישי; many Hebrew MSS, LXX[L], Vg: קושי "Kushi." Cf. 1 Chr 15:17 קושיהו "Kushaiah" and 2 Chr 29:12 קיש "Kish."

32 למשפחת; Josh 21:10 MT ממשפחת "from the families," but Joshua LXX and Syr also singular.

33 Syr, Arab., and Josh 21:10 add ריאשנה "first."

34 עיר with Josh 21:13; Chronicles MT ערי "cities." The same error occurs in v. 52. Joshua 21 identifies five cities as cities of refuge and apparently lost accidentally the designation for a sixth, Bezer.

35 ואת מגרשה with Josh 21:13; lacking in MT.

36 יתר; LXX exchanges "Jattir" with חילן "Hilen" in v. 43 (58).

37 ואת מגרשה with Josh 21:14; lacking in MT.

38 חילן with many Hebrew MSS, LXX (Σελνα from Εελνα in v. 42 [57]; see n. 36); MT חילז "Hilez." Josh 21:15 (cf. Josh 15:51) חלן "Holon."

39 את דביר; many Hebrew MSS, LXX, Syr, Vg., Josh 21:15: ואת דביר.

40 ואת עשן; cf. Josh 21:16 LXX[B]. Josh 21:16 MT ואת עין "Ain."

41 ואת יטה ואת מגרשיה, with LXX[B], Syr, Josh 21:16; lacking in Chronicles MT by homoioteleuton.

42 את גבעון ומגרשה with Josh 21:17; lacking in Chronicles by homoioteleuton.

43 עלמת; cf. Josh 21:18 LXX[gnpt], OL, and this is probably the correct spelling (Albright, "List," 67, n. x).

43 (58)/ Hilen[38] with its pasturelands, Debir[39] with its pasturelands, 44 (59)/ Ashan[40] with its pasturelands, Juttah with its pasturelands,[41] and Beth-shemesh with its pasturelands. 45 (60)/ From the tribe of Benjamin, Gibeon with its pasturelands,[42] Geba with its pasturelands, Alemeth[43] with its pasture-lands, and Anathoth with its pasturelands. All their towns throughout their families[44] were thirteen.[45]

46 (61)/ To the rest of the Kohathites were given by lot out of the families of the tribe of Ephraim, from the tribe of Dan, and from the half-tribe of[46] Manasseh, ten towns. 47 (62)/ The Gershomites[47] received[48] according to their families thirteen towns out of the tribe of Issachar, the tribe of Asher, the tribe of Naphtali, and the tribe[49] of Manasseh in Bashan. 48 (63)/ The Mera-rites received by lot[50] according to their families twelve towns from of the tribe of Reuben, the tribe of Gad, and the tribe of Zebulun. 49 (64)/ So the Israelites gave the Levites the towns[51] with their pasturelands. 50 (65)/ They also gave them by lot from the tribe of the Judahites, the tribe of the Simeonites, and the tribe of the Ben-jaminites[52] these towns that are mentioned by name.

51 (66)/ And some of the Kohathite families[53] of the Levites who were left from the Kohathites[54] received towns for their territory[55] out of the tribe of Ephraim. 52 (67)/ They gave them the city[56] of refuge: Shechem with its pasturelands in the hill country of Ephraim, Gezer with its pasturelands, 53 (68)/ Jok-meam[57] with its pasturelands, Beth-horon with its pasturelands, 54 (69)/ and out of the tribe of Dan: Elteke with its pasture-lands, Gibbethon with its pasturelands,[58] Aijalon with its pasturelands, Gath-rimmon with its pasturelands; 55 (70)/ and out of the half-tribe of Manasseh, Taanach[59] with its pasturelands, Ibleam[60] with its pasture-lands, for the rest of the families of[61] the Kohathites.

56 (71)/ To the Gershomites: out of their families from the half-tribe[62] of Manasseh: Golan[63] in Bashan with its pasturelands and Ashtaroth[64] with its pasturelands, 57 (72)/ and out of the tribe of Issachar: Kishion[65] with its pasturelands, Daberath with its pasturelands, 58 (73)/ Ramoth[66] with its pasturelands, and En-gannim[67] with its pasturelands; 59 (74)/ out of the tribe of Asher: Mishal[68] with its pasturelands, Abdon with its pasturelands, 60 (75)/ Helkath[69] with its pasturelands, and Rehob with its pasturelands; 61 (76)/ and out of the tribe of Naphtali: Kedesh in

44 במשפחותיהם; Josh 21:19 ומגרשיהם "pasturelands." The reading in Joshua is better, but there is no evidence that it ever appeared in Chronicles.

45 With the restoration of Juttah and Gibeon, this number corresponds to the number of individual towns listed for the Aaronites.

46 ממשפחת מטה אפרים וממטה דן ומחצית מטה; cf. Josh 21:5. MT ממשפחת המטה ממחצית מטה חצי "out of the family of the tribe from the half." The final חצי in Joshua MT (not in the versions) is a correction or explanation for the word ממחצית (HALOT 2:571). Japhet, 161, concludes that Joshua is also already corrupt and that the first two words there were originally למשפחותם ממטה "according to their fami-lies. From the tribe of."

47 גרשום; Josh 21:6 גרשון "Gershonites." Cf. 1 Chr 5:27 (6:1).

48 Josh 21:6 adds בגורל "by lot." BHS suggests restoring it here, but there is no evidence this word was ever in the text of Chronicles.

49 וממטה; Josh 21:6 ומחצי מטה "half-tribe." The Chroni-cler may have thought that "in Bashan" was suffi-cient to indicate that he was describing the Transjordanian portion of the tribe of Manasseh.

50 בגורל with Chronicles MT, LXX, Josh 21:7 LXX; lacking in Josh 21:7 MT.

51 את הערים; cf. Josh 21:8 LXX, Vg. Chronicles Syr, Arab., and Josh 21:8 MT: את הערים האלה "these towns."

52 וממטה בני בנימן; cf. Josh 21:9 LXX. Lacking in Josh 21:9 MT. Cf. Josh 21:4.

53 וממשפחות בני קהת; LXX[L], Vg, Josh 21:20: ולמשפחות בני קהת.

54 הלוים הנותרים מבני קהת, with Josh 21:20; lacking in Chronicles by homoioteleuton.

55 גבולם; cf. Josh 21:20 LXX[Amss.]. Josh 21:20 MT גורלם "by their lot." Josh LXX[B]: "their priests" (ἰερέων for ὁρίων). A. Graeme Auld, Joshua Retold (Edinburgh: T. & T. Clark, 1998) 31, argues that "their territory" is the original reading and points to the use of this term in v. 39 (54).

56 את עיר, with Josh 21:21; Chronicles ערי את "cities." Cf. v. 42 (57).

57 יקמעם; Josh 21:22 קבצים "Kibzaim." Mazar, "Cities," 198, believes there was a change of names from Kibzaim to Jokmeam (1 Chr 23:19; 24:23). Harry Orlinsky, according to Albright, "List," 67, n. aa, thought that Kibzaim was a corruption of קמעם, an alternate spelling for Jokmeam. Albright, "List," 53, 55; and Boling, "Levitical Cities," in Biblical and Related Studies Presented to Samuel Iwry (ed. A. Kort and S. Morschauser; Winona Lake, IN: Eisenbrauns,

Galilee with its pasturelands, Hammon[70] with its pasturelands, and Kiriathaim[71] with its pasturelands. 62 (77)/ To the rest[72] of the Merarites out of the tribe of Zebulun: Jokneam with its pasturelands,[73] Rimmon[74] and its pasturelands, Tabor[75] with its pasturelands, and Nahalal with its pasturelands;[76] 63 (78)/[77] and across the Jordan from Jericho, on the east side of the Jordan, out of the tribe of Reuben: Bezer in the steppe with its pasturelands, Jahzah with its pasturelands, 64 (79)/ Kedemoth with its pasturelands, and Mephaath with its pasturelands; 65 (80)/ and out of the tribe of Gad: Ramoth[78] in Gilead with its pasturelands, Mahanaim with its pasturelands, 66 (81)/ Heshbon with its pasturelands, and Jazer[79] with its pasturelands.

1985) 24, include both of these city names. According to Albright, Jokmeam was accidentally lost in Joshua and Kibzaim was accidentally lost in Chronicles. See also Kallai, *Historical Geography,* 470, who suggests that both of these were Levitical cities, but only one of them was preserved in Joshua and one in Chronicles.

58 וממטה דן את אלתקא ואת מגרשה את גבתון ואת מגרשה, with Josh 21:23; lacking in MT. Dan is lacking here, in v. 46, and in the present shape of chap. 7. The towns in v. 54 (69) are Danite, not Ephraimite, which makes our restoration likely.

59 תענן, with Josh 21:25; MT ענר "Aner." The *tāw* was lost by haplography and the *kāp* was miswritten as a *rêš.*

60 יבלעם, with two Hebrew MSS, LXX, Syr, Tg, Arab.; MT בלעם "Bileam." Josh 21:25 גת רמון "Gath-rimmon," which has been copied from Josh 21:24= 1 Chr 6:54 (69).

61 למשפחות בני קהת with Josh 21:26; Chronicles MT למשפחת לבני קהת (sg.). Chronicles also omitted from Josh 21:26: "The towns and their pasturelands were ten in all." The words "two towns" (after "Gath-rimmon and its pasturelands") were also omitted from Josh 21:25.

62 למשפחתם מחצי מטה; cf. Curtis and Madsen, 141; and Rudolph, 62. MT ממשפחה חצי מטה; Josh 21:27 ממשפחת הלוים מחצי מטה "from the families of the Levites from the half-tribe."

63 גולן; cf. Josh 21:27 Q. Josh 21:27 K גלון.

64 עשתרות; Josh 21:27 בעשתרה "Be-eshterah," an abbreviation for Beth-ashteroth.

65 קשיון as in Josh 21:28; Chronicles MT קדש "Kedesh." Cf. Kedesh in Galilee in v. 61. Albright, "List," 62, 70, n. ss קישון.

66 ראמות. Albright, "List," 70, n. xx, explains the *'ālep* by analogy with the historical (rather than phonetic) spelling of Ramoth in Gilead, and he believes the initial *yôd* in Josh 21:29 (ירמות) was added by analogy with the better known Jarmuth of Judah. Cf. Josh 19:21 רמת "Remeth."

67 עין גנים, with Josh 21:29; Chronicles MT ענם, which Kallai, *Historical Geography,* 472, interprets as a corrupt abbreviation for En-gannim. Albright, "List," 22, n. א, reconstructed a hypothetical original עין ענם.

68 משאל, with Josh 19:26; 21:30; Chronicles MT משל "Mashal."

69 חלקת, with Josh 21:31 (cf. 19:25); MT חוקק "Hukkok." In Josh 19:34 Hukkok is in Naphtali.

70 חמון; Josh 21:32 חמת דאר "Hammoth-dor." Josh 19:35 חמת "Hammath." On the basis of Josh 21:32 LXX, Albright, "List," 53, 64, 71–72, concludes that the list originally included both Hammon and Hammoth-dor. It seems more likely, however, that

Hammoth-dor and Hammon are ancient variants that have been conflated in Joshua LXX.

71 קריתים; Josh 21:32 קרתן "Kartan." Albright, "List," 72, n. l, understands the latter as a Galilean dialectical form meaning "two towns," and the reading in Chronicles as a Hebraic version of the same name.

72 Braun, 98, believes this expression is inappropriate here. Cf. Josh 21:34.

73 את יקנעם ומגרשה, with Josh 21:34; lacking in Chronicles by homoioarchton.

74 רמון, with LXX (cf. Josh 19:13); *BHS* suggests רמונה. MT רמונו. The final *wāw* results from dittography. Josh 21:35 דמנה "Dimnah," representing the frequent *dālet/rêš* interchange.

75 תבור; Josh 21:34 קרתה, apparently replaced תבור by an assimilation to קרתן in Josh 21:32. If Rimmon and Tabor are equivalent to Kartah and Dimnah

76 (see the previous note), their order in Chronicles is reversed from that in Joshua.

76 את נהלל ואת מגרשה with Josh 21:35; lost in Chronicles by homoioteleuton.

77 The corresponding verses to vv. 63-64 (78-79) in Josh 21:36-37 are missing from Cairo Codex of the Prophets, Codex Leningradensis, other Hebrew MSS, Bohairic, and Tg. They do appear in many Hebrew MSS, LXX, some Tg MSS, and Vg. Many printed Bibles omit these verses and they are printed in small type in *BHS*. The cause of the omission is homoioteleuton in Joshua 21 from "and their pasturelands four" at the end of v. 35 to the same expression at the end of v. 37.

78 ראמות; Josh 21:46 רמה.

79 יעור; Josh 21:39 יעזר.

5:27—6:66 (6:1-81)

Structure

Note: The Hebrew Bible includes the genealogy of the immediate descendants of Levi and the high priests from Aaron to Jehozadak (the high priests) in chap. 5, but English versions put this material at the beginning of chap. 6. Chapter 6:1 in Hebrew is 6:16 in English versions. Consequently, in our discussion of 5:27—6:66 (6:1-81), there will always be a difference of fifteen verses between the Hebrew and the English verse references.

The Chronicler has placed the genealogies of the clergy at the center of the great genealogical introduction in chaps. 1–9 (see the genealogical chart "Descendants of Levi-1"). The sections in this unit include:

I. 5:27-41 (6:1-15). Genealogy of the high priests, beginning with the words, "The sons of Levi." The first three verses of this unit are a segmented genealogy of the three sons of Levi, the four sons of Levi's second son Kohath, and the three children of Kohath's oldest son Amram, while the last twelve verses are a linear genealogy of the high priests, beginning with Amram's eldest son Aaron and ending with Jehozadak.

II. 6:1-15 (16-30). Genealogy of the regular Levites, beginning with the words, "The sons of Levi." The first four verses are a segmented genealogy of the first and second generations after Levi, while the next eleven verses are linear genealogies of Levi's sons Gershom (vv. 5-6 [21-22]), Kohath (7-9 [22-24]), and Merari (vv. 14-15 [29-30]), through their oldest sons (see the commentary), ending with the heads of these three families, who are named Jeatherai, Shaul, and Asaiah. Inserted into the genealogy of Kohath is another linear genealogy leading to the prophet Samuel and his two sons Joel and Abijah (vv. 10-13 [25-28]).

III. 6:16-34 (31-49). Three linear pedigrees of the Levitical singers, beginning with the three heads of the singer guilds, Heman (18-23 [33-38]), Asaph (vv. 24-28 [39-43]), and Ethan (vv. 29-32 [44-47]), and leading back to the second or third sons of Kohath, Gershom, and Merari. Heman, who is in the twenty-first generation after Levi, stands in the middle; Asaph, who is in the fourteenth generation after Levi, is on the right of Heman; and Ethan, who is in the thirteenth generation after Levi, is on his left. Interspersed with these genealogies are brief descriptions of the duties of the Levitical singers (vv. 16-17 [31-32]), the regular Levites (v. 33 [48]), and the priests (v. 34 [49]).

IV. 6:35-38 (50-53). An excerpt from the high priestly genealogy (cf. section I), containing the twelve names from Aaron to Ahimaaz. This excerpt is intended to set the chronological context for the following cities of the priests and Levites (section V) to the time of David since it ends with Zadok and Ahimaaz, who were David's contemporaries.

V. 6:39-66 (54-81). Cities of the priests and Levites.

This list was taken from Josh 21:1-40, although the Chronicler omitted an equivalent for Josh 21:1-4, and moved Josh 21:5-9//1 Chr 6:46-50 (61-65) to a position after Josh 21:19//1 Chr 6:45 (60). There are numerous differences between the lists in Joshua and Chronicles as the textual notes indicate. Some differences will also be discussed in the commentary. The list originally referred to forty-eight cities, with four cities contributed by each of the twelve tribes. The origins and date of this list will be discussed below. Chapter 6 concludes with a list of the dwelling places for the priests and Levites, similar to the last part of the genealogy of Judah, in chap. 4, focused on the dwelling places for various segments of that tribe.

Pride of place is given to the genealogy of the high priests by its initial position and by setting the two lists of the high priests (sections I and IV) as an *inclusio* around the other lists of Levites (sections II-III). The excerpt, part IV, is cast in the form "X, his son Y, his son Z," and so on, instead of "X became the father of Y, Y became the father of Z," and so on, as in the master list in section I.

5:27-41 (6:1-15) and IV. 6:35-38 (50-53) Genealogy of High Priests

All or parts of the genealogy of the high priests occur in six different contexts, which I have called A—F in table 6.[1] These six lists, while clearly related to one another, do not agree on the length of the genealogies or on specific names. All scholars admit that there is a certain amount of artificiality in these lists and considerable ignorance on our part about why some names were

included and others excluded. The intent of at least lists A and B is to claim that the priests in Jerusalem were descendants of Aaron and of Zadok. The list of eleven or twelve names from Aaron through Zadok or Ahimaaz is, of course, scarcely long enough to bridge the three hundred years from the exodus to the building of the temple (1 Kgs 6:1),[2] nor are the eleven names from Zadok to Jehozadak sufficient to cover the time from the erection of Solomon's temple to the destruction of Jerusalem in 586 BCE. Some names seem to have been omitted in both cases especially in the middle of the genealogy in a process called telescoping. Particularly baffling is the omission in all of the lists of some prominent high priests from the narratives of Kings and/or Chronicles, namely, Amariah during the reign of Jehoshaphat (2 Chr 19:11); Jehoiada during the reigns of Athaliah and Joash (2 Chronicles 22–24//2 Kings 11–12), Azariah during the reign of Uzziah (2 Chr 26:17, 20); and Uriah during the reign of Ahaz (2 Kgs 16:10, 11, 15, 16).

How do the six lists relate to one another? John R. Bartlett proposed that the Chronicler put together a number of sources that were available to him.[3] The first of these sources, stemming from the Chronicler or some unique tradition, consisted of the names from Aaron to Meraioth (nos. 1-8) and appears in the first four lists (A, B, C, D), all of which agree except for minor differences in transliteration. The first three names are well known from pentateuchal tradition; the other five are just as equally unknown. The pair of names Azariah and Amariah (nos. 15-16) constituted for Bartlett a second source[4] and appear in lists A, C, and D.[5] The third source contained the names Ahitub, Zadok, Shallum/

---

1   Column G is my reconstruction of the list of high priests. I have given numbers to all the names in list A and used those numbers for corresponding priests in the other five lists in order to facilitate the discussion and avoid confusion. The word "high priest" does not appear in this unit at all and the word "priest" occurs only in the comment on Azariah, which I have moved to 5:35 (6:9); see textual note 1. The term "high priest" will be discussed below.

2   The genealogists may have assigned forty years to each generation, but historically such extraordinarily long tenure is highly unlikely if not impossible.

3   "Zadok and His Successors at Jerusalem," *JTS*, n.s.

19 (1968) 1–18. Bartlett included a seventh list from 1 Esdr 8:1-2, which is the translation of Ezra 7:1-5, but the publication of the Göttingen LXX has made clear that what Bartlett saw as further variants were simple haplographies in the text of Vaticanus. See Robert Hanhart, *Esdrae liber I* (Septuaginta 8/1; Göttingen: Vandenhoeck & Ruprecht, 1974) 115.

4   Bartlett, "Zadok," 5, tentatively associated these priests with the people named in 1 Kgs 4:2 and 2 Chr 19:11. I would associate Azariah with 2 Chr 31:10, 13 and leave this Amariah without a biblical parallel.

5   Bartlett, "Zadok," 5, says that they were inserted at three different places: between Meraioth and Ahi-

Table 6. High Priests

Other Biblical References and Contemporaneous Kings	Omitted Priests[6]	A 1 Chr 5:29-41//6:3-15	B 1 Chr 6:35-38//50-53	C Ezr 7:1-5	D 2 Esd. 1:1-3	E Neh 11:10-11	F 1 Chr 9:10-11	G Reconstructed List of High Priests
		1. Aaron	1. Aaron	1. Aaron	1. Aaron			1. Aaron
Exod 6:23; Num 3:2; 26:60		2. Eleazar	2. Eleazar	2. Eleazar	2. Eleazar			2. Eleazar
Exod 6:25		3. Phinehas	3. Phinehas	3. Phinehas	3. Phinehas			3. Phinehas
		4. Abishua	4. Abishua	4. Abishua	4. Abishua			4. Abishua
		5. Bukki	5. Bukki	5. Bukki	5. Borith			5. Bukki
		6. Uzzi	6. Uzzi	6. Uzzi	6. Uzzi			6. Uzzi
		7. Zerahiah	7. Zerahiah	7. Zerahiah	7. Arna			7. Zerahiah
		8. Meraioth	8. Meraioth	8. Meraioth	8. Meraioth			8. Meraioth
		9. Amariah	9. Amariah					9. Amariah I
2 Sam 8:17		10. Ahitub	10. Ahitub					10. Ahitub I
2 Sam 8:17; 1 Kgs 2:35—David-Solomon		11. Zadok	11. Zadok					11. Zadok I
2 Sam 15:27—David		12. Ahimaaz	12. Ahimaaz				12. Ahimaaz	
1 Kgs 4:2—Solomon		13. Azariah						13. Azariah I
2 Chr 19:11—Jehoshaphat		Amariah						Amariah II
2 Kgs 11//2 Chr 24—Athaliah-Joash	Jehoiada							Jehoida
2 Chr 26:17, 20—Uzziah	Azariah							Azariah II
		14. Johanan						14. Johanan
2 Chr 31:10, 13—Hezekiah	Uriah							Uriah?
		15. Azariah		15. Azariah	15. Azariah			15. Azariah III
		16. Amariah		16. Amariah	16. Amariah			16. Amariah III
					Eli			
					Phinehas			
					Ahijah			
		17. Ahitub		17. Ahitub	17. Ahitub	17. Ahitub	17. Ahitub	17. Ahitub II
						Meraioth	Meraioth	
		18. Zadok		18. Zadok	18. Zadok	18. Zadok	18. Zadok	18. Zadok II
		19. Shallum		19. Shallum	19. Shallum	19. Meshullam	19. Meshullam	19. Shallum
2 Kgs 22:4—23:4—Josiah		20. Hilkiah		20. Hilkiah	20. Hilkiah	20. Hilkiah	20. Hilkiah	20. Hilkiah
		21. Azariah		21. Azariah	21. Azariah		21. Azariah	21. Azariah IV
2 Kgs 25:18—Zedekiah		22. Seraiah		22. Seraiah	22. Seraiah	22. Seraiah		22. Seraiah
Hag 1:1		23. Jehozadak						
				Ezra	Ezra			

Meshullam, Hilkiah, Azariah, and Seraiah (nos. 17-22). These names occur in lists A, C, D, E, and F. Bartlett noted that all of these priests, except Shallum/Meshullam, are mentioned elsewhere in the Deuteronomistic History, but not, in his opinion, in the order given in the genealogy.[7] In his opinion, this Ahitub (no. 17) was the father of Zadok (no. 18), who served under David and Solomon, and Hilkiah (no. 20) and Seraiah (no. 22) are referred to in 2 Kgs 22:4–23:4 and 2 Kgs 25:18, respectively. To Bartlett, only Azariah (no. 21 in table 6), connected by him with 1 Kgs 4:2, seemed out of place. The Chronicler added Jehozadak (no. 23) to this source in list A, appended the name Ezra to list C[8] (followed naturally also in list D),[9] and one or more postexilic priests were added to the version of this source in lists E and F.[10] These three sources were put together by the Chronicler in Ezra 7:1-5, list C, and were used there to provide the pedigree for Ezra whose name was added to the third source, which had originally ended with Seraiah. In order to create the genealogy of the high priests themselves, the Chronicler then added the "Zadokite group" (nos. 9-14), which, according to Bartlett, was the Chronicler's own composition. It was made up of members of the priestly family of David's day.

Subsequent writers have affirmed and clarified Bartlett's proposal. In his book on the biblical genealogies, Marshall D. Johnson concluded that the lists in Nehemiah 11 (E) and 1 Chronicles 9 (F) formed the core of the genealogies in 5:27-41 (6:1-15; A) and Ezra 7:1-5 (C) and were prior to them.[11] Braun, 83–86, follows Johnson and identifies Zadok (no. 18) as the priest of David and Solomon. This purportedly complete genealogy in nos. 17-22, however, does little to establish the pedigree of Zadok[12] and has only one priest between the tenth (Zadok) and the seventh (Hilkiah) centuries. Johnson also judged that Ezra 7:1-5 (C), which had added ten names (nos. 1-8, 15-16) to the old lists E and F,[13] was shorter and older than 1 Chr 5:27-41 (6:1-15; A), and he found each of the six additional names in A (nos. 9-14) "somewhat suspicious."[14] He noted that Amariah, Ahitub, and Zadok (nos. 9-11) repeat names from a later part of the list (nos. 16-18), without carefully considering whether this might have taken place historically, but correctly observed that Ahimaaz (no. 12) was actually the brother rather than the father of Azariah (no. 13; cf. 1 Kgs 4:2).[15] Johnson also found it suspicious that the name of the last priest in this list of six, Johanan (no. 14), is mentioned as a predecessor of Jaddua in Ezra 3:2.[16] He further concluded that the late list A exhibits chronological speculation, dividing the priests into two groups of twelve, each generation forty years long, with

---

tub in list C, after the "Zadokite group" (see below) in list A, and before the group of the house of Eli in list D. This actually overstates the case, since in A and C they come right before Ahitub (#17) and in D they would come in the location were it not for the clearly secondary mention of Eli-Phinehas-Ahijah. The result of the positioning in list C, where Amariah (#16) is the father of Ahitub (#17), may have caused the addition of Amariah (#9) in A (and B).

6 Spelling throughout this table is taken from the NRSV.

7 Bartlett, "Zadok," 5.

8 Bartlett believed that the Chronicler was the author of Chronicles, Ezra, and Nehemiah.

9 List D is dependent on C, but has been supplemented with three members of the house of Eli between Amaraiah (#16) and Ahitub (#17).

10 These two lists also agree in adding "the ruler of the house of God" to the name Ahitub (#17), in having the name Meshullam instead of Shallum (#19),

and in inserting Meraioth between Ahitub (#17) and Zadok (#18).

11 Johnson, *Purpose*, 38-41.

12 In fact, it inserts Meraioth between Zadok and his father.

13 See ##1-8, 15-16. Braun notes that Uzzi #6 and Amariah #16 were the names of leading priests of the postexilic period although the second name at least is so common that this observation carries little force. He also felt that Meraioth was moved from its position between #17 and #18 to #8 in order to bring Zadok's genealogy at #18 into total conformity with 2 Sam 8:17. While the early part of the list was supposedly growing, the list of high priests during the monarchical period remained impossibly short.

14 *Purpose*, 40.

15 So also Bartlett, "Zadok," 5.

16 This is apparently a *lapsus calami*, since this information is actually in Neh 12:22. Bartlett, "Zadok," 3, connected Johanan the son of Azariah to Jonathan

the priest of the exile not being named.[17] While Rudolph, 53–54, believed that Jehoiada had been unintentionally omitted in the second half of the list so that there would be twelve priests in both halves of the list, I will propose below that the list was probably originally somewhat longer and that the number twelve has no significance for it. Japhet, 151, who believes that Ezra and Chronicles had separate authors, understands Ezra 7 as an initial attempt to produce an Aaronide genealogy without making a full adjustment to the history of the monarchical period as portrayed in the historical books, and that this attempt was adapted and elaborated in 1 Chr 5:27-41 (6:1-15), where the house of Zadok was integrated into the Aaronide line. Despite the alleged artificiality of most of the list, she concludes that the mention of Jehozadak (no. 23) as the final member of the genealogy came from a dependable source. Apparently she means a source in addition to Hag 1:1, Zech 6:11, and Ezra 2. It seems more likely to me that the Chronicler added this name precisely to connect the postexilic priest Joshua, the son of Jehozadak, with the preexilic high priestly line. Jehozadak occurs in no other form of this genealogy (lists E and F link the genealogy to one or more postexilic priests, and C and D add Ezra here).

I do not find the hypothesis that list A is made of a bundle of fragmentary sources convincing since it is hard to imagine a segment like nos. 17-22 (Nehemiah 11, E; and 1 Chronicles 9, F) would be considered sufficient to cover the whole monarchical period, and I would therefore like to propose an alternate reconstruction. List B, as all of the above scholars agree, is an excerpt from the long genealogy in A, designed to attribute the list of Levitical cities (1 Chr 6:39-66 [54-81]) to the time of David. If the conclusion that this list is an excerpt is correct, and I think it is, then other shorter genealogies

may be excerpts as well, and I believe this is indeed the case for Nehemiah 11 (E) and 1 Chronicles 9 (F). Both of these genealogies begin awkwardly, probably representing a corrupt text:

> Neh 11:10-11 "Jedaiah, the son of Joiarib, Jachin, Seraiah, the son of Hilkiah . . ."
> 1 Chr 9:10-11 "Jedaiah, and Jehoiarib, and Jachin and Azariah, the son of Hilkiah . . ."

The relationship of the first three names to one another and to the high priestly line is not clear and has led to a wide variety of emendations, none of which is fully convincing.[18] In any case, one or more postexilic priests is being legitimatized by relating him (or them) to an excerpt from the main high priestly line. This excerpt consisted of seven names: the six names of Ahitub–Seraiah (nos. 17-22) and the name Meraioth, which had been inserted between Ahitub and Zadok.[19] Nehemiah 11 lost Azariah (no. 21) and 1 Chronicles 9 lost Seraiah (no. 22), both by haplography. Surely no one would have thought that a sequence of seven names, with Zadok in the third position, was long enough to have covered the whole monarchical period (contra Johnson, Braun).

Note that Ezra 7 (C) contains names nos. 1-8 and nos. 15-22. Rather than proposing that Ezra is a combination of three fragmentary sources—nos. 1-8, nos. 15-16, and nos. 17-22—as in Bartlett and the other scholars noted above, I believe that this genealogy is haplographic, with a scribe skipping from Azariah (no. 15) to Meraioth (no. 8),[20] leaving out Johanan, Azariah, Ahimaaz, Zadok, Ahitub, and Amariah (nos. 14-9) because of the similarity between Azariah and the last name omitted, Amariah. This same haplography is presupposed in the genealogy

---

the son of Abiathar, but of course both the name itself and the name of the father are different. Braun, 85, observed that Johanan was an exceedingly important name in postexilic families implying that his presence at #14 was fictitious.

17 Johnson, *Purpose,* 41; similarly Braun, 85. Both conclude correctly that the parenthesis about Azariah in 5:36b (6:10b) was intended to apply to the Azariah of 5:35 (6:9).

18 See the commentary at 1 Chr 9:10-11.

19 Since Meraioth (#8) is the immediate ancestor of the sequence Amariah-Ahitub-Zadok (nos. 9-11), I

propose that someone added his name marginally to the second sequence of these names at nos. 16-18 in the original form of the genealogy (the master list), and that he was later entered incorrectly after Ahitub (#17) instead of before Amariah (#16).

20 This genealogy, like E and F, is an ascending genealogy, from Ezra to Aaron, in contrast to lists A and B. A scribe therefore skipped from the end of Azariah ([#15], the son of Johanan [#14]) to the end of Amariah ([#9] the son of Meraioth [#8]). Similarly, Frank Moore Cross, "The Priestly Houses of Early Israel," in *Canaanite Myth,* 196, although he

of Ezra in 2 Esdr 1:1-3,[21] and in the two Greek translations of Ezra 7 (Esdras β and 1 Esdr 8:1-2). Whether this haplography happened early in the textual history of Ezra or already in his source is impossible to say.

I have concluded therefore that the five shorter genealogies—B-F—presuppose the longer and more original genealogy in 1 Chr 5:27-41 (6:1-15). Genealogies B, E, and F are *excerpts* from that genealogy (E and F are also haplographic at the end), and genealogies C and D are *copies* of that genealogy that have been damaged by haplography. On this basis I would like to make a somewhat more speculative proposal about the history of genealogy A, the subject of this chapter. If lists C and D are haplographic, is it not plausible that list A is haplographic as well? Note that the names Amariah, Jehoiada, and Azariah that follow Azariah no. 13 are well-regarded high priests attested in 2 Chronicles, and that Jehoiada is arguably the most outstanding high priest in the monarchical period. Would he—and his two colleagues for that matter—have been omitted from the high priestly genealogy? The book of Chronicles has him live to one hundred thirty years (the same as Jacob), and affords him a burial site among the kings (2 Chr 24:15-16), an honor denied to his contemporary King Joash. These three high priests fit chronologically *after* Azariah no. 13, and the sequence of names Amariah-Jehoiada-Azariah could easily be lost by homoioteleuton after Azariah no. 13.[22] The case with Uriah, a fourth priest mentioned in 2 Kgs 16:10, but not in Chronicles, is not so clear. The name does not resemble either Johanan no. 14 or Azariah no. 15 so that there is no ready cause for haplography. The

genealogists may have been loathe to include him in any case since he built an alien altar from plans Ahaz had sent back from Damascus (2 Kgs 16:10-16), and the temple doors were shut up by Ahaz during his reign (2 Chr 28:24). In addition, the name of this priest is not mentioned in the Chronicler's account of Ahaz. It also cannot be determined if Zechariah was in a longer form of this genealogy, after Jehoiada, just as it is not clear that he actually served as a high priest (2 Chr 24:20-22).

I conclude, therefore that the longest genealogy (1 Chr 5:27-41 [6:1-15]) antedates the five other, shorter genealogies, and that it is plausible to consider that it might once have been even longer before being damaged by haplography. This conjecture explains why the sequence Amariah-Jehoiada-Azariah is not included in the present form of the genealogy in 5:27-41 (6:1-15), and it provides chronologically coherent names to which Amariah and Azariah, in 2 Chr 19:11 and 26:17, respectively, can be applied. My reconstructed earlier form of the high priestly genealogy, outfitted with Roman numerals I, II, III, and IV, where appropriate, appears in column G of table 6.[23]

6:1-15 (16-30). Genealogy of Regular Levites

The Chronicler could have found most of the first and second generation of the descendants of Levi in other biblical sources (Exod 6:16-19 and Num 3:17-20).[24] In sections I and II the sons of Levi are listed in the standard order: Gershom, Kohath, and Merari (1 Chr 5:27; 6:1 [16]), while in section III they are given in the order of Kohath, Gershom, and Merari (vv. 23, 28, 32 [38, 43,

---

slightly misstates the words that were omitted. This proposal is rejected by Japhet, 151, arguing that all the names connected explicitly with Zadok have been omitted.

21 The insertion of the names Eli—Phinehas—Ahijah after Amariah #16 is also haplographic, since Ahitub should be inserted between Phinehas and Ahijah.

22 In addition, a scribe's eye could have skipped from one הוליד to the next. H. J. Katzenstein, "Some Remarks on the Lists of the Chief Priests of the Temple of Solomon," *JBL* 81 (1962) 377–84, also wanted to restore these names, but he did not detect the cause of the loss in homoioteleuton, nor can I endorse all the proposals in his article, including the correlation with the high priestly list of Josephus.

23 W. Boyd Barrick, "Genealogical Notes on the 'House of David' and the 'House of Zadok,'" *JSOT* 96 (2001) 29–58, accepts my reconstruction of the "master list," but goes on to reconstruct the "actual" list of high priests that involves a number of conjectures and finally does not persuade.

24 Both sources spell the name of the oldest son of Moses as Gershon, instead of Gershom, as in 1 Chr 5:28 (6:1). In Num 26:28 we find a divergent and presumably older genealogy of Levi that refers to the Libnites, Hebronites, Mahlites, the Mushites, and the Korahites, without relating them to the three sons of Levi, Gershom, Kohath, and Merari. The first generation of Levi's descendants is also given in Gen 46:11 and Num 26:57.

47]) in order to give preeminence to Kohath's descendant Heman. The names for the second through the seventh generations after Gershom and Merari in section II are not derived from any biblical source. The genealogies for the regular Levite descendants from Gershom and Merari in section II are clearest in their structure, listing in both cases seven generations after Gershom and Merari, proceeding through the oldest son of Gershom and Merari, and listing only one child for each generation. Presumably these genealogies served at some time to legitimatize the roles of Jeatherai (6:6 [21]) and Asaiah (6:15 [30]). For their possible identification, see the commentary on the relevant verses.

The genealogy of Kohath in section II is more complicated and more difficult both because it has been secondarily expanded to give the lineage of Samuel and because of uncertainties regarding Amminadab, Assir, Elkanah, Ebiasaph, and Assir that will be discussed in the commentary.[25] The secondary expansion that includes Samuel, perhaps found by the Chronicler in some genealogical source, since Samuel does not play a significant role in his work,[26] provides a genealogical pedigree for Samuel and his two sons. While this extends the genealogy provided for Samuel in 1 Sam 1:1 for many generations and changes him from an Ephraimite to a Levite, this genealogy has not been fully integrated into Kohath's genealogy and forms a kind of sidebar to it. That is, it traces Samuel's genealogy from Elkanah, a fourth-generation descendant of Kohath and ancestor of Shaul the Kohathite leader of the regular Levites, rather than beginning the genealogy of Samuel with Levi or Kohath himself.

6:16-34 (31-49). Pedigrees of Levitical Singers

Chronicles identifies the singers as Levites, in distinction from Ezra 2:41 and Neh 7:44, where they have not yet been included among the Levites, but the status of the singers in Chronicles is different from the other, regular Levites, and the work of both kinds of Levites is dif-

ferent from that of the priests, the sons of Aaron (1 Chr 6:34 [49]). The genealogies of the Levitical singers differ from those of the regular Levites in three significant ways.

1. The genealogy of the Kohathite singer Heman is given first, extends for twenty-one generations after Levi, and actually includes Israel (Jacob), the father of Levi, for a grand total of twenty-three generations. Heman is placed liturgically in the middle, with Asaph from the Gershomites on the right in the fourteenth generation after Levi, and Ethan from the Merarites on the left in the thirteenth generation after Levi. Hence the guild associated with Heman is clearly longer and in the ascendancy and the guild associated with Asaph seems to have declined and ranks lower. The high rank of the Kohathites is stressed in sections I (the genealogy of the high priests), III (the singers), IV (the excerpt from the genealogy of the high priests), and V (the cities of the priests and the Levites) of this chapter.[27]

2. These genealogies begin with the last member in each case—Heman, Asaph, and Ethan—and proceed upward (ascending genealogy) to the first member of the genealogy, which is Israel in the case of Heman, and Levi in the case of Asaph and Ethan.

3. These genealogies connect to Levi through the second son in the case of Kohath and Merari or the third son in the case of Gershom. One would expect therefore that the descendants of the second son would be totally different from the names given for the regular Levites, but that is not true for the descendants of Kohath since there is a large amount of overlap in the pedigree of Heman and of Samuel. That is, the genealogy of Samuel, which appears intrusive in the Kohathite line of the regular Levites, has been reused in the genealogy of Heman (see under v. 18 [33] below).

The Levites appear in a late, domesticated form in Chronicles.[28] There is nothing here of the militant Yahwism that is evident in Exod 32:25-29. While the Levites were to follow Yahweh without attention to family rela-

---

25 In the MT there are ten rather than seven generations after Kohath, but I suggest in the commentary that a more original length of seven can be reconstructed.

26 Samuel is mentioned only in 1 Chr 9:22; 11:3; 26:28; 29:29; and 2 Chr 35:18. Perhaps the Chronicler only wanted to make sure that this prominent

cultic official in early Israel's history had a proper Levitical genealogy.

27 In the latter case the Aaronide cities from Judah, Simeon, and Benjamin are listed first.

28 Oeming, *Wahre Israel,* 149–50.

tionships according to Deut 33:9, the family relationships in the genealogies of Chronicles are of the essence. The Chronicler has chosen to omit several items from his extensive material on the Levites: (a) The additional people descended from Izhar (Nepheg and Zichri) and Uzziel (Mishael, Elzaphan, and Sithri) mentioned in Exod 6:21-22; (b) and a genealogy for the priests who were not high priests.

6:39-66 (54-81). Cities of Priests and of Levites

A number of introductory questions face any interpreter of the cities of the priests and the Levites in 1 Chr 6:39-66 (54-81): (1) What is the relationship of the list of the cities of the priests and Levites in this chapter to the same list in Josh 21:1-40? (2) Were the cities of refuge always part of this list? (3) When is the list to be dated and on what bases? (4) Is the list historical, fictional, or utopian? (5) How might this list have arisen? (6) What is the function of the list in 1 Chronicles 6?

1. *Relationship to Josh 21:1-40.* The vast majority of scholars believe that the Chronicler's list of Levitical cities is dependent on or drawn from the parallel list in Josh 21:1-40. In a number of cases where the texts differ in MT, the text used by the Chronicler is closer to the *Vorlage* of the LXX of Joshua rather than to the MT.[29] Dissenting from this position and arguing for the priority of the text of Chronicles are J. P. Ross[30] and A. Graeme Auld,[31] both of whom wrote dissertations on the Levitical cities in the 1970s at Edinburgh. Auld concedes that the arrangement in Joshua 21 is more logical, but to him that points to its secondary character, as does its greater length.[32] A number of the shorter readings in 1 Chronicles 6, however, result from haplographies in MT and are therefore secondary. They have been restored in my translation.[33] Three times the Chronicler has omitted the reference to "the city of refuge for the slayer" (Josh 21:27, 32, 38),[34] and on two other occasions he retains "the city of refuge" but drops "for the slayer" (Josh 21:13//1 Chr 6:42 [57] and Josh 21:21//1 Chr 6:52 [67]).[35] Six cities with their pasturelands have also accidentally been omitted in the textual history of 1 Chronicles 6 and now restored in my translation—Juttah (v. 44 [59]), Gibeon (v. 45 [60]), Eltekeh and Gibbethon (v. 54 [69]), and Jokneam and Nahalal in Josh 21:34-35 (v. 62 [77]). In these cases, too, a shorter text in Chronicles MT does not indicate a more original text.

---

29 See esp. the detailed textual study by Albright, "List," 49–73.

30 "The 'Cities of the Levites' in Joshua XXI and I Chron VI" (Ph.D. diss., University of Edinburgh, 1973).

31 "The 'Levitical Cities': Text and History," *ZAW* 91 (1979) 194–206; idem, "The Cities in Joshua 21: The Contribution of Textual Criticism," *Textus* 15 (1990) 141–52. These two essays are reprinted in idem, *Joshua Retold: Synoptic Perspectives* (Edinburgh: T. & T. Clark, 1998) 29–36 and 49–57, respectively.

32 Of the twenty-one numerical totals given in Joshua 21, the Chronicler includes only four: the total for the detailed listing of the Aaronides (v. 45 [60]) and the totals for the summary of the cities assigned to Kohath, Gershom, and Merari (vv. 46-48 [61-63]). Having provided totals for each of the four Levitical groups in four consecutive verses, the Chronicler chose to omit the rest of the totals (Josh 21:4 [whole verse not included in Chronicles], 16, 18, 22, 24, 25, 26, 27, 29, 31, 32, 33 [whole verse not included in Chronicles], 35 [whole verse not included in Chronicles], 37, 39, 40-41 (both verses not included in Chronicles). Hence the Chronicler's shorter text in regard to numerical totals by no means indicates that Joshua 21 is secondary.

33 See textual notes 35 and 37 on "with its pasturelands"; textual note 46 on "out of the families of the tribe of Ephraim, from the tribe of Dan, and from the half-tribe of" (see the note for more details); textual note 54 on "of the Levites who were left of the Kohathites"; and textual note 58 on "and out of the tribe of Dan: Elteke with its pasturelands, Gibbethon with its pasturelands." There are also haplographies in Joshua 21 MT: v. 36: "and across the Jordan from Jericho, on the east side of the Jordan," and "the city of refuge for the slayer." Oeming, *Wahre Israel*, 155, and Braun, 10–11, 97, 99–100, have seen the omission of Dan as intentional in Chronicles; and Kallai, *Historical Geography*, 467, finds it hard to decide whether the omission of Dan is intentional or accidental. For the polemic against Dan see H. Hotzki, "Ein Beitrag zum Problem des Stierkultes in der Religionsgeschichte Israels," *VT* 25 (1975) 470–85; and Ch. Dohmen, "Das Heiligtum von Dan: Aspekte religionsgeschichtlicher Darstellung im deuteronomistischen Geschichtswerk," *BN* 17 (1982) 17–22.

34 1 Chr 6:56 (71); 6:61 (76); 6:65 (80).

35 The sixth city of refuge, Bezer, is not designated as such a city in either Josh 21:36 or 1 Chr 6:63 (78). It was probably lost by haplography in the sequence

The Chronicler also omitted the word "priest" twice (vv. 42, 45 [57,[36] 60[37]]) and "the Levites" three times (vv. 39, 56, 62 [54, 71, 77]), since the context in 1 Chronicles 6 made these identifications superfluous. In a number of other cases the Chronicler may have omitted a word or words, or they may have been added subsequently in the textual history of Joshua 21.[38]

Auld believes that 1 Chronicles 6 is a text that "grew" in at least four stages: (1) a list of Aaronide cities (vv. 39-45 [54-60]); (2) a summary of the Levitical settlements (vv. 46-49 [61-64]); (3) a summary of the Aaronide materials (v. 50 [65]); and (4) a detailed list of Levitical cities (vv. 51-66 [66-81]).

A columnar outline of the two chapters will facilitate our discussion of the Auld proposal and also reveal some of the Chronicler's intention in including this material.

Topic	Joshua 21	1 Chronicles 6
A. Introduction to the assignment of cities	vv. 1-3	Not included
B. Summary of the cities assigned to the Aaronides	v. 4	Not included
C. Summary of the cities assigned to the Kohathites	v. 5	v. 46 (61)
D. Summary of the cities assigned to the Gershomites[39]	v. 6	v. 47 (62)
E. Summary of the cities assigned to the Merarites	v. 7	v. 48 (63)
F. Conclusion to the summary presentation	v. 8	v. 49 (64)
G. Introduction to the detailed assignment of cities to the Aaronides	v. 9	v. 50 (65)
H. Detailed assignment of cities to the Aaronides	vv. 10-19	vv. 39-45 (54-60)
I. Detailed assignment of cities to the Kohathites	vv. 20-26	vv. 51-55 (66-70)
J. Detailed assignment of cities to the Gershomites[40]	vv. 27-33	vv. 56-61 (71-76)
K. Detailed assignment of cities to the Merarites[41]	vv. 34-40	vv. 62-66 (77-81)

These sections may be gathered into the following groups: A, introduction; B-F, summaries of assignments to the Aaronides and the three Levitical families; G-K, detailed assignments to the Aaronides and the three Levitical families. The Chronicler omits section A since his text is primarily a description of where the priests and Levites lived at the time of David rather than a part of a narrative of how their cities were assigned to the Levites at the time of Joshua, following Yahweh's command to Moses. Of far greater significance is his shifting of section H, the detailed assignment of cities to the Aaronides, to a position *before* sections C-G.[42] The net effect of this positioning, as Auld himself agrees, is to give far greater emphasis to the Aaronide cities, all of which come from the tribes of Judah, Simeon, and Ben-

---

אֵת עִיר מִקְלָט הָרֹצֵחַ אֵת בֶּצֶר when a scribe skipped from the first to the second אֵת. The longer, original reading is attested in Joshua LXX. Does this haplography explain why the designation was lost three additional times in Chronicles?

36 Here Chronicles may be following the LXX *Vorlage* of Joshua 21.

37 Instead of "all the cities of the sons of Aaron the priests" Chronicles reads "all their towns."

38 E.g., Josh 21:8 "these" and "just as Yahweh had commanded through Moses by lot" (cf. Josh 21:2). The latter clause may have been omitted since the Chronicler is describing the system of the cities of the priests and Levites and not how these cities were assigned as in Joshua. For similar reasons he omitted Josh 21:1-4. See Götz Schmitt, "Leviten-

städte," *ZDPV* 111 (1995) 37. See also Josh 21:10, "first"; 21:11, "Kiriath-arba, Arba being the father of Anak, that is"; 21:12, "as a possession"; 21:34, "families."

39 The spelling is that found in Chronicles. They are called "Gershonites" in Joshua.

40 The half-tribe of Manasseh appears last in the summary (D), but first in the detailed assignment. See Auld, *Joshua Retold*, 26.

41 Zebulun appears last in the summary (E), but first in the detailed assignment. See Auld, *Joshua Retold*, 26.

42 This shift also made Josh 21:4 superfluous, since its essential content is covered by 1 Chr 6:50 (65), and it was therefore omitted.

jamin in the southern half of the land, and to distinguish the Aaronide cities from the cities in north Israel and in Transjordan. Only the cities of the Aaronides overlap with the postexilic province of Yehud. In a similar fashion, the Chronicler presented the genealogy of the Aaronides themselves first among the Levitic genealogies (5:27-41 [6:1-15]) before giving the genealogy of the rest of the Levites in 6:1-32 (16-47). Auld's proposal to privilege the arrangement in Chronicles, however, runs into great difficulty in trying to understand v. 50 (65). He considers it a "clumsy continuation . . . which refers back to the allotment from the tribes of Judah, Simeon, and Benjamin" (p. 26). Rather, it was designed to be an introduction to the detailed list of Aaronide cities, quite at the right place at Josh 21:9, but awkwardly placed in Chronicles[43] because the Chronicler decided to start his account with section H. Instead of introducing the detailed list of Aaronide cities, v. 50 (65) now concludes the assignment to the Aaronides.[44] Auld also classifies Josh 21:4 as part of the introduction to that chapter rather than a summary comparable to Josh 21:5-7 and concludes that neither text has a four-sentence summary paragraph, but this is a denial of the obvious purpose of v. 4. Auld points to a series of longer readings in Joshua in an attempt to support his hypothesis, but some of these may have been subsequent expansions of Joshua after the Chronicler borrowed this text, and others may be haplographies in the text of Chronicles that need to be restored (see the textual notes). Ben Zvi[45] also notes that whereas the Chronicler shifted the setting from the time of Joshua to the time of David and

therefore made irrelevant the assignment of the cities to the various groups by lot, he did not thoroughly redact the account to fit its new context, leaving references to the lot in vv. 39, 46, 48, and 50 (54, 61, 63, and 65) and to the giving of cities in vv. 40, 42, 49, 50, 52 (55, 57, 64, 65, 67).[46] For all of these reasons I find the Auld proposal unconvincing.[47]

Once the six city-names lost by haplography have been restored,[48] a total of thirty-four cities are identical in the two lists.[49] In six cases the original name is better preserved in Chronicles:[50] Ashan (v. 44 [59]), Alemeth (v. 45 [60]), Ibleam (v. 55 [70]), Ramoth (v. 58 [73]), Rimmon (v. 62 [77]), and Kartah/Tabor (v. 62 [77]). In four cases the original name is better preserved in Joshua:[51] Taanach (v. 55 [70]), Kishion (v. 57 [72]), En-gannim (v. 58 [73]), and Helkath (v. 60 [75]). In four cases the lists contain ancient variants and I am unable to decide which reading is superior: Kibzaim/Jokmeam (v. 53 [68]), Beeshterah/Ashtaroth (v. 56 [71]), Hammoth-dor/Hammon (v. 61 [76]), and Kartan/Kiriathaim (v. 61 [76]). There are thirteen cities ascribed to the Aaronides, ten to the Kohathites, thirteen to the Gershomites, and twelve to the Merarites.[52]

2. *The cities of refuge.* Provisions for refuge or asylum cities for those accused of unintentional or unpremeditated killing are contained in the Covenant Code (Exod 21:13), Deuteronomistic materials (Deut 4:41-43; 19:1-13), priestly legislation (Num 35:9-15), and Josh 20:1-9. In Deut 19:1-7 Moses instructs the people to set aside three cities of refuge "in the land," that is, west of the Jordan, and in Deut 19:8-9 he proposes an additional

---

43 Note that the text refers to towns which are mentioned by name, but then does not mention any towns.

44 Auld notes that there is no mention of Judah in vv. 39-45 (54-60), but this would not be significant if v. 4, not included by the Chronicler, and v. 50, which is misplaced in Chronicles, were allowed to play their proper roles. Japhet, 143, 161, notes the awkward position of v. 50 (65) and suggests moving it after v. 39a (54), but there is no evidence that the Chronicler ever put it there. We should leave his awkward product the way it is.

45 Ehud Ben Zvi, "The List of the Levitical Cities," *JSOT* 54 (1992) 77–78, n. 1, where he cites additional arguments against Auld.

46 Cf. Japhet, 147; Nadav Na'aman, "A New Look at

the System of Levitical Cities," in *Borders and Districts in Biblical Historiography* (JBS 4; Jerusalem: Simor, 1986) 210–16.

47 See also the discussion of Auld in Kallai, *Historical Geography,* 464–65; Kartveit, *Motive und Schichten,* 69–77.

48 Juttah, Gibeon, Elteke, Gibbethon, Jokneam, Nahalal.

49 There are slight orthographic variants with Holon (textual note 38) and Mishal (textual note 68).

50 For details see the textual notes.

51 The verse numbers are from 1 Chronicles 6.

52 The splitting of the tribe of Manasseh gives two cities to the Kohathites (v. 55 [70]) and two to the Gershomites (v. 56 [71]). If Manasseh were considered as a unified tribe and all its cities ascribed to

three cities, presumably east of the Jordan, if Yahweh should enlarge their territory. This six-city system, half east and half west of the Jordan, is also mandated by Yahweh to Moses in Num 35:13-14. In Deut 4:41-43 Moses sets aside the three Transjordanian cities: Bezer in the wilderness on the tableland (Reuben), Ramoth in Gilead (Gad), and Golan in Bashan (Manasseh). In Josh 20:7-8 the Israelites set aside all six cities by name, the ones mentioned in Deuteronomy 4 and Kedesh in Galilee in the hill country of Naphtali, Shechem in the hill country of Ephraim, Kiriath-arba (i.e., Hebron) in the hill country of Judah.

These six cities are included in the list of Levitical cities in Joshua 21, where they are always the first city mentioned for their tribe and identified by the same descriptive phrase: "the city of refuge for the slayer," except for Bezer, v. 36:[53] v. 13, Hebron;[54] v. 21, Shechem;[55] v. 27, Golan;[56] v. 32, Kedesh;[57] v. 38, Ramoth in Gilead.[58] 1 Chronicles 6 also places each of these six cities first among the cities of their tribe, but only Hebron and Shechem, both in Cisjordan, are called a "city of refuge,"[59] and even they lack the expression "for the slayer." Japhet, 148, has proposed that the Chronicler considered Hebron a refuge city for the southern kingdom and Shechem for the northern kingdom. Both of these cities are in sections assigned to the Kohathites. It is also possible, of course, that the references to "the

city of refuge" were lost by haplography for Golan, Kedesh, and Ramoth in Gilead, as this reference was lost in Joshua for Bezer, and that the change from "city" to "cities" for Hebron and Shechem was a simple metathesis (עיר became ערי).

Albright thought that the cities of refuge were secondary to the Levitical cities, although he conceded that all but Hebron and Shechem were Levitical cities already apart from their role as refuge cities.[60] He thought that the correct total number of Levitical cities was retained after the addition of Hebron and Shechem by separate and fortuitous omissions in Joshua 21 and 1 Chronicles 6. Kallai, however, has argued convincingly that the cities of refuge are an inseparable part of the list.[61] He notes that the framework of the Levitical cities is so firm in assigning four cities to each tribe that it would be impossible to break up this frame by removing the cities of refuge from it. In any case, all six names of the cities of refuge were already present in Joshua, which makes the argument about their originality moot in a commentary on Chronicles.

3. *The date of the Levitical cities.* Both those who consider the document historical and those who consider it fictional or utopian have come up with a wide range of dates for the original document. Kaufmann noted the absence of Jerusalem and therefore located the document in the early years of Israel's occupation of the land

---

the Kohathites, their number would be twelve and the Gershomites eleven. And if Beth-shemesh, now ascribed to Judah and the Aaronides, was originally ascribed to the Gershomites and the tribe of Naphtali (v. 61 [76]; see discussion below), each group would have twelve cities.

53 As pointed out in n. 34 above, the expression was lost by homoioarchton in the MT of Joshua, though preserved in the LXX. Since 1 Chronicles 6 is dependent on Joshua 21, the expression therefore is not attested for Bezer in 1 Chr 6:63 (78) either.

54 Cf. 1 Chr 6:42 (57). The name Kiriath-arba, as in Josh 20:7, is used in Josh 21:11, where the writer explains the division of land between the Levites and Caleb the son of Jephunneh.

55 Cf. 1 Chr 6:52 (67).

56 Cf. 6:56 (71).

57 Cf. 6:61 (76).

58 Cf. 6:65 (80).

59 The MT designates them "cities of refuge" in vv. 42 and 52 (57 and 67). See textual notes 34, 56. Oem-

ing, *Wahre Israel*, 146–47, n. 15, takes the plural noun as an indication that multiple cities of refuge followed each name, but that seems highly unlikely. So also Kartveit, *Motive und Schichten*, 159, who states that the Chronicler considers more or less all of the Kohathite cities as asylum cities.

60 "List," 52. Boling, *Joshua*, 488, believes that the "updating" that included these cities was the work of Dtr². Noth, *Josua*, 127, also considers the cities of refuge secondary in this list. Oeming, *Wahre Israel*, 155–56, also believes the cities of refuge are to be separated from the original form of this list.

61 *Historical Geography*, 453. Cf. Götz Schmitt, "Levitenstädte," 33.

before the northern migration of the Danites, though he also held it to be a utopian program that was never implemented.[62] Albright sought a terminus a quo and a terminus ante quem on the basis of when cities came under Israelite control or passed out of Israelite control. He cited a number of cities that were fortified Canaanite locations during the period of the judges (Judges 1) and did not come into Israelite possession until the monarchy, such as Gezer (Judg 1:29), Aijalon (1:35), Taanach (1:27), Rehob (1:31), and Nahalol (1:30). He proposed the same analysis for other peripheral towns, without specific corroborating biblical evidence, such as Elteke and Gibbethon in the tribal territory of Dan, Mishal and Helkath in Asher, Jokneam in Zebulun, the towns of Reuben, and Heshbon and Jazer in Gad. He believed that David had reconquered the last six cities from the Ammonites and the Moabites. In his judgment Anathoth and Alemeth in Benjamin could not have become Levitical towns until after their foundation in the time of David. On the other hand, Gezer was destroyed by Shishak[63] and not reoccupied until the Persian period,[64] and Golan and Ashtaroth were lost to Ben-hadad after Solomon's death (1 Kgs 15:20).[65] Bezer and Jahaz were taken by Mesha of Moab by the mid-ninth century. Since the list was structured according to the tribal system, Albright placed it before the creation of Solomon's twelve, nontribal districts (1 Kings 4), or in absolute figures between 975 and 950 BCE.[66] By the ninth century, in his opinion, the list was only an ideal configuration of the past.

Albright took at more or less face value the descriptions of the kingdoms of David and Solomon as they are spelled out in Samuel and Kings. Many scholars today believe that the area actually controlled by these kings was much smaller than these texts imply. Benjamin Mazar cited arguments similar to Albright's but placed the origin of the list during the reign of Solomon because of Gezer, which had been given to Solomon by the Pharaoh as a dowry (1 Kgs 9:16). Mazar believed that Solomon followed Egyptian precedents in stationing loyal Levites in recently conquered territories or in border regions to collect taxes and manage royal estates.[67] Alt dated the list to the time of Josiah,[68] in which he was followed with some hesitancy by Noth.[69] Alt called attention to the gaps in the heart of Judah and in the hills of

---

62 Yehezkel Kaufmann, *The Biblical Account of the Conquest of Palestine* (trans. M. Dagut; Jerusalem: Magnes, 1953) 40–46.

63 So was Mahanaim according to Mazar, "Cities," 204.

64 Subsequent excavations have shown that the town did continue to exist even after the defeat by Shishak.

65 Nadab, the second king of the northern kingdom, laid siege to Gibbethon, which was then under Philistine control (1 Kgs 15:27). Aharoni, *Land of the Bible,* 302, proposes that Rehob and probably also Abdon were among the twenty towns Solomon returned to Hiram.

66 Chris Hauer Jr., "David and the Levites," *JSOT* 23 (1982) 33–54, adduced anthropological arguments in support of Albright's position. Aharoni, *Land of the Bible*, 302, also placed it in the reign of David. Tryggve N. D. Mettinger, *Solomonic State Officials* (ConBOT 5; Lund: Gleerup, 1971) 98–99, dates the cities to the reign of Solomon and used this list as part of his argument to demonstrate the existence of royal estates. Kallai, *Historical Geography*, 458, dates the list to the latter half of Solomon's reign.

67 Most of the cities in Judah for example are in the southern hills, but Libnah is on the border with the Philistines and Beth-shemesh was on the northern edge of the Shephelah. Mazar cites 1 Chr 26:30-32 as an example of how this administrative scheme worked. Mazar, "Cities," 199, believed that when the Levites fled the northern kingdom (2 Chr 11:13-17), Rehoboam settled them in the fortified cities he built in the western and southern borderlands of the kingdom (2 Chronicles 11). He found Egyptian parallels in the Papyrus Harris coming from the time of Ramesses III (205). Aharoni, *Land of the Bible*, 305, concludes: "The Levitical cities were established probably principally as royal Israelite centres near the borders intended for strengthening the kingdom's authority by promulgating Yahwistic worship, national solidarity, and loyalty to the Davidic dynasty at Jerusalem, besides their administrative functions." It is important to remember that the lists themselves specify no function for the Levitical cities.

68 Alt, "Bemerkungen zu einigen judäischen Ortslisten des Alten Testaments," in *Kleine Schriften zur Geschichte des Volkes Israel* (Munich: Beck, 1953) 2:301, believed the Josianic document was based on an earlier document, which was not a great deal older.

69 Noth, *Josua*, 131–32, also considered a late dating in the Persian period, but finally rejected it because he

Ephraim,[70] the very areas affected by Josiah's removal of local sanctuaries to Jerusalem.[71]

The most extensive attempt to invoke archaeological data in dating the list was carried out by John L. Peterson.[72] From surface surveys and archaeological reports he tried to find a century when all of the cities in this list were occupied at the same time. For nineteen cities he found evidence of occupation from the tenth through the eighth centuries; for eleven cities only for the ninth and eighth centuries; for one city, Qishion, only in the ninth century; and for six cities—Geba, Hebron, Hammoth-dor, Jattir, Qedesh, and Rimmon—only in the eighth century.[73] Peterson and, following him, Robert Boling concluded that the date of the list was in the eighth century. Perhaps Peterson's most original and surprising finding was that for fully half the cities there was no occupational level for the tenth century.[74]

A number of smaller and greater difficulties, however, challenge the validity of his conclusion. (1) The surface survey was completed a generation ago, in 1971, and badly needs updating in view of further excavations and surveys and the current debate about how to date tenth-century remains in Palestinian archaeology. In at least one case, Elteke, the site proposed by Peterson and Boling has now been definitively identified as the site of Ekron, and the excavators found evidence of occupation for all three centuries, whereas Peterson limited the range to the ninth-eighth century.[75] (2) In several cases the archaeological conclusions are in serious conflict with biblical or extrabiblical evidence. While Peterson found evidence for occupation in Hebron only in the eighth century, this city played a major role as the first capital of David for seven and one-half years in the tenth century.[76] Similarly, Anathoth and Gibeon, which Peterson limited to the ninth-eighth centuries, played significant roles in the tenth century. Solomon exiled Abiathar to Anathoth, and Solomon also sought out the high place at Gibeon where he received his famous dream (1 Kgs 3:3-15).[77] Peterson also found no evidence for tenth-century occupation at Eshtemoa and Jattir, but dealings of David with them are recorded in 1 Sam 30:27-28. (3) The most telling problem with Peterson's conclusion about the eighth century, however, is that the list makes little historical or sociological sense in that century. Until 722 BCE there were two distinct nations in the northern and southern kingdoms and no evidence that they had a common assignment of Levites throughout the two kingdoms.[78] Long before 722 the Assyrians had greatly reduced north Israel and formed parts of it into three provinces. It is hard to imagine Hezekiah

---

did not think the book of Joshua otherwise contained such late material. Na'aman, "Levitical Cities," 233, accepted the Josian dating and observed that the extension of Judean rule under Josiah "brought with it a widespread consciousness of the inauguration of a new era, and a feeling of restoration of former glory."

70 Mazar, "Cities," 200–202, explained the gap in Judah because David and Solomon already had strong control there, and the gap in the central part of the country he attributed to its strong tradition of tribal rule. I believe that the gaps are to be attributed to the restraints imposed by limiting the number of Levitical cities in any tribe, regardless of its size, to four.

71 Alt's point is not convincing since there are Levitical cities in both Ephraim and Manasseh, including Shechem, Beth-horon, and Taanach. Mettinger, *Solomonic State Officials*, 98, opposed Alt's idea as lacking proof and by no means necessary, and argued for a date in the reign of Solomon.

72 John L. Peterson, *A Topographical Surface Survey of the Levitical "Cities" of Joshua 21 and I Chronicles 6:*

Studies on the Levites in Israelite Life and Religion (Evanston, IL: Chicago Institute of Advanced Theological Studies and Seabury-Western Theological Seminary, 1977).

73 For twelve cities the sites were either inaccessible or the evidence unclear.

74 Peterson, *Topographical Survey*, 714, sets the number at thirty. In "Levitical Cities," *ABD* 4:311, he indicates that only twenty cities showed evidence of occupation in the 10th century.

75 See provisionally Trude Dothan and Seymour Gitin, "Ekron," *ABD* 2:415–22.

76 Other 8th-century-only sites also play a role in the David story: Jattir in 1 Sam 30:27 and Geba in 2 Sam 5:25.

77 The arguments raised by Albright and Mazar about the loss of Israelite control over some of these cities after the 10th century is also still valid, and it may be somewhat irrelevant that we can conclude that they were occupied in later centuries.

78 Boling, "Levitical Cities: Archeology and Texts," in *Biblical and Related Studies Presented to Samuel Iwry* (ed. A. Kort and S. Morschauser; Winona Lake, IN:

toward the end of the century being able to station Levites in large parts of the north and in Transjordan where the Assyrians were in control. Boling traced the institution behind the list all the way back to Moses, who had established teaching centers in the land for the Levites to spread the ethic of Yahwism, and he distinguished between this system as a sacred institution and the actual roster of names, but there is a great deal of speculation in his proposal.[79] To the extent that archaeologists could still argue today that the eighth century was the only time when these cities were all occupied at one time, the logical conclusion would seem that the list is not historical because internal politics and Assyrian presence would preclude that possibility. While Peterson's positive suggestion cannot be accepted, his negative conclusions with regard to the tenth century are telling. If the list is artificially created, primarily by using the cities of refuge and information from Joshua 13–19, including the order of the tribes in those chapters, it is futile to seek a particular century when the list could have served an administrative purpose.

4. *The list as history or fiction.* Proponents of both positions have sometimes assumed their position rather than demonstrating it and have castigated their opponents' opposite position. Oeming concludes, however, that the list of Levitical cities remains in large part an unsolved riddle and there is very little evidence on which to base a sure historical judgment.[80] Advocates of the text's historical character include Albright, Alt, Mazar, and Kallai, while those thinking it fictional include Na'aman, Ben Zvi, Kartveit, Kaufmann, and Wellhausen.[81]

Menahem Haran holds a mediating position. He believes the text is in part utopian, but that it also contains realistic, that is, historical, data.[82] Utopian elements include the identical measurements given for the pasture

lands of each city, an exact square of 2,000 cubits (Num 35:4-5), regardless of the geographical setting of the city, the idea that these cities were inhabited only by Levites, and the differentiation between priests and Levites that is unhistorical in the preexilic period. Also utopian are the contribution of four cities by each tribe and the Jubilee legislation that is interwoven with the Levitical cities. He believes, however, that the dispersion of the Levites throughout all Israel is realistic, as is the fact that not all the cities are shrine cities and that they are not all located within the traditional boundaries of the Holy Land given in Numbers 34. The implied equal social and economic status of priests and Levites in preexilic times he also believes to be historical, and the number of cities assigned to the Aaronides exceeds what one would expect from reading P and therefore gains in credibility. Haran concludes that there was an old historical document to which various utopian features were added. In any case, while the Levites received places to live and to pasture their animals, they remained essentially landless, that is, they did not own land.[83] I would add, however, that not only does the assignment of four cities per tribe seem artificial since some tribes were clearly much larger than others, but large parts of Ephraim, Manasseh, and Judah have no cities of the priests and Levites, which renders unlikely any administrative purpose attributed to this list.

Götz Schmitt has made a strong case that the order of the tribes in Joshua 21 is based on the order in Joshua 13–19, thus supporting the artificial character of the list.[84] He also notes that the cities of Dan in the southwestern part of Palestine were occupied by this tribe only in premonarchical times and only then on the edges of the region assigned to their cities in Josh 21:23-24//1 Chr 6:54 (69). He also believes that the order of

---

Eisenbrauns, 1985) 30, argues that the system flourished in the time of Jeroboam II and Uzziah.

79 "Levitical Cities," 27–31. See also Robert G. Boling, "Levitical History and the Role of Joshua," in *The Word of the Lord Shall Go Forth* (FS D. N. Freedman; ed. C. L. Meyers and M. O'Connor; Winona Lake, IN: Eisenbrauns, 1983) 258, where he assigned the cities of refuge and the Levitical cities to Dtr².

80 *Wahre Israel,* 154–55. He suggests that one could argue for the idea of Levitical cities from a passage in the Chronicler's narrative. In 2 Chr 23:2 we read of Levites who came from the cities of Judah to

Jerusalem; and Neh 12:27, which he considers part of the Chronicler's history, speaks of Levites who are brought together from all their places.

81 *Prolegomena,* 159–64.

82 "Studies in the Account of the Levitical Cities," *JBL* 80 (1961) 45–54, 156–65.

83 See Num 18:24; Deut 10:8-9; Josh 13:33; 18:7.

84 "Levitenstädte," 40–42.

the Transjordanian tribes, with Reuben south of Gad, corresponds to the arrangement of Joshua 13 and is not historical (cf. the earliest form of Num 32:34-38 and the Mesha stela, which place Gad south of Reuben).[85]

5. *Recent proposals on the origin of the list.* The attempts to date the list to a specific historical century have not been successful, and the schematic form of the list, assigning four cities to each tribe, regardless of that tribe's size, does not create confidence in the suggestions for an administrative purpose for the list.[86] The gaps south of Jerusalem and in large parts of Samaria also do not favor an administrative or historical origin for the list. Three of the twelve districts in Solomon's administrative document (1 Kgs 4:7-19) are from the Cisjordan part of Manasseh, but there are only two Levitical cities assigned to the same area.

Na'aman notes that the historical scheme of forty-eight cities, four from each tribe, has long been suspect and he casts doubt on whether the Levitical cities were ever connected with the administration of the country.[87] He also finds surprising the omission of many prominent cult centers: Dan, Bethel, Mizpah, Gilgal, Bethlehem, Beer-sheba, Arad, Nebo, and Ataroth.[88] One would

expect Levites to live in such cities. While rejecting the Auld proposal on the priority of 1 Chronicles 6, Na'aman agrees with him that the thirteen Aaronide cities, or at least the nine assigned to Judah and Simeon, have a ring of authenticity to them precisely because of their unusual number—nine instead of eight. In his opinion, the creator of the list of Levitical cities used these nine/thirteen Aaronide cities of the kingdom of Judah[89] and supplemented them with data from the list of tribal inheritances (Joshua 13–19)[90] and the list of the cities of refuge to create the forty-eight member list.

Ben Zvi accepts Na'aman's interpretation of the relationship between the lists of cities and the tribal inheritances,[91] but suggests a later origin for the list because of its dependency on the lists of the cities of refuge. He argues that Deut 19:1-7 is the oldest form of the list of the cities of refuge, which mandates only the selection of three unnamed cities, presumably in Cisjordan. He dates these verses to the time of Josiah, meaning that the later expansion of this pericope by vv. 8-9, which mandates the selection of three more towns, must be dated even later, that is, after the monarchical period, as an attempt to harmonize with the six-city system presupposed by the

---

85 Richard D. Nelson, *Joshua* (OTL; Louisville: Westminster John Knox, 1997) 236–37, also concludes that the list is not historical.

86 See esp. Schmitt, "Levitenstädte," 35. Mazar believed that Solomon stationed Levites in recently conquered territories or in border regions to collect taxes and manage royal estates. Boling, "Levitical Cities," 31, writes: "A support-system for the network of levitical torah-teachers which embraced north and south and extended to both sides of the Jordan is one which apparently had not acknowledged the permanence of political divisions and had not made peace with the redefinition of Israel in terms of the monarchic nation-states. There is nothing to gainsay a claim that the rationale is Mosaic in origin." In view of the "covenant silence" of the prophets, such a central role for the covenant in 8th-century Israel might be questioned. Aelred Cody, "Levitical Cities and the Israelite Settlement," in *Homenaje a Juan Prado* (ed. L. Alvarez Verdes and E. J. Alonso Hernandez; Madrid: Consejo Superior de Investagaciones Cientificas, 1975) 179–89, speculates on when the Levites could have become residents in various sections of the country. He notes, 183, that in both versions of the list it is considered a list of cities where Levites acquired some kind of

property rights, not as a list of towns where offices were being erected for a Levitical branch of the civil service.

87 "Levitical Cities," 203–36.

88 Ibid., 206–7.

89 Eight of the nine cities located in Judah and Simeon are mentioned in the province list of Judah (Josh 15:21-62), and we know from archaeology that the ninth, Beth-shemesh, continued to be occupied until the end of the monarchy. See Na'aman, "Levitical Cities," 228. Geba and Gibeon, assigned in the list of Levitical cities to Benjamin, are also mentioned in the province list of Judah (Josh 18:21-28). Anathoth is well attested in the monarchy, and Alemeth is mentioned with it in the genealogy of Benjamin (1 Chr 7:8). Na'aman, "Levitical Cities," 229, follows Alt in dating the Judean province list to the time of Josiah.

90 This is also considered by Na'aman as a purely literary composition, but a decision on this issue does not affect the overall validity of his argument.

91 "List of the Levitical Cities," 77–106.

Priestly writer in Num 35:9-15. Another author gave an alternate harmonization with Numbers by having Moses assign three cities of refuge east of the Jordan (Bezer in the wilderness, Ramoth in Gilead, and Golan in Bashan; Deut 4:41-43). On somewhat different grounds he argues for the postmonarchic date of the naming of all six cities in Josh 20:7-8 as well, reflecting Israelite claims for Transjordan that are also put forward in other post-monarchic texts: Deuteronomy 2; Judg 11:12-28; Num 21:10-30, 31-35.

Na'aman and Ben Zvi have proposed divergent under-standings of the nine (or thirteen) Aaronide cities, with Na'aman dating these cities to the time of Josiah, when he also dates the creation of the list of Levitical cities, while Ben Zvi holds the nine or thirteen cities came from a source but attributes the specific allocation of these cities to the Aaronides to the ideological concerns of an author writing in postmonarchic times.[92] This author proposed that the Aaronides are neither strangers nor newcomers in Judah, but legitimate residents since the time of the conquest.

The dependence of the list of the Levitical cities on the list of the cities of refuge and the tribal inheritances in Joshua 13–19 seems very probable. The nomenclature for the cities of refuge in Joshua 21 is identical with that in Josh 20:7-8, including the very unusual designation for Ramoth in Gilead. The relationship between the Levitical cities and the tribal inheritances will be out-lined in the next paragraphs. Where I part company with Na'aman and Ben Zvi is the historicity ascribed to the Judah-Simeon portion of the list merely because of its odd number—nine (increased to thirteen if Benjamin is included). The absorption of Simeon within Judah

itself is known from Josh 19:1 (cf. 1 Chr 4:28-33). In view of the numerous textual errors found in both Joshua 21 and 1 Chronicles 6, it seems unwarranted to build too much on the unique number nine. One reason for the odd number could be historicity, reflecting a time before four Levitical cities were assigned to each tribe, but there might be other reasons for this odd number. Y. Tsafrir, for example, has suggested that the extra Judahite city and the presence of only three cities in Naphtali might be related. If Beth-shemesh was origi-nally a reference to the city by that name in Naphtali, it might later have been included in Judah because of the greater renown of the town Beth-shemesh in Judah. That would reduce the Judahite-Simeon numbers to eight and increase the Naphtali numbers to four.[93] If the hypoth-ical core list of nine cities in Judah-Simeon is not the original form of the list, the whole list may have arisen by selecting four cities per tribe from the cities named in Joshua 13–19 to create a list that shows Levitical and priestly presence throughout the land.

Here is the dependence that Na'man suggests on Joshua 13–19:

Reuben: Jahaz, Kedemoth and Mephaath are taken from Josh 13:18 (and in that order); the fourth city, Bezer, is a city of refuge.[94]

Gad: Mahanaim, Heshbon, and Jazar are taken from the boundary description of Gad in Josh 13:25-27; the fourth city, Ramoth in Gilead, is a city of refuge. Includ-ing Heshbon in the tribal territory of Gad is a mistaken understanding of the boundary description in 13:26 since Heshbon belonged to Reuben (13:17).[95] Ramoth in Gilead belongs to the tribal territory of Manasseh (17:1, 6), but was probably assigned to Gad because of 20:8.[96]

---

92 Ben Zvi, ibid., 102–4, argues that Hebron, Libni, and Korah from Num 25:58 were originally associated with Judah. Aside from this list, there are almost no explicit traditions that relate the Aaron-ides to Judah except for Exod 6:23. Na'aman, "Levitical Cities," 228–29, notes that eight of the nine cities of Judah are mentioned in the province list (Josh 15:21-62), as are Geba and Gibeon in Josh 18:21-28.

93 Y. Tsafrir, "The Levitic City of Beth-Shemesh in Juda or in Naphtali," *ErIsr* 12 (1975) 44–45 (Heb.). See the discussion of this point in Schmitt, "Leviten-städte," 33.

94 Schmitt, "Levitenstädte," 25, suggests that the selec-tion of the seven Transjordanian cities that are not cities of refuge may have been influenced in part by the author's knowledge of the Pentateuch: Jahaz, Num 21:23; Deut 2:32; Kedemoth, Deut 2:26; Mahanaim, Gen 32:3; Jazer, Num 21:32; 32:1; Hesh-bon, Num 21:26-27; Deut 2:26; Ashtaroth, Deut 1:4. Only Mephaath is not mentioned, but it follows Jahaz and Kedemoth in Josh 13:18 and 21:37.

95 See Kallai, *Historical Geography*, 263.

96 Ibid., 266–68. Na'aman, "Levitical Cities," 220, sug-gests that the creator of the list wanted to assign a city of refuge to each of the three Transjordanian

Manasseh: Two cities from this tribe in Transjordan are assigned to the Gershomites: Ashtaroth (Beeshterah) was taken from Josh 13:31 and Golan was a city of refuge. Two other cities of Manasseh in Cisjordan were assigned to the Kohathites, Taanach and Ibleam, both taken from the boundary description in Josh 17:11.

Ephraim: Gezer and Beth-horon are taken from the boundary description in Josh 16:3, 5, 10, and Shechem was a city of refuge. Shechem actually belonged to Manasseh (17:2, 7),[97] but 20:7 locates it "in the hill country of Ephraim."[98] Where the creator of the list got Jokmeam or Kibzaim is anyone's guess (see the commentary and textual note 57).

Dan: Elteke, Gibbethon, Aijalon, and Gath-rimmon are taken from the heritage of this tribe in the southwestern part of Palestine (Josh 19:42-45).

Issachar: Kishion, Daberath,[99] Ramoth (Jarmuth),[100] and En-gannim were taken from the tribal heritage in Josh 19:20-21.

Zebulun: Jokneam, Rimmon, and Nahalal are taken from the tribal heritage (Josh 19:11-15). For Tabor/Qartah see textual note 75.[101] Jokneam actually belongs to Manasseh, according to Na'aman, but the creator of the list misunderstood the force of על פני in 19:11.[102]

Asher: Mishal, Abdon,[103] Helkath, and Rehob are taken from Asher's tribal inheritance (Josh 19:25-28).

Naphtali: To make up for the nine cities assigned to Judah and Simeon, there are only three cities assigned to this tribe: Kedesh in Galilee, Hammon, and Kiriathaim. The two names in addition to the refuge city, Kedesh in Galilee (Judg 20:7), are very uncertain (see textual notes 70 and 71). Na'aman follows Noth in wanting to reconstruct Hammath and Rakkath, both mentioned in 19:35, as the original cities assigned to Naphtali.[104] If the fourth city was originally Beth-shemesh, it could have been drawn from 19:38.

I would like to extend this dependence to the final three tribes:

Judah-Simeon: Hebron (Josh 15:13; also a city of refuge), Libnah (15:42), Jattir (15:48), Eshtemoa (15:50),[105] Hilen/Holon (15:51), Debir (15:7, 15, 49), Ashan (15:42), Juttah (15:55), Beth-shemesh (15:10; or 19:39 if a city in Naphtali is meant).

Benjamin: Gibeon (Josh 18:25), Geba (18:24). Alemeth/Almon and Anathoth are not mentioned in Joshua 13–19.[106]

6. *Significance of the list in Chronicles.* Japhet, 163–65, observes that in Joshua the Levitical cities indicate that the goals of the conquest have been accomplished (see Josh 21:43-45). The Chronicler, however, has deliberately changed the list from a distribution of land to the Levites to a description of where the priests and Levites lived at the time of David.[107] The Levites, mentioned at the center of the genealogical introduction to the books

---

97 Albright, "List," 53. In 1 Chr 7:28 it is listed among the settlements of Ephraim.

98 Na'aman, "Levitical Cities," 220, notes that Golan had already been assigned as a city of refuge to Manasseh.

99 See Josh 19:20 LXX; in MT it is miswritten as והרבית "Rabbith."

100 Remeth. See textual note 66.

101 If this is a reference to Chisloth-tabor, it would have been taken from the boundary description of Zebulun in Josh 19:12.

102 "Levitical Cities," 224.

103 See the apparatus in *BHS* to Josh 19:28.

104 Na'aman, "Levitical Cities," 225; Noth, *Josua*, 126, 129.

105 It is commonly agreed that אשתמה = אשתמע.

106 Schmitt, "Levitenstädte," 44–47, provides an interesting alternate possibility for the origin of the names of the Aaronide cities. He notes the presence

of Hebron and Libni in the old genealogy of Num 26:58 (and in 1 Chronicles 6), but notes that while the names of Jattir, Eshtemoa, Hilen, Debir, Ashan, and Juttah do appear in Joshua 15, they are assigned to three separate provinces there and Debir appears out of order. He observes that these six cities are not important, except for Debir, and that they lie in close geographic proximity. He adds, speculatively, that they are in the general region of the tribe of Simeon, who is associated with militant Levites in early tradition. Could these cities have become possessions of the Levites, and the author then used them as his base when constructing a list of Levitical cities to match the command of Moses in Num 35:1-8? He would have included Anathoth and Alemeth because they were well-known priestly cities (cf. Neh 3:22; 12:28).

107 Oeming, *Wahre Israel*, 155, also speaks of the panIsraelite claim of the Levites in this context, although he errs in my judgment in finding an antiSamaritan tenor in the list.

of Chronicles, are settled in the land as much as any tribe, and their distribution relates them to the all Israel theme. The other tribes have their territories and their land possessions; the priests and Levites have only their cities and their pasturelands. The genealogies and territories of both laity and clergy show the unity and completeness of Israel. The rights of the Levites are independent of the priests, and the priestly cities are listed first. The vast majority of the priestly and Levitical cities are outside Yehud, but this does not, in Japhet's opinion, represent a concrete demand for actual property rights. This holds true regardless of whether one holds that the list originally represented an administrative document from the time of the united monarchy, or, as I prefer, a list developed from the tribal inheritances of the other tribes and the list of the cities of refuge. According to Kartveit, the purpose of the list in 1 Chronicles 6 is to give a clerical interpretation of the entire land, and the Cisjordanian sites were all made into asylum cities.[108]

Literary Criticism of 5:27—6:66 (6:1-81)

Rudolph believed that of all the materials dealing with the clergy in 5:27—6:66 (6:1-81) only 6:1-9, 14-15 (6:16-24, 29-30) was original (the genealogy of the regular Levites without the sidebar tracing the ancestry of Samuel). The rest of the materials were added in several stages. At least three stages in the development of the Levitical genealogies were identified by Rudolph in this chapter: the genealogy of the sons of Kohath without the Samuel sidebar, the genealogy with this sidebar, and the present shape of the genealogy of the Levitical singer Heman, which has fully integrated the Samuel genealogy into the genealogy of Kohath-Heman. But there is no compelling reason to date these changes later than the Chronicler or even to attribute them to the Chronicler himself. These developments may all predate the writing of the Chronicler. Kartveit proposes a com-

plicated literary history for this pericope. In simplified form it puts 6:1-34 (16-49) on a first level, 5:27-41 (6:1-15) at the second level, and 6:35-66 (48-81) at a third level.[109] Oeming, on the other hand, sees in the entire pericope, 5:27—6:66 (6:1-81), clear structures and a well-planned arrangement, and I agree.[110]

Detailed Commentary

5:27-41 (6:1-15). Genealogy of High Priests

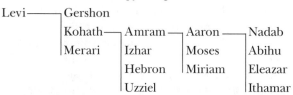

■ **27 (6:1)** *The sons of Levi: Gershon, Kohath, and Merari:* This is the standard list of the sons of Levi (cf. Gen 46:11; Exod 6:16; Num 3:17; 26:57; 1 Chr 6:1 [16]; 23:6; see the genealogical chart "Descendants of Levi-1"). A more archaic listing of the sons of Levi appears in Num 26:58: the clan of the Libnites, the clan of the Hebronites, the clan of the Mahlites, the clan of the Mushites, and the clan of the Korahites.[111] Gershon (גרשון), as in P,[112] is normally spelled Gershom[113] in Chronicles, including references within the genealogies of the ordinary Levites and the Levitical singers in 1 Chr 6:1, 2, 5, 28 (6:16, 17, 20, 43); 15:7,[114] but the spelling Gershon does appear in 23:6 and the word Gershonite(s) is used in 23:7 (see my translation); 26:21; 29:8; and 2 Chr 29:12. The Gershonites camped on the west side of the tabernacle during the wilderness period (Num 3:23), and they were responsible for carrying the textile and skin components of the tabernacle (3:25-26; 4:24-26). During the wilderness period the Merarites camped on the north side of the tabernacle (3:35), and they were charged with carrying the planks, pillars, stands, and so on, of the tabernacle (3:36-37; 4:31-32).

---

108 *Motive und Schichten,* 163.

109 *Motive und Schichten,* 69–87.

110 *Wahre Israel,* 144.

111 See the discussion of Korah in 1 Chr 6:22 (37).

112 Gen 46:11; Exod 6:16; Num 3:17; 26:57. *NRSV* and *NJPS* translate "Gershom" in this verse.

113 Gershom is also the oldest son of Moses (Exod

2:22). He may be the unnamed son of Moses who was circumcised by Zipporah (Exod 4:24-26). Cf. Exod 18:3 and Judg 18:30.

114 The Gershomites also receive thirteen cities in 1 Chr 6:47, 56 (62, 71).

The Gershonites and the Merarites were supervised by Ithamar, Aaron's youngest son (4:28, 33).[115] The Chronicler focuses here only on the line of Kohath, leading to Aaron and the high priests, and ignores all the side lines stemming from Gershon and Merari, in contrast to the genealogy in Exod 6:16-23.[116] While the Kohathites became the most important of the Levitical ancestors, their location after Gershon may reflect a time before the ascendancy of the Aaronides. Frank Cross has suggested that Gershom was once a Mushite (descendant of Moses) clan.[117] In 1 Chr 6:32 (47) Mushi is identified as a son of Merari, representing either a decline in status or the fact that Zadokite Aaronides are responsible for this genealogy. The Kohathites, except for the house of Amram (Num 3:38), camped on the south side of the tabernacle and they were responsible for transporting the ark, the table, the lampstand, the altars, and the vessels of the sanctuary (Num 3:29-31; 4:15-20;[118] 7:9).

■ **28 (6:2)** *And the sons of Kohath: Amram, Izhar, Hebron, and Uzziel:* Cf. Exod 6:18; Num 3:19; 26:58 (which mentions only that Kohath was the father of Amram); 1 Chr 6:3 (18); 23:12; 24:20-25. In Exod 6:18 Kohath is credited with a lifespan of one hundred thirty-three years. Only the line of Amram is followed in the genealogy of the high priests. For descendants of Izhar see the commentary on 1 Chr 6:23 (38), and for the descendants of another son of Kohath, Amminadab, see the commentary on 6:22 (37).

■ **29 (6:3)** *And the children of Amram: Aaron, Moses, and Miriam:* The Chronicler omits the marriage of Amram to Jochebed his father's sister (Exod 6:20; Num 26:59),[119] but he includes Miriam among Amram's children, with Num 26:59.[120] This is the first mention of Moses in Chronicles.[121] The linear genealogy that begins with Aaron and is segmented in the first generation can be diagrammed as follows:

```
Aaron ──┬─ Nadab
        │  Abihu
        │  Eleazar─Phinehas─Abishua─Bukki─Uzzi─Zerahiah─Meraioth─Amariah─
        │          Ahitub─Zadok─Ahimaaz─Azariah–Johanan–Azariah–Amariah–
        │          Ahitub─Zadok–Shallum–Hilkiah–Azariah–Seraiah–Jehozadak
        └─ Ithamar
```

And the sons of Aaron: Nadab, Abihu, Eleazar, and Ithamar: The Chronicler's genealogy is supported by Exod 6:23; Num 3:2; 26:60; 1 Chr 24:1. He does not refer here to the sins of Nadab and Abihu and their premature deaths (Lev 10:1-2; 1 Chr 24:2), nor to Ahimelech, who also served with Zadok as a priest during the reign of David, being descended from Ithamar (1 Chr 24:3), but keeps his attention solely on the line of Aaron.

■ **30 (6:4)** *Eleazar became the father of Phineas, Phinehas became the father of Abishua:* Eleazar and Phinehas are mentioned in the genealogy at Exod 6:25, where we are also told the name of Eleazar's wife, Putiel. The Penta-

115 For other references to Merari in Chronicles see 1 Chr 6:14 (29); 29-32 (44-47); 9:14; 23:21-23; 24:27-30; 26:10-11, 19; 2 Chr 29:12; 34:12. Twenty descendants of Merari joined Ezra in his return to Jerusalem (Ezra 8:19).

116 See also 1 Chr 15:5, where Uriel leads one hundred twenty Kohathite priests, and 2 Chr 29:12, where Joel the son of Azariah led the Kohathites in the days of Hezekiah. Josiah used Zechariah and Meshullam of the house of Kohath as musicians (2 Chr 34:12). In 1 Chr 9:32 Kohathites are in charge of the rows of bread for the Sabbath.

117 *Canaanite Myth*, 198.

118 The Kohathite Levites carry them only after the items have been wrapped by the sons of Aaron (Num 4:5-14).

119 Cf. the law on incest in Lev 18:12.

120 Cf. Exod 6:20 LXX and SP. In Exod 15:20 Miriam is called Aaron's sister, and in Num 12:1, 5 she and Aaron speak against Moses and she is punished with leprosy (Num 12:10, 15). Micah speaks about God sending Moses, Aaron, and Miriam before Israel during the wilderness period (6:4).

121 He also appears in 1 Chr 6:34 (49); 15:15; 21:29;

teuch reports the death of Aaron and the installation of Eleazar as his successor in Num 20:25-29, and it also records the covenant of perpetual priesthood that God made with Phinehas because of his decisive actions in spearing one of the Israelites, Zimri, and the Midianite woman Cozbi he had brought into his family in Num 25:6-9, 14-15 (cf. Num 31:6). Later Phinehas ministered before the ark at Bethel (Judg 20:28).

■ **34 (6:8)** *Ahitub became the father of Zadok, Zadok became the father of Ahimaaz:* In the subsequent narrative there is more about Zadok than any of the other priests mentioned in this genealogy, although there is little about character development or his lineage, and he is never called "high priest." Among the people rallying to David at Hebron is Zadok, a young warrior (נער גבור חיל) accompanied by twenty-two commanders from his ancestral house (1 Chr 12:29 [28]). The previous two verses mention four thousand six hundred Levites and Jehoiada, leader of the house of Aaron. Next the priests Zadok and Abiathar are summoned by David to bring the ark to Jerusalem (15:11), and David stationed Zadok before the tabernacle that was at the high place at Gibeon to offer burnt offerings (16:39). In the list of David's officers, Zadok son of Ahitub and Ahimelech son of Abiathar are identified as priests (18:16//2 Sam 8:17[122]). The organization of the priests in 1 Chronicles 24 takes place under David's direction along with Zadok of the sons of Eleazar and Ahimelech of the sons of Ithamar (v. 3, thus making also Ahimelech a descendant of Aaron through his fourth son;[123] cf. v. 6, where Ahimelech is called the son of Abiathar, and v. 31). Sixteen heads of ancestral houses came from the descendants of Eleazar and only eight from the descendants of Ithamar. Among the leaders of the tribes in chap. 27, Zadok is mentioned as leader (נגיד) of the "tribe" of Aaron

(27:17). In 29:22 the people anoint Solomon as Yahweh's prince and Zadok as priest.[124] Solomon and Zadok will carry out the temple plans made by David. Zadok could not be chief priest without a temple.[125] Zadok is not mentioned during the building and dedication of the temple, presumably because his name was not found in the Chronicler's *Vorlage.* Finally, during the reign of Hezekiah, the chief priest Azariah is said to be of the house of Zadok (2 Chr 31:10).[126]

The lineage of both Ahitub and Zadok has been vigorously debated among OT scholars. On the basis of 1 Sam 1:3; 2:34; 4:4, 11, 17, 21; 14:3, 22:9, 20 one could link Abiathar, Zadok, and Ahitub to the line of Eli, as the following diagram shows:

```
Eli───────Hophni
         │Phinehas───Ichabod
         │           │Ahitub────Ahijah
         │           │          Ahimelech───Abiathar
         │           │Zadok
```

This genealogy, which makes Zadok Abiathar's uncle, conflicts with 1 Sam 2:27-36 and 1 Kgs 2:26-27, which declare that the family of Zadok will succeed the family of Eli in the priesthood, with the family of the latter experiencing deep grief in the process. Historically this was realized with the banishment of Abiathar to Anathoth and the selection of Zadok as Solomon's sole priest (1 Kings 1–2). It is not at all certain, however, that the Ahitub mentioned in these verses in Samuel is the same as the Ahitub identified as Zadok's father in 2 Sam 8:17.[127] The MT of the latter verse is generally recognized as being corrupt: "Zadok son of Ahitub and Ahimelech son of Abiathar were priests." Wellhausen

---

22:13; 23:13-15; 26:24; and twelve times in 2 Chronicles.

122 This is Zadok's first appearance in the Deuteronomistic History.

123 According to 1 Sam 14:3 and 22:20 Abiathar is a son of Ahimelech and a descendant of Eli.

124 The anointing of the (high) priest is referred to in Lev 4:3, 5, 16, and 6:15. In 1 Kgs 1:39 Zadok anoints Solomon, but there is no mention of his own anointing.

125 Rooke, *Zadok's Heirs: The Role and Development of the*

High Priesthood in Ancient Israel (Oxford: Oxford Univ. Press, 2000), 203.

126 Zadok, the father of Jotham's mother, mentioned in 2 Chr 27:1//2 Kgs 15:33, is a different individual.

127 Chronicles makes explicit that they are not the same person, since Ahitub the father of Zadok is not a descendant of Eli. The ambiguity in Samuel may have caused some confusion since the priests descended from Zadok *replaced* the house of Eli.

emended that text to read: "Zadok, and Abiathar son of Ahimelech son of Ahitub," thus leaving Zadok without a father's name. Cross, on the other hand, proposed the emendation: "Zadok the son of Ahitub, and Abiathar the son of Ahimelech."[128] The genealogy of the high priests in Chronicles connects Ahitub the father of Zadok I not to Eli's son Phinehas but to Amariah, a descendant of Aaron.

Who was Zadok and what was his lineage? The first mention of Zadok in the Deuteronomistic History is in the list of David's officers (2 Sam 8:15-18), discussed in the previous paragraph, with no explanation of how he achieved his position as priest (2 Sam 8:17//1 Chr 18:16; cf. 2 Sam 20:25). Several passages describe Zadok and Abiathar as "the priests" (2 Sam 15:35; 17:15; 19:11; 1 Kgs 4:4; 1 Chr 15:11). In 2 Sam 15:24-29, 35, Zadok and Abiathar are identified as custodians of the ark of the covenant, which David tells them to take back to Jerusalem during his flight from Absalom. Zadok was made Solomon's sole priest after Abiathar sided with Adonijah in his failed coup d'etat in David's dying days (1 Kgs 2:35). For Zadok's role in Chronicles, see the discussion above.

Despite this paucity of information there has been no lack of proposals on the background of Zadok.[129] E. Auerbach put him at Gibeon prior to his service in Jerusalem (cf. 1 Chr 16:39), and suggested that David brought him to Jerusalem because of the oracle in 2 Sam 21:1.[130] There is no firm evidence, prior to the passage from 1 Chronicles 16 (see the commentary there), that Zadok was ever in Gibeon. Karl Budde, on the basis of a textual emendation, thought Zadok was an unnamed brother of Uzzah, the man who was killed for touching the ark (2 Sam 6:3-4).[131] He also identified Uzzah with Eleazar (1 Sam 7:1). But this brother is not mentioned when the ark comes to Jerusalem in 2 Samuel 6, and it is hard to imagine that he would still be functioning under Solomon if his brother had lived at the time of the cap-

ture of the ark, some sixty years earlier. A number of scholars have supposed that Zadok was a priest at a Jebusite shrine in Jerusalem, before David captured the city.[132] Cross has criticized this theory for a number of reasons, noting that the appellative ṣdq is not limited to Jerusalem and that the Bible nowhere directly attests this lineage. Cross sees no reason to doubt Zadok's descent from Aaron through Ahitub, as in this genealogy in Chronicles and in 2 Sam 8:17 (as emended above). Moreover, he believes that the rivalry between Zadok and Abiathar echoes that between the priestly family of Aaron and priests descended from Moses (the Mushites). The Aaronides have connections with Hebron (Josh 21:10, 13; 1 Chr 6:42 [57]), and Zadok, a young warrior, was among those who joined up with David at Hebron (1 Chr 12:29 [28]). In an attempt to balance the contending priestly houses, Jeroboam I set up an Aaronide temple at Bethel and a Mushite shrine in Dan, just as David had chosen as priests representatives from both leading priestly houses. Olyan has developed this idea in a different direction, suggesting that Zadok was the son and aide of the Aaronide priest Jehoiada mentioned in 1 Chr 12:28 (27). Jehoiada in his view was also the father of Benaiah, one of David's military leaders, who commanded the Cherethites and Pelethites (2 Sam 8:18; 20:23) or David's bodyguard (1 Chr 11:25), and who sided with Solomon, Zadok, and Nathan in the struggle against Adonijah. Zadok, Benaiah, and Jehoiada came from Kabzeel (MR 148071), not Hebron, a town in southern Judah that supported David (2 Sam 23:30//1 Chr 11:22).[133] But why does our genealogy of Zadok not go back through Jehoiada if he was a descendant of Aaron? This reconstruction, while plausible, has many uncertainties and does little to explain the genealogy of the high priests as it is presented here in Chronicles. Indeed, it is improbable that all the preexilic priests were Zadokites, let alone descendants of Aaron. Only the high priest Azariah in the reign

128 Cross, "Priestly Houses," in *Canaanite Myth*, 213–14.

129 For an excellent survey of the proposals see George W. Ramsey, "Zadok," *ABD* 6:1034–36.

130 "Die Herkunft der Ṣadokiden," *ZAW* 49 (1931) 327–28.

131 "Die Herkunft Ṣadok," *ZAW* 52 (1934) 42–50.

132 For details of this theory see Ramsey, "Zadok," 1035.

133 Saul Olyan, "Zadok's Origins and the Tribal Politics of David," *JBL* 101 (1982) 177–93.

of Hezekiah is said to be of the house of Zadok (2 Chr 31:10).

The biblical materials on Ahimaaz, no. 12 in our list of high priests, and the son of Zadok according to v. 34, indicate that he and Jonathan the son of Abiathar served as messengers who reported espionage from Absalom's camp to David (2 Sam 15:27, 36; 17:17-20). Ahimaaz brought David a positive or at least noncommittal message after the death of Absalom until another messenger showed up and told David the bitter truth (2 Sam 18:19-30). An Ahimaaz was one of Solomon's district officials in Naphtali, but there is no way of telling whether this is the same person (1 Kgs 4:15). In short, there is nothing that confirms that Ahimaaz actually served as a priest, let alone as the high priest.

■ **35 (6:9)** *Ahimaaz became the father of Azariah (it was he who served as priest in the temple that Solomon built in Jerusalem), Azariah became the father of Johanan:* In 1 Kgs 4:2 we read in the first line of a list of Solomon's high officials that Azariah was the son of Zadok. If "son" is to be taken literally and not in the sense of "descendant," Azariah and Ahimaaz were brothers, not son and father as in the present genealogy. The passage from Kings is not included in the Chronicler's narrative. The parenthesis identifying Amariah with the building of the temple has been moved here from v. 36 (6:10); see textual note 2. Amariah II, whose name I believe was lost from the genealogy at this point when three names fell out by haplography, served as high priest (כהן הראש) during the reign of Jehoshaphat, who put him over "all the matters of Yahweh" (2 Chr 19:11; see the commen-

tary there).[134] Amariah is the first to have this title, and three other priests have this title in Chronicles (Jehoiada, 2 Chr 24:11;[135] Azariah, who served under King Uzziah, 26:20; and Azariah, who served under King Hezekiah, 31:10), which appears to be the official name for the office before the exile.[136] The postexilic name for this office הכהן הגדול is only attested in the MT for Hilkiah, who served during the reign of Josiah (2 Chr 34:9//2 Kgs 23:4). Jehoiada's name was also lost through the same haplography, though the Chronicler glorifies his career by having him live to be one hundred thirty years old and by putting his grave with that of the kings (2 Chr 22:11—24:17; see the commentary there). Azariah is the third name that dropped out of the genealogy. He rebuked Uzziah for daring to offer a sacrifice in the temple and constrained the king to make a quick exit from it (26:17, 20; see the commentary there).[137] Uriah, the high priest under Ahaz, built an altar after the model Ahaz had sent from Damascus and did everything this highly criticized king asked of him. He was omitted from the genealogy and is not mentioned in the Chronicler's account of Ahaz in 2 Chronicles 28. Nothing is known about Johanan.[138]

■ **36 (6:10)** *Johanan became the father of Azariah:* Azariah is identified in 2 Chr 31:10 as coming from the house of Zadok, and in 31:13 he is called chief officer of the house of God (נגיד בית האלהים).[139] He is to be identifed as Azariah III in my reconstruction.[140] Hezekiah and Azariah appointed Levites to oversee the collection and storage of the tithe.

134 Rudolph, 55, associates the Azariah mentioned in 2 Chronicles 11 with the person mentioned in v. 37, who I believe served some time late in the reign of Hezekiah or in the time of one of his successors.

135 Steven J. Schweitzer, "The Presentation and the Function of the High Priest in Chronicles" (paper presented at the SBL annual meeting, Toronto, 2002) 19, n. 33, observes that the Chronicler has replaced הכהן הגדול from the *Vorlage* in 2 Kgs 12:11 (10) with this title, which he interprets as a diminishment of Jehoiada's role. But Chronicles LXX reads ἱερέως τοῦ μεγάλου, which may be the original reading and suggests that the change may have been made in the course of the textual transmission of Chronicles and not by the Chronicler himself.

136 Rooke, *Zadok's Heirs,* 214.

137 Rudolph, 55, is unable to assign this verse to any priest in the genealogy.

138 Schweitzer, "Presentation," proposed that the Chronicler inserted this name between the two Azariahs and took the name from the current high priest at the time the Chronicler was writing. This seems like a very mechanical view of the creation of ancient genealogies.

139 Rooke, *Zadok's Heirs,* 215, interprets this as a title implying administrative oversight over the temple. See also 1 Chr 9:11 and 2 Chr 35:8, and the genealogy of Hilkiah in 1 Chr 5:39 (6:13).

140 Rudolph, 55, says that the passages in chap. 31 do not fit the Azariah (III) mentioned in v. 36 (#15) or in v. 39 (= Azariah IV, #21), although Rothstein, 114, had opted for the latter option. Gary N.

■ 39 (6:13) *Shallum became the father of Hilkiah, Hilkiah became the father of Azariah:* Hilkiah was the high priest who found the book of the law during the reign of Josiah and who inquired of Huldah about its significance (2 Kgs 22:4–23:24//2 Chr 34:9–35:8). During the Passover celebration, Hilkiah, Zechariah, and Jeiel are referred to as the chief officers of the house of God. Bulla no. 27, excavated in Jerusalem and dated to the stratum destroyed by the Babylonians, reads: "To Azariah the son of Hilkiah," and may well offer physical evidence of these two high priests.[141]

■ 40 (6:14) *Azariah became the father of Seraiah, Seraiah became the father of Jehozadak:* When Jerusalem fell, Nebuzaradan the captain of the guard took Seraiah and many other officials to Riblah in Syria (MR 296427), where they were executed (2 Kgs 25:18-21). Seraiah is not mentioned in the Chronicler's narrative. Jehozadak is mentioned in the Bible only as the father of Joshua the high priest after the return from exile.[142]

■ 41 (6:15) *Jehozadak went into exile when Yahweh exiled Judah and Jerusalem by the hand of Nebuchadnezzar:* This is the first reference to Nebuchadnezzar and the fall of the southern kingdom in the book after three previous references to the exile in the north (vv. 6, 22, 26). Nebuchadnezzar will next be mentioned in 2 Chr 36:6-17.[143] Indeed, only 1 Chr 9:1 mentions the exile of Judah again, since 2 Chr 36:17-21 refers only to the exile of Jerusalem and then obliquely. While the exile is attributed to Yahweh's initiative,[144] no theological justification for this action is offered here. But, as Johnstone observed, "It is, then not accidental, that the line of the priesthood is traced . . . only as far as Johazadak, the high-priest carried off into exile by Nebuchadnezzar. Nothing could emphasize more clearly that the mere rites as such can neither suffice nor avail to expunge the guilt even of its

officiants."[145] Even the cult does not protect anyone *ex opere operato* from the judgment of God.[146]

6:1-15 (16-30). Genealogy of Regular Levites

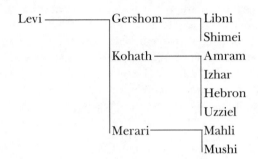

■ 1 (16) *The sons of Levi: Gershom, Kohath, and Merari:* For commentary on the sons of Levi, see 1 Chr 5:27 (6:1), where the name of the oldest son of Levi is spelled Gershon. The Chronicler now presents a genealogy for the regular Levites after presenting only the priestly line in 5:27-41 (6:1-15).

■ 2 (17) *These are the names of the sons of Gershom: Libni and Shimei:* Cf. Exod 6:17 and Num 3:18, 21 for the same information. The only exception to this genealogical listing for Gershom is in 1 Chr 23:7-9 and 26:21, where Ladan is listed as the oldest son of Gershom instead of Libni (see the commentary there). An old genealogical source identifies the families of Levi as the Libnites, Hebronites, Mahlites, Mushites, and Korahites (Num 26:58). That Libni and Libnites are always listed as the firstborn demonstrates their prominence. It is usually thought that Libni is related to the Judahite town Libnah.[147] On Libni the son of Mahli see the commentary on 1 Chr 6:14 (29).

Knoppers, "The Relationship of the Priestly Genealogies to the History of the High Priesthood in Jerusalem," in Lipschits and Blenkinsopp, *Judah and the Judeans,* 114, n. 19, denies this identification since Azariah III "appears after the time of Ḥilqiah." Unfortunately he has confused Azariah III and Azariah IV (see 5:39 [6:13]).

141 Tsvi Schneider, "Azariahu Son of Hilkiahu (High Priest?) on a City of David Bulla," *IEJ* 38 (1988) 138–41.

142 Hag 1:1, 12, 14; 2:2, 4; Zech 6:11.

143 The five references there are all written plene,

while the name here is spelled without a vowel letter (cf. 2 Kgs 24:1, 10; 25:1, 8; Jer 28:11, 14).

144 Cf. 1 Chr 5:26; 2 Chr 12:5-7; 28:5.

145 William Johnstone, "Guilt and Atonement: The Theme of 1 and 2 Chronicles," in *A Word in Season* (FS William McKane; ed. J. D. Martin and P. R. Davies; JSOTSup 42; Sheffield: Sheffield Academic Press, 1986) 130.

146 Oeming, *Wahre Israel*, 153.

147 Cf. the list of towns assigned to the sons of Aaron in 1 Chr 6:42 (57).

■ **3 (18)** *The sons of Kohath: Amram, Izhar, Hebron, and Uzziel:* The same sons of Kohath are listed in Exod 6:18 and Num 3:19. See also the commentary on 1 Chr 5:28 (6:2).

■ **4 (19)** *The sons of Merari: Mahli and Mushi:* The same sons of Merari are given in Exod 6:19; Num 3:20, 33; 1 Chr 23:21; 24:26. On Merari see the commentary on 5:27 (6:1). An old genealogy in Num 26:28 makes the Libnites, Hebronites, Mahlites,[148] Mushites, and Korahites clans of Levi. Cross has proposed that the Mushites were a priestly clan, descended from Moses, once attached to the sanctuary at Shiloh.[149]

These are the clans of the Levites according to their fathers: This clause has been taken from Num 3:20b and modified to fit the present context. In Numbers it served as a conclusion to Num 3:17-20, the introductory paragraph on the Levitical census, but here it introduces the following genealogical lists. The reference to the ancestral houses in Numbers (לבית אבתם)[150] has been replaced by a reference to the "fathers" (לאבותיהם), presumably because of people like Jeatherai, Shaul, and Asaiah, who headed Levitical groups when this genealogy was recorded (Japhet, 153).

■ **5-6 (20-21)** The linear genealogy of Gershom in these verses is:

Gershom—Libni—Jahath—Zimmah—Joah—Iddo—Zerah—Jeatherai

None of these individuals—except Gershom and Libni—is known elsewhere,[151] though some of these names are included among the ancestors of the singer Asaph. The names in the two genealogies will be compared in the commentary on the singers in vv. 24-28 (39-43). This linear genealogy places Jeatherai in the seventh generation after Gershom and serves to establish his status as some kind of Levitical official. See Shaul in v. 9 (24) and Asaiah in v. 15 (30).

■ **7-9 (22-24)** The linear genealogy of Kohath in these verses is:

Kohath—Amminadab—Korah—Assir—Elkanah—Ebiasaph—Assir—Tahath—Uriel—Uzziah—Shaul

The sons of Kohath: Amminadab his son, Korah his son, Assir his son, Elkanah his son, Ebiasaph his son, Assir his son: No completely satisfactory solution for the presence of Amminadab[152] as the son of Kohath in this genealogy has been achieved. He is not named among the four sons of Kohath in 1 Chr 5:28 (6:2) and 6:3 (18). On the basis of Exod 6:18, 21; Num 16:1, we might expect Izhar to be the son of Kohath and the father of Korah, and that name Izhar is attested by Codex Alexandrinus and a few other LXX manuscripts (see textual note 6).[153] The

---

148 Not in LXX.

149 *Canaanite Myth*, 190–215, esp. 196–98. Baruch Halpern, "Sectionalism and the Schism," *JBL* 93 (1974) 519–32; idem, "Levitic Participation in the Reform Cult of Jeroboam I," *JBL* 93 (1976) 31–41, believes that the Mushites were part of the opposition to Jeroboam's reform party.

150 At the same place in the genealogy, Exod 6:19 refers to "generations" (לתלדתם).

151 Joah son of Zimmah recurs in 2 Chr 29:12, as a contemporary of Hezekiah. Johnstone, 1:86, takes this as an indication that the list of names in this geneal-

ogy is incomplete. But the Chronicler in chap. 6 makes his Joah a predecessor of David, and hence the two sons of Joah the son of Zimmah are different individuals.

152 According to Exod 6:23, an Amminadab was the father-in-law of Aaron, and an Amminadab is listed among the sons of Uzziel who carried the ark in 1 Chr 15:10-11.

153 Rudolph, 55, favors Izhar and argues that this name was chosen since Amram was already the ancestor of the high priests in 1 Chr 5:27-41 (6:1-15). Rudolph's complicated proposal on how Ammi-

genealogy of the other two regular Levitical families, those descended from the other sons of Levi, Gershom and Merari, is passed on through their *oldest* son, while the genealogy of the Levitical singers passes through the second or third son, Jahath for Gershom,[154] Mushi for Merari, and Izhar for Kohath (1 Chr 6:23 [38]). The logical choice for this linear genealogy leading to Shaul, therefore, would be Amram, the oldest son of Kohath. We can understand why Amram was not the son of Kohath through whom this line is traced because the line of high priests had already been traced through Amram the oldest son of Kohath (5:30 [6:3]; cf. 23:13), but the reason behind the choice of the name Amminadab is not clear since he is nowhere else listed as a son of Kohath. Both Amram and Amminadab begin with the same two Hebrew letters, *'ayin* and *mêm*. Amminadab's son is Korah, who is the grandson of Kohath, just as Korah is the son of Izhar and the grandson of Kohath in the genealogy of the Levitical singers (v. 23 [38]). Are these two Korahs the same individual with a divergent genealogy, or are they to be understood as two separate individuals? Assir is the son of Korah here and his grandson in the pedigree of the singer Heman (v. 22 [37]).

Shaul is in the tenth generation after Kohath, always a favorable position in a genealogy. Assir, Elkanah, and Ebiasaph comprise the three generations after Korah, but they are listed as siblings and all sons of Korah in Exod 6:24. Perhaps they were changed from siblings to father, son, and grandson, to come up with ten names in the lineage. On the other hand, if we assume that only

the second name "Assir" is original, and that a marginal reference to Assir's brothers Elkanah and Ebiasaph was mistakenly included in the genealogy, with the expression "his son" placed after each name,[155] then the second Assir resulted from a conflation of the two variant genealogies: variant 1: Korah—Assir; and variant 2: Korah—Elkanah—Abiasaph—Assir were conflated to make Korah—Assir—Elkanah—Abiasaph—Assir. We can then reconstruct the following genealogy for Shaul that extends for only seven generations after Kohath:[156] Kohath—Amminadab—Korah—Assir—Tahath—Uriel—Uzziah—Shaul

■ **9 (24)** *Tahath his son, Uriel his son, Uzziah his son, and Shaul his son:* A Kohathite by the name of Uriel,[157] a chief, with one hundred twenty of his kindred, was among those assembled by David to bring up the ark to Jerusalem (1 Chr 15:5, 11), but since neither his father nor his son is given in chap. 15 it is impossible to tell whether the same individual was meant. The other individual Levites in this verse are unknown. The conjunction "and" before Saul indicates that he is the last in the series and the one for whose benefit the linear genealogy was preserved.[158]

---

nadab arose out of the reading Izhar is not convincing.

154 See the discussion of v. 28 (43) below, where I suggest that Shimei and Jahath have traded places, which would suggest that the line once went back through Shimei to Gershom.

155 The *wāw* conjunction, which would have been needed when the three names were considered brothers, is still retained before Ebiasaph. Rudolph, 54, deletes the last בנו in v. 7 (22) after Assir, and the first in v. 8 (23) after Elkanah (textual note 7), and changes the second בנו in v. 8 (23) to בניו "his sons" (textual note 9) and so reconstructs the three men as brothers. But the result is a text that reads: "Korah his son, Assir, Elkanah, and Ebiasaph, his sons, Assir his son." See André Lefèvre, "Note

d'exégèse sur les généalogies des Qehatites," *RSR* 37 (1950) 287–92; and Johnson, *Purpose*, 71–73.

156 Of course, in the present form of the list he is in the tenth generation after Kohath, also a favorable position. In the list of high priests (1 Chr 5:27-42 [6:1-15]), Zadok and Ahimaaz are in the twelfth and thirteenth generations after Kohath.

157 The son of Tahath in the Kohath-Heman genealogy is Zephaniah. See below.

158 Rudolph, 56, conjectures on the basis of this conjunction that Saul is secondary.

■ **10-13 (25-28)** The linear genealogy of Samuel is inserted after Assir from the genealogy of Kohath discussed above:

Kohath—Amminadab—Korah—Assir—

Elkanah I ⌐Amasai—Elkanah II—Zuphai—Nahath—Eliab—Jeroham—Elkanah III—Samuel ⌐Joel
          └Mahath   └Abijah

In these verses the genealogy of Kohath the son of Levi branches off to give Samuel a Levitical pedigree. The book of Samuel begins with the following genealogical notice (1 Sam 1:1): "There was a certain man of Ramath-aim, a Zuphite from the hill country of Ephraim, whose name was Elkanah, the son of Jeroham, the son of Elihu, the son of Toah,[159] the son of Zuph, an Ephraimite." Here is a graphic representation of that genealogy: Ephraim—unknown number of generations—Zuph—Toah—Elihu—Jeroham—Elkanah
Later tradition may have found it offensive that Samuel, an Ephraimite, not a Levite, "ministered to Yahweh under Eli" at the sanctuary of Shiloh (1 Sam 3:1). It seems probable that the priest Eli at Shiloh had a Mushite ancestry,[160] though the text in Samuel does not indicate the intervening links between Eli and Moses in that genealogy, nor would Eli's ancestry provide a Leviti-cal link for Samuel since the two men were not related to each another. It is sometimes proposed on the basis of Judg 12:5[161] and 17:7[162] that Samuel was in fact a Levite, who happened to reside in Ephraim.[163] But that seems unlikely, and earlier biblical tradition has no record of any explicit genealogical link of Samuel to the Levites, nor does the book of Samuel ever identify Samuel as a Levite. By giving Samuel a Levitical lineage the genealogy in Chronicles exonerates him from the possibility of inappropriate cultic activity. Samuel's enhanced status is then used in the genealogy of the Kohath-Heman singers to legitimate the priority position of Heman, who is identified as the grandson of Samuel (see below on v. 18 [33]; cf. Japhet, 155–56).

■ **10-11a (25-26a)** *The sons of Elkanah: Amasai and his brother Mahath. Elkanah his son:* The first Elkanah (Elka-nah I) is considered a brother of Assir and Ebiasaph in Exod 6:24, and all three men are identified there as sons of Korah, but in the pedigree of Shaul, just discussed, this Elkanah is the son of Assir and the father of Ebias-aph, who is in turn the father of another Assir (vv. 7-8 [22-23]). Samuel's genealogy is connected to the Leviti-cal line through this Elkanah I. We can surmise that the genealogy of Samuel was linked via Elkanah to the Kohathite line because Elkanah was also the name of Samuel's own father. We do not know the source for the pair of brothers, Amasai and Mahath,[164] identified as Elkanah I's sons, or of the Elkanah mentioned in the next generation after them, whom I would identify as Elkanah II.

159   תוה with LXX and LXX^L; MT תחו.

160   1 Sam 2:27. Cf. Cross, *Canaanite Myth,* 197–98, 207. In 1 Chr 24:3 the Chronicler traced Ahimelech, the descendant of Eli, back to Ithamar, the fourth son of Aaron (Exod 6:23). For discussion see the com-mentary there.

161   F. X. Kugler, "Angebliche Übertreibungen der bib-lischen Chronik," *Stimmen der Zeit* 109 (1925) 252–54, argued that fugitives from the Ephraimite army could claim that they were not descendants of Ephraim, but they only resided in Ephraim. Rudolph, 57, argues that Jephthah would not have been persuaded by such sophistry. If people were part of the Ephraimite army, they were Ephraimites.

162   "There was a young man of Bethlehem in Judah, of the clan of Judah. He was a Levite residing there." Rudolph, 57, points out that this text is probably corrupt and that the young man from Bethlehem came from the clan of Gershom. Boling, *Judges,* 256–57, construes the verse somewhat differently, but also confirms that the original text said that the Levite was a resident alien in Judah.

163   Kugler, 252–54; Williamson, 72.

164   These two names appear as father and son in the Kohath-Heman genealogy of singers (v. 20 [35]), dated by the Chronicler to the time of David. A dif-ferent Amasai-Mahath father-son pair shows up dur-ing the reign of Hezekiah, some two hundred fifty years later (2 Chr 29:12).

■ **11b-12 (26b-27)** *Zuphai his son, Nahath his son, Eliab his son, Jeroham his son, Elkanah his son, Samuel his son:* Samuel's father Elkanah (cf. 1 Sam 1:1) is Elkanah III in vv. 10-13 (25-28) and Samuel's grandfather is Jeroham both in this verse and in 1 Sam 1:1. Elihu (אליהוא) from 1 Sam 1:1 can be identified with Eliab (אליאב) of 1 Chr 6:12 (27),[165] Toah (תוח) from 1 Sam 1:1 can be identified with Nahath (נחת) in 1 Chr 6:11 (26),[166] and Zuph (or the Zuphite) from 1 Sam 1:1 with Zuphai in 1 Chr 6:11 (26).

■ **13 (28)** *The sons of Samuel: Joel his firstborn, the second Abijah:* According to the book of Samuel, Samuel appointed these two sons as judges over Israel, but they reportedly took bribes and perverted justice, leading the elders of Israel to request Samuel to appoint a king (1 Sam 8:1-5).

■ **14-15 (29-30)** The linear genealogy of Merari in these verses is:

Merari—Mahli—Libni—Shimei—Uzzah—Shimea—Haggaiah—Asaiah

■ **14 (29)** *The sons of Merari:*[167] *Mahli his son:* Cf. v. 4 (19); Exod 6:19; Num 3:20, 33; 26:58. In 1 Chr 23:21-22 the sons of Mahli the son of Merari are given as Eleazar (who died without sons) and Kish, whose sons married Eleazar's daughters.[168]

■ **15 (30)** *Asaiah his son:* None of the Levitical descendants of Merari, from Libni the son of Mahli through Haggaiah, is known.[169] Asaiah, a chief, from the sons of Merari, however, was one of the persons commanded by David to bring the ark to Jerusalem (1 Chr 15:6, 11), and his Levitical credentials are supplied by these verses.

6:16-34 (31-49). Genealogy of Levitical Singers and Duties of Clergy

■ **16 (31)** *These are the people whom David appointed over the song in the house of Yahweh, after the ark had come to a rest:*

With David's transfer of the ark to Jerusalem,[170] a marked change in the status of the Levites occurred according to the Chronicler. Since the Levites no longer had to carry the ark, David assigned them other duties, primarily their leadership in the service of song in the temple.[171] In 1 Chr 15:1—16:43 (cf. 2 Chr 35:3),[172] the Chronicler reports David's initiation of this new role,[173] at first on a provisional basis (1 Chr 15:16-24) and then more permanently (16:4-7, 37-42). David's association with music is also attested in the Psalter[174] and in the account of the transfer of the ark to Jerusalem (2 Sam 6:5),[175] so his leadership role in establishing the cultic music of the temple comes as no surprise. Cultic music and singing may well go back to the time of David, but it is highly probable that the particular organization of the singing guilds in 1 Chronicles 6 reflects the Chronicler's

---

165 Cf. Eliel in 1 Chr 6:19 (34).

166 This name is spelled Toah (תוה) in 1 Chr 6:19 (34).

167 In the transportation of the tabernacle, the sons of Merari were responsible for the structural elements of the court and tent (Num 4:29-33).

168 Cf. 1 Chr 24:26, 28, and 29.

169 Libni and Shimei, the son and grandson of Mahli, have the same names as the two sons of Gershom in v. 2 (17).

170 Jerusalem was its place of rest (1 Chr 22:9; 28:2).

171 Cf. 1 Chr 15:16-24; 16:4-36; 25:6, 7; 2 Chr 8:14; 19:8; 20:21-22; 23:18-19; 29:25, 28; 31:2; 35:2. Also Johnstone, 1:89.

172 Von Rad, *Geschichtsbild*, 98–115. David's appointment of Levites is also treated in 1 Chronicles 23–26.

173 Cf. 1 Chr 15:16-17; 22:2; 2 Chr 8:14; 11:22; 19:5, 8; 20:21; 23:10, 19; 24:13; 29:25; 30:5; 31:2; 34:32; 35:2. See also Johnstone, 1:89.

174 See also the reference to David inventing musical instruments (Amos 6:5; cf. Neh 12:36; 1 Chr 23:5; 2 Chr 29:26, 27) and to David as the "singer of Israel's songs" (2 Sam 23:1 *NIV;* but see *NRSV*). In the History of David's Rise (1 Sam 16:14—2 Sam 5:10), David is reported to be a skilled player of the lyre, though this music is apparently without cultic connotation (1 Sam 16:14-23).

175 "David and all the house of Israel were dancing before the LORD with all their might, with songs and lyres and harps and tambourines and castanets and cymbals."

own time and is merely backdated to the tenth century to establish its legitimacy.[176] The singers David appointed were divided into three guilds[177] taken from each of the great Levitical families of Kohath, Gershom, and Merari and headed by Heman,[178] Asaph, and Ethan.[179]

Hartmut Gese proposed the following stages of development of the singers in the postexilic period:[180]

I. At the beginning of the postexilic period temple singers were not considered Levites (Ezra 2:41; Neh 7:44). They were known only as "the sons of Asaph" (2 Chr 35:15; Ezra 3:10).

II. In Neh 11:3-19//1 Chr 9:1-18, which can be dated to the time of Nehemiah, the singers are identified as Levites. The two singer groups at this time are the sons of Asaph and the sons of Jeduthun.

III A. The Levitical singers were divided into three groups: Asaph, Heman, and Jeduthun (1 Chr 16:4-7; 2 Chr 5:12; 29:13-14; 35:15).

III B. Jeduthun was replaced by Ethan, and and sons of Heman had become the most prominent group of singers (1 Chr 6:16-32 [31-47]; 15:16-24).

Gese held that the Chronicler was at stage III.A and that III.B was a post-Chronistic layer; Williamson, 121, on the other hand, located the Chronicler at III.B.[181] The genealogies of the singers below, showing the preeminence of Heman and identifying Ethan as the third leader of a singing group, are at stage III.B.

■ 17 (32) *They were also the ones ministering in song before the tabernacle of the tent of meeting until Solomon built the house of Yahweh in Jerusalem; and they carried out their service according to their custom:* Two elements in the Chroni-

176 David's interest in cultic change is shown by his transfer of the ark to Jerusalem, and the importance of cult to his rule is shown by the inclusion of Zadok in the lists of his officials (2 Sam 8:16-18; 20:23-26).

177 Sigmund Mowinckel, *The Psalms in Israel's Worship* (trans. D. R. Ap-Thomas; 2 vols.; Nashville: Abingdon, 1962) 2:80, refers to similar groups of singers in Babylonia, Assyria, Egypt, and Ugarit.

178 The length of Heman's genealogy emphasizes Heman's high status. This results in large part from the inclusion within this genealogy of the genealogy of Samuel. In the genealogy of the high priests, there are only thirteen generations from Levi to Zadok while there are twenty-one generations from Levi to Heman.

179 In the Psalter there are references to groups of singers connected with Asaph and Korah. The name Jeduthun occurs thirteen times, all in the books of Chronicles. Twelve psalms are assigned to Asaph (50, 73–83), one to Heman (88), and one to Ethan (89).

180 "Zur Geschichte der Kultsänger am zweiten Tempel," in *Vom Sinai zum Zion: Alttestamentliche Beiträge zur biblischen Theologie* (BEvT 64; Munich: Kaiser, 1974) 147–58.

181 In the commentary on chap. 15, under Structure, I show that the data on the Levitical singers within Chronicles is more complex than Gese believed, and that there are at least five levels of singer configurations within materials now in Chronicles itself. Antri Laato, "The Levitical Genealogies in 1 Chronicles 5–6 and the Formation of Levitical Ideology in Postexilic Judah," *JSOT* 62 (1994) 77–99,

argues that both singers and gatekeepers were Levites already at the beginning of the Persian period. He notes that some passages stress the cultic function of the group in question while other passages speak explicitly of their genealogical descent. In this view Ezra 2:41//Neh 7:44 speak of cultic function and simply do not discuss or identify genealogical descent. He also suggests that the ancient genealogy of the Levites in Num 26:58 MT (Libnites, Hebronites, Mahlites, Mushites, and Korahites) or LXX (Libnites, Hebronites, Korahites, and Mushites) can be coordinated with the genealogies of the Levites in 1 Chronicles 5–6. The genealogy extending from Gershom to Jeatherai (6:5-6 [20-21]) passes through *Libni* the son of Gershom, and many of the names in the pedigree of Asaph (6:24-28 [39-43]) are similar so that both of these can be associated with the *Libnites*. The genealogy extending from Merari to Asaiah passes through *Mahli* (6:14-15 [29-30]), while the pedigree of Ethan the singer goes back to *Mushi* the son of Merari (6:29-32 [44-47]). The descendants of the two grandsons of Kohath (both called *Korah*) are given in the pedigree of Heman (6:18-23 [33-38]) that goes back to Korah the son of Izhar, and in the genealogy extending from Kohath to Joel the son of Samuel or from Kohath to Shaul (6:7-13 [22-28]) that goes back to Korah the son of Amminadab. No descendants for Hebron are given in this chapter, but there is a close connection in the Bible between Aaron and the city of Hebron (Josh 21:13//1 Chr 6:42 [57]; cf. also the genealogy of the descendants of Aaron in 1 Chr 5:27-41 [6:1-15]).

cler's reconstruction of the cultic history of Israel are prominent here. First, he states that there was a fully operative worship program during the time of David, even before the erection of the temple, including the service of song that was obviously central to the worship life of his own day. Second, he uses a pleonastic title for the tabernacle erected in the desert by Moses, "the tabernacle of the tent of meeting," also found at Exod 39:32; 40:2, 6, 29; but the Chronicler applies it now to the tent shrine that was present at Gibeon. This ministry of song was "according to their custom" (כמשפטם), or, as Kleinig translates it, "according to their ritual statute."[182] Kleinig argues that music, according to this verse, was performed before the tabernacle in Gibeon, led by Heman and Jeduthun/Ethan (1 Chr 16:41), as well as in the service at the tent where David had deposited the ark in Jerusalem (15:1; 16:1), led by Asaph (16:37),[183] until the services were united at the dedication of Solomon's temple (2 Chr 5:5). "Service" (עבודה) refers to liturgical actions in this verse and apparently to altar rites in v. 33 (48; so Johnstone, 1:89). Just as the duties of the Levitical singers are outlined in the introduction to this genealogy of the singers, so the duties of the regular Levites and the priests will be outlined at its conclusion (vv. 33-34 [49-49]).

■ **18-23 (33-38)** The linear genealogy of Heman in these verses is:

Israel—Levi—Kohath—Izhar—Korah—Ebiasaph—Assir—Tahath—Zephaniah—Azariah—Joel—Elkanah I

Amasai—Mahath—Elkanah II—Zuph—Toah—Eliel—Jeroham—Elkanah III—Samuel—Joel—Heman

■ **18 (33)** *Heman, the singer, the son of Joel, son of Samuel:* Heman, the only singer who is explicitly given this title in these genealogies,[184] is prominent throughout the books of Chronicles.[185] As a son of Joel in this genealogy, Heman is made the grandson of Samuel, a connection that in itself establishes his preeminence. This genealogy integrates almost the whole pedigree of Samuel into its pedigree of Heman.[186] Heman is the twenty-second member of the genealogy from Levi to himself (twenty-third from Israel to himself). This compares with twelve or thirteen from Levi to Zadok or Ahimaaz in the genealogy of the high priests. There are only twenty-three generations from Aaron to Jehozadak, the high priest who went into exile, but, as we have seen, this genealogy is haplographic. Japhet, 157, proposes that the original form of the Heman genealogy, before the inclusion of the Samuel pedigree, numbered only eleven generations (Levi–Kohath–Izhar–Korah–Ebiasaph–Assir–Tahath–Zephaniah–Azariah–Joel–Heman), with Asaph running to fifteen and Ethan to fourteen generations. In that "original" genealogy, she believes that Joel was also Heman's father, but Joel had no relationship to Samuel. For comparison of the spelling of the names from Eliel to Elkanah the father of Amasai (vv. 19-21 [34-36]) in the genealogy, see the commentary on vv. 10-13 (25-28) above.

182 Kleinig, *Lord's Song*, 43.
183 David's tent is anachronistically described in v. 16 (31) as "the house of Yahweh." See Kleinig, *Lord's Song*, 43; Goettsberger, 68; and Becker, 35. This justifies the addition of the word "also" in my translation of v. 17 (32). Cf. also 16:4-6, 37-42, and the commentary there. Keil, 125, identified the tent of meeting in v. 17 with the tent David had erected for the ark.
184 But this title is used in the plural in 1 Chr 15:19 for Heman, Asaph, and Ethan.
185 1 Chr 15:17, 19; 16:41, 42; 25:1, 4, 5, 6; 2 Chr 5:12; 29:14; 35:15. He is, however, associated with only one psalm (Psalm 88).
186 The Chronicler begins with Heman and works backward to Israel, whereas with Samuel he begins with Elkanah I and follows the line of descent to Samuel.

Pedigree of Heman	Pedigree of Samuel
Heman (v. 18 [33])	
Joel	Joel (v. 13 [28])
Samuel	Samuel
Elkanah III (v. 19 [34])	Elkanah III
Jeroham	Jeroham
Eliel	Eliab (v. 12 [27])
Toah	Nahath
Zuph (v. 20 [35])	Zuphai
Elkanah II	Elkanah II (v. 11 [26])
Mahath[187]	Amasai, Mahath (v. 10 [25])
Amasai	
Elkanah I (v. 21 [36])	Elkanah I

■ **21 (36)** *Joel, son of Azariah, son of Zephaniah:* These three names from the genealogy leading from Levi to Heman show the greatest divergence from the genealogy of the regular Levites in v. 9 (24) leading to Shaul, where the corresponding names are: Shaul, Uzziah, and Uriel.[188] The alternation between Azariah and Uzziah mirrors that of the king of Judah referred to as Azariah in 2 Kings 14–15 and as Uzziah in 2 Chronicles 26. There is a similarity in three of the Hebrew letters in Shaul (שָׁאוּל) and Joel (יוֹאֵל), and one of these names may have developed out of the other. But there is no obvious explanation for the alternation between the names Zephaniah and Uriel.

■ **22 (37)** *son of Tahath, son of Assir, son of Ebiasaph, son of Korah:* This segment of the genealogy (Tahath—Assir—Ebiasaph—Korah) presupposes that contained in the pedigree of Shaul in vv. 7-9 (22-24) (Tahath—Assir—Ebiasaph—Elkanah—Assir—Korah), although it omits the third and second last names from that genealogy.[189] The relationship of Korah to Ebiasaph and Assir in the vari-

ous traditions can be outlined as follows (listed here as descending genealogies; see also the discussion at vv. 7-8 [22-23]):

Exod 6:24 Korah——┐Assir
　　　　　　　　　│Elkanah
　　　　　　　　　│Abiasaph

1 Chr 6:7-8 (22-23)
　　Korah—Assir—Elkanah—Ebiasaph—Assir

1 Chr 6:22 (37)
　　Korah—Ebiasaph—Assir

In Num 26:58 the Korahites are one of the five clans of Levi. In Exod 6:16-21 Korah, Nepheg, and Zichri are identified as sons of Izhar the son of Kohath the son of Levi. Korah the son of Izhar son of Kohath son of Levi was an opponent of Moses and Aaron according to Num 16:1.[190] Korah's sons (or the guild named after him) are associated with Psalms 42–49, 84, 85, 87, and 88. In 1 Chr 9:19 and 26:1, 19, the Korahites are identified as gatekeepers and temple bakers (9:31).

■ **23 (38)** *son of Izhar, son of Kohath, son of Levi, son of Israel:* In Exod 6:18, Num 3:19,[191] 1 Chr 5:28 (6:1), 6:3 (18), and 23:12, Amram, Izhar, Hebron, and Uzziel are listed as sons of Kohath. Izharites were officers and judges according to 26:29.

187　The genealogist treats Amasai and Mahath as father and son instead of as brothers in the pedigree of Samuel.

188　The names actually appear in reverse order in v. 9 (24), since that genealogy starts with the oldest ancestor and works down, while the genealogy in vv. 18-23 (33-38) starts with Heman and works up.

189　I earlier raised the possibility that the two mentions of Assir in the genealogy of Shaul may be the result of a conflation of variant readings.

190　In 1 Chr 23:18 Shelomoth is listed after "the sons of Izhar," and he is later identified as the father of Jahath (24:22). See the commentary there.

191　Note the clans attributed to Kohath in Num 3:27: the Amramites, the Izharites, the Hebronites, and the Uzzielites. They camped on the south side of the tabernacle and were in charge of the ark, table, lampstand, altars, and vessels of the sanctuary (Num 3:29, 31).

■ **24-28 (39-43)** The linear genealogy of Asaph in these verses is:

Levi—Gershom—Jahath—Shimei—Zimmah—Ethan—Adaiah—Zerah—Ethni—Malchijah—Baaseiah—Michael

Shimea—Berechiah—Asaph

■ **24-25 (39-40)** *and his brother Asaph, who stood on his right, namely, Asaph son of Berechiah, son of Shimea, son of Michael, son of Baaseiah, son of Malchijah:* Asaph has clearly declined among the guilds of singers and is now in the second position,[192] standing at Heman's right hand. His onetime importance, however, is indicated by the fact that twelve psalms are associated with him (50, 73–83).[193] The only individual that is known from these verses, aside from Asaph himself, is his father Berechiah, who is also identified as the father of Asaph in the story of the ark (15:17).

■ **26 (41)** *son of Ethni, son of Zerah, son of Adaiah:* Beginning with the name Ethni, six generations before Asaph, the names in Asaph's genealogy are similar to those descended from Gershom among the regular Levites: Ethni (אתני) here corresponds to Jeatherai (יאתרי)[194] among the regular Levites descended from Gershom (v. 6 [21]); Zerah is identical in both lists; Adaiah (עדיה) here corresponds to Iddo (עדו) there.

■ **27-28 (42-43)** *son of Ethan, son of Zimmah, son of Shimei, son of Jahath, son of Gershom, son of Levi:* Ethan (איתן) among the Asaphite singers corresponds in the genealogical order to Joah (יואח)[195] among the regular Levites descended from Gershom through Libni (v. 6 [21]), and Zimmah is identical in both lists. Note the parallels between Shimei the son of Jahath the son of Gershom and Shimei the son of Gershom, and between Jahath the son of Gershom and Jahath the son of Libni the son of Gershom. Six of the last seven names in the Gershomite singer pedigree are identical, or quite similar, to the first six descendants of Libni among the regular Levites. The seventh, Shimei, as the second oldest of Gershom's sons, might have once been the person through whom the list of singers was traced.[196] In columnar form:

Generic Levites	Singers
	Jahath
Jahath	Shimei
Zimmah	Zimmah
Joah יואח	Ethan איתן
Iddo עדי	Adaiah עדיה
Zerah	Zerah
Jeatherai יאתרי	Ethni אתני

■ **29-32 (44-47)** The linear genealogy of Ethan in these verses is:

Levi–Merari–Mushi–Mahli–Shemer–Bani–Amzi–Hilkiah–Amaziah–Hashabiah–Malluch–Abdi–Kishi–Ethan

Only the beginning and ending of this list can be explicated. Ethan, who is called the Ezrahite in Ps 89:1 (S), is called the son of Kushaiah (קושיהו) in 1 Chr 15:17 (cf. v. 19), clearly only an orthographic difference from the name of Ethan's father Kishi (קישי) in v. 29 (44). At the other end of the genealogy, Mushi is Merari's second son among the regular Levites, while Mahli, Merari's first son, has become the son of Mushi and therefore

---

192 Cf. Gese's stage III B.

193 See also Ezra 2:41//Neh 7:44; Ezra 3:10; Neh 11:17, 22; 12:46.

194 Rudolph, 56, proposes that Jeatherai is a corruption of Joel. See 1 Chr 15:7: "Of the sons of Gershom, Joel the chief, with one hundred thirty of his kindred."

195 Of the four letters in each name two are identical, and the *tāw* resembles the *ḥêt*. The order of the letters, however, is quite different.

196 Heman and Ethan are linked to the second sons of Kohath and Merari, respectively.

Merari's grandson in this genealogy of the third singer guild.[197] This probably indicates that Mushi in some circles has become more important than Mahli. Frank Cross has proposed that the Mushites originally claimed descent from Moses.[198] Gershom, identified in this chapter as the oldest son of Levi, may once have been a Mushite clan. The assignment of Mushites to the third son of Levi, Merari, may indicate either a decline in their status or that this genealogy represents the viewpoint of the Zadokite Aaronides. The other eight names in this genealogy have no correspondence with the five other names in the genealogy of Merari in vv. 14-15 (29-30). Since the names in the three genealogies of the singer guilds have quite disparate relationships to the three corresponding genealogies of the regular Levitical families, it seems probable that these genealogies had been developed independently of the Chronicler and are only included by him here from a source available to him.

■ **33 (48)** *and their kindred the Levites were being dedicated for all the service of the tabernacle of the house of God:* While the principal duty of the Levitical singers was described in vv. 16-17 (31-32), the duties of their kindred, the regular Levites, are described broadly as being dedicated (נתוני; lit. "given")[199] to the "service" (עבודה) of the tabernacle of the house of God. This is the only time that the expression "the tabernacle of the house of God" is used in the Bible. Of the fifty-one occurrences of the "house of God" in the OT, thirty-three are in Chronicles. Elsewhere in Chronicles the duties of the Levites include: stripping the hide off animals in the burnt offering (2 Chr 29:34)[200] and handing the blood of the sacrifices to the priests (2 Chr 30:16).[201] Occasionally Levites functioned as prophets under the influence of the spirit (1 Chr 25:1-3; cf. 2 Chr 20:14-17). Outside the temple

cult, Levites were counted among the troops of David, 4,600 strong (1 Chr 12:27 [26]), and formed a bodyguard around Joash (2 Chr 23:7). According to 2 Chr 34:12-13, some of the Levites had oversight and were musicians, while others were scribes (סופרים), officials (שטרים), and gatekeepers (שוערים). Jehoshaphat appointed Levites, priests, and family heads to give judgment for Yahweh and to decide disputed cases (2 Chr 19:8). According to 1 Chr 23:4, the 38,000 Levites were divided as follows: 24,000 for temple service, 6,000 officers and judges, 4,000 gatekeepers, and 4,000 musicians. The Levites gathered the temple tax (2 Chr 24:5-6) and taught the people the law (2 Chr 17:8). Japhet, 158, finds a chiastic arrangement in the listing of Levites in this verse and of priests in the next verse, since priests were listed first in 1 Chr 5:27-41 (6:1-15) and Levites were listed second (6:1-33 [16-48]).

■ **34 (49)** *But Aaron and his sons made offerings on the altar of burnt offering and on the incense altar, performing all the work of the most holy place, to make atonement for Israel:* This verse refers to the duties of all the priests (for whom no genealogy is supplied in this context) and not just of the high priests, whose genealogy was given in 1 Chr 5:27-41 (6:1-15). The sons of Aaron had the exclusive right in the Pentateuch to offer burnt offerings in the temple courtyard (Num 18:1-5), burn incense in the tabernacle,[202] and make atonement for Israel.[203] In Chronicles, as in P and Ezekiel, Yahweh grants atonement, the priests perform the atoning rites, and Israel is the beneficiary.[204] Only the high priests were allowed to enter the most holy place, which housed the ark of the covenant, and then only once a year on the Day of Atonement.

according to everything that Moses the servant of God commanded: While the singers were appointed by David, the Chronicler recognizes that the duties of the priests were

---

197 Cf. 1 Chr 24:30.

198 *Canaanite Myth*, 190–215.

199 Cf. Num 3:9; 8:16-19. They should not be confused, however, with the Nethinim (1 Chr 9:2), who performed menial temple service and did not have Levitical status.

200 According to this verse, they were more conscientious/willing than the priests in sanctifying themselves.

201 See von Rad, *Geschichtsbild*, 98–115. Cf. 1 Chr 9:17-32; 2 Chr 35:11.

202 Exod 30:7-8 prescribes that Aaron is to make the

incense offering. Cf. Lev 16:12-13. In Chronicles the word "incense" is used at 1 Chr 9:29; 28:18; 2 Chr 2:3 (4); 13:11; 14:5; 26:16, 19; 29:7; 30:14; 34:4, 7.

203 E.g., Leviticus 4–5; 9:7; 16.

204 At the time of Hezekiah, the king gave impetus to the sacrifice of atonement and to the atonement itself (2 Chr 29:5, 21, 23-24). Hezekiah prayed for atonement for those who had not cleansed themselves before the Passover celebration (2 Chr 30:18). See F. Maas, *TLOT* 2:624–35.

set by Moses himself. The epithet "servant of Yahweh" or "servant of God" is used of Moses in 2 Chr 1:3; 24:6, 9; cf. Neh 10:30 (29), probably to indicate his prophetic status (cf. Amos 3:7). This is the first time, aside from the genealogical reference in 1 Chr 5:29 (6:3), that Moses is introduced as an authority behind a given worship practice.

6:35-38 (50-53). Excerpt from High Priestly Genealogy

■ **35-38 (50-53)** *These are the sons of Aaron:* Chronicles repeats the genealogy of Aaron and his first descendants, using the same names as those employed in 5:29-34 (6:3-8). This excerpt from the high priestly genealogy takes the reader chronologically to the time of David, when we find references to Ahimaaz, the son of Zadok, in the Succession Narrative, although there are no references to his functioning as high priest but only to his role as a courier (2 Sam 15:36; 17:17-29; 18:19-29). The result of the citation of this excerpt from the list of high priests is that Chronicles has shifted the date of the cities of the priests and Levites from the time of Joshua (Joshua 21) to the time of David himself. The Levitical cities are no longer cities that fell by lot, but rather settlements occupied by priests and Levites. While the content of the list of the high priestly descendants of Aaron is the same as in the master list, the person who included these words[205] changed the form from "X became the father of Y, and Y became the father of Z, and so on," to "X, his son Y, his son Z, his son, and so on."

6:39-66 (54-81). Cities of Priests and of Levites

■ **39 (54)** *These are their dwelling places according to their encampments within their borders:* "Dwelling places" (מושבות) are also listed in the genealogies for Simeon (1 Chr 4:33) and Ephraim (7:28).[206] "Encampments" (טירת) is used only seven times altogether in the OT and only here in Chronicles. In Gen 25:16 it is used of the seminomadic Ishmaelites, and in Ps 69:26 (25) it is used in parallelism with "tents."[207] This fits quite well the picture of the Levites in this list, who do not possess land but live in their cities and use their pasturelands presumably to raise animals (see below). The term "border" suggests the tribal territory to which each group of cities is assigned (cf. 1 Chr 6:51 [66]). With this opening clause, the Chronicler establishes a new context for the list: it names the places where the priests and Levites lived at the time of David; it is not a narrative of how the cities were assigned in the days of Joshua.

to the sons of Aaron of the Kohathite clan: Under Structure I have noted the prominent place given to the Aaronides in this list in Chronicles. The Chronicler omits from the *Vorlage* in Josh 21:10 the words "from the sons of Levi." This is one of three such omissions in this list (cf. vv. 56, 62 [71, 77])—or additions to the text of Joshua after the creation of 1 Chronicles 6. Since the Chronicler clearly sets this list within a context of the genealogy of the Levites and surely does not object to the Aaronides also being considered descendants of Levi, there is no reason to propose any specific ideological significance to this omission.[208]

For each tribal section I provide a list of the cities from that tribe, the probable modern Arabic name of that site, and the map references that help locate it precisely on the map.

---

205 Williamson, 74, holds this excerpt to be secondary because the context has been dealing with all the priests, not just high priestly duties. If the primary function was to establish a new date for the list of the cities of the priests and Levites, this objection loses some of its force.

206 Japhet, 159-60, cites uses of this term in priestly contexts.

207 Cf. also Num 31:10, where it is used of Midian, and Ezek 25:4, where it is used of the sons of the east.

208 So also Oeming, *Wahre Israel*, 146–47, n. 15.

Judah/Simeon (vv. 39-44 [54-59])

City	Modern Name	Map Reference
Hebron	Jebel er-Rumeidah	159103
Libnah	Tell Bornât	138115
Jattir	Khirbet 'Attîr	151084
Eshtemoa	es-Samû'	156089
Holon/Hilen	Khirbet 'Alîn[209]	152118
Debir	Khirbet Rabûd	151093
Ashan	Khirbet Asan[210]	ca. 133073
Juttah	Yaṭṭā	158095
Beth-shemesh	Tell er-Rumeileh[211]	147128

■ **40-41 (55-56)** *to them they gave Hebron in the land of Judah and its pasturelands surrounding it, but the fields of the city and its villages they gave to Caleb the son of Jephunneh:* In both Joshua (21:11-12) and 1 Chronicles, there is a double reference to Hebron (see v. 42 [57]//Josh 21:13), with this first reference adjudicating the fact that Hebron is both a Levitical city and a place assigned to Caleb the son of Jephunneh (Josh 14:13-14; 15:13-14). Hence the Aaronides get the pasturelands, but the fields and the villages still belonged to Caleb.[212] After "Jephunneh," Josh 21:12 adds "as a possession." The Chronicler calls the city "Hebron" in both verses, while in the first case Josh 21:11 reads "Kiriath-arba (Arba being the father of Anak), that is, Hebron" (cf. Josh 14:15; 15:13, 54; 20:7). The Chronicler also changed "the hill country of Judah" in Joshua to "the land of Judah." One hundred four of the one hundred fourteen biblical references to "pasturelands" occur in the two parallel lists of priestly and Levitical cities, with all but

one of the rest of occurrences appearing in laws relating to the Levitical cities.[213] These pasturelands may actually refer to open or common land around the city.

Benjamin[214] (v. 45 [60])

City	Modern Name	Map Reference
Gibeon	Tell el-Jîb	167139
Geba	Jeba'	175140
Almon/Alemeth	Tell 'Almît	176136
Anathoth	Râs el-Kharrûbeh	174135

■ **46 (61)** *To the rest of the Kohathites were given by lot out of the families of the tribe of Ephraim, from the tribe of Dan, and from the half-tribe of Manasseh:* MT lacks mention of both the tribe of Ephraim and the tribe of Dan. Braun, 97, 101, Oeming,[215] and Schmitt[216] have suggested that the Chronicler or a later writer deliberately omitted Dan here, in v. 54 (69), and in 7:12. But the MT here is clearly corrupt (see textual note 46), and the loss of the name Dan in v. 54 (69) is also explainable by homoioteleuton (textual note 58). For the absence of Dan in chap. 7 see the commentary there.

209 For a discussion of this city and its location, see John L. Peterson, "Holon," *ABD* 3:257–58.

210 According to Peterson, *Topographical Survey,* 548, this site now lies under the suburbs of the modern Israeli city of Beer-sheba. This is the only city that is clearly associated with Simeon (Josh 19:7). Kartveit, *Motive und Schichten,* 160, puts it either at Khirbet 'Asan or Khirbet Muleḥ (MR 116077). At either location it is the most southern of these nine cities.

211 Also known as 'Ain Shems. In Josh 19:41 Ir-shemesh is assigned to Dan. As noted under Structure, Y. Tsafrir has made the interesting suggestion that this city originally referred to a city in Naphtali by the same name (MR 181271). In the present list it is 10 kilometers farther north than any other Judahite or Simeonite city.

212 For Caleb the son of Hezron and Caleb the son of Jephunneh in Chronicles, see the commentary to 1 Chr 2:9, 18, 21, and 4:15.

213 The only exception is 1 Chr 5:16, a reference to the pasturelands of the Gadites. See the discussion in Lienhard Delekat, "Zum hebräischen Wörterbuch," *VT* 14 (1964) 7–66.

214 Note that these Benjaminite towns are clustered just north of Jerusalem (MR 172131).

215 *Wahre Israel,* 148.

216 Schmitt, "Levitenstädte," 39, notes that Joshua 21 describes premonarchical conditions, when Dan is still in the south, but the Chronicler, who ascribed the list to the time of David, knew that Dan was no longer in the southwest at that time and therefore deleted this reference.

Ephraim (vv. 52-53 [67-68])

City	Modern Name	Map Reference
Shechem	Tell Balâtah	176179
Gezer	Tell Jezer	142140
Kibzaim	Tell el-Mazâr[217]	195171 or
Jokmeam (Lower)	Tell esh-Sheikh Dhiâb[218]	190161
Beth-horon (Upper)	Beit 'Ûr et-Taḥtā	158144[219] or
Beth-horon	Beit 'Ûr el-Fôqa	160143

■ 53 (68) *Jokmeam with its pasturelands:* At this point Josh 21:22 has "Kibzaim." Albright proposed that both names were original, with Kibzaim accidentally dropping out of Chronicles and Jokneam out of Joshua (see textual note 57). In his view Shechem was secondary, but there is no compelling reason to follow this proposal. Mazar and Tsafrir conjectured that the name Kibzaim was changed to Jokmeam. Orlinsky thought that the names were accidentally confused in the course of textual transmission, with the original being either יקמעם or קבצים. If Jokneam and Kibzaim represent only one city originally—and only one of the Beth-horons was included—the total of four for Ephraim can be retained.

Dan (v. 54 [69])

City	Modern Name	Map Reference
Elteke	Tell esh-Shallâf[220]	128144
Gibbethon	Tell Malât[221]	137140
Aijalon	Yālô[222]	152138
Gath-rimmon	Tell Jerîsheh[223]	132166

Manasseh (vv. 55-56 [70-71])[224]

City	Modern Name	Map Reference
Taanach	Tell Ti'innik	171214
Ibleam	Khirbet Bel'ameh	177205
Golan	Saḥm el-Jōlân	238243
Ashtaroth	Tell 'Ashtarah	243244

Issachar (vv. 57-58 [72-73])

City	Modern Name	Map Reference
Kishion	Tell el-Muqarqash[225]	194228 or
	Khirbet Qasyûn[226]	187229
Daberath	Debûriyeh	185233
Jarmuth/ Ramoth	Kôkab el-Hawā'	199222
En-gannim	Khirbet Beit Jann	196235

217 Boling, "Levitical Cities," 25. Aharoni, *Land of the Bible*, 437, identifies this tell hesitantly with Jokmeam. Peterson, *Topographical Survey*, 273–74, was unable to identify a tell for Kibzaim and associated this tell with Ataroth (Josh 16:7).

218 Kartveit, *Motive und Schichten*, 160, identifies Jokmeam with Tell Qemun (MR 160230).

219 It is not clear which of the two Beth-horons is meant, with the territory of Joseph extending to Lower Beth-horon in Josh 16:3, but the territory for Ephraim extending only as far as Upper Beth-horon in Josh 16:5.

220 Aharoni, *Land of the Bible*, 434. Boling, "Levitical Cities," 25; and Peterson, "Eltekeh," *ABD* 2:483–84, identified Elteke with Khirbet el-Muqenna' (MR 136133), about 10 miles to the southeast. But that site has now been decisively identified with Ekron.

221 Peterson, *Topographical Survey*, 330, considers an alternate location at Ras Abu Hamid, but finally rejects it.

222 Peterson, *Topographical Survey*, 343–51, also consid-

ers the nearby Tell Qoqa as a possible site for Aijalon.

223 Aharoni, *Land of the Bible*, 434, makes this identification with a question mark. Peterson, *Topographical Survey*, 357–76, wavers between this site and Tell Abu Zitun (MR 134167).

224 Taanach and Ibleam are assigned to the western half of Manasseh and the Kohathites, while Golan and Ashtaroth are assigned to the Transjordanian half of Manasseh and the Gershomites.

225 Peterson, *Topographical Survey*, 165

226 Aharoni, *Land of the Bible*, 438.

Asher (vv. 59-60 [74-75])

City	Modern Name	Map Reference
Mishal/Mashal	Tell Kīsân[227]	164253 or
	Tell Keisan[228]	194253 or
	Tell Bîr er-jarbi[229]	166256
Abdon	Khirbet 'Abdon[230]	165272
Helkath	Tell el-Qassîs[231]	160232 or
	Tell el-Harbaj[232]	158240
Rehob	Tell el-Gharbi[233]	166256

Naphtali (v. 61 [76])

City	Modern Name	Map Reference
Kedesh	Tell Qades	199279
Hammoth-dor/Hammon	Tell Raqqat[234]	199245
Kartan/Kiriathaim	Khirbet et-Qureiyeh[235]	ca. 1944.2800
	Khirbet el-Quneiṭireh	199245[236]

Zebulun (v. 62 [77])

City	Modern Name	Map Reference
Jokneam	Tell Qeimûn	160230
Rimmon	Rummâneh	179243
Chisloth-tabor	Iksâl[237]	180232
Nahalal	Tell en-Nahl	1568.2450

Reuben (vv. 63-64 [78-79])

City	Modern Name	Map Reference
Bezer	Umm el-'Amad[238]	235132
Jahzah	Khirbet el-Medeiniyeh al-Themed[239]	236110
Kedemoth	es-Saliyeh[240]	No MR number in Peterson or *ABD*
	'Aleiyān[241]	233104
Mephaath	Tell Jâwah[242]	239140

---

227 Ibid., 439; David W. Baker, "Mishal," *ABD* 4:871.

228 Peterson, *Topographical Survey*, 21.

229 Kartveit, *Motive und Schichten*, 161.

230 Abdon has now shown up on an 11th-century BCE arrowhead. See Frank Moore Cross, "A Note on a Recently Published Arrowhead," *IEJ* 45 (1995) 188–89.

231 Boling, "Levitical Cities," 25. Cf. Peterson, *Topographical Survey*, 43, who notes that Tell Qeimun, identified with Jokneam of Zebulun (v. 62 [77]), is only 2 miles south of Tell el-Qassîs.

232 Peterson, *Topographical Survey*, 46–51; idem, "Helkath," *ABD* 3:125–26.

233 Boling, "Levitical Cities," 25.

234 Ibid.; Peterson, *Topographical Survey*, 84–90. Kartveit, *Motive und Schichten*, 161, suggests Umm el-Amad (MR 164281).

235 Peterson, *Topographical Survey*, 93, observes that it is close to Aytarun (MR 194280), 6 kilometers west and 1 kilometer north of Tell Qades. Cf. Boling, "Levitical Cities," 25.

236 Aharoni, *Land of the Bible*, 441. This site is located 1 kilometer north of modern Tiberias. Kartveit, *Motive und Schichten*, 161, locates this tell at 179243. Is this a mistake?

237 Aharoni, *Land of the Bible*, 432; Peterson, *Topographical Survey*, 112. Boling, "Levitical Cities," 25, provides no identification for Qartah/Tabor.

238 Kartveit, *Motive und Schichten*, 162, considers this identification improbable. He prefers Buṣra eski-šâm (MR 289214) or Khirbet Bir Zeit (MR 168152).

The first suggestion is much too far to the north.

239 Boling, "Levitical Cities," 25; Aharoni, *Land of the Bible*, 437, with a question mark. For a discussion of other possible locations see J. Andrew Dearman, "Jahaz," *ABD* 3:612.

240 Peterson, *Topographical Survey*, 679; idem, "Kedemoth," *ABD* 4:10–11; Boling, "Levitical Cities," 25. This site is just north of the Arnon River.

241 Aharoni, *Land of the Bible*, 438, with a question mark.

242 Kartveit, *Motive und Schichten*, 162, suggests Umm er-Rasas (MR 237101). John L. Peterson and Michele Piccirillo, "Mephaah," *ABD* 4:696, list three possibilities: Tell Jawah, about 10 kilometers south of Amman (MR 239146); Khirbet Nefa'ah, about 1.5 kilometers north of Jawah; and Umm er-Rasas (MR 237101), some 45 kilometers south of Amman. A mosaic in the floor of an 8th-century church identified this last site as Kastron Mefaa. A seal bearing the name Mephaath has been published by Nahman Avigad, "The Seal of Mefa'ah," *IEJ* 40 (1990) 42–43.

Gad (vv. 65-66 [80-81])

City	Modern Name	Map Reference
Ramoth in Gilead	Tell Rāmîth[243]	244210
Mahanaim	Tell edh-Dhahab el-Gharbi[244]	214177 or
	Tell Hejjaj[245]	215173
Heshbon	Tell Ḥesbân	226134
Jazer	Khirbet Jazzir[246]	219156 or
	Khirbet Aṣṣār[247]	228150

Conclusion

1 Chronicles 5:27-41 (6:1-15) is a master list of the genealogy of the high priests that is at points haplographic. Rooke proposes that the primary aim in including the line of priests in Chronicles is to demonstrate that there had been an unbroken line of chief priests prior to the exile and that this line had been resumed in the postexilic period.[248] The issue, therefore, is more continuity than legitimacy. But the Chronicler has also made all of the priests contained in the genealogy sons of Zadok and therefore sons of Aaron, and this surely gives legitimacy to the Zadokite claim on the high priesthood in the postexilic period. Jeshua, the first priest after the return, is given the patronymic "son of Jozadak,"[249] and I have argued that it was the Chronicler himself who appended this name on to the master genealogy. The high priests in the books of Chronicles are not examples of priests who ruled a hierocratic society in its entirety. While the king has lost sacral privilege, there is no corresponding rise in civil power or privilege for the chief priest.[250] Thus the high priest in Chronicles did not have a particularly significant office outside the cultic sphere. All the chief priests mentioned in Chronicles serve alongside a king, but not all the kings are accompanied by a high priest. Since the people

as a whole in Chronicles are heirs to the Davidic promise, the chief priest continues to exercise a stabilizing influence, only now in the context of the whole community.

However much the Chronicler is an advocate for the Levites, he still gives pride of place in the genealogy of the Levites to the line of chief priests, beginning with Aaron, Eleazar, and Phinehas, continuing throughout the monarchic period, and ending with the father of the first known postexilic high priest. At roughly the midpoint of this line of high priests come Zadok and Ahimaaz, priests at the time of David. The Chronicler, however, chose not to trace the line of postexilic priests as they are found in Neh 12:10-11, 22-23, even though those verses are stated in the same format: "X became the father of Y."

The genealogy of the regular or generic Levites through Gershom, Kohath, and Merari ends with the heads called Jeatherai, Shaul, and Asaiah (1 Chr 6:1-15 [16-30]). These genealogies were no doubt designed to give legitimacy to these three heads, but in Chronicles they are used to provide a more robust genealogy for Levi himself. Inserted into the genealogy of Kohath-Shaul is another linear genealogy making a Levite of the prophet Samuel and his two sons. In the books of Samuel he was an Ephraimite. By including the Levitical genealogy of Samuel, the Chronicler may well be dependent on another source, since he does not seem to be a particular advocate of Samuel himself. The genealogy exonerates Samuel of any suspicion of inappropriate cultic activity.

The pedigrees of the Levitical singers, beginning with the heads of the singer guilds, Heman, Asaph, and Ethan, and going back to Kohath, Gershom, and Merari (6:16-34 [31-49]), gives prominence to the role of the singers in the Chronicler's understanding of the worship

---

243 Aharoni, *Land of the Bible,* 441; Patrick M. Arnold, "Ramoth-Gilead," *ABD* 5:620–21. This identification is based on a suggestion by Nelson Glueck, "Ramoth-Gilead," *BASOR* 92 (1943) 10–16.

244 Aharoni, *Land of the Bible,* 439; Boling, "Levitical Cities," 25. On p. 29, n. 16, Boling says that John Peterson puts Mahanaim at T. Hejjaj. Cf. also Diana Edelman, "Mahanaim," *ABD* 4:472–73, who rules out other proposals.

245 Peterson, *Topographical Survey,* 612–14.

246 See ibid., 641–43; idem, "Jazer," *ABD* 3:650–51.

247 Kartveit, *Motive und Schichten,* 162. This site is called Khirbet Sar in Peterson, "Jazer," 651.

248 *Zadok's Heirs,* 199.

249 Cf. Ezra 3:2, 8, 9; 4:3; 5:2; 8:33.

250 Rooke, *Zadok's Heirs,* 213. Cf. also idem, "Kingship as Priesthood," 198–206.

of Israel. A relatively late form of these three musical guilds is represented by these genealogies, with the guild of Heman emerging as preeminent. Hence the assignment of these guilds to the time of David is anachronistic. The Chronicler is trying to establish a niche for the Levites in the postexilic cult, since their role in carrying the ark had become obsolete.

The incidental notices about the responsibility of the clergy anticipates in large part what the Chronicler will state elsewhere: 6:16-17 (31-32) duties of Levitical singers; 6:33 (48) duties of regular Levites; 6:34 (49) duties of the priests.

In 6:35-38 (50-53) the Chronicler uses an excerpt from the high priestly genealogy in order to ascribe the cities of the priests and Levites to the time of David rather than to the time of Joshua. This fits in with his general idea that many of the features of the Israelite cult, including its clergy, were established during the reigns of David and Solomon.

The cities of the priests and Levites (6:39-66 [54-81]) has been revised from the source document in Josh 21:1-40. The Chronicler repositioned the cities assigned to the Aaronides, thereby giving them greater emphasis, just as he gave the high priests preeminence among the Levites by putting them at the head of the Levitical genealogies. By being spread throughout all twelve tribes, the Levites also represent an all-Israel theme. There may be incorporated in this list an implicit hope by the Chronicler for a restoration of Israel to a territory approximating the dimensions of Israel in the era of David and Solomon. The six cities of refuge are always placed first among the cities assigned to a given tribe. The list of the cities of the priests and Levites is not a historical or administrative document, but it was created by using the cities of refuge and information from Joshua 13–19 in order to show Levitical and priestly presence throughout the land.

Translation

1/ The sons of[1] Issachar: Tola, Puah,[2] Jashub,[3] and Shimron, four. 2/ The sons of Tola: Uzzi, Rephaiah, Jeriel, Jahmai,[4] Ibsam, and Shemuel,[5] heads of their ancestral houses, namely of Tola, mighty warriors of their generations, their number in the days of David were twenty-two thousand six hundred. 3/ The son of[6] Uzzi: Izrahiah. And the sons of Izrahiah: Michael, Obadiah, Joel, and[7] Isshiah, five,[8] all of them chiefs; 4/ and alongside them, by their generations, according to their ancestral houses, were troops[9] of the war force, thirty-six thousand, for they had more wives and sons than 5/ their kindred.[10] For all the families of Issachar there were altogether eighty-seven thousand mighty warriors, enrolled by genealogy.

6/ The sons of[11] Benjamin:[12] Bela,[13] Becher, and Jediael,[14] three. 7/ The sons of Bela: Ezbon, Uzzi, Uzziel, Jerimoth, and Iri, five, heads of ancestral houses, mighty warriors; and their enrollment by genealogies was twenty-two thousand thirty-four. 8/ The sons of Becher: Zemirah,[15] Joash, Eliezer, Elioenai, Omri, Jeremoth, Abijah, Anathoth, and Alemeth. All these were the sons of Becher; 9/ and their enrollment by genealogies, according to their generations, as heads of their ancestral houses, mighty warriors, was twenty thousand two hundred.

10/ The son[16] of Jediael:[17] Bilhan. And the sons of Bilhan: Jeush,[18] Benjamin, Ehud, Chenaanah, Zethan, Tarshish, and Ahishahar. 11/ All these were the sons of Jediael, the heads[19] of their ancestral houses, mighty warriors, seventeen thousand two hundred, ready for service in war. 12/ And Shuppim and Huppim[20] were the sons of Ir, Hushim[21] the son[22] of Aher.[23]

13/ The descendants of Naphtali: Jahziel,[24] Guni, Jezer, and Shallum.[25] These were[26] the descendants of Bilhah.

14/ The sons of Manasseh: Asriel,[27] whom his Aramean concubine bore;[28] she bore Machir the father of Gilead. 15/ And Machir[29] took a wife for Huppim and for Shuppim.[30] The name of his sister[31] was Maacah.[32] And the name of the second[33] was Zelophehad; and Zelophehad had only daughters. 16/ Maacah the wife of Machir[34] bore a son, and she named him Peresh; the name of his brother was

1 ולבני; cf. 1 Chr 6:47, 56, 62 (62, 71, 77). LXX[Aal], Syr, Vg: ובני. See the commentary for a discussion of the syntax.

2 ופואה, also at Gen 46:13 SP, Syr; cf. Judg 10:1. Gen 46:13 MT; Num 26:23, ופוה "Puvah." The spelling in Chronicles and Judg 10:1 may be a combination of פוה and פוא.

3 ישוב with Q, LXX, Vg, Num 26:24; cf. Syr, K: ישיב "Jashib." Chronicles Tg, Gen 46:13: יוב Iob (haplography of the šin).

4 ויחמי; LXX[Aal] ויחמו "Jahmou."

5 The spelling in Hebrew is the same as the man traditionally called "Samuel" in the Bible.

6 ובן Sebir; MT ובני "sons of."

7 Conjunction lacking in MT.

8 Syr, Arab.: "four." This is a harmonistic change because of the apparent contradiction between the number of names given and this total. See the commentary.

9 גדודי; LXX, Syr, Vg, Arab.: גבורי "mighty men."

10 מאחיהם and connect with v. 4. See Curtis and Madsen, 145; BHS. MT ואחיהם.

11 בני with some Hebrew MSS, LXX[L], Syr, Tg, Vg, Arab.; lost by haplography (homoioarchton) in MT.

12 LXX[i] reads "The sons of Zebulun." Curtis and Madsen, 147–49, proposed that this was indeed originally a genealogy of Zebulun. For discussion see the commentary.

13 Omitted accidentally by LXX.

14 Syr adds "and Ashbel." This is a harmonization here and in v. 10 with Gen 46:21.

15 זמירה; LXX[Lal], Rudolph, 66: זמריה "Zemariah," thus adding a theophoric element to the name and eliminating a name with a feminine ending.

16 ובן Sebir; MT ובני "The sons of."

17 Syr adds 'škl "and Ashkel" for "and Ashbel." Cf. textual note 14.

18 יעוש with Q, many Hebrew MSS, and the versions; cf. 1 Chr 1:35. K יעיש "Jeish."

19 ראשי with LXX, Vg; MT לראשי. The lāmed arose by dittography of the last letter on the previous word.

20 שפם וחפם; Num 26:39 ושפופם וחופם "Shephupham and Hupham." Gen 46:21 מפים וחפים "Muppim and Huppim."

21 חשם; Gen 46:23; Num 26:42 שחם "Shuham."

22 בן with BHS, following LXX. MT בני "the sons of."

23 אחר. Perhaps a corrupt gloss related to ארד "Ard" (Gen 46:21) or אחירם "Ahiram" (Num 26:38).

24 יַחֲצִיאֵל; some Hebrew MSS, Gen 46:24, Num 26:48: יַחְצְאֵל. The variation in vocalization arose because of the addition of the vowel letter yôd in MT. Cf. also the next note.

25 ושלום. A few Hebrew MSS, LXX[L], Gen 46:24, Num 26:49 ושלם "Shillem." In a text written without a vowel letter, this difference in vowels is easy to

Sheresh, and his sons were Ulam and Rakem. 17/ The son[35] of Ulam: Bedan. These were the sons of Gilead son of Machir, son of Manasseh. 18/ And his sister Hammolecheth bore Ishhod, Abiezer, Mahlah, and Shemida.[36] 19/ The sons of Shemida: Ahian, Shechem, Likhi, and Aniam.

20/ The sons of Ephraim: Shuthelah, and Bered[37] his son, Tahath[38] his son, Eleadah his son, Tahath his son, 21/ Zabad his son, Shuthelah his son. As for his sons, Ezer[39] and Elead, the people of Gath, who were born in the land, killed them, because they came down to take their cattle. 22/ And their father Ephraim mourned many days, and his relatives came to comfort him. 23/ Ephraim went in to his wife, and she conceived and bore a son; and he called[40] his name Beriah, because disaster had befallen[41] his house.[42] 24/ His daughter was Sheerah, who built both Lower and Upper Beth-horon, and Uzzen-sheerah. 25/ Rephah his son, Shuthelah,[43] his son, Tahan his son, 26/ Ladan his son, Ammihud his son, Elishama his son, 27/ Non his son, Joshua his son. 28/ Their possessions and settlements were Bethel and its towns, and eastward Naaran,[44] and westward Gezer and its towns, Shechem and its towns, as far as Ayyah[45] and its towns; 29/ also along the borders of the Manassites, Beth-shean and its towns, Taanach and its towns, Ibleam and its towns,[46] Megiddo and its towns, Dor and its towns. In these lived the sons of Joseph son of Israel.

30/ The sons of Asher: Imnah, Ishvah, Ishvi, Beriah,[47] and their sister Serah. 31/ The sons of Beriah: Heber and Malchiel, who was the father of Birzaith.[48] 32/ Heber became the father of Japhlet, Shomer,[49] Hotham,[50] and their sister Shua. 33/ The sons of Japhlet: Pasach, Bimhal, and Ashvath. These are the sons of Japhlet. 34/ The sons of Shemer[51] his brother:[52] Rohgah,[53] Hubbah,[54] and Aram. 35/ The sons[55] of Helem[56] his brother: Zophah, Imna, Shelesh, and Amal. 36/ The sons of Zophah: Suah, Harnepher, Shual. The sons of Imna:[57] 37/ Bezer, Hod, and Shamma. [The sons of][58] Shilshah, Ithran,[59] and Beera. 38/ The sons of Jether: Jephunneh, Pispa, and Ara. 39/ The sons of Ulla:[60]

explain. The slight spelling variations on two names in any case do not indicate that the Chronicler had any other source than those noted in the commentary.

26 אלה; lost in MT. *BHS* inserts שניהם "the two of them were."

27 אשריאל. Rudolph, 68, considers this a dittography or a remnant of the original superscription standing before the Asher genealogy. According to Josh 17:1-2, Asriel is not the firstborn of Manasseh, and according to Num 26:30-31 he is not even a son of Manasseh. See the commentary.

28 אשר ילדה. Some would delete these words as a dittograph of אשריאל "Asriel." See the commentary.

29 ומכיר. Japhet, 176, גלעד "Gilead." For discussion see the commentary.

30 ומכיר לקח אשה לחפים ולשפים. *BHS* replaces this clause with ובני גלעד איעזר בכורו חלק אשריאל חפר שכם ושמידע "And the sons of Gilead were Iezer his firstborn, Helek, Asriel, Hepher, Shechem, and Shemida." Cf. Num 26:30-32.

31 אחתו; one Hebrew MS אשתו "his wife." *BHS* emends to אחתם "their sister"; cf. LXX[L], Tg.

32 מעכה. *BHS* inserts ובני חפר הבכור "and the sons of Hepher the firstborn." Japhet, 167, replaces Maacah with המלכת "Hammolecheth" and transfers this sentence to the end of v. 14. See the commentary.

33 השני; a few Hebrew MSS, LXX[B]: השנית, interpreting Zelophehad as a woman.

34 מכיר; Curtis and Madsen, 152; Japhet, 167: גלעד "Gilead." See the commentary.

35 ובן with *Sebir*, Vg; MT ובני "sons."

36 Add ואת שמידע "and Shemida."

37 וברד; Syr, Arab. (Num 26:35 MT): ובכר "Becher." An original *bkr* > *brk* > *brd*.

38 ותחת; cf. LXX[L]; LXX[B] *Noome*.

39 בנו ובניו עזר. This is a conjectural reconstruction proposed by Nadav Na'aman, "Sources and Redaction in the Chronicler's Genealogies of Asher and Ephraim," *JSOT* 49 (1991) 99–111. MT ובני. בנו ועזר was lost by haplography and a conjunction was then applied to the next word.

40 ויקרא; a few Hebrew MSS, Syr, Tg, Arab.: ותקרא "she called."

41 היתה; *BHS* emends to הרתה "because she had become pregnant" (in an unfortunate time).

42 בביתו. Is this a dittograph of ובתו "his daughter" at the beginning of the next verse?

43 שתולה with *BHS*; MT רשף ותלח "Resheph and Telah." Resheph is a strange name for an Israelite, since it is the name of a Canaanite deity. The *pê* and *rêš* may have been added from the preceding name ורפח "Rephah" to the original *wāw* and *šîn* that began the name Shuthelah to create "Resheph and Telah." Japhet, 167, retains Resheph and suggests

Arah, Hanniel, and Rizia. 40/ All of these were men of Asher, heads of ancestral houses, select mighty warriors, chiefs of the princes. Their number enrolled by genealogies, for service in war, was twenty-six thousand men.

adding (with a question mark) בנו "his son" after this name, with ten Hebrew MSS and LXX$^{bye}_2$. LXX^B reads "his sons" after Telah, making Resheph and Telah brothers.

44 נערן; Josh 16:7 נערתה "[toward] Naarah."

45 עיה; many Hebrew MSS, LXX^{Aal}, Tg, Vg: עזה "Gaza."

46 יבלעם ובנתיה with LXX; lacking in MT by homoioteleuton. Cf. Josh 17:11.

47 *BHS* proposes to insert ארבעה "four." Cf. vv. 1, 3, 6, 7.

48 ברזית with Q, a few Hebrew MSS, and the versions; K ברזות "Birzoth."

49 שׁומר; *BHS* emends to שׁמר "Shemer." Cf. LXX.

50 חותם; v. 35 חלם "Helem."

51 שׁמר. One Hebrew MS, LXX^{Aal}, Vg: שׁומר "Shomer," as in v. 32 MT. See textual note 49.

52 אחיו; cf. Curtis and Madsen, 156. MT אחי ו "Ahi and. . . ."

53 ורהגה with Q; K ורוהגה "Rohagah."

54 וחבה with Q, LXX, Vg; K יחבה "Jahbah." "Jehubbah" in *KJV* combines K and Q. Cf. Jehovah.

55 ובני with some Hebrew MSS, LXX^L, Vg; MT ובן "The son of."

56 חלם; *BHS* emends to חותם "Hotham." This name appears in v. 32. While *BHS* produces a "correct" text, there is no evidence that this reading was ever present in a MS of Chronicles.

57 ובני ימנע; cf. v. 35. MT וברי וימרה "Beri and Imrah." Since there is no conjunction before Bezer in v. 37, Rudolph, 74, following Noth, *Personennamen*, 240, 246, proposed this conjectural emendation based on v. 35, where Imna occurs.

58 בני, a conjectural addition. See the commentary on v. 37.

59 ויתרן. See the commentary. This name is a variant spelling of יתר "Jether" in the next verse, and that spelling occurs here in one Hebrew MS and LXX^{Aal}. This reading, however, is to be understood as a correction.

60 עלא. For a discussion of what might be the original reading, see the commentary.

Structure

The genealogies of the tribes in this chapter can be outlined as follows:

I. 7:1-5. Genealogy from Issachar (see the genealogical chart "Descendants of Issachar")

II. 7:6-12. Genealogy from Benjamin (see the genealogical chart "Descendants of Benjamin," which also includes materials from chap. 8),[1] perhaps once followed by genealogies for Dan and Zebulun that are now lost (see the commentary on v. 12)

III. 7:13. Genealogy from Naphtali (see the genealogical chart "Descendants of Naphtali")

IV. 7:14-19. Genealogy from Manasseh (cf. the Manassehite territory in v. 29 [see the genealogical chart "Descendants of Manasseh," which reflects changes proposed in the commentary])

V. 7:20-27. Genealogy from Ephraim (cf. the Ephraimite territory in v. 28 [see the genealogical chart "Descendants of Ephraim"])

VI. 7:30-40. Genealogy from Asher (see the genealogical chart "Descendants of Asher")

These six sections can be divided into three parts. Section A is part of the military census list detected already in 5:23-24 (Issachar, Benjamin, and Asher); section B consists of Naphtali, a tribe descended from Bilhah, the concubine supplied to Jacob by Rachel, which logically should also include Dan;[2] and section C, which provides genealogical information for the descendants of the two tribes stemming from Joseph (Manasseh and Ephraim).

The genealogies of the tribes of Issachar and Benjamin (cf. the tribe of Asher) begin with a genealogical citation from the Pentateuch, usually from Numbers 26. Each of them is further characterized by references to ancestral houses (vv. 2, 3, 7, 9, 11; cf. v. 40), military terminology (vv. 2, 4, 5, 7, 9, 11; cf. v. 40), and a lack of any reference to tribal settlements. The genealogies of these two tribes (perhaps also Asher) appear to come from a military census list that gives totals for each tribe: 87,000 for Issachar, 61,434 for Benjamin, and 26,000 for Asher (cf. 5:18). At least one principle that accounts for the order of these census-list genealogies, therefore, is numerical, beginning with the highest number and moving to the lowest. The existence of the census materials may explain why genealogical material for Benjamin is given twice (in vv. 6-12 and in chap. 8) and why Benjamin in this chapter is linked to Issachar (data for these two tribes come from the partially preserved military census list consulted by the Chronicler). In general, the order of tribes in this chapter is from north to south. Benjamin and Asher are the exceptions. Benjamin's position may come because of its ties to Issachar in the census list. Asher's unusual position may be related to the unusual southern references in this paragraph (see the commentary) and to its small total in the census list.

One of the unsolved problems in this chapter is the absence from the MT of the tribes of Zebulun and Dan and the meager data supplied for the tribe of Naphtali. Numerous commentators have tried to explain the absence of Dan as a polemical reaction to the cult of Jeroboam that was practiced at the sanctuary of Dan, but that explanation does not account at all for the absence of Zebulun. I am attracted by the idea that the genealogies for Zebulun and Dan were lost by textual accident (Williamson, 78), but proof, of course, is impossible, and I believe that a later hand may have filled in genealogical data from Genesis 46 for Naphtali. In the commentary I discuss the proposal that a highly corrupted version of the genealogy of Dan can be retrieved from v. 12, although I finally reject that proposal. A related factor is that the Chronicler may have had very little genealogical data for the northern tribes in general, but this would account only for the brevity of his treatment of a tribe like Naphtali, not for the absence of all information for

---

1   The Chronicler included a lengthy genealogy of Benjamin in chap. 8 (plus a genealogy of the descendants of the Benjaminite King Saul in 8:29-40//9:35-44), but he also utilized this shorter genealogy, apparently because it was part of the military census source he used for this chapter. Curtis and Madsen, 145–49, interpreted this genealogy as originally belonging to Zebulun, but this opinion has found few followers. See the commentary. Does this show Benjaminites living in the north? See Abraham Malamat, "*Ummatum* in Old Babylonian Texts and Its Ugaritic and Biblical Counterparts," *UF* 11 (1979) 527–36.

2   The absence of Zebulun and Dan will be discussed in the commentary on v. 12.

Zebulun and Dan, since the Chronicler could easily have included some data for them from the Pentateuch.

The genealogies for the sons of Joseph, Manasseh (vv. 14-19) and Ephraim (vv. 20-29), make up nearly half of this chapter. Neither of these genealogies contains the military terminology contained in the genealogies of Issachar, Benjamin, and Asher, nor do they have genealogical information to be found elsewhere in pentateuchal sources.[3] On the other hand, areas of settlement are provided for both Ephraim (v. 28) and Manasseh (v. 29). Important geographical information can also be found in the genealogy of Asher. Since vv. 14-19 report the descendants of Manasseh and vv. 20-27 those of Ephraim, the verses devoted to the sons of Joseph are chiastically arranged: descendants of Manasseh (vv. 14-19), descendants of Ephraim (vv. 20-27), settlement areas of Ephraim (v. 28), and settlement areas of Manasseh (v. 29). The genealogy for Manasseh requires the most conjectural emendation of any of the genealogies in chaps. 1–9, whereas the genealogy for Ephraim is made up of two linear genealogies (vv. 20-21a, 25aγ-27) and an anecdote dealing with Ephraim's tribal history (vv. 21b-25aβ).

Detailed Commentary

7:1-5. Genealogy from Issachar

Issachar—Tola——— Uzzi———— Izrahaiah— Michael
         Puah   Rephaiah   Obadiah
         Jashub   Jeriel   Joel
         Shimron Jahmai   Isshaiah
                   Ibsam
                   Shemuel

■ **1** *The sons of Issachar: Tola, Puah, Jashub, and Shimron, four:* For the first generation of the sons of Issachar, the Chronicler draws on Num 26:23-24[4] (cf. Gen 46:13), but the source of his information for succeeding generations is unknown. The verse begins with a *casus pendens:* "As for the sons of Issachar . . ."[5] One of the "minor judges" from Issachar seems to owe his existence to an interpretation of this genealogy: "Tola son of Puah[6] son of Dodo, who lived at Shamir in the hill country of Ephraim" (Judg 10:1). The names Tola and Puah are identical with the first two sons of Issachar. "Shamir" has the same root consonants as Shimron, and Jashub (ישׂוב) has the same consonants as "who lived" (ישׁב). Hence four of the words in Judg 10:1 seem to be dependent on the genealogy of Issachar in Num 26:23-24 and in this verse.[7] Levin has suggested that we can conclude from Judg 10:1 that Issachar's clans originally settled in the hill country and moved into their inheritance only at a later date.[8] This may explain the absence of Issachar in the Barak-Sisera story of Judges 4[9] or the Gideon story in Judges 6–7. Only the descendants of the firstborn son in each generation are followed in this genealogy. The number of sons is explicitly noted in this verse and also in vv. 3, 6, and 7 (cf. textual note 47 to v. 30).

■ **2** *The sons of Tola: Uzzi, Rephaiah, Jeriel, Jahmai, Ibsam, and Shemuel, heads of their ancestral houses, namely of Tola, mighty warriors of their generations:* For each of the genealogies in section A, the names refer to heads of ancestral houses and not simply to individuals. In this case six heads are named for the sons of Tola, none of whom is known outside the genealogy of Issachar, and the names Jeriel, Jahmai, and Ibsam appear only here in

---

3 Descendants for Manasseh and Ephraim are lacking in Gen 46:20 MT, but two generations for both Manasseh and Ephraim are given in Gen 46:20 LXX.

4 "The descendants of Issachar by their clans: of Tola, the clan of the Tolaites; of Puvah, the clan of the Punites; of Jashub, the clan of the Jashubites; of Shimron, the clans of the Shimronites."

5 Cf. GKC §143e.

6 The spelling of this name agrees with 1 Chr 7:1 against Gen 46:13 and Num 26:23. See textual note 2.

7 See Ran Zadok, "Notes on the Prosopography of the Old Testament," *BN* 42 (1988) 44. Or was this genealogical notice created from Judg 10:1?

8 "Understanding Biblical Genealogies," 30. Zvi Gal, "The Settlement of Issachar: Some New Observations," *TA* 9 (1982) 79–86, concludes that none of the sites of Issachar were occupied prior to the 10th century BCE.

9 But Issachar is present in Judg 5:15.

the Bible. The category "mighty warriors" (גבורי חיל),[10] with slight spelling variations, is used throughout section A, the excerpts from the military census list. The term "generations" (תלדות) is used also in the census of Numbers 1, the "toledoth" formulas in Genesis, and in some of the genealogies of Chronicles.[11]

their number in the days of David were twenty-two thousand six hundred: The reference to the days of David calls to mind the census David took and for which Israel was punished in 1 Chronicles 21//2 Samuel 24.[12] Other administrative changes in the time of David are noted in the genealogical introduction to Chronicles at 1 Chr 4:31 and 6:16 (31). The total number given for the clans of Issachar in Num 1:29 is 54,400; in Num 26:25 it is 64,300. The warriors of the tribe of Issachar alone are not numbered with those of other tribes in 1 Chronicles 12; the total of the chiefs (ראשיהם) of Issachar there is given as 200 (12:33 [32]). Oeming notes the contrast between the large tribal numbers in chap. 7 and the mere 500 Simeonites recorded at 4:42, but his conclusion that the numbers here are meant as criticism of the north for lacking trust in God is not warranted.[13] The presence of these numbers here, rather, is neutral since they came from the military census list used here by the Chronicler. If they do have any specific message, it is of the full participation of Issachar in the reality called Israel.

■ **3** *The son of Uzzi: Izrahiah. And the sons of Izrahiah: Michael, Obadiah, Joel, and Isshiah, five:* If Izrahiah and his four sons are all considered "descendants" of Uzzi, the number "five" is congruent with the rest of the verse. Rudolph, 64, however, deletes "the sons of Izrahiah" as a partial dittography and therefore makes all five men *actual* sons of Uzzi.

■ **4-5a** *troops of the war force, thirty-six thousand, for they had more wives and sons than their kindred:* While the martial vocabulary is similar for the three tribes in section A, it is not uniform, and the variant reading attested in the versions and discussed in textual note 9 is an attempt to

correlate the terminology here ("troops") more closely with that of the other tribes. The word "troops" (גדודי) is used with some frequency by the Chronicler (1 Chr 12:19, 22 [18, 21]; 2 Chr 22:1; 25:9, 10, 13; 26:11). The greater size of the number of the descendants of Uzzi (36,000) in comparison with the sons of Tola in v. 2 (22,600) is explained by the greater number of wives and children among the descendants of Uzzi, with the clear suggestion that this total was reached two generations after the number achieved by the sons of Tola.

■ **5b** *For all the families of Issachar there were altogether eighty-seven thousand mighty warriors enrolled by genealogy:* No date is suggested for this total for the whole tribe. Is this number in addition to the figures in vv. 2 and 4? If so, the total is 145,600, far more than any other tribe in 1 Chronicles 1–9, Numbers 1 and 26, and 1 Chr 12:25-38. If it *includes* the numbers given for the descendants of Tola and Uzzi in vv. 2 and 4,[14] or if it is a third total for the tribe from an unspecified time (which I think is the most reasonable conclusion), Issachar is still larger than any tribe except Judah (470,000 in 1 Chr 21:5// 500,000 in 2 Sam 24:9). This total suggests that the tribe had multiplied almost fourfold since the time of David in v. 2.[15] The last verb in this verse התיחשׂם is a *hitpael* infinitive construct with suffix, functioning as a substantive (*HALOT* 2:408; cf. vv. 7, 9, 40): literally: "their registration."

---

10   1 Chr 7:2, 5, 7, 9, 11, 40. Cf. 5:24 and 8:40.

11   1 Chr 1:29; 5:7; 7:2, 4, 9; 8:28; 9:9, 34; 26:31.

12   There has clearly been telescoping in this genealogy since historically the second generation after the patriarch would not bring us to the 10th century.

13   *Wahre Israel,* 166.

14   This calculation would suggest that the descendants

of Puah, Jahub, and Shimron totaled 28,400 in addition to those assigned to the son and grandson of Tola.

15   Oeming, *Wahre Israel,* 159, observes that 87,000 less 22,600 is 64,400, suggesting that there may be some connection with the number given in Num 26:25 (64,300).

7:6-12. Genealogy from Benjamin

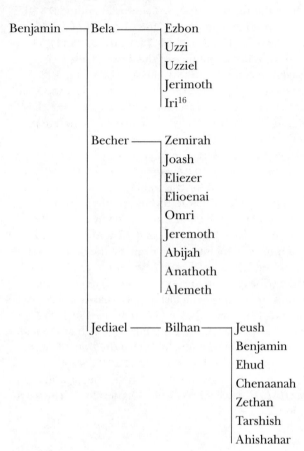

Benjamin	Bela	Ezbon
		Uzzi
		Uzziel
		Jerimoth
		Iri[16]
	Becher	Zemirah
		Joash
		Eliezer
		Elioenai
		Omri
		Jeremoth
		Abijah
		Anathoth
		Alemeth
	Jediael — Bilhan	Jeush
		Benjamin
		Ehud
		Chenaanah
		Zethan
		Tarshish
		Ahishahar

Gen 46:21 MT	Num 26:38-39	1 Chr 8:1-2
Bela	Bela	Bela
Becher	Ashbel	Ashbel
Ashbel[18]	Ahiram	Aharah
Gera	Shephupham	Nohah
Naaman	Hupham	Rapha
Ehi		
Rosh		
Muppim		
Huppim		
Ard		

■ **6** *The sons of Benjamin: Bela, Becher, and Jediael, three:* We have three[17] other witnesses to the immediate children of Benjamin:

Bela is common to all four genealogies as the oldest son of Benjamin, but Becher, the second son of Benjamin in 1 Chr 7:6, is known elsewhere as a son of Benjamin only in Gen 46:21. The remaining parts of each of the genealogies of Benjamin go their own separate ways.[19] Jediael, the third child here, who seems to have replaced Ashbel, also appears in vv. 10-11, but nowhere else as a descendant of Benjamin.[20] The genealogy gives a total of fourteen sons for Benjamin's first two sons, Bela (five) and Becher (nine); for the third son, Jediael, the genealogy provides an intermediate generation Bilhan and then a list of Bilhan's seven sons, for a total of eight descendants of Jediael.

It is strange that Benjamin is listed in this chapter among the northern tribes,[21] especially since a full genealogy for Benjamin follows in chap. 8.[22] Perhaps the best explanation for this is that the Chronicler continued citing the military census list he had already used for Issachar (Williamson, 77; cf. also the sequence of Reuben in 5:1-10 and Gad in 5:11-17). Curtis and Madsen, 147,[23] however, noted that Zebulun follows Issachar

---

16 For Shupphim and Huppim see the commentary on v. 12.

17 While totals for the descendants of Benjamin are given in Num 1:36-37, no sons of Benjamin are named there.

18 Only these first three names are immediate children of Benjamin in Gen 46:21 LXX.

19 In Gen 46:21, Num 26:38, and 1 Chr 8:1 the next child is Ashbel. That makes him the second son in Numbers 26 and 1 Chronicles 8, and the third in Genesis 46.

20 The name appears three other times in the OT, all in Chronicles: 1 Chr 11:45; 12:21 (20); 26:2.

21 The Chronicler often distinguishes between Benjamin and the northern tribes (Oeming, *Wahre Israel,* 160). Note how Benjamin and Levi are the only two tribes not included in the census (1 Chr 21:6).

22 Both Rudolph, 65, and Kartveit, *Motive und Schichten,* 107–9, consider Benjamin secondary here, but it is difficult to explain why anyone would want to insert this tribe here.

23 See also G. Richter, "Zu den Geschlechtsregistern 1 Chr 2–9," *ZAW* 50 (1932) 130–41, esp. 133–34; A. M. Brunet, "Le chroniste et ses sources," *RB* 60 (1953) 481–508, esp. 485 and n. 6.

in thirteen out of seventeen OT lists,[24] including 2:1, and they suggest that the genealogy in vv. 6-11 should be ascribed to Zebulun rather than Benjamin. In their opinion this mistake began when a text like Gen 46:14 "The children of Zebulun: Sered, Elon, and Jahleel" (ובני זבלון סרד ואלון ויחלאל) was miswritten to the text in v 6: בנימין בלע ובכר וידיעאל. But the correspondence between the names in these verses is not particularly close and the hypothesis requires that several Benjaminite names

were added later, such as Bela and Becher in vv. 7-8, Anathoth and Alemeth in v. 8, and Ehud in v. 10. See Curtis and Madsen, 149, for the text of the reconstructed Zebulunite genealogy.[25]

■ **7** *The sons of Bela: Ezbon, Uzzi, Uzziel, Jerimoth, and Iri, five:* Descendants of Bela are also given in Gen 46:21 LXX, Num 26:40, and 1 Chr 8:3-5, but not in Gen 46:21 MT.

Gen 46:21 LXX (with some corrections in spelling)

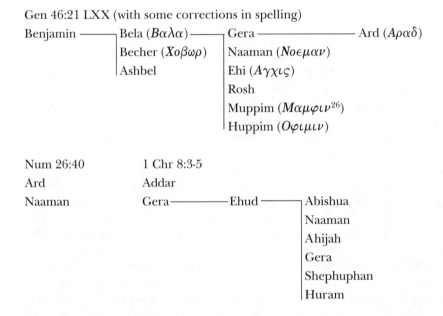

Bela's sons in Num 26:40 are Ard and Naaman, but these two persons are identified as the ninth and the fourth *brothers,* respectively, among Bela's nine brothers in Gen 46:21 MT.[27] Two sons, one grandson, and six great-grandsons of Bela are given in my reconstruction of the genealogy of Benjamin in 1 Chr 8:3-5,[28] all of

them different from those named here. So none of the sons of Bela in 7:7 is listed as a direct son or even as a descendant of Benjamin elsewhere.

and their enrollment by genealogies was twenty-two thousand thirty-four: The total number of Benjaminites in vv. 7, 9, and 11 is 59,434.[29] This compares with 35,400 in

---

24 See, e.g., Deut 33:18-19; 1 Chr 12:34, 41 (33, 40); 27:18-19; 2 Chr 30:18.

25 Oeming, *Wahre Israel,* 161–63, argues that in the pre-state, divided monarchy, and postexilic times there were ties between Benjamin and the north, but this still leaves unexplained the reason for locating the genealogy of Benjamin right after Issachar.

26 Cf. 1 Chr 7:15 LXX.

27 In Gen 46:21 LXX Naaman is listed as a son of Bela, and Ard is Bela's grandson via Gera.

28 For a comparison of these with the sons of Bela mentioned in Gen 46:21 LXX see the commentary on chap. 8.

29 Oeming, *Wahre Israel,* 159, has 59,830, but this results from his misreading the number in this verse as 22,430.

Num 1:37 and 45,600 in Num 26:41. Three thousand Benjaminites are listed among those who rallied to David in 1 Chr 12:30 (29). The census of the Benjaminites seems to have been recorded at one unspecified time whereas that of Issachar happened at two different periods (the time of David and two generations later; vv. 2, 4).

■ **8** *The sons of Becher: Zemirah, Joash, Eliezer, Elioenai, Omri, Jeremoth, Abijah, Anathoth, and Alemeth:* No sons of Becher are given at Gen 46:21.[30] Anathoth (MR 174135) and Alemeth (MR 176136) are place names rather than personal names (see the list of Levitical cities, 1 Chr 6:45 [60], where they are two of the four Benjaminite cities).[31] Japhet, 173, suggests these two names might be regarded as a literary irregularity and hence secondary, or the people inhabiting these two sites were homogeneous and therefore regarded as one family. However, a mixture of persons/clans and localities appears throughout the genealogies. Layton has parsed the word Alemeth as a verbal adjective with the meaning "lass, young girl."[32]

■ **9** *their enrollment by genealogies, according to their generations, as heads of their ancestral houses, mighty warriors, was twenty thousand two hundred:* The technical terms "enrollment by genealogies," "according to their generations," "heads of their ancestral houses," and "mighty warriors" also appeared in vv. 4–5. For the total number see v. 7.

■ **10** *The son of Jediael: Bilhan. And the sons of Bilhan: Jeush, Benjamin, Ehud, Chenaanah, Zethan, Tarshish, and Ahishahar:* Jeush appears as a descendant of Saul[33] and therefore of Benjamin in 1 Chr 8:39, and Ehud the son

of Gera is a well-known judge from Benjamin (Judg 3:15-30). A Chenaanah is listed as the father of Zedekiah in 1 Kgs 22:11, 24//2 Chr 18:10, 23, but he is not identified there as a Benjaminite. Zethan and Ahishahar are hapax legomena. The name Benjamin is plausible as a descendant of the patriarch Benjamin, but this particular Benjamin is unattested elsewhere. This is the only time Tarshish is identified as a descendant of Benjamin.

■ **12** *And Shuppim and Huppim were the sons of Ir, Hushim the son of Aher:* Shuppim (שפים) is similar to Muppim (מפים), the eighth son of Benjamin in Gen 46:21, and Huppim (חפים) is identical with the ninth son of Benjamin there. Compare also Shephupham (שפופם)/Shupham (שופם) and Hupham (חופם), the ancestors of the fourth and fifth clans of Benjamin in Num 26:39. The two names are probably a corrective gloss here,[34] and were also falsely entered in v. 15 (q.v.).

More than a century ago, August Klostermann suggested emending the rest of the present verse (בני עיר חשם בני אחד "[were] the sons of Ir, Hushim the son of Aher") to read: בני דן חשם בנו אחד "The sons of Dan: Hushim his son one."[35] Hushim is listed as the only son of Dan in Gen 46:23.[36] The use of a number after the listing of descendant(s) also occurs in vv. 1, 3, 6, and 7.[37] This emendation recovers a genealogy for Dan, which would seem to be required by the words "These were the descendants[38] of Bilhah" that come after the genealogy of Naphtali in the next verse. The greatest difficulty with this suggestion is that Dan דן and Ir עיר bear almost no resemblance to one another in Hebrew.[39] Williamson understands the verse as a fragmentary series of Benjami-

---

30 Becher and the Becherites in Num 26:35 are part of the tribe of Ephraim.

31 Anathoth occurs as a personal name in Neh 10:20 (19), and Alemeth occurs as a personal name in 1 Chr 8:36 and 9:42, both times among the descendants of Saul.

32 Scott C. Layton, "The Semitic Root *Ǵlm and the Hebrew Name 'Ālæmæt*," *ZAW* 102 (1990) 80–94.

33 He is the second son of Eshek, the brother of Azel, in the last generation after Saul.

34 Japhet, 174, suggested that this gloss was intended to supplement the names of Benjamin's sons in 1 Chr 7:6.

35 "Chronik," *RE* 4.94. Oeming, *Wahre Israel*, 163, suggests that the last two words could be read בנים אחרים "other sons" and be a gloss on Shuppim and Huppim.

36 Cf. Num 26:42, where Dan's sole son is named שוחם "Shuham," clearly a result of metathesis.

37 Williamson, 378, notes, however, that the latter numbers are in the context of a census list. Rudolph and *BHS* add such a number in v. 30. See textual note 47.

38 Note the plural.

39 W. Bacher, "Zu 1 Chron. 7,12," *ZAW* 18 (1898) 236–38, attempted to meet this difficulty by proposing that the genealogist wrote "city" because he did not want to write the name of the city where idolatry was practiced. This is highly unlikely, however, since the Chronicler elsewhere uses the name Dan without objection: 1 Chr 2:2; 12:36 (35); 21:2; 27:22; 2 Chr 2:14 (13; the *Vorlage* in 1 Kgs 7:14 reads "Naphtali"); 16:4; 30:5. Bacher proposed that a later hand added בני אחר, which Bacher understood as a

nite names added without connection to the preceding.[40] Huppim and Shuppim, as we saw, can be compared to Benjaminite names attested elsewhere. Williamson compares "Ir" to "Iri" in v. 7; cites the presence of Hushim in 8:8, 11;[41] and emends אחר to "Ard," a name that follows Muppim and Huppim in Gen 46:21, or a person who is the son of Bela and therefore the grandson of Benjamin in Num 26:40.[42] If Klostermann's proposal can be accepted, we have an explanation for the absence of Dan if not for Zebulun. If his suggestion cannot be followed, as I believe, then the absence of Dan can be explained either as an accident (the genealogy of Naphtali originally followed the genealogies of Dan and Zebulun, but the latter two were accidentally lost) or as intentional.[43] The "original" genealogies for Dan and Zebulun, as far northern tribes, may have been quite brief.

7:13. Genealogy from Naphtali

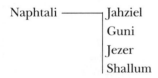

■ 13 *The descendants of Naphtali: Jahziel, Guni, Jezer, and Shallum:* The Chronicler here follows Gen 46:24 and Num 26:48-49, with the slight spelling changes noted in the first and last names that were discussed in textual notes 24 and 25. The shortness of this genealogy has led some to suspect that the original genealogies of Dan, Zebulun, and Naphtali were lost but only that of Naphtali (and perhaps Dan; see v. 12) was restored. The shortness of this genealogy corresponds to the general lack of detailed genealogical information the Chronicler has for the northern tribes.

These were the descendants of Bilhah: Cf. Gen 46:23-25, where the two sons of Bilhah, Rachel's maid, are given as Dan and Naphtali. This summary does indeed seem to presuppose the presence of Dan.

7:14-19. Genealogy from Manasseh (cf. v. 29)

The genealogy from Manasseh elsewhere in the Bible shows some fluidity about the location of Machir and Hepher within the descendants of Manasseh. According to the genealogy of Manasseh in Josh 17:1-3 (see the graphic), Manasseh had seven sons. Machir was his first-born and the father of Gilead, and the other sons of Manasseh were Abiezer, Helek, Asriel, Shechem, Hep-

---

somewhat clearer reference to Dan for ancient readers. Kartveit, *Motive und Schichten,* 99–100, 188, reads: "Huppim and Shuppim were the sons of Ir, Hushim was the son of another." He also takes "another" as a code word for Dan. Rudolph, 68–69, proposed that a marginal gloss, לפנים לעיר שם אחר "formerly the city had another name," referring to Judg 18:29, led to the corrupt present text. Noth, *Chronicler's History,* 37, 40–42, took vv. 12-13 as the basis for his theory that the lists in chap. 7 originally followed the information in Numbers 26 both in order and in length. This order consisted of Issachar, Zebulun, Manasseh, Ephraim, Benjamin, Dan, Asher, and Naphtali. Zebulun was accidentally lost, and Manasseh, Ephraim, and Benjamin were subsequently displaced to the end of the list. He read v. 12 as follows: "and Shupham and Hupham" [a remnant of the original genealogy of Benjamin]. The sons of Dan: Shuham" (Num 26:42; Gen 46:23; this is basically Klostermann's suggestion, although he followed the spelling of Dan's son found in Num 26:42). Noth believed that the text continued as follows: "The sons of Asher . . ." (reading אשר for אחר and continuing with material from Num 26:44-45).

The title for Asher was left here, but the rest of Asher's genealogy was greatly expanded and relocated at 7:30-40. According to Noth, the extract for Naphtali in 7:13 (drawn from Num 26:48-49; cf. Gen 46:24) formed the original conclusion to Chronicler's information about the tribes of Israel.

40 "A Note on 1 Chronicles VII 12," *VT* 23 (1973) 375–79.

41 In 1 Chr 7:12 and 8:11 the name is written defectively, while in 8:8, it is written plene.

42 Williamson, "Note," 377, observes that this person is called "Addar" in Num 26:40 LXX and in 1 Chr 8:3.

43 Braun, 107, cites an "aversion" to Dan in 1 Chr 6:46, 54 (61, 69). In his view v. 12 represents a fragment of an earlier genealogy of Benjamin and Dan related to Gen 46:21, 23. Braun, 109, argues that an original genealogy of Benjamin based on Genesis 46 has now been replaced with another based on a military census, which has also influenced the genealogy of Issachar. Japhet, 174, considers that v. 12 might be a continuation of the Benjaminite genealogy. She states that "Aher" could be a corruption of a name like Ehi (Gen 46:21), Ahiram (Num

her, and Shemida.[44] In Num 26:29-34, however, Machir is the sole son of Manasseh and he is again the father of Gilead. The remaining six sons of Manasseh known from Joshua are classified as sons of Gilead.[45] Both passages also include Zelophehad and his five daughters (cf. Num 27:1 and 36:11), possibly secondarily, and Zelophe-

had in both cases is considered the son of Hepher, the son of Gilead the son of Machir the son of Manasseh. In Joshua this creates a tension since in v. 2 Hepher is the son of Manasseh whereas in v. 3 he is the great-grandson of Manasseh (through Gilead and Machir).

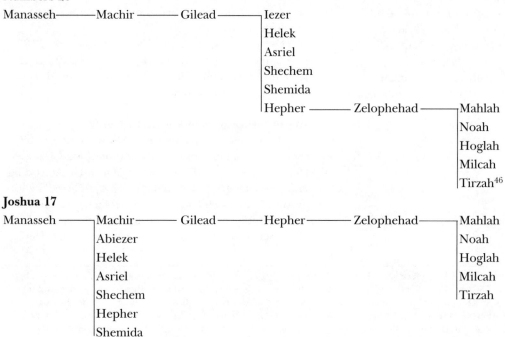

Numbers 26

Manasseh——Machir———Gilead——Iezer
Helek
Asriel
Shechem
Shemida
Hepher———Zelophehad——Mahlah
Noah
Hoglah
Milcah
Tirzah[46]

Joshua 17

Manasseh——Machir——Gilead——Hepher——Zelophehad——Mahlah
Abiezer
Helek
Asriel
Shechem
Hepher
Shemida
Noah
Hoglah
Milcah
Tirzah

26:38), Aharah (1 Chr 8:1), or Adar/Ard (1 Chr 8:3; Gen 46:21). Finally, however, she adopts Klostermann's proposal. Rudolph, 65–66, concluded that the original order of tribes in chap. 7 was Issachar, Zebulun, Benjamin, Dan, Naphtali, Gad, Asher, Manasseh, and Ephraim. He believed that the Chronicler followed the order of tribes outlined in 1 Chr 2:1-2, except that he moved Judah to the beginning and the sons of Joseph to the end. The first two words of v. 12 are in his opinion the ending to the original genealogy of Benjamin (cf. Num 26:38-39), but the rest of the genealogy of Benjamin and the preceding genealogy of Zebulun were lost by textual corruption. What we now have in vv. 6-11 comes from a specific postexilic context. Rudolph

also denied the genealogy of Benjamin in chap. 8 to the Chronicler and believed that the original materials on Asher were lost and replaced by what we find in 7:30-40. He denied the genealogy of Gad in 5:11-16 to the Chronicler as well. He also held part of v. 2, from לתולע to the end of the verse, and vv. 4-5 in Issachar to be secondary.

44   The relationship of Machir and his six brothers is implied, rather than stated explicitly.

45   Hence they are great-grandsons of Manasseh instead of sons.

46   In Num 36:11 the daughters are given in the following order: Mahlah, Tirzah, Hoglah, Milcah, and Noah.

The genealogy of Manasseh in 1 Chronicles 7 presents such severe difficulties that one must suppose textual corruption and the need for conjectural changes. It is impossible to tell whether these difficulties existed already in the sources consulted by the Chronicler and therefore included by the Chronicler in his text, or whether the genealogy of the Chronicler has been damaged by subsequent copyists' errors. These difficulties include:[47]

a. In v. 14 there are two parallel verbal clauses, the first of which apparently lacks a subject: "Asriel whom she bore" and "his [Manasseh's] Aramaic concubine bore Machir the father of Gilead." Are Asriel and Machir brothers, as in Josh 17:1-2, where Machir is the firstborn and Asriel the fourth son of Manasseh? In Num 26:31 Asriel is the third son of Gilead and the grandson of Machir, the son of Manasseh. The syntactical relationship of the two clauses is also awkward.

b. In v. 15 we are told that Machir took a wife for Huppim and Shuppim, but no children are assigned to them in this genealogy. We have already seen that the presence of these names in v. 12 is probably the result of a gloss.

c. In v. 15 the text refers to "his sister Maacah," and the antecedent of the pronoun "his" is probably Machir, since we have recognized Huppim and Shuppim as secondary. In v. 16, however, we read that Maacah is Machir's *wife*. Maacah is mentioned before Zelophehad in v. 15, but her children appear only in vv. 16-17.

d. Zelophehad is mentioned in v. 15 without any explicit connection to the genealogy of Manasseh and is called "the second," but there is no indication who "the first" is. As we saw above, Zelophehad is identified elsewhere as the son of Hepher the son of Gilead the son of Machir the son of Manasseh (Num 26:32-33; Josh 17:3). While his daughters are named in both Numbers and Joshua, as we have seen above, 1 Chronicles 7 states only that he is the father of daughters, but their names and even their number are not given.

e. The children of Machir and Maacah are listed in vv. 16-17, but in a summary clause at the end of v. 17 they are called "sons of Gilead the son of Machir the son of Manasseh."

f. Verse 18 mentions another sister, Hammolecheth. Is she the sister of Machir (vv. 14-16) or of Gilead (v. 17)?

g. Shemida is mentioned in v. 19, with no explicit connection to the genealogy of Manasseh. In Num 26:29 he is the fifth son of Gilead; in Josh 17:2 he is the seventh and youngest son of Manasseh.

No way out of these problems has been found without more or less radical surgery. Three proposals may be considered as representative. Rudolph, 68–71, introduced the following changes in an attempt to bring this genealogy into line with Numbers 26:

a. He deleted "Asriel" (אשריאל) from v. 14 as a dittograph of the Hebrew words "which she bore," (אשר ילדה) but added the words "and the sons of Gilead Abiezer" (cf. Num 26:30) at the beginning of the next verse. He believed these words were lost when a scribe's eye skipped from "father of Gilead" (אבי גלעד) at the end of v. 14 to the end of the name "Abiezer" (אביעזר) at the beginning of v. 15.

b. He changed "and Machir" at the beginning of v. 15 to "his firstborn." The next four Hebrew words ("he took a wife for Huppim and Shuppim") were understood to be a corruption of the next four sons of Gilead from Num 26:30-32. The final son of Gilead, Shemida (שמידע), in his opinion, was lost by homoioarchton before "and the name of" (ושם). He included all six sons of Gilead in his reconstructed text. Rudolph also changed "his sister" to "their sister" in v. 15.

c. After Maacah in v. 16, he inserted: "And the sons of Hepher the firstborn X," where X represented a lost name.

d. He moved v. 19 between v. 15 and v. 16. Rudolph believed it had been moved to its present position because it clearly involved Cisjordan, just as Abiezer does in v. 18.

---

47   For the following see Japhet, 175; Rudolph, 69. Shechem (Josh 17:1) and Abiezer (Judg 16:11) point to Cisjordan for the land of Manasseh.

e. The husband of Maacah in v. 16 is unknown; Machir in MT is a correction of another name.

The result is a text that reads very much like Numbers 26, but many of Rudolph's changes seem arbitrary and unnecessary:

14/ The sons of Manasseh whom his Aramean concubine bore: she bore Machir the father of Gilead. 15/ And the sons of Gilead: Abiezer his firstborn, then Helek, Asriel, Hepher, Shechem, and Shemida, and the name of their sister was Maacah. And the sons of Hepher the firstborn X, and the name of the second was Zelophehad; and Zelophehad had only daughters. 19/ The sons of Shemida were Ahian, Shechem, Likhi, and Aniam. 16/ Maacah the wife of Y bore a son, and she named him Peresh; the name of his brother was Sheresh, and his sons were Ulam and Rakem. 17/ The sons of Ulam: Bedan. These were the sons of Gilead son of Machir, son of Manasseh. 18/ And his[48] sister Hammolecheth bore Ishhod, Abiezer, and Mahlah.

Here is the reconstruction of Rudolph listed in genealogical form:

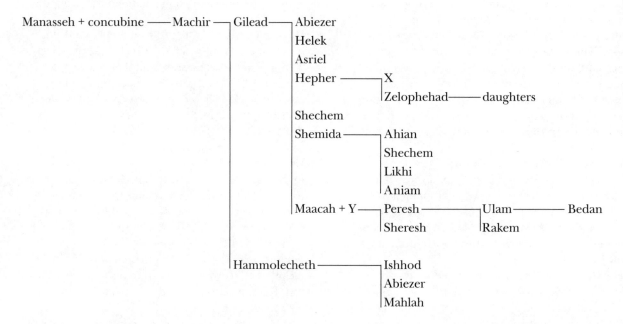

In an article on this genealogy,[49] Diana Edelman introduced the following changes to the Hebrew text:

a. She deleted "Asriel" from v. 14.
b. She concluded that "Huppim and Shuppim" were mistakenly added to v. 15.
c. She changed אחתו "his sister" in v. 15 to האחת "the first," and השני "the second" (a masculine adjective) in the same verse to השנית (a feminine adjective), with the result that Zelophehad is changed from a man to a woman, and Maacah and Zelophehad are identified as Machir's wives.
d. She emended אחין "Ahian" in v. 19 to אחיו "his brother" and deleted the wāw before "Shechem." Shemida then becomes the brother of Machir (or

48 The antecedent in Rudolph's opinion, 71, is Gilead.
49 "The Manassite Genealogy in 1 Chronicles 7:14-19: Form and Source," *CBQ* 53 (1991) 179–201.

Gilead) in v. 17, and he has three instead of four children.

While the smaller number of changes is certainly commendable, a number of difficulties with the text remain. "Sons" (plural) of Manasseh's concubine are mentioned in v. 14, but only one, Machir, is named in that verse. Machir takes *a* wife, but then two are named, Maacah and Zelophehad, with the already mentioned change in Zelophehad's gender.[50] Shemida and his sons are not well integrated into the genealogy. Edelman assigns vv. 16-19 to a separate source, with vv. 14-15 based on Numbers 26 and Joshua 17. But the resulting three children of Manasseh—Machir, Shemida, and Hammolechet—are radically different from those listed in other biblical passages.[51] Her reconstructed text reads as follows:

14/ The sons of Manasseh whom his Aramean concubine bore: she bore Machir the father of Gilead. 15/ And Machir took a wife. The name of the first was Maacah. And the name of the second was Zelophehad; and Zelophehad had only daughters. 16/ Maacah the wife of Machir bore a son, and she named him Peresh; the name of his brother was Sheresh, and his sons were Ulam and Rakem. 17/ The son of Ulam: Bedan. These were the sons of Gilead son of Machir, son of Manasseh. 18/ And his sister Hammolecheth bore Ishhod, Abiezer, and Mahlah. 19/ The sons of Shemida his brother: Shechem, Likhi, and Aniam.

In genealogical form (p. 190):

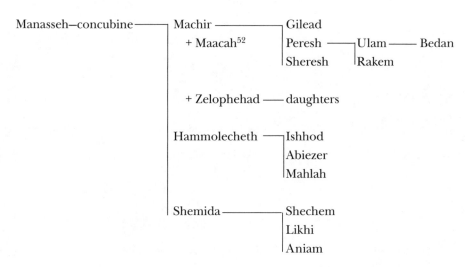

---

50 This is perhaps a bigger problem than she recognizes since Zelophehad is a rather prominent male in Numbers 27 and 36.

51 Edelman attempts to date the two sections of the genealogy, assigning vv. 14-15 with some hesitancy to the united monarchy and attributing vv. 16-19 to the reign of Joash.

52 In her diagram Edelman indicates with a parenthesis that Gilead may be the parent of Peresh and Sheresh.

In her commentary Japhet, 176, introduces the following emendations:

a. She deletes "which she bore" אשר ילדה in v. 14 as a dittograph instead of deleting "Asriel," as Rudolph and Edelman had done.[53]

b. "Huppim and Shuppim" are deleted as a gloss, originally intended for v. 6, that has been inserted both here in v. 15 and in v. 12.

c. She proposes a lengthy lacuna after the word "wife" in v. 15 that is to be filled in as follows: "and she bore him X [possibly Hepher]. X had two sons; the name of the first was Y."

d. She changes "Machir" to "Gilead" in both v. 15 and v. 16, and she moves "and the name of his sister was Maacah" from v. 15 to the end of v. 14 and the name Maacah is changed in this clause to Hammolecheth. The change of Machir to Gilead in vv. 15-16 might seem arbitrary, but v. 15 in her reconstruction makes Gilead the father of Hepher, as in Num 26:32-33; 27:1; and Josh 17:3, and the change in v. 16 is justified by the summary statement, "these are the sons of Gilead son of Machir, son of Manasseh," in v. 17.

e. She adds "and Shemida" at the end of v. 18, which was lost by homoioarchton.

Japhet's translation:

14/ The sons of Manasseh: Asriel. His Aramean concubine bore Machir the father of Gilead, and his sister's name was Hammolecheth. 15/ And Gilead took a wife and she bore him X (Hepher?). X had two sons; the name of the first was Y and the name of the second was Zelophehad; and Zelophehad had only daughters. 16/ Maacah the wife of Gilead bore a son, and she named him Peresh; the name of his brother was Sheresh, and his sons were Ulam and Rakem. 17/ The sons of Ulam: Bedan. These were the sons of Gilead son of Machir, son of Manasseh. 18/ And his sister Hammolecheth bore Ishhod, Abiezer, Mahlah, and Shemida. 19/ The sons of Shemida: Ahian, Shechem, Likhi, and Aniam.

Japhet's reconstruction in genealogical form:

```
Manasseh ──────────── Asriel
 + Aram. concubine ─┬─ Machir── Gilead + wife ──────X (Hepher?)──┬Y
                    │                                            │Zelophehad────────daughters
                    │           Gilead + Maacah ─┬Peresh ────────┬Ulam──── Bedan
                    │                            │Sheresh        │Rakem
                    │
                    │ Hammolecheth ───┬ Ishhod
                    │                 │ Abiezer
                    │                 │ Mahlah
                    │                 │ Shemida ──────┬ Ahian
                                                      │ Shechem
                                                      │ Likhi
                                                      │ Aniam
```

---

53 Alternately, she considers it possible that the clause is original and that the name of Asriel's mother has dropped out.

In Japhet's reconstruction Asriel and Machir are the only two children of Manasseh from Josh 17:2 who maintain their place in the genealogy. Abiezer and Shemida, the second oldest and the youngest son, become sons of Hammolecheth and grandsons of Manasseh. Helek (חלק = Likhi לקחי) and Shechem become sons of Shemida and therefore great-grandsons of Manasseh. Hepher's reconstructed position as a son of Gilead corresponds to his position in Josh 17:3.

Japhet's text is drastically different from the MT, and the genealogy of Manasseh is considerably different from that provided in Numbers and Joshua, but that may just represent the fluidity that has been so frequently noticed in segmented genealogies. The changes proposed in a, b, and e are the easiest to accept. Perhaps the change in point a is unnecessary, but without this deletion the syntax is awkward. The extra words she proposed in point c are of course a conjecture, but plausible. The name changes of Machir to Gilead proposed in point d are the most drastic but justified by the context. My commentary will follow her reconstructed text, but I choose not to move the clause about Machir's sister Hammolecheth,[54] retaining her as the sister of Gilead rather than a sister of Machir.[55] I have decided to consider Hepher as indeed the son of Gilead and his wife, and Hepher as the father of Y and Zelophehad, and I have therefore included him in the text. The wording of each verse in the commentary reflects the changes made by Japhet and/or me. A graphic for my own tentative reconstruction of this genealogy, based largely on Japhet, follows:

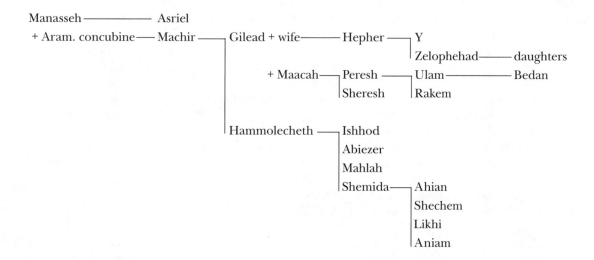

■ **14** *The sons of Manasseh: Asriel. His Aramean concubine bore Machir the father of Gilead:* In Num 26:30-31 Asriel is a son of Gilead and consequently a great-grandson of Manasseh (Manasseh–Machir–Gilead–Asriel). In Josh 17:2, on the other hand, Asriel is the fourth son of Manasseh.[56] The genealogical link of Machir, the father of Gilead, to the Arameans is more historically realistic than the notice in Gen 50:23 that implies that Gilead

---

54 I accept her change of the name of this sister from Maacah to Hammolecheth.
55 This requires a slight rewording of Japhet's insertion (point c) and placing it after the name Hammolecheth.
56 A. Lemaire, "Asriel, Šr'l, Israel et l'origine de la con-

federation Israelite," *VT* 23 (1973) 239–43, claimed that the three names in the title of his article were identical and that the name of the Israelite confederation בני ישראל came from one of its first confederate clans, בני אשריאל.

was born in Egypt. Rudolph, 70, surely errs in finding in the report of Manasseh's marriage to an Aramean concubine a polemic against the Samaritans for practicing mixed marriage like their ancestor Manasseh. The parenting of Machir by Manasseh and his Aramean concubine is also attested in Gen 46:20 LXX (lacking in MT). For Machir as the father of Gilead, see 1 Chr 2:21, 23; Josh 17:1, 3; Num 36:1.

■ **15** *And Gilead took a wife, and the name of his sister was Hammolecheth. His wife bore him Hepher. Hepher had two sons; the name of the first was Y and the name of the second was Zelophehad. Zelophehad had only daughters:* This well-integrated text is the result of a considerable amount of textual surgery. Changing Machir to Gilead here and in v. 16 keeps the parentage of Hepher in line with other biblical passages and is congruent with "these were the sons of Gilead" in v. 17 (cf. Japhet, 167, 176; and Curtis and Madsen, 151–52). Changing Maacah to Hammolecheth as the name for Gilead's sister enables Maacah to be Gilead's wife in v. 16 rather than his sister, and harmonizes with the genealogical relationship of Hammolecheth in v. 18.

■ **16** *Maacah the wife of Gilead bore a son, and she named him Peresh:* Maacah is a small Aramean kingdom east of the Sea of Galilee, near Mount Hermon, either adjoining the territory of Manasseh (Deut 3:14) or included in it (Josh 13:11).[57] The word Peresh appears six times in the OT with the meaning of "content of the intestines" or "feces," which, as *HALOT* 3:977 notes, is hardly possible in a personal name.[58] Rudolph, 70, suggests a vocalization פֶּרֶשׁ meaning "rider." Note the wordplay between Peresh and his brother Sheresh.

the name of his brother was Sheresh: Noth interprets Sheresh as "clever" or "cunning," but observes that it could also mean "weak" or "impotent."[59] *HALOT* 4:1659 prefers the meaning "root" or "offshoot," and suggests the name could be part of a sentence name meaning "the foundation [is secure]," as in an Akkadian parallel.

his sons were Ulam and Rakem: Ulam the son of Eshek is identified as a descendant of Saul and therefore a descendant of Benjamin in 1 Chr 8:39-40. Rakem/Rekem is a town associated with Benjamin in Josh 18:27. These are clearly different individuals. In short, nothing more can be known about Ulam and Rakem. I have taken Peresh as their father, but the Hebrew would also permit Sheresh to be their father.

■ **17** *The son of Ulam: Bedan:* The only other reference to the name Bedan is in 1 Sam 12:11, but the text there is quite uncertain and there is no reason to identify the two names.[60]

■ **18** *And his sister Hammolecheth bore Ishhod, Abiezer, Mahlah, and Shemida:* It is not clear why the mother rather than the father is cited in the genealogy. Hammolecheth means "the reigning one," and I am construing her as the sister of Gilead and the granddaughter of Manasseh and his Aramean concubine (see v. 15 as reconstructed above).[61] Abiezer אֲבִיעֶזֶר is designated as a son of Manasseh in Josh 17:2; he should also be identified with Jezer יֶצֶר, the firstborn of the descendants of Gilead in Num 26:30.[62] In short, his place in the genealogy shows a considerable amount of fluidity. Abiezer and Shemida are attested in the Samaria ostraca.[63] Mahlah is the first of the daughters of Zelophehad in

---

57 Curtis and Madsen, 151. Cf. 2 Sam 10:6 and Gen 22:24. According to Josh 12:5, Og ruled up to the boundary of the Maacathites.

58 Oeming, *Wahre Israel*, 169, takes it as a polemic against the north.

59 *Personennamen*, 228, n. 13.

60 Y. Zakovitch, "בדן = יפתח," *VT* 22 (1972) 123–25, proposed that Bedan and Jephthah are identical, but as Howard Jacobson, "The Judge Bedan (1 Samuel xii 11)," *VT* 42 (1992) 123–24, points out, Jephthah's father is Gilead (Judg 11:1-2) and Bedan's in this verse is Ulam.

61 Aaron Demsky, "The Genealogies of Manasseh and the Location of the Territory of Milcah Daughter of Zelophedad," *ErIsr* 16 (1982) 70–75, identifies Hammolecheth with Milcah the daughter of Zelophehad.

62 In Judg 6:11, 24, 34, Gideon is said to be of the clan of the Abiezrites, from the tribe of Manasseh (6:15). In defending himself against the accusations of Ephraim, Gideon appeals to his Abiezrite heritage (8:2).

63 Aharoni, *Land of the Bible*, 367. Frank Moore Cross, "Epigraphic Notes on Hebrew Documents of the Eighth-Sixth Centuries B.C: I. A New Reading of a Place Name in the Samaria Ostraca," *BASOR* 163 (1961) 12–14, has suggested a location for Shemida west of Samaria and north of the Wadi et-Tin. According to Levin, "Understanding Biblical Genealogies," 29, ostracon 28 refers to the village of Elmatan in the district of Abiezer, south of Samaria.

Num 26:33; 27:1; 36:11; and Josh 17:3. In Num 26:32 Shemida is the fifth of Gilead's six sons. In Josh 17:2 Shemida is the last of the six clans listed for Manasseh in addition to Machir. That is, Shemida was Manasseh's seventh son. My reconstruction therefore would give him a third genealogical location.[64] Only in 1 Chronicles 7 does he have descendants.

■ **19** *The sons of Shemida: Ahian, Shechem, Likhi, and Aniam:* Many scholars identify Likhi לקחי with Helek חלק, the second son of Gilead (Num 26:30; cf. Josh 17:2), and Aniam אניעם with Noah נעה, one of the daughters of Zelophehad (Num 26:33). Myers, 1:54, notes that Shemida, Abiezer, Helek, Shechem, Hoglah, and Noah occur in the Samaria ostraca. In Josh 17:2 Shechem is the fifth son of Manasseh and in Num 26:31 the fourth

son of Gilead but here he is only the son of Shemida. Levin has suggested that Shechem's lower status in this verse may reflect the city's status in the Chronicler's era, since the site of Tell Balatah was practically abandoned by 480 BCE.[65] Williamson, 66–67, 79, believes that 1 Chr 5:23-26 (the genealogy of the Transjordanian Manasseh) originally followed this verse.

7:20-27. Genealogy from Ephraim (cf. v. 28)

This genealogy consists of two linear genealogies at the beginning and end of the paragraph, and genealogical information on the new descendants of Ephraim after their defeat. The first of the linear genealogies can be depicted as follows:

Ephraim—Shuthelah I—Bered—Tahath—Eleadah—Tahath—Zabad—Shuthelah II[66]┬Ezer[67]
└Elead

■ **20** *The sons of Ephraim: Shuthelah, and Bered his son, Tahath his son, Eleadah his son, Tahath his son:* The first three generations after Ephraim in this linear genealogy seem to derive from Num 26:35, where the three clans/descendants of Ephraim are identified as Shuthelah, Becher[68] (בכר, vs. Bered ברד in Chronicles; see textual note 37), and Tahan (תחן[69] vs. Tahath תחת in Chronicles). In short, a segmented genealogy has been reinterpreted as a linear genealogy. If Bered in this verse is indeed derived from Becher, Zabad זבד in v. 21 may be a corruption of וברד ("and Bered") itself.[70] The name in

the fourth generation after Ephraim in Chronicles, Eleadah (אלעדה), seems to be a corruption of Eran, the son of Shuthelah, in Num 26:36.[71] The MT there reads "of Eran" לערן while some Hebrew manuscripts, SP, LXX, and Syr read לעדן "Ladan." Ladan is also the name of the son of Tahan and the grandson of Shuthelah in my reconstruction of vv. 25-26 below. The misinterpretation of the *lāmed* as part of the name led to the spelling of the name Eleadah in this verse, perhaps under the influence of Elead (אלעד) in 7:21. Galil has pointed out the artificial symmetry of this part of the genealogy, that

---

64 Levin, "Understanding Biblical Genealogies," 27, makes Shemida the son of Manasseh in 1 Chr 7:18 as well.

65 Yigal Levin, "Chronological Aspects of the Chronicler's Genealogies" (paper presented at the SBL annual meeting, Toronto, 2002) 13; idem, "Who Was the Chronicler's Audience? A Hint from His Genealogies," *JBL* 122 (2003) 242.

66 Rudolph, 72, begins the narrative with the words: "Shuthelah was his son, but also Ezer and Elead." When he resumes the linear genealogy after the narrative, he makes Rephah the son of Zabad.

67 Ezer and Elead may be sons of either Shuthelah II or Ephraim himself.

68 Becher and his clan are not attested in Num 26:35 LXX. Becher is listed as Benjamin's second son in

Gen 46:21. Hope W. Hogg, "The Ephraim Genealogy," *JQR* 13 (1901) 149, suggested that Becher was lost accidentally from the Benjaminite list in Num 26:38 and a marginal correction was placed in Num 26:35 that was the source of Bered in 1 Chr 7:20.

69 The SP reads תחם as does Gen 46:20 LXX, while Num 26:35 LXX reads תנה. With such textual fluidity, the derivation of Tahath from Tahan seems quite plausible.

70 So Curtis and Madsen, 153.

71 Rudolph, 72, finds Eran in either Ezer (עזר) or Elead (אלעד).

is, in the seven generations following Ephraim:[72] Eleadah is put in the middle and is surrounded by Tahath on both sides, Bered/Zabad in the next ring, and the two Shuthelahs in a third ring.[73] The chiastic duplication of the three names: Shuthelah I—Bered—Tahath and Tahath—Zabad—Shuthelah II, around Eleadah (A-B-C-D-C′-B′-A′) would seem to rule out understanding the names of Shuthelah through Elead as a list of the sons of Ephraim. Na'aman proposes that this genealogy was composed by the Chronicler to introduce the narrative about Beriah by putting the name of Shuthelah, the oldest son of Ephraim, just before Ezer and Elead.[74]

■ **21a** *Zabad his son, Shuthelah his son.* For the name Shuthelah see the commentary on v. 20. The name Zabad occurs eleven times, only in the books of Chronicles and in Ezra, but it is probably a corrupt reading for Bered, as noted in the commentary on the previous verse.

```
Ephraim ─────┬── Beriah
             │   Sheerah[75]
             │   Rephah
```

■ **21b** *As for his sons, Ezer and Elead:* Ezer is a common name, occurring three times in the Edomite genealogy in Genesis (36:21, 27, 30), five times in Chronicles (1 Chr 1:38, 42; 4:4; 7:21; 12:10 [9]), and twice in Nehemiah (3:19; 12:42). None of these sheds any light on Ezer in this verse. The narrative regarding Beriah begins with a *casus pendens* related to Ezer and Elead.

The relationship of Elead to Eleadah in v. 20 and Ladan in v. 26 is unclear, since the names Ezer and Elead were part of a separate tradition history in the following narrative. The antecedent of "his" in the present context would be the second Shuthelah, but in the story itself, it may have referred to Ephraim. In either case the high status of Ezer and Elead would be designated either by their connection to the linear genealogy going back through Shuthelah to Ephraim, or their being sons of Ephraim himself.

the people of Gath, who were born in the land, killed them: Gath (probably Tell es-Sâfi; MR 135123) is so far away from the Ephraimite cities that some scholars understand the reference to Gath as actually a reference to Gittaim (2 Sam 4:3; Neh 11:33; MR 140145), within about 12 or 13 miles of Beth-horon.[76] The insistence that these Gathites "were born in the land" is apparently meant to identify them with the pre-Israelite inhabitants of the land and to guard against the idea that this was an intra-Israelite feud (Rudolph, 72).[77] The people of Gath were part of the pre-Israelite population that still remained after the "conquest." Gittaim remained independent of Israel at least into early monarchical times (2 Sam 4:3). The antecedent of "them" and "they" in this verse and of "their" in v. 22 is Ezer and Elead or, more broadly, the Ephraimites.

because they came down to take their cattle: Since the attackers "came down" to raid the cattle of the citizens of Gath or Gittaim, this cannot refer to a raid by Ephraimites who were still living in Egypt before the conquest, since one characteristically "goes up" from

72 Gershon Galil, "The Chronicler's Genealogies of Ephraim," *BN* 56 (1991) 11–14. See also N. Na'aman, "Sources and Redaction in the Chronicler's Genealogies of Asher and Ephraim," *JSOT* 49 (1991) 107–8; idem, "The Genealogy of Asher (1 Chron. 7:30-40)," in *Archaeological, Historical, and Geographical Studies: Avraham Malamat Volume* (ed. S. Ahituv and B. A. Levine; *ErIsr* 24; Jerusalem: Israel Exploration Society, 1993) 68–73.

73 If Ezer and Elead are interpreted as the sons of Ephraim in v. 21, then the two Ephraims form a fourth ring. But they are probably part of the beginning of the narrative about Beriah.

74 "Sources," 108.

75 Or Sheerah and Rephah may be children of Beriah.

76 Benjamin Mazar, "Gath and Gittaim," *IEJ* 4 (1954) 227–35. Anson F. Rainey, "The Identification of

Philistine Gath," *ErIsr* 12 (1975) 69, concedes this possibility but also says the passage may refer to the pre-Philistine population of Gath itself.

77 Japhet, 182, however, writes: "The individual Ephraim, his sons, brothers, wife and daughter, are all here in the land, and as a person he could not have lived in both Egypt and Israel. The close bond established between Joseph and the land should be regarded as the Chronicler's alternative to the Hexateuch tradition. It is probably no coincidence that this bond is so emphasized for the sons of Joseph—traditionally the most 'Egyptian' of the tribes, giving expression to the Chronicler's idiosyncratic views in this matter." In other words, she feels that the Chronicler denied the Egypt-conquest tradition and asserted that the Ephraimites were native-born in the land.

Egypt to Palestine. Geographically, too, a raid from distant Egypt would make little sense. Albright understood this incident as evidence for the presence of Israelite tribes in central Palestine before the invasion of Joshua (cf. Gen 48:22 and chap. 34).[78] In my judgment this narrative describes a hostile relationship, after the "settlement," involving Ephraimites who made a raid on their neighbors and who were defeated by them. The chronological uncertainty comes from the built-in ambiguity in the story: Was it the personified tribe that mourned for this event and produced new children in its wake, or were those actions of mourning and population expansion undertaken by the patriarch himself?[79] In any case this laconic clause preserves a historical memory of hostile relationships between the Ephraimites and the local residents during which the Ephraimites had attempted to steal their cattle.

■ **22** *And their father Ephraim mourned many days, and his relatives came to comfort him:* Rudolph, 73, understands "Ephraim" as a reference to the tribe of Ephraim that mourns for one of its lost members (cf. Jer 31:15, where Rachel [the Northern Kingdom] weeps for its perished children). The text seems to treat Ephraim as an individual, however, since "Ephraim" has sexual congress with his wife in the next verse. If the narrator understood "Ephraim" as the patriarch himself, it would imply that the patriarch once lived in Palestine, whereas the Bible has him and his sons born in Egypt and presumably dying there, since there are four hundred years between the time of Joseph and the exodus (Gen 41:50-52; 46:20;[80] 48:1-22; 50:23). If I am correct in placing this anecdote after the "settlement," the character of Ephraim represents tribal history. Since elsewhere in the Bible Ephraim has only one brother, Manasseh, I have chosen to translate "his relatives came to comfort him," rather than "his brothers came to comfort him." Any similarity between this and the "comforting" of the friends or relatives of Job seems incidental (Job 2:11 and 42:11).[81]

---

78   William F. Albright, *From the Stone Age to Christianity* (2d ed.; Garden City, NY: Doubleday, 1957) 277.

79   The Tg to the Song of Songs (2:7) from the 7th century CE reports that the Ephraimites had offended God by leaving Egypt thirty years before the appropriate time of the exodus and that the Philistines who lived in Gath killed them. Tg to Chronicles tells that the Ephraimites had calculated four hundred years between the covenant of Genesis 15 and the exodus but they should have calculated that four-hundred-year period from the birth of Isaac, which took place thirty years after the events of Genesis 15. Cf. also Exod 12:41. Hence the Ephraimites left Egypt thirty years early, with two hundred thousand people. Tg Pseudo-Jonathan to Exod 13:17 relates that Israel was told not to go by way of the Philistines, since on that route they might see the bodies of the Ephraimites on that road, take fright, and return to Egypt. The bones of the Ephraimites who were slain were interpreted as the dry bones God restored to life through Ezekiel (37:1-14). Finally, Tg to Ps 78:9 accuses the Ephraimites, who had left Egypt thirty years prematurely, of violating the covenant of God. For discussion of these Targumim and their interpretation by medieval commentators, see Martin J. Mulder, "1 Chronik 7,21b-23 und die Rabbinische Tradition," *JSJ* 6 (1975) 141–66. For a different interpretation of these traditions see J. Heinemann, "The Messiah of Ephraim and the Premature Exodus of Ephraim," *HTR* 8 (1975) 1–15. Heineman believes that the legend of the premature exodus arose originally as an attempt to make sense of several obscure passages noted above (as well as information drawn from 2 Chr 17:16-17, which refers to Benjamin and Eliada, a mighty warrior with two hundred thousand armed with bow and shield). The Ephraimites had possessed a burning desire for redemption, for which they had sacrificed their lives. While sinners, the Ephraimites deserved compensation, which took the form of resurrection before its time for those who had died. In his opinion the notion of the Messiah of Ephraim was similarly modified after the Second Jewish Revolt to have this messiah die in battle, but have him also raised up like the Ephraimites before his time. This was an attempt to remove any hint of condemnation of the revolt of Bar Kochba.

80   LXX adds a son and a grandson for Manasseh and two sons and a grandson for Ephraim. Cf. Gen 50:23 (Joseph saw Ephraim's children of the third generation) and Num 26:28-29 and 26:34-36.

81   See Wilhelm Rudolph, "Lesefrüchte," *ZAW* 93 (1981) 291–92, who offers a sharp critique of the parallel proposed by R. E. Hoffmann, "Eine Parallele zur Rahmenerzählung des Buches Hiob in 1 Chr. 7:20-29?" *ZAW* 92 (1980) 120–32.

■ 23 *Ephraim went in to his wife, and she conceived and bore a son; and he named him Beriah:* Keil, 140, and Williamson, 80, deny that this is the patriarch Ephraim, at least in the view of the Chronicler,[82] but the story creates an ambiguity between a personified tribe and the patriarch himself.[83] Beriah, the new child of Ephraim and his wife, is a replacement for the two descendants of Ephraim, Ezer and Elead, killed by the people of Gath or Gittaim. Elsewhere the name Beriah is given to a descendant of Asher (Gen 46:17; Num 26:44-45; 1 Chr 7:30-31), to a descendant of Benjamin (1 Chr 8:13-16),[84] or to a Levite (23:10-11). Beriah may have been a large ethnic group that infiltrated its way into two or more tribes in addition to Ephraim. Or it may have been a clan or family that altered its tribal affiliation over the years. On the basis of an Arabic root, Noth suggested an etymological meaning for the name Beriah of "outstanding."[85]

because disaster had befallen his house: This folk etymology explains the name Beriah as a commentary on the defeat of the Ephraimites. There is a pun between the person Beriah (בריעה) and a neologism ברעה "disaster." The latter word is made up of the preposition *bêt* and the word רעה ("evil" or "calamity"). This contrived word ברעה "disaster" is construed as the subject of the verb

היתה.[86] There is some similarity between this etiological explanation for the name Beriah and that for the name Jabez in 1 Chr 4:10, except that the potentially negative name of Jabez was given a positive treatment in chap. 4. Mulder sees here anti-Ephraimite or even an anti-Samaritan intention: in Ephraim's house, things are evil.[87] The Chronicler, however, has no animus against the north, let alone against the Samaritans, and the name is an etymological etiology of one incident, not a durative characterization of Ephraim.

■ 24 *His daughter was Sheerah, who built both Lower and Upper Beth-horon, and Uzzen-sheerah:* Sheerah is to be considered as either the daughter of Ephraim or the daughter of Beriah. Her name is obviously chosen because of the third city she founded, Uzzen-sheerah, whose location is unknown. The name "Uzzen" (אזן) means "little ear" or "corner." Sheerah's founding[88] of the two Beth-horons[89] may mean that there was a sizable Ephraimite immigration into these two previously existing cities. The border of Benjamin is south of the Beth-horons so that they are within Ephraimite territory (Josh 18:13-14).[90] This is the only place in the OT where a woman is named as the founder of a city.[91] She is blessed, but disaster is associated with her brother Beriah.[92]

---

82 Their position may be supported by the inclusion of the linear genealogy from Ephraim to Ezer and Elead, which puts a considerable chronological distance between the patriarch and this incident. See also Gershon Galil, "Notes on the Genealogy of Ephraim," *Beth Mikra* 36 (1990–1991) 139–43.

83 Levin, "Chronological Aspects," 15, thinks the solution lies in the fluidity of genealogies. The ancients saw no problem in an Asherite clan like Beriah (1 Chr 7:30-31) being adopted into the tribe of Ephraim through this story and then into the tribe of Benjamin (8:13-16).

84 Mulder, "1 Chronik 7,21b-23," 165, sees in these verses from chap. 8 the kernel from which the story in chap. 7 with its present etymological etiology developed. These verses report that Beriah and Shema, heads of ancestral houses of Aijalon, had put to flight the inhabitants of Gath. He attributed the transfer of this tradition to Ephraim and the change to a defeat for the Israelites to an attempt to date the anti-Samaritan bias to the early days of Israel.

85 *HALOT* 1:157.

86 Mulder, "1 Chronik 7,21b-23," 145, suggests an

alternate translation: "because she [Ephraim's wife] had been present in his house in a disastrous way." A few Hebrew MSS and versions support this by having Ephraim's wife give the child its name. See textual note 40.

87 Mulder, "1 Chronik 7,21b-23," 159. So also Oeming, *Wahre Israel,* 168.

88 Other cities are built by notable figures of the past (Enoch, Gen 4:17; Nimrod, 10:11; the man who showed the house of Joseph the way into Bethel and later founded Luz in the land of the Hittites, Judg 1:23-26; Hiel, who built Jericho, 1 Kgs 16:34), but this is the only reference in the Bible to a woman building a city.

89 Lower Beth-horon (MR 158144); Upper Beth-horon (MR 160143).

90 Cf. Josh 10:10-11; 1 Sam 13:18.

91 For men as city builders see Gen 4:17; Josh 19:50; Judg 1:26; and 1 Chr 8:12 (the only reference to a man building a city in Chronicles).

92 Lea Mazor, "The Origin and Evolution of the Curse upon the Rebuilder of Jericho," *Textus* 14 (1989) 1–26, has proposed that in an LXX plus at Josh 6:26 Ozan was the father of Sheerah. In the context here

■ **25a** *and Rephah his son:* Na'aman suggests that Rephah is still part of the anecdote begun in v. 21aγ, balancing the mention of Ephraim's or Beriah's daughter Sheerah.[93] Rephah's father is either Ephraim (Sheerah's father) or Beriah (Sheerah's brother). Rephah is otherwise unknown.[94] Na'aman has also proposed that Rephah may originally have been the name modified by "who was the father of Birzaith" in v. 31.[95]

Shuthelah—Tahan—Ladan—Ammihud—Elishama—Non—Joshua

■ **25b-27** *Shuthelah his son, Tahan his son. Ladan his son, Ammihud his son, Elishama his son. Non his son, Joshua his son:* This seven-member, linear genealogy in vv. 25-27[96] culminates in Joshua the leader of the conquest (the first reference to Joshua in the Bible is made in Exod 17:9 and the first reference to Non/Nun as his father in Exod 33:11). This emphasis on Joshua may mean that the Chronicler does not deny the importance of the conquest as much as Japhet sometimes insists.[97] The sequence Shuthelah—Tahan—Ladan seems to have derived from Shuthelah—Bered—Tahath—Eleadah in v. 20. This Ladan (לעדן) is otherwise unknown,[98] but I have argued in v. 20 above that this name and Eleadah are derived from "of Eran" (לערן), the son of Shuthelah in Num 26:36. Elishama the son of Ammihud is a leader (נשיא) of the tribe of Ephraim mentioned in Num 1:10; 2:18; 7:48, 53; and 10:22, without any explicit connection with Joshua. Father and son have now been incorporated just before Joshua's father Non/Nun in this linear genealogy, thus enhancing the pedigree of Joshua. An Ephraimite contemporary of Joshua in the book of Numbers has become his grandfather. Joshua's father's name is always spelled elsewhere נון "Nun" (Exod 33:11; Numbers 28; etc.) instead of נון "Non."[99] Consonantally there is no difference between the two names.

■ **28** *Their possessions and settlements were Bethel and its towns, and eastward Naaran, and westward Gezer and its towns, Shechem and its towns, as far as Ayyah and its towns:* While this verse itself lists settlements only for Ephraim, the conclusion to the next verse, "the sons of Joseph son of Israel," seems to refer to both sons of Joseph. Bethel (MR 172148), Gezer (MR 142140), and Shechem (MR 176179) are well known and their ancient sites are securely identified. Naaran (נערן) is usually identified with Naarah (נערה; Tel el-Jisr, MR 190144), near Jericho (MR 192142; Josh 16:7). Ayyah (עיה), Aija (עיה, Neh 11:31), and Aiath (עית, Isa 10:28) are thought to be variants of Ai (העי; MR 174147).[100] If these identifications

there are three unusual features: Uzzen-Sheerah is unknown, Sheerah is the only woman in the Bible to build a city, and Rephah his son is not well integrated into the genealogy. On the basis of Chronicles LXX καὶ υἱοὶ Οζαν Σεηρα "and the sons of Ozan Sheerah," she reconstructs an earlier form of this genealogy with Ozan also being the father of Sheerah, and with Rephah, Shuthelah, etc., following as further descendants, thus resolving all three difficulties. This is an attractive proposal, although her suggestions on how ובני אזן became ואת אזן שארה, on the development of ובתו "and his daughter," and on the switch from ויבן to ותבן involve a good deal of conjecture.

93 Na'aman, "Sources," 107; cf. Galil, "Chronicler's Genealogies," 11–14; Oeming, *Wahre Israel*, 165. If the narrative ends with v. 24, one could construe Rephah as the son of Shuthelah the son of Zabad in v. 21. But this presupposes that the narrative has awkwardly interrupted the genealogy.

94 Hogg, "Ephraim Genealogy," 151, suggested that Rephah (רפח) may be a corruption through metathesis of an original "Hepher" (חפר). Cf. Josh 12:17.

95 "Sources," 108. This suggestion is based on a hypothetical original connection between this narrative and vv. 31b-39.

96 Shuthelah could be construed as Shuthelah I (v. 20), the son of Ephraim, or as Shuthelah II (v. 21), the son of Zabad, or even as Shuthelah III, the son of Shuthelah II. In the latter case, Joshua would be depicted as being in the fourteenth generation after Ephraim.

97 See also 1 Chr 4:34-43; 5:25.

98 For a Gershonite Levite by this name see 1 Chr 23:7-8; 26:21.

99 Pauline A. Viviano, "Nun," *ABD* 4:1155, suggests the name might originally have been a tribal designation.

100 Rudolph, 74, denies this identification and seeks Ayyah in the vicinity of Shechem. See also Aaron Demsky, "The Chronicler's Description of the Com-

are correct, the territory described ranges from Gezer in the southwest, to Naaran in the southeast, and to Shechem in the north, with Bethel and Ai in the middle of the triangle formed by the other three sites. Bethel and Ai are usually considered to be Benjaminite cities (Josh 18:22 [Bethel only]; Neh 11:31), but in Joshua 16 Bethel (vv. 1-2), Gezer (v. 3; cf. v. 10), and Naarah (v. 7) are listed as border points for Ephraim. Shechem belongs to the tribe of Manasseh in 1 Chr 7:19 (cf. Josh 17:7), but Shechem and Gezer are considered Ephraimite in the cities of the Levites (6:51-52 [66-67]). The territory for Ephraim outlined here is somewhat larger than that described in Joshua 16. In Josh 16:9 and 17:9 we read of unnamed towns within the inheritance of Manasseh that were set aside for Ephraim.

■ **29** *also along the borders of the Manassites, Beth-shean and its towns, Taanach and its towns, Ibleam and its towns, Megiddo and its towns, Dor and its towns:* All of these cities are well known: Beth-shean (MR 197212), Taanach (MR 171214), Ibleam (MR 177205), Megiddo (MR 167221), and Dor (MR 142224) are listed moving roughly from southeast to northwest. These five cities, plus En-dor (MR 187227), are listed as Manassite possessions "within Issachar and Asher" in Josh 17:11, which probably served as the Chronicler's source for this verse. Note that the towns' questionable linkage to Manasseh is signaled here by "also along the borders of the Manassites." The author of Judges 1 concedes that the Manassites were not able to drive the Canaanites out of Beth-shean, Taanach, Dor, Ibleam, and Megiddo (v. 27), but these same towns are described as "possessions and settlements" of Manasseh here (see v. 28). Taanach and Ibleam are considered part of Manasseh in the list of Levitical cities (6:55 [70]).

In these lived the sons of Joseph son of Israel: Ephraim and Manasseh are here considered together as the sons of Joseph. This brings the chiastically arranged section on Manasseh (v. 29) and Ephraim (v. 28) to a satisfying conclusion and is surely not evidence for the secondary character of the geographical notes in vv. 28-29 (*pace* Rudolph, 73). As is his custom, the Chronicler calls the patriarch Jacob "Israel" here.

7:30-40. Genealogy from Asher[101]

■ **30** *The sons of Asher: Imnah, Ishvah, Ishvi, Beriah, and their sister Serah:* These five descendants of Asher are identical with those given in Gen 46:17, including the mention of the daughter Serah; Num 26:44 is similar, lacking only the name "Ishvah," which may be a mistaken dittograph of "Ishvi,"[102] or Num 26:44 could be haplographic. The name Beriah, listed here as a descendant of Asher, is also used for the head of a Benjaminite father's house in 1 Chr 8:13, where he and Shema, both sons of Elpaal, are identified as heads of the ancestral houses of the inhabitants of Aijalon (MR 152138), who put to flight the inhabitants of Gath. Hence Aijalon, which was originally part of the territory of Ephraim, had later become part of the expanding tribe of Benjamin. In 7:23, as noted above, a Beriah is born to Ephraim after the men of Gath or Gittaim had killed Ezer and Elead.[103] Are all three Beriahs the same person/clan, whose genealogical identification is fluid? If so, this would support the argument of those who contend that there is evidence for the tribe Asher in a southern location. But if Beriah refers to two or three separate individuals,[104] then there may be another way to understand this genealogy, as I will argue below. Serah is mentioned after Asher's sons in Gen 46:17 and is called their sister; in Num 26:46 she is mentioned after the two clans descended from Beriah and is called

mon Border of Ephraim and Manasseh," in *Studies in Historical Geography and Biblical Historiography Presented to Zecharia Kallai* (ed. G. Galil and M. Weinfeld; VTSup 81; Leiden: Brill, 2000) 8–15, who changed עיה to עזה on the basis of versional evidence and identified the latter with the modern town of 'Azzun, north of Nahal Qanah, placing it at the northwest corner of the territory of Ephraim.

101 This reconstruction incorporates several conjectures that are explained in the commentary. There are also variant spellings of several names as indicated by the textual notes.

102 Ishvi also appears as a son of Saul in 1 Sam 14:49.

103 Steuernagel concluded that the presence of Beriah here indicates that the tribe of Asher originally came from the region of Mt. Ephraim. Cf. Curtis and Madsen, 155.

104 It seems to me that Beriah the son of Asher should at least be distinguished from the Beriahs in 1 Chr 7:23 and 8:13. The latter two names may refer to the same person/clan.

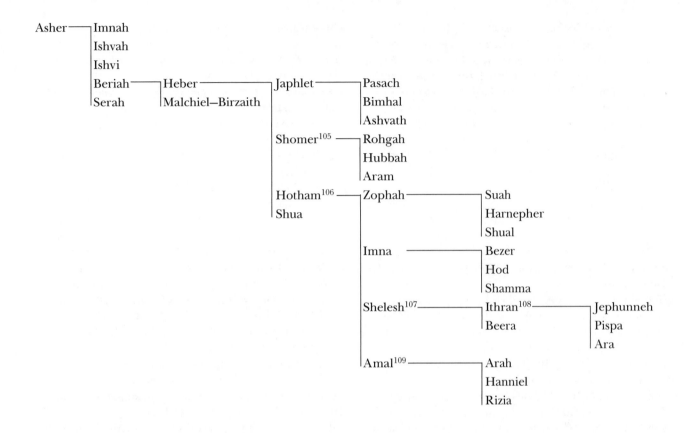

Asher's daughter. The genealogy of Asher is similar to that of Issachar in that it follows only the line of Beriah and his firstborn Heber and ignores the descendants of three of Asher's sons and of his daughter Serah.

■ **31** *The sons of Beriah: Heber and Malchiel, who was the father of Birzaith:* Heber and Malchiel are identified as sons of Beriah the son of Asher in Gen 46:17 and Num 26:45. Heber is also the name of a lesser family of Benjamin in 1 Chr 8:17, the Kenite husband of Jael (Judg 4:11), and the son of Mered and grandson of Ezrah the

Judahite (1 Chr 4:18). Japhet, 185, believes that Heber should be located in the western part of the hill country of Ephraim, and not in the northwest part of Israel where the tribe of Asher is traditionally located (but see the commentary on the next verse).[110] Only in this verse is Malchiel called the father of Birzaith. "Father" here means founder, colonizer, and so on, as frequently in chap. 2 (see n. 8 there) and chap. 4 (see n. 1 there). Should Birzaith be identified with the city north of Tyre, which would probably be within the tribal territory of

---

105 Or Shemer (see commentary on v. 34).

106 Or Helem (see commentary on v. 35).

107 Or Shilshah (see commentary to v. 37). The name may originally have been Shalishah (see commentary to v. 35).

108 Or Jether (see commentary to v. 38).

109 Or Shaalim (see commentary on v. 35), or Ulla (see commentary on v. 39).

110 According to 1 Chr 7:23 and 8:13, 17, Heber was regarded as Ephraimite or Benjaminite. Aijalon to which Heber's father Elpaal is connected in 8:13, also once belonged to Dan (Josh 19:42; 21:4).

Asher (Josh 19:25-29),[111] as proposed by J. Randall O'Brien,[112] or is it to be identified with the modern site of Bir Zeit, about 3-4 miles northwest of Bethel (modern Bīr Zēt; MR 168152)?[113] If Malchiel, the grandson of the northern patriarch Asher, is the father of Birziath, I prefer the northern location for that city (for map references see commentary on v. 31). If Rephah, the Ephraimite, is the father of that city in an earlier stage of the tradition (see commentary on v. 25), the southern location is preferable. The context in the MT favors the northern location.

■ 32 *Heber became the father of Japhlet, Shomer, Hotham, and their sister Shua:* Japhlet can be identified with the Japhletites, who lived north of the Beth-horons (Josh 16:3), towns that were on the border between Benjaminite and Ephraimite territory.[114] Japhlet's prominence is shown by the fact that Shomer/Shemer and Hotham/Helem[115] are identified by being called his brothers in vv. 34-35. Shomer (v. 32) and Shemer (v. 34) are the same person and may be identical with Shemed (1 Chr 8:12), a Benjaminite who built Ono (MR 137159)[116] and Lod (MR 140151),[117] or Shamir in the hill country of Ephraim, whose exact location is unknown (Judg 10:1-2). The only other occurrence of the name Shua is in Gen 38:2, where the daughter of Shua is the Canaanite wife of Judah. One of Saul's sons has the name Malchishua (1 Sam 14:49).

■ 33 *The sons of Japhlet: Pasach, Bimhal, and Ashvath:* None of these names is known elsewhere. On the basis of the transliteration of Bimhal in the LXX, Müller suggests an etymology of "In truth by/with/in God," and cites an Old South Arabic parallel name *bml* from the eighth or seventh century.[118]

■ 35 *The sons of Helem his brother: Zophah, Imna, Shelesh, and Amal:* Helem and Hotham are probably the same person (see v. 32), the son of Heber and the grandson of Beriah. Zophah (צופח), Imna (ימנע), and Shelesh (שלש) are similar to three of the four towns/lands Saul visited in his search for his father's asses: the land of Zuph (צוף, 1 Sam 9:5), the land of ימיני (NRSV "the land of Benjamin"; 1 Sam 9:4), and the land of Shalishah (שלשה, 1 Sam 9:4). Edelman associates Shelesh with the region around Baal-shalishah (2 Kgs 4:42), which she locates either at Khirbet Marğame (MR 1816.1554) or Khirbet Ğib'it (MR 1846.1598),[119] and thinks that Shalishah was a long narrow strip comprising the desert fringe region near the Jordan. Na'aman identifies Shelesh (שֶׁלֶשׁ) in this verse with Shilshah (שלשה) in v. 37 and proposes that the name originally was Shalishah (שְׁלִישָׁה).[120] Edelman identifies Imna (ימנע) with the land of ימיני (1 Sam 9:4) in the region of Bethel (MR 172148) and Ai (MR 1749.1587).[121] She places the land of Zuph in the vicinity of Khirbet Raddāna (perhaps Ramathaim [1 Sam 1:1]; MR 1693.1466) and Rās eṭ-Ṭāhūne (Zemaraim; MR 1702.1462).[122] All these proposals are plausible, with the identification of Shalishah being the most likely.

111 See the discussion of Asher's allotment in Kallai, *Historical Geography*, 204–24.

112 *ABD* 1:750.

113 See Diana Edelman, "The Asherite Genealogy in 1 Chronicles 7:3-40 [sic]," *BR* 33 (1988) 15. Na'aman, "Sources," 108, favors the location in Mt. Ephraim (see also F. M. Abel, "Une mention biblique du Birzeit," *RB* 46 [1937] 223–24), but he also surmises that vv. 32-39 once continued the narrative about Ephraim in vv. 21aγ-25aα and that the clause "the father of Birzaith" once modified Rephah.

114 Lower Beth-horon is located at Beit 'Ûr et-taḥta (MR 158144) and Upper Beth-horon at Beit 'Ûr el-Fôqā (MR 160143).

115 Hotham in v. 32 and Helem in v. 35 are clearly the same name, but it cannot be determined which is correct.

116 Benjaminites lived in Lod during the Persian period (cf. Neh 11:35). The location of the tribe of Benjamin this far west in preexilic times is problematic. Ono seems once to have been within the territory of Dan and then later Ephraim. See Rodney H. Shearer, "Ono," *ABD* 5:24–25.

117 The town's earliest association may have been with the tribe of Dan and later with the tribe of Ephraim. See Melvin Hunt, "Lod," *ABD* 4:346–47.

118 Walter W. Müller, "Zum biblischen Personennamen Bimhāl (1 Chr 7,33)," *BN* 91 (1998) 11–15.

119 Diana Edelman, "Saul's Journey through Mt. Ephraim and Samuel's Ramah (1 Sam. 9:4-5; 10:2-5," *ZDPV* 104 (1988) 44–58, esp. 51.

120 Na'aman, "Sources," 101.

121 "Saul's Journey," 49, 53–54.

122 Ibid., 56. Edelman, 49, indicates that the distinction between Zuph (צוף) and Zophah (צופח) involves

Na'aman reconstructs Shaalim (שעלים) as the original name behind "Amal" (עמל).[123] Shaalim is mentioned in 1 Sam 9:4 as another region Saul passed through in the search for his father's asses. Edelman locates it east of Shalishah in the vicinity of eṭ-Ṭaiyibe (Ophrah; MR 178151). What is clear is that the "Asherite" names listed in this verse were located much to the south of the traditional tribe of Asher, within the region normally associated with Mount Ephraim.[124]

Two conclusions have been drawn from this. Edelman argues that the entire Asherite genealogy in 1 Chr 7:30-40 should be assigned to a southern Asherite group.[125] Na'aman, on the other hand, distinguishes between the genealogy of Asher drawn from the Pentateuch (vv. 30-31) and the genealogy of Heber, whose descendants are in the Ephraim area (vv. 32-39). The Chronicler or the source on which he was drawing, in this view, created this genealogy of Asher by (wrongly) identifying Heber the father of Japhlet, Shomer, Hotham, and Shua and their descendants (vv. 32-39) with Heber the son of Beriah and the grandson of Asher (vv. 30-31).[126] This solution, which I favor, eliminates the need to identify an Asherite group dozens of miles to the south of its traditional home in the northwest corner of Israel. Instead, the genealogy of Heber and his descendants, who lived in Ephraim, has been incorrectly connected to Heber, the son of Beriah and grandson of Asher.

■ 36 *The sons of Zophah: Suah, Harnepher, Shual:* Harnepher is an Egyptian name ("Horus is good").[127] Edelman associates Shual שועל with the land of Shual in 1 Sam 13:17 and the land of Shaalim (שעלים) in 1 Sam

9:4.[128] She places eṭ-Ṭaiyibe (Ophrah; MR 1784.1513) and Rammūn (MR 1785.1484) in this land. The names Suah and Harnepher are attested only in this verse.

The sons of Imna: This reading, which is the result of a conjectural emendation (see textual note 57) introduces the descendants of Imna, the second son of Hotham/Helem. If the MT is retained (ובְרי וימרה "Beri and Imrah), vv. 36-37 give eleven sons of Zophah. Edelman, who does retain the MT, makes a dubious identification of Beri (ברי) with Beriah (בריעה) in 7:30.[129]

■ 37 *Bezer, Hod, and Shamma. [The sons of Shilshah:] Ithran, and Beera:* Shilshah (שלשה) should be identified with Shelesh (שלש) in v. 35, and Ithran (יתרן) with Jether (יתר) in v. 38. Whether the changes in spelling reflect actual changes over the generations or just the vagaries of textual transmission cannot be determined. Na'aman makes the plausible proposal that we should insert "the sons of" before Shilshah. If this is correct, Ithran and Beera would be descendants of Shelesh/Shilshah, as in the graphic of the genealogy above.[130]

■ 38 *The sons of Jether: Jephunneh, Pispa, and Ara:* Jether (יתר) is to be identified with Ithran (יתרן) in v. 37. The only other Jephunneh in the Bible is the father of Caleb (Num 14:6). Pispa and Ara (ארא; see the similar name in the next verse) are attested only here.

■ 39 *The sons of Ulla: Arah, Hanniel, and Rizia:* Taking the MT without change or emendation, Edelman interprets this verse as an unconnected genealogical fragment from the time of the restoration. A man by the name of Arah (ארח) is mentioned without a patronymic in Ezra 2:5//Neh 7:10, but it is not clear to me why that Arah

only the alternation between a final *hê* and a final *ḥêt*, but it is not clear how a final *hê* relates to Zuph.

123 "Sources," 101. He argues that *šʿlm* lost its initial *šîn* by haplography after Shelesh (*šlš*) and then the *mêm* and *lāmed* were transposed.

124 Zecharia Kallai, "The Settlement Traditions of Ephraim," *ZDPV* 102 (1986) 68–74, concludes that the "Ephraimite" clans in the genealogy of Asher represent families that started their settlement in the central parts of the country before moving north.

125 "Saul's Journey," 49. Edelman divides this genealogy into three independent strands, vv. 30-35, 36-37, and 38-39, which she dates respectively to the 10th century, to the late monarchy, and to the postexilic period. Levin, "Understanding Biblical Genealogies," 30, comes to similar conclusions.

126 Na'aman, "Sources," 102–4.

127 Edelman, "Asherite Genealogy," 19, proposes that Harnepher represents an Egyptian garrison in the Asherite territory established by Neco II. It seems doubtful that this name alone is enough to date vv. 36-37 to the reign of Jehoiakim. Na'aman, "Sources," 105, points out that Egyptians in these genealogies are not restricted to one particular time.

128 "Saul's Journey," 48, 53, though she errs in stating that it is east of the land of Shalishah. It is west of this land.

129 "Asherite Genealogy," 15.

130 Cf. Na'aman, "Sources," 101. He also conjectures that the name of a son of Shelesh/Shilshah has been lost.

should be identified with this one.[131] Most scholars assume a textual error in this verse since Ulla is not mentioned in the previous verses. Some scholars would add Ulla to the three sons of Jether in the previous verse, and this would make Arah, Hanniel, and Rizia into Jether's grandsons through his son Ulla. Richter[132] and Japhet, 187, conjecturally emended Ulla (עלא) to Shua (שועא), a woman mentioned in v. 32.[133] This change would mean that descendants are provided in this genealogy for all of Heber's children. Rothstein, 584, n. i, suggested identifying Ulla with Shual (שועל) in v. 36, making Shual the only descendant of Zophah for whom descendants are traced, but in his longer commentary, 151, he suggested identifying Ulla with Ara (ארא) in v. 38,[134] making the names in v. 39 grandsons of Ithran/Jether. Noth[135] changed Ulla to Amal (עמל), v. 35,[136] making the sons of this verse grandsons of Hotham/Helem. This is similar to the proposal of Na'a-man, who identifies Ulla with Shaalim/Amal.[137] I have somewhat arbitrarily settled on this solution. This means that descendants are provided for one generation for each son of Hotham/Helem. Clearly no one can be certain on how to construe the names in this verse.

■ **40** *All of these were men of Asher, heads of ancestral houses, select mighty warriors, chiefs of the princes:* This summary verse contains many of the terms associated with the genealogies of Issachar and Benjamin that are thought to have come from a military census list.[138] Lacking is the expression "in their generations." The word translated "select" (ברורים) is used in 9:22 for those who are chosen as gatekeepers. In 16:41 the Chronicler refers to Heman and Jeduthun and the rest of those who are chosen (הברורים) to render thanks. In Neh 5:18 the word is used to describe six choice sheep.

Their number enrolled by genealogies, for service in war, was twenty-six thousand men: The numbers given for Asher elsewhere are much higher: 41,500 (Num 1:41; 2:28), 53,400 (Num 26:47), or 40,000 (1 Chr 12:37 [36]). Curtis and Madsen, 156, and Braun, 119, conclude that the census here is limited to the clan of Heber (cf. 7:2, 4, 7, 9, 11).

Conclusion

Genealogies for six Cisjordanian tribes are provided in this chapter: Issachar, Benjamin, Naphtali, Manasseh, Ephraim, and Asher. The content of these genealogies ranges from repetition of only the pentateuchal data available (Naphtali), to use of pentateuchal data and information from a military census list (Issachar and Benjamin), to selective use of pentateuchal data and fragmentary genealogical material (Manasseh), to two linear genealogies (the second of which leads to Joshua, the leader of the conquest) and a historical anecdote telling of a defeat of the Ephraimites and their subsequent growth (Ephraim), and to use of pentateuchal data, the genealogy of clans residing in Ephraim (and mistakenly connected to Asher), and material apparently from the military census list (Asher). Clearly the Chronicler attempted to make maximal use of the mixed data that were available to him. His all-Israel theme would seem to require the inclusion of Zebulun and Dan, but these genealogies, for whatever reason, no longer appear.

The high numbers recorded from the military census for Issachar, Benjamin, and Asher show, at least in the first and last cases, strong participation in Israel by tribes that were no longer part of the postexilic community. It is possible that placing the northern tribes of

---

131 So also Na'aman, "Sources," 105. A Shecaniah son of (this or another?) Arah is mentioned in Neh 6:18 as the father-in-law of Tobiah.

132 Georg Richter, "Zu den Geschlechtsregistern I Chronik 2–9," *ZAW* 50 (1932) 137.

133 In Hebrew two of the four letters of Shua are the same as two of the three letters of Ulla.

134 Both names end in *'ālep* but otherwise are spelled completely differently.

135 *Personennamen*, 253.

136 In Hebrew two of the three letters of Amal are identical with two of the three letters of Ulla.

137 "Sources," 101. In v. 35 I noted that Na'aman considers Shaalim the original form of the name Amal. For different reasons Noth and Na'aman affix Arah, Hanniel, and Rizia at the same point in the genealogy.

138 Na'aman, "Sources," 103–4, makes the Chronicler responsible for this verse. The Chronicler formulated the verse according to the pattern of the summaries in Numbers 26 and therefore, in his opinion, it has nothing to do with a genuine military census.

Issachar and Asher first and last in this chapter was meant to show the inclusion of the entire north in the Chronicler's view of Israel.

Whatever his theological intention, the Chronicler's preservation of these data, however corrupted they were already were for him and remain so for us, also provides significant information about tribal structures and history, and even tribal territories, that can be correlated with other information from the Bible and from modern research.

8

Translation

1/ **Benjamin became the father of Bela his first-born, Ashbel[1] the second, Aharah[2] the third, 2/ Nohah the fourth, and Rapha the fifth. 3/ Bela had sons: Addar[3] and Gera, that is, the father of Ehud.[4] 4/ These are the sons of Ehud:[5] Abishua, Naaman, Ahijah,[6] 5/ Gera,[7] Shephuphan,[8] and Huram.[9] 6/ They were heads of the ancestral houses of the inhabitants of Geba, and they sent them into exile[10] to Manahath. 7/ As for Gera,[11] he sent them into exile,[12] and he[13] became the father of Uzza and Ahihud.[14]**

8/ **And Shaharaim[15] became the father of sons in the field of Moab after he had sent away/divorced[16] his wives Hushim[17] and Baara.[18] 9/ Through his wife Hodesh he became the father of Jobab, Zibia, Mesha, Malcam, 10/ Jeuz, Sachia,[19] and Mirmah. These were his sons,[20] heads of ancestral houses. 11/ Through Hushim[21] he had become the father of Abitub[22] and Elpaal. 12/ The sons of Elpaal: Eber,[23] Misham, and Shemed[24]—he is the one who built Ono and Lod with its towns— 13/ and Beriah, Elpaal,[25] and Shema[26] (they were the heads of ancestral houses of the inhabitants of Aijalon, who put to flight the inhabitants of Gath); 14/ and their brothers,[27] Shashak[28] and Jeremoth.[29]**

15/ **Zebadiah, Arad, Eder, 16/ Michael, Ishpah, and Joha were the sons of Beriah. 17/ Zebadiah, Meshullam, Hizki, Heber, 18/ Ishmerai, Izliah, and Jobab were the sons of Elpaal. 19/ Jakim, Zichri, Zabdi, 20/ Elienai,[30] Zillethai, Eliel, 21/ Adaiah, Beraiah, and Shimrath were the sons of Shimei.[31] 22/ Ishpan, Eber,[32] Eliel, 23/ Abdon, Zichri, Hanan, 24/ Hananiah, Omri,[33] Elam, Anthothijah,[34] 25/ Iphdeiah, and Penuel[35] were the sons of Shashak. 26/ Shamsherai,[36] Shehariah, Athaliah, 27/ Jaareshiah, Elijah, and Zichri were the sons of Jeroham.[37] 28/ These were the heads of ancestral houses, according to their generations, chiefs.[38] These lived in Jerusalem.[39]**

29/ **But Jeiel[40] the father of Gibeon lived[41] in Gibeon, and the name of his wife was Maacah. 30/ His firstborn son:[42] Abdon, then Zur, Kish, Baal, Ner,[43] 31/ Gedor, Ahio,[44] Zecher,[45] and Mikloth.[46] 32/ And Mikloth became the father of Shimeah.[47] Now these also lived alongside their kindred, in Jerusalem, with their kindred.[48]**

33/ **And Ner became the father of Kish,[49] Kish became the father of Saul, Saul became the father of Jonathan, Malchishua, Abinadab,[50] and Esh-baal; 34/ and the son of Jonathan was Merib-baal;[51] and Merib-baal became the father of Micah. 35/ The sons of Micah: Pithon, Melech,[52] Tarea,[53] and Ahaz.[54]**

1 Syr has additional names from Gen 46:21.

2 וְאַחְרַח; Num 26:38 לַאֲחִירָם "Ahiram." *BHS* prefers the latter reading.

3 אַדָּר; cf. Num 26:40 LXX. A few Hebrew MSS, LXX[Aal]: אַרְדְּ "Ard"; cf. Gen 46:21, Num 26:40. 1 Chr 7:12 אַחֵר "Aher."

4 Reading וַאֲבִי אֵהוּד with Curtis and Madsen, 158; Rudolph, 76; Williamson, 83. Cf. Judg 3:15, "Ehud, son of Gera," and the name Ehud in 1 Chr 8:6. Without this change and the one in the next note, there would be two sons of Bela named Gera. D. W. Baker, "Further Examples of the *Waw Explicativum*," *VT* 30 (1980) 133, attributes explicative force to the *wāw*. MT וַאֲבִיהוּד "and Abihud."

5 וְאֵלֶּה בְּנֵי אֵהוּד. Rudolph, 76, and Williamson, 83, move these words from v. 6a to this position and remove the conjunction from the next name, Abishua, in MT. This makes the names Abishua through Huram sons of Ehud instead of sons of Bela. This clause was probably lost by homoioteleuton, inserted as a correction in the margin, and then reinserted at the beginning of the wrong verse. Note that I read אֵהוּד instead of MT אֵחוּד. Cf. v. 3.

6 וַאֲחִיָּה with LXX[B], Syr, Arab., and v. 7; MT וַאֲחוֹחַ "Ahoah."

7 Lacking in Syr. Was this a harmonistic deletion since in MT this would be the second Gera among the sons of Bela?

8 וּשְׁפוּפָן. A few Hebrew MSS, Tg: וּשְׁפוּפָם "Shephupham." Cf. Num 26:39. LXX[A] καὶ Σωφαν; Syr וּשְׁפִים.

9 וְחוּרָם. Syr, Arab., Num 26:39: חוּפָם "Hupham." Rudolph, 76, notes that there are strong departures from Numbers 26 elsewhere in this chapter.

10 Cf. GKC §144f-g.

11 וְגֵרָא, following Williamson, 84; MT וְנַעֲמָן וַאֲחִיָּה וְגֵרָא "and Naaman, Ahijah, and Gera." Gera was the original subject of this clause and the names Naaman and Ahijah have been filled in from v. 4. Japhet, 189, proposes that Naaman is the original name and that Ahijah and Gera have been filled in from vv. 4-5. Braun, 120–21, retains all three names and even proposes that one or more additional names may have been omitted.

12 הוּא הֶגְלָם. *RSV* and *NRSV*: "that is, Heglam." Rudolph, 76, emends to לֹא הֶגְלָם ["And as for Naaman, Ahijah, and Gera], they did not lead them into exile."

13 Rudolph, 76, believes a name has fallen out. LXX[L] inserts Gera.

14 וְאֵת אֲחִיחֻד; some Hebrew MSS: וְאֵת אֲחִיהֻד.

15 וּשְׁחָרַיִם; some have proposed וַאֲחִירָם "Ahiram" (cf. note 2 above). Rudolph, 76, opposes this change

36/ Ahaz became the father of Jehoaddah;[55] and Jehoaddah became the father of Alemeth, Azmaveth,[56] and Zimri; Zimri became the father of Moza. 37/ Moza became the father of Binea;[57] Raphah[58] was his son, Eleasah his son, Azel his son. 38/ Azel had six sons, and these are their names: Azrikam, his firstborn,[59] Ishmael, Sheariah, Azariah,[60] Obadiah, and Hanan; all[61] these were the sons of Azel. 39/ The sons of his brother Eshek:[62] Ulam his firstborn, Jeush the second, and Eliphelet the third. 40/ The sons of Ulam were mighty warriors, archers, having many children and grandchildren, one hundred fifty.[63] All these were Benjaminites.

since in his opinion the names in vv. 13 and 19 also have no connection with preceding names. See also v. 29.

16   שְׁלְחוֹ. Is this an unusual form of the *piel* infinitive construct (GKC §52o) or should it be emended to יְשַׁלְחוֹ?

17   אֹתָם חוֹשִׁים; MT אֹתָם חוּשִׁים. Rudolph, 76, notes that the anticipation of the direct object in MT (אֹתָם) seems awkward, and Hushim is elsewhere always a man's name. He proposes to read her name either as אֶת מַחֲשָׁם "Mahsham" or אֶת מַחְשָׁם "Mahsam." See the commentary.

18   בֶּעְרָא; one Hebrew MS, LXXms 127: בַּעְרָא. Cf. LXXB.

19   שְׂכְיָה; many Hebrew MSS, LXX, Tg: שִׁבְיָה "captivity" or "captive."

20   בָּנָיו; lacking in LXX. *BHS* suggests adding בְּמוֹאָב "in Moab," which was lost in Hebrew by haplography (cf. v. 8).

21   וּמֵחֻשִׁים. Rudolph, 78, changes to וּמִמַּחְשָׁם "Mahsham," as in v. 8, note 17. LXXL, Vg, and perhaps Syr, Arab. also link the *mêm* to the name.

22   אֲבִיטוּב. Some Hebrew MSS, Syr: אֲחִיטוּב "Ahitub."

23   עֶבֶר; some Hebrew MSS עֹבֵד. LXX Ωβηδ. See v. 22.

24   וּשְׁמַר; many Hebrew MSS, LXX, Syr, Tg: וְשֶׁמֶר "Shemer."

25   וְאֶלְפַּעַל, with *BHS*; lacking in MT and versions. With this emendation vv. 15-27 lists the descendants of Beriah, Elpaal, Shimei, Shashak, and Jeroham according to the order of the sons of Elpaal in vv. 13-14. Japhet, 188–89, inserts "And the sons of Eber" before Beriah, which makes Beriah, Shema, Sheshak, and Jeremoth sons of Eber and grandsons of Elpaal.

26   וְשֶׁמַע. Cf. v. 20 שִׁמְעִי "Shimei."

27   וְאַחְיֹהֶם with *BHS*; cf. LXXL. MT וְאַחְיוֹ "and Ahio."

28   שָׁשָׁק; LXXA σωσηκ; LXXL σισαχ.

29   וִירֵמוֹת. Rudolph, 78, emends to וְיֶרֹחָם "Jeroham." Cf. v. 27. Braun, 121, favors either this change or changing "Jeroham" in v. 27 to "Jeremoth." Rudolph, 78, moves the last four words of v. 28 to this position: רָאשִׁים אֵלֶּה יָשְׁבוּ בִירוּשָׁלַ͏ִם "heads, these lived in Jerusalem."

30   וְאֵלִיעֵנִי; *BHS* וְאֶלְיוֹעֵינַי "Elioenai." Cf LXXAal, Tg, Vg.

31   Cf. שֶׁמַע "Shema" in v. 13.

32   וְעֶבֶר. Some Hebrew MSS, LXX: וְעֹבֵד "Ebed." Cf. v. 12.

33   וְעֹמְרִי; cf. LXX. Lacking in MT.

34   וְעֲנָתֹתִיָּה. *BHS* and Rudolph, 78, וְעֲנָתְיָה.

35   וּפְנוּאֵל with Q, many Hebrew MSS, LXX, Tg, Vg; K וּפְנִיאֵל "Peniel." Cf. LXXB.

36   וְשִׁמְשְׁרִי. Rudolph, 78, interprets this as a conflation of שִׁמְשִׁי (cf. LXXL) and שִׁמְרִי (Syr, Arab.).

37   יֶרֹחָם; cf. ירמות "Jeremoth" in v. 14.

38   רָאשִׁים "chiefs" repeats רָאשֵׁי "heads" earlier in the verse. Perhaps this results from the conflation of

two concluding formulas.

39 Rudolph, 78, transfers this sentence to the end of v. 14. Cf. v. 13aβ.

40 יעיאל, with LXX[L] and 9:35 Q, LXX, Tg, Vg. The name was apparently lost accidentally in MT.

41 ישבו; cf. 9:35 MT. One Hebrew MS, LXX, Syr: שב.

42 ובנו הבכור; LXX ובנה הבכור "Her firstborn son."

43 ונר with LXX[Aal]; cf. 9:36. Lost in MT by haplography before "Nadab."

44 ואחיו; LXX וְאֶחָיו "and brother(s)."

45 וזכר; 9:37 וזכריה "Zechariah."

46 ומקלות; cf. LXX[B], Syr, Vg, Arab., and 9:37. This name was lost in MT.

47 שמאה; 9:38 שמאם "Shimeam." Samuel Krauss, "Text-kritik auf Grund des Wechsels von ה und ם," *ZAW* 7 (1930) 324, collected a number of examples of confusion in the square script of *hê* and final *mêm*.

48 עם אחיהם; lacking in Syr.

49 קיש; some have proposed אבנר "Abner." See the commentary.

50 אבינדב; LXX Αμιναδαβ. Syr, Arab.: ישוי "Ishvi" (cf. 1 Sam 14:49), but this may be a euphemism for the following name אשבעל "Esh-baal."

51 מריב בעל; cf. 1 Chr 9:40a. LXX, Syr, and 9:40b: מרי בעל "Meribaal" ("man of Baal"). The same spelling variant also occurs in its next appearance

here in 8:34 in LXX, Syr, LXX[L] and in 9:40 μεμφιβααλ "Mephibaal."

52 ומלך; LXX[BL] καὶ Μελχ(ε)ηλ. "Melch(e)al. Cf. 9:41 LXX.

53 ותארע; 9:41 ותחרע "Tahrea."

54 This name is lacking in 9:41 MT.

55 יהועדה; 9:42 יערה "Jarah." Cf. 8:36 LXX[B] Ιαδα "Jada"; 8:36 LXX[Aal] Ιωιαδα = יהוידע "Jehoiadah."

56 עזמות; LXX[ALal], Syr, Vg: עַזְמָוֶת "Azmoth."

57 בנעא; LXX Βα(α)να = בענא.

58 רפה; LXX and 1 Chr 9:43 רפיה "Rephaiah."

59 בכרו with some Hebrew MSS, LXX, Syr, Arab., Tg, and *BHS*; MT בכרו "Bocheru." See also the next note.

60 ועזריה, following a suggestion in *BHS*. Cf. LXX[L], which reads "Azariah, Obadiah, and Sheariah" instead of MT ושעריה ועבדיה "Sheariah, Obadiah." Or is LXX[L] a correction in order to come up with six sons for Azel? The name Azariah is also missing from 1 Chr 9:44. If one reads "his firstborn," the verse is one name short. If the strange name "Bocheru" is retained, there are enough names.

61 כל; lacking in 9:44.

62 עשק; LXX[B] Ασηλ; LXX[Aal] Εσελεκ; LXX[min] Εσηλ.

63 וחמשים; LXX[AV] "ninety."

8:1-40

Structure

In the final form of Chronicles this complex genealogy of Benjamin forms an *inclusio* with the complex genealogy of Judah (1 Chr 2:3–4:23) around the tribal genealogies in chaps. 2–8, with the complex genealogy of Levi and the Levitical cities located approximately in the center of these genealogies (5:27–6:66 [6:1-81]). The Chronicler gives Judah and Benjamin prominence because of their past loyalty to David and the temple and because they are the two main tribes that returned from the exile (Ezra 1:5). This chapter demonstrates that Benjamin has strong ties with Jerusalem and Judah (1 Chr 8:28, 32).[1] This genealogy also prepares the way for

listing the inhabitants of Jerusalem in chap. 9. I see no evidence for designating this chapter as secondary. The duplication between this genealogy of Benjamin and that found at 7:6-12 has been discussed in the commentary on the latter passage. This chapter begins (v. 1) and ends (v. 40) with the word "Benjamin."

This chapter contains a number of obscure references and requires emendation, sometimes conjecture, at several points to achieve a coherent genealogy (see the genealogical chart "Descendants of Benjamin").[2] My reconstruction of this Benjaminite genealogy, which I explain and defend in the commentary and already partially justify in the textual notes, may be outlined as follows:

I. 8:1-7. Descendants of Benjamin through his first-born, Bela, to the fifth generation. The family heads

---

1 Oeming, *Wahre Israel*, 175.
2 Such emendation must be done with due caution. Contrast Hope W. Hogg, "The Genealogy of Benjamin: A Criticism of 1 Chronicles VIII," *JQR* 11

(1899) 102–14, who concludes presciently (113): "It is not likely that all the suggestions we have made will commend themselves to other students."

244

in this part of the genealogy are connected to the town of Geba.

II. 8:8-14. Descendants of Shaharaim, through two of his wives, Hodesh and Hushim. Shaharaim's connection to the main Benjaminite genealogy is not provided (see the genealogical chart "Descendants of Jeiel"). Verses 9-10 list seven sons born to Shaharaim and Hodesh in Moab. Verse 11 lists the two sons, Abitub and Elpaal, born to Shaharaim and his wife Hushim, at an unspecified location. Verses 12-14, as reconstructed in this commentary, list the eight descendants of Elpaal, the son of Shaharaim and Hushim, who are broken up into three sets of names by descriptive clauses. The third of these descendants, Shemed, is linked by a descriptive clause to the towns of Ono and Lod (v. 12) while the fourth through the sixth sons, Beriah, Elpaal, and Shema, are linked to Aijalon, and they are credited with putting the (Philistine?) inhabitants of Gath to flight (vv. 13-14).

III. 8:15-28. Descendants of the fourth through eighth sons of Elpaal—Beriah, Elpaal, Shimei (Shema), Shashak, and Jeroham (Jeremoth)—are listed and are all said to live in Jerusalem. This part of the genealogy follows a common form: a list of names who are said to be the sons of X (where X stands for one of the five sons of Elpaal).

IV. 8:29-32. Descendants of Jeiel, the father of Gibeon, and his wife Maacah are listed. The context suggests that Jeiel is a Benjaminite, but how his family traced their genealogy back to the patriarch Benjamin is not given (see the genealogical chart "Descendants of Jeiel"). All of these Gibeonites are living in Jerusalem at the time of the composition of this genealogy. This genealogy is repeated in 9:35-38,

where it forms the penultimate list of inhabitants of Jerusalem in postexilic times.[3]

V. 8:33-40. These verses, which also are repeated in 9:39-44,[4] provide a genealogy beginning with Ner, the grandfather of King Saul, and continuing for twelve (or thirteen) generations after Saul. Ner is identified in this genealogy with the fifth son of Jeiel in the previous genealogy. Ner may even have been added to the sons of Jeiel because of the presence already of Kish among his sons (cf. Braun, 127, 138). In comparison with the genealogy in chap. 9, the genealogy in chap. 8 has two additional verses (vv. 39-40), which provide information on a brother of Azel by the name of Eshek in the eleventh generation, three sons for Eshek in the twelfth generation, and one hundred fifty military descendants of Ulam, the son of Eshek, in the thirteenth generation after Saul.

Parts I-IV of the Benjaminite genealogy offer information on the expansion of the Benjaminites at various, unspecified periods. Geographical references scattered throughout the chapter (6b, 8a, 12-13, 28-29, 32b) provide evidence for such movement within the Benjaminite family. Tribal genealogies in the strict sense appear in vv. 1-6a, 7b-12a, 14-28, and 29-32; episodes of the tribal history appear in vv. 6b-7a, 12b, and 13. Part V, vv. 33-40, in the version provided by 1 Chronicles 8, traces the ancestry of a military group called the "sons of Ulam" all the way back to the grandfather of Saul. The present form of parts I-IV has been dated to the time of Josiah or even to postexilic times, though elements within these genealogies may be considerably older (note the various episodes in vv. 6, 13, and 40).[5] The "sons of Ulam" in part V are a military unit dating no earlier than late preexilic times.

---

3   Braun, 122, 142, believes that 1 Chr 9:34-44 has been transferred secondarily to 8:28-38, where it is inappropriate in that context. Obviously someone thought it appropriate in the context of chap. 8 (see discussion below), and the addition of the information about Eshek (vv. 39-40) is unexplained by Braun's hypothesis.

4   Pseudo-Rashi concluded that whenever the author of Chronicles had two sources that only differed in minor matters he included both of them (Eisemann, 132).

5   Rudolph, 77, thinks of the time of Josiah or even more preferably the time after Nehemiah. Oeming, *Wahre Israel*, 177–78, thinks that the traditions come from various times. The move into Moab and the use of the name Baal would be early. The tradition of the important role of Gibeon could come from monarchical times. The tradition of the settling/rebuilding of Ono and Lod by Benjamin is postexilic.

Detailed Commentary

8:1-7. Descendants of Benjamin through His Firstborn, Bela

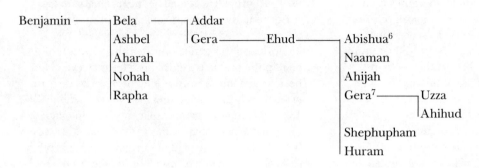

Gen 46:21 MT

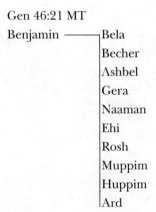

Gen 46:21 LXX (with some corrections in spelling)

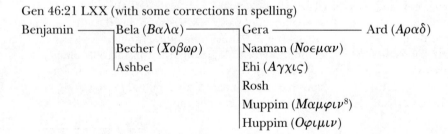

---

6   I follow Rudolph, 76, and Williamson, 83, and make
     the following six names sons of Ehud (cf. textual
     note 5); in MT they are sons of Bela and there are
     two Geras who are sons of Bela. The MT is retained
     by Braun, 120–21, and Japhet, 191.

7   Rudolph leaves a blank for the name of the father
     of Uzza and Ahihud.

8   Cf. 1 Chr 7:15 LXX.

Num 26:38-41

```
Benjamin ──────┬── Bela ──────────────┬── Ard (LXX Αδαρ)
               │   Ashbel              │   Naaman
               │   Ahiram
               │   Shephupham
               │   Hupham
```

1 Chr 7:6-7 See the commentary to chap. 7

■ **1-2** *Benjamin became the father of Bela his firstborn, Ashbel the second, Aharah the third, Nohah the fourth, and Rapha the fifth:* The five children in Benjamin's first generation need to be compared with the genealogies of Benjamin elsewhere in the Bible. In Gen 46:21 MT ten children of Benjamin are named:[9] Bela, Becher, Ashbel, Gera, Naaman, Ehi, Rosh, Muppim, Huppim, and Ard.[10] In Num 26:38-41 the first-generation children of Benjamin include Bela, Ashbel, Ahiram, Shephupham, and Hupham. Ard and Naaman are designated as sons of Bela. Finally, in 1 Chr 7:6 the children of Benjamin are Bela, Becher, and Jediael, while in 7:7 the children of Bela are Ezbon, Uzzi, Uzziel, Jerimoth, and Iri.[11] Bela alone therefore appears in all three parallel passages, and Ashbel appears in two of the three (not in 1 Chronicles 7). Bela is the only name the two genealogies of Benjamin in chaps. 7–8 have in common in the first generation. The "firstborn" in 8:1 is an alternate vocalization of "Becher" in two of the other passages (Genesis 46 and 1 Chronicles 7). Aharah in this verse is probably a variant of "Ahiram" in Numbers 26. Nohah and Rapha are not known elsewhere, but there is a Raphah among the descendants of Saul in v. 37. Nohah (נוחה) is sometimes thought to be variant of Naaman (נעמן), but they have only their first letter in common.

■ **3** *Bela had sons: Addar and Gera, the father of Ehud:* "Addar" (אדר), the son of Bela and the grandson of Benjamin, would appear to be the same name as "Ard" (ארד), who is the tenth son of Benjamin in Gen 46:21 MT, the great-grandson of Benjamin via Bela and Gera in Gen 46:21 LXX, and the oldest son of Bela in Num 26:40. The reconstructed genealogy of Gera—Ehud (see textual note 4) would seem to be an allusion to Ehud the son of Gera, a Benjaminite deliverer against the Moabites in Judg 3:15-30, dating this part of the genealogy to the premonarchical period. "Father" may be used here in its literal sense and not as a metaphor for settling or founding a city (cf. Gen 11:29). A Benjaminite clan Ehud is attached to Bilhan and the subtribe of Jediael in 1 Chr 7:10. Knauf holds that Ehud in the Judges' story also represents a clan.[12]

■ **4-5** *These are the sons of Ehud: Abishua, Naaman, Ahijah, Gera, Shephuphan, and Huram:* I have followed the conjecture of Rudolph and Williamson (see textual note 5) that moves "These are the sons of Ehud" from v. 6 to v. 4 and makes the six names from Abishua through Huram the sons of Ehud. Gera in v. 5 is the grandson of the Gera in v 3. These names in MT are listed as additional sons of Bela, although this means that Bela has two sons by the name of Gera. In its Masoretic location, in v. 6, the clause "These are the sons of Ehud" is followed by no proper names.[13] Naaman and Shephupham in this reconstruction are the great-great-grandsons of Benjamin, while in Gen 46:21 MT Naaman is a son of Benjamin and in Num 26:40 and Gen 46:21 LXX he is the grandson of Benjamin. In Num 26:39 Shephupham is the fourth son of Benjamin. It is not clear whether these variations reflect sociological changes or only textual corruption.[14]

---

9   Cf. *Jub.* 44:25, which lists these ten names, but gives the total as eleven.

10 In Gen 46:21 LXX only the first three are considered children of Benjamin, with Gera through Huppim construed as children of Bela. Ard in the LXX is the son of Gera and grandson of Benjamin.

11 Cf. the commentary on 1 Chr 7:6-12 and J. Marquart, "The Genealogies of Benjamin (Num. 26:38-40, I Chron. 7:6ff., 8:1ff.)," *JQR* 14 (1902) 345.

12 Ernst Axel Knauf, "Eglon and Ophrah: Two Toponymic Notes on the Book of Judges," *JSOT* 51 (1991) 30.

13 Japhet, 191, proposes that a few names have been lost following this heading.

14 M. Patrick Graham, "Shephupham," *ABD* 5:1205, notes that the relationship among the names Shephupham, Muppim, Shuppim, and Shephuphan remains uncertain (cf. textual note 8), as does their relationship to the patriarch Benjamin.

6 *They were heads of the ancestral houses of the inhabitants of Geba:* The designation of the preceding names as family heads of a specific location occurs again in v. 13 (cf. vv. 10 and 28 for heads of ancestral houses). Geba is a Levitical city of Benjamin (Josh 21:17; 1 Chr 6:45 [60]; cf. Josh 18:24) and is customarily identified with Jabaʻ (MR 175140), about 6 miles north-northeast of Jerusalem.[15] King Asa had carried out building activities at Geba (1 Kgs 15:22). After the exile it was occupied by Benjaminites (Ezra 2:26; Neh 7:30; 11:31; 12:29).

and they sent them into exile to Manahath: In this episode, a portion of the tribe of Benjamin was exiled or the Benjaminites exiled their opponents.[16] The antecedent of "them" may be the heads of the ancestral houses of Geba. Manahath may be identified with el-Mâlḥah (1 Chr 2:52, 54; MR 167128), 3 miles southwest of Jerusalem outside the Benjaminite tribal territory.[17] Rudolph, 79, argues that the verb גלה implies an exile away from Palestine and therefore this verse cannot refer

to the Manahath identified above, but Ezek 12:3 provides counterevidence since the prophet in his symbolic action was commanded to go from one place to another as an act of exile. Rudolph prefers an Edomite site, as in 1 Chr 1:40.[18]

7 *As for Gera, he sent them into exile:* The verb הגלם ("he sent them into exile") presupposes a singular subject, and I have selected for that role Gera, who also may be the subject of the verb in the second half of this verse. In MT the names Naaman and Ahijah have been filled in from the same sequence of names in vv. 4-5 (see textual note 11).

and he became the father of Uzza and Ahihud: The Benjaminite clans Uzza[19] and Ahihud, about whom nothing is known, are probably to be seen as contemporaneous with the original compilation of this section of the genealogy.

8:8-14. Descendants of Shaharaim through Two of His Wives, Hodesh and Hushim

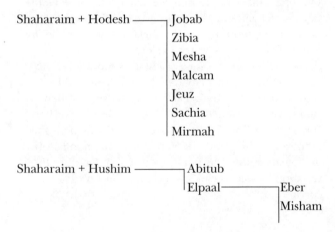

---

15 J. Maxwell Miller, "Geba/Gibeah of Benjamin," *VT* 25 (1975) 145–66, suggests that Geba and Gibeah are linguistic variants of the same toponym.

16 ויגלום אל מנחת. "They" may be a circumlocution for the passive. Hogg, "Genealogy of Benjamin," 107, reconstructs from this clause the names Iglaam and Alemeth.

17 Ernst Axel Knauf, "Manahath," *ABD* 4:493, identifies Manahath with Maḥnah in Gilead (MR 221193,

7 kilometers north of ʻAjlûn) and believes that this verse deals with Benjaminite colonization of the mountains of Gilead before the monarchy. See also idem, "Eglon and Ophrah," 25–44.

18 Tg places Manahath "in the land of the house of Esau."

19 Uzza עזא resembles Bela's son Uzzi עזי in 1 Chr 7:7.

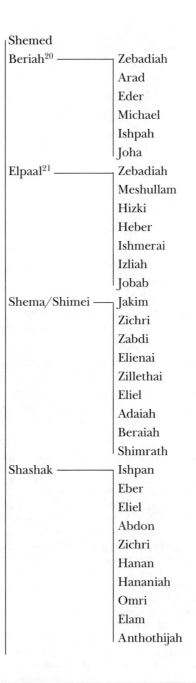

Shemed
Beriah[20] ———— Zebadiah
Arad
Eder
Michael
Ishpah
Joha
Elpaal[21] ———— Zebadiah
Meshullam
Hizki
Heber
Ishmerai
Izliah
Jobab
Shema/Shimei —— Jakim
Zichri
Zabdi
Elienai
Zillethai
Eliel
Adaiah
Beraiah
Shimrath
Shashak ———— Ishpan
Eber
Eliel
Abdon
Zichri
Hanan
Hananiah
Omri
Elam
Anthothijah

20   Japhet, 194, inserts "and the sons of Eber" at the
beginning of v. 13. In her view Eber, Misham, and
Shemed are sons of Elpaal, and Beriah, Shema,
Shashak, and Jeremoth are the sons of Eber. She
does not add a second Elpaal in v. 13 (see textual
note 25).

21   Added by Rudolph, 78, and Williamson, 84–85 (see
textual note 25).

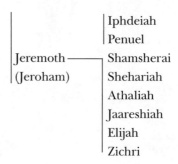

```
                         ┌ Iphdeiah
                         │ Penuel
  Jeremoth  ─────────────┤ Shamsherai
  (Jeroham)              │ Shehariah
                         │ Athaliah
                         │ Jaareshiah
                         │ Elijah
                         └ Zichri
```

■ **8** *And Shaharaim became the father of sons in the field of Moab after he had sent away/divorced his wives Hushim and Baara:* In the MT, Shaharaim (שחרים) is not explicitly connected to any of the preceding members of the Benjaminite genealogy.[22] In an effort to connect Shaharaim to the line of Benjamin, Japhet, 192, proposed that Shaharaim is a variant of Huram (חורם; v. 5) or Aharah (אחרה, v. 1; cf. Ahiram אחרים, Num 26:38).[23] Without versional support, there can be little confidence in these conjectures, but on the genealogical chart of Benjamin I have identified him with Huram. In any case the Chronicler identified Shaharaim as a Benjaminite who is followed by three successive generations. According to this verse Shaharaim was the ancestor of a clan of Benjaminites who lived in Moab.[24] Other Israelites who lived at least temporarily in Moab include the family of Elimelech and Naomi, the great-grandparents of David (Ruth 1), the parents of David who were sent to Moab by David (1 Sam 22:3-4),[25] and a number of Judeans at the time of Jeremiah who had fled there during the attack of Nebuchadnezzar (Jer 40:11-12). Shaharaim's presence in Moab may have taken place when Moab was under Israel's control after the victory of the judge Ehud over Eglon[26] (Judg 3:15-30; Myers, 1:60) or in the ninth century before the rise of Mesha. The smallness of the Benjaminite territory may have led to tribal expansion to Moab in the east and to Lod and Ono in the west (v. 12). Shaharaim's "divorce" from his earlier wives may indicate the uprooting of his portion of the tribe of Benjamin and its emigration to Moab.[27] His wife Baara is

---

22 Jeiel, the ancestor of Saul, also lacks such a link in v. 29.

23 Marquart, "Genealogies of Benjamin," 347, following Hogg, replaces "Shaharaim" with "Ahihor": "And Ahihor begat in the plateau of Moab of his concubine whose name was Baara, Hushim." Tom Wayne Willett, "Shaharaim," *ABD* 5:1152, mentions that Shaharaim could be a copyist's error for Shehariah, his great-grandson (שחריה; 1 Chr 8:26), but even if that were true it would not facilitate a connection to the lineage of Benjamin. Johnstone, 1:115, raises the possibility that Shaharaim had been lost by haplography at the end of v. 7. This would make him the brother of Uzza and Ahihud.

24 Despite Curtis and Madsen, 157, there is no reason to associate this with the postexilic family Pahathmoab (Ezra 2:6; 8:4). The "field of Moab" occurs elsewhere only in the Edomite king list (Gen 36:35//1 Chr 1:46) and in the book of Ruth (1:6; 2:3, 8, 9, 17, 22).

25 Does the Benjaminite presence in Moab in this genealogy offer a defense against any criticism of David's great-grandmother Ruth being from Moab or his parents spending time there?

26 This is dated by S. Yeivin, "The Benjaminite Settlement in the Western Part of Their Territory," *IEJ* 21 (1971) 150, to the second half of the 13th century, but a date a century or more later seems to be more likely if this is a premonarchical tradition. Knauf, "Eglan and Ophrah," dates the story to the 8th century, but basically denies its historical character.

27 Oeming, *Wahre Israel*, 172, concludes that שלח does not mean "divorce" but "set free." He would add a *mēm* to "Hushim" and "Baara" (מחושים ומבערא; lost by haplography) so that this sentence could be translated: "Shaharaim became the father of sons in the country of Moab—after he had released them [referring to the Moabites he had captured in v. 6]—through his wives Hushim and through Baara."

```
```

unknown elsewhere, but the children of Shaharaim and Hushim are listed in v. 11. In Gen 46:23 Hushim is listed as the only *son* of Dan and in 1 Chr 7:12 as the son of Aher, although that is no reason, *pace* Rudolph, to change this name here as if it were inappropriate for a woman (cf. textual note 17). If this Hushim and the name in Gen 46:23 refer to the same clan, the genealogical point might be that a portion of the tribe of Dan was associated with (married to) a part of Benjamin.[28] But the appearance of Hushim as a Benjaminite name in 1 Chr 7:12 obviates the need to connect Benjamin with Dan (cf. Williamson, 78). Many, of course, have followed Klostermann's emendation in 7:12 and connected this Hushim also to Dan (see the commentary on 7:12).

■ **9-10** *Through his wife Hodesh, he became the father of Jobab, Zibia, Mesha, Malcam, Jeuz, Sachia, and Mirmah:* Hodesh means "new moon," but Myers, 1:57, suggests that "his wife Hodesh" could be translated "his new wife," that is, the one after his divorce. Presumably, according to v. 8, these children were born in Moab. The name of the second son of Shaharaim and Hodesh, Mesha, is the same as that of the Moabite king made famous by the Moabite Stone (*ANET,* 320–21). A Jobab also appears as the seventh son of Elpaal in v. 17. All of these sons are identified as heads of ancestral houses in v. 10.

■ **11** *Through Hushim he had become the father of Abitub and Elpaal:* The reduced status of Hushim and her sons may be indicated by the facts that she had been "divorced" by Shaharaim (v. 8), that she and her sons are mentioned after the children of Shaharaim and Hodesh, and that her sons are not called heads of ancestral houses.[29] The

location of these births is not indicated. Subsequent descendants of Shaharaim and Hushim are traced through Elpaal in the next three verses.

■ **12** *The sons of Elpaal: Eber, Misham, and Shemed–he is the one who built Ono and Lod with its towns:* Elpaal's third son Shemed[30] is credited with rebuilding or fortifying Ono and Lod. Both towns are well outside usual Benjaminite territory.[31] This may indicate that parts of Benjamin claimed territory to the northwest during the Persian period. Ono (MR 137159) lay 7 miles southeast of Joppa (MR 126162), and Lod (MR 140151) is 11 miles southeast of Joppa. Ono appears in a list of cities under Thutmose III at Karnak (*ANET,* 243). The book of Nehemiah assumes that Ono (and Lod) are outside the postexilic province of Yehud (Neh 6:2). Seven hundred twenty-five inhabitants of Lod, Hadid, and Ono appear in the list of returnees (Ezra 2:33; Neh 7:37).[32] The people of Benjamin occupied Lod and Ono in postexilic times (Neh 11:35); in fact, this is the only period when these towns are mentioned in the Bible.

■ **13** *and Beriah, Elpaal, and Shema (they were the heads of ancestral houses of the inhabitants of Aijalon, who put to flight the inhabitants of Gath):* According to this reconstruction,[33] these three sons of Elpaal the son of Shaharaim and Hushim[34] were inhabitants of Aijalon (Yâlō, MR 152138), which was assigned to Dan in Josh 19:42, but apparently ruled by Ephraim in certain periods (Judg 1:35). Aijalon was the location of one of Rehoboam's fortresses and hence belonged to the southern kingdom (2 Chr 11:10), but it was taken by the Philistines during the reign of Ahaz (2 Chr 28:18). As

---

28   Yeivin, "Benjaminite Settlement," 149, writes: "A splinter clan of the Danite Hushim . . . became involved by intermarriage with Shaharahimite clans . . . hence its appearance in their genealogy as an eponymous 'mother' on the western end of Benjaminite territory."

29   Laban and Ben Zvi, "Observations," 468, suggest that she held the structural role of the concubine.

30   Curtis and Madsen, 160, make Elpaal responsible for these building activities and consider Eber, Misham, and Shemed a transcriber's blunder. Cf. vv. 17-18. Tg also connects Elpaal to Ono and Lod.

31   Oeming, *Wahre Israel,* 172, notes that according to Joshua 16, Ono and Lod would fall within the territory assigned to Ephraim, though their names are not mentioned there. Earlier they would have been

within the territory assigned to Dan when it was still in the south; later they would have been under the control of the Philistine states.

32   Rudolph argues that Ezra 2 and Nehemiah 7 represent the land possessed by Judah just before the exile.

33   See textual note 25 for an alternate possibility favored by Japhet that would make Beriah, Shema, Sheshak, and Jeremoth descendants of Eber and therefore grandsons of Elpaal.

34   Rudolph, 75–76, sees here a new genealogical fragment not connected to Elpaal, since vv. 15-27 provide descendants for the names mentioned in vv. 13-14, not for those in v. 12a. So also Williamson, 84.

one of the Levitical cities, it is assigned to Dan (Josh 21:24; cf. 1 Chr 6:54 [69]). Since the inhabitants of Gath (Tell es-Safi, MR 135123), who were put to flight (cf. the exiling mentioned in v. 6), would both be far away from Benjamin and under Philistine domination, a number of scholars, following Mazar,[35] have identified "Gath" with Gittaim ("double Gath"; Râs Abū Ḥumeid, MR 140145; cf. the same possible confusion at 7:21).[36] It was at Gath or Gittaim that the sons of Ephraim died (7:21). The people of Beeroth, a Benjaminite city, had fled to Gittaim and remained there as resident aliens until the time of David (2 Sam 4:2-3). In Neh 11:33 Gittaim appears in the list of towns inhabited by the Benjaminites at the time of Nehemiah. Building on Neh 11:33-35 and Ezra 2:3//Neh 7:37, which mention Lod and Ono, Rudolph, 77, ascribes the incidents mentioned in 1 Chr 8:1-32 to late monarchic times (Josiah) or even to the Persian period. In the postexilic period the people of Yehud would first have expanded to Aijalon, then to Gittaim, and then to Ono and Lod. Judahites and Benjaminites lived in Jerusalem (cf. vv. 28 and 32) both in preexilic (Jer 6:1) and postexilic times (Neh 11:4//1 Chr 9:3). But an expansion of Benjaminites into Moab (v. 8) is hard to prove for either the time of Josiah or the postexilic period. Japhet, 194–95, prefers a context in the monarchical period. Shema (שמע) is apparently the same as Shimei (שמעי) in v. 21. Is there any relationship between Beriah the son of Elpaal in this verse and Beriah the son of Ephraim mentioned in 7:23?

■ **14** *and their brothers, Shashak and Jeremoth:* In my reconstruction these are the seventh and eighth sons of

Elpaal.[37] Jeremoth (ירמות) is apparently the same person as Jeroham (ירחם) in v. 27. Rudolph, 79, thinks that these two brothers were settlers in Jerusalem (v. 28), but that location is clear for their sons in vv. 25-27, not for themselves.

8:15-28. Descendants of Elpaal—Beriah, Elpaal, Shimei (Shema), Shashak, and Jeroham (Jeremoth)—Live in Jerusalem

In these verses six sons are listed for Beriah (vv. 15-16),[38] seven for Elpaal (vv. 17-18),[39] nine for Shimei (vv.19-21),[40] twelve[41] for Shashak (vv. 22-25),[42] and six for Jeroham (vv. 26-28).[43]

■ **28** *These were the heads of ancestral houses, according to their generations, chiefs. These lived in Jerusalem:* I take the forty names in vv. 15-27 as the antecedent of "these." Thus at the time of the final compiling of this genealogy, forty Benjaminite families lived in Jerusalem. The different localities identified in vv. 6, 8, 12, 13 relate to movements of various segments of the tribe of Benjamin at an earlier date and do not contradict v. 28 (*pace* Braun, 126). Although Jerusalem is assigned to Benjamin in Josh 18:24, the city was on the border between Judah (Josh 15:63) and Benjamin (Judg 1:21), and these verses reflect an attempt to expand the territory of Benjamin to include Jerusalem. According to chap. 9 there were four Benjaminite heads of fathers' houses in Jerusalem in postexilic times (Sallu, Ibneiah, Elah, and Meshullam, vv. 7-8), and only one of them is related to the Benjaminites recounted in chap. 8 (Ibneiah the son of Jeroham, 9:8; cf. the sons of Jeroham in 8:27). I sus-

35 Benjamin Mazar, "Gath and Gittaim," *IEJ* 4 (1954) 223–33. Cf. Japhet, 194.

36 See Joe D. Seger, "Gath," *ABD* 2:908–9; Wesley I. Toews, "Gittaim," *ABD* 2:1030.

37 *NEB* connects Ahio (see textual note 27), Shashak, and Jeremoth with vv. 15-16 and makes them sons of Beriah. So also Johnstone, 1:112.

38 The names Arad and Ishpah occur only here in the Bible.

39 I take this Elpaal to be the one inserted into v. 13 by Rudolph in *BHS* (textual note 25). Since the names of Elpaal's sons in vv. 12-14 and vv. 17-18 show no relationship to one another, one must assume either that there were two Elpaals or that the name Elpaal reflects a strong clan name whose branches developed independently. See Williamson, 84. The

names Hizki, Ishmerai, and Izliah occur only here in the Bible.

40 The names Elienai and Beraiah occur only here in the Bible. With Elienai compare Elioenai (1 Chr 3:23-24; 4:36; 7:8; Ezra 10:22, 27; Neh 12:41).

41 Japhet, 195, counts eleven, since she does not restore Omri (textual note 33).

42 The names Ishpan, Anthothijah, and Iphdeiah occur only here in the Bible.

43 The names Shamsherai, Shehariah, and Jaareshiah occur only here in the Bible.

pect that this verse conflates ancient synonymous variants: "heads of ancestral houses" and "chiefs [of their ancestral houses]."[44] While this sentence summarizes the Benjaminite families here, a highly similar sentence based on it summarizes the Levitical families in 9:34.

8:29-32. Genealogy from Jeiel and Maacah

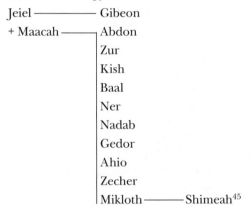

Jeiel ————— Gibeon
+ Maacah ——— Abdon
　　　　　　 Zur
　　　　　　 Kish
　　　　　　 Baal
　　　　　　 Ner
　　　　　　 Nadab
　　　　　　 Gedor
　　　　　　 Ahio
　　　　　　 Zecher
　　　　　　 Mikloth ——— Shimeah[45]

■ **29** *But Jeiel the father of Gibeon lived in Gibeon, and the name of his wife was Maacah:* The Hebrew word order makes an important contrast between "in Jerusalem" (at the end of v. 28) and "in Gibeon" (which begins v. 29). Jeiel (יעיאל) is an early settler ("father")[46] of Gibeon, but his relationship to the Benjaminite genealogy itself is not specified.[47] It is unclear whether his role as father of Gibeon reflects a preexilic tradition or refers to the refounding of Gibeon in postexilic times. If the latter is

the case, this would serve as additional proof that Saul's genealogy has been grafted into that of Gibeon (see below on v. 33). Gibeon (el-Jîb, MR 167139)[48] is 6 miles northwest of Jerusalem, and men from this city assisted Nehemiah in rebuilding Jerusalem's walls (Neh 3:7).[49] Earlier, in the years when David and Ishbaal were competing for the kingship, Gibeon was the scene of a battle between the men of Joab and the men of Abner (2 Sam 2:12-17). Gibeon is assigned to the tribal territory of Benjamin (Josh 18:15). In fact, of the four cities associated with the Hivites of Gibeon, three—Gibeon, Beeroth, and Chephira—are listed as Benjaminite (Josh 18:25-26), while the fourth, Kiriath-baal/Kiriath-jearim, is Judahite (Josh 15:60). Jeiel's marriage to Maacah could imply a tie of part of the tribe of Benjamin to the Aramean kingdom south of Mount Hermon in Transjordan (2 Sam 10:6, 8; 23:34; 1 Chr 19:7),[50] although there are nine individuals, both men and women, who are called Maacah in the OT.[51] Jeiel's name and that of Ner in 8:30 and Mikloth in 8:31 have been restored in my translation on the basis of 9:35-37 (see textual notes 40, 43, and 46).

■ **30-31** *His firstborn son: Abdon, then Zur, Kish, Baal, Ner, Nadab, Gedor, Ahio, Zecher, and Mikloth:* These ten names represent families or clans related to Jeiel and/or Gibeon.[52] The names Zur (צור), Kish, and Ner are identical or similar to names in the genealogy of Saul (Zeror [צרור],1 Sam 9:1; Kish, 1 Sam 9:1; 14:51; Ner 1, Sam 14:50, 51).[53] Williamson, 85, suggests that the presence of the name Baal implies the relative antiquity of this

---

44　ראשים לבית אבותם . . . ראשי אבותם; cf. 1 Chr 7:2.

45　1 Chr 9:38 has Shimeam.

46　Cf. the reference to Machir father of Gilead in 1 Chr 2:21 and n. 8 in the commentary on that chapter.

47　There is some similarity to Jediael (ידיעאל), the third son of Benjamin in 1 Chr 7:6.

48　J. Maxwell Miller, "Notes on Benjaminite Place Names," *JNSL* 25 (1999) 68–69, identifies Gibeon with Nebi Samwil (MR 167137).

49　Ninety-five people from Gibeon are recorded in the list of those who returned (Neh 7:25). But the parallel verse in Ezra 2:20 reads "Gibbar."

50　Marc Z. Brettler, "Jeiel," *ABD* 3:675, following N.-E. A. Andreason, "The Role of the Queen Mother in Israelite Society," *CBQ* 45 (1983) 179–94, suggests

that this ancestor of Saul might function as a queen mother.

51　Yeivin, "Benjaminite Settlement," 151, points out that the name Maacah always represents a non-Israelite, or a person of non-Israelite descent.

52　Marquart, "Genealogies of Benjamin," 346, makes them descendants of Becher and he moves vv. 30-40 after v. 3. Becher, of course, does not appear in the MT of chap. 8.

53　Aaron Demsky, "The Genealogy of Gibeon (I Chronicles 9:35-44): Biblical and Epigraphic Considerations," *BASOR* 202 (1971) 17, suggests a relationship between [Abi] Baal and Abiel (1 Sam 9:1). Rudolph, 80–81, argues that Kish and Ner are not the same persons known from the family of Saul since vv. 29-32 are much later than the days of Saul

section of the Benjaminite genealogy (cf. 1 Chr 5:5).[54] Demsky notes that Kish is a clan in its own right in the horizontal (segmented) genealogy and therefore argues for the lateness of v. 30.[55] He also observes that vv. 29-40 combine horizontal (segmented) and vertical (linear) elements. Kish in v. 30 is part of a horizontal or segmented genealogy, whereas in v. 33 he is part of a vertical or linear genealogy.[56] Demsky further calls attention to possible connections between the names of Ner and Gedor in this genealogy and the jar handles found at Gibeon.[57] Zecher occurs only here in the Bible, but in 9:37 the name is spelled "Zechariah."

■ **32** *And Mikloth became the father of Shimeah:* In vv. 29-32 this is the only time a descendant is mentioned beyond the first generation of the descendants of Jeiel and Maacah, and in this case the descendant comes from the youngest son. For the descendants of Ner see the commentary on v. 33.

Now these also lived alongside their kindred, in Jerusalem,

with their kindred: The antecedent of "these" is unclear: it could refer to Mikloth and Shimeah his son in v. 32 or to all the people mentioned in vv. 30-32, though the latter seems unlikely in this context. At least some of the Benjaminites associated with Gibeon had migrated to Jerusalem. Japhet, 196, notes the repetitious prepositional phrases "alongside their kindred" and "with their kindred." Perhaps the Hebrew text has conflated ancient variants.[58] Note that the second prepositional phrase is missing from Syr (textual note 48). "Their kindred" could refer to other Benjaminites or other Israelites. The association of Gibeon and Jerusalem appears already in 1 Kgs 3:4, 15//2 Chr 1:3-6, 13 (Solomon went to Gibeon to sacrifice and returned to Jerusalem) and is further developed in 1 Chr 16:37-42 (where David stationed Asaph and Obed-edom before the ark in Jerusalem and Zadok, Heman, and Jeduthun by the tabernacle at Gibeon). The tabernacle and the altar of burnt offering were stationed at Gibeon (21:29).

8:33-40. Ancestors and Descendants of King Saul

Ner—Kish—Saul┬Jonathan—Merib-baal—Micah— *(continued on next page)*
⎜Malchishua
⎜Abinadab
┕Esh-baal

---

and since the family of Saul was associated with Gibeah, not Gibeon. Edelman, *ABD* 4:1073–74, argues that Ner in v. 30 is among the postexilic settlers of Gibeon and that the Chronicler has falsely identified him with Saul's uncle Ner. Braun, 127, believes that Ner in 9:36 is an addition and is an attempt to bring the data in vv. 29-32 and vv. 33-38 closer together. He therefore does not restore Ner in 8:30.

54 Braun, 127, argues that the name Baal indicates that the genealogy is either quite early or quite late. In the early monarchy a place was named Baal-perazim because "Yahweh has broken through" (2 Sam 5:20). One of David's heroes was named Beeliah (1 Chr 12:6 [5]). Cf. Baal, a Reubenite (5:5), and Beeliada (14:7). Note also Saul's son Esh-baal (v. 33). All these references show the acceptability of "Baal" in the early monarchy. Rudolph, 80, notes that by the time of Nehemiah the name "Baal" had come to mean "lord" or "owner" and therefore this name could be used without giving offense.

55 "Genealogy of Gibeon," 19, n. 12.

56 Williamson, 85; Demsky, "Genealogy of Gibeon"; and Malamat," King Lists of the Old Babylonian Period and Biblical Genealogies," *JAOS* 88 (1968) 168–73, favor the unity of vv. 29-32 and vv. 33-40. Japhet, 197, and many others see them as separate.

57 On those handles, however, Ner is spelled נראל and there is a debate whether the other name at Gibeon is גדר or נדד. Demsky's proposed link between Hanan, the youngest son of Azel, and Hananiah חניהו of the jar handles ("Genealogy of Gibeon," 23) is not strong evidence since it is dealing with such a common name. On the name Gedor see 1 Chr 4:4.

58 Williamson, 86, suggests that the second phrase clarifies the first and that without it one might conclude that none of the families but only their kinsmen lived in Jerusalem.

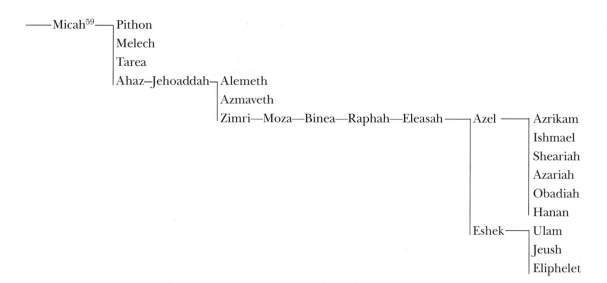

Genealogy of Saul in 1 Sam 9:1-2

a Benjaminite—Aphiah—Becorath—Zeror—Abiel—Kish—Saul

Genealogy of Saul in 1 Sam 14:50-51

Abiel——Ner——┌Abner   or   Abiel——┌Ner—— Abner
              └Kish——Saul   └Kish——Saul

■ **33** *And Ner became the father of Kish, Kish became the father of Saul, Saul became the father of Jonathan, Malchishua, Abinadab, and Esh-baal:* According to 1 Sam 9:1 Abiel was the grandfather of Saul and Kish was his father. There is an ambiguity in 1 Sam 14:50, "Abner the son of Ner the uncle of Saul," since the expression "the uncle of Saul" could modify either Abner or Ner. If Abner is the uncle of Saul, then Abner and Kish are brothers, sons of Ner, who is the son of Abiel (cf. 1 Sam 14:51). If Ner, on the other hand, is the uncle of Saul, Abner and Saul are cousins, sons of the brothers Ner

and Kish, respectively. In 1 Sam 14:51 MT Ner alone is identified as the son of Abiel, but *BHK* suggested emending בן to בני, making both Ner and Kish sons of Abiel (cf. Josephus *Ant.* 6.130).[60] While I believe that the latter option is the more likely construal of the text (that Abner and Saul are cousins and Ner is the father of Abner[61]), the genealogy preserved in 1 Chr 8:33 presupposes the former interpretation (that Abner is Saul's uncle) and makes Ner the father of Kish.[62] The result conflicts with 1 Sam 9:1, which makes Abiel, and not Ner, Saul's grandfather. Rudolph, 81, therefore inserts

---

59 This Micah is the same as the one listed in the fifth generation after Ner above. He is listed separately only because of the length of this genealogy.

60 Japhet, 197, who considers Abner the uncle of Saul, favors this emendation in 1 Sam 14:50, without realizing that it is meant to support the other interpretation.

61 So also Diana V. Edelman, "Abner," *ABD* 1:26.

62 Of course in 1 Chr 8:30//9:36 Kish and Ner are also brothers. Curtis and Madsen, 165, try to ease the problem by replacing the first Kish in v. 33 with Abner. Hence: "Ner became the father of Abner and Kish became the father of Saul."

"the son of Ner" into 1 Sam 9:1 after Kish, but this would require the further identification of Abiel and Jeiel.[63] The Chronicler incorrectly made Ner the son of Jeiel the father, rather than the brother, of Kish.[64] Hence the Chronicler grafted the genealogy of Saul into the Gibeonite genealogy. An antagonism between Saul and the Gibeonites is reflected in 2 Samuel 21 (where the Gibeonites execute seven descendants of Saul), but many argue that Gibeon was that capital of Saul.[65] According to 1 Sam 10:26 Gibeah, not Gibeon, was the home of Saul. This grafting of the genealogy of Saul into that of Gibeon forced the Chronicler to omit Aphiah, Becorath, Zeror, and Abiel from Saul's ancestry (1 Sam 9:1).

Saul's sons according to 1 Sam 14:49 were Jonathan, Ishvi, and Malchishua,[66] and in 1 Sam 31:2//1 Chr 10:2 we are told the Philistines killed Saul's sons Jonathan, Abinadab, and Malchishua. Ishbaal survived this battle. Ishvi (ישוי) is apparently the same person as Esh-baal

(אשבעל) in 1 Chr 8:33 and 9:39 and Ishbaal (אישבעל) in 2 Sam 2:8 LXX.[67] Chronicles does not contain the story of Esh-baal's rival reign since Yahweh turned the kingdom over immediately after the death of Saul to David the son of Jesse (1 Chr 10:14).

Oeming believes that the extended genealogy of Saul, which is repeated in chap. 9, plays an important role.[68] In 2 Sam 16:7-8 Shimei the son of Gera called David a murderer and a scoundrel and charged him with violence against the house of Saul. The Deuteronomistic History also gives the impression that many circles held David accountable for the murder of seven Saulides by the Gibeonites (2 Sam 21:1-14). But the Chronicler omits both of these passages and preserves the genealogy of Saul to twelve generations. David is no murderer of the house of Saul (cf. 1 Chr 10:6)!

■ **34** *and the son of Jonathan was Merib-baal; and Merib-baal became the father of Micah:* Merib-baal,[69] the son of Jonathan, is called Mephibosheth[70] in 2 Sam 4:4—21:7.[71]

---

63 Tg harmonizes in its own way: "Ner, who was called Abiel, became the father of Kish. They called him Ner because he used to light the lamps in the schools and synagogues, and this merit enabled Saul, his grandson, to become king."

64 So also Diana Edelman, "Did Saulide-Davidic Rivalry Resurface in Early Persian Yehud?" in *The Land that I Will Show You* (FS J. Maxwell Miller; ed. J. A. Dearman and M. P. Graham; JSOTSup 343; Sheffield: Sheffield Academic Press, 2001) 78, though she errs in stating that Ner is listed as Saul's uncle in 1 Sam 9:1, since neither Ner nor Abner appears there. Edelman, 90, makes the interesting suggestion that the genealogy of Saul preserved in chaps. 8–9 may in its noncanonical context have represented an attempt to advocate for a Benjaminite rather than a Judahite governor of Yehud. In a later essay, "Gibeon and the Gibeonites Revisited," in Lipschits and Blenkinsopp, *Judah and the Judeans,* 164–65, Edelman proposes that the non-Golah group living in Gibeon hoped for the restoration of the Saulide dynasty. Once the pro-Davidic Golah group had consolidated their power they may have filled in the Gibeon pool and weakened the city's defensive wall. In her view Gibeon, not Gibeah, was the capital of Saul.

65 Edelman, "Rivalry," 77; and Joseph Blenkinsopp, "Did Saul Make Gibeon His Capital?" *VT* 24 (1974) 1–7. See also P. J. Kearney, "The Role of the Gibeonites in the Deuteronomistic History," *CBQ* 35 (1973) 1–19.

66 Had Abinadab not been born when this genealogical notice was recorded?

67 The name in MT is changed to Ish-bosheth. McCarter, *II Samuel*, 254, is cautious about identifying Ishvi with Ishbosheth. Gordon J. Hamilton, "New Evidence for the Authenticity of *bšt* in Hebrew Personal Names and for Its Use as a Divine Epithet in Biblical Texts," *CBQ* 60 (1998) 228–50, argues that the element *bšt* is not the word "shame," but an element in the Amorite onomasticon meaning "protective spirit."

68 *Wahre Israel,* 179.

69 The etymology of Merib-baal is "Baal contends" (cf. Jerubbaal, the alternate name for Gideon in Judg 6:31-32), but the parallel passage in 1 Chr 9:40 has both this form and "Meri-baal," whose etymology is "man of Baal." See also textual note 51 to 8:34. Does the change in name suggest religious sensibility (Williamson, 86) or only haplography? M. Tsevat says that clusters of identical letters at mutual boundaries of two words are frequently simplified and not necessarily as a result of scribal error ("Ishbosheth and Congeners: The Names and Their Study," *HUCA* 46 [1975] 81). Cf. J. D. Fowler, *Theophoric Personal Names in Biblical Hebrew* (JSOTSup 49; Sheffield: Sheffield Academic Press, 1988) 61.

70 The name originally would have been "Mephibaal." See Diana V. Edelman, "Mephibosheth," *ABD* 4:696–97.

71 In 2 Sam 21:8 another Mephibosheth is mentioned, the son of Saul and his concubine Rizpah.

In 2 Samuel 9 the lame Mephibosheth was invited to eat at the king's table. During Absalom's revolt, Ziba, the servant of Mephibosheth, indicated that his master hoped to be restored to the kingship of his (grand)father (2 Sam 16:1-4). After the death of Absalom, Mephibosheth claimed that Ziba had slandered him, and he and David are reconciled (2 Sam 19:24-30). None of these stories is included in Chronicles. Micah (מיכה) the son of Merib-baal/Mephibosheth is also mentioned in 2 Sam 9:12, where the name is spelled with a different final *mater lectionis* (מיכא).

■ **35** *The sons of Micah: Pithon, Melech, Tarea, and Ahaz:* From here on out, the descendants of Saul are unknown elsewhere in the Bible. This is the only time, aside from the name of the king at the time of Isaiah (Isa 1:1; 7:1-12), where "Ahaz" appears in the OT as a personal name. Because the names are unknown, it is impossible to say what social situation lay behind this segmented genealogical list of four brothers in a genealogy that is primarily linear. Note only that the line of descent in this verse passes through the youngest son Ahaz.

■ **36** *Ahaz became the father of Jehoaddah; and Jehoaddah became the father of Alemeth, Azmaveth, and Zimri; Zimri became the father of Moza:* Demsky speculates that the original form of Jehoaddah (יהועדה) was Ya'rāh (יערה), which suggests a move of part of Saul's family to Kiriath-jearim (Deir el-'Âzar, MR 159135).[72] However that may be, Alemeth and Azmaveth are indeed towns in southern Benjamin. Alemeth is probably the same as Almon in the list of Levitical cities (Josh 21:18;[73] Khirbet 'Almît, MR 176136), and Azmaveth may be located at Hizmeh (MR 175138), both within the tribal territory of Benjamin. Forty-two descendants of (Beth-) Azmaveth are in the list of returnees (Ezra 2:24//Neh 7:28; cf. Neh 12:29), where Beth-azmaveth is linked to Geba (Ezra

2:26//Neh 7:30; MR 175140) and Anathoth (Ezra 2:23//Neh 7:27; MR 174135). Zimri is unknown, but his fathering of Moza represents a move of another part of the tribe of Benjamin to the town of Moza (מוצא), spelled Mozah (מצה) in its only appearance in a list of Benjaminite towns in Josh 18:26 (Qâlunyah, MR 165134).[74]

■ **37-38** *Moza became the father of Binea; Raphah was his son, Eleasah his son, Azel his son. Azel had six sons, and these are their names: Azrikam, his first born, Ishmael, Sheariah, Azariah, Obadiah, and Hanan; all these were the sons of Azel:* Note that the form of the genealogy changes after Moza fathers Binea by listing all the subsequent names followed by "his son."[75] While none of these individuals is known elsewhere,[76] this genealogy may originally have found its goal in Azel and his six sons,[77] who could trace their ancestry back to Saul and his ancestors (cf. 1 Chr 9:43-44). This family asserted its claim to prestige by linking itself to Israel's first king. One can surmise that Saul's genealogy was also preserved for four centuries because some of his descendants hoped for a restoration to power.[78] Since the sons of Azel are in the twelfth generation after Saul, they may be dated to late preexilic or even postexilic times. This genealogy, of course, is in considerable tension with the narrative in 1 Chr 10:6, which states that the whole house of Saul perished on Mount Gilboa.

■ **39** *The sons of his brother Eshek: Ulam his firstborn, Jeush the second, and Eliphelet the third:* The addition of vv. 39-40 in chap. 8 is an expansion of the genealogy of Saul and makes the genealogy in chap. 8 apparently typologically later than that in chap. 9. Or, more likely in my judgment, the Chronicler may have decided not to incorporate 8:39-40 into chap. 9 since he may have thought the final sentence—"All these were Benjaminites"—is not

---

72   Demsky, "Genealogy of Gibeon," 19, n. 13.

73   The parallel in 1 Chr 6:45 (60) reads Alemeth. In 7:8 Alemeth is a grandson of Benjamin through Becher.

74   In 1 Chr 2:46 a different Moza is a child of Caleb and his concubine Ephah.

75   In vv. 34 and 35 a third form is used where "son of" or "sons of" precedes the father's name.

76   Levin, "Chronological Aspects," 16, states that Eleasah and Azel are well-known toponyms in the postexilic period, but Azel appears only in the two copies of the genealogy of Saul, and Eleasah

appears there and among the descendants of Judah in 1 Chr 2:39-40.

77   As observed in textual note 60, Bocheru may have been one of those sons, or if that word is read as "his firstborn," we need to add another name, such as "Azariah."

78   J. Flanagan, "Genealogy and Dynasty in the Early Monarchy of Israel and Judah," *Proceedings of the Eighth World Congress of Jewish Studies. Division A: The Period of the Bible* (Jerusalem, 1982) 25, suggests that the preservation of the Saulide genealogy may reflect a hope that they would return to power.

what he wanted to emphasize at that point. The name Ulam is attested only here and 7:16-17, where he is a son of Peresh, the son of Machir and Maacah, descendants of Manasseh. Japhet, 199, concludes that Ulam would be living about the end of the seventh century (cf. the list of high priests and Davidic kings).[79] A later date is of course not excluded.

■ **40** *The sons of Ulam were mighty warriors, archers, having many children and grandchildren, one hundred fifty:* The report on the sons of Ulam apparently comes from a military census list (cf. 7:2, 5, 7, 9, 11; 49; 5:24). Oeming concludes from the number of troops assigned to Ulam that with a small number of troops one can, with God's help, achieve great victories.[80] The troops of the northern kingdom, on the other hand, had great numbers but no success. This may be overinterpretation. The number of the troops from this family is similar to the number of people attributed to families in Ezra 2//Nehemiah 7 (Curtis and Madsen, 167). The military forces of Ulam in this genealogical notice are claiming prestige by identifying themselves as descendants of Israel's first king.

Conclusion

The long genealogy of the Benjaminites brings the genealogy of the sons of Israel to an end and forms an *inclusio* with the genealogy of Judah in chaps. 2–4. At forty verses it is exceeded only by that of Judah (one hundred verses) and the Levites (eighty-one verses). These three tribes form the core of the postexilic community. Already in the Pentateuch Benjamin was the second child of Jacob's favorite wife (Gen 29:30), and Joseph showed special favor to Benjamin by giving him five times as much food as he gave to his brothers (Gen 43:34). According to the present genealogy, Shaharaim, a Benjaminite, had expanded into Moab, creating a Benjaminite/Israelite presence in the former territory of Reuben and Gad. Not incidentally, some Benjaminites are said to reside in Jerusalem (vv. 28, 32) which anticipates what will be said in 9:3, 34, and 38. These families

in Jerusalem include the five families outlined in vv. 15-27 and (some of) the Gibeonite descendants of Jeiel. The inclusion of the genealogy of the house of Saul, which survived for twelve generations after the first king died in battle, subtly exonerates David from the accusation that he is somehow responsible for violence against the house of Saul.

Stanley Walters proposed that the genealogy of Saul links Saul back not to Benjamin but to Jeiel, the "father" of Gibeon. Saul in this view is a geographic but not an ethnic Benjaminite, and the city to which he is connected has primarily negative connotations in the Former and Latter Prophets.[81] He added that Saul was unsuitable to be king because he was not connected by blood to Israel (cf. Deut 17:15). But the Chronicler makes no such charge in his narrative, and his additional material in 1 Chr 10:13-14 focuses squarely on the issue of Saul's unfaithfulness, not his genealogical illegitimacy. I suspect that the lack of genealogical connection to Benjamin results from the limitations of the genealogical materials that were available to the Chronicler in vv. 29-32 and vv. 33-40.[82] The first of these paragraphs documented the presence of Benjaminites in Jerusalem, surely something that the Chronicler welcomed. He decided to connect the second paragraph to this information, identifying Ner from (the reconstructed) v. 30 with Ner the father of Kish in the (primarily) linear genealogy of vv. 33-40. The advantage of this genealogy of Saul over that in 1 Sam 9:1-2 is that it followed the descendants of Saul to the twelfth generation, which as Oeming observes, exonerates David from the accusation of wiping out the house of Saul. Lengthening the genealogical materials on Benjamin by twelve verses provides a more robust genealogy for Benjamin that now could be paired with the genealogy of Judah in chaps. 2–4. Associating Saul with Gibeon would hardly have a negative connotation for the Chronicler, since he located the tabernacle at that spot in premonarchical and even Davidic times.

---

79 The genealogy in 1 Chr 4:34-41 is dated to the late 8th century, the time of Hezekiah.
80 *Wahre Israel,* 178.
81 Stanley D. Walters, "Saul of Gibeon," *JSOT* 52 (1991) 61–76, esp. 71.

82 The Chronicler also seems not to be bothered by the fact that Shaharaim in v. 8, who introduces the lengthy genealogy leading to v. 28, also could not be explicitly tied to Benjamin himself.

9

Translation

1/ So all Israel was enrolled by genealogies; and these are written in the Book of the Kings of Israel.[1] And Judah was taken into exile to Babylon because of their unfaithfulness. **2/** The first[2] settlers[3] who were in their possessions in their towns were Israel, the priests, the Levites, and the temple servants.[4]

3/ And in Jerusalem lived some of the people of Judah, some of the people of Benjamin, and some of the people of Ephraim and Manasseh.[5] **4/** Uthai[6] son of Ammihud, son of Omri, son of Imri,[7] son of Bani, from[8] the sons of Perez son of Judah. **5/** And of the Shelanites:[9] Asaiah[10] the firstborn[11] and his sons.[12] **6/** Of the sons of Zerah: Jeuel[13] and their kin, six hundred ninety. **7/** Of the Benjaminites: Sallu[14] son of Meshullam, son of Hodaviah,[15] son of Hassenuah,[16] **8/** Ibneiah[17] son of Jeroham, Elah son of[18] Uzzi, son of Michri,[19] and Meshullam son of Shephatiah, son of Reuel, son of Ibnijah; **9/** and their kindred according to their generations, nine hundred fifty-six.[20] All these were[21] heads of families according to their ancestral houses.

10/ Of the priests: Jedaiah, Jehoiarib, Jachin,[22] **11/** and Azariah[23] son of Hilkiah, son of Meshullam, son of Zadok, son of Meraioth, son of Ahitub, the chief officer of the house of God; **12/** and[24] Adaiah[25] son of Jeroham,[26] son of Pashhur, son of Malchijah, and Maasai[27] son of Adiel,[28] son of Jahzerah,[29] son of Meshullam,[30] son of Meshillemith,[31] son of Immer; **13/** besides their kindred, heads of their ancestral houses, one thousand seven hundred sixty, valiant warriors for the work[32] of the service of the house of God.

14/ Of the Levites: Shemaiah son of Hasshub, son of Azrikam, son of Hashabiah, of the sons of Merari;[33] **15/** and Bakbakkar, Heresh, Galal,[34] and Mattaniah son of Mica, son of Zichri,[35] son of Asaph; **16/** and Obadiah[36] son of Shemaiah,[37] son of Galal, son of Jeduthun,[38] and Berechiah son of Asa,[39] son of Elkanah, who lived in the villages of the Netophathites.

17/ The gatekeepers were: Shallum,[40] Akkub, Talmon, Ahiman;[41] and their brother[42] Shallum was the chief, **18/** stationed until now in the king's gate on the east side. These were the gatekeepers of the camps of the Levites. **19/** Shallum son of Kore, son of Ebiasaph, son of Korah, and his kindred of his ancestral house, the Korahites, were in control of the work of the service, guardians of the thresholds of the tent, as their ancestors had been in control of the camp of Yahweh, guardians of the entrance. **20/** Phinehas son of Eleazar was leader[43] over them previously; Yahweh was with him.[44] **21/** Zechariah[45] son of

1 I retain this name for the source document used by the Chronicler (see the commentary). A reference to "the Book of the Kings of Israel" occurs only at 2 Chr 20:34. LXX, Vg, Tg connect "and Judah" from the next sentence to this first sentence, creating the "Book of the Kings of Israel and Judah" (cf. also Pseudo-Rashi). A reference to this source appears in 2 Chr 27:7; 35:27; 36:8. If this change is made, however, as Rudolph, 82, notes, "and Judah" must be added to the beginning of the next sentence, where it is indispensable. Braun, 130, assumes that both Israel and Judah have been lost. Hence he reads: "the book of the kings of Israel and Judah. But Israel and Judah were exiled. . . ."

2 הראשנים; *BHS* notes that LXX, Syr, Arab. presuppose בראשנה; cf. Neh 7:5.

3 והיושבים; some propose השבים "the first returnees," but this list in Chronicles refers to the settlers "of old." See the commentary.

4 Neh 11:3 adds ובני עבדי שלמה "and the sons of the slaves of Solomon." Cf. Neh 7:57, 60//Ezra 2:55, 58.

5 "and some of the people of Ephraim and Manasseh" is omitted in Neh 11:4.

6 עותי; Neh 11:4 עתיה "Athaiah." Neh 11:4 adds at the beginning מבני יהודה "of the sons of Judah." Knoppers, "Sources," 153, suggests that this may represent haplography in Chronicles. It seems more likely that this phrase has been replaced redactionally in 9:4 by adding the word "son of Judah" to the mention of Perez at the end of this verse.

7 אמרי; Neh 11:4 אמריה "Amariah." "Son of Imri" is missing from LXX because of homoioteleuton.

8 בני מן ("Bani, from"), with Q, some medieval Hebrew MSS, Tg, Vg (cf. LXX^min); K בנימן ("Benjamin") has incorrectly joined the two words into one name.

9 השלני; MT השילוני "the Shilonites," but a person from Shiloh would not be a Judahite. The reference is to descendants of Shelah, the son of Judah. Cf. Num 26:20; 1 Chr 4:21; and Japhet, 201. Braun, 131, retains "Shilonites."

10 עשיה; Neh 11:5 (ו)מעשיה "Maaseiah."

11 הבכור; LXX πρωτότοκος αὐτοῦ = בכרו "his firstborn."

12 ובניו; Syr, Arab.: ובציה אחיו "and Bezai his brother." Cf. the name בצי in Ezra 2:17//Neh 7:23; Neh 10:19 (18). Chronicles LXX^Baghc2 lack a translation for "and his sons," apparently because of homoioteleuton in Greek (from αὐτοῦ to αὐτοῦ). See the previous note. Knoppers, "Sources," 147, suggests that this minus might be a significant agreement between Chronicles LXX and the text of Nehemiah. If so, it would support my own proposal in the commentary that בניו was added after a significant

Meshelemiah[46] was gatekeeper at the entrance of the tent of meeting. 22/ All these, who were selected as gatekeepers at the thresholds,[47] were two hundred twelve. They were enrolled by genealogies in their villages, but they[48] were the ones whom[49] David and Samuel the seer installed on account of their trustworthiness.[50] 23/ So they and their descendants were in control of the gates of the house of Yahweh, that is, the house[51] of the tent, as guards.[52] 24/ The gatekeepers[53] were on the four[54] sides,[55] toward the east,[55] west, north, and south. 25/ And their kindred who were in their villages were required to come in for seven days, in turn,[56] to be with them;[57] 26/ for the four chief gatekeepers were on permanent duty;[58] they were the Levites,[59] and they had supervision over the chambers and the treasuries[60] of the house of God. 27/ They would spend the night near[61] the house of God; and it was they upon whom was the responsibility for watching it,[62] and they were responsible for opening it every morning.[63]

28/ Some of them were responsible for the utensils of service, for they were required to count them when they were brought in and taken out. 29/ Others were appointed over the furniture and over all the holy utensils, also over the choice flour, the wine, the oil, the incense, and the spices. 30/ Others, of the sons of the priests, prepared the mixing of the spices, 31/ and Mattithiah, one of the Levites, the firstborn of Shallum the Korahite,[64] was responsible for making the flat cakes.[65] 32/ Also some of the sons of the Kohathites[66] were responsible for the rows of bread, to prepare them for each sabbath.

33/ Now these[67] singers, the heads of ancestral houses of the Levites, (living) in the chambers of the temple, were free from other service,[68] for they were on duty day and night. 34/ These were the heads of ancestral houses of the Levites, according to their generations, chiefs.[69] These lived in Jerusalem.

35/ And in Gibeon lived[70] Jeuel[71] the father of Gibeon, and the name of his wife[72] was Maacah. 36/ His firstborn son was Abdon, then Zur, Kish, Baal, Ner, Nadab, 37/ Gedor, Ahio,[73] Zechariah,[74] and Mikloth; 38/ and Mikloth became the father of Shimeam;[75] and these also lived opposite their kindred in Jerusalem, with their kindred. 39/ Ner became the father of Kish, Kish became the father of Saul, Saul became the father of Jonathan, Malchishua, Abinadab, and Eshbaal; 40/ and the son of Jonathan was Merib-baal; and Meri-baal[76] became the father of Micah. 41/ The sons of Micah: Pithon, Melech, Tahrea,[77] and Ahaz;[78]

textual loss because of homoioteleuton in this genealogy. See the commentary for further discussion.

13 יעואל; LXX^{ALal}, Tg: יעיאל "Jeiel." Cf. v. 35.

14 סלוא; Neh 11:7 סלא.

15 בן הודויה; Syr hwdy'. In Neh 11:7 Meshullam is the son of Joed (יועד), but Chronicles has been damaged by haplography here. See the commentary.

16 הַסְּנָאָה; LXX^L, Vg: סנאה "Senaah." Cf. Ezra 2:35 and Neh 3:3.

17 The first and last names in v. 8 are spelled the same way consonantally, but they are vocalized differently.

18 וְאֵלֶּה בֶן; some Hebrew MSS, LXX^B: וְאֵלֶּה בְּנֵי "and these are the sons of."

19 מכרי; LXX, Syr: מכיר "Machir."

20 Syr "nine hundred ninety-nine."

21 כל אלה; MT adds אנשים "men." Rudolph, 84, suggests it is a miswritten marginal correction of ראשים (לבית אבות).

22 ידעיה בן יויריב יכין; Neh 11:10 ידעיה ויהויריב ויכין "Jedaiah son of Joiarib, Jachin." At Neh 11:10 Rudolph, *Esra und Nehemia*, 184, reconstructs the original reading in Nehemiah as ידעיה בן יויקים בן "Jedaiah the son of Jehoiakim the son of [Seraiah]," and he favors the same reading here, p. 84, with Azariah replacing Seraiah (see the next note). In Maccabean times he believes Jehoiakim was replaced by Joiarib (the ancestor of the Maccabees; 1 Chr 24:7), and this led to the further change of the second "son of" to "Jachin" on the basis of 24:17. Japhet, 201, reads ידעיה בן יהויריב בן שריה בן עזריה "Jedaiah the son of Jehoiarib the son of Seraiah the son of Azariah." Williamson, *Ezra, Nehemiah*, 343, reconstructs Neh 11:10 as ידעיה ויויריב בני שריה "Jedaiah and Joiarib, the sons of Seraiah." See the commentary.

23 ועזריה; Neh 11:11 שריה "Seraiah."

24 Neh 11:12 adds the following words: "and their associates who did the work of the house, eight hundred twenty-two."

25 ועדיה; a few Hebrew MSS, Syr: ועזריה "Azariah."

26 Neh 11:12 adds "son of Pelaliah son of Amzi son of Zechariah." This was lost because of homoioarchton in Chronicles.

27 ומעשי; Neh 11:13 ועמשסי "Amashsai."

28 עדיאל; Neh 11:13 עזראל "Azarel."

29 יחזרה; Neh 11:13 אחזי "Ahzai."

30 בן משלם; lacking in the parallel text at Neh 11:13 because of homoioarchton.

31 משלמית; LXX, Syr, Neh 11:13: משלמות.

32 חֵיל לִמְלָאכֶת (cf. Rudolph, 86, and LXX, Tg, Vg); MT חֵיל מְלָאכֶת. The preposition *lāmed* was lost by haplography, requiring חיל to be vocalized as a construct.

42/ and Ahaz became the father of Jarah,[79] and Jarah of Alemeth, Azmaveth, and Zimri; and Zimri became the father of Moza. 43/ Moza became the father of Binea;[80] and Rephaiah[81] was his son, Eleasah his son, Azel his son. 44/ Azel had six sons, and these are their names: Azrikam, his firstborn,[82] Ishmael, Sheariah,[83] Obadiah, and Hanan; these[84] were the sons of Azel.

33 מן בני מררי ;Neh 11:5 בן בוני "son of Bunni."

34 חרש וגלל ;Neh 11:17 ובקבקיה "Bakbukiah." Rudolph, 86 (cf. *BHS*), suggests following Syr, Arab., and reading ובקבק בן חרש בן גלל "Bakbuk the son of Heresh the son of Galal," or ובקבק רב חרשי גלל "Bakbuk the head of the stone carvers."

35 זכרי ; a few Hebrew MSS, Syr, Arab., and Neh 11:17: זבדי "Zabdi."

36 ועבדיה ;Neh 11:17 ועבדא "Abda."

37 שמעיה ;Neh 11:17 שמוע "Shammua."

38 ידותון ; cf. Neh 11:17 Q. 1 Chr 9:16 LXX^min, Syr, Vg, and Neh 11:17 K: ידיתון.

39 אסא ; Cairo Genizah fragments, many Hebrew MSS, Syr, Arab.: אסף "Asaph."

40 שלום ; omitted in Neh 11:19.

41 ואחימן . A fourth name is needed because of v. 26a but this name may be a dittography of the following word ואחיהם, or its spelling may have been affected by that word.

42 וַאֲחֵיהֶם ; a few Hebrew MSS, editions, LXX, Tg, Arab., and Neh 11:19: וַאֲחֵיהֶם "and their brothers." Braun, 131, adopts this reading. Neh 11:19 lacks "Shallum was the chief."

43 נגיד ; cf. v. 11, where it is translated "chief officer."

44 Or "may Yahweh be with him."

45 זכריה ; *BHS* suggests adding the conjunction "and," which has been lost by haplography.

46 מְשֶׁלֶמְיָה ; LXX^A min, Syr: משלם "Meshullam."

47 בספים ; Syr במספר "by number."

48 המה ; LXX^L adds before this word "and he numbered them and."

49 Rudolph, 88, interprets the rest of this sentence as a relative clause without the relative pronoun.

50 באמונתם ; or, Braun, 131, "in their office of trust." See vv. 26, 31, and 2 Chr 19:9; 31:12, 15, 18; 34:12. *BHS* cites two proposals: באמונת אבתם "according to the faithfulness of their fathers," or באבותם "according to their fathers."

51 לבית ; *BHS* notes a proposal to emend to לעמת "alongside."

52 למשמרות ; perhaps "in observation posts." Braun, 130–31, "by watches." LXX "to guard." Syr *zbn'* "[the tent] of meeting."

53 הַשֹּׁעֲרִים ; Rudolph, 88, emends to הַשְּׁעָרִים "gates." Cf. LXX, Syr, Arab.

54 לארבע ; Rudolph, 88, adds before this word, which is the first word in the verse, לארבעת גבורי השערים "to the four supervisors of the gatekeepers" (were the gates assigned).

55 מזרח ; *BHS*: מזרחה ; cf. v. 18. The final *hê* was lost by haplography.

56 מעת אל עת . Japhet, 217, cites Ezek 4:10 as a closely parallel expression and suggests that the meaning here is from the beginning of one week to the beginning of the next.

57   עם אלה. This is an unusual use of אלה as an object of the preposition עם, but see Neh 5:18 וזה עם.

58   באמונה. Rudolph, 88, "dauernd" (constantly). Braun, 130–31, "Because of their faithfulness" (though the noun lacks a possessive suffix) or "Because they were in office." Piet B. Dirksen, "1 Chronicles 9,26-33: Its Position in Chapter 9," *Bib* 79 (1998) 93, defends "on permanent duty."

59   הם הלוים. Rudolph, 88, emends to הם מן הלוים or גם הם לוים "they belong to the Levites." Japhet, 201: המה הלוים.

60   האצרות should be vocalized as absolute plural instead of construct plural, in which case the following בית is an accusative of place, or the definite article should be dropped. Cf. Rudolph, 88.

61   *BHS* emends ומהם סביבות to וסביבות, citing its own emendation in v. 26c (note 61 above) and the MT of vv. 28-29.

62   משמרתו; MT lacks the *wāw* suffix because of haplography before והם. Cf. Rudolph, 90.

63   LXX adds: "to open the doors of the temple." For והם על המפתח ולבקר, lit. "and they were over the key and for the morning," Rudolph, 90, reads: ועליהם מפתחו לבקר, with a translation similar to mine. See Judg 3:25 and Isa 22:22. Cf. GKC §123c. My translation follows Dirksen, "1 Chronicles 9,26,33," 93, who reads: והם עלהם פתחו לבקר.

64   הקרחי; lacking in Syr.

65   החבתים. Cf. Rudolph, 90. Japhet, 202: "What is baked on the griddle." Cf. Lev 2:5; 7:9. Chronicles LXX: "meat offering of the pan belonging to the high priest."

66   ומן בני הקהתי. Rudolph, 90, emends to ובניה הקהתי (cf. LXX) and translates: "The Kohathite Benaiah [was]." He thinks that the final *hê* was lost by haplography and ובני was then assimilated to the beginning of v. 30.

67   ואלה. Rudolph, 90, emends to ואלם "on the other

hand" since he feels that this verse cannot link back to vv. 15b-16. He also claims that אלה "these are" is usually at the end rather than at the beginning of a list, but see Gen 6:9.

68   פטורים (*qal* passive participle) with some Hebrew MSS, Tg, and Q; K פטירים (Aramaic participle or adjective?).

69   ראשים "chiefs" repeats ראשי "heads" earlier in the verse. Perhaps this results from the conflation of two concluding formulas.

70   ישבו; LXX^S, Syr: singular.

71   יעואל with K; some Hebrew MSS, LXX, Q, Vg, Tg: יעיאל "Jeiel."

72   אשתו; cf. 8:29. A few Hebrew MSS: אחתו "his sister." Cf. Maacah the sister of Machir in 7:15.

73   ואחיו; LXX "and his brother"; cf. Syr.

74   וכריה; 8:31 וזכר "Zecher."

75   שמאם; LXX and 8:32: שמאה "Shimeah."

76   ומרי בעל; 8:34 ומריב בעל. See the discussion at 8:34.

77   תחרע; 8:35 תארע "Tarea."

78   ואחז; added with 8:35 (cf. LXX^L, Syr, Tg, Vg, Arab.). The name is lacking in MT by haplography.

79   יערה; *BHS* emends with some Hebrew MSS (cf. LXX^L) to יעדה "Jadah." 1 Chr 8:36 יהועדה "Jehoaddah."

80   בנעא; LXX Β$α(α)$να; cf. 8:37 LXX.

81   רפיה; 8:37 רפה "Raphah."

82   בכרו, with Chronicles LXX and 8:38 LXX, Syr. Cf. Japhet, 201. Chronicles MT at both spots reads בכרו "Bocheru." LXX MSS djpqtz add, harmonistically, a sixth name here, "Asa." Perhaps no emendation is required (Rudolph, 90; *BHS*). At 8:38 we read "his firstborn" and added, tentatively, a sixth name "Azariah." If "firstborn" is the original reading, the list of names is one short.

83   *BHS* inserts with a question mark ועזריה "Azariah."

84   אלה; 8:38 כל אלה "all these."

9:1-44

Structure

The final chapter in the genealogical introduction consists primarily of a list of people who lived in Jerusalem.[1] The majority of the chapter—27 of 44 verses—repeats materials that also appear elsewhere in the Bible. Verses 2-17 are parallel to Neh 11:3-19, while vv. 34, 35-38, and 39-44 repeat nearly verbatim 1 Chr 8:28, 29-32, and 33-40. The relationship between 8:28-40 and 9:34-44 has already been discussed in the commentary on chap. 8. The relationship between 1 Chronicles 9 and Nehemiah 11 is much more complex, since the two chapters differ

---

1   Rudolph, 85, held this chapter to be secondary and believed that it was added by a redactor who thought that the mention of Benjaminites living in Jerusalem in 8:28, 32 gave this tribe an unjustified preference. For a rebuttal of Rudolph's position see Oeming, *Wahre Israel,* 195–96.

in their overall intention and to a considerable extent also in the content of individual verses. While some of the differences in content arise from the type of variations that are common in text-critical studies of ancient documents, the complexities of the question have led to commentators proposing a bewildering array of possible relationships of one chapter to the other (see below).

1 Chronicles 9 may be outlined as follows:

I. 9:1. Conclusion to the genealogies of the tribes of Israel

II. 9:2-34. List of those who lived in the land and especially in Jerusalem

    A. 9:2. Fourfold division of those who lived in the land: Israelites, priests, Levites, and temple servants

    B. 9:3. Heading to a list of the inhabitants of Jerusalem

    C. 9:4-9. List of lay inhabitants of Jerusalem, who are here called "Israel." Verses 4-6 name descendants of Judah, and vv. 7-9 name descendants of Benjamin.

    D. 9:10-13. List of the priestly inhabitants of Jerusalem. All those mentioned in vv. 10-34, my sections D and E, are members in some fashion of the clergy.

    E. 9:14-34. List of Levitical inhabitants of Jerusalem and their duties. Verses 14-16 list generic Levites, while vv. 17-18 list gatekeepers, who are included among the Levites in this chapter.[2] Verses 19-33 focus on the duties of the Levites, and especially of the gatekeepers, with v. 34 bringing the discussion of the Levites to its conclusion.[3]

III. 9:35-44. Genealogy of Benjamin repeated. This consists of two parts: a list of Gibeonites who lived in Jerusalem (vv. 35-38//8:29-32)[4] and a genealogy of the ancestors and descendants of Saul (vv. 39-44//8:33-38).[5] Oeming proposes that the list of Gibeonites is included since they belonged to the (lowest ranks of the) temple personnel (Josh 9:23, 27),[6] and some of them at least lived in Jerusalem (1 Chr 9:38//8:32). By repeating the genealogy of the ancestors and descendants of Saul, the author prepares for the narrative of Saul's death, which follows in the next chapter.

Much of the material in 9:2-18 (part of section II) is related in some fashion to the material in Neh 11:3-19. Gary Knoppers has outlined the bewildering array of possibilities that have been proposed in earlier studies for the relationship between the two chapters.[7] Some (e.g., Myers, 1:66–73, Williamson, 87–88) have posited an independent source from which the authors of Nehemiah and Chronicles selectively drew. Keil, 152–68, thought that 1 Chronicles 9 represented a preexilic register of Jerusalem's citizens while Nehemiah 11 is a postexilic register of the same citizens. Hölscher thought that Nehemiah 11 was dependent on 1 Chronicles 9,[8] but a great number of scholars (Braun, 132–26; Curtis and Madsen, 168; Japhet, 202–4; Kellermann;[9] and Kalimi[10]) believe that 1 Chronicles 9 is dependent on

---

2   In Nehemiah 11 the singers are among the Levites, but the gatekeepers and temple servants (נתינים) are not.

3   According to Japhet, 204, vv. 18-29 deal with the functions of the gatekeepers, v. 30 with the functions of the priests; vv. 31-33 with the functions of the Levites and singers, and v. 34 is a conclusion.

4   Japhet, 205, thinks that these verses may have been included for the sake of completeness, or inserted secondarily under the influence of chap. 8.

5   Japhet, 205, concludes that these verses in 1 Chronicles 9 offer a genealogical portrait of the house of Saul, whereas in chap. 8 they legitimatize the Benjaminite sons of Ulam.

6   *Wahre Israel*, 204.

7   "Sources," 141–68. Oded Lipschitz, "Literary and Ideological Aspects of Nehemiah 11," *JBL* 121 (2002) 429, n. 25, endorses the findings of Knoppers, but adds no new text-critical arguments.

8   G. Hölscher, *Die Bücher Esra und Nehemia* (4th ed.; HSAT; Tübingen: Mohr, 1923) 551–55.

9   Ulrich Kellerman, "Die Listen in Nehemia 11: Eine Dokumentation aus den letzten Jahren des Reiches Juda?" *ZDPV* 82 (1966) 209–27.

10 "The View of Jerusalem in the Ethnographical Introduction of Chronicles (1 Chr 1–9)," *Bib* 83 (2002) 556–62.

Nehemiah 11. I join myself to this latter group. Nehemiah 11 lists those who transferred their residence from the countryside to Jerusalem after Nehemiah's completion of the wall,[11] with vv. 20 and 25 referring to those who lived on the land, that is, in the countryside. Nehemiah 11:1 indicates that 10 percent of the population was chosen by lot to move to Jerusalem. Verse 2 indicates either that those so chosen were voluntarily glad to make this move, or it signifies that there were volunteers who were willing to move to Jerusalem in addition to those who were forced to go there by lot. The similar material in 1 Chronicles 9 identifies those who lived in Jerusalem at an unspecified time although with the strong suggestion that this represents Davidic times. Nehemiah 11 is typologically later than Ezra 2//Nehemiah 7, since the singers are now included among the Levites (vv. 15-17), although the gatekeepers have not yet attained Levitical status in this document (Neh 11:19). This needs to be contrasted with 1 Chr 9:26 and chaps. 23–26, where the gatekeepers also have attained the status of Levites. In Neh 11:3-4a the writer distinguishes between those people who continued to live throughout the land (v. 3b) and the leaders who subsequently lived in Jerusalem (vv. 3a, 4). These verses, therefore, describe the situation in Yehud after Nehemiah's completion of the wall and are especially appropriate to the era of Nehemiah.[12] These verses were modified when they were included in Chronicles as vv. 2-3 and no longer make a significant distinction between the leaders and the rank and file. This is one of the clearest pieces of evidence that the author of 1 Chronicles 9 copied from Nehemiah 11, and not vice versa.

Knoppers himself sees an even more complex relationship of the two chapters. He identifies a large number of minuses in Nehemiah LXX over against Nehemiah MT, largely unnoticed in the past, and finds as many differences between the lists in 1 Chronicles 9 and Nehemiah 11 as there are parallels.[13] He views Nehemiah LXX as a shorter and earlier form of the text that has been expanded in Nehemiah MT, but he also recognizes that Nehemiah and Chronicles represent two distinct literary editions. While Knoppers has made many excellent observations about the relationships of these chapters, in my judgment he has erred particularly with regard to the significance of the minuses in Nehemiah LXX, but also with regard to a number of other differences (listed in n. 13 below). As will be demonstrated in the commentary, in many cases these minuses in Nehemiah do not represent an earlier or superior text, but are the result of textual damage due to homoioarchton, homoioteleuton, or similar processes. Knoppers has indeed shown that the comparison should not be made just on the basis of MT alone, but he has not shaken my conclusion that some form of the text in

---

11   The materials in Neh 11:1-2 connect back to Neh 7:1-5a and Nehemiah's discovery of the population shortage in Jerusalem. The intervening verses contain the list of those who returned (Neh 7:5b-72a [73a], itself parallel to Ezra 2:1-70) and a section that I have entitled "Torah, Confession, and Firm Agreement," Neh 7:72b (73b)—10:40 (39), dealing with Ezra's reading of the law and its repercussions. See my commentary on "Ezra & Nehemiah," 794–821.

12   Neither Gunneweg's proposal to date Nehemiah 11 to Maccabean times (*Nehemia* [KAT 19/2; Gütersloh: Mohn, 1987] 142–50), nor Mowinckel's attempt to date Nehemiah 11 a generation or more later than Nehemiah (Sigmund Mowinckel, *Studien zu dem Buche Ezra-Nehemia*, vol. 1: *Die nachchronistische Redaktion des Buches. Die Listen*, SUNVAO [Oslo: Universitetsforlaget, 1964] 48–49, 145–51), nor Kellermann's attempt to prove that it is a list of arrangements made for the defense of Jerusalem at the time of Josiah (Ulrich Kellermann, "Die Listen

in Nehemia 11 eine Dokumentation aus den letzten Jahren des Reiches Juda?" *ZDPV* 82 [1966] 209–27; idem, *Nehemia: Quellen, Überlieferung und Geschichte* [BZAW 102; Berlin: de Gruyter, 1967] 103–4) has proved successful. For a critique of Mowinckel and Kellermann see Williamson, *Ezra, Nehemiah*, 347–48; and for Kellermann see Oeming, *Wahre Israel*, 197. Williamson calls attention to five types of data in this list that relate to the time of Ezra or Nehemiah, or, more generally, to postexilic times. Oeming argues strongly against Kellermann's militaristic interpretation of the list. For a critique of Gunneweg see Oeming, *Wahre Israel*, 196–97.

13   He also documents minuses in Chronicles LXX, pluses in Nehemiah LXX, pluses in Nehemiah MT and LXX vs. Chronicles, pluses in Chronicles compared with Nehemiah, pluses shared by Chronicles MT and Nehemiah MT vs. Nehemiah LXX, minuses in Nehemiah LXX that also do not appear in Chronicles MT and LXX, and variations in kinship, sequence, and number between the two lists.

Nehemiah is the basis for the composition in 1 Chr 9:2-17 even if the present state of the text in both books is not the same as when this chapter was composed.

The first nine chapters of Chronicles deal with an outer circle of the nations (chap. 1), a second circle dealing with the tribes of Israel (chaps. 2–8), and finally the innermost circle dealing with the holy city and its inhabitants and the temple with its personnel (chap. 9).[14] Thus the genealogical introduction ends with a focus on that city and that institution which will be the major concern of the narrative in the rest of 1 and 2 Chronicles.

Detailed Commentary

9:1. Conclusion to the Genealogies of the Tribes of Israel

■ **1** *So all Israel was enrolled by genealogies; and these are written in the Book of the Kings of Israel:* This verse sums up the preceding seven chapters dealing with the genealogy of Israel.[15] Here, as elsewhere, the reference to a sourcebook comes at the end of a pericope. We have no way of determining whether there was such a single book of genealogies or whether the Chronicler has assembled the genealogies from a variety of sources, including those found in the Pentateuch. A reference to the source called "the Book of the Kings of Israel" occurs elsewhere only at 2 Chr 20:34 (at the end of the reign of Jehoshaphat), where it is said to contain the acts

of Jehu the son of Hanani.[16] The first section in many of the preceding tribal genealogies had come from the Pentateuch, as far as we can tell. It is possible, of course, that the Chronicler was drawing on a genealogical source that was based in turn in part on the Pentateuch. The reference to "All Israel" harks back to the list of the twelve sons of Israel in 1 Chr 2:1-2. The emphasis on "all Israel" also suggests that the absence of genealogies for Zebulun, and probably Dan, in chap. 7 is accidental.

And Judah was taken into exile[17] to Babylon because of their unfaithfulness: The Chronicler had previously referred to the exile of Reuben, Gad, and the half-tribe of Manasseh to Assyria in the days of Pul/Tilgath-pilneser (5:26; cf. 5:6), the exile of Judah and Jerusalem by the hand of Nebuchadnezzar (5:41 [6:15]), and to an (internal?) exile involving Benjamin (8:6-7).[18] While the Chronicler nowhere explicitly refers to the exile of the northern kingdom, his reference here—and in 5:41 (6:15)—to the exile of Judah is not to be denied to him, even if this exile in his view was only temporary, that is, until the decree of Cyrus.[19] The mention of the exile in v. 1 at the end of the genealogical introduction anticipates the mention of the exile at the end of the Chronicler's narrative in 2 Chr 36:20. This is the first reference in Chronicles to the noun "unfaithfulness," which is one of the most crucial terms for the indictment made against Israel by the Chronicler.[20]

---

14 See Oeming, *Wahre Israel,* 200. This climax is anticipated by references to Jerusalem in 1 Chr 3:4-5; 5:36, 41; 6:17 (6:10, 15, 32); 8:28, 32. See also Kalimi, "View of Jerusalem," 556–62.

15 For "enrolled" (יהשׁ), see 1 Chr 4:33 and Curtis and Madsen, 30, #49.

16 Cf. the similar דברי מלכי ישׂראל "the Acts of the Kings of Israel" in 2 Chr 33:18 (at the end of the reign of Manasseh). The *Vorlage* at 2 Kgs 21:17 refers to "the chronicles of the kings of Judah." As indicated in the introduction to this commentary, it is not at all clear how this source citation in 1 Chr 9:1 is related to the royal source citations that are at the same places in Kings and Chronicles. Ehud Ben Zvi, "Shifting the Gaze: Historiographic Constraints in Chronicles and Their Implications," in *The Land that I Will Show You* (FS J. Maxwell Miller; ed. J. A. Dearman and M. P. Graham; JSOTSup 343; Sheffield: Sheffield Academic Press, 2001) 57, comments: "'All Israel was enrolled by genealogies and these were written in the Book of the Kings of

Israel. But Judah [i.e. the "Israel" whose kings were noted in the previous clause] was taken into exile because of their unfaithfulness.' Significantly, the text then moves to a description of [the] new community of Israel formed by the returning exiles (1 Chron. 9.2-38) in Judah."

17 This is the only use of נלה in the *hophal* in Chronicles.

18 For discussion of this tribal conflict see the commentary. Cf. also the reference to the Babylonian exile at 2 Chr 36:20; Ezra 2:1//Neh 7:6.

19 Japhet, 206, argues that in Chronicles Israel continued to dwell in its own territory (2 Chronicles 30) and suggests that v. 1b may be a gloss.

20 Cf. 1 Chr 10:13; 2 Chr 21:11, 13. The related verb has occurred at 1 Chr 2:7 (the sin of Achar) and 5:25 (the unfaithfulness of the Transjordanian half-tribe of Manasseh. Cf. Curtis and Madsen, 31, #68.

9:2-34. List of Those Who Lived in the Land and Especially in Jerusalem

9:2. Fourfold Division of Those Who Lived in the Land

■ **2** *The first settlers who were in their possessions in their towns were Israel, the priests, the Levites, and the temple servants:* This verse is parallel to, though remarkably different from, Neh 11:3: "These are the chiefs of the province who lived in Jerusalem, but in the towns of Judah every person lived in his possession in their towns: Israel, the priests, the Levites, the temple servants, and the sons of the servants of Solomon." Nehemiah referred to the people in the following list as the "chiefs" (ראשי) of the province, who moved to Jerusalem at the time of the building of the wall in Nehemiah (cf. Neh 7:3-4), in implicit criticism of the rest of the people living in the various towns of Judah (cf. Neh 11:20, 25-36).[21] In v. 2 the Chronicler lists the four types of people who lived *throughout the land:* Israel, the priests, the Levites, and the temple servants; and beginning with v. 3

he documents the postexilic settlers *in Jerusalem.*[22] The meaning of "their" in its two occurrences in this verse should be understood as "their own" and refer back to the first settlers.[23] Verses 3 and 34 make clear that all the people named in the list are inhabitants of Jerusalem, despite the reference in this verse to the towns. Even the inhabitants of Gibeon are now placed in Jerusalem (9:35-38; cf. 8:29-32). In distinction from Nehemiah 11, however, there is no implied criticism of the people who continued to live on their possessions in their towns in v. 2 or any evaluative contrast between them and the inhabitants of Jerusalem. "Israel" here refers to laypeople (cf. Ezra 10:5).

The categories of those who lived in the countryside are followed in the next verses by a listing of the laity (vv. 3-9), priests (vv. 10-13), and Levites (vv. 14-27) who lived in Jerusalem. The "temple servants" (נתינים), probably mentioned only here in Chronicles,[24] are not included in the following list, in contrast to Neh 11:21.[25] The Chronicler also omits the "sons of the servants of

---

21 The Chronicler may have constructed והיושבים הראשנים "the first settlers" in 1 Chr 9:2 out of ואלה ראשי . . . ישבו "These are the chiefs . . . who lived" in the *Vorlage.*

22 Japhet, 207–8, prefers "the old settlers" or "the dwellers of old" to "the first settlers." This conforms with her idea that only the two and one-half Transjordanian tribes were exiled. *NRSV* links this verse closely to the restoration: "Now the first to live again in their possessions. . . ." "Again" does not appear explicitly in Hebrew, and the *NRSV* translators were apparently guided to this interpretation by the reference to the exile in v. 1 and by the postexilic setting of the list in Nehemiah 11. In Johnstone's opinion (1:121), by relating contemporaries of Nehemiah to the time of David (v. 22), the Chronicler is linking the generations: "All are involved in the one perpetual cult of the Temple, whether in the age of David in the tenth century, or of Nehemiah in the fifth." I believe Johnstone misconstrues the reference to David. It indicates that the gatekeepers were installed in their office by David, but that does not mean the present list is meant to refer to that time. Rudolph, 84, understood the list to refer to postexilic inhabitants of Jerusalem and even emended the text to make that clearer (see textual notes 2-3). Levin, "Chronological Aspects," 22, also favors a postexilic setting. He argues that the Chronicler would not try to pass off

a clearly postexilic document, such as his source in Nehemiah, as if it came from the time of David. He also contends that an inclusive view of Israel would serve the Chronicler well in describing the present inhabitants, but of course it would also help his cause if Davidic Jerusalem were already inclusive of the northern tribes.

23 Rudolph, 82, understood these demonstrative pronouns as referring back to those who had been exiled from Judah.

24 But see the emendation proposed at 2 Chr 35:3 in *BHS* (note 5a).

25 The Chronicler breaks off his use of Nehemiah with Neh 11:19. The "temple servants" are also referred to in fourteen other verses in Ezra and Nehemiah. See Joseph P. Healey, "Nethinim," *ABD* 4:1085–86. Knoppers, "Sources," 147, notes that Nehemiah LXX lacks a reference to the temple servants, perhaps by haplography, but he suggests that this minus is related to the absence of the list of the Nethinim in Neh 11:21 LXX. Nehemiah LXX actually omits both vv. 20 and 21 (homoioarchton from καὶ at the beginning of v. 20 to καὶ at the beginning of v. 22). The Nethinim may have been deleted from Neh 11:3 LXX subsequent to this haplography. Knoppers, "Sources," 160 and n. 64, notes that these "temple servants" later suffered a decline in status.

Solomon" from Neh 11:3.[26] Neither 1 Chr 9:2 nor Neh 11:3 mentions the gatekeepers in the heading, although gatekeepers are mentioned in 1 Chr 9:17//Neh 11:19, and their duties are elaborated in 1 Chr 9:17-27.[27] They were presumably incorporated under the category of Levites (see also v. 34).[28] Neither this verse nor its parallel in Neh 11:3 mentions singers, though a list of singers is anticipated but not recorded in 1 Chr 9:33. For the Levitical singers mentioned in Neh 11:17, see the commentary on 1 Chr 9:15.

The genealogical introduction to Chronicles emphasizes that Solomon was born in Jerusalem (3:4-5), and that this city was the residence for David and his descendants in an almost uninterrupted sequence. Jerusalem will be the setting of the subsequent narrative, that is, during the reigns of David and Solomon in the united monarchy, and during the reigns of all the Judean kings. The Jerusalem temple is emphasized in the genealogy of Levi, and it is in the Jerusalem temple that the musicians performed their service (5:36, 41; 6:17 [6:10, 15, 32]). Now, in the postexilic period, Jerusalem is inhabited by Judah, Benjamin, and even remnants of the northern tribes of Ephraim and Manasseh. Also there are priests, Levites, gatekeepers, singers, and even the Gibeonites (9:1-38). While the Jerusalem population has been inserted between the genealogy of Saul (8:33-40) and the account of his death in 10:1-14, the Chronicler brings these two events together again by repeating the account of Saul's genealogy in 9:39-44.

9:3. Heading to List of Inhabitants of Jerusalem

■ **3** *And in Jerusalem lived some of the people of Judah, some of the people of Benjamin, and some of the people of Ephraim and Manasseh:* This verse is parallel to Neh 11:4a,[29] where, as one would expect, representatives of the two prominent postexilic tribes, Judah and Benjamin, are among those who volunteered to live in Jerusalem. The Chronicler has added a reference to the people of Ephraim and Manasseh,[30] which in the book of Chronicles is a kind of shorthand for all the northern tribes. Northerners often participate in the religious life of Jerusalem in Chronicles,[31] and the Chronicler in general seems to invite all Israel to participate in the temple worship at Jerusalem. He did not, however, add any specific names of people hailing from Ephraim or Manasseh in the following list.

C. 9:4-9. List of Lay Inhabitants of Jerusalem

■ **4** *Uthai son of Ammihud, son of Omri, son of Imri, son of Bani, from the sons of Perez son of Judah:*

Chronicles: Judah—Perez—Bani—Imri—Omri—Ammihud—Uthai

Nehemiah 11:4: [sons of] Judah—Perez—Mahalel—Shephatiah—Amariah—Zechariah—Uzziah—Athaiah

---

26 They are not included in the body of the list itself in Nehemiah 11, and they may have been added to this heading from Ezra 2:55, 58//Neh 7:57, 60. They never appear elsewhere in Chronicles.

27 Cf. Neh 12:25, which mentions by name a number of the gatekeepers in this chapter.

28 The gatekeepers were not considered to be Levites in Neh 11:19. Note that they are listed *after* the summary total for Levites in v. 18. Cf. Blenkinsopp, *Ezra-Nehemiah*, 324–26; and Williamson, *Ezra, Nehemiah*, 347.

29 Chronicles writes the preposition מִן ("some of") as a separate word while in Nehemiah it is prefixed to the following word בְּני.

30 Rudolph, 85, believed they were dropped from Nehemiah because of the animosity of the Chronicler to everything dealing with Samaria. Knoppers, "Sources," 155–56, raises the possibility that these words were added already to the Chronicler's *Vorlage*, which seems unlikely to me since Nehemiah otherwise does not seem favorably inclined toward the north.

31 2 Chr 30:1, 10, 11, 18 (representatives from Ephraim, Manasseh, Issachar, and Zebulun participated in Hezekiah's Passover at the king's invitation, albeit without proper preparation), and 34:9 (money was collected at the time of Josiah from Manasseh, Ephraim, and all the remnant of Israel). Cf. also 31:1. Allen, 362, calls attention to the gates of the new Jerusalem being named after all twelve

The corresponding pedigree in Neh 11:4 reads: "Of the Judahites: Athaiah son of Uzziah son of Zechariah son of Amariah son of Shephatiah[32] son of Mahalel, from the sons of Perez." Uthai עותי and Athaiah עתיה are more similar in Hebrew than in English, and a copyist's error could account for the different spelling.[33] Athaiah, however, is in the sixth generation after Perez, while Uthai is in the fifth. While Amariah אמריה (Neh 11:4) and Imri אמרי (1 Chr 9:4) could well be the same individual, in the third and second generation after Perez, respectively, all of the other intervening names in the two pedigrees are quite different.[34] Uthai and Athaiah, therefore, could be different people and the Chronicler may have picked

a contemporary, similar name, with a different pedigree, to represent the descendants of Perez; or, as Japhet, 209, suggests, the pedigrees between Perez and Uthai/Athaiah may have once been much longer and each writer selected different intervening generations. Nehemiah puts the expression "from the sons of Judah" first, while Chronicles puts "the son of Judah" *after* Perez, without essentially changing the meaning.[35] In vv. 4-6 Chronicles mentions a descendant for each of the surviving sons of Judah—Perez, Shelah, and Zerah; Nehemiah 11 lists descendants only for Perez (v. 4) and Shelah (v. 5). Perez was no doubt the most important clan of Judah and an ancestor of David (cf. 2:4, 6).[36]

■ **5** *And of the Shelanites: Asaiah the firstborn and his sons:*

Chronicles: Shelanites—the firstborn Asaiah

Nehemiah 11:5: Shelanites—Zechariah—Joiarib—Adaiah—Hazaiah—Col-hozeh—Baruch—Maaseiah

The corresponding pedigree of Maaseiah in Neh 11:5 reads: "And Maaseiah son of Baruch son of Col-hozeh[37] son of Hazaiah son of Adaiah son of Joiarib son of Zechariah from the Shelanites."[38] Asaiah עשיה (cf. 1 Chr 4:36) and Maaseiah מעשיה are probably the same individual, with only the additional *mêm* in Nehemiah distinguishing them, and "the firstborn" הבכור in Chronicles

and "son of Baruch" בן ברוך in Nehemiah are close enough to be accounted for by scribal variation (see also textual note 11). Instead of the pedigree going back to the seventh generation for Maaseiah in Nehemiah 11, Chronicles mentions only "his sons" for Asaiah, thus referring to his descendants rather than his ancestors.[39] If the emendation from Shilonite to Shelanites in both

---

tribes of Israel in Ezek 48:30-35, a similar inclusive view.

32 Knoppers, "Sources," 153, labels "son of Shephatiah" an addition in Nehemiah over against 1 Chronicles 9, but he also notes later, 164–65, that Athaiah and Uthai have *different* pedigrees.

33 See also the similarity of Meshelemiah (1 Chr 9:21; 26:1, 2, 9) with Meshullam (Neh 12:25) and Shelemiah (1 Chr 26:14), and of Asaiah (1 Chr 9:5) with Maaseiah (Neh 11:5).

34 In Nehemiah 11 עמרי "Omri" might be a corrupt variant of the preceding name אמרי "Imri." Ran Zadok, "Notes on the Prosopography of the Old Testament," *BN* 42 (1988) 47, suggests that עמיהוד "Ammihud" is a combination of עם and יהוד "people of Judah."

35 Knoppers, "Sources," 153, 156, labels these as alternate independent additions in Nehemiah and

Chronicles, respectively, without noting that they modify the exact same genealogy.

36 David is in the tenth generation beginning with Perez (1 Chr 2:5, 9-15; Ruth 4:18-22).

37 This person may also be the father of Shallum, from Mizpah, who worked on the wall at the time of Nehemiah (Neh 3:15).

38 מן־הַשֵּׁלָנִי, following the emendation suggested in *BHS*; MT בֶּן־הַשִּׁלֹנִי "son of the Shilonite."

39 Knoppers, "Sources," 153, 165, considers the pedigree of Maaseiah both an addition in Nehemiah and different from that of Asaiah in Chronicles. Note, however, that the Maaseiah//Asaiah and Baruch//the firstborn may be only textual variants, and in both texts the person comes from the same phratry of Shelah. The Chronicler may only have falsely abridged the pedigree by replacing the last part of it with the words "and his sons." Or, more

texts is correct,[40] we must note that this reference to the Shelanites appears *before* Asaiah and his descendants in Chronicles and after Maaseiah and his ancestors in Nehemiah, so that one of the texts has been revised. Shelah was the third son born to Judah and Shua (Gen 38:5).[41] The clans of the Shelanites, Perezites, and Zerahites are mentioned in Num 26:20.

■ **6** *Of the sons of Zerah: Jeuel and their kin, six hundred ninety:* Zerah was the second of twin sons born to Judah and Tamar in Gen 38:30 (cf. 1 Chr 2:4, 6). Neither he nor Jeuel[42] is mentioned in Nehemiah 11,[43] but they are probably original in the list.[44] The number of generations between Jeuel and Zerah is unstated. The numerical total in Chronicles (690) could refer to Jeuel and his relatives, that is, all the sons of Zerah, or it could refer to all of the descendants of Judah in vv. 4-6 (cf. the number

for the Benjaminites in v. 9, and for all the priests in v. 13).[45] In Neh 11:6, which has no parallel in 1 Chronicles 9, we are told that 468 of the descendants of Perez lived in Jerusalem. This probably includes Athaiah, the Perezite, from Neh 11:4 since I believe v. 6 once followed v. 4.[46] The larger number in Chronicles has been seen by some to indicate an increase in the population by the time of the Chronicler,[47] but it is inappropriate to compare the two numbers since they refer to different entities.[48]

■ **7-9** *Of the Benjaminites: Sallu son of Meshullam, son of Hodaviah, son of Hassenuah, Ibneiah son of Jeroham, Elah son of Uzzi, son of Michri, and Meshullam son of Shephatiah, son of Reuel, son of Ibnijah; and their kindred according to their generations, nine hundred fifty-six. All these were heads of families according to their ancestral houses:*

likely in my judgment, the Chronicler's text lost the rest of the ascending genealogy of Asaiah by haplography when a scribe's eye wandered from בכורו (see Chronicles LXX) to the end of בן זכריה "the son of Zechariah," leaving out everything in between. The addition of "and his sons" would then be a subsequent correction, which was either lost by homoioteleuton in the LXX (textual note 13), or the LXX was translated from a *Vorlage* to which this correction had not yet been made.

40 So also Knoppers, "Sources," 165, n. 76. Oeming, *Wahre Israel,* 201, rejects this emendation and finds here a tie to the old cultic traditions of Shiloh. Note the association of Shiloh with the tent of meeting (Josh 18:1) and the ark (1 Samuel 1–4). It is also a religious center of the Northern Kingdom (Judg 21:19-23) with which prophets had important ties (1 Kgs 11:29; 12:15; 14:2-16; 15:29; 2 Chr 9:29). But Shiloh was never part of Judah.

41 See the list of the sons of Shelah in 1 Chr 4:21-23. Cf. 2:3.

42 This name is also attested for two other individuals (2 Chr 29:13 and Ezra 8:13).

43 But see Neh 11:24, which does mention Pethahiah of the descendants of Zerah son of Judah.

44 1 Chronicles 9 and Nehemiah 11 may have experienced haplographies at this point, with 1 Chronicles 9 losing the equivalent of Neh 11:6, and Nehemiah 11 losing the equivalent of 1 Chr 9:6. Note that *BHS* suggests that Neh 11:6 belongs after Neh 11:4 as the completion to the mention of the sons of Perez. It may have been lost in the Nehemiah textual tradition that was the Chronicler's *Vorlage,* and then restored in the wrong position in Nehemiah MT

and LXX (after v. 5 instead of after v. 4). Nehemiah may have lost the equivalent of 1 Chr 9:6 when a scribe's eyes strayed from ומן בני זרח to כל בני פרץ at the beginning of Neh 11:6 where it had been placed at its secondary location. See Knoppers, "Sources," 153, 156, who explains Neh 11:6 and 1 Chr 9:6 as alternate additions. My solution explains the incorrect location of Neh 11:6 and obviates the need (*pace* Knoppers) to say that Nehemiah made the Shelanites subordinate to the phratry of Perez. This also explains the divergence in number between 690 (1 Chr 9:6) and 468 (Neh 11:6) —they are counts of the different phratries of Zerah and Perez, respectively. The original text contained totals for *both* the sons of Judah and Tamar (contrast Knoppers, "Sources," 166).

45 The words giving the numerical total in v. 6 are the shortest of these three enumerations and may be truncated.

46 Braun, 134, observes that 486 (read 468) is too large to include only chiefs resident in Jerusalem.

47 Curtis and Madsen, 170.

48 Oeming, *Wahre Israel,* 199, points out that the numbers in general are larger in 1 Chronicles 9 than in Nehemiah 11. 1 Chr 9:6, 690//Neh 11:6, 468; 1 Chr 9:9, 956//Neh 11:8, 928; 1 Chr 9:13, 1,760//Neh 11:12-14, 1,192 (822 + 242+128); 1 Chr 9:16, sum lacking//Neh 11:18, 284; and 1 Chr 9:22, 212//Neh 11:19, 172. Hence the community has become larger between the time of Nehemiah 11 and the time of 1 Chronicles 9.

1 Chronicles 9:7: Hassenuah—Hodaviah—Meshullam—Sallu
        9:8: Jeroham—Ibneiah
        Michri—Uzzi—Elah
        Ibnijah—Reuel—Shephatiah—Meshullam

Nehemiah 11:7-9: Jeshaiah—Ithiel—Maaseiah—Kolaiah—Pedaiah—Joed—Meshullam—Sallu
        Gabbai
        Sallai
        Zichri–Joel
        Hassenuah–Judah

The corresponding material in Neh 11:7-9 reads: "And these are[49] the Benjaminites: Sallu son of Meshullam son of[50] Joed son of Pedaiah son of Kolaiah son of Maaseiah son of Ithiel son of Jeshaiah. And his brothers Gabbai, Sallai: nine hundred twenty-eight. Joel son of Zichri was their overseer; and Judah son of Hassenuah was second in charge of the city." Chronicles lists four Benjaminite heads,[51] with the first and the last, Sallu and Meshullam, traced back to the fourth generation; while Ibneiah[52] and Elah are listed only with the name of their father or father and grandfather, respectively. In Neh 11:7 Sallu,[53] the only one of the four family names that is preserved in Nehemiah, is traced back to the seventh generation, but only the name of Sallu's father, Meshullam, is the same as the pedigree in Chronicles.[54] "Son of Hodaviah (הודויה), son of Hassenuah" in Chronicles closely resem-

bles "Judah (יהודה)[55] son of [Hassenuah]" in Neh 11:9,[56] suggesting that a scribe may have skipped, by homoioarchton, from "Joed (יועד) the son of" to "Judah (יהודה; the latter word is corrupted in Chronicles to 'Hodaviah' הודויה) the son of Hassenuah" and omitted all of the intervening material, including Gabbai, Sallai, and Joel the overseer.[57] The source of the Benjaminite names in 1 Chr 9:8 is unknown since there is no parallel in Nehemiah 11. After the haplography just discussed, 1 Chr 9:7 would list only one Benjaminite despite the caption "of the Benjaminites" (plural) with which v. 7 begins, and so the Chronicler may have added additional Benjaminite names from an unknown source. Verse 9 too contains material different from Neh 11:8-9, except that the total 956 resembles, but is slightly larger than, the 928 in Neh 11:8.[58] As Rudolph, 86, points out,

---

49 Note ואלה בני in Nehemiah instead of ומן בני in Chronicles.

50 בן; absent from LXX. Knoppers, "Sources," 148, believes that "Joed" in Nehemiah LXX begins a new ascending genealogy, but if so a conjunction would be expected before "Joed." I propose that the word "son" was inadvertently lost.

51 Five Benjaminites are named in Neh 11:7-9: Sallu, Gabbai, Sallai, Joel, and Judah.

52 Some have compared יבניה "Ibneiah" with גבי "Gabbai" of Neh 11:8. Cf. Curtis and Madsen, 171; Braun, 140.

53 A Sallu is also named in Neh 12:7 among those priests who returned to Jerusalem with Zerubbabel.

54 Japhet, 210, notes that the Chronicler regularly omits pedigrees and the names and functions of officials throughout the list. She also thinks that the Chronicler in vv. 7-9 was using a different *Vorlage* than Nehemiah 11.

55 "Hodaviah" in Ezra 2:40 is miswritten as "Judah" in Ezra 3:9.

56 Judah is identified in Neh 11:9 as "second in charge of the city." Ran Zadok, "A Note on SN'H," *VT* 38 (1988) 483–86, suggests that סנאה "Senaah" in the list of returnees (Ezra 2:35//Neh 7:38) and הסנאה "Hassenuah" are probably the same name. Cf. also the sons of הסנאה "Hassenaah" among the builders of the wall in Neh 3:3.

57 The modifying phrase "the second in charge of the city" was dropped after the haplography. Knoppers, "Sources," 154, identifies Neh 11:7-9a as a plus in Nehemiah.

58 As Japhet, 210, points out, terms such as "heads of families" and "according to their ancestral houses" are unknown in the rest of Nehemiah 11 and therefore may represent an independent development in 1 Chronicles 9.

numbers in Ezra 2//Nehemiah 7 are also not faultlessly preserved. Verse 9a summarizes vv. 7-8, and v. 9b forms a conclusion to all the laity listed in vv. 4-9. In Allen's (362) view, the reference to "their generations" (v. 9; cf. v. 34) implies clan ancestry even though the family heads are not explicitly distinguished by clan.

Priestly Inhabitants of Jerusalem

■ **10** *Of the priests: Jedaiah, Jehoiarib, Jachin:* With the possible exception of this verse, the names in vv. 10-12 are closer to Nehemiah (Neh 11:10-13) than elsewhere in these two parallel chapters. The three priests in this verse are matched by only two priests in Neh 11:10: "Jedaiah son of Joiarib, Jachin," but the relationship of these three or two names, if any, to Azariah (1 Chr 9:11) or Seraiah (Neh 11:11) and their ancestors is not given. The MT lists three priests in v. 10, one priest, Azariah, in v. 11, and two priests, Adaiah and Maasai, in v. 12. For Rudolph's reconstruction of the original list, which makes Jedaiah the first name in a priestly pedigree going back through Jehoiakim and Azariah to Ahitub in 1 Chr 9:12//Neh 11:11, see textual note 22.

Japhet's reconstruction: Azariah/Seraiah ⎤ Jehoiarib/Joiarib — Jedaiah
⎣ J(eh)ozadak ——— Jeshua

Japhet's plausible reconstruction, 210–11, makes Jedaiah the son of Jehoiarib/Joiarib, who in turn is the son of Azariah/Seraiah in 1 Chr 9:10-11 and Neh 11:10-11 (cf. 1 Chr 5:40 [6:14]). Since Jeshua is listed as a son of Jozadak in Ezra 3:2, 8; 10:18, and Jehozadak is listed as the son of Seraiah in 1 Chr 5:40 (6:14), J(eh)ozadak and Jehoiarib/Joiarib are brothers, and Jeshua and Jedaiah are cousins. Despite the plausibility of Japhet's reconstruction, it may reflect a form of the list that is earlier than what was ever attested in either Chronicles or Nehemiah. There is no versional evidence in Chronicles for an earlier form of v. 10.

We know from elsewhere that Jedaiah belongs to the house of Jeshua, one of the four priestly houses of the restoration in Ezra 2:36-39//Neh 7:39-42. In Neh 12:6-7 two Jedaiahs are listed and one Joiarib among the first repatriates who came up with Zerubbabel and who were the leaders of the priests in the days of Jeshua.[59] According to Neh 11:10, Jedaiah would presumably be a contemporary of Nehemiah. Jedaiah is assigned to the second priestly course in 1 Chr 24:7, and Jehoiarib is assigned to the first priestly course in the same verse.[60] Joiarib is listed as an ancestor of the Maccabees in 1 Macc 2:1. Jachin is assigned to the twenty-first priestly course in 1 Chr 24:17.[61]

■ **11** *and Azariah son of Hilkiah, son of Meshullam, son of Zadok, son of Meraioth, son of Ahitub, the chief officer of the house of God:*

Ahitub — Meraioth — Zadok — Meshullam — Hilkiah — Azariah

The only difference in Neh 11:11 is that "[and] Azariah" ועזריה is replaced by "Seraiah" שריה. In 1 Chr 5:40 (6:14) Azariah is the father of Seraiah, suggesting that the texts of 1 Chronicles 9 and Nehemiah 11 have suffered alternate haplographies, but that is only a conjecture and without versional support.[62] The original pedigree may

---

59 See also the "master list" of priestly houses and the name of the head of that house in the time of the high priest Joiakim, in Neh 12:19, 21, from which this list derives. A Joiarib also went up to Palestine with Ezra (Ezra 8:16).

60 Is a different ranking presupposed in 1 Chr 9:10 by listing Jedaiah first?

61 John R. Bartlett, "Zadok and His Successors at Jerusalem," *JTS* 19 (1968) 4, n. 1, observed that "Jachin," the fourth son of Simeon in Gen 46:10, is replaced by "Jarib" in 1 Chr 4:24 and suggested that the name Jachin in 1 Chr 9:10 is a gloss on the word "Jehoiarib."

62 Japhet emends "Azariah" in this verse to "Seraiah." Braun, 140, believes the reading in 1 Chr 5:40 (6:14) is conflate. Knoppers, "Sources," 154, n. 43, suggests that עזריה was miswritten as שריה when *'ayin* followed by *zayin* was taken as a *śin*.

have read: "Seraiah son of Azariah son of Hilkiah," etc. The other names in this verse, with the exception of Meraioth,[63] are an excerpt taken from the standard genealogy of the high priests.[64] Since this Azariah in MT is linked to the high priestly genealogy, he is appropriately called "chief officer of the house of God."[65] A different Azariah, six generations earlier in my reconstruction, is called "high priest" הכהן הראש in

2 Chr 31:10 and "chief officer of the house of God" in 31:13, during the reign of Hezekiah. Three chief officers of the house of God are listed in 35:8, of whom Hilkiah the high priest הכהן הגדול (34:9) is one.

■ **12** *and Adaiah son of Jeroham, son of Pashhur, son of Malchijah, and Maasai son of Adiel, son of Jahzerah, son of Meshullam, son of Meshillemith, son of Immer:*

Chronicles:

Malchijah—Pashhur—Jeroham—Adaiah

Immer—Meshillemith—Meshullam—Jahzerah—Adiel—Maasai

Nehemiah 11:12-13:

Malchijah—Pashhur—Zechariah—Amzi—Pelaliah—Jeroham—Adaiah

Immer—Meshillemoth—Ahzai—Azarel—Amashai

The corresponding verses in Neh 11:12-13 read: "and their associates who did the work of the house, eight hundred twenty two; and Adaiah son of Jeroham son of Pelaliah son of Amzi son of Zechariah son of Passhur son of Malchijah, and his associates,[66] heads of ancestral houses, two hundred forty-two; and Amashai son of Azarel son of Ahzai son of Meshillemoth son of Immer."[67] Chronicles lacks the clause giving numerical totals for groups of priests attested in Neh 11:12-13—and

in Neh 11:14 as well—although it adds a total for *all* the priests in 1 Chr 9:13. It also lacks three generations in the middle of the pedigree of Adaiah, namely, Pelaliah, Amzi, and Zechariah, presumably because of haplography.[68] In 1 Chr 24:9 a Malchijah is assigned to the fifth priestly course. The pedigree of Maasai is at first glance quite different from that of Amashai in Neh 11:13 though the differences *may* be attributable primarily to scribal error. Compare the following pairs of words in

---

63 In my earlier discussion of the high priests (under Structure in 1 Chr 5:27–6:66 [6:1-81]), I argued that since Meraiaoth (#8 in my numbering of the high priests) is the immediate ancestor of the sequence of high priests Amariah—Ahitub—Zadok (##9-11), someone added his name marginally to the second sequence of these names at ##16-18, and that he was later entered incorrectly after Ahitub (#17) instead of before Amariah (#16).

64 1 Chr 5:37-40 (6:11-14). Seraiah was one of the officials put to death by the Babylonians (Jer 52:24-27; 2 Kgs 25:18-21). A different Seraiah is listed with those who returned with Zerubbabel in Neh 12:1, and in Neh 12:12 Meraiah is named as head of the priestly family of Seraiah at the time of the high priest Joiakim, Jeshua's successor. The names in 1 Chr 9:11 are all preexilic.

65 Japhet, 212, makes Jedaiah the "chief officer of the house of God," but notes there is no high priest by the name of Jedaiah in the Persian period. She concludes, therefore, that the chief officer could have

been high priest, but was not necessarily so. This option becomes unnecessary if Azariah or Ahitub is assigned the title. Japhet also observes that this is the only title that was not omitted in the Chronicler's version of this list.

66 Knoppers, "Sources," 5, notes that there is no translation for ואחיו in LXX, but the next word, ראשים "heads," requires a plural antecedent, whereas the defective LXX reads: "Amzi the son of Zechariah the son of Pashur the son of Malchijah," referring to one person. Hence it is hard to consider the shorter LXX reading earlier than or superior to MT.

67 Knoppers, "Sources," 148, notes that there is no translation for "son of Ahazi son of Zechariah son of Immer" in Nehemiah LXX, but I suspect this is not a better or earlier text, but a text damaged by homoioarchton as a scribe's eyes shifted from בן אחזי to ואחזי (see LXX for the first word in Neh 11:14) and left out the intervening text.

68 Knoppers, "Sources," 148, notes that Nehemiah

Chronicles and the corresponding words in Nehemiah: Maasai מעשׁי vs. Amashsai עמשׁסי; Adiel עדיאל vs. Azarel עזראל; Jahzerah יחזרה vs. Ahzai אחזי; and Meshillemith vs. Meshillemoth. Meshullam, an extra generation in Chronicles, may simply be the result of dittography of Meshellemith. The ultimate ancestor in both cases is Immer. Pashhur and Immer are two of the four priestly houses of the restoration: Jeshua, Immer, Pashhur, and Harim (Ezra 2:36-39//Neh 7:39-42). Immer belongs to the sixteenth priestly course in 1 Chr 24:14,[69] and in Ezra's day, two of his descendants, Hanani and Zebadiah were forced to divorce their foreign wives (Ezra 10:20).[70]

■ **13** *besides their kindred, heads of their ancestral houses, one thousand seven hundred sixty, valiant warriors for the work of the service of the house of God:* Neh 11:14 differs substantially: "besides their kindred, valiant warriors, one hundred twenty-eight; their overseer was Zabdiel son of Haggedolim." The reading מלאכת עבודת בית ("the work of the service of the house") in Chronicles[71] may have been developed from המלאכה לבית "the work of the house" in Neh 11:12, the reading "heads of their ancestral houses" may have been taken from Neh 11:13, and the reading "their kindred, heads of . . . ancestral houses . . . valiant warriors" may have been taken from Neh 11:12 and 14. The mention of warriors in this verse suggests that the original form of this list may once have documented Jerusalem's military strength (cf. Neh

11:6).[72] The total number in 1 Chr 9:13 (1,760) exceeds the total of the individual numbers given in Neh 11:12-14 (1,192), and may indicate that the list in 1 Chronicles 9 is typologically later than that in Nehemiah 11. Japhet, 211, suggests that the larger number in Chronicles is calculated on the basis of the inclusion of the fourth priestly house of the restoration, Harim,[73] which has been lost otherwise in both 1 Chronicles 9 and Nehemiah 11. She concedes, however, that numerical errors are quite common in textual transmission. Perhaps the Chronicler's decision to put the numerical summary at the end, instead of scattered throughout the list of priests, as in Neh 11:12-14, led to the omission of "Zabdiel the son of Haggedolim in v. 13 in Chronicles."[74] Nothing else is known about this person in any case.

Levitical Inhabitants of Jerusalem and their Duties

■ **14** *Of the Levites: Shemaiah son of Hasshub, son of Azrikam, son of Hashabiah, of the sons of Merari:* The only difference between this verse and Neh 11:15 is that בן בוני "son of Bunni" in the latter verse has been replaced by מן בני מררי "of the sons of Merari" in the fourth generation before Shemaiah. It is likely that Chronicles replaced the obscure and otherwise unknown "son of Bunni" with the third of the Levitical families, the sons of Merari.[75] Knoppers observes that בן בוני "son of Bunni" and מן בני "of the sons of" are consonantally the

---

LXX omits "eight hundred twenty-two. And Adaiah son of Jeroham son of Pelaiah son of" and suggests that this represents an earlier form of Nehemiah 11. The minus, however, seems to have been caused by homoioteleuton when a scribe's eye skipped from οἴκου ("house," the eighth word in the verse) to υἱοῦ ("son," the translation for the last word in the omission). Knoppers (ibid., 154) suggests that "Amzi son of Zechariah" is an addition in Nehemiah MT.

69 Allen, 362, mistakenly refers to Immer in "Neh 10:20"; the correct reference is Ezra 10:20. Pashhur does not appear among the twenty-four priestly courses and is lacking in the MT's list of priests at Neh 12:2 and 14, though *BHS* suggests restoring it at both places.

70 1 Esdr 9:20-21 adds four additional descendants of Immer among those who divorced their wives, but in Ezra 10:21 these men are linked to Harim, not Immer.

71 In 1 Chr 6:33 (48) the Levites are appointed "for

the work of the tabernacle of the house of God." Cf. 23:28. Williamson, *Israel*, 57, #25, noted that עבודה occurs with this meaning thirty-six times in Chronicles, but only once in Ezra-Nehemiah (Neh 10:33).

72 See Klein, "Ezra & Nehemiah," 825.

73 The priestly house of Jeshua is represented by Jedaiah in v. 10, the houses of Pashhur and Immer are mentioned in v. 12.

74 Knoppers, "Sources," 148, observes that "son of Haggedolim" is absent from Nehemiah LXX, which suggests to him that this expression may be secondary.

75 The mention of Merari, Asaph, and Jeduthun in vv. 14-16 contrasts with chap. 6, where the three Levitical families are Gershom, Kohath, and Merari. See Oeming, *Wahre Israel*, 189. Knoppers, "Sources," 148-49, observes that Nehemiah LXX omits "son of Hashabiah son of Bunni" and all of Neh 11:16. There are no reasons, such as homoioteleuton, that explain this omission. Is the shorter text more original, or is it another haplography in a text that is

same except for the frequent *bêt/mēm* confusion.[76] Might this suggest that מררי ("Merari") has been accidentally lost in Nehemiah[77] instead of added in Chronicles?

■ **15** *and Bakbakkar, Heresh, Galal, and Mattaniah son of Mica, son of Zichri, son of Asaph:*

Chronicles: Asaph—Zichri—Mica—Mattaniah

Nehemiah 11:17: Asaph—Zabdi—Mica—Mattaniah

Verse 15b (from Mattaniah on) is very similar to the first part of Neh 11:17: "and Mattaniah son of Mica[78] son of Zabdi son of Asaph." The variation between Zabdi זבדי and Zichri זכרי represents two common confusions in Hebrew letters, between *dālet* and final *kāp* and between *bêt* and medial *kāp*. Nehemiah 11:16 ("And Shabbethai[79] and Jozabad[80] of the leaders[81] of the Levites, who were over the outside work of the house of God"[82]) and the rest of 11:17a ("who was the leader to begin the thanksgiving in prayer, and Bakbukiah, the second among his associates") are not represented in 1 Chronicles 9, though it seems likely that Bakbukiah[83] בקבקיה in Neh 11:17 and Bakbakkar בקבקר in 1 Chr 9:15 are the same person.[84] In any case, by omitting the two relative clauses, the Chronicler omitted all references to the roles of the people mentioned in Neh 11:16-17. Heresh and Galal have no parallel at this place in Nehemiah 11, but a Galal is mentioned both in 1 Chr 9:16 and Neh 11:17b and his name may be a dittograph here. Mattaniah[85] was a (Levitical) singer, as is clearer from the function given for him in Neh 11:17: "the leader of the praise[86] who gave thanks in prayer." Hence the Chronicler's source in Nehemiah 11 already regarded the singers as Levites, in contrast to Ezra 2:41//Neh 7:44, which makes a clear distinction between singers and Levites. Mattaniah traced his ancestry back to Asaph, the head of one of the Levitical singer guilds at the time of David (1 Chr 6:24-28 [39-43]; 25:1-2; Ezra 2:41). Asaph also was a descendant of Gershom, Levi's oldest son.

■ **16** *and Obadiah son of Shemaiah, son of Galal, son of Jeduthun, and Berechiah son of Asa, son of Elkanah, who lived in the villages of the Netophathites:*

Chronicles: Jeduthun—Galal—Shemaiah—Obadiah
Elkanah—Asa—Berechiah

Nehemiah 11:17: Jeduthun—Galal—Shammua—Abda

---

demonstrably frequently haplographic elsewhere? Might the fact that Shabbethai was one of the opponents of Ezra's divorce decree in Ezra 10:15, or that Jozabad (Ezra 10:23) was the first of the Levites who divorced his foreign wife, have led to the deletion of v. 16 in the text tradition behind Nehemiah LXX? The absence of this verse in Nehemiah LXX may explain why it is also absent from 1 Chronicles 9.

76   "Sources," 161.

77   A medial vowel letter was subsequently inserted into בני in Nehemiah in an attempt to interpret it as a personal name.

78   Knoppers, "Sources," 149, observes that Nehemiah LXX omits from "son of Zabdi" to the end of v. 17 and suggests that this represents a shorter and more original form of the text. It seems likely, however, that a scribe's eye veered from בן זבדי "son of Zabdi" to ועבדא "and Abda" at the start of the next verse (homoioarchton) and accidentally omitted the words in question.

79   Shabbethai was a Levite who opposed Ezra's divorce edict, perhaps because it was not exclusivist enough (Ezra 10:15). He provided interpretive help when Ezra read the law (Neh 8:7).

80   Jozabad was a Levitical official in the Jerusalem temple at the time of Ezra (Ezra 8:33; 10:23; Neh 8:7). Judging by his presence in Nehemiah 11, as one of those transferred to Jerusalem, his career spanned the tenures of both Ezra and Nehemiah.

81   Rudolph, 87, notes that the singers in Nehemiah 11 were not only included among the Levites, but were even considered Levitical heads.

82   Perhaps this refers to the temple treasuries. See 1 Chr 26:20-32.

83   In Neh 12:8-9, 27-42, Bakbukiah is the leader of a choir that sang antiphonally (cf. Ezra 3:11).

84   In Neh 11:17, however, he is identified as "the second among his associates," who are presumably Levitical singers.

85   Nehemiah mentions Mattaniah the son of Mica, of the descendants of Asaph (11:22), and Mattaniah the son of Micaiah the son of Zaccur the son of Asaph (12:35). Cf. Neh 12:8, which mentions Mattaniah, without a patronymic, among four Levitical singers.

86   Reading תהלת for תחלת.

Verse 16a (through Jeduthun) is nearly identical with Neh 11:17b: "and Abda son of Shammua son of Galal son of Jeduthun." Abda son of Shammua עבדא בן שמוע and Obadiah son of Shemaiah עבדיה בן שמעיה again represent minor variations in spelling.[87] Verse 16b ("and Berechiah . . . Netophathites") shows no relationship to Neh 11:18: "All the Levites in the holy city were two hundred eighty-four." Verse 16b, therefore, was either added by the Chronicler himself, or more likely, found by him in a form of his *Vorlage* that differed from Neh 11:18. In any case, the Chronicler did not include the total number for the Levites who were in Jerusalem. Obadiah's ancestor Jeduthun is a prominent leader of a singer guild, along with Asaph and Heman.[88] A certain Berechiah is the father of Asaph among the singers (1 Chr 6:24 [39]; cf. 15:17), but that Berechiah's father is Shimea, not Asa. Three men by the name of Elkanah appear among the ancestors of Heman the Kohathite (6:19-21 [34-36]), and Japhet, 213, suggests that between the time of Nehemiah 11 and 1 Chronicles 9 Berechiah affiliated with a group of singers who would eventually be known as the sons of Heman. Berechiah lived in the villages of the Netophathites, making his presence in a list of inhabitants of Jerusalem awkward.[89] Netophah (MR 171119)[90] is located 3.5 miles southeast of Bethlehem.

■ **17** *The gatekeepers were: Shallum, Akkub, Talmon, Ahiman; and their brother Shallum was the chief:* This verse is clearly related to, though different from, Neh 11:19: "The gatekeepers, Akkub, Talmon and their brothers, who kept watch at the gates,[91] were one hundred seventy-two."[92] Thus Nehemiah mentions only two of the four gatekeepers found in 1 Chr 9:17. The individuals (vv. 17b, 26) Shallum, Akkub, and Talmon are among six *families* of gatekeepers in Ezra 2:42//Neh 7:45.[93] Shallum's absence from Neh 11:19 may be an accident; he is present, in the spelling Meshullam,[94] with Talmon and Akkub, among the six gatekeepers in Neh 12:25.[95] Shallum's son Zechariah later replaced him at the east gate (1 Chr 9:21; cf. v. 18).[96] Four gatekeepers are referred to in v. 26 below and Ahiman אחימן is that fourth person here, but his name may be a corruption, because of the following ואחיהם "their brothers." This name may originally have been spelled אטר "Ater" (Ezra 2:42//Neh 7:45; Ezra 10:24[97]), or the name was invented on the basis of the following "their brothers" to meet the required four gatekeepers of v. 26. It is not explicit in this verse that the gatekeepers are Levites, as they also

87 Knoppers, "Sources," 149, observes that "the son of Galal the son of Jeduthun" and the first part of v. 18, "All the Levites in the holy city were," are missing from Nehemiah LXX. Note that the first of these readings is present not only in Nehemiah MT but also in Chronicles MT (with the spelling variations noted above). Without the second reading, the number given in Neh 11:18—284—would hang in midair and have nothing to modify.

88 1 Chr 16:38, 41-42; 25:1, 3, 6; 2 Chr 5:12; 29:14; 35:15. See discussion at 1 Chr 16:38.

89 Allen, 362, suggests Jerusalem was his part-time residence when he was on duty (cf. vv. 25, 33).

90 See 2 Sam 23:28-29//1 Chr 11:30; Ezra 2:22//Neh 7:26 (where it is listed right after Bethlehem); 1 Chr 2:54 (where Netophah is a "brother" of Bethlehem); 27:13, 15; and Neh 12:28. The latter verse mentions that singers from Netophah participated in the dedication of the wall of Jerusalem.

91 השמרם בשערים; lacking in LXX. Is this a synonymous variant for והשוערים "the gatekeepers" that has been conflated in MT?

92 From this point on the Chronicler no longer follows Nehemiah 11. Allen, 362, believes that the Chronicler follows a different source, beginning with this verse. So also Williamson, 90.

93 The sons of Shallum, Ater, Talmon, Akkub, Hatita, and Shobai. They are listed between the singers (Ezra 2:41//Neh 7:44) and the temple servants (Nethinim; Ezra 2:43//Neh 7:46).

94 Cf. Meshelemiah in v. 21 and 1 Chr 26:1, 2, 9, and Shelemiah in 1 Chr 26:14.

95 This list is dated to the time of Joiakim the son of Jeshua the son of Jozadak (Neh 12:26) and also to the time of Nehemiah and Ezra. Also present in this verse as gatekeepers are Mattaniah, Bakbukiah, and Obadiah. Talmon appears in Ezra 2:42//Neh 7:45; Neh 11:19; 12:25. Cf. also the postexilic gatekeeper Telem (Ezra 10:24).

96 This assumes that Meshelemiah (v. 21) and Shallum (v. 17) are the same person.

97 His name in Ezra 10:24 is spelled אורי "Uri." Other gatekeepers mentioned there are Shallum and Telem.

were not in Ezra 2:42//Neh 7:45 or Neh 11:15, 19, but they are clearly Levites in vv. 18 and 26 below, as well as in 1 Chr 23:3-5 and in the primary level of chap. 26.[98] Thirty-four of the thirty-seven biblical references to gatekeepers occur in Chronicles and Ezra-Nehemiah. The only exceptions are 2 Sam 18:26 and 2 Kgs 7:10-11.[99]

■ **18** *stationed until now in the king's gate on the east side:* The text refers to the present day of its author ("until now"), but this could have come from the source used by the Chronicler and not from the Chronicler himself. Elsewhere this pericope refers to the time of the desert (vv. 19-20) and the time of David (v. 22). The king's gate is probably the entrance by which the king entered the sanctuary.[100]

These were the gatekeepers of the camps of the Levites: This sentence explicitly includes the gatekeepers among the Levites (cf. also vv. 19-20, 26 and 23:3-5; chap. 26).[101] The reference to the camps of the Levites suggests that already in the wilderness period, at the time of Moses, the gatekeepers practiced their craft.[102] The tent of meeting is associated with the camp of the Levites in Num 2:17.[103]

■ **19** *Shallum son of Kore, son of Ebiasaph, son of Korah, and his kindred of his ancestral house, the Korahites:*

Korah—Ebiasaph—Kore—Shallum

According to 1 Chr 6:22-23 (37-38), the pedigree of the singer Heman, Korah קרח was a son of Izhar[104] and a grandson of Kohath, the son of Levi (cf. also Exod 6:16-

21).[105] The Korahites are also considered singers in 2 Chr 20:19 and in the Psalms. The pedigree in this verse, however, reinforces the Levitical status of the gatekeepers. Shallum[106] the son of Kore is apparently the same as Meshelemiah the son of Kore (1 Chr 26:1; cf. Shelemiah in 26:14 and Meshullam in Neh 12:25). This information is important for understanding the reference to Zechariah the son of Meshelemiah/Shallum in 1 Chr 9:21.

were in control of the work of the service, guardians of the thresholds of the tent, as their ancestors had been in control of the camp of Yahweh, guardians of the entrance: Historically the priests seem to have been guardians of the threshold in preexilic times (2 Kgs 12:10 [9]; 23:4; 25:18; Jer 35:4; 52:24), but the Chronicler assigns that responsibility to the Levites in 2 Chr 34:9 (//2 Kgs 23:4). This verse and vv. 20-21 distinguish the functions of the gatekeepers (under the Davidic dispensation) from that of their ancestors in the desert who were in control of the camp of Yahweh and guardians of the entrance.[107] The tent referred to in this verse would be the tent David had pitched in Jerusalem (2 Sam 6:17//1 Chr 16:1).[108] The tabernacle had one gate on the east side (Exod 27:16; cf. Num 25:6). The terms "guardians of the thresholds" and "guardians of the entrance" are used interchangeably in this verse. The entrance was the entrance into the court of the tabernacle. There is no other evidence that the ancestors of the Korahites played this role, but the Korahites were descended from Kohath (Exod 6:18, 21), and the Kohathites had high rank among the servants of

---

98 Japhet, 214, notes that the gatekeeper Shallum becomes Shelemiah or Meshelemiah in 1 Chr 26:1, etc., and that new families emerge: Obed-edom and the sons of Merari (26:8, 19). The other names of gatekeeper families from Ezra-Nehemiah disappear.

99 See Curtis and Madsen, 34, #116.

100 This preexilic custom is reflected in Ezekiel's vision of the future (Ezek 46:11-18). Cf. 2 Kgs 16:18.

101 The gatekeepers are also called "guardians of the thresholds of the tent" and "guardians of the entrance" (v. 19). Zechariah is a gatekeeper at the entrance of the tent of meeting (v. 21).

102 Curtis and Madsen, 175, consider vv. 18b-21 a gloss since by making the gatekeeper office an institution of Moses they contradict v. 22, which connects the institution to David and Samuel.

103 The temple is designated as the "camp of Yahweh" in 2 Chr 31:2.

104 Izhar was the younger brother of Amram, the father of Moses and Aaron (Exod 6:18, 20). Izhar also had younger brothers, Hebron and Uzziel.

105 In 1 Chr 6:7-8 (22-23) Ebiasaph is the son of Elkanah the son of Assir the son of Korah, and Korah is the grandson, through Amminadab, of Kohath.

106 Rudolph, 89, distinguishes this Shallum from the Shallum mentioned in v. 17.

107 Num 1:53: "The Levites shall perform the guard duty of the tabernacle of the covenant."

108 So Rudolph, 89. Curtis and Madsen, 174–75, believed it could also refer to the tabernacle or the temple. Allen, 363, finds a reference to the tabernacle here and allusions to it in vv. 18, 19, 21, and 23.

the holy place and were responsible for the holiest vessels (Num 4:4-15).[109]

■ **20** *Phinehas son of Eleazar was leader over them previously; Yahweh was with him:* The gatekeepers mentioned in the previous verses were those appointed by David and Samuel (v. 22),[110] while their ancestors had Phinehas the son of Eleazar[111] as their ruler (נגיד; cf. Num 25:7-12). In the Pentateuch the Levites in general guarded the tabernacle and their supervisor was Eleazar the son of Aaron (Num 3:32),[112] but the Chronicler limits that responsibility for guarding the sanctuary to the Levitical gatekeepers.

■ **21** *Zechariah son of Meshelemiah was gatekeeper at the entrance of the tent of meeting:* Zechariah the son of Meshelemiah (= Shallum), apparently the same person mentioned in 1 Chr 26:2, 14 (Zechariah the son of Shelemiah), takes us back to the time of David.[113] David had assigned him to the north gate (26:14); Zechariah's father Shelemiah (Meshelemiah) had been assigned to the east gate, a position now taken over by Zechariah. The "tent of meeting" in this verse could be either David's tent that he pitched in Jerusalem (16:1) or the tabernacle that the Chronicler located at Gibeon (16:39; 2 Chr 1:2-6).

■ **22** *All these, who were selected as gatekeepers at the thresholds, were two hundred twelve:* Rudolph, 89, concluded from this number that a gatekeeper was on duty every two to three weeks.[114] Johnstone, 1:126, calculates that there was one gatekeeper from each group at each gate in a fifty-two-week year (4 × 52 = 208), and these generic gatekeepers, with the four leading gatekeepers, total 212. The total given for the gatekeepers in Neh 11:19 is 172.

They were enrolled by genealogies in their villages, but they were the ones whom David and Samuel the seer installed on account of their trustworthiness: The general gatekeepers are identified as commuters here and in v. 25,[115] although the rest of the chapter (esp. vv. 3, 34) speaks about the gatekeepers as permanent residents in Jerusalem. The four chief gatekeepers of vv. 17 and 26 were permanent residents in Jerusalem (v. 24). While v. 20 had reported the activities of the gatekeepers already in the desert period, their present assignment is credited to David[116] and Samuel. The reference to Samuel is an anachronism since Samuel died long before David became king (1 Sam 25:1; 28:3), but his and David's authorization give the gatekeepers high status even if the gatekeepers were living in the countryside and not in Jerusalem. For the Chronicler, of course, Samuel was not only a seer ראה (1 Chr 26:28, 29:29;[117] 1 Sam 9:9) but a Levite as well (1 Chr 6:12-13 [27-28]). David's appointment of the gatekeepers to their duties is also reported in 23:5.[118] Installation by David and Samuel applies to the subordinate gatekeepers in vv. 22, 25, but the chief gatekeepers, who actually resided in Jerusalem (v. 27), traced their office back to Moses himself (vv. 19-20).

■ **23** *So they and their descendants were in control of the gates of the house of Yahweh, that is, the house of the tent, as guards:* Verses 23-29 spell out the gatekeepers' responsibilities,[119] with vv. 23-26a describing their service at the gates, and vv. 26b-29 listing specific items for which they were responsible. The term "the house of the tent" is unique to this passage[120] and apparently combines in

---

109 Cf. Curtis and Madsen, 175.

110 By comparison, the singers were established by David, Gad the king's seer, and Nathan the prophet (2 Chr 29:25).

111 1 Chr 5:30 (6:4); Ps 106:30-31.

112 He was chief over the leaders (נְשִׂיא נְשִׂיאֵי) of the Levites.

113 Braun, 141, thinks this should be dated to postexilic times.

114 He calculated from 1 Chr 26:12-18 that there were twenty-four posts to maintain, and since gatekeepers could not work twenty-four hours a day, that number should be tripled or quadrupled.

115 Cf. the singers in Neh 12:28-29.

116 In 1 Chr 6:16-17 (31-32), 25:1-6, David appointed the singers to their present assignment. The appointment of the singers is also credited to David, Gad the king's seer (חזה), and Nathan the prophet in 2 Chr 29:25. David also appointed the priests (1 Chr 24:3) and the Levites (23:27; 24:31).

117 Cf. Hanani the seer in 2 Chr 16:7, 10.

118 See also 1 Chr 16:38 and 26:1-19.

119 Cf. 1 Chr 26:12-18.

120 Cf. "the tent of meeting and the sanctuary" in 1 Chr 23:32 and "the tent" (K) in 1 Kgs 7:45.

one term the complete history of the sanctuary, both as tent and as temple.

■ **24-25** *And their kindred who were in their villages were required to come in for seven days, in turn, to be with them:* According to vv. 24-25, the leaders among the gatekeepers lived in Jerusalem, and their assistants resided in surrounding villages (cf. v. 22). Apart from this passage there is no indication elsewhere that the gatekeepers lived outside Jerusalem, but some singers did according to v. 16. The antecedent of "them" is the four leading gatekeepers of v. 17 (cf. v. 26).

■ **26** *for the four chief gatekeepers were on permanent duty:* In distinction from their assistants, who lived in the villages, the chief gatekeepers (גברי השערים) were on permanent duty in Jerusalem. "On permanent duty" is a unique meaning for באמונה and in some tension with the use of the same noun in vv. 22 and 31, where on both occasions it refers to faithfulness.[121] According to 26:13-16 the four chief gatekeepers were assigned to one of the four gates of the temple court.

they were the Levites, and they had the supervision over the chambers and the treasuries of the house of God: With these clauses the writer moves on to a more general description of Levitical functions, leading Dirksen to identify v. 26b-c and vv. 28-33 as secondary.[122] Supervision over the chambers (storehouses in which tithes and offerings were kept; 2 Chr 31:5, 11, 12; Neh 13:4-9) and treasuries elsewhere is often assigned to the Levites in general and not to the gatekeepers (1 Chr 23:28-29 and 26:20-28). In 2 Chr 31:14, however, Kore, the keeper of the east gate, was in charge of the freewill offerings to God, and he and his staff apportioned them to the priestly and Levitical workers on the temple. He controlled the temple payroll.[123] The chambers (לשכות) were rooms in which tithes and offerings were kept and which opened onto

the temple courts (2 Chr 31:5, 11, 12; Neh 10:38-40 [37-39]; 13:4-9). Japhet, 217, suggests that the actual administration of the guard duty was carried out by (generic) Levites.

■ **27** *They would spend the night near the house of God; for on them was the duty of watching it, and it was they upon whom was the responsibility for opening it every morning:* The subject has returned to the four leading gatekeepers.

■ **28** *Some of them were responsible for the utensils of service, for they were required to count them when they were brought in and taken out:* The emphasis on counting the utensils or vessels as they were taken in and out suggests they might be made up of gold or silver (1 Chr 28:13-18; Ezra 1:9-11; Dan 1:2; 5:2-3). The gatekeepers here perform sentry duty (in 1 Chr 26:15 Obed-edom's sons are assigned to the storehouse, and in 26:17 four [two and two] Levites are assigned to the storehouse).[124]

■ **29** *Others were appointed over the furniture*[125] *and over all the holy utensils, also over the choice flour,*[126] *the wine, the oil, the incense*[127] *and the spices:* The gatekeepers were responsible for receiving and storing the offerings in kind from the people, not including, at least here, animals. Curtis and Madsen, 173, believe this verse deals with the Levites in general (cf. v. 26b).

■ **30** *Others, of the sons of the priests, prepared the mixing of the spices:* The spices (בשמים) were the last item mentioned in the previous verse, and their preparation is here reserved for the priests (cf. Exod 30:22-38). In Num 4:16 Eleazar the high priest had responsibility for oil for the light and for anointing, incense (קטרת), and the cereal offering, although it is not said whether he also prepared these items.[128] In Chronicles all of these duties except for the spices are transferred to those Levites who were not priests (cf. 1 Chr 23:27-29).

121 See Piet B. Dirksen, "1 Chronicles 9,26-33: Its Position in Chapter 9," *Bib* 79 (1998) 91–96. Dirksen notes that "permanently" is related to the meaning of the root אמן, and he cites Exod 17:12 as an inexact parallel.

122 Allen, 363, suggests that the Chronicler shifted to another source or another part of the same source.

123 See Wright, "Guarding the Gates," 77. Wright also notes that the gatekeepers (שמרי הסף) were responsible for collecting funds in 2 Chr 34:8-13.

124 Allen, 363, notes that this is not a reference to the administrative posts of 1 Chr 26:20-28.

125 Or vessels. Rudolph, 90: "die (profanen) Gefässe" ("the [secular] vessels").

126 The noun סלת "choice flour" appears 53 times in the OT, but only here and in 23:29 in the book of Chronicles.

127 The word לבונה is only used here in Chronicles. Cf. Neh 13:5, 9. The Chronicler always uses two other words that are usually translated "incense": קטרת, 1 Chr 6:34 (49); 28:18; 2 Chr 2:3 (4); 13:11; 26:16, 19; 29:7; cf. 2 Chr 30:14; and חמן, 2 Chr 14:5; 34:4, 7.

128 Moses himself prepared the initial anointing oil,

■ **31** *Mattithiah, one of the Levites, the firstborn of Shallum the Korahite, was responsible for making the flat cakes:* Mattithiah was either the eldest son of Shallum mentioned in vv. 17, 19, 21, whose son Zechariah was discussed in v. 21,[129] or Mattithiah's father Shallum was a different Shallum than the one mentioned in the earlier verses.[130] The word "flat cakes" החבתים is used only here in the Bible. These cakes were presumably made from the fine flour mentioned in v. 29 and may be the same as the "griddle cakes" described in Lev 6:19-23.[131]

■ **32** *Also some of the sons of the Kohathites were responsible for the rows of bread, to prepare them for each sabbath:* The Kohathites were descendants of Kohath, the second son of Levi, through his son Izhar. Aaron was a descendant of Kohath through Kohath's son Amram (see Num 3:17, 19, 27). The regulations for the rows of bread, or showbread, are given in Lev 24:5-9, where the high priest on the Sabbath removes the old bread and replaces it with the new. He then distributes the old bread to the other priests, who must eat it within the sanctuary complex.[132] In Num 4:7 and 15 the Kohathites, that is, the Levites, are prohibited from touching "the holy things," presumably including the bread of the Presence. This verse in Chronicles, therefore, shows the increasing role of the Levites in the cult by assigning them the task of preparing the rows of bread. This is the only reference to the Sabbath in 1 Chronicles, but there are four references to it in 2 Chronicles (23:4, 8 [twice]//2 Kgs 11:5, 9; 2 Chr 36:21). The last two words of the sentence could also be translated "every Sabbath," which raises the question whether preparation of the rows of bread would violate the Sabbath prohibitions. Milgrom remarks, however, that the Sabbath prohibitions were suspended within Yahweh's sphere.[133]

■ **33** *Now these singers, the heads of ancestral houses of the Levites, living in the chambers of the temple, were free from other service, for they were on duty day and night:* This verse is frequently translated "Now these are the singers, etc.," and has led a number of commentators to conclude that the Chronicler is here depending on another source that has been broken off abruptly without actually naming the singers (Braun, 137; Williamson, 91). Dirksen has suggested an alternate translation, which I have followed, that does not require a subsequent list of names.[134] Dirksen also proposed that the reference to the singers here was required by the reference to the Kohathites in the previous verse, where they were assigned the showbread. The writer wanted to emphasize that the majority of the Kohathites were free from such menial service and were singers (1 Chr 6:18 [33]; 2 Chr 20:19). Psalm 134:1 refers to the servants of Yahweh "who stand by night in the house of Yahweh" (cf. Isa 30:29). Rudolph, 91, notes that the singers did not have rest periods like the gatekeepers (1 Chr 9:27a). Instead, they were on duty day and night.

■ **34** *These were heads of ancestral houses of the Levites, according to their generations, chiefs. These lived in Jerusalem:* As Williamson, 91, has shown, 9:34-44 is dependent on 8:28-38.[135] He notes that the immediate context in chap. 9 has dealt with Levitical functions more than lists of ancestral houses, and the reference to living in Jerusalem, altogether consistent with the context in

---

incense, and the bread of the Presence (Exod 30:22-25, 34-36; Lev 24:5-7).

129 I assume that Shallum and Meshelemiah (v. 21) are the same person. In 1 Chr 26:2 Zechariah is designated as the firstborn of Meshelemiah, which may represent a change in status for Zechariah from 1 Chr 9:21, where his rank among Meshelemiah's sons is not indicated. Note that Mattithiah in 9:31 is designated as the firstborn of Shallum.

130 Dirksen, "1 Chronicles 9," 96, thinks the reference is to the Shallum of v. 17, who he believes is not the same as the Shallum mentioned in vv. 19, 21, and 26:1. I cannot follow Dirksen in his proposal that the primary purpose of v. 31 is to give a Levitical ancestry for the Shallum in v. 17. The name Mattithiah also occurs in 15:18, 21; 16:5; 25:3, 21; Ezra 10:43; Neh 8:4.

131 Chronicles LXX translates חבתים by τῆς θυσίας τοῦ τηγάνου τοῦ μεγάλου ἱερέως "the sacrifices of the frying pan of the high priest," thus associating this rite with the grain offering (מנחה) of the high priest in Lev 6:14.

132 See Paul V. M. Flesher, "Bread of the Presence," *ABD* 1:780–81.

133 Jacob Milgrom, *Leviticus 23–27* (AB 3B; New York: Doubleday, 2001) 2099.

134 "1 Chr 9,26-33," 96.

135 For the opposite view see Braun, 123. A. Demsky, "The Genealogy of Gibeon (I Chronicles 9:35-44): Biblical and Epigraphic Considerations," *BASOR* 202 (1971) 17, feels that 9:35-44 is older and better preserved than 8:29-40.

chap. 8, is contradicted by vv. 16, 22, and 35 here. In Japhet's view, 218, the first sentence of this verse forms a conclusion to the list of the Levites in vv. 14-32, while the second sentence forms a conclusion to the larger unit beginning with v. 3. Japhet has also pointed out the neat chiasm with which vv. 3-34 begin and end: ובירושלם ישבו ("and in Jerusalem they lived") at the beginning of v. 3 and ישבו בירושלם ("they lived in Jerusalem") at the end of v. 34. The present form of the chapter asserts that all the preceding names lived in Jerusalem[136] even though that is in tension with vv. 16, 22, and 25. This verse is based on 8:28, with the additions of the word "Levites" and the removal (in Hebrew) of the article from "ancestral houses." The Chronicler brought over this verse from chap. 8, with its sequels in 9:35-38//9:29-32 and 9:39-44//8:33-38.[137]

9:35-44. Genealogy from Benjamin Repeated

■ **35** *And in Gibeon lived Jeuel the father of Gibeon, and the name of his wife was Maacah:* For a general discussion of the list of the Benjaminites in Gibeon (vv. 35-38)[138] and the genealogy of Saul (vv. 39-44), see the commentary at 8:29-38. The names Jeuel, Ner, and Mikloth have been preserved in vv. 35-37, but lost in the corresponding parts of the MT in chap. 8. Variants in spelling of personal names between the two lists are discussed in the notes to the translation.[139]

■ **36-38** *His firstborn son was Abdon, then Zur, Kish, Baal, Ner, Nadab:* Braun, 127, 138, concludes that Ner was added to the list of the sons of Jeuel, under the influence of the name Kish, whose name is the same as the father of Saul in v. 39, to identify vv. 35-38 as part of the genealogy of Saul.

The Ancestors and Descendants of Saul

■ **39** *Saul became the father of Jonathan, Malchishua, Abinadab, and Esh-baal:* Saul and his three oldest sons were

killed in the battle with the Philistines at Mount Gilboa. Esh-baal is mentioned only in 1 Chr 8:33 and 9:39, but the Chronicler did not include the narrative about the period of his rival kingship during David's early years as king (2 Samuel 2–4). There are fourteen references to Ishbaal in 2 Sam 2:8—4:12.

■ **40** *and the son of Jonathan was Merib-baal; and Meri-baal became the father of Micah:* The tracing of Saul's posterity through Jonathan is in tension with 1 Chr 10:6, which indicates that Saul, his three sons, and his whole house died together. On the basis of this twelve-generation posterity of Saul, however, David could hardly be charged with wiping out the house of Saul.[140]

■ **44** *Azel had six sons, and these are their names: Azrikam, his firstborn, Ishmael, Sheariah, Obadiah, and Hanan; these were the sons of Azel:* Kingship passed to the house of David, but Azel enjoyed the blessings of six sons (cf. Ps 127:3). The genealogy of the ancestors and descendants of Saul prepares the reader for the narrative of Saul's death in 1 Chronicles 10. The Chronicler here may have omitted 8:39-40, which end with the words: "All these were Benjaminites," lest he give the impression that Saul's unfaithfulness recounted in chap. 10 applies to the Benjaminites in general.

Conclusion

This chapter completes the genealogical introduction to Chronicles in chaps. 1–9. After setting Israel within the context of the nations in chap. 1, the Chronicler used chaps. 2–8 to provide genealogical information for all the tribes of Israel, indicating that the small size of Israel in the author's day, which was subject to the great Persian Empire, was indeed all Israel, at least in promise or in eschatological perspective. Representatives of the tribes beside Judah, Benjamin, and Levi, which were

---

136 See 1 Chr 9:27, 33, and 38.

137 He did not bring over 8:39-40, which lists Ulam and his warriors and ends with the sentence "All these were Benjaminites." This forms a fitting conclusion to chap. 8, but may have been deemed inappropriate in chap. 9.

138 Braun, 143, believes these verses may have been suggested by Neh 11:25-36, a list of Israelites living throughout the land rather than in Jerusalem. Oeming, *Wahre Israel*, 204, argues that the Gibeonites were part of the temple personnel (cf. Josh 9:23, 27)

and therefore were added at the end of this list of temple personnel as the group with the lowest rank.

139 Allen, 366, connects this list of Benjaminites and the genealogy of Saul with 10:1-14 as a redactional unit.

140 Oeming, *Wahre Israel*, 205.

part of the original Israel, were also welcome to be part of the Chronicler's Israel and to participate in its temple cult.

The center of Israel is the temple and the city of Jerusalem. That city had been named already in the genealogy of David (3:4, 5) in the genealogies of chaps. 5–6 (5:36, 41; 6:16-17 [6:10, 15, 31-32]), and in the final part of chap. 8 (vv. 28, 32), but after the conclusion of the genealogical listing of the twelve tribes, the Chronicler speaks of the inhabitants of Jerusalem (the first settlers) that consisted of laypeople from at least Judah, Benjamin, Ephraim, and Manasseh, as well as clergy of various ranks: priests and Levites, including Levitical gatekeepers and Levitical singers or musicians. It also included the Gibeonites, who were among the lowliest of temple personnel.

The final segment of the chapter lists the ancestors and the descendants of Saul. While in chap. 8 this genealogical material adds significant size to the genealogical materials on Benjamin and links the Benjaminites from the time of the ancestors to the present day, the same genealogical material in chap. 9 prepares for the beginning of the Chronicler's narrative with the death of Saul. It also indicates that while Saul's family suffered a severe blow at Gilboa, the whole family was not wiped out, least of all by David. Excision of the final two verses from chap. 8 (vv. 39-40) prevents ending the genealogy with the ringing words, "All these were Benjaminites." However unfaithful the Benjaminite Saul had proven to be, the indictment against him did not make all the members of his tribe guilty.

10

Translation

1/ When the Philistines fought[1] against Israel, every person of Israel fled before the Philistines and they fell slain[2] on Mount Gilboa.[3] **2/** The Philistines pursued[4] closely after Saul and his sons, and the Philistines smote Jonathan and Abinadab and Malchishua, the sons of Saul. **3/** The battle went badly for Saul and the archers[5] found him with [their] bows; he was in severe pain[6] from the archers.[7]

4/ Saul said to his weapon carrier, "Draw your sword and thrust me through with it lest these uncircumcised come and mock me." But his weapon carrier refused, for he was very afraid. Then Saul took his sword and fell on it.

5/ When the weapon carrier saw that Saul had died, he also fell on his sword[8] and died.[9] **6/** Saul died and his three sons;[10] his whole household together died. **7/** After every person of Israel who was in the valley saw that they[11] had fled and that Saul and his sons were dead, they abandoned their[12] cities and fled. So the Philistines came and lived in them.[13]

8/ On the next day the Philistines came to plunder the slain, and they found Saul and his sons[14] fallen on Mount Gilboa. **9/** They stripped him[15] and took his head and his weapons and sent messengers[16] around in the land of the Philistines to spread the good news to their idols[17] and the people. **10/** They put his armor in the temple of their gods and his skull they affixed to[18] the temple of Dagon.

11/ All the inhabitants of[19] Jabesh-gilead heard what the Philistines had done to Saul.[20] **12/** All the men of war rose and took the corpse of Saul and the corpse of his sons, and they brought them[21] to Jabesh. They buried their bones under the terebinth[22] at Jabesh, and they fasted seven days.

13/ Saul died because of his unfaithfulness whereby he acted unfaithfully against Yahweh, in that he did not keep the word of Yahweh, and also by consulting a medium.[23] **14/** He did not seek Yahweh, and so he [Yahweh] killed him and transferred the kingdom to David the son of Jesse.

1 נלחמו *niphal* perfect; 1 Sam 31:1 MT נלחמים *niphal* participle "were fighting." The imperfect tense in Samuel LXX could represent either reading. Peter R. Ackroyd, "The Chronicler as Exegete," *JSOT* 2 (1977) 26, n. 13, regards the perfect/participle interchange as a mere scribal variant, but see the commentary. In readings discussed below in textual notes 12, 17, and 21 (cf. n. 14), Chronicles presupposes a text of Samuel other than MT.

2 חללים. This might also be translated "wounded." See *HALOT* 1:320.

3 בהר גלבע; 1 Sam 31:1 בהר הגלבע. S. Noah Lee, "The Use of the Definite Article in the Development of Some Biblical Toponyms," *VT* 52 (2002) 337–39, attributes the loss of the definite article on "Gilboa" to the transition from Standard Biblical Hebrew to Late Biblical Hebrew.

4 וַיַּדְבְּקוּ. Rudolph, 93 (cf. G. Bergsträsser, *Hebräische Grammatik* [2 vols.; Leipzig: Hinrichs, 1918–1929] 2:104ʰ), identifies this as a mixed form: *qal* and *hiphil*. Cf. *HALOT* 1:209.

5 המורים; cf. the last word in the verse (n. 6).

6 וַיָּחֶל, *qal* imperfect with *wāw* consecutive from חיל (BDB, 297); or וַיָּחֶל *niphal* or וַיֶחֱלֶה *hophal* "he was wounded," from חלה (*NRSV*; *HALOT* 1:310; Rudolph, 92; cf. Chronicles LXX and 2 Kgs 1:2).

7 מן היורים; cf. n. 4. 1 Sam 31:3 מהמורים.

8 חרבו, with Chronicles LXX and 1 Sam 31:5; Chronicles MT החרב "the sword." The *wāw* suffix may have been lost by haplography, precipitating the addition of the definite article in Chronicles MT.

9 וימת; missing in Chronicles LXX because of haplography with the following identical word.

10 LXX adds "on that day" (= ביום ההוא), as in 1 Sam 31:6.

11 The Chronicler did not explicitly identify the subject, but "every person of Israel" is implied from v. 1 (Rudolph, 92). Chronicles LXX adds "Israel" and Chronicles LXXᴮ "all Israel." 1 Sam 31:7 אנשי ישראל "the men of Israel."

12 עריהם; cf. 1 Sam 31:7 LXX. Samuel MT את הערים "the cities."

13 בהם. The pronominal suffix in MT is masculine whereas the antecedent "cities" is feminine. Chronicles LXX and 1 Sam 31:7 MT and LXX have a feminine pronoun.

14 ואת בניו; cf. 1 Sam 31:8 LXX a₂ c₂ and Eth. Samuel MT ואת שלשת בניו.

15 Rudolph, 92, proposed inserting ויראשוהו "and they decapitated him," which he believed was lost before the following clause. As indicated in the commentary, however, I believe the Chronicler omitted Saul's decapitation when he recast vv. 9 and 12 to make the actions of the Philistines and the Jabesh-

gileadites parallel. Tg also adds decapitation in this verse.

16 וישלחו. "Messengers" has been supplied to complete the sense. Curtis and Madsen, 183, suggest vocalizing the verb וישלחו as a *qal* instead of the *piel* as in MT.

17 את עצביהם; cf. 1 Sam 31:9 LXX. A few Hebrew MSS, Syr, Tg: בית עצביהם "the temple of their idols" as in Samuel MT.

18 תקעו; *HALOT* 4:1784. McCarter, *1 Samuel*, 442, "nailed." Cf. 2 Sam 21:12 (the account of David burying the bones of Saul and Jonathan), where the verb תלא (Q) "hang" is used instead of תקע. Many emend to הקעו "they exposed," following Lagarde.

19 ישבי with one Hebrew MS, Syr; cf. LXX. The word is lacking in MT by haplography before יבש. LXX pre-

serves a translation for ישבי ("inhabitants") but not for יבש ("Jabesh") and hence has lost the latter word by haplography.

20 LXX adds "and to Israel."

21 ויביאום; cf. 1 Sam 31:12 LXX. Samuel MT ויבאו "they came."

22 האלה; 1 Sam 31:13 האשל "tamarisk."

23 The last three words of the verse לשאול באוב לדרוש are apparently a conflation of synonymous readings לשאל באוב "by asking a medium" and לדרוש באוב "by seeking a medium" (cf. לא דרש at the beginning of v. 14). It is impossible to tell which of these is more original. Chronicles LXX adds: "and Samuel the prophet answered him," alluding to 1 Sam 28:15-19.

10:1-14

Structure

The Chronicler begins the narrative portion of his work by including an account of Saul's death based on 1 Samuel 31.[1] This narrative may be outlined as follows:

I. 10:1-7. Death of Saul and his house (1 Sam 31:1-7)
II. 10:8-12. Benevolent acts of the people of Jabesh-gilead, introduced by a time notice, "On the next day" (1 Sam 31:8-13)
    A. 10:8-10. Philistines display head of Saul in temple of Dagon
    B. 10:11-12. People of Jabesh-gilead bury the bodies of Saul and his sons

III. 10:13-14. Theological reason for Saul's death (without a *Vorlage* in 1 Samuel).

The Chronicler omitted not only the story of Saul's early kingship in 1 Samuel 9–15, but also most of the materials on Saul from the so-called History of David's Rise in 1 Sam 16:14–2 Sam 5:10[2] (except for 2 Sam 5:1-3, 6-10//1 Chr 11:1-3, 4-9, on which see the appropriate sections of this commentary). He also subsequently omitted other sections from the Deuteronomistic History dealing with the heirs of Saul (including David's kindness toward Mephibosheth, 2 Sam 9:1-13, and the slaughter of Saul's seven sons by the Gibeonites and David's reburial of the bones of Saul and Jonathan, 2 Sam 21:1-14). Thus from the voluminous materials on Saul, the Chronicler selected only the chapter dealing

---

1 Craig Y. S. Ho, "Conjectures and Refutations: Is 1 Samuel xxxi 1-13 Really the Source of 1 Chronicles x 1-12?" *VT* 45 (1995) 82–106, proposes that 1 Chronicles 10 does *not* depend on 1 Samuel 31, but that both chapters are drawing on a common source. I find his proposal completely unconvincing, as will be clear throughout the commentary on this chapter. Also unconvincing is his proposal that although 1 Chronicles 10 is consistent with some of the episodes in 1 Samuel 1–18 and 28, the redactor responsible for composing 1 Samuel 31 also added the chapters dealing with the struggle between Saul and David in 1 Sam 19:1–27:4. In an appendix to this article Ho even proposes that 1 Chr 10:13-14 was in the common source used by the two authors of 1 Samuel 31 and 1 Chronicles 10! For an under-

standing of this chapter from a reader-oriented theoretical perspective, see James M. Trotter, "Reading, Readers and Reading Readers Reading the Account of Saul's Death in 1 Chronicles 10," in Graham and McKenzie, *Chronicler as Author*, 294–310. Christine Mitchell, "The Dialogism of Chronicles," in ibid., 311–26, uses the literary theories of Bakhtin and Lotman to read 1 Chr 10:1–11:9 on its own terms and then in dialogue with the *Vorlage* in Samuel. Readers can understand the message of Chronicles without knowledge of its *Vorlage*, but readers who also know Samuel-Kings can appreciate the dialogue between it and Chronicles. See also Christopher T. Begg, "The Death of King Saul According to Josephus," *ASE* 16 (1999) 485–505.

2 Klein, *1 Samuel*, xxxi–xxxii.

with Saul's death.[3] Except for the preceding genealogy of the ancestors and descendants of Saul in 1 Chr 9:35-44 (//8:29-40), the Chronicler provides the reader with no introduction to Saul or any historical context to aid in understanding or appreciating his retelling of 1 Samuel 31.

The Chronicler appended to the account taken from his *Vorlage* in 1 Sam 31:1-13 two verses that give the theological significance of the life and death of Saul (1 Chr 10:13-14). Here he castigates Saul for his unfaithfulness, described as not keeping the word of Yahweh and consulting a medium and, more generally, as not seeking Yahweh (see commentary). The result was that Yahweh killed Saul and turned the kingdom over to David.

Japhet, 229–30, emphasizes the continuity between the kingship of Saul and David, and she and others have seen the evident contrast in Chronicles between the terrible days of Saul and the glorious days of David. Saul's "unfaithfulness" anticipates the unfaithfulness of a number of his successors on the throne, which eventually would lead to the Babylonian exile. Rudolf Mosis has gone beyond this and posited a threefold typology in which Saul's death and its consequences stand for God's judgment and exile, David's reign stands for a period of *praeparatio*, and Solomon's reign stands for the eschatological future or final redemption anticipated by the postexilic community.[4] It is doubtful, however, whether the Chronicler himself would distinguish much between the significance of David and Solomon. In many ways, both of these rulers of the united kingdom initiated the temple, its clergy, and its cult, which the Chronicler invites his readers to support enthusiastically. According to Mosis, the narrative of Saul is a paradigm for the exilic situation and thus loses its historical character. King Ahaz is a second Saul and Hezekiah is a second David. Zalewski has pointed out that subsequent royal unfaithfulness is not merely a reprise of Saul, since Ahaz, for example, is specifically criticized for practicing idolatry and walking in the ways of the kings of Israel, not for repeating the sins of Saul.[5] The significance of Saul is that he acted unfaithfully (see below), and this necessitated his death and the extermination of his house. Those who subsequently acted unfaithfully put themselves in similar peril. Zalewski is correct in detecting links and allusions in 1 Chr 10:13-14 to specific misdeeds of Saul recounted in 1 Samuel, even though the Chronicler did not include these narratives themselves in his own story. Presumably the Chronicler assumed his readers' knowledge of the whole Saul story.

David is the legitimate successor to Saul because Yahweh himself transferred the kingdom to David the son of Jesse (1 Chr 10:14).[6] The inauguration of David's reign is Yahweh's doing and the Chronicler passed over in silence the many stories about David that showed him as the aggressive opponent and rival of Saul, with sometimes questionable motives and actions.

Detailed Commentary

10:1-7. Death of Saul and His House

■ **1** *the Philistines fought against Israel:* The Philistines were previously mentioned in 1 Chronicles only in the Chronicler's version of the Table of Nations (1 Chr 1:12). By replacing the participle in his *Vorlage* (נלחים) with a verb in the perfect tense (נלחמו), the Chronicler detached this narrative from the previous history in 1 Samuel and focused solely on this one battle.[7] The Deuteronomistic Historian, on the other hand, by his choice of a participle ("were fighting"), connected this battle with preparatory events leading up to it, including

---

3   There are also passing references to Saul in 1 Chr 11:2; 12:1-2, 20 (19), 30 (29); 13:3; 15:29; 17:13; and 26:28, but these were not taken from 1 and 2 Samuel. The reference in 1 Chr 26:28 alludes to booty won by Saul in warfare.

4   Mosis, *Untersuchungen*, 42–43, 122.

5   Saul Zalewski, "The Purpose of the Story of the Death of Saul in 1 Chronicles X," *VT* 39 (1989) 449–67. The last explicit reference to Saul in the Chronicler is in 1 Chr 26:28, though Zalewski, 452, finds an allusion to him in Solomon's prayer at the dedication of the temple in 2 Chr 6:4-6.

6   As De Vries, 119, points out, this is the only time that Yahweh directly intervenes in Chronicles to substitute one king for another. I find it extremely doubtful, however, when Zalewski, "Purpose," 465, proposes that the Chronicler, more than five hundred years after the death of David, had to combat traditions that said that David had collaborated with the Philistine enemy. Such traditions, of course, did have to be addressed by the author of the History of David's Rise, who probably wrote during the reigns of David or Solomon.

7   Mosis, *Untersuchungen*, 25, argues that the

specifically 1 Sam 28:4 and 29:11. Other changes from 1 Samuel 31 in this verse are stylistic and of little significance.

every person of Israel fled: The Chronicler makes the panic of the Israelite army vivid by replacing the more generic "the men of Israel fled" from 1 Sam 31:1 (Curtis and Madsen, 180). The same substitution takes place in v. 7.

Mount Gilboa: Mount Gilboa (Jebel Fuquʿah) is some 6 miles west of Beth-shan (MR 197212), overlooking the valley of Jezreel (cf. 1 Sam 28:4; 2 Sam 4:4). Whoever controlled this mountain would control the cities below (v. 7).

■ **2** *the Philistines smote Jonathan and Abinadab and Malchishua:* After the general routing of the Israelite army in v. 1, the narrative turns to the peril faced by Saul himself and notes first the killing of his three sons.[8] The Chronicler does not mention the friendship of David and Jonathan, let alone the covenant between them, or Jonathan's symbolic ceding of the right of succession to him (1 Sam 18:3-4). Nothing is known about Abinadab and Malchishua, who are otherwise mentioned only in genealogical references (1 Chr 8:33; 9:39; cf. 1 Sam 14:49). A fourth son, Esh-baal, is mentioned in the genealogies of Saul in Chronicles (1 Chr 8:33; 9:39), but neither Samuel nor Chronicles mentions him in this verse. The Chronicler also omitted the *Vorlage*'s extensive description of Esh-baal's/Ishbaal's two-year reign as a rival king to David (2 Sam 2:8—4:12).

■ **3** *he was in severe pain from the archers:* The text reports the results of the wounding and not the wounding itself (despite *NRSV:* "he was wounded by the archers"). Saul's distress helps explain his suicide in the subsequent verses. Saul was one of five kings of Israel and Judah who were severely wounded by archers.[9] It is more than a little ironic that Saul the Benjaminite is killed by archers, since his tribe was famed for its soldiers who could shoot arrows or throw stones with either hand (1 Chr 12:2).[10] For the Chronicler, health is a sign of life in harmony with God; disease or wounds are a sign of a breakdown of that relationship.[11]

■ **4** *lest these uncircumcised come and mock me:* Because of the highly selective use of materials from 1 Samuel, this is the only reference in Chronicles to the Philistines as being uncircumcised.[12] The irony of the narrative is that Saul's suicide does not accomplish its purpose since the Philistines do in fact use his head and weapons for propagandistic purposes and, possibly, mockery after his death.[13]

he was very afraid: In Chronicles the weapon carrier's fear and refusal to kill the king is understandable but not explicitly explained. His piety and loyalty stand in marked contrast to the impiety of Saul. In Samuel the reader might think of David's own repeated reticence to kill Yahweh's anointed (1 Sam 24:6-7; 26:11, 23). Saul himself was afraid before the battle and his heart trembled according to the Deuteronomistic narrative, which led him to resort to the medium at Endor (28:5). When she managed to bring up Samuel from the dead, the deceased prophet's words only increased Saul's panic (28:20).

Then Saul took his sword and fell on it: The Chronicler

<hr/>

Philistines represent in general the "heathen" rather than the political enemies of Israel.

8   At the battle of Ramoth-gilead the Aramean king had also focused on attacking the king of Israel himself (2 Chr 18:30//1 Kgs 22:31).

9   These kings include Ahab (1 Kgs 22:34//2 Chr 18:33) and Joram (2 Kgs 9:24//2 Chr 22:5-6) of the Northern Kingdom, and Ahaziah (2 Kgs 9:27//2 Chr 22:7-9) and Josiah (2 Chr 35:23) of the Southern Kingdom. According to Kings, Joram was fatally wounded by Jehu, but according to Chronicles he was wounded by the Arameans under Hazael and taken to Jezreel to recuperate. His death is not reported in Chronicles. Ahaziah was fatally wounded by the followers of Jehu in 2 Kings, but in 2 Chronicles he was arrested and executed by Jehu.

On the divergent description of the deaths of Jehoram and Ahaziah see now the Tell Dan inscription (*COS* 2:161–62) and my commentary on 2 Chronicles 22.

10   Another tradition reported that seven hundred left-handed Benjaminites could sling a stone at a hair and not miss (Judg 20:16). By etymology, the word "Benjamin" means "son of the right hand."

11   See Asa (2 Chr 16:12), Jehoram (21:15, 18), Joash (24:25), and Josiah (35:23).

12   See 1 Sam 14:6; 17:26, 36.

13   Suicide is rare in the OT. In addition to Saul and his weapon carrier, see Abimelech (Judg 9:54), Samson (Judg 16:29-30), Ahithophel (2 Sam 17:23), and Zimri (1 Kgs 16:18). Cf. also Ptolemy (2 Macc 10:13) and Razis (14:41-46).

chose to include the account of Saul's suicide rather than the alternate account in 2 Sam 1:1-10, where Saul was killed by one of his own warriors, at least according to the Amalekite who carried the news to David.

■ **5** *he also fell on his sword and died:* Once Saul had taken his own life, the weapon carrier quickly followed suit. The Chronicler omitted the words "with him" that follow "died" in 1 Sam 31:5, and so he made the death of the weapon carrier and Saul separate events, with the emphasis clearly on the death of Saul.[14] The main theme in the chapter remains the death of Saul, not the death of his sons or his weapon carrier.[15]

■ **6** *his whole household together died:* Both Samuel and Chronicles report the death of Saul and his three sons, but Samuel goes on to mention the death of Saul's weapon carrier and all of Saul's warriors.[16] The Chronicler, however, emphasizes that this battle marked the end of any thought of Saul having a dynasty: "his whole household together died." This somewhat awkward word order emphasizes the chiastic nature of this verse: "Saul died . . . his whole household . . . died." As Williamson, 93, notes, Saul's dynasty was judged by Yahweh and was therefore to all purposes at an end. Even though Chronicles (twice) includes a lengthy list of Saul's descendants, this continuation is only genetic and not dynastic (Japhet, 225).[17] Though the Chronicler surely knew about the rival rule of Saul's son Ishbaal and that David's kingship was at first only over Judah, he chose to omit these stories in order to concentrate on the transition from one legitimate, if evil, king to another king, who was both legitimate and righteous. The Targum, sensing the inaccuracy of the reference to the death of Saul's whole household, adds the words after

"house(hold)": "who were there." The obliteration of other survivors of the house of Saul, except for Mephibosheth, is also recorded in 2 Sam 21:1-14, a passage not included by the Chronicler.

■ **7** *every person of Israel who was in the valley:* The narrative in 1 Sam 31:7 identifies the witnesses of Israel's defeat as those who were across the valley (of Esdraelon) *and* those on the other side of the Jordan. In part, the Chronicler may have simplified the description available to him in 1 Samuel because he was uncertain of the meaning of its geographical terms. The text of Samuel more realistically presents the location of the Israelite residences since historically the Canaanites retained the plains while the Israelites dwelled in the hill country (cf. Judg 1:27).

saw that they had fled and that Saul and his sons were dead: The subject of the verb "fled" is unclear. In 1 Sam 31:7 we are told that the "men of Israel" had fled, repeating the subject from the first part of the verse and thereby creating some redundancy: "The men of Israel who were across the valley and who were across the Jordan saw that the men of Israel had fled and that Saul and his sons were dead." Presumably this would mean that those on the other side of the Esdraelon Valley and in Transjordan observed that the soldiers on the battlefield had fled. The same sort of interpretation may work in Chronicles as well. In paraphrase: the men in the valley saw that their comrades on Mount Gilboa had fled. Japhet, 225, however, proposes that the verb "fled" anticipates the subject after the next verb.[18] Hence: the men in the valley saw that Saul and his sons (= they) had fled. That is, the flight and subsequent deaths of Saul and his sons led *other* Israelites to abandon their cities. But Saul

---

14 Zalewski, "Purpose," 461. Chronicles LXX also lacks "and died," which makes the focus on the death of Saul even clearer, but this is probably only a textual error (see textual note 9).

15 Cf. Zalewski, "Purpose," 461.

16 In 1 Sam 31:6 a prepositional phrase, "on that day," gives the verse an epitomizing force. The Chronicler regularly omits this phrase when it occurs. See De Vries, 118–19. The presence of this prepositional phrase in Chronicles LXX (textual note 10) may mitigate the strength of this observation.

17 Japhet notes that the line continues through Meribbaal the son of Jonathan, and that no royal pretensions are reported of him. In 2 Samuel this son is

called Mephibosheth and he was seriously injured as a child (2 Sam 4:4). David's kindness to him in 2 Sam 9:1-13 also was a way to keep an eye on him. Mephibosheth's servant Ziba claimed that Mephibosheth remained in Jerusalem during the revolt of Absalom because he hoped to regain his grandfather's kingdom (16:1-3), but Ziba was apparently lying (19:24-30; 21:7).

18 Williamson, 93, favors an impersonal subject as in *RSV:* "they had fled." Mosis, *Untersuchungen,* 23, believes all the people fled. Cf. Ackroyd, "The Chronicler as Exegete," *JSOT* 2 (1977) 5.

and his sons died on the battlefield and did not flee. Therefore I believe that the antecedent of "they" is, implicitly, the Israelites who were in the army. In v. 1 they are referred to as "every person of Israel," but that expression in v. 7 designates the residents in the valley.

they abandoned their cities and fled, and the Philistines came and lived in them: Historically this clause, taken virtually unchanged from the *Vorlage,* shows the strong presence of the Philistines in the Esdraelon Valley[19] (and even in Transjordan?) at the end of Saul's reign. Because the plain is unidentified in Chronicles and "all the men of Israel" are mentioned at the beginning of the verse, Mosis concluded that Israel abandoned all their cities ("die Städte Israels ingesamt") creating an "exilic" situation.[20] But Japhet, 224, argues, correctly in my judgment, that the Chronicler has minimized the consequences of the war since only those who were in the valley abandoned their cities to the Philistines.[21] The downfall is limited to Saul and his house. The Chronicler in any case does not suggest that Canaanites had lived in the valley previously. The Israelites' presence is replaced by that of the Philistines.

10:8-12. Benevolent Acts of the People of Jabesh-gilead
10:8-10. Philistines Display Head of Saul in Temple of Dagon

■ **8** *On the next day the Philistines came to plunder the slain:* This new scene is set off from the death of Saul itself by the time designation at the beginning of the verse ("On the next day"). Saul's effort to avoid humiliation at the hands of the Philistines by committing suicide failed, since they administered their humiliation after his death. There may be alliteration in the words פלשתים "Philistines" and לפשט "to plunder."

■ **9** *They stripped him and took his head and his weapons:*

The Chronicler has reworded his *Vorlage* in 1 Sam 31:9, which read: "They cut off his head and stripped off his weapons." The rest of the Chronicler's account, in any case, presupposes that Saul's head had been cut off, and no further attention is given to the stripping of the king. The Chronicler's changes may result from his attempt to bring clarity to the text of his *Vorlage,* since the cutting off of Saul's head played no role later in the account in 1 Samuel 31. Both the Deuteronomistic Historian and the Chronicler focus on the desecration of Saul himself, with no attention given to the bodies of his sons who were also slain.

to spread the good news to their idols and the people: This clause, taken over without change from the *Vorlage,* shows that the Philistines saw both theological and political significance in the defeat of Saul and the Israelites. The only other use of the root בשׂר "spread the good news" in Chronicles is in 1 Chr 16:23, also taken over from his *Vorlage* (Ps 96:2).

■ **10** *They put his armor in the temple of their gods:* The sword of Goliath, according to the Deuteronomistic History, was deposited at the sanctuary of Nob (1 Sam 21:9). The Chronicler likewise has the Philistines place Saul's armor in a sanctuary, and he has replaced the reference to the בית עשתרות "temple of Astarte" in 1 Sam 31:10 with the more generic "temple of their gods." Christian Frevel suggests that the Chronicler could not allow something to exist—such as a goddess—that he did not think was permitted.[22] The divine name Astarte, used in 1 Sam 31:10 as a plural of majesty or excellence (*HALOT* 2:899) appears only five other times in the Bible, all in parts of the Deuteronomistic History not incorporated by the Chronicler.[23] It would also be possible to translate the word "god" in the singular, making the two halves of the verse synonymous.

---

19 See Trude Dothan and Moshe Dothan, *People of the Sea: The Search for the Philistines* (New York: Macmillan, 1992) 172.

20 *Untersuchungen,* 23.

21 So also Ackroyd, "Chronicler as Exegete," 5, who attributes the Chronicler's changes with regard to the valley and Transjordan to his uncertainty about the meaning of the geographic terms. Samuel had predicted in 1 Sam 28:19 that the army of Israel would be handed over to the Philistines.

22 Christian Frevel, "Die Elimination der Göttin aus dem Weltbild des Chronisten," *ZAW* 103 (1991) 270.

See also the Chronicler's replacement of "the carved image of Asherah" (2 Kgs 21:7) by "the carved image of the idol" (2 Chr 33:7).

23 Judg 2:13; 10:6; 1 Sam 7:3, 4; 12:10.

his skull they attached to the temple of Dagon: The *Vorlage* in 1 Sam 31:10 reads, "his corpse they attached to the wall of Beth-shan." For the Chronicler Beth-shan was an Israelite city (1 Chr 7:29; for its location see v. 1) and therefore Saul's head could not be hung up there. The Chronicler implies that the royal bodies were left on the battlefield but states that Saul's skull was placed in Dagon's temple, presumably somewhere in Philistia.[24] In the only other biblical references to Dagon, Samson performs his heroic suicide in the temple of Dagon (Judg 16:23; perhaps at Gaza [MR 099101]), and the temple of Dagon at Ashdod (MR 117129)[25] was the site for the confrontation between the ark of Yahweh and Dagon (1 Sam 5:2-7), where the statue of Dagon fell on its face before the ark of Yahweh, in defeat and in homage. The Philistines had presumably adopted this Mesopotamian and West Semitic deity after their arrival in the land.[26] Japhet, 227–28, points out the graphic similarity in Hebrew between the words "corpse" (גויתו) and "skull" (גלגלתו) and between "temple of Dagon" (בית דגן) and "Beth-shean" (בית שן), as part of the Chronicler's stylistic device of mimicking words in his *Vorlage* even as he changed them. Saul's skull was taken as a trophy to Philistia just as the head of Goliath was taken to Jerusalem after David had killed him (1 Sam 17:50-54).[27] The Philistines, in contrast to Achar in 1 Chr 2:7, did not act unfaithfully with regard to "things put under the ban" but dedicated them to their god. Mosis detects a reversal of the ark narrative in this verse since Saul's head is now placed before Dagon whereas in 1 Sam 5:1-4 Dagon's head and his arms fell off in homage before Yahweh.[28] This reversal will be itself reversed in the Chronicler's version of the ark narrative in 1 Chronicles 13–16.

10:11-12. People of Jabesh-gilead Bury the Bodies of Saul and His Sons

■ **11** *All the inhabitants of Jabesh-gilead:* Since the Chronicler did not include earlier chapters from 1 Samuel, the relationship between Saul and the people of Jabesh-gilead, clarified especially by 1 Samuel 11, where Saul rescued them from Nahash the Ammonite, is not made explicit for the reader, and the reason why they should be the ones to save Saul's honor is not provided. But the reader who did remember Saul's deliverance of the people of Jabesh-gilead would be affected emotionally by the knowledge that these loyal people performed these last rites; those who had been saved by him now deliver him by reverently laying his body to rest.[29] The roles had been reversed. The rejoicing at Saul's coronation after his deliverance of the Jabesh-gileadites (1 Sam 11:14-15) has been turned into lamentation. Jabesh-gilead was probably located on the Wadi el-Yabis in northern Gilead.

■ **12** *and took the corpse of Saul and the corpse of his sons:* The action of the Jabesh-gileadites echoes and reverses the action of the Philistines in v. 9 (both use the verb וישאו for "took"). The Philistines took Saul's head as part of their delirious victory celebration; the Jabesh-gileadites took the corpses of the royal family to give them proper burial. The paralleling of actions probably accounts for the Chronicler's replacement of וילכו כל הלילה ויקחו "they traveled all night and took" from 1 Sam 31:12 with one word: וישאו "they took."

The head and weapons of Saul were inaccessible to the Jabesh-gileadites because these items had been moved to sanctuaries within the territory of the Philistines (v. 10). The term for "corpse," גופת, is used only in this verse in the Bible (an Aramaism according to

---

24 1 Samuel 31 implies that his head was left on the battlefield.

25 Jonathan the Maccabee burned down the temple of Dagon in Azotus = Ashdod (1 Macc 10:83-84).

26 J. J. M. Roberts, *The Earliest Semitic Pantheon* (Baltimore: Johns Hopkins Univ. Press, 1972) 18–19, suggested that Dagon had an underworld role, and an inscription of Shamshi-Adad I connects the temple of the funerary ritual in Terqa with Dagon.

27 Cf. also 2 Sam 4:7-8, where the assassins of Ishbaal bring Ishbaal's severed head to David.

28 *Untersuchungen,* 24–26. In the Tg to this verse, Saul's skull is raised on a pole facing the idol of Dagon.

29 In this chapter the Chronicler presupposes knowledge of Saul's favor to the Jabesh-gileadites (1 Samuel 11), the confrontation of Samuel and Saul at Gilgal (chap. 13), Saul's violation of holy war in his battle with the Amalekites (chap. 15), and the incident of Saul and Samuel with the medium at Endor (chap. 28), although he incorporates none of these stories in his account.

HALOT 1:184) and it replaces the word גויה from Samuel. The Chronicler makes mention of the corpses of both the king and his sons, just as in v. 12 of the *Vorlage*.[30] In the Chronicler's understanding, the corpses were probably still on the battlefield while in Samuel they were hanging on the wall of Beth-shan. The Deuteronomistic story reported additionally that the bodies were burned with fire before burial. This is quite different than capital punishment by fire, which appears in four OT contexts.[31] Japhet, 228, proposes that the Jabesh-gileadites had burned the bodies to avoid pollution from bodies that were hanged (Deut 21:22-23), but again there is a difference between hanging up corpses for ridicule or celebration, as in this case, and hanging someone as a means of execution. The Chronicler may have been as ignorant of the significance of burning the bodies as we are and therefore omitted the reference to it, or he may have omitted it because of revulsion against cremation.[32] With this omission, there was no need to repeat the first word from 1 Sam 31:13 וישאו "they took," since it refers to taking the residue from the burning of the bodies.

They buried their bones under the terebinth at Jabesh: The omission of the burning of the bodies leaves unexplained why the word "corpse" is replaced by "bones." The Jabesh-gileadite burial of Saul was an act of piety (Tob 1:18; 2:8). The Chronicler gives no indication that burial under a tree at Jabesh is to be considered as any kind of judgment.[33] Hence his choice of burial place was dictated by the *Vorlage*. Certainly burial at Jerusalem would have been impossible, even inappropriate, since according to the Chronicler it was only captured by David in the next chapter. It is not clear why the Chronicler replaced אשל "tamarisk"[34] by אלה "terebinth" or

"oak" unless it was to change a rare word for a more common one.

they fasted seven days: Fasting often accompanied periods of mourning. David himself fasted for one day for Saul and Jonathan (2 Sam 1:11-12; cf. 2 Sam 3:35), and he fasted for seven days (2 Sam 12:7-8) when his illegitimate son lay dying.

III. 10:13-14. Theological Reason for Saul's Death

■ **13** *Saul died because of his unfaithfulness whereby he acted unfaithfully against Yahweh:* The *Vorlage* in 1 Samuel 31 offers no judgment at Saul's death, and the Chronicler makes up for this in vv. 13-14. The Chronicler mentions two specific misdeeds of Saul: he did not keep the word of Yahweh and he consulted a medium. The verb מעל "acted unfaithfully" appears thirty-five times in the OT, eleven of which are in Chronicles and always from the Chronicler's pen itself rather than from the *Vorlage*. The noun מעל appears twenty-nine times in the OT, six of which are in Chronicles. The verb and noun are used in a cognate accusative relationship twenty times in the OT and three times in Chronicles.[35] The Chronicler had already indicted the two and one-half Transjordanian tribes for "unfaithfulness" that led to their exile in 1 Chr 5:25. Judah too had been taken into exile because of the "unfaithfulness" of the priests and the people (9:1; cf. 2 Chr 36:14).[36] The word is never used in the accounts of David and Solomon and next appears in 2 Chr 12:2, in the account of Rehoboam.

Mosis has interpreted this verse and the next one typologically, and he argues against any close connection to the sins of Saul mentioned in 1 Samuel.[37] Furthermore, Mosis identified Ahaz as a second Saul just as he considered Hezekiah a second David. As Zalewski has

---

30   Only the skull of Saul was mentioned in 1 Sam 31:10.

31   Gen 38:24; Lev 20:14; 21:9; Josh 7:15, 25.

32   According to 1 Kgs 13:2 priests' bones could be burned on an altar in order to pollute it, and Amos castigates Moab for burning the bones of the king of Edom (Amos 2:1). Diana V. Edleman, "Jabesh-gilead," *ABD* 3:594, suggests that cremation followed by subsequent interment of the remaining bones shows the non-Semitic background of the people of Jabesh-gilead (1 Sam 31:12-13).

33   Contra Mosis, *Untersuchungen,* 27–28.

34   Abraham planted a tamarisk in Beer-sheba (Gen

21:33), and Saul held court at Gibeah under such a tree (1 Sam 22:6).

35   In addition to the present passage, see 2 Chr 28:19 and 36:14.

36   The first reference to unfaithfulness in Chronicles comes already in 1 Chr 2:7, where Achar acted unfaithfully with regard to things put under the ban.

37   *Untersuchungen,* 33–34, 41.

pointed out, however, Ahaz's unfaithfulness is shown by his idolatry and severe damage to the worship of Yahweh (2 Chr 28:19, 22-25), whereas Saul's unfaithfulness is tied to his sins in 1 Samuel 13, 15, and 28.[38] Ahaz also walked in the ways of the kings of Israel, again distinguishing him clearly from Saul. Saul as a paradigm of evil is not a theme that runs throughout the books of Chronicles—the last explicit mention of Saul comes in 1 Chr 26:28. Saul's "unfaithfulness" of course anticipates unfaithfulness that will be practiced by many other kings[39] and by the people as well.[40]

he did not keep the word of Yahweh: The only exact parallel in Chronicles is 2 Chr 34:21, where Josiah confesses: "Our ancestors did not keep the word of Yahweh," with the result that the wrath of Yahweh had been poured out on them. Josiah based this conclusion on what he had read from "the words of the law" (34:19) and "all that is written in this book" (34:21). While Mosis is correct that "not keeping the word of Yahweh" is a frequent motif in Deuteronomy and Psalm 119, this hardly justifies interpreting v. 13 abstractly, without any reference to the Saul traditions in 1 Samuel. In addition to the incident with the medium at Endor,[41] Saul's disobedience toward the word of Yahweh might be an allusion to his inappropriate sacrifice in 1 Sam 13:13-14 (because Saul had not "kept" the commandment of Yahweh he was to lose his kingship),[42] his disobedience in sparing the animals of the Amalekites in 1 Samuel 15 (cf. vv. 1-3 with vv. 23, 26), or even his killing of the priests of Nob (1 Sam 22:18-19).[43] While keeping the word of Yahweh in Deuteronomy resulted in life, rest, and possession of the land, observance of God's commandment is rewarded in similar terms in Chronicles, and failure to observe divine commands results in foreign invasion and exile.[44]

consulted a medium: This second accusation against Saul must refer to the incident with the medium at Endor in 1 Samuel 28. That account in its entirety would have caused the Chronicler some difficulty, since we are told there that Saul consulted the medium only after he had attempted to inquire of Yahweh by every other possible means, but Yahweh had given no dreams to Saul nor had he revealed his will through the Urim or prophets (v. 6). Elsewhere the Chronicler insists: "If you seek him [God], he will be inquired of by you" (2 Chr 15:2).[45] Inquiring of a medium at a time of military danger seems to be comparable in the Chronicler's judgment to reliance on military alliances, which he uniformly rejected for theological reasons.[46] There also seems to be a negative pun in this line: Saul (שָׁאוּל) inquired of (לִשְׁאוֹל) a medium.[47] The conflation of the roots דרשׁ and שָׁאַל in this line (see textual note 23) also anticipates the charge of not "seeking" Yahweh in the next verse. As Zalewski has pointed out, three of the passages in Samuel dealing with Saul's sinfulness, to which the Chronicler alludes, also point forward to David replacing Saul as king (1 Sam 13:13-15; 15:26-28; and 28:16-19).[48] This connection between the sins of Saul and the transfer of kingship to David is obviously central to the purpose of the Chronicler, as the next verse makes clear.

■ **14** *He did not seek Yahweh:* Here the Chronicler shifts from accusations against Saul that might be linked to

---

38   Zalewski, "Purpose," 452.

39   Uzziah (2 Chr 26:16, 18), Ahaz (28:19, 22; 29:19), and Manasseh (33:19).

40   1 Chr 5:25; 2 Chr 12:2; 29:6; 30:7; 36:14 (including the leaders of the priests).

41   1 Samuel 28 has links forward to the death of Saul (cf. vv. 16-19).

42   Cf. 1 Sam 10:8, where Samuel commanded Saul to wait for him at Gilgal.

43   Tg already sensed this allusion (McIvor, *Targum*, 84–85): "the word of the Lord which he had not observed *when he waged war against those of the house of Amalek,* and, as well, because he had consulted *necromancers, seeking instruction from them;* but he had not sought *instruction* from *before* the Lord *through the Urim and the Thummim, because he had killed the priests who were at Nob.*" Zalewski, "Pur-

pose," 460, finds an allusion to 1 Sam 15:28 and 16:1-13 in 1 Chr 11:3.

44   See 2 Chr 12:1, 4; 13:11 and 13-18; 14:4-5; 33:8; 34:2; 36:16. Cf. the discussion of the doctrine of retribution in the Introduction.

45   Tg sensed this difficulty and added that Saul had not inquired in the proper way, i.e., through Urim and Thummim, since that was impossible once Saul had killed the priests at Nob, who were in charge of these devices. Cf. McIvor, *Targum,* 85.

46   See also the indictment of Manasseh in 2 Chr 33:6 for dealing with mediums and wizards. Cf. Lev 19:31; 20:6, 27; Deut 18:11.

47   Cf. the puns contrasting Samuel and Saul in 1 Sam 1:28, and Klein, *1 Samuel,* 10–11.

48   "Purpose," 458–59.

specific incidents in Saul's life to a general indictment of his entire life. De Vries, 121, points out that in older writings דרש "seek" refers narrowly to seeking an oracle from Yahweh, but later it connotes devoting oneself to Yahweh. Saul should not have "sought" a medium (v. 13); instead, he should have "sought" Yahweh.[49] "Not seeking Yahweh" is synonymous with being unfaithful. Saul's neglect of the ark could also be seen as evidence for not seeking Yahweh.[50] The priests of Nob, whom Saul killed, were the national custodians of the ark (1 Sam 22:16-19).

and so he [Yahweh] killed him: The Chronicler's doctrine of retribution requires that unfaithfulness and "not seeking Yahweh" be punished. Saul's defeat by the Philistines and his suicide, therefore, are transformed into Yahweh's act of judgment upon him.[51] This interpretation of Saul's death was already adumbrated in 1 Sam 28:19: "Tomorrow you and your sons will fall at the same time, and Yahweh will also give the camp of Israel into the hand of the Philistines."[52] Consulting a medium is identified as a capital crime in Lev 20:6.

and transferred the kingdom to David the son of Jesse: This is the first mention of David within the Chronicler's narrative,[53] and the story of David's reign will occupy the rest of 1 Chronicles. The Chronicler's theological observation about Yahweh giving the kingship to David would not conflict with reports in 1 Samuel about the prophet Samuel anointing David or about many individuals and groups endorsing his election as king. But those earlier accounts in 1 Samuel, and in large part in 2 Samuel 1–5, are also replete with other, more troubling stories of David's quest for the monarchy, and with his defensive

assertions that he was not involved in this or that questionable practice. The change from the kingship of Saul to that of David is as momentous for the Chronicler as the change from the age of the united monarchy under David and Solomon to the divided monarchy thereafter, and both of them were "turns of affairs" brought about by God (2 Chr 10:15).[54] Japhet, 230, may well be right that for the Chronicler there was no transformation of the political system at this time, but I believe she downplays the momentous character of this verse in seeing here only a transition from Saul, who failed, to David, whose kingdom would be established forever.

Conclusion

What happened in the transition from Saul to David in the Chronicler's account was not Realpolitik or even something as tragic, selfish, and individualistic as a desperate act of suicide. No, this was divine retribution at work and, even more, divine providence. Yahweh's endorsement of David's kingship is soon ratified in the Chronicler's narrative by various segments of all Israel (see 1 Chr 11:1-3), and David and his son Solomon, under divine guidance, will inaugurate, define, and legitimize the temple cult, which is the Chronicler's central passion and to which he invites his readers so enthusiastically.[55] Verse 14 is a theological interpretation of the people's installation of David as king in 11:1-3. These subsequent human actions were merely a carrying out on the human plane what the word of Yahweh had already accomplished (11:3; 12:23).

---

49   According to 1 Sam 28:6, Yahweh did not answer Saul when he "inquired" (שאל) of him. Cf. 2 Chr 14:3 (4), where Asa commanded Judah to seek Yahweh and to keep the law and the commandment. Johnstone, 1:131, notes that 43 of 163 uses of דרש are in Chronicles.

50   "We did not seek it [the ark] in the days of Saul" (1 Chr 13:3). Note also that Michal the daughter of Saul continued this sin of Saul by despising David, who was leaping and dancing *before the ark* (1 Chr 15:29). Johnstone, 1:132, points out that the Chronicler sometimes delays the full reason for his condemnation to a later chapter. Hence David's own fault in 1 Chronicles 13 is not unexplained until 15:13-15, and the reason why he is forbidden to build the temple in chap. 17 becomes fully clear only in 22:7-10.

51   Zalewski, "Purpose," 465, errs, in my judgment, when he concludes that the Chronicler was trying to exonerate David from complicity in the death of Saul because of traditions preserved in the tribe of Benjamin. That may have been an issue for the author of the History of David's Rise or even 1 Samuel 31, but certainly no longer at the time of the Chronicler.

52   Klein, *1 Samuel*, 268.

53   But see the genealogical references to David in 1 Chr 2:15 and 3:1 and the commentary there.

54   Cf. the verb ויסב in 1 Chr 10:14 with the noun נסבה in 2 Chr 10:15. Cf. also 1 Chr 12:24 (23).

55   For reflections on how modern religious leaders might preach on such a text see Klaus Koch, "Das Verhältnis von Exegese und Verkündigung anhand eines Chroniktextes," *ThLZ* 90 (1965) 659–70.

11

Translation

1/ Then all Israel gathered together[1] to David at Hebron, saying,[2] "We are your bone and your flesh. 2/ Formerly even when Saul was king, you were[3] the one who brought out and brought in Israel, and Yahweh your God[4] said to you: "It is you who should shepherd my people Israel, and you will be prince over my people[5] Israel." 3/ All the elders of Israel came to the king[6] at Hebron, and David[7] made for them a covenant at Hebron before Yahweh, and they anointed David king over Israel according to the word of Yahweh by the agency of Samuel.

4/ David and all Israel[8] went to Jerusalem, that is, Jebus, and there were the Jebusites, the inhabitants of the land. 5/ The inhabitants of Jebus said to David, "You cannot come here," but David captured the fortress of Zion, that is, the city of David. 6/ David said, "Whoever is the first to smite the Jebusites will be head and commander." And Joab the son of Zeruiah went up first, and he became a head. 7/ David dwelled in the fortress; therefore they call it the city of David. 8/ He built[9] the city[10] round about from the Millo and all around,[11] while Joab repaired/kept alive the rest of the city.[12] 9/ David constantly grew greater and Yahweh of hosts[13] was with him.

10/ These are the heads of David's warriors who gave him strong support in his kingdom, together with[14] all Israel, to make him king, according to the word of Yahweh concerning Israel. 11/ These are the number[15] of the warriors who belonged to David: Jeshbaal,[16] son of[17] a Hachmonite,[18] was head over the Thirty;[19] he wielded his spear[20] over three[21] hundred men whom he killed at one time. 12/ After him was Eleazar son of Dodo,[22] the Ahohite. He was included among the three mighty men.[23] 13/ He was[24] with David at Pas-dammim[25] when the Philistines were gathering there for battle.[26] A portion of the field was full of barley.[27] The people had fled from the Philistines, 14/ but he[28] took his stand in the middle of the portion, he[29] defended it, and smote[30] the Philistines; Yahweh brought victory[31] by a great act of salvation.

15/ Three[32] of the thirty chiefs went down from[33] the rock[34] to David at the cave of Adullam, and the army[35] of the Philistines was camping in the valley of Rephaim. 16/ David was at that time in the stronghold, and the garrison[36] of the Philistines was at that time at Bethlehem. 17/ David said longingly, "Oh, that someone would give me water to drink from the cistern[37] at Bethlehem that is at the gate." 18/ The Three broke through the camp of the Philistines, and they drew water from the well at Bethlehem that is at the

1   ויקבצו; Chronicles LXX and 2 Sam 5:1 ויבא "came." Is Chronicles MT a secondary change, or has Chronicles LXX been corrected to Samuel? In readings discussed in textual notes 2, 9-10, 13, 16-17, 24-25, 32, 34, 38, 40, 47, 51, 53-55, 57, 62, 67, 69, 72, 74, 78, and 80, Chronicles presupposes a text of Samuel other than MT.

2   לאמר; cf. 2 Sam 5:1 4QSam[a], LXX[MNrell], OL, Vg. Samuel MT ויאמרו לאמר; Samuel LXX ויאמרו. Chronicles preserves one of the two synonymous readings in Samuel; Samuel MT is conflate.

3   In contrast to 2 Sam 5:2, this verb is not explicit in Chronicles. Johnstone, 1:143, suggests that this implies "you were and still are the one."

4   אלהיך; lacking in Chronicles LXX and 2 Sam 5:2.

5   עמי; lacking in Chronicles LXX and 2 Sam 5:2.

6   אל המלך. Rudolph, 94, proposed להמלכו "to make him king"; see the commentary.

7   One Hebrew MS, LXX, Syr add המלך "king"; cf. 2 Sam 5:3.

8   דויד וכל ישראל; Chronicles LXX המלך ואנשיו "the king and his men," a correction to 2 Sam 5:6.

9   ויבן. The subject is implied through the verb form in MT; cf. 2 Sam 5:9 LXX, 4QSam[a]. Samuel MT ויבן דוד "David built."

10 ויבן העיר; cf 2 Sam 5:9 LXX[L]. 4QSam[a], Samuel LXX: ויבנה עיר "and he built [it; or is this just a long form of the *wāw* consecutive?] a city" (same letters as LXX[L], but different word division). Samuel MT lacks "city": ויבן דוד סביב "And David built round about."

11 ועד הסביב. Rudolph, 94, proposes an original reading עד הבית "toward the palace" (cf. 2 Sam 7:9), which became corrupted to the reading in Chronicles MT. Japhet, 242, translates Chronicles MT "(from the Millo) outward." Chronicles LXX omits "from the Millo and all around" because of homoioteleuton.

12 ויואב יחיה את שאר העיר; LXX "and he [David] fought and took the city." Allen, *Greek Chronicles*, 1:130, suggests that the translator may have read the text as ויארב ויחח את העיר. A few Hebrew MSS (cf. Syr, Arab.) read העם "the people" instead of העיר "the city."

13 ויהוה צבאות; cf. 2 Sam 5:10 LXX. Samuel MT ויהוה אלהי צבאות "And Yahweh God of hosts."

14 עם; Syr, Arab., Vg: על "over."

15 ואלה מספר; 2 Sam 23:8 אלה שמות "These are the names." The Chronicler substituted "number" for "names," but awkwardly left the plural demonstrative pronoun, apparently construing the noun as a collective. Sometimes the Chronicler includes "these are the names" from his *Vorlage* (1 Chr 6:2 [17]; 14:4) and sometimes he omits the expression (1:29, 35, 51).

16 ישבעל; cf. Chronicles LXX (Ιεσεβαδα from Ιεσε-

gate. They picked it up and brought it to David, but David refused to drink it. He poured it out to Yahweh. 19/ He said, "Far be it from me and from my God to do this. Am I to drink[38] the blood of these men at the risk of their lives? At the risk of their lives they brought it." He refused to drink it. The three warriors did these things.

20/ Abshai[39] the brother of Joab[40] was head of the Thirty;[41] he wielded his spear against three hundred and killed them, but he did not get a place[42] among the Three. 21/ He was honored among the Thirty,[43] and he became their commander; but he did not enter among the Three.

22/ Benaiah son of Jehoiada was a hero[44] from Kabzeel, a doer of great deeds; he killed two[45] warriors[46] of Moab, and he went down and killed a lion in a pit on a day when snow had fallen. 23/ He killed the Egyptian,[47] a man of stature,[48] five cubits tall. In the hand of the Egyptian was a spear like a weaver's beam.[49] But Benaiah went down to him with a staff, and snatched the spear from the hand of the Egyptian and slew him with his own spear. 24/ These are the things Benaiah the son of Jehoiada did, and he did not get a place[50] among the three mighty men. 25/ He was renowned among the Thirty, but he did not become part of the Three. David set him over his bodyguard.

26/ The valiant warriors were Asahel the brother of Joab, Elhanan the son of Dodo from Bethlehem,[51] 27/ Shammoth[52] the Harodite,[53] Helez the Pelonite,[54] 28/ Ira the son of Ikkesh the Tekoite, Abiezer the Anathothite, 29/ Sibbecai[55] the Hushathite, Ilai[56] the Ahohite, 30/ Mahrai the Netophathite, Heled[57] the son of Baanah the Netophathite, 31/ Ithai[58] the son of Ribai from Gibeah of the Benjaminites, Benaiah[59] the Pirathonite,[60] 32/ Hurai[61] from the brooks of Gaash, Abiel[62] the Arbathite, 33/ Azmaveth the Bahurimite,[63] Eliahba the Shaalbonite, 34/ Hashem[64] the Gizonite,[65] Jonathan[66] the son of[67] Shagee[68] the Hararite, 35/ Ahiam the son of Sachar[69] the Hararite,[70] Eliphal[71] the son of Ur,[72] 36/ Hepher[73] the Mecherathite,[74] Ahijah the Pelonite,[75] 37/Hezro[76] the Carmelite, Naarai the son of Ezbai,[77] 38/ Joel the brother of Nathan,[78] Mibhar[79] the son of Hagri,[80] 39/ Zelek the Ammonite, Naharai the Beerothite,[81] the weapon carrier[82] of Joab the son of Zeruiah, 40/ Ira the Ithrite, Gareb the Ithrite, 41/ Uriah the Hittite,[83]

Zabad the son of Ahlai, 42/ Adina the son of Shiza the Reubenite, a leader of the Reubenites and thirty with him, 43/ Hanan the son of Maacah, and Joshaphat the Mithnite, 44/ Uzzi the Ashterathite, Shama and Jeiel the sons of Hotham the Aroerite, 45/

$\beta\alpha\alpha\lambda$) and 2 Sam 23:8 LXX[L] and OL. Chronicles MT has ישבעם "Jashobeam" (cf. 1 Chr 27:2). Was "Jeshbaal" changed to "Jashobeam" because a scribe took offense at the mention of Baal in this name? 2 Sam 23:8 MT ישב בשבת "Josheb-basshebeth"; Samuel LXX $\iota\epsilon\beta o\sigma\vartheta\epsilon$ = ישבשת. See also textual note 2 to 1 Chr 27:2.

17 בן; cf. 2 Sam 23:8 LXX[L]. Lacking in Samuel MT and LXX.

18 McCarter, *II Samuel*, 489, suggests that בן החמני "son of a Hachmonite" is a conflation of החמני "the Hachmonite" (which he reconstructs in 2 Sam 23:8) and בן החמן "the son of Hachmon." The same patronymic occurs, however, in 1 Chr 27:32.

19 השלושים with Chr K, LXX, Syr, Vg; Chronicles Q השלישים "officers." It is difficult to choose between these readings. Cf. 2 Sam 23:8 MT השלשי "the third part" (of the army?). 2 Sam 23:8 LXX[L] "the Three."

20 עורר את חניתו. For the corresponding, corrupt text in 2 Sam 23:8 (עדינו העצנו "Adino the Ezenite") see McCarter, *II Samuel*, 489–90.

21 2 Sam 23:8 MT "eight"; Samuel LXX[L], Josephus *Ant.* 7.308: "nine." See C. T. Begg, "The Exploits of David's Heroes according to Josephus," *LASBF* 47 (1997) 167.

22 דודו; cf. 2 Sam 23:9 Q. Chronicles LXX and Samuel K: דדי "Dodai."

23 הגברים; cf. 2 Sam 23:9 LXX[L]. The initial *hê* was lost by haplography in Samuel MT K, but retained by Q.

24 הוא היה. Cf. 2 Sam 23:9 LXX[L]; lacking in Samuel MT.

25 בפס דמים; cf. 2 Sam 23:9 LXX[L]. The place name was lost in Samuel MT by haplography, although Samuel MT retains the word בחרפם "when they defied them," which was lost in the Chronicles' MS tradition. See McCarter, *II Samuel*, 490.

26 A long section of text from 2 Sam 23:9bβ-11bα is lost in Chronicles because of haplography. A scribe skipped from "the Philistines were gathering there for battle" in 2 Sam 23:9 to the end of "the Philistines gathered together at Lehi" in 2 Sam 23:11. It is not clear whether this haplography happened in the text of Samuel used by the Chronicler or in the text of Chronicles itself.

27 שעורים; Chronicles LXX[L], 2 Sam 23:11: עדשים "lentils." There is no basis for choosing between these graphically similar readings. Chronicles Tg conflates the two readings: "There was a plot of ground, full of crops, half of it in lentils, half of it in barley." Cf. McIvor, *Targum*, 87.

28 ויתצב with Chronicles LXX, Arab., 2 Sam 23:12; Chronicles MT plural. Hence *NRSV* translates "but he and David."

29 ויצילה with Chronicles LXX, Arab., 2 Sam 23:12; Chronicles MT plural.

Jediael the son of Shimri, and Joha his brother the Tizite, 46/ Eliel the Mahavite,[84] Jeribai and Joshaviah the sons of Elnaam, and Ithmah the Moabite, 47/ Eliel and Obed and Jaasiel the Mezobaite.[85]

30 וֹיָדְ with Chronicles LXX, Arab., 2 Sam 23:12; Chronicles MT plural.

31 וַיֹּושַׁע; Chronicles LXX, Syr, Arab., 2 Sam 23:12: וַיַּעַשׂ "performed (a great act of salvation)." Japhet, "Interchanges," 41–42, suggests that Chronicles MT arose by metathesis because of the noun תְּשׁוּעָה that follows.

32 שְׁלוֹשָׁה. Cf. 2 Sam 23:13 LXX, Syr, Tg, Vg; Samuel MT שְׁלֹשִׁים "thirty."

33 מֵעַל; MT עַל.

34 הַצֻּר, also attested by 2 Sam 23:13 LXX[L]. 2 Samuel MT קָצִיר "[at] harvest [time]."

35 וּמַחֲנֵה; 2 Sam 23:13 וְחַיַּת "the band."

36 וּנְצִיב; 2 Sam 23:14 וּמַצַּב "outpost."

37 מִבּוֹר; 2 Sam 23:15 מִבְּאֵר "well." Curtis and Madsen, 189, suggest that the change was intentional since no well is found at the gate of Bethlehem today.

38 אֶשְׁתֶּה; retained in 2 Sam 23:17 LXX, but lost in Samuel MT. For a possible reconstruction of the original Samuel text, see McCarter, *II Samuel*, 491.

39 וְאַבְשַׁי; cf. 1 Chr 2:16 MT; 18:12; 19:11, 15. Tg, Vg, and 2 Sam 23:18: וַאֲבִישַׁי "Abishai."

40 יוֹאָב; cf. 2 Sam 23:18 LXX[L]. Samuel MT, LXX add בֶּן צְרוּיָה "the son of Zeruiah."

41 הַשְּׁלוֹשִׁים with Syr; MT הַשְּׁלוֹשָׁה "the Three." 2 Sam 23:18 K שָׁלִשִׁי "the third"; Sam Q "the Three"; 2 Hebrew MSS "the Thirty."

42 וְלֹא שָׂם "he was not set" (note revocalization of the second word, following *BHS*). Chronicles MT וְלֹא שֵׁם "there was not [to him] a name." Many Hebrew MSS, Q, the versions, and 2 Sam 23:18 (שֵׁם) וְלוֹ "he had a name." My translation is supported by v. 21.

43 מִן הַשְּׁלוֹשִׁים with Syr; MT מִן הַשְּׁלוֹשָׁה "among the three." MT also adds בַּשְּׁנַיִם, which, according to Rudolph, 98, means "by the second three one should read thirty." In any case it seems to be secondary and corrupt. McCarter, *II Samuel*, 491, notes that 2 Samuel LXX[L] reflects מִשְׁנִים, derived from מִן הַשְּׁלוֹשָׁה "above the Three." The reading "Thirty" is supported by v. 25 (cf. also 1 Chr 27:6).

44 בֶּן אִישׁ חַיִל. The Chronicler copied this conflate expression (a mixture of בֶּן חַיִל [cf. 1 Sam 14:52] and אִישׁ חַיִל [cf. 1 Kgs 1:42]) from 2 Sam 23:20. Samuel LXX, however, lacks a translation for בֶּן.

45 בְּנֵי. 2 Sam 23:20 LXX and LXX[L] add "sons of." בְּנֵי was lost by haplography after שְׁנֵי in 2 Samuel MT and in the text taken over by Chronicles. Cf. Driver, *Notes*, 368.

46 אֲרִאֵלִי with *BHS*, Rudolph, 98–99; and *HALOT* 1:82, following Syr and Tg. The etymology of this word might suggest a translation "lion of god." The word אראל appears in the Mesha inscription, *KAI* 1:33 (no. 181), l. 12, where it is often translated "hearth." MT אֲרִיאֵל "Ariel" (a proper noun). For this name see Ezra 8:16, where Ariel was a member of a delegation sent by Ezra to Iddo.

47 את האיש המצרי; cf. 2 Sam 23:21 LXX. Samuel MT lacks the definite article on both words.

48 איש מדה. 2 Sam 23:21 Q איש מראה "a man of [imposing] appearance" (McCarter, *II Samuel*, 491); cf. Chronicles LXX ἄνδρα ὁρατόν.

49 כמנור ארגים; cf. 2 Sam 23:21 LXX "like the wood of a ladder," which McCarter, *II Samuel*, 491, reconstructs tentatively as כעץ מעלה; the phrase is lacking in Samuel MT. This gloss in Chronicles is based on 1 Sam 17:7 or 2 Sam 21:19, and may have been added already in the text of Samuel used by the Chronicler.

50 שים; cf. textual note 42 in v. 20. MT שם "name."

51 מבית לחם; cf. also 2 Sam 23:24 LXX^L ἐκ Βαιϑλεεμ. Samuel MT lacks the preposition. Samuel LXX ἐν Βαιϑλεεμ.

52 שמות; 2 Sam 23:25 שמה "Shammah."

53 החררי, with 2 Sam 23:25; Chronicles MT החרורי "Harorite." Chronicles LXX ο Αδι. Samuel MT also adds "Elika the Harodite" after "the Harodite," but this was lost by homoioteleuton (already in Samuel LXX and Syr) and appears in no textual witnesses for Chronicles.

54 הפלוני; cf. 2 Sam 23:26 LXX^L. Samuel MT הפלטי "Paltite."

55 סבכי; cf. 2 Sam 23:27 LXX^L. Samuel MT מבני "Mebunnai."

56 עילי; 2 Sam 23:28 צלמון "Zalmon." Rudolph, 100, proposed that צילי "Zilai," a short form of Zalmon, was corrupted to עילי "Ilai." There is no indication that Chronicles ever read anything but "Ilai."

57 חלד; cf. 2 Sam 23:29 LXX^L αλλαν from αλδαν (McCarter, *II Samuel*, 492). Cf. 1 Chr 27:15 חלדי "Heldai." 2 Sam 23:29 MT חלב "Heleb."

58 איתי; 2 Sam 23:29 אתי "Ittai."

59 בניה; 2 Sam 23:30 בניהו.

60 הפרעתני. The definite article is lacking in 2 Sam 23:30.

61 חורי; 2 Sam 23:30 חדי "Hiddai."

62 אביאל; cf. 2 Sam 23:31 LXX^MN. 2 Sam 23:31 MT אבי עלבון "Abialbon."

63 הבחורמי, with *BHS*, McCarter, *II Samuel*, 492; MT הבחרומי "the Baharumite." 2 Sam 23:31 הברחמי "the Barhumite."

64 השם. MT prefaces this word with בני, which is a dittography of the last three letters of the preceding word השעלבני. This dittography is already present in 2 Sam 23:32 MT, but lacking in Samuel LXX^L. 2 Sam 23:32 reads the name as ישן "Jashen."

65 הגזוני. *BHS* makes two conjectural proposals: הגמזוני ("the Gimzonite"; cf. Karl Elliger, "Die dreissig Helden Davids," *PJ* 31 [1935] 53–54) or הגוני "the Gunite" (cf. LXX^AL).

66 יונתן; 2 Sam 23:32 יהונתן.

67 בן; cf. 2 Sam 23:32 LXX^L. Lacking in Samuel MT.

68 שגא. 2 Sam 23:33 שמה "Shammah." Shagee may be a

combination of שמה "Shammah" and אגא "Agee" from 2 Sam 23:11. See Elliger, "Dreissig Helden Davids," 35, n. 5.

69 שכר; cf. 2 Sam 23:33 LXX^L. Samuel MT שרר "Sharar."

70 ההררי, the gentilic of the preceding name Shagee; for 2 Sam 23:33 האררי see McCarter, *II Samuel*, 493.

71 אליפל; 2 Sam 23:34 אליפלט "Eliphelet."

72 אור; cf. 2 Sam 23:34 LXX^L. 2 Sam 23:34 MT אחסבי בן "Ahasbai, the son of."

73 חפר. An extra name in Chronicles, resulting from textual corruption. The Chronicler apparently deciphered אהסבי from the *Vorlage* as אור חפר. See Rudolph, 102.

74 המכרתי, a secondary spelling of the gentilic, which it shares with 2 Sam 23:34 LXX^L; Samuel MT בן המעכתי "the son of the Maacathite."

75 אחיה הפלני. The name and the patronymic are corruptions of אחיתפל הגלני "Ahithophel the Gilonite" from 2 Sam 23:34 (McCarter, *II Samuel*, 493). "Eliam the son of," which precedes Ahitophel in 2 Samuel was lost accidentally in Chronicles.

76 חזרו; cf. 2 Sam 23:35 K. Chronicles LXX, Syr, Arab. presuppose חזרי "Hezrai," with Samuel Q.

77 נערי בן אזבי; 2 Sam 23:35 MT פערי הארבי "Paarai the Arbite."

78 יואל אחי נתן; cf. 2 Sam 23:36 LXX^L. Samuel MT יגאל בן נתן "Igal son of Nathan."

79 מבחר. 2 Sam 23:36 MT מצבה "from Zobah," modifying Igal the son of Nathan (see the previous note). McCarter, *II Samuel*, 493, reconstructs a title רב צבא "commander of the army" for the text of Samuel. He proposes that מבחר "Mibhar" is miswritten from מבחרי "elite troops" and considers this an ancient variant of his own reconstruction. In any case the Chronicler here has an additional name.

80 בן הגרי. Cf. 2 Sam 23:36 LXX^L. Samuel MT בני הגדי "Bani the Gadite." The original reading may be בני הגרי "the sons of Hagri."

81 Read הבארתי with 2 Sam 23:37. Chronicles MT הברתי.

82 נשא כלי; cf. 2 Sam 23:37 Q; Chronicles LXX^L, Tg.: plural (נשאי), as in 2 Sam 23:37 K.

83 Here 2 Sam 23:39 adds: כל שלשים ושבעה "Thirty-seven in all."

84 המחרים. Rudolph, 103, finds this name uninterpretable and suggests emending to the המחנימי "Mahnaimite" or המחני "the Mahnite" (from Mahanaim, east of the Jordan).

85 המצבאי. Rudolph, 103, finds this name uninterpretable and thinks it is a conflation of מצבה "from Zobah" and הצבתי "the Zobathite." Cf. Goettsberger, 107.

Structure

The materials in 1 Chronicles 11 may be outlined as follows:

I. 11:1-9. Early days of David's rule (2 Sam 5:1-3, 6-10)
   A. 11:1-3. David anointed as king over Israel at Hebron (2 Sam 5:1-3)
   B. 11:4-9. David captures Jerusalem (2 Sam 5:6-10)[1]
II. 11:10-25. Heroic acts of David's mighty men (2 Sam 23:8-25)[2]
   A. 11:10. Introduction to the heads of the warriors (without *Vorlage*)
   B. 11:11-14. Two heroes, Jeshbaal and Eleazar (2 Sam 23:8-12)
   C. 11:15-19. Exploits of anonymous threesome (2 Sam 23:13-17)
   D. 11:20-25. Two additional heroes (2 Sam 23:18-23)
III. 11:26-41a. Primary list of mighty men (2 Sam 23:24-39)
IV. 11:41b-47. Additional list of mighty men (without *Vorlage*)

The vast majority of this material is taken from 2 Samuel but with significant omissions, rearrangements, and additions. There are numerous textual prob-lems with many of the names and with the numbers conventionally translated as "three" or "thirty." All of 2 Samuel 1–4 is missing from Chronicles, with its tales of the rival kingship of Ishbaal, the son of Saul, and David's initial rule over the tribe of Judah from Hebron.[3] The political infighting in this period led to the murders of the soldiers Asahel and Abner, and the execution of an Amalekite, who claimed he had killed Saul. In this section of 2 Samuel, David also delivered a moving lament over the deaths of Saul and Jonathan (2 Sam 1:19-27). The general picture in the first chapters of 2 Samuel is that of a highly divided country and of a David whose hold on the throne is contested. The Chronicler had asserted that the entire house of Saul fell on Mount Gilboa and that the kingdom was transferred immediately to David (1 Chr 10:1-14), making his omission of 2 Samuel 1–4 understandable. David faced no opposition in Chronicles from Saul's heirs or anyone else.

The materials in 2 Sam 23:8-39 are part of a complicated appendix to the books of Samuel (2 Samuel 21–24), coming between the Last Words of David in 2 Sam 23:1-7 (not included in Chronicles), and the story of the failed census in 2 Samuel 24//1 Chronicles 21. The relationship of the men recounted in 2 Sam 23:8-39 to the Three and the Thirty has been much discussed in recent years, although this is a problem more for the list

---

1   2 Sam 5:4, giving David's age at his accession and the overall length of his rule, is not included in Chronicles, although similar information appears at 1 Chr 29:27//1 Kgs 2:11. A somewhat different version of 2 Sam 5:5, giving the length of David's reigns in Hebron and Jerusalem, appears in 1 Chr 3:4. There it is appended to 3:1-3, a list of David's children born in Hebron (= 2 Sam 3:2-5), and it precedes 1 Chr 3:5-9, a list of David's children born in Jerusalem (= 2 Sam 5:13-16). This latter list also appears a second time in 1 Chr 14:3-7. The text of 4QSam[a] and the OL seem not to have contained 2 Sam 5:4-5, and this probably accounts for its absence from Chronicles. See McCarter, *II Samuel*, 131; and McKenzie, *Chronicler's Use*, 42–43. David A. Glatt, *Chronological Displacement in Biblical and Related Literatures* (SBLDS 139; Atlanta: Scholars Press, 1993) 174–78, notes that David's conquest and settlement of Jerusalem (1 Chr 11:4-9) should follow, rather than precede, the account of his coronation at Hebron in 11:10–12:40. He proposes that

in order to give two "firsts" to David's kingship—the conquering of Jerusalem and the transfer of the ark there—the Chronicler furnished a description of the coronation twice, in v. 3 and in 12:39-41 (38-40).

2   Christopher T. Begg, "The Exploits of David's Heroes According to Josephus," *LASBF* 47 (1997) 139–69, demonstrates that Josephus used both Kings and Chronicles and that his textual affinities were with LXX.

3   David's years in Hebron are noted in Chronicles in a list of his children born there (1 Chr 3:1-3) and in regnal summaries (29:27; 3:4)

in Samuel than for the list as it is redacted in Chronicles. A central question in Samuel has been how a series of nouns derived from the root שלש should be translated.[4] No consensus has emerged from this discussion.

The heroic acts of David's mighty men in Chronicles (section II) consist of a series of three anecdotes (II.B-D; vv. 11-25) introduced by a verse authored by the Chronicler (II.A; v. 10).[5] Verses 11-14 (cf. 2 Sam 23:8-12) present anecdotes about two heroic fighters, Jeshbaal and Eleazar, compared to three fighters in 2 Samuel. A textual loss at this point in Chronicles has reduced the number of heroes and assigned the deeds of the third (Shamma) to the second (Eleazar). While Jeshbaal and Eleazar were probably part of a group known as "the Three" originally, the first man, Jeshbaal, is called the head of the Thirty in Chronicles (v. 11), and the second, Eleazar, is said to be among the "three mighty men" (v. 12). Verses 15-19 (cf. 2 Sam 23:13-17) recount the efforts by an anonymous threesome to get water from David's hometown of Bethlehem, although David refuses to accept their gift of water. Verses 20-25 (cf. 2 Sam 23:18-23) contain information on two additional heroes. Verses 20-21 describe Abshai, who was chief or commander of the Thirty[6] (cf. Jeshbaal above) and honored among the Thirty, but who was not included in the Three. Verses 22-25 describe Benaiah, who also was honored among the Thirty, but who also was not included in the Three.

The primary list of the mighty men (section III) had been joined to the series of anecdotes about the heroic acts of David's mighty men already in the text of 2 Samuel. In distinction from 2 Samuel, the Chronicler calls them "valiant warriors" (v. 26) and omits the words "among the Thirty" (2 Sam 23:24) after the first of these valiant warriors, Asahel. In neither 2 Samuel nor in 1 Chronicles are there exactly thirty men.

Section IV (vv. 41b-47), the additional list of mighty men, is new material that is not contained in the *Vorlage*

---

4   Elliger, "Dreissig Helden Davids," 69–75, proposed that 2 Sam 23:24b-35 was a list of twenty-three men in a bodyguard called the Thirty, built on an Egyptian model, that formed when David was at Ziklag, while the seven men listed in vv. 36-39 joined David during his reign at Hebron. Similarly, Benjamin Mazar, "The Military Elite of King David," *VT* 13 (1963) 310–20, dated 2 Samuel 23 to David's reign at Hebron and proposed that it consisted of two groups of military elite. One was a list of thirty heroes, including the Three, and the other was a group of seven officers over foreign mercenary units (p. 319). B. A. Mastin, "Was the šāliš the Third Man in the Chariot?" in *Studies in the Historical Books of the Old Testament* (ed. J. A. Emerton; VTSup 30; Leiden: Brill, 1979) 125–54, believed that the word שליש described officers of the "third rank" in the armies of Israel. The only persons who outranked them were officers of the second rank (officials around Solomon) and the king. Nadav Na'aman, "The List of David's Officers (šālīšîm)," *VT* 38 (1988) 71–79, also concluded that שליש referred to officers and retained or restored that word in 2 Sam 23:8, 13, 19a, 23, and 24. He identified Ish-bosheth (= Jeshbaal in my translation) as chief of the officers, followed by the naming of the "Three"—Eleazar, Shammah, and Abishai. He proposed that Abishai, in the present text, has been separated from the other members of the Three by the secondary interpolation of the water anecdote in vv. 13-17. Verse 19b is also judged by him to be secondary. Na'aman identified the list as the organization of the professional army dating to shortly after David had made Jerusalem his capital. Donald G. Schley, "The *Šālīšîm*: Officers or Special Three-Man Squads?" *VT* 40 (1990) 321–26, interpreted שליש as three-man squads, although the only example he could cite was from the water anecdote in vv. 13-17. The rest of the men in the chapter act independently of one another and the vast majority are not arranged in triads. Finally, Pekka Särkiö, "'The Third Man'—David's Heroes in 2 Sam 23,8-39," *SJOT* 7 (1993) 108–24, interpreted שלש as elite mercenaries in the service of the king. They got the name שלש because sometimes they were assigned as the third person in a chariot. Since the king chose his commanders from these elite mercenaries, the word שליש later acquired the meaning of "adjutant" or "officer."

5   A similar list of heroes appears in 2 Sam 21:15-22// 1 Chr 20:4-8, where the deeds of Ishbi-benob, Abishai (the first two appear only in 2 Samuel), Sibbecai, Elhanan, and Jonathan are recounted.

6   The text here is uncertain. See textual note 41.

and that differs somewhat in form and content from the list in section III. It consists of sixteen additional mighty men. Scholars have debated whether this list was lost by accident in 2 Samuel,[7] composed by the Chronicler,[8] or added by the Chronicler from a source that was available to him. The third option seems to be the most likely since the list, in distinction to the previous verses, frequently puts the men into pairs, and reports that a surprising number of them came from Transjordan. The latter fact especially does not seem likely in a list composed originally in the postexilic period.

Williamson, 96–97, 105 (cf. Allen, 376),[9] has detected a convincing chiastic arrangement of 1 Chronicles 11–12 that implies that both of these chapters in their entirety were part of the Chronicler's original work:

A. The full number of those at Hebron who made David king (11:1-3)

B. David's coronation according to the word of Yahweh and the military personnel at Hebron (11:10-47)

C. Military support for David when he was at Ziklag (12:1-8 [1-7])

D. Support for David when he was in the wilderness "at the stronghold" (12:9-16 [8-15])

D′. Support for David when he was in the wilderness "at the stronghold" (12:17-19 [16-18])

C′. Military support for David when he was at Ziklag (12:20-23 [19-22])

B′. David's coronation according to the word of Yahweh and the military personnel at Hebron (12:24-38 [23-37])

A′. The full number of those at Hebron who made David king (12:39-41 [38-40])[10]

The overall message of 1 Chronicles 11–12 consists of four primary points:

1. A unanimous Israel made David king at Hebron (11:1-3; 12:38-40).

2. David's coronation was in accord with the word of Yahweh (11:10; 12:23).

3. David's first act as king was to make Jerusalem his capital (11:4-9). As soon as the festivities surrounding his coronation were over, David initiated efforts to bring the ark to Jerusalem (chaps. 13–16). Note that in Chronicles the materials dealing with the transfer of the ark in 2 Sam 6:1-11 (1 Chr 13:4-14) *precede* the materials in 2 Sam 5:12-25 (1 Chr 14:1-16) dealing with Hiram's support, the list of David's wives and children, and the defeat of the Philistines.

4. Various military groups rallied to David's cause already at Hebron (11:10–12:41).

In both chapters 10 and 11, the writer shows the complete correspondence between the rise of David and the will and word of Yahweh (10:14; 11:3).

The relationship of chap. 12 to possible sources will be discussed in the commentary on that chapter.

Detailed Commentary

11:1-9. Early Days of David's Rule
11:1-3. David Anointed as King over Israel at Hebron

■ **1** *all Israel gathered together:* The unanimous participation of Israel in the coronation of David at Hebron, reported by the Chronicler, is quite different from the context of this verse in the *Vorlage*. There (2 Sam 5:1) it was all the *northern* "tribes of Israel" that gave David his second public anointing, after the people of Judah had already anointed him as their king in 2 Sam 2:4.[11] The Chronicler ignores this earlier anointing in Judah and makes it appear as if a united Israel backed David right from the beginning (cf. also 1 Chr 12:38). Israel is treated as a whole—"all Israel"—and not as a sum of its individual parts ("all the tribes of Israel").[12] The Chronicler replaces the word "came" in his *Vorlage* (cf. textual

7   Rothstein, 220, 241.

8   Noth, *Chronicler's History*, 136; Elliger, "Dreissig Helden Davids," 78.

9   See also H. G. M. Williamson, "'We Are Yours, O David': The Setting and Purpose of 1 Chronicles xii 1-23," *OTS* 21 (1981) 168–70.

10 Allen, 376; and Willi, *Chronik als Auslegung*, 224, n. 30, note another scheme dealing with a roll call of the army in these chapters: Joab the commander

(11:6); the Three, the Thirty, and other leaders (11:10-47); veterans who were mighty warriors (12:1-21); rank and file of the great army (12:22-37).

11 Similarly, "all the elders of Israel" (1 Chr 11:3//2 Sam 5:3) refers in Samuel only to the northern delegation.

12 Johnstone, 1:142.

note 1) with "gathered together," a verb used in Chronicles at the inauguration of many important events in Israel's history.[13]

Hebron: This city was David's capital for seven years and six months (MR 160103). It is located some 19 miles south-southeast of Jerusalem.

We are your bone and your flesh: In 2 Sam 19:12-13 David uses this language of kinship ("you are my bone and flesh") to urge the elders of Judah to restore him to the throne after the death of Absalom, lest the tribes of northern Israel, who were unrelated to him, should restore David to the kingship before his own tribe of Judah. This sentence of loyalty expresses fictive kinship since neither northern Israel nor the entirety of Israel in David's day was in any way related to David.

■ **2** *Formerly even when Saul was king:* The Chronicler omitted the word עלינו "over us" from the text of Samuel. Is this a subtle challenge to Saul's legitimacy as king over Israel?

you were the one who brought out and brought in Israel: Israel's accolade for David, taken over from 2 Sam 5:2, contains some hyperbole. According to tradition, women ascribed to David ten times as many battle kills as they attributed to Saul, much to the latter's displeasure (1 Sam 18:7-8).[14] The list of heroes, soldiers, and military leaders in 1 Chr 11:10—12:41, who pledged their loyalty to David on the basis of their previous experience with him, provides concrete examples of the leadership David offered in the past. There is, however, no evidence that David actually led the army of Israel during the reign of Saul.

Yahweh your God said to you: The Chronicler[15] has added "your God," thus stressing the strong bond between Yahweh and King David.

"It is you who should shepherd my people Israel": The source of this divine oracle is not given, either here or in the *Vorlage,* nor is there any information on how the divine oracle was communicated. Its closest parallel is in the oracle of Nathan in 1 Chr 17:6//2 Sam 7:7: "Did I ever speak a word with one of the judges of Israel, whom I commanded to shepherd my people Israel?"

"you will be prince over my people Israel": The Hebrew term נגיד means "king designate" or "crown prince."[16] The closest parallel to this promise is also found in the oracle of Nathan: "I took you . . . to be prince over my people Israel" (1 Chr 17:7//2 Sam 7:8).[17] The Chronicler[18] added "my people" to this clause (cf. the previous clause in Chronicles and in 2 Sam 5:2).

■ **3** *All the elders of Israel came to the king:* The word "king" is somewhat of an anachronism at this point in Chronicles since David only became king when they anointed him later in the verse. Rudolph, 94, therefore, proposed to read: "The elders of Israel came to make him king." But "the king" is a quotation from 2 Sam 5:3, where David is in fact king because of his earlier anointing by the people of Judah. And one might note that Yahweh had already turned the kingdom over to David in 1 Chr 10:14.

David made for them a covenant at Hebron before Yahweh: David agreed to certain obligations as the king of Israel. This is to be clearly distinguished from the "everlasting covenant" God made with David, which expresses God's loyalty to the Davidic king (2 Sam 23:5).[19] The expression "before Yahweh" implies that the action took place in a sanctuary.[20]

they anointed David king: This ritual of anointing expressed the people's acceptance of the covenant David had made with them and their pledge of loyalty to him.

---

13 1 Chr 13:2; 16:35; 2 Chr 13:7; 15:9-10; 20:4; 23:2; 24:5; 25:5; 32:4, 6.

14 Note that David is also credited with fighting Yahweh's battles (1 Sam 18:17; 25:28).

15 Or it was added during the transmission of the text of Chronicles. See textual note 4.

16 1 Sam 9:16; 10:1; 13:14; 25:30; 2 Sam 6:21. Cf. Klein, *1 Samuel,* 88.

17 Cf. also 1 Sam 13:14; 16:11-13.

18 Or it was added during the transmission of the text of Chronicles? See textual note 5.

19 Other covenants in Chronicles include: a covenant at the time of Asa to seek Yahweh (2 Chr 15:12), the

covenant with Joash (23:1, 3), the covenant initiated by Jehoiada (23:16), the covenant initiated by Hezekiah (29:10), and the covenant initiated by Josiah (34:31-32). Cf. also 1 Chr 16:15, 17, where references to the covenant are taken from Ps 105:8 and 10, and the reference to Yahweh as keeper of the covenant in 2 Chr 6:14//1 Kgs 8:23. For the reference to the "covenant of salt" in 2 Chr 13:5, see the commentary there. The covenant that Yahweh made with David is mentioned in 2 Chr 21:7, where this term has been added by the Chronicler to the *Vorlage* (see 2 Kgs 8:19).

20 Johnstone, 1:145, suggests that the ark and the

according to the word of Yahweh by the agency of Samuel:
The Chronicler believed that history was guided by the
prophetic word, and so he added these words to his *Vorlage.* He may have been alluding to two texts in the
Deuteronomistic History, which he chose not to include
in his own work: 1 Sam 15:28, where Samuel tells Saul
that God has given the kingdom to someone better than
Saul; and 1 Sam 16:1-13, where Samuel anoints David
(cf. also 1 Chr 11:10 and 12:23).[21]

11:4-9. David Captures Jerusalem

■ **4** *David and all Israel:* The Chronicler ignores a passage in Judges that suggests that Jerusalem had been
captured by Judah in the era of the conquest (Judg
1:8).[22] When David captured Jerusalem in the Deuteronomistic History, it was David and "his men," that is, his
private army, that made the attack (2 Sam 5:6). The
Chronicler attributed the capture to David and all Israel
in order to lend more authority and prestige to this city
and its temple. It was David's first royal act even before
the completion of the celebration of his coronation
(1 Chr 12:38-40).

Jerusalem, that is, Jebus, and there were the Jebusites: The
Chronicler has added to his *Vorlage* (2 Sam 5:6) the
words "that is, Jebus,"[23] but 2 Sam 5:6—in a reading

retained also in Chronicles—also stated that the attack
was against "the Jebusites, the inhabitants of the land."
The name "Jerusalem" is known already in the Execra-
tion Texts of the nineteenth century BCE and in the
Amarna Letters of the fourteenth century BCE.

the inhabitants of the land: The reference is to the original inhabitants of the land (1 Chr 22:18; 2 Chr 20:7);
Israel itself is later dubbed "the people of the land"
(2 Chr 23:13).

■ **5** *The inhabitants of Jebus said to David, "You cannot come
here":* The prohibition decreed by the Jebusites proved to
be futile against David's attack. In the *Vorlage,* 2 Sam 5:6,
however, the prohibition was placed into the mouth of
an individual Jebusite, who added to the simple prohibition an etiological explanation that has baffled subsequent commentators with its obscurity.[24] Apparently
because of this obscurity, the Chronicler omitted this
sentence referring to the blind and the lame and its
sequel, also referring to the lame and the blind, in 2
Sam 5:8//1 Chr 11:6.[25] This omission of the Jebusite
taunt also lessens the potential threat offered by the
Jebusites to the Israelite attackers.

David captured the fortress[26] *of Zion, the city of David:*
Zion was originally an alternate name for what is known

---

tabernacle were at Hebron before the tabernacle's
transfer to Gibeon and the ark's transfer to
Jerusalem (1 Chr 16:1, 29).

21 According to Josephus *Ant.* 7.53, the people
"declared that he [David] had been chosen king by
God through the prophet Samuel." It is doubtful
whether this is sufficient evidence to claim that the
Chronicler found this phrase in a text of Samuel.
See McKenzie, *Chronicler's Use,* 42.

22 That passage, of course, is contradicted in Judg
1:21, which states that the Benjaminites could *not*
drive out the Jebusites who dwelled in Jerusalem.
Cf. also Josh 11:63. The story about David taking
the head of Goliath to Jerusalem in 1 Sam 17:54 is
anachronistic. See Klein, *1 Samuel,* 181. For a thorough study of 1 Chr 11:4-9 see Isaac Kalimi, "The
Capture of Jerusalem in the Chronistic History," *VT*
52 (2002) 66–79.

23 Aside from vv. 4-5, the name Jebus occurs elsewhere
only at Josh 18:28; 19:10-11, but the word
"Jebusites" appears forty-one times. In Josh 15:8
"Jebusites" is glossed with "that is, Jerusalem." J.
Maxwell Miller, "Jebus and Jerusalem: A Case of
Mistaken Identity," *ZDPV* 90 (1974) 115–27, argues

that the ancient city of Jebus should be located at
the modern village of Sha'fât just north of
Jerusalem. It is clear, in any case, that the Jebusites
did occupy Jerusalem before David's conquest (Josh
15:63). Johannes P. Floss, *David und Jerusalem*
(Arbeiten zu Text und Sprache im Alten Testament
20; St. Ottilien: Eos, 1987) 17–18, determines that
the Chronicler drew the wrong conclusion from the
fact that the people in Jerusalem were called
Jebusites.

24 McCarter, *II Samuel,* 137, interprets it as a gloss
added after 2 Sam 5:8 was no longer understood.
He translates: "For the blind and the lame had
incited them saying, David shall not come in here."

25 The omission of the phrase from 2 Sam 5:6 can also
be explained by homoioteleuton, with a scribe's
eyes skipping from the first הנה "here" to the second. R. Murray, "The Origin of the Aramaic ʿ*īr,*
Angel," *Or* 53 (1984) 312, believes that the words
"blind" and "lame" referred to protective deities
and so were omitted by the Chronicler.

26 מצד may be an Aramaism for מצודה (Japhet, 241).
Cf. vv. 5 and 16.

in Chronicles and today as the "city of David" (the area south of the southeast corner of the Old City of Jerusalem). "Zion" has a variety of uses in the OT, including as a poetic synonym for Jerusalem. In modern times the name Zion refers to the southwestern area of the city of Jerusalem. The Chronicler's only other use of this name is in 2 Chr 5:2 (= 1 Kgs 8:1). The appositional expression "the city of David" (cf. 2 Sam 5:7) replaces "the city of Jebus" that the Chronicler had added in the previous verse. The Jebusites, descended from Ham (1 Chr 1:8-14), are now replaced in Jerusalem by Israel.

■ **6** *David said, "Whoever is the first to smite the Jebusites will be head and commander." And Joab the son of Zeruiah went up first, and he became a head:* Joab, David's nephew, appears frequently in 2 Samuel 2–3, but those chapters are omitted in Chronicles, so this is the first mention of him in Chronicles aside from an early genealogical notice.[27] The Chronicler had to introduce Joab somewhere because of future references to him (18:15; 19:8, 10, 14-15; 20:2; 21:2-6; 26:28; 27:7, 24, 34), and this may have seemed to be an appropriate place. He is listed only incidentally in the rest of the chapter as one of the heads of David's mighty men or as the relative of other warriors (11:8, 20, 26, 29).[28] The Chronicler does not

refer to the curse that was put on Joab by David on his deathbed (1 Kgs 2:5-6, 28-34).[29] Indeed, the idea that Joab first rose to military prominence through the capture of Jerusalem is actually contradicted by traditions recorded in 2 Samuel. Joab was at the head of David's soldiers already in 2 Sam 2:12-13 (cf. 3:23), and his murder of Abner in 3:26-27 probably stemmed from his fear of being replaced by the latter as commander of the united army of north and south. These traditions seem historically reliable, and the Chronicler's alternate account of Joab's rise results from his literary methods.[30]

The Chronicler took "whoever strikes the Jebusite" from his *Vorlage* in 2 Sam 5:8,[31] and then he added the remaining words of the verse on his own after the word "Jebusite." Since Joab was the first to attack, meeting the criterion David had proposed, he gained the rank of head[32] and commander.[33] In the era of the judges, the Gileadites made a similar promise that whoever would begin the fight against the Ammonites would be head (ראש) over all the inhabitants of Gilead, and this resulted in the elevation of Jephthah (Judg 10:18; 11:11). Similarly, Caleb promised his daughter in marriage to anyone who would capture Kiriath-sepher, a promise redeemed by Othniel (Judg 1:12-13; cf. 15:16-17). Joab was the first

---

27   1 Chr 2:16: "And their sisters were Zeruiah and Abigail. The sons of Zeruiah: Abshai, Joab, and Asahel, three."

28   His brothers Abshai and Asahel are introduced in 1 Chr 11:20, 26.

29   Cf. also 2 Sam 3:19; 16:10; 19:22.

30   See Kalimi, "Capture," 76, and contrast the alternate position argued by numerous scholars in his n. 45.

31   In 2 Sam 5:8 these words are followed by instructions on how that feat should be accomplished. But the words after "Jebusites" in 2 Sam 5:8 are obscure and this may have been the reason for their omission in Chronicles. For a thorough review of the history of the interpretation of 2 Sam 5:8, see McCarter, *II Samuel,* 140. He paraphrases his own innovative interpretation as follows: "Whoever strikes down a Jebusite must deal a fatal blow [hit the Jebusites in the windpipe (צנור)], for otherwise the city will be filled with mutilated men whom we have wounded but not slain, and I [David] find such men intolerable." See also Manfred Oeming, "Die Eroberung Jerusalems durch David in deuteronomistischer und chronistischer Darstellung (II Sam 5,6-9 und I Chr 11,4-8)," *ZAW* 106 (1994) 408–15,

who believes that the Chronicler's omission of this material is part of his idealization of David, who would not participate in the mutilation of the genitals of his enemies. Svend Holm-Nielsen, "Did Joab Climb 'Warren's Shaft'?" in *History and Traditions of Early Israel* (ed. A. Lemaire and B. Otzen; VTSup 50; Leiden: Brill, 1993) 38–49, believes that these words mean that David cut off the water supply of the Jebusites. Kalimi, "Capture," 71, notes that by this omission the Chronicler avoids mentioning the animosity of David toward the blind and the lame and their being allowed to enter the house of God. For a defense of the translation "water shaft," see Terence Kleven, "The Use of Ṣnr in Ugaritic and 2 Samuel V 8: Hebrew Usage and Comparative Philology," *VT* 44 (1994) 195–204.

32   The Chronicler puns on the root ראש in this verse through the two uses of בראשונה "first" and the two uses of ראש "head."

33   Myers, 1:84, notes that Amenemheb was the first to breach the wall of Kadesh during the campaign of Thutmose III. See *ANET,* 241b.

to go up against Jerusalem and he became a head.[34] The emphasis on Joab here may reflect the prominence of his family in postexilic times.[35] In any case the Chronicler leaves out Joab's murder of Abner from 2 Sam 3:22-39 and ignores the role of this murder in Joab's rise to power. As the first to "go up," Joab was the first to make the aliyah to Jerusalem (cf. 2 Chr 36:23).

■ 7 *therefore they call it the city of David:* The Chronicler added the word "therefore" to his *Vorlage,* and this addition relates the etiology of "the city of David" to David's dwelling in, rather than his conquest of, the city. In the *Vorlage* (2 Sam 5:9) David himself, not the anonymous "they," gave the city his name. The Assyrian king Sargon called his city *dūr šarru-kīn* (Sargonsburg) and another Assyrian, Tukulti-Ninurta I (1244–1208 BCE), also named a city after himself.[36] Alexandria was named for Alexander the Great.

■ 8 *He built the city:* This is the first report of building projects by an Israelite king, which is a topos to which the Chronicler frequently returns.[37] Normally only pious kings engaged in building, and their productivity is seen as appropriate recompense for their behavior.

the Millo: While the text following the word "Millo" is very unsure (see textual notes 11-12), the Millo itself may be the stepped-stone structure in the city of David, uncovered in twentieth-century archaeology (cf. 2 Chr 32:5).

Joab repaired/kept alive the rest of the city: The Chronicler supplemented his *Vorlage* with this clause, but two interpretations of his addition are possible. In the first the Chronicler attributed other building projects in the rest of the city to Joab. The verb חיה (*piel*) "repaired" might be translated more literally as "salvaged." The same verb is used contemptuously by Sanballat of Nehemiah's building efforts (Neh 3:34 [4:2]).[38]

Williamson, 100, on the other hand, retains the literal meaning of the verb and suggests that v. 8 qualifies v. 6. While Joab killed the first Jebusites he met in v. 6, he kept the rest of the population alive. Edelman notes that building projects would normally be done by corvée labor rather than by the army. Joab attacked the acropolis and decimated it, but the rest of the city was left more or less intact.[39] Hence any mixed population that was in Jerusalem, in her view, was laid at Joab's feet rather than at David's.

■ 9 *and Yahweh of hosts was with him:* This "assistance formula" indicates the real authority that was behind David's capture of Jerusalem. The title "Yahweh of hosts," used here for the first time in Chronicles,[40] would indicate that divine power was behind the conquering armies of David (v. 5) and Joab (v. 6). This divine military title also anticipates or foreshadows the long list of military figures later in this chapter and in chap. 12.

11:10-25. Heroic Acts of David's Mighty Men
11:10. Introduction

■ 10 *These are the heads of David's warriors who gave him strong support:* This verse is an addition by the Chronicler. In chaps. 11–12 the Chronicler includes a variety of ancient lists of army officers, heroes, and soldiers that provide concrete demonstration of the widespread "strong support" (המתחזקים) for David at his coronation. Good kings in Chronicles often grew strong or showed themselves strong. The word חזק in the *hitpael* is a favorite of the Chronicler's.[41] Regardless of what the following names in 1 Chr 11:11-47 may have represented in Samuel or in the list's precanonical setting, in Chronicles they are the heads—officers, chiefs—of David's warriors.

---

34 I take "head" and "commander" as a hendiadys, so that David kept his promise fully. If one distinguishes between these words, David only partially kept his promise. See Kalimi, "Capture," 72, n. 23. The capture of the city is related to the Othniel tradition, and the reward of becoming a head is related to the Jephthah tradition.

35 Ezra 2:6//Neh 7:11; Ezra 8:9. Cf. 1 Chr 4:14. See also Welten, *Geschichte und Geschichtsdarstellung,* 59–63; Oeming, "Eroberung Jerusalems," 417.

36 See references in McCarter, *II Samuel,* 140–41.

37 2 Chr 11:5-12; 14:5-6; 17:12-13; 26:9-10; 27:3-4; 32:5-

6; 33:14. De Vries, 125, believes that only the reports about David and Rehoboam are historical.

38 "Will they revive the stones?" Japhet, 242, cites 1 Kgs 18:30 as a parallel: "He [Elijah] 'healed' the altar that had been thrown down."

39 Edelman, "Deuteronomist's David," 73.

40 Cf. 1 Chr 17:7, 24. David confronted Goliath in the name of Yahweh of hosts (17:45).

41 1 Chr 11:10; 19:13; 2 Chr 1:1; 12:13; 13:7, 8, 21; 16:9; 17:1; 21:4; 27:6; 32:5. All but 1 Chr 19:13// 2 Sam 10:12 are in material peculiar to the Chronicler. The verb often occurs in contexts dealing with

together with all Israel: This phrase links the list of military people quite closely to the "all Israel" theme with which the chapter began.

to make him king: The verb מלך in the *hiphil* is used of humans making someone king in 12:32, 39 (31, 38); 23:1; 29:22; 2 Chr 10:1; 11:22; 22:1; 23:11; 26:1; 33:25; 36:1, 4, 10,[42] but it is also used of God making a person king in 1 Chr 28:4 and 2 Chr 1:8-9, 11.

according to the word of Yahweh concerning Israel: Balancing the unanimous support of the people and the military personnel list is the word, or promise, of Yahweh that brought the kingship of David to pass (cf. 1 Chr 10:14; 11:3). The human support of David proves valid because of divine authorization.

11:11-14. Two Heroes, Jeshbaal and Eleazar

■ **11** *These are the number of the warriors who belonged to David:* The Chronicler replaced the word "names" in his *Vorlage* with "number"[43] to indicate the size of the support for David. Because of his additional material in vv. 41b-47, the Chronicler lists many more names than in his *Vorlage*—and even more names than will be listed in chap. 12.

Jeshbaal son of a Hachmonite: If the name Jeshbaal is correctly reconstructed (see textual note 16), it has the meaning of "Baal exists." Does "Baal" stand for the great Canaanite storm deity, or is בעל used in its more generic sense of "lord," referring to Yahweh? In 27:2 Jeshbaal[44] son of Zabdiel was in charge of the first division in the first month. "Hachmonite" is either a reference to an unknown place called Hachmon, or "Hachmoni" is a personal name ("wise one"?). Jehiel son of a Hachmonite

(or son of Hachmoni) attended to David's sons according to 27:32.

head of the Thirty: McCarter may well be correct that the original text of this list read "the Three" at this point,[45] but there is no evidence for such a reading in the Chronicles' textual tradition. As textual note 19 indicates, however, there is also good textual support in Chronicles for a reading "the head of the officers." The number "thirty" appears frequently in chaps. 11–12: 11:42; 12:4 (twice), 19 (18); cf. 27:6 (twice).

three hundred men whom he killed at one time: The fame of Jeshbaal and the others depended on their great accomplishments or their great courage. This man's prowess with the spear enabled him to beat overwhelming odds by single-handedly killing three hundred of an unidentified enemy.[46] Even that was five hundred less than he killed according to the *Vorlage* in 2 Sam 23:8.[47]

■ **12** *Eleazar the son of Dodo the Ahohite:*[48] Because of the long haplography in the materials taken from the *Vorlage* in 2 Sam 23:9bβ-11bα (see textual note 26), Eleazar's own deed[49] and the name of the third member of the Three, Shamma the Hararite, were lost. In Chronicles Eleazar is credited with the heroic deed of Shamma in 2 Sam 23:11-12. His enemy, like the enemy in the section that was lost, was the Philistines. When the people of Israel fled, he took the field by himself and defeated the Philistines. Despite these human heroics, it was finally Yahweh who gained a great victory (v. 14; cf. 2 Sam 23:10).[50] Eleazar may have been a member of the clan of Ahoah, listed genealogically as the grandson of Benjamin through his firstborn son Bela (1 Chr 8:4).

---

the establishment of the king in power. See Curtis and Madsen, 29–30, #38; Williamson, *Israel*, 54, §F.5.

42 It is also used of the Edomites setting up a king in 2 Chr 21:8.

43 The word "number" appears twenty-five times in the books of Chronicles. Cf. Johnstone, 1:152.

44 This follows LXX. See textual note 2 in chap. 27.

45 *II Samuel*, 489.

46 Johnstone, 1:153, calls attention to the promise at the end of the Holiness Code: "Five of you shall give chase to a hundred, and a hundred of you shall give chase to ten thousand" (Lev 26:42).

47 The lower number may result from harmonization with the similar heroic deed of Abshai in v. 20.

48 Dodai (cf. 2 Sam 23:9 K) the Ahohite (thus lacking

"Eleazar the son of") was in charge of the division of the second month in 1 Chr 27:4, and Ilai the Ahohite is mentioned in 11:29.

49 When the Israelites retreated, he stood his ground. Despite a weary arm, he clung to his sword until the end. Yahweh won the victory that day and the people came back to strip the dead.

50 See also 1 Chr 18:6, 13//2 Sam 8:6, 14.

Though a member of Saul's own tribe, he was part of the troops gathered around David. Elliger, however, interpreted "Ahohite" as referring to a place "Ahoah" in the region of the Wadi el-Khôkh, perhaps near the site of Etam (Khirbet el-Khôkh; MR 166121), one of Rehoboam's fortresses (2 Chr 11:6).[51]

■ **13** *He was with David at Pas-dammim:* Pas-dammim, added to the *Vorlage* by the Chronicler, is apparently the same as Ephes-dammim, where the Philistines gathered before the battle between David and Goliath (1 Sam 17:1). McCarter locates it at modern Damun, 4 miles northeast of Socoh (MR 147121).[52]

■ **14** *he defended it, and smote the Philistines:* The verb translated "defended" (נצל; elsewhere "deliver" or "rescue") appears in the *hiphil* eleven times in Chronicles, eight of which are in 2 Chronicles 32.

Yahweh brought victory by a great act of salvation: The text sees the victory as the joint product of the prowess of Eleazar and the intervention of Yahweh.[53]

11:15-19. Exploits of Anonymous Threesome

After the heroic acts performed by the two heroes in the text now preserved in vv. 11-14, vv. 15-19 describe an exploit by another group of three acting as a unit. There is confusion about the location of David (at the cave of Adullam [MR 150117], v. 15; or in the stronghold, v. 16). Japhet, 245, makes the plausible suggestion that 1 Chr 11:15a (= 2 Sam 23:13a) is a torso of a separate incident, in which three men made their way to David at Adullam, in the Shephelah (1 Sam 22:1). This has now been combined with a second incident, the water raid of the three at Bethlehem (MR 169123).

The water raid story describes the daring deeds of a threesome in an effort to fulfill a wish of King David for a drink of water from his hometown, but the story is really told to the greater glory of David, who would not drink water obtained at the risk of the lives of these three men. David's nostalgic wish for water from his hometown when it was occupied by the Philistines seems rather trivial, but the action of the anonymous group of three was needlessly reckless, however well intentioned. Unfortunately, we are not told how the three reacted to David's response to their dangerous mission.

■ **15** *to David at the cave of Adullam:* During his protracted struggle with Saul, according to 1 Sam 22:1, David fled to the cave of Adullam, some 10 miles east-southeast of Gath (MR 135123) and about 13 or 14 miles southwest of Bethlehem. At that time all sorts of malcontents had gathered around David. The torso of the first incident ends here and was combined with a second incident, both apparently involving the anonymous three heroes.

the army of the Philistines was camping in the valley of Rephaim: This refers to one of the two battles between David and the Philistines that took place when the Philistines were in this valley southwest of Jerusalem *after* David had already taken the city (2 Sam 5:17-25// 1 Chr 14:8-17).[54]

■ **16** *David was at that time in the stronghold:* This refers to the stronghold in the city of David (cf. vv. 5 and 7), not to a location in or near Adullam (1 Sam 22:4). McCarter, who places the stronghold at the Adullam location, situates the battle early in David's career, before the capture of Jerusalem and the battles recounted in 2 Sam 5:17-25//1 Chr 14:8-17.[55] While historically the battle may have taken place before David's conquest of Jerusalem, the Chronicler places it *after* David's anointing as king (v. 3) and *after* his capture of Jerusalem (vv. 4-9).

the garrison of the Philistines was at that time at Bethlehem: The Philistines had mounted an attack in the valley of Rephaim, southwest of Jerusalem (cf. 1 Chr 14:9), but their main base was at Bethlehem, David's hometown![56]

51   Elliger, "Dreissig Helden Davids," 45–46; cf. Wade R. Kotter, *ABD* 2:643.

52   *II Samuel,* 290.

53   The verb ישע also appears at 1 Chr 16:35; 18:6, 13; 19:12, 19; 2 Chr 20:9; 32:22. Cf. the nouns formed from the same root at 1 Chr 16:23; 2 Chr 6:41; 20:17.

54   See Christian E. Hauer Jr., "Jerusalem, the Stronghold and Rephaim," *CBQ* 32 (1970) 574–75. The Chronicler relocates the second battle to a nameless valley. See the commentary on 1 Chr 14:13-17.

55   *II Samuel,* 495. Klaus-Dietrich Schunck, "David's 'Schlupfwinkel' in Juda," *VT* 33 (1983) 110–13, has proposed that מצודה "stronghold" in this verse should be translated as "hiding place." But he admits that the occurrences of the same noun in vv. 5 and 7 should be translated "stronghold," referring to Zion. My decision to identify this stronghold with the city of David makes his proposal for this verse moot.

56   Hauer, "Jerusalem," 575, suggests that the Philistine garrison was a blocking force designed to prevent reinforcement, resupply, or relief of Jerusalem from the south.

■ **18** *David refused to drink of it. He poured it out to Yahweh:* According to Israelite law, blood of edible animals was to be poured out upon the ground like water since life is in the blood (Lev 17:10-13; Deut 12:23-25; 15:23). In David's eyes the water was obtained at such high mortal risk that life was in it, and it had to be poured out as if it were blood[57] despite the fact that he had expressed a strong desire for water from Bethlehem in v. 17. This verse does not refer therefore to a sacrificial water libation, as in 1 Sam 7:6.

■ **19** *The three warriors did these things:* McCarter[58] takes the corresponding sentence in 2 Sam 23:17 as a misplaced reference to the deeds of the Three in 2 Sam 23:8b-12; Japhet, 245, interprets it as a reference to the two incidents she has reconstructed in v. 15a and vv. 15b-19a. It may actually be a summary of everything recounted in vv. 11-19a (= 2 Sam 23:8-17a).

11:20-25. Two Additional Heroes

I follow McCarter, who interprets Abshai (vv. 20-21) and Benaiah (vv. 22-25) as two highly honored members of the Thirty who never attained entrance to the Three. This is based on somewhat precarious textual criticism in vv. 20-24. Japhet, 246, employing a more conservative textual criticism, believes there was a second group of three, and Abshai was the chief of this second group. As important as this debate is for reconstructing the shape of the military under David, it does not affect the message of the Chronicler.

■ **20** *Abshai the brother of Joab:* I have followed the unconventional vocalization of this hero's name in MT, although "Abishai" is no doubt the "correct" spelling (cf. textual note 39).[59] Chronicles omits "son of Zeruiah" from the *Vorlage* in 2 Sam 23:18, perhaps because the author had already identified Joab as the son of Zeruiah in 1 Chr 11:6. Joab the son of Zeruiah is mentioned again in 1 Chr 11:39//2 Sam 23:37. Abshai, Joab, and Asahel are identified as sons of Zeruiah in 1 Chr 2:16.

was head of the Thirty: Abshai was in charge of the group of Thirty, or, if we follow the MT (textual note

41), he was the chief person in (a second or third group of) the Three. The same information—with the same textual problems—recurs in v. 21. The word "Thirty" may be a round number, since 2 Sam 23:39 (not included in Chronicles) notes that there were actually thirty-seven warriors.

he wielded his spear against three hundred: Abshai's heroic act was the same as Jeshbaal's (v. 11), but without the textual uncertainty of that verse. According to 1 Chr 18:12 Abshai also killed eighteen thousand Edomites in the Valley of Salt,[60] and on another occasion Joab put troops in his charge (1 Chr 19:11, 15//2 Sam 10:10, 14). In the Deuteronomistic History Abishai and Joab are credited with the murder of Abner (2 Sam 3:30) and the slaughter of three hundred sixty of his Benjaminite men (2 Sam 2:31; neither passage is included in Chronicles).[61] Abishai also killed Ishbi-benob, a Philistine giant (2 Sam 21:15-17; another passage not included in Chronicles). Both Joab (see v. 6) and Abshai are treated positively by the Chronicler.

but he did not get a place among the Three: Despite Abshai's heroic action, he was not allowed into the select group of the Three.[62]

■ **22** *Benaiah son of Jehoiada was a hero:* The warrior Benaiah appears as captain of the Cherethites and Pelethites in 2 Sam 8:18//1 Chr 18:17 and 2 Sam 20:23 (not included in Chronicles), a group of mercenary soldiers who remained loyal to David in the revolts of Absalom and Sheba (2 Sam 15:18 and 20:7; neither passage appears in Chronicles). He may have attained this position after the events described in vv. 22-25. After Joab had supported Adonijah as David's successor, and Solomon, backed by Benaiah, had prevailed and become king, Solomon ordered Benaiah to execute Joab, who had sought refuge in the sanctuary (1 Kings 1–2). Benaiah then replaced Joab as commander of the army. Benaiah hailed from Kabzeel (Josh 1:21; Neh 11:25) in the extreme south of Judah (MR 148071), midway between Arad (MR 162076) and Beer-sheba (MR

---

57   Cf. Deut 12:16: "The blood [of a slaughtered animal] you must not eat; you shall pour it out on the ground like water."

58   *II Samuel*, 496.

59   For further information about him see 1 Chr 18:12//2 Sam 8:13; 1 Sam 26:6-9; 2 Sam 16:9; 18:2; 21:16-17.

60   According to the *Vorlage* of this passage (2 Sam 8:13), it was David who performed this deed.

61   Other passages omitted by the Chronicler portray him as a reckless hothead (1 Sam 26:6-11; 2 Sam 16:9; 19:21-22).

62   The text of v. 20 is quite uncertain; see textual notes 39-42.

134072; Josh 15:21). Because of the prominence of Benaiah, both McCarter[63] and Japhet, 247, following Zeron,[64] conclude that the list (2 Sam 23:8-39) reached its present form during the reign of Solomon, even though parts of it may be earlier. Benaiah's foes come from outside Palestine (Moab, Egypt). Benaiah was in charge of the division in the third month according to 1 Chr 27:5-6, where he is also designated as a mighty man of the Thirty and in command of the Thirty.

he killed two warriors of Moab: This is the first of three anecdotes about Benaiah, who is described in this verse as "a doer of great deeds." The reference is laconic and the translation "warriors" is unsure (see textual note 46). In any case Benaiah's foes came from Transjordan.

killed a lion in a pit on a day when snow had fallen: This is a heroic deed, but it has nothing directly to do with militaristic actions. Numerous commentators have compared this to the lion Samson killed with his bare hands in a vineyard (Judg 14:5-6). There is an interesting possible wordplay between "lion" (אֲרִי) and the word used for the two warriors in the previous clause (אֲרָאֵלִי). Snow is relatively rare in Palestine and helped to fix this deed in memory.[65]

■ 23 *He killed the Egyptian, a man of stature:* Armed only with a staff against his opponent's spear, Benaiah approached this giant. The reader is reminded of the confrontation of David and Goliath, especially because of two additions made by the Chronicler to the *Vorlage.* He compares the Egyptian's spear to a weaver's beam (cf. 1 Sam 17:7; 2 Sam 21:19 // 1 Chr 20:5) and gives the giant's height as five cubits (seven feet six inches).

Goliath was even taller at six cubits and a span—nine feet nine inches (1 Sam 17:4). Like David, Benaiah defeated the nameless Egyptian with the opponent's own weapon, in this case a spear rather than a sword (1 Sam 17:51). Hence the first two feats pun on אֲרָאֵלִי/אֲרִי and the second and third seem to make allusions to the legendary feats of Samson and David.

■ 24 *he did not get a place among the three mighty men:* Despite his great accomplishments, Benaiah, like Abshai, never attained to the rank of the Three.

■ 25 *David set him over his bodyguard:* David had held the same position in the reign of Saul (1 Sam 22:14).[66]

11:26-41a. Primary List of Mighty Men

This list, based on a list of the Thirty in the Chronicler's *Vorlage* at 2 Sam 23:24-39, omits the number "thirty" from 2 Sam 23:24[67] and actually contains forty-seven[68] names if vv. 41b-47 are included in the totals. McCarter proposes that the men are listed in rank order, with a tendency for places closer to Bethlehem to appear earlier in the list.[69] He argues that the list presupposes a time before David had been crowned king of the northern tribes. The warriors' homes that can be identified come from Judah or immediately adjacent tribes to the north, with the exception of the mercenary groups in Transjordan in vv. 36-39 (= 1 Chr 11:38-41a).[70]

The thirty-one names in 1 Chr 11:26-41a appear in one of six forms:

A. *X the Y* (in which Y is a gentilic or place name): Shammoth the Harodite, Helez the Pelonite, Abiezer the Anathothite, Sibbecai the Hushathite,

---

63 *II Samuel*, 496.

64 A. Zeron, "Der Platz Benajahus in der Heldenliste Davids (II Sam 23 20-23)," *ZAW* 90 (1978) 20–28.

65 For an attempt to employ this verse and the next in Christian proclamation, see J. A. Ross MacKenzie, "Valiant against All: From Text to Sermon on 1 Chronicles 11:22, 23," *Int* 22 (1968) 18–35.

66 See Klein, *1 Samuel*, 219–20, 225.

67 But see the Chronicler's addition of the number "thirty" in v. 42.

68 McCarter, *II Samuel*, 500, reconstructs thirty names in 2 Sam 23:24-39, and my reconstructed text of 1 Chr 11:26-41a has thirty-one names. The Chronicler omits "Elika the Harodite" from 2 Sam 23:25, but his two additional names derive from textual corruption: Hepher (v. 36) and Mibhar (v. 38). There

are sixteen names in vv. 41b-47.

69 *II Samuel*, 501. In my own calculations of the geographic locations, I have excluded the names Asahel (v. 26), Eliphal (v. 35), Naarai (v. 37), Joel (v. 38), and Mibhar (v. 38) because they contain no place names (unless Hagri the father of Mibhar is to be associated with the Transjordanian Hagrites), and Hashem (v. 34) and Ahiam (v. 35) are excluded because their place names are unknown. Of the other twenty-four names only Benaiah the Pirathonite (v. 31) and Hurai from the brooks of Gaash (v. 32) are north of Bethel, and only Zelek the Ammonite (v. 39) is from Transjordan.

70 See McCarter, *II Samuel,* 500–501, for a thorough discussion of earlier suggestions by Elliger and Mazar.

Ila the Ahohite, Mahurai the Netophathite, Benaiah the Pirathonite, Abibaal the Arbathite, Azmaveth the Bahurimite, Eliahba the Shaalbonite, Hashem the Gizonite, Hepher the Mecherathite, Ahijah the Pelonite, Hezro the Carmelite, Zelek the Ammonite, Naharai the Beerothite; Ira the Ithrite, Gareb the Ithrite, Uriah the Hittite. Nineteen names.

B. *X the son of Y the Z* (in which Y is the father's name and Z is a gentilic or place name): Ira the son of Ikkesh the Tekoite, Heled the son of Baanah the Netophathite, Jonathan the son of Shagee the Hararite, Ahiam the son of Sachar the Hararite. Four names.

C. *X the son of Y* (in which Y is the father's name): Eliphal the son of Ur, Naarai the son of Ezbai, Mibhar the son of Hagri. Three names.[71]

D. *X from Y* (in which Y is a place name): Hurai from the brooks of Gaash. One name.

E. *X son of Y from Z* (in which Y is the father's name and Z is a place name): Elhanan the son of Dodo from Bethlehem, Ithai the son of Ribai from Gibeah of the Benjaminites. Two names.

F. *X brother of Y:* Asahel the brother of Joab, Joel the brother of Nathan. Two names.

■ **26** *The valiant warriors:* The words וגבורי החילים were added by the Chronicler to the text taken from 2 Sam 23:24, perhaps because he needed a title to replace "the Thirty" (see the next comment) or to designate the following list as independent from the names mentioned above. It is a characteristic of Late Hebrew to put both the nouns in a construct chain into the plural (cf. 1 Chr 7:5; GKC §124q).

Asahel the brother of Joab: Since Asahel's death is recounted in 2 Sam 2:18-23, while David was still ruling from Hebron, his appearance in the list supports the early dating of the list proposed by McCarter.[72] The *Vorlage* adds after the word Joab "among the thirty" (2 Sam 23:24), which stands in some tension with the number "thirty-seven" in 2 Sam 23:39.[73] According to 1 Chr 27:7, Asahel was in charge of the division in the fourth month. Since Asahel's mother was Zeruiah, the sister of David, we assume he came from Bethlehem.

Elhanan the son of Dodo from Bethlehem: According to 2 Sam 21:19//1 Chr 20:5, he was the one—not David!—who killed Goliath, or at least the brother of Goliath.[74]

■ **27** *Shammoth the Harodite:* While many exegetes identify Shammoth's hometown with the spring Harod (Judg 7:1), near Mount Gilboa, where Gideon selected his men for the battle against the Midianites, Elliger proposed a location at Khirbet el-Ḥarēdān, almost 4 miles southeast of Jerusalem.[75] Elika, who is not mentioned in Chronicles (see textual note 53), came from the same location. Shammoth/Shammah (שמות) is probably to be identified with Shamhuth (שמהות) the Izrahite, who was in charge of the division in the fifth month (1 Chr 27:8).

Helez the Pelonite: Pelonite[76] is the unanimous reading in Chronicles and attested already in the Lucianic text of Samuel, but it is probably derived secondarily from "the Paltite" (2 Sam 23:26 [a person from Pelet or a descendant of the Calebite Pelet, 1 Chr 2:47]). Elliger located Beth-pelet (MR 141079; Josh 15:27; Neh 11:26) in the vicinity of Beer-sheba and related it to the Calebite clan of Pelet mentioned in 1 Chr 2:47.[77] No convincing geographic location for "Pelonite" has been offered. In 27:10 Helez the Pelonite is linked to the Ephraimites and placed in charge of the seventh month.

■ **28** *Ira the son of Ikkesh the Tekoite:* Tekoa (MR 170115), a city of Judah (2 Sam 14:2; cf. 1 Chr 2:24), is located about 10 miles south of Jerusalem. Its most famous son

---

71   All of these are very uncertain textually. See textual notes 71-72, 77, 79-80.

72   Japhet, 248, believes the death of Asahel provides a terminus a quo for the establishment of the Thirty and that the list contains names that are no longer part of the Thirty. The latter conclusion seems doubtful. There is no other evidence to support the idea that the list contains names that are no longer part of the Thirty. See my comment on Uriah below.

73   Rudolph, 100, proposed that Asahel should be included with the two heroes discussed in vv. 20-25,

namely, his brother Abishai and Solomon's army commander Benaiah, and he further proposed that the report of his deeds was accidentally lost. Both proposals seem arbitrary.

74   See the commentary on 1 Chr 20:5.

75   Elliger, "Dreissig Helden Davids," 40–41.

76   Cf. Ahijah the Pelonite in 1 Chr 11:36 and the textual note there.

77   Elliger, "Dreissig Helden Davids," 41–43.

is the prophet Amos. This Ira was in charge of the division in the sixth month (1 Chr 27:9).[78]

Abiezer the Anathothite: In 27:12 Abiezer is in charge of the ninth month. Anathoth (MR 174135), the birthplace of Jeremiah and the town to which Abiathar was banned, is some 3 miles north-northeast of Jerusalem (cf. 6:45 [60]).

■ **29** *Sibbecai the Hushathite:* Husha, modern Ḥûsān (MR 162124), is about 4 miles west of Bethlehem. Sibbecai is also called Sippai (or Saph), who was one of the descendants of the giants (1 Chr 20:4//2 Sam 21:18). In 1 Chr 27:11 Sibbecai is in charge of the eighth month and related to the Zerahites.[79] Cf. Mahrai, two names below.

Ilai the Ahohite: On "Ahohite" see v. 12.

■ **30** *Mahrai the Netophathite:* According to 1 Chr 27:13, Mahrai was in charge of the division in the tenth month and, like Sibbecai, from the Zerahites. Netophah (cf. 2:54) is probably to be located at Khirbet Bedd Fālûḥ (MR 171119), southeast of Bethlehem.

Heled the son of Baanah the Netophathite: In 27:15 Heldai the Netophathite is in charge of the twelfth month and traced his ancestry to the judge Othniel, the son of Kenaz, Caleb's brother.[80] On Netophah see the previous name.

■ **31** *Ithai son of Ribai from Gibeah of the Benjaminites:* Gibeah (MR 172136) is located about 3 miles north of Jerusalem.[81]

Benaiah the Pirathonite: According to 27:14 Benaiah was in charge of the eleventh month;[82] he is to be distinguished from Benaiah the son of Jehoiada in vv. 22-25. Pirathon (MR 165177) is a town in Ephraim (27:14) and home of the minor judge Abdon (Judg 12:13-15). It is about 5 miles southwest of Shechem (MR 176179).

■ **32** *Hurai from the brooks of Gaash:* The brooks, or wadis, of Gaash are to be associated with Mount Gaash (Josh 24:30 = Judg 2:9), south of Timnath-heres, and about 15 miles southwest of Shechem.

Abiel the Arabathite: Beth-arabah (MR 197139) is southeast of Jericho (MR 192142) on the border between Benjamin (Josh 18:18, 22) and Judah (15:6, 61).

■ **33** *Azmaveth the Bahurimite:* Bahurim, a Benjaminite city, modern Râs eṭ-Ṭmin (MR 174133), is just east of Mount Scopus in Jerusalem (see 2 Sam 3:16; 16:5; 17:18; 19:17; 1 Kgs 2:8). An Azmaveth[83] son of Adiel had charge of David's treasuries (1 Chr 27:25).

Eliahba the Shaalbonite: Elliger proposed identifying Shaalbon with Selbīṭ (MR 148141; cf. Josh 19:42), 3 miles northwest of Aijalon (MR 152138) and 8 miles north of Beth-shemesh (MR 147128).[84]

■ **34** *Hashem the Gizonite:* The place name Gizon is unknown.[85]

Jonathan the son of Shagee the Hararite: Jonathan is probably the son of Shammah, a member of the Three who is missing from the text of 1 Chronicles 11 by haplography (2 Sam 23:11). McCarter, commenting on 2 Sam 23:11, calls the Hararites an otherwise unknown mountain clan.[86]

■ **35** *Ahiam the son of Sachar the Hararite:* On "Hararite" see the previous comment.

Eliphal the son of Ur: Instead of this name and its patronymic, 2 Sam 23:34 reads Eliphelet the son of Ahitophel the Gilonite. On Giloh see my discussion of Ahijah in v. 36.

■ **36** *Hepher the Mecherathite:* A town Mecherath is unknown, and the reading in Chronicles is probably a corruption of Maacathite, a person from Maacah. Maacah is either the Aramaic state by this name or the Judean clan of Maacah.[87]

Ahijah the Pelonite: On Pelonite see v. 27. The original reading, "Gilonite," preserved in 2 Sam 23:34, points to a city Giloh, which is listed with a group of ten other towns in the Judean hills south of Hebron (Josh 15:48-51).

78 The names Helez and Ira are cited in reverse order in 1 Chronicles 27.
79 The names Abiezer and Sibbecai are cited in reverse order in 1 Chronicles 27.
80 1 Chr 4:13; Josh 15:15-19; Judg 1:11-15; 3:7-11.
81 J. Maxwell Miller, "Geba/Gibeah of Benjamin," *VT* 25 (1975) 145–166, locates it at Jeba' (MR 175140), about 4.5 miles northeast of Jerusalem. See Patrick M. Arnold, *ABD* 2:1007–9.
82 The names Heled (Heldai) and Benaiah are cited in reverse order in 1 Chronicles 27.
83 Cf. also 1 Chr 12:3.
84 Elliger, "Dreissig Helden Davids," 49–52.
85 Cf. ibid., 31, 53, who conjectured a reading of Gimso. Cf. John C. Endres, *ABD* 2:1030; and textual note 65.
86 *II Samuel*, 295.
87 Cf. Elliger, "Dreissig Helden Davids," 56–58, referring to 1 Chr 4:19, "Eshtemoa the Maacathite." Cf. also 1 Chr 2:48, identifying Maacah as Caleb's concubine.

■ **37** *Hezro the Carmelite:* Carmel (MR 162092) is a town south of Hebron in Judah and was the place where David had his encounter with Abigail and Nabal (1 Samuel 25).

■ **38** *Naarai the son of Ezbai:* McCarter reconstructs "[Paarai] the Archite" in 2 Sam 23:35 and identifies it as a clan located in northwest Benjamin, south of Bethel.[88] Hushai was a famous Archite (2 Sam 15:32). Ezbai אזבי is a miswriting of הארבי "the Arbite" in 2 Sam 23:35.

Mibhar the son of Hagri: The MT construes Hagri as a person's name, but perhaps we are to take it as a gentilic. The Hagrites were Transjordanian nomads living east of Gilead. Cf. 1 Chr 5:10, 19-22. According to 27:30 a Hagrite was in charge of David's flocks.

■ **39** *Zelek the Ammonite:* Another representative from across the Jordan.

Naharai the Beerothite: Beeroth (MR 167137) is 4-5 miles northwest of Jerusalem and 2 miles south of el-Jîb, ancient Gibeon (MR 167139).

■ **40** *Ira the Ithrite, Gareb the Ithrite:* The Ithrites (היתרי) were among the indigenous clans associated with Kiriath-jearim (MR 159135; 1 Chr 2:53). Since 2 Sam 23:38 LXX shows an *i* vowel in the second syllable ($I\epsilon\vartheta\iota\rho\alpha\iota\upsilon\varsigma$), Elliger[89] suggested vocalizing the gentilic as הַיִּתִּירִי "the Jattirite." Jattir (MR 151084) is near Debir (MR 151093; Josh 15:48). Jattir is also among the Levitical cities in Josh 21:14//1 Chr 6:42 (57).[90]

■ **41a** *Uriah the Hittite:* The first husband of Bathsheba and a foreigner, Uriah was killed by David through the agency of Joab. Neither David's adultery with Bathsheba nor his execution of Uriah is mentioned in Chronicles. The Chronicler omits "thirty-seven in all," which comes after "Uriah the Hittite" in 2 Sam 23:39. McCarter, who counts thirty names in 2 Sam 23:24-39, reaches the sum of thirty-seven by adding the Three from 2 Sam 23:8-12, Abishai and Benaiah from 2 Sam 23:18-23, an extra name in 23:36 MT (Bani the Gadite), and either Joab (1 Chr 11:39//2 Sam 23:37)[91] or "Adino the Ezenite" from v. 8.[92] Similarly, Japhet, 248, gets a list of thirty-two by including both Elika (2 Sam 23:25 only) and Hepher (1 Chr 11:36 only). To this she adds the Three and the pair of Abishai and Benaiah. She also believes that the list probably contains the names of men who were no longer members of the "Thirty." McCarter notes, however, that it is futile to try to guess what the editor meant by "thirty-seven."[93] Is there any significance to the fact that the first name (Asahel) and the last name (Uriah) in the primary list of thirty men are people whose violent death is recorded in 2 Samuel?

11:41b-47. Additional List of Mighty Men

The sixteen names in this section appear in one of three forms:

A. *X the Y* (in which Y is a gentilic or place name): Joshaphat the Mithnite, Uzzi the Asherathite, Eliel the Mahavite, Ithmah the Moabite, Eliel, Obed, and Jaasiel the Mezobaite. Seven names.

B. *X the son of Y the Z* (in which Y is the father's name and Z is a gentilic or place name): Adina the son of Shiza the Reubenite, Shama and Jeiel the sons of Hotham the Aroerite, Joha (the son of Shimri)[94] the Tirzite. Four names.

C. *X the son of Y* (in which Y is the father's name): Zabad the son of Ahlai, Hanan the son of Maacah, Jediael the son of Shimri, Jeribai and Joshaviah the sons of Elnaam. Five names.[95]

---

88 *II Samuel*, 493, 499.

89 "Dreissig Helden Davids," 62–63.

90 Saul Olyan, "Zadok's Origins and the Tribal Politics of David," *JBL* 101 (1982) 191, suggested that Jether, the father of Amasa (2 Sam 17:25), Absalom's general, should be identified with Nabal, the first husband of Abigail (1 Samuel 25). He also identified Ira the Jairite, one of the priests of David (2 Sam 20:26), with Ira the Ithrite/Jattirite (2 Sam 23:38//1 Chr 11:40). He believed that David appointed Ira as a priest to mollify the anger of the Calebites and other Judahites.

91 Elliger, "Dreissig Helden Davids," 79, n. 21.

92 *II Samuel*, 499. This would create four members of the Three! My reconstructed text has thirty-one names. It adds Hepher and Mibhar to McCarter's list, but omits Elika.

93 *II Samuel*, 499.

94 Joha is the brother of Jediael the son of Shimri.

95 A comparison of the primary and additional lists gives the following results:

Form	Primary List	Additional list
A	61.3%	43.7%
B	12.9%	25%
C	9.7%	31.2%
D	3.2%	
E	6.45%	
F	6.45%	

The conjunction "and" is used in this additional list of mighty men in ways different than in the primary list. In vv. 44b and 46a "Shama and Jeiel" and "Jeribai and Joshaviah" are paired as the sons of their fathers. In v. 45 Jediael is listed with Joah his brother. Two other entries are unclear. Does v. 43 speak of Hanan the son of Maacah and Joshaphat the Mithnite, as in my translation above, or are both Hanan and Joshaphat Mithnites? Does v. 47 speak of Eliel and Obed without patronymics and a third man named Jaasiel the Mezobaite, or are all three men Mezobaites?

An analysis of the topographical information in this additional list reveals the following results:

■ **42** *Adina the son of Shiza the Reubenite, a leader of the Reubenites and thirty with him:*[96] Reuben was assigned land in Transjordan in Josh 13:15-23. Was Adina the only soldier who brought troops with him? If others did, the number supporting David would be geometrically increased.

■ **43** *Hanan the son of Maacah:* If Maacah is a place name rather than a personal name, it may be identified with a kingdom south of Mount Hermon in northern Transjordan assigned to the tribe of Manasseh (Josh 13:11; cf. 2 Sam 10:6-8//1 Chr 19:6-9).[97]

the Mithnite: This location is unknown.

■ **44** *Ashterathite:* The city of Ashtaroth (MR 243244) is a Levitical city in Bashan, east of the Sea of Galilee (Deut 1:4; Josh 9:10; 13:12, 31; 21:27//1 Chr 6:56 [71]).

Aroerite: Aroer (MR 228097) is a site in the tribe of Reuben, on the Arnon River, east of the Dead Sea (cf. 1 Chr 5:8).

■ **45** *The Tizite:* This location is unknown.

■ **46** *Mahavite:* The name is unknown, but Japhet, 252, conjectures it may be a corruption of "Mahanaim" (MR 214177), a site on the Jabbok River, in the territory of Gad, east of the Jordan.

Ithmah the Moabite: Moab, a country east of the Dead Sea, was conquered by David (2 Sam 8:2, 12//1 Chr 18:2, 11). Ithmah was probably a mercenary soldier.

■ **47** *Mezobaite:* The text is uncertain (see textual note 85). If the site is Zobah, it may refer to the kingdom of Aram-Zobah, in the northern Biqa' Valley and eastward, which fought a battle with David (2 Sam 8:3-8//1 Chr 18:3-8; 2 Sam 10:1-19//1 Chr 19:1-19).

Of the nine possible geographical references, seven[98] are probably to be located in Transjordan and two are unknown.

Conclusion

Chapter 11 emphasizes the immediate and untroubled nature of David's rise to power. It ignores David's initial rule over Judah alone, and has all Israel rally to David at Hebron and anoint him as king (11:1-3). The anointing recorded in 2 Sam 5:1-3, by way of contrast, was only after the rival kingship of Ishbaal had been vanquished after some years and was only by the northern tribes of Israel. David's quick ascent to power in Chronicles was fully in accord with the word of Yahweh (1 Chr 11:10; cf. 12:24 [23]). The first act of the new king, accompanied by all Israel, was to capture Jerusalem, and build and repair it (11:4-9). He did this even before the celebration of his coronation had been completed (12:39-41 [38-40]). In all this Yahweh of hosts was with him (11:9).

In a reuse of a list of military heroes taken from 2 Samuel 23 (1 Chr 11:10-41a), supplemented by sixteen other names from another source (11:41b), the Chronicler identifies the strong support given David's rule by the warrior heads, who are again joined by all Israel (v. 10), and all this took place already during David's reign (over all Israel) at Hebron.

---

96 This is the only remaining trace of the "Thirty" in vv. 26-47, since the Chronicler does not record "thirty" from 2 Sam 23:34 (= 1 Chr 11:26) or "thirty-seven" from 2 Sam 23:39 (= 1 Chr 11:41). There are sixteen names in vv. 41b-47. Was this originally an additional list of thirty from the eastern side of the Jordan? See Japhet, 252.

97 Maacah is also a Judean clan name. See discussion of v. 36 above.

98 Two of these result from emendation (Mahanaim and Zobah), and one (Maacah) may be a personal name or even a Judean clan.

1/ These are those who came to David at Zik-lag, while he was kept back by Saul the son of Kish. These were among the warriors, who helped him in war. 2/ They were people armed with a bow, who could sling stones or shoot arrows with the bow, with right or left hand; they were kinsmen of Saul, from Benjamin. 3/ The chief was Ahiezer, then Joash, [both] sons[1] of Shemaah[2] the Gibeathite; also Jeziel and Pelet sons of Azmaveth; Beracah,[3] Jehu of Anathoth, 4/ Ishmaiah the Gibeonite, a warrior among the Thirty and a leader over the Thirty;[4] 5 (4b)/ Jeremiah, Jahaziel, Johanan, Jozabad the Gederathite, 6 (5)/ Eluzai, Jerimoth, Bealiah, Shemariah, Shephatiah the Haruphite;[5] 7 (6)/ Elkanah, Isshiah, Azarel, Joezer, and Jashobeam, the Korahites; 8 (7)/ and Jaelah[6] and Zebadiah, sons of Jeroham from Gedor.[7]

9 (8)/ From the Gadites there separated themselves to David at the stronghold[8] in the wilderness powerful and experienced warriors,[9] skilled with shield and lance,[10] whose faces were like the faces of lions, and who were swift as gazelles on the mountains: 10 (9)/ Ezer the chief, Obadiah second, Eliab third, 11 (10)/ Mishmannah fourth, Jeremiah fifth, 12 (11)/ Attai sixth, Eliel[11] seventh, 13 (12)/ Johanan eighth, Elzabad ninth, 14 (13)/ Jeremiah tenth, Machbannai eleventh. 15 (14)/ These Gadites were officers of the army; the least was equal to a hundred and the greatest to a thousand. 16 (15)/ These are the men who crossed the Jordan in the first month, when it was flooding its banks, and it made impassable[12] all the valleys, to the east and to the west.

17 (16)/ Some Benjaminites and Judahites came to David at the stronghold. 18 (17)/ David went out before them[13] and said to them, "If you have come to me in peace to help me, then my heart will be eager for an alliance with you. But if you have come to betray me to my enemies, even though my hands are without violence, may the God of our fathers see and give judgment. 19 (18)/ The spirit[14] clothed itself around Amasai the chief of the Thirty,[15]

"We are yours,[16] David, and we are with you,[17] son of Jesse.

Peace, peace to you, and peace to those who help you,

for your God has helped you."

Then David received them, and made them heads of his troops.

20 (19)/ Some of the Manassites defected[18] to David when he came with the Philistines for the battle against Saul. But he did not help them,[19] because the rulers of the Philistines took counsel and sent him away, saying,

1 בני; a few Hebrew MSS, LXX: בן "son."

2 שמעה. *BHS* suggests emending to יהשמע "Jehoshamah."

3 וברכה; LXX, Syr: וברכיה "Berechiah."

4 English versions do not begin a new verse at this point, with the result that all the rest of the verse numbers in English are one less than in Hebrew.

5 החריפי Q; K החריפי "Hariphite."

6 וַיַּעְלָה, with Hebrew MSS (cf. Rudolph, 104); MT יוֹעֵאלָה "Joelah."

7 מן הגדור. Rudolph, 104 (also *BHS*), suggests that this is probably a dittography of ומן הגדי, which begins the next verse. This conjecture is based in part on his opinion that Gedor, as a town of Judah, is inappropriate in a list of Benjaminite warriors. See the commentary. LXX בני הגדור "sons of the Gedor"; some Hebrew MSS מן הגדוד "from Gedud" or "from the band."

8 למצד; lacking in LXX.

9 גברי החיל אנשי צבא למלחמה; lit. "mighty warriors, men of service/host for battle." Cf. 1 Chr 7:11 גבורי חילים . . . יצאי צבא למלחמה "mighty warriors . . . ready for service in war/battle."

10 ורמח; one Hebrew MS and many editions: ומגן "and shield."

11 אליאל; a few Hebrew MSS, LXX: אליאב "Eliab."

12 Rudolph, 105, emends ויבריחו ("they put to flight") to the sg. וַיַּבְרֵחַ and translates the verb as denominative from בריח ("bar"). *JPS:* "they put to flight all the lowlanders to the east and west."

13 לפניהם; MT, but not LXX, adds ויען "and he answered." Rudolph, 105, proposed that this verb was originally a gloss to v. 19 after the introductory formula from Amasai's speech had fallen away (see the next note).

14 ורוח. Translation with the definite article seems necessary, although it is lacking in Hebrew. Because of this unusual construction, Paul Joüon, "Notes philologiques sur le texte Hébreu de 1 et 2 Chroniques," *Bib* 13 (1932) 87, wanted to add conjecturally אלהים or יהוה.

15 השלשים; cf. K, LXX, Syr, Vg. Q השלשים "officers." *BHS* suggests inserting וַיֵּשֶׁב לְדָוִד "and he answered David." Cf. versions and 2 Chr 10:16.

16 לך; LXX πορευου (לֵךְ) "go."

17 וְעִמְּךָ; LXX καὶ ὁ λαός σου (וְעַמְּךָ) "and your people."

18 נפלו. The verb is also used in this sense in 2 Chr 15:2; 2 Kgs 25:11; Jer 21:9; 37:14; 39:9; 52:15.

19 עֲזָרָם; cf. LXX[AL], Vg, MT: עֲזָרָם "they did not help them."

20 עדנה, following a few Hebrew MSS; cf. LXX, Vg. MT עדנח "Adnach."

21 לעזרו; lacking in LXX.

22 מספרי; LXX שמי "names."

"He will defect to his master Saul at the price of our heads." 21 (20)/ When he came to Ziklag, there defected to him some of the Manassites: Adnah,[20] Jozabad, Jediael, Michael, Jozabad, Elihu, and Zillethai, chiefs of the thousands who were in Manasseh. 22 (21)/ They provided help to David against the band of raiders, for they were all warriors and commanders in the army. 23 (22)/ Indeed, day after day, people kept coming to David to help him,[21] until there was a great army, like an army of God.

24 (23)/ These are the numbers[22] of the divisions of the army who came to David at Hebron in order to transfer the kingdom of Saul to him in accordance with the word of Yahweh. 25 (24)/ The people of Judah bearing shield and lance numbered six thousand eight hundred armed troops. 26 (25)/ Of the Simeonites, mighty warriors, seven thousand one hundred. 27 (26)/ Of the Levites, four thousand six hundred. 28 (27)/ Jehoiada, chief officer of Aaron, and with him three thousand seven hundred. 29 (28)/ Zadok, an aide, mighty in valor, and twenty-two commanders from his own ancestral house. 30 (29)/ Of the Benjaminites, the kindred of Saul, three thousand, of whom the majority until now had continued to keep their allegiance to the house of Saul.

31 (30)/ Of the Ephraimites, twenty thousand eight hundred, mighty warriors, people of renown in their ancestral houses. 32 (31)/ Of the half-tribe of Manasseh, eighteen thousand who were designated by name to come and make David king. 33 (32)/ Of the children of Issachar, those who had understanding of the times, to know what Israel ought to do, two hundred heads, and all their kindred under their command. 34 (33)/ Of Zebulun, fifty thousand troops fit for military service, lining up for battle with all the weapons of war, to help[23] David[24] with singleness of purpose.[25] 35 (34)/ Of Naphtali, a thousand commanders, with whom there were thirty-seven thousand armed with shield and spear.[26] 36 (35)/ Of the Danites, twenty-eight thousand six hundred equipped for battle. 37 (36)/ Of Asher, forty thousand seasoned troops ready for battle. 38 (37)/ From beyond the Jordan, from the Reubenites, Gadites, and the half-tribe of Manasseh, with all the weapons of[27] war, one hundred and twenty thousand.

39 (38)/ All these warriors, helpers[28] of the battle line, came to Hebron with full intent to make David king over all Israel; and likewise all the rest of Israel were of one mind to make David king. 40 (39)/ They were there with David three days, eating and drinking, for their kindred had provided for them.

23 ולעדר; an Aramaicism (*HALOT* 2:793). A few Hebrew MSS read the more common Hebrew verb ולעזור. LXX, Syr, Vg, Arab. omit the copula. The verb עדר appears also in v. 39 (38).

24 דויד, with LXX; lacking in MT.

25 בלא לב ולב. Contrast Ps 12:3 (2) בלב ולב "with a double or false heart."

26 וחנית; vv. 9, 25: ורמח "lance."

27 כלי מלחמה, with LXX. MT inserts צבא between the two nouns. The expression כלי מלחמה also occurs in Judg 18:11; 2 Sam 1:27; Jer 51:20.

28 עדרי; cf. v. 34 (33). A few Hebrew MSS, LXX: ערכי "drawing up."

29 הקרובים אליהם; *JPS* "relatives."

30 לחם; on the basis of Cairo Genizah fragments and LXX, *BHS* suggests emending to להם "to them."

41 (40)/ And also their neighbors,[29] from as far as Issachar and Zebulun and Naphtali, came bringing food[30] on donkeys, camels, mules, and oxen—abundant supplies of meal, cakes of figs, clusters of raisins, wine, oil, oxen and sheep, for there was joy in Israel.

12:1-41 (1-40)

Structure

Chapter 12, without a canonical *Vorlage*, continues the theme of widespread support of David by the military (cf. 11:10-47) and may be outlined as follows:

I. 12:1-13 (1-12). Soldiers who rallied to David during the days of Saul

    A. 12:1-8 (1-7). Representatives of Benjamin who joined David at Ziklag

    B. 12:9-16 (8-15). Representatives of Gad who joined David at the stronghold

    C. 12:17-19 (16-18). Representatives of Benjamin and Judah who joined David at the stronghold

    D. 12:20-22 (19-21). Representatives of Manasseh who joined David at Ziklag

    E. 12:23 (22). Conclusion

II. 12:24-38 (23-37). Report of tribal muster at Hebron to make David king

    A. 12:24 (23). Introduction

    B. 12:25-30 (24-29). Delegations from Judah, Simeon, Levi, and Benjamin

    C. 12:31-37 (30-36). Delegations from the northern tribes of Ephraim, half-tribe of Manasseh, Issachar, Zebulun, Naphtali, Dan, and Asher

    D. 12:38 (37). Delegation from Transjordanian tribes

III. 12:39-41 (38-40). Enthronement festival at Hebron

Several earlier commentators judged vv. 1-23 (22) to be secondary or, as in the case of Noth,[1] tertiary, that is, subsequent to the secondary addition of vv. 24-41 (23-40). These commentators were persuaded that vv. 1-23 (1-22) interrupted the transition between 11:10-47 (the list of military heroes who joined Israel in making David king at Hebron) and 12:24-41 (23-40) (the tribal muster at Hebron that came to make him king). The secondary verses, in their opinion, were out of order since they harked back to a time before the death of Saul when David was stationed either at Ziklag or in the Judean stronghold. Noth also felt that vv. 24-41 (23-40) were an expansion based on 11:10-47.

In a penetrating study Williamson was able to show that the order of chaps. 11–12 was chiastic, rather than chronological, and that the paragraph at the center of the chiasm was indeed the high point of this literary unit.[2] The results of his study may be presented as follows:

    a. 11:1-9 David's coronation at Hebron and the subsequent conquest of Jerusalem

    b. 11:10-47 Support for David at Hebron by individual military heroes

    c. 12:1-8 (7) Support of tribal groups for David at Ziklag

    d. 12:9-16 (8-15) Support of tribal groups for David at the stronghold

    d′. 12:17-19 (16-18) Support of Benjamin and Judah for David at the stronghold

    c′. 12:20-23 (19-22) Support of tribal groups for David at Ziklag

    b′. 12:24-38 (23-37) Support of tribal groups for David at Hebron

    a′. 12:39-41 (38-40) Festive celebration of David's coronation at Hebron

While a chiasm could be created by the original author or a later redactor, the evidence of a clear, nonchronological arrangement undercuts the arguments of those who judged some of these materials to be secondary

---

1   *Chronicler's History*, 34.

2   "'We are Yours, O David': The Setting and Purpose of 1 Chronicles xii 1-23," *OTS* 21 (1981) 164–76.

because they were out of chronological order (see also the discussion under Structure in 1 Chronicles 11).

The four main divisions in section I of my outline each begins in a similar way, naming the tribal group(s), their defection to David, and the place where they joined up with David. In the first, second, and fourth divisions (A, B, and D), this is followed by a list of a relatively small group of soldiers—twenty-three, eleven, and seven, respectively. The third division (C) finds David meeting the delegation and questioning their loyalty, to which the leader Amasai, clothed with the spirit, responded with a stirring poem. Other structural elements in the individual divisions will be discussed in the detailed commentary.

Although 1 Samuel may overstate the amount of support for David during the reign of Saul in the course of its apology for David, it seems reasonable to suppose that a growing number of people did identify with the cause of David. First, there is the song of the women, "Saul has slain his thousands and David his ten thousands," which appears in three separate contexts (1 Sam 18:7; 21:12 [11]; and 29:5) and shows evidence of popular support for David against Saul. Second, there is the not altogether complimentary comment at 1 Sam 22:2 about his growing numbers: "Everyone who was in distress, and everyone who was in debt, and everyone who was discontented gathered to him." This took place when he was at the cave of Adullam, also described as the period when David was in the stronghold (22:1, 4). The condescending attitude toward those who were joining David's cause nevertheless provides solid evidence for his popularity in the society.

The report of the tribal muster at Hebron in 1 Chr 12:24-38 (23-37), section II, has a decidedly different character. It describes the numbers for the military units of the twelve tribes, beginning from the south and moving north in Cisjordan, and then naming the tribes in Transjordan. The number twelve is achieved, despite the inclusion of both Levi and the two Joseph tribes, Ephraim and Manasseh, by lumping together the two and a half Transjordanian tribes under one census number. The numbers of troops, however, for most of the tribes and for Israel as a whole are enormous and unrealistic for this period in Israel's history, and especially for the history of David before his coronation, when according to 1 Samuel the troops connected to him numbered between four hundred and six hundred. In addition, the coronation of David at Hebron in 2 Sam 5:1-3//1 Chr 11:1-3 has a private, almost secret character—not the gathering of hundreds of thousands of people.

Three strategies have been pursued in attempting to render these numbers more meaningful in a military census list (Williamson, 110–11). The word אלף (normally "thousand") has been interpreted as a military unit. Instead of twenty-eight thousand six hundred for the tribe of Dan in v. 36 (35), for example, this number would be construed as twenty-eight military units and a total of six hundred men.[3] A second approach proposes that each clan was *theoretically* to provide one thousand men, but the number provided in fact was far smaller.[4] A third strategy somewhat resembles the first, but revocalizes אלף as 'allūp or "chief." Hence Dan would have twenty-eight chiefs and six hundred troops.[5]

There is no positive evidence for the second strategy, and I have provided a number of reasons in a separate article why the first—and by analogy the third—strategy will not work, to which the reader is referred for the complete argument.[6] In three cases I was able to show that when the Chronicler cites numbers from the Deuteronomistic History, he parsed them as multiple

---

3 George Mendenhall, "The Census Lists of Numbers 1 and 26," *JBL* 77 (1958) 61–62; adopted completely by Myers, 1:98–99. Saul Olyan, "Zadok's Origins and the Tribal Politics of David," *JBL* 101 (1982) 186, recognized some of the deficiencies of the argument and tried to rescue it by interpreting "hundreds" as a military unit smaller than a "thousand" rather than as a number as Mendenhall did. The same criticisms that can be raised against Mendenhall's hypothesis, however, apply in large part to this subsequent modification.

4 De Vaux, *Ancient Israel*, 216.

5 J. W. Wenham, "Large Numbers in the Old Testament," *TynBul* 18 (1967) 19–53.

6 Ralph W. Klein, "How Many in a Thousand?" in Graham, Hoglund, and McKenzie, *Chronicler as Historian*, 270–82.

thousands and not as multiple (military) units.[7] Numbers for nonhuman objects are also extremely large and unrealistic in Chronicles, and in this case the invocation of an alternate understanding of אלף will not work at all. Before his death, for example, David gathered for the house of Yahweh one hundred thousand talents of gold (about 3,365 tons) and one million talents of silver (33,000 tons; 1 Chr 22:14). Or again the Transjordanian tribes captured from the Hagrites fifty thousand camels, two hundred fifty thousand sheep, and two thousand donkeys (1 Chr 5:21; the passage also mentions one hundred thousand captives). If the Chronicler used exorbitant numbers for nonhuman objects, why should we remove or reinterpret his similarly large numbers when he writes about soldiers or other human beings?

Mendenhall's specific proposal to understand the numbers in 1 Chr 12:24-38 (23-37) as a tribal military muster, with אלף designating a military unit, runs into major obstacles:

1. To get units for all twelve tribes, Mendenhall had to split up the number one hundred twenty thousand for the two and one-half Transjordanian tribes into three equal sets of forty thousand each. In order to limit the tribes to twelve, he had to count the two parts of Manasseh as one tribe and ignore the data for Levi and the priests.

2. Of the twelve tribes in his reconstructed list, only four contain figures for both the units and the total number of soldiers. For seven of the other eight, his list contains only a total for units, with the actual number of men lacking (e.g., for Zebulun, v. 34 [33], fifty military units). For the eighth tribe, Issachar, v. 33 (32), only two hundred chiefs (ראשים) are listed, and there are neither units nor a total number of troops.

3. Naphtali (v. 35 [34]), in Mendenhall's reckoning, would have thirty-seven units consisting of an unspecified number of men, but it had one thousand officers, or twenty-seven officers for each unit.

4. Mendenhall dated this list not to the time of David's coronation, but somewhat later in the united monarchy. In other words, in his reconstruction it is mis-

placed and not historical. But even in its hypothetical chronological position, Mendenhall has major problems. Why would Judah at the time of David be represented by six units while the vastly less significant tribe of Zebulun had fifty units and the Transjordanian tribes had one hundred twenty units?

Instead of removing or reducing the large numbers, we need to interpret the muster list in its present form as a group of twelve tribal groupings, signifying the united, all-Israel interpretation for which the Chronicler always strives. His numbers are to be taken according to the plain sense of the Hebrew, as "thousands," but their significance is symbolic, not literal, just as the arrangement of these two chapters is chiastic, not chronological. The Chronicler mentions the presence of Judah, Simeon, Levi, and Benjamin—southern tribes and/or tribes present in the postexilic community—but their numbers are relatively small, ranging from three thousand for Benjamin to seven thousand one hundred for Simeon. The tribes from the heartland of the old northern kingdom were there too: eighteen thousand men from Manasseh and twenty thousand eight hundred from Ephraim, three to six times as many as from Judah, Simeon, Levi, and Benjamin. But the most remote tribes had the greatest representation: Dan numbered twenty-eight thousand six hundred; Naphtali thirty-seven thousand; Asher forty thousand; Zebulun fifty thousand; the Transjordanian tribes one hundred twenty thousand, while Issachar brought its whole tribe (v. 33 [32]). The principle seems to be, the more remote the tribe, the larger its delegation at David's coronation. Hence David was by no means a king representing only Judah. All tribes supported him, and the tribes that were most distant—or long since forgotten or grown insignificant by the time of the Chronicler—were far and away the most supportive. The tribes of Judah, Benjamin, and Levi at the time of the Chronicler needed no special justification to be part of Israel, nor did the small community of Yehud exhaust what might be meant by "Israel." The Chronicler gives significant importance to the tribes other than Judah and expresses thereby a broader hope for what Israel might become.

---

7   1 Chr 19:7//2 Sam 10:6, 32,000 chariots; 1 Chr 21:5//2 Sam 24:9, 1,100,000 men who drew the sword; 2 Chr 2:1, 16-17 (2, 17-18)//1 Kgs 5:29-30

(15-16), 70,000 laborers, 80,000 stonecutters, 3,600 overseers, 153,600 aliens.

The numbers are the following:

Judah 6,800

Simeon 7,100

Levi 8,300 (4,600 Levites and 3,700 people with Jehoiada, Zadok, and twenty-two commanders)

Benjamin 3,000

Ephraim 20,800

Half Manasseh 18,000

Issachar 200 "heads" and all their kindred under their command

Zebulun 50,000

Naphtali 37,000, with 1,000 chiefs

Dan 28,600

Asher 40,000

Tribes east of the Jordan 120,000

Total: 339,600 (plus 1,222 commanders and however many came with Issachar)

While the list may imitate more realistic muster lists and is rich with military vocabulary, I believe its value is primarily theological and provides another example of the Chronicler's all-Israel agenda. Saul Olyan has suggested that vv. 25-30, with their modest, plausible numbers for the southern tribes and with their identification of two specific Levitical leaders, may contain authentic information.[8] This may be true, especially with the individuals involved, but even for the time of David the numbers for Simeon seem too high. I will, however, treat this paragraph separately as possibly stemming in whole or in part from a source that was available to the Chronicler.

Detailed Commentary

12:1-13 (1-12). Soldiers Who Rallied to David during the Days of Saul

12:1-8 (1-7). Representatives of Benjamin Who Joined David at Ziklag

■ **1** *These are those who came to David at Ziklag:* Toward the end of Saul's reign David became allied with Achish the Philistine king of Gath, who ceded to him the city of Zik-

lag (1 Sam 21:10-14; 27:2-12). Ziklag (MR 119088) is located about forty to forty-five miles southwest of Jerusalem.[9] When Achish asked David to separate himself from the Philistine troops just before their battle with Saul, in which Israel was badly defeated and King Saul committed suicide, David returned to Ziklag only to discover it had been raided by Amalekites (1 Sam 29:1–30:3). David gathered his six hundred troops,[10] won a total victory against the Amalekites, and recovered his wives Ahinoam and Abigail, who had been taken captive (1 Sam 30:4-31). According to 1 Chr 12:1-8 (1-7), the troops who joined up with David at Ziklag deserted Saul in the final days of his reign. In 1 Sam 22:1-2 David's army was made up of those who were in distress or in debt, or who were discontented. In 1 Chronicles 12, however, the cream of the crop from all twelve tribes rallies around David.

while he was kept back by Saul the son of Kish: The Chronicler seems to assume that readers would know the story of the contest between David and Saul in the Deuteronomistic History. Despite the fact that Samuel had anointed David at Yahweh's direction in 1 Sam 16:1-13 and despite the fact that many groups and individuals had rallied to his cause, David was prevented from being king (עצור "kept back" or "constrained") because Saul still ruled as king and was in fact pursuing David wherever possible.

the warriors who helped him in war: "Help" is a leitmotif of this chapter, occurring seven times and in both of its major sections (vv. 1, 18 [17], 19 [18 twice], 20 [19], 22 [21], 23 [22];[11] an Aramaic synonym עדר appears in vv. 34 and 39 [33 and 38]). See also Ahiezer ("my divine brother is help") in v. 3 and several additional names in the subsequent verses.

■ **2** *They were people armed with a bow, who could sling stones or shoot arrows with the bow, with the right or left hand:* The word "Benjamin" means "son of the right hand" (or southerner) in Hebrew, but the Bible contains two passages that describe Benjaminites as left-handed (Judg 3:15; 20:16). In the present verse the Benjaminites

---

8   Olyan, "Zadok's Origins," 186. Christian E. Hauer, "Who Was Zadok?" *JBL* 82 (1963) 89–94, had earlier argued for the antiquity of v. 29 alone.

9   Wade R. Kotter, "Ziklag," *ABD* 6:1090, identifies it with Tell esh-Shariʻa.

10   Cf. 1 Sam 22:2; 27:2.

11   Cf. 1 Chr 5:20.

(see the next comment) are either ambidextrous or composed of some right-handed and some left-handed men. Their military ability may have compensated for their small numbers. Their role in the army was to do long-range, rather than hand-to-hand, fighting.

they were kinsmen of Saul, from Benjamin: The first group of deserters from King Saul to David were members of Saul's own tribe of Benjamin, with twenty-three individuals mentioned by name. The irony of their desertion is emphasized by not mentioning the tribe's name first, as in vv. 9, 17, and 20, but by delaying its mention until the very end of v. 2. Meir Malul has used this verse and the references to Benjaminites later in the chapter (vv. 17, 30 [16, 29)] and 1 Sam 31:3 to raise the possibility that David had formed a fifth column from Saul's closest relatives while David was still at the court of Saul. In his view these allies may even have been responsible for Saul's death.[12]

■ **3** *Ahiezer:* The motif of help offered to David (see the comment on v. 1) also echoes in this name ("my divine brother is help"), as well as in Azarel ("God has helped") and Joezer ("Yahweh is help"; v. 6 [5]), and Ezer ("help"; v. 10 [9]). Two names in chap. 11 anticipate this motif: Eleazar ("God [El] has helped"; v. 12) and Abiezer ("my divine father is help"; v. 28).

the Gibeathite: The first two Benjaminites even came from Saul's hometown of Gibeah (for its location see 1 Chr 11:31).

Jeziel and Pelet sons of Azmaveth: One of David's warriors in 1 Chr 11:33//2 Sam 23:31 also had the name Azmaveth. Azmaveth, however, might also be a town, modern Hizmeh (MR 175138; cf. 1 Chr 8:36).

Jehu of Anathoth: For the location of the Benjaminite city of Anathoth, which was also a Levitical city, see 1 Chr 6:45 (60). It is not clear in vv. 3-6 (3-5) whether the gentilics "the Anathothite," "the Gederathite," and "the Haruphite" refer only to the last name mentioned, in this case Jehu, or to all the names listed since the last gentilic or patronymic.

■ **4** *Ishmaiah the Gibeonite:* For the location of Gibeon see 8:29. The genealogies of Saul in chaps. 8 and 9 connect Saul with Gibeon rather than Gibeah. Hence Ishmaiah too could be considered to come from Saul's hometown. The defection of a Gibeonite might also be related to Saul's harsh treatment of the Gibeonites (2 Sam 21:1-6).

a warrior among the Thirty and a leader over the Thirty: No doubt the members of the Thirty and its leadership changed over the years, and there is no way to determine when Ishmaiah was their commander. There are several other leaders of the Thirty mentioned in Chronicles: Abshai (1 Chr 11:20), probably Adina the Reubenite (11:42), and Amasai (12:19 [18]).[13]

■ **5 (4b)** *Jozabad the Gederathite:* A place named Gederah is listed among the towns of the tribe of *Judah* in Josh 15:36 and 1 Chr 4:23.[14] If this is the place intended by this gentilic, the list in vv. 3-8 (3-7) may be composite, with the following names and places stemming from Judah.[15] Myers, 1:96, identifies it with Jedireh near Gibeon in Benjamin. The evidence for both Benjaminite and Judahite identifications will be given for the following names.

■ **6 (5)** *Eluzai, Jerimoth, Bealiah, Shemariah, Shephatiah the Haruphite:* The inclusion of בעל in the personal name Bealiah ("Yahweh is lord" or "Yahweh is Baal") may show the relative antiquity of this list when "baal" was considered an epithet meaning "lord," rather than the name of a deity competing with Yahweh. Cf. 5:4-6; 8:30, 33; 9:39; 11:11; 14:7. It is not clear whether "Haruphite" refers to all five names or only to Shephatiah. Hareph (חָרֵף) is mentioned among the descendants of Caleb, in Judah, in 2:51, and Hariph (Neh 7:24)[16] is mentioned as a place name near Gibeon, in Benjamin (Neh 7:25), in the list of returnees. A personal name Hariph appears in Neh 10:20 (19).

■ **7 (6)** *Azarel, Joezer:* Both names contain the root עזר, meaning "help." See the discussion in v. 3.

Jashobeam: Cf. 1 Chr 11:11 and 27:2.

12 Meir Malul, "Was David Involved in the Death of Saul on the Gilboa Mountain?" *RB* 103 (1996) 517–45.
13 Cf. Jeshbaal in 1 Chr 11:11.
14 See Carl S. Ehrlich, *ABD* 2:925, where four possible locations are given. Etymologically, the name means something like "(animal) shelter" or "wall," and so it may have been used for a number of locations.
15 Cf. Curtis and Madsen, 196, who suggest the introductory words for the tribe of Judah may have fallen out.
16 The parallel passage in Ezra 2:18 has "Jorah."

the Korahites: This could refer to a group of cultic leaders attested in genealogical references from Edom,[17] Levi,[18] and Judah.[19] J. Maxwell Miller proposed that the Edomite Korahites entered Palestine early in Israel's history and settled among Calebites in the vicinity of Hebron.[20] These cultic leaders may have competed with the Mushites in southern Judah (cf. Numbers 16).[21] The Korahite psalms are attributed to them. In the Chronicler's day they were gatekeepers and bakers, residing in Jerusalem (1 Chr 9:17-32; 26:1, 19).[22] Rudolph, 104, interprets "Korahites" as a reference to citizens of an unknown town קרח in Benjamin, but one would think that the writer would make this clearer since readers would more likely associate "Korah" with the religious leaders known by this name.

Jaelah and Zebadiah, sons of Jeroham of Gedor: The town of Gedor (MR 158115), southwest of Bethlehem (MR 169123), belonged to Judah (cf. 4:4). Rudolph (see textual note 7) wanted to delete the reference to Gedor as a dittograph of the beginning of the next verse, but the preceding Korahites are also probably from Judah, as is (are) the Haruphite(s) before them.

12:9-16 (8-15). Representatives of Gad Who Joined David at the Stronghold

■ **9 (8)** *From the Gadites there separated themselves to David:* As part of the Transjordanian tribes, the Gadites may have been cited to show the widespread support for David. These men separated themselves, presumably, from those Gadites who supported Saul.

at the stronghold in the wilderness: David's stay at the wilderness stronghold (cf. also v. 17) near Adullam (MR 150117), during his struggles against Saul (1 Sam 22:1, 4-

5; 24:22), was earlier than his stay at Ziklag (MR 119088).[23] But as we saw under Structure above, the arrangement of the various military groups is chiastic, not chronological.

powerful and experienced warriors, skilled with shield and lance: The high quality of the soldiers from Gad is underlined in this and subsequent clauses (cf. also v. 15 [14]). Their weapons[24] are primarily for fighting at close range, thus complementing the armaments of the Benjaminites.

whose faces were like the faces of lions, and who were swift as gazelles on the mountains: Gad's leonine fighting ability is noted in the Blessing of Moses: "Gad lives like a lion; he tears at arm and scalp" (Deut 33:20), and Jacob observed in his testament, "Gad shall be raided by raiders, but he shall raid at their heels" (Gen 49:19).[25] Asahel, one of the sons of Zeruiah, was "as swift of foot as a wild gazelle" (2 Sam 2:18). The lover in the Song of Songs is compared to a gazelle leaping upon the mountains and bounding over the hills (Song 2:8-9). There is no other biblical passage, however, that speaks directly about the fierce appearance of a lion or of someone who looks like a lion. In his lament over Saul and Jonathan, David mentions that these two men were swifter than eagles and stronger than lions (2 Sam 1:23).

■ **10 (9)** *Ezer the chief:* The eleven Gadites in vv. 10-14 (9-13) are referred to by ordinal numbers (chief, second, third, etc.), which are normally used to enumerate a sequence of children from one father (3:1-3, 13-15, etc.). Is this a literary device or a mnemonic aid, or did their numerical order serve some social purpose? The name Ezer is formed from עזר ("help"; cf. v. 1).

---

17 Gen 36:5, 14, 16, 18.

18 Exod 6:21.

19 1 Chr 2:43. Cf. also Num 26:57-58.

20 J. Maxwell Miller, "The Korahites of Southern Judah," *CBQ* 32 (1970) 58–68.

21 "Sons of Korah" are also attested in a late-8th-century inscription from Arad (Ostracon 49), found at the entrance to the temple. See Johannes Renz, *Die althebräischen Inschriften,* part 1: *Text und Kommentar* (Handbuch der althebräischen Epigraphik; Darmstadt: Wissenschaftliche Buchgesellschaft, 1991) 153–55.

22 Miller, "Korahites," 67–68, suggests they found their way to Jerusalem in connection with Josiah's reform.

23 Other sites during his days fighting with Saul are also possible: Ziph (1 Sam 23:14; MR 162098), Maon (1 Sam 23:24; MR 162090), and En-gedi (1 Sam 23:29; MR 187097).

24 Cf. Jer 46:3 for a similar use of the verb ערך with such weapons. The more usual verb is נשא, as in v. 25 (24).

25 There is alliteration and punning in this verse with the letters גד featured in four of the words: גד גדוד יגד . . . יגודנו. David commented on the speed and strength of Saul and Jonathan: "They were swifter than eagles, they were stronger than lions."

■ **15 (14)** *the least was equal to a hundred and the greatest to a thousand:* One of the blessings for obedience cited in Lev 26:8 speaks of soldiers capable of overcoming twenty-to-one or even hundred-to-one odds.[26]

■ **16 (15)** *crossed the Jordan in the first month:* The capability and determination of the Gadites were shown by their crossing the Jordan in the spring (April) when the river was at its height.

it made impassable all the valleys: This translation, based on a hypothetical denominative verb from ברית ("bar"), indicates the power of the Jordan at flood stage,[27] which the Gadites were able to overcome. This clause can also be rendered "they made all the valleys flee," in which case "valleys" stands for the people who inhabited the valleys.[28] Such a routing of the enemy by the Gadites might reflect their fierce appearance, their prowess as warriors, or their ability to overcome great numerical odds.

12:17-19 (16-18). Representatives of Benjamin and Judah Who Joined David at the Stronghold

This paragraph adds a strong theological message to the information about the military support shown for David. David exhorted God to uncover any treachery used against him, and Amasai responded to David's query about the loyalty of Benjamin and Judah with prophetic authority and with a confession that God had indeed helped David.

■ **17 (16)** *Some Benjaminites and Judahites came to David at the stronghold:* David's fear of treachery from these troops echoes the situation in the book of Samuel, where the Judahites of Keilah (1 Sam 23:10-12; MR 150113) and Ziph (1 Sam 23:19-24; 26:1; MR 162098) were ready to betray David to Saul.[29] Japhet, 263, believes that only the reference to the Judahites is original here and that the Benjaminites were added later,

since it is unlikely that these two tribes would have had a common leader at the time of Saul. In addition, an account of the troops coming from Benjamin had already been given in vv. 3-8 (9).

If you have come in peace to help me: David posed two "if" clauses (for the second "if" clause, see below) to this band of troops to test their loyalty. The word "peace" here might connote integrity or truth (cf. Judg 9:15[30]). The key to understanding the intentions of the Benjaminites and the Judahites was their willingness to help David, which has been a theme throughout the chapter.

my heart will be eager for an alliance with you: Talmon has argued that יחד, here translated "alliance," is a synonym for covenant.[31]

if you have come to betray me to my enemies even though my hands are without violence, may the God of our fathers see and give judgment: As soldiers come from other tribes, David needs to know whether they have come to help (1 Chr 12:1) or to betray him. David has no way to cross-examine the intentions of this band of troops and therefore he calls upon their mutual God to see and give judgment (cf. Exod 5:21). David claims that he is innocent of violence in words that are remarkably close to Job 16:17 ("There is no violence in my hands, and my prayer is pure"). The title "God of the fathers" is common in Chronicles and probably betrays the Chronicler's own hand.[32] Japhet, 265, calls the Chronicler's method of availing himself of already existing poetical phrases and interlacing them, with minor changes, into his own literary expression, his "anthological style."

■ **19 (18)** *The spirit clothed itself around:* Endowment with the spirit is a sign of someone who speaks with prophetic authority in Chronicles (cf. Azariah the son of Oded, 2 Chr 15:1; Jahaziel a Levite, 20:14; and Zechariah the son of the priest Jehoiada, 24:20).[33] The

---

26 Cf. Deut 32:30: "How could one have routed a thousand and two put a myriad to flight?" and Isa 30:17: "A thousand shall flee at the threat of one."

27 Cf. Josh 3:15: "Now the Jordan overflows all its banks throughout the time of harvest." In the account of Joshua's conquest, the Transjordanian tribes contributed decisive assistance, as here (Josh 4:12).

28 Traditionally, the Canaanites were said to live in the valleys (Josh 17:16; Judg 1:19).

29 Doeg the Edomite also betrayed David (1 Samuel 21–22).

30 "The bramble said to the trees, 'If in good faith (באמת) you are anointing me king over you. . . .'"

31 Shemaryahu Talmon, "The Sectarian יחד—a Biblical Noun," *VT* 3 (1953) 136.

32 For the "God of the ancestors" see 1 Chr 5:25.

33 2 Chr 18:21-23//1 Kgs 22:22-24 speaks of a lying spirit that causes the false prophets to prophesy.

closest parallel in phraseology to this verse is in 24:20, where the spirit also "clothes itself around" Zechariah, a priest. Schniedewind calls the figures who give inspired speeches but who are not designated as prophets "inspired messengers."[34]

Amasai the chief of the Thirty: This officer is otherwise unknown, and the attempt of Zeron to identify him with Amasa, the general of Absalom, has not met with wide acceptance.[35]

"We are yours, David, and we are with you, son of Jesse": The speech of Amasai was composed from language used in critical comments about David or the Davidic dynasty in Samuel and Kings[36] and from an anthology of other expressions from the Hebrew Bible. Nabal, for example, complained about David: "Who is David? Who is the son of Jesse? There are many servants today who are breaking away from their masters" (1 Sam 25:10). The Benjaminite Sheba led a revolt against David during his reign and highlighted his opposition in these words: "We have no portion in David, no share in the son of Jesse! Everyone to your tents, O Israel!" This opposition comes to a climax in 1 Kgs 12:16//2 Chr 10:16, when the people answered King Rehoboam: "What share do we have in David? We have no inheritance in the son of Jesse. To your own tents, O Israel! Look now to your own house, O David." The Chronicler composed the first part of Amasai's speech using language that was precisely the opposite of the negative slogans against David that were preserved in Samuel and Kings.

"Peace, peace to you, and peace to those who help you": This continuation of Amasai's reply picks up the word "peace" from David's initial "if" clause (v. 18 [17] "If you have come in peace to help me") and repeats the wish for peace for David three times. Amasai thereby demonstrated decisively that he and his men indeed did come

in peace. He also offered his blessing to those who had rallied to David's cause already in the days of Saul.

for your God has helped you: Amasai affirms that the military and political support shown to David by the troops joining his cause is ratified and enabled by the help previously shown him by God. Amasai's reference to David's God—"your God"—in contrast to "the God of our fathers" (v. 18 [17]), acknowledges David's status.

David received them: This clause resolves the tension created by v. 18 (17), when David met the delegation from Judah and Benjamin outside the camp and posed two "if" clauses. That delegation had demonstrated its own fidelity, and in the process they wished those other tribal contingents well who were helping David, and they confessed that David was the recipient of divine help.

and made them heads of his troops: There is a logic to David's choice. He appointed supervising officers from the tribes that were most closely related to him (Judah and Benjamin) and, not incidentally, that were the heart of the Chronicler's postexilic community.

12:20-22 (19-21). Representatives of Manasseh Who Joined David at Ziklag

■ **20 (19)** *Some of the Manassites defected to David:* The paragraph beginning with this verse has a repetitive resumption later; the words "there defected to him some of the Manassites" are repeated in chiastic order in v. 21 (20). The troops from Manasseh provide evidence for defection to David from the northern tribes, just as Gad played that role for the Transjordanian tribes. Manasseh frequently serves in Chronicles as a representative, or one of several representatives, of the northern tribes.[37]

when he came with the Philistines for the battle against Saul: In 1 Sam 27:2-6 David entered into the service of Achish king of Gath, and in 1 Sam 28:1-2 Achish invited David to go along in the Philistines' battle against Israel

---

34 *Word of God,* 70–74, 108–11. In Judg 6:34 the spirit's clothing itself around Gideon initiates his military leadership against the Midianites. A number of tribal groups joined him after the spirit's possession.

35 Alexander Zeron, "Tag für Tag kam man zu David, um ihm zu helfen: 1 Chr. 12,1-22: Ein versprengtes Stück einer Abschalom-Tradition?" *ThZ* 30 (1974) 257–61.

36 Williamson, 108; idem, "'We Are Yours, O David': The Setting and Purpose of 1 Chronicles xii 1-23," *OTS* 21 (1981) 174, believes that this first part of

Amasai's speech is an old authentic saying from the time of David, which was challenged by contrary negative assertions now preserved in the Deuteronomistic History. Since this positive saying is not preserved in the Deuteronomistic History, and since in any case Williamson concedes that the second part of his speech was created by the Chronicler, it is probably advisable to credit the Chronicler with the entire speech.

37 2 Chr 15:9; 30:1, 10, 11, 18; 31:1; 34:6, 9.

and even appointed him his permanent bodyguard. If David had participated in the battle of Gilboa, in which Saul died, his political career might well have been over. The Manassites defected from Saul at the time of his final defeat.

But he did not help them: As important as the help of God and of the groups of defecting soldiers are for David, it is also crucial that David did not provide any help for the Philistines, Israel's enemy. Similarly, the kings of Israel were not to help the wicked or to seek help from others.[38] It is hard to follow Halpern, however, in reconstructing a source used by the Chronicler that indicated that the Manassites defected to David at Apheq, *before* the battle at Jezreel.[39] The specific mention of the Manassites seems to be part of the Chronicler's agenda to show northern support for David from the beginning and should not be credited to a hypothetical source containing embarrassing information about David.

"He will defect to his master Saul at the price of[40] *our heads":* The Philistine rationale for dismissing David from the battle of Gilboa repeats the substance of their speech in the narrative of that event in 1 Sam 29:4: "He shall not go down with us to battle, or else he may become an adversary to us in the battle. For how could this fellow reconcile himself to his lord? Would it not be with the heads of the men here?" When he left the Philistines just before the battle of Gilboa, David would have passed through the territory of Manasseh on his way to Ziklag.

■ **21 (20)** *When he came to Ziklag:* Cf. 1 Sam 30:1. The Chronicler has returned to the setting of vv. 1-8 (1-9), thus completing this segment of the chiasm. After the repetitive resumption of the defection of the Manassites he lists seven men from Manasseh without any patronymics or other additional information.

■ **22 (21)** *They provided help to David against the band of raiders, for they were all warriors and commanders in the*

army: When David returned to Ziklag in 1 Samuel 30, he discovered that a band of the Amalekites had burned Ziklag down and had taken captive all of its inhabitants, including David's wives Ahinoam and Abigail.[41] David pursued the Amalekites, defeated them—except for four hundred who escaped on camels—and recovered all the captives. All this David did with only four hundred men from his army of six hundred, and they were reinforced, according to Chronicles, by seven men from Manasseh, all of whom were "warriors and commanders." As with the groups from Gad and Benjamin-Judah, the seven soldiers from Manasseh became officers in David's army.

E. 12:23 (22). Conclusion

■ **23 (22)** *people kept coming to David to help him:* With this, the seventh reference to "help" in vv. 1-23 (1-22), the Chronicler completes his account of those soldiers who sided with David during the period of his struggles with Saul.

a great army, like an army of God: JPS renders: "an army as vast as the army of God." Others take "army of God" as a metaphorical phrase best rendered in English as "an immense army." According to the Chronicler, therefore, the size of David's army had increased many-fold beyond the four hundred to six hundred of 1 Samuel. Just how big that army had become is shown in the following verses (vv. 24-41 [23-40]). The human and divine participation in David's military adventures is emphasized by comparing the human troops with an army of God. The Chronicler elsewhere links the army of Israel with the army (or camp, מחנה) of Yahweh (2 Chr 14:12 [13]).

12:24-38 (23-37). Report of Tribal Muster at Hebron to Make David King

12:24 (23). Introduction

■ **24 (23)** *These are the numbers of the divisions of the army:* Something like "divisions" or "companies" needs to be used for ראש since the conventional translation "heads"

---

38 Jehu admonished Jehoshaphat not to help the wicked (2 Chr 19:2); Ahaz sought help from the king of Assyria and the gods of the kings of Aram (28:16, 23).

39 *David's Secret Demons,* 78–79.

40 This interpretation of ב as a designation of price seems preferable to construing it as an oath formula (Myers, 1:95): "By our heads, he will defect to his

master Saul." On the latter suggestion see the note by Virgil M. Rogers, "The Use of ראש in an Oath," *JBL* 74 (1955) 272.

41 Cf. 1 Sam 30:8, 15, 23.

does not fit this context.[42] Throughout vv. 24-41 (23-40) the Chronicler uses varied terminology for the army, including its leadership and its common combatants. This verse is parallel to 11:11, which introduces the list of individual heroes.

who came to David at Hebron: The Chronicler now returns to the setting of David's coronation (11:1-3) and prepares to list the wholehearted rallying to David of the various Israelite tribal armies.

in order to transfer the kingdom of Saul to him: These warriors complete de facto the "transfer" (להסב) of the kingdom of Saul to David even though that had been done de jure by Yahweh's transfer (ויסב) of the kingdom to David at the death of Saul (10:14). The transfer is done peacefully and not by civil war. Saul is mentioned seven times in the chapter.[43] Since four of these occur in section I and three in section II, this may provide additional evidence against considering vv. 1-23 (22) secondary.

in accordance with the word of Yahweh: Cf. 10:14; 11:3, 10.

12:25-30 (24-29). Delegations from Judah, Simeon, Levi, and Benjamin

■ **25 (24)** *The people of Judah bearing shield and lance:* Judah is mentioned first—before the Simeonites and Levites—following a general pattern from south to north, although Simeon, of course, was really the southernmost tribe. But Judah's role as the tribe of David and as central to the identity of the postexilic community raises it to the first position. Like the tribe of Gad in vv. 9-16 (8-15), the soldiers from Judah were armed for fighting at

close quarters. The large shield, צנה, referred to here and in vv. 9, 35 (8, 34), covered the whole body, while the small shield, מגן (5:18), was used to fend off arrows.

■ **27 (26)** *Of the Levites four thousand six hundred:* The Levites here seem to be from the nonpriestly section of the tribe although a priest is mentioned in the following verse. Rooke has proposed that this verse and the next two are in an ascending hierarchical order.[44] The Levites are listed first as the most numerous, but least exalted, class.

■ **28 (27)** *Jehoiada, chief officer of Aaron, and with him three thousand and seven hundred:* Jehoiada and Zadok (see the commentary on the next verse) are the only individuals mentioned in vv. 24-41 (23-40). Rudolph, 109, used this fact to argue that the Levites originally had no place in the list, since the presence of two individuals conflicts with the superscription in v. 24 (23): "These are the numbers of the divisions of the army."[45] According to 11:22 Jehoiada was the father of Benaiah, one of David's heroes, from the southern town of Kabzeel, whom David put in charge of his personal bodyguard (11:25).[46] In 27:5 Benaiah, again identified as the son of Jehoiada, was the commander in charge of the third month. Later in that chapter the Chronicler mentions (another) Jehoiada, the *son* of Benaiah, the successor to Ahithophel as the king's counselor (27:34).[47] Olyan suggested that Jehoiada's bringing troops to David resulted in Zadok, Jehoiada's son and aide (נער),[48] being appointed to the position of one of David's priests, another son Benaiah to a high military position (11:22, 25), and Jehoiada's grandson, also named Jehoiada, to

---

42   BDB, 911, and *HALOT* 3:1166 suggest a meaning of "military units" at Judg 7:16, 20; 9:34, 37, 43, 44; 1 Sam 11:11; 13:17-18; and Job 1:17.

43   Vv. 1, 2, 20 (19, twice), 24 (23), 30 (29, twice).

44   Deborah W. Rooke, *Zadok's Heirs: The Role and Development of the High Priesthood in Ancient Israel* (Oxford: Oxford Univ. Press, 2000) 67.

45   He even speculated that the presence of the Levitical names led to the reading "names" in LXX for מספרי "numbers" in v. 24. More likely, in my judgment, the translator used the word "names" because of his difficulty in understanding what is meant by ראשי, which he took in its more common sense as "heads."

46   Since Benaiah killed Joab in the tent of Yahweh (1 Kgs 2:28-34), the Chronicler may have thought that

such access to the sanctuary required that he be a Levite. A later Jehoiada was high priest in the time of Joash (2 Chr 22:11–24:25).

47   See textual note 33 in chap. 27.

48   But the word נער refers to his social status and conspicuously lacks a suffix relating him to Jehoiada. See Carolyn Leeb, *Away from the Father's House: The Social Location of the nʿr and nʿrh in Ancient Israel* (JSOTSup 301; Sheffield: Sheffield Academic Press, 2000) 86, n. 38.

the office of the king's counselor (27:34).[49] Because of the relationship between Jehoiada and Zadok, Olyan also proposed that the twenty-two commanders accompanying Zadok were in charge of the military units connected with Jehoiada.[50] Olyan's suggestion about the relationship between Jehoiada and Zadok fails, however, since it depends on "his ancestral house" in v. 29 (28) having Jehoiada as its antecedent,[51] whereas the most natural antecedent is Zadok himself, as in my translation: "from his own ancestral house." Rooke questions the antiquity of 12:25-30 (24-29), central to Olyan's position, because of the ascending hierarchy in vv. 27-29 (26-28). Zadok is presented at the climax of vv. 27-29 (26-28), only after references to the Levites and Aaron, and thus gets introduced into the narrative much earlier than in the Deuteronomistic History, where he is first mentioned in 2 Sam 8:17//1 Chr 18:16.[52] Jehoiada, as chief officer (נָגִיד) of Aaron, presided over the priests, who are somewhat less numerous than the Levites (three thousand seven hundred to four thousand six hundred).

■ **29 (28)** *Zadok, an aide, mighty in valor, and twenty-two commanders from his own father's house:* Zadok is associated with, although apparently distinguished from, the Aaronides mentioned in the previous verse. His identity is militaristic: he is mighty in valor. The word translated "aide" (נער) might also indicate his relative youth.[53] While Zadok is not identified as a priest here, the Chronicler makes no effort to distinguish him sharply from Zadok the priest. If Rooke is right in detecting a hierarchy in vv. 27-29 (26-28), with Zadok at the peak,

these verses may not be ancient and in any case would add very little or no historical information to the already somewhat obscure history of Zadok. These verses merely provide an opportunity for the Chronicler to introduce Zadok.[54] If these verses, or at least v. 29 (28), do have some historical basis, it could clarify how Zadok rose to the position as David's chief priest by recording that he was involved with David as a military supporter already during David's Hebron days. Hauer, for example, argued that Zadok was a young priest from Jerusalem who deserted to David's cause prior to the capture of Jerusalem.[55] Hauer's position is related to the Jebusite hypothesis in which Zadok is regarded as a pre-Israelite priest of El Elyon in Jerusalem whom David appointed as his own priest in order to cement relationships between the native Jebusite population and his own regime.[56] Since Jerusalem is not mentioned in this passage, however, Zadok's early loyalty need not be related to the Jebusite hypothesis, and Cross has raised serious problems with that hypothesis in any case.[57] Cross does see evidence in these verses that members of the house of Aaron rallied to David in Hebron. Among these Aaronides were Jehoiada, whose name recurs later in the high priestly line,[58] and his aide Zadok.[59] The slender gain in knowledge about Zadok depends on whether vv. 28-29 (27-28) are old, and in my judgment there is not enough evidence to make a final decision on that question. Is there any connection between the twenty-two commanders who accompanied Zadok and the fact that there were twenty-two priestly houses in the days of

---

49 For the roles played by Jehoiada and Benaiah, see Olyan, "Zadok's Origins," 177–93. The only other Jehoiada in the Bible is the high priest during the reign of Joash. Perhaps he was named after his ancestor of the same name.

50 The Hebrew text, correctly in my judgment, puts 3,700 with Jehoiada. Olyan, "Zadok's Origins," 185–186, interprets this as meaning three larger and seven smaller military units.

51 Olyan, "Zadok's Origins," 188–89.

52 Rooke, *Zadok's Heirs,* 202–3.

53 Leeb, *Away from the Father's House,* 86, n. 38, suggests that Zadok was a נער warrior or a נער of a warrior.

54 In addition to the present passage, see references to Zadok in 1 Chr 15:11; 16:39; 24:3, 6, 31; 27:17; 29:22 (cf. 1 Kgs 1:38-39); and 2 Chr 31:10. In 1 Chr

18:16 Zadok is called the son of Ahitub. In other genealogical notices Chronicles puts him among the descendants of Eleazar (24:3) and even Aaron (24:31). The Chronicler explains Zadok's rise to power by his early loyalty to David and by his serving in a priestly capacity at Gibeon (16:39-40).

55 Hauer, "Who Was Zadok?" *JBL* 82 (1963) 89–94.

56 See S. Mowinckel, *Ezra den Skriftlaerde* (Kristiania: Universitets Forlaget, 1916) 109, n. 2; and H. H. Rowley, "Zadok and Nehushtan," *JBL* 58 (1939) 113–41.

57 Cross, *Canaanite Myth,* 209–11.

58 1 Kings 11–12//2 Chronicles 22–24.

59 *Canaanite Myth,* 212–15. See also the discussion of Ahitub as the father of Zadok at 1 Chr 18:16// 2 Sam 8:17.

Jeshua and Joiakim, the first two high priests after the return from the exile (Neh 12:1-7, 12-21)?

■ **30 (29)** *Of the Benjaminites, the kindred of Saul:* Judah and Benjamin form an *inclusio* at the beginning and end of the paragraph in vv. 25-30 (24-29). Benjamin has the smallest delegation, and the list explains this by noting that the majority of the tribe, not surprisingly, continued to keep their allegiance to the house of Saul. That would have been true during Saul's lifetime, but also after his death when his son Ishbaal maintained a rump kingdom for several years (2 Samuel 2–4).[60]

12:31-37 (30-36). Delegations from Ephraim, the Half-Tribe of Manasseh, Issachar, Zebulun, Naphtali, Dan, and Asher

I have already discussed, under Structure, the implausible character of the numbers. Additional nonspecific information is given for most of the tribes and listed immediately below; those tribes with more specific information will be discussed in the commentary on individual tribes.

Tribes with nonspecific information:

Ephraimites (v. 31 [30]): mighty warriors, people of renown in their ancestral houses.

half-tribe of Manasseh (v. 32 [31]): designated by name to come and make David king. Since the eighteen thousand had been designated by name, they did not comprise the entire tribe of Manasseh. This information refers to the tribe of Manasseh located west of the Jordan River.

Zebulun (v. 34 [33]): troops for military service, lining up for battle with all the weapons of war to help David with singleness of purpose.

Naphtali (v. 35 [34]): commanders . . . armed with shield and spear.

Danites (v. 36 [35]): equipped for battle. The Danites

are here part of all Israel while they were absent at least from the present form of the genealogies in 1 Chronicles 2–8. Dan is located at the northern boundary of Israel (cf. "from Beer-sheba to Dan" in 21:2; 2 Chr 30:5).

Asher (37 [36]): troops ready for battle.

Tribes with specific information:

■ **32 (31)** *Of the half-tribe of Manasseh . . . designated by name to come and make David king:* The purpose clause dealing with the coronation of David is also included in the Chronicler's summary of the significance of the list in v. 39 (38). Although we are told that the Manassites were designated by name, the only names of individuals actually given in the list are from the tribe of Levi (see above).

■ **33 (32)** *Of the children of Issachar, those who had understanding of the times, to know what Israel ought to do:* The combination of verb and noun יודעי בינה ("those who had understanding") is used elsewhere for those with special understanding or insight.[61] The only other reference to those who know "the times" is in Esth 1:13, where the king consults wise men who know the times. They are described later in the same verse as those well-versed in law and custom. The perceptive reading of the times by the Issacharites implies that there was one thing Israel should do—rally to the cause of David at Hebron.[62] This is therefore an ideological comment, not reflecting any specific information about the tribe of Issachar. Comments about the characteristics of Issachar in other biblical contexts have no relationship to this saying.[63]

two hundred heads, and all their kindred under their command: Issachar is the only tribe whose officers are designated by the title "heads." It is also the only tribe for which "all their kindred" are mentioned. This could mean that the whole tribe dedicated itself to David,

---

60   Braun, 169, suggests that the small numbers for Judah, Simeon, Levi, and Benjamin result from two lists being combined in the chapter.

61   Prov 4:1; Job 38:4; 2 Chr 2:11 (12), dealing with Solomon.

62   The expression is so appropriate to this context that I doubt there was a more original saying that credited the Issacharites with (astrological) knowledge about when to fight or go to war, which was then modified by the Chronicler adding "to know what Israel ought to do" (see Williamson, 112).

63   Gen 49:15, "He saw that a resting place was good

. . . so he bowed his shoulder to the burden, and became a slave at forced labor"; Deut 33:18, "Rejoice . . . Issachar in your tents"; Judg 5:15, "The chiefs of Issachar came with Deborah, and Issachar faithful to Barak."

which would seem appropriate according to the Chronicler's ideology in this chapter, where the more remote the tribe is the more people it sends to David's coronation.[64]

■ **34 (33)** *Of Zebulun, fifty thousand troops fit for military service:* Cf. v. 37 (36) and 5:18.

lining up for battle: Cf. vv. 36-37 (35-36) and 19:9-17; 2 Chr 13:3.

to help David with singleness of purpose: David had posed questions to the representatives of Benjamin and Judah on whether they were coming to help or to betray him (v. 18 [17]). Their answer was decisively positive, and the soldiers from remote Zebulun, which sent more people than any other single tribe, were similarly resolute.[65] "Helping" David is one of the themes of this chapter, though expressed here and in v. 39 (38) in Aramaic rather than Hebrew. "Singleness of purpose" is a paraphrase of בלא לב ולב (lit. "without a heart and a heart"), that is, not double-minded people.[66]

■ **35 (34)** *Of Naphtali, a thousand commanders . . . armed with shield and spear:* The only other reference to "commanders" שרים is in connection with Zadok (v. 29 [28]).[67] The weapons of Naphtali, "shield and spear" (בצנה וחנית), are similar to those of the Gadites, "shield and lance" (v. 9 [8] צנה ורמח), and of Judah (v. 25 [24] צנה ורמח), though a different word is used for lance/spear is used here (חנית).

12:38 (37). Delegation from Transjordanian Tribes

■ **38 (37)** *one hundred twenty thousand:* The Transjordanian tribes always had an uncertain status in Israel and were not included in Ezekiel's eschatological picture of the Holy Land (chap. 47).[68] By combining the two and a half tribes into one unit and assigning them the highest number of people of all the units, more than twice as big as

the largest single tribe, Zebulun, the Chronicler shows the desirability of including them in his picture of all Israel.

12:39-41 (38-40). Enthronement Festival at Hebron

■ **39 (38)** *All these . . . came to Hebron with full intent to make David king over all Israel:* The military personnel assembled at Hebron with a single purpose (cf. v. 34 [33]), to make David king (cf. vv. 24 and 32 [23 and 31]).

all the rest of Israel were of one mind to make David king: The military personnel represented all Israel at David's coronation (cf. 11:1). After expending so much space in demonstrating military loyalty, from 11:10–12:38 (37), the Chronicler affirms that all the civilian population ("all the rest of Israel") had the same singlemindedness.[69]

■ **40 (39)** *They were there with David, eating and drinking:* The Chronicler adds a celebratory feast to David's coronation that was lacking in the account of the coronation he had taken from 2 Sam 5:1-3 in 1 Chr 11:1-3. This may imply a covenant meal (cf. Gen 26:26-30; 31:43-53; Josh 9:11-15).[70] The festival of David, however, lacks any additional religious or ritualistic dimensions, which the Chronicler may have purposefully omitted, since in his opinion there was no appropriate sanctuary at Hebron. When the people made Solomon king in Jerusalem, on the other hand, they ate and drank *before Yahweh* (1 Chr 29:22).

their kindred had provided for them: The generosity of the Israelites who were not present explains how such a mighty army could be provisioned during their stay in Hebron, and it reinforces the civilian population's full commitment to David.

■ **41 (40)** *their neighbors, from as far as Issachar and Zebulun and Naphtali:* The distant tribes again do not lack in

---

64 The text might also mean that two hundred commanders brought all their own troops, without denying that there were additional commanders and additional troops.

65 The psalmist criticizes those who have a double or false heart (Ps 12:3 [2]). In the Song of Deborah Zebulun is characterized as a people that jeopardized their lives to the death (Judg 5:18).

66 Cf. also Ps 12:3 (2).

67 See also the two hundred "heads" from Issachar.

68 Ralph W. Klein, *Ezekiel: The Prophet and His Message* (Columbia: Univ. of South Carolina Press, 1988)

183–84. Cf. Josh 22:26-29.

69 Note the potential tension with v. 30 (29), dealing with the tribe of Benjamin, but the Chronicler may mean to suggest that by the time of David's coronation the Benjaminites may have changed their minds.

70 As E. W. Nicholson, "The Interpretation of Exodus xxiv 9-11," *VT* 24 (1974) 85–86, notes, not every occasion of eating and drinking in the OT is to be understood in covenantal terms.

commitment to David. These three tribes were located in the region west of the Sea of Galilee. Only Asher and Dan were more remote in Cisjordan.

bringing food on donkeys, camels, mules, and oxen: By mentioning all the standard beasts of burden, the Chronicler emphasizes the generosity of the people—and the size of the army now assembled.

abundant supplies of meal, cakes of figs, clusters of raisins, wine, oil, oxen and sheep: On cakes of figs see 1 Sam 25:18; 30:12. On raisins see 1 Sam 25:18; 30:12; 2 Sam 16:1.

there was joy in Israel: There is the first mention of joy in 1 Chronicles, and this begins a favorite motif of the Chronicler, to be repeated at such occasions as the appointment of the Levitical singers (15:16), the bringing of the ark to Jerusalem (15:25; 16:10, 31), Solomon's coronation (29:9, 17, 22), the dedication of the temple (2 Chr 6:41; 7:10), Asa's covenant with Yahweh (15:15), Jehoshaphat's victory celebration (20:27), the death of Athaliah (23:13, 18, 21), the offerings for the repair of the temple (24:10), and Hezekiah's reform (29:30, 36; 30:21, 23, 25, 26).

Conclusion

This chapter continues the widespread support for David noted already in chap. 11. Numerous individual warriors joined David even during Saul's kingship, from Benjamin and Judah, but also from Transjordanian Gad and from Manasseh in the north.

But a vast army showed up at Hebron to make the transfer of kingship, already accomplished de jure in chap. 10, de facto. While the numbers from Judah, Simeon, Levi, and Benjamin were relatively modest, the delegations from the north and from the Transjordanian tribes knew no bounds. The more remote the tribe, the more numerous was their delegation to David's coronation. Among the Levitical delegates were two individuals, Jehoiada and Zadok, who may be related to later officials under David and Solomon. In any case the all-Israel character of David's kingship is made crystal clear by this military support.

The final paragraph indicates that the military commitment to David was matched in the civilian population. For three days they celebrated the new king, eating and drinking from abundant supplies brought by distant tribes like Issachar, Zebulun, and Naphtali. For the first time the Chronicler refers to joy in Israel, but this theme will recur again and again at significant military, political, and religious/cultic events.

13

Translation

1/ David consulted with the commanders of the thousands and the hundreds, yes,[1] with every leader. 2/ David said to the whole congregation of Israel, "If it seems good to you, and if there is a breakthrough[2] brought about by Yahweh our God, let us send to our kindred who remain in all the regions of Israel[3]—and among them to the priests and[4] the Levites in their pastureland cities—and let them be gathered together to us. 3/ Let us bring around[5] the ark of our God to ourselves for we did not seek it in the days of Saul." 4/ All the congregation agreed to do this, for the proposal was appropriate in the eyes of all the people.

5/ David assembled all Israel, from the Shihor of Egypt up to Lebo-hamath, to bring the ark of God from Kiriath-jearim. 6/ So David and all Israel went up toward Baalah,[6] to Kiriath-jearim, which belongs to Judah,[7] to bring up from there the ark of the God Yahweh,[8] who sits enthroned on the cherubim, where he is invoked.[9] 7/ They made the ark of God ride on[10] a new cart from the house of Abinadab, with Uzzah[11] and Ahio[12] driving the cart.[13] 8/ David and all Israel were reveling in the presence of God with all their strength,[14] with songs,[15] lyres, harps, tambourines, cymbals, and trumpets.

9/ When they came to the threshing floor of Chidon,[16] Uzzah put out his hand[17] to seize[18] the ark, for the oxen had let it slip.[19] 10/ But Yahweh became angry with Uzzah and struck him because he had put out his hand against the ark;[20] and he died there in the presence of God.[21] 11/ David became angry because[22] Yahweh had broken forth against Uzzah, and so people call the name of that place Perez-uzzah until this day. 12/ David was afraid of God on that day, saying,[23] "How can I bring the ark of God to myself?" 13/ So David did not turn aside the ark to himself to the city of David, but he placed it at the house of Obed-edom the Gittite. 14/ The ark of God stayed in the house of Obed-edom[24] three months, and Yahweh blessed the house of Obed-edom and everything that belonged to him.[25]

Textual Notes

1 See BDB, 514, s.v. ל, definition 5 f (d). In readings discussed in textual notes 6-8, 10, 13-15, 17-18, 20-23, 25, Chronicles presupposes a text of Samuel other than MT.

2 נפרצה. According to the Masoretic accents, this verb goes with the following clause, but *NEB* and some recent commentators (Williamson, 114; Allen, 384) interpret it as part of the previous, second, conditional clause. Cf. Allen, *Greek Chronicles*, 1:128. If it is taken with the following verb נשלחה (cf. GKC §120h), we would translate: "Let us burst forth and send (to our kindred)." Johnstone, 1:169, adopts this translation and suggests that this verb expresses the unconsidered way in which David attempted at first to bring the ark to Jerusalem, without the Levites carrying it. The ark should only have been handled in the way proposed in the Mosaic tradition (1 Chr 15:15). In either interpretation the verb פרץ forms a unifying motif in the ark narrative (1 Chr 13:11; 14:11; 15:13). In 2 Chr 31:5 it is used to describe the dispersion of a word or message, which would favor the second interpretation. G. R. Driver, "Some Hebrew Roots and Their Meanings," *JTS* 23 (1922) 72–73, connected פרץ to Akkadian *parāṣu* ("decide") and proposed: "Let us issue an edict, let us send."

3 בכל ארצות ישראל; each tribe had its own "land" (cf. Judg 21:21; 1 Sam 13:7; 2 Chr 11:23; 15:5; 34:33). LXX attests a text with a more common reading: בכל ארץ ישראל "in all the land of Israel."

4 והלוים; LXX lacks "and." See the term הכהנים הלוים "Levitical priests" in Deut 17:9 and frequently in Deuteronomy.

5 ונסבה. Or "transfer." Cf. "Yahweh transferred (ויסב) the kingdom from Saul to David" (1 Chr 10:14). Cf. also להסב in 12:24 (23). The prepositional phrase "to us" presupposes that David and his followers are already residents of Jerusalem.

6 בעלתה. Chronicles presupposes the reading of 2 Sam 6:2 4QSam[a]: בעלה היא קר[י]ת יערים [. Samuel MT מבעלי יהודה "from the lords of Judah"; Samuel LXX is conflate: ἀπὸ τῶν ἀρχόντων Ἰούδα ἐν ἀναβάσει. Kalimi, *Geschichtsschreibung*, 63, proposes that the composer of 4QSam[a] was perhaps influenced by the text of Chronicles, which is highly doubtful in my judgment.

7 אשר ליהודה; cf. 2 Sam 6:2 4QSam[a] ליהודה [אשר]. See Ulrich, *Qumran Text*, 204. Samuel MT [מבעלי] יהודה.

8 יהוה. Chronicles and 2 Sam 6:2 4QSam[a] (judging by space requirements) lack צבאות, which follows in Samuel MT. See also the next note.

9 אשר נקרא שם. Vocalize the last word שָׁם instead of MT שֵׁם "name" in order to make sense of a difficult text. Comparison with 2 Sam 6:2 suggests that the

327

words preceding this lemma, יהוה יושב הכרובים עליו "Yahweh, who sits enthroned on the cherubim," which belong *after* שם, were omitted accidentally at some point and then the first three of these words were inserted by a corrector at the wrong place in Chronicles MT (or in its Samuel *Vorlage*), *before* אשר נקרא שם. For the textual problems in 2 Samuel see McCarter, *II Samuel*, 163. Japhet, 278, emends to אֲשֶׁר נִקְרָה שָׁם and translates, "which happened to be there," following the suggestion of I. L. Seeligmann, "Indications of Editorial Alteration and Adaptation in the Massoretic Text and the Septuagint," *VT* 11 (1961) 204–5. Jack M. Sasson, "'The Lord of Hosts, Seated over the Cherubs,'" in *Rethinking the Foundations: Historiography in the Ancient World and in the Bible: Essays in Honour of John Van Seters* (ed. S. L. McKenzie et al.; BZAW 294; Berlin: de Gruyter, 2000) 229, translates the last part of this verse as follows: "the ark of God, 'The Lord, Seated over Cherubs,' who has a name." The main point of Sasson's article is to propose that the Samuel text describes a label on the ark identifying the invisible Deity (pp. 232–34).

10 על; cf. 2 Sam 6:3 4QSam[a] and Samuel LXX; Samuel MT אל.

11 עזא; also in 2 Sam 6:3, or in a few MSS עזה. The Chronicler continues this spelling with a final א also in vv. 9-11, though the MS used by Vannutelli employed a final ה.

12 וְאֶחָיו; LXX, Syr, Arab.: וְאָחִיו "and his brothers." Cf. Vg *et frater ejus* (וְאָחִיו).

13 בעגלה. Samuel MT adds one word in v. 3 and five in v. 4: חדשה וישאהו מבת אבינדב אשר בגבעה "new. And they carried it away from the house of Abinadab, which was on the hill." This plus is a clear dittography of a clause that appears later in the verse. It is lacking not only in Chronicles but also in 4QSam[a] and Samuel LXX.

14 בכל עז. McCarter, *II Samuel*, 163–64, reconstructs an original reading in 2 Sam 6:5 בכלי עז "with sonorous instruments." Samuel MT בכל עצי "with every kind of (cypress) wood." See the next note. Samuel LXX conflates the two variant readings.

15 ובשירים; cf. 2 Sam 6:5 LXX and 4QSam[a]. Samuel MT ברושים "cypress."

16 כידון. Cf. Vg "Chidon" and Josephus *Ant.* 7.81 Χειδωνος. Lacking in Chronicles LXX; 2 Sam 6:6 נכון "Nacon"; 4QSam[a] נודן "Nodan." C. L. Seow,

Myth, Drama, and the Politics of David's Dance (HSM 46; Atlanta: Scholars Press, 1989) 97–98, interprets the reading in Samuel MT as an adjective "prepared," rather than as a proper noun. See also Arthur W. Marget, "גורן נכון," *JBL* 39 (1920) 70–76, "a permanent threshing floor"; Morgenstern, "נכון," *JBL* 37 (1918) 144–48, "a certain threshing floor"; and H. Tur-Sinai, "The Ark of God at Beit Shemesh (2 Sam 6) and Peres 'Uzza (2 Sam 6; 1 Chr 13)," *VT* 1 (1951) 279, "the threshing floor of the stroke (pestilence or affliction)."

17 את ידו; cf. 2 Sam 6:6 4QSam[a] and Samuel versions; lacking in Samuel MT.

18 לאחז; cf. 2 Sam 6:6 4QSam[a]. Samuel MT ויאחז; Samuel LXX is conflate: κατασχεῖν αὐτὴν καὶ ἐκράτησεν αὐτήν. See the commentary.

19 שמטו; MT שָׁמְטוֹ "had stumbled."

20 על אשר שלח ידו על הארון; cf. 2 Sam 6:7 4QSam[a]. Samuel MT על השל, which is probably a fragment of the longer reading found in 4QSam[a] and Chronicles. Samuel LXX[AL] interpreted the Hebrew found in MT as "on account of (his) rashness." See McCarter, *II Samuel*, 165.

21 לפני אלהים; cf. 2 Sam 6:7 4QSam[a]. Samuel MT עם ארון האלהים "with the ark of God"; Samuel LXX conflates both readings.

22 כי; 2 Sam 6:8 על אשר.

23 לאמר; cf. 2 Sam 6:9 4QSam[a] and Samuel LXX; Samuel MT ויאמר "and he said."

24 Chronicles MT partially conflates two synonymous readings עם בית עבד אדם (MT) and בבית עבד אדם (LXX; cf. 2 Sam 6:14) by adding בביתו from the second phrase after the first phrase. It is lacking in a few Hebrew MSS, LXX, Vg. Braun, 173, interprets MT's "in its house" as an indication that the ark was not kept in an ordinary house. Cf. Curtis and Madsen, 206.

25 את בית עבד אדם ואת כל אשר לו; cf. 2 Sam 6:11 LXX[L] and Samuel LXX[B]. Chronicles LXX omits a translation for בית (haplography?). Samuel MT את עבד אדם ואת כל ביתו "Obed-edom and his whole house."

Structure of the Ark Narrative (1 Chronicles 13–16)

The Ark Narrative in Chronicles extends from 1 Chr 13:1 through 16:43 and includes material written by the Chronicler himself, as well as material drawn from 2 Samuel and the Psalter and from lists that were presumably available to the Chronicler. The Chronicler's dependence on and departures from his *Vorlage* may be diagrammed as follows:

Chronicles	*Vorlage*	Content
1 Chr 13:1-4		Chronicler's introduction
13:5-7	2 Sam 6:1-3	the ark's journey begins
	6:4	brief note about Ahio
13:8-14	6:5-11	Uzzah killed for touching the ark
14:1-2	5:11-12	Hiram's support; David's kingdom established
14:3-7	5:13-16	David's wives and children from Jerusalem
14:8-16	5:17-25	Philistines defeated
14:17		David's fame
15:1-3		preparations for moving the ark
15:4-10		six Levite chiefs
15:11-15		clergy ordered to carry the ark
15:16-24		installation of Levitical musicians
	6:12a	house of Obed-Edom blessed
15:25–16:3	6:12b-19a	ark brought to Jerusalem
16:4-7		David appoints Levites to thank and praise
16:8-22	Ps 105:1-15	Israel's praise
16:23-33	96:1b-13a	international and cosmic praise
16:34-36	106:1b, 47-48	thanksgiving and petition
16:37-42		regular worship established
16:43	2 Sam 6:19b-20a	David's blessing
	6:20b-23	David rebuked by Michal

The narrative exhibits many of the compositional techniques and the problems that typify this book from beginning to end. The structure of individual chapters within the Ark Narrative will be discussed with the commentary on that chapter.

Structure of 1 Chronicles 13

I. 13:1-4. Chronicler's introduction to the Ark Narrative

II. 13:5-7. First stage of bringing the ark to Jerusalem (2 Sam 6:1-3)

III. 13:8-14. Uzzah killed for touching the ark; it remains at the house of Obed-edom for three months (2 Sam 6:5-11[1]).

Twentieth-century study of the ark in the books of Samuel has been dominated by the hypothesis of a precanonical Ark Narrative, including all or parts of 1 Samuel 4–6 and, at least in some cases 2 Samuel 6.[2] Whatever the truth about that precanonical source and its extent is, the Chronicler surely knew this account as it had been incorporated into the books of Samuel. In any case, the first three-quarters of the Ark Narrative, in 1 Samuel 4–6, are passed over in silence by the Chronicler.[3] The Chronicler either presupposes, or ignores as irrelevant, the reader's knowledge of how the ark was lost to the Philistines and how it was eventually returned to Kiriath-jearim.

---

1   The rest of 2 Samuel 6 is incorporated into 1 Chr 15:25–16:3 and 43.

2   See Leonhard Rost, *Die Überlieferung von der Thronnachfolge Davids* (BWANT 3/6; Stuttgart: Kohlhammer, 1926) 4–47. For the history of research into this hypothesis, see A. F. Campbell, *The Ark Narrative* (SBLDS 16; Missoula, MT: Scholars Press, 1975); and P. D. Miller Jr. and J. J. Roberts, *The Hand of the Lord: A Reassessment of the "Ark Narrative" of I Samuel* (Baltimore: Johns Hopkins Univ. Press, 1977). Miller and Roberts include 1 Sam 2:12-17, 22-25, and 27-36 in the narrative, but exclude from it 2 Samuel 6.

3   The word "ark" appears in 1 Chr 13:3 for the first time in Chronicles, except for the genealogy of the singers in 6:16 (31). There are forty-seven references overall to the ark in Chronicles, of which twenty-nine are found in the Ark Narrative itself. Cf. also 17:1. The ark is mentioned twelve times in the reign of Solomon and only once thereafter, in the reign of Josiah (2 Chr 35:3).

In Chronicles, the transfer of the ark to Jerusalem is David's first act as king after his coronation in 11:1-3// 2 Sam 5:1-3 and his capture of Jerusalem in 11:4-9// 2 Sam 5:6-10. This provides one of several reasons why the Chronicler shifts 2 Sam 5:11-25 and its account of David's building himself a house, the list of his family, and the account of his battles with the Philistines to a position between the two attempts to bring the ark to Jerusalem (at 1 Chr 14:1-17) rather than its position in 2 Samuel, where it precedes the *first* attempt to bring the ark to Jerusalem (in 2 Sam 6:1-11 = 1 Chr 13:4-14; for other reasons for this shift, see note 4 and the commentary on chap. 14).[4] After the coronation of David and his capture of Jerusalem, the rest of chaps. 11 and 12 had listed the soldiers and others who rallied to David's cause. The transfer of the ark is a direct continuation of these celebrations in Hebron. David's early attention to the ark is similar in timing to Hezekiah's religious reform that took place at the beginning of his reign, and the Chronicler's strategy of having good kings initiate faithful cultic actions without delay also explains why Josiah in Chronicles began to seek the God of his ancestor David in his eighth year, when he was only sixteen years old, and not wait until his eighteenth year, when he was twenty-six years old, as in 2 Kings. Just as Jerusalem was the home for the Davidic king, David made sure that Yahweh's dwelling place would be there as well.[5]

Detailed Commentary

13:1-4. Chronicler's Introduction to the Ark Narrative

■ **1** *David consulted with the commanders of the thousands and the hundreds:* Whereas the focus of the story about the movement of the ark to Jerusalem in the Deuteronomistic History is on the efforts of David, the journey of the ark in Chronicles is the work of all Israel.[6] David sought the support of his military officers, who had gathered around him at Hebron,[7] as well as with every leader (נגיד), before making his proposal to the assembly to move the ark. Jehoshaphat (2 Chr 20:21) and Hezekiah (30:2, 23; 32:3) also consulted with their staff or with the people before major decisions, and Rehoboam erred not by consulting but by following the advice of the iron-fisted young men rather than their more politically astute and moderate elders (10:6, 8, 9).[8] Consulting was primarily a positive virtue for the Chronicler.[9]

■ **2** *David said to the whole congregation of Israel:* This is the first mention of the "congregation" or "assembly" (קהל) in Chronicles, though this term appears some forty times throughout both books. David proposes that this representative assembly should bring together all those citizens who had not been part of the military assembly at Hebron in 1 Chr 12:39 (38).

---

4   Historically and according to the chronology in 1 and 2 Samuel, David's defeat of the Philistines made it physically possible for him to move the ark to Jerusalem. Japhet, 285, argues that in Chronicles David's building activities, his progeny, and his victories over the Philistines accrued to him precisely because of his first efforts for the ark. These actions are a sign of God's favor and are part of David's actions in Jerusalem to receive the ark. For similar ideas see David A. Glatt, *Chronological Displacement in Biblical and Related Literatures* (SLBDS 139; Atlanta: Scholars Press, 1993) 57–61. See also Peter Welten, "Lade—Tempel—Jerusalem: Zur Theologie der Chronikbücher," in *Textgemäss: FS für Ernst Würthwein zum 70. Geburtstag* (ed. A. H. J. Gunneweg and O. Kaiser; Göttingen: Vandenhoeck & Ruprecht, 1979) 169–83.

5   Gerrie Snyman has written two studies that use 1 Chronicles 13 to illustrate the Constance school of reception theory and the rhetorical features of this chapter. See "Fictionality and the Writing of

History in 1 Chronicles," *OTE* 3 (1990) 171–90; idem, "Who Is Responsible for Uzzah's Death? Rhetoric in 1 Chronicles 13," in *Rhetoric, Scripture and Theology* (ed. S. E. Porter and T. H. Olbricht; JSNTSup 131; Sheffield: Sheffield Academic Press, 1996) 203–17.

6   This point is made in six of the first eight verses in this chapter and is reinforced by 1 Chr 15:25–16:3.

7   Commanders of thousands are mentioned in 13:1; 15:25; 26:26; 27:1; 28:1; 29:6; 2 Chr 1:2; 17:14; 25:5, and in all but two cases (1 Chr 15:25; 2 Chr 17:14) the commanders of hundreds are mentioned with them.

8   For another negative consultation see 2 Chr 25:17, where Amaziah of Judah takes counsel and sends a message to Joash of the Northern Kingdom.

9   Cf. 1 Chr 28:1 (David); 2 Chr 1:2 (Solomon).

If it seems good to you, and if there is a breakthrough brought about by Yahweh our God: In a short speech (vv. 2-3), David asked the assembly to support his proposed transfer of the ark to Jerusalem, and to determine whether this proposal was also God's will. We are not told how the congregation was to decide whether the proposal was "from Yahweh." The death of Uzzah by Yahweh's intervention later in this chapter might cast doubt on the wisdom of transferring the ark, but the effect of Uzzah's death is mitigated by the many positive reports about David in chap. 14 that come as a retributive consequence of his first, though failed, attempt to transfer the ark. In the Chronicler's opinion the idea of transferring the ark to Jerusalem was God-pleasing even if the proper procedure for the Levites' carrying the ark had not been followed. The word "breakthrough" נפרצה anticipates the positive use of this verb to describe the victory over the Philistines in 14:11 (cf. also the commentary on 13:11).[10]

to our kindred who remain . . . and among them to the priests and Levites in their pastureland cities: David's invitation to transfer the ark sought the participation of those who had not attended the coronation ceremony in Hebron ("our kindred who remain[11] in all the regions of Israel") and clearly alludes to 12:39 [38] "all the rest of Israel were of one mind to make David king." David's invitation also included the priests and the Levites who lived in the Levitical cities scattered throughout the land (6:39-66 [54-81]).[12] Chronicles assumed, surely contrary to historical reality, that these clergy were already settled in their cities at the beginning of David's reign. David showed an inclusive spirit by identifying the people to be invited as "kindred" (אחינו "our brothers") of the groups with whom he consulted.

■ **3** *we did not seek it in the days of Saul:* David included himself and the people in a confession that they had not sought the ark in the days of Saul. In 15:13 David observes that "Yahweh had burst forth against us (פרץ . . . בנו) on this first attempt to bring the ark to Jerusalem because the Levites did not carry it and *we* did not seek it correctly." According to the Chronicler, not seeking Yahweh was the major reason why Saul fell to the Philistines (10:13-14).[13] In chap. 10 that charge was substantiated by noting that Saul had sought, or consulted, a medium (an allusion to 1 Samuel 28). Here, on the other hand, Saul's evil reign is characterized as a time when the *ark* was not sought. By leaving the ark in Kiriath-jearim, Saul neglected the ark, and, in the eyes of the Chronicler, did not appropriately seek God. Seeking the ark is, therefore, synonymous with seeking God. The book of 1 Samuel reports nothing about the failure of Saul to seek the ark, and in fact records one occasion when Saul, according to the MT, commanded that the ark be brought to the battlefield (1 Sam 14:18).[14] By describing David as seeking the ark, the Chronicler was building on a tradition present also in the Psalter. The psalmist celebrated David's vow to go sleepless until he had found a place for the ark (Ps 132:1-6).

■ **4** *All the congregation:* The assembly,[15] presumably consisting here of laypeople, unanimously endorsed the plan because it seemed appropriate (ישר).[16] The whole-hearted support of the clergy becomes clear in chaps. 15–16.

---

10   But see also textual note 2 for the uncertainty about how this Hebrew word is to be translated.

11   Braun, 173, considers it possible, but not certain, that this refers to the postexilic "remnant." Japhet, 87, however, denies this is such an anachronism and argues that the reference to שרית ישראל "the rest of Israel" in 1 Chr 12:39 (38) suffices to explain this vocabulary.

12   About 90 percent of the use of the expression "pasturelands" occurs in the parallel list of Levitical cities in 1 Chr 6:39-66 (54-81)//Josh 21:1-40. For discussion of its meaning see the commentary on 1 Chr 6:40 (55).

13   The psalm quoted in 1 Chr 16:11 (Ps 105:4) urges readers to "seek Yahweh and his strength." Cf. C. T. Begg, "'Seeking Yahweh' and the Purpose of Chronicles," *LS* 9 (1982) 128–41.

14   The LXX, however, reads "ephod" for "ark" and is to be preferred. See Klein, *1 Samuel*, 132.

15   The expression כל הקהל occurs six times in Chronicles (1 Chr 13:4; 29:10, 20; 2 Chr 23:3; 30:4, 23).

16   Similarly, the Passover proposal of Hezekiah seemed good (ויישר) to the king and the whole assembly (2 Chr 30:4).

13:5-7. First Stage of Bringing the Ark to Jerusalem

■ **5** *David assembled all Israel from the Shihor of Egypt up to Lebo-hamath:* The Chronicler used ויקהל "assembled," from the same root as קהל "congregation," instead of ויסף, which was present in the *Vorlage*. Even in 2 Samuel, David's procession with the ark involved a large crowd of thirty thousand people,[17] identified there as those selected from Israel, that is, military people (2 Sam 6:1); but the Chronicler's David included all Israel in the project (see also vv. 6, 8). The inclusive dimensions of Israel's participation is evidenced by the Chronicler's grandiose description of the land, not included in his *Vorlage* in 2 Sam 6:1,[18] that seems to equate the promised land with the extent of the Davidic-Solomonic empire.[19] The land constituting Yehud in the days of the Chronicler himself was vastly smaller. The book of Joshua uses "Shihor" to designate the southwestern extremity of the land that Joshua was to divide among the tribes (Josh 13:3).[20] It may be identified with the Wadi el-Arish (*NRSV* Wadi of Egypt;[21] Num 34:5, 8), the Nahal Bezor,[22] or even with an eastern branch of the Nile. Lebo-hamath (possibly modern Lebweh [MR 277397]), located some forty-five miles north of Damascus (MR 272324), forms the northern border of the land here and in the account of the spies (Num 13:21; cf. Ezek 47:15-17).[23] The assembly at the dedication of Solomon's temple in Chronicles came from a territory extending from Lebo-hamath to the Wadi of Egypt (2 Chr 7:8//1 Kgs 8:65).

from Kiriath-jearim: Judging only by the MT of 2 Sam 6:2, which does not mention this city, one might conclude that the Chronicler himself picked up this city name from the other part of the Ark Narrative in 1 Sam 6:21–7:2, which he otherwise omitted, where we are told that the ark stayed for twenty years at Kiriath-jearim,[24] but a reference to Kiriath-jearim was already included in the text of 2 Sam 6:2 by 4QSam[a] (see textual note 6). Kirith-jearim (Tel Qiryat Ye'arim [MR 159135]) is about eight miles west of Jerusalem and is a site where the ark had been left under the control of Eleazar the son of Abinadab, according to 1 Sam 7:1.[25]

■ **6** *So David and all Israel went up to Baalah, to the city of Kiriath-jearim, which belongs to Judah:* In Chronicles David took all Israel with him;[26] only thirty thousand had gone with David according to 2 Sam 6:1-2. Baalah is an alternate name for Kiriath-jearim (Josh 15:9),[27] and Johnstone, 1:170, remarks that a place named Baalah seems no place for the ark to remain. The ascription of Kiriath-jearim to Judah is explicit already in 4QSam[a].[28]

the ark of the God Yahweh, who sits enthroned upon the cherubim: The relationship between the cherubim and the ark first appears in the battle of Ebenezer, where the ark functions as a war palladium (1 Sam 4:4). Since Chronicles omits the divine epithet צבאות from his *Vorlage* in this verse (cf. 2 Sam 6:2), the martial overtones in the Ark Narrative in Chronicles are not as evident as in 2 Samuel.[29]

---

17 This number may have been chosen because it is the number of Israelites who fell to the Philistines in the earlier battle of Ebenezer (1 Sam 4:10).

18 All the materials from "from the Shihor" to the end of the verse have been added by the Chronicler.

19 Contrast the Chronicler's more common "from Beer-sheba to Dan" (1 Chr 21:2; 2 Chr 30:5).

20 Its only other occurrences are in Isa 23:3 and Jer 2:18 (where *NRSV* translates it as "Nile").

21 In 2 Chr 7:8 the congregation of all Israel at the dedication of Solomon's temple extends from Lebo-hamath to the Wadi of Egypt.

22 Nadav Na'aman, "The Brook of Egypt and Assyrian Policy on the Border of Egypt," *TA* 6 (1979) 68–90; idem, "The Shihor of Egypt and Shur that Is Before Egypt," *TA* 7 (1980) 95–109.

23 The kingdom of Hamath is the first nation beyond David's kingdom to the north according to 1 Chr 18:9-10.

24 So De Vries, 137, referring to 1 Sam 7:1.

25 The people of Kiriath-jearim consecrated Eleazar the son of Abinadab to have charge of the ark.

26 Isaac Kalimi, "Paranomasia in the Book of Chronicles," *JSOT* 67 (1995) 32–33, calls attention to the punning or alliteration introduced by the Chronicler in this verse: ויעל . . . בעלתה . . . להעלות.

27 In Josh 15:60 and 18:14 Kiriath-baal is identified with Kiriath-jearim.

28 See textual note 7. The ascription of Kiriath-jearim to Judah is supported by Josh 15:9. Josh 18:14 puts it on the border between Judah and Benjamin. Even Samuel MT refers to the "lords of Judah" at this point.

29 The Chronicler does use this epithet for Yahweh elsewhere, when appropriate, as in 1 Chr 11:9; 17:7, 24.

where he is invoked: Though the text is difficult (see textual note 9), the ark as the sign of God's presence is also the place where people call upon him. Yahweh's name is later invoked on the temple itself (2 Chr 6:33//1 Kgs 8:43): "your name has been invoked on this house that I have built."

■ 7 *They made the ark of God ride on a new cart from the house of Abinadab:* In 2 Samuel the use of a new cart recapitulated the decision of the Philistines to send the ark back to Israel on a new cart drawn by oxen that had never before been yoked (1 Sam 6:7). Presumably only a previously unused cart would be appropriate for transporting the Deity, but the Chronicler never uses the term "new" elsewhere with a similar connotation.[30] The Chronicler omits the verb וישאהו "and they carried it" from 2 Sam 6:3, perhaps because such carrying was the sole province of the Levites (1 Chr 15:2, 15),[31] and this first attempt to bring the ark to Jerusalem did not employ them in this function.[32]

with Uzzah and Ahio driving the cart: The two men who drove the cart are introduced in Chronicles without mentioning other details about them contained in 2 Samuel 6. According to Samuel, but not in Chronicles,[33] the two men were sons of Abinadab, at whose house the ark had stayed, and Ahio walked in front of the ark (2 Sam 6:4).[34] Abinadab's house is also said in that context to be on "the hill" (2 Sam 6:3-4, though the

latter reading is part of a dittography [see textual note 13]). "Driving" in Chronicles could indicate a position in front of or alongside[35] the cart, but a position behind or alongside the ark would be a more natural place for trying to catch the ark when it was about to fall.

13:8-14. Uzzah Killed; Ark Remains at the House of Obed-edom for Three Months

■ 8 *David and all Israel were reveling in the presence of God:* While those who were celebrating may also have been dancing (so *NRSV*), the verb שׂחק ("reveling") seems to have a wider meaning here since David and all Israel also sang and played musical instruments. Chronicles uses the same verb as its *Vorlage* in 2 Sam 6:5, but see also 1 Chr 15:29, where the Chronicler replaces the two verbs in his *Vorlage* at 2 Sam 6:16 and uses שׂחק again.[36]

with songs, lyres[37], harps,[38] tambourines, cymbals, and trumpets:[39] The musical instruments cited here, with the exception of the tambourines בתפים,[40] are assigned to be played by specific priests and Levites in chap. 15.[41] The Chronicler has added the priestly trumpets[42] to the *Vorlage* at the end of the verse because of the role of the priests in 15:24, 28; 16:6, 42, and he replaced the reference to the hapax legomenon ובמנענעים "castanets" from 2 Sam 6:5 with the more common word ובמצלתים "cymbals," perhaps reflecting which instruments were more widely used in his day.[43] The Deuteronomistic History

---

30 1 Chr 23:31; 2 Chr 2:4 (3); 8:13; 20:25; 31:3.

31 Deut 10:8; Num 3:31; Josh 3:3.

32 Cf. Fishbane, *Biblical Interpretation*, 393.

33 Snyman, "Who Is Responsible," 212, states that in Chronicles the name Uzzah appears as part of the Merari kinship of Levites (1 Chr 6:14 [29]). But there seems to be no reason to connect the Uzzah in this genealogy with the Uzzah who died for touching the ark.

34 Chronicles did not incorporate anything from 2 Sam 6:4, and about half that verse in MT is dittographic. See textual note 13.

35 See the reconstruction of 2 Sam 6:4 in McCarter, *II Samuel*, 163.

36 See also 2 Sam 6:21, where David responds to Michal's criticism of his lewd dancing by saying that he would indeed revel (שׂחק) before Yahweh. This verse is not included in Chronicles.

37 ובכנרות. Lyres are also mentioned in 1 Chr 15:16, 21, 28; 16:5; 25:1, 3, 6; 2 Chr 9:11//1 Kgs 10:12; 2 Chr 20:28; 29:25.

38 ובנבלים. See also 1 Chr 15:16, 20, 28; 16:5; 25:1, 6; 2 Chr 5:12; 9:11//1 Kgs 10:12; 2 Chr 20:28; 29:25. Note the highly similar distribution of the uses of lyres and harps. I have chosen to retain the translation "harps," although David P. Wright, "Music and Dance in 2 Samuel 6," *JBL* 121 (2002) 203, argues that this word is really the name of a different kind of lyre.

39 1 Chr 15:24, 28; 16:6, 42; 2 Chr 5:12, 13; 13:12, 14; 15:14; 20:28; 23:13 (twice)//2 Kgs 11:14; 29:26-28. All of these come from the Chronicler's own material. The word appears only one other time in the Deuteronomistic History: 2 Kgs 12:14.

40 The Chronicler got this item from his *Vorlage* in 2 Sam 6:5. Tambourines do not appear elsewhere in Chronicles.

41 In 1 Chr 15:16 the Levites play harps, lyres, and cymbals (for the latter see also v. 19).

42 See Num 10:8; 2 Chr 29:26-27; Ezra 3:10; Neh 12:35, 41.

43 The word occurs eleven times in Chronicles and

does not mention specifically who the musicians were who played these instruments, and it certainly does not associate them at this point with the Levites.[44] The anonymous, non-Levitical character of these musicians in the *Vorlage* may have seemed to the Chronicler like not giving the ark proper care (cf. 1 Chr 15:13).

■ **9** *When they came to the threshing floor of Chidon:* Are there cultic overtones to this threshing floor?[45] Note that David later purchased the threshing floor of Ornan as a site for the sacrificial altar (1 Chronicles 21) and that the threshing floor of Chidon is called מָקוֹם "place,"[46] that is, a sanctuary, in v. 11.

to seize the ark: Japhet, 280, proposes that Uzzah's seizing of the ark was a human attempt to protect the ark and hence an expression of disbelief (cf. v. 10). Since Chronicles here is dependent on a non-Masoretic form of the text of 2 Sam 6:6 (see textual notes 17 and 18), any attempt to attribute to the Chronicler a change in the nature of the infraction from touching the ark to attempting to touch the ark is ill advised; the Chronicler's divergent reading is attested already in 4QSam[a] and Sam LXX.[47]

■ **10** *Yahweh became angry with Uzzah and struck him because he had put his hand against the ark:* The holiness of the ark led to terrifying consequences when that holiness was compromised.[48] This is a typical example of immediate retribution in Chronicles.[49] Theological justification for this death sentence is found in Num 4:15, 20, where the Kohathites, who are assigned to carry the

tent of meeting, are forbidden to touch or "look on" its "holy things" or they will die.

he died there in the presence of God: The text of Chronicles, which is dependent on a non-Masoretic alternate reading from 2 Samuel (see textual note 21), suggests that the ark is the visible manifestation of the divine presence. Uzzah did not die "beside the ark" as in 2 Sam 6:10 MT, but by the hand of the affronted Deity, who was immediately present.[50]

■ **11** *David became angry:* David's anger matched Yahweh's earlier anger (v. 10), when Yahweh broke forth against Uzzah for failing to observe the boundaries between the sacred and the profane. David's anger at the Deity here and his expression of fear in v. 12 indicate that the Chronicler was not averse to finding some faults in David (cf. 1 Chronicles 21).

and so people call the name of that place Perez-uzzah until this day:[51] The text provides a folk etymology for the name of the town Perez-uzzah (פֶּרֶץ עֻזָּא; "breaking forth of[52] Uzzah"), that is, it is the place where Yahweh had broken forth (פֶּרֶץ)[53] against Uzzah.[54] An otherwise unknown place or sanctuary got its name from the divine attack on Uzzah, just as the place where David defeated the Philistines was later called Baal-perazim (בַּעַל פְּרָצִים; 1 Chr 14:11//2 Sam 5:20). The author of 2 Samuel had linked these two events by citing the two similar etiologies, but because the Chronicler put his equivalent of 2 Sam 5:11-25 at 1 Chr 14:1-17, the etiologies now appear in reverse order, that is, the attack on

---

once each in Ezra and Nehemiah, but nowhere else in the OT.

44   But see 1 Chr 15:16 (Levites as musicians), 24 (priests as trumpeters), and 28. Cf. also 25:1: "David and the officials of the liturgical host set apart the sons of Asaph, Heman, and Jeduthun, who were to prophesy to the accompaniment of lyres, harps, and cymbals."

45   Seow, *David's Dance*, 101–2, believes that a mock battle (the cosmogonic battle) took place at the "prepared threshing floor" (2 Sam 6:6).

46   *HALOT* 2:627, meaning 6.

47   Lemke, "Synoptic Problem," 350–51; and McKenzie, *Chronicler's Use*, 49.

48   Cf. the seventy descendants of Jeconiah who were killed for not rejoicing with the people of Beth-shemesh when they greeted the ark of Yahweh (1 Sam 6:19-20). In the narrative of the conquest, the people were urged to put two thousand cubits

between themselves and the ark (Josh 3:4).

49   Cf. the discussion of immediate retribution in the Introduction.

50   See also the reference to David and all Israel celebrating in the presence of God in v. 8.

51   Similar uses of the phrase "until this day" occur in 1 Chr 4:41, 43; 5:26; 17:5//2 Sam 7:6; 2 Chr 5:9/ 1 Kgs 8:8; 2 Chr 8:8//1 Kgs 9:21; 2 Chr 10:19// 1 Kgs 12:19; 2 Chr 20:26; 21:10//2 Kgs 8:22; 35:25.

52   Objective genitive.

53   See also 1 Chr 15:13.

54   Seow, *David's Dance*, 83, calls attention to the use of the verb פרץ in other similar contexts, such as the incident of Baal of Peor (Ps 106:29; Num 25:1-13).

Uzzah and the name Perez-uzzah now come *before* the battle with the Philistines and the giving of a name to Baal-perazim. The Chronicler later indicates that it was not Uzzah's error but the failure to have the Levites carrying the ark that led to the failure of this attempt to bring the ark to Jerusalem (cf. 15:13).

■ **12** *David was afraid of God on that day:* Because of a combination of anger (v. 11) and fear (cf. 21:30, where David fears the sword of the angel of Yahweh), David decided not to continue with the procession of the ark to Jerusalem and interrupted this procession for three months.[55]

"How can I bring the ark of God to myself?": The Chronicler repeated—and recast—David's rhetorical question from 2 Sam 6:9, "How can the ark of Yahweh come to me?" Is the change of the subject of the verb to the first person in Chronicles an attempt to magnify the role of David? David answers his own question about how he can bring the ark by the changes he effects in his second attempt to bring the ark to Jerusalem in chap. 15. While it is not clear in Samuel why David dared to make a second effort to take the ark to Jerusalem, in Chronicles the king's decision comes after he noted that God had blessed Obed-edom (v. 14) and David himself (chap. 14). As we will see, David subsequently commissioned the Levites to carry the ark.

■ **13** *So David did not turn aside the ark to himself to the city of David:* In 2 Sam 6:10 we read that David was unwilling (ולא אבה) to turn aside the ark to himself, which may have struck the Chronicler as too critical of his hero David. In any case he omitted at this point David's psychological reason for stopping the procession. Jerusalem had already been captured according to 1 Chr 11:4// 2 Sam 5:6, and it was at that time it had been named the city of David (1 Chr 11:5, 7//2 Sam 5:7, 9). According

to the implications of this clause, David had already taken up residence in Jerusalem ("to himself"; cf. vv. 3, 12, and 11:7).

but he placed it at the house of Obed-edom the Gittite: Neither the author of 2 Samuel 6 nor the Chronicler comments on the fact that the ark is again under the control of someone with Philistine connections (cf. 1 Samuel 5–6). A Gittite is a person who hails from the (Philistine) city of Gath (MR 135123). Obed-edom was apparently a Philistine expatriate who was loyal to David.[56] His name means something like "servant" or "worshiper of the god 'Adm."[57] In the remaining parts of the Ark Narrative in Chronicles a man by the name of Obed-edom appears as a Levitical singer, a gatekeeper, and even a son of the lead singer Jeduthun.[58] The Chronicler's several references to this Obed-edom in chap. 15 may be[59] an attempt to explain and even justify the ark's staying at Obed-edom's house.[60]

■ **14** *The ark of God stayed in the house of Obed-edom three months:* This interval was not long enough historically to carry out all the activities recorded in chap. 14, but it provided the Chronicler with a break in the action, into which he could put what seemed to him to be theologically appropriate materials. The presence of the ark brought Yahweh's blessings to Obed-edom and also to David, who had initiated the transfer of the ark in the first place (chap. 14).

Yahweh blessed the house of Obed-edom: Yahweh's blessing on this foreigner, who housed the ark for three months, foreshadows the far greater blessings that will come to the city of Jerusalem where David will pitch a tent for the ark (16:1) and where Solomon will include it in his lavish temple (2 Chr 5:2-7). In 1 Chr 26:5 the Chronicler lists eight sons for Obed-edom the gatekeeper and adds, "for God blessed him."

---

55 The two uses of "God" in this verse replace "Yahweh" in the *Vorlage*.

56 2 Sam 15:18-22; 18:2. Another Obed-edom occurs later in the history of Israel (2 Chr 25:24), where he is a keeper of the temple storehouses during the reign of Amaziah.

57 For a good summary of what little is known of this putative deity, see E. A. Knauf, "Edom," *DDD*, 273–74.

58 1 Chr 15:18, 21, 24; 16:5, 38, all texts not found in the Chronicler's *Vorlage*. An Obed-edom also appears in the genealogy of the gatekeepers (26:4,

8, 15). An Obed-edom also takes part in Joash's raid on Judah in 2 Chr 25:24. Did the ark sojourn with a Philistine just as David had sojourned among them (1 Sam 21:10-15)? Abinadab, with whom the ark stayed for twenty years, did not receive Levitical status, perhaps because of the offense committed by his son Uzzah.

59 See the commentary on 1 Chr 15:18.

60 Josephus *Ant.* 7.81 makes Obed-edom a Levite, apparently associating him with the man of the same name in chap. 15.

Conclusion

At the beginning of the Chronicler's Ark Narrative, the text of 1 Chr 13:5-14 is highly similar to the *Vorlage* in 2 Sam 6:1-11. The most significant change from the earlier account is in the first four verses, composed by the Chronicler himself, in which he makes it clear that the invitation to bring the ark to Jerusalem went out to kindred in all regions of Israel who had not come to the coronation at Hebron, including priests and Levites. The whole congregation agreed to David's proposal. The Chronicler also adds a confession in v. 3 that the people had not sought the ark in the days of Saul. One senses that the burden of this confession is an accusation directed against the kingship of Saul.

The other major change from the *Vorlage* is the placement of the first attempt to bring the ark to Jerusalem immediately after the ending of the coronation festivities in Hebron. This required the relocation of 2 Sam 5:12-25, which now become the first sixteen verses of chap. 14. The net effect, of course, is to show the exceedingly high priority given by David to Israel's worship life. Jerusalem was from David's time on the home for the Judean kings; David made sure that Yahweh's dwelling place would be there as well.[61]

---

61 Christopher T. Begg, "The Ark in Chronicles," in Graham, Mckenzie, and Knoppers, *Chronicler as Theologian*, 133–46, has raised the intriguing possibility that the Chronicler's focus on the ark does not just offer legitimation for the temple and the role of the Levites in the temple cult, but that the Chronicler may also have hoped that Israel would turn its attention to the ark once more and even restore it to the Second Temple.

14

Translation

1/ Hiram[1] the king of Tyre sent ambassadors to David and cedar wood, and masons and carpenters[2] in order to build a palace for him. 2/ Then David knew that Yahweh had established him as king over Israel, for his kingdom was exceedingly exalted[3] on account of his people Israel.

3/ David took more wives in Jerusalem, and David became the father of more[4] sons and daughters. 4/ These are the names of those who were born[5] to him in Jerusalem: Shammua,[6] Shobab, Nathan, Solomon, 5/ Ibhar, Elishua,[7] Eliphelet,[8] 6/ Nogah,[9] Nepheg, Japhia, 7/ Elishama, Beeliada,[10] and Eliphelet.

8/ When the Philistines heard that David had been anointed[11] king over all Israel, all the Philistines went up in search of David. When David heard that, he went out against them. 9/ The Philistines came and made raids[12] in the Valley of Rephaim. 10/ David made an inquiry of God, "Shall I go up against the Philistines, and will you give them into my hand?" Yahweh responded to him, "Go up and I will give them[13] into your hand." 11/ They attacked[14] at Baal-perazim, and David smote them there. David said,[15] "God has burst out against my enemies by my hand like a smiting against water." Therefore they call the name of that place Baal-perazim. 12/ They left their gods[16] there, and David commanded that they should be burned with fire.[17]

13/ Once more the Philistines[18] made a raid[19] in the valley.[20] 14/ And David again inquired of God, and God said to him,[21] "You shall not go up behind them. Circle around them[22] and attack them in front of the balsam trees.[23] 15/ When you hear the sound of marching in the top of the balsam trees, then you go out to battle,[24] for Yahweh has gone out before you to smite the camp of the Philistines." 16/ David did[25] just as Yahweh commanded him. He smote[26] the camp of the Philistines from Gibeon[27] to Gezer.[28] 17/ The reputation of David went out in all the lands, and Yahweh put the fear of him on all nations.

---

1 חירם K; Q חורם "Huram." In 2 Chr 2:2, 10-11; 4:16; 8:2, 18; 9:21 the name is spelled Huram. This alternate spelling will be discussed at 2 Chr 2:2. In readings discussed in textual notes 2-4, 9-13, 15-17, 19, 21-22, 24-25, 27-28, Chronicles presupposes a text of Samuel other than MT.

2 וחרשי קיר וחרשי עצים. The Chronicler reverses the order of the craftsmen found in the *Vorlage* at 2 Sam 5:11. For "masons" 4QSam[a] has וחרשי קיר (as in Chronicles), while Samuel LXX[B] presupposes וחרשי אבן(ים). These synonymous readings for "masons" have been conflated in Samuel MT and Samuel LXX[L] וחרשי אבן קיר. For "carpenters" Samuel MT וחרשי עץ, but Samuel LXX presupposes וחרשי עצים, as in Chronicles.

3 נשאת (*niphal* fem. sg. participle according to BDB, 671; and *HALOT* 2:726); cf. 2 Sam 5:12 LXX and LXX[L]. Samuel MT נשא (*piel* perfect).

4 דויד עוד; cf. 2 Sam 5:13 4QSam[a], Samuel LXX[B], and other versions. Samuel MT עוד לדויד.

5 הילודים; 2 Sam 5:14 הילדים; 1 Chr 3:5 נולדו.

6 שמוע; cf. 2 Sam 5:14. Chronicles LXX and 1 Chr 3:5 שמעא.

7 ואלישוע; cf. 2 Sam 5:15. 1 Chr 3:6 ואלישמע "Elishama." This is probably an assimilation to the same name later in the list (14:7//3:8//2 Sam 5:16).

8 ואליפלט with many Hebrew MSS, the versions, and 1 Chr 3:6. The name in 14:5 MT lacks the internal *yôd*.

9 Eliphelet and Nogah are also attested in 2 Sam 5:15 LXX and LXX[L] (but not in 2 Sam 5:15 MT) and in the parallel list of David's children at 1 Chr 3:6-7. Space considerations suggest they were present in 2 Sam 5:15 4QSam[a]. McCarter, *II Samuel*, 148, suggests that a scribe omitted by haplography the four original names between Elishua and the final Eliphelet (Nepheg, Japhia, Elishama, and Beeliada), and that a corrector reinserted the last five names, leading to the repetition of Eliphelet. Nogah may be a corrupt dittography of Nepheg. Japhet, 97, argues for the originality of Eliphelet and Nogah and attributes their omission in the text of Samuel to textual corruption. In any case there is no reason to think that Chronicles ever had a shorter list of David's sons born in Jerusalem.

10 ובעלידע; cf. 2 Sam 5:16 LXX and LXX[L]. In 2 Sam 5:16 MT and 1 Chr 3:8 this name has been changed to אלידע Eliada, possibly because of offense that was taken at the reference to the god Baal in the name of one of David's children.

11 נמשח; cf. 2 Sam 5:17 LXX. Samuel MT משחו "they had anointed him."

12 ויפשטו; cf. 2 Sam 5:18 LXX. Hence this reading was present already in the Chronicler's *Vorlage*. Samuel

MT וינטשו "they spread out." The variant may have arisen because of the graphic confusion of *nûn* and *pê* and the interchange of *šîn* and *ṭêt* (McCarter, *II Samuel*, 151). The same variation in verbs occurs in 1 Chr 14:13//2 Sam 5:22, and again Samuel LXX agrees with Chronicles. Johnstone, 1:178, detects assonance between פשט and פלשתים "Philistines."

13 ונתתים; cf. for the suffix 2 Sam 5:19 LXX[L] and Syr. Samuel MT and LXX כי נתן אתן את הפלשתי "for I will surely give the Philistines."

14 ויעלו. A few Hebrew MSS, LXX, Syr, Arab.: ויעל "he attacked." Contrast the *Vorlage* at 2 Sam 5:20: ויבא דוד "David entered."

15 ויאמר דויד; cf. 2 Sam 5:20 LXX, Syr. Samuel MT ויאמר.

16 אלהיהם; cf. 2 Sam 5:21 LXX. Samuel MT עצביהם "their idols." For this and the next note see Lemke, "Synoptic Problem," 351–52.

17 ויאמר דויד וישרפו באש; cf. 2 Sam 5:21 LXX[L] "And David said, 'Burn them with fire'"; Samuel MT וישאם דוד ואנשיו "and David and his men carried them off."

18 2 Sam 5:22 adds לעלות "(the Philistines continued) to go up." Chronicles LXX adds τοῦ ἀναβῆναι. Is this the preservation of the original reading or an assimilation to 2 Sam 5:22?

19 ויפשטו; cf. 2 Sam 5:22 LXX. Samuel MT וינטשו "spread out." Cf. v. 9, textual note 12.

20 בעמק. One Hebrew MS, LXX, Syr, Arab. add רפאים, apparently an assimilation to the text of 2 Sam 5:22. Cf. Allen, *Greek Chronicles*, 1:177.

21 ויאמר לו האלהים; cf. 2 Sam 5:23 LXX[L] "And Yahweh said to him (לו)"; and Samuel LXX "And Yahweh said." Samuel MT ויאמר "And he said." This shortened reading results from homoioarchton when the scribe's eye skipped from לו to לא.

22 אחריהם הסב מעליהם "behind them. Circle around them"; cf. 2 Sam 5:23 LXX εἰς συνάντησιν ἀποστρέφου ἀπ᾽ αὐτῶν. Samuel MT הסב אל אחריהם "Circle to their rear." Chronicles seems to conflate the two synonymous prepositional phrases that follow הסב in Samuel MT and Samuel LXX.

23 הבכאים. LXX "pear trees." *HALOT* 1:129 suggests "baka' shrubs." McCarter, *II Samuel*, 155–56, interprets this word as a town or region "Bachaim" north or northwest of Jerusalem. Seow, *David's Dance*, 89, retains the traditional understanding of the word as some form of trees. Ps 84:7 (6) describes pilgrims to Jerusalem passing through the valley of Baca, perhaps referring to a valley with lush vegetation (*HALOT* 1:129).

24 תצא במלחמה. Cf. 2 Sam 5:24: LXX[L] "go down into battle" = תרד במלחמה; Samuel MT תחרץ "get set" (for battle; cf. Seow, *David's Dance*, 89). See also the commentary.

25 ויעש דויד; cf. 2 Sam 5:25 LXX. Samuel MT and LXX[L] add כן "so."

26 ויך, with Chronicles LXX, Syr, Vg, Arab.; cf. 2 Sam 5:25. Chronicles MT ויכו "They smote."

27 מגבעון; cf. 2 Sam 5:25 LXX. Samuel MT מגבע "from Geba." Perazim and Gibeon are mentioned together in Isa 28:21 as locations of great Israelite victories. Aaron Demsky, "Geba, Gibeah, and Gibeon—an Historico-Geographic Riddle," *BASOR* 212 (1973) 26–31, argues that the author of 2 Sam 5:25 used "Geba" but was referring to el-Jib/Gibeon. He credits the change/updating of the name to the Chronicler, but we can see that this replacement already took place in Samuel textual tradition (LXX).

28 ועד גזרה; cf. 2 Sam 5:25 LXX[L]. Samuel MT עד באך גזר "until you come to Gezer."

14:1-17

Structure

The chapter may be outlined as follows:

I. 14:1-2. International recognition of David (2 Sam 5:11-12)

II. 14:3-7. Sons born to David in Jerusalem (2 Sam 5:13-16)

III. 14:8-16. Wars against the Philistines (2 Sam 5:17-25)
   A. 14:8-12. Battle in the Valley of Rephaim
   B. 14:13-16. Battle in the valley

IV. 14:17. Final observation

Three units in this chapter (the recognition of David by Hiram king of Tyre, vv. 1-2; the list of David's children born in Jerusalem, vv. 3-7; and his twofold defeat of the Philistines, vv. 8-17) are the Chronicler's reediting of three units from 2 Samuel 5 (vv. 11-12, 13-16, and 17-25). The biggest difference between the Chronicler's text and that of his *Vorlage* is that the Chronicler has chosen to place these events *after* David's first (failed) attempt to bring the ark to Jerusalem rather than before it. Historically, David would have had to defeat the Philistines even *before* he conquered Jerusalem (1 Chr 11:4-9//2 Sam 5:6-10), so that the sequence of events in both Samuel and Chronicles is to be attributed to literary or theological reasons and not to historical reality.[1] These three units in Chronicles show the manner in which Yahweh blessed David, the one who attempted to bring the ark to Jerusalem, as he had blessed Obed-edom at whose house the ark was placed,[2] and they demonstrate that David had the strength and organizational ability to complete the transfer of the ark on his second try. David, therefore, had been correct to seek the ark the first time, even if his procedure was faulty, and thus he had made up for the error he had confessed for himself and the people in not seeking the ark in the days of Saul (1 Chr 13:3). Not seeking Yahweh had led to the downfall of Saul's house (10:6, 14), but David's seeking the ark leads to the expansion of David's house.[3] The book of Chronicles had already used the account of David's children born in Jerusalem (section II, 14:3-7) as part of the genealogy of David in 3:5-9. There it was prefaced in vv. 1-4 (cf. 2 Sam 3:2-5) by a list of David's sons born in Hebron, but that list of sons born in Hebron was irrelevant to the Chronicler's purpose in showing how David the ark seeker was blessed in chap. 14.

The new literary position for the two battles against the Philistines makes Jerusalem, which had been captured only in name in 1 Chr 11:4-9 (2 Sam 5:6-10), ready to function as the cultic center of Israel. These battles secure the western approaches to Jerusalem from the direction of Kiriath-jearim and thus permit a safe transfer of the ark of the covenant. Finally, this new, later position for the materials from 2 Sam 5:11-25 brings the coronation of David and the capture of Jerusalem as close as possible to David's next official act: attempting to bring the ark to Jerusalem. The inclusion of these materials from 2 Samuel 5 at this point also emphasizes

that three months passed before a second attempt at bringing the ark to Jerusalem was made.[4]

The Chronicler concludes this chapter with an additional verse (v. 17) that sums up what has happened to David's reputation through the prior three units (cf. the similar function of 10:13-14).

Detailed Commentary

14:1-2. International Recognition of David

■ **1** *Hiram king of Tyre:* The Phoenician king, who ruled over the city state of Tyre (MR 168297), supported David's building projects with building materials and with skilled workmen, as he would later provide help to Solomon for the building of the temple. It is unlikely that Hiram's support took place near the beginning of David's forty-year reign, as the location of this account in 2 Samuel and 1 Chronicles implies, since Hiram is active well into Solomon's reign.[5] For the Chronicler Hiram was no longer merely the friend and treaty partner of David he had been in the Deuteronomistic History (1 Kgs 5:15 [1]); now he had become a vassal of David's who sent him raw materials and workmen.[6] According to the older account in Kings, Solomon, who needed materials for the temple, sent annual and abundant deliveries of grain and fine oil to Hiram (1 Kgs 5:25 [11]) and even ceded cities to him (1 Kgs 9:11).[7] In 1 Chr 14:1 Hiram is the one who initiates the gift giving. According to the Chronicler, Hiram (or Huram) assisted Solomon with building supplies for the temple (2 Chr 2:3-16//1 Kgs 5:15-27 [4-23]; 7:13-14)[8] and in supplying and staffing trading fleets in the Red Sea (2 Chr 8:18// 1 Kgs 9:27-28) and in the Mediterranean (2 Chr 9:21// 1 Kgs 10:22).

---

1   Seow, *David's Dance*, 80–90, believes that the battles against the Philistines in 2 Samuel 5 are a necessary liturgical preface to the victory parade of the ark recorded in 2 Samuel 6. In Chronicles the need to show David's blessing as a result of his efforts on behalf of the ark prevailed over any faded memories of the liturgical celebration that Seow has tried to reconstruct.

2   Myers, 1:106, suggests that the events in chap. 14 showed that Yahweh was still with David and so partially offset David's disconcerting failure to deal properly with the ark.

3   King Asa sought God and was victorious (2 Chr

14:4, 7, 9-15), and Jehoshaphat obtained tribute and riches after seeking Yahweh (17:4-5).

4   See Edelman, "Deuteronomist's David," 79.

5   Galil, *Chronology*, 163, 165, dates Hiram I to 980–946. Myers, 1:106, put his accession somewhat later, in the last decade of David's reign.

6   In 2 Chr 2:14, in a letter to Solomon, Huram refers to "my lord, your father David."

7   For the Chronicler's treatment of these cities, see the commentary on 2 Chr 8:1-2.

8   The text in Chronicles is significantly different from its *Vorlage* in this pericope. See the commentary.

in order to build a palace for him: In Chronicles Jerusalem did not fully function as David's capital until the defeat of the Philistines in 1 Chr 14:8-17. Hence the Chronicler changed the reading in 2 Sam 5:11, "they built a palace for David," into a purpose clause, "in order to build a house for David." The completion of David's building projects in Jerusalem is reported in 1 Chr 15:1. David's palace may have been constructed over the stepped-stone structure in the city of David that has been excavated by modern archaeologists. David's building a palace is the first sign in this chapter of his being under God's blessing.

■ **2** *Then David knew that Yahweh had established him as king over Israel, for his kingdom was exceedingly exalted:* Hiram's recognition of David provided convincing evidence for David that Yahweh also had established him as king over Israel and that his kingdom was exalted for the sake of Israel.[9] In Chronicles Hiram appears more as a vassal paying tribute than as an equal treaty partner (cf. 2 Chr 2:10, 14; 18:1-2). Although the word "established" was taken over from the *Vorlage,* it is part of a widespread motif in its new home in Chronicles.[10] Note also the Chronicler's addition of the word למעלה "exceedingly" to give emphasis to the exaltation of David's kingdom. The word used in this sense is found only in Chronicles.[11] Saul had lost his kingship (1 Chr 10:14), but David's was exceedingly exalted.[12]

on account of his people Israel: Rudolph, 114, has suggested that the suffix on the word "people" has David as its antecedent, but the Deity is also a possibility. Hence David's kingship was exalted either for the sake of his own people or for the sake of God's people.

14:3-7. Sons Born to David in Jerusalem

■ **3-7** *David took more wives in Jerusalem, and David became the father of more sons and daughters:* See also the commentary on 3:5-9. The gift of children is the second blessing David received for trying to bring the ark to Jerusalem. This marks a contrast with Saul, who lost all his sons at Gilboa (10:6). The Chronicler omitted the word "concubines" that was present in his *Vorlage* (2 Sam 5:13),[13] possibly to protect the moral character of David and the legitimacy of his children,[14] but he retained the report that David took *more* wives in Jerusalem. While both Samuel and Chronicles report that David fathered[15] sons and daughters, only sons are reported in the following list.[16] The use of the word "more" twice in v. 3 is a relic of a time when this list was preceded by the list of the wives and sons born in Hebron.[17] Though the Chronicler omitted the reference to the children born in Hebron here, just as he passed over the idea that David once ruled only Judah from Hebron, he (carelessly?) continued to use the word "more" from the text's earlier context. Solomon is listed as the fourth of thirteen royal

---

9   The Chronicler omitted the "and" from וכי in 2 Sam 5:12. Hence he makes the exaltation of David's kingdom evidence for Yahweh's establishment of David rather than it being a second fact that David knew: "David knew that Yahweh had established him as king . . . and that he had exalted his kingdom."

10   The verbal root is used with regard to the Davidic dynasty in 1 Chr 17:11-12; 22:10; 28:7; 2 Chr 17:5.

11   1 Chr 22:5; 23:17; 29:3, 25; 2 Chr 1:1; and 20:19; with עד also in 1 Chr 16:12; 17:12; 26:8. See Curtis and Madsen, 208.

12   Cf. Hezekiah, who was exalted in the sight of all nations (2 Chr 32:23).

13   For the role of these concubines in 2 Samuel see 2 Sam 15:16; 16:21-22; 19:5; 20:3. Nothing of 2 Sam 5:13 is included in the genealogy at 1 Chr 3:5-9, although concubines are mentioned in v. 9.

14   But note the reference to Rehoboam's concubines in 2 Chr 11:21. McKenzie, *Chronicler's Use,* 46, raises the possibility of loss by homoioteleuton if the

Chronicler was following the order of the nouns preserved in 2 Sam 5:13 LXX γυναίκας καὶ παλλακάς. The Chronicler also omitted the expression "after David had come from Hebron" in 2 Sam 5:13.

15   Chronicles uses the active form of the verb ויולד (*hiphil*), 2 Sam 5:13 the passive form ויולדו (*niphal*).

16   In 1 Chr 3:9 the Chronicler mentions a list of David's sons by his concubines and he also mentions their (one) sister Tamar. Though not mentioned elsewhere in Chronicles, Tamar was raped by her half-brother Amnon according to 2 Samuel 13.

17   This is currently the case only in 1 Chr 3:1-4 (sons born in Hebron) followed by 3:5-9 (sons born in Jerusalem). At an earlier time 2 Sam 3:2-5 (sons born in Hebron) followed by 2 Sam 5:13-16 (sons born in Jerusalem) may have been part of a single document.

sons born in Jerusalem.[18] Clearly, all these children were not born in the three months between the two processions of the ark, and like the reference to Hiram, belong historically much later in David's reign. We are not told how many women were involved in producing these children. The names of the mothers and the activities of the other ten sons are unknown, and none of the other sons appears later in Chronicles.

Beeliada: The name of the tenth son of David means "The Lord knows," with "Lord" (Heb. בעל) probably referring originally to Yahweh or another deity rather than to the god known as Baal. The name has been changed to "God knows" in 2 Sam 5:16 and 1 Chr 3:8, perhaps to avoid the implication that David gave his son a "Baal" name. But note the place name Baal-perazim in v. 11, which was retained without objection.

14:8-16. Wars against the Philistines
14:8-12. Battle in the Valley of Rephaim

■ **8** *When the Philistines heard that David had been anointed king over all Israel:* By the addition of the word "all" to the *Vorlage* from 2 Sam 5:17 the Chronicler makes clear that the change from David being king over only Judah in the Deuteronomistic History to king over all Israel turned David into a threat to the Philistines. David is never king over Judah alone in Chronicles (cf. 1 Chr 11:1-3).

he [David] went out against them: Two victories over the Philistines (in vv. 8-12 and 13-17) provide the third piece of evidence that David was rewarded for seeking the ark, while Saul, who did not seek the ark, had been badly beaten by the Philistines. After defeating Saul at Mount Gilboa (1 Chronicles 10), the Philistines responded with a renewed attack when they heard of David's anointing as king over all Israel (11:1-3).[19] Japhet, 287, suggests that since the Philistines had to search for David, he was not yet in Jerusalem, and that the correct historical sequence would be war with the Philistines, conquest of Jerusalem, and transfer of the ark. Though that may be true historically, the Deuteronomistic Historian and the Chronicler clearly placed David in Jerusalem *during* these two battles. David's response to the Philistine attack is more vigorous in Chronicles: ויצא לפניהם "he went out against them" versus וירד אל המצודה "he went down to the stronghold" in 2 Sam 5:17.

■ **9** *the Valley of Rephaim:* David was faced with an attack from the Valley of Rephaim, modern-day Baq'ah, near the modern-day Jerusalem railway station and extending southwest from Jerusalem.[20] Welten points out that it would not be possible to bring the ark from Kiriath-jearim to Jerusalem unless the belligerent Philistines would have been cleared out of the intervening territory.[21]

■ **10** *David made an inquiry of God:* This kind of inquiry (וישאל) before a holy war is exactly what Saul failed to do (1 Chr 10:13, לשאל). Yahweh responded positively to both of David's questions ("Shall I go up? Will you give them into my hand?"[22]) and thus authorized the beginning of a holy war against the Philistines. David also inquired of God before the second battle (14:14).

■ **11** *They attacked at Baal-perazim, and David smote them there:* The reference to the place name Baal-perazim at

---

18 In 1 Chr 3:5 Bathshua (= Bathsheba) is listed as the mother of the first four children born in Jerusalem. According to 2 Sam 11:27 Bathsheba bore an unnamed son who later died (12:14-23). Solomon seems to be the second son she bore to David (12:24). If we follow the context in 2 Samuel, this son was born during or after the Ammonite campaign. The exact number of sons born in Jerusalem is uncertain (see textual note 9).

19 References to the Philistines also appear in the list of David's mighty men in 1 Chr 11:13-18.

20 Seow, *David's Dance,* 81; cf. Aharoni, *Land of the Bible,* 293. For other references to the Valley of Rephaim, see Josh 15:8; 18:16; 2 Sam 23:13; 1 Chr 11:15. It was probably during one of these battles that three of David's heroes went to the cistern at

Bethlehem, which was then under Philistine control (1 Chr 11:15-19//2 Sam 23:13-17).

21 Peter Welten, "Lade—Tempel—Jerusalem: Zur Theologie der Chronikbücher," in *Textgemäss: Aufsätze und Beiträge zur Hermeneutik des Alten Testaments* (FS Ernst Würthwein; ed. A. H. J. Gunneweg and O. Kaiser; Göttingen: Vandenhoeck & Ruprecht, 1979) 175–76.

22 "Go up and I will give them into your hand." Yahweh also fights for Israel in 2 Chr 13:15; 17:10; 20:15, 17, 29; 25:8; 32:8.

this point in the verse is anachronistic, since this site would only receive its name and its etiological explanation as a *consequence* of the battle this verse describes. Of course the place name may well be older and is only given a new etymological etiology here.

"God has burst out against my enemies by my hand like a smiting against water": David compared God's smiting of the enemies (פרץ . . . אֶת אֹיְבַי) with God's smiting of the (cosmic) waters (כְּפֶרֶץ מָיִם).[23] Divine and human cooperation is expressed since *God's* smiting takes place through *David's* hand. The place name Baal-perazim ("Baal of [or lord of] the breaches/burst outs") is not attested aside from this reference and the *Vorlage* in 2 Sam 5:20. Isaiah refers to this battle and locates it at *Mount* Perazim (28:21), which may explain why the Chronicler has Israel[24] "going up" for this battle in v. 11 rather than David merely "going against" them as in 2 Sam 5:20.[25]

■ **12** *They left their gods there:* The Philistines abandoned their gods[26] into Israelite hands, thus allowing the Israelites to reverse the humiliation of Saul when the Philistines had put his weapons in the temple of their gods and hung his skull in the temple of Dagon (1 Chr 10:10).

David commanded that they should be burned with fire: Following the instructions of Deut 7:5, 25-26; 12:3,[27] David gave orders that the gods of the Philistines should be burned in fire. As textual note 17 shows, this change had already been made in a non-MT form of the Samuel *Vorlage,* but it is of course also now part of the Chronicler's interpretation of this event. The Chronicler has also changed the imperative of his *Vorlage* (שָׂרְפוּם "burn them") into a narrative verb form (וַיִּשָּׂרְפוּ "that they should be burned"). In 2 Sam 5:21 MT David and his men only "carried off" the Philistine idols.

14:13-16. Battle in the Valley

■ **13** *the Philistines made a raid in the valley:* When the Philistines attacked a second time, they were merely "in the valley," not in the Valley of Rephaim, as in 2 Sam 5:22. This new location for the Philistines reflects the poetic parallelism of Isa 28:21, where the first colon locates a battle at Mount Perazim, while the second colon places it in the valley of Gibeon (cf. below on v. 16).[28]

■ **14** *attack them in front of the balsam trees:* David once more inquired of God, but this time God advised against a direct attack ("You shall not go up"; contra v. 10) and instructed David instead to circle around and meet the Philistines by the balsam trees. The reason for this ambiguous geographical reference becomes clear in v. 15.

■ **15** *When you hear the sound of marching in the top of the balsam trees:* The cue for the Israelite army to attack was the sound of God's heavenly army moving through the

---

23　This follows Seow, *David's Dance*, 82–83, who demonstrates that in the analogous expression פֶרֶץ עֻזָּה (2 Sam 6:8//1 Chr 13:11) the second element is also the object rather than the subject of the verb פרץ. Earlier commentators explained כְּפֶרֶץ מָיִם as a reference to waters breaking through a dam or a similar barrier. See also Moshe Garsiel, "David's Warfare against the Philistines in the Vicinity of Jerusalem (2 Sam 5,17-25; 1 Chron 14,8-16)," in *Studies in Historical Geography and Biblical Historiography Presented to Zecharia Kallai* (ed. G. Galil and M. Weinfeld; VTSup 81; Leiden: Brill, 2000) 162. Cf. also the commentary at 1 Chr 13:2.

24　The first word in v. 11, "They," is ambiguous. It could refer to Israel, just as the *Vorlage* 2 Sam 6:20 had David going to Baal-perazim, and it would then indicate Israel's response to the command "go up" in the previous verse. "Them" later in the verse refers to the Philistines. Or "they" could refer to the Philistines, which would be consistent with "them" later in this verse.

25　Various suggestions have been put forward for locating Baal-perazim, including Mt. Abu Tor, just south of the railway station in Jerusalem. For this proposal and critique of earlier suggestions, see Garsiel, "David's Warfare," 160.

26　The Chronicler is following a non-MT of Samuel now attested by Samuel LXX (see textual note 16). In Samuel MT a redactor has denigrated the deities of the Philistines to idols. This versional evidence is ignored by Johnstone, 1:179, who attributes the change to the Chronicler, and by Fishbane, *Biblical Interpretation*, 71.

27　"The images of their gods you shall burn with fire."

28　The battle at Gibeon is no doubt an allusion to Josh 10:10. See Mosis, *Untersuchungen*, 119.

top of the trees. The verb צעד "march" is used in several holy war contexts to describe Yahweh's marching from the southern wilderness (Judg 5:4; Ps 68:8 [7]; cf. Hab 3:12).

then you go out to battle, for Yahweh has gone out before you: After he had heard the marching in the balsam trees, David was supposed to *go out* (תצא) to battle since God had already *gone out* (יצא) to smite the Philistine camp. The Chronicler has replaced the rare verb in 2 Sam 6:24, תחרץ (get set [for battle]), with a more common expression, תצא במלחמה (a reading partially anticipated in תרד במלחמה ["you will go down to battle] of Sam LXX[L]).[29] This change also allowed the Chronicler to make a wordplay between David's going out and Yahweh's going out.

■ **16** *He smote the camp of the Philistines from Gibeon to Gezer:* David followed God's instruction to the letter, and the people smote the Philistines along the road that passes through Beth-horon (MR for Upper Beth-horon: 160143), from Gibeon (MR 167139) and ends up in the vicinity of Gezer (MR 142140), a distance of about seventeen or eighteen miles as the crow flies. The second battle, or at least its conclusion, therefore, is located northwest of Jerusalem, and the pursuit follows a line north of Kiriath-jearim (MR 159135). The Chronicler has therefore used these two battles to erase any danger from the Philistines when the ark would come from Kiriath-jearim to Jerusalem. Since the rout of the Philistines began at Gibeon, the Chronicler may also have wanted to show that the tabernacle was made safe at that site (see comment on 1 Chr 16:39). Gibeon was also the hometown of Saul (8:29-33; 9:35-39).

14:17. Final Observation

■ **17** *The reputation of David went out in all the lands:* The Chronicler added this verse to the materials he had taken over from 2 Samuel 5 to drive home his central point: David's reputation for military prowess went out to all the lands. "Lands" may refer at once to both other

nations and to the lands of Israel (1 Chr 13:2) he had invited to bring the ark to Jerusalem. The emphasis is surely on the non-Israelite nations. The spread of David's name anticipates and justifies the conclusion drawn in 17:8//2 Sam 7:9: "I [Yahweh] was with you wherever you went, and I cut off all your enemies before you. I will make for you a name like the name of the great ones who were in the land." This verse also confirms what was stated earlier (v. 2) about the exaltation of his kingdom through Hiram.

the fear of him: David, who was afraid of God after his plan to bring the ark to Jerusalem had gone astray (1 Chr 13:12), now found that Yahweh had put "his fear" on all the nations.[30] De Vries, 140, notes that this could mean the fear of David or the fear of Yahweh, though he favors the latter interpretation.[31] Perhaps it is best to let the ambiguity and ambivalence of the text stand.

on all nations: Mosis is right therefore in seeing in these two Philistine defeats a paradigm for God's support for Israel against all enemies as long as the king and the nation would seek Yahweh or the ark.[32] The Chronicler may have been influenced in this interpretation by Isa 28:21, where the battles against the Philistines had already become paradigmatic for Yahweh's military power: "Yahweh will rise up as on Mount Perazim, he will rage as in the valley of Gibeon."[33] The Chronicler later refers to David taking booty from such nations as Edom, Moab, the Ammonites, the Philistines, and Amalek (1 Chr 18:11).[34]

Conclusion

While we have seen in the textual notes and the commentary that the Chronicler had a text of Samuel that diverged from MT at a number of places, his main difference from his *Vorlage* is that he moved the equivalent of 2 Sam 5:11-26 *after* the first attempt to bring the ark to Jerusalem, that had ended with the death of Uzzah. This shift accomplished several things. From a chronological

---

29   See textual note 24.

30   The Chronicler uses "Yahweh" in this sentence, although in several earlier references in this chapter (vv. 10, 11, 14, 15, 16) he replaced that divine name with "God." "Yahweh," however, also appears in vv. 2 and 10.

31   See 2 Chr 14:13; 17:10; 20:29.

32   *Untersuchungen,* 62.

33   The reference to Gibeon in Isaiah reflects the geographical reference to this town already contained in 2 Sam 5:25 LXX (cf. textual note 27).

34   Cf. also 2 Chr 17:10-11 and 20:29, the military successes of Jehoshaphat; and 32:22-23, the military success of Hezekiah.

perspective, these verses signified the three-month period during which the ark had remained at the house of Obed-edom, whereas in 2 Samuel the narrative of David's decision to make a second try comes right after the failed attempt. Of even more importance is the effect on the verses taken from 2 Samuel 5. Now the international recognition of David, the children born to him in Jerusalem, and his double victory over the Philistines are blessings on David for his initial, if failed, attempt to bring the ark to Jerusalem.

The Chronicler's own addition, in v. 17, notes the international renown of David, and how Yahweh had put fear or awe of him—himself or David—on all the nations. Regardless of how we interpret this ambivalent "him," it is clear from this verse that Yahweh is in full support of David.

15

Translation

1/ He [David] made for himself houses in the city of David, and he prepared a place for the ark of God, and he pitched for it a tent. 2/ Then David commanded that no one should carry the ark of God except the Levites, for Yahweh had chosen them to carry the ark of God and to serve him forever. 3/ David assembled all Israel to Jerusalem to bring up the ark of Yahweh[1] to its place, which he had established for it.

4/ David gathered the sons of Aaron and the Levites. 5/ Of the sons of Kohath: Uriel the chief, with one hundred twenty of his kindred. 6/ Of the sons of Merari: Asaiah the chief, with two hundred twenty of his kindred. 7/ Of the sons of Gershom: Joel the chief, with one hundred thirty of his kindred. 8/ Of the sons of Elizaphan: Shemaiah the chief, with two hundred of his kindred. 9/ Of the sons of Hebron: Eliel the chief, with eighty of his kindred. 10/ Of the sons of Uzziel: Amminadab the chief, with one hundred twelve of his kindred.

11/ David invited Zadok and Abiathar the priests, and the Levites Uriel, Asaiah, Joel, Shemaiah, Eliel, and Amminadab, 12/ and he said to them, "You are the heads of the ancestral houses of the Levites. Sanctify yourselves, you and your kindred, and bring up the ark of Yahweh[2] the God of Israel to [the place which][3] I have prepared for it. 13/ For at the first time[4] you[5] did not carry it. Yahweh[6] our God has burst out against us for we did not seek him correctly."[7] 14/ The priests and the Levites sanctified themselves to bring up the ark of Yahweh[8] the God of Israel. 15/ The Levites carried the ark of God on their shoulders[9] with carrying poles on them, just as Moses had commanded by the word of Yahweh.[10]

16/ David commanded the chiefs of the Levites to appoint[11] their kindred the singers to proclaim with musical instruments—harps, lyres, and cymbals—and to raise sounds of joy.[12] 17/ The Levites appointed Heman son of Joel; and of his kindred Asaph the son of Berechiah; and of the sons of Merari their kindred Ethan the son of Kushaiah.[13] 18/ And with them were their brothers of the second rank, Zechariah,[14] and Jaaziel, and Shemiramoth, and Jehiel, and Unni, and Eliab,[15] and Benaiah, and Maaseiah, and Mattithiah, and Eliphelehu, and Mikneiah, and Obededom and Jeiel and Azaziah[16] were gatekeepers.[17]

19/ The singers Heman, Asaph, and Ethan were to sound bronze cymbals. 20/ And Zechariah, and Jaaziel,[18] and Shemiramoth, and Jehiel, and Unni, and Eliab, and Maaseiah, and Benaiah[19] were to play harps according to Alamoth. 21/ And Mattithiah, and

1 Many Hebrew MSS "God." In readings discussed in textual notes 26 and 32-37, Chronicles is based on a text of Samuel different from Samuel MT.

2 Lacking in LXX.

3 אל. A few Hebrew MSS, Syr, Tg, Vg, Arab. add אשר (ה)מקום. *BHS* suggests adding האהל ה, which could have been lost by haplography after אל "to."

4 בראשונה. MT למבראשונה. Was this originally למה בראשונה ("Wherefore, at the first"; so Curtis and Madsen, 214)? Rudolph, 116, interprets the MT as "Since at the first time. . . ."

5 אתם. Add נשאתם, which was lost by homoioteleuton. *BHS* proposes to add אתנו "[you were not] with us."

6 Lacking in LXX.

7 כי לא דרשנהו כמשפט. *NRSV* translates: "We did not give it proper care," thus hiding the word "seek" from the reader.

8 Lacking in LXX.

9 בכתפם; lacking in LXX because of homoioarchton.

10 LXX "God."

11 Johnstone, 1:184, favors a translation of "put into operation," "reinstate," or "install." This harmonizes well with 1 Chr 6:16-32 (31-47), where David had already designated those who were to be singers.

12 שמחה; MT לשמחה (dittography of final letter in preceding word).

13 קושיהו; 1 Chr 6:29 (44) קישי "Kishi."

14 MT adds בן, which is lacking in 3 Hebrew MSS and LXX and clashes with the conjunction before "Jaaziel." Delete with *BHS*. Cf. "Zechariah" in v. 20 and 1 Chr 16:5.

15 ואליאב, with a few Hebrew MSS, LXX, Syr; the conjunction is lacking in MT. Cf. v. 20.

16 ועזזיהו with LXX; lacking in MT. Cf. v. 21.

17 It is not clear how many names the word "gatekeepers" applies to. Many commentators consider "gatekeepers" to be a secondary gloss on the basis of v. 24. See Structure.

18 ויעזיאל; cf. v. 18. MT ועזיאל, a misspelling.

19 Maaseiah and Benaiah appear in reverse order in v. 18.

20 במשא. Cf. Kleinig, *Lord's Song*, 47, who cites 2 Chr 35:3. Chenaniah was responsible for the physical and musical transportation of the ark. See *HALOT* 2:639, "transport" (or singing). Cf. M. Gertner, "The Masorah and the Levites," *VT* 10 (1960) 252, who suggests "head of the carrying." The word is lacking in LXX.

21 יסר. Rudolph, 119, and Kleinig, *Lord's Song*, 47, conclude that this is an active noun. Cf. Isa 28:26; GKC §84k.

22 מחצרים, with Q; K מחצצרים.

23 לארון; LXX לארון אלהים "ark of God."

345

Eliphelehu, and Mikneiah, and Obed-edom and Jeiel and Azaziah were to lead with lyres according to the Sheminith.

22/ Chenaniah was chief of the Levites with regard to transportation;[20] he was an instructor[21] in transportation, for he was a skilled person. 23/ Berechiah and Elkanah were gatekeepers for the ark. 24/ Shebnaiah, and Joshaphat, Nethanel, Amasai, Zechariah, Benaiah, and Eliezer, the priests, were to blow[22] trumpets in front of the ark of God. And Obed-edom and Jehiah were gatekeepers for the ark.[23]

25/ David and the elders of Israel and the commanders of the thousands, were going along[24] to bring up the ark of the covenant of Yahweh[25] from the house of Obed-edom with joy. 26/ Because God helped the Levites, who were carrying the ark of the covenant of Yahweh, they[26] sacrificed seven bulls and seven rams.[27] 27 And David was vested[28] in a fine linen mantle, as were all the Levites who were carrying the ark,[29] and the singers, and Chenaniah, the chief[30] of transportation,[31] and David wore a linen ephod.[32] 28/ And all Israel[33] was bringing up the ark of the covenant of Yahweh with a shout and the sound of the horn, and with trumpets and cymbals; they proclaimed with harps and lyres. 29/ And as[34] the ark of the covenant of Yahweh was coming into[35] the city of David, Michal the daughter of Saul looked down through the window, and saw King David skipping and reveling;[36] and she despised him in her heart.

16:1/ And they brought the ark of God and set it up[37] in the middle of the tent, which David had pitched for it, and they offered burnt offerings and peace offerings[38] before God. 2/ When David had finished offering the burnt offerings and the peace offerings, he blessed the people in the name of Yahweh. 3/ And David distributed to each person in Israel, both men and women, a loaf of bread, a portion of meat,[39] and a raisin cake.

24 הלכים; the prefixed article in MT arose by dittography.

25 2 Sam 6:12 MT "the ark of God"; Samuel LXX, Syr, Tg: "the ark of Yahweh." Chronicles LXX "ark of the covenant."

26 2 Sam 6:13 "he." See the commentary.

27 שב[עה] פר[ים] ושבע[ה] אילים = 2 Sam 6:13 4QSamᵃ Chronicles. Samuel MT שור ומריא "a bull and a fatling" or, via hendiadys, "a fattened bull."

28 The participle מכרבל may have been chosen because of its similarity to מכרכר ("strumming") in 2 Sam 6:14 (Rudolph, 119). This change may have been facilitated by the reference to David's being clothed in a linen ephod in 2 Sam 6:14b. Japhet, "Interchanges," 12, n. 13, sees Aramaic influence in the word chosen in Chronicles. See also textual note 35 below.

29 Chronicles LXX adds "of the covenant of Yahweh."

30 Read שׂר for MT השׂר (dittography of the last letter of the previous word). *BHS* suggests emending the following word המשׂא to במשׂא, but that is unnecessary once the dittography is recognized.

31 MT mistakenly adds המשׁררים "the singers."

32 Braun, 191, deletes this last clause as a secondary correction from 2 Sam 6:14.

33 וכל ישׂראל; cf. 2 Sam 6:15, a few Hebrew MSS, LXXᴸ, Syr. 2 Sam 6:15 MT ודוד וכל בית ישׂראל "And David and all the house of Israel." *BHS* emends to ודויד וכל ישׂראל "And David and all Israel."

34 ויהי; cf. 2 Sam 6:16 4QSamᵃ and Samuel LXX. Samuel MT והיה.

35 עד with 2 Sam 6:15 LXX; lacking in Samuel MT and in many Hebrew MSS of Chronicles (homoioarchton).

36 ומשׂחק. Cf. 2 Sam 6:16 LXXᴸ, which is partially conflate and is based on the following Hebrew *Vorlage:* משׂחק ומפזז ומכרכר "reveling and leaping and strumming." Samuel MT מפזז ומכרכר "leaping and strumming." The choice of the verb שׂחק in Chronicles depends on an alternate reading in the Samuel *Vorlage.*

37 2 Sam 6:17 MT adds במקומו "in its place." This reading is lacking in Chronicles, 4QSamᵃ, and Samuel Syr.

38 ושׂלמים with 2 Sam 6:17 Syr. Samuel MT and LXX place ושׂלמים at the end of the verse. This noun was added secondarily in texts of Samuel at two different positions (McCarter, *II Samuel,* 167), and Chronicles used the text type now preserved only in Samuel Syr.

39 *JPS* "cake made on fire."

15:1—16:3

Structure

To understand the structure of this unit we must survey the content of chaps. 15 and 16. The first twenty-four verses of chap. 15, without a parallel in the Deuteronomistic History, describe various kinds of preparations David made to bring the ark from the house of Obed-edom to Jerusalem, and the narration in 15:25—16:3, based on 2 Sam 6:12-19a, describes the actual procession of the ark. In 1 Chr 16:4-7 and 37-42, without parallels in previous biblical texts, priests and Levites are assigned to duties at Gibeon and Jerusalem. A medley of psalms drawn from the Psalter is in 1 Chr 16:8-36. Chapter 16 ends (v. 43) with a final excerpt from the Deuteronomist's Ark Narrative (2 Sam 6:19b-20a). We may put these materials in the following outline:

15:1—16:3

I. 15:1-3. David prepares to bring the ark to Jerusalem

II. 15:4-10. David assembles the sons of Aaron and the Levitical chiefs

III. 15:11-15. David arranges for Levites to carry the ark

IV. 15:16-24. Appointment of Levitical singers

    A. 15:16. David orders the appointment of singers

    B. 15:17-18. Levitical chiefs appoint heads of singer guilds and singers of second rank

    C. 19-21. Musical instruments are assigned to musicians

    D. 22-24. Description of the procession itself: a Levitical chief, two gatekeepers for the ark, seven priests with trumpets, and two more gatekeepers for the ark

V. 15:25—16:3. The ark processes to Jerusalem (2 Sam 6:12-19a)

16:4-43

I. 16:4-7. David appoints a group of clergy (consisting of a head of one singer guild, singers of the second rank, and priests) to praise Yahweh before the ark

II. 16:8-36. Song of the Levites

    A. 16:8-22 (Ps 105:1-15)

    B. 16:23-33 (Ps 96:1-10)

    C. 16:34-36 (Ps 106:1, 47-48)

III. 16:37-42. David assigns a head of a singer guild and two gatekeepers to ongoing ministry before the ark at Jerusalem; and he assigns priests, two heads of singer guilds, singers of the second rank, and gatekeepers to ongoing ministry for the tabernacle at Gibeon

IV. 16:43. Conclusion to the Ark Narrative: David and the people return to their homes (2 Sam 6:19-20a)

The transfer of the ark from the house of Obed-edom to Jerusalem (1 Chr 15:25—16:3 //2 Sam 6:12-19a; 1 Chr 16:43//2 Sam 6:19b-23) takes place after the ark's three-month stay in the house of Obed-edom. The Chronicler inserted forty-one verses between the first and second attempts to move the ark in 2 Samuel 6 (vv. 1-11 and vv. 12-19a), with more than enough events to fill the three months the ark stayed at the house of Obed-edom. Sixteen of these verses are taken from the Deuteronomistic History, where they were located *before* the Ark Narrative (1 Chr 14:1-16//2 Sam 5:11-25), but twenty-five verses (14:17 and 15:1-24) were supplied by the Chronicler himself. The Chronicler then inserted another thirty-nine verses without a *Vorlage* in the Deuteronomistic History (16:4-42; primarily drawn from the Psalter) before appending the final verse from the Deuteronomist's Ark Narrative (16:43//2 Sam 6:19b-20a). The net effect of this major addition in chap. 16 is to give detailed attention to the day on which the ark was installed in the tent in Jerusalem.[1] The Chronicler also omitted the incident with Michal, at the end of the Ark Narrative, which reports her criticism of David's dancing and his angry retort to her (2 Sam 6:20b-23).

Repetition and conflicting data within these materials have led to a wide variety of proposals for identifying secondary materials in these chapters.

A. There is repetition between the list of six Levitical heads of ancestral houses ראשׁי האבות[2] in 1 Chr 15:11

---

1   Cf. Tamara Eskenazi, "A Literary Approach to Chronicles' Ark Narrative (1 Chronicles 13–16)," in *Fortunate the Eyes That See* (FS D. N. Freedman; ed. A. B. Beck et al.; Grand Rapids: Eerdmans, 1995) 269.

2   This title comes from v. 12.

and the list of the six Levites identified as "chief" השׂר in 15:4-10. The latter list relates these names to one of the three main Levitical families (Kohath, Merari, and Gershom).[3] David "gathered the group" in v. 4 and "called" to them in v. 11. Many commentators feel that a secondary hand has added the genealogical materials in vv. 5-10 to show why the six Levites mentioned in v. 11 were considered heads or chiefs and to relate Zadok and Abiathar, the priests named in v. 11, to the Aaronide family.[4] Because of the allegedly secondary vv. 4-10, v. 11 strikes many modern readers as repetitious and redundant. The sixfold division of the Levites in vv. 5-10, which is not found elsewhere in Chronicles, and the relatively small numbers of Levites have convinced other scholars that the list in vv. 5-10 is older than Chronicles and is not likely to have been added later when the threefold division of the Levites had become standard.[5] If we can grant the Chronicler the right to a somewhat repetitive style, there is no necessity to identify a secondary hand in these verses.

B. A second repetition has been detected in 15:16-24, which reports the appointment of the Levitical singers after the generic Levites, who had been directed by David to carry the ark in vv. 12-13, had already purified themselves and put the ark on their shoulders in vv. 14-15.[6] Again, tolerance may be necessary toward the repetitive character of the Chronicler's style, and v. 15 itself does not so much describe the actual beginning of the procession as the manner in which the ark was to be transported when the procession would begin.[7] Much more serious in this case is the contradiction between the three Levitical families (or guilds) of singers listed in vv. 16-24 and those found elsewhere in Chronicles and even in chap. 16. The Chronicler's standard three guilds of singers are Asaph, Heman, and Jeduthun, but in

vv. 16-24 the three families are Heman (note his listing in first position), Asaph, and Ethan. This configuration of families is also found in the genealogy of the singers in 6:16-33 (31-48).[8]

Since the 1970s discussion of this problem has centered on a classic article by Hartmut Gese in which he attempted to arrange the postexilic materials about the singers into a series of stages.[9]

Stage I. Shortly after the exile, the singers are called "sons of Asaph" and are not yet considered Levites (Ezra 2:41; Neh 7:44).

Stage II. About the time of Nehemiah (second half of the 5th century), the singers *are* considered Levites and have been divided into the groups of Asaph and Jeduthun (Neh 11:3-19//1 Chr 9:1-18).

Stage III A. At the time of the Chronicler, the Levitical singers are in three groups: Asaph, Heman, and Jeduthun (1 Chr 16:4-7, 38-42; 2 Chr 5:12; 29:13-14; 35:15).

Stage III B. At a later time, Jeduthun has been replaced by Ethan, and Heman is more prominent than Asaph (1 Chr 6:16-33 [31-48] and 15:16-24), hence Heman, Asaph, and Ethan.

Since Gese considered the materials in stage III B to be secondary in Chronicles for literary-critical reasons, he assigned this stage to a time later than the Chronicler, whom he located at stage III A.

Japhet, 296, has called attention to the crucial role of Gese's literary-critical decisions in coming to his chronological conclusions, and therefore she alleges circular reasoning in his argumentation. She has also proposed that Ethan and Jeduthun were alternate names for the same individual. Williamson, 121, has located the Chronicler himself at stage III B and argued that the older materials about Asaph, Heman, and Jeduthun

---

3   Kohath, v. 5; Merari, v. 6; Gershom, v. 7. Shemaiah from the sons of Elzaphan, Eliel from the sons of Hebron, and Amminadab from the sons of Uzziel in vv. 8-10 are Kohathites. See the commentary on these verses.

4   See Paul D. Hanson, "1 Chronicles 15–16 and the Chronicler's Views on the Levites," in *"Sha'arei Talmon"* (ed. M. Fishbane and E. Tov; Winona Lake, IN: Eisenbrauns, 1992) 70–72.

5   Williamson, 121. Japhet, 295, proposes that these verses reflect a census of the central Levitical families at some juncture.

6   See Hanson, "1 Chronicles 15–16," 73–74.

7   Piet B. Dirksen, "The Development of the Text of I Chronicles 15:1-24," *Hen* 17 (1995) 272.

8   Heman, 1 Chr 6:16-23 (31-38), Asaph, 6:24-28 (39-43), and Ethan, 6:29-32 (44-47).

9   Hartmut Gese, "Zur Geschichte der Kultsänger am zweiten Tempel," in *Vom Sinai zum Zion: Alttestamentliche Beiträge zur biblischen Theologie* (Munich: Kaiser, 1974) 147–58.

were incorporated by the Chronicler from earlier sources. This, of course, does not completely alleviate the tension within the materials, especially between 1 Chronicles 15 and 16, and it does not explain why, in narrative contexts that he composed (2 Chr 5:12; 35:15), the Chronicler chose Asaph, Heman, and Jeduthun as heads of the singer guilds.

Gese made two other points in his article that bear repeating. First, he argued that the "family of Jeduthun" originally meant something like "those who were not of Asaph's family" and that its boundaries were somewhat fluid. He mentions the Korahite gatekeeper Obed-edom (1 Chr 26:4, 8, 15) who is reckoned among the singers in 15:18, 21, and 16:5, but who in 15:24 and 16:38 is numbered among the gatekeepers. Gese believed that when the guild of Heman rose in numbers and prestige,[10] another group of singers identified themselves as descendants of (their eponymous ancestor) Ethan, who is mentioned in the same verse with Heman in 1 Kgs 5:11 (4:31), and the amorphous group of Jeduthun singers gradually disappeared. While his attribution of the growth of the guild of Heman to the Korah incident is very speculative, the indefinite parameters of the Jeduthun group may be part of the solution to the present problem.

A second point is that Gese admitted that the situation was more complicated in Chronicles than might be indicated by his listing of stages III A and III B. In the listing of the singers in 1 Chronicles 25, Heman's power is already stronger than the other heads of the guilds,[11] but this list still mentions the family of Jeduthun as the third singer guild. This marks a position midway between Gese's stages III A and III B. Similarly, Gese found two families of Levitical singers in 2 Chr 20:19, those aligned with Asaph and those aligned with Korah. Gese places this tradition *before* III A, when the singers became divided into three groups, but later than stage

II. Gese's article was written at a time when he and many others denied 1 Chronicles 9 to the original draft of the book of Chronicles. If, however, 1 Chronicles 9 was included in the book of Chronicles from the start, as argued in this commentary, the data on the Levitical singers within Chronicles is even more complex and diverse than Gese admitted, and it is very difficult to say what *the* position of the Chronicler on the Levitical singers is. That is, there are at least five levels of singer configurations within materials now in Chronicles itself:[12]

1. 1 Chr 9:1-18 (Gese's stage II), Asaph and Jeduthun
2. 2 Chr 20:19, Asaph and Korah
3. the materials in Gese's stage III A, Asaph, Heman, and Jeduthun
4. 1 Chronicles 25, Heman, Asaph, and Jeduthun
5. the materials in Gese's stage III B, Heman, Asaph, and Ethan

I do not believe these five stages can be convincingly assigned to five separate authors or redactors by literary-critical methods. What is more, the Chronicler thus seems to be able to tolerate a considerable amount of tensions in his traditions about the Levitical singers.

On the basis of these arguments, I propose that the tension between the Ethan and Jeduthun references in chaps. 15 and 16 is typical of the multiple-singer traditions in 1 and 2 Chronicles, and that the Chronicler has not harmonized all of the data at his disposal. There is no need or justification, therefore, to excise 1 Chr 15:16-24.

C. Another apparent contradiction with literary-critical consequences is found in the references to Obed-edom in this chapter. In 15:21 he is among the players of the lyre (or one of the singers), and that role is implied in 16:5 as well. But in 15:18,[13] 15:24, and 16:38 he is called a gatekeeper. The latter tradition is also preserved in 26:4, 8, 15.[14] Williamson, 130, proposes that the core

---

10   Gese thought that when the Korahites were excluded from the priesthood (Num 16:8-11), they sought refuge and status in the Heman group of singers.

11   Four sons are listed for Asaph, six for Jeduthun, and fourteen for Heman.

12   Stage I, where the singers are called "sons of Asaph," but are not yet Levites, appears only in Ezra and Nehemiah.

13   As mentioned in textual note 17, it is not clear which names are modified by the word "gatekeepers." Some of the names, possibly including even Obed-edom in the present text, could be construed as singers.

14   The reference to an Obed-edom in the reign of Amaziah (2 Chr 25:24) is dependent on this tradition of Obed-edom as gatekeeper.

of 16:38 must be ascribed to the "corrector" who, as in 15:18 and 24, wanted to record Obed-edom's later (and hypothetical!) demotion from singer to gatekeeper. But a subsequent scribe offered a rejoinder to the corrector, noting that Obed-edom was the son of (the singer) Jeduthun. Japhet, 303, deletes the word "gatekeeper" in 15:18, but retains it in 15:24 and 16:38. In 15:24 Japhet, 305, emends Jehiah (ויחיה) to "and his brothers" (ואחיו) in order to create *more* gatekeepers, and in 16:38 she, 320, tentatively offers two reconstructions of the original text, either "Obed-edom and his brethren sixty-eight, were to be gatekeepers" or "Obed-edom and Hosah were to be gatekeepers." In either case she believes the reference to Jeduthun in 16:38 is secondary. Japhet correctly observes that there seems to be no escape from the conclusion that 16:38 has undergone some interpolation. She also considers 15:23 a gloss, where Berechiah and Elkanah are listed as gatekeepers for the ark, but she cannot ascertain the purpose of this gloss.

Here is my own attempt to bring order to this chaotic information. The references to Obed-edom as a singer/musician in 15:18, 21, and 16:5 are original. The mention of "gatekeepers" as the last word in v. 18 is to be identified as a gloss caused by the references to "gatekeepers" later in chaps. 15 and 16. As I observed in the textual notes, it is by no means certain which names in this verse are referred to as gatekeepers in any case. Hence limiting the gatekeepers to the last two or three names is arbitrary. The gatekeepers are not mentioned in 15:16-21 if the word "gatekeepers" in v. 18 is in fact secondary.

The materials in 15:22-24 need to be seen as different in genre from the lists of the heads of the singer guilds in 15:17 and the singers of the second rank in 15:18, to whom instruments are assigned in vv. 19-21. Note that vv. 22-24 identify Chenaniah, a leader (שׂר) not heard of before, two sets of gatekeepers (Berechiah and Elkanah in v. 23 and Obed-edom and Jehiah in v. 24), and between these sets of gatekeepers are listed seven

priests. I believe that this paragraph (vv. 22-24), which comes after the lists of singers (vv. 16-21) and immediately before the resumption of the Ark Narrative (in v. 25), describes the way part of the procession lined up in the Chronicler's opinion:[15]

Chananiah, the leader of the procession
Gatekeepers in front of the ark (Berechiah and Elkanah)
Seven priests with trumpets in front of the ark
Gatekeepers behind the ark (Obed-edom and Jehiah)

Presumably, the gatekeepers in front of and behind the ark were to make sure that no one touched the ark (cf. Uzzah in 13:9-10). The ark therefore must be imagined to come after the first set of gatekeepers and the priests with trumpets and before the second set of gatekeepers. One might surmise that the Levitical singers came at the end of the procession.

In chap. 16, as we will see, the Chronicler combined the two types of materials (type A, 15:17-21;[16] and type B, 15:22-24) as he created a distribution of the priests and Levites to the ark in Jerusalem, on the one hand, and to the tabernacle in Gibeon, on the other. For the ark (16:5-6, 37-38) he lists Asaph as head of a singer guild (cf. 15:17, type A[1]), followed by nine singers (cf. 15:18-21, type A[1 and 2]), two priests with trumpets (cf. 15:24a, type B), and finally gatekeepers (cf. 15:24b, type B). Similarly, for the sanctuary at Gibeon (16:39-42) the Chronicler first names Zadok and his kindred priests (cf. 15:24a, type B),[17] then he lists Heman and Jeduthun as heads of singer guilds (cf. 15:17, type A[1]),[18] followed by unnamed singers (15:18-21, who are by implication of type A[2]), and finally gatekeepers, who are assigned to Jeduthun, the least significant of the heads of the gatekeepers (cf. 15:24b, type B).

For the development of 16:38 itself I would propose the following. The first draft of the verse read, "Obed-edom and Hosah were gatekeepers." They represent, respectively, the two types of gatekeepers in chap. 26, Korahites and Merarites. This was glossed marginally by

---

15   In this I adopt the position of Kleinig, *Lord's Song*, 48. However, I cannot go along with his decision to read vv. 17-18 in reverse order in order to make the singers listed there part of the procession.

16   I designate the simple list of names in vv. 17-18 as A[1] and the assignment of instruments to these names in vv. 19-21 as A[2].

17   These were added because of the ongoing sacrificial cult at Gibeon.

18   Thus he utilizes his normal three families of Asaph, Heman, and Jeduthun, with Asaph retaining the first position. Both trumpets and cymbals are said to be "with" (stored with?) these two heads of singer guilds.

"And Obed-edom was the son of Jeduthun"[19] and by a second note "and their brothers were sixty-eight." This second gloss was based on a totaling of the sons of Obed-edom (sixty-two) and Jeduthun (six) in 26:8 and 25:3, respectively. The text of 16:38 represents a confused amalgamation of these readings.

D. We move on to other passages that have been considered secondary. The priests in 15:4, 11, 14, 24; 16:6 and 16:39 have seemed out of place in contexts that focus on the duties of the Levites. According to my reconstruction, the priests in 15:24 are part of a paragraph (vv. 22-24) describing how the procession lined up and so must be retained. In my opinion this reference to priests influenced the Chronicler in his composition of 16:6, where the priestly trumpeters before the ark in Jerusalem are named. Zadok is also essential in 16:39 because of the sacrificial character of the cult conducted by the tabernacle at Gibeon. Evidence on the first three mentions of priests in chap. 15 (vv. 4, 11, and 14) is less compelling. Japhet, 298, argues that it is highly unlikely that the Chronicler would ignore the priesthood altogether in preparing for the procession of the ark. While the text of v. 26 is ambiguous about who carried out these sacrifices, I propose that the sacrifices of the Levites mentioned there would actually have been offered through the cultic leadership of the priests. In light of this fragmentary, if inconclusive, evidence about 15:4, 11, and 14, I have chosen to retain the references to the priests in these verses.

E. Rudolph, 127, argued that since the observations about the trumpeters and the singer Obed-edom stand side by side in 15:24, chap. 16 should have the same arrangement, with v. 6[20] and v. 38[21] standing next to one another. Rudolph believed that v. 6 had been added to the original composition first and only a subsequent hand added vv. 7-37.[22] Japhet, 312, seems more on target when she notes that the materials from the second ark

procession (2 Sam 6:12b-20a) provide a frame for the whole unit, which is arranged in chiastic fashion:

A. Second ark procession (1 Chr 15:25-16:3 [2 Sam 6:12b-19a])
B. Permanent Levitical arrangments (1 Chr 16:4-6)
C. Connecting link related to Asaph (16:7)
D. Psalm (16:8-36)
C′. Connecting link related to Asaph (16:37)
B′. Permanent priestly and Levitical arrangements concluded (16:38-42)
A′. Second ark procession concluded (16:43 [2 Sam 6:19b-20a])

Detailed Commentary

15:1-3. David Prepares to Bring the Ark to Jerusalem

■ **1** *He made for himself houses:* David now built the houses for which Hiram had sent him materials and workmen (1 Chr 14:1//2 Sam 5:11), although he does not seem to move into these dwellings until 1 Chr 17:1. The single palace of 14:1 has now become multiple houses.

he prepared a place for the ark of God and he pitched for it a tent: At the same time that David was building secular houses, he prepared a "place" or sanctuary (מקום) for the ark and pitched a tent for it (cf. Ps 132:2-5). This verse anticipates 1 Chr 16:1 (2 Sam 5:17) by recording the actual pitching of the tent into which David will later put the ark.[23] David's preparation of a place for the ark is repeated in vv. 3 and 12.

■ **2** *Then David commanded that no one should carry the ark of God except the Levites for Yahweh had chosen them to serve him forever:* David's designation of the Levites as those chosen to carry the ark follows pentateuchal legislation (Num 4:15; Deut 10:8) and also appears in 2 Chr 29:11. But the two chronological designations, "then" and "forever," concede that others had carried the ark before the

---

19 This gloss was influenced by the mention of the sons of Jeduthun as gatekeepers in 1 Chr 16:42.

20 "And the priests Benaiah and Jahaziel were to blow the trumpets regularly before the ark of the covenant of God."

21 "And Obed-edom—and their brothers sixty-eight—and Obed-edom was a son of Jeduthun—and Hosah were gatekeepers."

22 Willi, *Chronik als Auslegung,* 196, omitted vv. 4-38, 41-42.

23 De Vries, 141, surely errs in denigrating this work: "David had built . . . palaces for himself . . . but had only established . . . a *māqôm,* 'shrine,' and a tent at that, for the ark."

time of David, or at least that it had been transported in a different way, that is, on a new cart. The everlasting service of the Levites echoes Deut 18:5: "For Yahweh your God has chosen Levi out of all your tribes to stand and minister in the name of Yahweh, him and his sons for all time" (cf. Deut 10:8).

■ **3** *David assembled all Israel to Jerusalem:* The Chronicler insists that the second procession of the ark, surely no less than the first, was the work of all Israel. The assembly gathered in 1 Chr 13:5 had presumably scattered during the three-month hiatus when the ark had stayed at the house of Obed-edom. The original decision to move the ark (13:1-5), as well as its actual transfer to Jerusalem, is the work of all Israel.

15:4-10. David Assembles the Sons of Aaron and the Levitical Chiefs

■ **4** *David gathered the sons of Aaron and the Levites:* The reference to the "sons of Aaron"[24] anticipates the mention of the priests Zadok and Abiathar in v. 11 and provides them with a connection to the main priestly genealogy, although Abiathar in the Deuteronomistic History is descended from Eli (and Moses?) rather than Aaron (see also comment on v. 11). "The Levites" anticipates the Levitical names in v. 11; their connection to the three main Levitical families is provided in vv. 5-10.

■ **5-10** *Uriel, Asaiah, Joel, Shemaiah, Eliel, Amminadab:* The three main Levitical families according to 6:1-15 (16-30) are Gershom, Kohath, and Merari. In vv. 5-10 the Chronicler identifies the six leading Levites mentioned in v. 11 as descendants of one of these sons of Levi.

• *Uriel* (v. 5) is in the fifth[25] generation after Kohath according to the (reconstructed and very uncertain) genealogy in 6:7-9 (22-24), through Kohath's second son, Amminadab (see the commentary on 6:7-9 [22-24] for the reconstruction of this genealogy and the uncertain identity of this Amminadab).

• *Asaiah* (v. 6) is in the seventh generation after Merari, through Merari's oldest son Mahli (6:15 [30]).

• *Joel.* The evidence available to the Chronicler for the ancestry of Joel (v. 7) was not so clear. The Chronicler assigned him to the sons of Gershom despite the fact that Joel's name does not appear in Gershom's genealogy in 6:2, 15-16 (17, 20-21). According to 23:7-8 Joel was the grandson of Gershon through Ladan, Gershon's oldest son, while in 26:21-22 Joel was the great-grandson of Gershon.

• *Shemaiah* (v. 8) traced his lineage through Elizaphan the son of Uzziel, the fourth son of Kohath (Exod 6:22; Lev 10:4; Num 3:30; cf. 1 Chr 6:3 [18]; 2 Chr 29:13).

• *Eliel* (v. 9) traced his lineage to Kohath as well, through Kohath's third son Hebron (1 Chr 5:28 [6:2]; 6:3 [18]; 23:12).[26]

• *Amminadab* (v. 10) is assigned to the sons of Uzziel, the fourth son of Kohath.[27]

Hence four of the chiefs are traced back to Kohath: one from Amram, one from Hebron, and two from Uzziel. Two other chiefs came from Merari and Gershom, respectively. The total number of persons associated with Kohath is five hundred twelve, with two hundred twenty assigned to Merari and one hundred thirty to Gershom. It is from Kohath's oldest son Amram that the sons of Aaron traced their ancestry. The reason for assigning four of the chiefs to Kohath probably results from the fact that the Kohathites were assigned responsibility for the ark in Num 3:31 (cf. Num 4:15).

15:11-15. David Arranges for Levites to Carry the Ark

■ **11** *David invited Zadok and Abiathar the priests:* This is the only clear reference to Abiathar serving as a priest in Chronicles, since elsewhere the non-Zadokite high priest

---

24 This is the first reference to the sons of Aaron in Chronicles. See 1 Chr 23:28, 32; 24:1, 31; 2 Chr 13:9, 10; 26:18; 29:21; 31:19; 35:14.

25 Johnstone, 1:182, follows the MT in 1 Chronicles 6 literally and puts Uriel in the ninth generation of Kohath (= the eighth after Kohath).

26 Another Eliel is in the fifth generation before Heman in the list of singers (1 Chr 6:19 [34]), tracing his own ancestry from Kohath.

27 In 1 Chr 6:7 (22) MT Amminadab is listed as the

son of Kohath. *BHS* emends "Amminadab" to "Izhar." Others would emend it to "Amram." Braun, 187–89, argues that 15:4-10 is late partly because it presupposes an error in 6:7 (22). The reading "Amminadab" in 15:10 seems unrelated to this error, since he is here listed in the ancestry of Uzziel.

at the time of David is called Ahimelech the son of Abiathar (1 Chr 18:16; 24:6; cf. 27:34). The Chronicler implies that Abiathar is a descendant of Aaron (v. 4). The name Zadok appears seventeen times in Chronicles, though this is his first mention outside the opening genealogies and the obscure reference in 12:29 (28). Zadok's Aaronide lineage was mentioned in v. 4 before the lineage of the leading Levites was given in vv. 5-10.

■ **12** *"You are the heads of the ancestral houses of the Levites. Sanctify yourselves":* The term "Levites" in Chronicles normally refers to those clergy who are second in rank to the priests, but it also is used in a wider sense, as here, to designate all clergy, including the Aaronides, who were also descended from Levi.[28] Note that both the priests and Levites sanctified themselves to bring up the ark of Yahweh according to v. 14, which supports the wider meaning of "Levites" here. David's first assignment to the Levitical family heads was to sanctify themselves[29] so that they and their kindred could bring the ark to the place prepared for it in Jerusalem. Such rites of sanctification apparently included at least bathing, the washing of clothes, and refraining from sexual intercourse (Exod 19:10, 15; 1 Sam 21:5).

■ **13** *"For at the first time you did not carry it":* David interprets the failure of the Levites to carry the ark from the house of Abinadab as the reason for the miscarriage of the first attempt to bring the ark to Jerusalem, leading to the death of Uzzah and the ark's stay at the house of Obed-edom for three months. This explanation removes the need for David to fear or to be puzzled on how he could bring the ark to Jerusalem, which the Chronicler had recorded earlier in a verse he had taken over from the *Vorlage* (1 Chr 13:12//2 Sam 6:9).

Yahweh our God has burst out: Yahweh's judgment is described as "bursting out," a play on the word פרץ that unites the whole Ark Narrative (see the discussion at 1 Chr 13:2).

"we did not seek him correctly": David includes himself and the whole community among the guilty; the guilt did not rest on Uzzah alone. The Chronicler makes the failure of the Levites to carry the ark the central issue. David's words addressed to the Levites, "you did not carry it," are more a statement of fact than an accusation against the Levites. After all, it was the decision of the whole congregation that was the decisive factor behind the first attempt to move the ark. The use of the term "correctly" (כמשפט) is the first use of what De Vries calls the "regulation formula." Wherever this regulation formula refers to David or the reigning Davidic king, it is specifically the rights and duties of the Levites that are in question.[30]

■ **15** *The Levites carried the ark of God on their shoulders, with carrying poles:* This verse describes a proper way to move the ark and explains what is meant by not seeking Yahweh "correctly" in v. 13—that is, the ark was not carried by the Levites, on their shoulders (Num 7:9), with poles. The word for poles (במטות) in Chronicles has replaced the word בדי used in Exod 25:13-14//37:4-5.[31] The poles would presumably provide a margin of safety so that the Levites would not touch the ark and die.

as Moses had commanded by the word of Yahweh: David's dramatic change in the way the ark was to be carried finds its authority in the "command of Moses" and the "word of Yahweh,"[32] both references to the pentateuchal

---

28   This interpretation depends on the reference to the priests in v. 11 not being secondary. See the discussion of this and other references to the priests under Structure.

29   The *hitpael* of קדש appears only twice in 1 Chronicles (see v. 14) and 11 times in 2 Chronicles (2 Chr 5:11; 29:5, 15, 34 [twice]; 30:3, 15, 17, 24; 31:18; 35:6). None of these is attested in the *Vorlage*. The root קדש is used here for the first time in the narrative section of 1 Chronicles (see 1 Chr 6:34 [49] and 9:29).

30   See also 1 Chr 23:31; 24:19; 2 Chr 4:7, 20; 8:14;

23:18; 29:15, 25; 30:6, 12, 16; 35:4, 10, 13, 16; and Simon J. De Vries, "Moses and David as Cult Founders in Chronicles," *JBL* 107 (1988) 619–39.

31   Japhet, 302, raises the possibility that the ark was carried in some form of frame otherwise used for smaller vessels (cf. Num 4:10, 12).

32   1 Chr 11:3, 10; 12:23; 15:15; 2 Chr 35:6.

legislation. This is the first reference to Moses in the narrative of Chronicles.[33]

15:16-24. Appointment of Levitical Singers
15:16. David Orders the Appointment of Singers

■ **16** *David commanded the chiefs of the Levites to appoint their kindred the singers:* David now ordered the six leading Levites, who had been identified in vv. 4-11, to appoint singers, or musicians, from among their kindred. By the use of the word "kindred" (אחיהם) the Chronicler recognizes the Levitical status of the singers and fosters good relationships between them and the chiefs of the generic Levites.

to proclaim with musical instruments: The musical role of these Levites supplements their other duties, including the carrying of the ark, a duty that continues until the time of Josiah in Chronicles (2 Chr 35:3). "Proclaim" is a more accurate rendering of the participle משמיעים than the *NRSV*'s paraphrastic "to raise loud sounds of joy." Since there was no ark in the Second Temple, the Levites of the Chronicler's day no longer carried it. The ad hoc singing during the procession became a regular part of the cult according to the Chronicler already at the time of the dual sanctuaries at Gibeon and at Jerusalem in 1 Chr 16:37-42.[34] In 6:16-32 (31-47) David put the singers in charge of the service of song in the house of Yahweh after the ark had come to a rest. In the commentary on that passage I argued, following Kleinig, that the service of song took place already at the tabernacle in Gibeon and at the tent where David had deposited the ark in Jerusalem. Dancing and trumpets had played a role in the transport of the ark according to 2 Sam 6:14-15, though these activities were carried on

by David and the house of Israel there, and not by the Levites. Liturgical joy is a frequent motif in Chronicles.[35]

15:17-18. Levitical Chiefs Appoint Heads of Singer Guilds and Singers of Second Rank

■ **17** *Heman the son of Joel . . . Asaph the son of Berechiah . . . Ethan the son of Kushaiah:* The Levitical chiefs appointed the three heads[36] of the guilds of singers, listing the father's name of this person in each case according to the genealogy in 1 Chr 6:16-33 (31-48). The order of the names reflects the dominance of the Heman guild as shown in his long genealogy in 6:18-23 (33-38). Only Ethan is identified explicitly with one of the three great Levitical families (Merari) in v. 17, which may indicate the Chronicler's, or his source's, awareness of the newness of this particular guild.

■ **18** *and with them were their brothers of the second rank:* The other fourteen[37] singers who were appointed were subordinate to the singer heads, but somehow above or distinguished from the general lot of singers,[38] of which there must have been dozens if not hundreds. The names of these singers, which appear frequently in Chronicles, are (partially) repeated when they are assigned musical instruments (vv. 18-21) or when they are distributed between the cult centers of the ark and of the tabernacle (16:37-42). The singer Obed-edom is presumably meant to be the same person as Obed-edom the Gittite in 13:14. A Philistine has become a Levitical singer in Chronicles!

15:19-21. Musical Instruments Are Assigned to Musicians

■ **19-21** *bronze cymbals . . . harps . . . lyres:* Heman, Asaph, and Ethan, the three leaders of the guilds of singers, were assigned to the bronze cymbals.[39] The first eight names among the singers of second rank (v. 20) were to

---

33   Earlier references to him appear in the genealogies at 1 Chr 5:29 (6:3) and 6:34 (49). See also 21:29; 22:13; 23:13-15; 26:24, and twelve times in 2 Chronicles.

34   Williamson, 120, argues that historically this change did not happen until after the dedication of the temple in 2 Chr 5:2–7:10.

35   See the discussion at 1 Chr 12:41 (40). The noun שמחה occurs twelve times and the verb שמח appears thirteen times in Chronicles. In the Ark Narrative see also 15:25; 16:10, 31.

36   No specific title is given to their role at this point in Chronicles.

37   See textual note 17 on v. 18. Following my argument under Structure I consider all the people named in v. 18 singers, not gatekeepers.

38   The next verse assigns specific musical instruments to them.

39   Eleven of the thirteen biblical occurrences of the word מצלתים "cymbals" are in Chronicles, and they appear during the reigns of David, Solomon, and Hezekiah. The other two references are in Ezra 3:10 and Neh 12:27.

play harps "according to Alamoth," and the last six (v. 21) were to lead with lyres "according to the Sheminith." Zechariah, Jeiel, Shemiramoth, Jehiel, Mattithiah,[40] Eliab, Benaiah, and Obed-edom appear again in 16:5. It has been customary to interpret עלמות "Alamoth" as a higher-pitched instrument because of its relationship to the word עַלְמָה "young woman,"[41] and to interpret השמינית "Sheminith" (lit. "the eighth [string?]")[42] as its opposite or a bass sound, but Kleinig points out the lyre was actually a higher tuned instrument.[43] It is impossible to determine the exact reason for assigning certain Levites to specific instruments. Were they skilled on that instrument? Did the other Levitical musicians merely sing?[44]

15:22-24. Description of the Procession

■ **22** *Chenaniah:* This person, otherwise unknown, was a chief (שֹׁר) among the Levites (cf. vv. 5-10), but his leadership was in matters of transportation, music, or even contributions. The difficult word מַשָּׂא is derived from the root נשׂא "to lift up," and could refer to the lifting or carrying of the ark (2 Chr 35:3), or, if it connotes the lifting up of the voice, to music. Johnstone, 1:185, suggests a third possibility, contributions, and notes that Chenaniah is in charge of overseeing contributions in 1 Chr 26:29. Because of the context in vv. 22 and 27, I favor the first of these alternatives. Chenaniah is not supplied with a patronymic or connected genealogically to the major Levitical families of Gershom, Kohath, and Merari.

■ **23** *Berechiah and Elkanah were gatekeepers for the ark:* The office of gatekeepers for the ark appears only in this paragraph in the Bible (vv. 23-24; see the discussion under Structure of vv. 22-24 describing the order of the procession), although the same role seems to apply to the two gatekeepers in 16:38, who were assigned by David to the ark. Elsewhere the term "gatekeeper" always refers to gatekeepers of the tabernacle or the temple.

■ **24** *were to blow trumpets in front of the ark:* Seven priests were assigned to the trumpets in the procession. This instrument is assigned to priests throughout the book of Chronicles.[45] Trumpets were played during the first abortive attempt to move the ark (13:8).

15:25—16:3. The Ark Processes to Jerusalem

■ **25** *the elders of Israel and the commanders of thousands:* The Chronicler leaves out an equivalent for 2 Sam 6:12a: "It was told King David, 'Yahweh has blessed the house of Obed-edom and everything he owns on account of the ark of God.'" These words might have given the impression that David acted opportunistically in bringing the ark to Jerusalem in order to gain for himself some of the "blessing" that had accrued to Obed-edom. In a gloss to Samuel retained by 4QSam[a], a reviser made this motivation explicit: "And David said, 'I will bring back this blessing to my own home.'" Without this half verse, however, the all-Israel theme prevails in Chronicles. The commanders of thousands were part of the group David consulted when he proposed to bring up the ark to Jerusalem (1 Chr 13:2), although "the commanders of hundreds" are not repeated here. The "elders of Israel" were not mentioned in 13:2 and are relatively rare in the Chronicler.[46] The Chronicler seems to have added them here in order to harmonize this account with Solomon's bringing up the ark from the city of David to the temple, where the elders are involved (2 Chr 5:2, 4//1 Kgs 8:1, 3).

were going along: Eskenazi points out a grammatical shift in vv. 25-29 that underlines the unique importance of the event.[47] Verbs change from the perfect tense to

---

40   Mattithiah also appears in 1 Chr 25:3, 21 among the sons of Jeduthun.

41   See Ps 46:1 (S): "To the leader. Of the Korahites. According to Alamoth. A Song." Cf. Ps 48:15 (14) and the suggested emendation to the last two words in that verse in the notes in *BHS*.

42   Cf. Pss 6:1 (S); 12:1 (S).

43   *Lord's Song*, 46.

44   Lyres and harps were also mentioned in the first attempt to bring the ark to Jerusalem (1 Chr 13:8).

45   1 Chr 16:42 MT might seem to form an exception since the trumpets and cymbals are "with" Heman and Jeduthun. But textual note 29 at 16:42 indicates that the names Heman and Jeduthun are secondary. Cf. also Num 10:10.

46   Only 1 Chr 11:3; 21:16; 2 Chr 5:2, 4.

47   Eskenazi, "Literary Approach," 267.

participles, emphasizing continuous action. In addition to the present case, see "vested," v. 27; "was bringing up," v. 28; and "was coming," v. 29. Naturally, the procession takes place with joy (cf. v. 16).[48]

the ark of the covenant of Yahweh: Only now, as the account of the last stage of the ark's movement begins, and with the Levites finally carrying the ark, does the Chronicler call it the "ark of the covenant of Yahweh" in harmony with Deut 10:8. Six of the twelve uses of this phrase in Chronicles occur in this context: 1 Chr 15:25, 26, 28, 29//2 Sam 6:12, 13, 15, 16; 1 Chr 16:6, 37.[49] Where the passages have a parallel in the *Vorlage,* in each case the Chronicler has added the word "covenant."[50] For the Chronicler the ark is the symbol of the covenant relationship between Yahweh and Israel and also the symbol of Yahweh's presence in Jerusalem (cf. 17:1, 4).

■ **26** *Because God helped the Levites, who were carrying the ark of the covenant:* In the *Vorlage* a group of unnamed

people carried the ark (2 Sam 6:13); here that task is assigned explicitly to the Levites. Previously in Chronicles, the two and one-half Transjordanian tribes were given divine help against the Hagrites (1 Chr 5:20), and Amasai, endowed with the spirit, referred to God as the one who helps David (12:19 [18]).[51] The addition of the notion of God's help is a theological change made by the Chronicler.[52]

they sacrificed seven bulls and seven rams: In 2 Sam 6:13, after the ark bearers had gone six steps, David sacrificed a bull and a fatling, or a fatted bull. The Chronicler notes explicitly that the sacrifice in this verse was in response to God's helping the Levites,[53] and the sacrifice itself was performed by persons designated as "they," that is, by all the people and not just by David.[54] As textual note 26 demonstrates, the expanded list of sacrificial animals ("seven bulls and seven rams"[55]) was taken over by the Chronicler from a text of Samuel divergent from the MT.

---

48 Cf. Ps 68:4 (3), which also describes a procession of the ark: "But let the righteous be joyful; let them exult before God; let them be jubilant with joy."

49 Cf. also 1 Chr 17:1, where Chronicles reads "the ark of the covenant of Yahweh," and 2 Sam 7:2 reads "the ark of God." Other passages where the Chronicler uses this expression are 1 Chr 22:19; 28:2, 18, and two occasions when he repeats this expression from his *Vorlage* (2 Chr 5:2, 7//1 Kgs 8:1, 6). Sabine van den Eynde, "Chronicler's Use of the Collocation ארון ברית יהוה," *ZAW* 113 (2001) 429, notes that all the changes in the terminology used for the ark happen before it is deposited in the temple in 2 Chr 5:2, 7//1 Kgs 8:1, 6. She adds: "The stories of the ark gradually lead to a culminating point: its placement in the temple that is built to provide it a place of rest."

50 The two verses from chap. 16 are themselves additions by the Chronicler. Chronicles LXX adds "of the covenant of Yahweh" to the word "ark" in v. 27 (see textual note 28). Eskenazi, "Literary Approach," 270–71, remarks: "At the surface level of the text, the Levites—not the ark itself—are perceived as the actual bearers of the covenant. Only when the two combine—when the Levites and the ark meet—does the ark constitute a covenantal symbol." I find some tension between these two sentences and believe that the second is the more helpful articulation. Van den Eyde, "Chronicler's Usage," 422–30, has made a thorough study of the ark of the covenant in Chronicles. I do not think

her thesis that this term must be connected to the covenantal promises to David is convincing. Rather, the ark functions to demonstrate Yahweh's presence in the sanctuary (17:1, 4, as well as the purpose of transporting the ark to Jerusalem in chaps. 13–16), and it is called "the ark of the covenant" because it contains the two tablets of the law (2 Chr 5:10; 6:11//1 Kgs 8:9). The ark in Chronicles combines therefore the older meaning of the ark as symbolizing God's presence and the Deuteronomic interpretation that it is a box to hold the tablets of the law, without Deuteronomy's polemic against the view of the ark as symbolizing God's presence.

51 Cf. the prayer of Asa requesting divine help in 2 Chr 14:10, God's help for Jehoshaphat (18:31) and Uzziah (26:7), and Hezekiah's confession about Yahweh's help in warfare (32:8). See also 25:8: "God has power to help or to overthrow."

52 Japhet, "Interchanges," 14–15, suggests that the Chronicler misread צעדו ("stride") in 2 Sam 6:13 as סעדו ("support," "sustain") and then replaced it with the more common word for help. This misreading seems doubtful to me.

53 Contrast 1 Chr 13:10-12, where God opposed the movement of the ark by bursting out against Uzzah and intimidating David.

54 So Johnstone, 1:187. It is possible, of course, that "they" could refer to the Levites or even to the priests.

55 The only sacrifices with mention of the same animals are in Num 23:1, 29, and Job 42:8.

■ **27** *David was vested in a fine linen mantle:* The Chronicler omitted the references to the music making and the dancing[56] of David, which were contained in his *Vorlage* at 2 Sam 6:14, 16, and 20. In the latter verse, Michal accused David of shamelessly uncovering himself before his maids. Instead of this questionable behavior, according to the Chronicler, David, the Levites who were bearing the ark, the musicians, and Chenaniah were dressed in liturgical vestments—a fine linen mantle (במעיל בוץ).[57] The singers at the dedication of the temple were similarly attired in fine linen (בוץ; 2 Chr 5:12). Remarkably, the Chronicler retained the notice that David was wearing a linen[58] ephod, although here it presumably refers to a garment worn over the מעיל (as with the high priest's vestments; cf. Exod 28:6-14) and not to a loincloth as in 2 Sam 6:14 (cf. 1 Sam 2:18).

■ **28** *all Israel was bringing up the ark of the covenant of Yahweh with a shout and the sound of the horn:* Despite the fact that the Levites are explicitly identified as the ark bearers, the Chronicler insists on all Israel's participation in this rite. The people's shout acclaims Yahweh's presence with the ark (cf. 2 Chr 13:12; 15:14).[59] The Year of Jubilee also begins with the sound of the horn (שופר; Lev 25:9).

trumpets and cymbals . . . with harps and lyres: To the sounds of shouting and the ram's horn, inherited from his *Vorlage* in 2 Sam 6:15, the Chronicler added references to musical instruments that had been assigned to the priests and Levitical musicians in the previous verses (1 Chr 13:8; 15:19-21, 24; cf. 16:5).

■ **29** *Michal . . . looked down through the window . . . and she*

despised him in her heart: Michal's disapproval of David in Chronicles is not a rebuke for his inappropriate dancing, but represents the continued failure of Saul and his house to seek Yahweh and the ark. The Chronicler thus continues to draw a moral contrast between the first two kings.[60]

and saw King David skipping and reveling: David's actions here seem tame in comparison with his dance in 2 Sam 6:16 and the way it was interpreted by Michal in 2 Sam 6:20: "How the king of Israel honored himself today before the eyes of his servants' maids, as any vulgar fellow might shamelessly uncover himself!" "Reveling" (ומשחק) is based on an alternate, non-MT of Samuel (see textual note 36). "Skipping" (מרקד) is a replacement for מפזז, a root used only once in the Bible outside this passage.[61]

■ **16:1** *set it up in the middle of the tent:* The Chronicler does not make explicit in this verse where David pitched the tent for the ark. The implication of 2 Chr 8:11 is that David pitched the tent in his own house. By omitting the word במקומו "in its place," or "in its sanctuary," which follows "set it up" in 2 Sam 6:17, the author may have wanted to signal that the ark was not the site of an ongoing sacrificial cult.

they offered burnt offerings and peace offerings: Those who offered these sacrifices would be either the priests, thus providing a small argument for their original presence throughout this pericope, or it could refer to the people as a whole. In the latter case, it does not necessarily mean that they took over the liturgical rights of the priests, but again affirms all Israel's participation in

---

56 While the Michal incident (2 Sam 6:20-23), which is perhaps a secondary elaboration of the Ark Narrative, suggests that David's dancing bordered on the obscene, Seow, *David's Dance,* 116, suggests that the dancing in the Ark Narrative itself was originally intended to dramatize the dance of nature before the Divine Warrior. David P. Wright, "Music and Dance in 2 Samuel 6," *JBL* 121 (2002) 223, compares David's dancing to various forms of self-affliction designed to attract the Deity's attention and prepare the way for a gracious response.

57 Cf. Exod 28:4, 31, 34, where the מעיל is one of the garments worn by the high priest. This is the only time this word is used in Chronicles, but Ezra was wearing this garment and tore it when he heard about the mixed marriages (Ezra 9:3, 5).

58 בד. Note that two different words for linen are used within this verse.

59 See also Lev 23:24 and Ps 47:6 (5).

60 Curtis and Madsen, 219, miss this point: "It is a mark of the unskillful art of the Chronicler that this single verse of the episode of Michal's judgment on David should be here introduced when the story as a whole with its reflection on David is omitted."

61 See Gen 49:24, where it appears in the *qal. HALOT* 3:921 judges this reading to be uncertain. See also Japhet, "Interchanges," 14.

the movement of the ark. In the *Vorlage* (2 Sam 6:17) the offerings were made by David himself. These sacrifices beside the ark were one-time occurrences on the occasion of the ark's installation in the tent. David did not acquire the threshing floor of Ornan, the site of the future altar of burnt offering and the temple in Jerusalem, until 1 Chronicles 21. This is the first occasion when burnt offerings and peace offerings were made in Chronicles. The only other occasions are when David built an altar on the threshing floor (1 Chr 21:26// 2 Sam 24:25), at Solomon's dedication of the temple (2 Chr 7:7//1 Kgs 8:64[62]), and during the Passover of Hezekiah (2 Chr 30:22).[63]

■ **2** *When David completed the burnt offerings and the peace offerings.* According to 2 Sam 6:17-18, David himself was the one who performed the sacrifices, but in Chronicles the sacrifices according to the previous verse were offered either by the priests or the people as a whole. This notice in Chronicles signifies only that David was the king under whose reign priests or the people carried out these sacrifices.

he blessed the people in the name of Yahweh:[64] David's blessing echoes Yahweh's own blessing of the house of Obed-edom in 1 Chr 13:14, and it anticipates David's blessing of his own household at the end of the ceremony in 16:43. David as cult founder is in many ways a second Moses. Moses also pitched a tent (Exod 33:7) and blessed the people (Deut 33:1).[65]

■ **3** *David distributed to each person in Israel . . . a loaf of bread, a portion of meat, and a raisin cake:* David distributed foodstuffs to everyone, both men and women, as a kind of symbolic banquet to celebrate the accession of

Yahweh to his home in Jerusalem. Seow compares the symbolic banquet described in Samuel to the banquet in the Ugaritic texts that Baal held after his victory over his enemies and the completion of his temple.[66]

Conclusion

This chapter ends with the resumption of the procession of the ark to Jerusalem, taken from the *Vorlage* in 2 Sam 6:12-19a. But the twenty-four verses before that, composed by the Chronicler himself without a biblical *Vorlage*, show David's meticulous preparation for this procession. The most important part of this preparation is the decree of David that no one but the Levites should carry the ark, in conformity with pentateuchal legislation and as a correction to the procedure in the first effort to bring the ark to Jerusalem. That failure was designated as not seeking Yahweh correctly. David also commanded the chiefs of the Levites to appoint Levitical singers, and so this additional duty of the Levites, also in the cult of the Chronicler's day, is given the authority of Israel's first king.

In recounting the procession itself, the Chronicler omits David's exotic/erotic dancing, including Michal's rebuke of his behavior, and adds information that has both David and the Levites in appropriate liturgical vestments. A number of departures from the MT of 2 Samuel, as the textual notes show, however, are based on alternate readings in the Samuel tradition, as evidenced primarily by 4QSam[a] and the LXX. David in this chapter is a second Moses, who also pitched a tent and blessed the people.

---

62   Instead of "burnt offerings and peace offerings," the text of Kings has "burnt offerings and the grain offerings and the fat pieces of the peace offerings."

63   The "fat of the peace offerings" is mentioned during the reign of Hezekiah at 2 Chr 29:35 (without a *Vorlage* in Kings).

64   The Chronicler again omits the word צבאות from his

Vorlage. Cf. 1 Chr 13:6. Seow, *David's Dance*, 132, argued that David blessed the people on behalf of the Divine Warrior. This interpretation no longer applies in Chronicles.

65   Johnstone, 1:190.

66   *David's Dance*, 133.

Translation

4/ He put in front of the ark[1] of Yahweh some of
the Levites as servants and, indeed, to invoke,
to thank, and to praise Yahweh the God of
Israel. 5/ Asaph the head, and those second to
him[2] were Zechariah, and Jaaziel,[3] and Shemiramoth, and Jehiel, and Mattithiah, and Eliab,
and Benaiah, and Obed-edom, and Jeiel, with
instruments consisting of harps and lyres.[4]
Asaph was to sound the cymbals. 6/ And the
priests Benaiah and Jahaziel were to blow the
trumpets regularly before the ark of the
covenant of God. 7/ At that same time David
inaugurated thanksgiving to Yahweh by the
hand of Asaph and his kindred.

8/ Thank Yahweh,[5] call upon his name,
Make known his deeds among the peoples.

9/ Sing to Yahweh, chant to him,
Meditate on all his marvelous acts.

10/ Glory in his holy name;
Let the heart of those who seek Yahweh[6]
rejoice.

11/ Seek Yahweh[7] and his strength,
seek his face regularly.

12/ Remember his marvelous deeds that he has
done,
his signs and the judgments of his mouth,

13/ O seed of Israel his servant,
children of Jacob his chosen ones.

14 He is Yahweh our God;
his judgments are in all the earth.

15/ Remember[8] his covenant forever,
The word that he commanded for a
thousand generations.

16/ [The covenant] that he made with Abraham,
his oath to Isaac.[9]

17/ He ratified it for Jacob as a precept,
for Israel as an everlasting covenant,

18/ saying, "To you I give the land of Canaan,
as a portion for your inheritance.

19/ When you were[10] few in number,
insignificant and sojourners in it,

20/ They walked from nation to nation,
and from one kingdom to another people.

21/ He did not allow a person to oppress them,
he reproved kings on their account,

22/ "Do not touch my anointed ones;
do no harm to my prophets."

23/ Sing to Yahweh, all the earth,
announce day after day his victory.

24/ Tell among the nations his glory,
among all peoples his marvelous deeds.[11]

25/ For great is Yahweh and to be praised
exceedingly,
he is to be feared above all the gods.

26/ For all the gods of the peoples are idols,
but Yahweh[12] made the heavens.

27/ Honor and majesty are before him,
strength and joy[13] are in his place.

1 LXX "ark of the covenant of Yahweh."

2 והמשנים with LXX; MT והמשנהו "and his second." In
1 Chr 15:18 those of second rank (המשנים) include
everyone from Zechariah through Azaziah (see
textual note 16 in that chapter).

3 ויעזיאל, with 15:18. Cf. 15:20, textual note 18. MT
ויעיאל "Jeiel."

4 וכנרות; cf. LXX, Tg. MT prefixes this noun with ב.

5 Divine name lacking in LXX.

6 So also Ps 105:3. Chronicles LXX "those who seek
his good pleasure." This reading is also found in a
Psalms MS from Qumran, 11QPsᵉ [ישמח לב מבקש
רצונו].

7 Divine name lacking in LXX.

8 זכרו; Ps 105:8 זכר "He remembered." *NIV* harmonizes the text of Chronicles with this *Vorlage:* "He
remembers."

9 All five occurrences of this name in Chronicles are
spelled יצחק (1 Chr 1:28, 34; 16:16; 29:18; 2 Chr
30:6); Ps 105:9 ישחק.

10 בהיותכם; Ps 105:12 בהיותם "when they were." Chronicles LXX, Vg are corrections to the text of the
Psalter.

11 The whole verse is missing in LXX by homoioteleuton, from one αὐτοῦ to the next.

12 LXX "our God."

13 וחדוה; LXX, Syr, Arab.: ותפארת "beauty," a correction to Ps 96:6.

14 This colon lacking in LXX. Note that three straight
cola begin with "Ascribe."

15 לפניו; Ps 96:8 לחצרותיו "into his courts."

16 בהדרת קדש. Or, "the theophany of the holy one."
Chronicles LXX presupposes בהצרות קדשו "in his
holy courts"; Ps 95:9 LXX has "in his holy court."
Peter R. Ackroyd, "Some Notes on the Psalms," *JTS*
17 (1966) 393–96, notes that *ḥlm* "dream" and *hdrt*
appear in poetic parallelism in the Keret text from
Ugarit, justifying the translation "theophany" here.

17 מלפניו; Ps 96:9 מפניו.

18 ויאמרו. The third person form results from its position in the present context. Ps 96:10 אמרו (2d masc.
pl. imperative). See the next note.

19 According to Ps 96:10, this colon belongs between
v. 30a and v. 30b. It seems to have been lost at that
original position by haplography and inserted in
the text of Chronicles at the wrong place. It is not
possible to tell whether this happened before or
after the composition of Chronicles. Howard N.
Wallace, "What Chronicles Has to Say about
Psalms," in Graham and McKenzie, *Chronicler as
Author,* 270, attributes the shift in location of this
colon and the change documented in the previous
note to the Chronicler, since "it might be more
appropriate [for the Chronicler's audience] to hope

28/ Ascribe to Yahweh, O families of the peoples,
    Ascribe to Yahweh honor and strength.

29/ Ascribe to Yahweh the honor of his name,[14]
    Lift up an offering and come into his presence.[15]
    Worship Yahweh in his holy theophany.[16]

30/ Writhe before him,[17] all the earth;
    aye, the world is established, it shall not be moved.

31/ Let the heavens rejoice,
    let the earth be glad,
    let them say[18] among the nations, Yahweh is king![19]

32/ Let the sea roar and its fullness,
    Let the field and everything in it exult.

33/ Then the trees of the forest will give a ringing cry,
    before[20] Yahweh for he comes[21] to judge the world.

34/ Give thanks to Yahweh for he is good,
    for his loyalty lasts forever.

35/ And say,
    "Save us, O God of our salvation,
    Gather us[22] and deliver us[23] from the nations
    to thank your holy name,
    and glory in your praise.

36/ Blessed be Yahweh the God of Israel,
    From everlasting to everlasting."

And all the people said,[24] "Amen," and they praised[25] Yahweh.

37/ He [David] left there, before the ark of the covenant of Yahweh, Asaph and his kindred to serve before the ark regularly, as each day required. 38/ And Obed-edom—and their brothers,[26] sixty-eight—and Obed-edom was the son of Jeduthun[27]—and Hosah were gatekeepers.

39/ And [he left] Zadok the priest and his kindred the priests before the tabernacle of Yahweh in the high place at Gibeon 40/ for offering burnt offerings to Yahweh on the altar of burnt offering regularly, morning and evening, according to everything written in the law of Yahweh that he commanded Israel.[28] 41/ And with them were Heman and Jeduthun and the rest of those selected who had been designated[29] by name to thank Yahweh, for his loyalty lasts forever. 42/ And with them[30] were the trumpets and the cymbals for the musicians[31] and instruments for the song of God. And the sons of Jeduthun were at the gate.

43/ All the people went—each one to his house—and David turned to bless his own house.

for some manifestation of the Lord's sovereignty in nature than to see the people themselves declaring it convincingly before their political and military masters." Cf. Johnstone, 1:195. The Chronicler also omits an equivalent for Ps 96:10b: "He will judge the peoples with equity"; and 96:13b "He will judge the earth with righteousness and the peoples in his truth." See the commentary on v. 30.

20 מלפני; Ps 96:13 לפני.

21 כי בא. Ps 96:10 כי בא כי בא "for he comes, for he comes." A haplography has taken place in Chronicles, but it is impossible to tell whether that was before or after the composition of Chronicles.

22 Lacking in LXX, but probably lost by homoiarchton from καὶ to καὶ.

23 והצילנו; lacking in Ps 106:47.

24 ויאמרו; LXX and Ps 106:48: ואמר "Let [all the people] say."

25 והלל, pointed as an infinitive absolute or a *piel* 2d masc. sg. imperative. I have translated it as an infinitive absolute that replaces a finite verb. In Ps 106:48 the form is *piel* 2d masc. pl. imperative with a 3d masc. sg. object suffix ("praise Yahweh").

26 ואחיהם; LXX, Vg: "his brothers."

27 ידותון, with some Hebrew MSS, Q; K ידיתון "Jedithun."

28 על ישראל; LXX על בני ישראל "the sons of Israel." LXX adds ἐν χειρὶ Μωυσῆ τοῦ θεράποντος τοῦ θεοῦ "by the hand of Moses the healer of God."

29 אשר נקבו; lacking in LXX.

30 ועמהם, with MT and LXX. MT adds הימן ידותון "Heman and Jeduthun" secondarily on analogy with v. 41. See the commentary.

31 למשמיעים; cf. *HALOT* 4:1574. Rudolph, 128, suspects that it is a correction entered wrongly, since it separates the cymbals from the other instruments.

16:4-43

Structure

In the previous chapter I proposed the following out-line for the materials in 16:4-43:

I. 16:4-7. David appoints a group of clergy to praise Yahweh before the ark.
II. 16:8-36. The Song of the Levites
  A. 16:8. General call to thanksgiving
  B. 16:9-22. Israel's praise (Ps 105:1-15)
    1. 16:9-11. Call to musical praise
    2. 16:12-22. Double call to remembrance
      a. 16:12-14. Remembrance of Yahweh's works
      b. 16:15-22. Remembrance of Yahweh's covenant
  C. 16:23-30. International praise (Ps 96:1-10)
    1. 16:23-27. The praise of the whole earth
    2. 16:28-30. The praise of its peoples
  D. 16:31-33. Cosmic praise
  E. 16:34. Final call to thanksgiving (Ps 106:1)
  F. 16:35-36. Summary petition (Ps 106:47-48)
    1. 16:35. Petition for Israel's deliverance
    2. 16:36a. Doxology
III. 16:37-42. David assigns a head of a singer guild and two gatekeepers to ongoing ministry before the ark at Jerusalem, and he assigns priests, two heads of singer guilds, singers of the second rank, and gate-keepers to ongoing ministry for the tabernacle at Gibeon
IV. 16:43. Conclusion to the Ark Narrative: David and the people return to their homes (2 Sam 6:19-20a)

The Chronicler added his own new materials in 16:4-7 and 37-42, dealing in the first instance with the appointment of cultic officials to serve in the presence of the ark (vv. 4-7),[1] and in the second case with regularizing these appointments for the ark (vv. 37-38) and with making similar appointments for the sanctuary of the tabernacle at Gibeon (vv. 39-42). The final verse of the chapter comes from the Ark Narrative in 2 Sam 6:19b-20a.

In the middle of the chapter the Chronicler[2] has placed selections from the Psalter: 1 Chr 16:8-22 = Ps 105:1-15;[3] 1 Chr 16:23-33 = Psalm 96; and 1 Chr 16:34-36 = Ps 106:1, 47-48.[4]

Psalm 105 is a psalm of thanksgiving that recounts Yahweh's efforts on Israel's behalf in the past, especially in the exodus and in the trek through the wilderness; Psalm 96 celebrates Yahweh's kingship, established in creation and expected to be fulfilled at Yahweh's coming; Psalm 106 is a community lament confessing Israel's national sin, God's judgment, and God's compassionate deliverance of the people. Linking these psalms to the transfer of the ark is similar to the assignment of certain psalms to David in the titles of the Psalms. Keil consid-

---

1 The Chronicler took note of this innovation already in 1 Chr 6:16-17 (31-32).
2 Noth, *Chronicler's History,* 35, suggested that vv. 5-38 and 41-42 were secondary to the work of the Chronicler, with vv. 7-36 added later than the other verses. Rudolph, 127, proposed a complicated series of additions, with vv. 7-37 being the last. For a review of these opinions and counterarguments, see James W. Watts, *Psalm and Story: Inset Hymns in Hebrew Narrative* (JSOTSup 139; Sheffield: JSOT Press, 1992) 162–64. Hans-Peter Mathys, *Dichter und Beter: Theologen aus spätalttestamentlicher Zeit* (OBO 132; Göttingen: Vandenhoeck & Ruprecht, 1994) 214–15, has also noted how closely the theological emphases in this psalm medley cohere with the emphases of the Chronicler himself.
3 The Chronicler omitted vv. 16-45 from Psalm 105, which deal with the story of Joseph, Moses and the exodus, the wilderness wandering, and the conquest. These themes are virtually ignored throughout Chronicles. Did such themes appear too revolutionary to the Chronicler? In quoting Ps 105:1-15 the Chronicler was drawing a comparison between the small postexilic community and the few but well-protected ancestors of Israel. Sara Japhet, "Conquest and Settlement in Chronicles," *JBL* 98 (1979) 205–18, has also emphasized that the Chronicler downplays the breaks in the habitation of the land, between the patriarchs and the monarchy, and during the exile. 1 Chronicles 1–9 portrays the people of Israel in the land of Israel as an uninterrupted reality since the time of Jacob/Israel. Cf. also Trent C. Butler, "A Forgotten Passage from a Forgotten Era (1 Chr xvi 8-36)," *VT* 28 (1978) 144.
4 Cf. the use by the Chronicler of Ps 132:8-10 and Isa 55:3 at 2 Chr 6:41-42. The remaining parts of Psalm 106 deal with Israel's history of sin, which is irrelevant to the present context.

ered these selections as a composition in its own right and believed that it had been composed by David, with the corresponding canonical psalms derived from this composition.[5] Most subsequent studies, however, acknowledge that vv. 8-36 are derived from the canonical psalms indicated above,[6] although a number of more recent studies have recognized the integrity of this composite psalm in its new position. That is, this poem is more than a careless pastiche of psalm fragments, but a piece of psalmic literature in its own right.[7] Psalms 24 and 132, like this composite psalm here, are also often thought to be associated with processions of the ark.

J. A. Loader called attention to the functional coherence of this new psalm,[8] and Butler demonstrated that the content and intention of this psalm are much like that of the Chronicler's history as a whole.[9] Andrew Hill pointed out a number of conventions and devices from classical Hebrew poetry in this psalm.[10] Howard N. Wallace has noted two primary themes in this new psalm: Israel among the nations and Yahweh's sovereignty over the other gods and nations.[11] In its present context, the form of the new psalm is that of thanksgiving, drawing on the first verses of Psalm 105. The context of this psalm is the worship of the temple and it conveys a feeling of national vulnerability. John Kleinig has suggested an outline that I adopt with minor changes:[12]

16:8 General call to thanksgiving
16:9-22 Israel's praise
  16:9-11 Call to musical praise
  16:12-22 Double call to remembrance
    16:12-14 Remembrance of Yahweh's works
    16:15-22 Remembrance of Yahweh's covenant
16:23-30 International praise
  16:23-27 The praise of the whole earth
  16:28-30 The praise of its peoples
16:31-33 Cosmic praise
16:34 Final call to thanksgiving
16:35-36a Summary petition
  16:35 Petition for Israel's deliverance
  16:36a Doxology

---

5 Keil, 211–18. Cf. Ackroyd, 64–65, who of course does not endorse Davidic authorship: "It is a misunderstanding to say that the Chronicler here quotes a group of psalm passages. . . . It is more accurate to say that he here includes a psalm, no doubt well-known to himself and his readers, which may be paralleled in the Psalter."

6 Note that 1 Chr 16:36 is the conclusion to Book IV of the Psalter (Ps 106:48), not really part of the psalm itself. Myers, 1:121, refers the reader to the standard Psalms commentaries to understand this poem.

7 A number of studies in the 1990s have investigated the phenomenon of inset poems within prose narrative in the OT. See Watts, *Psalm and Story;* idem, "'This Song': Conspicuous Poetry in Hebrew Prose," in *Verse in Ancient Near Eastern Prose* (ed. J. C. de Moor and W. G. E. Watson; AOAT 42; Neukirchen-Vluyn: Neukirchener Verlag, 1993) 345–58; Mathys, *Dichter und Beter;* and Steven Weitzman, *Song and Story in Biblical Narrative: The History of a Convention in Ancient Israel* (Bloomington: Indiana Univ. Press, 1997). Mathys, *Dichter und Beter,* 203–4, n. 9, calls attention to a few linguistic items that indicate that the text of the psalm is later than its canonical counterparts: v. 12 פיהו vs. פיו in Ps 105:5; v. 33 עצי היער vs. עצי יער in Ps 96:12; and v. 32 השדה vs. Ps 96:12 שדי. Chronicles has an additional את, the sign of the definite direct object, in vv. 24 and 33, but in v. 18 Chronicles likes this sign, which is present in Ps 105:11. See also Pierre Auffret, *Merveilles à nos yeux: Étude structurelle de vingt psaumes dont celui de 1 Chr 16,8-36* (BZAW 235; Berlin: de Gruyter, 1995) 289–307.

8 J. A. Loader, "Redaction and Function of the Chronistic 'Psalm of David,'" in *Studies in the Chronicler* (Ou-Testamentiese Werkgemeenskap in Suider Afrika 19; ed. W. C. van Wyk; Johannesburg: Univ. of Pretoria, 1976) 67–75. He corrects the sequence in vv. 30-33 to read 30a, 31b-30b, 31a-32a, 32b-33a, 33b. In other words, v. 31b is out of place in MT. So also Mathys, *Dichter und Beter,* 202. Cf. textual note 19.

9 Butler, "Forgotten Passage," 142–50.

10 A. E. Hill, "Patchwork Poetry or Reasoned Verse? Connective Structure in 1 Chronicles XVI," *VT* 33 (1983) 97–101.

11 Henry W. Wallace, "What Chronicles Has to Say about Psalms," in Graham, Hoglund, and McKenzie, *Chronicler as Author,* 267–91.

12 Kleinig, *Lord's Song,* 143–44. See also the helpful observations of R. Mark Shipp, "'Remember His Covenant Forever': A Study of the Chronicler's Use of the Psalms," *ResQ* 35 (1993) 29–39. Watts, *Psalm and Story,* 166, argues that the Chronicler's insertion of a psalm into this narrative context may have been prompted by the inclusion of 2 Samuel 22 in the Deuteronomistic History.

Verse 36b, which is itself a rewritten excerpt from Ps 106:48b, indicates the people's endorsement of what the singers had prayed for in this psalm. This psalm and the final prayer of David in 1 Chr 29:10-19 form a framework around the preparations by David for the building of the temple.[13]

While I still need to comment on how individual cola have been transformed by the Chronicler from their setting in his *Vorlage* (see the commentary below), this outline makes clear that in the present context these quotations are no longer mere excerpts from three canonical psalms, but that they are now a new reality, a new coherent psalm. In the commentary I will show some of the internal relationships within the psalm and will demonstrate its allusions to or support for the Chronicler's message in the wider context. Williamson, 186, points out many parallels between this psalm medley and the *prose* prayer of David in 29:10-19. Both prayers deal with the patriarchs and with Yahweh's kingship, and both end with petitions. This new psalm establishes continuity between the worship life established by David and that of the Chronicler's own day. David's authority now stands both behind the role of the Levites and the use of psalmody in worship. The Levites' participation in the temple cult of the Chronicler's day is justified by their appointment by Israel's first, and arguably greatest, king of the united monarchy. Since this act took place before the erection of the temple, the legitimacy of cultic worship was not dependent on the temple's physical structure.[14] The Chronicler's credibility in claiming Davidic authority for this practice was no doubt enhanced by his reuse of well-known psalms.

Detailed Commentary

16:4-7. David Appoints a Group of Clergy to Praise Yahweh before the Ark

■ **4** *to invoke, to thank, and to praise:* David gave three assignments to the Levites who served at the ark sanctuary: invoking,[15] thanking,[16] and praising.[17] As the three preceding footnotes indicate, each of these verbs is repeated in the subsequent psalmic composition.[18] Invoking is normally the duty of the priests (Num 10:10), and thanking and praising the duty of the Levitical singers (1 Chr 23:30-31). Hence "Levites" in this verse is used in its inclusive sense to refer to both priests and Levites. Japhet has pointed out a neat chiasm, with the verbs referring to the priests (invoking) and singers (thanking and praising) being picked up by the appointment, respectively, of priests in v. 6 and of singers in v. 5. There is also an *inclusio* between "Yahweh the God of Israel" in this verse and in v. 36.

■ **5** *Asaph the head, and those second to him:* The Chronicler names nine Levitical singers who are second in rank to Asaph. They are to perform with harps and lyres. If the instrumental assignments are the same as in 15:20-21, Zechariah, Jaaziel, Shemiramoth, Jehiel, Eliab, and Benaiah would play the harps, and Mattithiah, Obed-edom, and Jeiel the lyres. Instead of the order of Mattithiah, Eliab, and Benaiah, 15:20-21 would have led us to expect Eliab, Benaiah, and Mattithiah. Thus Mattithiah has moved up two places in the list.[19] Obed-edom is a musician in this verse (cf. 15:18 [as corrected], 21), but a gatekeeper in v. 38.[20]

---

13 So Wallace, "What Chronicles," 277.

14 See esp. Weitzman, *Song and Story*, 102.

15 ולהזכיר "to invoke" might also be translated "to cause to remember." Cf. vv. 12, 15, where the verb occurs in the *qal* pattern. Williamson, 127, linked "invoking" to the Lament Psalms, "thanking" to the Thanksgiving Psalms, and "praising" to the Hymns. "Invoking" is used in the titles of two psalms of lament: 38:1 and 70:1. Others link "invoking" to the blowing of trumpets on festival days (Num 10:9-10). See Johnstone, 1:191; and Kleinig, *Lord's Song*, 36.

16 See vv. 8, 34, 35 within the psalm. Cf. also vv. 7 and 41 in the narrative context.

17 ולהלל. See vv. 10, 25, 36. Cf. תהלה in v. 35.

18 See also Shipp, "Remember His Covenant Forever,"

34–35. Shipp claims that invoking, thanking, and praising from v. 4 appear in reverse order in vv. 8-14. It would be more correct to speak of an alternate order: thanking, praising, and remembering.

19 Is this merely a text-critical issue, or does it indicate a change in rank?

20 Cf. 1 Chr 15:18, 24.

Asaph the head . . . Asaph was to sound the cymbals: As a head of a singer guild, Asaph is called "the head" (הראש)[21] and is also assigned to the cymbals (cf. 15:19 and 16:42). The Chronicler omits the names Heman and Ethan, two other leading singers mentioned in 15:17.

■ **6** *the priests Benaiah and Jahaziel were to blow the trumpets regularly:* Benaiah the priest is known from 15:24, where he is among seven priests with trumpets; the addition of Jahaziel rather than one of the other six priests from 15:24 is unexplained. The word "regularly" (תמיד) here and in vv. 37 and 40[22] signifies the ongoing and enduring character of the Davidic appointments, including also the era of the Chronicler. The ministry of music and song for the temple is described in 23:30-31, but it was initiated already in David's time according to vv. 7 and 37.

■ **7** *At that same time David inaugurated thanksgiving to Yahweh by the hand of Asaph:* David does not sing the song himself, but he orders Asaph and the singers to perform the song. The function of the singers whom David appointed is illustrated by the psalm composition the Chronicler has inserted, which begins with the verb "Thank." This is likely an example of typical singing of Levites in the Chronicler's day, a practice rooted in David's authority.[23] Nielsen notes that the insertion of the psalm proves that the Levites did what David appointed them to do with great care.[24] None of the three psalms that have been incorporated into 1 Chronicles 16 is ascribed to Asaph in the Psalter.[25]

16:8-36. Song of the Levites
16:8. General Call to Thanksgiving
■ **8** *Thank Yahweh:* The opening imperative in this verse forms an *inclusio* with the same imperative in v. 34.[26] But while this thanksgiving at the beginning of the psalm is for past actions, the verb at the end of the medley introduces the need for Yahweh's intervention now.[27]

call upon his name: There are references to Yahweh's name in the psalm at vv. 10, 29, and 35, in addition to fifteen uses of the Tetragrammaton itself.[28]

make known his deeds among the peoples: The word עמים "peoples" forms a significant theme throughout this new composition.[29]

16:9-22. Israel's Praise
16:9-11. Call to Musical Praise
■ **9** *Sing to Yahweh, chant to him:* The first imperative (from Psalm 105) forms an *inclusio* with the same imperative in v. 23 (from Psalm 96). The verb זמר, translated "chant," can mean either "sing" or play a musical instrument (Curtis and Madsen, 222).

his marvelous deeds: A reference to Yahweh's miraculous, saving intervention into Israel's history recurs in vv. 12 and 24.[30]

■ **10** *Glory in his holy name:* The holiness of Yahweh's name is also mentioned in v. 35 (Psalm 106).

Let the heart of those who seek Yahweh rejoice: The verb "rejoice" (שׂמח) reappears again with the rejoicing of the cosmos in v. 31.[31] Other synonyms for rejoicing are used in vv. 27 (חדוה "joy"), 31 (גיל "be glad"), 32 (עלץ "exult"), and 33 (רנן "give a ringing cry").[32]

■ **11** *Seek Yahweh and his strength . . . seek his face:* Hebrew uses two different words for "seek" in this verse (דרש and בקש), the second of which occurs in v. 10 as well. Both verbs are central to the Chronicler's theology, and David had earlier confessed in the Ark Narrative that Yahweh had not been sought (דרש) correctly in the days of Saul and in his own first efforts to bring the ark to Jerusalem.[33] "Strength" in this context is apparently an

---

21   In 1 Chr 15:17 no title is given to the leaders of the guilds of singers.
22   See also its presence within the psalm composition at v. 11: "Seek Yahweh and his strength, seek his face regularly."
23   So Watts, *Psalm and Story,* 156.
24   Kirsten Nielsen, "Whose Song of Praise? Reflections on the Purpose of the Psalm in 1 Chronicles 16," in Graham and McKenzie, *Chronicler as Author,* 332.
25   The Asaph psalms are Psalms 50, 73–83.
26   In the *Vorlage* these imperatives are in the first

verses of Psalms 105 and 106, respectively.
27   Nielsen, "Whose Song of Praise?" 334.
28   Vv. 8, 10, 11, 14, 23, 25, 26, 28 (twice), 29, 31, 33, 34, 36 (twice).
29   Vv. 20, 24, 26, 28. Cf. v. 36.
30   The first two occurrences are from Psalm 105, the third from Psalm 96.
31   Cf. 1 Chr 15:16, 25.
32   For joy in Chronicles see the list of passages in Mathys, *Dichter und Beter,* 209, n. 25.
33   1 Chr 13:3 (cf. 10:14); 15:13. Cf. also 28:8-9; 2 Chr 34:3.

allusion to the ark.[34] All the kings of the earth "sought the face of Solomon" (מבקשים את פני שלמה) to hear his wisdom (2 Chr 9:23//1 Kgs 10:24).

regularly: The adverb תמיד is anticipated by the *regular* playing of the trumpets in 1 Chr 16:6 and echoed by the *regular* service of Asaph and his kindred before the ark (v. 37) and by the *regular* sacrifice of burnt offerings before the tabernacle (v. 40).

16:12-22. Double Call to Remembrance
16:12-14. Remembrance of Yahweh's Works

■ **12** *Remember his marvelous deeds . . . his signs:* This is an allusion to the exodus from Egypt in Ps 105:5, but in this context in 1 Chronicles 16 it may refer primarily to the accomplishments of David and his army.

the judgments of his mouth: This refers to Yahweh's sentences against his enemies or against those who have wronged him.[35] These judgments are *universally* effective according to v. 14b,[36] and this is complementary to the *particular* confession: "He is Yahweh *our* God" (v. 14a).

■ **13** *seed of Israel his servant, children of Jacob his chosen ones:* The Chronicler has created a parallelism between "Israel" and "Jacob" (cf. v. 17), with "Israel" being the name of choice to designate this patriarch throughout 1 and 2 Chronicles.[37] In the canonical psalm (105:6), there is a contrast between the seed of *Abraham* and the children of Jacob.[38] Rudolph, 120, proposed that the term "Abraham" was avoided here in Chronicles because it would include non-Israelites such as Ishmael, but the Chronicler employs the name Abraham in v. 16 and refers to the seed of Abraham in 2 Chr 20:7. In any case, the Chronicler's change of his *Vorlage* focuses the exhortation on the faithful community, Israel, whereas the *Vorlage* in Psalm 105 itself refers to those genealogically descended from *two* different ancestors.

16:15-22. Remembrance of Yahweh's Covenant

■ **15** *Remember his covenant forever:* The structure of the psalm in Chronicles, with its double call to remembrance in vv. 12 and 15, indicates that the opening imperative in v. 15, addressed to the Chronicler's audience (cf. also v. 19), is not to be changed back to the indicative, as in Ps 105:8, where it refers to *Yahweh's* remembrance of the covenant. Both the divine covenant with Israel in this verse and Yahweh's (covenantal) loyalty in v. 34 are confessed as everlasting, while his word is said to last for a thousand generations (v. 15). This reference to the covenant is echoed by the frequent designation of the ark as the "ark of the covenant" in these chapters (15:25-26, 28-29; 16:6, 37).

■ **16-17** *the covenant with Abraham . . . his oath to Isaac . . . for Jacob as a precept . . . for Israel as an everlasting covenant:* Both Psalm 105 and the Chronicler refer to a divine covenant or oath with all three of Israel's patriarchal ancestors, even though, strictly speaking, only a covenant with Abraham is recorded in Genesis (17:7, 13, 19; cf. 15:18). The oath to Isaac is attested in 26:2-5. For God's promises to Jacob see 28:13-15 and 35:9-13. According to this verse, the promise of the land is given to the three patriarchs at the same time. This is the only passage in Chronicles that mentions the covenant with the patriarchal ancestors, and here it is taken over from the *Vorlage* in the Psalter.[39] The promise to the Davidic dynasty in 1 Chronicles is also everlasting (1 Chr 17:13-14), though it is not termed a covenant in that chapter.

■ **18** *"To you I give the land of Canaan":* The everlasting divine covenant, as in P,[40] guarantees to Israel the possession of the land.

■ **19** *"When you were few in number":* The Chronicler, if the text is correct,[41] addresses his audience[42] ("you") and

---

34 Johnstone, 1:193, calls attention to "strength" as a title of the ark in Ps 78:61 and in 132:8//2 Chr 6:41 "the ark of your strength."

35 Cf. the verdict on Pharaoh in Exod 6:6; 7:4, and God's judgments against Israel in Jer 1:16; 4:12.

36 They are "in all the earth." Cf. vv. 23 and 30.

37 Cf. 1 Chr 1:1–2:2; 1:34. The two occurrences of Jacob in this psalm are the only references to him in all of 1 and 2 Chronicles. For the parallel between Israel and Jacob, see Isa 41:8.

38 Cf. Isa 63:16; Mic 7:20. *RSV* restores "Abraham" to the text of 1 Chr 16:13.

39 Japhet, *Ideology,* 117, writes: "According to the Chronicler, the history of the people begins with its creation, in other words: with Adam. . . . The bond between Israel and God is not created—it already exists." And again, p. 124: "Israel's relationship with YHWH is unconditional and unlinked to any historical event."

40 Gen 17:8; cf. Exod 6:8.

41 See textual note 10. Note that even in Chronicles the patriarchs are referred to in the third person in vv. 20-22.

42 Cf. "Remember" in v. 15.

their own experience as exiles or sojourners, few in number, whereas Ps 105:12 refers to the patriarchs themselves ("they," the third person") as the sojourners.[43] In the world of the text, the worshipers of David's day are also addressed. The addressees in any case are called to identify themselves with the experience of the patriarchs.

■ **21** *"He did not allow a person to oppress them"*: The change from אדם in Ps 105:14 to איש here is of no apparent significance. Curtis and Madsen, 223, point to the relationship of Abraham to the Canaanites, of Isaac to the men of Gerar, and of Jacob to Laban and Esau as occasions for possible violence to the ancestors. The Chronicler's readers would surely have seen a contrast in this verse between the patriarchs' freedom from the oppression of kings and their own current experience under the Persians. But the promises made to vulnerable Abraham freed him from harm; and that, ultimately, would be Israel's fate as well.

"he reproved kings on their account": The psalmist may have been thinking of Pharaoh in Gen 12:17 or of Abimelech in Gen 20:3-7.

■ **22** *"Do not touch my anointed ones; do no harm to my prophets"*: The value placed on the patriarchs by the Chronicler is exemplified by these distinctive titles: "anointed ones" and "prophets." The Chronicler may have also applied this verse to his present situation, treating Israel as a royal and prophetic people and thus democratizing these terms;[44] in the context of Ps 105:15 the reference of both terms is clearly to the patriarchs themselves.[45] Only Abraham of all the patriarchs is explicitly called a prophet in the Bible (Gen 20:7), and it is unlikely that all the prophets were anointed.[46] The

special protection of those who are anointed is reflected in David's refusal to lay a hand on Saul, the "anointed of Yahweh."[47] The Chronicler expected his politically insignificant audience to identify with the patriarchs.[48]

16:23-30. International Praise

16:23-27. Praise of the Whole Earth

■ **23-26** *Sing to Yahweh, all the earth:* The Chronicler omits Ps 96:1a, "Sing to Yahweh a new song." If this is not a textual error, the Chronicler may have thought a new song would be inappropriate in an invitation to praise addressed to a non-Israelite audience, or he considered such an invitation inappropriate in the middle of a psalm.[49] He also omitted an equivalent for Ps 96:2a[50] and thus created a new bicolon in v. 23, from Ps 96:1a and 2b, with appropriate parallelism. The Chronicler here invites the nations and peoples (vv. 24, 28) to celebrate in advance Yahweh's eschatological victories.[51] Even creation as a whole is invited to praise Yahweh (vv. 31-33). This song is an example of the song of praise of the Levites, but this command to sing also makes the reader part of the everlasting song of praise.[52] As Japhet, notes, "The covenant with the patriarchs is consummated in their time. There is no break, not even any 'history' between Jacob and salvation!"[53]

■ **27** *strength and joy are in his place:* The Chronicler replaced תפארת ("beauty") from Ps 96:6 with חדוה ("joy") for no apparent reason,[54] but his use of מקום ("place") instead of מקדש ("sanctuary") coheres with his frequent reference to Jerusalem as a "place" (e.g., 1 Chr 13:11; 14:11; 15:1, 3, 12) and with his description of Jerusalem's cult at David's time, when there were no sacrifices at Jerusalem, but only the ark[55] and a tent and the service of song. The *Vorlage,* of course, clearly presup-

---

43 Gen 15:13; 23:4.

44 Shipp, "'Remember His Covenant Forever,'" 36, believes that the anointed ones are the kings (cf. 2 Chr 6:42).

45 Braun, 192, notes that the Chronicler has turned Ps 95:15 into a timeless principle: "It is the people Israel, reduced in number and without a homeland, which is protected by God."

46 But see 1 Kgs 19:16; Isa 61:1.

47 1 Sam 24:7, 11; 26:9, 11, 16, 23. Cf. 2 Sam 1:14.

48 Cf. Ezek 33:24; Isa 51:1-3.

49 Note how it appears at the beginning of a number of psalms: 96:1; 98:1; 149:1.

50 "Sing to Yahweh, bless his name."

51 By contrast, the exhortation to sing in v. 9 was directed toward Israel.

52 Nielsen, "Whose Song of Praise?" 335.

53 "Conquest and Settlement," 218.

54 Though joy and rejoicing are frequent in Chronicles, even in 1 Chr 16:10, this is the only time he uses the word חדוה. Its only other occurrence in the OT is in Neh 8:10. Williamson, *Israel,* 47–48, suggests it may have been an Aramaism the Chronicler found in his *Vorlage.*

55 The ark symbolized Yahweh's presence (1 Chr 13:8, 10; 16:1).

posed the existence of the temple (cf. also v. 29). This "place" is the location where the temple will stand.

16:28-30. Praise of Its Peoples

■ **28-29** *Lift up an offering and come into his presence:* Verses 28-30 explicitly invite the nations of the world to praise Yahweh. The Chronicler changed לחצרותיו ("his courts," Ps 106:8) to לפניו ("before him") to avoid the anachronism of inviting people at the time of David to worship in the temple that was first erected by Solomon. Their offering (מנחה) is tribute they are to bring to the divine king.[56] This exhortation is partially fulfilled when David's institution of burnt offerings to Yahweh at Gibeon (vv. 39-40).

■ **30** The Chronicler omits an equivalent for Ps 96:10b, "He will judge the peoples with equity." Though text-critical reasons for this omission are not impossible,[57] political considerations (not wishing to alarm the Persians about Israel's international goals) may have led the Chronicler to omit this and a similar bicolon in Ps 96:13b:[58] "He shall judge the world in righteousness and the peoples in his truth." Yahweh's judging of the earth in v. 33, on the other hand, is retained, perhaps because it is general enough not to sound threatening to any particular nation.

16:31-33. Cosmic Praise

■ **31-33** *Let the heavens rejoice, let the earth be glad . . . let the sea roar:* In a text affected by a displacement of a colon (see textual notes 18 and 19), the Chronicler invites the whole tripartite cosmos to join in the celebration of Yahweh's kingship.

field . . . forest: Agricultural land and stands of trees in the forest, too, are urged in an apostrophe to join in the chorus that celebrates Yahweh's coming to judge, or rule, the earth.

16:34. Final Call to Thanksgiving

■ **34** *Give thanks to Yahweh for he is good:* The words "give thanks" form an *inclusio* with the first words of v. 8, even though in the Chronicler's *Vorlage* they were the first

words of a new psalm (106), from which he omitted the opening "Hallelujah." For Yahweh's goodness see also 2 Chr 30:18.

his loyalty lasts forever: This confession appears frequently in Chronicles and therefore fits well with the hypothesis that the inclusion of this psalmic composition was done by the Chronicler himself.[59]

16:35-36. Summary Petition
16:35. Petition for Israel's Deliverance

■ **35** *And say, "Save us, O God of our salvation":* By adding "and say" to the *Vorlage*, the Chronicler emphasizes that his audience is to utter the following prayer. The Chronicler also replaced the divine name found in Ps 106:47 ("Yahweh our God") by a reference to a saving God ("O God of our salvation"), which may have seemed more appropriate in a petition asking God to save or deliver the people. Both "save" and "salvation" are built on the root ישע.[60]

"Gather us and deliver us from the nations": In Ps 106:47 the imperative "gather" reflects the scattered or exiled condition of the people. Exile had been threatened already in the wilderness (106:27) and became a reality later in the psalm (vv. 40-46). To this *Vorlage* the Chronicler added "deliver us."[61] Deliverance from Persian domination may have been a bigger issue than Israel's dispersal at the Chronicler's time even if, for political reasons, the author avoided a direct criticism of or an attack upon the Persians. Gathering Israel from the nations, from the Diaspora, of course, is appropriate for almost any time when the Chronicler may have been writing. Curtis and Madsen, 224, suggest that the addition of "deliver us" was an attempt to make this verse more appropriate for the time of David. Deliverance from the nations might point forward to the wars in 1 Chronicles 18–20.

"to thank your holy name": Deliverance would lead the people to offer thanks, and such thanksgiving was a central assignment of the Levitical singers (v. 4).

---

56   מנחה is a technical term for tribute brought to David, Solomon, Jehoshaphat, Uzziah, and Hezekiah (1 Chr 18:2, 6; 2 Chr 9:24; 17:5, 11; 26:8; 32:23).

57   *BHK* suggested deleting the clause from Psalm 96 on the basis of 1 Chr 16:31.

58   This omission comes at the end of 1 Chr 16:33.

59   Cf. v. 41 and 2 Chr 5:13; 7:3, 6; 2 Chr 20:21. In 2

Chr 5:13 and 7:3 we also find the clause "for he is good." The longer formula, including "for he is good," appears in Pss 100:5; 106:1; 107:1; 118:1, 29; 136:1-26; Jer 33:11; Ezra 3:11. The shorter formula occurs in Pss 118:2, 3, 4, and 138:8.

60   Cf. v. 23 and 1 Chr 11:14; 18:6, 13.

61   "Gather" is used in 1 Chr 11:1; 13:2; and "deliver" is used in 11:14.

16:36. Doxology

■ **36a** *"Blessed be Yahweh the God of Israel"*: The Chronicler's psalm concludes with a blessing of "Yahweh the God of Israel," the same divine title that was the object of invocation, thanking, and praise of the singers in v. 4. This blessing also occurs in the mouth of Huram (2 Chr 2:11 [12]) and of Solomon (2 Chr 6:4).

■ **36b** *And all the people said, "Amen," and they praised Yahweh:* All the people, who had joined David in bringing the ark to Jerusalem, endorsed the song of the Levites. The Chronicler has changed the final doxology of Psalm 106 into a bridge passage leading back to his Ark Narrative. Since this doxology closes book IV of the Psalter, it has been assumed that at least the fourth book of Psalms was completed by the time of the Chronicler.[62]

16:37-42. Regular worship established

■ **37** *He left there before the ark of the covenant of Yahweh Asaph and his kindred to serve before the ark . . . regularly:* This verse picks up the narrative from v. 7 and assigns Asaph and his kindred, the Levitical singers, to permanent duty before the ark.

■ **38** *Obed-edom—and their brothers, sixty-eight . . . and Hosah:* David assigned two gatekeepers, Obed-edom and Hosah, from the families of Korah (26:1-4) and Merari (26:10), respectively, to the ark in Jerusalem (see the discussion of gatekeepers in general and this verse in particular under Structure in chap. 15 above). In the Pentateuch the Merarites have duties in connection with the tabernacle (Num 4:29-33). Merarites are assigned by the Chronicler to both parts of the divided sanctuary—tabernacle (v. 41) and ark—expressing an ideology of unity

even if the sanctuary is to be temporarily located at two different places. A later hand identified Obed-edom the gatekeeper as the son of Jeduthun,[63] the singer, and this led to the calculation that he and Jeduthun had sixty-eight kindred.[64] Hosah reappears in 1 Chr 26:10-19.

■ **39** *And [he left] Zadok the priest and his kindred the priests before the tabernacle of Yahweh in the high place at Gibeon:* Here for the first time the Chronicler mentions that the tabernacle was located at Gibeon,[65] where he has David install Zadok[66] and other priests, Levitical singers, and gatekeepers, and where burnt offerings continued until the building of Solomon's temple. Locating the tabernacle at Gibeon may be an attempt to justify Solomon's pilgrimage to the high place at Gibeon in 1 Kgs 3:4-5//2 Chr 1:3-7. This city was originally part of the Gibeonite league (Josh 9:17). Earlier biblical references place the tabernacle at Shiloh (Josh 18:1; 19:51), not at Gibeon. A reference to the "doorpost of the temple of Yahweh" at Shiloh may indicate that historically the tabernacle had already been replaced by a more permanent building by the time of Eli.[67]

■ **40** *for offering burnt offerings to Yahweh . . . morning and evening, according to everything written in the law of Yahweh:* The sacrifices conducted at Gibeon were offered by Zadok and other priests on a timetable set by the Pentateuch.[68]

What is the character of this Gibeonite motif, and why did it arise? In 1 Chr 21:26-29 the Chronicler reports that David built an altar at the threshing floor of Ornan and conducted sacrifices there despite the fact that the tabernacle and the altar of burnt offering were at that time in Gibeon. Fear of the sword of the angel

---

62 This may need to be reevaluated because of the unusual order of the psalms in 11QPs[a].

63 See the argument for the secondary character of "and Obed-edom was the son of Jeduthun" under Structure in chap. 15.

64 In 1 Chr 26:8 sixty-two gatekeepers are assigned to Obed-edom, and in 25:3 there are six sons of Jeduthun. For a similar reconstruction of this verse, see Piet B. Dirksen, "1 Chronicles 16:38: Its Background and Growth," *JNSL* 22 (1996) 85–90. My primary difference with Dirksen is that he assigns the core of v. 38, "and Obed-Edom and Hosah as gatekeepers," to the redactor responsible for adding chaps. 23–27 to Chronicles, whereas I attribute the core of v. 38 and most of chaps. 23–27 to the

Chronicler himself. He and I agree that subsequent glosses identified Obed-edom as the son of the singer Jeduthun and that the addition of sixty-eight brothers depends on that earlier gloss.

65 Cf. 1 Chr 21:29; 2 Chr 1:2-6.

66 The Chronicler makes no mention of Abiathar at this point. See 1 Chr 15:11.

67 See Klein, *1 Samuel*, 8.

68 Exod 29:38-42; Lev 1:3-9; 4:1–5:19; Num 4:5-15; 18:5; 28:2-8.

kept David from going to Gibeon (21:30). When Solomon visited the cult site at Gibeon in 2 Chr 1:3-13, he sacrificed a thousand burnt offerings on its bronze altar. After Solomon had completed the building of the temple, the priests and Levites brought up the ark, the tent of meeting (an alternate term for the tabernacle), and all the holy vessels that were in "the tent" to the new building. The ark was already in the city of David; the tabernacle and its paraphernalia were brought from Gibeon.

Japhet, 323, points out that the main purpose of the tradition about the tabernacle at Gibeon is to claim unbroken continuity of the cult from the time of Moses to the time of David and Solomon. The Chronicler is asserting the Israelite character of Gibeon against the evidence of Joshua 9. Above all, the Chronicler is explaining why Yahweh granted Solomon wisdom, riches, possessions, and honor at such an otherwise questionable site (see Braun, 193–94). The legitimacy of Solomon's visit to the high place of Gibeon is shown by the presence there of the tabernacle, the altar for burnt offerings, and Zadok and other appropriate clergy. In my judgment, it is doubtful that we must construct a long midrashic process to explain this Chronistic apologetic.[69]

■ **41** *And with them were Heman and Jeduthun:* With the priests at Gibeon were two leaders of the singer guilds, Heman and Jeduthun, whose Levitical ancestry goes back to Kohath and Merari, respectively.[70] Hence in vv. 37-42 the Chronicler utilizes all three elements of his standard listing of the heads of the singer guilds—Asaph, Heman, and Jeduthun.

the rest of those selected who had been designated by name: The other singers named in 15:20-21, who had not been assigned to the ark in Jerusalem (16:5), were now appointed to the cult of the tabernacle in Gibeon. This includes Unni and Maaseiah with harps, and Eliphelehu and Mikneiah with lyres. The verb הברורים "selected" is

used twice elsewhere in Chronicles for select mighty warriors (7:40) and for those who had been chosen as gatekeepers (9:22).

for his loyalty lasts forever: This is a frequent refrain in the Psalter (100:5; 106:1; 107:1; 118:1-4, 29; and esp. 136:1-26).[71] Watts suggests that this refrain indicates the liturgical response of the community and also one of its members, the narrator.[72]

■ **42** *And with them were the trumpets and the cymbals for the musicians:* In my reconstructed text of this verse (see textual note 29), the pronoun "them" refers, as in v. 41, to Zadok and the priests and to Heman, Jeduthun, and the rest of the singers mentioned in vv. 39 and 41. Only the musical instruments of the priests and the heads of the singer guilds are listed, namely, trumpets and cymbals. The reconstructed text, without narrowing "them" down to Heman and Jeduthun, avoids the confusion of the MT, where the cult in Gibeon apparently had the heads of the singer guilds entrusted with both the priestly trumpets and their own instruments, the cymbals.[73] The Chronicler assigned gatekeepers to the tabernacle at Gibeon, on analogy with 15:23-24 and 16:38, and then linked them to the weaker of the two singer groups, namely Jeduthun.

16:43. Conclusion to the Ark Narrative

■ **43** *David turned to bless his own house:* The Chronicler closes his account with his last quotation from 2 Samuel 6 (vv. 19b-20a), which there introduced the episode with Michal in which she criticized David's provocative dancing and in which David responded equally sharply, with the result that Michal had lifelong infertility (vv. 20b-23). Just as Yahweh had turned (ויסב) the kingdom of Saul over to David (1 Chr 10:14), David now turns (ויסב)[74] to bless his whole house. This forms a double *inclusio:* with 16:2, where David blessed the people in the name of Yahweh after the completion of sacrifices, and with 13:14, where Yahweh blessed the house of Obed-edom.

---

69   For a contrary opinion see Japhet, 321–23, who forcefully demonstrates that such a cult at Gibeon is a historical impossibility. Hence there does not seem to be reason, with Williamson, 131, to leave open the question of whether the Chronicler was here basing himself on an earlier tradition. Japhet, 321, clearly outlines previous conclusions.

70   Heman is a Kohathite (1 Chr 6:18 [33]), and

   Ethan/Jeduthun is a Merarite (6:29 [44]).

71   Cf. 1 Chr 16:34; 2 Chr 5:13; 7:3, 6; 20:21.

72   *Psalm and Story*, 157.

73   According to Williamson, 128, the Chronicler assumes the Levites blew the trumpets and hence Williamson wants to delete the references to priests throughout chaps. 15–16.

74   Note the change from 2 Sam 6:20 וישׁב.

Later Solomon blessed the assembly of Israel at the dedication of the temple (1 Kgs 8:55), though this verse is lacking in Chronicles. After David blesses his own house in this verse, he expresses a desire in the next chapter to build a house for Yahweh. This verse anticipates the blessing of David's house through the oracle of Nathan in 1 Chronicles 17.

Conclusion

The central part of this chapter, vv. 8-36, is a song of the Levites, a new composition, made up of elements from three of the canonical psalms. These excerpts have become a new entity in Chronicles and are not to be understood just as elements of canonical psalms. The new psalmic entity expresses Israel's own praise, international praise, and even cosmic praise.

The first four verses of this pericope (1 Chr 16:4-7) give Davidic authority to the Levites who praise Yahweh before the ark. At the end of the pericope, in 16:37-42, David creates appropriate ministries at two locations. Before the ark he regularizes the placement of Asaph and the other singers, and also Obed-edom and Hosah as gatekeepers. But in an attempt to document the legitimacy of the high place at Gibeon, the Chronicler assigns Zadok to that location, as well as Heman and Jeduthun, the Levitical singers.

At the end, in v. 43, the Chronicler includes the last verse of the Ark Narrative from the Deuteronomistic History. He omitted Michal's rebuke of David and the sentence of infertility that David imposed on Michal. David blessed his own house just as Yahweh had blessed the house of Obed-edom. How Yahweh blessed the house of David is recounted in 1 Chronicles 17.

By these appointments and by putting the psalm medley in the mouth of the singers, the Chronicler establishes a continuity between the worship life established by David and that of his own day.

17:1-27[1] Promise of Dynastic Succession and Temple Building

Translation

1/ When David had taken up residence in his house, David said to Nathan the prophet, "I[2] am dwelling in a house of cedar, but the ark of the covenant of Yahweh is under tent curtains." 2/ Nathan replied to David, "Do[3] everything your heart desires for God[4] is with you."

3/ That night the word of God came to Nathan, saying: 4/ "Go say to David my servant: Thus says Yahweh: You are not the one to build[5] for me the house[6] to dwell in.[7] 5/ For I have not dwelled in a house from the time when I brought Israel up[8] until this day, but I have traveled about[9] from tent to tent and from tabernacle to tabernacle.[10] 6/ Wherever I have moved about in all Israel,[11] did I ever speak a word with one of the judges[12] of Israel, whom I appointed[13] to shepherd my people, saying, 'Why have you not built for me a house of cedar?' 7/ Now, thus you shall say to my servant David: Thus says Yahweh of hosts: I took you from the pasture, from following the flock, to be ruler[14] over my people Israel.[15] 8/ I have been with you wherever you went, and I have cut off all your enemies before you, and I will make for you a name[16] like the name of the great ones who are in the earth. 9/ I will make a place for my people Israel, and I will plant them so that they may dwell in their own place, and not be disturbed anymore, nor shall wicked people continue to wear them out[17] as they did formerly, 10/ from the time[18] I appointed judges over my people Israel; and I will subdue all your[19] enemies. I declare[20] to you that[21] Yahweh will build[22] for you a house. 11/ When[23] your days are complete[24] to go to be[25] with your ancestors, I will raise up your seed after you, who will be from your sons,[26] and I will establish his kingdom. 12/ He will build for me a house and I will establish his throne[27] forever. 13/ I will be to him a father, and he will be for me a son. I will not remove[28] my loyalty from him, as I removed it from the one who was before you.[29] 14/ I will install him in my house and my kingdom forever, and his throne[30] will be established forever." 15/ According to all these words and all this vision, so Nathan spoke to David.

16/ King David went and sat before Yahweh, and he said, "Who am I, Yahweh God, and what is my house, that you have brought me to this place? 17/ And this[31] is a small thing in your eyes, God, for you have also spoken of your servant's house in a distant time, and you have let me look upon the generation of humankind to come,[32] O Yahweh God. 18/ What more can David add to you in order to make you honor[33] your servant?[34] It is you, Yahweh,[35] who have known your ser-

---

1   H. van den Bussche, "La texte de la prophétie de Nathan sur la dynastie davidique (II Sam. VII-I Chron. XVII)," *ETL* 24 (1948) 354–94; and Hartmut Gese, "Der Davidbund and und die Zionserwählung," *ZTK* 61 (1964) 10–26, give preference to the text of Chronicles and believe that in many instances it is earlier than the text of 2 Samuel 7. I do not believe this conclusion is warranted. I note, instead, that Chronicles, in readings discussed in textual notes 3, 4, 5, 8, 11, 15, 16, 18, 22, 23, 27-31, 33, 36, 39, 40, 42, 43, 45, and 48, presupposes a text of Samuel other than MT. I also note that in this chapter Chronicles LXX has frequently been corrected toward the text of Samuel, as discussed in notes 6, 10, 12, 17, 25, 26, 34, and 43.

2   This is the only time Chronicles uses אנכי. Everywhere else, some thirty times, it uses אני.

3   עשה; cf. some Hebrew MSS and Syr of 2 Sam 7:3; Samuel MT and LXX put לך "Go" before this word.

4   האלהים; cf. 2 Sam 7:3 LXX[L]. Samuel MT, LXX: יהוה "Yahweh."

5   לא אתה תבנה; cf. 2 Sam 7:5 LXX, Syr. Samuel MT האתה תבנה "Will you build?"

6   הבית; Chronicles LXX 2 Sam 7:5 MT בית "a house." See the list of corrections of Chronicles LXX toward Sam listed in n. 1. GKC §126q suggests that the indefinite article would be an appropriate translation for הבית in a Western language. But see the commentary.

7   לשבת; one Hebrew MS, LXX , and 2 Sam 7:5 read לשבתי "for me to dwell." Chronicles LXX adds ἐν αὐτῷ "in it."

8   2 Sam 7:6 MT adds "from Egypt." This phrase is in two different positions in Samuel LXX MSS, suggesting that it may be a later addition and not part of the Samuel *Vorlage* used by the Chronicler.

9   מתהלך restored with Chronicles Tg and 2 Sam 7:6; lacking in Chronicles MT, LXX. It was probably lost by homoioarchton before מאהל (three letters are the same).

10 וממשכן אל משכן. The last two words are a conjectural addition, based on the preceding מאהל אל אהל, and were lost in MT by homoioteleuton. Chronicles LXX "in a tent and in a tabernacle," apparently a correction to 2 Sam 7:6 MT באהל ובמשכן.

11 בכל ישראל; cf. 2 Sam 7:7 LXX. Samuel MT בכל בני ישראל "among all the Israelites."

12 שפטי; Chronicles LXX שבט "tribe" (the final *yôd* was lost by haplography) = 2 Sam 7:7 MT LXX שבטי. For a defense of the text of Samuel see Philippe de Robert, "Juges ou Tribus en 2 Samuel VII 7," *VT* 27 (1977) 116–18. McCarter, *II Samuel*, 192, repoints

vant. 19/ For the sake of your servant,[36] and according to your own heart, you have done all these great deeds, making known to your servant all these great things.[37] 20/ Yahweh, there is no one like you and no God besides you, according to[38] all we have heard with our ears. 21/ Who is like your people Israel,[39] one nation on the earth, whom God[40] has gone[41] to redeem to be his people, by making[42] for yourself[43] a reputation[44] for great and awe-inspiring things, by driving out[45] nations from before your people whom you have redeemed from Egypt. 22/ And you made[46] your people Israel to be your people forever, and you were, Yahweh, their God.

23/ And now, Yahweh,[47] let the word that you spoke concerning your servant and concerning his house be made sure[48] forever, and do just as you have spoken. 24/ Let your name be made sure and magnified forever in the saying, 'Yahweh of hosts the God of Israel is Israel's God, and the house of David your servant will be established before you.' 25/ For you, my God, have revealed to your servant that you will build for him a house. Therefore your servant has dared[49] to pray before you. 26/ Now, Yahweh, you are God[50] and you have spoken to your servant this good thing. 27/ And now, you have decided[51] to bless the house of your servant so that it may continue forever before you. For you, Yahweh, have blessed, and it is blessed forever."

the Samuel text and translates it "staff bearers." Cf. earlier Patrick V. Reid, "*šbṭy* in 2 Samuel 7:7," *CBQ* 37 (1975) 17–20.

13 אשר צויתי, as in 2 Sam 7:7; lacking in Chronicles LXX.

14 נגיד; Tg "king."

15 על עמי ישראל; cf. 2 Sam 7:8 LXX[L], Syr, Tg, Vg. Samuel MT על עמי על ישראל "over my people over Israel."

16 שם; cf. 2 Sam 7:9 LXX. In Chronicles a few Hebrew MSS and Syr add גדול "great" with Samuel MT.

17 לבלתו; Chronicles LXX, 2 Sam 7:10: לענותו "to afflict them." Japhet, "Interchanges," 29, observes that the Talmud seems to know the form לכלותו here and suggests that Chronicles MT is corrupt.

18 ולמימים; cf. 2 Sam 7:11 LXX. Samuel MT ולמן היום "from the day." The *wāw* on this word is explicative and need not be translated (Japhet, 332).

19 Rudolph, 130, changes "your" to "its."

20 ואגיד. For the present tense see Rudolph, 130. LXX "I will magnify you" (ואגדלך); cf. I. L. Seeligmann, "Indications of Editorial Alteration and Adaptation in the MT and the LXX," *VT* 11 (1961) 208–10, who argues that it is the original reading. 2 Sam 7:11 והגיד "[Yahweh] declares."

21 Some scholars have proposed כי בית for ובית (loss of *kaph* by haplography and *wāw/yôd* confusion) = 2 Sam 7:11. Rudolph, 131, suggests MT may be parataxis instead of hypotaxis. Cf. GKC §120c.

22 יבנה; cf. 4Q174 (4QFlor) l. 10 and 2 Sam 7:11 LXX[L] (see also Samuel LXX). Samuel MT יעשה "will make." Despite the readings in Samuel LXX and LXX[L], Japhet, "Interchanges," 13, attributes the change to the Chronicler.

23 The last word in v. 10 and the first word in v. 11 (יהוה והיה) are a conflation of ancient variants in Samuel: the last word in 2 Sam 7:11 MT is יהוה (not attested in Samuel LXX) and the first word translated in 2 Sam 7:12 LXX presupposes a reading והיה.

24 ימלאו; Chronicles MT מלאו (the initial *yôd* was lost by haplography). Cf. 2 Sam 7:12 and Japhet, 326.

25 ללכת. Chronicles LXX 2 Sam 7:12 ושכבת "and you lie down." Is Chronicles MT a secondary change, or has Chronicles LXX been corrected to Samuel? Japhet, "Interchanges," 27, n. 66, observes that the influence of one translator upon the other can be sensed in the entire verse.

26 מבניך; Chronicles LXX, Syr, Arab., 2 Sam 7:12: ממעיך "from your body."

27 את כסאו; cf. 2 Sam 7:13 LXX. Samuel MT את כסא ממלכתו "the throne of his kingdom."

28 לא אסיר; cf. 2 Sam 7:15 LXX, Syr. Samuel MT לא יסור "[My loyalty] will not depart."

29 מאשר היה לפניך; cf. 2 Sam 7:15 LXX ἀφ᾽ ὧν

ἀπέστησα ἐκ προσώπου μου "from him whom I removed from before me" = מאשר הסרתי מלפני. Samuel MT מעם שאול אשר הסרתי מלפניך "from Saul whom I removed before you." For full discussion see McCarter, *II Samuel*, 194–95.

30 וכסאו; cf. 2 Sam 7:16 LXX. Samuel MT כסאך "your throne."

31 זאת; cf. 2 Sam 7:19 LXX, OL, Syr. Samuel MT עוד זאת "yet this."

32 וראיתני כתור האדם המעלה. Chronicles MT וראיתני בתור האדם המעלה. The consonants וראיתני are derived from Chronicles LXX, though pointed as a *hiphil* rather than a *qal*. I also conjecturally emend כתור to בתור. McCarter, *II Samuel*, 233, interprets תור as "turn (in a succession)," and therefore understands the last three words as "the turn of mankind to come" or "the generation to come." The text and meaning are very uncertain. Rudolph, 130–31, "You have allowed me to see [cf. my emendation above] the future [המעלה or העלם] more than other people can fathom [מתור]." Willi, *Chronik als Auslegung*, 154, emended כתור to בתוך (following ten Hebrew MSS), changed המעלה to ותעלני, and translated: "And you have looked me out in the middle of the human race and raised me up." Earlier suggestions in Willis J. Beecher, "Three Notes," *JBL* 8 (1899) 138; Shlomo Marenof, "A Note on 1 Chron. 17:17," *AJSL* 53 (1936–1937) 47; and Julius A. Bewer, "Textkritische Bemerkungen zum A. T.," in *FS für Alfred Bertholet* (ed. W. Baumgartner et al.; Tübingen: Mohr [Siebeck], 1950) 65–76.

33 אליך לכבד = LXX; cf. Syr, Tg. MT אליך לכבוד "to you for honor" (followed by את, the sign of the definite direct object). The *Vorlage* in 2 Sam 7:20 reads: לדבר אליך "[What more can David] say to you?" McCarter, *II Samuel*, 234, explains Samuel MT as a result of the omission of לכבד את עבדך by homoioteleuton (after אליך) and subsequent correction by the addition of לדבר. In short, Chronicles MT presupposes a text of Samuel other than Samuel MT.

34 את עבדך; lacking in Chronicles LXX, a partial correction toward 2 Sam 7:20.

35 Read יהוה as the last word in the verse; cf. 2 Sam 7:20 LXX or Samuel MT אדני יהוה "my lord Yahweh." Chronicles MT has incorrectly ended the verse *before* יהוה. Chronicles LXX lacks יהוה.

36 עבדך; cf. 2 Sam 7:21 LXX. Samuel MT דברך "your word." Samuel LXX[L] conflates the two variants.

37 את עבדך את כל הגדלות. את עבדך is added with Chronicles Syr, Tg, and 2 Sam 7:21; lacking in Chronicles MT, LXX by homoioarchton, with the scribe skipping from the first to the second את.

V. 19b is lacking in Chronicles LXX due to homoioteleuton in its *Vorlage*.

38 ככל with many Hebrew MSS, LXX, Syr, Tg, and 2 Sam 7:22. Chronicles MT בכל. Rudolph, 132, judges these to be equivalent expressions and argues against changing the text.

39 כעמך ישראל; cf. 2 Sam 7:23 LXX, Syr, Tg. Samuel MT כעמך כישראל "like your people, like Israel."

40 האלהים; cf. 2 Sam 7:23 LXX. Samuel MT אלהים.

41 הלך. The Chronicler uses a singular verb instead of the plural in 2 Sam 7:23 MT. McCarter, *II Samuel*, 234, repoints Samuel MT הלכו "led him along."

42 לשום; cf. 2 Sam 23:23 LXX. Samuel MT ולשום.

43 לך; cf. 2 Sam 7:23 LXX[L]. Chronicles LXX is corrected to 2 Sam 7:23 MT לו "for himself."

44 I construe שם as a construct noun instead of the absolute vocalization in MT. In 2 Sam 7:23 שם is followed by ולעשות: "(by making for himself a name) and by doing for you (great and awesome things)." The additional לכם in Samuel MT is absent from Samuel LXX.

45 לגרש; cf. 2 Sam 7:23 LXX. Samuel MT לארצך "to your land."

46 ותתן; 2 Sam 7:24 והכונן לך ("you established for yourself"). Japhet, "Interchanges," 11, notes that the *polel* is limited almost exclusively to poetry, with the exception of 2 Sam 7:13, 24, and that the Chronicler has replaced one of these occurrences.

47 יהוה. 2 Sam 7:25 LXX κύριέ μου; Samuel MT יהוה אלהים.

48 יאמן; cf. 2 Sam 7:25 LXX[L]. Samuel MT הקם "cause it to stand." Japhet, "Interchanges," 36–37, suggests that the reading in Chronicles arose because the writer did not want to use the imperative in reference to God, but she does not note that the reading arose already in the Samuel textual tradition.

49 מצא. Translation after Rudolph, 132, and *HALOT* 2:620. 2 Sam 7:27 adds את לבו; hence: "your servant has found his courage."

50 האלהים. 2 Sam 7:28 adds ודבריך יהיו אמת "and your words are true." Rudolph, 132, suggests the clause was lost by homoioarchton (before ותדבר) in Chronicles. But this may have happened already in the *Vorlage* of Samuel and hence never have been in the text of Chronicles.

51 הואלת. Cf. *HALOT* 2:381.

Structure

The oracle of Nathan and David's prayer in response to it may be outlined as follows:

I. 17:1-15. Oracle of Nathan (2 Sam 7:1-17)
  A. 17:1-2. Opening dialogue between David and Nathan on David's plan to build a temple
  B. 17:3. Report of Nathan receiving the word of God
  C. 17:4-14. Nathan reports the word of God to David, which prohibits David from building the temple (vv. 4-6), promises David dynastic succession (vv. 7-11), and designates David's son as the temple builder (vv. 12-14)
  D. 17:15. Conclusion to the words of Nathan
II. 17:16-27. David's prayer in response to the oracle (2 Sam 7:18-29)
  A. 17:16a. Introduction
  B. 17:16b-27. The prayer itself (prayer of thanksgiving [v. 16b-22] and supplication [vv. 23-27]

Except for the omission of 2 Sam 7:1b and 7:14b, the Chronicler presents a text that is virtually identical in length and content with his *Vorlage*, although he has introduced a number of small changes, and textual variants have arisen in both Samuel and Chronicles (see textual note 1 for a list of readings where Chronicles is based on a Sam text other than MT).

This closeness to the *Vorlage* has important implications for the work of interpretation, since the text in Samuel gives evidence of internal inconsistency that has led to numerous attempts to reconstruct its diachronic history. While there have been notable attempts by Mowinckel[1], Herrmann[2], and McKenzie[3] to understand the text of 2 Samuel 7 as a unity, the vast majority of

scholars have concluded that beneath the present Deuteronomistic text they can discover earlier sources or layers. The principal issue is the tension between the divine promise of a dynasty to David and the equally clear criticism of David's proposal to build a temple. McCarter's reconstruction of the redactional history is representative, and while not everyone would subscribe to its details, there would be general agreement that he has accurately diagnosed the problem and proposed a reasonable solution.

McCarter isolates a first layer in 2 Samuel 7 (vv. 1a, 2-3, 11b-12, 13b-15a), which he dates to Solomonic times.[4] Here Yahweh responds to David's offer to build a temple with a promise that he will build a dynasty for David. Both temple and dynasty are expressed by the Hebrew word בית (lit. "house"). Yahweh says in effect: "You [David] have promised to build me a house; therefore, I shall build you a house." Hence Yahweh had approved David's proposal and reciprocated with the promise of a dynasty.

In a second, prophetic layer (vv. 4-9a, 15b), Yahweh judges the temple unnecessary and unwanted and suggests that David's proposal is uncalled for and presumptuous. David, nevertheless, is promised the abiding kingship of which Saul had been deprived. The dynastic promise was not a response to David's plan to build a temple. Rather, Yahweh says: "You will not build a temple (house); instead I will build you a house (dynasty)."

The third, seventh-century, Deuteronomistic stage included the addition of vv. 1b, 9b-11a, 13a, and 16 and represents the present configuration of the text. This makes the refusal of the plan to build a temple a temporary one. David did not build the temple because the time was not right, but his son would build a temple. With the establishment of the dynasty would come the

---

1   S. Mowinckel, "Natansforjettelsen 2 Sam. kap. 7," *SEÅ* 12 (1947) 220–29.

2   S. Herrmann, "Die Königsnovelle in Ägypten und in Israel," *Wissenschaftliche Zeitschrift der Karl-Marx-Universität, Leipzig 3. Gesellschafts- und sprachwissenschaftliche Reihe 1*, FS A. Alt (1953–1954) 51–62.

3   Steven L. McKenzie, "Why Didn't David Build the Temple? The History of a Biblical Tradition," in *Worship and the Hebrew Bible: Essays in Honor of John T. Willis* (ed. M. P. Graham, R. R. Marrs, and S. L.

McKenzie; JSOTSup 284; Sheffield: Sheffield Academic Press, 1999) 205–24.

4   *II Samuel*, 209–31. An exhaustive history of research is given by W. Dietrich and T. Naumann, *Die Samuelbücher* (ErFor 287; Darmstadt: Wissenschaftliche Buchgesellschaft, 1995) 143–56.

erection of the temple. Yahweh says: "You will not build a temple (house), but your son will."[5]

Even if this diachronic analysis is accurate,[6] I assume that the Chronicler knew only the final form of 2 Samuel 7, which turns the prohibition of temple building into a temporary delay, since the promised "rest" had not yet been achieved.[7] In the final form of the Deuteronomistic History, David, as a faithful king, proposed building the temple, which Nathan did not forbid, but only delayed it until the time of Solomon, who represented the establishment of David's dynasty. The Chronicler's message, too, is that the prohibition of the temple building was only temporary and due, in his judgment, to David's warlike character, which made it ritually inappropriate for him to build the temple. By his omission of 2 Sam 7:1b[8] and 7:14b,[9] the Chronicler avoids the implication that Solomon committed sins that were worthy of retribution, and he puts a much greater stress on Solomon as the fulfillment of the dynastic promise given through Nathan and the one who is to build the temple.

The Ark Narrative in Chronicles had ended with David going home to bless his house (1 Chr 16:43), which leads smoothly into David's reflections over the incongruity between his own, lavish home and the tent within which the ark was housed (17:1). After an initial affirmation of David's intentions, Nathan receives a word of God at night and delivers this "oracle of Nathan" to David, ending with v. 15.

Between the oracle of Nathan and the conclusion of the chapter comes a prayer of David dealing exclusively with the dynastic promise and not even mentioning the temple. Rudolph has called attention to the bright light that shines on David's piety in this prayer, though some commentators have been critical of its wordiness and even challenged its necessity.[10] The prayer, however, does reinforce the surety of the dynastic promise and therefore, at least by implication, the greatest accomplishment of that dynasty, namely, the erection of the temple and the initiation of its cult. The prayer begins with David recounting his own insignificance and Yahweh's beneficence to the house of David. After hailing Yahweh's uniqueness and his acts on behalf of Israel, David urges Yahweh to keep his promises and establish the Davidic dynasty. McCarter[11] proposes a complicated precanonical history for these verses in 2 Samuel 7 as well: vv. 18 and 29 were the original conclusion to the Ark Narrative; vv. 19, 22a, 27-28, and perhaps 29bα were written in the time of Solomon; vv. 20-21 are a prophetic insertion; and vv. 22b-26 were the contribution of the Deuteronomistic editor. Others challenge our ability to get behind the final editing.[12] Interpreters of Chronicles in any case can assume that the author of Chronicles knew the prayer of David only in its final form, and it is this form that provides the measure for assessing the Chronicler's own affirmation of or reinterpretation of this passage.[13]

---

5 For a substantially similar proposal see T. Veijola, *Die Ewige Dynastie: David und die Entstehung seiner Dynastie nach der deuteronomistischen Darstellung* (AASF B193; Helsinki: Suomalainen Tiedeakatemia, 1975) 69–79.

6 McKenzie, "Why Didn't David?" 207–8, has thrown that into considerable doubt.

7 The passages mentioning rest in the period of Joshua (Josh 1:13, 15: 21:44; 22:4; 23:1) were all considered secondary in Noth's discussion (*Deuteronomistic History,* 40).

8 "Yahweh had given him rest from all his enemies around him."

9 "When he commits iniquity, I will punish him with the kind of rod that mortals use, with blows inflicted by human beings."

10 Perhaps no one has been harsher in this judgment than Robert H. Pfeiffer, *Introduction to the Old Testament* (New York: Harper, 1948) 370–73, who called 2 Sam 7:23 "the worst instance of illiterate inanity" and regarded the whole chapter as "a mire of unintelligible verbiage," and, citing W. R. Arnold, "monkish drivel."

11 *II Samuel*, 240.

12 McKenzie, "Why Didn't David?" 208–9; and John Van Seters, *In Search of History: Historiography in the Ancient World and the Origins of Biblical History* (New Haven: Yale Univ. Press, 1983) 274–76.

13 McKenzie, "Why Didn't David?" 219, notes that 1 Chr 22:6-16 and 28:2-10 make allusions to the oracle of Nathan in both the versions of 2 Samuel 7 and 1 Chronicles 17. Japhet, 398, shows that 1 Chr 22:10 relies in two instances on 2 Samuel 7 rather than 1 Chronicles 17. Thus the words "(he shall build a house) for my name" and "the throne of his kingdom" conform to 2 Sam 7:13 rather than 1 Chr 17:12.

17:1-15. Oracle of Nathan (2 Sam 7:1-17)

17:1-2. Opening Dialogue between David and Nathan

■ **1** *When David had taken up residence in his house:* The word "house" occurs fourteen times in this chapter, with the following meanings: David's residence; the temple David plans to build; the dynasty that Yahweh will establish; and the temple that Solomon will build and that Yahweh will recognize. The Chronicler had previously noted that Hiram had sent cedar logs and workers to build David a house (1 Chr 14:1//2 Sam 5:11), and also reported that David had built houses and pitched a tent for the ark in Jerusalem (1 Chr 15:1 without *Vorlage*). The Chronicler omits from his *Vorlage* at this point the Deuteronomistic observation that "Yahweh had given rest to him all around from all his enemies" (2 Sam 7:1b). According to Deut 12:9-11 Israel was to go to the place that Yahweh has chosen when they had been given rest from their enemies.[14] "Going to Yahweh's place" implied the construction of the temple, and Solomon made this connection explicit in 1 Kgs 5:18-19 (4-5). The Chronicler's omission of 2 Sam 7:1b may have been caused in part by sensitivity to the wars that follow in chaps. 18–20, although that did not bother the Deuteronomistic Historian, who records the same wars right after this chapter in 2 Sam 8:1-18; 10:1-19; 11:1-2; and 12:26-31.[15] Much more important for the Chronicler, however, is that it is only with Solomon that rest was achieved: "A son will be born to you [David]; he will be a man of rest, and I will give to him rest from all his enemies" (1 Chr 22:9, without *Vorlage*).[16] Solomon was a man of peace, as even the etymology of his name affirms (22:9). David, on the other hand, was a warrior who had shed much blood, and hence was prohibited from building the temple (22:8; 28:3).

David said to Nathan the prophet: As in 2 Samuel 7, Nathan arrives on the scene without introduction or patronymic. His only other appearances in Chronicles are in the regnal summaries of David and Solomon (1 Chr 29:29 and 2 Chr 9:29; both references to Nathan added by the Chronicler), where the reader is referred to sources ascribed to him for more information about the two kings. His more memorable roles in the incident with Bathsheba (2 Samuel 12) and in the transfer of power to Solomon when David was on his deathbed (1 Kings 1 and 2) are not included in Chronicles. The only other references to the word "prophet" in 1 Chronicles are in 1 Chr 16:22//Ps 105:15 and in 1 Chr 29:19, again referring in the latter case to Nathan.

"I am dwelling in a house of cedar, but the ark of the covenant of Yahweh is under tent curtains": The contrast drawn between a solid house of cedar and a flimsy tent implies that David is contemplating building a temple for the ark, and this implication is confirmed by Nathan in v. 2 and especially by Yahweh's word in v. 4. Ever since the Levites began to carry the ark on its procession to Jerusalem, the Chronicler has frequently called the ark "the ark of the covenant of Yahweh" (see the commentary at 15:25). Johnstone, 1:200, detects in the preposition "under" a contrast with 2 Sam 7:2, where the ark was "within" the tent curtains. In Chronicles the tent is a mere awning. As in chaps. 13 and 21, David begins a significant cultic action on his own terms and soon runs into complications.

■ **2** *"Do everything your heart desires":* Nathan's strong endorsement of David's plans—virtually a blank check—and Yahweh's apparent subsequent prohibition of temple building in vv. 4-6—has led to the diachronic reconstruction of the prehistory of 2 Samuel 7 discussed above under Structure. In the final form of the text of 2 Samuel 7, which the Chronicler uses, Nathan says yes to David's plans, then Yahweh raises a question whether David should be the one to build the temple, and then Yahweh says that the plans for building the temple will be deferred to the next generation of David's family. As Nathan here encourages David to go ahead, he adds the

---

14 A secondary observation in Josh 21:44 implied that such rest was achieved within the lifetime of Joshua. See other passages listed in n. 7.

15 Myers, 1:125–26, observes that the Chronicler wanted to omit any lapse of time between the bringing of the ark to Jerusalem and the desire to build a temple.

16 McKenzie, "Why Didn't David?" 220, notes that rest was also enjoyed in the reign of Asa (2 Chr 15:15) and Jehoshaphat (20:30).

assistance formula, "God[17] is with you" (cf. v. 8, where Yahweh states that he has been with David in the past, and 1 Chr 11:9, where David became greater, for Yahweh was with him).

17:3. Report of Nathan Receiving the Word of God

■ **3** *That night the word of God came to Nathan:* This divine revelation changes considerably the initial response of Nathan to David's plans, and is identified in v. 15 as a vision (חזון). The young Samuel also received an important revelation at night (1 Samuel 3, an incident not included in Chronicles).

17:4-14. Nathan Reports the Word of God

■ **4** *"Go say to David my servant":* Even though Yahweh modifies Nathan's earlier exuberant advice, David is still addressed with the honorific title of "my servant."[18] Only Moses,[19] Joshua,[20] and David[21] are called "my servant" or "the servant of Yahweh" in the Deuteronomistic History, but the Chronicler restricts the title to David, with both of his uses coming from his *Vorlage* (cf. v. 7).[22] Verses 4-6 prohibit David from building the temple, while vv. 7-14 are positive words about David and his dynasty and authorize David's son to build the temple. Both of these sections begin with the messenger formula "Thus says Yahweh [of hosts]."

"You are not the one to build for me the house to dwell in": While 2 Sam 7:5 MT expressed this oracle in a rhetorical question, the difference between it and the wording in Chronicles may not be as great as often assumed.[23] The Samuel reading is not necessarily a categorical rejection of temple building, but only questioning whether David

should be the one to build it: "Will *you*[24] build for me a house for me to live in?" The issue for the Chronicler is also a matter of timing—the promised rest has not yet been achieved. David himself is not to be the actual builder, as both this indicative prohibition and v. 12 make clear.[25] Yahweh did not question the building of the temple itself, but only whether David was the person to do it. The emphasis given to the pronoun "you" by its location at the beginning of this clause is to be compared with the emphasis on "I" (referring to Yahweh) in v. 7. The addition of the definite article to the word "house" may be the Chronicler's attempt to emphasize that it is a question of building not *a* temple, but *the* temple that was in Jerusalem.[26] This initial deferral, until the next generation, of David's proposal to build a temple will be followed by a blessing on his "house" or "seed" in vv. 11-14.

■ **5** *"For I have not dwelled in a house":* Yahweh rejects the proposal of David to build a temple both because of David being a man of blood (22:8; 29:3) and because he has not found such permanent accommodations necessary in the past. According to 1 Sam 3:3, the tabernacle may have been replaced by a more permanent building or temple (היכל) at Shiloh in premonarchical times, although that possibility is ignored here.

"from the time I brought Israel up": In the material he has written on his own the Chronicler generally does not refer to the exodus, and he sometimes avoids it even when it is in his *Vorlage*.[27] In this chapter, however, he retains the reference, as well as the references to the period of the judges in vv. 6 and 9-10, and to the con-

---

17 In this chapter the Chronicler frequently changes the divine name used in the *Vorlage,* although without any apparent theological significance. In this case 2 Sam 7:3 reads: "Yahweh is with you."

18 Chronicles changes the word order from 2 Sam 7:5 ("to my servant to David"), again without apparent significance.

19 Josh 1:2, 7; 2 Kgs 21:8.

20 Josh 24:29.

21 2 Sam 3:18; 7:5, 8; 1 Kgs 11:13, 32, 34, 36, 38; 14:8; 2 Kgs 19:34; 20:6.

22 The word "servant" is used by David in a self-deprecating reference to himself a number of times (1 Chr 17:17, 18, 19, 23, 24, 25 [twice], 26, 27; 21:8).

23 And the wording of Chronicles is not an innovation of the Chronicler, but is the result of the copy of Samuel he was using (see textual note 5).

24 Note that the pronoun is explicit and put in the first position in the sentence. See McKenzie, "Why Didn't David?" 213.

25 See also 2 Chr 6:8-9 (//1 Kgs 8:18-19): "Yahweh said to my father David, 'You did well to consider building a house for my name; nevertheless you shall not build the house, but your son . . . shall build the house for my name.'"

26 So Eckhard von Nordheim, "König und Tempel," *VT* 27 (1977) 450. But see also textual note 6.

27 See the detailed discussion in Japhet, *Ideology,* 379–86. In this case Japhet, 330, believes that the Chronicler narrows the role of the exodus by omitting "from Egypt" from his *Vorlage*. LXX[Bhnva2] and Ethiopic place "from Egypt" before "the sons of Israel" in 2 Sam 7:6, while all the rest of the MSS follow the location in MT. Might this double loca-

quest of Canaan in v. 21. Johnstone, 1:202, finds a reference to the perpetual unity and destiny of the people in the word "Israel," which Chronicles has substituted for the "descendants of Israel" in 2 Sam 7:6. But the exodus is mentioned in 2 Chr 5:10; 6:5; 7:22 and the wilderness wandering (or at least the tabernacle made at that time) appears in 1 Chr 16:39; 21:29; 2 Chr 1:3-5.[28] The latter texts, of course, presuppose the exodus.

I have traveled about from tent to tent and from tabernacle to tabernacle: Since the people have not yet settled down in one place (Deut 12:9; cf. 1 Chr 17:9), Yahweh has remained similarly mobile. Does the Chronicler's recasting of his *Vorlage* and his reference to both tent and tabernacle mean to take account both of the tradition of the wilderness tabernacle (Exod 39:32; cf. 1 Chr 16:39) and of David's recently erected tent?[29] For Samuel and for Chronicles, Yahweh's sanctuary has had a number of temporary stopping places,[30] even if some sort of more permanent building had replaced the desert tent at Shiloh. As McKenzie remarks, the issue is between permanence and transience.[31] As the next verse notes, there was not to be a fixed shrine in the period of the judges because Israel's leadership was also not fixed in that period when leadership passed through a series of non-dynastic tribal leaders.

■ **6** *Did I ever speak a word with one of the judges of Israel:* Only in this verse and in vv. 9-10 does the Chronicler explicitly refer to the period of the judges. Because he sticks relatively close to his *Vorlage* in this chapter, he retains aspects of Israel's history that he downplayed elsewhere.[32] In the time of the judges, when there were no permanent leaders, there was no need for a permanent house. In the Deuteronomistic History Solomon explained David's inability to build the temple as a result of his preoccupation with war (1 Kgs 5:17 [3]).

Why have you not built for me a house of cedar?: Yahweh's rhetorical question implies a rejection of the necessity or even desirability of a temple in the period of the judges. The Chronicler has mechanically taken over this question from his *Vorlage,* and the final message there and here is that the temple is to be delayed but not prohibited. The mention of cedarwood harks back to David's initial reflections in v. 1.

■ **7** *Now, thus you shall say to my servant David . . . I took you from the pasture, from following the flock:* The new section, dealing with the promise of dynastic succession, is introduced by the transitional word "Now." With the beginning of the positive or promissory section of the oracle, the Chronicler has Yahweh allude to David's anointing by Samuel in 1 Sam 16:1-13 and David's occupation as a shepherd at that time, although he chose not to include that passage in his own narrative. He could presuppose, of course, that his readers would understand the allusion.

to be ruler: The Chronicler himself used the word נגיד ("ruler" or "king-designate") of David before his coronation (1 Chr 11:2//2 Sam 5:2), but the reader might also think of 1 Sam 13:14 and 25:30, passages not included in Chronicles, where this technical term is used of David. In any case, David, the onetime shepherd of sheep, was chosen to "shepherd" the people as their permanent leader in the place of the judges (v. 6), and he was given the title of "king-designate."

■ **8** *I have been with you wherever you went:* God's accompaniment of David was also affirmed in the account of the conquest of Jerusalem in 1 Chr 11:9//2 Sam 5:10. A number of other references to this assistance formula in the Deuteronomistic History are not included in Chronicles (1 Sam 16:18; 17:37; 18:14, 28). David's journeying (הלכת) is expressed in similar terminology to that of Yahweh in v. 6 (התהלכתי).

I have cut off all your enemies before you: This may be an

---

tion indicate its secondary character at least in some MSS?

28 This was pointed out helpfully in a draft of an article sent to me by Michael Avioz, "Nathan's Prophecy in II Sam 7 and in I Chr 17: Text, Context, and Meaning."

29 1 Chr 15:1, 3; 16:1. In its paraphrase Tg summarizes the history of the tent shrine: "*I caused my Shekinah to dwell from the* tent *of meeting to Nob, and from Nob to Shiloh, and from Shiloh to the* tent *at*

Gibeon" (McIvor, *Targum,* 104–5). Historically, the reference to Nob should *follow* Shiloh.

30 There had been sanctuaries at least at Gibeon, Shiloh, and Nob. Cf. Myers, 1:126.

31 "Why Didn't David?" 214–15.

32 Japhet, 330, calls attention to the implicit reference in "2 Chr 15:13ff," by which she must mean 2 Chr 15:3-5.

allusion to the struggles of David with Saul (1 Samuel 16–29) or even with Ishbosheth (2 Samuel 2–4). Neither of these accounts was included in the Chronicler's narrative. It could also refer, at least in part, to the defeat of the Philistines in 1 Chr 14:8-17.

I will make for you a name like the name of the great ones who are in the earth: The Chronicler (and his *Vorlage* before him), switches from a recounting of past benefactions to promises of future blessings.[33] David's name is referred to in 2 Sam 8:13 ("David won a name for himself") and 1 Kgs 1:47 ("May God make the name of Solomon more famous than yours [David's]"), neither of which appears in the Chronicler's narrative. Does "the great ones" refer to people like Abshai (1 Chr 11:20// 2 Sam 23:18) or Benaiah (1 Chr 11:24//2 Sam 23:22), who through their heroics won a name for themselves?

■ **9** *I will make a place for my people Israel, and I will plant them so that they may dwell in their own place:* The promise to David has implications also for the people. Though McCarter[34] proposes that a place of worship or a cult place is being referred to,[35] we need to note that this is a place where Israel is to be planted and where Israel will dwell. Hence the reference, at least in Chronicles, is to the gift of the land. The land will belong fully to Israel only when Yahweh will have given "rest" to Solomon from all his enemies round about (1 Chr 22:9).

nor shall wicked people continue to wear them out: This is a quite general and inclusive reference to the various enemies who oppressed Israel during the period of the judges, entities like Aram-naharaim (Judg 3:8), the king of Moab (3:12), King Jabin of Canaan (4:2), the Midian-ites (6:1), and the Philistines and Ammonites (10:8). McCarter[36] identifies the oppressors as Hophni and Phinehas, but the reference seems to be far more general, especially in Chronicles.

■ **10** *I will subdue all your enemies:* David's coming military victories were credited to the promise of divine intervention. The Chronicler, however, has replaced the verb "give rest to" from 2 Sam 7:11 with "subdue," since "rest" will not be achieved in David's day, but only during the reign of Solomon.[37] The Chronicler may also have chosen this verb in anticipation of the battles fought by David just ahead in 1 Chronicles 18–20. See especially 18:1//2 Sam 8:1: "Some time afterward, David attacked the Philistines and subdued them."

I declare to you: In 2 Sam 7:11 Yahweh is the subject of the verb. The first person pronoun in Chronicles could also refer to Yahweh, who has been speaking in the first person in vv. 7-10a. But it could also refer to Nathan, which would ease the transition to the next clause, where Yahweh is referred to in the third person. In 2 Sam 7:11, however, Yahweh declares that Yahweh will build a house.

Yahweh will build for you a house: Building a house here refers primarily to Yahweh establishing the dynasty of David.[38] In Hebrew, both in Samuel and Chronicles, the word "house" is given emphasis by being in the first position in the clause. The Chronicler's use of "build" instead of "make" in 2 Sam 7:11 was a change made

---

33 The change is from *wāw* consecutive with the imperfect to *wāw* consecutive with the perfect.

34 *II Samuel*, 203–4.

35 McCarter, 190, translates: "I shall fix a place for my people Israel and plant it, so that it will remain where it is and never again be disturbed." David Vanderhooft, "Dwelling Beneath the Sacred Place: A Proposal for Reading 2 Samuel 7:10," *JBL* 118 (1999) 630, shows that "my people Israel" is the object of the verb "plant" and the subject of "remain" and "be disturbed." He goes on to argue that the final word in this lemma תחתיו should be translated "beneath it [= the place]."

36 *II Samuel*, 204.

37 Cf. 1 Kgs 5:18 (4), where Solomon says: "And now, Yahweh my God has given me rest on every side."

This passage is not included by the Chronicler in his account of Solomon.

38 Tg here substitutes "kingdom" for "house": "the Lord will establish a kingdom for you." On the pun on the word "house," see the extensive discussion of punning in Chronicles by Isaac Kalimi, "Paranomasia in the Book of Chronicles," *JSOT* 67 (1995) 27–41. Pancratius C. Beentjes, "Transformations of Space and Time: Nathan's Oracle and David's Prayer in 1 Chronicles 17," in *Sanctity of Time and Space in Tradition and Modernity* (ed. A. Houtman, M. J. H. M. Poorthuis, and J. Schwartz; Leiden: Brill, 1998) 38, believes that "my house" in v. 14 compels the reader to consider the possibility that the noun "house" in v. 10 refers to the temple instead of a dynasty. Riley, *King and Cultus*, 183,

already in the textual history of Samuel,[39] and it makes for a clearer contrast: "You are not the one to build" (v. 4), but "Yahweh will build" in this verse.

■ **11** *When your days are complete to go to be with your ancestors:* The clause "to go to be with your ancestors" has replaced a more common expression in 2 Sam 7:12 MT: "you shall lie down with your ancestors."[40] The reason for this change is unclear; perhaps it is just a synonymous variant. Note that Chr LXX has been harmonized with 2 Samuel (see textual note 25).

I will raise up your seed after you, who will be from your sons: The Chronicler may have thought that the expression "from your sons" referred to Solomon more clearly than "from your loins/body" (2 Sam 7:12), which might imply that the word "seed" referred to all future descendants of David.[41] Japhet also observes that this reference to David's sons is in more refined language.[42]

■ **12** *He will build for me a house:* This clause here and in the *Vorlage* makes explicit that the collective promise of offspring has been narrowed to one person, still unnamed (Solomon), and that he, not David, will be empowered to build the temple.[43] Chronicles replaces the Deuteronomistic cliché "for my name" (2 Sam 7:13) with "for me," creating a closer literary relationship

between "he" and "for me." Note also the parallel between "he will build for me a house" and "Yahweh will build for you a house" in v. 10. Solomon's temple building leads to the divine dynastic promise in the second half of this verse.

William Schniedewind has argued that Chronicles was written in the early Persian period (539–460 BCE) and that the Chronicler's royalist and pro-temple message would be applicable solely in that time.[44] He believes that the Chronicler's reading of the promise to David states that God will give David a kingdom[45] and that Chronicles uses the promise of Nathan to build an apology for the temple that responded to those who resisted or were apathetic toward the rebuilding of the temple in postexilic times. He further proposes that this text of Chronicles was influential in Zerubbabel's role in the reconstruction of the Second Temple. The text of Nathan's oracle, however, promises the kingdom to Solomon rather than to David, and it is difficult to see why Yahweh's commissioning of Solomon to build the temple would require its rebuilding in postexilic times. In addition, Schniedewind's early dating depends on his judgment that the genealogies in chaps. 1–9 are secondary and added only when Chronicles was "attached

---

entertains the possibility that "house" here pertains to the temple even more than to the dynasty.

39 See textual note 22. Beentjes, "Transformations," 35, emphasizes the importance of the root בנה here, but does not note that this change was already made in the text of Samuel.

40 For "lie down with your ancestors," cf. Gen 47:10; Deut 31:16. It is also used in 2 Chronicles for nine of the kings of Judah: Rehoboam, 12:16; Abijah, 13:23; Asa, 16:13; Jehoshaphat, 21:1; Amaziah, 26:2; Uzziah, 26:23; Jotham, 27:9; Ahaz, 28:27; Hezekiah, 32:33; Manasseh, 33:20.

41 Cf. Isa 39:7: "and your sons who come out from you"; 1QIsaᵃ: "and your sons who come out from your loins." For discussion see Williamson, "Dynastic Oracle," 305–9. Tg takes away all ambiguity: "I shall raise up *your son* after you, *your very own son*" (McIvor, *Targum*, 106).

42 "Interchanges," 17.

43 Cf. 2 Chr 6:8-9: "But Yahweh said to my father, 'You did well to consider building a house for my name; nevertheless you shall not build the house, but your son who shall be born to you shall build the house for my name.'"

44 William M. Schniedewind, *Society and the Promise to*

David: The Reception History of 2 Samuel 7:1-17 (New York: Oxford Univ. Press, 1999) 125–34.

45 Schniedewind speaks of royalist propaganda in Chronicles (ibid., 128), and of the hope for a restoration of the Davidic kingdom (p. 139). I believe that Donald F. Murray, "Dynasty, People, and the Future: The Message of Chronicles," *JSOT* 58 (1993) 71–92, has shown decisively that while Chronicles values highly the dynastic promise in the context of the preexilic kingdom, it does not foster a hope for the future restoration of the Davidic dynasty. Riley, *King and Cultus,* 203, remarks: "The Edict of Cyrus forms an integral part of the Chronicler's work and is given by the Chronicler as a clear indication that the Davidic rule, having finished its cultic task, has given way to a new regime with God's approval because of the dynasty's unfaithfulness." Perhaps the best, guarded case for such a future restoration is that of Williamson, "Dynastic Oracle," 305–18.

to" Ezra and Nehemiah.[46] It seems much more likely to me that this chapter endorses the ongoing validity of the temple's cultus, which was initiated by the actions of both David and Solomon. The Second Temple shared in the legitimacy of Solomon's temple, but I sense no effort here to justify the construction of the Second Temple itself.

I will establish his throne forever: Yahweh promises here and twice in v. 14 that Solomon's throne will be established forever. This fits particularly well in Chronicles, where David and Solomon are often treated equally as model kings during the united kingdom.[47] The adverbial expression "forever" is used eight times[48] between here and the end of the chapter. This promise to David's son Solomon is expressed elsewhere as God's covenant with David (2 Chr 13:5, in the time of Abijah; 2 Chr 21:7// 2 Kgs 8:19, in the time of Jehoram; 2 Chr 23:3, in the time of Joash). God's forbearance with regard to this dynasty, despite its deleterious effects on temple and cult, results from the commitment God had made to David and Solomon. The promise to David and Solomon maintains the dynasty during its long history, but the Chronicler is silent about the fate of that promise when the dynasty finally fell.[49]

■ **13** *I will be to him a father, and he will be for me a son:* This adoption formula (cf. Ps 2:7)[50] is followed in 2 Sam 7:14 by a sentence that makes all subsequent Davidic kings subject to retribution for their misdeeds, but not to the same loss of divine favor experienced by Saul: "When he commits iniquity, I will punish him with a rod such as mortals use, with blows inflicted by human

beings."[51] The Chronicler's focus is primarily on Solomon in vv. 11-15, and the Chronicler's Solomon commits no such iniquity (1 Kings 11 is not included in his narrative), and therefore the Chronicler did not bring this sentence into his text. Nevertheless, the Chronicler does not make the continuation of the dynasty unconditional as in 2 Samuel 7.[52] After all, David prays that Solomon will have the wisdom to keep the law of Yahweh, and he states that Solomon will prosper *only if* he is careful to observe the decrees and ordinances of Yahweh (1 Chr 22:12-13). The Chronicler also quotes a clearly retributive statement of Yahweh: "I will establish his kingdom forever if he continues resolute in keeping my commandments and my ordinances" (28:7).[53] The Chronicler, therefore, announces a conditional promise that is concentrated almost exclusively on Solomon as the temple builder. Eventually, with Zedekiah, the Chronicler brings the story of the Davidic dynasty to an end. Its ultimate significance lay in the establishment of the temple and its cultus by David and Solomon.

I will not remove my loyalty from him: The Chronicler follows a reading in Samuel different from Samuel MT, which states that Yahweh's loyalty itself "will not depart from him" (see textual note 28). Thus the departure of this divine loyalty from Solomon in Chronicles would require the intervention of Yahweh, just as Yahweh had intervened in the case of Saul to remove his loyalty from him. It is not clear whether this change results from a desire to coordinate both cases, or whether the reading followed by the Chronicler is an effort to assert that Yah-

46   *Society and the Promise,* 128.

47   Cf. 1 Chr 14:2: "Yahweh had established him [David] as king over Israel." See Braun, "Solomonic Apologetic."

48   See also vv. 14 (twice), 22, 23, 24, 27 (twice). Cf. K. Seybold, *Das davidische Königtum im Zeugnis der Propheten* (FRLANT 107; Göttingen: Vandenhoeck & Ruprecht, 1972) 33, n. 52; McCarter, *II Samuel,* 206, though he cites Seybold, mistakenly says that the word occurs only seven times.

49   Murray, "Dynasty, People, and the Future," 90–91.

50   Gerald Cooke, "The Israelite King as Son of God," *ZAW* 73 (1961) 202–25.

51   H. van den Bussche, "Le texte de la prophétie de Nathan sur la dynastie Davidique (II Sam., VII-I Chron., XVII)," *ETL* 24 (1948) 388–89, thought

that the shorter reading in Chronicles was the original text also in 2 Samuel 7.

52   Elsewhere in the Deuteronomistic History the promise to David is made conditional. See 1 Kgs 2:3-4 and 9:5-7. Cf. also Deut 17:18-19. Beentjes, "Transformations," 39, finds conditional promises also in 1 Chr 22:11-13; 28:9; 2 Chr 7:17-18.

53   Cf. 1 Chr 28:9, where the king will be rejected if he fails to seek (דרש) Yahweh; 2 Chr 7:17-22//1 Kgs 9:4-9 states that Solomon's kingdom will be established if he observes all of God's statutes.

weh's "loyalty" cannot act independently of the Deity himself. In any case, this change had already taken place in the Chronicler's *Vorlage*.

as I removed it from the one who was before you: The reference is still clearly to Saul, even though the Chronicler follows a text of 2 Sam 7:15 that did not mention Saul explicitly.[54]

■ **14** *I will install him in my house and my kingdom:* The two nouns could be understood as a hendiadys: "in my royal house." Thus Solomon would be appointed[55] as an officer of God's kingdom, namely, Israel.[56] More likely, the two nouns are to be distinguished, with Solomon installed both in Yahweh's house/temple and in Yahweh's kingdom.[57] Thus the Chronicler has deftly changed the *Vorlage* in 2 Sam 7:16, which promised that David's house (dynasty) and David's kingdom would be made sure[58] forever. As Riley remarks, "The gift of the dynasty is not simply occasioned by David's desire to build the Temple, but is given primarily for the purpose of temple-building."[59] Installing Solomon in Yahweh's kingdom de-emphasizes the political kingdom, which was a thing of the past in any case by the Chronicler's time (cf. 2 Chr 36:23). Ackroyd, 67–68, adds that it is God's rule that is being established, not that of a line of earthly kings. Solomon will sit on the throne of Yahweh (1 Chr 29:23).

his throne will be established forever: It is the throne of

Solomon—not of David as in 2 Sam 7:16—that will be established forever. The Chronicler thus makes his account more internally consistent with v. 12.[60]

17:15. Conclusion to the Words of Nathan

■ **15** *According to all these words and all this vision:* The Chronicler, except for minute differences in vocalization, cites this verse verbatim from his *Vorlage*. He thereby declares that the message of vv. 4-14 is divine revelation, thus distinguishing it from v. 2, which is Nathan's own opinion. The only other use of חזון "vision" in Chronicles is in the regnal summary of Hezekiah, where the reader is referred for further information to the "vision of Isaiah the son of Amoz the prophet" (2 Chr 32:32).[61]

17:16-27. David's Response to Oracle of Nathan
17:16a. Introduction

■ **16a** *King David went and sat before Yahweh:* This is not the usual posture of prayer in the OT,[62] but the point may be that in the first half of the chapter David "sat" in his house (v. 1) while in the second half he "sat" in God's presence, probably at the tent shrine of the ark. The Talmud concluded from this verse that kings were allowed to sit while they prayed.[63] This is the first explicit reference to David as king in this chapter, following the divine promise of a dynastic house in vv. 15-10.[64]

---

54 See textual note 29. Chronicles Tg restores the mention of Saul: "I shall not withdraw my goodness from him as I withdrew it from Saul, who reigned before you."

55 Compare this use of עמד in the *hiphil* with 1 Chr 6:16 (31). Riley, *King and Cultus,* 74, suggests a translation of "stationed for duty."

56 Cf. Curtis and Madsen, 228; and von Nordheim, "König und Tempel," 452. On God's kingdom see 1 Chr 28:5; 29:11, 23; 2 Chr 9:8; 13:8. Of the other twelve uses of "house" in this chapter, one refers to David's palace (v. 1), four refer to the temple (vv. 4, 5, 6, 12), and seven to the Davidic dynasty (vv. 10, 16, 17, 23, 24, 25, 27). For this equation of the earthly kingdom with the kingdom of Yahweh, see 1 Chr 28:5; 29:23; 2 Chr 13:8. Rudolph, 135, understands "my house" here to be a reference to the temple. A better example of this meaning is 1 Chr 28:6.

57 Beentjes, "Transformations," 36–37, interprets "my house" as the temple and "my kingdom" as the kingdom of God. William M. Schniedewind, "King

and Priest in the Book of Chronicles and the Duality of Qumran Messianism," *JJS* 45 (1994) 73, states that these terms refer to the two institutions of the bicephalic leadership: temple and monarchy.

58 ונאמן. See 1 Chr 17:23-24 for the Chronicler's use of the verb אמן in this chapter.

59 Riley, *King and Cultus,* 71. Cf. Dennis J. McCarthy, "Covenant and Law in Chronicles-Nehemiah," *CBQ* 44 (1982) 26.

60 In 1 Chr 28:5 David indicates that Yahweh has chosen Solomon to sit on the throne of Yahweh's kingdom over Israel.

61 This is apparently identified with the "book of the kings of Judah and Israel." The vision of Isaiah was not mentioned in the *Vorlage* at 2 Kgs 20:20.

62 Elsewhere worshipers stand (Gen 18:22), kneel (1 Kgs 8:54), or prostrate themselves (Num 16:45). Tg paraphrases: "Then King David came and *lingered in prayer.*"

63 *b. Yoma* 25a.

64 David is given the title of king in 2 Sam 7:1-3.

17:16b-27. The Prayer Itself

■ **16b** *"Who am I"*: David expresses his humility and his unworthiness of the honor Yahweh has bestowed on him (self-abasement formula), following the example of Moses (Exod 3:11) and Gideon (Judg 6:11). The Chronicler uses this same rhetorical question in his own composition at 1 Chr 29:14. Note that David also calls himself by the deferential title "your servant" in vv. 17, 18 (twice), 19 (twice), 23, 24, 25 (twice), 26, and 27.[65]

Yahweh God: In the *Vorlage* of this chapter, David uses the divine title אדני יהוה ("Lord Yahweh") six[66] times, but in each case the Chronicler has replaced it with "Yahweh God,"[67] "God,"[68] or "Yahweh."[69] A similar replacement is made in 2 Chr 18:5 (//1 Kgs 22:6).[70]

■ **17** *you have spoken of your servant's house in a distant time, and you have shown me the generation of humankind to come:* Though the text is quite uncertain (see textual note 32), the message of the verse is clear: David praises Yahweh for bringing him to the office of the king, but even more amazing to him is the dynastic promise contained in vv. 10-15.

■ **18** *What more can David add to you in order to make you honor your servant?:* Since David cannot give God anything he does not already have, Yahweh's decision to honor David flows solely from his own, unmotivated divine favor.[71]

it is you, Yahweh, who have known your servant: The verb "know" in this clause has the connotation of "chosen" or "elected."[72] Yahweh has chosen David, not vice versa.

The election of Solomon, using the verb בחר, is affirmed three times in chap. 28 (vv. 5, 6, 10).

■ **19** *For the sake of your servant and according to your own heart:* The Chronicler detects a double reason behind God's great deeds: first, his loyalty to and concern for David, and second, his own divine merciful disposition and intention ("according to your own heart"). The divine intention/heart is to be contrasted with the advice of Nathan to David in v. 2: "Do everything *your* heart desires."[73] In emphasizing God's concern for his servant David, the Chronicler is following a version of 2 Sam 7:21 retained now in Sam LXX. The MT of Samuel, on the other hand, puts the emphasis on the fidelity of God to his promises—"for the sake of your word."[74] In 1 Chr 14:2//2 Sam 5:12 the Chronicler affirms that God had established David as king for the sake of his people Israel. Ackroyd, 68, suggests revocalizing וּכְלִבְּךָ ("according to your own heart") as וְכַלְבְּךָ ("and your dog"), with "dog" being in apposition with "servant."[75] The Masoretic vocalization in both 2 Sam 7:21 and 1 Chr 17:19 is to be preferred.

making known to your servant all these great things: There is a play on words with v. 18. The God who *knew*/elected David now makes him *know* "all these great things." This direct object, "all these great things," which was only implicit at 2 Sam 7:21 (*NRSV* "it"), has been supplied by the Chronicler.[76] The great thing is not the dynastic promise, but the revelation to David itself.

---

65 The first reference in v. 18 and the second reference in v. 19 were added by the Chronicler. The first reference in v. 19 (cf. 2 Sam 7:21) is based on a non-MT text of Samuel (see textual note 36).

66 2 Sam 7:18, 19 (twice), 20, 28, and 29. In two additional cases, 2 Sam 7:22, 25, the MT has "Yahweh God," and the Chronicler has "Yahweh" in both of these cases (1 Chr 17:20, 23).

67 1 Chr 17:16, 17. This divine name appears ten other times in Chronicles: 1 Chr 22:1, 19; 28:20; 29:1; 2 Chr 1:9; 6:41 (twice)//Ps 132:8-9 (for the first name Psalms has "Yahweh"; the second name is an addition in Chronicles), 42//Ps 132:10 (but the divine name has been added in Chronicles); 26:18; 32:16. Hence none of these occurrences was taken from the *Vorlage*.

68 1 Chr 17:17.

69 1 Chr 17:19, 26, 27.

70 Cf. Japhet, *Ideology*, 20–23. I am dubious about her

idea that the Chronicler was reluctant to write down אדני "my lords."

71 McCarter, *II Samuel*, 236.

72 Cf. Gen 18:19; Jer 1:5; Hos 13:5; Amos 3:2.

73 In 2 Sam 7:27 David says: "Therefore your servant has found his heart/courage (את לבו) to pray to you." The Chronicler has omitted this word. See textual note 48 for the translation of מצא without a direct object.

74 Cf. textual note 36.

75 This suggestion goes back to N. H. Tur-Sinai. See McCarter, *II Samuel*, 234.

76 כל הגדלות is clearly related to על כן גדלת ("Therefore you are great") from 2 Sam 7:22, which is not included in the Chronicler's version of that verse.

■ **20** *Yahweh, there is no one like you and no God besides you:* The Chronicler here affirms the incomparability of Yahweh (cf. Jer 10:7) and monotheism as well (cf. 1 Sam 2:2; Isa 64:4).[77] In 2 Sam 7:22 these statements are used to support the confession "You are great, Yahweh God," but these words were not picked up in Chronicles.

according to all we have heard with our ears: "We" and "our" here are the only first person plural forms David employs in his prayer. He frequently refers to himself in the third person (e.g., "your servant"), but also uses first person singular pronouns in vv. 16, 17, and 25. The content of this verse is remarkably similar to Isa 64:4: "No ear has perceived, no eye has seen any God besides you, who works for those who wait for him." Later in the prayer (v. 25) David confesses that God has "uncovered his ear" = "has revealed himself to him."

■ **21** *Who is like your people Israel . . . whom God has gone to redeem to be his people:* The author of Deuteronomy saw Israel's incomparability in its having a God so near to it (Deut 4:7) and in its righteous law (Deut 4:8). According to the Chronicler and the author of 2 Samuel 7, God's uniqueness consists in God performing the redemptive acts of the exodus (cf. also v. 5) and conquest.

by making for yourself a reputation for great and awe-inspiring things: David breaks out of a recital of God's redemptive deeds in the third person and addresses God in the second person. This phenomenon also takes place in Ps 23:4.

by driving out nations: What are we to make of the Chronicler's omission from his *Vorlage* of the additional ואלהיו "and their gods?" Is this a monotheistic correction of his *Vorlage,* since what does not exist cannot be driven out?

whom you have redeemed from Egypt: This is another, rare reference to the exodus in Chronicles, but this time,

in distinction from v. 5, Chronicles retains the explicit mention of Egypt.[78]

■ **22** *you made your people Israel to be your people forever, and you were, Yahweh, their God:* This variation on the "covenant formula"[79] appears in a somewhat different form also elsewhere in Chronicles (2 Chr 23:16//2 Kgs 11:17; 2 Chr 34:31//2 Kgs 23:3).

■ **23** *And now. . . let the word that you spoke concerning your servant and his house be made sure forever:* "And now" marks the transition between thanksgiving and supplication.[80] Chronicles uses the verb אמן ("be made sure"), which it had avoided at 1 Chr 17:14 (//2 Sam 7:16).[81] Here it is following a text of Samuel different from the MT (see textual note 48). The same verb is also used in v. 24.[82] After his stirring confession of Yahweh's uniqueness, David prays that the divine dynastic promise would be confirmed.

■ **24** *Let your name be made sure and magnified forever:* David prays that God's name or reputation, which was won through the acts of the conquest (v. 21), might endure and grow in importance. The verb ויאמן "be made sure" has been added to the *Vorlage* by the Chronicler (cf. the use of this verb in the previous verse, where the Chronicler was following a non-MT of 2 Sam 7:25).

Yahweh of hosts the God of Israel is Israel's God: The title "Yahweh of hosts" is used one other time in this chapter (v. 7)[83] and one other time in Chronicles outside this chapter (11:9//2 Sam 5:10). In each case the Chronicler retains the divine title from his *Vorlage.* The tautological confession in the present verse[84] affirms David's exclusive allegiance to the God who raised him up as king and established Israel as his people.

the house of David your servant will be established before you: This is the second use of the participle נכון in this chapter. The first, in v. 14, was with God's promise that

---

77 This is the only explicit statement of monotheism in Chronicles.

78 The Exodus is also mentioned in 2 Chr 5:10; 6:5; 7:22; and 20:10.

79 Cf. Jer 7:23 ("I will be your God, and you shall be my people"); 11:4; Ezek 36:28. Cf. Deut 29:9-12 (10-13).

80 This "and now" transitional formula also appears in v. 7 in the oracle of Nathan and two additional times in the prayer of David, vv. 26-27.

81 The *Vorlage* at 2 Sam 7:25 reads הקם "establish" (imperative addressed to Yahweh).

82 Allen, 408, claims incorrectly that the root אמן is used three times in these verses.

83 It is used in the messenger formula introducing the recital of God's actions to raise David up as king.

84 2 Sam 7:26 reads: "Yahweh of hosts is God over Israel." Was "God of Israel" added marginally in Samuel, now showing up as an apposition to "Yahweh of hosts" in 2 Sam 7:27 MT and in this confession in 1 Chr 17:24?

the throne of Solomon would be established. Here David prays for the same thing to happen to his own house or dynasty, as God's name is made sure and magnified.

■ **25** *For you, my God:* The text of Chronicles makes David's confession much more personal, although not really different in content from the *Vorlage*. In 2 Sam 7:27 we read: "For you, Yahweh of hosts, the God of Israel."[85]

have revealed to your servant that you will build for him a house: The Chronicler puts the oracle in indirect discourse, whereas 2 Sam 7:27 reads: "I will build a house for you."

Therefore your servant has dared to pray before you: David's boldness in prayer is based on God's prior revelation to him. Chronicles omits את התפלה הזאת "this prayer" from 2 Sam 7:27.

■ **26** *Now, Yahweh, you are God:* The repetitious character of David's prayer has long been observed. This is the third of four times he uses the expression ועתה, and the confession "you are God" seems unnecessary (to us). Did the Chronicler also sense the redundancy and therefore omit "and your words are true" from the *Vorlage,* or were these words merely lost by homoioarchton (cf. textual note 50)?

■ **27** *You have decided to bless the house of your servant:* David here recognizes that God has already blessed him with a dynastic promise, whereas the *Vorlage* in 2 Sam 7:29 reiterates once more David's request: "May it please you to bless the house of your servant."

For you . . . have blessed, and it is blessed forever: David's final confession sums up what the Chronicler has said

previously in his eightfold repetition of the word "forever." God has already blessed David with the promise of dynastic succession. This is also another way of saying that the word of Yahweh has been "made sure" (cf. the wish in v. 23). Japhet, 341, proposes that the Deity is the subject of the final participle.[86] Hence: "you are blessed forever" (cf. *JPS* and *NRSV*). In this understanding David blesses the God who has blessed him (cf. Ps 113:2; Job 1:21). Both translations seem equally possible. Is this a double entendre?[87]

Conclusion

After his anointing (1 Chr 11:1-3), capture of Jerusalem (11:4-9), and bringing the ark of the covenant of Yahweh to Jerusalem (chaps. 13–16), the first thing David mentions is his desire to build a temple there (17:1). The Chronicler follows closely the final redaction of 2 Samuel 7, although in more than twenty cases he follows a reading other than Samuel MT. The oracle of Nathan in its present form (1 Chr 17:1-15) prohibits David from building the temple, promises David dynastic succession, and designates David's son as the temple builder. The emphasis in Chronicles is more clearly on Solomon, though he is not mentioned by name.

In response (vv. 16-27), David expresses his thanks for God's revelation to him about his future dynasty, emphasizing both his own insignificance and Yahweh's beneficence. David confesses the incomparability of Yahweh demonstrated in his saving actions for Israel. His prayer ends with the plea for God to confirm his dynastic promise.

---

85   For "God of Israel" see the previous note.
86   See also Beentjes, "Transformations," 43.
87   The *Vorlage* in 2 Sam 7:29 went a third way. After asking Yahweh to be pleased to bless, it continues: "For you, Lord Yahweh, have spoken, and with your blessing the house of your servant will be blessed" (or "may the house of your servant be blessed").

Translation

1/ It happened after this that David defeated the Philistines and subdued them. He took Gath and its daughter villages[1] from the hand of the Philistines. 2/ David also defeated Moab, and the Moabites became[2] tribute-bearing slaves of David. 3/ David defeated Hadadezer[3] king of Zobah toward Hamath[4] when he[5] went to set up his monument on the river Euphrates.[6] 4/ David captured from him one thousand chariots and seven thousand cavalry,[7] and twenty thousand infantry, and David hamstrung all the chariot horses, but left one hundred of them. 5/ When the Arameans of Damascus came to help Hadadezer king of Zobah, David killed twenty-two thousand Arameans. 6/ Then David put garrisons[8] in Aram Damascus and the Arameans became tribute-bearing slaves to David.[9] Yahweh gave victory to David wherever he went.

7/ David took the golden bow cases that were on[10] the servants of Hadadezer, and he brought them to Jerusalem. 8/ From Tibhath[11] and from Cun,[12] cities of Hadadezer, David took very much[13] bronze. With it Solomon made the bronze sea and the pillars and also the vessels of bronze.[14]

9/ When Tou[15] the king of Hamath heard that David had defeated the whole army of Hadadezer king of Zobah,[16] 10/ he[17] sent Hadoram[18] his son to King David to ask him for peace and to congratulate him because he had fought against Hadadezer and defeated him. Tou had often been at war with Hadadezer. And as for all[19] kinds of vessels of gold, silver, and bronze, 11/ these also King David dedicated to Yahweh with silver and gold that he had carried off from all the nations, from Edom,[20] and Moab, and the Ammonites, and the Philistines, and Amalek. 12/ Abshai[21] the son of Zeruiah defeated Edom[22] in the Valley of Salt, with eighteen[23] thousand casualties. 13/ He put garrisons in Edom[24] and all the Edomites became[25] slaves to David, and Yahweh gave David victory wherever he went.

14/ David ruled over all Israel, and he[26] executed justice and righteousness for all his people. 15/ Joab the son of Zeruiah was over the army, and Jehoshaphat the son of Ahilud was recorder.[27] 16/ Zadok the son of Ahitub and Ahimelech[28] the son of Abiathar were priests; Shavsha[29] was secretary. 17/ Benaiah the son of Jehoiada was over the Cherethites and the Pelethites,[30] and David's sons were the chief officials[31] by the side of the king.

1 את גת ובנתיה. 2 Sam 8:1 has an obscure and unidentifiable reading, מתג האמה "Metheg-ammah," instead of "Gath and its daughter villages." Allen, 414, notes that the Chronicler may have derived Gath by a transposition of the last two letters of מתג, and that אמה suggested to him a mother city and so he created a reading ובנתיה "daughter villages." In readings discussed in textual notes 2, 7, 9, 10, 13, 14, 15, 17, 20, 25, 26, and 29 (cf. also 6 and 16), Chronicles presupposes a text of Samuel other than MT.

2 ויהיו מואב. The singular noun must be understood as a collective since the verb in Chronicles is plural. Cf. the partial reading in 2 Sam 8:1 4QSam^a: . . . היו. Samuel MT ותהי.

3 הדדעזר with Codex L and 2 Sam 8:3 MT; but many Chronicles Hebrew MSS, LXX, and 2 Sam 8:3 LXX read הדרעזר. Historically the correct spelling of this man's name is Hadadezer, but the alternate spelling arose already in the Samuel texts represented by Samuel LXX. Hadarezer appears throughout this chapter in some Hebrew MSS (vv. 3, 5, 7, 8, 9, 10) and in 1 Chr 19:16, 19.

4 צובה חמתה. Japhet, 343, צובה חמת "Zobah-Hamath." חמתה is lacking in Chronicles Syr, Arab., which is apparently a correction to 2 Sam 8:3.

5 The Hebrew is ambiguous and commentators have supplied the name of either David or Hadadezer. Since Hadadezer lived southwest of the Euphrates, but north of the kingdom of David, there is no way that Hadadezer would have encountered David on a trip to the Euphrates. Hence David is the correct antecedent. Cf. McCarter, *II Samuel*, 242.

6 בנהר פרת; cf. 2 Sam 8:3 Q, LXX; Samuel K lacks the name פרת "Euphrates."

7 אלף רכב ושבעת אלפים פרשים; cf. 2 Sam 8:4 4QSam^a LXX; Samuel MT אלף ושבע מאות פרשים "one thousand seven hundred cavalry," with no mention of chariots. The Chronicler's larger number here is not his own exaggeration but derives from his copy of the text of Samuel that was different from MT. D. R. Ap-Thomas, "A Numerical Poser," *JNES* 2 (1943) 198–200, proposed that the original reading in Samuel was one thousand chariots, seven hundred cavalry, and twenty thousand infantry, but there is no indication the proposed smaller number of cavalry ever appeared in a text of Chronicles. Cf. also textual note 31 at 1 Chr 19:18//2 Sam 10:18.

8 נציבים with one Hebrew MS, versions, and 2 Sam 8:6; Chronicles MT lacks this word.

9 עבדים לדויד; cf. 2 Sam 8:6 4QSam^a. Samuel MT לדויד לעבדים.

10 על; cf. 2 Sam 8:4 LXX. Samuel MT אל.

11 טבחת; 2 Sam 8:8 בטח "Betah." Rudolph, 134, may be right that the correct historical name of the city is

טבח "Tebah," but there is no evidence that this spelling ever appeared in Chronicles.

12 ומכון; 2 Sam 8:8 ומברתי "Berothai." Chronicles LXX ἐκ τῶν ἐκλέκτων "from the elect [cities of Hadadezer]" preserves a corrupt form of the reading in Samuel ומבחרי. At the time of Chronicles MT, Cun was a better known site (Rudolph, 135) and replaced Berothai.

13 רבה; cf. 2 Sam 8:8 4QSam[a]; Samuel MT הרבה. This initial ה arose as a false dittograph of the last letter on the preceding word.

14 Cf. 2 Sam 8:8 LXX, OL, Josephus *Ant.* 7.106; Samuel MT lacks this whole sentence, perhaps due to homoioteleuton when a scribe's eyes skipped from נחשת רבה מאד "very much bronze" at the end of 2 Sam 8:8 MT to ואת כלי הנחשת "and also the vessels of bronze" (see esp. Samuel LXX[L]; partial homoioteleuton), or, less likely, the sentence in Samuel LXX may be a secondary addition to the text of Samuel. Unfortunately, this section of 4QSam[a] has not been preserved. This sentence seems to be presupposed by the initial גם in 2 Sam 8:11//1 Chr 18:11 and hence I count it among the places where Chronicles presupposes a text of Samuel other than MT. McCarter, *II Samuel*, 245; and McKenzie, *Chronicler's Use*, 65, note this plus in parts of the Samuel textual witness but do not suggest it was lost by haplography in Samuel MT. Chronicles itself does not have a plus attested in 2 Sam 8:7 LXX, OL, 4QSam[a], and Josephus that reports that Shishak king of Egypt took the golden shields when he attacked Jerusalem in the days of Rehoboam the son of Solomon. Pisano, *Additions or Omissions*, 47–48, believes that Samuel LXX has been glossed from Chronicles.

15 תעו; cf. 2 Sam 8:9 LXX. Samuel MT תעי "Toi."

16 מלך צובה. "King of Zobah" is not attested in 2 Sam 8:9, but the identical phrase appears in 2 Sam 8:7 LXX. Was this originally a marginal gloss that was entered at two different places in the manuscript tradition?

17 The proper name "Tou/Toi" is lacking in Chronicles and in 2 Sam 8:10 LXX[L]; it is attested in 2 Sam 8:10 MT, LXX.

18 הדורם; Chronicles Syr, Arab. are corrected to 2 Sam 8:10 יורם "Joram."

19 *BHS* suggests tentatively an emendation: בכל for MT וכל. The awkwardness of the sentence results from the loss of ובידו היו "and in his hand were" from the immediately preceding context in 2 Sam 8:10. Piet B. Dirksen, "Chronistic Tendency in 1 Chr 18, 10-11," *Bib* 80 (1999) 269–71, has proposed that the Chronicler intentionally omitted ובידו היו from the *Vorlage* and added וכל so that the following articles used for the temple were not gifts

from Toi/Tou, but items taken as spoil. "And as for all kinds of vessels of gold, silver, and bronze" is construed by him as a *casus pendens*.

20 מאדום; cf. 2 Sam 8:12 LXX, Syr, Samuel MT: מארם "from Aram." McCarter, *II Samuel*, 245, adopts "Edom" as the original reading in Samuel. The difference of Chronicles from Samuel MT, in any case, is based on an alternate reading preserved in texts of Samuel and is not a change introduced by the Chronicler (*pace* Dirksen, "Chronistic Tendency," 270). Dirksen is right in noting that reading "Aram" at this point in Chronicles would duplicate the reference to this country already made in vv. 8 and 11a.

21 This is the spelling of this name throughout Chronicles. In the books of Samuel he is called Abishai. Cf. 1 Chr 11:20.

22 McCarter, *II Samuel*, 246, proposed that the clause ואבישי בן צרויה הכה את אדום ("And Abishai [the spelling used in Samuel] the son of Zeruiah defeated Edom") was once part of the text of 2 Sam 8:13 after ויעש דוד שם בשבו מהכותו את ארם ואבישי בן צרויה הכה את אדום ("David built a monument/made a name for himself when he returned from defeating Aram. And Abishai the son of Zeruiah defeated Edom"). He suggested that this last clause was omitted in Samuel because of homoioteleuton when a scribe's eye skipped from the end of "Aram" to the end of "Edom." Note that Samuel LXX skips from מהכותו ("defeating") to הכה ("defeated") in the reconstructed text (McCarter has an alternate proposal), leaving a text that reads: ". . . when he returned he defeated Edom." Ps 60:2 seems to be based on this reading, although the text has filled in the proper name: "Joab returned and defeated the Edomites in the Valley of Salt." In Chronicles, or its *Vorlage*, a scribe skipped from ויעש to ואבישי, leaving out everything in between. It is possible that Chronicles MT is based on an even larger haplography, omitting everything from ומשלל in 2 Sam 8:12 through את ארם in 2 Sam 8:13. Unfortunately, neither homoioarchton nor homoioteleuton would account for this larger omission. Dirksen, "Chronistic Tendency," 270–71, attributes this latter omission to the changes noted in connection with the *casus pendens* in v. 10. Benzinger, 58–59, proposed that the Chronicler omitted "And David made a name for himself" for some unknown reason and that בשובו was inadvertently miswritten as ואבשי בן, with "Zeruiah" being added to complete the identification. Diana Edelman, "Deuteronomist's David," 75–76, argues that Chronicles preserves the original text and that the author of 2 Samuel 8 substituted the name David because this incident appeared in the segment of his narrative showing David under the blessing. In view of my

text-critical proposal, her conclusion that the Chronicler used a source different from 2 Samuel seems unlikely and unnecessary. Rudolph's conjecture, 135, that we should read ובשבו מצובה "when he returned from Zobah" instead of ואבשי בן צרויה "Abishai the son of Zeruiah" is very unlikely. Cf. *BHK* on 2 Sam 8:13.

23 Ps 60:2 (S): "twelve."

24 וישם באדום נצבים. 2 Sam 8:14 has conflated synonymous variants ("And he put garrisons in Edom; in all Edom he put garrisons"), and Chronicles represents the first half of the conflation. Or Chronicles has dropped the second half of the conflation because of homoioteleuton. LXX in both Chronicles and Samuel has a singular noun, which would presuppose נציב rather than נצבים.

25 ויהיו; cf. 2 Sam 8:14 LXX. 2 Sam 8:14 MT ויהי.

26 A proper noun is lacking in Chronicles and in 2 Sam 8:15 LXX; דוד "David" is attested in Samuel MT.

27 מזכיר. Rudolph, 135, "Sprecher." McCarter, *II Samuel*, 253, "remembrancer."

28 ואחימלך with some Hebrew MSS, LXX, Syr, Vg, Arab., and 2 Sam 8:17; Chronicles MT ואבימלך "Abimelech." Abimelech and Ahimelech are occasionally interchanged in MSS (e.g., 1 Sam 21:2 LXX[B]). Ahimelech as the son of Abiathar is a historically inaccurate genealogical reference, derived from 2 Sam 8:17, and is reflected also in 1 Chr 24:6, where Ahimelech is mentioned as the son of Abiathar, and in 24:3, where Ahimelech is listed as a priest in the time of David. In 15:11 and 27:34, however, both without a parallel in Samuel, Abiathar does function as David's priest. Cross, *Canaanite Myth*, 212–14, proposed that the corruption took place in 2 Sam 8:17, when an original "Zadok the son of Ahitub and Abiathar the son of Abimelech" became "Zadok the son of Ahitub and Abimelech" (homoioarchton). Abiathar was then written in the margin and was mistakenly made the father of Abimelech/Ahimelech instead of his son. Wellhausen proposed that the original reading was "Abiathar the son of Ahimelech the son of Ahitub and Zadok."

29 ושושא; cf. 2 Sam 8:17 LXX[B] ασα and 2 Sam 20:25 σουσα, both apparently reflecting "Shavsha." 2 Sam 8:17 MT ושריה "Seraiah." For a full discussion see McCarter, *II Samuel*, 254.

30 והפלתי. Many Hebrew MSS ועל הפליתי. A literal translation of 2 Sam 8:18 would make Benaiah and the Cherethithes and Pelethites priests, in addition to the sons of David (for the latter see the commentary). But McCarter, *II Samuel*, 254, is probably right in reconstructing על before the Cherethites and ו or ועל before the Pelethites.

31 הראשנים. Instead of "the chief officials," 2 Sam 8:18 MT reads כהנים "priests." McCarter, *II Samuel*, 255, concludes that 1 Chr 18:17 is an interpretive paraphrase of 2 Sam 8:18 by someone who considered it impossible that there should be non-Levitical priests. J. Alberto Soggin, "The Davidic-Solomonic Kingdom," in *Israelite and Judaean History* (ed. J. H. Hayes and J. M. Miller; OTL; Philadelphia: Westminster, 1977) 357, notes the use of the verb היו "were" in 2 Sam 8:18, which suggests to him that this appointment was something unusual, belonging to time past. Gordon J. Wenham, "Were David's Sons Priests?" *ZAW* 87 (1975) 79–82, proposed that the Hebrew behind LXX's reading in Samuel (αὐλάρχαι ["chiefs of the court"]) is סכנים, a title attested in the singular for Shebna in Isa 22:15. This office was entrusted to princes in the early days of the monarchy, and he proposed that David's sons had roughly the same role as Ahishar (1 Kgs 4:6), who was in charge of the palace. ה was miswritten for ס in the Old Hebrew script and then there was a metathesis of the first two letters. Chronicles, therefore, does not represent a taking of offense at the idea of David's sons serving as priests, but only a paraphrase of a word that had become obsolete or rare at his time. Wenham also notes that David's sons are separated from the priests mentioned earlier in the previous verse, with no indication of how the two types of priests relate to one another, and the Chronicler elsewhere does not take offense at David performing ritual acts (cf. 1 Chr 15:27; 16:2-3). In this interpretation כהנים "priests" is an incorrect copying of סכנים "administrators." Rooke, "Kingship as Priesthood," 190, n. 10, doubts whether a controversial reading like "priests" would have replaced the less provocative "administrators." Willi, *Chronik als Auslegung*, 127, believes that this reading in Chronicles is not a result of cultic correctness, but that the Chronicler used 1 Kgs 4:5 to explain the reading from 2 Samuel. In Kings Zabud son of Nathan was priest and king's friend, just as David's sons were interpreted as chief officials in the service of the king. Edelman, "Deuteronomist's David," 76–78, wavers between the opinion of Wenham and the conclusion that the Chronicler replaced the word "priests" because membership in the priesthood in the Second Temple period was limited by lineage and genealogy. McKenzie, *Chronicler's Use*, 65, suggests that Samuel LXX αὐλάρχαι and Chronicles LXX διαδόχοι are attempts by the translators to get around the difficulty of David's sons being priests.

18:1-17

Structure

Between 1 Chronicles 17 (//2 Samuel 7), containing the oracle of Nathan about the temple and the Davidic dynasty and David's subsequent prayer, and 1 Chronicles 21 (//2 Samuel 24), reporting David's purchase of the threshing floor of Ornan the Jebusite as the location of the future temple, the Chronicler inserted materials from 2 Samuel dealing with David's wars. 1 Chr 18:1-17 is parallel to 2 Sam 8:1-18; 1 Chr 19:1—20:3 is parallel to 2 Sam 10:1—11:1a, 12:26, 30, 31; and 1 Chr 20:4-8 is parallel to 2 Sam 21:18-22.[1] Each of these units begins in the same way: ויהי אחרי כן ("It happened after this"), and fulfills the promise made in 1 Chr 17:10 that Yahweh would subdue all of David's enemies.[2] These wars, including the exploits of David's mighty men in 20:4-8,[3] also provide evidence for why David was barred from building the temple as someone who had shed much blood (22:8; 28:3). The word "hand" serves as a frame around the whole unit: in 18:1 we read that David "took Gath and its daughter villages *from the hand of* the Philistines," and in 20:8 that the Philistines "fell *by the hand of* David and *by the hand of* his servants." The Chronicler omitted many passages from this portion of 2 Samuel, which is part of the Succession Narrative (2 Samuel 9–20; 1 Kings 1–2). The omissions include a number of famous stories, such as David's affair with Bathsheba and his murder of her husband Uriah (2 Sam 11:2—12:25), his son Amnon's rape of Tamar, Absalom's murder of Amnon, the revolt and eventual death of Absalom (2 Samuel 13–19), the revolt of Sheba (2 Samuel 20), and the execution of the house of Saul (2 Sam 21:1-14).[4] Whether these omissions resulted from a single-minded focus on David's military activities to the exclusion of all other materials, a tendency not to report events from the private lives of his characters (Japhet, 343), or other reasons,[5] the net effect is to present a much more positive image of David. The Chronicler also omitted David's controversial military and political actions during the reign of Saul (1 Samuel 16–30; 2 Sam 1:1—4:12) as well as the account of Solomon's wives who led him to apostasy (1 Kings 11). Nevertheless, the Chronicler still does report David's sin in regard to the census (1 Chronicles 21//2 Samuel 24), and so an effort to clean up the image of David is not the sole or perhaps even the primary reason for these omissions from 2 Samuel.

David's victories in chap. 18 extend to all points of the compass: the Philistines on the west (v. 1), Moab in the east (v. 2), Hadadezer and the Arameans of Damascus in the north and northeast (vv. 3-8), and Edom in the southeast (vv. 12-13). Tou of Hamath in the far north also made peace with David and congratulated him for defeating Hadadezer (vv. 9-10). A summary verse (18:11) also mentions booty David garnered from victories over Edom, Moab, and the Philistines, and over the Ammonites and Amalek, though the actual battles in the latter two cases are not reported in this chapter. These military gains take place in wide stretches of the ideal limits of the Holy Land, from the Shihor in Egypt to

---

1. The Chronicler omitted 2 Sam 21:15-17, which reports that David was exhausted by his battles and that his men asked him not to engage in battles anymore. As a result of this omission, the number "four," referring to the number of "votaries to the Rapha-in-Gath," is omitted from 1 Chr 20:8, since there are only three such votaries in the Chronicler's telling.

2. As a counterpart to this theme are those passages that identify Solomon, David's son and successor, as a man of peace and promise him peace on every side (1 Chr 22:9-10, 18-19).

3. Cf. the similar material in 1 Chr 11:11-41a//2 Sam 23:8-39.

4. For a complete list of the parallels between 1 Chr 17:1—20:8 and 2 Sam 7:1—21:22, see Ralph W.

Klein, "Narrative Texts: Chronicles, Ezra, and Nehemiah," in *The Blackwell Companion to the Hebrew Bible* (ed. L. G. Perdue; Oxford: Blackwell, 2001) 387–88.

5. Tomotoshi Sugimoto, "Chronicles as Independent Literature," *JSOT* 55 (1992) 61–74, notes that incidents dealing with Saul, such as 2 Sam 9:1-13 and 21:1-14, were omitted not only because they report conflict with Saul, but also and even primarily because the Chronicler decided to restrict his account of Saul to his death, which is a type of the fate that will befall all those who do not seek Yahweh. The affair with Bathsheba, the account of Absalom, and Sheba's revolt may have been omitted so that the Chronicler could relate the temple building activities in the reigns of David and Solomon

Lebo-hamath (13:5). Some students of 2 Samuel 8 have proposed that at least some of the battles in that chapter are chronologically subsequent to the battles in 2 Sam 10:1–11:1, since the defeat of Hadadezer is more extensive in chap. 8.[6]

In his recent book on David,[7] Baruch Halpern has identified the genre of 2 Samuel 8 as a "display inscription," which is organized by topic or geography rather than by chronological sequence. He argues that such inscriptions often make modest claims at an *explicit* level, but imply much greater achievements to the naive reader.[8] He seeks to find the minimum achievements of David that would justify the assertions in the text. The net effect is that Halpern believes that historically David never campaigned north of Dan and therefore did not extend his frontier anywhere near the Euphrates River. While I find the identification of this chapter as a display inscription doubtful or at least quite hypothetical and believe that McCarter is on safer ground in classifying it as a catalogue of Davidic victories,[9] Halpern may well be right that at least in 2 Samuel the victories explicitly claimed are much more modest than often understood. The specifics of Halpern's observations about the text will be noted in the commentary on individual verses. As Halpern himself observes, the Chronicler often affirms the greater extent of David's victories, only implied in 2 Samuel 8, with the result that Halpern's proposal is more relevant to students of the books of Samuel and of the history of David than for the meaning of Chronicles.

1 Chronicles 18 may be outlined as follows:

I. 18:1-6. David's victories over the Philistines (v. 1), Moab (v. 2), and Hadadezer of Zobah and his Aramean allies (vv. 3-6)
II. 18:7-8. Spoil taken from Hadadezer and his men and its use for the temple
III. 18:9-13. Peace delegation from Tou king of Hamath and defeat of the Edomites
IV. 18:14-17. Officials in David's government

Detailed Commentary

18:1-6. David's Victories over the Philistines, Moab, and Hadadezer and His Allies

■ **1** *David defeated the Philistines:* The Chronicler had earlier reported two battles of David with the Philistines at Baal-perazim in which he had emerged victorious (1 Chr 14:8-16//2 Sam 5:17-25). The verb נכה ("defeat") is used eleven times in chaps. 18–20 and forms a steady drumbeat announcing David's victories in each of the three units into which the text is divided (18:1-17 [vv. 1, 2, 3, 5, 9, 10, 12]; 19:1–20:3 [20:1]; and 20:4-8 [vv. 4, 5, 7]). Halpern notes that the text, particularly in 2 Samuel, refers to the "Philistines" in general but does not explicitly claim victory over *all* the Philistines. He also notes that the Philistines consisted of a number of separate city-state entities and were not a single nation.[10] McCarter believes that the *Vorlage* of 18:1 in its context, that is, in 2 Sam 8:1, refers to a victory or a series of victories over the Philistines subsequent to 2 Sam 5:25.

much more closely. By omitting the Bathsheba-Uriah incident, the unit from 1 Chr 18:10–20:8 reports only the victories of David that fulfill 17:10 ("I will subdue all your enemies") and that are David's reward for seeking the ark.

6   See McCarter, *II Samuel*, 247, 252. McCarter proposes that chronologically the events of 8:3-5 fit between 2 Sam 10:19 and 11:1.

7   Halpern, *David's Secret Demons*. His discussion of 2 Samuel 8 extends from 107 to 226.

8   Ibid., 126–32. Because of its different genre, Halpern believes that 2 Samuel 8 need not be harmonized chronologically with 2 Samuel 10. A somewhat similar proposal is put forward by Robert M. Good, "2 Samuel 8," *TynBul* 52 (2001) 129–38. He identifies the genre of the chapter as a royal

encomium as apology. He notes a similar repetitive mentioning of the king's name in the Behistun inscription and observes that the latter was not only preserved on stone but circulated on papyrus. Good takes the assertions in the text more at face value than Halpern does.

9   *II Samuel*, 251. McCarter also identifies it as a Deuteronomistic composition (for him = late 7th century), whereas Halpern and Good date it *early* in the reign of David himself.

10   *David's Secret Demons*, 144–59.

and subdued them: There are only two other occurrences of the verb כנע in 1 Chronicles. In 17:10 God promised to subdue all of David's enemies, and in 20:4 we learn that the Philistines were subdued. This is the only one of the three passages where the verb is also found in the *Vorlage*. It functions here as a fulfillment of 17:10.

Gath and its daughter villages: The exact location of Gath is unknown, although Tell es-Safi (MR 135123) is frequently proposed and seems to have been confirmed by the present excavation at this site.[11] This site is about 6 miles south of Tel Miqne/Ekron (MR 136131). Lawrence Stager earlier suggested a location further to the south at Tel Haror, on the Wadi Besor.[12] The mention of Gath here may be no more than the Chronicler's valiant attempt to make sense of a difficult reading in his *Vorlage* (see textual note 1), and it would represent a significant extension of David's hegemony to the west that seems improbable historically.[13] Halpern sets David's western border at the approaches to Gezer (MR 142140), considerably north and east of Gath.[14] According to 1 Kgs 9:16, Gezer itself was first presented to David's successor Solomon by a pharaoh as a dowry for his daughter. Early in the reign of Solomon we hear of a Philistine king still reigning in Gath by the name of Achish (1 Kgs 2:39-40), and Solomon's borders did not include the land of the Philistines even in a passage that

has a quite glorified image of his reign (1 Kgs 5:1 [4:21]).

■ **2** *David also defeated Moab, and the Moabites became tribute-bearing slaves to David:* This entire verse is taken from 2 Sam 8:2, although Chronicles omits the central part of that verse, which reports that David made the Moabites lie down in rows and that he executed two rows of these Moabites and spared one row. Perhaps the Chronicler did not want to mention David's participation in this "war crime."[15] There is no reason to think the report of his severe measures against Moab dropped out through textual corruption (contra Japhet, 346). Halpern notes that no major settlements were taken by David in Moab and that the tribute may have been a one-time occurrence.[16] Earlier in his career, according to the Deuteronomistic History, David had good relationships with Moab. During the time when he was fleeing from Saul, David settled his father and mother in Moab for safekeeping (1 Sam 22:3-4; not included in Chronicles). The Moabite woman Ruth was also his great-grandmother (Ruth 4:18-22). The Moabites in any case are the first of the nations in this chapter to become vassals and to send tribute to David. Nations that send tribute to Israel or its kings are a sign of God's blessing in Chronicles (1 Chr 18:6; 2 Chr 17:5 and 11 [tribute to Jehoshaphat from Judah and the Philistines, respectively]; 26:8 [tribute from Uzziah from the Ammonites]).[17] In the days of Mesha,

---

11 See the Web site of the current excavation of this site at http://faculty.biu.ac.il/~maeira.

12 Lawrence E. Stager, "The Impact of the Sea Peoples in Canaan (1185–1050 BCE)," in *The Archaeology of Society in the Holy Land* (ed. T. E. Levy: New York: Facts on File, 1995) 342–43. For a critique see William M. Schniedewind, "The Geopolitical History of Philistine Gath," *BASOR* 309 (1998) 69–77; and Halpern, *David's Secret Demons,* 146. For other proposed locations for Gath see Joe D. Seger, "Gath," *ABD* 2:908–9.

13 Halpern, *David's Secret Demons,* 145, suggests that Metheg-ammah may refer to booty or even be a Philistine term, but it is not a reference to a city and definitely not to Gath.

14 *David's Secret Demons,* 150.

15 Curtis and Madsen, 233, thought this incident might have been omitted because it conflicted with the kindness shown David by the king of Moab in 1 Sam 22:3-4. They argued that the author of 2 Samuel 8 would not have known of that incident

(basing their opinion on Smith's ICC commentary on the books of Samuel), but the Chronicler did. McKenzie, *Chronicler's Use,* 64, notes that the Chronicler does mention David's shedding of blood in 1 Chr 22:8; 28:3, and that therefore this minus is a result of haplography, but he admits that "the mechanism for haplography is inexact." Good, "2 Samuel 8," 138, n. 34, thinks that the Samuel account presents David's treatment of Moab as especially magnanimous since David spared one line out of three!

16 *David's Secret Demons,* 160–63.

17 2 Chr 28:21 and 36:3 note tribute demanded from Israel by foreign powers (Assyria and Egypt, respectively).

Moab's tribute consisted of one hundred thousand lambs and wool of one hundred thousand rams (2 Kgs 3:4).

■ **3** *David defeated Hadadezer king of Zobah toward Hamath:* As a leading Aramean king, Hadadezer was a rival with David in attempting to control trade routes that ran through Syria-Palestine. Zobah was the leading Aramean state at the time of David[18] and was located between Hamath[19] (MR 312503) and the northern border of Israel at Dan (MR 211294), on the eastern slope of the Anti-Lebanon mountain range, and it extended far to the east, north of Damascus (MR 273324). In the *Vorlage,* 2 Sam 8:3, Zobah is called "the son of Rehob," which led Malamat to propose that Hadadezer hailed from the country of Rehob in the southern Beqaʿ, north of Dan at the foot of Mount Hermon. Later, according to Malamat, Hadadezer became king of Zobah, and he united the two countries in ways that resembled David's unification of Judah and Israel in a personal union.[20] The two countries of Beth-rehob and Zobah each provided one contingent of soldiers in 2 Sam 10:6 (1 Chr 19:6-7 has a different text). Halpern, on the other hand, understands "Rehob" in 2 Sam 8:3 to be the name of a king from the land of Zobah who was also Hadadezer's physical father.[21] Hamath pointed with a *hê* directive is attested in Chronicles but not in the *Vorlage* in 2 Sam 8:3. Hamath

is located on the Orontes River, at modern Ḥam? (MR 312503), north of the country of Zobah and about 115 miles north of Damascus (MR 272324). According to Chronicles, Hadadezer controlled a vast area extending well to the north, toward Hamath on the Orontes, making his defeat by David all the more remarkable. Tou, mentioned in v. 9 below, was apparently not only Hadadezer's enemy but probably a rebellious vassal as well.[22]

A number of scholars (Ackroyd, Soggin, and Wellhausen) understand the battle in 2 Sam 8:3-5 (//1 Chr 18:3-5) as a parallel account of the battle also reported in 2 Sam 10:16-19 (//1 Chr 19:16-19). Others (Bright, McCarter, Noth, and Pitard) believe that the battle in 2 Sam 8:3-5 is chronologically later than 2 Samuel 10, since in 2 Samuel 8 Hadadezer is soundly defeated while in 2 Samuel 10 he still acts as a leader of an independent nation.[23] In the aftermath of the battle in 1 Chr 18:3-5// 2 Sam 8:3-5, David received tribute from Hadadezer and later captured the Ammonite capital (1 Chr 20:2-3// 2 Samuel 11–12). The battles reported with the Ammonites and Arameans in 1 Chr 19:6-15 and 16-19//2 Sam 10:6-15 and 15-19 may reflect a two-stage engagement or totally separate wars.[24]

when he went to set up[25] his monument on the river Euphrates: As explained in textual note 5, the antecedent

18   Zobah is also mentioned during the reign of Saul (1 Sam 14:47), but Wayne T. Pitard, *Ancient Damascus* (Winona Lake, IN: Eisenbrauns, 1987) 90, doubts the reliability of this verse. Pitard provides a map showing the relationship of Aram Zobah, Damascus, and Israel on p. 82. See also his article "Zobah," *ABD* 6:1108.

19   In vv. 9-10 the king of Hamath is clearly not under the control of Hadadezer and thanks David for attacking Hadadezer.

20   Abraham Malamat, "Aspects of the Foreign Policies of David and Solomon," *JNES* 22 (1963) 1–6. Beth-rehob is mentioned in Judg 18:28 in connection with the northern migration of the Danites. Nadav Naʾaman, "Hazael of ʿAmqi and Hadadezer of Beth-rehob," *UF* 27 (1995) 381–94, also understands Rehob as Hadadezer's country of origin rather than as his biological father. As Halpern has pointed out, *David's Secret Demons,* 170–71, Naʾaman errs in identifying the country of ʿAmqi with Beth-rehob. This undercuts Naʾaman's argument that Hazael of Damascus was a descendant of Baasha of Beth-rehob

mentioned in Shalmaneser III's account of the battle of Qarqar in 853 BCE.

21   *David's Secret Demons,* 183.

22   According to 2 Chr 8:3 (without *Vorlage*), Solomon went to Hamath of Zobah and captured it. This probably rests on an inference drawn from the present passage about what territory the Israelite kings controlled in Syria. See Halpern, *David's Secret Demons,* 178.

23   See Pitard, *Ancient Damascus,* 93; and John Bright, *A History of Israel* (3d ed.; Philadelphia: Westminster, 1981) 202–5. While Bright places 2 Samuel 8 after 2 Samuel 10, he is unsure whether 2 Samuel belongs before or after the battles in Transjordan.

24   See Randall C. Bailey, "Hadadezer," *ABD* 3:12–13.

25   In the Chronicler's substitution of להציב for להשיב in 2 Sam 8:3, Kalimi, "Paranomasia," 34–35, finds a pun on the word צובה "Zobah." Japhet, "Interchanges," 41, suggests that Chronicles has preserved the original reading and that Samuel is the result of textual corruption.

of the pronoun "he" is probably David, since it would not make geographical sense for Hadadezer to confront David at the Euphrates.[26] Many historians today doubt whether David's power extended that far north. In the world of the text, David was eager to stake out the widest possible claim in Aramean territory.[27] The word "Euphrates" was already added in some texts of Samuel (see textual note 6) and was found by the Chronicler in his *Vorlage*. Only in Chronicles and in Ezra 6:22 does David's empire reach explicitly to the Euphrates. The use of יד for "monument" also occurs at 1 Sam 15:12, 2 Sam 18:18, and Isa 56:5.[28]

■ **4** *David captured from him one thousand chariots and seven thousand cavalry, and twenty thousand infantry:* David took twenty-seven thousand prisoners of war in addition to the capture of chariots and horses, but the text does not tell us what David did with the human prisoners. David did hamstring all but one hundred of the horses that came with the chariots, presumably because this instrument of warfare had not yet been incorporated into his army, as it would be under Solomon (1 Kgs 5:6 [4:26]).[29] The Chronicler presumably would have been happy that David's destruction of most of the horses would have enabled David to escape the Deuteronomic polemic against kings' acquiring horses (Deut 17:16). The numbers of those captured, while exceedingly high, and higher than those in Samuel MT, had been increased already in at least one version of Samuel (see textual note 7). In the battle with the Arameans reported at 1 Chr 19:18//2 Sam 10:18, David killed seven thousand charioteers[30] and forty thousand cavalry.

■ **5** *When the Arameans of Damascus came to help Hadadezer:* Damascus, always spelled דרמשק instead of דמשק in Chronicles,[31] did not emerge as a significant power until Rezon the son of Eliada, a servant of Hadadezer, captured it after fleeing from his master Hadadezer, during the reign of Solomon (1 Kgs 11:23-24, a passage not included in Chronicles) and was made king of Damascus. The exact political relationship of these earlier Damascene Arameans to Hadadezer is not specified, but it was probably either that of an ally or a vassal state. They attacked David from a second front, much as the Arameans in 1 Chr 19:9-15.[32] They paid for their intrusion into this war with high, I would say exaggerated, casualties: David allegedly killed twenty-two thousand Arameans. The numbers in 2 Sam 8:5 are the same.

■ **6** *David put garrisons in Aram Damascus:* The word נציב can mean "governor" or "prefect" in the singular and "garrisons" in the plural.[33] If the singular noun attested in the LXX texts of Samuel and Chronicles were preferable, David installed a governor in Damascus; if we follow the plural in MT, David stationed troops there. In any case the text claims that Aram Damascus became a fully occupied territory, part of the empire of David, and that it, like the Moabites in v. 2, paid tribute to David. Halpern notes that the text does not claim that Damascus itself was captured. He believes that David occupied some of the territory of Aram Damascus, perhaps ceded to David by Rezon of Damascus in order to secure his own dominance in Damascus.[34]

Yahweh gave victory to David wherever he went: The

---

26   Na'aman, "Hazael of 'Amqi," 390, makes Hadadezer the antecedent of "he."

27   Halpern, *David's Secret Demons,* 189, 196, has proposed that historically the river where David set up his monument was the Jordan.

28   A monument may also be referred to by the word שם "name" in 2 Sam 8:13, a reading not preserved in Chronicles (see textual note 22). Cf. McCarter, *II Samuel,* 245–46; and Halpern, *David's Secret Demons,* 195–96.

29   Cf. Josh 11:6, 9. At Yahweh's command Joshua also hamstrung captured horses.

30   The number in Chronicles is supported by Josephus *Ant.* 7.128. 2 Sam 8:18 MT and LXX read seven hundred. For fuller discussion see textual note 31 in the next chapter.

31   1 Chr 18:6; 2 Chr 16:2; 24:23; 28:5, 23. See Kutscher, *Language,* 3–4; Willi, *Chronik als Auslegung,* 82; *HALOT* 1:232.

32   Indeed, Halpern, *David's Secret Demons,* 187–94, would insist that the battle against this Aramean coalition is really what is behind the report of the battle in 2 Sam 8:5. That is, a group of Aramean kingdoms were allied with Ammon when it fought with David in northern Transjordan.

33   See *HALOT* 2:716–17.

34   *David's Secret Demons,* 197–98.

author attributes David's success to divine assistance and with this summary statement brings this section to a fitting conclusion (see also v. 13 for the same God-given victory; cf. 1 Chr 11:14; 2 Chr 32:22).[35]

18:7-8. Spoil Taken from Hadadezer and His Men and Its Use for the Temple

■ **7** *David took the golden bow cases:* The word שלט ("bow case") is obscure and conventionally translated as "shields" (*NRSV*; BDB, 1020). R. Borger studied an inscription in the tomb of Aspathines, a dignitary of Darius I, in which a bow case carried by Aspathines is represented by the Babylonian word *šaltu*, a loanword from Aramaic.[36] The traditional understanding of the word as "shields" may have led a supplementer to add a sentence to the end of the *Vorlage* in 2 Sam 8:7 that is based on Shishak's taking of the gold shields (מגן) that had been made by Solomon (1 Kgs 14:26): "Shishak king of Egypt took them [= the shields/bow cases] when he went up to Jerusalem in the days of Rehoboam the son of Solomon." The sentence is attested in 4QSam[a], LXX, OL, and Josephus, but not in Samuel MT (see textual note 14).

■ **8** *From Tibhath and from Cun . . . David took very much bronze:* The name Tibhath may be a corruption of Tebah (see textual note 11). According to Gen 22:24, Tebah was a son of Nahor, the brother of Abraham, and his concubine Reumah, and he was the eponymous ancestor of an Aramaic tribe and the founder of Tebah/Tibhath. His city is mentioned in several Egyptian documents, including the Amarna Letters (*ṭubiḫi*),[37] and was located

in the Beqaʻ, south of modern Ḥoms, though its exact location is unknown.[38] Cun (probably modern Râs Baʻalbek) is attested in MT, and Berothai (probably modern Bereitan, a few miles south of Râs Baʻalbek)[39] is presupposed by the translation in Chronicles LXX. Tebah, Berothai, and Cun were probably leading cities in the kingdom of Zobah. From both of these cities David seized additional spoils.

With it Solomon made the bronze sea and the pillars and also the vessels of bronze: This sentence, which is lacking in 2 Sam 8:8 MT, is one of the few additions by the Chronicler in 18:1—20:3. My first inclination would be to say that the Chronicler added this sentence to show another way in which David made preparations for the temple before he died. This is indeed how the sentence functions here.[40] But since it appears in LXX, OL, and Josephus in the text of Samuel, it is more appropriate to say that this idea had occurred to someone who wrote or transmitted the book of Samuel, even though it was lost in Sam MT (see textual note 14). Whether original to Samuel or added secondarily, in any case it was a reading in Samuel prior to the composition of Chronicles.[41]

18:9-13. Peace Delegation from Tou King of Hamath and Defeat of the Edomites

■ **9** *Tou the king of Hamath:* This king, with a Hurrian name,[42] was a long-time enemy of Hadadezer (v. 10) and possibly also his vassal (if it is correct to make Hamath part of a hyphenated country name in v. 3 [see textual note 4]). According to vv. 9-10, Tou decided to switch sides and wager his future on David.[43] This league with

35   A similar statement appears in 2 Sam 3:18, a passage not included in Chronicles.

36   R. Borger, "Die Waffenträger des Königs Darius," *VT* 22 (1972) 385–98; *HALOT* 4:1522.

37   EA 179:15, 24, 26, 28.

38   Edwin C. Hostetter, "Tibhath," *ABD* 6:343. See also Halpern, *David's Secret Demons*, 175, n. 21.

39   Cf. Halpern, *David's Secret Demons*, 175, n. 21; and McCarter, *II Samuel*, 150. Berothai is probably the same as Berothah in Ezek 47:16. Mitchell Dahood, "Philological Observations on Five Biblical Texts," *Bib* 63 (1982) 390, finds both names listed in a gazetteer from Ebla.

40   For a description of the bronze furnishings see the discussion at 2 Chr 4:1-6, 11-18.

41   Curtis and Madsen, 234, identified it as an addition

by the Chronicler that had made its way into Samuel LXX. Pisano, *Additions or Omissions*, 47–48, also argues that this sentence arose in Chronicles and was later incorporated into the text of Samuel.

42   McCarter, *II Samuel*, 250.

43   Halpern, *David's Secret Demons*, 195, thinks it unlikely that Hamath submitted to David and interprets the gifts from Hamath as part of an alliance between Israel and Hamath against Zobah.

Hamath makes David's expansion to the Euphrates more geographically plausible even if it seems historically unlikely.

■ **10a** *he sent Hadoram his son to King David:* This incident may imply the creation of a parity treaty between Hamath and Israel ("to ask him for peace and to congratulate him").[44] The importance of this diplomatic initiative undertaken by Tou is shown by the fact that he chose his own son to head it. Hadoram's name means something like "Hadad is exalted," but the same person is called Joram in 2 Sam 8:10, with the meaning "Yahweh is exalted." A scribal error in Samuel MT is a possibility,[45] but it is also possible that Tou's son took a Yahwistic name in order to curry the favor of David, or even that there were Yahweh worshipers in Hamath at that time.[46] However that may be, this Yahwistic name is not attested in the Hebrew text of Chronicles.

■ **10b-11** *And as for all kinds of vessels of gold, silver, and bronze, these also King David dedicated to Yahweh:* "These also" (גם אתם) refers back to the sentence in v. 8, which describes Solomon's manufacture of cultic vessels from the captured bronze. The text of Chronicles is quite different from the *Vorlage,* which mentioned tribute or gifts from Tou (the vessels were in his hand; see textual note 19), and the various vessels now refer to spoils that David had taken from a number of nations. David now dedicated these spoils for cultic use. Later Solomon brought into the temple the things his father David had dedicated (קדשי דויד אביו, 2 Chr 5:1//1 Kgs 7:51).

with silver and gold that he had carried off from all the nations: The Chronicler replaced the word "dedicated"

(הקדיש) from his *Vorlage* with "carried off" (נשא). This makes a clear distinction (not observed in Samuel) between the taking of spoils in war (v. 11aβ) and their subsequent dedication to the Deity (v. 11aα). This is related to the change (recorded in textual note 19) by which the Chronicler made the vessels of gold, silver, and bronze into things taken by David as the spoils of war and not items contributed to the temple by a foreign king. Of the five nations enumerated in this verse (// 2 Sam 8:12), Moab and the Philistines have already been mentioned in this chapter (vv. 1-2), and the defeat of Edom will be discussed in the next two verses, while the defeat of the Ammonites will be described in chap. 19. There is no other evidence for David fighting Amalek while he was king, although he did wage war against the Amalekites, according to the Deuteronomistic History, in the final days of his struggle with Saul, when he was in the service of Achish king of Gath (1 Samuel 30).[47] Chronicles does not include a phrase from the end of 2 Sam 8:12, "and from the spoil of Hadadezer son of Rehob king of Zobah." If the Chronicler did not omit this phrase, it may have been added secondarily to the text of Samuel (Japhet, 350), or it may be part of a larger haplography in Chronicles (see textual note 22).

■ **12** *Abshai the son of Zeruiah defeated Edom:* Zeruiah was the sister of David and mother of three men who served David in a military capacity: Joab, Abshai, and Asahel. Abshai's foray against the Edomites would have been undertaken on behalf of David, although one has to infer this in the truncated text of Chronicles. If this sentence about Abshai was once part of a longer reading in

44   Brian Peckham, "Israel and Phoenicia," in *Magnalia Dei: The Mighty Acts of God* (FS G. E. Wright; ed. F. M. Cross, W. E. Lemke, and P. D. Miller Jr.; Garden City, NY: Doubleday, 1976) 231, 243, n. 78.

45   Codex Vaticanus reads Ιεδδουραν in Kings and Ιδουρααμ in Chronicles. Malamat, "Aspects of Foreign Policies," 6; and McCarter, *II Samuel,* 245, take the Greek readings as corrupt mixtures of the two names. They could also be construed as showing that Hebrew texts of both Kings and Chronicles once read Hadoram. Cf. Driver, *Notes,* 282. Halpern, *David's Secret Demons,* 194–95, n. 12, observes that an original הדרם would easily have become ידרם in Paleo-Hebrew script. A later scribe replaced ה with ו and so created the name Joram.

46   Stephanie Dalley, "Yahweh in Hamath in the 8th

Century BC: Cuneiform Material and Historical Deductions," *VT* 40 (1990) 21–32, points to cuneiform evidence for two Yahwistic names, Azri-Yau and Yau-bi'di, in Hatarikka/Hazrak and Hamath, respectively, in the second half of the 8th century.

47   This verse may supply a stereotypical list of enemy nations. According to 1 Sam 14:47, Saul also fought against all his enemies on every side—against Moab, against the Ammonites, against Edom, against the kings of Zobah, and against the Philistines.

the book of Samuel (see textual note 22), it would have been balanced by a sentence speaking of David's own defeat of the Arameans. Joab, however, is also associated with the defeat of the Edomites in 1 Kgs 11:15-16 and in Ps 60:1-2 (S). Given the uncertainty of the textual reading, we are best advised not to come to a final decision on who led the attack on the Edomites during the reign of David.

in the Valley of Salt: The exact location of this valley is unknown, but since the opponent was Edom, it should be sought south and east of the Dead Sea. King Amaziah later fought a battle in this valley as well (2 Chr 25:11).

■ **13** *He put garrisons in Edom:* The Chronicler repeats the claim he found in Samuel that Edom became part of the Davidic empire.

and all the Edomites became slaves to David: Earlier the Moabites (v. 2) and the Arameans (v. 6) had become slaves of David. Nothing is said in this case about these slaves bringing tribute.

and Yahweh gave David victory wherever he went: This sentence, as in v. 6, brings a unit to its end and emphasizes a primary theme in this chapter.

18:14-17. Officials in David's Government

This is a copy of one of two lists in 2 Samuel that name the officers of David (2 Sam 8:15-18).[48] The other, in 2 Sam 20:23-26, was not included in Chronicles. This second list is usually interpreted as coming from a later period in David's reign since it includes an official in charge of the forced labor (2 Sam 20:24).[49] Listing the officers right after the battle account lends a sense of stability to the reign of David.

■ **14** *he executed justice and righteousness for all his people:* Perhaps the closest parallel in a royal context comes in Jeremiah, where the prophet praises Josiah for these

traits, which were lacking in Jehoiakim (22:15).[50] Jeremiah also ascribes these traits to the coming righteous Branch (23:5).

■ **15** *Joab the son of Zeruiah was over the army:* Joab achieved this rank because of his heroism in the conquest of Jerusalem (1 Chr 11:6), and he remained David's general in Chronicles throughout David's reign. In 2 Samuel, after the revolt of Absalom, he was replaced for a time by Amasa (2 Sam 19:13). Joab was executed at the command of Solomon and with the advice of David, after he supported Adonijah in his attempt to take over the kingdom as David lay on his deathbed (1 Kgs 2:5-6, 22-35, not included in Chronicles). The last reference to him in Chronicles is 1 Chr 27:34.

Jehoshaphat the son of Ahilud was recorder: This office has been compared to that of the *whmw* (speaker) in Egyptian sources who proclaimed royal decrees and made reports to the king.[51] He continued to serve into the reign of Solomon (1 Kgs 4:3, without a parallel in Chronicles). The recorder is mentioned again in Chronicles only in 2 Chr 34:8 during the reign of Josiah.

■ **16** *Zadok the son of Ahitub and Ahimelech the son of Abiathar were priests:* The faulty genealogy of Abiathar (see textual note 28) is also reflected in 1 Chr 24:3, 6, where Ahimelech is identified as one of David's priests and the son of Abiathar. Historically, Abiathar was the only priest who escaped when Saul massacred the priests of Nob (1 Sam 22:11-23), and both he and Zadok served as priests throughout David's reign (see 1 Chr 15:11). Solomon banished him to Anathoth after he had sided with the supporters of Adonijah in an attempt to install this son of David as David's successor instead of Solomon (1 Kgs 2:27, not included in Chronicles).

---

48   A list of the sons, daughters, wife, and single officer of Saul is given in 1 Sam 14:49-50.

49   Mettinger, *Solomonic State Officials*, 8, cites an ingenious proposal of Joachim Begrich that the list was once presented in two columns that were meant to be read across: (1) Joab, (2) Shavsha, (3) Jehoshaphat, (4) Benaiah, (5) Zadok and Ahimelech, (6) David's sons. A copyist read down the first column and then down the second, leading to the present order: 1-3-5 and 2-4-6. One advantage of this proposal is that it brings the two groups of priests together in the fifth and sixth positions. De

Vries, 162, detects a chiasm in this list, but he is forced to ignore the two sons of David to make the chiasm work.

50   See Keith W. Whitelam, *The Just King* (JSOTSup 12; Sheffield: JSOT Press, 1979) 17–37.

51   Mettinger, *Solomonic State Officials*, 52–62.

Shavsha was secretary: In Egypt the holder of this office was the personal secretary of the pharaoh and his chief of staff.[52]

■ **17** *Benaiah the son of Jehoiada was over the Cherethites and the Pelethites*: Benaiah was in charge of this group of mercenaries loyal to King David (2 Sam 15:18; 20:7, 23; 1 Chr 11:24). Under Solomon Benaiah replaced Joab as the commander of the army after he had executed Joab on Solomon's orders (1 Kgs 2:34-35). The Cherethites and Pelethites backed Solomon during Adonijah's unsuccessful coup attempt (1 Kgs 1:38, 44). The Cherethites possibly hailed originally from Crete, but a region near David's dwelling at Ziklag is called the Negeb of the Cherethites (1 Sam 30:14), and they may have been recruited into David's service during his residence at Ziklag. The identity of the Pelethites is unknown.[53] Neither group is mentioned elsewhere in Chronicles.

David's sons were the chief officials by the side of the king: As explained in textual note 31, the "office" (הראשנים) assigned to these princes is probably the Chronicler's paraphrase of the word for "administrators" (סכנים), which he did not understand and/or which had become obsolete. Some commentators, however, believe that the Chronicler took offense at the notion that the king's sons, who were not of the house of Aaron, would serve as priests. But the Chronicler elsewhere assigns priestly functions to David and Solomon without criticism.[54]

Conclusion

The narratives in this chapter, as well as 1 Chr 19:1–20:8, describe a number of victorious battles David fought against surrounding nations—Philistines, Moab, Hadadezer of Zobah and his Aramean allies, Edom, Ammon, and Amalek. The king of Hamath also made peace with David and congratulated him for defeating Hadadezer. These battles imply the blessing David was under because he had successfully brought the ark to Jerusalem (chaps. 13–16) and because God had promised to establish his dynasty (chap. 17).

David took much booty in these battles, and the Chronicler notes that booty from these encounters was used by Solomon to make various items for the temple (v. 8) or was dedicated to Yahweh by David himself (vv. 10-11). Yahweh's support of David is underscored in vv. 6 and 13 by this conclusion: "Yahweh gave victory to David wherever he went."

The final paragraph of the chapter (vv. 14-17) emphasizes that David ruled over "all Israel," that he executed justice and righteousness for the people, and that his rule was stable because of the officials in his administration.

---

52 See Mettinger, *Solomonic State Officials*, 35–51. Aelred Cody, "Le titre égyptien et le nom propre du scribe de David," *RB* 71 (1965) 387, believes that this name is a corruption of an Egyptian title, consisting of the words "scribe" and "letter."

53 Various possibilities are surveyed by Carl S. Ehrlich, "Pelethites," *ABD* 5:219.

54 In 1 Chr 15:27 David was clothed with fine linen and wore a linen ephod; in 16:2-3 David offered burnt offerings and offerings of well-being; in 16:43 David went home to bless his household. According to 21:26 David built an altar to the Lord on the threshing floor of Ornan and presented burnt offerings and offerings of well-being. In 2 Chr 6:3, 13 Solomon turned and blessed the assembly, stood on a bronze platform, and uttered a public prayer from that position.

19:1/ It[1] happened after this that Nahash[2] king of the Ammonites died, and[3] his son ruled in his stead. 2/ David said, "I will deal loyally with Hanun the son of Nahash, for[4] his father dealt loyally with me." David sent messengers[5] to comfort him concerning[6] his father, and the servants of David came to[7] the land of the Ammonites to Hanun, to comfort him. 3/ And the officials of the Ammonites said to Hanun,[8] "Do you think that David is honoring your father because he has sent people to offer comfort to you? Is it not for the sake of exploring[9] and looking over[10] and spying out the land that these servants of David have come to you?" 4/ Hanun then took the servants of David and shaved them, and he cut their garments in half up to their hips and sent them away. 5/ They went[11] and told David about the men,[12] and he sent [messengers] to meet them for the men were exceedingly ashamed. The king said, "Stay in Jericho until your beard grows. Then you can return."

6/ The Ammonites were afraid because they had made themselves odious to[13] David, and Hanun and the Ammonites sent one thousand talents of silver[14] to hire for themselves—from Aram-naharaim, Aram-maacah, and Zobah—chariots and cavalry.[15] 7/ They hired for themselves thirty-two thousand chariots[16] and the king of Maacah and his troops,[17] and they came and encamped before Medeba.[18] The Ammonites gathered together from their cities[19] and came for the battle. 8/ When David heard, he sent Joab and all the host of the warriors.[20] 9/ The Ammonites went out and drew up a battle line at the entrance of the city,[21] and the kings who had come were by themselves in the field.

10/ When Joab saw that the line of battle was set against him both in front and in the rear, he chose some of all the best picked men[22] in Israel and arranged them opposite Aram. 11/ The rest of the troops he put in the command of Abshai[23] his brother, and they arranged themselves[24] opposite the Ammonites. 12/ He said, "If Aram is stronger than I, then you will save me. But if the Ammonites are stronger than you, then I will save you. 13/ Be strong and let us show ourselves to be courageous on behalf of our people and on behalf of the cities of our God. Yahweh will do what he deems right." 14/ Joab and the troops who were with him drew near before Aram for battle, and they fled before him. 15/ When the Ammonites saw that Aram had fled, they also fled from before Abshai his brother,[25] and they

1 Beginning in 2 Samuel 10 and continuing through 1 Kgs 2:11—i.e., through the Samuel *Vorlage* for the rest of 1 Chronicles—LXX[B] is no longer a direct witness to the OG, but is part of the *kaige* recension. LXX[L], the 4th-century Lucianic recension, does provide some indirect access to the proto-Lucianic recension of the 1st century BCE and therefore indirect access to some OG readings (see Textual Criticism in the Introduction). In readings discussed in textual notes 6-7, 12-16, 19, 21-22, 24, 26, 29-30, and 35, Chronicles presupposes a text of Samuel other than MT.

2 נחשׁ. The name is lacking in Chronicles LXX and in 2 Sam 10:1.

3 A few Hebrew MSS, LXX, Syr, and 2 Sam 10:1 add חנון "Hanun."

4 כי; Chronicles LXX and 2 Sam 10:2 have כאשׁר "(just) as." Johnstone, 1:215, sees here a "downgrading" of the relationship by the Chronicler whereas in Samuel there was reciprocity of action between equals. This may be overinterpretation, and in any case Chronicles LXX suggests that Chronicles MT may be a secondary development.

5 מלאכים "messengers" replaces ביד עבדיו "by the hand of his servants" in 2 Sam 10:2, but the term "servant" is used in both texts at 2 Sam 10:3-4// 1 Chr 19:3-4.

6 על; cf. 2 Sam 10:2 LXX. 2 Sam 10:2 MT אל.

7 אל, with a few Hebrew MSS of 2 Sam 10:2 and Samuel LXX; lacking in Samuel MT, perhaps by homoioarchton.

8 לחנון with 2 Sam 10:3; Chronicles Syr and 2 Sam 10:3 add אדניהם "their lord."

9 לחקר; Chronicles LXX, Syr, 2 Sam10:3 add את העיר "the city." Chronicles MT supplies a different direct object, "land," later in the sentence.

10 ולהפך. This word is lacking in LXX, Syr, possibly by haplography, and its position in Chronicles MT is different from 2 Sam 10:3, where it is the last word in the clause. *BHK, BHS,* and Rudolph, 37, emend to לחפר (exploring). Cf. also Fincke, *Samuel Scroll,* 185–86. See the commentary.

11 וילכו; lacking in Syr and in 2 Sam 10:5.

12 על האנשׁים; cf. 2 Sam 10:5, 4QSam[a], LXX. Lacking in Chronicles LXX, Vg, and 2 Sam 10:5 MT.

13 עם. Cf. Chronicles LXX and 2 Sam 10:6 LXX, both of which, however, interpret incorrectly the unpointed preposition עם as עם "people." Samuel MT replaces עם with the preposition ב.

14 אלף ככר כסף; cf. 2 Sam 10:6 4QSam[a]. These words are lacking in Samuel MT, LXX. The rest of 1 Chr 19:6-7 diverges greatly from 2 Sam 10:6 MT (cf. LXX), which reads: "and they hired Aram Beth-rehob and Aram-zobah, twenty thousand infantry,

entered the city while Joab came to Jerusalem.[26]

16/ When the Arameans saw that they had been beaten before Israel, they sent messengers and brought out the Arameans who were across the river, with Shophach, the commander of the army of Hadadezer at their head. **17/** After David had been told, he gathered all Israel and crossed the Jordan. Coming to them,[27] he set up battle lines against them,[28] with David positioned opposite the Arameans[29] for battle, and they fought with him. **18/** The Arameans fled before Israel, and David killed seven thousand Aramean charioteers and forty thousand infantry.[30] He also put to death Shophach, the commander of the army. **19/** When the servants of Hadadezer saw that they had been defeated by Israel, they made peace with David and became subject to him. Aram refused to give assistance to the Ammonites anymore.

20:1/ At the time of the turning of the year, at the time when kings[31] go out to war, Joab led the armed forces, ravaged the land of the Ammonites, and came and besieged Rabbah. But David remained at Jerusalem. Joab attacked Rabbah,[32] and overthrew it. **2/** David took the crown of Milcom[33] from his head; he found it weighed a talent of gold, and in it[34] were precious stones; and it was placed on the head of David. He also brought out the booty of the city, a very great amount. **3/** He brought out the people who were in it and he ripped[35] the city apart with saws, iron cutting tools, and axes.[36] Thus David did to all the cities of the Ammonites, and David and all the people returned to Jerusalem.

and the king of Maacah, one thousand men, and the men of Tob, twelve thousand men." 4QSam[a] is very fragmentary here, but appears to follow the text of Chronicles except for its retention of וא[יש טוב] from 2 Sam 10:6. See also the next note.

15 וֹמֵן אֲרָם מַעֲכָה וּמִצּוֹבָא רֶכֶב וּפָרָשִׁים; cf. 4QSam[a] [אֲרָם מִ]עֲכָה [. . .] וּמִצּוֹבַ]ה רֶכֶב וּפָרָשִׁים "[Aram-m]aacah [. . . and from Zoba]h chariots and cavalry." Herbert, *Reconstructing*, 137, has suggested that the first letter after the second set of brackets should be a *bêt* or final *kāp* rather than a *hê*. He therefore fills in the gap with וּמִבֵּית רְחוֹב "and from Beth Rehob" (cf. 2 Sam 10:6 MT) rather than וּמִצּוֹבָה "and from Zobah" (as in Fincke, *Samuel Scroll*, 187). The tiny fraction of the contested letter preserved on the leather, however, allows no certainty, and it would seem strange to introduce Beth-rehob instead of Zobah when this alternate text has apparently already replaced "Beth-rehob" from 2 Sam 10:6 MT, LXX with "Aram-naharaim."

16 שְׁנַיִם וּשְׁלוֹשִׁי[ם] אֶלֶף רֶכֶב; cf. 4QSam[a] אֶלֶף רֶכֶב. See Herbert, *Reconstructing*, 135, 137; and Ulrich, *Qumran Text of Samuel*, 154–55. Fincke, *Samuel Scroll*, 187, reconstructs the Hebrew of 4QSam[a] as [עֶשְׂרִי]ם אֶלֶף רֶכֶב רֶכֶב "twenty thousand chariots" = 2 Sam 10:6 MT. The number "thirty-two thousand" is apparently a sum of twenty thousand (infantry) and twelve thousand (men) in 2 Sam 10:6 MT, LXX.

17 וְאֶת עַמּוֹ. Cf. 2 Sam 10:6 אֶלֶף אִישׁ וְאִישׁ טוֹב "one thousand troops and the men of Tob." Ulrich, *Qumran Text of Samuel*, 155, notes that "one thousand troops" is not included by Josephus and may be secondary. The Chronicler also seems not to have known it since his total of thirty-two thousand is a combination of twenty thousand (infantry) and twelve thousand (men of Tob) from 2 Sam 10:6. See the commentary.

18 מֵידְבָא. Rudolph, 137, following earlier commentators, proposes a conjectural reading, מֵי רַבָּה "waters of Rabbah." Cf. 2 Sam 12:27, where Joab reports to David that in capturing Rabbah he has captured "the city of waters." Medeba is both too far south in general for Aramean penetration and too distant from Rabbah if Joab and Abishai are going to be able to offer assistance to one another. Herbert, *Reconstructing*, 135; and Fincke, *Samuel Scroll*, 187, include the whole clause from Chronicles in their reconstruction of 4QSam[a]; McCarter, *II Samuel*, 268, believes that space considerations preclude this and proposes that there was an empty space on the scroll before 2 Sam 10:7.

19 וּבְנֵי עַמּוֹן נֶאֶסְפוּ מֵעָרֵיהֶם. These words are not attested in 2 Sam 10:6 MT, LXX, but 4QSam[a] reads: [וּבְנֵי] עַמּוֹן נֶאֶסְפוּ מִן הֶ[עָרִים] "The Ammonites gath-

ered together from the cities." See Herbert, *Reconstructing*, 135, 137. Fincke, *Samuel Scroll*, 187, fills in the final lacuna differently: מן הרי ארם "from the mountains of Aram."

20 צְבָא הגברים (construct chain) with Chronicles LXX, Syr, Vg, and 2 Sam 10:7 LXX[L], Syr, Tg, OL; Chronicles MT צְבָא הגברים (absolute). Samuel MT and LXX read הצבא הגברים "the host the warriors," in apposition to each other, which Curtis and Madsen, 239, believe is the original text.

21 העיר; cf. 2 Sam 10:8 LXX[LN]. Chronicles Syr, Samuel MT, LXX[BAM], Syr: השער "the gate."

22 בחור. This noun is collective singular in Chronicles and in 2 Sam 10:9 LXX[L] νεανίου (υἱῶν); Samuel MT, LXX בחורי (construct plural). The ב following the construct is an archaic construction. See GKC §130a.

23 Throughout Chronicles the name is actually spelled Abshai rather than Abishai (1 Chr 2:16; 11:20; 18:12; 19:15).

24 ויערכו; cf. 2 Sam 10:9 LXX. Samuel MT ויערך.

25 מפני אבשי אחיו. Chronicles LXX ἀπὸ προσώπου Ιωαβ καὶ ἀπὸ προσώπου ἀδελφοῦ αὐτοῦ = מפני יואב ומפני אחיו "from the face of Joab and from the face of his brother." Leslie C. Allen, "Cuckoos in the Textual Nest," *JTS* 22 (1971) 144, explains the origin of the LXX by proposing that "Joab" was originally inserted interlinearly to explain the suffix on "his brother" and then later was understood as a correction for Abishai and replaced that name. Since a scribe realized that Abishai was the actual opponent of the Ammonites, a second "and from" was inserted to harmonize the text with its context. *BHS* proposes a haplography in MT and emends אחיו "his brother" to אחי יואב "the brother of Joab."

26 ויבא יואב ירושלם. 2 Sam 10:14 LXX[L] retains a synonymous variant וישב יואב מעל בני עמון אל ירושלם "And Joab returned from against the Ammonites to Jerusalem." Both readings have been conflated in Samuel MT and LXX.

27 אלהם. This defectively written preposition with a suffix is apparently an error for חלאמה "to Helam" in 2 Sam 10:17. Chronicles did not include ויבאו חילם "they came to Helam" from 2 Sam 10:16 in its equivalent verse, 1 Chr 19:16. Perhaps the Chronicler did not understand Helam as a place name.

28 ויערך אלהם. This reading was lost in two Hebrew MSS, Syr, Arab. by homoioteleuton. Was it also lost in the Hebrew text of 2 Sam 10:17, or is it a synonymous variant of the next sentence that has been preserved in a conflate MT in Chronicles? See also the next note.

29 ויערך דויד לקראת ארם; cf. 2 Sam 10:17 LXX. Chronicles LXX, Syr, Samuel MT, LXX[L] ויערכו ארם לקראת דוד "with the Arameans positioned opposite David."

30 מארם שבעת אלפים רכב וארבעים איש רגלי; cf. Josephus *Ant.* 7.128, "seven thousand cavalry and forty thousand infantry," and 2 Sam 10:18 LXX[L] and OL: "seven hundred Aramean charioteers and forty thousand infantry." Samuel MT and LXX מארם שבע מאות רכב וארבעים אלף פרשים "seven hundred Aramean charioteers and forty thousand cavalry." McCarter, *II Samuel*, 269, reconstructs "seven hundred Aramean charioteers and forty thousand cavalry" as the best text in Samuel. He mistakenly says that 1 Chr 19:18 and Josephus agree, whereas Chronicles divides the troops into charioteers and infantry while Josephus divides them into cavalry and infantry. The numbers in Chronicles and Josephus do agree. In short, Chronicles depends at least partially on a non-MT reading in its *Vorlage*. D. R. Ap-Thomas, "A Numerical Poser," *JNES* 2 (1943) 198–200, reconstructs the "original text" as one thousand chariots, seven hundred cavalry, and twenty thousand infantry. Only the first two letters of the word "seven" are preserved in 4QSam[a]; space leads Herbert, *Reconstructing*, 138, to reconstruct "seven hundred."

31 המלכים; cf. 2 Sam 11:1 Q, LXX, OL, Vg; K המלאכים "messengers." Curtis and Madsen, 241, proposed that "messengers" was the more original reading in Samuel and referred to the time when David had sent messengers to Hanun (2 Sam 10:2).

32 ויך יואב את רבה. LXX[iy] add: "and Joab sent messengers to David, saying, 'Go, seize Rabbah lest I capture it and my name be called over it.' David gathered the troops and went to Rabbah and captured it." Rudolph, 138, restored this lemma, which incorporates parts of 2 Sam 12:27-29, to the text of Chronicles, arguing that it was lost by homoioteleuton (from "Rabbah" to "Rabbah"; for the text see *BHS*, note 1[b]). He deletes וילכדה from the end of the lemma in order to make the homoioteleuton work. LXX[g] has a very similar addition after the last word in the verse. I take these pluses as harmonizations. See the commentary.

33 מלכם; cf. Chronicles LXX, Vg, Arab., and 2 Sam 12:30 LXX "Molech/Melchol their king" (double translation). Chronicles MT and Samuel MT מַלְכָּם "their king." The suffix in MT lacks an antecedent; and "Milcom," god of the Ammonites, is surely the correct reading, since the crown is too heavy for a human king. Cf. 1 Kgs 11:7 MT וּלְמֹלֶךְ "and to Molech"; LXX τῷ βασιλεῖ αὐτῶν "to their king."

34 ובה; accidentally lost in 2 Sam 12:30, but see Samuel Tg, Syr.

35 וישר; cf. 2 Sam 12:31 LXX[L]. Lit. "he sawed," with "the city" as the implied object. 2 Sam 12:31 MT

וישם "he put" (them to work at saws, etc.). Rudolph, 140, and many others emend Chronicles to agree with Samuel, but the Samuel LXX^L reading suggests that this reading was in the original text of Chronicles.

36 ובמגרות, with one Hebrew MS and 2 Sam 12:31; Chronicles MT ובמגרת "saws" is a duplication of a

word earlier in the sentence. Chronicles also omits והעביר אותם במלכן from 2 Sam 12:31, perhaps because the author did not understand these words. They are difficult for modern readers to understand as well. *NRSV*: "He sent them to the brickworks." McCarter, *II Samuel*, 313, "He sent them to work with the brick mold."

19:1—20:3

Structure

The point of the war stories in 1 Chr 19:1—20:3 (cf. also chap. 18) is that God is thereby rewarding David for his faithfulness, especially in bringing the ark to Jerusalem, and is keeping his promise to subdue all of David's enemies (17:10). The Chronicler does not include the materials from 2 Samuel 9, David's kindness to Mephibosheth, the lame son of Jonathan and grandson of Saul, since here and elsewhere he does not comment on David's relationship to Saul, and because Saul and his whole household purportedly died at Gilboa (1 Chr 10:6). He draws his materials in this unit from 2 Samuel 10–12, but he omits 2 Sam 11:2–12:25, which reports David's affair with Bathsheba and the murder of her husband Uriah the Hittite, apparently because of the extremely bad light it cast on the character of David. 1 Chr 20:1 is parallel to 2 Sam 11:1, except that the last four words of 1 Chr 20:1 paraphrase 2 Sam 12:26, and 1 Chr 20:2-3 are parallel to 2 Sam 12:30-31. The Chronicler omits 2 Sam 12:26-29 in which Joab instructs David on the taking of Rabbah.

The materials in this pericope may be outlined as follows:

I. 19:1-5 (2 Sam 10:1-5). Ammonite provocation. Hanun the new Ammonite king humiliates a delegation David had sent to comfort him, but which Hanun interpreted as a group of spies.

II. 19:6-9 (2 Sam 10:6-8). Ammonites hire Aramean troops to help in their war against Israel.

III. 19:10-15 (2 Sam 10:9-14). Joab wins an initial victory over the Arameans in a battle possibly fought near Rabbah. Joab returns to Jerusalem either because he has been weakened by this battle or because he had not taken a big enough part of the army along in the first place.

IV. 19:16-19 (2 Sam 10:15-19). David wins a decisive victory over the expanded Aramean coalition in northern Transjordan or Gilead. The Arameans are now isolated from the Ammonites, and David himself leads the troops. The sequel to this battle historically takes place in 1 Chr 18:3-8 (see the discussion of Structure in 1 Chronicles 18).

V. 20:1-3 (2 Sam 11:1; 12:26, 30-31). Joab and David defeat the Ammonites and capture the city of Rabbah.

Detailed Commentary

19:1-5. Ammonite Provocation

■ **1** *It happened after this:* This is the stereotypical beginning of the units in these stories of David's wars (cf. 1 Chr 18:1; 20:4).

King Nahash of the Ammonites died: King Saul had decisively defeated Nahash and the Ammonites when they had threatened the people of Jabesh-gilead (1 Sam 11:1-11), a passage not included in Chronicles. Hence this is the first mention of Nahash in Chronicles. This verse indicates that Nahash remained on the Ammonite throne into the first part of David's reign. Nahash may have sided with David in his rivalry with Saul in order to check the rising power of Judah/Israel to his west.

■ **2** *David said, "I will deal loyally with Hanun the son of Nahash, for his father dealt loyally with me":* David vowed to act loyally toward the new Ammonite king Hanun in response to the loyalty Nahash Hanun's father had shown toward David. When David had fled from Absalom, he was met at Mahanaim in Transjordan by three men who provided him with abundant food and supplies. One of these three was Shobi the son of Nahash (2 Sam 17:27-29; an account not included in Chronicles). If this is the act of loyalty to which David is referring, although that is by no means certain, it would mean that the Absalom incident and its aftermath in 2 Samuel

13–20 preceded chronologically David's wars with the Ammonites and Arameans (so McCarter, *II Samuel*, 270). We have already seen that the battles in 1 Chr 19:1–20:3 probably preceded the wars in 18:3-6. In the present text of Samuel, David's affair with Bathsheba provides the theological rationale for the many troubles he has in the following chapters (see esp. 2 Sam 12:11-12). Any chronological or other relationship between the brothers Shobi and Hanun is unknown. Nahash's loyal actions may refer more generally to the mutual obligations and duties between allies; such loyalty is frequently cited in vassal and parity treaties. No reliable additional details of the relationship with Nahash or his family are provided in Samuel or Chronicles. According to 2 Sam 17:25 (not included in Chronicles), however, only two verses before the reference to Shobi, Abigail, the sister of Zeruiah,[1] is identified as the daughter of Nahash although it is not stated explicitly whether this was the Ammonite king by that name. Many commentators believe this apparent relationship between Abigail and Nahash is the result of textual corruption from 2 Sam 17:27.[2] If the reading in 2 Sam 17:25 is authentic information, this Nahash could also be either the mother of Abigail and Zeruiah or an earlier husband of Jesse's wife.[3]

David sent messengers to comfort him concerning his father: Here and in v. 16 Chronicles makes a stylistic addition of the word "messengers" to the words "David sent" taken from 2 Samuel. In this verse "messengers" replaces "by the hand of his servants" in 2 Sam 10:2, though the reference to David's servants is retained in v. 3//2 Sam 10:4.

to Hanun, to comfort him: This clause has been added by the Chronicler. It substantially repeats a clause earlier in the verse ("to comfort him concerning his father")

that was based on a similar clause in 2 Sam 10:2.[4] David's embassy was probably also intended to maintain and renew his treaty relationship with the Ammonites rather than just to express sympathy over Hanun's personal loss of his father. Hiram sent a similar embassy to Solomon when he had become king (1 Kgs 5:15 [1]; not included in Chronicles).

■ **3** *The officials of the Ammonites said to Hanun:* The narrator here is omniscient, revealing the strategic conversations that took place between the Ammonite king and his advisors (cf. the narrator's knowledge of what David thought or said in the previous verse). Hanun's advisors scornfully interpreted David's messengers as a group of spies rather than a delegation paying respects to Nahash and his successor.

"Do you think that David is honoring your father": By placing the participle "honoring" in the initial position in Hebrew, the narrator gives it special emphasis.

Is it not for the sake of exploring and looking over and spying out the land: Chronicles rearranges the order of the second and third verbs taken over in this clause from Samuel and makes the object of the espionage the land instead of just the city (except for Chr LXX; see textual note 9). McCarter, *II Samuel*, 270, following Ehrlich, argues that הפך (which is translated here as "looking over") means "overthrow" only when Yahweh is the subject and notes that Tg Jonathan to Samuel understands this verb here in the sense of espionage activities.[5] Ehrlich also observes that the position of this word in Chronicles—before "spying out"—would rule out a translation "overthrowing."[6] This understanding of the present text obviates the need for the emendation proposed by Rudolph (see textual note 10).

■ **4** *Hanun then took the servants of David and shaved them, and he cut their garments in half up to their hips:* Hanun's

---

1. In 1 Chr 2:15-16 Abigail and Zeruiah are also identified as sisters of David and children of Jesse.
2. For discussion, see Driver, *Notes,* 326.
3. So Hertzberg, *I and II Samuel,* 357. For discussion see McCarter, *II Samuel,* 392, 394, who believes that this reference to Nahash is simply an error; and Driver, *Notes,* 326. Richard D. Nelson, "Nahash," *ABD* 4:966, speculates that this earlier husband of Jesse's wife could be the Ammonite king, thereby explaining Nahash's friendly relations to David.
4. This may be the conflation of a synonymous variant.
5. "Is it not rather to reconnoiter, discover its secrets, and spy out the land that his servants have come to you?"
6. Ehrlich, *Randglossen,* 3:294.

insulting treatment of David's servants[7] would provoke a military attack by David and may have been a strategy designed to distance himself from David, who was no longer a friendly rival who could hold Saul in check, but who in his own right had become a threat to Ammon. According to 2 Sam 10:4 MT Hanun shaved off half their beard while in Sam LXX the whole beard was removed.[8] By replacing "beard" with "them" the Chronicler apparently makes the shaving include the removal of all body hair. By cutting off their garments Hanun exposed David's ambassadors to the shame of nakedness (cf. Isa 47:2-3; Nah 3:5, where exposed nakedness is mentioned as being shameful for women). In Isa 20:4 the prophet Isaiah announced that Israel's Egyptian allies would be led away in shame, with bared buttocks, by the Assyrians, using the same word for buttocks as in 2 Sam 10:4 (שֵׁת). The word used for "hip" in Chronicles (מִפְשָׂעָה) is used only here in the OT and may be a euphemism or a slightly less coarse term (Rudolph, 136) than the one employed in the *Vorlage*.[9]

■ **5** *The king said, "Stay in Jericho until your beard has grown"*: Jericho (MR 192142) was the natural stopping off point on a return trip from Rabbath-ammon (MR 238151) to Jerusalem (MR 172131). David shows compassion to his servants just as he had attempted to offer condolences to Hanun on the death of his father.

19:6-9. Ammonites Hire Aramean Troops to Help in War against Israel

■ **6** *The Ammonites were afraid because they had made themselves odious*: Chronicles replaces the *niphal* of 2 Sam 10:6 נִבְאֲשׁוּ with a *hitpael* הִתְבָּאֲשׁוּ, showing even more dramatically the insult perpetrated by the Ammonites.

Hanun and the Ammonites sent one thousand talents of silver to hire for themselves chariots and cavalry from Aram-

naharaim, Aram-maacah, and Zobah: The extravagantly large tribute or bribe (about 67,300 pounds of silver)[10] sent by Hanun[11] and the Ammonites to their Aramean allies indicates that they knew that their provocative action against David's servants would lead to war and require more troops on their part. Because the words "one thousand . . . Zobah" are attested by 4QSam^a, though not by Sam MT (see textual notes 14-15), we may conclude that this information was already found in the text of Samuel, which the Chronicler was rewriting.

Aram-naharaim: "Aram of the two rivers" or "Aram of Mesopotamia"[12] is a replacement for Beth-rehob in 2 Sam 10:6. Beth-rehob was a state located between Israel and Hamath, in the area of the southern Beqa' north of Dan, west of Damascus. A town Rehob, near the entrance of Hamath, was the northernmost extent of the spies' journey (Num 13:21).[13] Verse 16 refers to the participation of Arameans from "beyond the river," that is, the Euphrates. Aram-naharaim was the home of Balaam according to Deut 23:5 (4).

Zobah: This country, ruled by Hadadezer, lay north of Beth-rehob and extended from the Anti-Lebanon mountains east into the plain of Ḥoms, north of Damascus. It was the main Aramean power in 1 Chr 18:3-8, and it was invaded, according to that passage, by David with heavy losses.

Aram-maacah: Maacah was a country north of Geshur and south of Beth-rehob and Damascus.[14] Maacah joined the Aramean coalition, whereas Geshur was united through marriage to David and hence was not part of this anti-David coalition.[15] Absalom fled for three years to Geshur, his mother's country, after he had killed his half-brother Amnon (2 Sam 13:38; not included in Chronicles).

---

7   Cf. the harsh reply of Rehoboam to those who asked him to lighten the burden his father Solomon had imposed on the people, 2 Chr 10:14.

8   Shaved beards is often a sign of mourning (cf. Isa 15:2; Jer 41:5; 48:37). McCarter, *II Samuel*, 270, observes that this may have been a symbolic castration.

9   Cf. Ludwig Köhler, *ZAW* (1940/1941) 228; and *HALOT* 2:618, which defines the word in Chronicles as "place requiring a covering, seat, buttocks."

10   In 2 Chr 25:6 Amaziah hires one hundred thousand mighty warriors from Israel for one hundred talents

of silver, roughly one ounce of silver for each man.

11   Chronicles has added the king's name.

12   See also Gen 24:10; Deut 23:5 (4); Judg 3:8; Ps 60:2 (S).

13   See the map in Pitard, *Ancient Damascus*, 83.

14   Cf. Josh 13:11 and 1 Chr 2:48; 7:15-16; 8:29; 9:35. See D. G. Schley, "Maacah," *ABD* 4:430; and McCarter, *II Samuel*, 271, and map 6. Halpern, *David's Secret Demons*, 202–3, associates Maacah with Abel-beth-maacah (MR 20296), directly west of Dan (MR 211294).

15   David married Maacah, the daughter of King Tal-

7 *They hired for themselves thirty-two thousand chariots and the king of Maacah with his army:* This text, largely supported by the fragmentary 4QSam[a], summarizes and abbreviates the information in 2 Sam 10:6 MT. The number thirty-two thousand is the sum of the figures of twenty thousand and twelve thousand (both referring to infantry) in the corresponding verse in Samuel MT. The Chronicler apparently considered the king of Maacah and the men of Tob as one unit and did not mention separately the one thousand men assigned to the king of Maacah or the twelve thousand men of Tob in 2 Sam 10:6. Hence the number of troops who came with the king of Maacah is unspecified. Thirty-two thousand infantrymen would be a large army in antiquity; a chariot corps of thirty-two thousand would be gargantuan. The vast number of chariots, of course, indicates the severity of the battle and the threat posed by the enemy rather than any kind of numerical accuracy. This is the largest chariot force in the Bible.[16] No numbers are given for the Israelite armies, but one assumes they were much smaller and much more poorly equipped.

the king of Maacah and his troops: Instead of "the king of Maacah . . . and the men (אִישׁ) of Tob" (2 Sam 10:6), Chronicles speaks of "the king of Maacah and his troops." Similarly, "Arameans of Zobah, of Rehob, the men of Tob and Maacah" from 2 Sam 10:8 disappear in v. 9 into the generic "the kings who had come." Tob is mentioned as a place where Jephthah lived (Judg 11:3, 5) and is usually identified with eṭ-Ṭaiyibeh (MR 266218), 12 miles southeast of the Sea of Galilee. Tob is also mentioned in 1 Macc 5:13, where it may be refer to either a geographical place or a group.[17]

They came and camped before Medeba: From here to the end of the verse the Chronicler supplies material not in the *Vorlage*. Medeba (MR 225124) was in Moab, about 20 miles southwest of Rabbath-ammon (MR 238151) and about 6 miles south of Heshbon (MR 226134; Num 21:30; Josh 13:9, 16; Isa 15:2; Mesha inscription, l. 8).

Thus it is too distant from Joab to make the mutual support of Joab and Abshai envisioned in v. 12 possible. Rudolph, 137, emended Medeba (מידבא) to "the waters of Rabbah" (מי רבה), and calls attention to 2 Sam 12:27, where Rabbah is named in a line parallel with עיר המים "the city of waters." Japhet, 359, who thinks that the Ammonites would not have chosen their home city as a battle ground, suggests that Medeba is an unidentified city near the Israelite border. Or is the mention of Medeba by the Chronicler meant to show Moabite complicity in the war against David?

The Ammonites gathered together from their cities: Ironically, it is these cities themselves that David later destroyed (1 Chr 20:3).

9 *The Ammonites . . . drew up a battle line at the entrance of the city:* The city is apparently Rabbath-ammon (modern Amman; MR 238151).

and the kings who had come were by themselves in the field: Chronicles summarizes the text in 2 Sam 10:8, which listed as enemies the Arameans of Zobah and Rehob, and the men of Tob, and Maacah (cf. the diverse order of these names in 2 Sam 10:6).[18] The separate location of the Aramean kings means that Joab was facing an attack from two directions (v. 10), just as David had in 1 Chr 18:5.

19:10-15. Joab Wins Initial Victory over Arameans

10 *He chose some of all the best picked men[19] in Israel and arranged them opposite Aram:* Joab took the best troops to confront the Arameans, who were presumably the stronger force; the rest of the army, under the leadership of his brother Abshai, took on the Ammonites.

11 *The rest of the troops he put in the command of Abshai his brother:* Abshai, Joab, and Asahel were brothers, sons of Zeruiah (1 Chr 2:16; cf. 11:20; 18:12). Abshai is mentioned frequently in 1 Sam 26:6–2 Sam 23:18, where his name is spelled אֲבִשַׁי "Abishai." See also v. 15 below.

13 *"Be strong and let us show ourselves to be courageous on*

---

mai of Geshur (2 Sam 3:3; not included in Chronicles), and she was the mother of Absalom and Tamar (2 Sam 13:1-22).

16   The Philistines mustered an equally astonishing thirty thousand chariots in 1 Sam 13:5.

17   See Paul L. Redditt, "Tob," *ABD* 6:583.

18   Johnstone, 1:217, believes that the explicit mention of kings implies the cosmic struggle going on

behind the scenes. It seems more likely that this is a generic description of the enemy in Chronicles, partly because the names of the enemy nations no longer made good sense to him.

19   Note the cognate accusative: ויבחר . . . בחור.

20   The Chronicler "corrects" the cohortative form of his *Vorlage* (ונתחזק) by adding a final *hê* (ונתחזקה).

behal of our people and on behalf of the cities of our God": Joab's speech in vv. 12-13 lays out a strategy that Abshai will help Joab if he is losing and vice versa. "I will help you" in v. 12 replaces "I will go to help you" in 2 Sam 10:11. Joab's summons to battle and his exhortation to have courage[20] add a nationalistic motive ("on behalf of our people") and a theological one ("on behalf of the cities of our God"). His exhortation is similar to the one Moses gave Joshua (Josh 1:6-9; cf. 1 Chr 11:10). The Mesha stela indicates that even as late as the ninth century Yahweh was worshiped in the old Reubenite city of Nebo (*ANET,* 320; cf. Num 32:3, 38).[21] This may have justified designating the Ammonite cities as "the cities of our God."

"Yahweh will do what he deems right": Joab puts his reliance on the intervention of Yahweh and not on his own muster of troops, making this a holy war. This is an indicative sentence and not a wish as the *NRSV* ("and may the Lord do what seems good to him") and other English translations propose.

■ **14** *Joab and the troops who were with him drew near before Aram for battle, and they fled before them*: The Chronicler puts emphasis on the Aramean enemy by locating the phrase "before Aram" before the phrase "for battle," whereas the *Vorlage* read "for battle against Aram." Fright and flight are characteristic activities of the enemies of Yahweh in holy war,[22] and the Arameans flee even before the battle begins. The flight of the Ammonites follows in the next verse (the word "fled" is used three times within eight Hebrew words), inspired apparently by their fright over what Yahweh had done to the Arameans. Hence neither alternative laid out by Joab in v. 12 proved to be necessary—neither brother had to come to the rescue of the other. In line with the holy war ideology, no physical activities of the Israelite army are mentioned in regard to either enemy. By way of contrast, the Arameans flee away from David's army only *after* a battle (v. 18).

■ **15** *they entered the city while Joab came to Jerusalem:* The Ammonites retreated to the city, presumably Rabbah,[23] which will be the object of Israelite attack in 1 Chr 20:1-3. Since Joab only had the "host of the warriors" (v. 8) and not the whole army, he returned back to the capital in Jerusalem, from which David would launch a full-scale war with all Israel at his command. It is also possible that Joab's forces had been considerably weakened in this battle. This verse brings this initial battle to a close.

19:16-19. David Wins Decisive Victory over Expanded Aramean Coalition

■ **16** *When the Arameans saw that they had been beaten before Israel, they sent messengers and brought out the Arameans who were across the river:* The Arameans realized that an expanded force was necessary to try to hold their position against Israel and therefore they summoned allies from related Aramean groups across the river Euphrates. According to the *Vorlage* in 2 Sam 10:16, Hadadezer himself sent for these reinforcements. The Chronicler also omits from 2 Sam 10:15 a clause, "they [the Arameans] gathered together." Na'aman argues that "across the river/Euphrates" is a territorial name by which the areas *west* of the Euphrates were known from the eighth century on.[24] If that is the presupposition of the author of the text of Samuel, then at least the *Vorlage* may not be claiming as much territory for the Aramean forces as a literal reading of "across the Euphrates"—that is, east of the Euphrates—might suggest. Halpern argues that the historical reference behind the text in Samuel (2 Sam 10:16) would have been the Jordan River.[25] In the light of 1 Chr 18:3, the text in Chronicles seems clearly to refer to territory beyond—to the northeast of—the Euphrates.

Shophach, the commander of the army of Hadadezer: Shophach שׁופַך, spelled Shobach שׁובַך[26] in 2 Sam 10:16, will be directly attacked by an army under David himself, and his death in v. 18, by the hand of David, is the

---

21 Raphael Giveon, "'The Cities of Our God,' (II Sam 10 12)," *JBL* 83 (1964) 115–16, cites extrabiblical evidence for possible Yahweh sanctuaries in southern Transjordan. See also Frank Moore Cross, "Reuben, First-Born of Jacob," *ZAW* 100 (1988) 46–65.

22 See Exod 14:27; 23:27; Deut 7:23; Josh 10:11.

23 Johnstone, 1:218, identifies it as Medeba.

24 Na'aman, "Hazael of 'Amqi and Hadadezer of Beth-rehob," *UF* 27 (1995) 390.

25 Halpern, *David's Secret Demons,* 189, 196.

26 For a list of the sound shift *b/p* in Semitic languages, see Manfred Weippert, *The Settlement of the Israelite Tribes in Palestine* (SBT 2/21; London: SCM, 1971) 78–79.

climactic moment of defeat for the Arameans. The Chronicler omits the site of this battle, "Helam," mentioned in 2 Sam 10:16, 17, perhaps because he did not understand this geographical reference. McCarter, *II Samuel*, 273, locates Helam as a region east of the Sea of Galilee in northern Transjordan (cf. 1 Macc 5:26, where Alema is probably the same as Helam).

■ **17** *he gathered all Israel and crossed the Jordan:* When David heard about the approach of Shophach, he brought out the whole army—or even the whole people of Israel— to meet the expanded Aramean challenge.

Coming to them: In 2 Sam 10:17 the text reads "(he came) to Helam." It is possible that "to them" (אלהם) in 1 Chr 19:17 is a miswritten form (intentional or unintentional) of the obscure geographical term (חלמה Q), which was omitted by the Chronicler in the preceding verse. Yigael Yadin proposed that David crossed the Jordan at Adamah/Adam (Tell ed-Dâmiyeh, just south of the mouth of the Jabbok) to cut the Arameans off so that he would not be trapped as Joab was, with enemies on two sides (v. 9).[27]

with David positioned opposite the Arameans: As many commentators have noted, we would expect "with the Arameans positioned opposite David" after the prior clause, as in 2 Sam 10:18 (MT, LXX[L]) and Chronicles LXX. The textual note indicates, however, that this "error" was already present in one version of the text of Samuel (Sam LXX), and the Chronicler no doubt copied it from there (see textual note 29). In any case, David is given pride of place over against the Arameans in Chronicles.

■ **18** *David killed seven thousand Aramean charioteers and forty thousand infantry:* These same numbers are already known in one text tradition of Samuel (Josephus; cf. the proto-Lucianic recension; see textual note 30). 2 Sam 10:18 MT reads: "Seven hundred charioteers and forty thousand cavalry." "Seven hundred" may have become "seven thousand" by simple textual attraction to the word "thousand" later in the verse. The military classification of the second group as infantry seems more proportionate to what we would expect, that is, that infantry would number more than chariots, rather than that the cavalry would number more than chariots. Does this

indicate a more original reading or a correction? The Chronicler changed the description of the death of Shophach from "he wounded (Shophach) and he died there" (2 Sam 10:18) to "he also put to death Shophach." In addition to the forty-seven thousand killed by David in this verse, he captured twenty-eight thousand in 1 Chr 18:4 and killed twenty-two thousand Arameans in 18:5. These numbers are clearly not realistic.

■ **19** *the servants of Hadadezer . . . made peace with David and became subject to him:* The "servants of Hadadezer" are the vassal rulers who had been part of the Aramean coalition, although the Chronicler omitted the word "the kings" from the *Vorlage.* The Chronicler, in line with his stress on David, changed the name of the Arameans' new suzerain from "Israel" in 2 Sam 10:19 ("they made peace with Israel and they served them") to David himself ("they made peace with David and became subject to him"). These servants of Hadadezer assumed the same vassal status with David as they had had with Hadadezer before him. Hadadezer, however, survived this battle and appears again in the chronologically later battle reported in 1 Chr 18:3-5.

Aram refused to give assistance to the Ammonites anymore: This sentence brings the second battle to a close and also indicates that the Ammonites would now have to stand alone against the forces of Israel. The Chronicler changed the verb in the *Vorlage* at 2 Sam 10:19 from "were afraid" (ויראו) to "refused" (ולא אבה).

20:1-3. Joab and David Defeat Ammonites

■ **20:1** *Joab led the armed forces:* Joab alone led this attack against Ammon, and he was accompanied only by "the armed forces," whereas in 2 Sam 11:1 "all Israel" went with him and his servants. This change was necessitated by the fact that David stayed in Jerusalem and therefore, ipso facto, all Israel could not be on the battlefield. If the Chronicler had included 2 Sam 12:28, with Joab's instructions to David to gather "the rest of the people," the term "all Israel" would seem self-contradictory. Joab's initiative in this battle in Chronicles is in contrast with 2 Sam 11:1, where he is explicitly sent on this mission by David himself.

---

27   Yigael Yadin, "Some Aspects of the Strategy of Ahab and David," *Bib* 36 (1955) 347–51.

ravaged the land of the Ammonites: The verb שחת "ravage" will become increasingly important in Chronicles, even being used to refer to the defeat of Israel in 1 Chr 21:12. The addition of "land" to the text of 2 Sam 11:2 echoes the same addition made to the text of 2 Sam 10:3 by the Chronicler in 1 Chr 19:3.

But David remained at Jerusalem: In Chronicles this explains why Joab alone led the attack on Rabbah, whereas in 2 Sam 11:1 this notice introduces David's affair with Bathsheba in Jerusalem while Uriah her husband and the army of Israel are on the battlefield. The omission of the Bathsheba incident (2 Sam 11:2–12:25) creates an awkward situation, since while David is present in Jerusalem in this verse, in subsequent verses he is on the battlefield. In 2 Sam 12:27-28, omitted by the Chronicler, Joab invites David to the battlefield, after his affair with Bathsheba and the murder of Uriah, lest Joab get undue credit for taking Rabbah. According to the chronology in 2 Samuel, the siege of Rabbah lasted more than a year.[28] In the Chronicler's drastically shorter account, the assault on Rabbah by Joab and then by David seems to happen in quick succession.

Joab attacked Rabbah and he overthrew it: According to 2 Sam 12:26-29—summarized in the four Hebrew words translated in this lemma—Joab fought against Rabbah of the Ammonites and seized the royal city (עיר המלוכה) or the city of water (עיר המים; a fortification protecting the water supply?), but then he urged David himself to capture the city lest the victory redound to Joab's credit and the city be named after Joab. David in fact subsequently captured the city (2 Sam 12:29). Chronicles omits 2 Sam

10:27-29[29] and clarifies Joab's role by saying he "overthrew" (or "ruined") the city rather than he seized it, as in 2 Sam 12:26. The verb הרס ("overthrew") was apparently derived from 2 Sam 11:25, a verse omitted in Chronicles, in which David sent a messenger to urge Joab to continue the battle after the death of Uriah.[30] Rabbah is 28.5 miles east of the Jordan.

■ **2** *David took the crown of Milcom:* The transition to this verse is awkward in Chronicles because of the omission of 2 Sam 10:27-29, which explains how David came to join Joab on the battlefield. How did David take a crown from the Ammonites when he was staying in Jerusalem (1 Chr 20:1)?[31] I suggest it was this awkwardness that led to the reintroduction of parts of 2 Sam 12:27-29 as two divergent harmonistic additions in minor Chr LXX MSS, as detailed in textual note 32. Milcom was the god of the Ammonites. This god is known from the Bible[32] and from extrabiblical sources.[33] Ironically, while David deprived Milcom of his crown, this was one of the same deities his son Solomon worshiped according to the Deuteronomistic History (1 Kgs 11:5, 33; 2 Kgs 23:13). Some eight sculptures in the round of Ammonite crowned heads have been discovered near Amman, though none in a stratified archaeological context. They all wear the so-called *'atef* crown of Osiris, which in Egypt is only worn by Egyptian gods or non-Egyptian goddesses. It is not clear whether the person depicted on the sculptures is the Ammonite king or the god Milcom.[34] Booty (שלל, 1 Chr 20:2) taken from Ammon was already referred to in a list of the silver and gold David had taken from a variety of nations in 18:11.

---

28 It took nine months for David and Bathsheba's child to be born and die. Then Joab summoned David to the battlefield and the city itself was taken.

29 Johnstone, 1:220, believes the Chronicler omitted these verses so that an underling like Joab would not be giving directions to the Lord's anointed.

30 החזק מלחמתך אל העיר והרסה "Press your attack on the city, and overthrow it." This is a clear example in which the Chronicler knew the longer text of Samuel and Kings (contra Auld).

31 Willi, *Chronik als Auslegung*, 57, cites this as a case where the Chronicler presupposed knowledge of 2 Sam 12:29. While Willi's point about the Chronicler assuming his readers knew the stories of Samuel in Kings in general seems valid, in this case they would have to know that story exceedingly well

and fill in the gap in the text of Chronicles itself. Rudolph, 141, cites the following passages where the Chronicler assumed his readers would know the earlier sources: 1 Chr 10:13-14; 13:5; 20:5.

32 1 Kgs 11:5, 33; 2 Kgs 23:13; מלכם in Jer 49:1 is almost universally emended to מלכם. Cf. also the versions in Amos 1:15; Zeph 1:5; 1 Kgs 11:7.

33 E. Puech, "Milkom," *DDD*, 575–76.

34 See Siegfried H. Horn, "The Crown of the King of the Ammonites," *AUSS* 11 (1973) 170–80, who favors the identification with the Ammonite king. Horn remarks that David would not likely wear the crown of a pagan deity; or, I might add, we might not expect the Chronicler to have him do so. Wearing the crown of a pagan deity could be interpreted, of course, as a polemical act against that god.

Booty gained by Israel becomes a prominent theme in Chronicles from this point on (26:27; 2 Chr 14:12; 15:11; 20:25).[35]

it weighed a talent of gold: This would be an extremely heavy crown, wearing nearly seventy pounds. The weight may be exaggerated, but if it is not, the weight alone might favor identifying this crown as coming from a statue of a god, even though the end of the verse says that the crown wound up on David's head.

*in it were precious stone*s: By adding "in it" to the text of 2 Sam 12:30[36] Chronicles makes clear that the weight was that of the crown alone and not the total of the crown and the precious stone(s), and that it was the crown and not the precious stone(s) that was on the head of David. The noun אבן is to be understood as a collective (so *JPS*).

■ **3** *he ripped the city with saws, iron cutting tools, and axes:* David tore apart the defenses of the city of Rabbah so that it would not have to be besieged again in the near future. The text of 2 Sam 12:31 MT and LXX has David putting the inhabitants of Rabbah to hard labor (וישׂם) with saws, iron picks, and axes. There is no evidence that that reading was ever in Chronicles, and in fact the text of Chronicles may be more original and is preserved by the LXX[L] reading in the *Vorlage* (see textual note 35).

Thus David did to all the cities of the Ammonites: This is the last mention of the Ammonites in Chronicles until 2 Chr 12:13//1 Kgs 14:21 (cf. 1 Kgs 11:1), where we learn that Rehoboam's mother—Solomon's wife—was Naamah the Ammonite, suggesting a reestablishment of more peaceful relationship between the two kingdoms.

and David and all the troops returned to Jerusalem: David returns from an expedition against the Ammonites on which—in Chronicles—he never explicitly set out (see above on the omission of 2 Sam 12:27-29). But his return to Jerusalem echoes that of Joab in v. 15 and brings the whole account of the Ammonite and Aramean wars of David to a satisfying conclusion.

Conclusion

This second pericope on David's wars shows how David prospered because of his bringing the ark to Jerusalem (1 Chronicles 13–16) and because Yahweh had promised that he would subdue all of David's enemies (17:10). David also demonstrates in these successful campaigns his legitimacy as king and founder of a dynasty. In these victories Yahweh does what he deems right (19:13). The Chronicler omits completely from the *Vorlage* any mention of David's adultery with Bathsheba and his murder of her husband Uriah.

The conflict with the Ammonites was triggered by an insult to a delegation sent by David to greet the new Ammonite king Hanun. Hanun hired a large Aramean mercenary force, which fled before the battle with the forces of Joab had begun. Joab then returned to Jerusalem, and David later decisively defeated the Arameans, killing forty-seven thousand Aramean troops in the process. At the end of this conflict the servants of Hadadezer made peace with David and become subservient to him.

In a final battle against Rabbah, the capital of the Ammonites, Joab overthrew the city, and David took the crown of Milcom and ripped apart this city and other Ammonite cities before himself returning to Jerusalem.

---

35 In 2 Chr 24:23 and 28:8, 15, enemy nations take booty away from Israel.

36 Cf. textual note 34.

20

Translation

4/ After this there was again[1] war with the Philistines at Gezer;[2] then Sibbecai the Hushathite killed Sippai,[3] one of the descendants of[4] the Rephaim;[5] and they were subdued. 5/ There was again war with the Philistines, and Elhanan the son of Jair[6] killed Lahmi the brother of Goliath the Gittite, and the shaft of his spear was like a weaver's beam. 6/ Again there was war at Gath, where there was a man of great size,[7] and there were six digits on each of his extremities, twenty-four in number; he was also descended from the Raphah.[8] 7/ When he taunted Israel, Jonathan the son of Shimea[9] the brother of David killed him. 8/ These[10] were descended[11] from the Raphah in Gath;[12] they fell by the hand of David and by the hand of his servants.

1 ותהי עוד, with Chronicles LXX, Syr, 2 Sam 21:18; Chronicles MT ותעמד "[war] stood," a miswriting of the original reading; contra Japhet, "Interchanges," 17. In readings discussed in textual notes 2-4 and 9 Chronicles presupposes a text of Samuel other than MT. In textual note 7 I suggest that Chronicles preserves the original reading in Samuel, though it is not now present in the Hebrew or versions of Samuel.

2 בגזר; cf. 2 Sam 21:18 LXX[L]. This reading may be the original one in 2 Sam 21:18: MT בנב "Gob" (anticipating v. 19) and LXX "Gath" (anticipating v. 20). Note that the final part of the name of Ishbi-benob (בנב) in 2 Sam 21:16 is very similar to the name of the city (בנב) in 2 Sam 21:18, 19.

3 ספי; cf. 2 Sam 21:18 LXX[L]. Samuel MT סף "Saph."

4 מילדי; cf. 2 Sam 21:18 LXX[L]. Samuel MT אשר בילדי "who was among the descendants of."

5 הרפאים. Some editions of the Hebrew Bible have הרפא "the Rapha" (2 Sam 21:18 הרפה). See vv. 6 and 8 and the commentary.

6 יעיר Q, LXX, Syr, Arab.; יעור K "Jaur." 2 Sam 21:19 MT ארגים יערי "[son of] Jaare-oregim." The second word, lit. "weavers," anticipates the last word in the verse and is secondary. Chronicles Q יעיר and the first name in 2 Sam 21:9, יערי, differ only in the metathesis of the last two letters.

7 מדה; 2 Sam 21:20 MT איש מדין "a man of Midian/Madon," or "a man of strife." The reading in Chronicles may have been the original one in Samuel (McCarter, *II Samuel*, 449). For the usage see 1 Chr 11:23.

8 להרפא; 2 Sam 21:26 להרפה.

9 שמעא; cf. 2 Sam 21:21 LXX[L] (McCarter, *II Samuel*, 449). 2 Sam 21:21 Q שמעה; K, LXX שמעי. In 1 Sam 16:9 the name is spelled שמה. The spelling שמעא also occurs in 1 Chr 2:13.

10 אלה Sebir; cf. 2 Sam 21:22. Chronicles MT אל.

11 נולדו; cf. 1 Chr 3:5. One would expect נולדו. Cf. GKC §69t; and Curtis and Madsen, 244.

12 בגת. Chronicles LXX adds "all were four giants" after "Gath." This addition, entered wrongly, is a correction made on the basis of a comparison with the text of 2 Sam 21:22.

Structure

The Chronicler concludes his account of David's wars by including three anecdotes found at 2 Sam 21:18-22,[1] in which Israelite heroes defeated Philistine heroes in one-to-one combat. These incidents should probably be related historically to David's Philistine wars recounted in 2 Sam 5:18-25//1 Chr 14:8-16. Each of these anecdotes is structured in a similar way:

- There was war again with the Philistines
- An Israelite hero kills a Philistine hero
- Characteristics of the Philistine hero and/or his relationship to the Rapha

Within this structure there is some minor variation. The third Philistine hero is unnamed, and the second's relationship to the Rapha is not given. A final sentence in v. 8 serves as a summary for the whole account. These three accounts are taken over with minor changes from the *Vorlage* in 2 Sam 21:18-25. They show both how the blessing of Yahweh gave David victory and they indicate the bloodshed that prevented him from building the temple (1 Chr 22:8; 28:3). Even in these three accounts, where David does no actual fighting, the conclusion is still drawn that these men fell by the hand of David and the hand of his servants (20:8).

Three omissions from the context of the *Vorlage* deserve comment. The first is a major one, including the lengthy account of the rape of Tamar, Absalom's murder of Amnon, his revolt and death, and the aftermath of that rebellion (2 Samuel 13–20).[2] While on the one hand the Chronicler's omission of these materials could be explained because of the Chronicler's focus on the temple and its worship, which is not discussed in these chapters, or because these chapters do not show how God's blessing lay on David as in his victories in wars, the Chronicler also could not have been pleased that the troubles in David's household in 2 Samuel 13–20 are seen as a fulfillment of Nathan's words that the sword would never depart from his house (2 Sam 12:10), that there would be trouble against him from within his house, and that a "neighbor" (רֵעַ) would lie with his wives openly (12:10-11). Absalom in fact did lie with his father's concubines in a tent pitched upon the roof (16:21-22). The revolt of Absalom would stand in tension with the Chronicler's own idea that "All the sons of King David pledged their allegiance to King Solomon" (1 Chr 29:24). So for both positive and negative reasons the omission by the Chronicler is understandable.

The second omission, of 2 Sam 21:1-14, also makes eminent sense. David's role in handing the descendants of Saul over to the Gibeonites who impaled them is hardly his finest ethical hour. In addition, the Chronicler wrote in 1 Chr 10:6: "Saul died and his three sons; his whole household died together." There would be no point, therefore, in including this account about the fate of Saul's survivors. For the same reason the story of Mephibosheth in 2 Samuel 9 was not included in Chronicles.

The reasons for the third omission, the anecdote in 2 Sam 21:15-17, in which David is captured and nearly killed, are less clear, but three possibilities can be identified. First, the structure of 1 Chronicles 18–20 is marked by the repeated formula, ויהי אחרי כן "it happened after this" (18:1; 19:1; 20:4), and the third and last use of the formula begins the second anecdote in 2 Sam 21:15-25 at v. 18, which is the first anecdote in Chronicles. Second, the Chronicler may not have been happy that David grew faint in this first anecdote and had to be rescued by one of his men (2 Sam 21:15),[3] or that the soldiers vowed at the completion of the anecdote that David would not fight again lest his life be put in danger. Third, Rudolph, 139, n. 1, notes that haplography through homoioarchton is not completely impossible, especially if the Chronicler had inserted ויהי אחרי כן "it happened after this" at the beginning of the first anecdote taken over from 2 Sam 21:15-17. The first two reasons, however, are sufficient grounds for me to believe that the Chronicler intentionally omitted an equivalent for 2 Sam 21:15-17.

1　An additional anecdote is recounted in 2 Sam 21:15-17. For its omission see below.

2　The omission of David's adulterous affair with Bathsheba and his murder of Uriah (2 Samuel 11–12) were discussed in the previous chapter.

3　Curtis and Madsen, 243.

Detailed Commentary

■ **4** *There was again war with the Philistines at Gezer:* While Gezer (MR 142140) was not a Philistine city, it abutted Philistine territory so that a clash between Israelites and Philistines there is not implausible. The books of Joshua and Judges recognized that Canaanites continued to live there (Josh 16:10; Judg 1:29). Earlier the Chronicler had noted that David struck down the Philistine army from Gibeon to Gezer (1 Chr 14:16//2 Sam 5:25).[4] Gezer is listed among the cities of refuge (1 Chr 6:52 [67]).

Sibbecai the Hushathite killed Sippai: Hushah (cf. 1 Chr 4:4)[5] was a small city a few miles southwest of Bethlehem (modern Ḥūsān; MR 162124). McCarter, *II Samuel*, 450, raises the possibility that Sibbecai may be identifiable with Mebunnai the Hushathite, one of the Thirty (2 Sam 23:27), who in fact is called Sibbecai in the parallel text at 1 Chr 11:29 (cf. 2 Sam 23:27 LXX^L). Sibbecai is put in charge of the military division for the eighth month in 1 Chr 27:11.

one of the descendants: Conrad E. L'Heureux has argued that ילד in these verses does not mean descendants, but rather "votaries" and that these men had entered the group of the divine patron Raphah by adoption, initiation, or consecration.[6] His argument is convincing for the original list and even for its inclusion in Samuel. But is it not likely that by the time of the Chronicler that specialized meaning might have been forgotten? McCarter, translated the *qal* passive[7] forms of ילד in 2 Sam 21:20, 22 as "were devoted to," but those forms have been replaced in Chronicles by *niphal* perfect forms of ילד in 1 Chr 20:6, 8. Does not this indicate that the Chronicler understood that these two men were "born"

or "descended from" the Raphah? For this reason I have kept the traditional translation "descendants" for the substantives as well.

of the Rephaim: This reading (see textual note 5) would indicate that the Chronicler associated the Philistine heroes with the legendary pre-Israelite gigantic inhabitants of the land (Gen 14:5; 15:20; Deut 2:10-11, 20-21; 3:11-13; Josh 12:4; 13:12; 15:8// 17:15; 18:16; 2 Sam 5:18, 22). In some editions of the Hebrew Bible and in vv. 6, 8 of Leningradensis, the word is spelled הרפא, which L'Heureux[8] takes as a stative participle with a definite article: "The Hale One"[9] or "Raphah." In v. 8 Raphah is associated with the city of Gath.

and the Philistines were subdued: The use of the verb כנע (here in the *niphal*) signals a fulfillment of Yahweh's promise to subdue (כנע) all of David's enemies (1 Chr 17:10). This verb is an addition by the Chronicler, not found in the text of Samuel. The verb is used later in Chronicles also to indicate defeat in battle for Israel (2 Chr 13:18; 28:19).

■ **5** *There was again war with the Philistines:* The Chronicler omitted the geographic reference "at Gob" attested in the *Vorlage* at 2 Sam 21:19. This place name is attested only in 2 Sam 21:18-19 MT and appears in no extrabiblical source. I proposed in textual note 2 that Gezer was the more original reading in 2 Sam 21:18. Perhaps the Chronicler did not recognize the name of this town. See also the next comment for another reason for the omission of Gob.

Elhanan the son of Jair killed Lahmi the brother of Goliath the Gittite: Discussion of this reading generally begins with its parallel in 2 Sam 21:19: "Elhanan the Jearite[10]

---

4 In 1 Chr 18:1 the Chronicler even had David taking Gath from the Philistines, even though it was south and west of Gezer, but that notice was probably the Chronicler's valiant attempt to make sense of an obscure reading.

5 This genealogical notice links Hushah to Ezer and the sons of the Judahite Hur, the firsborn of Ephrathah. Cf. Curtis and Madsen, 243.

6 Conrad E. L'Heureux, "The *yĕlîdê hārāpā'*—a Cultic Association of Warriors," *BASOR* 221 (1976) 83–85; idem, "The Ugaritic and Biblical Rephaim," *HTR* 67 (1974) 265–74.

7 Traditionally called *pual* imperfects, as in BDB.

8 Conrad E. L'Heureux, *Rank Among the Canaanite Gods: El, Ba'al, and the Repha'im* (HSM 21; Missoula, MT: Scholars Press, 1979) 217.

9 In Samuel the same word is spelled with final *hê*. Is this name polemical: "The one who has grown weak"?

10 In 1 Chr 2:19 Caleb and his second wife Ephrathah become parents of Hur. According to 2:50 Hur fathered Shobal, who in turn fathered Kiriath-jearim, while in 2:51 Hur fathered Salma, who is the parent of Bethlehem. Hence Kiriath-jearim and Bethlehem are "cousins" genealogically since their fathers were brothers and sons of Hur. This shows a

from Bethlehem killed Goliath the Gittite."[11] To relieve the apparent conflict of 2 Sam 21:19 and the present form of 1 Samuel 17 about who killed Goliath,[12] including the notice that "the shaft of his [Goliath's] spear was like a weaver's beam" (1 Sam 17:5), some scholars, beginning with the rabbis and the Tg, have considered Elhanan and David two names for the same person. In the mid-twentieth century Honeyman proposed that Elhanan was David's personal name and David his throne name.[13] Aside from this passage, of course, there is no evidence of such double names for David, and an earlier theory that the word "David" was a title meaning "chief" has failed because the Akkadian word in question actually means "defeat." It seems most likely, therefore, that 2 Sam 21:19 preserves an alternate tradition about the victory of Elhanan, an obscure hero from Bethlehem (2 Sam 21:19),[14] that was transferred to David, the much more famous citizen of Bethlehem. Whatever the case may be, the Chronicler harmonized the data of 2 Sam 21:19 with the data from 1 Samuel 17, which, though he did not include it, his readers were sure to know. A look at the Hebrew texts that identify the hometown of Elhanan and the person whom he killed clarifies the Chronicler's procedure:

2 Sam 21:19: בית הלחמי את גלית הגתי "[Elhanan the son of Jaare-oregim] the Bethlehemite [smote] Goliath the Gittite."

1 Chr 20:5: את לחמי אחי גלית הגתי "[Elhanan the son of Jair smote] Lahmi the brother of Goliath the Gittite."

From בית הלחמי "the Bethlehemite" in 2 Sam 21:19 the Chronicler created the sign of the direct object את

and the name Lahmi לחמי, and from the subsequent sign of the direct object in 2 Samuel את he created the word brother אחי.[15] As seen elsewhere in Chronicles, the Chronicler sometimes used graphically similar letters from his *Vorlage* to create his revised text.

Finally, the Chronicler's reason for omitting "Gob," the name of the city where this battle was fought in 2 Sam 21:19, may not only be due to this town's obscurity. Perhaps this omission in Chronicles was also a harmonization since the battle in 1 Sam 17:1 took place at Socoh, and the Chronicler may have reckoned that Goliath and Lahmi died in the same battle. By omitting Gob the reader might infer the location of the fight was at Socoh.

and the shaft of his spear was like a weaver's beam: The Chronicler retained this descriptive clause, even though in his *Vorlage* it referred to Goliath himself, not to his brother Lahmi.

■ 6 *a man of great size:* Chronicles seems to preserve the superior text here.[16] Samuel calls this anonymous warrior "a man of strife." Goliath's height was six cubits and a span (1 Sam 17:4).[17]

there were six digits on each of his extremities, twenty-four in number: The Chronicler simplifies the text of 2 Sam 21:20: "six fingers on each of his hands and six toes on each of his feet."[18]

■ 7 *When he taunted Israel:* The verb חרף "taunt" is used frequently of Goliath (1 Sam 17:10, 25, 26, 36, 45) and

---

clear association between the city of Kiriath-jearim and Bethlehem in Israelite tradition. The epithet "Jearite" refers to Kiriath-jearim.

11 1 Sam 17:4, 23; 21:10 (9); 22:10; 2 Sam 21:19; Sir 47:4.

12 McCarter, *II Samuel*, 450, has argued that the Philistine hero in 1 Sam 17:4 was originally anonymous.

13 A. M. Honeyman, "The Evidence for Regnal Names Among the Hebrews," *JBL* 67 (1948) 23–24. For criticism of this idea see Johann Jakob Stamm, "Der Name des Königs David," in *Congress Volume: Oxford 1959* (VTSup 7; Leiden: Brill, 1960) 167–68, 182. R. Weiss, "Ligatures in the Hebrew Bible," *JBL* 82 (1963) 194, argued that one name was a corruption of the other.

14 1 Chr 11:26 mentions Elhanan son of Dodo of Bethlehem.

15 Williamson, 142, suggests that the Chronicler may have faced a corrupt or unclear text in his *Vorlage* and that therefore the Chronicler did not deliberately harmonize the text. Japhet, 369, also conjectures that Chronicler's reading could have emerged earlier in his *Vorlage,* but there is no evidence either from Qumran or LXX to support this.

16 Cf. textual note 7 and McCarter, *II Samuel*, 449.

17 Nine feet, nine inches. See Klein, *1 Samuel*, 175.

18 For a discussion of polydactylism see Richard D. Barnett, "Polydactylism in the Ancient World," *BARev* 16, no. 3 (1990) 47.

of Sennacherib in his attack on Hezekiah (2 Chr 32:17; cf. 2 Kgs 19:4, 16, 22, 23//Isa 37:4, 17, 23, 24). His taunt no doubt touched on the supposed inability of Israel—and/or Israel's God—to meet his challenge.

Jonathan the son of Shimea the brother of David: Jonathan was the full brother[19] of Jonadab, who advised Amnon on how to have sexual relations with his sister (2 Sam 13:3). Jonathan was David's nephew.

■ **8** *These were descended from the Raphah in Gath:* In 2 Sam 21:22 "the Raphah" was a reference to the divine patron of the four warriors who were killed by the Israelites.[20] The Chronicler probably thought that the warriors were all descendants of the Rephaim. The Chronicler omitted the number "four" from 2 Sam 21:22 because he only included three of the anecdotes.[21]

they fell by the hand of David and by the hand of his servants: This clause explains why these anecdotes were important to the Chronicler, although strictly speaking none of the giants in these three anecdotes fell to David but only to his servants.[22] Even in the anecdote omitted by the Chronicler, it was David's nephew Abishai (Abshai) who killed the Philistine giant who intended to kill David (2 Sam 21:15-17).

Conclusion

The three anecdotes recounted in this pericope show how the blessing of Yahweh gave David victory, and they fulfill the promise that Yahweh would subdue David's enemies (1 Sam 17:10). They may also indicate some of the bloodshed that prevented David from building the temple (1 Chr 22:8; 28:3). While the heroic actions were done by Sibbecai, Elhanan, and Jonathan, the Chronicler concludes that these enemies fell by the hand of David and by the hand of his servants. The Chronicler also attempted to resolve the conflict between 1 Samuel 17 and 2 Sam 23:19 on who killed Goliath by making a harmonistic

---

19 Robert D. Miller II, "Jonadab," *ABD* 3:936, raises the possibility that Jonadab and Jonathan were the same person. So also Curtis and Madsen, 243.

20 McCarter, *II Samuel,* 451.

21 As textual note 12 indicates, this number was restored in Chronicles LXX.

22 This hardly justifies Rudolph's attempt to "improve" this text by a conjectural emendation (p. 140).

Satan stood up against Israel and incited David to number Israel. 2/ David said to Joab and to the commanders of[1] the people, "Go,[2] number Israel from Beer-sheba to Dan, and bring me a report[3] so that I may know their number." 3/ Joab said, "May Yahweh add to his people[4] like them[5] a hundredfold! Are not, my lord the king,[6] all of them servants to my lord? Why should my lord seek this? Why should this bring retribution for Israel?" 4/ The word of the king prevailed over[7] Joab. Joab went forth and traveled through all Israel and came to Jerusalem. 5/ Joab gave the number of the census of the people to David. All Israel amounted to one million one hundred thousand who drew the sword. Judah amounted to four[8] hundred seventy[9] thousand who drew the sword. 6/ He did not number Levi and Benjamin among them, for the command of the king was abhorrent to[10] Joab. 7/ This matter was displeasing to God and he struck Israel. 8/ David said to God, "I have sinned exceedingly against God in that I have done this matter.[11] Now take away the iniquity of your servant, for I have behaved very foolishly." 9/ Yahweh spoke to Gad the seer of[12] David, 10/ "Go and say to David, saying,[13] 'Thus says Yahweh: Three things I am offering[14] to you. Choose one of them for yourself so that I may do it to you.'" 11/ Gad came to David and said to him, "Thus says Yahweh, 'Take your choice:[15] 12/ either three[16] years of famine or three months of your fleeing[17] from before[18] your foes while the sword of your enemies overtakes you, or three days of the sword of Yahweh, pestilence in the[19] land, and the angel of Yahweh destroying throughout the territory of Israel.' And now,[20] consider what I should respond to the one who sent me." 13/ David said to Gad, "This is exceedingly stressful for me."[21] Let me fall[22] into the hand of Yahweh, for his mercies are exceedingly[23] manifold, but let me not fall into human hands." 14/ Yahweh caused a pestilence in Israel,[24] and there fell from Israel seventy thousand persons. 15/ God sent an angel to Jerusalem[25] to destroy it, but when he was about to destroy[26] it, Yahweh looked and changed his mind about[27] the calamity and said to the destroying angel, "Enough! Now let your hand drop." The angel of Yahweh was standing[28] by the threshing floor of Ornan[29] the Jebusite. 16/ David looked up and saw the angel of Yahweh standing between earth and heaven, with his drawn sword in his hand stretched out against Jerusalem. David and the elders, covered with sackcloth, fell on their faces.[30] 17/ David said to God, "Was it

1 ‏ואל שרי‏; cf. 2 Sam 24:2 LXX[L]. Samuel MT ‏שר‏ (singular, referring to Joab). Samuel MT continues ‏החיל אשר אתו‏ "of the army, who was with him," as does Samuel LXX and LXX[L], though the latter adds "in Jerusalem." Samuel LXX[L] agrees with Chronicles in making the leaders a group distinct from Joab. See also the next note. In readings discussed in textual notes 1-5, 7-8, 11-13, 15-16, 18-20, 22-23, 25, 27-28, 30-33, and 36-40, Chronicles presupposes a text of Samuel other than MT.

2 While 2 Sam 24:2 LXX[L] probably translates a different Hebrew verb, it agrees with Chronicles in putting the verb in the plural, since its subject is Joab *and* the commanders.

3 ‏והביאו אלי‏; cf. 2 Sam 24:2 LXX[L]. Lacking in Samuel MT, LXX.

4 ‏על עמו‏; cf. one Hebrew MS of 2 Sam 24:3, LXX[L]. Samuel MT, LXX: ‏אל העם‏ "to the people." The text of Chronicles MT, therefore, is not a theological change effected by the Chronicler, but a change based on a divergent text of Samuel.

5 ‏כהם‏; cf. 2 Sam 24:3 LXX[ALMN]. Samuel MT ‏כהם וכהם‏.

6 ‏הלא אדני המלך‏. Instead of this initial clause, Chronicles LXX agrees with 2 Sam 24:3 ‏ועיני אדני המלך ראות‏ "And the eyes of the king see." Because the next words in Chronicles LXX follow Chronicles MT, it is likely that the initial clause has been corrected from Samuel.

7 ‏על‏; cf. 2 Sam 24:4 few Hebrew MSS, LXX[L]. Samuel MT, LXX: ‏אל‏.

8 ‏ארבע‏; cf. 2 Sam 24:9 LXX[L], Josephus, *Ant.* 7.320. Samuel MT, LXX: ‏חמש‏ "five."

9 Chronicles LXX "eighty."

10 ‏אל‏, with some Hebrew and LXX MSS. MT ‏את‏, the sign of the definite direct object.

11 ‏את הדבר הזה‏; cf. 2 Sam 24:10 LXX[ALMN]. Lacking in Samuel MT.

12 ‏גד חזה‏; cf. 2 Sam 24:11 LXX[L]. Samuel MT ‏גד הנביא חזה‏ "Gad, the prophet, the seer of." Japhet, 380, argues that Samuel MT conflates the original Samuel reading ("the prophet Gad") with the reading in Chronicles ("Gad the seer of David"), but in light of LXX[L] it seems more likely that Samuel MT conflates two variant readings in Samuel MSS.

13 ‏לאמר‏; cf. 2 Sam 24:12 LXX and LXX[L]. Lacking in Samuel MT.

14 ‏נטה‏; some Hebrew MSS, LXX[BL], and 2 Sam 24:12: ‏נוטל‏ "imposing [upon]." The reading in Chronicles MT may have arisen in the course of textual transmission of Chronicles, although Wellhausen preferred this reading as the original in Samuel (see discussion in McCarter, *II Samuel*, 505). Japhet, "Interchanges," 21, notes that ‏נטל‏ in Rabbinic Hebrew means "carry off," and this linguistic change may have been known already by the

not I who gave the command to number the people. It was I who sinned and acted very wickedly.[31] But these sheep, what have they done? Yahweh my God, let your hand be against me and against my father's house, but let not the plague be against your own people."
18/ The angel of Yahweh had commanded Gad to tell David that David should go up to establish an altar for Yahweh[32] at the threshing floor of Ornan the Jebusite. 19/ David went up at the word of Gad, which[33] he had spoken in the name of Yahweh. 20/ And Ornan turned[34] and caught a glimpse of the king[35] and his four sons who were with him hiding themselves.[36] Ornan was threshing wheat. 21/ As David came closer to Ornan, Ornan got a better look and recognized David[37] and left the threshing floor and prostrated himself before David, with his nose to the ground. 22/ David said to Ornan,[38] "Give me the site of the threshing floor so that I may build an altar to Yahweh. Give it to me at full price so that the plague may be prevented for the people." 23/ Ornan replied to David, "Take[39] it for yourself, and may my lord the king do[40] that which is good in his eyes. See, I have given the cattle for the burnt offerings and the threshing sledges for the wood and the wheat for the grain offering. I have given everything." 24/ But King David said to Ornan, "No, but for the full price I will acquire it, for I will not take what is yours for Yahweh to offer up burnt offerings that cost me nothing." 25/ So David paid Ornan six hundred shekels of gold by weight. 26/ David built there an altar to Yahweh, and he offered up burnt offerings and peace offerings.[41] When he called to Yahweh, he answered him by fire from heaven on the altar of burnt offering. And it consumed the burnt offering.[42] 27/ Then Yahweh commanded the angel and he returned his sword to its sheath.[43]
28/ When David saw that Yahweh had answered him at the threshing floor of Ornan the Jebusite, and when he offered a sacrifice there 29/ (but the tabernacle of Yahweh, which Moses had made in the wilderness, and the altar of burnt incense were at that time at the high place in Gibeon; 30/ David had not been able to go before it to seek God because he was afraid of the sword of the angel of Yahweh), 22:1/ David said, "This will be the house of Yahweh God,[44] and this will be the[45] altar for burnt offering for Israel."

15 קבל לך; cf. 2 Sam 24:13 LXX[BLMN]. Lacking in Samuel MT.

16 שלוש; cf. 2 Sam 24:13 LXX. Samuel MT שבע "seven."

17 נסכה, with Chronicles LXX and 2 Sam 24:13. Chronicles MT נספה ("being swept away"?). Japhet, "Interchanges," 42, proposes that Chronicles MT arose because of an orthographic interchange of *kāp* and *pê*.

18 מפני; cf. 2 Sam 24:13 LXX[L]. Samuel MT לפני.

19 בארץ; cf. 2 Sam 24:13 LXX[L]. Samuel MT בארצך "in your land."

20 ועתה; cf. 2 Sam 24:13 few Hebrew MSS, LXX[L]. Samuel MT עתה.

21 צר לי מאד. Chronicles LXX Στενά μοι καὶ τὰ τρία σφόδρα; 2 Sam 24:14 LXX[L] Στενά μοι πάντα σφόδρα ἐστιν καὶ τὰ τρία. McCarter, *II Samuel*, 506, suggests that an original כלו was lost in Samuel after לי and that השלשה was a variant for כלו. In any case Chronicles LXX is related to the variant reading in 2 Sam 24:14 LXX[L].

22 אפלה; cf. 2 Sam 24:14 LXX. Samuel MT נפלה "let us fall."

23 מאד; cf. 2 Sam 24:14 LXX. Lacking in Samuel MT.

24 For the plus in 2 Sam 24:15 LXX, see textual note 37 and the extended discussion in Pisano, *Additions or Omissions*, 61–65.

25 וישלח האלהים מלאך לירושלם. Cf. 2 Sam 24:16 וישלח ידו המלאך ירושלים "The angel put forth its hand [to] Jerusalem"; Samuel LXX καὶ ἐξέτεινεν ὁ ἄγγελος τοῦ θεοῦ τὴν χεῖρα αὐτοῦ εἰς Ιερουσαλημ. האלהים was added secondarily in the *Vorlage* of Samuel LXX and shows up in a different position in Chronicles, where it became the subject of the sentence and turned the angel into the direct object, with the consequent omission of ידו. BHS proposes וישלח מלאך האלהים לידו לירושלם "the angel of God put forth his hand to Jerusalem," but there is no reason to believe that reading was ever present in Chronicles.

26 וכהשחיתו, with LXX; MT וכהשחית. Cf. *BHS*.

27 על; cf. 2 Sam 24:16 few Hebrew MSS, LXX. Samuel MT אל.

28 עמד; cf. 2 Sam 24:16 4QSam[a] עומד. Samuel MT, LXX היה "was." Japhet, "Interchanges," 17, 31, notes this change from Samuel MT in Chronicles, but does not observe that this change had been made already in the Samuel textual tradition.

29 ארנן. 2 Sam 24:16 K הארונה; Q ארונה (see v. 20); 4QSam[a] ארנא. For the possible Hurrian etymology of this name see McCarter, *II Samuel*, 506 and 512.

30 This verse, which has been lost in 2 Samuel by homoioarchton (a scribe's eyes skipped from וישא דוד "And David lifted up" to ויאמר דוד "and David

Chronicler, who therefore replaced the verb.

said" in 2 Sam 24:17), has been preserved in 4QSam[a]: וישא [דויד את עיניו וירא את מלאך יהוה עומד בין ה[אר]ץ ובין [השמ]ים וחר[ב]ו שלופה בידו נטויה על ירושלם ויפל דויד והזקנים על פנ[יהם מתן]כסים בשק[י]ם. Chronicles differs in reading מכסים for מתכסים and in placing על פניהם after בשקים. Note that in 4QSam[a] על פניהם appears before מתכסים בשקים. Cf. also Josephus *Ant.* 7.327–28. Paul Dion, "The Angel with the Drawn Sword (II Chr 21, 16): An Exercise in Restoring the Balance of Text Criticism *and* Attention to Context," *ZAW* 97 (1985) 114–17, rightly calls attention to the fact that even if the Chronicler derived this verse from a manuscript of Samuel he was still responsible for developing the motif of the angel with the drawn sword throughout the pericope. Contra Lemke, "Synoptic Problem," 357.

31 הרעתי הרע; cf. 2 Sam 24:17 and 4QSam[a]: הרע הרעתי "I, the shepherd, did wrong." These readings are closely related and 4QSam[a] is probably superior. Samuel MT העויתי "I have acted iniquitously." Most Samuel LXX MSS are conflate: ἐγὼ ἐδίκεσα καὶ ὁ ποιμὴν ἐκακοποήσα. Japhet, 385, concludes that Samuel MT evolved from the reading in Chronicles, but McCarter, *II Samuel,* 507, provides a more convincing reconstruction: הרעה was lost by haplography and then הרעתי became העויתי in Samuel MT. A. Rofé, "4QSam[a] in the Light of Historico-Literary Criticism: The Case of 2 Sam 24 and 1 Chr 21" in *Biblische und judaistische Studien: FS für Paolo Sacchi* (ed. A. Vivian; Judentum und Umwelt 29; Frankfurt am Main: Peter Lang, 1990) 116, suggests that the MT reading in 2 Samuel was a secondary alteration to make David's word conform to a standard confession of sins (e.g., 1 Kgs 8:47//2 Chr 6:37).

32 מזבח ליהוה; cf. 2 Sam 24:18 LXX[L]. Samuel MT ליהוה מזבח.

33 אשר; cf. 2 Sam 24:19 LXX[L]. Samuel MT כאשר.

34 וישב. This seems to be a misreading of 2 Sam 24:20 וישקף ("looked down"), but there is no evidence that there was ever another reading here in Chronicles. See also textual note 36.

35 המלך, with one Hebrew MS, LXX, and 2 Sam 24:20. Chronicles MT המלאך "the angel." Curtis and Madsen, 252–54, retain the MT and translate: "And Ornan turned about and saw the angel; and his four sons who were with him hid themselves."

36 וישב ארנן וירא את המלך וארבעת בניו עמו מתחבאים; 2 Sam 24:20 וישקף ארונא וירא את המלך ואת עבדיו עברים עליו "and Araunah looked down and saw the king and his servants passing by him." 4QSam[a] supports Samuel on the first word (see textual note 34) but then is followed by a long lacuna that has been reconstructed diversely, e.g., McCarter: וירא ארנא [מתחבאים מתכסים] את המלך ואת עבדיו באים אליו

[ארנא וירא את המלאך וארבעת בניו בשקים; Fincke: [ארנא] עמו מתחבאים ומכסים בשקים; and Herbert: [ארנא] וירא את המלך ואת עבדיו עוברים עליו מתכסים] בשקים. Fincke's reconstruction presupposes the greatest dependence of Chronicles on a non-MT text of Samuel and McCarter presupposes that one word in Chronicles, מתחבאים, is based on a Samuel variant. Pisano, *Additions or Omissions,* 114, remarks: "4Q contains a later addition to the text which agrees with Chr, but which was not necessarily part of the older text of Sam as contained in MT." He does not seem to question whether Chronicles depended on the type of reading preserved in 4QSam[a], but rather whether that reading was a secondary development in the text of Samuel.

37 וארנן דש חטים ויבא דויד עד ארנן וירא את דויד; cf. 2 Sam 24:20 4QSam[a] וארנא דש חטים [ויבוא דויד עד ארנא ויבט ארנא וירא את דויד ואת עבדיו מתכ]סים בשקים בא[י . . .]ם. "Orna was threshing wheat. As David came closer to Orna, Orna got a better look and recognized David and his servants, covering themselves with sackcloth coming. . . ." For the reconstruction of 4QSam[a] see McCarter, *II Samuel,* 507; Herbert, *Reconstructing,* 194–96; and Fincke, *Samuel Scroll,* 268–69 (who reads והזקנים instead of ואת עבדיו). Lacking in 2 Sam 24:20 MT, LXX. The last four Hebrew words in the Qumran reading are themselves an expansion. The reading on the leather and space considerations in the lacuna show that Chronicles was based on a non-MT text of Samuel. 2 Sam 24:15 LXX contains a secondary plus that anticipates the reference to threshing wheat: "And David chose for himself the plague (death). And in the days of the wheat harvest. . . ." Japhet, "Interchanges," 16, notes the replacement of וישקף by ויבט in Chronicles, but fails to notice that this change was already made in one of the textual traditions of Samuel.

38 אל ארנן; cf. 2 Sam 24:21 LXX[L] αὐτῷ. Lacking in Samuel MT.

39 קח; cf. 2 Sam 24:22 LXX[L]. Samuel MT יקח "May he take."

40 ויעש; cf. 2 Sam 24:22 LXX[L]. Samuel MT ויעל "let [my lord the king,] offer up." Japhet, "Interchanges," 42, proposes that Chronicles MT preserves the original reading, but does not note that the same reading appears in the Samuel textual tradition.

41 2 Sam 24:25 LXX contains a plus here indicating that Solomon enlarged David's altar because it was too small. Pisano, *Additions or Omissions,* 65–66, sees it as an addition inspired by the Chronicler's account of the temple construction.

42 והאכל את העלה, with Chronicles LXX (cf. Syr, Arab.); lacking in Chronicles MT by homoioteleuton.

43 נדנה. Curtis and Madsen, 254, identify this as a Persian loanword. Cf. *HALOT* 2:674.

44 יהוה האלהים. For this double divine title see also 1 Chr 22:19 and 2 Chr 32:16. יהוה אלהים occurs in 1 Chr 17:16, 17; 28:10; 2 Chr 1:9; 6:41 (twice), 42; 26:18.

45 המזבח. The definite article was lost in Chronicles MT by haplography after זה.

21:1—22:1

Structure

This passage is parallel to 2 Sam 24:1-25, though the Chronicler has considerably changed the focus of that passage and added an important concluding paragraph of his own (1 Chr 21:26b—22:1).[1] In addition, the discovery of 4QSam[a], a copy of 2 Sam 24:16-20, has shown that many of the differences between the two accounts are due to an alternate text of Samuel that was available to the Chronicler as his *Vorlage*.[2] This is the last time that the Chronicler quotes from the books of Samuel, and we need to review what he has selected for inclusion and what he has omitted from the final chapters of these books, 2 Samuel 21–24.

- 2 Sam 21:1-14: David turns the descendants of Saul over to the people of Gibeon, who impale them; David buries Saul and his descendants. The Chronicler omitted this passage, which has nothing to do with the temple and with his cultic interests, and which indicates (contra 1 Chr 10:6) that some members of the house of Saul survived for a time. The Chronicler may also have been offended by David's turning over the descendants of Saul to the Gibeonites for execution.
- 2 Sam 21:15-17: The reasons for the Chronicler omitting this anecdote about a battle with a Philistine hero are discussed in the commentary on 1 Chr 20:4-8.
- 2 Sam 21:18-22: This pericope, which recounts three anecdotes about battles with Philistine heroes, is included in 1 Chr 20:4-8.
- 2 Sam 22:1-51: This royal song of thanksgiving is not included by the Chronicler, but a slightly divergent copy appears in the Bible as Psalm 18.
- 2 Sam 23:1-7: The Chronicler does not include this poem called "The Last Words of David," but he presents his own much longer version of David's last words in 1 Chronicles 22, 28–29.
- 2 Sam 23:8-39: This list of David's warriors is included at 1 Chr 11:10-47.
- 2 Sam 24:1-25: This final chapter of 2 Samuel is included at 1 Chr 21:1—22:1. While David incurs guilt in this chapter and therefore we might expect it to be omitted,[3] the Chronicler uses this account to indicate how the place for the temple and the altar of burnt offerings were obtained by David at divine direction.[4] The David who sins in this chapter is also one who trusts in the manifold mercies of God (v. 13), which would also be available to the Chronicler's audience through the temple.

This chapter in Chronicles may be outlined as follows:

I. 21:1-6. Military census undertaken by David (2 Sam 24:1-9)

II. 21:7-15. Divine punishment because of the census (2 Sam 24:10-15)

III. 21:16-17. David's intercession with Yahweh (2 Sam 24:16-17)

---

1   Johnstone, 1:238, includes 1 Chr 22:2-4 with this pericope. In these verses David makes additional provisions for the temple.

2   For a thorough study of Josephus's treatment of this chapter and its *Vorlage,* including comparison with the ancient versions, see Christopher T. Begg, "Josephus' Version of David's Census," *Hen* 16 (1994) 199–226.

3   In his prayer at the dedication of the temple Solomon concedes that there is no one who does not sin (2 Chr 6:36).

4   See Piet B. Dirksen, "Why Was David Disqualified as Temple Builder? The Meaning of 1 Chronicles 22:8," *JSOT* 70 (1996) 53.

IV. 21:18-27. David purchases a threshing floor and builds an altar (2 Sam 24:18-25)

V. 21:28–22:1. David designates the site as the future place for the temple and the altar of burnt offering (without a parallel in 2 Samuel 24)

Detailed Commentary

21:1-6. Military Census Undertaken by David

■ **1** *Satan stood up against Israel:* According to 2 Sam 24:1, "The anger of Yahweh was again kindled against Israel and he [Yahweh] incited David to number the people." Chronicles omits the clause about Yahweh's anger being kindled "again" from the *Vorlage,* since this links back to 2 Sam 21:1-14, a passage not included in Chronicles, which told of a three-year famine because of the blood-guilt stemming from the house of Saul. Chronicles also replaces the problematic idea of Yahweh's anger leading to his temptation of David to number the people, and it attributes this temptation instead to Satan.[5] Satan's motivation is unknown and irrelevant to the Chronicler's purpose, but Satan plays a similar accusatory role in his other two occurrences in the OT: the prologue to the

book of Job (chaps. 1–2) and the postexilic prophet Zechariah (3:1-2). Only in Chronicles, however, does this word lack the definite article and therefore function as a personal name.[6] Japhet, 374–75, notes that the figure of Satan does not appear elsewhere in Chronicles and that angels appear in this work only when they are already present in the Chronicler's sources (in this chapter and 2 Chr 32:21). Since this figure in v. 1 does not appear in the divine realm and his incitement is against David rather than against God, she proposes that what is meant is a human adversary.[7] But the use of the verb "stand" (עמד) in a legal sense, used also with "the adversary" in Zech 3:1, and the use of the verb "incited" (סות), also used with "the adversary" in Job 2:3,[8] suggest that a supernatural tempter/accuser is indeed intended.[9] A similar use of Satan to lessen problematic actions by Yahweh can be seen in the later book of *Jubilees,* where it was Mastema (= Satan) who suggested to God that he test Abraham by having him sacrifice Isaac (Gen 22:1; *Jub.* 17:15-18), and who replaced Yahweh as the agent who tried to kill Moses on his way to Egypt (Exod 4:24; *Jub.* 48:2). Rudolph, 143, notes that the Tg conflates and harmonizes the contrasting notions of the cause of the

5   John Sailhamer, "1 Chronicles 21:1—A Study in Inter-Biblical Interpretation," *TJ,* n.s. 10 (1989) 37–38, following in part Willi, *Chronik als Auslegung,* 156, sees the Chronicler's version not as an alternative view intended to replace the view of 2 Samuel 24, but as an *explanation* of 2 Samuel 24 itself. Willi believed this understanding was facilitated by the presence of the verbs סות and שום in 2 Sam 24:1-4 and in Job 2. The Chronicler was then merely making explicit a sense he already found in 2 Samuel 24. Sailhamer himself sees "the adversary" as "the enemies of Israel" (p. 42). Hence he interpreted 2 Samuel 24 as stating that the anger of Yahweh meant a threat of foreign invasion.

6   GKC §125f. האדם "the man" in Gen 2:7 becomes אדם "Adam" in Gen 5:1. Japhet, *Ideology,* 145–49, argues that השטן would denote a proper noun, appealing to GKC §126d, but overlooks what was said in GKC §125f.

7   Cf. 1 Kgs 11:14, 23, 25 or Ps 109:6. John W. Wright, "The Innocence of David in 1 Chronicles 21," *JSOT* 60 (1993) 87–105, identifies the adversary as an anonymous enemy, who threatens Israel's national security. In the publication of her dissertation on the topic, Peggy L. Day, *An Adversary in Heaven: śāṭān in the Hebrew Bible* (HSM 43; Atlanta: Scholars

Press, 1988) 127–45, wavers between identifying this figure as an unspecified human enemy of the Israelite state (p. 143) or a divine accuser who brings an unspecified charge against Israel to the heavenly assize, finally settling on the latter (p. 144). But, of course, what Satan does here is no such thing, but rather he incites David to number Israel. Sailhamer, "1 Chronicles 21:1," 33–48, after reviewing and criticizing Willi's interpretation of this verse as an *explanation* of 2 Samuel 24 itself, argues that the Chronicler was looking for a term from the Deuteronomistic History that would express his understanding that Yahweh's wrath meant the threat of foreign invasion, and hit upon the word שטן. See especially 1 Kgs 11:14, 23. He believes that this harmonistic reading is true to the original intention of the author of 2 Samuel 24.

8   Yahweh is the object of the verb "incited" in Job, and David is the object of that verb in 1 Chronicles.

9   Kirsten Nielsen, *Satan: The Prodigal Son? A Family Problem in the Bible* (Biblical Seminar 50; Sheffield: Sheffield Academic Press, 1998) 100–105, rejects a legal understanding of Satan in this passage and an understanding of Satan as adversary, but prefers a father-son relationship between Yahweh and Satan. In Job, too, the God-Satan relationship offers a

census in Samuel and Kings by having Yahweh cause Satan to stand up against Israel.[10] In tempting David, Satan puts Israel itself at risk.

and incited[11] *David to number Israel:* Censuses were ordinarily taken for purposes of taxation or military conscription.[12] The latter is clearly intended here since it is conducted by Joab, David's chief army officer and the commanders of the troops, and the results are listed according to those "who drew the sword." The Chronicler changed the name of the group to be numbered from "Israel and Judah" in 2 Sam 24:1 to "Israel" alone in 1 Chr 21:1—that is, the whole nation of Israel (the numbers for Judah in v. 5 are secondary; see below). He also omitted from the *Vorlage* בהם "against them," which would imply that David engaged in hostile action against Israel.

■ **2** *David*[13] *said to Joab and to the commanders of the people:* For Joab see 1 Chr 2:16; 11:6-39; 18:15; 19:8-15; 20:1-2. The phrase "commanders of the people" has replaced the description of Joab as the commander of the army in 2 Sam 24:2. But the plural word "commanders" already showed up in some versions of Samuel (see textual note 1),[14] thus diminishing the importance of this change for understanding the text of Chronicles.

"Go, number[15] *Israel from Beer-sheba to Dan":* The ideal limits of the land are given in reverse order in Chronicles (cf. also 2 Chr 30:5),[16] perhaps because of a preference for the south/Judah over the north.[17] Beer-sheba is located at MR 134072 and Dan at MR 211294. The verb "go" (from הלך) has replaced שוט in the *Vorlage* at 2 Sam 24:2, perhaps because of the rarity of the latter verb.[18] A similar substitution is made in v. 4 where הלך in the *hitpael* replaces שוט.

"bring me a report so that I may know their number": The idea of a report is already contained in one text tradition of Samuel (see textual note 3). The Chronicler speaks of "their number" rather than "the number of the people" (2 Sam 24:2).

■ **3** *"May Yahweh add to his people like them a hundredfold":* Joab's wish indicates that an increase of numbers in itself would be considered a good thing and would in fact result from divine blessing. David's decision to take a census, however, might imply a considerably greater amount of self-reliance. In 1 Chr 27:16-24, a paragraph perhaps added to diminish David's guilt for this census, the Chronicler notes that Yahweh had promised to make Israel as numerous as the stars of heaven.[19]

---

proximity between God and what is happening in the world as well as a certain distance from the misfortunes that people must suffer. This is not the place to debate her interpretation of God and Satan as the image of a father and a son, though I believe she seriously underplays Satan's prosecutorial or adversarial role in the divine council. Her interpretation of Satan as a supernatural being related to temptation in 1 Chronicles 21 is closer to the traditional view—and my view—than to that of Japhet.

10 "The Lord raised up Satan against Israel, and he [Satan] incited David to number Israel."

11 In Job 2:3 the verb סות is used of Satan's inciting God against Job, while in 1 Sam 26:19 David asks if Yahweh has incited Saul against David. Cf. 1 Kgs 22:20-22//2 Chr 18:19-21, where Yahweh considers how to entice (פתה) Ahab.

12 Cf. Exod 30:11-16; Numbers 1.

13 David's name replaces the title "the king" in 2 Sam 24:2.

14 These "commanders of the army" recur in 2 Sam 24:5 (twice), a verse not incorporated by the Chronicler.

15 Japhet, "Interchanges," 24, notes that the Chroni-

cler has replaced פקד from 2 Sam 24:2 with ספר in line with usage in Late Biblical Hebrew.

16 2 Sam 24:2, "from Dan to Beer-sheba." Directions from south to north are also given at 1 Chr 13:5, "from the Shihor of Egypt to Lebo-hamath" (an addition not contained in the *Vorlage* at 2 Sam 6:1), and 2 Chr 19:4, "from Beer-sheba to the hill country of Ephraim" (again without *Vorlage*). Neh 11:30 refers to territory from Beer-sheba to the valley of Hinnom.

17 A. Hurvitz, "'Diachronic Chiasm' in Biblical Hebrew," in *J. Liver Memorial Volume* (ed. B. Uffenheimer; Tel Aviv: Tel Aviv University, 1971) 253–54, sees it as a linguistic development, not limited to Chronicles.

18 So Japhet, "Interchanges," 15. The verb שוט was used to describe Satan's movements through the world in Job 1:7; 2:2. Did this verb suggest to the Chronicler the idea of introducing Satan into his account (so Johnstone, 1:226)?

19 Cf. Gen 15:5; 22:17.

"Are not all of them, my lord the king, servants to my lord?" Joab's objection to the census is stronger in Chronicles than in Samuel. This sentence replaces one in 2 Sam 24:3 that completed Joab's wish about Yahweh multiplying the people a hundredfold by adding that this should take place within the king's lifetime ("while the eyes of my lord the king can still see it"). Joab argues instead in Chronicles that the people are already totally on David's side ("servants to my lord") so that there is no point in taking a census, with its connotations of centralization and improved administration.

"Why should this bring retribution for Israel?" Even with Joab's stronger objections in Chronicles, the reader has to infer what is wrong with this census, especially since censuses are listed elsewhere in Chronicles with no hint of criticism.[20] The problem Joab found with the census is even less clear in 2 Samuel 24. McCarter, *II Samuel*, 512–14, concludes that people enrolled in a census were subject to military rules of purity, such as Deut 23:10-15 (9-14), and the onset of the plague in this chapter suggests that taboos may have been violated (cf. also Exod 30:11-16). But the context in Chronicles suggests a different interpretation. David has just conducted a number of military campaigns in 1 Chronicles 18–20 in which Yahweh had given him victory wherever he went (18:6, 13). In 19:14-15 the Arameans and the Ammonites fled without the Israelite armies even engaging in combat. A census implies, however, that numbers count,[21] and therefore taking a census is an indication of a lack of trust in God's role in bringing about victory.[22] The military purpose of the census is its central error. The Chronicler also uniformly criticizes any reliance on alliances as if they were the source of strength (e.g., in the case of Jehoshaphat, 2 Chr 18:1; 20:35-37). "Guilt," as in NRSV and other English versions, is not a correct translation for אשמה ("retribution") in this verse, and the noun can mean both guilt and the consequence of guilt, or punishment, as is clearly intended here.[23] The term אשם becomes a key term in Chronicles (2 Chr 24:18; 28:10, 13; 33:23).[24] In any case Joab's question is well taken since any guilt of David should redound on the king himself and not on the people.[25] Perhaps the Chronicler calculated that the people became liable to such retribution by participating in the census.

■ **4** *Joab went forth and traveled through all Israel and came to Jerusalem:* Joab's objections were overruled by David ("The word of the king prevailed over Joab"),[26] and Joab therefore carried out the census as an obedient soldier. The Chronicler summarizes and abbreviates the corresponding account in 2 Samuel (24:4-8), which traces the route of the census, beginning in Transjordan and proceeding in a counterclockwise direction that wound up in Jerusalem, where Joab also finishes the census in Chronicles. In 2 Samuel 24 the census took two hundred

20 Wright, "Innocence of David," cites 1 Chr 11:11; 23:1; 2 Chr 2:17; 17:13b-19; 25:5; 26:11-13. The general thesis of this article, that David is an innocent victim of Joab's failure to complete the census, is, however, unacceptable. See the articles by Gary N. Knoppers, "Images of David in Early Judaism: David as Repentant Sinner in Chronicles," *Bib* 76 (1995) 449–70; and Noel Bailey, "David's Innocence: A Response to J. Wright," *JSOT* 64 (1994) 83–90, for details.

21 Common wisdom says that numbers do count: "The glory of a king is a multitude of people" (Prov 14:28). But in Chronicles the invasion of a million Ethiopians during the reign of Asa is easily turned back (2 Chr 14:9-15).

22 For a similar line of argument see Knoppers, "Images of David." Joshua J. Adler, "David's Last Sin: Was It the Census?" *JBQ* 23 (1995) 91–95, supports the unlikely hypothesis that David's sin was his failure to oust the seven nations who inhabited Canaan (Deut 20:17) and specifically his failure to capture Mount Moriah.

23 J. Milgrom, *Cult and Conscience: The Asham and the Priestly Doctrine of Repentance* (Studies in Judaism in Late Antiquity 18; Leiden: Brill, 1976) 3–12. Milgrom, 3, remarks: "It has long been recognized that the biblical terms for good and bad behavior also connote their respective reward and punishment."

24 See also the use of the verb אשם twice in 2 Chr 19:10.

25 Noel Bailey, "David and God in 1 Chronicles 21: Edged with Mist," in Graham and McKenzie, *Chronicler as Author,* 339–40, cites only Amos 8:14 and Lev 4:3 as possible parallels.

26 2 Sam 24:4 adds "and over the commanders of the army." In 2 Samuel these commanders go out with Joab to take the census.

days to complete (no duration for the census taking is given in Chronicles). The Chronicler may have considered these details irrelevant, and/or he may not have understood all of the geographic data in the itinerary. In Chronicles Joab merely travels (lit. walks "back and forth" [הלך in *hitpael*]) throughout the land.

■ **5** *Joab gave the number of the census of the people to David:* The word for "census," מפקד, provides a link to the law of the census in Exod 30:11-16, where the root פקד is used frequently.[27] David neglected to require the payment of the half-shekel tax, which was to serve as an indemnity for the life of all whose lives were put in jeopardy by war.[28]

All Israel amounted to one million one hundred thousand who drew the sword: The results of Joab's military census invite comparison with the numbers recorded in 2 Sam 24:9: eight hundred thousand for Israel and five hundred thousand for Judah.[29] "Israel" for the Chronicler can mean the nation as a whole, also in this chapter (see 1 Chr 21:1, 2, 3, 4, 7, 12, 14; 22:1) the Northern Kingdom,[30] or even the kingdom of Judah.[31] In the original draft of this verse, I believe "Israel" referred to the entire nation. The list of the tribes in 2:1-2 numbers twelve, and there would be thirteen tribes in chaps. 2–8, since Joseph is divided into Ephraim and Manasseh, were it not for the unexplained lacuna involving Zebulun and possibly Dan in chap. 7. If the Chronicler calculated that these thirteen tribes totaled one million three hundred thousand in 2 Samuel 24, adding the sums for Israel (eight hundred thousand) and Judah (five hundred thousand), each tribe would contribute roughly one hundred thousand soldiers. Since Levi and Benjamin were explicitly excluded from this census in Chronicles (v. 6), the Chronicler reduced the overall total by two hundred thousand.[32]

Judah amounted to four hundred seventy thousand who drew the sword: This sentence is generally recognized as a correction by a later hand that understood "Israel" to include *only* the territory of the Northern Kingdom and not that of Judah. Where the supplementer got the number four hundred and seventy thousand is not completely clear. Did he take five hundred thousand from 2 Sam 24:9 and reduce it by thirty thousand, since Judah in his day would include the tribal territories of both Judah and Benjamin and therefore he had to reduce the total by a number appropriate for Benjamin, which was not included in the census?[33] Or did he take four hundred thousand for Judah from the text of Samuel now represented by 2 Sam 24:9 LXX[L] (see textual note 8) and then add seventy thousand, so that after the plague, in which seventy thousand lives were lost (v. 14), the overall total would remain the same? In either case this secondary reading has departed from the idea that there were roughly one hundred thousand in a tribe, since Judah had four hundred seventy thousand and Benjamin, possibly, had only thirty thousand. The overall number in the present text also goes up to one million five hundred seventy thousand.

■ **6** *He did not number Levi and Benjamin among them:* In this addition made by the Chronicler, the reason given for the omission of these two tribes—that the command of the king was abhorrent (נתעב) to Joab—explains why Joab did not fully carry out David's census, but not why these two tribes in particular were left out.[34] Two references in Numbers (1:49; 2:33) excuse Levi from any military census and include the expression בתוך "among" (the Israelites) that is also used in this verse (with "them" as a suffix).[35] The explanation for Benjamin's exclusion

---

27   Exod 30:12 (3 times), 13, 14.

28   So Johnstone, 1:228.

29   According to 1 Chr 5:18 the two and one-half Transjordanian tribes numbered 44,760 warriors.

30   2 Chr 10:16 (3 times), 18, 19; 11:1; 13:4, 12; 21:6; 25:7.

31   2 Chr 10:17; 11:3; 12:1, 6; 13:5; 15:17; 19:8; 20:29; 21:2, 4; 24:5, 16; 28:19, 23; 28:27; 29:24 (2 times).

32   LXX[L] in 2 Sam 24:9 assigns nine hundred thousand to Israel and four hundred thousand to Judah, with the overall total remaining at one million three hundred thousand.

33   When Saul mustered the people (1 Sam 11:8), there were three hundred thousand from Israel and thirty (MT; 4QSam[a], LXX, and Josephus: seventy) thousand from Judah. The supplementer may have calculated that the tribes of Judah and Benjamin at the time of the united monarchy would have been about the same size.

34   Mosis, *Untersuchungen*, 110, following Galling, 61, proposed that Chronicles originally excluded Judah and Benjamin from the census.

35   The Levites could be numbered for religious purposes (Num 3:15; 26:57).

is not so clear.[36] An earlier suggestion[37] that the Chronicler attributed Jerusalem to the tribal territory of Benjamin is unlikely despite such passages as Josh 18:28 and Judg 1:21, since the temple site had not yet been sanctified by the sacrifices of David.[38] It is more likely that it was because the tabernacle was located at Gibeon (1 Chr 16:39; 2 Chr 1:3; cf. 5:5 and Josh 18:25) in Benjaminite territory that the Chronicler had Joab exclude this tribe from the census.[39] This verse is the last reference to Joab in a narrative context in Chronicles (but see the lists in 1 Chr 26:28; 27:7, 24, 34). His role in the attempted coup by Adonijah and his subsequent execution by Benaiah at Solomon's behest (1 Kings 1–2) go unmentioned in Chronicles.

21:7-15. Divine Punishment Because of the Census

■ **7** *This matter was displeasing to God:* Allen, 423, notes that this disapproval of David's actions is very similar to the judgment recorded in 2 Sam 11:27 about David's adultery with Bathsheba. The Chronicler, of course, did not include that word of judgment about the king's adultery since he omitted the entire incident with Bathsheba. "This matter," in vv. 7-8, does not refer, *pace* Day[40] and Wright,[41] to Joab's omitting Levi and Benjamin from the census, but to the king's command in v. 6, as David himself affirms in vv. 8 and 17.[42] The king's command was abhorrent to Joab and also evil in the eyes of Yahweh. This verdict anticipates the negative evaluative formula used with later kings (2 Chr 21:6; 22:4; 33:6, 22, etc.).

he struck Israel: This clause does double duty. On the one hand it anticipates the judgment of God through pestilence in v. 14, and the intervening verses explain why that specific catastrophe was the one that occurred. But on the other hand it functions as punishment prior to that to bring David to his senses and lead him to confess his sin in v. 8. Similarly, Pharaoh came to his senses when Yahweh unleashed plagues on Pharaoh and his household after he had taken Sarai, Abram's wife (Gen 12:17-18). In the *Vorlage* at 2 Sam 24:10 David's heart struck him (conscience pangs that anticipate God's punishment?) after the report of Joab's census, but, as the Chronicler would have noticed, no reason is given for his sense of guilt. The Chronicler now supplies one.

■ **8** *David said to God,*[43] *"I have sinned exceedingly in that I have done this matter":* The word "exceedingly" and the word "very" later in the verse,[44] both translations of מאד, anticipate the double use of the same adverb in v. 13.[45] The expression "this matter" on the other hand points

---

36 According to Pseudo-Rashi, Joab omitted the Benjaminites because they had been stricken in the episode of the concubine from Gibeah (Judges 19–21). If they were to be afflicted now by military obligations, what would be left for them? Curtis and Madsen, 248, cite older commentators who suggested that Benjamin was omitted because the census was interrupted by a countermand from David: "Joab the son of Zeruiah began to count but did not finish. Wrath came upon Israel for this, and the number was not entered in the book of the Chronicles of King David" (1 Chr 27:24).

37 By Wellhausen and Benzinger, cited by Curtis and Madsen, 248.

38 Japhet, 378, believes that Joab left both Levi and Benjamin out because of their connections—as priests and geographically, respectively—with Jerusalem.

39 So Curtis and Madsen, 248.

40 Day, *Adversary in Heaven,* 137, relates "this matter" to Joab's omission of Levi and Benjamin, but her only argument is an appeal to 1 Chr 27:24. That passage, however, is a late corrective to chap. 21, attempting to exonerate David for taking a census and operating on entirely different premises. In

chap. 21 Joab finishes the census; in 27:24 he does not. In chap. 21 Joab raised objections to David ordering a census; in 27:24 he undertook a census against the will of David.

41 "Innocence of David," 99.

42 See Bailey, "David's Innocence." Bailey suggests that this clause has the force of "This matter was *also* distressing to God."

43 "God" replaces "Yahweh" in 2 Sam 24:10, and the second use of "Yahweh" in that verse is also omitted in Chronicles.

44 "I have behaved very foolishly."

45 Even though each of the four uses of מאד in Chronicles is inherited in one form or another from the Samuel text tradition (three from Samuel MT and one from LXX[L]), they have a synchronic function in the present text of Chronicles.

back to the same words in the previous verse. In any case the king, who was supposed to be wise,[46] now admits that he has acted very foolishly.[47] The only other reference to folly in Chronicles occurs when Hanani describes Asa's alliance with Ben-hadad as a foolish action (2 Chr 16:9). This is the first occurrence of the verb חטא "sin" in Chronicles.[48]

"Now take away the iniquity of your servant": The use of עון "inquity" is based on 2 Sam 24:10 and comprises the only use of this noun in the books of Chronicles. David again assumes full responsibility for taking the census.

■ **9** *Yahweh spoke to Gad, the seer of David:* The Chronicler rephrases the way the divine word was revealed to Gad in 2 Sam 24:11,[49] making the divine communication more direct, and he also omits from 2 Sam 24:11 the clause, "and David got up in the morning," which may have seemed like an extraneous comment. Gad is later credited as being the author of one of the three prophetic sources dealing with David (1 Chr 29:29), and he and David alike are cited, in the days of Hezekiah, as the authors of the commandment on how to station the Levites (2 Chr 29:25).[50] Zevit argues that the term חזה "seer" designates a person as a court prophet.[51] In 2 Sam 24:11 MT and LXX Gad is also called a נביא "prophet," but Chronicles is dependent on a manuscript of Samuel that lacks this word (see textual note 12).

■ **10-11** *"Go and say"*: For the first word the Chronicler has substituted an imperative for an infinitive absolute in his *Vorlage,* following a regular pattern in the Chronicler (Japhet, 380, for references).

"Thus says Yahweh, 'Take your choice'": Gad's message begins with the messenger formula (cf. v. 10), and announces three possible judgments without giving the reasons for the judgments that one usually finds in pre-exilic prophets. There is irony in that the name Gad means something like "good luck" or "good fortune," but his message threatens quite the opposite. Gad's message implies that despite David's contrition in v. 8, retributive punishment will have to take place.

■ **12** *"either three years of famine or three months of your fleeing from before your foes"*: Seven years of famine is a more conventional time period for a famine (cf. Pharaoh's dream in the Joseph story [Gen 41:27]) than three years and perhaps led to the reading in 2 Sam 24:13 MT (textual note 16), but the Chronicler's "three years" existed in the Samuel text tradition (see textual note 16) either as the original reading or by assimilation to three months in the next proposed judgment.

"three days of . . . pestilence in the land": The Chronicler surrounds these words taken from his *Vorlage* in 2 Sam 24:13 with two expressions, "the sword of Yahweh" (cf. vv. 16, 27) and "the angel of Yahweh destroying [משחית;[52] cf. v. 15] throughout the territory of Israel," that anticipate the angel with the drawn sword who is so central to this narration, and he indicates much more clearly than in Samuel that the third choice is a punishment that will be administered directly by Yahweh[53]—through the sword or the angel of Yahweh—and not through human

---

46 See Solomon's prayer in 2 Chr 1:10: "Give me now wisdom and knowledge to go out and come in before this people."

47 De Vries, 171–72, suggests, implausibly in my opinion, that David's confession of sin here is inadequate.

48 Cf. v. 17 and 2 Chr 6:22, 24, 26, 36, 37, 39; 25:4; 29:24.

49 "And the word of Yahweh came to Gad." The title "seer" is used only here in the books of Samuel and Kings.

50 In 1 Sam 22:5, not included in Chronicles, the prophet Gad served as a counselor to David while he was fleeing Saul.

51 Ziony Zevit, "A Misunderstanding at Bethel: Amos VII 12-17," *VT* 25 (1975) 783–90. In 1 Chr 25:5 Heman is designated as the king's seer, and in 2 Chr 35:15 Asaph, Heman, and Jeduthun are

called royal seers. Cf. 2 Chr 29:30, where this title is given to Asaph. Schniedewind, *Word of God*, 44, proposes that the singers were called "royal seers" because David had established the Levitical singers in their office.

52 The angel who destroyed the Egyptian firstborn is also designated by this participle (Exod 12:13, 23). Hence the role of this angel has been drastically reversed to bring judgment to Israel rather than to its enemies. The verb שחת "destroy" appears a number of times in Chronicles: 1 Chr 20:1; 2 Chr 12:7, 12; 20:23; 21:7; 22:4; 24:23; 25:16; 26:16; 27:2; 34:11; 35:21; 36:19.

53 None of the choices is particularly good. Pseudo-Rashi observed that such choices are like telling a sick person, "Behold, you are going to die. Now in which grave do you wish to be buried: beside your father or beside your mother?"

agents.[54] Rofé sees these additions as extensions of the angelological interpretation of the plague, first introduced in 2 Sam 24:16 4QSam[a], which he considers to be secondary.[55]

"And now, consider what I should respond to the one who sent me": By omitting the word "know" from Gad's request for a reply in 2 Sam 24:13,[56] the Chronicler leaves David alone, with no thought that an answer would be revealed to him so that he might know it.

■ **13** *"Let me fall into the hand of Yahweh, for his mercies are exceedingly manifold"*: David takes the initiative as the primary recipient of the judgment—"let me fall into the hand of Yahweh" rather than "let us fall into the hand of Yahweh"—although that change from plural to singular was already made in some manuscripts of Samuel (see textual note 22). By choosing what could be the most devastating punishment delivered by Yahweh himself, even if for the shortest duration, David counts on the fact that the one delivering these blows is the same one whose mercies are exceedingly manifold. One might think of the characteristic confession that appears several times in the OT: "Yahweh, Yahweh, a God merciful and gracious, slow to anger, and abounding in loyalty and faithfulness" (Exod 34:6-7; Joel 2:13; Jonah 4:2). The Chronicler may also thought of the divine characteristics reported in Psalm 103: Yahweh is merciful; he does not deal with us according to our sins; he knows how we were made; he remembers that we are dust (vv. 8-14).

"but let me not fall into human hands": Such human agents might overstep their bounds as Assyria did in Isa 10:5-12 or 37:26-39 (cf. also Hab 1:17). David never seems to consider the first choice, three years of famine.[57]

■ **14** *there fell from Israel seventy thousand persons:* Chronicles omits from 2 Sam 24:15 the duration of the plague (from the morning to the appointed time)[58] and its geographical extent (from Dan to Beer-sheba). Hence the plague did not last for three days, but only until Yahweh had changed his mind about the calamity. As Bailey notes, the death of seventy thousand shows Yahweh's mercy to be debatable and the amount of the punishment seems out of proportion.[59] David himself is not punished for his sin.

■ **15** *God sent an angel to Jerusalem:* The Chronicler indicates that the angel was acting at God's direction, not on its own initiative.[60] This contrasts with 2 Sam 24:16 ("The angel put out its hand toward Jerusalem"). In textual note 25 I outlined a process by which this reading could have resulted from the addition of האלהים in some Samuel witnesses. This, however, could also be a change introduced by the Chronicler himself.[61] We saw a similar tendency to emphasize God's direct involvement in Yahweh's direct address in the divine oracle to Gad in v. 9 and in the Chronicler's modifying "pestilence on the land" by a preceding reference to the "sword of Yahweh." In any case the angel appears suddenly and unex-

---

54 Famine, sword, and pestilence are also mentioned in Solomon's prayer at the dedication of the temple (2 Chr 6:28) and by Jehoshaphat in his prayer at 2 Chr 20:9.

55 A. Rofé, "4QSam[a] in the Light of Historico-literary Criticism: The Case of 2 Sam 24 and 1 Chr 21," in *Biblische und judaistische Studien: FS für Paolo Sacchi* (ed. Angelo Vivian; Frankfurt am Main: Peter Lang, 1990) 113.

56 "Now know and consider what I should respond to the one who sent me."

57 Bailey, "David and God," 346, believes that David offers God a choice between famine and a combination of plague and the sword of the angel.

58 McCarter, *II Samuel*, 503, "from morning until dinnertime."

59 Bailey, "David and God," 345–46. Bailey also suggests that the people, as represented by Joab, had resisted the idea of a census, thus adding bitter irony to the fact that they receive the full weight of

the divine punishment. For his own disobedience Asa suffers from a foot problem (2 Chr 16:12), and Uzziah contracts leprosy (26:19).

60 A. A. da Silva, "A Comparison between the Avenging Angel of 1 Ch 21 and Analogous 'Angel-like' Figures in the Ugaritic Ba'al Cycle," *JSem* 6 (1994) 154–69, draws a comparison between this avenging angel and the "punishment-gods" found in the Ugaritic texts. Resheph killed through pestilence and Anat brought death and destruction. The paired gods Qodesh and Amrur delivered messages (cf. v. 18). Da Silva notes, however, that these figures at Ugarit are real, if often minor, deities.

61 Japhet, *Ideology*, 140.

pectedly in 2 Sam 24:16, with no indication in the *Vorlage* of how it got there. The text in Chronicles remedies that problem by recording God's sending of the angel. After the death of seventy thousand throughout Israel, the plague now threatens the capital itself.

when he was about to destroy it, Yahweh looked and changed his mind about the calamity: David's wager, in the Chronicler's mind, had paid off. He had chosen punishment delivered by one whose mercies were exceedingly manifold. The words "when he was about to destroy it, Yahweh looked" were added by the Chronicler to the text of the *Vorlage* and indicate that Yahweh's compassion arose precisely when he saw the people's devastation taking place. Similarly, when God had *looked* on the Israelites in Egypt, he thoroughly understood their condition (Exod 2:25). The psalmist prayed, "Look down from heaven and see" (Ps 80:15 [14]). Elsewhere Yahweh changed his mind when he saw how people had repented (Jer 26:3, 13, 19).[62] The double use of the *hiphil* infinitive construct of the verb שחת in this verse ("to destroy it"; "when he was about to destroy it") and the use of the *hiphil* participle of the same verb to modify the angel ("the destroying [angel]") recall the danger posed by the "destroyer" (*hiphil* participle of the same verb) in the Passover account (Exod 12:23). While the destroying angel now stopped his killing, he remains as a threatening presence up to v. 27.

standing by the threshing floor of Ornan the Jebusite: Ornan's name in 2 Samuel 24 is spelled אֲרַוְנָה or ארונה instead of ארנן[63] as here.[64] While the spelling in Samuel is probably more original and comes from a Hurrian or Hittite provenance, the spelling in Chronicles resembles that in the LXX of both Kings and Chronicles and in Josephus.[65] The verb "standing" was taken from the Samuel textual tradition (see textual note 28) and does not represent a change introduced by the Chronicler.

The Jebusites are listed generically with other pre-Israelite inhabitants of the land in twenty-two biblical lists, or they are identified as the pre-Davidic inhabitants of Jerusalem (e.g., Josh 15:63; 18:16; Judg 1:21; 2 Sam 5:6). While there is some doubt about the historical identification of Jebus with Jerusalem,[66] by the time of the Chronicler everyone would understand that Ornan was a resident in Jerusalem.[67]

21:16-17. David's Intercession with Yahweh

■ **16** *David looked up and saw the angel of Yahweh standing between earth and heaven:* All of v. 16 was once part of the Samuel tradition, despite its absence from Samuel MT, and does not reflect exclusively the thoughts of the Chronicler (see textual note 30). The angel hovering in midair seems to represent a mediating role between God and the world (see the references in much later texts in Dan 8:16; 10:4; and 12:6). Some scholars detect a great tension between the angel standing by the threshing floor (v. 15) and the angel standing between earth and heaven (v. 16). The first reference, however, initiates the role of the threshing floor in the account, and the second emphasizes the threat that hangs over the city until David's penance is completed. Rofé detects two phases in the cessation of the pestilence: when Yahweh repented or changed his mind, he told the angel, "Let your hand drop"; and when David had built the altar and offered a sacrifice, the angel was commanded to put the sword into its sheath.[68]

with his drawn sword in his hand: This awesome posture of the angel not only threatens Jerusalem, but it makes puny by comparison the hundreds of thousands of men Joab had counted "who drew the sword."[69]

David and the elders, covered with sackcloth, fell on their faces: David performed proper penance in line with the usual penitential demeanor (for sackcloth see 1 Kgs

---

62   See also Gen 6:6; Exod 32:14; 1 Sam 15:11; Jer 18:8, 10; 42:10; Jon 3:10. The *Mekilta* explains God's look in this way: "What did He behold? He beheld the blood of Isaac's *Akedah*, as it says, 'the Lord God will provide Himself the lamb.'" See Bernard Grossfeld, "The Targum to Lamentations 2:10," *JJS* 28 (1977) 63.

63   See textual note 29.

64   The threshing floor of Ornan is also mentioned in the account of Solomon's building the temple in 2 Chr 3:1.

65   Ορνα in LXX; Ορονναϛ in Josephus.

66   Stephen A. Reed, "Jebus," *ABD* 3:652–53.

67   Cf. 1 Chr 11:4, "Jerusalem, that is, Jebus."

68   Rofé, "4QSamᵃ," 113.

69   Hollis R. Johnson and Svend Holm-Nielsen, "Comments on Two Possible References to Comets in the Old Testament," *SJOT* 7 (1993) 100–103, propose that the sword might refer to the tail of a comet and believe that the Chronicler transformed the original idea of an angel with a sword into a heavenly phenomenon. This observation is based on no credible

425

21:27; Jonah 3:5, 8; for falling on one's face, see Num 16:22; Josh 7:6, 10; Ezra 10:1). The presence of the elders is attested already in 4QSam[a].

■ **17** *"it is I who sinned":* David repeats his confession from v. 8. In the previous sentence he admitted his initiative in taking the census: "Was it not I who gave the command to number the people?"[70] David's repentance follows Yahweh's merciful command for the angel to stop his destruction.

"But these sheep, what have they done?" David affirms that the people are innocent of wrongdoing in the census and he takes full responsibility.[71] The people, therefore, have been suffering unjustly. While there is no evidence that the reading "I the shepherd have acted very wickedly" at the end of the previous verse in 4QSam[a] ever appeared in Chronicles (see textual note 31), the Chronicles reading is clearly derivative from that better reading of the Samuel text. That more original reading makes an excellent contrast between David the shepherd and the people he ruled, who are the sheep.

"Yahweh my God": This address to God has been added by the Chronicler to his *Vorlage;* "my God" is used by David twice previously in 1 Chronicles. In 11:19 he used it when he declined to drink the water obtained by his men through a dangerous mission, and he used it in 17:25 when he was emboldened to pray because God had promised him a dynasty. David offers to accept the punishment on himself and his family and asks that it not be visited anymore on Israel as a whole: "Let your hand be against me and against my father's house, but let not the plague be against your own people." Unfortunately, David's plea comes after the divine judgment has already ceased (cf. Japhet, 383), although that decision may only be known by the narrator and not by David himself. David still saw the angel with the drawn sword

(v. 16).[72] The final result of the divine change of mind in v. 15 does not become reality until Yahweh orders the angel to sheathe his sword in v. 27. David's confessions in vv. 8 and 17 are followed by his sacrifice or cultic atonement in v. 26.[73] Only then does the divine judgment cease.

21:18-27. David Purchases a Threshing Floor and Builds an Altar

■ **18** *The angel of Yahweh had commanded Gad to tell David:* The Chronicler rewords his *Vorlage*[74] in order to make clear that Gad is speaking on divine authority and not just on his own initiative (cf. comments above on vv. 9 and 15). The content of this oracle is that David should build an altar for Yahweh on the threshing floor of Ornan; that is, it gives divine and prophetic warrant to the altar site. By acquiring the site and building an altar David does penance for his sin and initiates sacrifice at the site of the future temple. Mosis has called attention to several parallels between this chapter and Josh 5:13-15. There Joshua meets a man with a sword in his hand who is revealed as the commander of Yahweh's army. This "man" also indicates a spot that is a sanctuary when he commands Joshua to remove his shoes.[75]

■ **19** *David went up at the word of Gad, which he had spoken in the name of Yahweh:* No longer the headstrong initiator of the census, David acts only on the prodding of the prophet Gad, who spoke in the name of Yahweh. The relative clause in Chronicles replaces "just as Yahweh had commanded" in 2 Sam 24:19.

■ **20** *And Ornan turned and caught a glimpse of the king and his four sons who were with him hiding themselves:* This reading has been corrupted from the original reading in Samuel, especially with the mention of the four sons. They have developed from a misreading of an original

evidence and is innocent of the textual history discussed in textual note 30 that shows that this is no innovation of the Chronicler.

70 While parts of 1 Chr 21:15-17 are based on divergent texts of Samuel (see the textual notes), there is no reason to doubt that it was the Chronicler himself who added this question.

71 Contra Japhet, 377, who argues that to submit to a census is in itself a sin. This results from her translation of אשמה in v. 3 as "guilt."

72 See P. E. Dion, "The Angel with the Drawn Sword (II [*sic*] Chr 21, 16): An Exercise in Restoring the

Balance of Text Criticism and Attention to Context," *ZAW* 97 (1985) 115.

73 Cf. Lev 4:3, where an anointed priest offers a bull as sacrifice because he had brought guilt on the people.

74 "And Gad came to David on that day and he said to him" (2 Sam 24:18).

75 *Untersuchungen*, 115–16.

"and his servants." The reading in 4QSam^a indicates that the Chronicler's text should be construed as meaning that the king and his sons were still in a state of mourning (covering themselves in sackcloth) as they approached Ornan. If the reading of the MT, "the angel" instead of "the king," should prove to be original (see textual note 35), then the four sons might be those of Ornan, who would be hiding because they had seen the supernatural appearance of the angel. With the deep corruption in the text of Chronicles, it is pointless to put too much weight on either option.[76]

Ornan was threshing wheat: In another reading taken from a non-MT Samuel tradition, the Chronicler anticipates the gift of wheat Ornan will make in v. 23. This reference may also date this incident to the time of the normal wheat harvest in late May or early June.[77] The mention of the threshing floor leads to a number of associations with the meeting of Gideon and the angel of Yahweh at a threshing floor (Judg 6:11-24):[78] the angel appears on the threshing floor and at the winepress (1 Chr 21:16-27; Judg 6:11); both there and here "hiding" plays a role (1 Chr 21:20; Judg 6:11); Ornan turned and the angel waited for Gideon to return (1 Chr 21:20; Judg 6:18); fire from God consumed the sacrifice (1 Chr 21:26; Judg 6:21); Ornan caught a glimpse of the king/angel and Gideon saw the angel (Judg 6:22); Ornan was generous toward David and Gideon generously presented food to the angel (1 Chr 21:23; Judg 6:19); and David built an altar and Gideon was commanded to build one (1 Chr 21:26; Judg 6:26).

■ **21** *prostrated himself before David, with his nose to the ground:* Ornan shows proper respect before the king and thereby indicates that David had not lost the confidence of the people by his sinful census. See also Ornan's words "my lord the king" in v. 23.

■ **22** *David said to Ornan:* The Chronicler omits Araunah's question from 2 Sam 24:21,[79] with the result that David, appropriately, begins the conversation.

"Give me the site of the threshing floor": The negotiations of David with Ornan seem patterned after those of Abraham for the cave of Machpelah in Genesis 23.[80] David, like Abraham, takes the initiative in the bargaining (cf. Gen 23:3-4). The use of the imperative "give"[81] (from נתן) echoes the use of the same verbal root in Gen 23:4, 9. The word מקום "site" often has the connotation of religious site or sanctuary in the OT.[82] It may also indicate a broader area than the threshing floor, with enough space to build the temple. Abraham also bought more than the grave site he originally desired (Gen 23:11).

"at full price": See Gen 23:9, where the same prepositional phrase refers to Abraham's purchase of a burial place, and the repetition of the term בכסף מלא later in 1 Chr 21:24. In the first case it is an addition by the Chronicler to the *Vorlage* of 2 Sam 24:21, and in the second it replaces the word במחיר ("for a price"; 2 Sam 24:24).

"so that the plague may be prevented for the people": While the chief interest of the Chronicler was in the purchase of the site for the temple and the altar, David's efforts to acquire the threshing floor and to build an altar for Yahweh are also part of his penance that will free the people from further suffering. This "plague" (מגפה) as a consequence of David's census corresponds to the "plague" (נגף) that was threatened in the census law on all those who did not pay a ransom for their lives (Exod 30:12).[83]

■ **23** *"See, I have given the cattle for the burnt offerings and the threshing sledges for the wood and the wheat for the grain offering. I have given everything":* The cattle and the

---

76   Mosis, ibid., 114, surely goes too far in identifying the fourth of these sons with Solomon.

77   See Oded Borowski, "Agriculture," *ABD* 1:97.

78   See Willi, *Chronik als Auslegung*, 157.

79   "And Araunah said, 'Why has my lord the king come to his servant?'" Rudolph, 142, proposed that the Chronicler omitted this question because he believed that the king and not a subordinate should begin the conversation.

80   Willi, *Chronik als Auslegung*, 158; Williamson, 149. This is already true in 2 Samuel, since in both 2 Samuel 24 and Genesis 23 a Gentile landowner is

ready to give a piece of land without price, but the Israelite figure insists on paying full value. In both cases the final price paid is also noted. See also the remarks of Yair Zakovitch, "Assimilation in Biblical Narratives," in *Empirical Models for Biblical Criticism* (ed. J. H. Tigay; Philadelphia: Univ. of Pennsylvania Press, 1985) 181.

81   It replaces the infinitive לקנות "to acquire" in 2 Sam 24:21. Cf. also 1 Chr 21:25//2 Sam 24:24.

82   Cf. v. 25 and Josh 5:15.

83   Cf. Johnstone, 1:228.

threshing sledges given by Ornan are taken over from the *Vorlage*, omitting the word "harnesses,"[84] but the Chronicler adds "the wheat for the grain offering" at the end. A grain offering was often added to a burnt offering (cf. Exod 29:1-2, 38-41; Num 15:2-20; 2 Chr 7:7; this offering is mentioned three other times in 1 and 2 Chronicles[85] in addition to the use of the word מנחה to designate tribute). In 1 Sam 26:19 David mentioned that if Yahweh had stirred up (הסיתך, the same verbal root used in 1 Chr 21:1) Saul against David, then he should accept a grain offering. Perhaps the Chronicler reckoned that such an offering was needed in recompense for what Satan had stirred up. The word "give" is used three times by Ephron the Hittite in Gen 23:11. The Chronicler puts the words "I have given everything" into the mouth of Ornan. In 2 Sam 24:23 these words are part of a third person summary description of everything Ornan gave: "Everything Araunah gave to the king."[86]

■ **25** *So David paid Ornan six hundred shekels of gold:* The price is different in 2 Sam 24:24: fifty shekels of *silver* for the threshing floor *and* the cattle.[87] Pseudo-Rashi explained the difference between the price in Samuel and that in Chronicles by saying that fifty shekels were paid for each tribe so that all Israel would have a share in the altar. His fifty-times-twelve explanation provides an all-Israel interpretation for the purchase of the altar. Since Abraham paid four hundred shekels of silver for his burial ground (Gen 23:15), the Chronicler may have wanted David to pay more for the site of the temple than Abraham had for the burial site.[88]

■ **26** *David built there an altar to Yahweh, and he offered up burnt offerings and peace offerings:* These same sacrifices were offered by David when he installed the ark in the tent he had pitched for it in Jerusalem (1 Chr 16:1).

When he called to Yahweh,[89] *he answered him by fire from heaven on the altar of burnt offering:* This addition by the Chronicler[90] indicates divine approval for the sacrifice and the altar and also indicates perhaps that this altar will replace that of the tabernacle which received similar divine approval when sacrifice was offered at it (Lev 9:24). An angel also ignited the fire of Gideon's sacrifice (Judg 6:11), and Elijah called down fire from heaven on his altar in his contest with the prophets of Baal (1 Kgs 18:24, 37-38). A fire from heaven, finally, also ignited the sacrifices when Solomon dedicated the temple (2 Chr 7:1, without a parallel in 1 Kings).[91] In making this emphasis the Chronicler omitted from 2 Sam 24:25 the following: "So Yahweh answered his supplication for the land, and the plague was averted from Israel" (see 1 Chr 21:27). The plague had actually been checked earlier; the ritual of sacrifice only served to avert a renewal of the angel's attack.[92]

and it consumed the burnt offering: This reading, restored from Chronicles LXX (see textual note 42), anticipates what will happen to Solomon's offering at the dedication of the temple (1 Chr 7:1). If it is not part of the original text of Chronicles, the account of Solomon's dedication rite is no doubt the source of the addition.

■ **27** *he returned his sword to its sheath:* By sheathing its sword at Yahweh's command, the angel effectively brings the plague to an end (cf. 2 Sam 24:25). God's command to the angel had ended the threat to Jerusalem in v. 15, and David's sacrifice freed the rest of the land from plague (Rudolph, 147). נדן "sheath" is a Persian loanword,[93] thus reflecting the Chronicler's chronological location in the postexilic period.

---

84 Johnstone, 1:235, suggests that this omission keeps the rhetorical balance.

85 1 Chr 16:29; 23:29; 2 Chr 7:7.

86 So Sam LXX; MT adds המלך after Araunah. For an alternate reconstruction see McCarter, *II Samuel*, 508.

87 2 Sam 24:24 LXX[L] adds the expression "for a price" after "threshing floor." Hence David acquired the threshing floor for an unspecified price and paid fifty shekels for the cattle alone.

88 Johnstone, 1:236, provides a list of comparative costs for mainly secular transactions: seventeen shekels of silver for a field at Anathoth (Jer 32:9);

thirty shekels of silver for a gored servant (Exod 21:32); two hundred shekels of silver and a gold bar of fifty shekels taken by Achan (Josh 7:21).

89 Jabez also called on the God of Israel (1 Chr 4:10).

90 All the material from here through 22:1 is the Chronicler's own composition.

91 Cf. also 2 Macc 2:10: "Just as Moses prayed to the Lord, and fire came down from heaven and consumed the sacrifices, so also Solomon prayed, and the fire came down and consumed the whole burnt offerings."

92 So Rofé, "4QSam[a]," 114.

93 *HALOT* 2:674.

21:28—22:1. David Designates the Site for the Temple and the Altar of Burnt Offering

■ **28** *When David saw:* Most English versions treat each of the next verses as single, independent sentences. I interpret v. 28 as a protasis followed by the apodosis in 22:1. Verses 29-30 are a parenthesis.[94]

and when he offered a sacrifice there: I take this to be a reference to the sacrifice in v. 26 rather than an additional sacrifice, though Japhet, 390, believes it refers to subsequent sacrifices.

■ **29-30** *David was not able to go before it to seek God:* The parenthesis in vv. 29-30 explains that David did not worship at the tabernacle at Gibeon during the crisis because of his fear of the sword of the angel (cf. Balaam's confrontation with the angel with the drawn sword in Num 22:23, 31).[95] But the Chronicler does not preclude that David might have worshiped there after this crisis was over, and Solomon did make a pilgrimage to this very sanctuary and offered a thousand burnt offerings on its altar (2 Chr 1:3-6). In the meantime, the Chronicler implies that David continued to sacrifice at the threshing floor of Ornan.

■ **22:1** *This will be the house of Yahweh God, and this will be the altar for burnt offering for Israel:* In this verse added by the Chronicler, David designates the threshing floor of Ornan as the site of the future temple. This is in some tension with the repeated notice in Deuteronomy about the place that *Yahweh* would choose (Deut 12:5 and often).[96] Rudolph, 148, notes the similarity to Jacob's confession after Yahweh had appeared to him at Bethel: "This is none other than the house of God" (Gen 28:17; cf. v. 22), but he errs in attributing this to an anti-Samaritan polemic. Rather, the Chronicler has made allusions to a number of storied characters and events in Israelite history—Abraham, Jacob, Balaam, Joshua, and Gideon—in drafting this account. When the Chronicler begins his account of the actual building of the temple, he alludes to God's appearance to David at the threshing floor of Ornan, as well as to the name Moriah, which linked this site back to Abraham (2 Chr 3:1, without parallel in 1 Kings). The sin and forgiveness David received at the threshing floor of Ornan will be replicated in the temple of Solomon, where Solomon prays that God would forgive the people when they repent and come and pray in this house (2 Chr 6:24-31, 36-40), to which Yahweh responds by promising to hear from heaven, forgive their sins, and heal the land (7:13-14).[97] As Kalimi notes, in Chronicles Yahweh chose the city of Jerusalem, the temple site, Solomon the temple builder (1 Chr 28:6, 10; 29:1), and the temple itself (2 Chr 7:16).[98]

Conclusion

This pericope is based on 2 Sam 24:1-25, but modifies it in a number of ways, in addition to the fact that there are twenty-nine cases where he seems to depend on a text of Samuel other than MT. This is a rare case of the preservation of an account mentioning a sin of David, and the seventy thousand who lost their lives because of David may be the cause of David being banned from building the temple because he had shed innocent blood (1 Chr 22:8; 28:3). But in addition to his discussion of sin and forgiveness, the Chronicler used this account to indicate that David had purchased the site of the future temple and had even initiated sacrificial worship at the altar at this site. Allusions are made to earlier worthies in Israelite history—Abraham, Jacob, Balaam, Joshua, and Gideon—that lend significance to this account and credibility to the actions of David. Fire from heaven kindles the first sacrifice on this altar, just as it had at the tabernacle in the wilderness, and just as it would in Solomon's dedication of the temple. Participation by all Israel is suggested by the price David paid for the site, twelve times as great as the price paid in 2 Samuel 24.

---

94 Contra Mosis, *Untersuchungen*, 118–19.
95 Johnstone, 1:237, notes that the way back to Eden was also blocked for humanity (Gen 3:24).
96 Cf. Bailey, "David and God," 356.
97 Im, *Davidbild*, 152.
98 "Jerusalem," 193–94.

Translation

2/ David gave orders to gather[1] the resident aliens who were in the land of Israel, and he appointed some of them[2] as stonecutters to prepare dressed stones for building the house of God. 3/ David also provided iron in abundance for nails for the doors of the gates and for the wooden beams, as well as bronze in abundance beyond weighing, 4/ and cedar logs beyond counting—for the Sidonians and Tyrians brought cedar logs in abundance for David. 5/ David thought to himself, [3] "My son Solomon is young and inexperienced, and the house to be built for Yahweh must be exceedingly magnificent, famous and an object of praise for all the lands; I will therefore make preparations for it."[4] So David made preparations in abundance before he died.
6/ Then he called Solomon his son and commissioned him to build a house for Yahweh the God of Israel. 7/ David said to Solomon, "My son,[5] I had it in my heart to build a house for the name of Yahweh my God. 8/ But the word of Yahweh came to me, saying, 'You have shed much blood and you have carried out great wars. You shall not build a house for my name, for you have shed much blood on the ground before me. 9/ See, a son shall be born for you. He will be a person of rest, and I will provide him rest from all his enemies round about, for Solomon will be his name, and peace and quietness I will give to[6] Israel in his days. 10/ He will build a house for my name, and he will be a son to me, and I will be a father to him. I will establish his royal throne over Israel forever.'
11/ "Now, my son, may Yahweh be with you and may you succeed, and may you build the house of Yahweh your God just as he has spoken concerning you. 12/ Only, may Yahweh give to you discretion and understanding—and may he commission you (as king) over Israel—to keep the law of Yahweh your God. 13/ Then you will prosper if you are careful to do the statutes and the ordinances which Yahweh commanded Moses for Israel. Be strong and of good courage. Do not be afraid or dismayed. 14/ See, with great effort I have provided for the house of Yahweh one hundred thousand talents of gold and one million talents of silver, and bronze and iron beyond weighing for they are so abundant; lumber and stone I have provided and you must add more to these. 15/ With you is an abundance of workers: stonecutters, masons, carpenters, and all kinds of artisans, skilled in working[7] 16/ gold, silver, bronze, and iron—without number. [8] Rise and get to work, and may Yahweh be with you."

1 LXX and other versions add "all"; cf. 2 Chr 2:16.

2 מהם, with Syr, Vg, Arab.; LXX[L] "them." Neither expression occurs in Chronicles MT, LXX. This prepositional phrase may not have been part of the Hebrew text, but it is necessary to supply something like this in translation. Cf. מהם in 2 Chr 2:17.

3 ויאמר. *HALOT* 1:66, meaning 4; BDB, 56, meaning 2.

4 לו. As Rudolph, 150, notes, this could also be translated "for him" (Solomon).

5 בני, with Q, many Hebrew MSS, LXX, and other versions; cf. v. 11. K בנו "his son." Either reading may be original. If the latter reading is chosen, the speech begins with the word "I."

6 אתן על; two Hebrew MSS, Syr: יהיה על "there will be over."

7 Vv. 15 and 16 are connected syntactically and therefore the verse division has been ignored in translating the sentence.

8 אין מספר. Rothstein, 404, and Rudolph, 152, point out that metals are weighed and workers are counted.

9 One would expect לאמר at this point to introduce the following quotation, and a translation of it appears in late minuscules of LXX and in Vg, but this may be the translator's decision and not a textual difference.

17/ David commanded all the leaders of Israel to assist Solomon his son.[9] 18/ "Is not Yahweh your God with you, and has he not given you rest on every side? For he has delivered into my hand the inhabitants of the land, and the land has been subdued before Yahweh and before his people.

19/ Now set your heart and your spirit to seek Yahweh your God. Rise up and build the sanctuary of Yahweh God in order to bring the ark of the covenant of Yahweh and the holy vessels of God to the house that will be built for the name of Yahweh."

22:2-19

Structure

From here to the end of 1 Chronicles, there is no canonical *Vorlage* on which the Chronicler depends, though he clearly used the materials describing the transition from Moses to Joshua in Deuteronomy 31 and Joshua 1 in constructing the speeches in 1 Chronicles 22 and 28, and he also utilized 1 Kgs 5:17-19 (3-5) as well as other materials from the Deuteronomistic History. Between the speeches of David in chaps. 22 and 28–29 he placed extensive materials on the gathering, numbering, and organizing of the cult personnel (chaps. 23–27). Braun deserves credit for demonstrating that the Chronicler gives nearly equal emphasis to both David and Solomon, in chaps. 22, 28–29, as patrons and builders of the temple, correcting an overemphasis on David alone in earlier scholarship.[1] The present chapter may be outlined as follows:

I. 22:2-5. David prepares building materials (cf. v. 14 in his subsequent speech) and organizes a labor force (cf. vv. 15-16 in the subsequent speech).

II. 22:6-16. David's private speech to Solomon (the public address to Solomon and the leaders comes in 28:1-10; cf. 28:19-21). This is the first of the farewell speeches of David.

   A. 22:6-13. David's disbarment from temple building and his designation of Solomon as the temple builder. Verses 7-10 look back to the past and report a word of Yahweh in vv. 8-10; vv. 11-13 are an admonition to Solomon about the future.

   B. 22:14-16. David provides materials and workers for the temple.

III. 22:17-19. David's preliminary exhortation to the leaders of Israel. Verse 17 is an introduction and

vv. 18-19 contain the speech itself, the second of David's farewell speeches.

Rudolph, 151–52, and Braun, 221–22, have argued that vv. 14-16 and 17-19 are secondary. Rudolph noted that the figures for materials in vv. 14-16 are extraordinarily high in comparison with 1 Chr 29:4, 7, and 2 Chr 9:13, and that the numerous workers in vv. 15-16 are only a heightening of the information in v. 2. He felt that one would not expect the speech to continue after v. 13. None of these reasons, however, is compelling. The Chronicler may well have used both exaggerated and realistic figures for different rhetorical effects and chosen to include some information both in his narration and in the speech he composed.

Braun observes that vv. 17-19 have often been considered a doublet of chap. 28 and there is no notice in chap. 22 of the convening of the Israelite leaders who are addressed in these verses. He believes that this public exhortation was inserted because the private speech in vv. 7-13 was so far separated from the public address in chap. 28 by the insertion of chaps. 23–27. If these latter chapters, at least not in their entirety, are not an insertion (see the commentary ad loc.), this argument collapses. The Chronicler may have wanted to insert a preliminary public exhortation to the leaders in vv. 17-19 before the long excursus narrating the gathering, numbering, and organizing of cult personnel.

The "last words of David" in chaps. 22, 28, and 29 contrast sharply with the poem called the Last Words of David in 2 Sam 23:1-7 and the final words of David to his successor Solomon in 1 Kgs 2:1-9, neither of which is incorporated by the Chronicler. The poem in 2 Samuel 23, narrated by David in the first person, compares a just ruler to the morning sun and asserts that God has made an everlasting covenant with David. The speech to Solomon in 1 Kings 2 urges him to keep the laws of

---

1   Braun, "Solomonic Apologetic."

Yahweh, but also urges him to deal violently with Joab and Shimei and to deal loyally with the sons of Barzillai. David is the only biblical king for whom final speeches are preserved.[2]

Detailed Commentary

22:2-5. David Prepares Building Materials and Organizes a Labor Force

■ **2** *David gave orders to gather the resident aliens who were in the land of Israel:* In 2 Chr 2:16-17 (17-18), building on the *Vorlage* in 1 Kgs 5:27-32 (13-18), the Chronicler reports that in preparation for building the temple Solomon took a census of the resident aliens in addition to the census of such resident aliens (implied in 1 Chr 22:2[3]) that David his father had made, and that Solomon used more than one hundred fifty thousand of these as laborers, stonecutters, and overseers. The Chronicler reinforces and expands this idea in 2 Chr 8:7-10 (// 1 Kgs 9:21-22), noting that for forced labor Solomon conscripted the survivors of the pre-Israelite inhabitants of the land and did not enslave the Israelites. The question in 1 Kings is whether Solomon also conscripted forced laborers from the Israelites themselves, which might seem to be implied by 1 Kgs 5:27 (13), which reports that Solomon conscripted thirty thousand for forced labor out of "all Israel." Mettinger has argued that Solomon conscripted the non-Israelites for an institutional, *permanent* levy (מס עבד), whereas the Israelites themselves were pressed into *temporary* service (מס) for work on the temple and perhaps the king's palace.[4] However that may be, the Chronicler did not include 1 Kgs 5:27 (13) in his account so that there is no ambiguity about what he intended, namely, that only non-

Israelites served as forced laborers.[5] The Chronicler is presumably historically correct in backdating the practice of forced labor to the time of David in 1 Chr 22:2, since there appears in the second list of Davidic officials in 2 Samuel (2 Sam 20:23-26, without parallel in Chronicles) an official named Adoram who was in charge of the forced levy (על המס). The conscription of forced laborers from the resident aliens follows logically after David's census of all Israel in the previous chapter. The repeated exhortations in Deuteronomy to deal justly with the resident aliens (Deut 1:16; 24:17; 27:19), to show them kindness (10:19; 26:12), and to refrain from oppressing them (24:14) indicates their precarious existence (Curtis and Madsen, 256). The "land of Israel" is used four times in Chronicles, and in every case it refers to a not clearly defined territory with set borders in which Israel lives. It indicates a territory far bigger than Yehud. It is the place where a people called Israel dwells, but non-Israelite inhabitants are not excluded, as can be seen by the resident aliens mentioned in this verse.[6]

he appointed some of them as stonecutters to prepare dressed stones: Such dressed or hewn stones were used for the foundations of Solomon's temple (1 Kgs 5:31 [17]; without a parallel in Chronicles) and for the four tables of the burnt offering in Ezekiel's description of the new temple (Ezek 40:42). Solomon assigned eighty thousand to quarry in the hill country (2 Chr 2:1 [2]). Nari limestone for ashlar masonry could have been quarried in the vicinity of Jerusalem. Archaeologists have noted that quarrying activities must have been quite extensive in the light of the large quantities of ashlar masonry discovered in excavations.[7]

---

2   For observations on the relatively late character of the Hebrew in this chapter, see Jean Margain, "Observations sur *I Chroniques*, XXII: À propos des anachronismes linguistiques dans la Bible," *Sem* 24 (1984) 35–43.

3   The census taken in 1 Chronicles 21 was of all Israel.

4   Mettinger, *Solomonic State Officials*, 128–39.

5   Japhet, *Ideology*, 346, argues that a "resident alien" in Chronicles "is a member of a foreign people who has joined the people of Israel, adopted their religion, and thus lost his foreign identity." Chronicles considers them as adjuncts to the Israelite community and eliminates their foreign affiliation. The

term גר, originally "resident alien," has become identical with "proselyte." In her commentary, 547, she writes: "Those who survived from the 'seven nations' are 'aliens' (*gērīm*), attached to the people of Israel and sharing their destiny."

6   See Thomas Willi, "Die alttestamentliche Prägung des Begriffs אֶרֶץ יִשְׂרָאֵל," in *Nachdenken über Israel, Bibel und Theologie* (ed. H. M. Niemann, M. Augustin, and W. H. Schmidt; BEATAJ 37; Frankfurt am Main: Peter Lang, 1994) 387–97.

7   Y. Shiloh and Aharon Horowitz, "Ashlar Quarries of the Iron Age in the Hill Country of Israel," *BASOR* 217 (1975) 23–24.

■ **3** *David also provided[8] iron in abundance for nails for the doors of the gates:* Iron may have been in much greater supply after David's defeat of the Philistines since they seem to have had an early monopoly on iron refining in Palestine (1 Sam 13:19-22). The leaders or commanders also contributed one hundred thousand talents of iron (1 Chr 29:7) in addition to David's contribution. According to the Chronicler, Solomon used golden nails, weighing fifty shekels each, in the construction of the Most Holy Place (2 Chr 3:9, without a canonical *Vorlage*).[9]

and for the wooden beams: Recent commentators and English versions have suggested a translation of "clamps" for ולמחברות, and Williamson has compared the strips of bronze on the gates of Shalmaneser III excavated at Balawat.[10] Piet Dirksen[11] notes that in its only other occurrence in Chronicles (2 Chr 34:11) מחברות refers to "wooden beams" (ועצים למחברות),[12] and he casts doubt on the idea that one word could refer both to large wooden beams and to (small) iron clamps. He plausibly proposes that the nails were used both for the doors and for the wooden beams. *HALOT* 2:567 defines the word as "brace" or "truss" and indicates that this building component is made of iron in 1 Chr 22:3 and of timber in 2 Chr 34:11.

bronze in abundance beyond weighing: The Chronicler had reported earlier that David had acquired vast quantities of bronze from the cities of Hadadezer, and that Solomon had used this bronze to make the molten sea, the pillars in front of the temple, and temple vessels (1 Chr 18:8). Tou king of Hamath had also sent to him bronze (18:10). The leaders of ancestral houses also contributed subsequently eighteen thousand talents of bronze (29:7). "Beyond weighing" is used elsewhere in the Bible only in 22:14, where it refers to David's abundant provisions of bronze and iron. See also 2 Chr 4:18//1 Kgs 7:47, where the weight of the bronze vessels

made by Solomon was "not determined." Bronze would be needed for the molten sea, the pillars in front of the temple, and for temple vessels (2 Chr 4:11-18//1 Kgs 7:15-47; cf. 2 Chr 2:7, 14, 16 [6, 13, 15]).

■ **4** *cedar logs beyond counting:* Huram, the king of Tyre, had earlier sent David cedar logs to build his own palace (1 Chr 14:1). Despite David's abundant supplying of cedar logs for the temple, Solomon later requested additional lumber supplies from Huram (2 Chr 2:7-8 [8-9]//1 Kgs 5:20, 24 [6, 10]), and the Phoenician king gladly supplied this (2 Chr 2:10-15 [11-16]; cf. the similar text, but with a divergent order in 1 Kgs 5:20-25 [6-11]). The Chronicler resolves this potential tension caused by David's inadequate provision of lumber by having David tell Solomon in v. 14: "You must add more to these." The expertise of the Sidonians in cutting timber is noted in 1 Kgs 5:20 (6), though this information is not incorporated in Chronicles. Ezra reports that the Sidonians and Tyrians sent wood for the Second Temple through the port of Joppa. Cedarwood was used for the roof and for the walls, from floor to ceiling, in the Holy Place and in the Holy of Holies (1 Kgs 6:9, 15-16 [not included in Chronicles]). For "beyond counting" see 1 Chr 22:16 and 2 Chr 12:3. Cypress (ברוש, 1 Kgs 5:22, 24 [8, 10]; 6:15, 34) and olivewood (1 Kgs 6:23, 31, 32, 33) were also used in the temple, though the Chronicler does not mention them. This reading is known in 4Q522, from the so-called Joshua Cycles at Qumran, where we read of "cedars and cypress" brought by David from Lebanon.[13]

■ **5** *David thought to himself:* Verse 5 describes the reflections which led David to assemble materials and organize the workers during his lifetime. Throntveit (mistakenly) identified this verse as an edict, even though he recognized that David is speaking to himself.[14] The narrator here is omniscient.

---

8   The *hiphil* of the verb כון is one of the favorite words of the Chronicler. See Curtis and Madsen, 30, #54.

9   Apart from these two references, "nails" do not appear elsewhere in Kings or Chronicles.

10   J. E. Curtis and J. E. Reade, eds., *Art and Empire: Treasures from Assyria in the British Museum* (New York: Metropolitan Museum of Art, 1995) 98–99.

11   "What Are the *mĕḥabbĕrôt* in 1 Chron. 22:3?" *BN* 80 (1995) 23–24.

12   *NRSV* "and timber for binders." The word also

appears several times in Exodus: 26:4-5; 28:27; 36:11 (two times), 12, 17; 39:20.

13   Kalimi, "History of Interpretation," 20.

14   Throntveit, *When Kings Speak*, 22–23.

"*Solomon is young and inexperienced*": It has long been recognized that נער does not necessarily mean "young" in a strictly chronological sense. Rehoboam was "young and irresolute" when he ascended to the throne at forty-one years (2 Chr 13:7; cf. 12:13//1 Kgs 14:21). Pseudo-Rashi calculated that Joshua, a נער, was forty-two in Exod 33:11 and concluded that the Chronicler therefore added the word "inexperienced" to 1 Chr 22:5 (see also 29:1) to indicate that Solomon was actually young, twelve years old.[15] Carolyn Leeb has now shown that Hebrew נער in most cases describes the social status of a person who is partially independent of parental control and therefore often incorrectly translated as "young."[16] Solomon calls himself a "small נער" in 1 Kgs 3:7. If Solomon needed David's preparations to complete the temple because of his inexperience, David needed Solomon's ability to carry out the construction itself, since David himself was barred from building the temple (1 Chr 22:8). The youth of Solomon is echoed in 4Q522: "and his youngest son [will build it]."[17]

"*the house to be built for Yahweh must be exceedingly magnificent, famous and an object of praise for all the lands*": Chronicles apparently does not distinguish between a house built for Yahweh (vv. 5-6, 11) and a house built for Yahweh's name (vv. 7, 8, 10). "Magnificent" (להגדיל)[18] is an adjective formed by the *hiphil* infinitive construct of the verb meaning "to be great" (cf. 2 Chr 2:4 [5]).[19] "Famous and an object for praise" is used elsewhere in the OT as a complimentary designation for Israel as the covenant people of God (Deut 26:19; Jer 13:11). The word "famous" (לשם) is used in Zeph 3:19-20 to describe the condition of the exiled people after they have been brought home. The Chronicler now has David apply these adjectives describing the people to the temple. David's praise of the temple also reverses the judgment pronounced by Ezekiel on Jerusalem: "Therefore I have made you a disgrace before the nations, and a mockery to all the countries" (Ezek 22:4). David's own fame had earlier gone out to all the lands (1 Chr 14:17).

David made preparations in abundance before he died: This is the second reference to David's preparations in this verse. Cf. 1 Chr 28:11-19, which recounts additional preparations. David also dedicated some of the booty taken in warfare for sacred use (18:11//2 Sam 8:11 and 2 Chr 5:1//1 Kgs 7:51).

22:6-16. David's Private Speech to Solomon

This is the only speech in Chronicles in which a king directly addresses his successor (but see 1 Chr 28:9-10, where David addresses Solomon within a speech to a larger assembly).[20] A number of studies have shown how vv. 11-13 in this speech and vv. 10-12, 20 in chap. 28 make extensive use of a form or genre dealing with the induction of a leader into his office.[21] Lohfink identified three elements in this form: (1) the formula of encouragement: "Be strong and courageous" (Josh 1:6; cf. 1 Chr 22:13; 28:10, 20); (2) the description of the task to which the individual is inducted (Josh 1:6; cf. 1 Chr 22:1; 28:10, 20); and (3) the formula of accompaniment: "Yahweh is with you" (Josh 1:9; cf. 1 Chr 22:11, 20). It is clear that in composing 1 Chronicles 22 and 28, which describe the installation of Solomon into the office of king, the Chronicler depended on the account of the installation of Joshua. This makes the relationship of

---

15   The age of Solomon at his accession or death is not given in the Bible (2 Chr 9:30//1 Kgs 11:42).

16   Carolyn Leeb, *Away from the Father's House: The Social Location of na'ar and na'arah in Ancient Israel* (JSOTSup 301; Sheffield: Sheffield Academic Press, 2000). Her study, 16–17, supplants that of John MacDonald, "The Status and Role of the Na'ar in Israelite Society," *JNES* 35 (1976) 147–70, who suggested the meaning of "squire" or "young knight."

17   Kalimi, "History of Interpretation," 20.

18   *HALOT* 1:179, "beyond all measure."

19   "The house that I am about to build will be great, for our God is greater than other gods."

20   Throntveit, *When Kings Speak*, 42–44, classifies this speech as an oration, or perhaps an edict.

21   Norbert Lohfink, "Die deuteronomistische Darstel-lung des Übergangs der Führung Israels von Moses auf Josue: Ein Beitrag zur alttestamentliche Theologie des Amtes," *Scholastik* 37 (1962) 32–44; Dennis J. McCarthy, "An Installation Genre?" *JBL* 90 (1971) 31–41; H. G. M. Williamson, "The Accession of Solomon in the Books of Chronicles," *VT* 26 (1976) 351–61; and esp. Braun in his commentary, 222–23, in "Solomon," and in "Solomonic Apologetic." McCarthy also calls attention to the presence of this form in 2 Chr 19:5-7 (Jehoshaphat's appointment of judges) and in 32:6-8 (Hezekiah's appointment of army leaders). Parts of this form also occur in 1 Kings 2.

David to Solomon much like the relationship of Moses to Joshua. The work of Moses, who led the people out of Egypt, was completed by Joshua. David's extensive preparations for the temple building were brought to completion by Solomon.[22] Other connections with Joshua will be noted in the commentary on individual verses.

Lohfink and McCarthy called attention to the parallel sequences in Deut 31:7-8 (Moses' speech to Joshua), Deut 31:23 (Yahweh's speech to Joshua), and Josh 1:2-9 (Yahweh's speech to Joshua) on the one hand and in 1 Chronicles 22 and 28 on the other. The twofold commissioning of Joshua in Deuteronomy 31 and Joshua 1 is paralleled by the private and public speeches of David commissioning Solomon in 1 Chronicles 22 and 28. McCarthy concluded from 1 Chronicles 22 and 28 that the Chronicler had studied the sequence between Deuteronomy 31 and Joshua 1 with great care. The final speeches of Moses and David, in Joshua 1 and 1 Chronicles 28, instruct Joshua and Solomon, respectively, to begin their tasks. Williamson has also detected allusions to the Joshua material in 1 Chr 29:23 (the obedience of Israel is noted on both occasions) and 29:25 (exaltation of Joshua and Solomon; see the commentary below ad loc.).

22:6-13. David's Disbarment from Temple Building and His Designation of Solomon as Temple Builder

■ **6** *he called Solomon his son and commissioned him to build a house for Yahweh:* For צוה in the sense of "commission," see Josh 1:9 and 1 Kgs 2:1. Cf. 4Q522.[23]

■ **7** *I had it in my heart*: For the expression "have something in the heart," see also 1 Chr 28:2; 2 Chr 24:4; 29:10. While the idea of David proposing to build a temple is already present in 1 Chr 17:1-2//2 Sam 7:1-3, the actual wording of this verse is built on Solomon's letter to Huram describing David's intent (2 Chr 6:7//1 Kgs 8:17).[24] Thus the Chronicler has David say now what Solomon quotes him later as saying.

to build a house for the name of Yahweh my God: This Deuteronomic (Deut 12:11) and Deuteronomistic (1 Kgs 8:16, 19, 20, 29) designation for God's presence in the temple appears also in v. 19 and in the Solomonic account at 2 Chr 1:18 (2:1); 2:3-4 (2:4-5); 6:7, 10.

■ **8** *the word of Yahweh came to me, saying:* In 1 Chr 17:3//2 Sam 7:4 the divine oracle came to Nathan. Here David himself functions as a prophetic recipient of the word, unless we are to supply the idea that the word of Yahweh came to him "through Nathan." But, as Schniedewind points out, both here and in 1 Chr 28:3, 6, the role of the prophet Nathan recedes into the background and David claims to be directly instructed by God.[25] In the Last Words of David in 2 Sam 23:1-7 David also claims the role of prophet: "The spirit of Yahweh speaks through me, his word is upon my tongue" (v. 2).

You have shed much blood and you have carried out great wars . . . you have shed much blood on the ground before me: The rationale given by Solomon in his letter to Hiram for David not building the temple (1 Kgs 5:17-19 [3-5], not included in Chronicles) was that his father had been too preoccupied with wars, apparently leaving him insufficient time for undertaking the construction of the temple. In the oracle of Nathan, the objection to David's proposal to build a temple was divine opposition in principle to the idea of building a temple instead of the tabernacle, but then this was changed to say that David's son rather than David himself would build it (1 Chr 17:4-12//2 Sam 7:5-13), with no indication of how these two ideas can be reconciled with one another or why Solomon could build when David could not.[26] The

---

22 Christine Mitchell, "Transformations in Meaning: Solomon's Accession in Chronicles," *JHS* (2002) 7, has summarized the similarities between David-Solomon and Moses-Joshua as follows: "1) David's disqualification as Temple builder linked to Solomon's succession parallels Moses' disqualification from entering the land of Israel linked to Joshua's succession; 2) the installation of Solomon parallels that of Joshua by including encouragement, the description of the task, and the assurance of divine aid; 3) both charges to Joshua and Solomon are first given in private and then in pub-

lic; 4) the obedience of the people is emphasized in both accounts; and 5) Joshua is magnified with respect to Moses, so too Solomon is magnified."

23 Kalimi, "History of Interpretation," 20.

24 "My father David had it in heart to build a house for the name of Yahweh, the God of Israel."

25 *Word of God,* 198.

26 Students of 2 Samuel 7 have often offered a diachronic solution to this conundrum. See the discussion under Structure in 1 Chronicles 17.

Chronicler now attributes David's exclusion from temple building to two ideas: his wars (cf. 1 Kings 5) and his shedding of blood. Commentators have struggled with this latter explanation since David's wars were carried out under divine favor and as sign of divine blessing (e.g., 1 Chr 14:10, 14-15; 18:6, 13). Japhet, 397–98, nevertheless comments that though these wars were carried out in fulfillment of God's plan, blood was shed in them and this was David's paradoxical and tragic flaw. The opposition between war and temple is absolute in her mind, and war is presented in a negative light when Asa is told that because of his alliances he would have wars in the future (2 Chr 16:9). Hence the "man of war" David is excluded from temple building not only in practice but in principle. The Chronicler interprets David's involvement in wars not just as making him too busy, but also turning him into a "man of wars" (1 Chr 28:3) who carried out great wars (22:8). In my judgment, the principal weakness in this argument is its equation of waging war with the shedding of blood.

Donald F. Murray has shown that outside of Chronicles "shedding blood" is never used for killing by Israelite warriors in the context of war.[27] Hence the use of this term three times in Chronicles with regard to David's wars (twice in 1 Chr 22:8 and once in 28:3) is an astounding charge. Murray also shows that shedding of blood pollutes the land, a condition that is totally incompatible with Yahweh's dwelling in the land (Num 35:33-34). The difficulty with this latter passage is that the shedding of blood being discussed does not involve an Israelite killing someone in war. Murray attempts to remedy this situation by showing that a military person who has killed (הרג) someone or has touched a corpse is ritually unclean and needs to be purified (Num 31:19-24). He then tries to make such killing equivalent to "shedding blood" by noting another synonym for killing in Num 35:30 (נכה), a term used frequently in military contexts. On this basis he equates the three terms for killing and this permits him to tie together the provisions for uncleanness of a soldier in Numbers 31 with those for a shedder of blood in Num 35:33-34. Earlier Williamson, 154, had claimed that David was ritually unclean through warfare and therefore unfit to build the temple.[28] But if David were ritually unclean in the Chronicler's mind for his warfare, then he could not have performed sacrifices either, as he did in 1 Chronicles 21. I am also not persuaded by his equation of הרג ("kill"), נכה ("smite"), and שפך דם ("shed blood").

Gabriel observes that "shedding blood" is repeated twice in this verse—making it the preeminent charge[29]—and that "shedding blood" always refers in the Bible to the violent death of one or more persons, not to the kind of killing done in war.[30] Shimei, part of the house of Saul, had called David a "man of blood"—and several other names: "Murderer! Scoundrel"—after the death of Absalom and the collapse of his revolt (2 Sam 16:7-8). At that time David had prevented Joab from executing Shimei and even stated that Yahweh had bidden Shimei to curse David. The Chronicler may have picked up the epithet "man of blood" (and hence "blood shedder") from the curses of Shimei, though he hardly fills it with the same content since he does not even mention the

---

27 "Under Yhwh's Veto: David as Shedder of Blood in Chronicles," *Bib* 83 (2001) 457–76. Joab's killing of Abner and Amasa were unlawful civil homicides (see 1 Kgs 2:5 [retaliating in time of peace for blood that had been shed in war], 31 [where Solomon speaks of shedding of blood]).

28 Allen, 430, notes that in the divinely initiated campaign against Midian (Num 31:3), any who killed someone else or touched a dead body became unclean (Num 31:19-20, 24), and that unclean people were barred by the high priest Jehoiada from going to the temple (2 Chr 23:19). See also Im, *Davidbild*, 139.

29 The mention of wars was picked up from Kings (1 Kgs 5:17-19 [3-5]).

30 Ingeborg Gabriel, *Friede über Israel* (ÖBS 10; Klosterneuburg: Österreichisches Katholisches Bibelwerk, 1990) 67–72. The charge of shedding blood is also repeated in 1 Chr 28:3. Gabriel bases her understanding of "shedding blood" on the monograph of H. Christ, *Blutvergiessen im Alten Testament: Der gewaltsame Tod des Menschen untersucht am hebräischen Wort dam* (Theologische Dissertationen 12; Basel: Friedrich Reinhardt Kommissionsverlag, 1977). Christ, however, holds that 1 Chr 22:8 is an exception to the rule.

revolt of Absalom, let alone his death, in his account.[31] Micheel suggests that David's shedding of blood refers to an incident like the death of Uriah, surely known by the Chronicler, though not included in his account.[32] Much more likely to me is the idea proposed by Gabriel and Kelly that by "shedding blood" the Chronicler has in mind the seventy thousand who died as punishment for and in consequence of David's sinful census in the immediately preceding chapter.[33] Kelly also notes that this census had been for military purposes and that it led not to military success but only to divine chastisement. Hence there is a logical connection between David's faulty war efforts and his shedding of blood. Finally, on the basis of Ezek 22:4, 9, 12, 13, Kelly holds that shedding blood need not be taken in the literal sense of spilling blood, but more metaphorically: You have culpably caused the death of innocent people. Shed blood pollutes the land (see Num 35:33, dealing with murder, and Ps 106:38-39, dealing with child sacrifice), and hence the Chronicler adds the words "on the ground before me" to his second statement of the blood-shedding charge.

■ **9** *See, a son shall be born for you:* This birth oracle for Solomon closely resembles that of Josiah (1 Kgs 13:2; cf. the birth of the messianic prince in Isa 9:1-6 [2-7]). The dynastic promise is now linked explicitly to Solomon (contrast 2 Sam 7:12-16//1 Chr 17:11-14). The transition from David to Solomon in Chronicles proceeds peaceably without any other contenders for the throne, such as Absalom, Amnon, and Adonijah, reported in the Succession Narrative (2 Samuel 9–20; 1 Kings 1–2).

He will be a person of rest, and I will provide him rest from all his enemies round about: This is the only use of "person of rest" in the OT, and might even be translated "ruler of rest."[34] By this title Solomon is contrasted to David, who in 1 Chr 28:3 is called a "person of wars" or a "ruler of wars" (איש מלחמות). According to Deut 12:9-11 Israel was to bring its sacrifices to the central sanctuary once Yahweh had given them rest from their enemies all around. In the book of Joshua "rest" designates the completion of the conquest as the fulfillment of divine promise (Josh 1:13, 15; 21:44; 22:4; 23:1).[35] Once such rest is achieved (Josh 11:23; see n. 36), the whole congregation assembled at Shiloh was supposed to set up the tent of meeting there (Josh 18:1), in line with Deut 12:8-11. In the books of Samuel, David himself had achieved the condition of rest, as we see in 2 Sam 7:1, 11. The first of these references indicating that Yahweh had given David rest[36] is omitted altogether by the Chronicler in 1 Chr 17:1; the second is changed by him from "I will give you rest from all your enemies" to "I will *subdue* all your enemies." In neither case, therefore, does David achieve rest according to the Chronicler. When the enemies are subdued in chap. 18, it is only through the military efforts of David. In the present verse Yahweh promises to give Solomon rest without any military effort on Solomon's part. The reference to rest in this verse is the only complete use of the rest formula in Chronicles, and it moves beyond the promise to David that he would defeat all his enemies (1 Chr 17:8, 10) by adding to the rest formula connected with Solomon the expression "round about." In Kings Solomon affirmed

---

31   Absalom is listed among David's children in 1 Chr 3:2 and as the father of Rehoboam's wife in 2 Chr 11:20-21.

32   Rosemarie Micheel, *Die Seher- und Propheten-Überlieferungen in der Chronik* (BBET 18; Frankfurt am Main: Peter Lang, 1983) 16. This idea was expressed already by the medieval Jewish commentator Kimḥi. One might also cite David's handing over of the descendants of Saul to the Gibeonites for impalement (2 Sam 21:1-6), though this incident is not included in Chronicles.

33   Brian E. Kelly, "David's Disqualification in 1 Chronicles 22:8: A Response to Piet B. Dirksen," *JSOT* 80 (1998) 53–61. Kelly criticizes Dirksen, "Why Was Solomon Disqualified as Temple Builder? The Meaning of 1 Chronicles 22," *JSOT* 70 (1996)

51–56, who held that the Chronicler had made an ad hoc adaptation of 1 Kgs 5:17 (3) in equating bloodshed and warfare. In his view this provided a theological explanation for the fact that Solomon, not David, was the temple builder. This opened the way for God to intervene and approve Solomon as temple builder.

34   Gabriel, *Friede*, 74, though she confuses things a bit by suggesting a translation of "ruler of peace" (*Friedensherrscher*). She notes that איש is used occasionally as a designation for the one who succeeds to the throne (2 Chr 6:16; 7:18; Jer 33:17).

35   Cf. the similar idea, but expressed with the verb שקט, in Josh 11:23 and 14:15.

36   For other references to Yahweh giving rest see Exod 33:14; Deut 25:19; Josh 23:1; 2 Sam 7:1, 11; 1 Kgs

in a letter to Hiram that Yahweh had given him rest on every side (1 Kgs 5:18 [4],[37] omitted in Chronicles) and this notion is picked up and developed by the Chronicler in this context while David's achievement of "rest" is removed.[38]

Solomon will be his name, and peace and quietness I will give to Israel: By divine revelation Solomon is given his name, whereas in the Deuteronomistic History David named this second child of Bathsheba himself (2 Sam 12:24, not included in Chronicles).[39] The name Solomon is then given an etiological etymology by connecting it to the word שלום.[40] The noun "quietness" (שֶׁקֶט) is used only here in the Bible, but the verbal root שקט functions in Judges to indicate the time of peace and quiet after the military activity of the judge (e.g., 3:11, 30; 8:28).[41]

■ **10** *He will build a house for my name, and he will be a son to me, and I will be a father to him. I will establish his royal throne over Israel forever:* David quotes here from the oracle of Nathan (1 Chr 17:12-13//2 Sam 7:13-14) that authorizes David's son (implicitly Solomon; see esp. 1 Chr 17:14 in contrast to 2 Sam 7:16) to build the temple and applies the dynastic promise to him.[42] In distinction from 1 Chronicles 17 and 2 Samuel 7, the second and the fourth clauses are interchanged while the first and the third remain in the same position. This means that the first two clauses start out with an emphasis on the third person pronoun: *he* will build a house; *he* will be a son to me, and the effect of this change is to put more emphasis on Solomon's sonship than on Yahweh as the divine parent and so exalt him as the equal to David. Yahweh's promise here is unconditional, though David adds a condition in 1 Chr 28:7[43] and David admonishes Solomon to be faithful in 28:9.[44] The Chronicler also adds the expression "over Israel" to the mention of "his throne" in 17:12//2 Sam 7:13.

■ **11** *may Yahweh be with you:* This is the third element in the form for the induction of a leader into office,[45] here placed in the first position.

---

37 5:18 (4). Cf. also 1 Chr 23:25; 2 Chr 14:5-6; 15:15; 20:30.

37 Cf. 1 Kgs 5:1 (4:24), also not included in Chronicles: "Solomon was ruler over all the kingdoms."

38 Braun, 225, notes two other utilizations of "rest" in Chronicles. First, the temple becomes the place where Yahweh will take up his rest in the midst of the people (1 Chr 28:2; 2 Chr 6:41//Ps 132:8). Later kings have rest as part of the prosperity that results from faithfulness. See the Chronicler's interpretation of Asa (2 Chr 13:23 [14:1]; 14:4-6 [5-7]; 15:15), Jehoshaphat (2 Chr 20:30), and Hezekiah (2 Chr 32:22, emended according to LXX and Vg; see *BHS*).

39 According to 2 Sam 12:25 Solomon was also called Jedidiah ("beloved of Yahweh").

40 Halpern, *David's Secret Demons*, 35, argues that the correct linguistic etymology of Solomon is "his replacement" or "[the God] made good his loss." For Solomon and peace see 1 Kgs 5:4 (4:24): "He had peace on all sides."

41 Cf. also 1 Chr 4:40; 2 Chr 13:23 (14:1); 14:4-5 (5-6); 20:30; 23:21.

42 This passage is not messianic, contra Theodor Lescow, "Das Geburtsmotiv in den messianischen Weissagungen bei Jesaja und Micha," *ZAW* 79 (1967) 205–7, who finds the first clear reference to the presence of a hope of the birth of the messiah in v. 9; or James D. Newsome Jr., "Toward a New Understanding of the Chronicler and His Purposes," *JBL* 94 (1975) 208–10, who finds a striking

similarity between the Chronicler and the views of Haggai and Zechariah 1–8.

43 "I will establish his kingdom forever if he is resolute in keeping my commandments and my judgments, as at this day."

44 According to Japhet, 398, the Chronicler in two cases in v. 10 chooses what is now the reading in 2 Samuel over that in his own account in 1 Chronicles 17: "a house for my name" (2 Sam 7:13) rather than "for me a house" (1 Chr 17:12), and "the throne of his kingdom" (or "his royal throne"; 2 Sam 7:13) rather than "his throne" (1 Chr 17:12). For the first of these, however, note that the Chronicler had already used the expression "a house for my name" in 22:8, which is not dependent on the wording in the oracle of Nathan. The Chronicler's use of the verb form והכינותי in 22:10 echoes 17:11//2 Sam 7:12, and neither his own composition in 1 Chr 17:12 nor its *Vorlage* in 2 Sam 7:13.

45 Cf. Deut 31:6, 8 (both verses speak of God "going" with Israel and Joshua, respectively), 23; Josh 1:5 (Yahweh will be with Joshua as he was with Moses), 9.

and may you succeed: The *hiphil* of the verb צלח is also found in Josh 1:8 and in1 Chr 22:13 and 2 Chr 7:11.[46] The passage from Joshua is part of the paradigmatic installation genre, which has formed the basis for the Chronicler's composition of this passage. In 2 Chr 7:11, as in 1 Chr 22:11, the verb describes the successful completion of the building of the temple.[47] Promised success also offers encouragement for Solomon to undertake the task (part one of the form). Success expressed by the verb שׂכל is also promised in Josh 1:7, 8, and 1 Kgs 2:3.

may you build the house of Yahweh your God:. This is the description of the main task that Solomon is to perform, but he is also given the assignment to keep the law (תורה, v. 12).

■ **12** *Only, may Yahweh give to you discretion and understanding:* The syntax of the verse is difficult, but the best solution seems to be to make the keeping of the law the sequence to and the result of Solomon's discretion and understanding. The restrictive "only" (אך) is somewhat parallel to Josh 1:7: "Only (רק), be strong and very courageous so that you are careful to act according to the law."[48] The words following "understanding," "and may he [Yahweh] commission you (as king) over Israel,"[49] are to be understood as a parenthesis that repeats Yahweh's commissioning of Solomon (v. 10). Huram praises Yahweh for giving Solomon discretion and understanding to build the temple (2 Chr 2:11 [12]), an addition the Chronicler made to the *Vorlage* in 1 Kgs 5:21 (7), which had only mentioned that Solomon was a wise son.[50] In Chronicles Solomon's discretion is shown in his building of the temple rather than in his rule in general.

to keep the law of Yahweh your God: This clause begins, unusually, with the conjunction *wāw* (lit. "and"), perhaps to indicate that this obedience is a consequence of his discretion and understanding rather than as a consequence of being commissioned as king. The obedience of Solomon is also urged in the next verse and in 1 Chr 28:7, 9,[51] as such obedience was also commanded at the installation of Joshua (Josh 1:7-8), which continues to exercise its influence in this passage. David also urged Solomon to abide by the law in 1 Kgs 2:1-4, a passage also influenced by the form for the induction of a leader into his office.

■ **13** *Then you will prosper:* While the same verb (*hiphil* of צלח) is used in vv. 11 and 13, the translation need not be the same. The first use promises success in Solomon's building program and this second use points to the positive blessings Solomon will receive under the principle of retribution if he obeys Yahweh's statutes and ordinances.[52] This verse is again inspired by Josh 1:8, the only other use of אז תצליח in the Bible.[53]

Be strong and of good courage. Do not be afraid or dismayed: This fourfold formula of encouragement occurs exactly in this form only in 2 Chr 32:7 (without a *Vorlage* in 2 Kings), when Hezekiah "installs" the combat commanders into their office. A similar formula, however, occurs in David's next speech (1 Chr 28:20), where the word "act" has been added between the first and the last pair of imperatives as a fifth imperative. The Chronicler would have found a fourfold encouragement formula in Josh 1:9,[54] where the third imperative is formed from the root ערץ, apparently replaced here by the more common root ירא.[55]

---

46 Braun, 223, demonstrates that its other uses in the Deuteronomistic History are incidental (e.g., 1 Kgs 22:12, 15; Deut 28:29).

47 For 1 Chr 22:13 see below.

48 Piet B. Dirksen, "1 Chron 22:12: The Chronicler in *Actu Scribendi,*" *JNSL* 20 (2000) 135–41.

49 Cf. v. 6. The same verbal root צוה is used also in the commissioning of Joshua in Deut 31:14, 23; cf. Josh 1:9.

50 Cf. 2 Chr 2:10//1 Kgs 3:9.

51 Cf. 2 Chr 7:17-18.

52 Other passages referring to blessings coming from the obedience of the king to the Torah include 1 Chr 28:7-8; 2 Chr 6:16; 23:18.

53 Dirksen, "1 Chron 22:12," 138. I do not subscribe to Dirksen's proposal that the Chronicler originally

wrote 1 Chr 22:12aα, 12b-13 and then corrected himself by adding v. 12bβ ("and may he commission you [as king] over Israel"), which made kingship rather than the temple contingent on keeping the law.

54 Cf. Josh 10:25, where the first and last pairs of imperatives are given in reverse order.

55 The first two imperatives are used frequently in passages shaped by the induction form: Deut 31:7, 23; Josh 1:6, 7, 9, 18.

22:14-16. David Provides Materials and Workers for the Temple

■ **14** *with great effort:* This translation of בעני is probable, but somewhat uncertain (cf. 1 Chr 29:2).[56] LXX and Vg: "in my poverty"; *NEB:* "in spite of all my troubles"; *JB:* "poor as I am"; *JPS:* "by denying myself" (with Tg); BDB, 777, "in spite of my frustration"; *HALOT* 2:856, "in my misery" or "in my oppressed situation"; Mason, "even in my own difficult circumstances."[57] "Poverty" hardly seems correct in view of the extravagant gifts David gives to the temple.

I have provided for the house of Yahweh one hundred thousand talents of gold: The amount of gold is enormous and unrealistic: roughly 6,730,000 pounds or 3,365 tons. At four hundred dollars an ounce, that much gold today would amount to more than forty-three billion dollars. The amount of gold David donates in 1 Chr 29:4 is three thousand talents, a reduction by 97 percent.[58] According to 2 Chr 9:13//1 Kgs 10:14 Solomon's annual income was a mere six hundred sixty-six talents of gold.[59] Allen, 434, calls these figures "rhetorical mathematics," and compares them to common expressions like "thanks a million" or "a thousand pardons." The intent in any case is to show the grandeur and magnificence of the temple (cf. 2 Chr 2:4 [5]). Neither gold nor silver is mentioned among the materials amassed by David earlier in the chapter (1 Chr 22:3-4).

one million talents of silver: Everything said about the exaggerated and hyperbolic character of the amount of gold applies to the silver as well—and more so.[60] The amount of silver would be 67,300,000 pounds or more than 33,000 tons. According to 1 Chr 29:7, the leaders contributed an additional ten thousand talents of silver.

bronze and iron beyond weighing, for they are so abundant: David's gifts of bronze and iron were already mentioned in v. 3.

lumber and stone I have provided: Stone may include jewels and fine building materials (Johnstone, 1:242; cf. 1 Chr 29:2). For wood see v. 4. In v. 2 David appointed stonecutters to prepare dressed stones for the temple.

you must add more to these: This pushes the hyperbole to the absurd. As I stated at v. 4, this clause may be an attempt to harmonize David's provision of cedar with Solomon's subsequent acquisition of cedar from Huram (2 Chr 7:7-15 [8-16]//1 Kgs 5:20-25 [6-11]). Verse 14 lists metals followed by lumber and stone, whereas vv. 15-16 chiastically list craftsmen with stone and lumber followed by metalworkers.

■ **15-16** *With you is an abundance of workers: stonecutters, masons, carpenters:* The Chronicler has added "masons and carpenters" to the stonecutters mentioned in v. 2. Perhaps the Chronicler calculated that they were needed for temple construction just as they were needed for temple repair in the days of Joash (2 Chr 24:12//2 Kgs 12:11-12) and Josiah (2 Chr 34:11//2 Kgs 22:6). In vv. 15-16 he notes that the workers were in "abundance" and "without number." In the previous verse bronze and iron were listed "beyond weighing" and in "abundance."

skilled: Literally "wise." This adjective is used for the workers on both the tabernacle (Exod 28:3; 31:6; 35:10; 36:1, 2, 4, 8) and the temple (2 Chr 2:6, 12, 13).

Rise and get to work, and may Yahweh be with you: These two clauses correspond to parts two and three of the installation form (description of the task and accompaniment formula). Chronologically this admonition to Solomon is premature since David has not yet died, but the intention is surely to encourage him to act quickly once he has become king.[61] The Chronicler may simply be following Josh 1:2, where Yahweh tells Joshua to proceed to cross the Jordan, that is, get to work on the assignment given to him. ועשה ("Get to work") is usually not used without a direct object, but the same usage appears in 1 Chr 28:10, 20.

---

56 Braun, 220–21, "by my hard work"; Rudolph, 152, "durch meine mühevolle Arbeit."

57 Mason, *Preaching the Tradition,* 19–20. "It may refer to the difficulties David had experienced in gathering all these resources when engaged in so many battles."

58 According to 1 Chr 29:7 the leaders contibuted five thousand talents and ten thousand darics of gold.

59 Solomon brought four hundred twenty talents of gold from Ophir (2 Chr 8:18//1 Kgs 9:28 [LXX: one hundred twenty]).

60 See also the discussion of large numbers in Chronicles under Structure at 1 Chronicles 12.

61 In the reign of Hezekiah the service of the temple was restored in the first sixteen days of his first month (2 Chr 29:17).

22:17-19. David's Preliminary Exhortation to the Leaders of Israel

■ **17** *David commanded all the leaders of Israel to assist Solomon:* In these last three verses David urges the leaders to provide general support for Solomon and for his building of the temple, whereas in 29:5-9 David requests the assembly only to give financial support, and the people respond generously to this request. The order of these requests is logical in my judgment and does not provide a reason for declaring vv. 17-19 secondary. Allen, 431, proposes that this is a kind of private lobbying before David makes his public address to the leaders in 28:1-8.

■ **18** *"Is not Yahweh your God with you":* The Chronicler continues to use elements from the installation form (formula of accompaniment), even though David's address to the leaders ("you" in Hebrew is plural) deals with *their* responsibilities and not the installation of Solomon.

"has he not given you rest on every side? For he has delivered into my hand the inhabitants of the land": The Chronicler seems to introduce a slight inconsistency into his narrative, since elsewhere he does not report the achievement of "rest" in the time of David. Even here the recipient of rest is the people, not David. These sentences return to a positive evaluation of David's wars. They also provide the theological rationale that will enable David in the next verse to urge the people to rise and build. The "inhabitants of the land," here and in two other references in Chronicles (1 Chr 11:4; 2 Chr 20:7), refer to the pre-Israelite population in Palestine.

"the land has been subdued before Yahweh and before his people": Japhet, 402–3, points out that Chronicles does not report the conquest of the land in the days of Joshua and in accordance with the promises of the Pentateuch (Deut 12:10; Josh 21:44), but it presupposes that the Israelites had multiplied in the land from the time of Jacob onward. Many of the expressions in this verse, such as "the land being subdued" (Num 32:22; Josh 18:1) or the "inhabitants of the land" (Exod 23:31), are known in the earlier sources from which the Chronicler mined his terminology, but the completion of the con-

quest of the land is dated by him to the time of David. The clause "the land was subdued before Yahweh" is cited from Num 32:22, where "before Yahweh" is mentioned in the context of vv. 20-22 four times. The Chronicler's addition of "before his people" harmonizes this passage with Num 32:29 ("the land shall be subdued before you") and Josh 18:1 ("The land lay subdued before them" [= the whole congregation of the Israelites]).

■ **19** *"Now set your heart and your spirit to seek Yahweh your God. Rise up and build the sanctuary of Yahweh God":* This unique exhortation introduces three specific tasks: seeking Yahweh (1 Chr 10:13-14; 13:1-3), building the temple, and bringing the ark of the covenant and the holy vessels to the new sanctuary. The way to seek Yahweh is to build the temple and carry out its rites. The term מקדש ("sanctuary") as a designation for the temple is used only here and in 28:10 in 1 Chronicles. There are five more uses of the noun in this sense in 2 Chronicles.[62]

"in order to bring the ark of the covenant of Yahweh": David had already brought the ark from Kiriath-jearim to the tent in Jerusalem (1 Chronicles 13–16), and later notes that he had planned to build a house of rest for it (28:2).[63] At the dedication of the temple Solomon prayed for Yahweh and his ark to rise and go to their place of rest in the temple (2 Chr 6:41-42, verses from Ps 132:8-10 that were added by the Chronicler to the Deuteronomistic prayer from 1 Kings 8). David's command to bring the ark into the temple was carried out in 2 Chr 5:2-10//1 Kgs 8:1-9. Solomon's manufacture of the bronze sea, the pillars, and the bronze vessels was also anticipated in the David narrative (1 Chr 18:8). All these connections help to put David and Solomon on the same level as equally responsible for the building of the temple.

"and the holy vessels of God": This refers to the holy vessels housed in the tent, which Solomon brought up to the temple (2 Chr 5:5//1 Kgs 8:4). In the next part of his farewell speeches, David also orders the manufacture of additional new vessels (1 Chr 28:13).

---

62   2 Chr 20:8; 26:18; 29:21; 30:8; 36:17. None of these references is found in the *Vorlage* of the Deuteronomistic History. In Deuteronomy–2 Kings the word appears only in Josh 24:26.

63   Cf. also 1 Chr 17:1.

Conclusion

This chapter contains the first two of David's farewell addresses and an account of his lavish gifts of material and workers for the building of the temple. In a private speech to Solomon, modeled after the transition from Moses to Joshua, David encourages Solomon, assigns him the tasks of building the temple and keeping the law of Yahweh, and promises that Yahweh will be with him. David himself had been prevented from building the temple because of his wars and especially because of his shedding of blood, which I take as an allusion to the seventy thousand who died in the previous chapter because of David's unfortunate census. David links the dynastic promise explicitly to Solomon and contrasts his son to himself as a person of rest and a person whose name connotes an era of peace and quietness. Solomon is made equal to David.

In an initial speech to the leaders, David urges support for Solomon and the temple and indicates that rest has now been achieved for the people. The leaders are to seek the Lord, build the temple, and bring the ark into it.

The legitimacy and authority of the temple in Jerusalem are here traced to the two kings of the united monarchy. David gets the materials and workers together for the construction and recognizes Solomon, the actual temple builder, as his equal and fully endorsed successor. With Solomon comes rest, which is the prerequisite for building the temple. Solomon's name is his destiny: he is a person of shalom, of peace.

23

Translation

1/ When David grew old and had reached the full limit of days, he made his son[1] Solomon king over Israel. **2/** Then he gathered together all the leaders of Israel and of the priests and the Levites. **3/** The Levites were counted from thirty years old and upward, and the head count for their men[2] was thirty-eight thousand: **4/** of these,[3] there were twenty-four thousand over the work of the house of Yahweh, six thousand officers and judges, **5/** four thousand gatekeepers, and four thousand to praise Yahweh with instruments I had made[4] for offering praises.[5] **6/** David distributed them[6] into divisions.

Concerning the sons of Levi: Gershon, Kohath, and Merari. **7/** Concerning the Gershonites[7]: Ladan and Shimei. **8/** The sons of Ladan the chief: Jehiel, Zetham[8], and Joel—three. **9/** The sons of Jehiel[9]: Shelomoth,[10] Haziel[11], and Haran—three. These were the heads of the families of Ladan. **10/** The sons of Shimei: Jahath, Zizah,[12] Jeush, and Beriah. These were the sons of Shimei—four. **11/** Jahath was chief and Zizah second. Jeush and Beriah did not have many sons, and so they were enrolled as a single family.[13]

12/ The sons of Kohath: Amram, Izhar, Hebron, and Uzziel—four. **13/** The sons of Amram: Aaron and Moses. Aaron, together with his sons, was set apart forever to consecrate the most holy things by burning offerings before Yahweh in service to him and to bless with his name forever. **14/** As for Moses, the man of God, his descendants were reckoned among[14] the tribe of Levi. **15/** The sons of Moses: Gershom and Eliezer. **16/** The sons of Gershom: Shubael[15] the chief. **17/** The sons of Eliezer: Rehabiah the chief. Eliezer had no other sons, but the sons of Rehabiah were exceedingly many. **18/** The sons of Izhar: Shelomoth[16] the chief. **19/** The sons of Hebron: Jeriah the chief, Amariah the second, Jahaziel the third; and Jekameam the fourth. **20/** The sons of Uzziel: Micah the chief and Isshiah the second.

21/ The sons of Merari: Mahli and Mushi. The sons of Mahli: Eleazar and Kish. **22/** Eleazar died and had no sons, but only daughters; the sons of Kish their kindred[17] married[18] them. **23/** The sons of Mushi: Mahli, Eder, and Jeremoth.

24/ These were the sons of Levi by their ancestral houses, the heads of families as they were enrolled,[19] with a list of names by their heads, from twenty years old and upward, who were to do[20] the work of the service of the house of Yahweh.

25/ For David had said, "Yahweh, the God of Israel, has given rest to his people, and he

1 LXX adds ἀντ᾽ αὐτοῦ "instead of him."

2 מספרם לגלגלתם לגברים, lit. "their number according to their heads of the men."

3 Should we preface these words with ויאמר דויד "And David said," in order to accommodate the first person reference in v. 5? Or is that first person reference secondary?

4 עשיתי; LXX, Vg: עשה "he made." See textual note 3.

5 להלל; a few Hebrew MSS ליהוה להלל. Cf. LXX, where, however, the divine name Yahweh follows the verb.

6 ויחלקם. The verb is vocalized as a *niphal* imperfect with *wāw* consecutive and 3d masc. pl. suffix (cf. 1 Chr 24:3); a *qal* or *piel* pointing would be preferable. Cf. *BHS* and BDB, 323b.

7 לגרשני. Other uses of this gentilic are at 1 Chr 26:21; 29:8; 2 Chr 29:12.

8 וזתם; Syr ויותם "Jotham."

9 יחיאל. This conjecture follows Kjell Hognesius, "A Note on 1 Chr 23," *SJOT* 1 (1987) 123–27, who bases himself on the structure of the genealogy. Rudolph, 154, also conjectures that שמעי "Shimei" (MT) is a corruption of one of the names in v. 8 without specifying which. See the commentary for additional discussion.

10 שלמות with K, Syr, Arab.; Q, many Hebrew MSS, LXX, Tg, Vg: שלמית: "Shelomith."

11 וחזיאל. LXX[B] καὶ Ειειηλ. A copyist mistakenly confused this name with "Jehiel" in the previous verse.

12 זיוא, with one Hebrew MS, LXX, Vg; cf. v. 11. MT זינא "Zinah." This is the only time Zinah appears as a name in the OT, and Zizah appears only in these verses as well. Cf. זמה Zimmah in 1 Chr 6:5, 27-28 (20, 42-43).

13 ויהיו לבית אב לפקדה אחת, lit. "And so they were a (single) father's house, one duty group." Cf. *HALOT* 3:958.

14 יקראו. Cf. *HALOT* 3:1131.

15 שובאל with LXX; cf. 1 Chr 24:20. MT שבואל "Shebuel." The name is written defectively—without a vowel letter—in 1 Chr 26:24.

16 שלמות with LXX, Syr, Arab.; cf. v. 9. MT שלמית "Shelomith."

17 אחיהם; Tg "their uncle" (אחי אביהם).

18 וישאום, *qal* 3d masc. pl. imperfect. The suffix on the word "kindred" is also 3d masc. pl. The use of נשא in the sense of "marry" is common in later materials: Ezra 9:2, 12; 10:44; Neh 13:2; 2 Chr 11:21; 13:21; 24:3.

19 לפקדיהם. Or: "according to their service groups." See 1 Chr 24:3, 19.

20 עשי with many Hebrew MSS (*qal* participle, construct pl.); MT עשה (*qal* participle construct sg.).

dwells forever in Jerusalem. 26/ And so the Levites have no need to carry the tabernacle and all its vessels or to do its service" — 27/ For according to the last words of David these were the number of the Levites from twenty years old and upward—[21] 28/ "but their duty[22] was to be at the side of the sons of Aaron in the service of the house of Yahweh, having oversight over the courts and the side chambers, the cleaning of[23] all that is holy, and the work for the service of the house of God 29/ involving the rows of bread,[24] the choice flour for the grain offering, the wafers of unleavened bread, the baked offering,[25] the offering mixed with oil, and all measures of quantity or size.[26] 30/ And they shall stand[27] regularly before Yahweh every morning to thank and to praise Yahweh, and also at evening, 31/ and whenever[28] burnt offerings, according to their prescribed number, are offered up to Yahweh on Sabbaths, new moons, and appointed festivals. 32/ Thus they shall observe the instructions about the tent of meeting and the sanctuary and the sons of Aaron, their kindred, in the service of the house of Yahweh."

21 I have construed vv. 28-32 as a continuation of the speech of David after the interruption by v. 27. Japhet, 406, notes that there is no indication in MT that these verses (28-29) are David's words. *NEB* ascribes all of vv. 28-32 to the narrator.

22 מעמדם; LXX ὅτι ἔστησεν αὐτοὺς "for he had appointed them." Cf. Syr.

23 For ל after the construct, see GKC §130a; Kropat, *Syntax,* 56.

24 ללחם המערכת, with LXX; MT prefixes ו "and."

25 ולמחבת. Braun, 230, "griddle cakes."

26 ולכל משׂורה ומדה; LXX καὶ εἰς πᾶν μέτρον "and for every measure." See Rudolph, 158, who claims that Greek has only one common word for "measure."

27 ולעמד, lit. "And to stand."

28 Rudolph, 158: v. 31a is parallel to 30b (Rothstein), not 30a.

23:1-32

Structure

The structure of chaps. 23–27[1] in their present form is as follows:

Chapter 23

I. 23:1. Introduction to the rest of 1 Chronicles, including both the lists of Levites, priests, and secular officials in chaps. 23–27 and the book's final two chapters, which contain speeches and prayers of David and the installation of Solomon (chaps. 28–29)

II. 23:2. Introduction to lists of Levites, priests, and secular officials (chaps. 23–27)

III. 23:3-6a. Census of Levites

IV. 23:6b-24. List of Levites in their divisions

V. 23:25-32. Description of Levites' duties

Chapter 24

I. 24:1-19. Twenty-four priestly courses

II. 24:20-31. Further genealogy of some Levites that extends five families of Kohath and one family of

---

1   For the history of interpretation of these chapters see John W. Wright, "From Center to Periphery: 1 Chronicles 23–27 and the Interpretation of Chronicles in the Nineteenth Century," in *Priests, Prophets and Scribes* (ed. E. Ulrich et al.; JSOTSup 149; Sheffield: Sheffield Academic Press, 1992) 20–42. Wright argues that an apologetic attempt in the 19th century to salvage the historicity of Chronicles by seeking the sources behind chaps. 23–27 had the unintended effect of marginalizing Chronicles in much of Western scholarship.

Merari by another generation and adds a new descendant of Merari and Levitical families descended from him.

Chapter 25

I. 25:1-6. Twenty-four sons of Asaph, Heman, and Jeduthun; families of Levitical singers

II. 25:7-31. Lot-casting ceremony distributed Levitical singers into twenty-four teams, consisting of the leader and eleven other musicians

Chapter 26

I. 26:1-19. Divisions of gatekeepers

II. 26:20-32. List of Levitical treasurers, officers, and judges

Chapter 27

I. 27:1-15. Twelve divisions, of twenty-four thousand each, that served on a monthly basis, under the leadership of one of the military heroes associated with David

II. 27:16-24. Chief officers of tribes of Israel

III. 27:25-31. Twelve supervisors over the king's property

IV. 27:32-34. Seven advisors or associates of David

Since the beginning of the twentieth century, scholars have taken three basic positions in regard to these chapters: (A) all of these lists, from 23:3 (or 2b) through 27:34, are secondary; (B) some of the lists are original and others belong to a secondary level; (C) all, or almost all, of the lists are original. I will describe each of these positions in turn.

A. All of the lists are secondary.[2] Advocates of this position hold that 28:1 is a repetition of 23:2, and it was added to resume the narrative after the lengthy interruption of five chapters of secondary material. This "interruption" of the narrative is the principal argument adduced by Noth.[3] Welch and Rudolph, in particular, have observed that there is no unity of form or coherence of content in these materials, suggesting that more

than one hand may be responsible for the addition of these lists. Many of the scholars cited in n. 2 have found contradictions in these lists with the content of Chronicles elsewhere. They hold that the lists in these chapters were not added all at one time, and once the addition of lists had been made here, subsequent additions were made throughout 1 and 2 Chronicles.

B. Some of the lists are original and the others belong to a secondary level. This position has been advocated most forcefully by Williamson.[4] He notes that 28:1 is not an exact duplicate of 23:2, but should rather be understood as a repetitive resumption of the mainstream of the narrative after the Chronicler himself had included some of the lists in these chapters. Through a study of the census list in 23:3-6a, Williamson identifies a fourfold division of the Levites according to their duties and believes that the Chronicler included a list corresponding to each of these divisions:

- 23:4a Those who had charge of the work in the house of Yahweh, correlated with the list of Levites in 23:6b-13a, 15-24.
- 23:4b The Levites who were officers and judges, correlated with the list of Levites in 26:20-32.
- 23:5a The Levitical gatekeepers, correlated with the list of Levites in 26:1-3, 9-11, and 19.
- 23:5b The Levitical singers or musicians, correlated with the list of Levites in 25:1-6.

All of these lists belonging to the primary level in the composition of Chronicles also make David responsible for the organization of the list and are genealogically based. Williamson retains for the Chronicler roughly one-third of the verses between 23:3 and 27:32. He observes that the divisions of the Levites in vv. 4-5 are listed in descending numerical order (24,000–6,000–4,000–4,000), while the order of the four lists of Levites themselves are arranged by their relationship to the center of worship in the temple.

---

2 See Welch, *Work,* chap. 4; Noth, *Chronicler's History,* 31–33; Rudolph, 152–85; Mosis, *Untersuchungen,* 95, n. 43; Braun, 231; Im, *Davidbild,* 145; and Throntveit, *When Kings Speak,* 5–7. Rudolph, 152–53, holds all of 1 Chr 23:3–27:34 to be secondary and ascribes the founding of temple service in the original edition of Chronicles itself to Solomon. According to pre-Chronistic material in Ezra 6:18, the divisions of the Levites were ascribed

to Moses, while in another pre-Chronistic passage, Neh 13:30, they are attributed to Nehemiah.

3 *Chronicler's History,* 31.

4 See "Origins," 251–68. This argument is also adopted by Allen, 437, and by De Vries, 188.

Williamson assigns the following materials to a secondary level:

- 23:13b-14 and 23:25-32. The list that comes from the primary level (23:6b-13a, 15-24) assigns the Levites to do the work of the house of Yahweh (vv. 4, 24), whereas vv. 25-32 include both this assignment (with much more specific detail) and the duties of the Levitical singers (vv. 30-31). In addition, Williamson interprets vv. 28, 29, and 32 as emphasizing the distinction between Levites and priests, just as in verses 13b-14, which Williamson also believes to be secondary.[5] With many scholars, Williamson holds v. 27, which interrupts vv. 26 and 28, to be an even later gloss (see the commentary).
- 24:1-19. This paragraph deals with the twenty-four *priestly* courses, whereas 23:3-6a limits its focus exclusively to the Levites. Verse 1 of chap. 24 shows ties to 23:32, already judged secondary. David does not act alone in creating these priestly courses, but he utilizes the help of Zadok and Ahimelech in v. 3, and the Levites organize themselves by lot in v. 5. Finally, the twenty-four divisions here and in 1 Chr 25:7-31 (in the list of the Levitical singers) are taken to be a sign of secondary status.
- 24:20-31. Tensions with the similar list of Levites in 23:6b-13a, 15-24 are seen in that this list of Levites contains no names for descendants of Gershon and in that it extends the genealogy of the Kohathites and the Merarites for one additional generation and adds a son of Merari and three Levitical families descended from him. The list is closely tied to 24:1-19, already deemed secondary, and these Levites also cast lots (v. 31).
- 25:7-31. In this supplementary list of singers, there is no mention of David, and the Levites decide their duties by casting lots. Verses 2, 3, and 6 from the original list of singers in 25:1-6 state that the musicians worked under the direction of their father, but in vv. 9-31, the musicians are divided into twenty-four courses (just like the priests in 24:1-19). The small differences in names between this list and the list in 25:1-6 are held to result from the actual circumstances at the time of composition. The word מספר in the original composition of the Chronicler (v. 1) means "list," while the same word in the secondary v. 7 is used in the sense of "total." The word שיר in the secondary v. 7 means "singing," whereas its use in the original vv. 1-6 puts the emphasis on music played by instruments.
- 26:4-8, 12-18. The materials on Obed-edom in vv. 4-8 interrupt v. 3 and v. 9 from the original list of Levitical gatekeepers, and Obed-edom is not linked genealogically to the Levites, as Meshelemiah (vv. 1, 2, 9) and Hosah (vv. 10, 11, 16) are. The presence of Obed-edom in vv. 12-18, where he is inextricably linked with the surrounding verses, marks these verses as secondary as well. In addition, David is not mentioned in these supplementary verses, and the gatekeepers named here got their positions by casting lots.
- 27:1-32. The four paragraphs in this chapter do not deal with Levites (hence they show no correlation with 23:3-6a), nor do they represent offices initiated at this point in David's reign. Rather, these lists could come from almost any time in David's reign.[6]

Central to the origin of Williamson's secondary level is the innovative arrangement of the priests into twenty-

---

5   Knoppers, "Hierodules," has downplayed the distinction between priests and Levites in these verses and sees them in a complementary relationship. He notes that the Chronicler's depiction of the Levites here departs in a number of ways from P and Ezekiel and represents a kind of via media between Deuteronomy, P, and Ezekiel. New roles for the Levites, in addition to those attested by P and Ezekiel, are noted particularly in regard to the baked products and the measures of capacity and length in v. 29, their responsibilities in the chambers (v. 28), and for the rows of bread (v. 29).

6   The date of the materials themselves will be discussed in the commentary to chap. 27.

four courses (24:1-19), which he believes may have risen in relation to the departure of a number of priests from Jerusalem for Shechem, where they played an important role in the development of the later Samaritan community.[7] Their departure necessitated the reorganization of the remaining priests. Persian intervention after the high priest Joannes had murdered his brother may also have been a precipitating factor.[8]

C. All, or almost all, of the lists are original. Japhet, 406–10, has built a clear but simple case for retention of all the lists.[9] Like Williamson and Wright, she denies that 23:2 and 28:1 are identical and that 28:1 was added as a resumption after the insertion of secondary materials. While she acknowledges some lack of unity of form and coherence in the materials in these chapters and a degree of tension with other materials in Chronicles, she relativizes these objections by arguing that they may stem from the variety of source documents that the Chronicler was using. She also notes that the Chronicler may have been able to tolerate more incompatibility in these materials than his recent commentators can. She also suspects that some critics want to make the Chronicler read more like the Deuteronomistic Historian,[10] or they want to play down his interest in the cult.[11] She sees the contrast between the emphasis on the military at David's coronation (11:10–12:39) and the focus on both

secular and clerical organization at the time of Solomon as resulting from a transition from a time of war under David to a time of peace under Solomon (409). For her (410), 23:13-14 merely indicates that the sons of Aaron, while descendants of Levi, are not included among the generic Levites. Once the Chronicler has finished with the generic Levites, he provides a genealogy for the sons of Aaron in chap. 24. This also accounts, in her opinion, for the unexpected position of the list of priests after that of the Levites.

I am convinced by Williamson and Japhet that the genealogy of the Levites who were in charge of the work (23:6b-24) was an original part of the Chronicler's history. Japhet's interpretation of vv. 13b-14 successfully counters Williamson's attempt to make these verses secondary. On the other hand, the broad interpretation of "work on the house of Yahweh" or temple maintenance in vv. 25-32 and the reference specifically to the duties of the musicians in 23:30-31 persuade me of the secondary character of these verses. The differences between these verses and the Chronicler himself are not major, however, and their identification as secondary is by no means an open and shut case.[12]

The identification of primary and secondary levels in chaps. 24–27 will be continued under Structure in the following chapters.

---

7   See H. G. Kippenberg, *Garizim und Synagoge: Traditionsgeschichtliche Untersuchungen zur samaritanischen Religion der aramäischen Periode* (Berlin: de Gruyter, 1971) 50–59; and Williamson, *Israel*, 137–38.

8   Josephus *Ant.* 11.297–301.

9   Cf. Knoppers, "Hierodules," 51–54. Wright adopts a similar position, for somewhat different reasons, in his dissertation, "The Origin and Function of 1 Chronicles 23–27" (Univ. of Notre Dame, 1989); and in "The Legacy of David in Chronicles: The Narrative Function of 1 Chronicles 23–27," *JBL* 110 (1991) 229–42. Wright calls attention to other passages in Chronicles that ascribe the ordering of the Levites to David (and in some cases also to Solomon): 1 Chr 6:16-17; 9:22; 2 Chr 8:14; 23:18; 35:4. Wright, who believes that the Chronicler included the Nehemiah Memoirs in his history (241, n. 31), also points to Neh 12:24-25. Curtis and Madsen, 260, argued for the originality of these chapters, since they found references to the enthronement of Solomon, the leaders of Israel, priests, and Levites in 23:1-5 and the same cate-

gories in reverse order in later chapters: chap. 23, Levites; chap. 24, priests; chap. 27, leaders of Israel; chaps. 28–29, the enthronement of Solomon. Unfortunately, the proposed chiasm does not account for chaps. 25–26.

10   See Noth, *Chronicler's History,* 33.

11   On the latter point she cites Adam Welch and Thomas Willi.

12   Japhet, 421, calls attention to the close link between 1 Chr 23:32 and 24:1 (both refer to the sons of Aaron) and between 23:32 and 24:31 (both refer to the sons of Aaron). These links could lead to either the conclusion that both 23:25-32 and chap. 24 are original or that both are secondary. Cf. also the link between vv. 6 and 31 in chap. 24 (David, Zadok, and Ahimelech occur in both verses).

Detailed Commentary

23:1. Introduction to Chapters 23–29

■ **1** *When David grew old and had reached the full limit of days:* Because שָׂבַע ("had reached the full limit"; lit. "be satisfied with," "have one's fill of") is pointed as a verb instead of an adjective, the word זָקֵן ("grew old") is to be interpreted as a stative verb rather than as an adjective as well. David is similarly described in 29:28 and 1 Kgs 1:1a.[13] The Chronicler uses very little material from 1 Kings 1–2 (see the commentary on chaps. 28–29), and his picture of David at the end of his life is of a person who is vigorous and in total control of the situation, hence in considerable contrast to 1 Kgs 1:1b-4.

he made his son Solomon king: This verse summarizes and anticipates the events of the next seven chapters, climaxing with the assembly's actually making Solomon king prior to David's death in 1 Chr 29:22.[14] The full sanctioning of Solomon as king entails his being made king by his father and predecessor David and by the people. In the process of making Solomon king, David organized the temple personnel for him and made lavish preparations for the building of the temple itself.

23:2. Introduction to Lists of Levites, Priests, and Secular Officials in Chapters 23–27

■ **2** *he gathered together all the leaders of Israel and of the priests and the Levites:* Many commentators distinguish between the preliminary character of this assembly and the more formal assembly in 28:1. Wright has argued that this initial assembly was designed to give the priests and Levites specific assignments, whereas David convoked the later civil and cultic assembly in 28:1 to establish and inaugurate Solomon as David's successor.[15] The

mention of "priests" in this verse makes their listing in 24:1-19 not quite as unexpected as Williamson's focus on 23:3-6a might lead one to conclude.

23:3-6a. Census of Levites

■ **3** *The Levites were counted:* On first reading one might conclude that a census of the Levites would be impossible since it seems to conflict with 21:6, where neither Levi nor Benjamin was counted in David's census, and there has been no subsequent divine oracle to make their inclusion permissible.[16] But censuses of the Levites in order to assign them to specific tasks were made in Num 3:14-39 and 4:1-49 despite the prohibition about including them in the census in 1:49. The latter census counted only those who were able to go to war (1:3), which presumably did not include the Levites.

from thirty years old and upward: According to the Chronicler (2 Chr 31:17), the Levites were enrolled during the reign of Hezekiah from twenty years old and upward. That age also appears later in this chapter (vv. 24, 27),[17] and the age given in v. 24 (twenty) is very likely from the Chronicler himself (see the commentary below), correcting the "thirty"[18] he found in his source. This would indicate that the census reported here by the Chronicler in vv. 3-5 was taken by him from some kind of source document. The age for entering Levitical service varies in the Bible, perhaps depending on issues of supply and demand. The book of Numbers reports that the age of Levitical service was from thirty to fifty (4:35-36, 39-40, 43-44, 47-48), but it also reports an alternate initial age of twenty-five and of Levitical service that extended to the age of retirement at fifty (8:24).[19]

the head count for their men was thirty-eight thousand: The number is exaggerated. The total for the census of

---

13 In 2 Chr 24:15 both verbs זָקֵן and שָׂבַע (with *wāw* consecutives) are used of the high priest Jehoiada.

14 For a discussion of the secondary character of the words "a second time" in the latter passage, see the commentary and textual notes ad loc. Important support for the Egyptian background of this co-regency of David and Solomon is supplied by E. Ball, "The Co-regency of David and Solomon (1 Kings I)," *VT* 27 (1977) 268–79.

15 "Legacy of David," 231. For "gather" (אָסַף) see 1 Chr 15:4; 19:17.

16 For this reason alone, Rudolph, 153, holds vv. 3-6a to be secondary.

17 Cf. also Ezra 3:8.

18 Like Keil, 253, before her, Japhet, 412, mentions the possibility of a textual corruption in the reading "thirty," under the influence of "thirty (thousand)" later in the verse. There is no evidence of such a reading, however, in the manuscript or versional evidence. Keil thought that "thirty" arose because of a scribe's memory of Numbers 4.

19 Those over fifty could help when the tabernacle was stationary (Num 8:26).

thirty-to-fifty-year-old Levites in Numbers was eight thousand five hundred eighty (4:36, 40, 44, 48), whereas the total for all Levites over one month old was given at twenty-two thousand in 3:39[20] or twenty-three thousand in 26:62. The number of Levites who rallied to David at Hebron according to the Chronicler was four thousand six hundred (1 Chr 12:27 [26]), with three thousand seven hundred priests accompanying them (12:28 [27]). The number of Levites in the list of returnees, including temple servants and the sons of Solomon's servants,[21] was seven hundred thirty-three (Ezra 2:40-58) or seven hundred fifty-two (Neh 7:43-60). Despite a special effort, Ezra was able to get only thirty-eight Levites and two hundred twenty temple servants (נתינים) to accompany him to Jerusalem (Ezra 8:18-20).

■ **4** *twenty-four thousand over the work of the house of Yahweh:* It may be just coincidence, but this number is the same as each of the twelve monthly military divisions during David's reign (1 Chr 27:4, 5, etc.). The Levites in vv. 4-5 are not divided by families or monthly divisions, but by the functions that they carried out. Curtis and Madsen, 262, err in making these Levites overseers of the building/construction of the house of Yahweh. More general administrative (9:19; 2 Chr 24:12; 34:12; Ezra 3:8) and maintenance duties in connection with the temple and Israel's worship life (2 Chr 29:5-11) seem to be in the author's mind.

six thousand officers and judges: The only other place that the words "officers" (שטרים) and "judges" (שפטים) appear together in Chronicles is in 1 Chr 26:29, where we are told that a family of the Izrahites was to serve as officers and judges. Williamson interprets this category

of Levites as applying to all those mentioned in 26:20-32.[22]

■ **5** *four thousand gatekeepers:* Compare the list of gatekeepers appointed by David in 26:1-19.

four thousand to praise Yahweh with instruments I had made: Williamson links this category of Levites to the singers or musicians mentioned in 25:1-6. Rudolph, 153, notes that while the singers are included among the Levites, they are relatively small in number and are listed last. He regards this census in vv. 3-5 as pre-Chronistic (but post-Ezra) since it does not reflect the enthusiasm of the Chronicler for the singers (1 Chr 16:4-5).[23] Regardless of whether David himself claimed to have made musical instruments in this verse[24] or the narrator ascribed this activity to him (see textual notes 3 and 4), we are dealing with a tradition attested elsewhere in Chronicles (2 Chr 7:6; 29:26-27), Nehemiah (12:36), and one of the apocryphal psalms (151:2 LXX) that traces musical instruments back to David.[25]

■ **6a** *David distributed them into divisions:* While David divided all the Levites into divisions, v. 24 indicates that vv. 6b-24 deal only with those generic Levites who performed the work of the service of the house of Yahweh.[26] David here acts alone, without using or presupposing the assembly mentioned in v. 2. Only traces of such Levitical divisions are attested in Ezra and Nehemiah.[27] Welch argued that the next words, לבני לוי ("concerning the sons of Levi"), begin a new document (cf. 24:20) and that v. 6a forms the conclusion to the document begun in v. 3.[28] Japhet, 413, however, proposed that organizing into divisions is the topic of vv. 7-24 and is an action distinct from the census itself[29] and

20 The total for the individual figures in this chapter (vv. 22, 28, 34) comes to 22,300.

21 Neither of these latter groups had yet attained full Levitical status.

22 "Origins," 260–61. See also the commentary below on 26:20-32.

23 Contra Welch, *Work*, 84, who ascribed 23:1-6 to the Chronicler.

24 Johnstone, 1:246, points to 28:19 as a similar first person interjection.

25 "My [David's] hands formed a musical instrument, and my fingers tuned a psaltery." Amos 6:5 is another possible parallel, though the Hebrew is obscure: "Like David, they invent musical instru-

ments for themselves." See Shalom M. Paul, *Amos* (Hermeneia; Minneapolis: Fortress Press, 1991) 199, 206–7. If Paul's interpretation is correct, this verse would take the tradition about David's responsibility for making musical instruments back to at least the 8th century.

26 Williamson, 161; Allen, 436.

27 Japhet, 413; idem, "Supposed Common Authorship," 344ff.

28 *Work*, 84.

29 The next use of the word "divisions," however, is in 24:1.

so this requires that this clause and indeed all of v. 6 be taken with the following unit.[30] I follow Rudolph and Williamson, who link v. 6a to the preceding verses and v. 6b to the following list of Levites.[31]

23:6b-24. List of Levites in Their Divisions

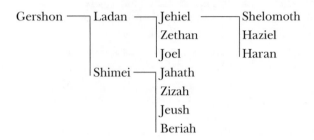

■ **6b** *Concerning the sons of Levi: Gershon, Kohath, and Merari:* The following verses contain a segmented genealogy for the three sons of Levi: Gershon, Kohath, and Merari (see the genealogical chart "Descendants of Levi–2"). This reference to the first generation of the sons of Levi (לבני לוי) and the reference to the Gershonites in the next verse (לגרשני) begin with a *lāmed,* translated here "concerning." For a discussion of the three main Levitical families—Gershon/m, Kohath, and Merari—see the commentary at 1 Chr 5:27 (6:1).[32] Since the Chronicler is quoting a source here, he spelled the first name Gershon instead of Gershom as in 5:27 (6:1).

While the persons named in the second-to-last and last generation under each main family are purportedly heads of a Levitical family at the time of David, these people are only two, three, or four generations past Levi himself. Hence many generations have been omitted in the genealogy. The twenty-two, twenty-three, or twenty-four families in this list (see the discussion in n. 31) are the divisions into which the Levites were divided at the time of the Chronicler, not the divisions at the time of David (cf. Rudolph, 155). Hence we should not be surprised that these names differ in detail from other genealogies in Chronicles.

■ **7** *Concerning the Gershonites:* The genealogist used the gentilic form of the name for Gershon (cf. 26:21), but not for Kohath (v. 12) or Merari (v. 21).

Ladan and Shimei: Elsewhere the firstborn son of Gershon is given as Libni (6:2 [17]; Exod 6:17; Num 3:18, 21; 26:58). The presence of Ladan here and in 1 Chr 26:21 indicates that this family has displaced the family of Libni in the genealogy and that the Chronicler took this information from a source.[33] Ladan may have once been a descendant of Libni, who later replaced him in the genealogy.[34] Shimei always appears as the second son of Gershon in genealogies (Num 3:21; 1 Chr 6:2 [17]), but the name is common, appearing more than forty times in the OT.

■ **8** *The sons of Ladan the chief: Jehiel, Zetham, and Joel– three:* The title "chief" is used seven times in this genealogy,[35] always elsewhere *after* the name it modifies. This

---

30 So also *NIV. RSV* and *NRSV* put all of v. 6 in a paragraph together with vv. 2-5. Cf. *NEB.*

31 Williamson, 157; Rudolph, 152–54. Ladan and Shimei, v. 7; Amram, Izhar, Hebron, and Uzziel, v. 12; Aaron, Moses, Gershom, and Eliezer, vv. 13-15; and Mahli and Mushi, v. 21, are significant divisions within the three Levitical families, but they are not counted as fathers' houses in this list since they are not modified by the word בני. Japhet, 413, counts twenty-four fathers' houses: ten from Gershon (she notes that there were four sons of Shimei, v. 10, despite the merger of Jeush and Beriah reported in the "afterthought," v. 11), nine from Kohath, and five from Merari. Williamson, 160, and Allen, 436, find only twenty-two houses: nine from Gershon (Jeush and Beriah are combined), nine from Kohath, and four from Merari (Eleazar is not counted; see v. 22); Curtis and Madsen, 263, count

twenty-three fathers' houses: nine from Gershon, nine from Kohath, and five from Merari, since they keep Eleazar as a separate family, even though he had no sons (v. 22).

32 Cf. Gen 46:11.

33 The only other Ladan mentioned in the Bible is an Ephraimite (1 Chr 7:26).

34 So Williamson, 161.

35 Vv. 8 (Ladan), 11 (Jahath), 16 (Shubael), 17 (Rehabiah), 18 (Shelomoth), 19 (Jeriah), 20 (Micah). Note also "the heads of families" in v. 9. No descendants of Merari are included in this list of chiefs.

would suggest that the title belongs to Ladan rather than to Jehiel.[36] Several times it is used when there is only one son (vv. 16-18), but in at least three cases it has the connotation of firstborn since it is followed by the words "second," "third," or "fourth" with other sons who are named (vv. 11, 19, 20). Zetham and Joel are listed as *sons* of Jehieli (rather than brothers of Jehiel) and in charge of the temple treasuries in 26:22;[37] Jehieli himself is in charge of the temple treasury in 29:8. The name Jehiel is restricted to Chronicles and Ezra; Zetham is used only here and in 26:22. Joel is a common name. Curtis and Madsen, 264, suggest that this Joel is possibly the same as the Gershonite Joel, also called the chief, in 15:7, 11. The number of families, here "three," is given three times for the Gershonites (vv. 8, 9, 10). A number is provided only once for the Kohathites[38] and not at all for the Merarites.

■ **9** *The sons of Jehiel: Shelomoth, Haziel, and Haran–three. These were the heads of the families of Ladan:* While the MT and the versions unanimously read "the sons of Shimei," instead of "the sons of Jehiel," the sons of Shimei are also listed in v. 10. Many scholars propose that the Shimei of v. 9 is a corruption of one of the three sons of Ladan listed in v. 8 (Jehiel, Zetham, and Joel), since the three names in v. 9 are identified as belonging to the family of Ladan. If the names in v. 9 are indeed members of the family of Ladan, as I believe (see textual note 9), that family becomes the largest of all the families in this genealogy with six members (three in each of two generations). Curtis and Madsen, 264, retained "Shimei" in this verse, deleted "these were the heads of the fami-

lies of Ladan," and emended the name Shimei in v. 10 to Shelomoth.[39] The net effect is to give Shimei, the youngest son of Gershon, the largest family, with seven descendants—Shelomoth, Haziel, and Haran in the first generation and Jahath, Zizah, Jeush, and Beriah in the second generation (the last four are sons of Shelomoth). Braun, 229, 232–33, proposes that v. 9 contains a second or alternate list of families of Shimei,[40] and he links "these were the heads of the families of Ladan,"[41] from v. 9, to the three names in v. 8. This listing of the three sons of Ladan would then begin[42] and end with a statement about the sons of Ladan, which seems quite unlikely. Although the reference to "family heads" in v. 9 is the only mention of these heads within the genealogy itself, the summary of the genealogy in v. 24 indicates that all of the names are to be so understood.

The name Shelomoth appears among the descendants of Izhar the son of Kohath (v. 18 and 24:22) and Amram (26:25-28). Haziel appears only here. Another Haran is a descendant of Caleb in 2:46.[43]

■ **10** *The sons of Shimei: Jahath, Zizah, Jeush, and Beriah. These were the sons of Shimei–four:* Jahath is the father of Zimmah in 6:5 (20) and the father of Shimei and the grandfather of Zimmah in 6:27-28 (42-43).[44] While Zizah occurs only in this context (see textual note 12),[45] the names Jeush and Beriah appear elsewhere in other families.

■ **11** *Jahath was chief and Zizah the second:* The title "the second" is also used in v. 19 (which also includes a name entitled "the third" and "the fourth") and in v. 20. The next two names, Jeush and Beriah, are not assigned an

---

36 *NRSV* and some commentators attribute this title to Jehiel, as does *NIV,* which translates it as the "first." In 26:21 we read of the heads of the families belonging to Ladan the Gershonite.

37 In 26:21-22 Jehiel (יחיאל) is spelled with a gentilic ending: Jehieli (יחיאלי).

38 See 23:12. In this case it refers to the sons of Kohath himself and not to the list of the heads of the families that the genealogy justifies.

39 For earlier suggestions see Curtis and Madsen, 263–64.

40 He places it in parentheses in his translation.

41 This clause is omitted in *NEB.* Cf. also Curtis and Madsen, 264, who emend "Shimei" in v. 10 to "Shelomoth" and thus create three sons and four grandsons for Shimei.

42 "The sons of Ladan the chief."

43 The name is also held by the brother of Abraham (Gen 11:26) and by the place from which Abraham and Sarah came (Gen 11:27-32; 12:4-5).

44 According to Curtis and Madsen, 264, Jahath in 1 Chronicles 6 and 23 may be the same person.

45 A זיזא is mentioned in 1 Chr 4:37 and 2 Chr 11:20.

ordinal number perhaps because of their small size.

Jeush and Beriah did not have many sons, and so they were enrolled as a single family: While there were originally two families here, they have been reduced to one in the Chronicler's day because of their small size. Japhet, 415, concludes that another house would eventually bifurcate to make up this gap. In any case Japhet, 413, thinks that there were potentially or originally ten sons of Gershon, but only nine were functioning at the time of the Chronicler.

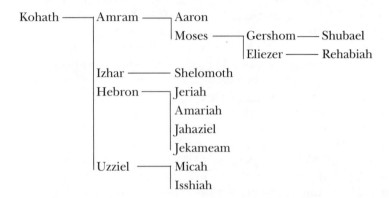

■ **12** *The sons of Kohath: Amram, Izhar, Hebron, and Uzziel–four:* These are the standard sons of Kohath (cf. 1 Chr 5:28 and 6:3 [6:2 and 18]; 26:23; cf. Exod 6:18; and Num 3:27).

■ **13** *The sons of Amram: Aaron and Moses:* Aaron and Moses appear as the children of Amram in genealogies at Exod 6:20 and, with their sister Miriam, at 1 Chr 5:29 (6:3).[46]

Aaron, together with his sons, was set apart forever to consecrate the most holy things by burning offerings before Yahweh: By burning incense and offering the daily sacrifices the priests carried out their responsibilities with regard to the temple and its ritual.[47] This articulation of priestly responsibilities has no exact parallel.[48] Elsewhere in the Bible "most holy things" (קדש קדשים) can describe the altar (Exod 29:37), the altar of incense (Exod 30:10), the tabernacle and all its furnishings (Exod 30:29), any of the offerings (e.g., Lev 2:3, 10), or the sanctuary itself (Ezek 45:3).[49] This is the only time the Chronicler employs the technical term in this way.[50]

to bless with his name forever: This is the second principal duty of the Aaronic priests after their consecration

---

46 Despite this preeminence of Aaron over Moses in the genealogies, Merlin Rehm has pointed out that Moses normally precedes Aaron in narrative contexts. See "Levites and Priests," *ABD* 4:299.

47 For the translation of this verse and for this interpretation, see Kleinig, *Lord's Song*, 105.

48 Kleinig, *Lord's Song*, 105, cites Exod 29:43-44, but this does not seem helpful since it is Yahweh's glory there that consecrates the tabernacle. Aaronic responsibility for offerings is outlined in Exod 29:38-42; 30:1-10; Lev 8:1–9:24; 18:8-20.

49 Johnstone, 1:248, adds: the incense (Exod 30:36); the cereal offering, the sin offering, and the guilt offering (Num 18:9); the showbread (Lev 24:9); and devoted objects (Lev 27:28).

50 Japhet, 415, believes this verse is a midrash on Exod 30:29-30, combining the ideas of anointing the tent and its vessels to be most holy and the anointing of Aaron of sons to serve as priests, and then projecting the meaning of one on the other. Her translation reads: "set apart forever to be consecrated as most holy." She has to admit, however, that nowhere else is "most holy" applied to humans. This term does appear elsewhere in Chronicles at 1 Chr 6:34 (49); 2 Chr 3:8, 10; 4:22; 5:7, where it refers to the Holy of Holies of the tabernacle or temple.

of the most holy things. See also their assignment to pronounce the Aaronic benediction in Num 6:22-27. The two uses of "forever" in this verse emphasize the continuity between preexilic and postexilic worship. Compare also the reference to Yahweh dwelling forever in Jerusalem in v. 25.

■ **14** *As for Moses, the man of God, his descendants were ascribed to the tribe of Levi:* This sentence explains why the descendants of Moses alone are followed in this genealogy of the heads of Levitical families. While Aaron is genealogically a Levite in the wider sense of the term, he and his descendants are distinguished from the rest of the Levites by the priestly responsibilities outlined in v. 13.[51] For the title "man of God" see 1 Sam 9:6 and 1 Kgs 17:24.

■ **15** *The sons of Moses: Gershom and Eliezer:* These two men are mentioned as the sons of Moses through his wife Zipporah in Exod 18:3-4.[52] According to Judg 18:30 Jonathan and his sons were descendants of Gershom, the son of Moses, and served as priests for the Danites until the time of the captivity (of the Northern Kingdom) in 722 BCE.

■ **16** *The sons of Gershom: Shubael the chief:* Even though only one son of Gershom is mentioned, he is called "chief."[53] In 1 Chr 26:24 Shebuel (Shubael)[54] is called the officer (נגיד) in charge of the treasuries. For the next generation after Shubael, see 24:20, where Shubael's ancestry is linked to Amram without mention of either Gershom or Moses.

■ **17** *Rehabiah the chief. Eliezer had no other sons, but the sons of Rehabiah were exceedingly many:* Eliezer, like Gershom, had only one son, but Rehabiah (רחביה) was prolific in engendering children, a feature of his life that apparently arose as an etymological interpretation of his

name: the root רחב means to be or grow wide or large. Isaac named one of his wells Rehoboth (רחבות, Gen 26:22) and interpreted it to mean: "Now Yahweh has made room for us (הרחיב יהוה לנו), and we shall be fruitful in the land." For the next generation after Rehabiah, see 1 Chr 24:21, where no mention is made of either Eliezer or Moses, and the link to Amram is derived only from the context. In 26:25 Rehabiah is identified as the son of Eliezer.

■ **18** *The sons of Izhar: Shelomoth the chief:* Izhar's sole son is called "chief" (cf. vv. 16-17). For the next generation after Shelomoth see 24:22. For other people by this name see the commentary on v. 9.[55] In Exod 6:21 the sons of Izhar are given as Korah,[56] Nepheg, and Zichri.

■ **19** *The sons of Hebron: Jeriah the chief, Amariah the second, Jahaziel the third; and Jekameam the fourth:* This is the only time in this genealogy where an ordinal number extends as far as the fourth position (cf. vv. 11, 20 [both end with the second]), and this list of names with the same ordinal positions is repeated in 24:23. The names Jeriah[57] and Jekameam appear only in these two passages, while Amariah and Jahaziel are names given to several individuals in the Bible.

■ **20** *The sons of Uzziel: Micah the chief and Isshiah the second:* Both Micah and Isshiah are names used of other individuals in the OT. For the next generation after Isshiah see 24:24-25. In Exod 6:22 the sons of Uzziel are Mishael, Elzaphan, and Sithri.

There are a total of nine sons of Kohath purportedly serving as heads of families at the time of David.[58]

---

51 Vv. 13b-14 are held by Williamson, 161, to be part of a pro-priestly redaction of 1 Chronicles 23–27, comprising roughly two-thirds of the material in these chapters. I take these verses in a more neutral sense and believe that the point of the genealogy is not so much advocating for the priests as explaining why the descendants of a major Levitical figure, Aaron, are not listed at this point. Chronicles recounts the twenty-four courses of the priests in 24:1-19, although I believe that passage is secondary.

52 Gershom's birth is recorded in Exod 2:22.

53 Cf. also Rehabiah and Shelomoth in 1 Chr 23:17, 18.

54 He is identified as the son of Gershom, son of Moses.

55 In 6:7 (22) the descendants of Izhar are Amminadab (? see commentary there), Korah, Assir, etc.

56 So also Num 16:1.

57 ירִיהוּ. Cf. ירִיה in 1 Chr 26:31.

58 Shubael, Rehabiah, Shelomoth, Jeriah, Amariah, Jahaziel, Jekameam, Micah, and Isshiah.

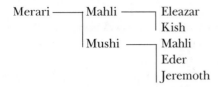

Merari —— Mahli —— Eleazar
| Kish
| Mushi —— Mahli
| Eder
| Jeremoth

■ **21** *The sons of Merari: Mahli and Mushi:* These two sons of Merari are also attested in 1 Chr 6:4 (19) and Exod 6:19; Num 3:20; cf. Num 3:33; 1 Chr 6:14 (29); and Ezra 8:18. This clause is repeated in 1 Chr 24:26a. For the difficult list of descendants of Mahli and Mushi in 24:26b-27 see the commentary there.

The sons of Mahli: Eleazar and Kish: Eleazar is an exceedingly common name, and Kish also is the name of several people, including most notably the father of Saul (8:33; 9:39; 12:1; cf. 1 Sam 9:1-2).[59]

■ **22** *Eleazar died and had no sons, but only daughters; the sons of Kish their kindred married them:* The case of Eleazar closely resembles that of Zelophehad and his daughters in Numbers. Zelophehad died, leaving only his five daughters as his heirs. In fact, the way of indicating his lack of sons is similarly expressed: Num 27:3: ובנים לא היו לו and here ולא היו לו בנים.[60] By marrying within the clan of their father's tribe (36:6) the daughters of Zelophehad were permitted to retain the name of their father and a possession of land (אחזה; 27:4) or an inheritance (אחזת נחלה; 27:7) among their father's brothers. It seems likely to some, therefore, that the descendants of the daughters of Kish would remain as an independent family within this Levitical genealogy.[61] In my opinion, however, these daughters would not have been able to serve as the head of a Levitical house.

■ **23** *The sons of Mushi: Mahli, Eder, and Jeremoth:* A Mahli is also listed as a son of Mushi in 1 Chr 6:32 (47). Eder is the name of a Benjaminite in 8:15, and Jeremoth is the name of a Benjaminite (7:8; 8:14), or a singer (25:22), and of three men who had married foreign wives in the days of Ezra (Ezra 10:26, 27, 29). This genealogical reference is repeated in 1 Chr 24:30a.[62] There are four family heads for Merari, one from Mahli (for Eleazar, see the

commentary on v. 22), and three from Mushi. Altogether therefore there are twenty-two functioning family heads mentioned in this chapter.

■ **24** *These were the sons of Levi by their ancestral houses, the heads of families:* This summation makes clear what had been implicit all along, namely, that this has been a list of Levitical families (ancestral houses) and indeed of the heads of those houses (see v. 9 for an earlier, passing reference to the heads of the houses). It remains somewhat confusing that while all of these persons are "heads" (ראשים), seven of them are also called "the chief" (הראש), apparently indicating their rank among their siblings.

by their ancestral houses, the heads of families as they were enrolled, with a list of names by their heads: It is interesting to see how closely the technical terminology of this verse corresponds to that of the census report in Num 1:2:

v. 24: לבית אבתיהם ראשי האבות לפקודיהם במספר שמות לגלגלתם

Num 1:2: לבית אבתם במספר שמות כל זכר לגלגלתם ("by their ancestral houses, with a list of names of every male by their heads")

Japhet, 417–18, points out that גלגלת ("by heads") is used in this sense only in Numbers 1 and 1 Chronicles 23 and that the word פקודיהם is best paralleled by Num 1:21, 23, 25, etc. "Men" (לגברים) in 1 Chr 24:3 replaces כל זכר in Num 1:2 and other passages in that chapter. 1 Chr 23:3, which shares some of this terminology, combines with v. 24 to form an inclusive framework around the genealogical unit.

from twenty years old and upward: Here the Chronicler corrects the age limit given in v. 3 to agree with his normal age limit for the beginning of Levitical service (see the passages cited at v. 3). Japhet, 418, on the other hand, thinks that the Chronicler is here making the age of the Levites agree with that of all other Israelites in the census lists from Numbers (e.g., Num 1:3, 18, 20).[63]

---

59 In 1 Chr 6:14 (29) the descendants of Mahli are Libni, Shimei, and Uzzah.

60 Eleazar's lack of sons is also noted in 1 Chr 24:28.

61 So Curtis and Madsen, 265; Japhet, 417.

62 For the spelling of Jeremoth as Jerimoth there, see the commentary ad loc. Cf. also 7:7.

63 Curtis and Madsen, 266–67, saw no contradiction between the data in vv. 24 and 27 and the data in v. 3. They believed that thirty-year-olds were needed for supervision of the work of building the temple, but that twenty-year-olds were fine after the completion of the temple.

the work of the service of the house of Yahweh: Braun, 235, has proposed that this reading conflates the expressions "the work of the house of Yahweh" (v. 4) and "the service of the house of Yahweh" (vv. 26, 28, 32). Such a conflation may be attributable to the Chronicler himself rather than to the conflation of textual variants. The rationale for the census in this verse replaces words in other census lists such as "all who are able to go to war" (used numerous times from Num 1:3-45). Knoppers points out that the "work" of the Levites includes both temple work and temple liturgy.[64]

23:25-32. Description of Levites' Duties

■ **25** *For David had said:* David's words here explain "the work of the service" rather than the age of the Levites at the beginning of their service.

"Yahweh, the God of Israel, has given rest to his people, and he dwells forever in Jerusalem": According to Williamson, 162, the person who added these verses did not maintain the position of the Chronicler himself that rest would come only with the reign of Solomon (see the commentary on 17:1, 10; 22:9). In citing a divine oracle, for example, David declared, "His name shall be Solomon, and I will give peace and quiet to Israel in his days" (22:9). But this point is considerably weakened if 22:18 is part of the Chronicler's work. There David asks, "Has he [Yahweh] not given you rest on every side? For he has delivered into my hand the inhabitants of the land, and the land has been subdued before Yahweh and before his people." Since Yahweh now dwells (שׁכן) in Jerusalem, he has no need for a tabernacle (משׁכן, v. 26). On "forever" see v. 13.

■ **26** *"the Levites have no need to carry the tabernacle or to do its service":* None of the other six references to the tabernacle in Chronicles refers to the Levites carrying the tabernacle.[65] Rather, it had been the responsibility of the

Levites to carry the ark (1 Chr 15:2, 12, 15, 26, 27; 2 Chr 5:4; 35:3; cf. Deut 10:8). This slight change reflects the secondary character of these verses. In any case the duties of the Levites regarding the tabernacle, outlined in Numbers 3–4, have become obsolete because of the plans to build the temple (Deut 12:10-11). This principle is reiterated by Josiah in 2 Chr 35:3, which refers to the requirement for Levites to carry the ark.

■ **27** *"For according to the last words of David these were the number of the Levites from twenty years old and upward":* This verse is widely held to be a misplaced gloss on v. 24. It interrupts the flow of thought between v. 26 and v. 28 and it ascribes Davidic authority to the change in age for the beginning of Levitical service described in v. 24. The Chronicler would probably have considered all the speeches of David in chaps. 22–29 as David's last words, but by identifying the content of this verse as David's final words this secondary hand made this ruling of David more authoritative than that made in v. 3.[66] The expression "the last words of David" was also used to introduce the poem in 2 Sam 23:1.

■ **28** *"their duty was to be at the side of the sons of Aaron":* In a section dealing with the rights of the Levites, this clause defines their status as "at the side of" (ליד)[67] the sons of Aaron. Priestly texts in the Pentateuch, on the other hand, refer to the Levites "serving" (שׁרת) the sons of Aaron.[68] Rudolph, 157, finds subordination of the Levites to the Aaronides here[69] and contrasts this passage with 1 Chr 15:2; 16:4, 41. There the duties of the Levites after they no longer needed to carry the ark were an advance in status and showed preferential treatment. Here he believes that the subordination of the Levites to the priests is strongly emphasized, as in P. Knoppers stresses the complementarity of the priests and Levites in this verse.[70] The Chronicler's narrative at the time of Josiah also seems more affirmative of their

---

64 "Hierodules," 64.

65 1 Chr 6:17 (32); 6:33 (48); 16:39; 17:5; 21:29; 2 Chr 1:5. In Num 10:17 we learn that the Gershonites and Merarites carried the tabernacle. The roles of the Gershonites, Kohathites, and Merarites with regard to the tabernacle are outlined in Num 3:21-37.

66 Strictly speaking, of course, v. 3 is not a word of David; contra Japhet, 419.

67 Subordination would be expressed by על יד.

68 Num 3:6; 8:26; 18:2.

69 He holds this in spite of his translation: "ihr Platz neben den Söhnen Aarons."

70 "Hierodules," 59.

rights: "He [Josiah] said to the Levites who taught all Israel and who were holy to Yahweh, 'Put the holy ark in the house that Solomon son of David, king of Israel, built; you need no longer carry it on your shoulders. Now serve Yahweh your God and his people Israel'" (2 Chr 35:3).

"in the service of the house of Yahweh": The duties of the Levites outlined in these verses are framed with references to the service of the house of Yahweh here and in v. 32. See also the reference to this service at the end of this verse.

"having oversight over the courts and the side chambers": The temple courts (חצרות) play a significant role in the Chronicler's account of the temple,[71] although the responsibility of the Levites with regard to them is not spelled out in detail. During the reform of Hezekiah the Levites took the unclean things, which the priests had removed from the temple to the court, and deposited them in the Wadi Kidron (2 Chr 29:16). Knoppers points out parallels between these Levitical responsibilities in the court and those mentioned for them in P (Num 3:26; 4:26-32)[72] and in Ezekiel (Ezek 46:21-24).[73]

There are only five references to the side chambers (לשכות) in Chronicles, including this passage. In 9:26 four Levitical gatekeepers were given charge of these chambers, and in 9:33 they are the dwelling place of the singers. The Levites in 2 Chr 31:11-12 were in charge of preparing the temple chambers for Israel's gifts.[74] The Levitical responsibility for the side chambers in this verse and in the other passages in Chronicles is not par-

alleled in other parts of the Bible. Knoppers observes that the "holy chambers" in Ezekiel (42:13-14) were reserved exclusively for the priests.[75] Chronicles, therefore, gives a new assignment to the Levites.

"the cleaning of all that is holy": There is nothing in Chronicles that helps us to explicate this unparalleled assignment of the Levites.[76] Rudolph, 157, observes that this probably had more to do with janitorial duties like keeping the sanctuary clean than with types of ritual purification. A passage in Nehemiah (12:45) refers to an unidentified group of people performing the service of purification, "as did the singers and the gatekeepers." The linking of cleaning with singers and gatekeepers may indicate the secondary character of vv. 25-32, since the genealogies of these groups first appear in chaps. 25 (singers) and 26 (gatekeepers).[77]

"and the work for the service of the house of God": Priestly texts speak of Levitical responsibility for the work of the tent of meeting and the work of the tabernacle (Num 3:7, 8) or the work of the sanctuary (Exod 36:1, 3).[78] The Chronicler has now transferred this terminology from the tent to the permanent temple,[79] though he has adapted it as well by adding "for the service" between "work" and "the house of God."

■ 29 *"involving the rows of bread"*: The Kohathites had charge of the rows of bread (1 Chr 9:32), a task that is also the responsibility of the priests and the Levites according to the sermon of Abijah in 2 Chr 13:11.[80] Knoppers notes that in P the bread of the Presence (לחם הפנים) is discussed only in regard to the obligations

71 1 Chr 28:6, 12; 2 Chr 4:9; 7:7; 20:5; 23:5; 24:21; 33:1. Johnstone, 1:249, states that the outer court was that to which laity were admitted while the inner court was the court of the priests (2 Chr 4:9).

72 These passages refer to the duties of the Gershonites and Merarites.

73 "Hierodules," 60–61.

74 Cf. also 1 Chr 28:12.

75 "Hierodules," 65.

76 In 2 Chr 30:19, the only other use of the noun, we read only about the "sanctuary's rules of cleanness." Knoppers, "Hierodules," 65, speculates that their work might guard against lay encroachment or it might deal with the purification of sacred utensils.

77 Japhet, 419–20, assigns the duties outlined in v. 28a to the gatekeepers. She notes the similarity of the gatekeepers' role to that outlined in Numbers 3–4.

See also her discussion of 1 Chr 9:17-20.

78 Ezekiel also assigns Levitical duties of a somewhat different sort for the work of the temple (Ezek 44:9-16). See Knoppers, "Hierodules," 61.

79 Cf. 1 Chr 23:32; 25:6; 28:21; 29:7; 2 Chr 29:35; 31:21; 35:2. In 1 Chr 6:33 (48) we read of the Levitical responsibility for the work of the tabernacle of the house of God.

80 It is somewhat uncertain whether this is the responsibility of the priests, the Levites, or both groups. Cf. also 2 Chr 29:18. Other passages dealing with these rows of bread in Chronicles are 1 Chr 28:16 and 2 Chr 2:3 (4). Rudolph, 157, notes that this verse does not explicitly limit the Levites to preparing the rows of bread as 1 Chr 9:32 does with the Levites, or at least the Kohathites. If the Levites were actually to place the rows of bread in the sanc-

of Aaron and his descendants and could be handled and eaten only by the priests.[81] While the exact duties of the Levites with regard to the rows of bread is unspecified, their link to this bread in Chronicles is a departure from P. The first five tasks in this verse have to do with Levitical responsibility for flour products during worship.

"the choice flour for the grain offering": According to 1 Chr 9:29, the Levites were appointed over several offerings, including choice flour (סלת), mentioned only in these two places in Chronicles, but fifty-one other times in the Bible.[82] As Knoppers points out, P speaks of fine flour for the cereal offering, the unleavened wafer(s), the griddle, and the well-mixed cakes, but only in priestly contexts, with no mention of the Levites.[83] The grain offering (מנחה) is mentioned, with no reference, however, to the Levites, in 1 Chr 16:29//Ps 96:8; 21:23//2 Sam 24:22 (where the word "grain offering" is not attested); and 2 Chr 7:7//1 Kgs 8:64.

"the wafers of unleavened bread": Mentioned only here in Chronicles, these wafers (רקיקי המצות) are part of the ceremony for ordained priests (Exod 29:2, 23) and also are constituent parts of other sacrifices (Lev 2:4; 7:12; 8:26; Num 6:15, 19). All these passages are from the Priestly parts of the Pentateuch.

"the baked offering": In its occurrences outside Chronicles, the word מחבת refers to a griddle made of clay or an iron pan.[84] My translation assumes that the Chronicler is referring to what is baked on such a griddle.

"the offering mixed with oil": This refers literally to the mixed, soaked, or kneaded offering. In its three occur-

rences, including here, the verb רבך is a *hophal* feminine singular participle.[85]

"and all measures of quantity or size": Leviticus warns about cheating in measures of length and quantity, reversing the order of these words (Lev 19:35). Curtis and Madsen, 268, surmise that the Levites may have been the keepers of standard measures. This attention to detail may have also been the reason they functioned as treasurers (1 Chr 26:20). Knoppers points out that Leviticus gives responsibility for standard measures to the entire community (19:3-36), Deuteronomy to "the Israelites" (25:13-16), and Ezekiel to the political authorities (45:9-12).[86] Hence this role for the Levites is an innovation in Chronicles. For "quantity" or "volume" (משורה) see Ezek 4:11, 16; for "size" or "length" (מדה) see 1 Chr 11:23; 20:6//2 Sam 21:20 (see the textual note on 1 Chr 20:6); and 2 Chr 3:3.

■ **30** *"they shall stand regularly before Yahweh every morning to thank and to praise Yahweh, and also at evening":*[87] The activity in this and the following verse would normally be performed by the singers or musicians, whose genealogy appears in chap. 25, again suggesting that the composer of vv. 25-32 is not the same person who included the genealogy in vv. 6b-24. The role of singing also presupposes that the Levites will no longer carry the ark/tabernacle (cf. 6:16-17 [31-32]). For תמיד "regularly" (v. 31) see 16:6, 37, 40; 2 Chr 2:3 (4); 24:14 (all without *Vorlage*). The official role of the Levites as musicians or singers is not mentioned in the Deuteronomistic History or P.

---

tuary, they would have to cross into territory from which they were usually barred.

81 "Hierodules," 66. See Exod 25:30; 35:13; 39:26; Lev 24:5-9.

82 The word occurs only in the Priestly writing and in Ezekiel. Milgrom, *Leviticus 1–16*, 179, points out that wheat flour was normally twice as expensive as barley flour. Semolina is the grainlike portions of wheat retained after the fine flour has passed through the bolting machine.

83 "Hierodules," 62. For the passages in P see Exod 29:1-30; Lev 2:17; 6:1–7:10; 7:11-21; 14:21-32; 23:9-21. Cf. Num 6:1-21; 15:1-16; 28:1-31; Ezek 46:11-14.

84 Lev 2:5; 6:14; 7:9; Ezek 4:3. In 1 Chr 9:31 Mattithiah is responsible for the making of "flat cakes" (חבתים). Knoppers, "Hierodules," 56, n. 33, retains the translation "griddle" because of the spelling (מחבת).

85 Cf. also Lev 6:14 (21); 7:12. Milgrom, *Leviticus 1–16*, 399–400, translates it "well soaked," but canvasses four meanings proposed by the rabbis and lexicographers and finds none of them completely satisfying.

86 "Hierodules," 62–63.

87 To produce an idiomatic translation, it has been necessary to consider vv. 30-31 together as one unit, permitting the shifting of the word order.

■ **31** *"whenever burnt offerings, according to their prescribed number, are offered up to Yahweh"*: The closest parallel to this duty of the Levites is in Ezra 3:4: "And they kept the festival of booths, as prescribed, and offered the daily burnt offerings by number according to the ordinance, as required for each day."[88] The Levites here are only singers or musicians, not directly involved with the burnt offering itself.[89]

"on Sabbaths, new moons, and appointed festivals": This is the Chronicler's regular formula for referring to the cycle of festivals that are in addition to the daily morning and evening times of worship (2 Chr 2:3 [4]; 8:13; 31:3, all without *Vorlage* in the Deuteronomistic History). On new moons see Num 28:11-15. The appointed festivals would include Passover (Num 28:16-25), Weeks (28:26-31), and Tabernacles (29:12-38).

■ **32** *"Thus they shall observe the instructions about the tent of meeting and the instructions about the sanctuary and the instructions about the sons of Aaron, their kindred"*: "Observe the instructions about" translates ושמרו את משמרת, with the noun משמרת appearing before each of the following objects—the tent of meeting, the sanctuary, and the sons of Aaron.[90] Two other passages in Chronicles use this verb and noun together (2 Chr 13:11; 23:6; cf. Num 3:5-8; 18:3-5). For the instructions about the tent of meeting see Num 18:3-4; for instructions about the sons of Aaron see 3:7; 18:1-2. For the instructions about the holy place

see 3:28,[91] 32.[92] Contrast 18:5.[93] Knoppers argues that the Chronicler contests priestly law by making the Levites guards of the shrine.[94] While some of the instructions about the tabernacle or tent of meeting became obsolete with the building of Solomon's temple, others, including those about Levitical responsibilities for particular types of offerings mentioned in vv. 25-31, continued.[95] The instructions about the sons of Aaron would include those that distinguish the roles and the duties of the sons of Aaron from those of the Levites. Subordination of the Levites to the Aaronides is forcefully put forward in Num 3:6-9; 4:15, 27, 33.[96] The Chronicler calls the Aaronides kinsmen of the Levites, with both the Aaronides and the Levites tracing their genealogy in Chronicles back to the ancestor Levi (1 Chr 5:27—6:38 [6:1-53]).

Japhet, 421, notes the following characteristic Chronistic ideas in vv. 25-32:

1. Division of Levites into Levites, singers, and gatekeepers. This may be true, but 23:6b-24 focuses on the generic Levites alone.
2. Gradual appropriation of priestly functions by the Levites.
3. Singing as accompanying sacrifices (cf. 2 Chr 8:14, without a *Vorlage* in the Deuteronomistic History).[97]
4. The Levites are viewed favorably, as kindred assigned to attend the sons of Aaron.

---

88 Cf. Num 3:24.
89 Rudolph, 157, calls this pre-Chronistic because it lacks the preferential treatment of the singers and the participation of the Levites in the slaughter of the offerings themselves. He also believes that 23:3-6a was pre-Chronistic, while vv. 6b-24 are post-Chronistic (p. 158). The author was using 23:3-6a and 23:25-32 as weapons against the singers.
90 Knoppers, "Hierodules," 61, interprets this as guard duty. Guard duty is assigned to the Levites in P (Num 1:53; 3:7-8; 18:3, 22-23) and in Ezekiel (Ezek 44:14).
91 The Kohathites were assigned the duties of the sanctuary (in transit). The duties with regard to the sanctuary are applied to all Levites in Chronicles.
92 Eleazar was to have oversight of those who had charge of the sanctuary.
93 The priests (= Aaron) are assigned the duties of the sanctuary and the altar. Ezekiel insists that only the priests should attend to the consecrated areas of

the temple (40:45-46; 43:18-27; 44:8, 15-16; 46:20; 48:11).
94 "Hierodules," 64.
95 Allen, 437, suggests that "tent of meeting" is used metaphorically for the temple in this verse. Japhet, 421, believes that "tent of meeting" is anachronistically retained and identified as the house of the Lord. Rudolph, 157, thought the author extended David's new regulations to the tabernacle, which stood at Gibeon in David's time.
96 Knoppers, "Hierodules," 62, argues that the Levites may also have protected the priests in P (Num 3:6-9; 8:13, 19; 18:2-6).
97 She writes "I Chron 8:14."

5. The new roles for the Levites are justified by the fact that the people have reached their rest and the role of Levites in carrying the ark (or tabernacle) has been abolished.

Conclusion

After the two farewell speeches in the previous chapter, David installed his son Solomon as king during his lifetime and appointed Levites to four different duties that reflect the roles of the Levites in the Chronicler's day: general Levites, officers and judges, gatekeepers, and musicians. In this chapter the author records a Levitical census and names leaders of Levitical families who had charge of the work in the house of Yahweh and who could trace themselves back genealogically to Gershon, Kohath, and Merari.

The final paragraph in this chapter (vv. 25-32) itemizes a number of Levitical duties after the need for them to carry the tabernacle or ark was over. These words set the beginning of Levitical service at the age of twenty and put the Levites and the priests in complementary roles. Directions for the Levitical musicians in vv. 30-31 support the argument of those who identify vv. 25-32 as secondary.

1/ The divisions of the sons of Aaron were these. The sons of Aaron: Nadab, Abihu,[1] Eleazar, and Ithamar. 2/ Nadab and Abihu died before their father. Since they had no sons, Eleazar and Ithamar became priests. 3/ Together with Zadok of the sons of Eleazar and Ahimelech of the sons of Ithamar, David divided them[2] according to their appointed duties in their service. 4/ Because the sons of Eleazar were more numerous in male heads than the sons of Ithamar, they organized them as follows: among the sons of Eleazar, sixteen heads according to their[3] families, and among the sons of Ithamar, eight according to their families. 5/ They divided them by lot, both alike, for there were sacred officials and officials of God among the sons of Eleazar and the sons of[4] Ithamar. 6/ The scribe Shemaiah the son of Nethanel, from the Levites,[5] wrote them down in the presence of the king, the leaders, Zadok the priest, Ahimelech the son of Abiathar, and the heads of the priestly and Levitical families, one father's house[6] being chosen for Eleazar and one being chosen[7] for Ithamar.

7/ The first lot fell to Jehoiarib, the second to Jedaiah, 8/ the third to Harim, the fourth to Seorim,[8] 9/ the fifth to Malchijah, the sixth to Mijamin,[9] 10/ the seventh to Hakkoz, the eighth to Abijah, 11/ the ninth to Jeshua, the tenth to Shecaniah, 12/ the eleventh to Eliashib, the twelfth to Jakim, 13/ the thirteenth to Huppah, the fourteenth to Jeshebeab,[10] 14/ the fifteenth to Bilgah, the sixteenth to Immer, 15/ the seventeenth to Hezir, the eighteenth to Happizzez, 16/ the nineteenth to Pethahiah, the twentieth[11] to Jehezkel, 17/ the twenty-first to Jachin, the twenty-second to Gamul, 18/ the twenty-third to Delaiah, the twenty-fourth to Maaziah. 19/ In accord with their appointed duty in their service, these were to enter the house of Yahweh, as was stipulated for them by the authority of Aaron their father, just as Yahweh the God of Israel had commanded him.

20/ The remaining Levites: the sons of Amram: Shubael; the sons of Shubael: Jehdeiah; 21/ Rehabiah: the sons of Rehabiah the chief: Isshiah. 22/ Izharites: Shelomoth. The sons of Shelomoth: Jahath. 23/ The sons of Hebron[12]: Jeriah the chief,[13] Amariah the second, Jahaziel the third, Jekameam the fourth. 24/ The sons of Uzziel: Micah. The sons of Micah: Shamir.[14] 25/ The brother of Micah: Issiah. The sons of Issiah: Zechariah. 26/ The sons of Merari: Mahli and Mushi.[15] 27/ The sons of Merari by Jaaziah his son:[16] Shoham,[17] Zaccur, and Ibri. 28/ Mahli:

1 On each of its twelve occurrences in the OT, LXX renders Abihu as Ἀβιούδ.

2 ויחלקם. The form is *niphal* imperfect. Cf. 1 Chr 23:6. It should probably be vocalized as *piel* or *hiphil*.

3 אבותם, with a few Hebrew MSS, Syr, Arab.; MT אבות. The suffixed form is also used with the sons of Ithamar later in the verse.

4 ומבני, with many Hebrew MSS, Syr, Tg, Vg; cf. מבני earlier in the verse. MT ובני. Rudolph, 160, concludes that no change is necessary.

5 הלוים, with a few Hebrew MSS; MT הלוי (sg.).

6 בית אב אחד. Rudolph, 160, proposed to insert a second בית אב אחד at this point and translate: "Each time a family and yet another family was drawn." Hence he believes the first two divisions were assigned to Eleazar, the third to Ithamar, the fourth and fifth to Eleazar, the sixth to Ithamar, etc.

7 ואחד אחז, with a few Hebrew MSS, LXX, Syr, Vg; MT ואחז אחז (the first word has been assimilated to the second).

8 לשערים. This name means "barley." Is שערים a corruption of שריה "Seraiah" (Neh 12:12)? Three of the four letters in "Seraiah" are the same as three of the five letters in "Seorim."

9 למימן; LXX (mistakenly) "to Benjamin" (= לבנימן).

10 לישבאב; LXX "Ishbaal." This name occurs fourteen times in 2 Samuel 2–4 as the name of the son of Saul who contested with David for the kingship of the northern tribes. It is unlikely that a man with Baal as the theophoric component of his name would be a member of the priestly courses.

11 העשרים. Instead of ordinals for numbers greater then ten, the Hebrew uses cardinal numbers, but here, unusually, with the definite article. Cf. 1 Chr 25:19; 27:15.

12 ובני חברון, with 2 Hebrew MSS (marginal reading); cf. LXX[L]. MT ובני "and my sons." *BHS* and Rudolph, 162, propose an original reading לחברני "the Hebronites," of which ובני is a remnant.

13 יריהו הראש; cf. 1 Chr 23:19 (note "the second," etc., with the following names). MT יריה. *BHS* inserts לבני יריהו "of the sons of Jeriah" after יריהו and suggests that other names have fallen out. Rudolph, 162, following Rothstein, believes a name from the next generation has been lost and then the rest of the verse, from "Amariah" to "the fourth," has been filled in from 1 Chr 23:19.

Eleazar,[18] who had[19] no sons. 29/ and Kish:[20] the sons of Kish: Jerahmeel. 30/ The sons of Mushi: Mahli, Eder, and Jerimoth. These were the sons of the Levites by their ancestral houses.

31/ These also cast lots like their kindred the sons of Aaron before King David, Zadok, Ahimelech, and the heads of the ancestral houses of the priests and Levites,[21] the chief as well as the youngest brother.

14 שָׁמִיר, with a Cairo Genizah MS, Q, many Hebrew MSS, and the versions; K שָׁמוּר "Shamur."

15 וּמוּשִׁי. MT adds בְּנֵי יַעֲזִיָּהוּ בְנוֹ "the sons of Jaaziah his son," which I take as a variant of v. 27bα לִיעֶזְיָהוּ בְנוֹ. Rudolph, 164, retains the phrase and emends בְּנֵי "sons of" to בְּבָנָיו "among his sons."

16 בְּנוֹ; LXX "his sons."

17 MT adds a *wāw* conjunction, but this is a dittography lacking in LXX.

18 LXX adds "and Ithamar and Eleazar died." A scribe apparently linked this Eleazar to Eleazar the son of Aaron in v. 1 and then added the note about Eleazar's death from 1 Chr 23:22.

19 הָיוּ with 1 Chr 23:22; MT הָיָה.

20 לְקִישׁ; *BHS* suggests וּקִישׁ.

21 וְלַלְוִיִּם. MT adds אָבוֹת. Is this a conflate variant of הָאָבוֹת "the ancestral houses" earlier in the verse?

24:1-31

Structure

This chapter may be outlined as follows:
I. 24:1-19. Twenty-four priestly courses
   A. 24:1-6. This introduction ascribes the division of the Aaronides to David, with the assistance of Zadok and Ahimelech, but it also indicates that these divisions or orders were assigned by lot, perhaps to indicate that they were God-given. Sixteen of the divisions were assigned to Eleazar, one of the sons of Aaron and the high priest who succeeded him; the other eight were assigned to his brother Ithamar. The proceedings were recorded by a Levite, Nethanel.
   B. 24:7-18. The lot casting is structured very systematically. After the opening clause, "The first lot fell to Jehoiarib,"[1] the next courses follow routinely, with two courses described in each verse: to B the second, to C the third, to D the fourth, etc. For courses higher than the "tenth," this list, as usual in Biblical Hebrew, construes the corresponding cardinal numbers as ordinal numbers. The numbers "first" through "tenth" and "twentieth" use the definite article; the numbers "eleventh" through "nineteenth" and the numbers "twenty-first" through twenty-fourth" do not.
   C. 24:19. The actual assignment of tasks to these courses is credited to Aaron, who received them by divine command.
II. 24:20-31. Further genealogy of some Levites
   A. 24:20-25. Kohathites
   B. 24:26-30a. Merarites
   C. 24:30b-31. Conclusion

Questions about the unity of this chapter and about what is original and what is secondary have long engaged commentators. Three typical examples will give an idea of the range of ideas that have been proposed.

Rudolph, 159, believed the chapter was a unity, coming from one hand, though he also held that the entire chapter was secondary in Chronicles itself and came from a person even later than the author of chap. 23, also held by him to be secondary.

---

1 The adjective "first" follows the noun "lot" in Hebrew and then comes *lāmed* followed by the name Jehoiarib. Subsequent courses put the name of the priestly family first (prefixed with a *lāmed*) and followed by the ordinal number.

As noted in the introduction to chap. 23, Williamson divided the whole of chaps. 23–27 into two layers, assigning 23:6b-13a, 15-24; 25:1-6; 26:1-3, 9-11, 19; 26:20-32 to the primary strand, which the Chronicler introduced with 23:1-6a.[2] The original sections from these four chapters correspond to one of the categories of Levites mentioned in 23:3-6a. All the rest of chaps. 23–27 is assigned by him to a pro-priestly redactor, who worked about a generation after the Chronicler himself. This date depends on the fact that the genealogy of the Kohathites and Merarites in 24:20-31 adds one generation to many of the names in the Levitical list of chap. 23.

Japhet, 410, believes that Williamson uses the categories of Levites in 23:3-6a too rigidly, and she attributes 24:1-20a and 31 from this chapter to the Chronicler but relegates vv. 20b-30b to a secondary level. In her view vv. 20a and 31 describe a ceremony parallel to that in vv. 1-19 in which the Levites who are not priests are appointed by lot following the example of the priests. Verses 20b-30 are held to be an independent unit, with its own conclusion, and, primarily because of her analysis of vv. 26-27, she doubts whether these supplemental materials can be dated as early as one generation after the Chronicler. Both she and Williamson note the close connection between 24:1 and 23:32, particularly the reference to the "sons of Aaron," but they draw diametrically opposite conclusions from this fact. Since Williamson assigns 23:25-32 to his pro-priestly (secondary) redactor, 24:1-19 must be assigned to that redactor as well. Japhet believes 23:25-32 to be original, and hence considers 24:1-19 original as well.

Since I believe that 23:25-32 is probably secondary, I lean toward that judgment also on chap. 24. The data are not overwhelming for either side of the argument,

however, and these materials, even if secondary, do not clash sharply with the overall message of the Chronicler.

Ten of the twenty-four names in the priestly courses in vv. 7-18 are also attested in lists of postexilic priests in Neh 12:1-7 and 12-21. The second of these lists, Neh 12:12-21, consists of a master list of priestly houses, followed in each case by the name of the head of that house in the time of the high priest Joiakim, who was the second high priest after the return from exile (first half of the 5th century BCE). Twenty-two priestly families appear in the present form of that list.[3] From this list is derived the list of "priests" from the time of Jeshua, the first high priest after the return from exile in 12:1-7 (last third of the 6th century BCE). This list artificially interprets the list of the priestly *houses* from vv. 12-21 as if it were a list of *individual* priests, and it backdates the list to the first generation after the return. The list in 12:12-21 also seems to be the basic source used to develop the roster of priestly signatories to the "firm agreement" in 10:3-9 (2-8), made in the time of Nehemiah.[4] Table 7 shows these three lists. The numbers listed before ten of the names correspond to their respective priestly course in 1 Chr 24:7-18. Minor spelling variations will be explained in the commentary on individual verses.

---

2 "Origins."

3 Apparently an original list of sixteen priestly families (vv. 12-18) has been expanded by the addition of the last six names (vv. 19-21). Note that none of the last six appears among the signatories in Neh 10:3-9 (2-8), and there is an unnecessary "and" before the name Joiarib in the Hebrew text of Neh 12:6 (part of the list in 12:1-7) and 19 (part of the list in 12:12-21). The date of this expansion would have had to be before the creation of the list of priestly courses in 1 Chronicles 24. See Klein, "Ezra & Nehemiah," 830–32, 834.

4 At least three priestly houses have been added to the list in the meantime: Daniel, Baruch, and Meshullam. A Daniel, whether this man or another, is associated with Ithamar in Ezra 8:2. Pashhur, who appears only in the list in Nehemiah 10, may have been omitted or lost accidentally from the earlier list in Neh 12:12-21, on which the list in 12:1-7 depends. See also n. 10 below.

Table 7. Postexilic Priests

Neh 12:12-21	Neh 12:1-7	Neh 10:3-9 (2-8)
High priest Joiakim (v. 12)	*High priest Jeshua (v. 1)*	*Time of Nehemiah*
Priestly house/head of house	Priest	Priestly signatories
Seraiah/Meraiah	Seraiah	Seraiah (v. 3 [2])
Jeremiah/Hananiah	Jeremiah	Azariah
Ezra/Meshullam (v. 13)	Ezra	Jeremiah
		Pashhur (v. 4 [3])
16. Amariah/Jehohanan	16. Amariah (v. 2)	16. Amariah
5. Malluchi/Jonathan (v. 14)	5. Malluch	5. Malchijah
Data missing[5]	Hattush	Hattush (v. 5 [4])
10. Shebaniah/Joseph	10. Shecaniah (v. 3)	10. Shebaniah
3. Harim/Adna (v. 15)	3. Rehum[6]	3. Harim (v. 6 [5])
Meraioth/Helkai	Meremoth	Meremoth
Iddo/Zechariah (v. 16)	Iddo (v. 4)	Obadiah
		Daniel (v. 7 [6])
Ginnethon/Meshullam	Ginnethon	Ginnethon
		Baruch
		Meshullam (v. 8 [7])
8. Abijah/Zichri (v. 17)	8. Abijah	8. Abijah
6. Miniamin/name missing	6. Mijamin (v. 5)	6. Mijamin
24. Moadiah/Piltai	24. Maadiah	24. Maaziah (v. 9 [8])
15. Bilgah/Shammua (v. 18)	15. Bilgah	15. Bilgai
Shelemaiah/Jehonathan	Shemaiah (v. 6)	Shemaiah
1. Joiarib/Mattenai (v. 19)	1. Joiarib	
2. Jedaiah/Uzzi	2. Jedaiah	
Sallai/Kallai (v. 20)	Sallu (v. 7)	
Amok/Eber	Amok	
Hilkiah/Hashabiah (v. 21)	Hilkiah	
Jedaiah/Nethanel	Jedaiah	

5 The name of the priestly house, Hattush, can be reconstructed from the other two lists, but the name of the head of this house is irretrievably lost.

6 רחם; metathesis of חרים "Harim."

Four priestly families are attested already in the list of returnees from Babylon: Jedaiah, Immer (= Amariah), Pashhur, and Harim (Ezra 2:36-39//Neh 7:39-42);[7] and three of these, Jedaiah, Immer/Amariah, and Harim, also appear in both lists of priests in Nehemiah 12 and as priestly courses #2, #16, and #3, respectively, in 1 Chronicles 24.[8] The fourth priestly family, Pashhur, which has the largest number of descendants in the list of returnees,[9] appears in neither of the lists in Nehemiah12 nor among the priestly courses in 1 Chronicles 24.[10] Either this family declined precipitately;[11] or, more likely, it has divided into two or more priestly houses and assumed new family names, or remained one family and taken on a new family name. In Ezra 2:61-63//Neh 7:63-65, the descendants of three priestly families, Habaiah, Hakkoz, and Barzillai, were excluded as unclean because they could not find their names among the priestly genealogies, and they were told they could not partake of the holy food until a priest arose who could consult the Urim and Thummim. A descendant of Hakkoz, Meremoth son of Uriah[12] son of Hakkoz (Neh 3:4, 21), appears among the builders of the wall in the time of Nehemiah, and this is usually taken to mean that he had attained the priestly rank by that time. Ezra turned over the temple vessels he had brought back from Babylon to Meremoth the son of Uriel (Ezra 8:33), presumably the descendant of Hakkoz mentioned in Nehemiah 3. Hakkoz appears as the name of the seventh priestly course in 1 Chr 24:10.

In summary, comparison of the list of priestly courses with that of the priestly houses in Neh 12:12-21 shows that the number of priestly houses had already reached twenty-two by the first half of the fifth century, and ten of these priestly houses appear among the priestly courses of chap. 24, though not in the same order. Subsequent to the time of the list in Neh 12:12-21, therefore, the list has been lengthened from twenty-two to twenty-four names, and fourteen new names appear among the priestly courses, one of which, Hakkoz, is already known from the list of returnees in Ezra 2//Nehemiah 7. The other thirteen arose either as the remaining priestly houses merged with one another or, if they were larger, divided into two or more priestly families, or completely new houses of priests worked their way into the list of twenty-four. Of these remaining thirteen names in 1 Chr 24:1-19, four (#9 Jeshua, #11 Eliashib, #20 Jehezkel, #21 Jachin) are known as priests elsewhere in the postexilic period, though we cannot be sure that these are the same individual. Four other names are attested elsewhere, but identified only here as priests (#12 Jakim, #17 Hezir, #19 Pethathiah, and #23 Delaiah). Finally, five are names attested only here in the Bible (#4 Seorim, #13 Huppah, #14 Jeshebeab, #18 Happizzez, and #22 Gamul).[13]

The reason for establishing the priestly courses resulted from the fact that there were more priests than could be used at one time in the temple service or that could be supported in the small postexilic community. Already in the list of returnees there were four thousand two hundred eighty-nine priests (Ezra 2:36-39//Neh 7:39-42), but only seventy-four Levites, one hundred twenty-eight[14] singers, one hundred thirty-nine[15] gate-

---

7 Only these four priestly families are listed in Ezra 10:18-22, a list of the priests who had married foreign wives.

8 Names #3 and #16 also appear among the signatories in Nehemiah 10.

9 Jedaiah, 973; Immer, 1,052; Pashhur, 1,247; and Harim, 1,017.

10 Rudolph, *Esra und Nehemiah*, 190, 192, restores Hattush and Pashhur to the list of priestly houses in Neh 12:14, between Malluchi and Shebaniah. The case for Hattush is stronger, since this name does appear in Neh 10:5 (4) and 12:2, both of which are dependent on 12:12-21. Rudolph restores Pashhur after Hattush in 12:2 since he observes this priestly family was clearly active at the time of Nehemiah (1 Chr 9:12; Neh 11:12). But since Pashhur does not appear among the priestly courses in 1 Chronicles 24 as well, it seems to me that his absence from Neh 12:2 and 14 is probably intentional.

11 Note that six men of the sons of Pashhur were among those who had to divorce their foreign wives in Ezra 10:22.

12 N. Avigad, "A New Class of *Yehud* Stamps," *IEJ* 7 (1957) 146–53, identified a "Urio" found on a stamp seal impression with this Uriah.

13 The names in courses 1, 2, 5, 16, and 21 (Jehoiarib, Jedaiah, Malchijah, Immer, and Jachin) appear in the list of priests in 1 Chr 9:10-12. Cf. Johnstone, 1:253.

14 Neh 7:44: one hundred forty-eight.

15 Neh 7:45: one hundred thirty-eight.

keepers, three hundred ninety-two temple servants and sons of Solomon's servants (Ezra 2:43-58//Neh 7:43-60). While the priests were too many for the community, the other clergy categories were too small. Eventually the singers and gatekeepers were included among the Levites, while the Nethinim and the sons of the servants of Solomon disappeared. Only one priestly course would serve at any one time, meaning that a given course would need to serve only about two weeks per year. Divisions of the priests are mentioned in 1 Chr 28:13, 21, and the list in 24:1-19 amplifies and clarifies what is meant by those divisions. Divisions of the Levites, implied in v. 31, without explicit mention of the total number of courses or divisions, are also attested in 2 Chr 8:14 (appointed by Solomon) and in 2 Chr 31:2 (appointed by Hezekiah).[16]

Once established in the form given in 1 Chr 24:1-19, the twenty-four priestly courses remain stable or fixed in Judaism. Josephus paraphrases this event and adds that one family of priests was to minister to God each week from Sabbath to Sabbath. He notes that the family that drew the first lot was the first to serve and that "this apportionment has lasted down to this day" (*Ant* 7.365–66).

The priestly courses are also mentioned in the documents from Qumran. In its calculation of the annual festivals, the document known as 4Q320 mentions the following courses in this order: Maaziah #24, Jedaiah #2, Sheorim #5, Jeshua #9, Maaziah #24, Jehoiarib #1, Jedaiah #2 (frg. 4 iii-vi) and Jedaiah #2, Hakkoz #7, Eliashib #11, Bilgah #15, and Pethahiah #19 (frg. 1 i 6—iii 10).[17] This document demonstrates that both the names of the orders and their assignment to a specific numerical order have remained the same.[18] Another document,

4Q319, refers to the orders of Gamul #22 and Shecaniah #10.[19]

Detailed Commentary

24:1-19. Twenty-four Priestly Courses
24:1-6. Division of Aaronides

■ **1** *The divisions of the sons of Aaron were:* "sons of Aaron" in this clause refers to all the priests, while in the next clause (see below) it refers to the actual sons of Aaron in the genealogical sense.

the sons of Aaron: Nadab, Abihu, Eleazar, and Ithamar: These four sons of Aaron, listed in this order, are the standard genealogical information about Aaron's descendants in the Bible (cf. 1 Chr 5:29 [6:3]; Exod 6:23; 28:1; Num 3:2; 26:60; cf. Exod 24:1, 9).

■ **2** *Nadab and Abihu died before their father:* The Chronicler is referring to an incident recorded in Lev 10:1-5; Num 3:2-4; and 26:61 in which Nadab and Abihu were killed by fire that came out from before Yahweh (Lev 10:2) because the two men had offered illicit fire (אש זרה, Lev 10:1; Num 3:4; 26:61), that is, an offering that Yahweh had not commanded (Lev 10:1). Moses ordered Mishael and Elzaphan, sons of Uzziel, the uncle of Aaron, to remove the bodies of Nadab and Abihu from the camp. We are also told that Eleazar and Ithamar served as priests during the lifetime of their father (Num 3:4). The Chronicler omits any reference to the sin of Nadab and Abihu and merely indicates that they died prematurely and without surviving sons. This omission and his changing of a local reference, "before Yahweh," to a temporal one, "before their father," indicate his desire to shift attention from their sin and their resultant punishment to a focus on Aaron's remaining heirs and their priestly descendants.

---

16   According to 2 Chr 23:18 David had organized the Levitical priests to be in charge of the house of Yahweh.

17   I have used the spelling of the names as they appear in my translation of 1 Chronicles 24 and have supplied the numbers for the courses. Because the festivals do not appear in consecutive weeks, many numbers are omitted and Maaziah and Jedaiah appear twice.

18   For full interpretation of this text see James C. VanderKam, *Calendars in the Dead Sea Scrolls: Measuring Time* (London: Routledge, 1998) 77–80. See also

Shemaryahu Talmon, "The Calendar Reckoning of the Sect from the Judaean Desert," *Scripta hierosolymitana* 4 (1958) 170–71. An earlier study by Paul Winter, "Twenty-six Priestly Courses," *VT* 6 (1956) 215–27, notes that the twenty-six priestly courses mentioned in the War Scroll reflect the solar rather than the lunar year.

19   Vanderkam, *Calendars,* 80–84. For a list of rabbinic references to these courses, see Emil Schürer, *The History of the Jewish People in the Age of Jesus Christ (175 B.C.–A.D. 135)* (rev. Geza Vermes et al.; 3 vols. in 4; Edinburgh: T. & T. Clark, 1979), 2:247, n. 36.

Since they had no sons, Eleazar and Ithamar became priests: Though Nadab and Abihu originally had had the right to priesthood through primogeniture, their early death and lack of male heirs passed that right on to Eleazar and Ithamar. According to biblical tradition Eleazar succeeded his father Aaron when he died (Num 20:25-28), and Phinehas succeeded his father Eleazar when he died (Josh 24:33; Judg 20:28). Eleazar was considered prince of the princes of the Levites (נשׂיא נשׂיאי הלוי) and had oversight of all who had charge of the sanctuary (Num 3:32).[20] The traditions about Ithamar are much more limited. See Exod 38:21 (the work of the Levites was under the supervision of Ithamar); Num 4:28 (the Gershonites were under the supervision of Ithamar); and 4:33 (the Merarites were under the super-

vision of Ithamar; cf. also Num 7:8). Among those returning with Ezra was a descendant of Ithamar by the name of Daniel (Ezra 8:2). Moses gave Eleazar and Ithamar jointly various cultic instructions (Lev 10:6, 12, 16).

■ **3** *Together with Zadok of the sons of Eleazar and Ahimelech of the sons of Ithamar, David divided them according to their appointed duties in their service:* In distinction to the manner of selecting the Levites in chap. 23, where David acted alone, David is assisted in making assignments to the twenty-four priestly courses by the two leading priests. The connection of Zadok with Eleazar is standard in the high priestly genealogies (1 Chr 5:29-35; 6:35-38 [6:3-9, 50-53]). Ahimelech and Ithamar are much more problematic.

Genealogy of Eli in 1 Samuel

```
Eli ── Phinehas ──┬─ Ichabod
                  │ Ahitub ──┬── Ahimelech ── Abiathar
                  │ Ahijah
```

According to 1 Samuel, Abiathar was the son of Ahimelech the priest at Nob, who was the son of Ahitub (1 Sam 22:20; 23:6; 30:7); Ahimelech's brother, presumably, was Ahijah.[21] Ahijah[22] was the son of Ahitub, the (older?) brother of Ichabod, the son of Phinehas, who was the son of Eli (1 Sam 14:3). Hence Abiathar was the great-great-grandson of Eli. According to Julius Wellhausen and Frank Moore Cross, Eli himself was probably a descendant of Moses.[23] In this reconstruction, there is no historical relationship between Ahimelech and

Eleazar,[24] or between Ahimelech and Ithamar, or for that matter between Ahimelech and Aaron. Abiathar was the only priest who escaped Saul's slaughter of the priests at Nob (1 Sam 22:20), and he and Zadok were priests under David (2 Sam 15:35; 17:15; 1 Chr 15:11; cf. 1 Kgs 4:4). The only exception to the relationship of Abiathar and Ahimelech, as son and father, in the books of Samuel is 2 Sam 8:17, which makes Zadok the son of Ahitub and Ahimelech the *son* of Abiathar.[25] While Wellhausen reconstructed this text to read "Abiathar the son

---

20   See also Numbers 3–4; 20:27; 27; 31; 32; 34; Josh 14:1; 19:51; 21:1; 22:13; 24:33; Judg 20:28.

21   This is the weakest link in this genealogy. Some scholars believe that Ahimelech and Ahijah are names of the same person (see F. T. Schumacher, *IDB* 1:67). But since other pairs of priests are known in this genealogy (Hophni and Phinehas; Ahitub and Ichabod [1 Sam 14:3]), Ahijah and Ahimelech may be brothers. See Klein, *1 Samuel*, 135.

22   And therefore Ahimelech was also the son of Ahitub.

23   Cf. Wellhausen, *Prolegomena*, 142; Cross, *Canaanite Myth*, 196–97. In 1 Sam 2:27 Moses is apparently

from the father's house of Eli in Egypt, although Propp, "Ithamar," *ABD* 3:579–81, considers the father's house of Eli Aaronic.

24   Contra Japhet, 427; and Williamson, 163, who concedes that the Chronicler here associated Ahimelech with Ithamar.

25   Syr and Ethiopic have "Abiathar the son of Ahimelech," but this may be a secondary correction. See McCarter, *II Samuel*, 253. The only son of Abiathar recorded elsewhere in the Bible is Jonathan, not Ahimelech (2 Sam 15:27, 36; 17:17, 20; 1 Kgs 1:42-43).

of Ahimelech the son of Ahitub and Zadok," Cross reconstructed the original text as "Zadok the son of Ahitub and Abiathar the son of Ahimelech."[26]

Whatever the correct reconstruction of 2 Sam 8:17 may be, the Chronicler took up this text in 1 Chr 18:16 and made Ahimelech[27] and Zadok the priests of David (cf. 24:3, 6, 31).[28] The Chronicler's connection of Ahimelech with the sons of Ithamar—and therefore a descendant of Aaron— is without precedent or any other attestation in the OT. Had the Ithamarite priests come to see themselves as heirs of the house of Eli?

■ **4** *Because the sons of Eleazar were more numerous in male heads than the sons of Ithamar:* Japhet, 426, observes that a census of all the sons of Eleazar indicated that they were more numerous and hence more preeminent than the descendants of Ithamar and therefore they were assigned more priestly houses. This does not conform to social reality in which members of a father's house were created by genealogical affiliation over a long period of time, not established by dividing up a larger population into smaller groups.

among the sons of Eleazar, sixteen heads according to their families, and among the sons of Ithamar, eight according to their families: The greater importance of the sons of Eleazar is reflected in that two-thirds of the priestly houses are attributed to them and only one-third of the priestly houses to the descendants of Ithamar.

■ **5** *They divided them by lot, both alike:* The casting of lots allows the results to be interpreted as divine selection (cf. the use of lots with the Levites in v. 31, with the singers in 25:8, and with the gatekeepers in 26:13).[29]

While the Eleazarites predominate over the Ithamarites, the author is intent on indicating by "all alike" the equity of the division into courses (cf. v. 31; 25:8; 26:13).

for there were sacred officials and officials of God among the sons of Eleazar and the sons of Ithamar: The terms "sacred officials" (שׂרי קדשׁ)[30] and "officials of God" (שׂרי האלהים) are in apposition,[31] and both terms designate the high status of all the priestly courses in both priestly lines of Eleazar and Ithamar. The "officials of God" might also be translated as "the highest officials," construing the noun אלהים in the absolute state as a way of expressing the superlative.[32]

■ **6** *The scribe Shemaiah the son of Nethanel, a Levite, wrote them down:* The authenticity of the materials purportedly stemming from the time of David is supported by this reference to their being recorded by an otherwise unknown Levite. The author thereby indicates that being a scribe was another role assigned to the Levites of his day. A similar quest for authenticity is reflected in the list of those who witnessed this event: the king, the leaders, Zadok, Ahimelech, and the heads of the priestly and Levitical families.

one father's house being chosen for Eleazar and one being chosen for Ithamar: One house was chosen from Eleazar and one from Ithamar until the number 16 was reached so that the final eight courses were all assigned to Eleazar. Houses 1, 3, 5, 7, 9, 11, 13, 15 and 17-24 were assigned to Eleazar and 2, 4, 6, 8, 10, 12, 14, 16 to Ithamar.[33] For the alternate proposal of Rudolph, see textual note 6.[34]

26 *Canaanite Myth*, 212–14. Propp, "Ithamar," *ABD* 3:580, proposes that Zadok's father was Ahitub and that Abiathar had a son named Ahimelech, who shared his father's duties toward the end of his reign. In short, 2 Sam 8:17 is not corrupt in his opinion.

27 I follow the reading of LXX; MT "Abimelech."

28 The only exception is 1 Chr 15:11.

29 For lot casting in the postexilic period, see also Neh 10:35 (34) and 11:1. Cf. also Esth 3:7 and 9:24. Lot casting was used to divide the land among the twelve tribes (Josh 19:51) and to allocate the Levitical cities (1 Chr 6:39-66 [54-81]; 25:9; 26:14). Cf. also 1 Sam 14:38-45.

30 Cf. Isa 43:28, where these words are characteristically translated as "the princes of the sanctuary."

31 Welch, *Work*, 87, believed that the two titles originally represented distinct groups and were evidence of priestly contentions that the author was here trying to resolve.

32 D. Winton Thomas, "A Consideration of Some Unusual Ways of Expressing the Superlative in Hebrew," *VT* 3 (1953) 209–24, who believed that there were no unambiguous examples of the use of the divine name as an intensifying epithet in the OT (p. 218). See also his later article, "Some Further Remarks on Unusual Ways of Expressing the Superlative in Hebrew," *VT* 18 (1968) 120–24.

33 Cf. Curtis and Madsen, 272; Japhet, 428. Japhet believes that her view is supported by the similar arrangement of the singers in chap. 25.

34 See also the translation in *JPS*: "one clan more

24:7-18. Lot Casting

■ **7** *The first lot fell to Jehoiarib, the second to Jedaiah:*
Jehoiarib (יהויריב) is spelled the same way in 1 Chr 9:10
but as Joiarib (יויריב)[35] in the parallel list of priests in
Neh 11:10. His exact genealogical relationship to the following excerpt from the high priestly genealogy is
unknown.[36] Joiarib is also listed as the priestly family to
which Mattathias, the head of the Maccabean family,
belonged (1 Macc 2:1; 14:29). Rudolph, 161, and others
have used this genealogical connection to date the list of
priestly courses to Maccabean times,[37] but there is no
evident or explicit propaganda for the Maccabees in this
list of priestly courses and the name Joiarib had achieved
prominence among the priestly houses by inclusion at
the end of the lists in Nehemiah 12. There also is no
indication that hierarchical rank was indicated by the
number of the priestly course to which a priestly name is
attached.[38] Rather, these numbers only assisted in assigning the priests of this family to a rotating schedule of
duties. Jedaiah appears in the confusing list in 1 Chr
9:10//Neh 11:10 and was among the four priestly families in the list of returnees from Babylon (Ezra 2:36-
39//Neh 7:39-42), where his descendants are linked to
Jeshua, the first high priest in the restoration.[39] Neither
Jehoiarib nor Jedaiah is among those who signed the
firm agreement in Neh 10:3-9 (2-8).

■ **8** *the third to Harim, the fourth to Seorim:* Harim also
appears in the list of returnees (Ezra 2:36-39//Neh 7:39-
42). The name Seorim, which appears only here in the
Bible, means "barley" in Hebrew and may be corrupt
(see textual note 8).

■ **9** *the fifth to Malchijah, the sixth to Mijamin:* Both of
these names appear in the lists of Nehemiah 10 and 12.
Malchijah (מלכיה; cf. Neh 10:4 [3]) is spelled Malluchi
(מלוכי K[40]) or Mallichi (מליכי Q) in Neh 12:14 and as
Malluch (מלוך) in Neh 12:2.[41] Mijamin (מימן) appears in
all three lists of Neh 10:8 (7); 12:5, 17, the last reference
with a significantly different spelling: Miniamin (מנימין).[42]

■ **10** *the seventh to Hakkoz, the eighth to Abijah:* Hakkoz is
the priestly family that was unable to establish its
genealogical credentials at first (see discussion of Ezra
2:61-63//Neh 7:63-65 above). Abijah appears in all three
lists of Neh 10:8 (7); 12:4, 17. Zechariah, the father of
John the Baptist, belonged to this priestly course (Luke
1:5). This NT story also indicates the function of these
courses, namely, to assign priests to a rotating schedule
(Luke 1:8).

■ **11** *the ninth to Jeshua, the tenth to Shecaniah:* Jeshua
(ישוע) was the first high priest after the return from
Babylon (Ezra 2:2; spelled Joshua יהושע in Hag 1:1; Zech
3:1), though it is unknown whether the ninth course
traced itself to him[43] or to another person known by this
common name. Shecaniah (שכניה) appears in the lists in
Neh 10:5 (4); 12:3, 14, twice under the alternate spelling
Shebaniah (שבניה).[44]

■ **12** *the eleventh to Eliashib, the twelfth to Jakim:* Eliashib

---

taken for Eleazar for each one taken of Ithamar."
This view is also supported by L. Dequeker, "1
Chronicles XXIV and the Royal Priesthood of the
Hasmoneans," *OTS* 24 (1986) 100. He proposed
that the preeminence of the line of Eleazar is shown
in that two families from Eleazar would always serve
in consecutive weeks, followed by one family from
Ithamar.

35 It is this spelling that also appears in the lists from
Neh 12:6 and 19 presented above. Such variation in
the spelling of the divine name in personal names
is widely known elsewhere.

36 See the commentary on 1 Chr 9:10.

37 See Dequeker, "1 Chronicles XXIV," 103. A lengthy
list of advocates of a Hasmonean date is given by
Schürer, *History,* 2:250, n. 50.

38 Later, however, Josephus asserts that it was a great
advantage to belong to the first of the twenty-four
courses, as his ancestors had (cf. *Life* 1 [1.2]).

39 Rudolph, 162, declines to identify the Jedaiah of the
priestly courses with the Jedaiah from the list of
returnees because the name occurs so commonly,
indeed, twice in Neh 12:6-7 and 12:19, 21.

40 LXX "Malluch." The gentilic ending arose because
of dittography of the first letter of the following
word.

41 Cf. also Malchijah in 1 Chr 9:12. A Malluch also
appears in Neh 10:5 (4) between Shebaniah and
Harim. Is this the conflation of an alternate
spelling for Malchijah?

42 The name in Neh 12:5, compared to 1 Chr 24:9,
adds a vowel letter: מימין.

43 This identification seems plausible to me, although
the descendants of Jedaiah, of the second course,
are said to be of Jeshua's house in Ezra 2:36-
39//Neh 7:39-42. There is a similar uncertainty
about Eliashib in v. 12.

44 In Neh 12:14 LXX reads Shecaniah (Σεχενια) for
MT Shebaniah.

was high priest at the time of Nehemiah,[45] though it is unknown whether this priestly course was linked to him or to other people known by this name (cf. Jeshua in the preceding verse). This name is common, though restricted to the books of Chronicles, Ezra, and Nehemiah. A Jakim is attested among the descendants of Benjamin in 1 Chr 8:19, but known as a priest only here.

■ **13** *the thirteenth to Huppah, the fourteenth to Jeshebeab:* Both of these names appear only here in the Bible.

■ **14** *the fifteenth to Bilgah, the sixteenth to Immer:* Bilgah (בלגה) occurs in the lists of Neh 10:9 (8); 12:5, 18, though in Neh 10:9 (8) his name is spelled Bilgai (בלגי). Immer was one of the four priestly families that appear in the list of returnees (Ezra 2:36-39//Neh 7:39-41). Immer (אמר) may also be identified with Amariah (אמריה) of the lists in Neh 10:4 (3); 12:2, 13, although there his name has a theophoric element referring to Yahweh.[46]

■ **15** *the seventeenth to Hezir, the eighteenth to Happizzez:* A Hezir appears among the lay signatories of the "firm agreement" in Neh 10:21 (20), but the name is only used of a priest here in biblical texts. While this name, which means "swine,"[47] seems strange for a priestly family, a well-known tomb of the Bene Hezir is in the Kidron Valley. The tomb itself is dated to the end of the Hasmonean period, and an inscription found in it can be dated to the beginning of Herod's reign. The unusual name Happizzez appears only here.[48]

■ **16** *the nineteenth to Pethahiah, the twentieth to Jehezkel:* Pethathiah is the name of a Levite in Ezra 10:23 and Neh 9:5 and a Judahite in Neh 11:24. The reference in this verse is the only time this name is used of a priest. Jehezkel is used elsewhere only as the name of the priest/prophet Ezekiel (Ezek 1:1; 24:24).

■ **17** *the twenty-first to Jachin, the twenty-second to Gamul:*

Jachin occurs as a priest in 1 Chr 9:10//Neh 11:10, where his genealogical relationship to the segment of the high priestly genealogy in 1 Chr 9:11//Neh 11:11 is unclear.[49] This is the only place in the OT where the name Gamul occurs.

■ **18** *the twenty-third to Delaiah, the twenty-fourth to Maaziah:* The descendants of Delaiah in the list of returnees were not able to prove whether they belonged to Israel (Ezra 2:60//Neh 7:62), while a certain Shemaiah the son of Delaiah[50] tried to get the layman Nehemiah to enter the temple in order to destroy his reputation (Neh 6:10).[51] It is possible that the last figure in Neh 6:10 is a priest, but if he is not, the only reference to Delaiah as a priest is in this list of priestly courses. Maaziah (מעזיהו) appears in the lists of Nehemiah 10 and 12. The name is spelled מעזיה in Neh 10:9 (8), lacking only the final *wāw*, but with variant spellings in the other two cases: Moadiah (מועדיה) in 12:17 and Maadiah (מעדיה) in 12:5.

24:19. Assignment of Tasks

■ **19** *these were to enter the house of Yahweh as was stipulated for them by the authority of Aaron their father:* Although David, with the assistance of Zadok and Ahimelech, cast the lots (v. 3), the obligations of the priests for their periodic times of service had been given by Aaron, who had received them in turn directly from Yahweh. In the Pentateuch such instructions are usually given to Aaron through Moses: "Yahweh spoke to Moses, saying, 'Command Aaron and his sons'" (Lev 6:8-9 [1-2]), although there are occasions when God speaks to Aaron alone (Exod 4:27; Lev 10:8; Num 18:1, 8, 20).[52] Detailed descriptions of Levitical tasks are given in 1 Chr 23:28-32; 15:1-6; 26:14-18; and 26:30-32, but the Chronicler does not supply such detailed descriptions of priestly tasks. The expression "their appointed duty in their service" in the first half of this verse reveals little.

---

45 Neh 3:1, 20-21; 12:22-23; 13:28.

46 Immer is cited as a priestly ancestor in 1 Chr 9:12//Neh 11:12-13.

47 BDB, 306, which notes slightly divergent spellings in the Talmud and Tg meaning pomegranate and apple; and *HALOT* 1:302.

48 See *HALOT* 3:954: "Yahweh/God has shattered" (this man's family).

49 See the commentary on 1 Chr 9:10.

50 A Delaiah son of Shemaiah appears in Jer 36:12, 25.

51 All three of these references are spelled דליה, but the name is spelled דליהו in 1 Chr 24:18.

52 Japhet, 432, says that in this verse there is no indication whether God's command came directly to Aaron or through the mediation of Moses, but the former is surely implied.

24:20-31. Further Genealogy of Some Levites
24:20-25. Kohathites

This genealogy is structured very much like 1 Chr 23:7-24, except that no data for Gershom are included and in five cases data from a later generation are included from the descendants of Kohath, as well as one new descendant and three Levitical families from a new branch of the Merarites (the descendants of Jaaziah). There are ten new names in all.[53] This section, therefore, has been added by a secondary hand. Instead of updating the data in chap. 23 itself or adding this section directly after chap. 23, the redactor inserted it here after the courses of the Aaronides. Verse 31 implies that the Levites too were divided into courses by lot and this provided a context for inserting this updated material.

Japhet indeed proposed that the Levites were also divided into courses by lot as part of the original version drafted by the Chronicler himself (vv. 20a and 31; see the introduction to this chapter). We can only speculate on the reason for the omission of the data on Gershom. Perhaps only a fragmentary genealogy was available to the person who added these materials, a view I prefer (note also that Kohath is not mentioned explicitly in the extant text), or the data on Gershom had not changed.[54] Because of the incomplete character of this genealogy, it is not clear what role the additional names play. Were the names from the next generation additional Levitical families, or did these names replace the families already listed?

Descendants of Kohath[55]

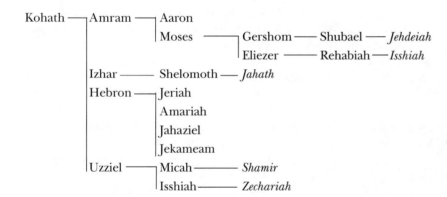

■ **20** *The remaining Levites:* This notice marks the following paragraph off clearly from vv. 1-19 and links it back to 23:7-24.

the sons of Amram: Shubael; the sons of Shubael: Jehdeiah: Shubael here is listed as a descendant of Amram, without indicating, as in 23:13, 15-16, that the intervening generations were Moses and his son Gershom. No additional information is available for Jehdeiah, the descendant of the sons of Shubael (cf. 27:30 for Jehdeiah the Meronothite).

■ **21** *the sons of Rehabiah the chief: Isshiah:* Most English versions give the title of chief to Isshiah, but its position immediately after Rehabiah indicates that it belongs to him, as at 23:17 (cf. also the commentary on Ladan the chief at 23:8). In chap. 23 Rehabiah, who had many sons, is connected to Amram through Eliezer the second son of Moses. Nothing more is known of his son Isshiah (but see v. 25).

■ **22** *Izharites: Shelomoth. The sons of Shelomoth: Jahath:* Izhar is the only son of Kohath whose name is spelled

---

53   Johnstone, 1:254, counts eleven, since he interprets "his son" in v. 27 as a name, Beno.

54   Revised data for Jehiel(i), the son of Ladan the son of Gershon, are provided at 1 Chr 26:21-22.

55   The basic genealogy of Kohath is taken from the commentary on chap. 23. New names are in italics.

with a gentilic ending—"Izharites." This genealogy is extended beyond the data in 23:18 by the addition of an otherwise unknown Jahath (he is to be distinguished from the Gershonite Jahath in 23:10-11).

■ 23 *The sons of Hebron: Jeriah the chief, Amariah the second, Jahaziel the third, Jekameam the fourth:* Since this repeats the information from 23:19, there has been no change in the genealogy of Hebron, the third son of Kohath.[56]

■ 24 *The sons of Uzziel: Micah. The sons of Micah: Shamir:* In 23:20 Micah is called the chief and his brother Isshiah the second. Shamir is only known here as a personal name; elsewhere it is the name of a Judahite (Josh 15:48) or Ephraimite (Judg 10:1-2) town.

■ 25 *The brother of Micah: Isshiah. The sons of Isshiah: Zechariah:* The unique feature of this notice is that a generation has been added to *both* sons of Uzziel. While the name Zechariah is very common, occurring more than forty times, nothing more is known of this particular Zechariah.

24:26-30a. Merarites

Descendants of Merari[57]

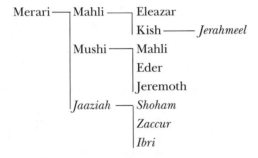

■ 27 *The sons of Merari by Jaaziah his son: Shoham, Zaccur, and Ibri:* In addition to the usual sons of Merari, Mahli

and Mushi (see v. 26), the genealogy adds a third son to this family[58] and then lists three descendants in the following generation. This major change in the genealogy leads Japhet, 434, to question whether this genealogy can be dated securely within a single generation after 1 Chr 23:7-24 (*pace* Williamson). Again nothing is known of the additional four names, the last three of whom are additional Levitical families. The names Jaaziah, Shoham,[59] and Zaccur occur only here in the Bible. Since the descendants of Jaaziah are given before those of Mahli and Mushi, one might infer that the descendants of Jaaziah have gained preeminence among the sons of Merari.

■ 28 *Mahli: Eleazar, who had no sons:* In 23:22 the house of Eleazar, which had no sons, was preserved by having the sons of Kish intermarry with the daughters of Eleazar. In this later genealogy the Levitical house of Eleazar has apparently died out.[60]

■ 29 *and Kish: the the sons of Kish: Jerahmeel:* The family of Kish, known from 23:21-22, is extended to a new generation by the addition of Jerahmeel. Nothing more is known of this Jerahmeel.[61]

■ 30a *The sons of Mushi: Mahli, Eder, and Jerimoth:* This sentence repeats 23:23.[62]

24:30b-31. Conclusion

■ 31 *These also cast lots like their kindred the sons of Aaron:* This clause makes explicit the comparison of the genealogy in vv. 20-31 with the list of priestly courses in vv. 7-19. If it implies that there were also twenty-four courses or divisions of Levites,[63] it is unclear exactly how which names should be included in the twenty-four. There are nine families assigned to Kohath, seven to Merari, and nine from Gershon in 23:7-17.

---

56 See textual note 13 for an alternate proposal, based on a conjecture that names of Jeriah's descendants have been accidentally lost.

57 The basic genealogy of Merari is taken from the commentary on chap. 23. New names are in italics.

58 Braun, 239, speculates that a new name may have been given to the family of Eleazar, the son of Mahli, but this seems to be contradicted by the following verse.

59 An Arabic etymology for his name is proposed by L. Kopf, "Arabische Etymologien und Parallelen zum Bibelwörterbuch," *VT* 8 (1958) 206.

60 Cf. Curtis and Madsen, 273; Japhet, 433.

61 See, however, the descendant of Judah (1 Chr 2:9, 25, 26, 27, 33, 42) and the son of Jehoiakim (Jer 36:26) who have the same name.

62 There Jerimoth is spelled within an internal *yôd* as a *mater lectionis*. Rudolph, 165, speculates, unnecessarily in my judgment, that the next generation has been lost after these names. He assumes that a generation must always be added, whereas a genealogy is not so much a birth record as an indication of social structures at any given time.

63 This is the way Josephus understands the passage (*Ant.* 7.367). Cf. also Schürer, *History,* 2:247.

before King David, Zadok, Ahimelech, and the heads of the ancestral houses of the priests and Levites: This list of witnesses closely parallels that in 24:6, omitting only the king's "leaders," whom Japhet, 428, considers "out of their element" in v. 6.

Conclusion

In materials that were probably added secondarily to the text of Chronicles, perhaps to lessen the emphasis of Levites over against priests, this chapter lists for the first time the twenty-four priestly courses. This division is credited to David, who was assisted in the casting of lots by Zadok and Ahimelech. The obligations of the priests for their times of service were given already by Aaron.

Sixteen of these courses are ascribed to Eleazar and eight to Ithamar. The names and order of these priestly courses persist throughout the rest of the Second Temple period.

Also secondary in this chapter is the listing of Levites in vv. 20-31. While this list does not repeat the data for Gershon from 23:7-11, it expands the data for Kohath from 23:12-20 by adding five names from the next generation; it also adds an additional son of Merari himself and three descendants from that son to the descendants of Merari from 23:21-23, and an additional descendant for Kish, the grandson of Merari. The chronological difference between this verse and the genealogies in chap. 23 suggests that these verses have been added secondarily.

25

Translation

1/ David and the officials of the liturgical host[1] set apart the sons of Asaph, Heman, and Jeduthun,[2] who were to prophesy[3] to the accompaniment of lyres, harps, and cymbals. The list[4] of the men for this work, according to their ritual duties, was: 2/ Sons of Asaph: Zaccur, Joseph, Nethaniah, and Asarel. These four[5] were the sons of Asaph under the direction of Asaph, who prophesied[6] according to the orders of[7] the king. 3/ Jeduthun—the sons of Jeduthun: Gedaliah, Zeri,[8] Jeshaiah, Shimei,[9] Hashabiah, Mattithiah—six people; they were under the direction of their father Jeduthun, who prophesied with the lyre,[10] and they were in charge of thanking and praising Yahweh. 4/ Heman—the sons of Heman: Bukkiah, Mattaniah, Uzziel,[11] Shubael,[12] Jerimoth,[13] Hananiah, Hanani, Eliathah,[14] Giddalti, Romamti-ezer, Joshbekashah, Mallothi, Hothir, and Mahazioth; 5/ all these were the sons of Heman the king's seer, according to the promises of God to raise up his horn.[15] God gave Heman fourteen sons and three daughters. 6/ All these were under the direction of their father (Heman) for music in the house of Yahweh, with the accompaniment of cymbals, harps, and lyres,[16] according to the orders of the king.[17]

7/ Their number, with their kindred, trained in music for Yahweh, all skilled, was two hundred eighty-eight. 8/ They cast lots,[18] watch with watch,[19] young and old alike, teacher and pupil[20] alike. 9/ The first lot fell out [for Asaph] to Joseph, his sons and his brothers, twelve;[21] Gedaliah the second,[22] him and his brothers and his sons, twelve; 10/ the third to Zaccur, his sons and his brothers, twelve; 11/ the fourth to Zeri,[23] his sons and his brothers, twelve; 12/ the fifth to Nethaniah, his sons and his brothers, twelve; 13/ the sixth to Bukkiah, his sons and his brothers, twelve; 14/ the seventh to Asarel,[24] his sons and his brothers, twelve; 15/ the eighth to Jeshaiah, his sons and his brothers, twelve; 16/ the ninth to Mattaniah, his sons and his brothers, twelve; 17/ the tenth to Shimei,[25] his sons and his brothers, twelve; 18/ the eleventh to Uzziel,[26] his sons and his brothers, twelve; 19/ the twelfth[27] to Hashabiah, his sons and his brothers, twelve; 20/ the thirteenth[28] to Shubael, his sons and his brothers, twelve; 21/ the fourteenth to Mattithiah, his sons and his brothers, twelve; 22/ the fifteenth to Jeremoth,[29] his sons and his brothers, twelve; 23/ the sixteenth to Hananiah, his sons and his brothers, twelve; 24/ the seventeenth to Josbekashah, his sons and his brothers, twelve; 25/ the eighteenth to Hanani, his

1 וְשָׂרֵי הַצָּבָא לַעֲבֹדָה, lit. "officers of the army for the ritual service" (Kleinig, *Lord's Song*, 151). See Rudolph, 164; Curtis and Madsen, 279. Cf. Num 8:25. Japhet, 439, believes that this expression is a synonym of "the chiefs of the Levites" (1 Chr 15:16). See also the commentary.

2 וִידוּתוּן. Here and in vv. 3, 6 LXX reads "Jeduthun" (יְדוּתוּן). Cf. K at Neh 11:17.

3 הַנִּבְּאִים with Q, many Hebrew MSS, LXX, Tg, Vg (*niphal* participle); K הַנְּבִיאִים "the prophets." There is some ambiguity about this reading and "prophesied" in the next verse, where the LXX, like K here, reads the noun "prophet." The use of "prophesied" in v. 3 is unambiguous, however, and probably indicates that the two readings in vv. 1-2 should also be understood as verbs.

4 LXX adds: "according to their head(s)," apparently interpreting מִסְפָּר as "number." See the commentary.

5 וְאִשְׂרָאֵל אַרְבָּעָה אֵלֶּה with *BHS*; Rudolph, 165; MT וְאִשְׂרָאֵלָה "Asarelah." Rudolph attributed the shorter MT to parablepsis. Japhet, 437, 442, makes a similar proposal, אִשְׂרָאֵל אֵלֶּה, but notes that Asarelah also appears in v. 14 as יְשַׂרְאֵלָה. A few Hebrew MSS point the second letter as a *śin*.

6 הַנִּבָּא; a few Hebrew MSS, LXX read הַנָּבִיא "the prophet." Cf. textual note 3 above.

7 עַל יְדֵי. This expression occurs also in v. 3 and twice in v. 6. I have translated it "according to the orders of" when it refers to the king, but "under the direction of" when it refers to the leadership of one of the chief musicians. It is not clear to me why עַל יַד is used instead earlier in this verse ("under the direction of Asaph").

8 וּצְרִי. The same name is given as "Izri" (יִצְרִי) in v. 11. Curtis and Madsen, 277, 279, read Izri in both places. LXX Σουρει = זוּרִי = וּרִי = יִצְרִי.

9 וְשִׁמְעִי. Inserted from v. 17 in order to make six people as required. It is attested by one Hebrew MS, LXX^BA, Arab.

10 הַנִּבָּא בְּכִנּוֹר; cf. *BHS* and Vg. MT has the words in inverse order.

11 עֻזִּיאֵל; LXX "Azarel" (עֲזַראֵל). Cf. v. 18. Rudolph, 166, notes that Uzziah and Azariah are alternate names for the same king, mirroring the difference in the initial syllable between these two names here.

12 שׁוּבָאֵל, with LXX; cf. v. 20 and 1 Chr 23:16 LXX and 24:20. MT שְׁבוּאֵל "Shebuel."

13 וִירִימוֹת; cf. 1 Chr 24:30. V. 22 לִירֵמוֹת "Jeremoth."

14 אֱלִיאָתָה; v. 27 אֱלִיָּתָה. The medial א between two vowels became *yôd* and is written with *dagesh forte*.

15 קַרְנוֹ. The suffix, whose antecedent was Heman, was lost in MT by haplography since the following word begins with a *wāw*.

16 וְכִנֹּרוֹת. MT, but not LXX, adds לַעֲבֹדַת בֵּית הָאֱלֹהִים

sons and his brothers, twelve; 26/ the nineteenth to Mallothi, his sons and his brothers,
twelve; 27/ the twentieth to Eliathah,[30] his
sons and his brothers, twelve; 28/ the
twenty-first to Hothir, his sons and his
brothers, twelve; 29/ the twenty-second to
Giddalti, his sons and his brothers, twelve;
30/ the twenty-third to Mahazioth, his sons
and his brothers, twelve; 31/ the twenty-
fourth to Romamti-ezer, his sons and his
brothers, twelve.

"for the liturgical service of the house of God." This
is a conflated synonymous variant of בשיר בית יהוה
"for music in the house of Yahweh" earlier in the
verse.

17 MT (cf. LXX) adds: "Asaph, Jeduthun, and Heman."
Rudolph, 166, identifies this as a gloss on the pronoun "these" at the beginning of the verse, interpreting it falsely as applying to all three groups
when it actually refers to the sons of Heman. Cf.
Japhet, 437; and Williamson, 168. By adding a conjunction before the names, LXX and Tg indicate
that the singers were following the orders of the
king and of Asaph, Heman, and Jeduthun. But this
implies, incorrectly, that "all these" at the beginning
of the verse applies to all three guilds. Kleinig,
Lord's Song, 151–52, translates: "Asaph and
Jeduthun and Heman were under the king." This
interpretation avoids the conjectural deletion and
understands "all these" at the beginning of the
verse as referring to the Hemanites.

18 גורלות. Five Hebrew MSS, Tg, Rudolph, 166, point
this noun as a construct; cf. LXX. All these are
attempts to make sense of a difficult text. See the
commentary.

19 משמרת לעמת משמרת, with a few Hebrew MSS, Tg.
MT lacks the second משמרת. See the commentary
for a discussion of the translation.

20 מבין עם תלמיד. Rudolph, 166, deletes these words as
a false interpretation of "young and old alike." He
believes they contradict v. 7: "trained in song . . . all
skilled." תלמיד ("pupil") occurs only here in the OT.

21 בניו ואחיו שנים עשר. These words are filled in from
the context (see the end of this verse and subsequent verses). Cf. LXX, which places these words
earlier in the verse, before Asaph.

22 השני. LXX has both a translation and a transliteration of this word. See Allen, *Greek Chronicles,* 1:163.

23 לצרי, emended to agree with v. 3. MT ליזרי "Izri."

24 אשראל. Emended to agree with name reconstructed
in v. 2; MT ישראלה "Jesarelah."

25 שמעי. Two Hebrew MSS, Vg: שמעיה "Shemaiah."

26 עזיאל with LXX[L], Syr (cf. v. 4). MT עזראל "Azarel."

27 השנים עשר. Cf. 1 Chr 24:16. The definite article is
used here to distinguish the ordinal number from
the immediately preceding cardinal number.

28 לשלשה עשר. From here to the end of the list all the
numbers are preceded by a *lāmed.*

29 לירֵמות. In v. 4 וירימות "Jerimoth." Cf. textual note
13.

30 לאליאתה. Emended to agree with spelling of name
in v. 4; MT לאליתה "Eliyyathah."

Structure

This chapter consists of a genealogical listing of twenty-four sons of Asaph, Heman, and Jeduthun, the heads of the families of singers (vv. 1-6), and an account of how these sons were arranged by casting lots into twenty-four divisions or duty groups (vv. 7-31). Curtis and Madsen, 275, suggest that the order of chaps. 23–25 may have been influenced by the duties of the three groups described: the Levites to prepare the sacrifices (chap. 23), the priests to make the offering (chap. 24), and the singers to offer praises to Yahweh (chap. 25). The structure of chap. 25 is as follows:

I. 25:1-6. Twenty-four sons of Asaph, Heman, and Jeduthun, who traced their lineage back to Gershon, Kohath, and Merari, the three sons of Levi (6:18-32 [33-47]). The listing of the sons of each father takes place in the order Asaph, Jeduthun, and Heman, for whom four, six, and fourteen sons are mentioned, respectively. The musicians are credited with prophetic activity and are under the authority of their father.
   A. 25:1. Introduction
   B. 25:2. Four sons of Asaph
   C. 25:3. Six sons of Jeduthun
   D. 25:4-6. Fourteen sons of Heman

II. 25:7-31. Lot-casting ceremony distributed the two hundred eighty-eight Levitical singers into twenty-four teams, with each team consisting of the leader and eleven other musicians. With only minor exceptions, the twenty-four divisions are described in a stereotypical manner that mentions the numerical rank of the division, its head or leader, a reference to his sons and brothers, and the total membership of twelve.
   A. 25:7-8. Introduction, describing the method and purpose of this lot casting
   B. 25:9-31. Description of the results of the lot casting

For Rudolph, 168, this chapter is a unity, but it did not come from the Chronicler himself. Rudolph notes that Asaph does not play the decisive role in this chapter that he has in original texts written by the Chronicler, for while he is mentioned first, he has the smallest number of sons, and Heman has more sons than the other two heads of the singers combined. Heman is also called "the seer of the king" (v. 5), whereas for the Chronicler, according to Rudolph, Asaph alone is "the seer" (2 Chr 29:30), or all three heads are given that title (2 Chr 35:15). The high position of Heman closely resembles that of other secondary pieces, such as 1 Chr 6:16-33 (31-48) or 15:16-24, although there Jeduthun has been replaced by Ethan. The person who added this chapter was himself a singer, in Rudolph's opinion, and therefore not to be identified with the redactor of chap. 24, who was a priest.

Japhet, 437–39, retains the whole of the chapter for the Chronicler, although she does not directly address the objections of Rudolph. While admitting a certain amount of stereotypical language in all such lists, she finds this feature to be especially true of this chapter, and holds it to be an artificial construction. She concludes, 438: "The theological motivation was the wish to provide a full analogy, down to the smallest detail, between the service of sacrifices and the service of song (cf. also on 23.30-31),[1] but there is no evidence that such a perfect parallelism actually existed at any time in the liturgy of the Second Temple." She also observes that the singers are arranged both by descent and by divisions in this chapter, while the Levites and the gatekeepers in chaps. 23 and 26 are arranged only by descent, and the priests in chap. 24 only by courses or divisions.

Williamson has used his identification of the controlling force of the heading in 23:3-6a[2] to ascribe 25:1-6 to the Chronicler. This passage, like the others in this section that he considers original, is genealogically based and has David as the person who separates out the singers. Williamson also notes the presence of musical instruments in this passage and in 23:5. The second part of this chapter, vv. 7-31, is assigned by him to a pro-

---

1   Japhet believes that the creation of the list of singers was made on the basis of the list of priests in 1 Chr 24:1-19.

2   See the discussion of his essay, "Origins," under Structure in 1 Chronicles 23.

priestly redactor, who provides twenty-four divisions for the singers, as he will for the gatekeepers in the next chapter, on the analogy of the twenty-four priestly courses in (the secondary) chap. 24. References to lot casting and to treating all the members alike are especially close in 25:8 and 26:13. Williamson detects considerable tension between the two sections of this chapter (vv. 1-6 and 7-31). In the first section, David sets apart the Levites; in the second David is not mentioned and the assignment to divisions is done by lots. In the first section the individual singers are under the direction of their father (Asaph, Heman, or Jeduthun), but it is difficult to see how this would function with twenty-four distinct divisions. The term מספר means "list" in v. 1 and "number" in v. 7; instruments are explicitly mentioned in the first six verses, while singing seems to be the understanding of music in vv. 7-31. Nevertheless, Williamson does not think that the secondary passage shows literary dependence on vv. 1-6, but rather holds that the second list shows actual, historical continuity, at a slightly later time.

In general, I am persuaded by Williamson's approach, although I would modify it in the following ways. The least compelling part of his argument to me is the unified character of the so-called pro-priestly redaction. Priestly proclivities play no role in this passage, which could be said to be favorable toward (pro) the Levitical singers, unless one considers the distribution of any cultic functionaries into twenty-four divisions to be "priestly." The ties to other secondary passages in chaps. 23–26 could well have been created by a redactor of this chapter who was different from the one in chap. 24 or 26. I do not deny the *possibility* of all the secondary

materials coming from one hand, but I also do not think their unity has been established.

Other details of Williamson's analysis of chap. 25 are open to further refinement. Already in 1870, H. Ewald noticed that the last seven names of the sons of Heman do not fit standard Hebrew onomastic patterns.[3] Three of them[4] consist of verbs in the perfect tense in the first common singular, the second of which is followed by a noun (עזר, "help") that is treated as part of the name (see v. 31). A fourth name is a *hiphil* perfect (third masc. sg.) or a *hiphil* infinitive construct (הותיר "Hothir"). A fifth is a feminine plural noun (מחזיאות "Mahazioth") and a sixth and a seventh are anomalous (אליאתה "Eliathah" and ישבקשה "Joshbekashah"). Scholars have noted that with relatively minor changes these unusual "names," to which they have also added the two preceding names, Hananiah and Hanani, could be understood as a poem, or a poetic fragment, and this has led to a flurry of subsequent proposals that have attempted to refine Ewald's basic insight.[5] While there would be much quibbling on details, the following Hebrew text and translation represents a broad consensus of understanding:

חנני יה חנני[6]
אלי אתה
שגדלתי רוממתי
עזרי מלאה בקשתי[7]
הותירה מחזיות[8]

Be gracious, Yah(weh), be gracious to me.
Oh my God, come[9] [or, You are my God].
I have magnified (you), I have exalted (you).
Oh, my helper, fulfill my request.
Give abundant visions.[10]

3   *Ausführliches Lehrbuch der hebräischen Spraches des Alten Bundes* (8th ed.; Göttingen: Dieterich'sche Buchhandlung, 1870) 680, §274b.

4   גדלתי "Giddalti"; יהממר "Romammti"; and מלותי "Mallothi."

5   H. Torczyner, "A Psalm by the Sons of Heman," *JBL* 68 (1949) 247–49, arranged the "poem" according to the order of names in vv. 23-31 instead of v. 4, but his proposal ignores the overall principles by which the names in vv. 23-31 have been arranged. Julius Böhmer, "Sind einige Personennamen 1 Chr 25,4 'künstlich geschaffen,'" *BZ* 22 (1934) 93–100; and E. Kautzsch, "Miscellen," *ZAW* 6 (1886) 260, suggested adding Hananiah and Hanani to the

poetic fragment; P. Haupt, "Die Psalmenverse in I Chr 25:4," *ZAW* 34 (1914) 142–45, has supplied the most detailed philological comments and most subsequent studies begin with his article as a baseline.

6   In distinction from MT, the first word חנניה has been divided in two words and the *yôd* doubled.

7   MT עזר ישבקשה מלותי.

8   MT הותיר מחזיאות.

9   Petersen, *Late Israelite Prophecy,* 91, n. 52, cited 2 Chr 35:21 (vocalized following LXX) as a parallel.

10 Petersen, ibid., 91, n. 57, suggests that מחזיאות is a plural form equaling מחזיות, which can be explained by analogy with משכית (sg.) and משכיות (pl.; cf. also משכיאת). In any event he prefers a translation of

While there are elements of a lament form in these lines, it is certainly not great poetry or stylistically impressive Hebrew.[11] For these reasons Myers, 1:172–73, analyzed it as a series of incipits or first lines of poems, but this analysis explained at best sixty percent of the poem.[12] Rudolph, 168, has proposed that individual singers were known for reciting a particular poem in which the word by which they are named occurred, but the Sumerian parallel on which this has been partially based has been sharply criticized by Petersen.[13] While many of the proposed reasons for this strange development from poetic fragment to list of names make some sense, no interpretation is fully convincing. What remains convincing to me, however, is that these are not normal names and that their names when viewed together can be understood as the language of prayer.

Scholars have also noticed that seven of the twenty-four names of the individuals in vv. 2-5 show a number of spelling differences from the names in vv. 9-31 (see the textual notes), which supports the notion of different authorship for the two sections. The variants can be arranged in parallel columns:

v. 2 אשראלה	v. 14 ישראלה
v. 3 צרי	v. 11 יצרי
v. 3 lacuna	v. 17 שמעי
v. 4 עזיאל	v. 18 עזראל
v. 4 שבואל	v. 20 שובאל
v. 4 ירימות	v. 22 ירמות
v. 4 אליאתה	v. 27 אליתה

The first six variants occur in the first fifteen names (hence 40 percent of those names show variation); the last name is the only variant among the nine names derived from the poetic fragment (11 percent variation).

While Heman occurs in the second position among the singer heads in the first verse, he is very highly honored in vv. 4-6. His fourteen sons and three daughters are directly attributed to divine promises that have "exalted his horn." He is also given the unusual title "seer of the king." I propose therefore that the redactor who created and added vv. 8-31, the twenty-four divisions of the singers, derived nine new names of singers from the poetic fragments and added them to the names of the sons of Heman in order to reach the number twenty-four (= the last ten words in v. 4). The names of Heman's sons originally numbered five, a number suitable for Heman's location in the second position. Because the redactor added these names to an older document, there was almost perfect agreement in spelling between the new names he supplied and these same names in the list of twenty-four divisions. To justify the great size of Heman's family, the redactor also added v. 5, giving Heman the exalted title of king's seer and attributing his prolific family to divine aid both by the reference to the divine promises and through the words "God gave" in v. 5. The "three daughters," also mentioned in v. 5, who seem irrelevant in a list of male singers, were a further explanation of Heman's fertility: God's gift to Heman was similar to God's establishment of Job's second family. The secondary character of v. 5 may also explain why both v. 5 and v. 6 begin with the words "All these." The redactor's further addition of v. 7 pulls together the data of vv. 1-6 and vv. 8-31 in which there are now twenty-four singers or singer groups, respectively. The number of singers in each group (twelve) appears only in the second section.

How should we explain the differences in order between the names in the first section and the names in the list of divisions in the second? The narrator attributes it to the casting of lots and therefore suggests divine origin to the rotation of singer groups. Is the

---

"visions" over "signs" or "noteworthy events" favored by Haupt and Rudolph (167).

11 Ehrlich, *Randglossen*, 7:350: "Aus den neun letzten Namen der Söhne Hemans macht man neuerdings ein Gebet. Aber was für Hebräisch da herauskommt!" (From the nine last names of the sons of Heman people recently make a prayer. But what sort of Hebrew results from this!)

12 Myers translated: "Be gracious to me, Yahweh, be gracious to me; / My god art thou; / I have magnified, and I will exalt [my] helper. / Sitting [in] adversity I said, / Clear signs give plentifully." For

parallels to the first line of his translation, Myers suggested Pss 51:3 (1); 56:2 (1); 57:2 (1); for l. 2, 63:2 (1); for l. 3, 34:4 (3) or 115:9-11 (where only the common word "help" occurs). He offered no parallels to the last two lines of his own translation.

13 *Late Israelite Prophecy*, 65–66.

divergence between the first and the second listing of the twenty-four names really the result of casting lots and therefore a random arrangement, or is there some rational principle by which the second list of names was rearranged?[14] Since the redactor did not reveal such a rational principle to us, we need to determine if it exists inductively. In the following discussion I will number every son by an abbreviation: the first two sons of Asaph would be A1 and A2, the first two sons of Jeduthun would be J1 and J2, the first two sons of Heman H1 and H2, with the rest of the abbreviations following the same pattern thereafter.

1. A2	Joseph		2. J1	Gedaliah
3. A1	Zaccur		4. J2	Zeri
5. A3	Nethaniah		6. H1	Bukkiah
7. A4	Asarel		8. J3	Jeshaiah
9. H2	Mattaniah		10. J4	Shimei
11. H3	Uzziel		12. J5	Hashabiah
13. H4	Shubael		14. J6	Mattithiah
15. H5	Jerimoth		16. H6	Hananiah
17. H11	Joshbekashah		18. H7	Hanani
19. H12	Mallothi		20. H8	Eliathah
21. H13	Hothir		22. H9	Giddalti
23. H14	Mahazioth		24. H10	Romamti-ezer

The redactor's strategy is apparently to select a son of Asaph and a son of Jeduthun until the sons of Asaph run out, and then select a son of Jeduthun and a son of Heman until the sons of Jeduthun run out. The final ten names are all sons of Heman, including the nine created from the poetic fragment. There are only two exceptions to this procedure: the first two names of the sons of Asaph are switched, and the first son of Heman is given position 6, which should have gone to the third son of Jeduthun. These two changes may be an attempt by the redactor to create the illusion of randomness that would be produced by lot casting.

I use the word "illusion" about the lot casting because the arrangement of the groups seems to follow a rational plan rather than the random results[15] that would be expected from the casting of lots or mere historical change (so also Curtis and Madsen, 281). The four sons of Asaph, for example, are given the first four odd numbers: 1, 3, 5, and 7 (vv. 9a, 10, 12, 14),[16] with the first three sons of Jeduthun and the first son of Heman[17] being given the first four even numbers: 2 = J1; 4 = J2; 6 = H1; and 8 = J3 (vv. 9b, 11, 13, 15). For the next eight numbers, the sons of Jeduthun continue to get the even numbers until their sons run out (10 = J4; 12 = J5; 14 = J6 [vv. 17, 19, 21]), and the next five sons of Heman get the next four odd numbers and the first available even number after the sons of Jeduthun have run out (9 = H2; 11 = H3; 13 = H4; 15 = H5; 16 = H6 [vv. 16, 18, 20, 22, 23]). Finally, the last eight sons of Heman take up the final eight places. The next four sons of Heman,

---

14 While Kleinig, *Lord's Song*, 58–60, outlines a plausible alternate procedure (see below), he also apparently believes that the lot casting was a historical act that took place in the time of David, thus ignoring the stereotypical and artificial features to which Japhet has called attention. Kleinig believes the lot was cast twelve times between pairs of singer groups: *1. A1 vs. A2*; 2. A3 vs. A4; *3. J1 vs. J2; 4. J3 vs. H1;* 5. H2 vs. H3; 6. H4 vs. H5; 7. J4 vs. J5; 8. J6 vs. H6; *9. H7 vs. H11; 10. H8 vs. H12; 11. H9 vs. H13; 12. H10 vs. H14.* In items printed in italics, the order of the two singer groups was reversed by the casting of the lot. What seems arbitrary to me in this proposal is the insertion of the first five Heman groups between Jeduthun group 3 and Jeduthun group 4. An earlier explanation of the order of the groups was made by P. Fr. v. Hummelauer, "1 Chr. 25: Ein Beitrag zum Gebrauch des Loses by den Hebräern," *BZ* 2 (1904) 254–59. He divided the singers into groups of nine, six, and nine, headed up, respectively, by Joseph (Asaph), Shimei (Jeduthun), and Hananiah (Heman). There is no evidence, however, for such a division into three groups.

15 If one were to number the sons in vv. 2-5 consecutively and compare them with the list of twenty-four divisions, the results would appear to be random (the first number in the following list is that of the son and the second is that of the position of this group as decided by lot): 1 = 3; 2 = 1; 3 = 5; 4 = 7; 5 = 2; 6 = 4; 7 = 8; 8 = 10; 9 = 12; 10 = 14; 11 = 6; 12 = 9; 13 = 11; 14 = 13; 15 = 15; 16 = 16; 17 = 18; 18 = 20; 19 = 22; 20 = 24; 21 = 17; 22 = 19; 23 = 21; 24 = 23.

16 Zaccur (A1) is in position 3 rather than position 1, with the latter position given to Joseph (A2).

17 This is the second exception referred to above.

H7–H10, are given the final even numbers (18 = H7; 20 = H8; 22 = H9; 24 = H10 [vv. 25, 27, 29, 31]), and the final four sons of Heman, H11–H14, are given the final odd numbers (17 = H 11; 19 = H12; 21 = H13; 23 = H14 [vv. 24, 26, 28, 30]). In my judgment this rational explanation is more convincing than attributing the order to the pure chance of lot casting.

The standard pattern for announcing the results of the lottery can be illustrated by v. 10: "The third to Zaccur, his sons and his brothers, twelve." The pattern consists of the ordinal number written with a definite article, a reference to the leader's sons and brothers, and the total head count. Beginning with v. 20 and continuing until the end, the definite article is replaced by the preposition *lāmed*, and beginning with v. 22 and continuing until the end the leader's name is also prefixed with a *lāmed*.[18] The first lottery result in v. 9a varies slightly from the pattern: "the first for Asaph to Joseph." *BHS* identifies Asaph as an addition, but without citing any evidence. Asaph could be construed as a miswritten dittography of Joseph[19] or it may have arisen as a simple anomaly. None of the other lottery picks is associated with one of the three great heads of the singers. The second lottery result, in v. 9b, differs from the pattern in two ways: the name of the singer comes before the ordinal number, and the pronoun "him" is inserted before "his sons and his brothers."[20]

Detailed Commentary

25:1-6. Levitical Singers
25:1. Introduction

■ **1** *David and the officials of the liturgical host set apart:* A literal translation of the Hebrew שרי הצבא would be "the commanders of the army" (see 1 Chr 26:26; 2 Chr 33:11), but it is difficult to understand why army officers would be involved in appointing the singers. Keil, 269, thought "the officials of the host" was a synonym for the leaders of the army or "the officials of Israel" (1 Chr 23:2; cf. 24:6); but Curtis and Madsen, 279, pointed out that when David appointed the twenty-four priestly courses he was assisted by two priests, Zadok and Ahimelech (24:2) and consequently we might expect that officials of the Levites would assist him in appointing singers. Curtis and Madsen also noticed that צבא is frequently used in Numbers (4:3, 23; 8:24-25) in connection with the age at which Levites were qualified for ritual service, and in Num 8:25 in a construct chain מצבא העבדה they translated "from the service of the work" or, as I would prefer, "from the host of those performing ritual service." The "officials of the liturgical host" would be a synonym for "the officials of the Levites" mentioned in 1 Chr 15:16, whom David directed to appoint singers at the time of the transfer of the ark.[21]

the sons of Asaph, Heman, and Jeduthun: This list of the head Levitical singers seems to be at first the stage Gese called III A (Asaph, Heman, and Jeduthun) in the development of the Levitical singers (cf. discussion at 15:1–16:3, Structure). In the next stage, III B, Heman becomes preeminent and the name Jeduthun is replaced by Ethan.[22] In the present (expanded) state of chap. 25, Heman has become preeminent, since he has more sons (fourteen) than the other two brothers combined (ten), but Jeduthun has not yet been replaced by Ethan. That is, the passage seems to be midway between stages III A and III B. If I am correct in proposing that nine of Heman's sons were added by the redactor who arranged the singers into twenty-four divisions, the material assigned to the original Chronicler is more clearly from the III A stage.[23]

---

18 This *lāmed* prefix also appears in three other isolated cases: vv. 9, 11, and 19.

19 One could also speculate that the insertion of "to Asaph" was intended for v. 2 in order to make the list of Asaph's sons begin just like those of Jeduthun (v. 3) and Heman (v. 4).

20 Japhet, 447, argues that all these differences are "premeditated stylistic technique." That seems exceedingly unlikely for at least the first, where I have restored the words "his sons and his brothers twelve," since the number of members assigned to Joseph is necessary for the calculation of the total of 288 in v. 7.

21 One might also take the word לעבדה in a genitival relationship to "host" and not as a description of the singers' duties.

22 See the genealogy at 1 Chr 6:16-33 (31-48).

23 The difference in the status of Heman between the primary and the secondary materials is additional confirmation of the literary-critical decision.

who were to prophesy to the accompaniment of lyres, harps,
and cymbals: Here the task of "prophesying" is assigned
to all twenty-four sons, whereas in vv. 2 and 4 only
Asaph and Jeduthun prophesy, and in v. 5 Heman alone
is called the seer of the king.[24] My translation of this
clause suggests that the musical instruments *accompanied*
the prophetic activity, but the Hebrew could also be construed to mean that the playing of the musical instruments was itself an act of prophesying. Rudolph,
170–71, suggests that the singing of the psalms was a
form of prophetic proclamation[25] and that it is only in
this passage that the cultic activity of the singers is
called prophesying. That may need to be modified
depending on how one defines "cultic activity." Jahaziel,
a descendant of Asaph and presumably therefore a
singer in the Chronicler's thinking, delivered a
prophetic oracle in the midst of the assembly (2 Chr
20:14). This cultic activity was surely considered prophesying.[26] Schniedewind has argued that "prophesying" is
attributed only to the *heads* of the Levitical singers and
not to all of the singers, but this is contradicted by v. 1,
which attributes prophesying to the *sons* of the three
heads of the singers.[27]

Music as an accompaniment of prophetic activity is
known from traditions about preexilic times. Samuel
told Saul he would meet a band of prophets playing
musical instruments and that they would be in a

prophetic frenzy. Samuel added that the spirit would
come on Saul and put him in such a prophetic frenzy as
well (1 Sam 10:5-6). Elisha received the power of Yahweh
while a musician was playing (2 Kgs 3:15).

While the playing of instruments alone might be
interpreted as prophesying, it is more likely that the
Chronicler has both vocal and instrumental music in
mind (cf. vv. 6-7) when he speaks of the prophesying of
the singers. Rothstein, 447, argued that the singing of
psalms to the accompaniment of instruments could be
described as prophetic proclamation.[28] King Hezekiah,
for example, commanded the Levites to praise Yahweh
in psalms, or as he put it, "with the words of David and
of the seer Asaph" (2 Chr 29:30). Nearly half the canonical psalms are ascribed to David in the MT, and Psalms
50 and 73–83 are ascribed to Asaph. Psalms 88 and 89
mention in their captions the singers Heman the
Ezrahite and Ethan the Ezrahite, and ten psalms are
assigned to the sons of Korah, who are probably also to
be numbered among the singers.[29] Both the psalms of
David and the psalms of the Levitical singers were probably considered prophetic by the Chronicler[30] so that in
singing these psalms the musicians would be repeating
prophetic words.

Commentators have speculated on the relationship
between the prophesying of the singers and the prophesying of the classical prophets or the so-called cult

24 P. Dirksen, "Prophecy and Temple Music: 1 Chron
    25:1-7," *Hen* 19 (1998) 259–65, argues that הנבאים
    modifies Asaph, Heman, and Jeduthun in v. 1 and
    that "prophesying" and "playing music" are to be
    kept totally distinct. He suggests that the singer-
    fathers used musical instruments in their prophetic
    role at court but were not musicians themselves.
    This seems to be directly contradicted by 1 Chr
    15:19.

25 I believe that Kleinig, *Lord's Song,* 156, goes too far
    in stating that the singers proclaimed the Lord's
    acceptance of the people with their burnt offerings
    and that they admonished them to act appropri-
    ately. He seems to read into the text a much later
    theological tradition.

26 Schniedewind, *Word of God,* 182–84, argues that the
    possession formula ("the spirit of Yahweh came
    upon Jahaziel") and the messenger formula ("Thus
    Yahweh has said to you") serve only to show that the
    speech of Jahaziel was inspired, not that the speaker
    was a prophet. On p. 118 he concludes that

Jahaziel's speech is essentially a human exegetical
voice empowered and authorized by God by the use
of inspiration formulas.

27 Schniedewind, *Word of God,* 186–87.

28 Rudolph, 171, added that the prophetic proclama-
    tion of the singers was probably limited to their cul-
    tic songs, but this again seems to be contradicted by
    2 Chr 20:14, cited above.

29 Psalms 42, 44–49, 84–85, 87–88. Petersen, *Late
    Israelite Prophecy,* 76, has made it likely that the
    Korahites were Levitical singers and may be virtu-
    ally identical with the sons of Jeduthun. See 2 Chr
    20:19.

30 Note that when Hezekiah stationed the Levitical
    musicians in the temple, this followed the com-
    mandment of Yahweh through his prophets (2 Chr
    29:25), or, as the Chronicler said earlier in the same
    verse, "according to the commandment of David
    and of Gad the king's seer and of Nathan the
    prophet." During Josiah's Passover the singers, here
    called the sons of Asaph, were in their place accord-

prophets. Evidence for the latter is itself very slender, with Mowinckel building much of his case on 1 Chr 15:22, 27. It is risky, of course, to reconstruct the offices that functioned in Solomon's temple from passages in Chronicles, since the Chronicler is more likely describing offices that functioned in his own day. And, as David Petersen has shown, the crucial word that Mowinckel translated as "oracle" (משא) more likely means "music."[31] Petersen's own proposal to see the singers as taking over the role of the classical prophets is also not convincing.[32] The Levite who delivers an oracle of salvation or encouragement in 2 Chr 20:14-17 could just as well be seen as a cultic functionary. When the Chronicler replaces "priests and prophets" from 2 Kgs 23:2 with "priests and Levites" in 2 Chr 34:30, this hardly makes the Levites prophets, but rather the Chronicler has replaced the word "prophets" with one of his favorite expressions and effectively removed the prophets from the scene.

For lyres, harps, and cymbals see the discussion at 1 Chr 13:8. Jeduthun prophesied with a lyre (v. 3; see textual note 10) and the sons of Asaph performed songs with cymbals, harps, and lyres—note the reverse or chiastic order—in v. 6.

The list of the men for this work: The word מספר is used here with the meaning "list" and in v. 7 with the meaning "number" or "total," and this is one of the reasons that led Williamson to identify vv. 7-31 as secondary.[33] The Chronicler used the word מספר in the sense of list in 11:11 (not attested in the *Vorlage* at 2 Sam 23:8), and Kleinig points to this sense in 1 Chr 27:1 as well.[34]

25:2. Four Sons of Asaph

■ **2** *Zaccur, Joseph, Nethaniah, Asarel. These four:* None of these names appears as a singer elsewhere, although Zaccur is listed as a descendent of Asaph in Neh 12:35. Zichri is the grandfather of the Levite Mattaniah in 1 Chr 9:15,[35] Zechariah appears as a singer in 15:18, 20; and Asaph the chief and Zechariah the second are singers in 16:5.[36] None of these latter three, of course,

actually bears the name Zaccur, and the name Zechariah is very common. The reading "These four" results from a textual conjecture by Rudolph (see textual note 5) and is therefore uncertain. Totals are given for Jeduthun in v. 3 and for Heman in v. 5, but according to my understanding of the passage the latter number was provided by the reviser.

under the direction of Asaph, who prophesied according to the orders of the king: "Under the direction of" translates על יד, whereas "according to the orders of" translates על ידי. The same double meaning within one verse recurs in v. 6. As far as I can determine there is no significant difference in meaning in this prepositional phrase between the singular or plural forms of the word "hand," and their synonymity is shown by the presence of the Ketib (sg.) and Qere (pl.) forms of the word in 2 Kgs 2:12. The meaning "under the direction of" finds a close parallel in 2 Chr 26:11, and the translation of "according to the orders of" or "by the directions of" is paralleled by 2 Chr 23:18 and Ezra 3:10. The sons of Jeduthun and Heman are also said to be under the authority of their father (vv. 3 and 6).

25:3. Six Sons of Jeduthun

■ **3** *the sons of Jeduthun: Gedaliah, Zeri, Jeshaiah, Shimei, Hashabiah, Mattithiah:* Only Mattithiah of the six sons of Jeduthun is known elsewhere as a musician. In connection with the transfer of the ark to Jerusalem, he played the lyre (1 Chr 15:18, 21; 16:5), as does Jeduthun later in this verse. Mattithiah's genealogical identification is unspecified in chaps. 15–16. Shimei (שמעי) may be the same person as Shemaiah (שמעיה), listed as a grandson of Jeduthun in 9:16 (cf. Shammua in Neh 11:17). The name Jeduthun was later replaced by "Ethan" in lists of singers (see 1 Chr 6:29 [44] and 15:17, 19).

and they were in charge of thanking and praising Yahweh: The verbs "thank" and "praise" are often used in tandem in connection with the musical activities of the singers (16:4; 23:30; 2 Chr 31:2). The musicians were responsible for both the instrumental and vocal aspects of sacred

---

ing to the command of David, Asaph, Heman, and Jeduthun. Either Jeduthun or even all three singers collectively are referred to here as "the king's seer" (2 Chr 35:15).

31 *Late Israelite Prophecy,* 6–64.
32 Ibid., 87, 100.
33 "Origins," 256.

34 *Lord's Song,* 149, n. 2.
35 The parallel text in Neh 11:17 reads "Zabdi."
36 Nethaniah is a Levite in 2 Chr 17:8.

song. The use of על ("in charge of") followed by infinitives construct (הדות והלל) is without precedent in Biblical Hebrew.[37]

25:4-6. Fourteen Sons of Heman

■ **4** *the sons of Heman: Bukkiah, Mattaniah:* A Mattaniah son of Mica is listed among the descendants of Asaph in Neh 11:17[38] (//1 Chr 9:15), 22. In Neh 12:8 Mattaniah and his brothers, without reference to Asaph, are in charge of the song of thanksgiving. Bakbukiah (בקבקיה) is listed as second among Mattaniah's associates in Neh 11:17 (cf. 12:9), and Mattaniah and Bakbukiah are listed together as gatekeepers in 12:25. Perhaps Bakbukiah is to be identified with Bukkiah (בקיהו).

Shubael, Jerimoth, Hananiah, Hanani, Eliathah, Giddalti, Romamti-ezer, Joshbekashah, Mallothi, Hothir, and Mahazioth: The last nine of these names are formed from the "poetic fragment." Hanani was the name of a chief musician in the time of Nehemiah (Neh 12:36). In its present form "Eliathah" is without meaning. Many scholars see it as a combination of two words, אלי and אתה, and translate either "you are my God" or "my God, come." A literal translation of Giddalti would be "I have exalted" and of Romamti-ezer "I have made help lofty." Joshbekashah is unexplained. For Mallothi, BDB, 576, suggests "I have uttered" and derives it from the root מלל. Hothir is a *hiphil* perfect or infinitive construct from יתר ("he made abundant") or, according to BDB, 452, possibly a noun meaning "abundance," or "superabundance." Mahazioth means, according to BDB, 303, "visions."

■ **5** *Heman the king's seer:* Other "seers" mentioned in Chronicles are Gad (1 Chr 21:9;[39] 29:29); Iddo (2 Chr 9:29; 12:15); Hanani (19:2);[40] and the seers who spoke to Manasseh in the name of Yahweh (33:18). More pertinent to this passage is that Asaph is called a seer in 29:30

and Jeduthun is called a seer in 35:15.[41] The reference in 1 Chr 25:5 to Heman the king's seer, therefore, means that all three ancestral heads of the musicians are called "seer" in Chronicles, and all three head singers, Asaph, Heman, and Jeduthun, are connected in vv. 2-5 with some kind of prophesying. Heman may be given this specific title in v. 5 because of the honor due to him as father of the largest group of musicians.

according to the promises of God to raise up his horn: The numerous offspring of Heman—more than the offspring of his two brothers combined—is interpreted as a sure sign of divine blessing, which is reinforced with the words "and God gave to Heman" in the next clause. As mentioned under Structure, the reviser's view of Heman is very close to that reflected in Gese's stage III B. Raising one's horn is a sign of strength or victory, and the antecedent of "his" is Heman.[42] In Deut 33:17 Joseph is compared to an animal that carries his horns high and is proudly conscious of his strength. In Ps 89:18 (17) the raising of the horn of the people or their king is the result of divine favor. Hannah prayed that God would exalt the power (lit. raise the horn) of the anointed king (1 Sam 2:10).[43] The psalmist also praises God for raising up a horn for his people (Ps 148:14).

God gave Heman fourteen sons and three daughters: The three daughters seem irrelevant in a description of Heman as the father of singers unless it hints that there were also female singers in the temple. Women drum players are mentioned in Exod 15:20; Judg 11:34; 1 Sam 18:6; and Jer 31:4. Meyers suggests that the absence of references to women musicians in later periods need not be taken as evidence that women's performance groups disappeared during the monarchy.[44] Job was fabled for being richly blessed with seven sons and three daughters

---

37 Dirksen, "Prophecy and Temple Music," 262, cites the meaning of על as "in addition to" in Lev 7:12-13; Num 6:20; 15:9; but he provides no clarification for its use here with the infinitive.

38 Mattaniah son of Mica son of Zabdi son of Asaph is similar to Mattaniah son of Micaiah son of Zaccur son of Asaph in Neh 12:35, where he is listed among the sons of the priests.

39 David's seer.

40 This verse refers to Jehu the son of Hanani "the seer" (החזה). "Seer" could refer to either Jehu or Hanani. Cf. also 2 Chr 16:7, where the title "seer" used with Jehu represents Heb. הראה. In 1 Kgs 16:7

41 Some commentators argue that the title "seer" refers to Asaph, Heman, and Jeduthun in this verse, as in LXX.

42 See Kleinig, *Lord's Song,* 150. Rothstein-Hänel, 450, interpreted בדברי האלהים as "in religious affairs" and considered it a modifier of "Heman the king's seer."

43 Cf. Klein, *1 Samuel,* 15.

44 Carol L. Meyers, "Of Drums and Damsels: Women's Performance in Ancient Israel," *BA* 54 (1991) 25.

Jehu the son of Hanani is called a "prophet" (נביא).

in both his first (Job 1:3) and second (42:13) families. Heman has as many daughters as Job and twice as many sons.

■ **6** *All these were under the direction of their father:* Without the supplementary material added by the reviser in v. 5, "All these" at the beginning of this verse would not sound as repetitious as it does in the MT, and the antecedent to "All these" would clearly be the sons of Heman, whose responsibility was to their own father. The *NIV* makes all three sons the antecedent of "All these"[45] and therefore interprets "father" collectively: "All these men were under the supervision of their fathers."

for music in the house of Yahweh, with the accompaniment of cymbals, harps, and lyres: "Music" includes words of thanking and praising (v. 3) as well as instrumental music. The author nicely ties vv. 1 and 6 together by repeating the list of instruments, only this time in reverse order. The MT conflates an alternate description of their activity into the main text: "for the liturgical service of the house of God."[46]

according to the orders of the king: As noted with the sons of Asaph, v. 1, the sons of Heman were established by royal decree.

25:7-31. Assignment of Levitical Singers to Twenty-four Teams

Since the structure and the order of the divisions or watches were discussed extensively above, and since all of the names correspond to names in vv. 2-5, the discussion can be brief.

25:7-8. Introduction

■ **7** *Their number, with their kindred, trained in music for Yahweh, all skilled, was two hundred eighty-eight:* This verse refers to the twenty-four divisions, each with twelve members, and the total of two hundred eighty-eight singers. This calculation also requires the restoration of the twelve associates of Joseph, as in textual note 21 to v. 9. In the list of returnees, the number of singers, who

were not yet considered Levites, is also relatively small: one hundred twenty-eight in Ezra 2:41 and one hundred thirty-eight in Neh 7:44. "Trained in music" and "all skilled" comprise the two factors that produce musical excellence: appropriate training and natural ability. As noted under Structure, מִסְפָּר "number" is used in a different sense here than in v. 1 ("list").

■ **8** *They cast lots, watch with watch, young and old alike, teacher and pupil alike:* The purpose of the lot casting, according to this translation, was basically twofold: first, to determine the order of the rotation of the watches or periods of service; second, to determine the makeup of the individual groups for each watch, which consisted of singers of mixed ages and mixed musical achievement levels. The central difficulty in this translation is "watch with watch" מִשְׁמֶרֶת לְעֻמַּת מִשְׁמֶרֶת, as in my reconstruction, or מִשְׁמֶרֶת לְעֻמַּת, as in MT.[47] The noun מִשְׁמֶרֶת can mean "duties" (so *NRSV* and *NIV*; cf. "instructions about" in 1 Chr 23:32), but if it is taken as a noun in the absolute state in a construct chain, the preceding word "lots" must then be revocalized as a construct (גּוֹרְלוֹת instead of גּוֹרָלוֹת), as Rudolph recommends in *BHS* and is apparently followed in *NRSV:* "lots for their duties." But מִשְׁמֶרֶת can also refer to the time when the duties are performed, thus "watch," as in 9:27.[48] The difficulty with either definition continues with the following preposition לְעֻמַּת. While Kropat suggested that the two following words prefixed with a *kap,* כְּקָטֹן כְּגָדוֹל ("young," "old"), could be construed as *nomina recta* in a construct chain,[49] he did not provide parallels, and it seems more likely that either the text read originally מִשְׁמֶרֶת לְעֻמַּת מִשְׁמֶרֶת (see textual note 19) or that the reading in the MT is to be understood as a truncated form of such a stock expression (cf. 26:16; Neh 12:24).[50] Rudolph, 166, deleted "teacher and pupil alike" as a mistaken interpretation of "young and old alike" because it seemed to him to contradict the preceding verse, where we read that "all were skilled." I believe that the context in v. 7 permits us to construe the participle מֵבִין as referring to

---

45 So also Kleinig, *Lord's Song,* 151. See also the gloss in MT, deleted in my translation: "Asaph, Jeduthun, and Heman." Cf. textual note 17.

46 See textual note 16.

47 See textual note 19.

48 כִּי עֲלֵיהֶם מִשְׁמֶרֶת "for their responsibility was the watch." *NRSV* "for on them lay the duty of watch-

ing"; *NIV* "because they had to guard it."

49 *Syntax,* 56.

50 So Kleinig, *Lord's Song,* 58.

natural ability ("skilled"), while the context in v. 8 allows us to understand it as referring to a teacher in contrast with a learner.[51] The latter noun, in any case, is a hapax legomenon in the Bible.[52] If v. 7 is redactional, tying together vv. 1-6 and vv. 8-31, as I have suggested,[53] the different construal of מבין in v. 7 as "skilled" and in v. 8 as "teacher" causes little difficulty.

25:9-31. Results of Lot Casting

■ **9** *The first lot fell out:* Cf. Josh 16:1; 19:1, 24; 21:4; 24:7. *his sons and his brothers, twelve:* In later periods, according to the Mishnah, each unit of twelve musicians consisted of nine lyre players, two harp players, and one cymbal player.[54] In 1 Chr 16:5-6 nine[55] Levitical names are associated with harps and lyres, one with cymbals, and two with trumpets.

Conclusion

In its present form chap. 25 presents a list of the twenty-four sons of Asaph, Heman, and Jeduthun, the heads of the families of singers or musicians, and an account of how these sons were arranged by casting lots into twenty-four divisions, each consisting of twelve musicians. Only vv. 1-4a and 6 are original to the Chronicler's account, and they listed four sons of Asaph, six sons of Jeduthun, and five sons of Heman as singers. The Chronicler granted Levitical status to the singers and considered their music as a type of prophesying.

The later supplement in vv. 4b-5 and 7-31 expands the sons of Heman by nine members and arranges the resultant twenty-four singer groups, each composed of twelve members, into a regular rotation that departs remarkably from the order of the sons in vv. 1-6. While the final form of the text attributes this to lot casting, I have identified rational principles that produced this divergent order. The division into twenty-four divisions echoes the twenty-four priestly courses that had been secondarily added in chap. 24. The large number of sons attributed to Heman in the final form of the text reflects his preeminence among the singers.

51 BDB, 107, lists both "understand" and "teach" as meanings of the *hiphil*, and these correspond to the way I have translated vv. 7 and 8, respectively. Cf. *HALOT* 1:122.

52 BDB, 541: "scholar." *HALOT* 4:1741, "pupil." *REB* and *NEB* "apprentice." Sidney B. Hoenig, "The Biblical Designation for 'Pupil,'" *JQR* 70 (1979) 176–77, notes that "pupil" elsewhere in the Bible is always למוד or לִמֻּד and suggests therefore that MT מבין עם תלמיד be emended to מבין עמת למוד.

53 See the discussion under Structure.

54 "They played on never less than two harps or more than six" (*m. ʿArak.* 2:3). "There were never less than nine lyres, and their number could be increased without end; but of cymbals there was but one" (ʿArak. 2:5). See Danby, *Mishnah,* 545.

55 Or ten if Asaph the chief is to be included among these musicians. Cf. Japhet, 447.

Translation

1/ The divisions of the gatekeepers:[1] from the Korahites: Meshelemiah son of Kore from the sons of Abiasaph.[2] 2/ Meshelemiah had sons: Zechariah the firstborn, Jediael the second, Zebadiah[3] the third, Jathniel[4] the fourth, 3/ Elam the fifth, Jehohanan the sixth, Eliehoenai the seventh.

4/ Obed-edom had sons: Shemaiah the first-born, Jehozabad the second, Joah the third, Sachar the fourth, Nethanel the fifth, 5/ Ammiel the sixth, Issachar the seventh, Peullethai the eighth, for God had blessed him. 6/ Also to his son Shemaiah sons were born,[5] who were leaders[6] in the house of their father,[7] for they were mighty warriors. 7/ The sons of Shemaiah: Othni, Rephael, Obed, and[8] Elzabad, and[9] his brothers were valiant men, Elihu[10] and Semachiah.[11] 8/ All these were some of the sons of Obed-edom; they and their sons and their brothers were valiant men,[12] with strength for the service. Sixty-two of Obed-edom.

9/ Meshelemiah had sons and brothers, valiant men, eighteen.

10/ Hosah, of the sons of Merari, had sons: Shimri the chief, although he was not the firstborn,[13] his father made him chief; 11/ Hilkiah the second, Tebaliah[14] the third, Zechariah the fourth. All the sons and brothers of Hosah were thirteen.

12/ These are the divisions of the gatekeepers, through their chief men, [who worked in] shifts, like their brothers, serving in the house of Yahweh. 13/ They cast lots for each gate, regardless of whether the father's house was young or old. 14/ The lot for the east gate fell to Shelemiah. For[15] Zechariah his son, a prudent counselor, they also cast lots, and his lot came out for the north gate. 15/ Obed-edom's lot came out for the south gate, and his sons were assigned to the vestibules.[16] 16/ Hosah's[17] lot came out for the west gate, namely, the gate of the chambers,[18] the gateway that leads upward. Watch corresponded with watch: 17/ On the east there were six each day,[19] on the north four each day, on the south four each day, and two each[20] at the vestibules. 18/ On the west[21] there were four at the gateway and two at the colonnade. 19/ These were the divisions of the gatekeepers for the Korahites[22] and the Merarites.

20/ The Levites their brothers[23] were over the treasuries of the house of God and the treasuries of the dedicated gifts. 21/ From the sons of[24] Ladan the Gershonite,[25] the heads of families belonging to Ladan the Gershonite: Jehieli. 22/ The sons of Jehieli:[26] Zetham and his brother Joel were in charge of the treasuries of the house of Yahweh. 23/ From the Amramites, the Izharites, the Hebronites,

1 לַשֹּׁעֲרִים with *BHS*. MT לְשֹׁעֲרִים. Cf. vv. 12, 19, where the definite article is used with "gatekeepers."

2 אביאסף with LXX; cf. 9:19 אביסף "Ebiasaph." Either spelling may be correct. MT אסף "Asaph." Abiasaph (or Ebiasaph) was a descendant of Korah and therefore also a descendant of Kohath (6:8, 22-23 [23, 37-38]). In Exod 6:24 Assir, Elkanah, and Abiasaph are listed as sons of Korah (as in the reconstruction of this genealogy in this commentary on 1 Chronicles 6), but in 1 Chronicles 6 MT they are the son, grandson, and great grandson of Korah. Asaph, in any case, was a descendant of Gershom, not of Kohath (6:24-28 [39-43]). Johnstone, 1:259, suggests that Asaph arose by contamination from the Gershonite line at 25:2, 6, 9. For the Levitical links of the gatekeepers, see the commentary on v. 1.

3 זבדיהו. A few Hebrew MSS, LXX[B], Syr: זכריהו "Zechariah."

4 יתניאל; LXX[L] "Nethanael." Cf. Syr, Arab.

5 נולד. For the singular of this verb with a plural subject see 2:9; 3:1.

6 Rudolph, 170 (cf. *BHS*), proposes הם משלים; MT הממשלים "the dominions." *HALOT* 2:596 interprets MT as the use of the abstract for the concrete ("dominions" = "rulers"), but also suggests following the emendation of Rudolph. Japhet, 456, argues that LXX presupposes a variant ראשים, which it has both translated and transliterated. But LXX reads τοῦ πρωτοτόκου "the firstborn" (הבכור), a gloss on "his son" taken from v. 4, and Ρωσαι, which Allen, *Greek Chronicles*, 2:142–43, explains as an abbreviation for ראשים, an explanatory gloss on the rare word הממשלים.

7 אביהם (distributive singular); some Hebrew MSS, Tg: אבותם "their fathers."

8 The conjunction is lacking in MT, but present in a few Hebrew MSS, LXX.

9 Conjunction lacking in MT.

10 Conjunction lacking in MT, but is present in one Hebrew MS, which apparently did not identify Elihu with the valiant men who were Elzabad's brothers.

11 LXX adds "Ishbakom," which Allen, *Greek Chronicles*, 1:163, interprets as a doublet.

12 Distributive singular.

13 הבכור. The definite article was lost in MT by haplography. Cf. *BHS*.

14 טבליהו. This name, which is unique in the Bible, is sometimes revocalized טֹבַלְיָהוּ and interpreted as "Beloved of Yahweh" or "Good for Yahweh." Cf. *HALOT* 2:368.

15 ולזכריהו; cf. LXX[L], Vg. MT lacks the preposition *lāmed*. It is possible that the versions were just translating idiomatically and that no change needs to be made.

16 בית האספים. Rudolph, 170, interprets this as a

and the Uzzielites: 24/ Shubael[27] the son of Gershom the son of Moses was the chief officer in charge of the treasuries. 25/ His brothers through Eliezer: Rehabiah his son,[28] Jeshaiah his son,[29] Joram his son, Zichri his son, and Shelomoth[30] his son. 26/ This Shelomoth and his brothers were over the treasuries of the dedicated gifts, which King David, and the heads of families, and the commanders of[31] the thousands and hundreds, and the commanders of the army had dedicated. 27/ From booty won in battles[32] they dedicated gifts for the maintenance of the house of Yahweh.[33] 28/ And all that Samuel the seer, Saul the son of Kish, Abner the son of Ner, and Joab the son of Zeruiah had dedicated—all dedicated gifts[34] were in the care of Shelomoth[35] and his brothers. 29/ From the Izharites: Chenaniah[36] and his sons were appointed[37] to outside duties over Israel as officers and judges. 30/ From the Hebronites: Hashabiah and his brothers, one thousand seven hundred valiant men, had oversight of Israel west of the Jordan for all the work of Yahweh and for the service of the king. 31/ From the Hebronites: Jerijah[38] was chief of the Hebronites according to the genealogical records of their families. In the fortieth year of the reign of David a search was made in the records, and mighty warriors were found in Jazer of Gilead. 32/ His brothers were two thousand seven hundred mighty men, heads of families, and King David appointed them over the Reubenites, and the Gadites, and the half-tribe of the Manassites for everything pertaining to God and to the king.

plural because of v. 17 (וֹלאספים) and Neh 12:25 (אספי השערים). See the commentary for the defense of this translation.

17 לחסה. MT adds ו לשפים "Shuppim and" before Hosah, but the name Shuppim is to be deleted as a corrupt dittography of האספים "vestibules" at the end of v. 15.

18 לשכות "chambers" or לשכת "chambers." Cf. LXX παστοφοριον. This gate is mentioned only here in the OT. MT here שער שלכת "Shalleceth gate." Vg quae ducit "which leads" = לכת + שׁ, but the syntax is awkward, if not forced. Johnstone, 1:262, who retains MT, speculates that the Shalleceth gate was the place where refuse was disposed of (שׁלך = "throw out").

19 למזרחה ליום ששה; cf. LXX and BHS. MT למזרח הלוים ששה ("on the east the Levites six"). Uziel Fuchs, "למצתחה ליום or למזרח הלוים: The Talmudic Evidence for 1 Chronicles 26:17," Textus 20 (2000) 169–72, showed that the original reading in the Talmud agreed with the reading reconstructed on the basis of LXX.

20 שנים שנים. The second שנים is lacking in a few Hebrew MSS and LXX by haplography. Cf. Rudolph, 172. Contra Japhet, 450.

21 למערב. Rudolph, 172; and Japhet, 450, suggest that the word לפרבר, which precedes this word in MT, is a dittograph of the last word in the verse. If this conjecture is not correct, one could translate the beginning of this sentence with a casus pendens: "As for the colonnade on the west."

22 LXX[B] "the Kohathites."

23 אחיהם with LXX (cf. 6:33 [48]); MT אחיה "Ahijah."

24 מבני with BHS; the initial mêm is lost in MT by haplography.

25 לעדן הגרשׁני, following the conjecture of Rudolph, 174, or only לעדן, following the conjecture of Japhet, 461. MT לעדן בני הגרשׁני ללעדן "Ladan the sons of the Gershonites of Ladan." Rudolph suggests deleting בני "the sons of," and ללעדן "of Ladan," as in my translation. He proposes that these words originally arose as a gloss לבני ללעדן "Libni for Ladan," indicating that elsewhere in the Gershon genealogy Libni stands in the place of Ladan. Japhet, 461, deletes בני הגרשׁני ללעדן "the sons of the Gershonites belonging to Ladan" as an expanded dittograph of the initial "sons of Ladan." Rudolph also deleted "the heads of families belonging to Ladan the Gershonite" as a secondary attempt at closer definition.

26 Japhet, 450, tentatively identifies "The sons of Jehieli" as a gloss.

27 ושובאל LXX, Syr; cf. 23:16. MT וּשְׁבָאֵל "Shebuel."

28 בנו; LXX "a son" (בן).

29 בנו. LXX lacks "his son" here and after all the

names in the rest of the verse, making the last four names—
Jeshaiah, Joram, Zichri, and Shelomoth—brothers of
Rehabiah.

30 וּשְׁלֵמוֹת, with K, LXX[BAal]; Q, some Hebrew MSS, LXX[L], Syr,
   Tg, Vg: וּשְׁלֹמִית "Shelomith." Cf. 23:9, 18; 24:22.

31 וְשָׂרֵי, with LXX, Vg; cf. 29:6. MT לְשָׂרֵי.

32 Hendiadys; lit. "from battles and from booty."

33 לְחַזֵּק לְבֵית יהוה; LXX paraphrases: "so that the building of the
   house of God should not want *supplies*."

34 הַמֻּקְדָּשׁ is vocalized as a *pual* participle or as הַמִּקְדָּשׁ, a noun
   with the definite article; MT הַמַּקְדִּישׁ = *hiphil* participle.

35 שְׁלֵמוֹת, with LXX and 26:25; MT שְׁלֹמִית.

36 כְּנַנְיָהוּ; LXX, Vg: כְּנַנְיָהוּ "Conaniah." Where the latter name
   occurs in K of 2 Chr 31:12, 13, and 35:9, Q always has
   "Chenaniah."

37 The verb does not appear in Hebrew.

38 יְרִיָּה; cf. 1 Chr 23:19. A few Hebrew MSS and editions: יְדָיָה
   "Jedaiah"; cf. LXX.

26:1-32

Structure

The first nineteen verses of this chapter deal with the
gatekeepers[1] and may be outlined as follows:

I. 26:1-19. Divisions of Gatekeepers

    A. 26:1-11. Genealogical list of gatekeepers

    B. 26:12-19. Assignment of gatekeepers to positions

The data on Obed-edom (vv. 4-8) interrupt in a secondary fashion the presentation of Meshelemiah (vv. 1-
3, 9) and, unlike Meshelemiah and Hosah (vv. 10-11),
Obed-edom is not linked genealogically to the Levites.
The numbers for Obed-edom (sixty-two) are also out of
proportion with those of Meshelemiah (eighteen) and
Hosah (thirteen). The uncertain status of Obed-edom
appears in chaps. 15–16, where the Chronicler listed
him both as a singer and as a gatekeeper.[2] Verses 12-18
also seem to be secondary because they also have data
about Obed-edom, who cannot easily be removed from

this paragraph since his sons are assigned to one of the
four gates, and without him the assignment to the gates
would make little sense. In this secondary unit
Meshelemiah is called Shelemiah, and the assignments
are made by casting lots,[3] whereas David himself is credited with assigning all the Levites in 23:3-6a, including
the gatekeepers. The numbers in vv. 17-18 total twenty-
four, though this refers to the number of men assigned
to the various gates and not to courses as in 24:1-19.
Without vv. 12-18, v. 19 serves as an appropriate conclusion to the genealogical listing of the Levitical gatekeepers in vv. 1-3 and 9-11. In this original material, vv. 1-3,
9-11, 19, corresponding to 23:5, we have a genealogical
list of gatekeepers, organized by David into divisions (cf.
23:5-6a). David, however is not mentioned in this section
of chap. 26 (but see vv. 26, 32), though his role may be
implied by the context.[4] According to these literary-critical judgments,[5] therefore, I believe that vv. 4-8 and 12-18
are secondary expansions.

---

1 The gatekeepers are normally listed after the
  singers (e.g., chap. 26 after chap. 25), but there are
  exceptions: 1 Chr 23:5; Neh 7:72 (73); 10:29, 40 (28,
  39).

2 See the commentary ad loc. Obed-edom is listed as
  a singer in 15:18 (except for the last word, "gatekeepers"), 21, and 16:5. His role as gatekeeper is
  spelled out in 15:24 and 16:38. In drafting 16:5 and
  38, the Chronicler combined separate traditions
  about Obed-edom that were available to him in
  15:18, 21, where he was a singer, and in 15:24,
  where he was a gatekeeper.

3 Cf. 24:7-19; 25:9-31.

4 In 9:22 David and Samuel assigned the gatekeepers
  on account of their trustworthiness. There is no

parallel verse in Nehemiah 11. David is expressly
mentioned in 1 Chr 24:3 (the assignment of priests)
and 25:1 (the assignment of singers).

5 These are also the conclusions of Williamson, 169,
  which are in substantial agreement with Rothstein,
  465; and von Rad, *Geschichtsbild*, 116. Rudolph,
  171–73, treats these verses as a unity but not stemming from the Chronicler. Welch, *Work*, 91–93,
  believed that vv. 4-8 and 14-18 were older material,
  incorporated into a later record that *may* derive
  from the Chronicler, but he thought that Obed-
  edom was later expelled from the gatekeepers
  rather than given Levitical descent.

Japhet, 451, considers the secondary character of the Obed-edom materials highly improbable and proposes that the materials on Meshelemiah have been arranged chiastically.[6] She notes that the link of Obed-edom to the Levites had not been explicitly worked out, without concluding from this that Obed-edom is secondary. I do not believe that her interpretation adequately meets the objections that have been raised to the presence of Obed-edom in the original genealogy. If this is granted, the objections raised to vv. 12-18, a paragraph that she also retains in the original edition of Chronicles, also still apply.

The descendants of Meshelemiah, Obed-edom, and Hosah are presented in a common pattern (vv. 2, 4, 10). The name is given, prefixed with the pronoun *lāmed*, and followed by the noun בנים "sons." This pattern is broken with the descendants of Shemaiah, the firstborn son of Meshelemiah in vv. 6-7, since בנים is preceded by the verb נולד "were born." All the sons of Meshelemiah, Obed-edom, and Hosah are modified by ordinal numbers, but again the pattern is broken with Shemaiah. Japhet, 456, takes this as evidence that the names of the sons of Shemaiah were added secondarily to the list to make the number twenty-four. She also notes that their special status is expressly justified in v. 6 (they were mighty warriors). If the Obed-edom materials are secondary, however, as I argued above, these are the names that were added to make the number twenty-four.

II. 26:20-32. List of Levitical Treasurers, Officers, and Judges
   A. 26:20-28. The Levites who were over the treasuries[7] of the house of God and of the dedicated gifts
   B. 26:29-32. Officers and judges

In part, this section provides supplementary information to the Levites listed in 23:6-23 and 24:20b-30. At first glance the division of sections A (vv. 20-28) and B (vv. 29-32) into separate categories makes good sense, with the recognition that the officials mentioned in B are of a miscellaneous sort. But the reference to the four sons of Kohath in v. 23 (A.3)—Amramites, Izharites, Hebronites, and Uzzielites—brings the two sections closer together. The Amramites mentioned in v. 23 appear again in vv. 24-28 (A.4 and A.5), while the Izharites in v. 23 relate to the Izharite Chenaniah in v. 29 (B.1), and the Hebronites in v. 23 relate to the two Hebronites Hashabiah and Jerijah in vv. 30-32 (B.2 and B.3). Furthermore, the reference to Shubael in v. 24, who is chief officer in charge of the treasuries, presupposes the information in vv. 20-22 (A.1 and A.2), the only detailed description of the treasuries of the house of Yahweh. There is, therefore, an overall unity to this passage.

There are also indications that the unit might once have been larger. The same v. 23 that helps us see the unity of the passage also mentions the Uzzielites, who are not mentioned again in the rest of the present passage. The unit may once have included information on one or more officers of the Uzzielites. The wording of the original introduction to the Gershonites in v. 21 is in some question (see textual notes 24-25), but if vv. 20-28 referred to both the Gershonites and the Kohathites, did it also once include material about the Merarites?

In any case, Williamson, 172, has pointed out that this paragraph (vv. 20-32) comes naturally after the reference to judges and officers in the text that introduces the materials on the various kinds of Levites (23:3-6a), and it is therefore part of the original document drafted by the Chronicler.[8] Less convincing to me is the proposal of Japhet, 461–62, who sees v. 23 as a secondary interpolation that created the unified passage. If this were so, why would Uzziel be mentioned and why would not the interpolator have clarified the introduction of the Gershonites? Finally, I am not persuaded by P. Dirksen,[9] who has proposed that vv. 20-21a, 25-28, and 31-32 are from the same secondary hand to which he has ascribed all of chaps. 23–27 and that the rest of the pericope (vv. 21b-24, 29-30) comes from a source available to

6   Rudolph, 172, proposes that the number for Meshelemiah has been put after that for Obed-edom in order to give Obed-edom's numbers more prominence.

7   The treasurers also follow the gatekeepers in 1 Chr 9:17-26. Cf. Curtis and Madsen, 282.

8   Johnstone, 1:262, notes that the list of the treasurers, dealing with the contributions of the laity, prepares the reader for the organization of the laity in chap. 27.

9   P. B. Dirksen, "The Composition of 1 Chronicles 26:20-32," *JNSL* 24 (1998) 145–55.

that interpolator. Dirksen argues that the two kinds of treasuries were introduced by this secondary author, but in the process he destroys the unity outlined above. What is unclear about this paragraph is whether it reflects actual circumstances at some point during the monarchical period, or whether it is a literary fiction. Because it does not seem to support clearly any of the Chronicler's objectives and because the discussion of the system of priests and Levites would be clearer without it, Japhet, 464, concludes that it comes from some ancient source whose full meaning is no longer clear.

Detailed Commentary

26:1-19. Divisions of Gatekeepers
26:1-11. Genealogical List of Gatekeepers

■ **1** *from the Korahites: Meshelemiah son of Kore from the sons of Abiasaph:* The first leader of the gatekeepers, Meshelemiah (משלמיהו), seems to be identical with Shelemiah (שלמיהו) in v. 14. Both have a son named Zechariah who is called "the firstborn" in v. 2 and "a prudent counselor" in v. 14. In 6:7 (22)[10] and 6:22-23 (37-38),[11] Korah, the ancestor of the Korahites,[12] is considered a descendant, through Amminadab[13] or Izhar,

respectively, of Kohath, one of the three sons of Levi. The same spelling of the name Meshelemiah is attested at 9:21, where Zechariah is identified as his son, but Meshelemiah seems to be identified as Shallum in 9:19.[14] A postexilic Shallum appears with five other gatekeepers—Ater, Talmon, Akkub, Hatita, and Shobai—in the list of returnees (Ezra 2:42//Neh 7:45), where the gatekeepers are not linked to the Levites, and where their numbers total one hundred thirty-nine and one hundred thirty-eight, respectively.[15] The gatekeepers are not identified as Levites in Ezra 10:24 and Neh 11:19, but they are considered Levites in 1 Chronicles 9.[16] The same genealogical ancestry, from Shallum/Meshelemiah through Kore (קרא)[17] and Ebiasaph to Korah (קרח) appears in 9:19.[18] In 6:8 (23), as reconstructed in this commentary, Ebiasaph (plus his brothers Assir and Elkanah) is in the third generation after Kohath[19] and is the son[20] of Korah. In 6:22 (37) Ebiasaph is also identified as the son of Korah.

■ **2-3** *Meshelemiah had sons: Zechariah the firstborn:* Zechariah's identification as a gatekeeper and his relationship to Meshelemiah are also supported by 9:21, where Zechariah the son of Meshelemiah is stationed at the tent of meeting. Most of the other names in vv. 2-3

---

10 This is part of the genealogy of Kohath that ends with Shaul in the seventh or tenth position (see the commentary).

11 This is part of the genealogical ancestry of Heman, one of the Levitical singers. In Num 16:1 the names from Korah through Levi are identical with the names in 1 Chr 6:22-23 (37-38). Cf. Exod 6:16, 18, 21, 24.

12 That some Korahites were included among the singers is shown by 2 Chr 20:19 and by the Korahite psalms: 42–49, 84, 85, 87–88. See also the inclusion of Korah among the Hemanite singers (1 Chr 6:18, 22 [33, 37]) and the Hemanites in 1 Chr 25:4-5.

13 See textual note 6 at 1 Chr 6:7 (22).

14 The Shallum mentioned in 1 Chr 9:17 is probably a postexilic individual, since he and at least two of his gatekeeper colleagues are listed among the returnees in Ezra 2:42//Neh 7:45. Hence the Shallum in 1 Chr 9:17 is to be distinguished from the Shallum in 9:19, who comes from the time of David. See also the commentary on 9:31. Japhet, 452, provides a helpful list of similar spelling variations from this period. Meshelemiah, Shelemiah, and Shallum may be the same as Meshullam in Neh 12:25 (Curtis and Madsen, 174). Japhet notes, 455,

15 that the Chronicler sometimes replaced dialectal forms of names with more classical spellings.

15 Meshullam, Talmon, and Akkub are mentioned as gatekeepers in Neh 12:25, together with Mattaniah, Bakbukiah, and Obadiah.

16 Cf. Rudolph, 173; and Allen, 450. See the commentary above on chap. 9.

17 Kore is otherwise unknown.

18 Rudolph, 173, concludes that the author of 1 Chr 9:19 put Shallum at the tent of meeting on the basis of chap. 26. In 9:31 the Korahite Mattithiah, the firstborn son of Shallum, is a baker, i.e., neither a singer nor a gatekeeper. It is unclear whether this Shallum is to be identified with Meshelemiah.

19 He is in the fifth generation after Kohath according to MT: "The sons of Kohath: Amminadab his son, Korah his son, Assir his son, Elkanah his son, Ebiasaph his son, Assir his son."

20 Great-grandson in MT.

are common, but they are not known elsewhere as gate-keepers. The name Jathniel (v. 2; see textual note 4) is unique, and the unusual name Eliohoenai[21] appears as a descendant of Pahath Moab in Ezra 8:4.

Secondary Expansion: 26:4-8

■ **4** *Obed-edom had sons: Shemaiah the firstborn:* For Obed-edom see the commentary at 1 Chronicles 15–16, where he is a Levitical singer (15:21; 16:5), but also a gate-keeper in three passages (15:18, 24; 16:38[22]).[23] Obed-edom and Hosah are in charge of the ark in its tent in Jerusalem (16:38). Verses 4-8 do not mention any genealogical link to Levi as Obed-edom's ancestor. The context suggests that he too was part of the Korah-Kohath lineage, but no intermediary links are given.[24] In 13:13//2 Sam 6:10-11, Obed-edom is called the Gittite (a person from Gath), and the ark stayed at his house after the death of Uzzah. The descendants of Shemaiah are listed in vv. 6-7, and they take their place among the sons of Obed-edom, so that the named descendants total thirteen altogether (seven sons and six grandsons of Obed-edom).

■ **5** *for God had blessed him:* The Chronicler picked up this clause from 1 Chr 13:14//2 Sam 6:11, where we are told that God blessed the house of Obed-edom because the ark had stayed with him for three months. Here in chap. 26 that blessing is viewed as fulfilled in Obed-edom's large family. Japhet, 455–56, notes that three of the names of his sons also may refer to the theme of divine reward, namely, Sachar,[25] Issachar,[26] and Peullethai,[27] and that other names of his sons, such as Jehozabad[28] and Nethanel,[29] imply the kind of thanksgiving for

the gift of children that is common to many Hebrew names.

■ **6-7** *for they were mighty warriors:* Wright[30] has called attention to the military implications of this clause (כי גבורי חיל המה) and the similar expressions in v. 7 (בני חיל "valiant men"), v. 8 (איש חיל בכח "valiant men, with strength"), and v. 9 (בני חיל "valiant men").[31] At the very least these references allude to the physical strength needed by the gatekeepers for at least some of their duties and suggest that they served as a security force. For this reason the Chronicler has them play important roles in the coup against Athaliah (2 Chr 23:4, 19). Other commentators and English versions have omitted the physical implications of these complimentary expressions.[32]

None of the sons or grandsons of Obed-edom is mentioned elsewhere as a gatekeeper. Shemaiah's son Obed (v. 7) is named after his grandfather (papponomy), and Elzabad has a name resembling Obed-edom's second son and therefore Elzabad's uncle, Jehozabad (v. 4), but with a different theophoric element in the name: El instead of Yahweh. As valiant men, Elihu and Semachiah, sons of Shemaiah, were distinguished from their brothers.

■ **8** *Sixty two of Obed-edom:* The relatives of Obed-edom far outnumber those of Meshelemiah (eighteen) or Hosah (thirteen), but their number is quite similar to the number given at 1 Chr 16:38: sixty-eight. It is possible to imagine a confusion between "two" (שנים) and "eight" (שמונה), but more likely sixty-eight there is the sum of the sixty-two sons of Obed-edom and the six sons of his

---

21 "On Yahweh are my eyes set." See *HALOT* 1:55. Cf. Pss 25:15; 123:2.
22 Here associated with Jeduthun.
23 The first of these is a gloss, the second is taken from a source dealing with the procession of the ark, and the third is a composition of the Chronicler. We do not know the final fate of Obed-edom, but some of the Korahites were considered singers in the final form of Chronicles (1 Chr 6:18, 22 [33, 37], where Korah is linked to the Hemanite singers) and 2 Chr 20:19.
24 Johnstone, 1:260, assigns him to the Merarites.
25 "Reward, wage" (*HALOT* 3:1331).
26 "There is a reward," or "El gives a reward" (cf. *HALOT* 2:443).
27 "Wage" plus a hypocoristic ending (*HALOT* 3:951–52). This name is a hapax legomenon.

28 "Yahweh has given" (*HALOT* 2:396).
29 "God has given."
30 "Guarding the Gates," 69–81. The military connotations are not so clear with לראשי הגברים in v. 12 (cf. 1 Chr 24:4), and Wright errs, 73, in stating that the exact phrase is found in 11:10, since the noun there is גִּבּוֹר instead of גֶּבֶר.
31 Cf. vv. 30-32.
32 *NRSV* renders these words as "able men"; *NIV* "able men" or "capable men." Braun, 251, suggests that the title is used in an honorary fashion.

father Jeduthun (25:3). The blessing of Obed-edom himself was attested by his eight biological sons; Meshelemiah in vv. 2-3 has only seven sons. The total of all the gatekeepers listed here is only ninety-three, which is to be compared with two hundred eighty-eight singers (25:7) and with the numbers attested earlier for the gatekeepers: Ezra 2:42, one hundred thirty-nine; Neh 7:45, one hundred thirty-eight; Neh 11:19, one hundred seventy-two; 1 Chr 9:22, two hundred twelve. The number given here, therefore, is significantly smaller than these earlier numbers. Perhaps not all the families of the gatekeepers were able to prove their right to be in the Levitical genealogies with the same speed. Or do the figures in this chapter only include the chiefs of the gatekeepers? None of these numbers bears any recognizable relationship with the four thousand gatekeepers reported in the census at 1 Chr 23:5.

■ **10-11** *Hosah, of the sons of Merari,*[33] *had sons:* According to 16:38 David assigned Obed-edom and Hosah the son of Jeduthun to be gatekeepers for the ark at Jerusalem, and this is the only other mention of Hosah in the Bible.[34] The genealogical links between Hosah and his ancestor Merari are not provided.

Shimri the chief, although he was not the firstborn, his father made him chief: At a number of points in chap. 23, "chief" is used in the implied sense of firstborn when other sons are known (vv. 8, 11, 19, 20; cf. 24:23), but it is also used of a son when only one son is named (vv. 16, 17, 18; cf. 24:21). In the latter cases the title conveys a sense of rank or prestige. Shimri's case indicates that "firstborn" and "chief" were not always interchangeable, and that a father could designate one of his younger sons "chief" in preference to his firstborn. Nevertheless, Hosah's subsequent sons in v. 11 are called the second, third, and fourth. Two of these names are common, Hilkiah and Zechariah, though not known as gatekeepers elsewhere; the fourth, Tebaliah, is unique (see textual note 14).

26:12-18. Assignment of Gatekeepers to Positions

■ **12** *[who worked in] shifts, like their brothers:* The Hebrew is compressed and is best translated with a paraphrase (cf. *JPS*). The word "shifts" (משמרות) is identical to the singular word I translated "watch" (משמרת) in 25:8, and the mention of "their brothers" may be either a reference to that passage or to the twenty-four priestly courses in 24:1-19 (cf. also 24:31). Unfortunately, we do not know how long the shifts of the gatekeepers lasted according to this chapter, although 9:25 implies that there was a weekly rotation even if the small numbers in this chapter make such a rotation unlikely.[35] The gatekeepers functioned in various forms of security control. According to 2 Chr 23:19, at the time of Jehoiada and Joash, they made sure that no one who was unclean would enter the temple grounds. The entrance liturgies that are known from several psalms may be related to their responsibilities.[36]

serving in the house of Yahweh: The service of the gatekeepers in the temple is not described in detail, but elsewhere they are caretakers of temple paraphernalia, used in the ritual of the temple (1 Chr 9:27-29, 31-32).[37] Since David is still king in 1 Chronicles until chap. 29, and since the temple was not built until the reign of Solomon, this verse is anachronistic. This problem is avoided in 9:21 because the gatekeepers there were assigned to the tent of meeting. But David is not mentioned in 26:1-19, and this reference to service in the temple appears in the section I have judged to be secondary. In any case the time that the writer is describing is his own postexilic situation.

■ **13** *They cast lots for each gate, regardless of whether the father's house was young or old:* The assignment process gave each father's house equal opportunity to be assigned to any gate, regardless of its age or size[38] (cf. 24:5, 31; 25:8), and the lot casting indicated also divine preference in these decisions. Rudolph, 175, judges the

---

33 Meshelemiah and his family in vv. 1-3 were descendants of Kohath. None of these gatekeepers is connected to the third son of Levi, Kohath.

34 A town named Hosah appears in Josh 19:29.

35 Another description of the duties of the gatekeepers appears in 1 Chr 9:18-29.

36 Cf. Psalms 15; 24:3-6; 118:19-20; Isa 33:14-16. Cf. Erhard S. Gerstenberger, *Psalms, Part 1; with an*

Introduction to Cultic Poetry (FOTL 14; Grand Rapids: Eerdmans, 1988) 249.

37 See Wright, "Guarding the Gates," 78.

38 The Hebrew—כקטן כגדול— can be interpreted in terms of age or size of the father's house.

lot casting to be fictional, as in chap. 25, because the first or most important family got the best gate on the east, and therefore the assignment does not appear to be mere luck.

■ **14** *The lot for the east gate fell to Shelemiah:* While spelling variations are common among names in this period (see the commentary on v. 1 and n. 14 there), it does not seem likely that a writer would change the spelling within a single chapter, and so the difference between Shelemiah here and Meshelemiah in vv. 1, 2, and 9 is additional evidence for the secondary character of vv. 12-18. Shallum, a postexilic gatekeeper (and another alternate spelling for Meshelemiah), was also stationed in the east gate and was called the chief of the gatekeepers (9:17-19).[39] The prestige of this gate is shown by its being called "the king's gate on the east side."[40] In Ezekiel's final vision, the east gate was the one through which Yahweh entered the temple (Ezek 44:1-3) and where the "prince" (נשיא) offered his burnt offering (Ezek 46:12).[41]

For Zechariah his son, a prudent counselor, they also cast lots, and his lot came out for the north gate: Zechariah was the firstborn son of Meshelemiah/Shelemiah (v. 2; 1 Chr 9:21) and through him the family receives its second gate. This may have been conditioned both by the fact that Zechariah had been assigned a gate at the tent of meeting (9:21), and that Meshelemiah as the first descendant listed among the Korahites may have been entitled to the double portion due a firstborn son (cf. Deut 21:15-17; 2 Kgs 2:9). According to v. 17 the family of Meshelemiah/Shelemiah and Zechariah would need ten persons to staff each watch—six at the east gate and four at the north gate—but their total number according to v. 9 is only eighteen. Either that number in v. 9 is corrupt, although there is no evidence for this in the ver-

sions,[42] or the number eighteen refers to fathers' houses and not to individuals. Zechariah's qualification for appointment as a "prudent counselor" (יועץ בשכל) seems to be in tension with or irrelevant to the idea that the gates were assigned by lots, but perhaps the author intended to indicate that Zechariah's character matched the responsibilities assigned to him by lot. The term "counselor" is used several other times in Chronicles, referring to the roles of Jonathan, the uncle of David (1 Chr 27:32), Ahithophel, who was a counselor to the king (27:33; cf. 2 Sam 15:12), and Athaliah, the evil counselor of her son Ahaziah (2 Chr 22:3), who was also counseled by the "house of Ahab" (2 Chr 22:40).[43] In all these cases it concerns giving advice to the king. David earlier prayed that Yahweh would give Solomon discretion (שכל; 1 Chr 22:12), and Huram recognizes Solomon as a "wise son" (בן חכם; 2 Chr 2:11 [12]). Hezekiah spoke to the Levites "who had shown good skill" (המשכילים שכל טוב), presumably like that possessed by the Levitical gatekeeper Zechariah here (2 Chr 30:22).

■ **15** *Obed-edom's lot came out for the south gate:* Despite the large size of his family, Obed-edom gets only the third gate, on the south. It may be doubted whether there was a south entrance to the temple in preexilic times.[44] Ezekiel cites divine criticism of the way in which the king's palace and the temple were separated only by a wall, and this proximity made possible all sorts of abominations by kings in the temple, suggesting that there was no defensive gate between palace and temple (Ezek 43:8).[45] In the coup against Athaliah, on the other hand, guards were stationed on both the north and south sides of the temple (2 Kgs 9:11), indicating that there may have been a preexilic south gate after all. Gatekeepers were also assigned to all four compass points according to 1 Chr 9:24.

---

39 In 2 Chr 31:14 Kore the son of Imnah is the keeper of the east gate.

40 Numbers 3 describes the placement of the Levites around the tabernacle. Merari is in the north, Kohath in the south, Gershon in the west, and the two most prestigious leaders, Aaron and Moses, in the east. Wright, "Guarding the Gates," 74–75, suggests that service at the gate of the king gave the gatekeepers a role in the administration of the state.

41 Neh 3:29 refers to Shecaniah, the keeper of the East Gate.

42 But Japhet, 459, regards textual corruption as the simplest solution.

43 Cf. also Amaziah, who sarcastically asked a prophet who criticized him if he had been made a royal counselor (2 Chr 25:16).

44 Curtis and Madsen, 285, note that the preexilic temple was protected on the south by the royal palace, confirming the anachronistic character of the arrangements described in these verses.

45 The south gates Ezekiel describes in 40:24-31 are for the future temple.

and his sons were assigned to the vestibules: The word בית האספים (cf. v. 17, ולאספים, without בית) has been conventionally understood from the etymology of the Hebrew word אסף ("gather") as a place for things that are gathered or stored.[46] A recent Hebrew dictionary also suggests that definition (*HALOT* 1:75), though it cites Akk. *asuppu* (anteroom), leading to my translation "vestibule" (cf. also Japhet, 459–60). In Neh 12:25 we read about people stationed at the "vestibules" (באספי) of the gates. Obed-edom's "sons" in this clause may include his grandsons, that is, the sons of Shemaiah (v. 7), who are not given special mention here.

■ **16** *Hosah's lot came out for the west gate, namely, the gate of the chambers:* The "gate of the chambers" (see textual note 18) appears only here in the OT, but see 9:26, which states that the four chief gatekeepers were in charge of the chambers (לשכות), and 23:28, which assigns to the Levites the care of the courts and the chambers. Hence assignment of Levitical gatekeepers to a gate with such a name makes good sense.

the gateway that leads upward: The conventional translation of במסלה העולה by "on the ascending road" (*NRSV*) faces difficulties, since a road would not be expected within the temple precincts. Some interpreters, therefore, have suggested the translation "track" (*HALOT* 2:606). David A. Dorsey has pointed out that "road" does not really fit any of the three uses מסלה in Chronicles (see also v. 18 and 2 Chr 9:11[47]) and interprets this noun instead on the basis of Akk. *mušlālu*, which means a gateway, sometimes accompanied by an outside stairway.[48] The latter detail may explain the use of the participle העולה, which is translated here as "which leads upward."

■ **17** *On the east there were six each day, on the north four each day:* Assuming that my textual reconstruction is correct (see textual note 19), these two gates would require ten guards per day from Meshelemiah/Shelemiah and his descendants, including especially Zechariah, who numbered only eighteen altogether according to v. 9. As noted above, under v. 9, the number is either a mistake or refers to families instead of individuals. With eighteen men, Meshelemiah/Shelemiah would not have had enough personnel for two complete shifts. The high importance of the east gate is shown in its having six gatekeepers instead of the usual four.

on the south four each day, and two each at the vestibules: There is some ambiguity in the number of men in Obed-edom's assignment. There were four gatekeepers in the south, and two gatekeepers for each of the vestibules. But the exact number of the vestibules is unspecified.

■ **18** *On the west, there were four at the gateway and two at the colonnade:* The family of Hosah would have to supply six guards each shift, out of a total membership of thirteen.[49] The word translated "colonnade," פרבר, transliterated as Parbar in *KJV*, has now been clarified by a use of the word פרור in the Temple Scroll in the sense of a colonnaded porch.[50] It is apparently the singular form of a word also appearing in 2 Kgs 23:11 in the form בפרורים (*NRSV* "precincts").[51]

---

46 Johnstone, 1:262, suggests "house of gathering," the collection point to which offerings in kind were brought. From this gate the Levites would transfer the offerings to the appropriate chambers. In 2 Chr 25:24 we are told that the temple vessels had been in the care of Obed-edom.

47 The word here appears in the plural (*NRSV* "steps"), which Solomon makes out of algum wood, which would be totally inappropriate for a road. A gateway could be lined with wood, which may be intended here.

48 David A. Dorsey, "Another Peculiar Term in the Book of Chronicles: מְסִלָּה, 'Highway'?" *JQR* 75 (1985) 385–91.

49 Cf. the discussion of these numbers under v. 14 above.

50 See Yigael Yadin, ed., *The Temple Scroll* (3 vols. in 4; Jerusalem: Israel Exploration Society, 1977–1983)

2:150: "And you shall make a place west of the *heikhal* around, a stoa of standing columns" (פרור עמודים עומדים), and the discussion in 1:235–39. Cf. *HALOT* 3:962, which cites Persian *frabar*, meaning "forecourt" or "vestibule." While it also notes the reading from the Temple Scroll, the definitions given are from commentaries written before the discovery of the scroll! Donna Runnalls, "The *Parwār*: A Place of Ritual Separation?" *VT* 41 (1991) 324–31, notes that the Temple Scroll shows that this building was a columned structure in which the purgation offerings of the priests could be kept separate from those of the people. She suggests the noun developed from a biconsonantal Semitic root *pr*.

51 *HALOT* 3:962, an annex on the west side of the temple. Cf. Ezek 41:12.

■ **19** *These were the divisions of the gatekeepers for the Korahites and the Merarites:* According to my interpretation of vv. 17-18, there were at least twenty-four gatekeepers required at any one time.[52]

26:20-32. List of Levitical Treasurers, Judges, and Officers
26:20-28. Levites Who Were over the Treasuries of the House of God and of the Dedicated Gifts

■ **20** *The Levites their brothers were over the treasuries of the house of God and the treasuries of the dedicated gifts:* The antecedent of "their" is the Kohathites and Merarites of vv. 1-19, and "the Levites" could refer to the treasurers in vv. 20-28 or, more likely, to all the officials mentioned in vv. 20-32. Braun, 253, on the other hand, believes that only the Gershonite Levites were identified as brothers here and that they originally supervised both types of treasuries—of the house of God and of the dedicated gifts—while the Kohathites and Merarites were gatekeepers. He attributes the assignment of the Amramites of vv. 24-28 to a later, or at least a different, strand. In addition to their work here with the treasuries, Levites elsewhere in Chronicles are responsible for collecting, storing, and distributing money (2 Chr 24:11, during the reign of Joash; 31:12-16, during the reign of Hezekiah; and 34:9-11, during the reign of Josiah). How their assignment in regard to the treasuries related to that of the priests and scribes in this regard is unknown (see Neh 13:13). These two types of treasuries are treated further in vv. 21-22 and vv. 24-28, respectively. The two types of treasuries—treasuries of the house of God and of the dedicated gifts—are also mentioned in 1 Chr 28:12. I do not believe that it is of much significance that the first treasury is called the treasury of the house of *Yahweh* in v. 22 (rather than the treasury of the house of God).

■ **21** *From the sons of Ladan the Gershonite:* For the substitution of Ladan for the more usual Libni as the son of Gershon, see the commentary at 23:7. Kohathites are

listed in the following verses (vv. 23-26, 29-31), but there are no Merarites among the treasurers.

Jehieli: Jehiel was identified as the first of the sons of Ladan in 23:8, and he was also the person in charge of the treasury of the house of Yahweh at the end of David's reign (29:8). Donations for the temple were entrusted to his care. The addition of what appears to be a gentilic ending on his name here is unexplained.

■ **22** *The sons of Jehieli: Zetham and his brother Joel were in charge of the treasuries of the house of Yahweh:* The source from which this information was taken can be dated to a generation later than 29:8, since the "sons" of Jehieli have taken over for their father. In 23:8 Jehiel, Zetham, and Jehiel are all listed as brothers, sons of Ladan. The difference in relationships may not indicate a significant social change,[53] but only a difference in the genealogist's perspective: in chap. 23 he was interested in recording the descendants of Ladan; here he narrates the genealogy from the point of view of who succeeded whom in office. The treasuries of the house of Yahweh would probably contain supplies needed for the regular functioning of the temple and the sacrificial system (see the commentary at 9:28-29). For "the treasuries of the dedicated gifts" see v. 26.

■ **23** *From the Amramites, the Izharites, the Hebronites, and the Uzzielites:* These are the standard four families of Kohath, the second son of Levi, who is not mentioned here by name. These four families are also mentioned in 23:12. Amramites are mentioned in vv. 24-26, Izharites in v. 29, and Hebronites in vv. 30-32.

■ **24** *Shubael the son of Gershom the son of Moses:* A Shebuel is identified as a chief in 23:16, where his ancestry is traced back through Gershom and Moses to Amram. Here the ancestor by whom Gershom is linked to Amram is not made explicit, although Moses is commonly identified elsewhere as the son of Amram and the father of Gershom. Since Shubael's son is listed in 24:20, the genealogical notice in 26:24 is presumably older than 24:20-32.[54]

---

52   If there were more than two vestibules in v. 17, the number would increase.

53   Contra Braun, 253.

54   Typologically speaking, 1 Chr 29:8 is older than 26:20-32 (see commentary on v. 22), and 26:20-32 is older than 24:20-32 (as noted in this verse). On the other hand, 24:20-32 is younger than 23:6b-23 (since the genealogy has been extended for another generation in chap. 24).

the chief officer in charge of the treasuries: The word נגיד ("chief officer") is used in Chronicles as a synonym for "king" (11:2; 17:7; 2 Chr 6:5), for an official of the temple (1 Chr 9:11; 31:13) or of the palace (2 Chr 28:7), for the role of Phinehas in his supervision of the gatekeepers (1 Chr 9:20), and for leaders in general (13:1; 27:16). The closest parallel to the use in this verse may be 2 Chr 31:12, where Conaniah is the chief officer (נגיד) in charge of the tithes and offerings. As the person in charge of both treasuries, Shubael would supervise the work of Zetham and Joel, on the one hand, and Shelomoth, on the other.

■ **25** *His brothers through Eliezer: Rehabiah his son, Jeshaiah his son, Joram his son, Zichri his son, and Shelomoth his son:* In 23:15, 17 Rehabiah is identified, as here, as the son of Eliezer the second son of Moses,[55] and he is said to have had many sons. The somewhat later genealogy in 24:21 names Isshiah (יִשִּׁיָּה) as Rehabiah's son, and this person is presumably the same as Jeshaiah (יְשַׁעְיָהוּ) in this verse. Shelomoth,[56] who is made head over the treasury of the dedicated gifts in the next verse, is listed in the fourth generation after Rehabiah, apparently in an attempt to put him at the time of David and Solomon, and in the tenth generation in a genealogy beginning with Levi.[57] Shubael in the previous verse is in the fifth generation of a genealogy beginning with Levi.[58] The intervening two people mentioned in this verse, Joram and Zichri, are unknown. Outside Exod 6:21, the name Zichri is used only in Chronicles and Nehemiah.

■ **26** *This Shelomoth and his brothers were over the treasuries of the dedicated gifts, which King David, and the heads of families, and the commanders of the thousands and hundreds, and the commanders of the army had dedicated:* The Chronicler had earlier reported that David had brought vast quantities of gold and silver, which he had taken from Hadadezer, to Jerusalem (1 Chr 18:7-8), and David also dedicated to Yahweh gifts that had been sent to him from Tou of Hamath, in addition to gold and silver he had taken from Edom, Moab, the Ammonites, the

Philistines, and Amalek (18:11). Elsewhere in 1 Chronicles, David claims to have made other staggeringly large gifts for the temple (22:14; 29:2). The Chronicler also stresses the generosity of the lay and military leaders at the time of David, without citing specific earlier passages in support, but the theme recurs in 29:6-9. The captains of hundreds and thousands in the wilderness period donated what they had captured for the tent of meeting as a memorial for the Israelites before Yahweh (Num 31:48-54). When Ezra returned from Babylon, he turned over the silver, gold, and the temple vessels to the priests Meremoth son of Uriah and Eleazar son of Phinehas, and to the Levites Jozabad son of Jeshua and Noadiah son of Binnui (Ezra 8:33-34).

■ **27** *they dedicated gifts for the maintenance of the house of Yahweh:* By dedication (הקדישו) booty from war was set aside for cultic purposes. "Maintenance" (so also *NRSV*) rather than "repair" (so *NIV*) seems a far better translation of לחזק, since the temple has not yet been built. In later passages in Chronicles, of course, the translation "repair" makes a great deal of sense (2 Chr 24:5, 12; 34:8, 10; cf. 2 Kgs 12:13).

■ **28** *And all that Samuel the seer, Saul the son of Kish, Abner the son of Ner, and Joab the son of Zeruiah had dedicated:* In addition to David's contemporaries, the Chronicler (or the source from which he draws) claims that earlier Israelite leaders had contributed or dedicated (הקדיש) booty from their wars for the maintenance of a temple that in fact they never saw nor presumably ever contemplated. In his enthusiasm the Chronicler (or his source) links people who were rivals to one another and to David in their lifetimes and who even, in the case of Saul, otherwise served in a completely negative capacity in Chronicles. The booty of Samuel would be from his war against the Philistines (1 Sam 7:7-14), while Saul's booty presumably was accumulated in his battles against the Ammonites (chap. 11), the Philistines (chaps. 13–14), and even the Amalekites (chap. 15), although in the latter case Samuel had severely criticized Saul for

---

55 For Eliezer see also Exod 18:4.
56 Shelomoth is to be distinguished from the Levite by that name in 1 Chr 23:9, who is a Gershonite, and Shelomoth of 23:18 or 24:22, who is a descendant of Izhar.
57 Levi–Kohath–Amram–Moses–Eliezer–Rehabiah– Jeshaiah–Joram–Zichri–Shelomoth. Zadok, the

high priest of David, is in the tenth generation *after* Aaron (cf. 5:34 [6:8]), and David himself is in the seventh generation *after* Ram and in the tenth generation *after* Judah.
58 Levi–Amran–Moses–Gershom–Shubael.

sparing the best of Agag's livestock, allegedly for sacrificial purposes (15:21).[59] This positive note about Saul in this verse is in sharp contrast with the Chronicler's harsh judgment on Saul in 1 Chr 10:13-14. Abner the son of Ner is only mentioned elsewhere in Chronicles in 27:21, where David appoints Jaasiel, Abner's son, as leader over Benjamin.[60]

26:29-32. Officers and Judges

■ **29** *From the Izharites: Chenaniah and his sons were appointed to outside duties over Israel as officers and judges:* This Chenaniah is unknown elsewhere, although a man by the same name is a musician in 15:22, 27. The outside duties (למלאכה החיצונה) of Chenaniah and his sons as officers and judges form a direct link between this paragraph and 23:4.[61] In Neh 11:16[62] two Levites are also appointed for "outside work" (המלאכה החיצנה) or what we might call secular duties. These Levites were apparently excused from temple duties to play a role in the community at large. "Officers and judges" listed together are nowhere else connected to the clergy or the temple, but only to the political bureaucracy.[63] Aside from the incidental reference to the officers in 1 Chr 27:1, the next time we read about them in the Chronicler's narrative is during the judicial reform of Jehoshaphat, where they are mentioned incidentally ("The Levites will serve you as officers"), after mentioning the high priest and the governor of the house of Judah (2 Chr 19:11). Maaseiah the officer is mentioned alongside the secretary Jeiel as the person responsible for the numbers in the muster of the army during the reign of Uzziah (26:11). In the repair of the temple at the time of Josiah, the officers are mentioned between scribes and gatekeepers (34:13). Levitical judges appear

only during the reform of Jehoshaphat (19:8). Despite the fact that the officers are mentioned first, the officers were probably subordinate to the judges.[64] No numbers are given here for the officers and judges, while the census reported in 1 Chronicles 23 identified six thousand of them. According to Deuteronomy, Moses had appointed officers throughout the tribes (Deut 1:15), and he commanded the Israelites to appoint both judges and officers throughout their tribes (Deut 16:18). Artaxerxes also instructed Ezra to appoint judges throughout the province (Ezra 7:25).

■ **30** *Hashabiah and his brothers, one thousand seven hundred valiant me*n, *had oversight of Israel west of the Jordan:* It is unclear how the officials in vv. 30-32 are related to the officers and judges in v. 29. If they exercise the same function, then the sum of the four thousand four hundred people mentioned in vv. 30-32 and the unknown number of Chenaniah and his sons in v. 29 might come close to the six thousand officers and judges mentioned in 1 Chr 23:4. It is surprising, however, that the number for Cisjordan is smaller than for the Transjordanian tribes.[65] The name Hashabiah, who had oversight of Israel west of the Jordan, is used for nine individuals in the OT,[66] but this particular person is not known elsewhere. Both he and Jerijah, the official mentioned in vv. 31-32, are Hebronites, that is, descendants of Hebron, the third son of Kohath. What is the relationship between such Hebronites and the fact that David's first capital was at Hebron? And what is the relationship between these Hebronites and those descended from the Israelite ancestor Judah in 2:42-43?

for all the work of Yahweh and for the service of the king: This expression and the parallel words in v. 32, "for

59 See also 1 Sam 14:47, where we are told that Saul fought against "Moab, Ammonites, Edom, the kings of Zobah, and the Philistines."

60 For the relationship of Ner to the genealogy of Saul, see the commentary on 1 Chr 8:33.

61 "Six thousand officers and judges."

62 A passage not included in the parallel text at 1 Chronicles 9.

63 K.-D. Schunck, *TDOT* 14:609, notes that these officers are also present as tribal representatives at cultic (covenantal) ceremonies: Deut 29:9 (10); Josh 8:33; 23:2; 24:1 (in the last two cases, judges are listed before the officers), but he believes the Chronicler is incorrect in designating them as

Levites. Schunck, 608, dates the origin of this office to premonarchic times and notes that it does not appear in any of the lists of officials (2 Sam 8:15-18; 20:23-26), nor anywhere in the books of Samuel and Kings or the prophetic books. He notes the use of this word in military, legal, and general administrative contexts.

64 Cf. J. van der Ploeg, "Les šōṭᵉrîm d'Israël," *OTS* 10 (1954) 185–96.

65 For Cisjordan there were 1,700 men, and for Transjordan there were 2,700 men (v. 27). Johnstone, 1:264, suggests that the area of the East Bank had been neglected until now.

66 See Gary S. Shorgren, "Hashabiah," *ABD* 3:64.

everything pertaining to God and the king," probably imply collection of taxes for both the religious and secular systems by one bureaucracy. Listing such officials just after the Levites who were in control of the treasuries makes eminent sense. How much of this procedure stems from ancient records and how much is invented to legitimate the collection of revenue for both religious and secular purposes at the Chronicler's time is hard to say. The latter purpose surely played into the reasons for the Chronicler recording it here. In any case the territory described in vv. 30-32 would be that of the united monarchy rather than that of the small province of Yehud.

■ **31** *Jerijah was chief of the Hebronites according to the genealogical records of their families:* Jerijah also appears as a "chief" in the lists of Levitical Hebronites in chap. 23 and chap. 24,[67] and it is these references that are probably meant by "the genealogical records (תלדת) of their families (v. 31)."

In the fortieth year of the reign of David: This was also the final year of David's kingship (1 Chr 29:27; 1 Kgs 2:11).

a search was made in the records, and mighty warriors were found in Jazer of Gilead: Jazer is probably to be located at Khirbet Jazzir (MR 219156), 4 kilometers south of es-Salt.[68] Jazer is one of the Levitical cities (Josh 21:39; 1 Chr 6:66 [81]), and this reference to Jazer was one of the clues that led William Foxwell Albright to seek the origin of these cities in the reign of David.[69] Rudolph, 177–79, on the other hand, calls attention to the fact that Judah the Maccabee conquered Jazer in the second century BCE (1 Macc 5:8) and later transferred a number of Jews from Gilead to Judea (1 Macc 5:45-54). Rudolph also points out that in Maccabean times the clergy took over some secular responsibilities, but he finally has to admit that while historical circumstances probably lie behind vv. 29-32, we do not have the means to say much about them. The reference to the "mighty warriors" in this verse led John L. Peterson to say that Jazer had been "garrisoned" by Judah from Hebron.[70] There is also a genealogical connection between Hebron and Gilead in 1 Chr 2:21-22, where we learn that Hezron, the father of Caleb (2:9), married the daughter of Machir "father" of Gilead. Their "grandson" Jair had twenty-three towns in Gilead.[71] Apparently Judahite families in Gilead later came to be considered Levites.

■ **32** *King David appointed them over the Reubenites, and the Gadites, and the half-tribe of Manassites:* David appointed the Hebronites stationed at Jazer to the same administrative responsibilities over the two and one-half Transjordanian tribes, as those of Hashabiah and his brothers west of the Jordan.

Conclusion

Chapter 26 contains references to gatekeepers and officers and judges, both anticipated by the census list in 23:4-5. I concluded that the list of gatekeepers was originally restricted to Meshelemiah and his descendants and Hosah and his descendants (vv. 1-3, 10-11, 19), with the references to Obed-edom and his sons as gatekeepers (vv. 4-8) and the assignments to the gatekeepers to their positions by lot (vv. 12-18) as secondary expansions. Verses 12-18 associate the four groups of gatekeepers from vv. 1-11 with each of the four temple gates. At least twenty-four gatekeepers were required at any one time.

The chapter closes with the listing of additional Levitical offices. Some Levites were treasurers of the house of God (Zetham and Joel, the sons of the Gershonite Jehieli) while others were treasurers of the dedicated gifts won by David and others through warfare (Shelomoth and his brothers, descendants of Eliezer the son of Moses the son of Amram from the Kohathites). Over all the treasuries was Shubael, the son of Gershom, the oldest son of Moses, who was from the Amramites. Chenaniah and his associates, descendants of Izhar from the Kohathite Levites, were officers and judges. The Kohathite Hebronites had oversight over Israel in both Cisjordan and Transjordan, with the latter having the bigger contingent.

---

67   Here is name is spelled יְרִיָּה, but in 1 Chr 23:19 and 24:23 it is spelled יְרִיָּהוּ.

68   Cf. John Peterson, "Jazer," *ABD* 3:650–51.

69   "List," 56. Mazar, "Cities," 197–99, also used this reference to date the list of Levitical cities to the united monarchy. For its location and for a discussion of the historical character of this list, see the commentary on 1 Chr 6:65-66 (80-81).

70   "Jazer," *ABD* 3:651.

71   See the commentary on 1 Chr 2:21-22.

Translation

1/ This is the list of the sons of Israel, the heads of families, the commanders of thousands and hundreds, the officers who served the king in every matter concerning the divisions,[1] as each month came and went away month by month for all the months of the year. Each division numbered twenty-four thousand. 2/ Ishbaal[2] the son of Zabdiel was in charge of the first division in the first month; in[3] his division were twenty-four thousand.[4] 3/ He was from the sons of Perez and was the chief for the first month over all the commanders of the hosts. 4/ Dodai the Ahohite was in charge of the division of the second month;[5] in his division were twenty-four thousand. 5/ The third army commander, for the third month, was Benaiah the son of Jehoiada the high priest;[6] in his division were twenty-four thousand. 6/ This was the Benaiah who was a mighty warrior of the Thirty[7] and was over[8] the Thirty; and over his division[9] was Ammizabad his son. 7/ Asahel the brother of Joab was fourth for the fourth month, and Zebadiah his son was after him;[10] in his division were twenty-four thousand. 8/ The fifth[11] for the fifth month was the commander Shamhuth[12] the Zerahite;[13] in his division were twenty-four thousand. 9/ The sixth for the sixth month was Ira son of Ikkesh the Tekoite; in his division were twenty-four thousand. 10/ The seventh for the seventh month was Helez the Pelonite from the sons of Ephraim; in his division were twenty-four thousand. 11/ The eighth for the eighth month was Sibbecai the Hushathite of the Zerahites; in his division were twenty-four thousand. 12/ The ninth for the ninth month was Abiezer the Anathothite, from the Benjaminites;[14] in his division were twenty-four thousand. 13/ The tenth for the tenth month was Maharai the Netophathite of the Zerahites; in his division were twenty-four thousand. 14/ The eleventh for the eleventh month was Benaiah the Pirathonite from the sons of Ephraim; in his division were twenty-four thousand. 15/ The twelfth for the twelfth month was Heldai[15] the Netophathite, of Othniel; in his division were twenty-four thousand.

16/ Over the tribes of Israel for the Reubenites, Eliezer son of Zichri was chief officer; for the Simeonites, Shephatiah the son of Maacah. 17/ For Levi, Hashabiah the son of Kemuel; for Aaron, Zadok. 18/ For Judah, Elihu[16] from the brothers of David; for Issachar, Omri the son of Michael. 19/ For Zebulun, Ishmaiah[17] son of Obadiah; for Naphtali, Jeremoth the son of Azriel. 20/ For the Ephraimites, Hoshea the son of Azaziah;[18] for the half-tribe of Manasseh, Joel the son of Pedaiah.

1 את המלך לכל דבר המחלקות. Rudolph, 178, proposes על דבר המחלקות לכל שרי המחלקות "concerning the divisions: of all the leaders of the divisions." LXX τῷ λαῷ καὶ εἰς πᾶν λόγον τοῦ βασιλέως κατὰ διαρέσεις εἰς πᾶν λόγον. LXX has a double translation of לכל דבר and apparently other inner-Greek corruption. Note λαῷ and τοῦ βασιλέως. Allen, *Greek Chronicles*, 1:145–46, posits two references to 26:32, which I do not find convincing.

2 ישבעל with LXX and 11:11 LXX; MT and 11:11 MT ישבעם "Jashobeam"; 2 Sam 23:8: ישב בשבת "Josheb-basshebeth," from an intermediate ישבשת (cf. LXX), from an original ישבעל. Cf. textual notes to 1 Chr 11:11. In both 27:2 and 11:11 MT has "Jashobeam" and LXX has "Ishbaal," with the latter more likely the original reading that has been corrected in both verses in the MT.

3 Johnstone, 1:266, here and in vv. 4-5 and 7-15, translates על with the word "over." As a result there are twenty-four thousand supervisors in each monthly division or two thousand per tribe per month.

4 ועל מחלקתו עשרים וארבעה אלף. Rudolph, 178, proposes to put these words at the end of v. 3.

5 MT, but not LXX, adds ומחלקתו ומקלות הנגיד "And his division, and Mikloth was the chief officer." Rudolph, 178, interprets this as a marginal notation calling attention to the name "Eleazar the son of Dodo the Ahohite" in 11:12. He translates: "As far as his division is concerned, there is corruption (מקלות) [of the name] of the chief officer." More likely in my judgment "Mikloth" (ומקלות) arose as a corrupt variant of ומחלקתו (see v. 6), and both variants were secondarily included in the text of this verse, with the addition of נגיד (see v. 16) to make sense. Japhet, 468, deletes the *wāw* from the name Mikloth, without recognizing the source of this reading. There is no apparent reason why Dodai would need a replacement or a second in command.

6 הכהן הראש, with *BHS*. Cf. 2 Chr 31:10; Ezra 7:5. MT הכהן ראש. In 1 Chr 12:28 (27) Jehoiada is called the leader (הנגיד) for Aaron. It would be tempting to translate "Benaiah the chief, the son of Jehoiada the priest," but Benaiah has already been designated the commander (שר) earlier in the verse. See the commentary.

7 השלשים. Many Hebrew MSS replace the article ה with ב "among," but the construct chain in Hebrew might be interpreted in a similar way without changing the text.

8 ועל. Rudolph, 178, wanted to insert וישם ("and he was placed") before this word, supposing that it had been lost by haplography, and then he also deleted the conjunction on the preposition, but these changes lack support in the versions and are unnecessary.

21/ For the half-tribe of[19] Manasseh in Gilead, Iddo the son of Zechariah;[20] for Benjamin,[21] Jaasiel the son of Abner. 22/ For Dan, Azarel the son of Jeroham;[22] these are the leaders of the sons of Israel. 23/ David did not take their number of those below twenty because Yahweh had promised to multiply Israel like the stars of the heavens. 24/ Joab the son of Zeruiah began to count but did not finish. Wrath came upon Israel for this, and the number was not entered in the book[23] of the Chronicles of King David.

25/ Over the king's treasuries[24] was Azmaveth the son of Adiel, and over the treasuries in the country, in the cities, in the villages, and in the towers was Jonathan the son of Uzziah. 26/ Over those doing the work of the field, tilling the ground, was Ezri the son of Chelub. 27/ Over the vineyard workers[25] was Shimei the Ramathite; over the wine cellars[26] was Zabdi the Shiphmite. 28/ And over the olive and sycamore trees in the Shephelah was Baal-hanan the Gederite;[27] over the stores of oil was Joash. 29/ Over the cattle grazing in Sharon was Shitrai[28] the Sharonite; over the cattle in the valleys was Shaphat the son of Adlai. 30/ Over the camels was Obil the Ishmaelite;[29] over the she-asses was Jehdeiah the Meronothite. 31/ Over the flocks was Jaziz the Hagrite; all these were the officials in charge of King David's property.

32/ Jonathan the uncle/kinsman of David[30] was a counselor, a man of discernment and a scribe.[31] Jehiel the son of Hachmoni took care of the king's sons. 33/ Ahitophel was a counselor to the king. Hushai the Archite[32] was the king's friend. 34/ After Ahitophel there came Jehoiada the son of Benaiah,[33] and Abiathar.[34] The commander of the king's army was Joab.

9 וּמַחֲלֻקְתּוֹ. The preposition is not explicit in Hebrew. Rudolph, 178, would add עַל before "Ammizabad," with LXX, Vg, judging that it is lacking in MT because of homoioarchton before עַמִּיזָבָד "Ammizabad." But the versions may be giving a dynamic equivalent of a difficult text.

10 אַחֲרָיו; LXX "and the [or his] brothers" (וְהָאַחִים or וְאֶחָיו).

11 הַחֲמִשִׁי; MT הַחֲמִישִׁי.

12 שַׁמְהוּת; 1 Chr 11:27 שַׁמּוֹת "Shammoth." Rudolph, 178, concludes that MT is a combination of Shammoth (11:27) and Shammah (2 Sam 23:25).

13 הַזַּרְחִי, with BHS; cf. vv. 11, 13. MT הַיִּזְרָח "the Izrah."

14 לְבֶן יְמִינִי, with Q. MT לִבְנִימִינִי. Normally the definite article is inserted before the second part of this compound word. See GKC §127d.

15 חֶלְדַי; 11:30 חֵלֶד "Heled."

16 אֱלִיהוּ; LXX אֱלִיאָב "Eliab" (cf. 2:13). As the *lectio difficilior*, "Elihu" may deserve preference. See also the commentary.

17 יִשְׁמַעְיָהוּ; LXX "Shemaiah," lacking the initial *yôd*.

18 עֲזַזְיָהוּ; a few Hebrew MSS, LXX עֻזִּיָּהוּ "Uzziah."

19 שֵׁבֶט, with a few Hebrew MSS, LXX, Vg; cf. v. 20. Lacking in MT.

20 זְכַרְיָהוּ; LXX, except for LXX^L, זְבַדְיָהוּ "Zebadiah."

21 לְבִנְיָמִן; LXX "to the sons of Benjamin" (dittography of the first three letters of בִּנְיָמִן "Benjamin").

22 יְרֹחָם; LXX יוֹרָם "Joram."

23 בְּסֵפֶר with LXX; MT בְּמִסְפַּר ("in the number" or "in the list"). The MT reading was precipitated by the immediately preceding word הַמִּסְפָּר "the number."

24 וְעַל אֹצְרוֹת הַמֶּלֶךְ. Rudolph, 180, and BHS add בְּעִיר הַמַּמְלָכָה "in the royal city," which was supposedly lost by homoioteleuton, though there is no evidence for this in the versions. The treasuries in this half verse in any case must be those in Jerusalem. Cf. v. 25b and 1 Sam 27:5.

25 הַכְּרָמִים with BHS; cf. Vg, the previous verse, and 2 Chr 26:10. MT הַכְּרָמִים "the vineyards."

26 וְעַל שֶׁבַכְּרָמִים לְאֹצְרוֹת הַיַּיִן, with BHS. MT וְעַל שֶׁבַּכְּרָמִים לְאֹצְרוֹת הַיַּיִן "and over what was in the vineyards [or 'over those who were in the vineyards'] for the wine cellars." According to Rudolph, 180, שֶׁבַּכְּרָמִים was originally a gloss on הַכְּרָמִים designed to make sure that the vocalization proposed in the previous note was followed.

27 הַגְּדֵרִי; LXX הַגְּדֹרִי "the Gedorite." Cf. 1 Chr 4:4, 18.

28 שִׁטְרַי; a few Hebrew MSS, Q, LXX^B, Tg: שִׁרְטַי "Shirtai."

29 הַיִּשְׁמְעֵלִי with Q; K הַיִּשְׁמְעָלִי. Q is the normal spelling (Rudolph, 182).

30 דּוֹד דָּוִיד. Rudolph, 182, tentatively adds לְדָוִיד "to David" ("[Jonathan . . . was a counselor] to David"), which was lost by haplography.

31 וְסוֹפֵר הוּא. LXX^B and c_2 lack "and a scribe" due to

homoioteleuton after συνετὸς [καὶ γραμματεὺς αὐτός].

32 LXX ὁ πρῶτος "the first." Allen, *Greek Chronicles*, 1:22, believes that the translator is using here a title from the Ptolemaic court.

33 יהוידע בן בניהו; two Hebrew MSS בניהו בן יהוידע "Benaiah the son of Jehoiada," as in v. 5.

34 ואביתר. Rudolph, 182, deletes the conjunction and inserts before this word יועץ למלך וכהנו "[Benaiah] the king's counselor, and his priest was," which he believes was lost by homoioteleuton after Benaiah.

27:1-34

Structure

This chapter contains four lists dealing with the secular administration of the land at the time of David and may be outlined as follows:

  I. 27:1-15. Twelve military divisions, of twenty-four thousand each, that served on a monthly basis, under the leadership of one of the military heroes associated with David (material derived from 11:10-31; see below).

  II. 27:16-24. Chief officers of the tribes of Israel. The listing of the tribes begins with the sons of Leah in their birth order, with the omission of the tribes coming from Leah's concubine Zilpah, namely, Gad and Asher. The second set of tribes (or parts of tribes) begins with Naphtali, the son of Bilhah, Rachel's maid, then the grandsons of Rachel (Ephraimites[1] and the two halves of the tribe of Manasseh), Rachel's son Benjamin, and the final son of Bilhah, Dan.[2] This list concludes with two verses providing historical and theological comments on the census undertaken by David and Joab in chap. 21.

  III. 27:25-31. Twelve supervisors over the king's property. Two of these officials supervised treasuries while the others had supervision over the raising and storing of crops and the tending of livestock.

  IV. 27:32-34. Seven advisors or associates of David.

Are these materials part of the original draft of the book of Chronicles? Are they authentic documents from the time of David?

This chapter is denied in its entirety to the Chronicler by Rudolph, 179, and Noth,[3] primarily because of their conclusion that 23:2 is continued by chaps. 28 and 29, and that everything in between is secondary. Williamson, 174, also denies the chapter to the Chronicler because of his prior decision that 23:3-6a is a caption that indicates the categories of lists of Levites that the Chronicler included.[4] He also notes that this chapter does not deal with David's final actions, but with his reign in general. He ascribes this chapter and other secondary materials to a pro-priestly redactor. I have noted on several occasions that the unity of the secondary materials and their attribution to one reviser are less persuasive than the distinction between the primary and secondary materials. The pro-priestly character of the materials in chap. 27 is not strong, aside from the identification of Benaiah as the son of the high priest Jehoiada in v. 5 and an identification of a tribal(?) division for Aaron, with Zadok as its leader, in v. 17. While the theological justification for David's census in vv. 23-24 is based on Numbers 1, part of the priestly materials in the Pentateuch, it would be difficult to characterize these two verses as pro-priestly. Hence if these materials are secondary, the case for them coming from a pro-priestly redactor is not strong.

Japhet, 468–74, argues that all of the materials in the chapter are original, except for vv. 23-24. The arguments for the secondary character of the latter verses are strong, since they offer a far different interpretation of the census of David than the Chronicler himself wrote in chap. 21. Japhet's central point is that 23:2, which reports David assembling the leaders of Israel, the priests, and the Levites, serves as a superscription that

---

1   Ephraim was younger than Manasseh but was given the firstborn's blessing by Jacob (Gen 48:8-22).

2   Johnstone, 1:269, suggests that the juxtaposition of Benjamin and Dan might imply the traditional location of Dan in the central part of the country west of Bethlehem before the migration of the tribe to the north reported in Judges 18. In 1 Chr 2:2 the order of the tribes is Dan (the second son of Bilhah, the maid of Rachel), Joseph, Benjamin, and Naphtali (the first son of Bilhah).

3   *Chronicler's History*, 31–33.

4   Cf. also "Origins," 261.

introduces the various lists of Levites[5] and of David's secular administration in chiastic order.[6] Just as David made provisions for the temple by providing for its clergy and the necessary materials for its construction, so in this chapter he anticipates the administrative structures that will be needed by Solomon and subsequent kings. This approach offers a good rationale for the Chronicler's omission of Solomon's own administrative innovation in 1 Kings 4. Such a purpose for the inclusion of the materials in chap. 27, however, could be ascribed to a secondary redactor as well as to the original author. The argument from the wording of 1 Chr 23:2 and from the omission of 1 Kings 4 causes me to lean toward Japhet's position, while recognizing that the case is by no means clear-cut. Whether these materials are primary or secondary, the transition to secular administration is eased by the reference to the Levites who performed secular duties in 26:30 and 32.

It is quite another question to ask whether these lists can be dated to the era of David himself or to some other period in preexilic Israel. Each list must be considered on its own merits, and I have come to three different conclusions. Before examining each list, however, we must first discuss some general considerations. How likely is it that lists written presumably on organic materials, such as leather and papyrus, would have survived for over four centuries and been available to the Chronicler? No Israelite or Judean royal inscriptions on clay or stone have yet been discovered in the land of Israel, although absence of evidence does not provide evidence of absence. One could appeal to the analogy of the Samaria ostraca, although they are both shorter and of a different genre than these lists. We also do not know whether such

administrative lists might have been recopied by priests or royal officials over the years. Again the Samaria ostraca are not analogous since they were buried in a destruction layer and only discovered almost three millennia later by modern archaeologists. They were not available to the Chronicler and his contemporaries.

Second, what was the historical character of David's kingship itself, and how sophisticated, extensive, or centralized was his administration? Historical debates rage in contemporary scholarship about the history of David both because of new sociological models to which his kingship has been compared and because of a general skepticism in some circles about the history of Israel before the time when there is contemporary extrabiblical information about it. While lack of supporting evidence does not justify nihilism toward the history of David or toward the possibility of administrative documents surviving from his reign, it also severely complicates the situation for those who try to demonstrate the character of his reign or the authenticity of documents in question.[7]

A third consideration is that a document might be preexilic, reflecting an administrative situation at a later time, while not going back to the time of David himself.

Finally, one must weigh how much the Chronicler or the redactor might have revised the document, so that we may need to distinguish between what came from a source and what came from an editorial hand.

The claim for the antiquity of the first list in 27:1-15 is the least persuasive for me.[8] The names of the leaders of the monthly divisions are derived from the list of David's military heroes in 1 Chronicles 11//2 Samuel 23, as the following comparison of the list with the first sixteen names in 1 Chronicles 11 demonstrates:

---

5   For my rationale for excluding the priests and some secondary lists of Levites from these chapters, see the sections on Structure in chaps. 23–26.

6   These administrative officers are also presupposed by 1 Chr 28:1 and 29:6, 24.

7   Some see David as a chief, ruling over a very limited geographical territory. See the studies by Halpern, *David's Secret Demons;* and Steven L. McKenzie, *King David: A Biography* (Oxford: Oxford Univ. Press, 2000). Both books have extensive bibliographies and discussions of the historical questions about David.

8   See also Welten, *Geschichte und Geschichtsdarstellung,* 93–94. Welten believes that the list of monthly pro-

visions for Solomon's court in 1 Kgs 4:7-19 provides the best analogy for this list. For a cautious counter-argument see Japhet, 469–71. Japhet notes that the organization of the priests and Levites that is attributed to David is similar to that which prevailed at the Chronicler's day. The fact that there was not a military force in the Chronicler's day in any way comparable to vv. 1-15 leads Japhet, 470, to conclude that it would be "rather much" to assume that the military organization is a product of the Chronicler's imagination. She notes that E. Junge, *Der Wiederaufbau des Heerwesens des Reiches Juda unter Josia* (BWANT 5; Stuttgart: Kohlhammer, 1937) 65–69, attributed the list to the time of Josiah so

1 Chronicles 27

A. Ishbaal[9] son of Zabdiel from the sons of Perez, vv. 2-3
B. Dodai the Ahohite, v. 4

C. Benaiah[11] son of Jehoiada the high priest, v. 5
D. Ammizabad, v. 6
E. Asahel brother of Joab, v. 7
F. Zebadiah son of Asahel, v. 7

G. Shamhuth the Zerahite, v. 8
H. Ira son of Ikkesh the Tekoite, v. 9
I. Helez the Pelonite from the sons of Ephrain, v. 10
J. Sibbecai the Hushathite[16] of the Zerahites, v. 11
K. Abiezer the Anathothite from the Benjaminites, v. 12

L. Maharai the Netophathite[19] of the Zerahites, v. 13

1 Chronicles 11

1. Ishbaal son of a Hachmonite, v. 11

2. Eleazar son of Dodo[10] the Ahohite, v. 12
3. Abishai brother of Joab, v. 20
4. Benaiah the son of Jehoiada from Kabzeel, v. 22

5. Asahel brother of Joab, v. 26[12]

6. Elhanan the son of Dodo from Bethlehem, v. 26
7. Shammoth[13] the Harodite,[14] v. 27
8. Helez the Pelonite,[15] v. 27

9. Ira son of Ikkesh the Tekoite, v. 28
10. Abiezer the Anathothite, v. 28
11. Sibbecai[17] the Hushathite, v. 29

12. Ilai[18] the Ahohite, v. 29
13. Maharai the Netophathite, v. 30

14. Heled[20] son of Baanah the Netophathite, v. 30

M. Benaiah the Pirathonite from the sons of Ephraim, v. 14
N. Heldai the Netophathite of Othniel, v. 15

15. Ithai[21] son of Ribai of Gibeah of the sons of Benjamin, v. 31
16. Benaiah the Pirathonite, v. 31

Four names from the list in chap. 11 are omitted from the list in chap. 27: #3 Abishai brother of Joab, #6 Elhanan the son of Dodo, #12 Ilai the Ahohite, and #15 Ithai son of Ribai of Gibeah; and three pairs of names toward the end of the list are recorded in reverse order: H. Ira son of Ikkesh and I. Helez the Pelonite in chap. 27 are ##9 and 8 in chap. 11; J. Sibbecai the Hushathite and K. Abiezer the Anathothite in chap. 27 are ##11 and 10 in chap. 11; M. Benaiah the Pirathonite and N. Heldai the Netophathite in chap. 27 are ##16 and 14 in chap. 11. The regularity of these changes—the tendency to omit every third name and reversing the order of six of the last seven names that were taken from the list[22]—suggests that chap. 27 is a literary development and not the product of sociological change. A few of the differences between the two lists may be the result of scribal errors, in addition to the ones already dealt with in my textual notes: Dodai (B) versus Dodo (2), the omission of "Eleazar son of" with this same name (B/2), and Shamhuth (G)[23] versus Shammoth (7). The most striking remaining difference between the two lists is that chap. 27 adds clan or tribal names to eight of the twelve

---

that all the Chronicler had to do was to provide earlier names.

9 See textual note 2.
10 Chronicles LXX and 2 Sam 23:9 K דדי "Dodai." Cf. 1 Chronicles 11, textual note 22.
11 In 18:17 Benaiah son of Jehoiada is over the Cherethites and the Pelethites.
12 Cf. 2:16, which lists the sons of Zeruiah as Abishai, Joab, and Asahel. That makes Joab and Asahel brothers.
13 שמות; 2 Sam 23:25 שמה "Shammah."
14 חהררי. Cf. 2 Sam 23:25. 1 Chr 11:27 ההרורי "the Harorite." 2 Sam 23:25 adds: "Elika the Harodite."
15 הפלוני. Cf. 2 Sam 23:26 LXX[L]; 2 Sam 23:26 MT הפלטי "the Paltite."

16 This warrior is also mentioned in 1 Chr 20:4//2 Sam 21:18. For Hushah (MR 162124) see 1 Chr 4:4.
17 סבכי; cf. 2 Sam 23:27 LXX[L]. Samuel MT מבני "Mebunnai."
18 2 Sam 23:28 "Zalmon."
19 For the association of Netophah with Bethlehem see Ezra 2:22//Neh 7:26.
20 חלד. 2 Sam 23:29 MT חלב "Heleb."
21 איתי. 2 Sam 23:29 אתי "Ittai."
22 The seventh, Maharai (L/13), is retained in its position between ##11-10 and 16-14.
23 The name שמהות conflates the ending of this name in 2 Sam 23:25 שמה and 1 Chr 11:27 שמות, respectively.

names: Perez (A); Zerah (G, J, L); Othniel (N); Benjamin (K), and Ephraim (I, M). Five of these clan names are from the tribe of Judah (A, G, J, L, N),[24] and may have been deduced from the hometown[25] of the heroes. The tribal names could also be deduced from city names in the case of Benjamin (K) and Ephraim (I, M).[26] Assuming that Dodai (B) is to be assigned to Benjamin,[27] Benaiah (C) and Ammizabad (D) to Levi, and Asahel (E) and Zebadiah (F) to Judah, the total for all fourteen names is: Judah eight, Benjamin two, Levi two, and Ephraim two. Once again we note the orderly distribution of tribes, with the tribes contemporary with the Chronicler occupying twelve of the fourteen positions. The two Ephraimite names show a convenient openness to the north. Other details of the names will be treated in the verse-by-verse commentary. Not only are the names derived from the list of military heroes in chap. 11 and assigned now as commanders of the monthly contingents,[28] but Asahel is a particularly inappropriate choice, since according to 2 Sam 2:23 he was killed before David was anointed by the ten northern tribes. His early death is taken account of by the addition of Zebadiah as his replacement, but Asahel's presence still presents a double historical difficulty: it could not come from the end

of David's reign as the Chronicler reports, nor is the list ever plausible for the united monarchy as long as it has Asahel's name associated with it, since he died before David became king of Israel.

Second, and more briefly, the numbers assigned to each monthly division presuppose a total army for David of two hundred eighty eight thousand that is unrealistically high,[29] and the presence of both twelve divisions and the repeated emphasis on the number twenty-four seems based on other lists in the wider context.[30] The total number of troops organized in this scheme is suspiciously similar to the two hundred eighty-eight singers described in 25:7 (cf. 25:9-31).[31] While assigning the military heroes as commanders of the monthly contingents implies that this is a militia,[32] not related to the tribal structure, its actual job description is not given and one suspects that the author is here giving David credit for organizing the whole kingdom in a way that preempts and even makes unnecessary Solomon's own establishment of new administrative districts, which also were not based on the twelve-tribe system and which supplied monthly food for the king and his household (1 Kgs 4:7-19; 5:7 [4:27]).[33] Lending credence to this line of inter-

24 Perez (A) and Zerah (G, J, L) were twin sons of Judah and Tamar (1 Chr 2:4; Gen 38:29-30); Othniel (N) is a son of Kenaz, the younger brother of Caleb (1 Chr 4:13; cf. Josh 15:15-19 and Judg 3:9). Johnstone, 1:268, notes that many of the leaders come from Bethlehem and its environs.

25 Son of a Hachmonite(A/1); the Harodites (G/7); Hushathite (J/11); two are Netopathites (L/13; N/14).

26 Pirathon, the city of Benaiah (M), is from the tribe of Ephraim. The obscurity of the reference to "the Pelonite" gave the author the opportunity to associate Helez (I) with Ephraim.

27 Johnstone, 1:267. Cf. 1 Chr 8:4, where Ahoah is mentioned among the descendants of Benjamin.

28 The monthly contingents are a militia while their leaders are part of David's permanent and personal armed force.

29 In 854 the great Assyrian king Shalmaneser III had no more than one hundred twenty thousand troops. Cf. Rudolph, 181. Similarly unrealistic are the four hundred thousand men that Ahijah sent against the eight hundred thousand of Jeroboam (2 Chr 13:3). The report that the northern king Pekah killed one hundred twenty thousand Judeans and carried off

another two hundred thousand captives is also unrealistic.

30 De Vaux, *Ancient Israel*, 227, noted these features but then remarked that if we suppress the figures and the names, the structure itself may have been in use at a later epoch. Of course without the numbers and names, the document only gives the barest outline for a monthly militia, for which there is no other confirming evidence.

31 David appointed twenty-four thousand Levites to work in the temple (1 Chr 23:4), and he organized the priests into twenty-four divisions (chap. 24).

32 In a spirited essay Yigael Yadin, *The Art of Warfare in Biblical Lands in the Light of Archaeological Study* (trans. M. Pearlman; 2 vols.; New York: McGraw-Hill, 1963) 2:279–84, attempts to show the strategic logic of David's establishing a militia, with a monthly rotation, as a basis for defense forces also in modern Israel. Yadin also argues that the following list of tribal leaders would supply the recruits from all the tribes to the central government, which would then assign them to a monthly contingent. Nowhere in the text is this role hinted at for the tribal leaders.

33 Solomon's list covered only northern Israel, not

pretation is the Chronicler's omission of the passage about Solomon's administrative innovation in 1 Kings 4.

This paragraph has an introduction in v. 1 that applies only to vv. 1-15, but it lacks a summary or concluding verse (contra 25:8-31). Beginning with the sixth month and continuing until the twelfth month (vv. 9-15), the form is very regular: the numerical rank of the division commander, the number of the month, the name of the leader, and a note that there were twenty-four thousand in his division. This pattern is already discernible in the third month, and, indeed, its beginning phrase, "the third commander for the third month," is presupposed in all the subsequent months. Verse 1 differs considerably from this pattern and v. 2 less so, especially as reconstructed in my textual notes.

Historicity of Verses 16-24

The arguments for and against the historicity of the list of tribal leaders in vv. 16-24 are thin and somewhat inconclusive on both sides.[34] The difficulties start with the number and the order of the "tribes" in these verses: Reuben, Simeon, Levi, Aaron, Judah, Issachar, Zebulun, Naphtali, Ephraimites, the half-tribe of Manasseh, the half-tribe of Manasseh in Gilead, Benjamin, and Dan.

There are thirteen names in this list, but since Aaron is nowhere else considered a tribe,[35] his name may have arisen because of a desire to include his descendant Zadok among the tribal heads,[36] with the result that there are in fact really only twelve tribes in this list. Elsewhere, when Levi is omitted from the tribal lists, the number twelve is achieved by dividing Joseph into Ephraim and Manasseh. Here Levi is present, and Joseph is divided into three tribes! The order of tribes seems to follow a scheme based on the birth mothers:[37] the six sons of Leah (Reuben–Zebulun) are followed by six descendants of Rachel (Naphtali, the second son of Rachel's handmaid Bilhah, Ephraim, the western half of Manasseh, the eastern half of Manasseh, Benjamin, and Dan the first son of Bilhah). The two sons of Bilhah form an envelope around the other sons of Rachel as they also do—but in reverse order—around Joseph and Benjamin in 1 Chr 2:1-2.[38] The reason for this equal distribution of tribes to the full wives of Jacob—attested nowhere else in the Bible—is not clear and seems stylized and artificial, reflecting no historical period. This unique distribution, in any case, convinces me that Gad and Asher were intentionally omitted. Japhet, 471, who believes that the Chronicler does not restrict himself rigidly to the number twelve[39]—since there are thirteen

---

including Judah, while the leadership of David's list is limited to only four tribes, three of which were part of the community within which the Chronicler wrote and the majority of them are Judah. Cf. also Welten, *Geschichte und Geschichtsdarstellung*, 93.

34 Even Myers, 1:184, admits that the only reflection of the period of the united monarchy is the reference to the tribal system that supposedly obtained in that period. He holds that the nucleus of the list could be quite old because of the presence of Reuben, Simeon, and Elihu, the brother of David, or the list could be a fabrication, which he considers unlikely.

35 Rudolph, 182, believes that Zadok was not an Aaronide for the Chronicler and only became a priest in 1 Chr 29:22, but he also mentions 18:16. Rudolph believes that Zadok was connected to Aaron only in the time of Ezra. See Ezra 8:2 and Rudolph, *Esra und Nehemia*, 79. If, however, the master genealogy of the high priesthood is presupposed by the Chronicler (1 Chr 5:27-41 [6:1-15]), Rudolph's argument about the lack of genealogy for Zadok is not convincing.

36 In 1 Chr 12:27-29 (26-28) numbers are given for the

Levites in general, for Jehoiada a leader of the house of Aaron, and for Zadok, a young warrior. Williamson, 176, argued that in the original list, the reference to Zadok would have been at the beginning of the list. Cf. Num 1:3, where both Moses and Aaron were instructed to conduct the census. Hence his pro-priestly reviser moved this phrase or added it himself with the purpose of drawing attention to the Aaronic family.

37 Zecharia Kallai, "The Twelve Tribe Systems of Israel," *VT* 47 (1997) 53–90, includes this in his category 1b. Other tribal lists in this category include: Gen 33:1-2; 35:23-26; 46:8-25; 49:3-27 (1-28); Exod 6:13-26?; Num 13:4-15?; Deut 27:12-13; 33:6-25; Ezek 48:31-34; 1 Chr 2:1-2; 1 Chronicles 2–9.

38 Was Dan placed last because of the tendency in some lists to list him late or because of his location in the north? This listing of the tribes is category 4 in Kallai's schema.

39 See also Martin Noth, *Das System der Zwölf Stämme Israels* (Stuttgart: Kohlhammer, 1930) 20–21.

tribes already in this list if one includes Aaron—believes that Gad and Asher were lost accidentally through textual error.[40]

Almost all commentators agree that vv. 23-24 are an attempt to exonerate David for the census he took in chap. 21. These verses therefore were added by someone later than the Chronicler and are not historical.[41] According to Numbers 1, the head of each tribe was to be involved in the taking of the census (Num 1:4; cf. vv. 5-16),[42] and this might explain the reason for listing the tribal heads just before, in vv. 16-22. According to v. 23, David only counted those over twenty years of age (cf. Num 1:3, 45, where this involves everyone able to go to war), and the reason given for that is that he trusted in the promises of God to give him as many descendants as the stars of the heavens (cf. Gen 15:5; 22:17; 26:4). But if he had really trusted those promises, why would he even count those over twenty? Verse 23, therefore, is an evident attempt to remove the guilt of David that permeates the account in chap. 21. In that chapter David ordered the census, which Joab carried out only with great reluctance, and Joab omitted Levi and Benjamin for reasons discussed in the commentary on 21:6-7. Joab shows a reverence for God's will in 21:3 that is credited instead to David in 27:24. In 27:24 Joab is implicitly criticized for not completing the census—presumably by not including Levi and Benjamin[43]—as a result of which the wrath of Yahweh came upon Israel. This is a reinterpretation of the plague that struck Israel and killed seventy thousand in Israel (21:14). The word used for divine anger in v. 24 (קֶצֶף) is taken from the census account in Num 1:53.[44] Verse 24 explains that the divine wrath is the reason why no numbers are given for the individual tribes in the "Chronicles of David," as they are in Numbers 1.[45] In this "midrashic"[46] understanding of vv. 23-24, the "Chronicles of David" would be a reference to 1 Chronicles 21 and possibly other narratives about David and not to some independent and otherwise unknown source.

The principal argument for the historicity of the list in vv. 16-22 is that the names of the tribal heads are not stereotyped nor is there a known analogous list from which they could have derived (see the discussion of vv. 1-15 above). Only three names of the tribal heads are known elsewhere, and none can be identified with certainty. The best candidate is Abner, who might be the cousin of Saul, representing the tribe of Benjamin, since no one else bears the name Abner in the OT. But Joab killed Abner in Hebron (2 Sam 3:27) before David became king over the ten northern tribes. Consequently, this list of the twelve tribes would have to come early in David's reign when he did not yet rule all Israel, and a list of twelve tribes would not be appropriate. For this reason I concluded in the commentary on 1 Chr 26:28 that a different Abner was intended here. Hashabiah could be identified with the person with the same name

---

40   Rudolph, 183, attributes their omission to textual corruption or carelessness. Curtis and Madsen, 291, note that Gad and Asher are the last tribes named in some lists (1 Chr 2:2; Gen 35:26) and so they were the ones omitted in order to keep the total at twelve.

41   Japhet, 473, notes the awkward connection between "their number" in v. 23 and the "leaders of the tribes of Israel" in v. 22.

42   The sons of Joseph have been divided into Ephraim and Manasseh in this census list. In first position come the five remaining sons of Leah, the three tribes attributed to Rachel, and then the four sons of the handmaids: Dan (the firstborn of Rachel's handmaid Bilhah), Asher (the second son of Leah's handmaid Zilpah), Gad (the firstborn of Zilpah), and Naphtali (the second son of Bilhah). Japhet, 471, alleges that 1 Chr 27:16-22 follows "strictly" the order of Num 1:5-15, but admits that Naphtali is out of position, Levi is included, and Manasseh is divided into two troops—not to mention that Gad and Asher are also missing! In the actual census (Num 1:20-43) Gad has been moved into Levi's old position, with the rest of the list remaining same.

43   These tribes are included in 1 Chr 27:17, 21.

44   In Numbers the Levites were stationed around the tabernacle so that there would not be wrath against the Israelites.

45   Williamson, 175–76, argues that the explanation of the lack of numbers causes tension if not contradiction with the numbers actually listed in 1 Chr 21:5. Those numbers are for all Israel (or Israel and Judah) and not for individual tribes.

46   Cf. De Vries, 214, who compares it to 1 Chr 5:1-2; Japhet, 474.

in 26:30, but Hashabiah is a relatively common name used for nine individuals in the OT. The reference to Elihu, the brother of David, is quite uncertain, since this brother is not mentioned elsewhere (see textual note 16 and the commentary to v. 18). Some commentators have appealed to the unique order of the tribes, but that order seems to be based on an equal division between the sons of Leah and Rachel, which seems more artificial than historical. The tension caused by the lack of numbers in the "Chronicles of David" and the numbers present in 21:5 may disappear if the lack of numbers here refers to those for the individual tribes, whereas the numbers in chap. 21 are for "all Israel" and for "Judah."[47]

As a result of this discussion I doubt the historical nature of vv. 16-24, and surely of vv. 23-24. My only caution, which keeps the option for historicity open, is my inability to explain the origin of the names of the tribal chiefs. The structure of the list is set already by v. 16: For the Reubenites, the title chief officer (נגיד), and the name of this leader with his patronym. For subsequent leaders the title "chief officer" is presupposed but not explicitly repeated.[48] Only Zadok and Elihu are not provided with patronyms (see the commentary). Some

tribes have gentilic endings (e.g., Reubenites, Simeonites), some have only the tribal name (e.g., Judah, Issachar), and Ephraim is prefaced with the words "sons of." Most of the personal names are used elsewhere in the OT for other people and little can be learned from such comparison. Iddo (ידו) is unknown elsewhere in this spelling of the Hebrew name, though the transliteration Iddo appears in the *NRSV* eighteen times.[49]

The claim for the historicity of vv. 25-31[50] and vv. 32-34 depends largely on the nonstereotypical names and the lack of obvious vocabulary or ideology of the Chronicler. Both lists seem plausible for the era of David, the first as a list of managers of David's properties and economic interests[51] and the second as a list of some of his personal staff in addition to the more formal list of officers in 1 Chr 18:15-17//2 Sam 8:16-18 or 2 Sam 20:23-26. Japhet, 472, notes that the geography is not restricted to the postexilic province of Yehud, but includes the Shephelah and the region of Sharon.[52] Rudolph, 183, held that vv. 25-34 were in the "Chronicles of King David" (27:24), but that claim is not contained in the text, and I have seen reason to doubt the historical character of that reference. There are twelve officials in the first list (vv. 25-31)[53] and seven[54] in the

---

47   Horst Seebass, "Erwägungen zum altisraelitischen System der zwölf Stämme," *ZAW* 90 (1978) 196–219, esp. 214–15, dated the list of tribes to the time of Ahab. He took "Manasseh in Gilead" (v. 21) as a reference to Solomon's sixth district, which had Ramoth-gilead as its administrative center. He explained the absence of Gad by its being included in Reuben, and the absence of Asher because of its uncertain status between the division of the kingdom and the increased power of the Omrides. The all-Israel dimension of the list would be related to the alliance between Ahab and Jehoshaphat. None of these points convinces.

48   V. 22 uses the word "leaders" (שרי) for all the tribes of Israel.

49   Various Hebrew spellings lie behind this name: אדו, עדו, עדא.

50   Braun, 262, refers to Frank Moore Cross and G. Ernest Wright, "The Boundary and Province Lists of the Kingdom of Judah," *JBL* 75 (1956) 202–26, who argued that the list of towns in Josh 15:21-26 reflects the organization of Judah during the days of the united monarchy. Earlier, William F. Albright, "The Administrative Districts of Israel and Judah," *JPOS* 5 (1925) 17–54, dated the cities of

refuge in Joshua 20 to the time of David. Cf. also Aharoni, *Land of the Bible,* 263–80.

51   These illustrate David's riches, also attested by 1 Chr 29:28. Cf. de Vaux, *Ancient Israel,* 124–26. Cf. also Michael L. Heltzer, "The Royal Economy of King David Compared with the Royal Economy in Ugarit" (Hebrew), *ErIsr* 20 (1989) 175–80, who observes that the main economic categories were in the territories David conquered from the Philistines. He also notes that the administration of David was more centralized than that of Ugarit in the 13th century.

52   Cf. Myers, 1:185. See Martin Noth, "Das Krongut der israelitischen Könige und seine Verwaltung," *ZDPV* 50 (1927) 217, 230–40. Galling, 76, dates these verses to the time of Josiah.

53   Johnstone, 1:271, notes that there are seven agricultural officials: two in charge of storage and five for agricultural production (one for grain, v. 26; two for wine, v. 27; and two for olives, v. 28). There are five officials for livestock (two for cattle, one for camels, one for donkeys, and one for sheep and goats).

54   Or six if Ahithophel and his replacement did not serve at the same time.

second (vv. 32-34). While these numbers may imply wholeness or completeness, the numbers are not stereotypical enough to justify calling the historicity of either list into question. The list in vv. 25-31 has the following structure: (a) an area of responsibility (over the treasuries, over the vineyard workers, etc.); (b) the official's name; (c) the name of the official's father or hometown. Only Joash in v. 28 lacks such an additional modifier. The list has no introduction, but concludes with the words, "all these were the officials in charge of King David's property." The possible identification of these officials with people otherwise identified in the Bible will be examined in the commentary. The list in vv. 32-34 lacks both an introduction and a conclusion. It gives the name of the person associated with David and a title for his[55] role in David's administration. Five of the names are provided with links to their family or clan, two of whom, Ahithophel and Hushai, are known from 2 Samuel 15–16, and the other three, Jonathan, Jehiel, and Jehoida, have links to persons attested elsewhere. The two persons named without family ties, Abiathar and Joab, are also well known from earlier books.

Detailed Commentary

27:1-15. Twelve Divisions That Served the King on a Monthly Basis

■ **1** *the heads of families, the commanders of thousands and hundreds, the officers who served the king in every matter concerning the divisions:* Rudolph, 180–81, took this as an introduction to the entire chapter, but the individuals listed in vv. 25-31 do not seem to be described by "the officers who served the king in every matter concerning the divisions," and "the heads of families" do not appear in vv. 16-24. No term from this verse alludes to vv. 32-34. To make "the commanders of thousands and hundreds" fit vv. 1-15, Rudolph identified the reference to "hundreds" as secondary (for the full title see 13:1; 26:26). Rudolph surely errs in wanting to ascribe a different order to the paragraphs in this chapter, moving vv. 16-24 to the head, on the basis of this verse. Instead, the verse refers verbosely to the monthly commanders mentioned in vv. 2-15.

Much has been said about the monthly militia that is envisioned in vv. 1-15, primarily because the head of each monthly division is one of David's military heroes, but the account gives little detail about the job description of these monthly divisions that had the grand total of two hundred eighty-eight thousand people, and the final clause quoted above suggests that it could easily include the supplying of provisions, much like the administrative divisions later created by Solomon.

■ **2** *Ishbaal the son of Zabdiel:* While this warrior may also have had the name Jashobeam (see textual note 2), I have chosen to restore the name Ishbaal. More puzzling is the patronymic, since in 11:11 he is said to be the son of a Hachmonite (cf. 2 Sam 23:8). Japhet, 474, proposes that his original name might have been Jeshbaal the son of Zabdiel the Hachmonite, thus conflating the alternate readings in chaps. 11 and 27, but we have no evidence in 1 Chronicles 11 or 2 Samuel 23 that those passages ever had information about Zabdiel. It may be significant that the two names added to the list by the Chronicler (Ammizabad in v. 5 and Zebadiah in v. 7) also have names derived from the root זבד ("bestow upon, endow with"). The implication would be that the author had a liking for this name and introduced it whenever necessary. Another possibility is that the author of this passage had a *Vorlage* that differed from 1 Chronicles 11 with regard to the father's name, but that does not seem likely. In truth, this change of father's names is inexplicable. A Jashobeam without a patronymic appears in 12:7 (6), a Zabdiel son of Haggedolim ("the big ones"?) in Neh 11:14, and Jehiel son of Hachmoni in 1 Chr 27:32. Was this change of Ishbaal/Jashobeam's father's name introduced to keep him and Jehiel in v. 32 from being considered brothers?

■ **3** *He was from the sons of Perez and was the chief for the first month over all the commanders of the hosts:* The writer linked Ishbaal/Jashobeam to the tribe of Judah by putting him among the sons of Perez, and he also provides a hint on how he thought these monthly contingents were organized by giving this man supervision over all the commanders of units or hosts.

■ **5** *Benaiah the son of Jehoiada the high priest:* Benaiah the son of Jehoiada was a well-known general in the reign of David, who succeeded to the top military position with

---

55   All of the names in this chapter are men.

the accession of Solomon (2 Sam 8:18; 1 Kings 1–2).[56] The reason for including him here, however, is the Chronicler's use of 1 Chr 11:22-25 (see the commentary on these verses). According to 12:28 (27) Jehoiada was a leader (נגיד) of the house of Aaron who brought three thousand seven hundred troops to David at Hebron. The Chronicler apparently interpreted Jehoiada's association with Aaron as implying that he was a priest. He may have become a "high priest" by confusion with Jehoiada the high priest in the Second Temple period (Neh 12:10, 11, 21).[57] Benaiah, the military leader, hailed from Kabzeel, a town in southern Judah near the Edomite border (MR 148071; 1 Chr 11:22; 2 Sam 23:20; cf. Josh 15:21).

■ **6** *Benaiah who was a mighty warrior of the Thirty and was over the Thirty:* According to 1 Chr 11:20-21, Abshai was the commander of the Thirty, but he is omitted from the list of monthly commanders in chap. 27 and his place is taken by Benaiah. This might mean that the author of this list had access to a later copy of the list of David's heroes, but that seems unlikely, since chap. 11 seems clearly to be based on 2 Samuel 23. Perhaps the author of this section of 1 Chronicles 27 concluded that Abshai had died by the end of David's reign, since he plays no role whatsoever in the revolt of Adonijah, reported in 1 Kings 1, in which his brother Joab was heavily involved. The last mention of Abishai[58] in 2 Samuel, outside the list in 23:8-39, is 20:6-7, where he appears as commander of the Cherethites and Pelethites. Ironically, this is an assignment that Benaiah had according to the record of David's cabinet officers in 8:18; 20:23. The Chronicler may also have been led to put Benaiah in charge of the Thirty because of 1 Chr 11:25: מן השלושים הנו נכבד הוא, which the NRSV translates as "he was renowned among the Thirty,"[59] but could eas-

ily be construed to mean "he was honored more than the Thirty."

and over his division was Ammizabad his son: This clause implies that when Benaiah became head of the Thirty, his position as leader of a monthly division was taken over by his son.[60] Since Benaiah continued his military service into the reign of Solomon, the author would not have thought Benaiah had died during the lifetime of David. Did the author have reliable historical information about the name of Benaiah's son, or has this name been constructed by him from the root זבד, as seems possible since two other new names in this list include this verbal root?[61]

■ **7** *Asahel the brother of Joab was fourth for the fourth month, and Zebadiah his son was after him:* Asahel's murder by Abner early in the reign of David (2 Sam 2:18-23) was one of the historical problems cited with this list under Structure above, since Asahel died before David had become king over the northern ten tribes.[62] The author of this passage takes account of this by providing a son, Zebadiah, to take his place as leader of a monthly division. Again the name of this son is formed from the root זבד.

■ **8** *the commander Shamhuth the Zerahite:* Unless the author had access to a different version of 1 Chr 11:27, he apparently replaced the obscure gentilic "the Harodite"[63] with one linking him to a prominent Judean family, Zerah (Gen 38:30; 46:12; Num 26:20).

■ **9** *Ira son of Ikkesh the Tekoite:* Ira's home town Tekoa (MR 170115, about ten miles south of Jerusalem) was in Judah and was also the birthplace of the prophet Amos.

■ **10** *Helez the Pelonite from the sons of Ephraim:* The meaning of the term "Pelonite" is unknown. The author takes advantage of this obscurity to attribute one of the monthly leaders to the Ephraimites (cf. v. 14). The

---

56 He is even credited with the execution of Joab (1 Kgs 2:33-34).

57 Or with Jehoiada, the high priest under Joash in 2 Chronicles 24. For הכהן הראש as the title of the high priest, see 2 Chr 19:11; 24:6, 11; 26:20; 31:10.

58 The usual spelling in Samuel.

59 So also my translation in chap. 11.

60 Johnstone, 1:267, surmises that Ammizabad's replacement of Benaiah may imply Benaiah's rise to take the place of Joab.

61 Zabdiel, v. 2, and Zebadiah, v. 7.

62 Japhet, 476, concedes that this is one of the weighti-

est arguments against the claim that this section is historically authentic. Asahel is mentioned among the descendants of Jesse in 1 Chr 2:16.

63 McCarter, *II Samuel*, 497, following Elliger and Dalman, connects "the Harodite" in 2 Sam 23:25 with a site a few miles southeast of Jerusalem.

apparently superior reading "the Paltite," in 2 Sam 23:26, would have connected Helez to the Calebites (1 Chr 2:47) and/or to the town of Beth-pelet in southern Judah (Josh 15:27).

■ **11** *Sibbecai the Hushathite of the Zerahites:* Hushah (MR 162124) is a city southwest of Bethlehem,[64] which has here been linked with the clan of Zerah.

■ **12** *Abiezer the Anathothite, from the Benjaminites:* Anathoth (MR 175135)[65] is the well-known town of the Benjaminites (Josh 21:17-18; 1 Chr 6:45 [60]), which permitted the author to make this tribal identification.

■ **13** *Maharai the Netophathite of the Zerahites:* Netophah (MR 171119) is located southeast of Bethlehem.[66] The author connected this site with Zerah (cf. 2:4, 6).

■ **14** *Benaiah the Pirathonite from the sons of Ephraim:* The only occurrence of Pirathon, outside this passage and its parallels in 2 Sam 23:30 and 1 Chr 11:31, is in Judg 12:15, where it is located in the land of Ephraim. The author therefore added a reference to the Ephraimites here.

■ **15** *Heldai the Netophathite, of Othniel:* Perhaps in order to distinguish this monthly commander from Maharai in v. 13, who also is called the Netophathite, the author assigned Heldai to a different clan of Judah, Othniel, a son of Kenaz, the younger brother of Caleb.[67]

27:16-24. Chief Officers of Tribes of Israel and Comment on Census

See the extensive comments under Structure above.

■ **16** *Eliezer son of Zichri was chief officer:* The title נגיד "chief officer," applied here to Eliezer[68] and implicitly to the following tribal leaders, is used elsewhere in Chronicles as a synonym for "king" (1 Chr 5:2; 11:2; 17:7; 28:4; 29:22; 2 Chr 6:5; 11:22), for officials of the temple (1 Chr 9:11; 2 Chr 31:13; 35:8), for a leader of the house

of Aaron (1 Chr 12:28 [27]), for financial officers (1 Chr 26:24; 2 Chr 31:12), for a governor of the house of Judah (2 Chr 19:11), for a commander of the palace (2 Chr 28:7), for the high priest (1 Chr 9:20), and in a generic sense (1 Chr 13:1; 2 Chr 11:11; 32:21).[69] The group of these chief officers together are called "leaders" or "officials" (שרי) of the tribes of Israel in v. 22. The tribal officials in Numbers 1 are known primarily by the title נשיא ("leader," 1:16, 44), but also as "heads of families" (1:4), the "chosen from the congregation" (1:16), and "heads of thousands" (1:16).

■ **17** *For Levi, Hashabiah the son of Kemuel:* Curtis and Madsen, 292, propose the possible identity of this Levite with the man mentioned in 1 Chr 26:30, who had the oversight over Israel west of the Jordan, but he is identified there as a Hebronite and hence probably a Judahite. No patronymic is given for the man in chap. 26.

■ **18** *For Judah, Elihu from the brothers of David:* Elihu and Zadok are the only names lacking patronyms in this list. Elihu could be an eighth son of Jesse (1 Sam 16:10-11; 17:12), whose name is not included among the other lists of Jesse's son (1 Sam 16:6-9; 17:13, 28; 2 Chr 11:18; and esp. 1 Chr 2:13-15). This name could also be a mistake for Eliab, otherwise known as the eldest son of Jesse, though this reading in the LXX may be an adjustment to the canonical information (see textual note 16); or Elihu may only be one of David's kinsmen, taking "brothers" in the wider sense (12:2, 30 [29]).[70]

■ **21** *Manasseh in Gilead:* Gilead can refer to all of Transjordan (Num 32:1, 26, 29) or only to the territory of the tribe of Manasseh/Machir (32:39-40).

■ **23** See the discussion under Structure above, where I established that vv. 23-24 were a secondary addition.

■ **24** *Wrath came upon Israel for this:* Cf. Johnstone, 1:270; 2 Chr 19:2, 10; 24:18; 29:8; 32:25-26.

---

64 See 1 Chr 11:29.

65 John L. Peterson, "Anathoth," *ABD* 1:227–28, locates the Iron Age city at Ras el-Kharrubeh.

66 See the discussion at 1 Chr 11:30. Cf. Ezra 2:22, which reports that fifty-six people returning from the exile hailed from Netophah. Netophah is relegated to Salmah the son of Hur in the genealogies (1 Chr 2:50, 54).

67 See the passages listed in n. 24.

68 Of the men listed in vv. 16-22, only Zadok is surely known. For Hashabiah and Elihu (the brother of David), see the commentary on vv. 17-18. Abner,

the father of Jaasiel (v. 21), is, of course, also known.

69 1 Chr 27:4 is secondary. See the textual note.

70 For Williamson, 176–77, the reference to David's brothers, instead of identifying the man by his father's name, shows that the author was drawing from a source.

and the number was not entered in the book of the Chronicles of King David: The phrase דברי הימים "Chronicles" is the same as the name of the book of Chronicles itself. While it occurs some thirty-eight times in the OT (e.g., 2 Kgs 12:20; 13:8, 12), this is its *only* use in the book of Chronicles itself aside from the title (but see 2 Chr 20:34;[71] 33:18[72]). Solomon is the first king for whom such records exist according to the Deuteronomistic History (1 Kgs 11:41). I suggested under Structure that the "book of the Chronicles of King David" may be an allusion to 1 Chronicles 21.

27:25-31. Twelve Supervisors of the King's Property

■ **25** *Over the king's treasuries was Azmaveth the son of Adiel:* The king's treasuries[73] listed here were probably located in Jerusalem as compared with the treasuries in towns and rural areas mentioned in v. 25b. This holds true regardless of how one evaluates the conjectural addition of "in the royal city" discussed in textual note 24. These treasuries may have dealt both with the king's estate and with collecting tax from the people, although taxation is not mentioned in David's reign in our sources. An Azmaveth from Bahurim (2 Sam 23:31)[74] was among David's warriors and may be the same person as this treasury supervisor. An Azmaveth was also a father of two of the Benjaminites, Jeziel and Pelet, who joined David at Hebron (1 Chr 12:3).

over the treasuries in the country, in the cities, in the villages, and in the towers was Jonathan the son of Uzziah: This person is otherwise unknown.[75] King Uzziah built towers in the wilderness (2 Chr 26:10) and Jotham built them in the wooded hills (27:4).

■ **26** *tilling the ground, was Ezri the son of Chelub:* Ezri,[76] also unknown, has a name that is an abbreviation for Azariah, just as Shimei is an abbrreviation for Shemaiah and Zabdi for Zebadiah in the next verse. A Judahite Chelub is also attested at 1 Chr 4:11.[77] For tilling the soil see David's instructions to Ziba about tilling the property of Saul for Mephibosheth (2 Sam 9:9-10).[78] It is not clear whether this tilling included the production of grain (so Johnstone, 1:271) in addition to the crops mentioned in the following two verses.

■ **27** *Over the vineyard workers was Shimei the Ramathite:* The hometown of this person could be Ramah in Benjamin (Josh 18:25; MR 172140) or Ramah of the Negeb (Josh 19:8; 1 Sam 30:27; MR 165068 or 138043[79]). Ramah in Benjamin seems more likely a place for a vintner.

over the wine cellars was Zabdi the Shiphmite: In the 1959 and 1960 excavations at el-Jib (Gibeon; MR 167139), sixty-three cellars were found for the storage of wine. The excavator estimated that these cellars would have provided storage space for jars containing ninety thousand liters of wine. They are apparently to be dated to the eighth and seventh centuries BCE.[80] In this and the following verse there is a supervisor both for the agricultural workers and for the storage of the product itself. Curtis and Madsen, 293, propose that Zabdi's gentilic "Shiphmite" (השפמי) may refer either to Shepham (שפם; Num 34:10-11), which seems too far north,[81] or to Siphmoth (שפמות) in the Negeb of Judah (1 Sam 30:28), though the sibilant in the latter case does not match.

■ **28** *over the olive and sycamore trees in the Shephelah was Baal-hanan the Gederite:* The excavators at Tel Miqne

---

71 בדברי יהוא . . . על ספר מלכי ישראל "in the acts of Jehu . . . in the book of the kings of Israel."

72 על דברי מלכי ישראל "in the acts of the kings of Israel."

73 A Masoretic note in the margin of the Hebrew Bible observes that this is the halfway point in terms of verses in the books of Chronicles (882.5 of 1,765). The middle in terms of words is approximately in 2 Chronicles 5 (Johnstone, 1:270).

74 Cf. 1 Chr 11:33 "Bahurum." For the location of this town in Benjamin, between Gibeah and Jerusalem, see 1 Chr 11:33.

75 In addition to the well-known King Uzziah (see 2 Chronicles 26), the Chronicler also refers to an Uzziah as a descendant of Kohath through Izhar,

who is the father of Shaul (1 Chr 6:9 [24]).

76 See the epithet עזרי "my help" used of God in the Psalms (70:6 [5]; 121:1-2).

77 Cf. Chelubai at 1 Chr 2:9 (LXX "Caleb") and Caleb at 1 Chr 2:18-24 and 42-55, both of whom may be the same as Chelub.

78 Cf. Gen 2:5, 25; 3:23; 4:2, 12.

79 See Klein, *1 Samuel*, 284.

80 James B. Pritchard, "Gibeon," *EAEHL* 2:512.

81 Some unknown site on the Upper Orontes (Sidnie Ann White, *ABD* 5:1203).

(Ekron), on the western edge of the inner coastal plain, have found evidence for massive production of olive oil in the seventh century, making it the largest olive-oil industrial center in the ancient Near East, producing at least one thousand tons of olive oil annually.[82] Sycamore trees are not the sycamore known in the United States, but the sycamore fig tree *ficus sycomorus L.* Oded Borowski proposes that the sycamore groves in the time of David were maintained for timber rather than for their figs, since they latter were mainly consumed by the poor.[83] The production of abundant sycamore trees in the Shephelah was proverbial (1 Kgs 10:27//2 Chr 1:15 and 9:27). Geder's location is disputed. Its proximity to Debir in Josh 12:13 might place it in the southern Judean foothills or Shephelah, while Josh 12:14 might suggest a location closer to the Negeb desert. Na'aman proposed Khirbet Jedur (MR 158115), between Bethlehem and Hebron.[84] If we follow the LXX and read Gedorite (see textual note 27), Gedor might be located as a district or suburb of Gibeon (167139).[85]

over the stores of oil was Joash: Since this official lacks a patronym, it is impossible to identify him. The name Joash is used for eight different people in the OT.[86] Rehoboam later put "stores of food, oil, and wine" in the fortresses he constructed (2 Chr 11:11).

■ **29** *Over the cattle grazing in Sharon was Shitrai the Sharonite:* A passage in Isaiah (65:10) promises that the plain of Sharon will be a place for flocks (of sheep and goats?) to pasture. Harry R. Weeks proposes that "Sharonite" meant not only a person from the plain of Sharon, but it intimates that people from this area in general were good at animal husbandry.[87] Shitrai is one of seven individuals identified with a gentilic rather than a patronym.

over the cattle in the valleys was Shaphat the son of Adlai: No specific valley is mentioned, but Rudolph, 183,

relates it to the plain of Jezreel. Adlai is otherwise unknown.[88]

■ **30** *Over the camels was Obil the Ishmaelite:* The presence of an Ishmaelite[89] in this verse and of a Hagrite in the next may be signs of relative antiquity, since such foreigners would not likely be included in a late or fictionalized list. Curtis and Madsen, 293, and many other commentators, however, have parsed "Obil" (אוביל) as "camel driver" or "camel manager" and related it to the Arabic word *ābil.* For Curtis and Madsen this pointed to the artificial character of the list.

over the she-asses was Jehdeiah the Meronothite: A man by the name of Jadon the Meronothite is associated with the men of Gibeon and Mizpah in the building of the wall under Nehemiah (Neh 3:7). Jehdeiah, a Levite, appears in 1 Chr 24:20.

■ **31** *Over the flocks was Jaziz the Hagrite:* The Hagrites were tent-dwelling people living east of Gilead, who had conflicts with the tribes of Reuben and Gad.[90] The name derives from Hagar, the maternal ancestor of the Ishmaelites (cf. v. 30).

in charge of King David's property: Borowski suggests that such land could have been acquired in six ways: military conquest (2 Sam 5:7, 9; 8:2, 6, 14; 10:19), taking possession of vacant land (2 Kgs 8:1-6), purchase (1 Chr 21:22-24), trading other commodities for it (1 Kgs 9:11-14), receiving either land or cities as presents (1 Sam 27:5-10), confiscating land from domestic enemies charged with treason (2 Sam 9:7), or confiscating it for no good reason (1 Sam 8:12-17).[91]

27:32-34. Seven Advisors or Associates of David[92]

■ **32** *Jonathan the uncle/kinsman of David was a counselor:* If Jonathan was in fact David's uncle, as a literal translation of דוד would suggest, he would have been the

---

82 Trude Dothan and Seymour Gitin, "Miqne, Tel (Ekron)," *EAEHL* 3:1057–58.

83 Oded Borowski, *Agriculture in Iron Age Israel* (Winona Lake, IN: Eisenbrauns, 1987) 128. He also notes that Solomon ignored this source of timber and preferred to bring cedarwood from Lebanon.

84 See Carl S. Ehrlich, "Geder," *ABD* 2:924–25.

85 See ibid., 925, where Ehrlich calls attention to the name *gdr* or *gdd* on the jar handles from Gibeon. See also Gederah in 1 Chr 12:5 (4).

86 Linda S. Shearing, "Joash," *ABD* 3:855–58.

87 Harry R. Weeks, "Sharon," *ABD* 5:1161–63.

88 Adlai E. Stevenson was the Democratic presidential candidate in the United States in 1952 and 1956, and both his father and son, who were also politicians, bore this biblical name.

89 Gen 37:25-28; 39:1; Judg 8:24; 2 Sam 17:25; Ps 83:7 (6); 1 Chr 2:17.

90 See 1 Chr 5:10, 19-21; 11:38; Ps 83:7 (6).

91 See Borowski, *Agriculture,* 27.

92 Johnstone, 1:272, notes the striking absence of the official known as "recorder" or "herald" (מזכיר; 1 Chr 18:15).

brother of Jesse or of Jesse's wife. If the word means more generally a relative or kinsman,[93] however, this Jonathan could be David's nephew, the son of Shimea (שמעא), David's brother, who killed a giant with twenty-four fingers and toes (1 Chr 20:7//2 Sam 21:21). Jonathan could also be the brother of Jonadab, the son of Shimeah (שמעה), David's brother, who assisted Amnon in his plans to rape Tamar (2 Sam 13:3). Curtis and Madsen, 294, translate as "lover" and believe that the Chronicler was here alluding to Jonathan, the son of Saul.[94] But since Jonathan died with his father in the battle of Gilboa, he would not have been a counselor to David during his actual kingship. For "counselor" see Isa 40:13.[95]

a man of discernment and a scribe: Jonadab, the putative brother of Jonathan (see the previous paragraph), is called an exceedingly wise or clever man (חכם), and so Jonathan himself is deemed a man of discernment.[96] Shavsha is named as a scribe in the list of David's officers (1 Chr 18:16//2 Sam 8:17; cf. 2 Sam 20:25), Elihoreph and Ahijah are scribes in the list of Solomon's officers (1 Kgs 4:3), and other scribes of the king appear later in Chronicles (2 Chr 24:11; 26:11; 34:18).

Jehiel the son of Hachmoni took care of the king's sons: In 1 Chr 11:11 Ishbaal/Jashobeam, one of David's warriors, is described as the son of a Hachmonite. If this Hachmoni is the same person named in v. 32, Ishbaal/Jashobeam and Jehiel were brothers.[97] The translation "took care of" is paraphrastic, since it represents the Hebrew preposition "with" (עם). Jehiel may have been their tutor, their counselor,[98] their companion, or their guardian. References to the "king's sons" could refer to the literal sons of the king or it could imply an administrative function or office performed by various members of the royal family.[99] Nineteen epigraphic references to "the king's son" (always in the singular) have also been discovered.[100]

■ **33** *Ahithophel was a counselor to the king:* This man is well known, since he switched from being David's counselor (2 Sam 15:12) to a counselor of Absalom during the latter's revolt against David, and he urged Absalom to sleep with David's concubines (16:21-23) and attack David quickly (17:1-3). His advice was opposed by Hushai the Archite, who was secretly representing David even as he offered advice to Absalom. Hushai urged Absalom to muster all Israel from Dan to Beer-sheba before attacking (17:8-13). When Ahithophel saw that his counsel had not been followed, he hanged himself. There is no trace of this dispute in this verse. See also the note on Jehoiada, the successor of Ahithophel, in the next verse.

Hushai the Archite was the king's friend: The Archites occupied territory west of Bethel (Josh 16:2). When Hushai (cf. 2 Sam 15:32, 37) supposedly defected to Absalom, though in fact he remained loyal to David, he told Absalom, "Long live the king," referring ostensibly to Absalom, although ironically he could have intended David by his remark (2 Sam 16:16). He is called "David's friend" in this verse, and in v. 17 Absalom asks, "Is this your loyalty to your friend? Why did you not go with your friend?"[101] Several scholars have proposed that the title "the king's friend" is more formal than might

---

93   Cf. Amos 6:10.

94   They believe that the translation "lover" is justified by 1 Sam 18:1, 3; 20:41-42; 2 Sam 1:16.

95   Cf. R. N. Whybray, *The Heavenly Counsellor in Isaiah xl 13–14* (SOTSMS 1; Sheffield: Sheffield Academic Press, 1989), *passim*.

96   Cf. 2 Chr 26:5; 34:12.

97   But see discussion of v. 2 above, where Jashobeam is described as the son of Zabdiel.

98   Cf. the elders who had stood before Solomon, Rehoboam's father, and the youths who stood before Rehoboam himself, both of whom offered advice to the new king (1 Kgs 12:6, 8).

99   Cf. the commentary on 1 Chr 18:17//2 Sam 8:18 and the sons of Athaliah in 2 Chr 24:7. Y. Avishur and M. Heltzer, *Studies on the Royal Administration in Ancient Israel in the Light of Epigraphic Sources* (Tel Aviv and Jaffa: Archaeological Center Publication, 2000) 62–74. Avishur and Heltzer refer to a man named Qanāma, who was responsible for the sons of Jehoiachin when they were prisoners in Babylon. They also argue against G. Brin, who held that the title was primarily an administrative one without implying a biological relationship to the dynasty.

100 See the list in Nahman Avigad, *Corpus of West Semitic Stamp Seals* (rev. Benjamin Sass; Jerusalem: Israel Academy of Sciences and Humanities, 1997) 467.

101 Cf. 2 Sam 15:32 LXX and 15:37, where Hushai is called David's friend. In 1 Kgs 1:8 LXX^L and Josephus construe the name Rei רעי as "his friend(s)."

appear on first reading. Early on it represented a court title, but later was connected with an official duty, probably as a counselor to the king.[102] Hence the titles for the contemporaries Ahithophel and Hushai are synonyms. Donner claimed that the corresponding Egyptian office of "friend" was *śmr*.[103] Mettinger showed that this parallel is inappropriate since the Egyptian word does not mean "friend," and he offered the Egyptian title *rḫ-nśw.t* ("king's acquaintance") as a more appropriate parallel.[104] He noted, however, that this title was used for several persons in Egypt at one time and it was used at court for persons of fairly low rank. He cited an Amarna letter as a possible parallel (EA 288:11), where the king of Jerusalem presents himself to the pharaoh as the *ru-ḫi šarri*, in which the first word could stand for *rḫ-nśw.t* or a translation for Heb. רֵעֶה, which Mettinger takes as a synonym for רֵעֶה "friend." In the list of Solomon's officers, Zabud is called a priest and king's friend (1 Kgs 4:5). This title is not used after Solomon but was superseded by the word יוֹעֵץ "counselor."

■ **34** *After Ahithophel there came Jehoiada the son of Benaiah:* This verse presupposes the death of Ahithophel and his replacement by another counselor, showing that the list had been updated, as would be appropriate for its position in Chronicles, late in the reign of David,[105] and hence that Ahithophel and Jehoiada did not serve at the same time.[106] The figure of Jehoiada, however, presents his own difficulties.[107] Benaiah the son of Jehoiada is mentioned as the commander of the third month in vv. 5-6 above, and his father is identified, falsely in my judgment, as the high priest Jehoiada (see 12:28 [27], where Jehoiada is called "leader of the house of Aaron,"[108] and the commentary above). The Jehoiada mentioned in v. 34 could be the son of the Benaiah mentioned in vv. 5-6 so that he was named after his grand-

father (papponomy) in a genealogy we might call Sequence I: Jehoiada I (the "high priest")—Benaiah (vv. 5-6)—Jehoiada II (the man in v. 34). Alternately, the Jehoiada of v. 34 could be the father of the Benaiah in vv. 5-6, so that three generations in Sequence II were named successively Benaiah I—Jehoiada (the man in this verse), and Benaiah II (the man in vv. 5-6). Benaiah the commander of the Cherethites and Pelethites in 1 Chr 18:17//2 Sam 8:18 would be the same as the Benaiah of Sequence I or the same as Benaiah II of Sequence II.

and Abiathar: Abiathar escaped from the slaughter of the priests of Nob and joined forces with David as one of his priests (1 Sam 22:20-22). He and Zadok are named as David's priests in 2 Sam 20:25. Because of the textual confusion engendered by 2 Sam 8:17/1 Chr 18:16, Ahimelech is usually listed by the Chronicler as the second priest who served with Zadok under David (1 Chr 18:16; 24:3, 6), but there is one exception, where Abiathar does play a role even in Chronicles (15:11).[109]

The commander of the king's army was Joab: There is no difficulty with the historical accuracy of this statement, but some scholars (e.g., Rudolph, 185; Williamson, 178; and Mettinger, *Solomonic State Officials,* 9), believe that this notice is secondary since the other people mentioned in these verses are only influential counselors, with a close personal relationship to the king, but not holders of specific state offices under David. This reflects an interpretation of 2 Sam 8:16//1 Chr 18:15 and 2 Sam 20:23 as an official list of officers, whereas 1 Chr 27:32-34 is taken as a list of influential persons or personal staff in the immediate entourage of the king. But Abiathar appears in the second list of officials in 2 Sam 20:25, and it is only because of textual error in the first list that he is listed as the father of Ahimelech (2 Sam 8:17//1 Chr 18:16) instead of his son. It seems

---

102 Mettinger, *Solomonic State Officials,* 69.

103 Herbert Donner, "Der 'Freund des Königs,'" *ZAW* 73 (1961) 269–77. Earlier A. van Selms, "The Origin of the Title 'The King's Friend,'" *JNES* 16 (1957) 118–23, proposed that the king's friend was the king's best man, active at royal weddings. For a critique see Mettinger, *Solomonic State Officials,* 64–65.

104 *Solomonic State Officials,* 63–69.

105 Myers, 1:186.

106 Hence it is inappropriate to talk about seven officials in this list, since at most six served at one time.

Japhet's question, 480, about a possible parallel with the seven counselors of the Persians seems to be moot.

107 Bertheau thought this was a mistake and read "Benaiah the son of Jehoiada." Curtis and Madsen, 295, however, opposed this.

108 Jehoiada's father's name is not given in this verse.

109 Apparently overlooked by Japhet, 480, who affirms that Abiathar plays no role whatsover in Chronicles and that therefore the role of Abiathar as counselor is devoid of historical value.

to me that if Joab is secondary in v. 34, Abiathar would be secondary here as well. The problem may lie with the presuppositions of the commentators, not with the secondary development of the text.

Conclusion

The four administrative lists in this chapter provide a picture of the secular administration of David's kingdom. Although I believe most of this chapter can be attributed to the Chronicler himself, that conclusion is by no means certain. The first list (vv. 1-15) provides the names of twenty-four military heroes (cf. 11:10-31), who were in charge of twelve monthly military divisions, each consisting of twenty-four thousand men. A second list (vv. 16-21) names the chief officers of each of the twelve tribes of Israel, although the selection of the tribes and the order in which they are listed are unusual. A third list (vv. 25-31) identifies twelve supervisors over the king's property, two of whom supervised treasuries while the rest dealt with the raising and storing of crops and the tending of livestock. A final list (vv. 32-34) names advisors or associates of David. The third and fourth list may well come from the time of David, but that is surely not true for the first list, and probably not true for the second.

Two verses, 23-24, are judged to be clearly secondary. These verses have a far different interpretation of the census taken by David in chap. 21. This paragraph removes the guilt from David and blames Joab for the wrath Israel experienced from this census since he began the census but did not finish the count. The reverence that Joab showed for God's will in 21:3 is credited to David in 27:24.

28

Translation

1/ David assembled to Jerusalem all the leaders of Israel—the leaders of the tribes,[1] the leaders of the divisions that served the king, the commanders of the thousands, the commanders of the hundreds, the stewards of all the property and cattle of the king, and his sons,[2] together with the eunuchs and the mighty warriors—and all the men of substance. 2/ King David stood on his feet[3] and said,

"Listen to me, my brothers and my people. I had it in my heart[4] to build a house of rest for the ark of the covenant of Yahweh and for the footstool of the feet of our God, and I had made preparations for building. 3/ But God said to me, 'You shall not build a house for my name, because you are a man of wars; you have shed blood.' 4/ Yahweh the God of Israel had chosen me from all my father's house to be king over Israel forever. For he chose Judah to be leader, and within the house of Judah the house of my father, and among the sons of my father he took pleasure in me to make me king over all Israel. 5/ And from all my sons—for Yahweh has given to me many sons—he has chosen Solomon my son to sit on the throne of the kingdom of Yahweh over Israel. 6/ He said to me, 'Solomon, your son—he will build my house and my courts,[5] for I have chosen him to be my son, and I will be his father. 7/ I will establish his kingdom forever if he is resolute in keeping my commandments and my judgments, as at this day.' 8/ And now in the sight of all the assembly of Yahweh,[6] and in the hearing of our God, [I say] keep[7] and seek all[8] the commandments of Yahweh your God so that you may possess the good land and leave it as an inheritance[9] to your children after you forever. 9/ And you,[10] my son Solomon, acknowledge the God of your father[11] and serve him with a perfect heart and a willing spirit, for Yahweh searches longingly all hearts and understands every motive behind thoughts. If you seek him, he will be found by you, but if you abandon him, he will cast you off forever. 10/ See now that Yahweh has chosen you to build a house for him[12] as a sanctuary. Be strong and do it."

11/ David gave to his son Solomon the plan of the vestibule and its rooms,[13] its treasuries, its upper rooms, and its inner chambers, and of the room of the mercy seat; 12/ and the plan of everything that he had in mind:[14] for the courts of the house of Yahweh and for all the surrounding chambers; for the treasuries of the house of God; for the treasuries of the dedicated gifts; 13/ for the divisions of the priests and the Levites and for all the work of the service of the house of Yahweh; for all

1 השבטים; LXX "judges" (השפטים).

2 That is, David's sons were among those assembled in Jerusalem. Cf. Braun, 265; and Curtis and Madsen, 296. Others, including *NRSV* and *NIV,* make the property and cattle jointly owned by the king and his sons. See the commentary.

3 על רגליו; LXX "in the middle of the assembly."

4 אני היה עם לבבי. Cf. 1 Chr 22:7 אני עם לבבי.

5 וחצרותי; LXX(with the exception of L) "my court" (וחצרתי).

6 כל ישראל קהל יהוה, with LXX; MT כל קהל יהוה "all Israel, the assembly of Yahweh."

7 ובאוני אלהינו שמרו; missing in LXX[B] because a copyist skipped from one καί to the next one and left out everything in between.

8 Lacking in two LXX MSS. πάσας τάς became τάς.

9 והנחלתם; missing in some LXX MSS because a scribe's eye skipped from end of the first to the end of the last of the following words: ἀγαθὴν καὶ κατακληρονομήσητε αὐτήν.

10 ואתה; LXX "and now" (ועתה). Braun, 266, follows LXX, arguing that the change to the MT reading was precipitated by what he judges to be the secondary insertion of v. 8, which also begins "and now."

11 אביך; LXX reads the pl. "fathers" (אבותיך). Perhaps this is a change made by the translator.

12 לו, with LXX; lacking in MT by homoioarchton before למקדש.

13 בתיו; *BHS* emends to תבנית הבית "the plan for the house." Cf. Dirksen, "1 Chronicles xxviii 11-18: Its Textual Development," *VT* 46 (1996) 429. But why would the Chronicler mention a portion of the house (vestibule) and the whole house in that order?

14 For the translation see the commentary.

15 לכל כלי הזהב במשקל זהב with *BHS,* to conform with the description of the weight of the silver vessels in the second half of the verse; MT לזהב במשקל לזהב.

16 הכסף. Rudolph, 186, and *BHS* add כסף after הכסף here and in vv. 15 and 17. But perhaps the Hebrew writer assumed that readers would supply this word as they read.

17 ולמנרות הזהב, with Rudolph, 186, and Rothstein, 497; MT ומשקל למנרות הזהב "and the weight for the golden lampstands."

18 See v. 14, textual note 16.

19 במשקל למנורה ומנורה with *BHS;* MT במשקל למנורה ומנרה.

20 במשקל instead of MT משקל. The initial ב was lost by haplography after the preceding word ואת הזהב, as noted by Rothstein, 497, and Rudolph, 186.

21 "The weight of" is to be supplied by the reader, or the word משקל was accidentally lost from the Hebrew text.

22 זהב "of gold" is to be supplied by the reader, or it was accidentally lost from the Hebrew text.

515

the vessels of the service of the house of Yahweh— 14/ the weight of gold for all the golden vessels[15] for each kind of service; the weight of silver[16] for all the silver vessels for each kind of service; 15/ for the golden lampstands[17] and their lamps, the weight of gold for each lampstand and its lamps; and for the silver lampstands the weight of silver[18] for each lampstand[19] and its lamps, according to the use of each lampstand in the service; 16/ the weight[20] of gold for each table for the rows of bread; the weight of[21] silver for the silver tables; 17/ and pure gold for the forks, the basins, and the cups; for the golden bowls the weight of gold[22] for each bowl; for the silver bowls the weight of silver[23] for each bowl; 18/ and the weight in refined gold for the altar of incense—and the plan[24] of the chariot,[25] that is, the cherubim of gold (which spread out [their wings][26] and covered the ark of the covenant of Yahweh).[27] 19/ All this was in a document—since the hand of Yahweh was upon him[28]—that[29] made clear all the details of the plan.

20/ David also said to his son Solomon, "Be strong and of good courage, and act. Do not be afraid or dismayed; for Yahweh[30] my God is with you. He will not fail or forsake you until all the work for the service of the house of Yahweh is finished.[31] 21/ Here are the divisions of the priests and the Levites for all the service of the house of God; and with you in all the work will be every volunteer who has skill for every kind of service;[32] also the officers and all the people will be completely at your command."

23 כֶסֶף "of silver" to be supplied by the reader or was accidentally lost from the Hebrew text.

24 ולהבנית. Rudolph, 188, suggests a translation of "form" rather than "plan," as in vv. 11-12. A translation of "structure" or "frame" is also possible.

25 המרכבה is in the absolute state, which makes the translation of *NRSV* impossible: "the golden chariot *of* the cherubim."

26 Insert כנפים with *BHS*; or is this word to be supplied by the reader?

27 Rudolph, 188, judges the parenthesis to be a secondary addition from 2 Chr 5:8 or 1 Kgs 8:7 (which uses the verb סכך), since it is separated in Hebrew by the word "gold" from its antecedent, "cherubim," and because the words in parenthesis are introduced by a *lāmed* (לפרשים).

28 עליו with LXX, referring to David. MT עלי "to me," also referring to David. The MT could be interpreted either as "since Yahweh's hand was upon me," much like my translation above, or, if Yahweh is the subject of השכיל (see the next note), as "Yahweh made clear to me all that was in the document from the hand of Yahweh." In my translation this verse completes the paragraph begun at v. 11. If one follows MT, the verse becomes a saying of David referring back to vv. 11-18. For an extensive discussion see Rothstein, 503–6. Julius A. Bewer, "Textkritische Bemerkungen zum Alten Testament," in *FS Alfred Bertholet zum 80. Geburtstag* (ed. Walter Baumgartner et al.; Tübingen: Mohr [Siebeck], 1950) 75–76, adopts the reading עליו but notes that על after the verb שכל always refers to content and not to a person. Bewer interprets the verse as follows: "All this was in a writing from the hand of Yahweh, on the basis of which (עליו) he (David) had exact knowledge about all the works of the plan." Rudolph, 188, however, calls attention to the connection of עליו with "the hand of Yahweh" in Ezra 7:6.

29 Cf. Rudolph, 188; Braun, 267. Braun appealed to the additional words, "David gave to Solomon," in the LXX that follow "the hand of Yahweh," and made David the subject of השכיל ("made clear") and made עליו refer to Solomon: "He (David) taught him (Solomon) everything in a writing from the hand of Yahweh." Curtis and Madsen, 300, and many others identify the subject of the verb as Yahweh.

30 יהוה, with LXX; MT adds אלהים.

31 LXX adds many words similar to vv. 11-12a: "The pattern of the temple, and its house, and its treasury, and the upper chambers, and the inner storerooms, and the place of propitiation, and the plan of the house of the Lord." This might have dropped out by homoioteleuton (Curtis and Madsen, 300),

but it is more likely a correction meant to harmonize the completion of the building project with the details of v. 11. Cf. Rudolph, 188, against Rothstein, 506–7, who equivocates on whether the LXX reading is original.

32   Braun, 267, cites parallels in Exod 35:5, 10.

Structure

After the long excursus in chaps. 23–27 in which David appointed priests, Levites, gatekeepers, and other officials, the Chronicler provides the final speeches of David before his death in chaps. 28–29. While Curtis and Madsen, 296, detected some correlations between David's speech at the completion of his temple preparations in 29:10-19 and Solomon's prayer at the dedication of the temple (1 Kgs 8:22-53), it is striking to see how little of the account of David's final days in 1 Kings 1–2 is represented in 1 Chronicles 28–29. I note only the way 1 Kgs 2:11 is taken up and changed in 1 Chr 29:26-27, and the ways in which 1 Kgs 2:2-4 is echoed in this chapter in David's speech to Solomon.[1] The people play a minor role in 1 Kings 1–2 but are the center of attention in 1 Chronicles 28–29. Japhet, 483, notes that the Chronicler puts the loyalty of the people at Solomon's disposal in these chapters and that Solomon himself does or says nothing in these chapters.

The present chapter may be outlined as follows:[2]

I.   28:1-2aα. Introduction to David's speeches.
II. 28:2aβ-10. David's address to officials. Within this address there are citations of divine oracles in vv. 3aβ-b and in 6aβ-7 and a direct address to Solomon in vv. 9-10.
III. 28:11-19. David's provision of the plan for the temple and related items (vv. 11-13, 18a) and his gift of gold and silver for the furnishings of the temple (vv. 14-18a).[3] Verse 19 indicates that the plan was written and was given by the hand of Yahweh.
IV. 28:20-21. David's third speech to Solomon (cf. the first in 22:6-16 and the second in 28:9-10).

As with the preceding chapters, there have been many attempts to identify secondary passages in this chapter. The references to various categories of officials in v. 1, for example, are closely correlated with the sections of chap. 27 (see the commentary), and if these sections of chap. 27 are secondary, which I doubt, so also are the references to them in this verse.

Other proposed secondary additions are also not convincing to me. Braun, 268, following Rothstein, 495, 499, identified vv. 4-5 as secondary, noting the concern with Solomon as a king rather than as temple builder in these verses, the reference to the election of Judah, the unusual use of the word רצה ("he took pleasure"), and the lengthy technical expression "the throne of the kingdom of Yahweh over Israel." Braun also calls attention to the way these verses break "the connection between vv 6 and 10" (*sic;* he apparently meant vv. 3 and 6). None of these reasons is compelling, however, and while we as modern editors might think that vv. 3 and 6 should be joined immediately together, the Chronicler may have wanted to give special emphasis to the election of David

---

1   See the commentary on vv. 7, 9, and 20.
2   M. Patrick Graham, "A Character Ethics Reading of 1 Chronicles 29:1-25," in *Character and Scripture* (ed. W. P. Brown; Grand Rapids: Eerdmans, 2002) 98–120, detects a chiastic arrangement in chaps. 28–29: (A) 28:1, report that David assembles people in Jerusalem; (B) 28:2-10, speech of David to the assembly and then to Solomon; (C) 28:11-19, report that David gave the temple plan to Solomon; (D) 28:20-21, speech of David that exhorts Solomon to build the temple and promises the people's help;

(D′) 29:1-5, speech of David to the assembly; (C′) 29:6-9, report of the people's generous response; (B′) 29:10-19, prayer of David; (A′) 29:20-25, report of the people's response. Throntveit, *When Kings Speak*, 45–47, classifies chap. 28 as an "oration."

3   See textual note 28 to v. 19. If one follows MT in that verse, v. 19 becomes a speech of David referring to vv. 11-18.

and Solomon, before dealing with Yahweh's choice of Solomon to build the temple and the father-son relationship of David and Solomon in the divine oracle of v. 6.

Braun, 268–69, labels as secondary all of v. 8, and Rudolph, 184, rejects most of it.[4] They follow Rothstein, 496, 500, in seeing a close connection between vv. 7 and 9, proposing that a secondary hand applied to the leaders of the people the moral expectations given to Solomon in v. 9. While the opening part of this verse is awkward (elliptical in Japhet's view, 490), there is no necessity to excise the admonition to the people in this verse even if in our own judgment David should have kept his attention focused on his son Solomon.

Finally, Rudolph, 185, and Braun, 269, consider vv. 14-18 as secondary. In this connection, Rudolph also labels vv. 12b-13a as secondary, while Braun wants to excise "12ab" (read: 12aβ-b) and "13b." Braun's reasons for deleting v. 13b depend on a prior conclusion that all references to temple vessels are secondary in this chapter. Rudolph's decision on vv. 12-13 seems to depend on v. 12aα being construed as a climactic summary statement and v. 13b being filled in from 26:20b. Verse 13a was offensive to Rudolph because of the isolated references to the priests and the Levites.[5] Rudolph's objection to vv. 14-18 stems from their detailed description of the (minor) temple vessels compared with the relatively brief references given to the temple itself and related items in vv. 11, 12a, and 13b. He also takes exception to the reference to the weight of the precious metals in vv. 14-18, a reference that is not necessary to describe their "plan."[6] Ackroyd, however, has shown the profound importance of the theme of the temple vessels as demonstrating a clear continuity between the first and the second temples,[7] and this may well account for the extended discussion devoted to them here.

Piet B. Dirksen has brought new arguments for the secondary character of vv. 14-18a and, in his judgment, probably also of vv. 12b-13.[8] He argues that the items in these secondary verses cannot be fitted under a building design (תבנית), but he retains v. 18b as part of the divinely revealed "plan" only by arbitrarily deleting the word "gold" (p. 435). He credits these supplementary verses to the same hand who, in his judgment, added 15:4-10, 17-18, 24b, and 23:2–27:34. Dirksen believes that this redactor had a predilection for cultic details and clear lines of demarcation among temple personnel (p. 434).

Since there is no manuscript evidence supporting these claims,[9] and since most of the arguments depend on imposing upon the Chronicler a consistency and a logical arrangement of materials that may have been foreign to him, it seems best to interpret the text as it stands, in full awareness that the Hebrew syntax sometimes seems awkward to us. If we can detect a measure of cohesion or coherence to the text, as I will argue in the commentary section, it seems quite arbitrary to create our vision of a better writing style by arbitrarily eliminating various Hebrew words, sentences, or verses. The materials in vv. 12b-18a do not seem to be of such compelling urgency that would lead a secondary hand to add them. This seems especially true for the silver lampstands and silver tables in vv. 15-16, which are mentioned nowhere else in the Bible.

Detailed Commentary

28:1-2aα. Introduction to David's Speech

■ 1 *David assembled:* Many commentators have noted how this verse picks up the basic content of 23:2 after the lengthy, excursus-like lists that we have been discussing

---

4   He keeps—and emends (see *BHS*, note 8[a])—only v. 28aα.

5   For the same reason, Rudolph, 185, holds v. 21a to be secondary, since it provides a link to chaps. 23–26.

6   Rudolph, 189, considers these verses an inept anticipation of 1 Chr 29:2.

7   Peter C. Ackroyd, "The Temple Vessels—a Continuity Theme," in *Studies in the Religion of Ancient Israel* (VTSup 23; Leiden: Brill, 1972) 166–81.

8   Piet B. Dirksen, "1 Chronicles xxviii 11-18: Its Textual Development," *VT* 46 (1996) 429–38.

9   Both Braun, 269, and Rudolph, 185, note the abbreviating tendencies in the versions in vv. 14-18, but these omissions may reflect nothing more than that the ancient translators experienced some of the same difficulties with the Hebrew text that we do.

in chaps. 23–27. But the makeup of the two assemblies differs—the priests and Levites are notably not among those convened in this verse[10]—and even the verbs used to describe David's convening of the assembly are different: אסף in 23:2 and קהל here.[11] Williamson, 179, identifies this verse as a *Wiederaufnahme* (repetitive resumption of the narrative), a literary device that allows the inclusion of material relevant to the author's main purpose, but that does not precisely fit in his narrative sequence.[12] Japhet, 486, proposes that David gathered two main groups in this verse: "all the leaders of Israel" and "all the men of substance." The rest of the groups are to be considered as subsets of the leaders of Israel. The description of the makeup of the assembly is the most detailed in all of Chronicles.

the leaders of the tribes: Compare 27:16-22.

the leaders of the divisions that served the king: Compare 27:2-15.

the commanders of the thousands, the commanders of the hundreds: Compare 27:1. "Commanders" here and "stewards" in the next group are translations of the same Hebrew word, שׂרי, which was translated "leaders" in the first two groups.

the stewards of all the property and cattle of the king: Compare 27:25-31, where the word "property" (רכוש) is explicitly mentioned in v. 31.[13]

and his sons, together with the eunuchs: The king's sons are certainly in place at this assembly (Curtis and Madsen, 296–97, citing 1 Kgs 1:9, 19, 25); as already noted, "and his sons" should not be read with the previous phrase, which would make them joint owners of the property and cattle of the king (see textual note 2). Both *NRSV* and *NIV* translate סריסים as "palace officials." The word is used elsewhere in Chronicles only in 2 Chr 18:8, where it is taken over from the *Vorlage* in 1 Kgs 22:9.[14] All eight references to סריסים in Kings are translated

"eunuchs" in LXX. This translation seems to be supported by 2 Kgs 9:32 (referring to the eunuchs attending Queen Jezebel); 20:19 (Israelite prisoners who become eunuchs to the king in Babylon); and 24:15 (where they are mentioned right after the king's wives). The reference to an individual סריס in charge of the fighting men (25:19) might support a more generic translation.

all the men of substance: This designation (גבור חיל) is used in Chronicles for distinguished military leaders or for fighting men themselves.[15]

■ **2aα** *King David stood on his feet:* In the Chronicler's account, the aged David (1 Chr 23:1) is much more vigorous than the feeble and even impotent David of 1 Kgs 1:1-4. Like Moses, David was vigorous to the end (Deut 34:7).

28:2aβ-10. David's Address to Officials

■ **2aβ** *"Listen to me":* This call to attention is found in other speeches by kings and prophets (cf. 2 Chr 13:4; 15:2; 20:20; 28:11; 29:5).

"my brothers and my people": This is the only use of this form of address in Chronicles. According to Deut 17:15, 20, the king was to be chosen from "among your brothers." Compare 1 Sam 30:23; 2 Sam 19:13 (12). For "my people" see 1 Chr 29:14; 2 Chr 18:3. The other twelve references to "my people" in Chronicles are from the mouth of God.[16]

"I had it in my heart to build": Compare 1 Chr 22:7, David's private speech to Solomon. The idea itself harks back in turn to 17:1, where David contrasted his own house of cedar with the tent in which the ark of the covenant was housed.

"a house of rest for the ark of the covenant of Yahweh": This phrase is unique in the Bible, though the use of "house of rest" in the Tg to Deut 12:9 shows that it reflects linguistic usage in the postexilic period.[17] The

---

10 They are mentioned, however, in vv. 13 and 21.

11 See Wright, "Legacy of David," 230–32.

12 See also his "Origins," 264–65.

13 Cf. also 2 Chr 31:3; 32:29

14 Robert North, "Postexilic Judean Officials," *ABD* 5:87, understands the term here as an official for minor errands, but states that the term is usually a higher and foreign official. He considers the translation "eunuch" outdated.

15 1 Chr 12:29 (28); 2 Chr 13:3; 17:16-17; 25:6; 32:21.

16 1 Chr 11:2 (twice); 17:6, 7, 9, 10; 2 Chr 1:11; 6:5 (twice), 6; 7:13-14.

17 Avi Hurvitz, "Terms and Epithets Relating to the Jerusalem Temple Compound in the Book of Chronicles: The Linguistic Aspect," in *Pomegranates and Golden Bells* (FS Jacob Milgrom; ed. D. P. Wright, D. N. Freedman, and A. Hurvitz; Winona Lake, IN: Eisenbrauns, 1995) 165–83.

temple as the resting place for Yahweh and the ark is a tradition known from Ps 132:8, a psalm that the Chronicler drew on elsewhere in composing his work.[18] In distinction from 1 Chr 22:9, where the rest achieved under Solomon is the prerequisite for the building of the temple, the use of the word rest here may be indebted to the Song of the Ark in Num 10:33-36. There the mobile ark sought out places of rest for Israel and when it rested, Yahweh rested with it. In the place where it rested, Yahweh was invited to return to the ten thousands of Israel.[19] In Chronicles the temple is a place of rest for the ark, not expressly for Yahweh.

"the footstool of the feet of our God": The ark itself is the footstool of the Deity in this unique reference in Chronicles, where "footstool" and "ark" are in apposition to one another and therefore equated with one another. Elsewhere in the OT, God's footstool can be the temple (Pss 99:5; 132:7, 13-14); Zion/Jerusalem (Lam 2:1, the temple may well be meant), or the earth itself (Isa 66:1). In v. 11 here the ark is referred to as the "mercy seat."

"I had made preparations for building": According to this verse, David made preparations for building the temple *before* Yahweh rejected his role in temple building, in distinction from 1 Chr 17:1-2; 22:2-14, where the idea of temple building is rejected right after David first proposed it. Allen, 460, attempts to work around this by proposing a harmonistic translation: "And subsequently I made preparations."

■ **3** *"But God said to me":* The Chronicler seems to heighten the significance of the oracle given to David by having it come directly from God. In 17:3-15 that oracle came through Nathan. In 22:8 David cast himself in the role of prophet by saying that the word of Yahweh came to him.

"because you are a man of wars; you have shed blood": Compare 22:8, where these two reasons for David's disqualification are given in reverse order *before* the prohibition against David's building of the temple. As Braun has noted, what was prohibited to David as a man of wars is permitted to Solomon, "the man of rest."[20]

■ **4** *"Yahweh the God of Israel had chosen me":* God's choice of David as king forever is attested already in the Deuteronomistic History and in the corresponding passages in Chronicles where they are extant (1 Sam 16:8-12 [by implication]; 2 Sam 6:21; 1 Kgs 8:16//2 Chr 6:6; 1 Kgs 11:34), just as Yahweh had chosen Saul before him (1 Sam 10:24, not included in Chronicles).[21] The choice of David here is spelled out in a narrowing-down process—"Judah, the house of my father, among the sons of my father"[22]— that resembles Achan's and Saul's selections by lot (Josh 7:16-18; 1 Sam 10:20-21[23]), and it probably alludes to the tradition of God rejecting David's elder brothers when Samuel anointed him as king (1 Sam 16:8-12).[24] Judah's election is attested in relationship to David's and Mount Zion's in Ps 78:68, 70, and is implied, without using the word "elect," in Gen 48:8-12. The use of the term "leader" (נגיד) for Judah is unparalleled. Normally this noun refers to a person designated for kingship before popular acclamation (1 Sam 9:16 and 10:1),[25] although it is used elsewhere in Chronicles in a more generic sense as here (cf. 1 Chr 12:28 [27]; 13:1). In 5:2 we read that a נגיד (David) came *from* Judah. The choice of David's father's house and of David himself among his brothers echoes the tradition of the book of Samuel (1 Sam 16:1, 6-13; David's brothers were not chosen, but by implication David was) and of Isa 11:1, although the word "choose" is not used in the latter passage.

---

18 See 2 Chr 6:41-42//Ps 132:8-10 and the classic study of Gerhard von Rad, "There Remains Still a Rest for the People of God: An Investigation of a Biblical Concept," in *The Problem of the Hexateuch and Other Essays* (Edinburgh: Oliver & Boyd, 1966) 94–102. Cf. also "The Levitical Sermon in I and II Chronicles," in *Problem of the Hexateuch*, 276.

19 See Braun, 270.

20 Braun, "Solomon," 583. In 1 Chronicles 22 I suggested that "bloodshed" might refer to those killed in the previous chapter because of David's census.

21 According to 1 Chr 15:2 the Levites were chosen by Yahweh to carry the ark and to minister before him forever.

22 Cf. 1 Chr 2:13-15.

23 Tribe, family, father, son.

24 Christine Mitchell, "Transformations in Meaning: Solomon's Accession in Chronicles," *JHS* 4 (2002) 9, notes that Saul is chosen by the casting of lots in 1 Sam 10:17-27 and in a very similar process. She errs, however, in asserting that David is not chosen according to Samuel-Kings (see the passages cited in the text above).

25 See Klein, *1 Samuel*, 88. See also the discussion at 1 Chr 27:16.

"he took pleasure in me to make me king over all Israel": "Took pleasure" (רצה) as a synonym for "choose" is used only here in Chronicles, but the usage is not far from that in Pss 147:11[26] and 149:4.[27] In 2 Sam 24:23 Araunah had prayed for David using the same verb: "May Yahweh your God receive you favorably" (ירצך).[28] David's kingship over Israel is mentioned twice in this verse, and on its second occurrence the word Israel is supplemented by the word "all."

■ **5** *"Yahweh has given to me many sons"*: The genealogy in 1 Chr 3:1-9 lists six sons born in Hebron and thirteen in Jerusalem, not counting the sons of the concubines and his daughter Tamar (cf. 14:3-7//2 Sam 5:13-16). The divine choice of Solomon obviates the need to say anything about the rebellion and attempted coups of Absalom and Adonijah. Aside from the lists of his children, none of them is mentioned in the narrative passages in Chronicles except for Solomon.

"he has chosen Solomon my son": In Deuteronomy there are frequent references to Yahweh's choice of Israel (e.g., Deut 4:32-40) and the site where his name would dwell (12:5), two mentions of the choice of the Levites (18:5; 21:5), and one reference to Yahweh's choice of David (17:15). In the Deuteronomistic History we find mentions of Yahweh's choice of his people (1 Kgs 3:8) and of Jerusalem (1 Kgs 8:44, 48; 11:13, 32, etc.) in addition to

passages mentioning the choice of Saul and David mentioned above in the commentary on v. 4.[29] Chronicles shares all of these,[30] except for the passages describing the choice of Saul and Israel itself (!),[31] but in the context of David's final speeches he makes four references to the choice of Solomon (1 Chr 28:5, 6, 10; 29:1). Here alone in the Bible is Solomon designated as the chosen king and temple builder.[32] The birth oracle cited in 22:9 means that Solomon, like Jeremiah, was chosen before his birth (Jer 1:5, where election is expressed by the verb "know"). For the Chronicler it is important that both the one who made preparations for the temple and provided a plan for its erection and the one who executed that plan were chosen by God. David and Solomon are chosen; later kings rule because of the promise that had been made to David.

"the throne of the kingdom of Yahweh over Israel": David and Solomon were earthly kings, but the real ruler of Israel in the Chronicler's eye was Yahweh.[33] This is the longest designation for this kingship in Chronicles (but surely not therefore one of the reasons for considering vv. 4-5 secondary, *pace* Braun, 268), and similar terminology is attested also in 17:14 ("I will confirm him . . . in my kingdom"; where 2 Sam 7:16 is rewritten); 1 Chr 29:23, where Solomon sits "on the throne of Yahweh"; and 2 Chr 9:8//1 Kgs 10:9, where Solomon has been set

---

26   "Yahweh takes pleasure in those who fear him."

27   "Yahweh takes pleasure in his people."

28   This passage is recast in 1 Chr 21:24.

29   See Vladimir Peterca, "Die Verwendung des Verbs BḤR für Salomo in den Büchern der Chronik," *BZ* 29 (1985) 94–96, who notes that the Chronicler omits the reference to the election of Israel (1 Kgs 3:8) in his reuse of this material in 2 Chr 1:9. This is a passage, however, in which the Chronicler departs significantly in every respect from the *Vorlage*.

30   Jerusalem (2 Chr 6:6, 34, 38; 12:13; 23:7), the temple (2 Chr 7:12, 16), the Levites (1 Chr 15:2; 2 Chr 29:11).

31   The text of 2 Chr 1:9-10 is quite different from the *Vorlage* in 1 Kgs 3:8-9, which affirms Israel's election. Another reference to Israel's election in 1 Kgs 8:51-53 is omitted by the Chronicler, who inserts instead a quotation from Ps 132:8-10 and v. 1.

32   Fishbane, *Biblical Interpretation,* 466, notes that the Oracle of Nathan (2 Samuel 7//1 Chronicles 17) is ambiguous or indeterminant and does not in fact

name the son who is to be David's heir. This speech of David is a proclamation after the fact, *vaticinium ex eventu.* In an important study of David's speeches, Mark A. Throntveit, "The Idealization of Solomon as the Glorification of God in the Chronicler's Royal Speeches and Royal Prayers," in *The Age of Solomon: Scholarship at the Turn of the Millennium* (ed. Lowell K. Handy; Studies in the History and Culture of the Ancient Near East 11; Leiden: Brill, 1997) 411–27, concludes that the glorification of God rather than the idealization of Solomon is the true thrust of the Chronicler's message to postexilic Israel. These ideas, however, might better be understood as complementary, and the emphasis on Solomon's election and the whole presentation of Solomon in 2 Chronicles 1–9 lead me to conclude that the Chronicler did indeed idealize him.

33   See Raymond Kuntzmann, "Le trône de Dieu dans l'oeuvre du Chroniste," in *Le Trône de Dieu* (ed. Marc Philonenko; WUNT 69; Tübingen: Mohr [Siebeck], 1993) 19–27.

on Yahweh's throne instead of the throne of Israel. The earthly, royal throne is also the throne of Yahweh.

■ **6** *"He said to me, 'Solomon, your son—he will build my house and my courts, for I have chosen him to be my son, and I will be his father'"*: This divine oracle was cited already in 1 Chr 22:10. Two significant changes are introduced in this verse. Solomon is to build both the temple and its courts, anticipating what will be said about the latter in v. 12.[34] The people celebrated the festivals in the courts of the temple rather than in the building itself,[35] and this accounts for their special mention here. Also, instead of the adoption formula in 22:10 ("he will be a son to me, and I will be a father to him") and as a slight modification of it, the Chronicler indicates that Yahweh has chosen Solomon as his son (cf. also v. 10 and 29:1). Braun notes that no other writer in the OT speaks of the election of any individual king after David,[36] and Solomon's remains the only case where election is applied to a king who rose to the throne through dynastic succession. Of course, Deuteronomy indicates that all kings of Israel are in principle chosen by Yahweh (Deut 17:15).

■ **7** *"'I will establish his kingdom forever if he is resolute in keeping my commandments and my judgments'"*: The Chronicler's major change to the oracle in 1 Chr 22:10 is that he makes Yahweh's eternal establishment of the kingdom conditional on Solomon's obedience. In 2 Sam 7:14-15 the Davidic kings were threatened with punishments ("a rod of men and with blows of humans"), but nothing would make Yahweh withdraw his loyal love from them. The Chronicler omitted these threatened punishments in 1 Chr 17:13 and only stated that Yahweh would not remove his loyal love from Solomon as he had

from Saul. In 17:11 Yahweh also promised only to establish Solomon's kingship, omitting the word "forever" from his *Vorlage* in 2 Sam 7:12. Obedience by Solomon is considered possible, as for people in general in Deut 30:11-14, and the Chronicler presents Solomon as meeting this requirement and therefore guaranteeing the continuation of the dynasty.[37] The Chronicler omits the accounts of Solomon's marriages with foreign women and his resulting apostasy, which was the cause for the division of the united kingdom (1 Kgs 11:31-34).[38] In 1 Chr 22:12-13 the Chronicler had made Solomon's success dependent on his obedience; now he extends this conditionality to the dynasty itself.[39] The unconditional dynastic promise to David in 2 Samuel 7 (note the use of "forever" in vv. 13, 16, 25, 29) was already made conditional in (some layers of) the Deuteronomistic History (1 Kgs 2:3-4; 6:12-13; 8:25; 9:4-5; cf. 3:14).[40]

"'as at this day'": The Chronicler indicates that at the time David was handing kingship over to Solomon, the latter had indeed kept God's commandments and judgments. The only other use of the expression "as at this day" in Chronicles refers to the fidelity of God's promises to David, cited at the dedication of the temple in 2 Chr 6:15, where it is taken from 1 Kgs 8:24. Solomon's carrying out of the other mandate at this time, namely the building of the temple, was abetted considerably by the preparatory works of David.

■ **8** *"And now in the sight of all the assembly of Yahweh, and in the hearing of our God"*: With the words "And now" David makes a transition from the divine oracle itself to his own application of its message to the people and not just to Solomon. Verses 2-7 introduced the reasons for

34 See the references to the courts of the temple in 2 Chr 23:5//2 Kgs 11:5, 6; Isa 62:9; and Ps 84:3 (2).

35 See Ps 84:3 (2) and Isa 62:9, and the tabernacle account in Exod 27:9-19. In the account of the coup against Athaliah the people gathered in the courts of the house of Yahweh (2 Chr 23:5, not mentioned in the parallel text, 2 Kgs 11:6).

36 "Solomon," 589.

37 This message is reaffirmed in 2 Chr 13:5; 21:7; 23:3.

38 Jeroboam's dynastic succession is also made conditional on his obedience in 1 Kgs 11:38. Solomon's sin with foreign women is also scored in Neh 13:26, demonstrating again the separate authorship of Chronicles and Ezra-Nehemiah.

39 Cf. also 2 Chr 6:16//1 Kgs 8:25; 7:17-18//1 Kgs

9:4-5; and the discussion by Williamson, "Dynastic Oracle," 313–18. As Williamson points out, 317–18, the whole future of the dynasty depends upon the obedience of Solomon, and with the completion of the period of David's and Solomon's rule, the dynasty has been eternally established. God will now maintain his promise (2 Chr 21:7; 23:3).

40 See Ralph W. Klein, *Israel in Exile: A Theological Interpretation* (OBT; Philadelphia: Fortress Press, 1979) 29–31.

the call to obedience issued in this verse, namely the legitimate passing of the throne to Solomon. There are two witnesses—Israel will see, and God will hear—to what the actions of the addressees will be. While the word קהל "assembly" is used some forty times in Chronicles, this is the only time that the construct chain "the assembly of Yahweh" is used.[41] Moses also addressed Joshua in the sight of all Israel (Deut 31:7).[42] As Johnstone, 1:277, has noted, the monarchy is not an end in itself. Rather, the final goal of God's gift of kingship is faithful obedience by all to Yahweh.

["I say] keep and seek all the commandments of Yahweh your God": The elliptical style of the Chronicler requires the insertion of something like the bracketed words. The two imperatives are in the plural, thus referring to the various leaders whom David has assembled. The verb שמרו "keep" is typical of Deuteronomic and Deuteronomistic passages,[43] whereas ודרשו "seek" is one of the favorite religious terms of the Chronicler himself.[44] A similar call to observe the statutes and ordinances of Yahweh was issued in 1 Chr 22:13, but then only to Solomon himself.

"so that you may possess the good land": The people's possession of the land is made conditional on their own obedience (cf. 2 Chr 33:8).[45] Later, the infidelity of the priests and the people, including their ignoring of the prophets, led eventually to the land's loss (2 Chr 36:14-16). The vocabulary is Deuteronomistic (Deut 1:8, 21; 4:21-22, 26; 6:18-20;[46] 30:18-20; and often), and this is the only use of ירש in the *qal* in Chronicles and the only use of "good land" outside of Deuteronomistic passages. Japhet points out that the Chronicler does not foresee a new conquest, but offers a challenge to each new generation to obey and thus possess the land.[47]

"and leave it as an inheritance to your children after you

forever": This is the only use of the verb נחל (hiphil) in Chronicles. In Deuteronomy it is God[48] who leaves the land as an inheritance to Israel (Deut 12:10; 19:13, 14; 32:8).

■ **9** *"And you":* David now applies v. 7 to Solomon (cf. 1 Chr 22:6-16). The alternate reading in LXX ("And now") marks a similar transition and would have the same effect. This public encouragement of Solomon echoes that privately delivered to him in 22:13.

"acknowledge the God of your father": Jeremiah 31:34 offers a parallel use of the verb "know" or "acknowledge."[49] Herbert B. Huffmon has argued persuasively that the connotation of recognizing Yahweh as sole legitimate God in the verb "know" can be traced back ultimately to usage in international treaties.[50] The letter from Elijah to Jehoram, drafted by the Chronicler, refers to "the God of David your father" (2 Chr 21:12). The "God of the fathers," attested here by LXX, is frequent in Chronicles (e.g., 2 Chr 13:18; 20:33).

"and serve him with a perfect heart and a willing spirit": The people offer freely to Yahweh "with a perfect heart" in 1 Chr 29:9, and David prays that Solomon would have such a heart in 29:19.[51] An earlier use of this expression appears in 1 Kgs 8:61, a passage not included by the Chronicler, and in other passages in Kings, one of which is paralleled in Chronicles.[52] The word שלם "perfect" may be a pun on the word שלמה "Solomon." The best two parallels to a "willing spirit" or "a spirit that delights to do God's will" (בנפש חפצה) are in negative contexts, referring either to evils people delight in (Isa 66:3) or to activities Yahweh does not delight in (Isa 66:4). In 1 Kgs 2:3-4 David also admonished Solomon to obey Yahweh, although the terminology used is not the same.

"for Yahweh searches longingly all hearts and understands every motive behind thoughts": These clauses follow logi-

---

41 The "assembly of Israel" occurs in 1 Chr 13:2; 2 Chr 6:3, 12, 13, "the (whole) assembly" in 1 Chr 29:1, 10, 20; and the "assembly of Judah" in 2 Chr 20:5; 30:35. The construct chain קהל יהוה does appear in Num 16:3; 20:4; Deut 23:1, 2, 8; Mic 2:5.

42 Cf. MT in 1 Chr 28:8 (textual note 6).

43 Cf. Deut 5:10 and often elsewhere.

44 Curtis and Madsen, 29, #23.

45 Cf. Fishbane, *Biblical Interpretation,* 466.

46 "Do what is right and good . . . so that you may go in and occupy the good land."

47 *Ideology,* 393.

48 In Deut 31:7 Moses instructs Joshua to put the people in possession of the land, using this verb in the *hiphil.*

49 Cf. 2 Chr 33:13, where Manasseh acknowledges that Yahweh is God and the use of "knowledge of God" in the book of Hosea.

50 Herbert B. Huffmon, "The Treaty Background of Hebrew *YĀDAʿ*," *BASOR* 181 (1966) 37.

51 Cf. also 2 Chr 15:17; 16:9; 19:9; 25:2.

52 Cf. also 1 Kgs 11:4; 15:3, 14//2 Chr 15:17; 2 Kgs 20:3

cally after the admonition to serve Yahweh with both heart and spirit. This passage has often been understood to mean that Yahweh knows what goes on in Solomon's and other human hearts and even the יצר מחשבות, the inclinations of one's thoughts.[53] The latter expression recalls Gen 6:5, where, before the flood, Yahweh saw that the inclination of the thoughts of humankind's hearts was only evil all day long (cf. Gen 8:21). Since Yahweh searches out hearts, Solomon seems thus to being bullied into obedience. J. G. McConville,[54] however, understands the word דרש to have a connotation of longing rather than judgment. As Solomon "acknowledges" Yahweh, Yahweh "understands human thoughts," and as Solomon serves Yahweh, Yahweh searches for a positive human response. After all, it is Yahweh's intention that Solomon's obedience will validate the promise made to David. In 1 Chr 29:17, I might add, David also confesses that God's knowledge about human moral conduct has a positive overtone: "I know, my God, that you search the heart, and take pleasure in uprightness."[55] Yahweh's searching or seeking with longing leads to Solomon's seeking Yahweh and being found by him.

"If you seek him, he will be found by you, but if you abandon him, he will cast you off forever": The Chronicler has David articulate clearly the positive and negative consequences of the doctrine of retribution. This is the second use of דרש "seek" in this verse, and this time with Solomon as subject and Yahweh as object. Here it is used in the Chronicler's characteristic sense of religious fidelity.[56] Close parallels to this statement of retribution appear in Deut 4:29; Jer 29:13; and Isa 55:6. The first two passages emphasize that God can be found only by those who seek him with their whole heart and spirit. The prophet Azariah proclaims to Asa two similar "if-then" statements in 2 Chr 15:2 ("If you seek him, he will be found by you") and 4 ("when the people turned to Yahweh and sought him, he was found by them"). The

Chronicler seems to be arguing against the position of the Deuteronomistic Historian, who wrote in 1 Kgs 11:4: "His [Solomon's] heart was not true to Yahweh his God, as was the heart of his father David." Such sins of Solomon would have led to his being cast off by Yahweh. Since he was not cast off, he must have sought Yahweh. To abandon or forsake (עזב) Yahweh is a major concern in Chronicles (see 1 Chr 28:20; 2 Chr 7:19, 22; 12:1, 5; 13:10, 11; 15:2; 21:10; 24:18, 20, 24; 28:6; 29:6; 32:31; 34:25; for זנח "cast off" see 2 Chr 11:14; 29:19[57]).

■ **10** *"See now that Yahweh has chosen you to build a house for him as a sanctuary":* Earlier David had referred to Yahweh's choice of Solomon to succeed him on the throne. Now he focuses on a specific purpose of that choice—the construction of the temple. For "sanctuary" (מקדש) see 1 Chr 22:19 and five occurrences in 2 Chronicles.[58]

Be strong and do it: David completes his address to Solomon with the formula of encouragement (cf. v. 20 and 1 Chr 22:13). The people conclude their speech to Ezra during the mixed marriage crisis in Ezra 10:4 with the same admonition.

28:11-19. David's Provision of the Plan for the Temple and His Gifts

■ **11** *David gave to his son Solomon the plan:* In Exod 25:9, 40, Yahweh instructed Moses to make the tabernacle and its vessels according to the plan (תבנית) that had been shown or revealed to him, and similarly Ezekiel was instructed by Yahweh to make known the plan[59] of the future temple (43:11). David is therefore a second Moses, communicating the plan of the temple (cf. 1 Chr 28:12-13) to Solomon as Moses had revealed the plan of the tabernacle to the Israelites.[60] Solomon, as the executor of the plan, is a second Bezalel, who was the craftsman who worked on the tabernacle in the wilderness.[61] In v. 19 the Chronicler claims that the plan had been revealed to David by God, just as the plan of the tabernacle had been revealed to Moses. As a result, the

53 Cf. 1 Chr 29:18.
54 "I Chronicles 28:9: Yahweh 'Seeks Out' Solomon," *JTS* 37 (1986) 105–8.
55 Cf. also 1 Sam 16:7; Jer 11:20; Pss 7:10 (9); 139:1.
56 It can also be used to describe infidelity, as in 1 Chr 10:14: Saul did *not* seek Yahweh.
57 Curtis and Madsen, 29, #30.
58 2 Chr 20:8; 26:18; 29:21; 30:8; 36:17.

59 Ezekiel, however, does not use the word תבנית (but see Ezek 8:3, 10; 10:8 for the prophet's use of this term in other contexts) for this plan, but צורה and תכונה.
60 The tabernacle was later housed within the temple according to the Chronicler (2 Chr 5:5).
61 See Exod 31:2–38:22.

temple shares the status of the tabernacle in Israelite cultic life. No such divinely revealed plan for the temple is known in the book of Kings.

of the vestibule and its rooms, its treasuries, its upper rooms, and its inner chambers and of the room of the mercy seat: The Chronicler first provides a summary list of rooms within the temple. For the vestibule see 2 Chr 3:4; 8:12; 15:8; 29:7, 17. The vestibule itself did not have other rooms, so unless there is a textual error,[62] we are probably to understand "vestibule" as synecdoche, letting a part of the temple stand for its entirety. Hence "the vestibule and its rooms" is equal to "the temple and its rooms." The Persian word for "treasuries," גנזך,[63] used only here in the Bible, anticipates the separation of these treasuries into two categories in the following verse. The "upper rooms" are also mentioned in 2 Chr 3:9, but there is no parallel mention for the inner rooms. The three parts of the temple were conventionally called the vestibule (אולם), the nave (היכל), and the inner sanctuary or Holy of Holies (דביר or קדש הקדשים). Instead of either of the Hebrew expressions for the Holy of Holies, however, the Chronicler uses a unique term, "the room of the mercy seat" (ובית הכפרת),[64] which would seem to describe the content of the room in the Chronicler's day, since the ark itself was not part of the Second Temple. The "mercy seat" is never mentioned elsewhere in connection with Solomon's temple, nor does it appear elsewhere in Chronicles. But there are twenty-seven references to it in the Priestly account of the tabernacle (Exodus 25–40), the Day of Atonement (Leviticus 16), and Num 7:89. Elsewhere, of course, the Chronicler makes clear that the First Temple was the resting place for the ark.[65]

■ **12** *the plan of everything that he had in mind:* The *NIV* translation, "the plans of all that the Spirit had put in his mind," seems to go counter to the intention of the Hebrew text[66] and imply divine inspiration. This verse refers instead to the plan that was in the mind of David. As v. 19 makes clear, of course, the ultimate source of this plan was the hand of Yahweh on David. The noun תבנית "pattern" also occurs in vv. 12, 18, 19.

the courts of the house of Yahweh . . . the surrounding chambers . . . the treasuries of the house of God and . . . the treasuries of the dedicated gifts: The plan included the various side buildings associated with the temple. For חצרות "courts" see 2 Chr 4:9, 7:7, and v. 6 above; for לשכות "chambers" see 1 Chr 9:26; 23:28; Ezra 8:29; 10:6; Neh 13:4-9. Levitical duties included caring for the courts and the chambers (1 Chr 23:28). A certain Ahijah had earlier been put in charge of the treasuries of the house of God and of the dedicated gifts (הקדשים; 26:20; cf. 18:11, which recounts the gifts David dedicated to Yahweh from the plunder taken from foreign nations).

■ **13** *for the divisions of the priests and the Levites:* The plan moves beyond the buildings of the temple complex itself to include plans for the clergy, but this change does not justify identifying this verse as secondary (*pace* Dirksen).[67] The divisions of the sons of Aaron were mentioned in 24:1 and the divisions of the Levitical gatekeepers in 26:1, 19. If this phrase is not an addition designed to make mention of materials that had been added in chaps. 24 and 26, it could anticipate David communicating these divisions of the priests and the Levites to Solomon in v. 21 of this chapter (cf. also 23:2).

and for all the vessels of the service of the house of Yahweh: This phrase summarizes what will be said about individual vessels in vv. 14-18.[68] The plan for the tabernacle in Exod 25:9 also included a plan for its vessels.

---

62   See textual note 13.

63   *HALOT* 1:199.

64   The term כפרת is used in Exod 25:18; 35:12; and frequently in Exodus, but only here in Chronicles. Hurvitz, "Terms and Epithets," points out that such expressions with בית in the construct are frequent in Second Temple texts.

65   1 Chr 22:19; 28:2; 2 Chr 6:10-11.

66   Rudolph, 186, and Myers, 1:188, 190, think that ברוח refers to the Spirit of God here. But R. N. Whybray, *The Heavenly Counsellor in Isaiah xl 13-14* (SOTSMS 1; Cambridge: Cambridge Univ. Press, 1971) 11-12, points out that היה עמו means "it was

his intention" (1 Kgs 11:11) and that ברוח therefore should be translated "in his mind." Rudolph and Myers claim that רוח never refers to the human spirit in Chronicles, but that is contradicted (see Braun, 266) by 2 Chr 21:16 (the spirit of the Philistines and the Arabs) and 36:22//Ezra 1:1 (the spirit of Cyrus).

67   Curtis and Madsen, 298, judge this verse to be ambiguous. It may refer to the plan for the divisions, etc., or it may refer to the uses of all the surrounding chambers in v. 12.

68   For the importance of the temple vessels see Ackroyd, "Temple Vessels."

14 *the weight of silver vessels:* Beginning with this verse and continuing through v. 18a, the Chronicler shifts from the plan David gave to Solomon to the gifts for the temple he gave to Solomon. Hence these materials are marked off by a dash in the translation. The silver vessels mentioned here and in subsequent verses are not included in the account of Solomon's temple in either Kings or Chronicles. Other passages about the First Temple, however, indicate the plausibility of their being listed here. In the account of the destruction of Jerusalem, we are told that the captain of the guard took silver items from the temple in order to use the silver that was in them (2 Kgs 25:15). When Joash repaired the temple he made dishes and other objects of gold and silver (2 Chr 24:14//2 Kgs 12:14[13]). There were also many bronze objects in the tabernacle and temple that are not mentioned here. Japhet, 496, wonders whether the silver vessels were left out of the account of the building of the First Temple as less valuable, or whether they were not part of the Second Temple and therefore also omitted anachronistically from the account of Solomon's temple.

15 *the golden lampstands and their lamps:* This is the first mention of the lampstands in Chronicles. In 2 Chr 4:7, 20-21//1 Kgs 7:49-50 (cf. Jer 52:19), Solomon constructs ten golden lampstands (cf. the golden lampstand mentioned in Abijah's sermon to the north in 2 Chr 13:11). These lampstands are to be distinguished from the multibranched lampstand of the tabernacle mentioned in the Pentateuch (Exod 25:31-40; 37:17-24; Lev 24:1-4).

and for the silver lampstands: Neither these silver lampstands nor the silver tables mentioned in the next verse appear anywhere else in the Bible.

16 *golden tables and the rows of bread for each table:* This is also the first mention in Chronicles of the tables for the showbread. In 2 Chr 4:8, 19 Solomon constructs these tables, but 2 Chr 13:11 and 29:18 refer to only one table in the First Temple (cf. 1 Kgs 7:48), and there was only one table for the bread of the Presence in the tabernacle

(Exod 25:23-30; 37:10; 40:22).[69]

17 *the forks, the basins, and the cups:* In 2 Chr 4:16 Solomon constructs the forks (מזלגות)[70] and in 4:8 the basins (מזרקות; cf. 4:11, 22).[71] The cups (קשׂות) are not mentioned elsewhere in Chronicles, but they do appear in the tabernacle account (Exod 25:29; 37:16; Num 4:7), where they are also made of pure gold and used for the pouring out of drink offerings.

the golden bowls: These appear neither in the tabernacle or First Temple accounts, but both golden and silver bowls are among the temple vessels given by Cyrus to Sheshbazzar to bring back from Babylon to Jerusalem (Ezra 1:10), and gold bowls were brought back by Ezra himself (Ezra 8:27).

18 *and the weight in refined gold for the altar of incense:* For the incense altar in the tabernacle see Exod 30:1-10 (cf. Lev 4:8; 16:12). Solomon's actual construction of the altar of incense is not recorded in Chronicles, but one of his express purposes in building the temple was the burning of incense before Yahweh (2 Chr 2:4).[72] Uzziah is severely criticized for attempting to make an offering on the altar of incense (2 Chr 26:16), which presupposes its existence in the First Temple. For "refined gold" (זהב מזקק)[73] the tabernacle account uses "pure gold" (זהב טהור; Exod 30:3).

and the plan of the chariot, that is, the cherubim of gold: The expression ולתבנית המרכבה הכרבים זהב is awkward in several ways and interpreters have to decide whether the Chronicler wrote so awkwardly or whether this awkwardness stems from secondary additions or textual corruption. Dirksen argues that gold would not be used for the plan for the chariot, but this presupposes a translation beginning "and gold for the plan of the chariot." The expression הכרבים זהב is to be understood as "cherubim of gold," as Exod 25:18 makes clear; that is, "gold" modifies the cherubim, not the plan.[74] In any case the writer is returning to a literal understanding of "plan" as in vv. 11-12, after the intervening verses when he has written about David's gifts of gold and silver.[75] "Cherubim"

---

69   See Curtis and Madsen, 299.
70   See Exod 27:3; 38:3; Num 4:14 for their connection to the tabernacle. Cf. 1 Sam 2:13-14, where the forks were used to retrieve the offerings due the priests from the rest of the sacrifices. These forks appear also in 2 Chr 4:16.
71   Johnstone, 1:281, says that the basins were used to

collect sacrificial blood that was dashed against the altar.
72   Cf. 1 Chr 6:34 (49); 2 Chr 26:16, 19.
73   David mentions ten thousand talents of refined silver in 1 Chr 29:4.
74   Dirksen, "1 Chronicles xxviii," 435, argues that the cherubim in the temple were made of "oleaster"

must be understood in apposition to "chariot" and not as part of a construct chain (as implied in *NRSV:* "the golden chariot of the cherubim"). In the Solomonic temple the cherubim were independent of the ark, since 1 Kgs 6:23-28 describes the construction of the cherubim and only later is the ark placed beneath them in 1 Kgs 8:6. In P, however, the cherubim were part of the cover over the ark (Exod 25:19-21; the cherubim were of one piece with the mercy seat). The cherubim are probably connected to the ark in this passage (so Japhet, 496–97; cf. 1 Chr 13:6). Ezekiel's visions of Yahweh by the river Chebar (chap. 1) and of Yahweh's leaving and returning to Jerusalem (chaps. 10 and 43) are often called visions of a throne chariot, and they were so taken in Jewish mysticism, but what Ezekiel saw is not explicitly called a chariot in the Bible.[76] According to Ps 18:11 (10), Yahweh flew on the cherubim.[77]

(which spread out [their wings] and covered the ark of the covenant of Yahweh): As indicated by the parentheses, this clause may be secondary, for the reasons given in textual note 27. The verb "spread out" (פרש)[78] is used with the cherubim in 2 Chr 3:13 and 5:8, but the verb "covered" (כסך) occurs only here in Chronicles. This verb is used with the cherubim in the tabernacle account in Exod 25:20 and 37:9, and with the cherubim in the temple account in 1 Kgs 8:7.[79] For "ark of the covenant of Yahweh" see 1 Chr 15:25, 26, 28, 29; 16:37; 22:19; 28:2.

■ **19** *All this was in a document–since the hand of Yahweh was upon him–that made clear all the details of the plan:* This short verse is difficult to translate and therefore difficult to interpret (see esp. textual notes 28–29).[80] Compare

the following translations: *NIV:* "'All this,' David said, 'I have in writing from the hand of the LORD upon me, and he gave me understanding in all the details of the plan.'" *NRSV:* "All this, in writing at the LORD's direction, he made clear to me—the plan of all the works." *JPS:* "All this that the LORD made me understand by His hand on me, I give you in writing—the plan of all the works." *REB:* "'All this was drafted by the LORD's own hand,' said David; 'my part was to consider the detailed working out of the plan.'"

Note that *NIV, JPS,* and *REB* insert words not in the Hebrew text: "David said," "I give you," and "said David," respectively. All four of these versions interpret David as the speaker. Rudolph, 188, however (cf. Braun, 266–67), believes this verse continues the narrative from the previous verses. My translation, "since Yahweh's hand was upon him" (מיד יהוה עליו), understands this phrase as a paraphrase for what we might call divine inspiration (cf. Ezek 1:3; 3:14). Despite several uncertainties in the phraseology, two things seem clearly intended by this verse: the plan for the temple and its furnishings was contained in a written document, and this plan had divine authorship even if it was mediated through David. According to the Chronicler the plans for the temple were not just ideas David had dreamed up. Moses had also received the pattern for the tabernacle from God (Exod 25:9, 40; 27:8). De Vries, 220, thinks that the Chronicler is trying to convince the reader that this revelation to David is as sure as the Decalogue given to Moses.

---

wood (= olive wood), not of gold, but they were overlaid with gold (2 Chr 3:10). He admits that the cherubim in the tabernacle were made of gold (Exod 25:18), but does not notice that the relationship between gold and cherubim is the same in this verse of Chronicles and the Exodus verse.

75   The preposition *lāmed* is prefixed to תבנית since it is the last item in a list. See Kropat, *Syntax,* 6.

76   In Ezekiel 10, but not in Ezekiel 1, the word "cherubim" is used for what Ezekiel saw.

77   Johnstone, 1:281, suggests that identification of the chariot with the cherubim is a polemical reference to the chariots of the sun in 2 Kgs 23:11, not included in Chronicles. If so, it is an exceedingly subtle polemic.

78   "Their wings" must be supplied (*HALOT* 3:975). G.

R. Driver, "Studies in the Vocabulary of the Old Testament, II," *JTS* 32 (1931) 250–57, suggested the meaning of "flew" for this verb in this passage and 2 Chr 3:13 on the basis of a parallel verb *parāšu* in Akkadian. It seems highly unlikely, however, that the cherubim in the temple flew anywhere.

79   The parallel text in 2 Chr 5:8 uses the verb כסה.

80   Yigael Yadin, *The Temple Scroll* (3 vols.; Jerusalem: Israel Exploration Society, 1983) 1:177, believed that the Temple Scroll from Qumran was intended by its author to be the document described in 1 Chr 28:11-19. That opinion is now affirmed by Dwight D. Swanson, *The Temple Scroll and the Bible* (STDJ 14; Leiden: Brill, 1995) 225–26; idem, "The Use of the Chronicles in 11QT: Aspects of a Relationship," in *The Dead Sea Scrolls: Forty Years of Research* (ed.

28:20-21. David's Third Speech to Solomon

■ **20** *"Be strong and of good courage, and act"*: This is the "formula of encouragement" that is a regular part of the form for induction into an office, as we have seen it previously in 1 Chr 22:13 (cf. Deut 31:7, 23; Josh 1:6; 1 Chr 28:10), supplemented here by the word "act" (ועשׂה).[81] David's address to Solomon in 1 Kgs 2:2 begins: "Be strong, play the man."

"Do not be afraid or dismayed": Compare 1 Chr 22:13; Deut 1:21; Josh 1:6, 9; 8:1.

"for Yahweh my God is with you": This is the "formula of accompaniment" from the form for induction into an office. This and the following clauses provide the rationale that makes possible the carrying out of the commands earlier in the verse. Compare 1 Chr 22:11.

"He will not fail or forsake you": Compare Deut 4:31; 31:6, 8; Josh 1:5.

"until all the work for the service of the house of Yahweh is finished": Outside Chronicles (1 Chr 9:13; 23:24), the expression "work for the service" occurs only in the tabernacle narrative (Exod 35:24; 36:1-3). Here it refers to the work of construction rather than the ongoing cultic rites.

■ **21** *"Here are the divisions of the priests and the Levites"*: David hands over to Solomon the plan for the divisions of the clergy, mentioned above in v. 13.[82] The groups of people mentioned in this verse shows that all are now ready to construct the temple.

"and with you in all the work will be every volunteer who has skill": While the Chronicler has emphasized the parallels between the transition from Moses to Joshua, on the one hand, and from David to Solomon, on the other, he also distinguishes between the two pairs of leaders. Japhet, 499, points out that Joshua alone is given responsibility to conquer the land, with the people following more or less passively. In Chronicles the people *actively* support Solomon in his work: "the officers and all the people will be completely at your command." This is an emphasis found also in the tabernacle account, where the terms translated here as "[every] volunteer (נדיב)[83] who has skill (חכמה[84] or חכם[85])" occur frequently, even if

in separate verses. The presence of these volunteers runs parallel to the presence of Yahweh promised in the previous verse.

Conclusion

In a first speech to various officials (vv. 2-10), David rehearses the reasons why he was not allowed to build the temple even though he had made preparations for it. David cites a divine oracle in v. 3 that forbade him to build the temple because of his wars and bloodshed. David also asserts that both he and his son Solomon have been chosen as kings over Israel and, indeed, Solomon was chosen to sit on the throne of *Yahweh's* kingdom over Israel. A second divine oracle in v. 6 identifies Solomon as the temple builder. In v. 7 Yahweh makes the dynastic promise conditional on Solomon's obedience, and David exhorts the whole assembly to obedience in v. 8. In the last two verses of this speech (vv. 9-10), addressed directly to Solomon, David exhorts him to obedience, with a promise of blessing for obedience and a threat of abandonment for disobedience. He urges Solomon to undertake the task of building the temple.

The Chronicler also reports David giving Solomon "the plan" for the temple and making massive donations of gold and silver for its furnishings. In handing over the written plan to Solomon, David is a second Moses, and the plan itself was revealed to David by God. In carrying out the plan, Solomon will play the role of Bezalel, who constructed the tabernacle. David gave to Solomon golden and silver vessels, lampstands, tables, and other paraphernalia in the temple, but the exact weight of the gold and silver is not specified in this chapter (vv. 11-19).

In a third speech to Solomon (vv. 20-21; cf. 22:6-16 and 28:9-10), David encourages his son and urges him to carry out the building of the temple. David also assures Solomon that he will have the wholehearted support of the people in this project. Both the people and Yahweh himself will be with Solomon.

Devorah Dimant and Uriel Rappaport; STDJ 20; Leiden: Brill, 1992) 290–99. The instructions for construction of the temple in the Temple Scroll follow the order of items in vv. 11-19.

81   Cf. 1 Chr 22:16, 19; 2 Chr 19:11; 25:8; Ezra 10:4.

82   This supports the idea that v. 13 is original.

83   Exod 25:2; 35:5, 21, 22, 29.

84   Exod 28:3; 31:3, 6; 35:26, 31, 35; 36:1-2.

85   Exod 28:3; 31:6; 35:10, 25; 36:1, 2, 4, 8.

29

Translation

1/ King David said to the whole assembly, "Solomon my son, whom alone God has chosen, is young and inexperienced and the work is great; for the temple[1] will not be for humans but for Yahweh God. 2/ With all my strength I have provided for the house of my God gold for gold things, silver for silver things, bronze for bronze things, iron for iron things, and lumber for wooden things, and great amounts of red carnelian, and [stones for] setting, colorful stones set into mortar to form a mosaic, and all sorts of precious stones, and stones of alabaster. 3/ In addition to all I have provided for the holy house, I have treasure of my own of gold and silver, and because I take pleasure in the house of my God, I give it to the house of my God: 4/ three thousand talents of gold from the gold of Ophir, and seven thousand talents of refined silver for overlaying the walls of the chambers of the house,[2] 5/ and for all the work to be done by artisans, gold for the things of gold and silver for the things of silver.[3] Who then will offer themselves willingly, consecrating themselves today to Yahweh?"

6/ Then the leaders of the ancestral houses offered themselves willingly, as did the leaders of the tribes[4] of Israel, and the commanders of the thousands and the hundreds, and the officers[5] over the work of the king. 7/ They gave for the service of the house of God[6] five thousand talents and ten thousand darics of gold, and ten thousand talents of silver, and eighteen thousand talents of bronze, and one hundred thousand talents of iron. 8/ Whoever had precious stones gave them to the treasury of the house of Yahweh through the hand of Jehiel the Gershonite. 9/ Then the people rejoiced because these have given voluntarily, for they had volunteered with a perfect heart to Yahweh, and also King David rejoiced with a great rejoicing.

10/ David blessed Yahweh before the whole assembly, and David said, "Blessed are you Yahweh, God of Israel our ancestor, forever and ever. 11/ To you Yahweh belong greatness, and power, and honor, and splendor, and majesty, indeed,[7] all things in heaven and earth; yours is the kingdom, Yahweh, and you are exalted as head above all.[8] 12/ Riches and wealth[9] come from you, and you rule over all, and in your hand are strength and power, and it is in your power to make great and to give strength to all. 13/ And now, our God,[10] we give thanks to you and we praise your magnificent name. 14/ For who am I and who is my people that we should have enough strength to make a freewill offering like this? For from you

1 הבירה; omitted by LXX, which paraphrases the second half of v. 19, where this term appears again. The LXX translator may not have known what to do with this Akkadian word, which usually means "palace" or the like. See the commentary and Polzin, *Late Biblical Hebrew*, 130, #12.

2 הבתים. For this construal see the commentary. LXX, Syr, Vg, Arab. read הבית "the house," the "less difficult" reading, and therefore probably secondary.

3 לזהב לזהב ולכסף לכסף ולכל מלאכה ביד חרשים. LXX omits the first six Hebrew words in this verse and makes the artisans responsible for the gold plate on the walls from the previous verse. This is the translator's (mistaken) attempt to make sense of the text and does not presuppose a different Hebrew *Vorlage* (cf. Allen, *Greek Chronicles*, 1:115; contra Throntveit, *When Kings Speak*, 34).

4 שבטי; LXX "sons" (בני).

5 ולשרי. The *lāmed* before the last noun in a series is emphatic and perhaps represents Aramaic influence. See Polzin, *Late Biblical Hebrew*, 66–68.

6 האלהים; LXX "Lord" (יהוה).

7 כי is an emphatic rather than a causative particle (Kropat, *Syntax*, 31; Curtis and Madsen, 306; BDB, 472). Others (including *BHS* with a question mark) follow Vg and add לך "(for) to you belong" to the text.

8 והמתנשא לכל לראש; LXX reads: "before your face every king and nation is troubled." Allen, *Greek Chronicles*, 1:130, observes that the translator rendered המתנשא in the sense of "rise up in revolt" (= "is troubled"). He judges "before your face" to be a misplaced literal rendering of מלפניך in v. 12 (1: 152). It is translated by παρὰ σοῦ in v. 12. "Every king and nation" is a paraphrastic translation of הממלכה.

9 והכבוד. See *HALOT* 2:457, meaning 2.a; BDB, 458: "splendor."

10 אלהינו; LXX "Lord" (יהוה).

11 הוא, with Q, in gender agreement with "abundance" and to be preferred; K היא.

12 אלהי; LXX "Lord" (יהוה).

13 הנמצאו. For the article with a finite verb functioning as a relative pronoun, see GKC §138i.

14 שמרה זאת לעולם ליצר; lit. "Keep this forever, namely, the inclination. . . ."

15 לשמור; LXX "to do" (לעשות). MT has conflated this variant reading by adding ולעשות הכל ("doing all of them") later in the verse (not attested in LXX). The synonymous variants "do" and "keep" with commandments as the direct object occur in 1 Chr 28:7 and 28:8, respectively.

16 At this point MT adds ולעשות הכל. See the previous note.

comes everything, and from what comes from your hand, we have given you. 15/ We are aliens before you and transients like all of our ancestors. Our days are like a shadow on the earth, and there is no hope. 16/ Yahweh our God, all this abundance that we have provided to build you a house for your holy name comes[11] from your hand and is all your own. 17/ I know, my God,[12] that you test the heart and take pleasure in uprightness. In the uprightness of my heart I have freely offered all these things, and now I have seen your people, who are present here,[13] offering themselves joyfully to you. 18/ Yahweh, God of Abraham, Isaac, and Israel, our ancestors, keep forever the inclination[14] of the thoughts of the heart of your people and direct their heart toward you. 19/ And give to Solomon my son a perfect heart to keep[15] your commandments, your decrees, and your statutes,[16] and to build the temple, for which I have made preparations."[17]

20/ David said to all the congregation, "Bless Yahweh your God," and all the assembly blessed Yahweh the God of their ancestors, and they bowed and prostrated themselves to Yahweh and to the king.

21/ On the next day they sacrificed[18] communion sacrifices to Yahweh[19] and they offered[20] burnt offerings to Yahweh, a thousand bulls, a thousand rams, and a thousand lambs, with their libations and sacrifices in abundance for all Israel. 22/ And they ate and drank before Yahweh on that day with great[21] joy, and they made Solomon, the son of David, king,[22] and they anointed him[23] as Yahweh's prince[24] and [they anointed] Zadok as priest. 23/ And Solomon sat on the throne of Yahweh as king in the place of David his father.[25] He prospered, and all Israel obeyed him. 24/ All the leaders, warriors, and all the sons of King David[26] pledged their allegiance to King Solomon. 25/ Yahweh magnified Solomon exceedingly in the eyes of all Israel, and he gave him royal majesty that had not been on any king more than on him.[27]

26/ David the son of Jesse reigned over all Israel. 27/ The days that he ruled over Israel[28] were forty years. In Hebron he ruled seven years, and in Jerusalem he ruled thirty-three years.[29] 28/ He died in good old age, full of days, riches, and wealth, and Solomon his son reigned in his place. 29/ The deeds of David, the first and the last, behold they are written in the acts of Samuel the seer, and in the acts of Nathan the prophet, and in the acts of Gad who saw visions, 30/ with accounts of all his rule and might and of the events that befell him and Israel and all the kingdoms of the earth.[30]

17 ולבנות הבירה אשר הכינותי. LXX, paraphrastically: καὶ τοῦ ἐπὶ τέλος ἀγαγεῖν τὴν κατασκευὴν τοῦ οἴκου σου "and to lead to the end the preparation of your house."

18 ויזבחו; LXX "David sacrificed" (ויזבח דויד).

19 Braun, 287, places the communion sacrifices on the first day.

20 ויעלו; LXX "he offered" (ויעל).

21 גדולה; lacking in LXX.

22 LXX[B], Syr., Arab.; MT adds שנית "for a second time." See the commentary.

23 וימשחוהו, with LXX; MT lacks הו־ ending by haplography.

24 לנגיד; LXX "king" (למלך).

25 על כסא יהוה למלך תחת דויד אביו; LXX "on the throne of David his father."

26 דויד; LXX adds "his father."

27 LXX; MT adds על ישראל "over Israel." See the commentary.

28 LXX omits this first clause because of homoioteleuton with the last words in v. 26.

29 שנים, with LXX; lacking in MT. Cf. 1 Kgs 2:11.

30 LXX adds a translation of 2 Chr 1:1, but it repeats a slightly different variant of that translation at 2 Chr 1:1.

530

Structure

This chapter, again lacking a *Vorlage* in Samuel-Kings (except for vv. 23 and 27),[1] may be divided into four parts:[2]

I. 29:1-9. Freewill offerings for the temple
   A. 29:1-5. David's speech inviting people to give generously to the temple
   B. 29:6-9. People's generous response
II. 29:10-20. David's final prayer
   A. 29:10-19. The prayer itself, praising the people's generosity and asking God to give the people and Solomon an obedient heart and to sustain Solomon in his assignment to build the temple
   B. 29:20. People's response: David exhorts the people to bless Yahweh, and they respond with worship and with submission to Yahweh and the king
III. 29:21-25. Enthronement of Solomon,[3] a ceremony that included the anointing of Solomon and of Zadok the priest. Verse 23 is dependent on 1 Kgs 1:46.
IV. 29:26-30. David's death and a summary of his reign. This is an expanded and highly revised version of 1 Kgs 2:10-12 in which the Chronicler uses for v. 27 only one verse from the three-verse summary of David's reign in 1 Kings (2:11; 2:10 and 2:12 are not directly quoted). We might have expected this paragraph to come before the enthronement of Solomon, but the Chronicler apparently wanted to link

that event as closely as possible to David's final prayer and to make David and Solomon co-regents. Both Solomon's anointing (1 Kgs 1:39) and his enthronement itself (1:46) are listed before David's death notice also in 1 Kings (2:10), where David and Solomon also share a brief co-regency. In Chronicles, however, the transition is made without any controversy or any hint of any rivalry for the throne.

Curtis and Madsen, 295–96, detect a parallel between Solomon's completion of the temple and 1 Chronicles 29: prayer of dedication (1 Kgs 8:22-53 parallels vv. 10-19), blessings (1 Kgs 8:54-61 parallels v. 20), dedicatory sacrifices (1 Kgs 8:62-64 parallels v. 21), and a concluding sacred feast (1 Kgs 8:65 parallels v. 22).

The Chronicler is dependent on the tabernacle account in the book of Exodus for the idea of contributions by the people for the temple and for many of the details about these contributions. There is no record of the people's contribution to the building of the temple in 1 Kings.[4] In Exod 25:1-7 and 35:4-9 Yahweh instructed Moses to take up an offering for the tabernacle, and everyone whose heart was stirred and whose spirit was willing then brought an offering in 35:20-29.[5] In Exod 35:25-26 women who could spin actually joined in the task of constructing the tabernacle. Since only Levites were permitted in the temple in the Chronicler's day (2 Chr 23:6), no mention is made of lay participation in construction of the temple.

In 1 Chr 29:1-5, called an oration by Throntveit,[6] David's previous generosity (22:2-5) is brought to public notice in his invitation to the people to give. His lavish

---

1   I will also note in the commentary other incidental references to 1 Kings 1–2 and the tabernacle account in Exodus.

2   For a careful and insightful theological reading of this chapter that pays special attention to the role of the community in the formation of character and ethics, see M. Patrick Graham, "A Character Ethics Reading of 1 Chronicles 29:1-25," in *Character and Scripture* (ed. W. P. Brown; Grand Rapids: Eerdmans, 2002) 98–120.

3   In an attempt to harmonize Kings and Chronicles, W. J. Beecher, "Note on the Proper Paragraph Division in I Chron. xxix.22," *JBL* 5 (1885) 73–75, made a paragraph division between v. 22a and v. 22b. He described the first paragraph as the first making of Solomon as king and the second paragraph, which

he took as a summary of 1 Kings 1, as the second making of Solomon as king. But, as the textual notes show, the reading "a second time" is secondary from a textual perspective, and the divergent presentation of Solomon's installation as king in Chronicles should be preserved without harmonization.

4   According to 1 Kgs 6:2 Solomon built the temple, and no mention is made of any contribution by the people for the building materials.

5   The people in fact gave too much, and Moses had to give an order that no more should be contributed (Exod 36:5-6).

6   *When Kings Speak*, 33–34. There and on pp. 89–96, however, Throntveit performs radical surgery on the Chronicler, identifying 22:14-19, all of chaps.

preparations were required by the youth and inexperience of Solomon and by the magnitude of the temple that was required by Yahweh. Unlike Moses, who merely commanded the people to give, David attempts to persuade the assembly to be generous, and the Chronicler may well be using these words of David to persuade his own intended audience to be generous in their support of the temple. The people responded to David's invitation with lavish offerings, stated in hyperbolic terms, that express their generosity, their joy, and their whole-hearted commitment to the task (29:6-9).

The final prayer of David consists of three parts: praise of Yahweh for his riches and power (vv. 10b-12), thanksgiving for God's generosity (vv. 13-17), and petitions for Yahweh to give the people and Solomon a perfect heart (vv. 18-19). Each of these parts begins with some form of the vocative: "to you Yahweh" (v. 11); "And now, our God" (v. 13); "Yahweh, the God of Abraham, Isaac, and Israel" (v. 18). Altogether there are six references to "Yahweh" and five to "God" in the prayer. The people's blessing of Yahweh (v. 20b) comes in response to an edict of David in v. 20a.[7] While there are many ties to the vocabulary of the Psalter (see Braun, 281–82) and even some use of parallelism (Japhet, 505), the prayer itself is in prose and does not conform exactly to any of the standard genres of the Psalter. Japhet may be right in proposing that the prayers of a layperson needed to be in prose to distinguish them from the liturgical singing done by the Levitical singers (1 Chr 16:8-36 and 2 Chr 20:21), but in any case the Chronicler has effectively used vocabulary and formulas from Israel's psalmic or liturgical traditions to construct a powerful and convincing final prayer for David.

Williamson, 185–86, has called attention to the fact that three themes appear in this prayer and in the psalm cited at 1 Chr 16:8-36. First, there is a reference in both cases to landless ancestors receiving the land (16:9 and 29:14-16). Next there is a celebration of Yahweh's kingship (16:23-33 [cf. 17:14] and 29:11-12). Finally, both prayers end with petitions (16:35 and 29:18-19). The first prayer of David, at 16:8-36, is placed after the ark had been safely brought to Jerusalem and just before the lengthy section, chaps. 17–29, dealing with David's support for the construction of the temple and the establishment of its staff. The final prayer comes at the end of that section. Therefore prayers frame this major section in 1 Chronicles. Japhet, 502, notes that this prayer contains no historical survey, either of God's deeds (contrast Neh 9:7-15) or of the people's sins (contrast Neh 9:10; 16:31).

The account of Solomon's accession in 1 Chr 29:21-25 little resembles the hasty, ad hoc rite performed in 1 Kgs 1:32-40, and in fact elements of the Chronicles account can be considered critical corrections of that account. Verse 23 is a significantly revised version of 1 Kgs 1:46.

David's death and the summary of his reign are also described in a different manner and with different vocabulary from the *Vorlage* in 1 Kgs 2:10-12. Only in v. 27 does the Chronicler explicitly use a passage from his *Vorlage*, 1 Kgs 2:11.

Detailed Commentary

29:1-9. Freewill Offerings for the Temple
29:1-5. David's Speech Inviting People to Give Generously to the Temple

■ **1** *"Solomon my son, whom alone God has chosen"*: I have previously noted the Chronicler's unique theme of Solomon's election as king and temple builder in Chronicles (1 Chr 22:9; 28:6, 10). In this verse the Chronicler delin-

---

23–27; 28:7b-18; 29:1-9, and 29:14b-16-17, 19 as secondary. In declaring 29:1-9 secondary, he follows the lead of Mosis, *Untersuchungen*, 105–7, and notes that David's speech in 29:1-5 does not follow exactly the characteristics of royal speech he had identified earlier in his dissertation, but this argument is circular and not convincing. Parts of David's prayer in vv. 10-19 are deleted by him (vv. 14b, 16-17, 19) because they link back to David's speech (in vv. 1-5). This argument, of course, is only as strong as that for the secondary character of David's speech itself. The differences from his "ideal form" can be

explained by the demands of the context and by the fact that the Chronicler's creativity cannot be constricted to what we may detect as his regular practices. The "clear and lucid" sequence Throntveit reconstructs on p. 91 ignores much of the complex and intricate structure that the Chronicler has painstakingly prepared.

7 Throntveit, *When Kings Speak*, 23. See now also Samuel E. Balentine, *Prayer in the Hebrew Bible* (OBT; Minneapolis: Fortress Press, 1993) 100–102.

eates Solomon's role among the many sons of David (cf. 28:5), with an implicit criticism of the account recorded only in 1 Kings 1–2 of the attempt by Adonijah to take over the throne while David was on his deathbed. This use of אחד in the sense of "alone" seems to be without parallel in the Bible, except perhaps in the Shema: "Yahweh is our God, Yahweh alone" (Deut 6:4).[8]

"is young and inexperienced and the work is great": Compare 1 Chr 22:5.[9] David's provisions of building materials were necessary because of Solomon's youth and inexperience and because of the size of the task itself. As Solomon notes in 2 Chr 2:4 (5), "The house that I am about to build will be great, for our God is greater than other gods." Solomon is referred to by name only in vv. 1 and 19 in this chapter. The focus elsewhere is on God, David, and the people.

"for the temple will not be for humans but for Yahweh God": The Chronicler chooses a word for "temple" (בירה) that is a loanword from Akkadian (*birtu*; *HALOT* 1:123), and means "citadel" or "acropolis" in its fourteen OT occurrences outside Chronicles.[10] This "citadel," however, is not for human use but for Yahweh himself, and hence it will demand enormous resources. The use of the word בירה in v. 19 forms an *inclusio* with this verse at the end of David's speeches. The divine name Yahweh God was also used in 28:20.

■ **2** *"With all my strength I have provided"*: David's previous efforts to contribute materials have been noted at 22:2-5, 14-16 and 28:2, including his "great effort" in 22:14. These contributions represented his efforts as king, perhaps drawing from public resources. In vv. 12 and 14 David acknowledges that his strength itself is a gift of Yahweh.

"gold for gold things, silver for silver things, bronze for bronze things, iron for iron things": David first lists metals in declining order of worth[11]—gold, silver, bronze, and iron—and then his contribution of precious stones. All the metals in this verse, except for iron, are found in the tabernacle account,[12] but 1 Kings also does not mention this metal in discussing Solomon's temple. Iron is mentioned in the Chronicler's account of Solomon's temple, 2 Chr 2:6, 13 (7,[13] 14), as it was mentioned earlier among David's contributions in 1 Chr 22:3 and 14.

"great amounts of red carnelian": Instead of the building stones that might be expected next (cf. 1 Chr 22:14-15), the Chronicler lists various kinds of gems that would have been part of vestments or furnishings in the temple. Most English versions and commentators translate this first stone, אבני שהם, as "onyx,"[14] but a cognate verb in Akkadian (*siāmum, sâmu*) means "to be red or brown," and the corresponding noun in Akkadian (*sāmtu*) means "carnelian" (*HALOT* 4:1424). Carnelian, attested eleven times in the OT altogether, appears in Exod 25:7 (the high priest's ephod and breastpiece) and at six other places in the tabernacle account,[15] but not in the account of the building of the temple itself either in 1 Kings or 2 Chronicles.

[*"stones for] setting"*: The noun מלואים occurs at Exod 25:7; 35:9, 27, together with "carnelian," in connection with offerings for the ephod or breastpiece.

"colorful stones set into mortar to form a mosaic": This is a conjectural translation proposed by Rudolph, 190 (אבני פוך ורקמה; lit. "stones of hard mortar and variegation"), and is listed as uncertain by *HALOT* 3:918. פוך usually means (black or red) eye makeup (2 Kgs 9:30; Jer 4:30), but may mean something like "hard mortar" here

---

8   See, however, also 1 Chr 17:21//2 Sam 7:23 (Israel as a unique nation), Isa 51:2 (Abraham was one when Yahweh called him), and 2 Chr 32:12 (before one altar you shall worship).

9   "David thought to himself, 'My son Solomon is young and inexperienced, and the house to be built for Yahweh must be exceedingly magnificent, famous and an object of praise for all the lands; I will therefore make preparations for it.'"

10 Cf. Curtis and Madsen, 28, #12; and Polzin, *Late Biblical Hebrew*, 130, #12.

11 The people contributed gold, silver, and bronze for the tabernacle (Exod 35:5).

12 In addition to individual passages on specific mate-

rials, there are comprehensive lists of the materials used in the tabernacle at Exod 25:3-7 and 35:5-9, 22-28.

13 This is a reference to the artisan Huram-abi, who only worked in bronze according to 1 Kgs 7:14.

14 BDB, 995, notes its definition is dubious, but suggests onyx or chrysoprasus. The latter is an apple-green form of chalcedony, apparently based on the adjective πράσινος used in the LXX.

15 Exod 28:9, 20; 35:9, 27; 39:6, 13. According to Gen 2:12 it was found in Havilah.

and in Isa 54:11. Other scholars consider פּוּךְ to be a by-form of נֹפֶךְ (a semiprecious stone, possibly turquoise, malachite, or garnet, *HALOT* 2:709).[16] רִקְמָה means colorful woven cloth everywhere else in the OT, except for Ezek 17:3, where it refers to the colorful plumage of the eagle (*HALOT* 3:1291). After reviewing similar options, Curtis and Madsen, 303, interpreted וְכָל אֶבֶן יְקָרָה ("and all sorts of precious stones"; see the next comment) as a gloss on the obscure word פּוּךְ that was entered in the wrong place in the text. רִקְמָה then became for them "variegated cloth"[17] and שֵׁשׁ (שֵׁשׁ III in *HALOT* 4:1663; see the discussion of "stones of alabaster" below) was interpreted by them as linen[18] (see the use of the word "linen" in Exod 25:4 and very often in the tabernacle account).

"and all sorts of precious stones": Compare 1 Chr 20:2// 2 Sam 12:30; 2 Chr 9:1, 9//1 Kgs 10:2, 10. The Hebrew is וְכָל אֶבֶן יְקָרָה. Japhet, 507, observes helpfully that the plural of this term (אֲבָנִים גְּדֹלוֹת אֲבָנִים יְקָרוֹת; *NRSV* "great, costly stones") is used in 1 Kgs 5:31 (17) and 7:9-11 (not included in Chronicles) for stones used in the building of the temple.[19]

"stones of alabaster": אַבְנֵי שַׁיִשׁ. שַׁיִשׁ, which is hapax legomenon, is a "later construction" of שֵׁשׁ II and means alabaster (*HALOT* 4:1483, 1663). Both שֵׁשׁ II and שֵׁשׁ III ("alabaster" and "linen" respectively; *HALOT* 4:1663) derive from the same Egyptian loanword (šš), with different determinatives. My tentative translation of the materials assumes that v. 2b refers only to various kinds of gems. Curtis and Madsen, 301–2, on the other hand, thought this verse contained a mixture of gems and various kinds of cloth, leading to their translation of "fine linen" for this term.

■ **3** *"In addition to all I have provided for the holy house"*: This is the last clause in the verse in Hebrew, but the sentence must be rearranged for a coherent English translation. "Holy house" (לְבֵית הַקֹּדֶשׁ) is used only here in Chronicles for the temple;[20] cf. בִּירָה in vv. 1 and 9.

"I have treasure of my own of gold and silver": In addition to his contributions as king, perhaps drawing on public resources (cf. 1 Chr 27:25-31), David also contributed from his personal wealth. "Treasure" (סְגֻלָּה) has a similar meaning in Eccl 2:8, but its more frequent use is as a designation for Israel as Yahweh's prized possession (e.g., Exod 19:5; Deut 7:6).[21]

"and because I take pleasure in the house of my God": The Chronicler uses the expression "the house of my God' three times in vv. 2-3. The verb רצה "take pleasure in" is used to describe God's choice of David in 1 Chr 28:4 and God's preference for uprightness in 29:17.

■ **4** *"Three thousand talents of gold from the gold of Ophir"*: The reference to gold from Ophir[22] is anachronistic, since it is only Solomon who began trading with this country, in league with Hiram (2 Chr 8:18; 9:10//1 Kgs 9:28; 2 Chr 10:11). Ophir is variously located in Arabia, India, or East or southern Africa. Gen 10:29 and 1 Chr 1:23 put it between Seba and Havilah. The amount of gold—about one hundred twelve and a half tons!—is hyperbolic. On one occasion Solomon imported four hundred twenty talents of gold from Ophir (1 Kgs 9:28; the parallel text in 2 Chr 8:18 reads four hundred fifty talents of gold). David's contribution is about seven times greater. The Queen of Sheba gave Solomon one hundred twenty talents of gold from Ophir (2 Chr 9:9//1 Kgs 10:10). Solomon's annual income was six hundred sixty-six talents of gold (2 Chr 9:13). Neco imposed tribute on Judah of only one hundred talents of silver and one talent of gold (2 Chr 36:3). David had already made preparations for the temple of one hundred thousand talents of gold and one million talents of silver (1 Chr 22:14). The cost of the entire tabernacle was twenty-nine talents and seven hundred thirty shekels

---

16 It is one of the jewels in the high priest's vestments in Exod 28:18; 39:11.

17 This noun does not occur in the tabernacle account, but the verb רקם ("weave colorful cloth") appears in Exod 26:36 and frequently.

18 They also regard the word "stones" before this word as secondary.

19 In 2 Chr 3:6, however, without *Vorlage*, the Chronicler has Solomon adorn the walls of the temple with gems (אֶבֶן יְקָרָה לְתִפְאָרֶת).

20 Cf. בֵּית קֹדֶשׁ הַקֳּדָשִׁים as a designation for the Holy of Holies in 2 Chr 3:8, 10//1 Kgs 6:19, 23, and בֵּית מִקְדָּשָׁם "the house of their sanctuary" in 2 Chr 36:17.

21 *HALOT* 2:742. See E. Lipiński, *TDOT* 10:144–48.

22 See also Isa 13:12; Job 28:16; Ps 45:10 (9).

of gold and one hundred talents and one thousand seven hundred seventy-five shekels of silver (Exod 38:24-25).

"seven thousand talents of refined silver": The amount (more than 235 tons) is staggering (but see v. 7). Ammon hired Aramean chariots and cavalry against David for one thousand talents of silver (1 Chr 19:6). King Amaziah was able to hire one hundred thousand mighty warriors from Israel for one hundred talents of silver (2 Chr 25:6). King Jotham had the Ammonites pay an annual tribute of only one hundred talents of silver (2 Chr 27:5). The word "refined" is used of gold in 1 Chr 28:18, of silver in Ps 12:7 (6), and of wine in Isa 25:6. The total of ten thousand talents in this verse may indicate that the Chronicler was creating a perfect round number.

"overlaying the walls of the chambers of the house": The verb "overlay" (טוח, *HALOT* 2:373) is used only here in Chronicles and is used elsewhere in the sense of plastering the wall of a house (e.g., Ezek 13:10). Other verbs (צפה, 1 Kgs 6:20-22, 2 Chr 3:4; and חצף, 2 Chr 3:9) are used for this process in the actual construction of the temple.[23] The word "house" is plural in Hebrew (הבתים) but construed in my translation to refer to the various rooms or chambers of the temple.[24] Other scholars follow the versions (see textual note 2) and read the singular הבית "house."

■ **5** *"and for all the work to be done by artisans":* "Work" (מלאכה) in the sense of workmanship appears also in 1 Chr 22:15 and 28:21. The artisans (חרשים) were respon-sible for manufacturing the temple vessels and other furnishings of the temple and for creating vestments and wall hangings.[25] Such people were also employed in the construction of the tabernacle.[26]

"Who then will offer themselves willingly, consecrating themselves today to Yahweh?" On the basis of his own public and private giving, David appeals to the people to commit themselves to generous contributions for the temple (cf. 2 Chr 35:8). Such generosity was also characteristic of those who contributed toward the tabernacle, though the verb "offer oneself" (נדב) is used in Exodus in the *qal* rather than in the *hitpael*.[27] This use of the *hitpael* is a characteristic of Late Biblical Hebrew.[28] Freewill offerings also took place at the building of the tabernacle (Exod 35:21–36:7) and the building of the Second Temple (Ezra 1:4, 6; 2:68-69; 7:15-16; 8:28). The technical term "consecrate" (lit. "fill the hand")[29] usually describes the setting aside or consecration of priests,[30] beginning with the instructions for the tabernacle and recurring with the designation of the first priests.[31] In Chronicles alone is it used for laypeople committing themselves to contribute for the temple.[32] L. A. Snijders paraphrases the meaning of this verse as follows: "Who now also wishes to increase his own 'strength' so as to be capable for the service of Yahweh?"[33] This verse is also then speaking of a kind of consecration. Japhet, 508, wonders whether this term, borrowed from the consecration of priests, might imply that the Israelites themselves were to be considered as a kingdom of priests (Exod 19:6).

23 This does not justify declaring this passage secondary, *pace* Throntveit, *When Kings Speak*, 90. See also Sara Japhet, "Interchanges," 19–20.
24 See also the commentary on 1 Chr 28:11.
25 1 Chr 14:1 (artisans sent by Hiram to work on David's palace); 22:15; 29:5; 2 Chr 24:12 (artisans commissioned by Joash and Jehoiada to repair the temple); 34:11 (artisans to repair the temple at the time of Josiah). Cf. also the description of Huram-abi in 2 Chr 2:13 (14)//1 Kgs 7:14.
26 Exod 28:11; 35:35; 38:23.
27 Exod 25:2; 35:5, 21-22, 29. Cf. also 1 Chr 29:6, 9, 14, 17; and 2 Chr 17:16. See J. Conrad, "נדב," *TDOT* 9:219–26.
28 Curtis and Madsen, 31, #70; Polzin, 135, #30. In addition to the seven occurrences in this chapter, it also appears in 2 Chr 17:16.
29 Snijders, *TDOT* 8:304, concludes that "fill the hand" is "either a general designation for the ordination of priests or constitutes an integral part of such ordination, namely, the application of blood, the apportionment of sacrificial flesh, and the meal." He adds: "The ritual of hand-filling is a ritual of strengthening one's efficacy as priest." "Hand" is to be understood as "efficacy" or "power."
30 Cf. 2 Chr 13:9; 29:31.
31 Exod 28:41; 29:9, 29, 33, 35; Lev 8:33; 16:32. There are sixteen references to the consecration of priests altogether.
32 In 2 Chr 29:31 Hezekiah says to the people, "You have now consecrated yourselves to Yahweh."
33 *TDOT* 8:305.

29:6-9. People's Generous Response

■ **6** *the leaders of the ancestral houses:* This is the only time שָׂרֵי אָבוֹת is used in Chronicles, but it does appear in Ezra 8:29. Everywhere else leaders of fathers' houses are referred to either as רָאשֵׁי אָבוֹת (with or without definite article; see 1 Chr 8:6, 10, 13, 28; 9:9, 33, 34; 15:12; 23:9, 24; 24:31; 26:21, 26, 32; 27:1; 2 Chr 1:2; 26:12) or as רָאשֵׁי בֵית אָבוֹת (1 Chr 7:40; 24:4).

the leaders of the tribes of Israel, and the commanders of the thousands and the hundreds: Compare 1 Chr 28:1.

the officers[34] *over the work of the king:* Compare the list of civic officials in 27:25-31.

■ **7** *They gave for the service of the house of God five thousand talents and ten thousand darics of gold:* The weight of the talents comes to about one hundred sixty-eight tons, but the darics to only about one hundred eighty-five pounds. Darics came into circulation at the time of Darius I (522–486 BCE), precluding the writing of Chronicles before that time. This passage and Ezra 8:27 ("twenty gold bowls worth a thousand darics") are the only biblical passages to mention the coin with this spelling with a prosthetic *'ālep* (אֲדַרְכֹנִים).[35] Whatever we make of its weight,[36] the appearance of darics in the time of David and Solomon—four centuries before their actual use—is a clear anachronism. Williamson, *Israel*, 84, argues convincingly that this coin provides a terminus ante quem for the date of Chronicles, since it is unlikely that this coin would be referred to much later than the Persian Empire itself. The lay contributions according to the Chronicler were in gold itself and in minted coins. The highly inflated numbers in this verse echo the extremely large gifts of David in 1 Chr 22:14-16.

ten thousand talents of silver: More than three hundred thirty-six tons. In v. 4 David contributed three thousand talents of gold.

eighteen thousand talents of bronze: More than six hundred five tons. In v. 4 David contributed seven thousand talents of silver.

one hundred thousand talents of iron: More than three thousand three hundred sixty-five tons. The amount of bronze and iron contributed by David (v. 2) was not specified.

■ **8** *Whoever had precious stones gave them:* This is the only time gems are referred to by the generic word for stones, אֲבָנִים.

to the treasury of the house of Yahweh through the hand of Jehiel the Gershonite: Jehiel was chief among the sons of Ladan and grandson of Levi, through Gershon, in 1 Chr 23:8. According to 26:22, Zetham and Joel, sons of Jehieli, were in charge of the treasuries of the house of Yahweh.

■ **9** *the people rejoiced . . . and also King David rejoiced with a great rejoicing:* The Chronicler characteristically reports joy at significant moments of Israel's history. Compare vv. 17 and 22 below and 1 Chr 13:8//2 Sam 6:5; 1 Chr 15:16, 29//2 Sam 6:16; 2 Chr 7:10; 15:15; 24:10; 29:30, 36; 30:21, 23, 25, 26.

because these have given voluntarily, for they had volunteered with a perfect heart: David had encouraged Solomon to serve Yahweh with a perfect heart (1 Chr 28:9), and he prays that God would give him such a heart in this chapter (v. 19; cf. v. 18).[37] In this verse the Chronicler characteristically combines the ideas of generosity, joy, and a perfect heart. The people's gifts flowed in without any reluctance.

29:10-20. David's Final Prayer
29:10-19. The Prayer Itself

■ **10** *David blessed Yahweh before the whole assembly:* In response to David's bidding the assembly blesses Yahweh in v. 20.[38] Other passages in which individuals or the people as a whole bless Yahweh in the Bible include Gen 24:48; Deut 8:10; Josh 22:33; 2 Chr 20:26; 31:8. When people bless Yahweh, they apply the blessing formula to

---

34   The Chronicler uses an emphatic לְ before the last element in this list. Cf. Polzin, *Late Biblical Hebrew*, 66–68.

35   See also Ezra 2:69; Neh 7:70-72 דַּרְכְּמוֹנִים. Curtis and Madsen, 29, #22; Williamson, *Israel*, 42, #10; 51, #24; Polzin, *Late Biblical Hebrew*, 133, #21.

36   Williamson, 184, remarks that this amount is not beyond reason.

37   See also 1 Chr 12:39 (38); 2 Chr 15:17; 16:9; 25:2.

38   The verb "bless" is used twice in both v. 10 and v. 20. Josef Scharbert, *TDOT* 2:292, attributes the prefixed לְ (לַיהוה) to Aramaic influence. Cf. Dan 2:19-20; 4:31 (34).

him, as in the following citation from v. 10. As Solomon will do in 2 Chr 6:14-42, David takes the lead in the praise of God.

"Blessed are you Yahweh, God of Israel our ancestor": While this second person blessing of Yahweh is common in contemporary synagogal worship today, the only other occurrence in the Bible is in Ps 119:12.[39] A formula offering a blessing to Yahweh in the third person appears in 1 Kgs 5:21 (7)//2 Chr 2:11 (12); 1 Kgs 8:15//2 Chr 6:4; 1 Kgs 10:9//2 Chr 9:8; Pss 28:6; 31:22 (21); 41:14 (13); 72:18; 89:53 (52); 106:48//1 Chr 16:36; Ps 135:21. "Israel" is always used instead of "Jacob" to designate the patriarch in Chronicles, except for 1 Chr 16:13, 17, where the Chronicler is quoting from Psalm 105. "Our ancestor" modifies Israel, not Yahweh.[40] The appeal to the tradition of Jacob in this context is appropriate, since Jacob was both rich and attributed his riches to the blessing of Yahweh (Gen 30:43; 31:7; and esp. 33:11). See v. 18 below.

"forever and ever": See Pss 41:14 (13); 90:2; 103:17; 106:48//1 Chr 16:36; Neh 9:5.

■ **11** *"To you Yahweh belong greatness, and power, and honor, and splendor, and majesty"*: Braun, 284, has demonstrated how indebted the Chronicler is to the Psalter for these epithets,[41] although the Chronicler may also have known them through personal liturgical use.

"indeed, all things in heaven and earth": Compare the references to Yahweh as the maker of heaven and earth in Pss 115:15; 121:2. Chronicles starts with an affirmation of Yahweh as the God of Israel (v. 10) and extrapolates from that to Yahweh's rulership over the whole world.

"yours is the kingdom, Yahweh": Compare 2 Chr 13:8: "the kingdom of Yahweh in the hand of the sons of David." The doxology appended to the Lord's Prayer in many late manuscripts of Matt 6:13 is dependent on vv. 11-12.

■ **12** *"Riches and wealth come from you"*: God promised riches and wealth to Solomon in a passage from Kings not included by the Chronicler (1 Kgs 3:13), and this passage may have led the Chronicler to make this reference here to this idea. Riches and honor are given to Solomon in another passage considerably revised from its *Vorlage* (2 Chr 1:12//1 Kgs 2:12), and David had both riches and wealth in his old age (v. 28). Both Jehoshaphat and Hezekiah, two of the Chronicler's favorite kings, had riches and wealth (2 Chr 17:5; 18:1; 32:27).

"you rule over all": In Jehoshaphat's prayer in 2 Chr 20:6, also composed by the Chronicler, the king proclaims: "You rule over the kingdoms of the nations." Compare Ps 89:10 (9): "You rule the raging of the sea."

"it is in your power to make great and to give strength to all": Compare v. 25, where Yahweh exalts Solomon, and especially 2 Chr 1:1: "Yahweh made him [Solomon] exceedingly great."

■ **13** *"And now, our God, we give thanks to you and we praise your magnificent name"*: David moves from general praise to specific expressions of thanksgiving, and signals this shift with the words "And now" (cf. 1 Chr 28:8). The two clauses cited here are in synonymous parallelism. Since the second clause would be shorter because the pronoun "we" is not repeated, the object of the praise in the second clause is lengthened from "you" to "your magnificent name" (a ballast variant). The word "magnificent" (תפארתך; a noun in Hebrew) is used of Yahweh's name in Isa 63:14 and of Yahweh's house in Isa 60:7 and 64:10.

■ **14** *"who am I and who is my people"*: For a similar self-deprecation see the prayer of David in 1 Chr 17:16//2 Sam 7:18 and the words of Solomon in 2 Chr 2:6 (without *Vorlage*).

"that we should have enough strength to make a freewill offering": The combination עצר כח ("have enough

---

39 Drawing on rabbinic sources, L. Finkelstein, "The Prayer of King David according to the Chronicler" (Hebrew), *ErIsr* 14 (1978) 110–16, English summary, 126–27, argued that a layperson like David would have to say two words ("Blessed you") before the Tetragrammaton outside the temple whereas a priest in the temple only had to say one word before the Tetragrammaton: "Blessed."

40 Contra Braun, 281, who bases his argument on 1 Kgs 1:48, on which this passage is dependent, but in that passage Israel refers to the nation/people of Israel, not to the ancestor.

41 For greatness see Ps 71:21; for power see Ps 89:14 (13); for honor see Ps 71:8; for splendor (*HALOT* 2:716) see 1 Sam 15:29; Isa 63:6; Lam 3:18 (in the Psalter, esp. with ל, this word frequently connotes permanence [e.g., Ps 9:19 (18)]); for majesty see Ps 96:6//1 Chr 16:27.

strength") is characteristic of Late Biblical Hebrew and is used in Chronicles and Daniel as a synonym of יכל.[42] The Chronicler's David, having praised and thanked God for his power and majesty, now declares on behalf of the whole assembly their own weakness and dependence. Balentine concludes, "The rhetoric of these prayers [of David, Asa, and Jehoshaphat] serves as proclamation."[43]

"from what comes from your hand, we have given you": This clause answers the rhetorical question with which the verse began. Graham notes that "freewill offering" is a bit of an illusion: "Whenever one is devoted to God and expresses it in practices, God is to be thanked for having made that disposition possible."[44] The thought of Paul is similar: "For who sees anything different in you? What do you have that you did not receive? And if you received it, why do you boast as if it were not a gift?" (1 Cor 4:7). The people are stewards of God's gifts, just as David's officials managed his properties (1 Chr 27:15-21).

■ **15** *"We are aliens before you and transients like all of our ancestors":* Daniel Estes has written, "The fact of sociopolitical sojourning of the previous generations is to the pious mind analogous to the unassimilated character of the righteous individual living in a world estranged from God."[45] "Aliens" and "transients" are also used elsewhere with a similar connotation, beginning with the

account of Abraham.[46] The transience of human life can be contrasted with Yahweh, who is blessed forever and ever (v. 10).

"Our days are like a shadow on the earth": The fleeting character of human life, classically expressed in the three score years and ten of Ps 90:9-10 (cf. v. 5), is often compared in the Bible to a passing shadow.[47]

"there is no hope": The ultimate expression of human frailty and dependence is our hopelessness in the face of our mortality.[48] Jeremiah spoke about Yahweh as the hope of Israel (14:8; 17:13; 50:7), and Shecaniah affirmed an adamant belief in hope despite the sin of intermarriage (Ezra 10:2). Rudolph, 192, finds the mention of hopelessness inappropriate in this context (why?) and therefore construes the noun מקוה to mean "security."[49]

■ **16** *"all this abundance that we have provided[50] to build you a house for your holy name comes from your hand and is all your own":* This repeats in different words what had been already expressed in v. 14b. For "your holy name" see 1 Chr 16:35//Ps 106:47. Deuteronomy frequently speaks of Yahweh putting his name in the temple (12:5 and often; cf. 2 Chr 6:5-10).

■ **17** *"you test the heart and take pleasure in uprightness":* The idea that Yahweh tests or tries the heart and the kidneys is widespread in the Bible,[51] with the contrast between Yahweh's testing and human innocence that

---

42   Curtis and Madsen, 33, #92; Polzin, 148, #74. See 2 Chr 2:5 (6); 13:20; 22:9; Dan 10:8, 16; 11:6; cf. 2 Chr 14:10 and 20:37, where it appears without כה. None of the passages from Chronicles has a *Vorlage* in the Deuteronomistic History.

43   See Balentine, *Prayer,* 102. This contrast between the power and might of Yahweh and human weakness and dependence is a major theme in the Chronicler's prayers (2 Chr 14:11; 20:6, 12).

44   "Character Ethics," 113.

45   Daniel J. Estes, "Metaphorical Sojourning in 1 Chronicles 29:15," *CBQ* 53 (1991) 45–49.

46   Gen 23:4; Lev 25:23; Ps 39:13 (12). In the last case the psalmist compares himself to all of his ancestors.

47   Job 8:9; 14:2; Pss 102:12 (11); 109:23; 144:4; Eccl 6:12; 8:13. J. Rendell Harris, "On an Obscure Quotation in the First Epistle of Clement," *JBL* 29 (1910) 190–95, argued that a quotation ascribed to Moses in *1 Clement* 17 ("I am smoke from a pot") should really be attributed to David and is based on

a variant text of 1 Chr 29:15 now preserved only in the Syriac version of that verse.

48   Cf. 2 Chr 20:12: "We are powerless against this great multitude that is coming against us. We do not know what to do, but our eyes are on you." Cf. Ezra 9:6-15.

49   M. Wallenstein, "Some Lexical Material in the Judean Scrolls," *VT* 4 (1954) 214, suggests a meaning "abode."

50   הכיננו from כון in the *hiphil.* Cf. Curtis and Madsen, 30, #54; Williamson, *Israel,* 53. See also vv. 2, 3, 19.

51   Pss 7:10 (9); 11:4-5; 17:3; Jer 11:20; 12:3; 17:10; 20:12; Prov 17:3.

David affirms here best paralleled in Ps 17:3: "If you try my heart, if you visit me by night, if you test me, you will find no wickedness in me; my mouth does not transgress." As we have seen before (see the commentary on 1 Chr 28:9), the attitude behind Yahweh's testing of the heart is linked to the Deity's hope in human piety. This third use of the verb רצה, translated "take pleasure," in the last two chapters—and only here in Chronicles—matches well with Yahweh's delight in making David king (28:4) and in David's devotion to (i.e., his delight in) the temple (29:3).

"*In the uprightness of my heart I have freely offered all these things*": By the use of the independent pronoun אני the Hebrew now emphasizes what David had done as a complement to what Yahweh characteristically does. This link is reinforced by the second use of the word "uprightness" (ישר) in this verse, though now in the singular instead of the plural.[52] David's uprightness was also affirmed by Yahweh in 1 Kgs 9:4,[53] although the Chronicler does not use the word "uprightness" when he cites this verse in 2 Chr 7:17. The possibility for humans to live uprightly is widely affirmed in the OT (Job 33:3; Ps 119:7; contrast Deut 9:5). The word "heart" is used five times in vv. 17-19.

"*and now I have seen your people, who are present here, offering themselves joyfully to you*": Introduced by the transitional and climactic words "and now," David's words acknowledge the joyful donations of the people recorded in vv. 6-9. The exemplary generosity of David and the people is surely meant to be an incentive for the audience of the Chronicler also to give generously to the temple.

■ **18** "*Yahweh, God of Abraham, Isaac, and Israel, our ancestors*": As David turns to the section of his prayer offering petitions, he uses the longest divine title in this chapter, naming Yahweh as the God of all three patriarchs. The prayer had begun with an appeal to "Yahweh, God of Israel our ancestor" (v. 10). This full invocation is attested elsewhere only at 2 Chr 30:6 (a nonsynoptic pas-

sage) and 1 Kgs 18:36 (not included by the Chronicler). Abraham (Gen 24:1) and Isaac (Gen 26:12-14) had received all their wealth from God, just like Jacob/Israel (see v. 10).

"*keep forever the inclination of the thoughts of the heart of your people and direct their heart toward you*": David prays that the present commitment of the people will be maintained forever, no doubt including the audience for whom the Chronicler was writing. Such commitment can come only through divine assistance.[54] The Chronicler was indebted to Gen 6:5 for "the inclination of the thoughts" (cf. 1 Chr 28:9), and his kerygmatic intention is reinforced by the use of the word "forever." The verbosity of this verse (Braun, 282) may stem from the Chronicler's attempt to emphasize both inward and outward piety toward Yahweh. Rehoboam is criticized by the Chronicler for not directing his heart toward Yahweh (2 Chr 12:14), while Jehoshaphat is praised for directing his heart to seek God (19:3). The people of Jehoshaphat's time had not yet directed their hearts to Yahweh (20:33), and Hezekiah prayed for all those who so directed their hearts in his day (30:19).[55]

■ **19** "*give to Solomon my son a perfect heart to keep your commandments, your decrees, and your statutes*": The first item for which David prays is Solomon's ability and determination to obey the law, with a pun between "Solomon" (שלמה) and "perfect heart" (לבב שלם; cf. v. 9). The only other time in Chronicles that these three words for "law"—מצותיך, עדותיך, וחקיך—are used in one verse is 2 Chr 34:31//2 Kgs 23:1, where Josiah made a covenant to keep Yahweh's commandments, decrees, and statutes.

"*and to build the temple, for which I have made preparations*": The second item for which David prays is Solomon's ability and determination to build the temple. By mentioning his own preparations one more time David emphasizes that the joint authority of both kings of the united monarchy has been placed behind the temple. As in v. 1, the Chronicler uses בירה to designate the sanctuary.

---

52 ישר instead of מישרים.

53 "As for you, if you will walk before me, as David your father walked, with integrity of heart and uprightness, doing according to all that I have commanded you, and keeping my statutes and my ordinances. . . ."

54 Cf. 1 Chr 22:12; 2 Chr 30:12.

55 Cf. 1 Sam 7:3: "If you are returning to Yahweh with all your heart. . . ."

29:20. People's Response

■ **20** *all the assembly blessed Yahweh the God of their ancestors:* This blessing took place in response to David's command and presumably consisted of the formula "Blessed are you . . ." (cf. v. 10). Only here is the object of blessing preceded by a ל. See also the parallel passages cited at v. 10 and especially 2 Chr 20:26 and 31:8.

and they bowed and prostrated themselves to Yahweh and to the king: The only unexpected thing in this verse is the prostration before the king.[56] One might argue that the assembly had followed David twice already in this chapter by donating to the temple (vv. 6-9) and by blessing Yahweh in this verse, and that therefore they would naturally honor him by prostrating themselves before him as well. Ornan had previously prostrated himself to David (1 Chr 21:21//2 Sam 24:20), and the officials of Judah will later do the same to Joash (2 Chr 24:17, without *Vorlage*).[57] It is proper to prostrate themselves before the king, since he sits on Yahweh's throne (see v. 23). This act also implies popular endorsement of David's plans and his generosity. The first celebration is for the completion of preparations for the temple before the people turn to the inauguration of the new king.

29:21-25. Enthronement of Solomon

■ **21** *On the next day:* While there is no textual evidence against this reading, its location in the Hebrew text is unusual—it comes late in the verse and separates the "burnt offerings" from the list of animals that were offered up. Japhet, 513, considers it a gloss by an editor who did not like the fact that sacrifices preceded Solomon's enthronement and hence transferred them to the day after the enthronement. But why then would the editor not shift the whole verse to make that clearer? Even after this proposed gloss, the sacrifices come before Solomon's installation. Braun, 286, and De Vries, 223, connect the communion sacrifices to the prayers of David and the people on the previous day, putting the burnt offerings on the second day, but this would be an odd distribution of the two kinds of sacrifices to separate days. Throntveit believes that both kinds of sacrifices had to be moved to the day after the events in vv. 1-19 because of the secondary insertion of the contributions by David and the people in vv. 1-9 after the presentation of Solomon to the assembly in 1 Chr 28:1-7a, 19-21.[58] Since an editor reckoned that the collection of gifts would take time, he postponed the sacrifices and Solomon's anointing to the next day. If 29:1-9 is original, as I believe, Throntveit's argument is moot. Perhaps we should admit that we have insufficient reasons to change the text and conclude that the Chronicler has used his temporal reference awkwardly. It was only on the second day, after the gifts of David and the people (vv. 1-9) and their blessing of Yahweh had taken place on the first day (vv. 10-20), that the people offered their sacrifices to Yahweh.

a thousand bulls, a thousand rams, and a thousand lambs: The large number of animals points to the significance of the occasion.[59] These three thousand animals pale in comparison with the twenty-two thousand oxen and one hundred twenty thousand sheep sacrificed at the dedication of the temple (2 Chr 7:4-5//1 Kgs 8:62-63),[60] with the nineteen thousand animals contributed by Hezekiah and his officials at his great Passover (2 Chr 30:23-27), and with the thirty-seven thousand six hundred lambs and kids and the three thousand eight hundred bulls at Josiah's Passover (2 Chr 35:7-9). Sacrifices of sheep, oxen, and fatlings had been offered up at Adonijah's abortive coronation (1 Kgs 1:9, 19, 25), and the Chronicler makes up for a lack of sacrificial ritual in Solomon's anointing by recording this massive sacrifice by the whole assembly.

with their libations: These libations or drink offerings that accompanied the burnt offerings are mentioned elsewhere in Chronicles only in the days of Hezekiah (2 Chr 29:35). Drink offerings for the daily sacrifices of lambs were one-fourth of a hin of wine for each lamb (Exod 29:40-41; Num 28:7-10).

56　Braun, 287, suggests 2 Chr 20:20 and 13:12 as parallels, but neither example is really apt. De Vries, 223, proposes that "the king" is a gloss and notes incorrectly that it is wanting in LXX[BA] and Syr.

57　In 1 Kgs 1:31 Bathsheba prostrates herself before David.

58　*When Kings Speak*, 90–91.

59　Johnstone, 1:291, notes that on this occasion there is no sin offering since the community shows complete solidarity. Contrast this with 2 Chr 29:21.

60　Solomon and the assembly offered an uncountable number of sheep and oxen at the installation of the ark (2 Chr 5:6).

for all Israel: This is the first of four references to "all Israel" in the latter part of this chapter (cf. vv. 23, 25, 26). The Chronicler does not grow weary of emphasizing how united the nation was in its support of David and Solomon.

■ **22** *they ate and drank before Yahweh on that day with great joy:* At David's coronation at Hebron his warriors ate and drank with him for three days (1 Chr 12:40 ([39]), and eating and drinking are also mentioned at Adonijah's coronation (1 Kgs 1:25), and the people rejoiced with great joy at the anointing of Solomon (1 Kgs 1:40). The Chronicler therefore puts echoes of David's coronation in the coronation of Solomon, and he has put elements from the coronations of Adonijah and Solomon in 1 Kings into his own description of Solomon's coronation.

they made Solomon, the son of David, king: The MT adds to the original text (see textual note 22) "for a second time." The first coronation might either have been 1 Chr 23:1, where we are told in a summary statement, anticipating the following chapters, that David made Solomon king; or it could be an allusion to 1 Kgs 1:38-49, where Zadok and Nathan made Solomon king in what might have seemed to the Chronicler as a hasty and excessively private manner.[61] Elsewhere in Chronicles it is either Yahweh himself or the people that make someone king. The people's actions here confirm what was done in a preliminary way by David.[62]

they anointed him as Yahweh's prince and [they anointed] Zadok as priest: The prince (נגיד) was either someone designated to be king, that is, a crown prince (as Rehoboam chose Abijah as king-designate, 2 Chr 11:22, without *Vorlage*) or the word is merely a synonym for the word "king" itself (as in 1 Chr 5:2). A divine oracle had indicated that David should be נגיד (1 Chr 11:2//2 Sam 5:2; 1 Chr 17:7//2 Sam 7:8). The Chronicler's use of the term here shows the influence of 1 Kgs 1:35. According to 1 Kgs 1:39, it was Zadok—not the people—who anointed Solomon to be king. David had been anointed king at Hebron (1 Chr 11:3; cf. 14:8).[63] A contrast between Solomon and Saul (cf. 1 Sam 9:16; 10:1) is implied, since only these two people were anointed to be נגיד.[64]

Much more surprising is the notice that the assembly anointed Zadok to be priest, which is sometimes considered secondary.[65] Zadok had already been serving as priest during David's reign (cf. 1 Chr 15:11, where he is named with Abiathar, and 1 Chr 16:39, where he is stationed before the tabernacle at Gibeon).[66] Perhaps this anointing of Zadok is the Chronicler's interpretation of 1 Kgs 2:35, where Solomon made Zadok priest in the place of Abiathar, whom he had banished to Anathoth.[67] It might also be an attempt to emphasize the joint roles of king and priest known from other postexilic passages, such as Hag 1:12-14; Zech 6:12-14; and Jer 33:17-18.[68] The Pentateuch, in any case, makes provisions for the

---

61   See also Beecher, "Note."
62   Christine Mitchell, "Transformations in Meaning: Solomon's Accession in Chronicles," *JHS* 4 (2002) 7: "In order to be fully sanctioned, he has to be made king by the people, not merely by his father."
63   Yahweh also anointed Jehu to destroy the house of Ahab (2 Chr 22:7), and Jehoiada and his sons anointed Joash in the temple (2 Chr 23:11).
64   See Mitchell, "Transformations in Meaning," 8, 10. She notes that in 2 Chr 19:11 Amariah is the high priest and Zebadiah is נגיד, and both officials are subject to the king, Jehoshaphat. So Solomon is subservient to David until the latter's death.
65   Williamson, 187.
66   Zadok is also mentioned in the high priestly genealogy (1 Chr 5:34 [6:8]; 6:38 [53]). See also 1 Chr 18:16; 24:3, 6, 31; 27:17.
67   Rudolph, 193, notes that 1 Kgs 2:35 comes after David's death. Since Zadok anointed Solomon at David's command (1 Kgs 1:34, 39), the Chronicler

would have concluded that Zadok must have been anointed priest already on Solomon's coronation day. Rudolph assigns the other references to Zadok during David's reign to a secondary stratum (1 Chr 5:34; 6:38; 12:29; 15:11; 24:3, 6, 31). Zadok also appears among the list of David's officers in 1 Chr 18:16//2 Sam 8:17.
68   See William Schniedewind, "King and Priest in the Book of Chronicles and the Duality of Qumran," *JJS* 45 (1994) 71–78; Klaus Baltzer, "Das Ende des Staates Juda und die Messiasfrage," in *Studien zur Theologie der alttestamentlichen Überlieferungen* (FS. Gerhard von Rad; ed. R. Rendtorff and K. Koch; Neukirchen: Neukirchener Verlag, 1961) 40–43. Cf. also the commentary to 2 Chr 19:11.

anointing of Aaron and his sons (Exod 40:15; Lev 8:1-12; 21:10).[69]

■ **23** *And Solomon sat on the throne of Yahweh:* This quotation of 1 Kgs 1:46[70] is one of only two direct uses of 1 Kings 1–2 by the Chronicler (cf. below on v. 27). Even here the Chronicler alters the reference to the throne from "the royal throne" (כסא המלוכה)[71] to the "throne of Yahweh" (כסא יהוה; cf. 1 Chr 17:14; 28:5; 2 Chr 9:8// 1 Kgs 10:9). In 1 Kgs 2:12 Solomon sat on the throne of David after his death.

He prospered, and all Israel obeyed him: The Chronicler reports that Solomon prospered already before his reign had begun, and such prosperity in Chronicles is a repeated sign of God's blessing on a reign.[72] The second clause, noting Israel's obedience, is an example of the way in which Solomon prospered. It might be a paraphrase of 1 Kgs 2:12, 46, which tell how Solomon's kingdom was firmly established. The Chronicler may also be continuing his comparison of the installation of Solomon with Joshua, for the Israelites also obeyed him (Deut 34:9; cf. Josh 1:16-20). In 1 Chr 22:13 David and the Chronicler had made Solomon's prosperity dependent on his keeping the Law of Moses. In any case the obedience of Israel shows that Solomon was equally ranked with David by his contemporaries (cf. 11:1, where all Israel indicates its subservience to David by identifying themselves as his bone and flesh).

■ **24** *All the leaders, warriors, and all the sons of King David pledged their allegiance:* The support of the warriors echoes their support for David in 1 Chr 12:39 (38).

David's own warriors had not sided with Adonijah in his attempted coup, nor did Adonijah invite the warriors to his royal ritual (1 Kgs 1:8, 10). The alleged support of all David's sons for Solomon, of course, is in direct contradiction to the story of Adonijah, who had invited all the king's sons, with the exception of Solomon himself, to the sacrificial ritual designed to make him king (1:9-10, 19, 25). Adonijah did subject himself to Solomon after the latter had been made king (1:43). In Kings, however, there was widespread, if not unanimous, support for Solomon (1:38-40).[73] For "pledge allegiance" (נתנו יד תחת) see 2 Chr 30:8, where it refers to allegiance to Yahweh.

■ **25** *Yahweh magnified Solomon exceedingly:*[74] David's prayer had anticipated this fulfillment when he had affirmed that Yahweh has the power "to make great" (v. 12) since to him belongs "greatness" (v. 11). In 1 Kings Benaiah had expressed the wish that Yahweh would make both the throne of Solomon (1:37) and the name of Solomon (1:47) greater than those of King David. The second book of Chronicles begins by noting that Yahweh had made Solomon exceedingly great (2 Chr 1:1). Only Solomon among the kings of Israel is so magnified in Chronicles. This exaltation of Solomon continues the parallels with the installation of Joshua.[75]

he gave him royal majesty that had not been on any king more than on him: "Majesty" is ascribed to Yahweh in v. 11, as well as in 1 Chr 16:27. The translation of לפניו by "more than on him" follows a suggestion by W. E. Barnes mentioned in Curtis and Madsen, 307.[76] If we

---

69 Japhet, 513, notes that except for these passages there is no biblical evidence from either the First or the Second Temple for the anointing of priests. There is indirect evidence, however, in the references to the anointed priest (הכהן המשיח) in Lev 4:3, 5, 16; 6:15.

70 1 Kgs 2:12 is similar: "So Solomon sat on the throne of his father David; and his kingdom was firmly established."

71 Other references to the throne in 1 Kings 1–2 have David refer to "my throne" (1:13, 17, 24, 30, 35), or others refer to "the throne of my lord the king" (1:20, 27, 37, 47) or "the throne of David his father" (2:12).

72 1 Chr 22:11, 13; 2 Chr 7:11; 14:7 (6); 26:5; 31:21; 32:30. When people are disobedient, they do not prosper (2 Chr 13:12; 24:20).

73 He is supported by Zadok, Nathan, and Benaiah, and "all the people" followed him and rejoiced.

74 למעלה. Cf. Curtis and Madsen, 32, #87; Williamson, 55, #7; Polzin, 140–41, #46.

75 Cf. Josh 3:7: "I will begin to exalt you in the sight of all Israel"; 4:14: "On that day Yahweh exalted Joshua in the sight of all Israel."

76 Barnes cited Job 34:19 as a parallel.

translate the suffixed preposition more conventionally by "before him," it would make Solomon exceed both Saul and David in majesty, perhaps in fulfillment of the prayer of Benaiah, who asked that Solomon's name would be greater than David's (1 Kgs 1:39, 47).[77] Mitchell finds here an intertextual relationship that contrasts Solomon to Saul without mentioning the latter.[78] She notes that Saul was anointed by Samuel (1 Sam 10:1), chosen as king and acclaimed by the people (10:20-26), and made king after his defeat of the Ammonites (11:14-15), but he is evaluated negatively by the Chronicler (1 Chr 10:13-14). In comparison, Solomon is made king twice (23:1 and 29:22) and highly evaluated in this verse. The MT adds the words "over Israel" at the end of the sentence (see textual note 25) to make explicit that Solomon is just being compared with kings of Israel.

29:26-30. David's Death and a Summary of His Reign

■ **26** *David the son of Jesse reigned over all Israel:* The reference to David as the son of Jesse means that a mention of David's father appears as a bracket around his reign (see 1 Chr 10:14) and that David's origins were as a commoner. In addition, the affirmation of David's rule over all Israel balances the reference to all Israel being witness to Solomon's exaltation in the previous verse, and it echoes the statement at the beginning of David's reign that all Israel had made David king already at Hebron (11:1, in distinction to 2 Sam 5:1, where the northern Israelite tribes alone made him king there).

■ **27** *The days that he ruled over Israel were forty years:* This verse is the second direct quotation from 1 Kings 1–2, namely 2:11. The emphasis in the previous verse that David had ruled over all Israel means that readers of Chronicles are meant to understand that his rule at Hebron was already over all Israel.

In Hebron he ruled seven years, and in Jerusalem he ruled thirty-three years: Actually, David ruled seven years and six months in Hebron (2 Sam 5:9).

■ **28** *He died in good old age, full of days, riches, and wealth:* The Chronicler corrects the impression gained from 1 Kings 1–2 that David was feeble and powerless in his final days.[79] Rather, David is described with words that were used of the blessed end of many OT worthies: Abraham (Gen 15:15; 25:8), Isaac (Gen 35:29), Gideon (Judg 8:32), and Job (42:17). The words "old and full of days" were used of David already in 1 Chr 23:1. Riches and wealth are signs of divine approval in Chronicles (see 2 Chr 1:11-12; 17:5; 18:1, both with Jehoshaphat; 2 Chr 32:27, with Hezekiah). As David had affirmed earlier in the chapter, riches and wealth are also to be understood as gifts of God (v. 12).[80] Japhet, 516, proposes a possible accidental omission of the burial notice for David that was lost by parablepsis after the word "wealth" (וכבוד): "And he was buried in the city of David" (ויקבר בעיר דויד; cf. 1 Kgs 2:10), but the Chronicler has expanded and changed the concluding summary from 1 Kgs 2:10-12 so radically that it is hard to accept this suggestion with any confidence. Neither Kings nor Chronicles provides an evaluation of David's reign, but the positive tone of this verse indicates where the Chronicler stood on this question: David excelled over all the other kings.

■ **29** *The deeds of David, the first and the last:*[81] The book of Kings did not have a formula citing sources for the reign of David. The formula "the first and the last" is used for nine kings by the Chronicler, and in none of these cases was it found in his *Vorlage* (Solomon, 2 Chr 9:29//1 Kgs 11:41; Rehoboam, 2 Chr 12:15//1 Kgs 14:29; Asa, 2 Chr 16:11//1 Kgs 15:23; Jehoshaphat, 2 Chr 20:34//1 Kgs 22:46; Amaziah, 2 Chr 25:26//2 Kgs 14:18; Uzziah, 2 Chr 26:22//2 Kgs 15:6; Ahaz, 2 Chr 28:26//2 Kgs

---

77 The Chronicler makes no mention here or elsewhere of Ishbosheth.

78 Mitchell, "Transformations in Meaning," 8–10. Saul is also alluded to without name in 1 Chr 17:13.

79 See esp. 1 Kgs 1:1-4, where the king is warmed by Abishag, whom he did not know sexually, perhaps because he was unable to.

80 In 1 Kgs 3:13, not included by the Chronicler, Yahweh promises Solomon riches and wealth. In 1826 Pastor Peter Whitney used this verse as the text for his sermon at the funeral of John Adams, the sec-

ond president of the United States: "He died in good old age, full of days . . . and honor."

81 Wilhelm Caspari, "Der Anfang von II Chron und die Mitte des Königsbuches," *ZAW* 39 (1921) 170–74, argued that this verse really begins 2 Chronicles. He related the words of David recorded by Samuel to 1 Sam 17:26 or 32, the words recorded by Nathan to 2 Sam 7:18-29, and the words recorded by Gad to 2 Sam 23:1-8.

16:19; Josiah, 2 Chr 35:26-27//2 Kgs 23:28). In fact, this formula is never used in any of the source citations in the book of Kings.[82]

in the acts of Samuel the seer: It is unlikely that the Chronicler is alluding to noncanonical sources in this and the following two references.[83] Rather, he is attributing prophetic authorship to 1-2 Samuel, which is included among the "Former Prophets" in the Jewish canon. A reference like 1 Chr 28:4 (Yahweh's choice of David among the sons of Jesse) might have led the Chronicler to think of Samuel's role in the anointing of David in 1 Sam 16:1-13. Samuel is called "the seer" (הראה) in 1 Sam 9:9, 11, 18, 19, but in 1 Sam 9:9 this title is equated with "prophet." Samuel plays a very minor role in Chronicles, though he is given Levitical ancestry (1 Chr 6:13 [28], 18 [33]; 9:22 [where he is also called "seer"]; 11:3; 26:28; 2 Chr 35:18 [where he is called "prophet"]). By using three prophetic terms for Samuel, Nathan, and Gad the Chronicler stresses the entire range of prophetic activity.

in the acts of Nathan the prophet: Here the Chronicler may have thought of 1 Chronicles 17//2 Samuel 7 (cf. 2 Chr 9:29; 29:25). Did Nathan's prominent role in 1 Kings 1–2, which the Chronicler knew but did not quote extensively, lead to the idea that Nathan had authored these chapters? For the title "the prophet" with Samuel, see 1 Chr 17:1//2 Sam 7:2.

in the acts of Gad who saw visions: Gad appears in the account of David's census, 1 Chronicles 21//2 Samuel 24. Gad is specifically called a "seer" (חזה) in 2 Sam 24:11[84]//1 Chr 21:9 and 2 Chr 29:25 (without *Vorlage*). A much later apocryphal source is called "The Words of Gad the Seer."[85] I have chosen the translation "who saw visions" in this verse to distinguish Gad from Samuel the seer (הראה) earlier in the verse.

■ **30** *with accounts of all his rule and might:* The Chronicler would have found references to a king's might in the regnal summaries of Asa in 1 Kgs 15:23 ("might" is omitted

in 2 Chr 16:11), Jehu in 2 Kgs 10:34, and Hezekiah in 2 Kgs 20:20 ("might" is omitted in 2 Chr 32:32).

the events that befell him: The best parallel to this usage within Chronicles may be 1 Chr 12:33 (cf. 2 Chr 15:5; neither passage has a *Vorlage*). Perhaps the Chronicler also thought of Ps 31:16 (15), one of the "David" psalms: "My times are in your hand."

all the kingdoms of the lands:[86] Here the Chronicler refers to nations with whom David interacted, such as the Philistines, Moab, the Arameans, Edom, Ammon, Sidon, and Tyre. All the families of the peoples were asked to bring an offering in 1 Chr 16:28-29//Ps 96:7-9a.

Conclusion

In the first speech in this chapter (vv. 1-5), David rehearses his own generous support of the temple and urges the Israelite assembly to offer themselves and their possessions for this project. The people responded generously, which led to rejoicing by themselves and by David (vv. 6-9). David's second speech (vv. 10-19) is a prayer in which David credited Yahweh with providing the people and himself with the power to give freely. He asks Yahweh to maintain these inclinations in the heart of the people forever, and to give to Solomon a perfect heart to keep the commandments and to carry out the building of the temple for which David had made preparations. In response to David's bidding, the people bless Yahweh and prostrate themselves before Yahweh and the king (v. 20).

On the next day, the people offered sacrifices to Yahweh and anointed Solomon as king and Zadok as priest. Their actions sanctioned David's actions in 1 Chr 23:1, where he had already made Solomon king. Yahweh also sanctioned Solomon by giving him greatness (vv. 21-25).

Finally, David died, and the book closes with a summary of his reign and with references to source docu-

---

82 See also the discussion of the source references in the Introduction to this commentary.

83 This does not mean, of course, that the Chronicler did not utilize other, noncanonical sources. Japhet, 517, points to the probability of sources for 1 Chr 11:41b-47 and 27:25-31.

84 "The prophet Gad, David's seer."

85 See Meir Bar-Ilan, "The Date of the Words of Gad the Seer," *JBL* 109 (1990) 475–92. This work comes from the first centuries CE.

86 ארצות. Curtis and Madsen, 28, #6; Williamson, 55, #8; Polzin, 127, #6. See 2 Chr 12:8; 17:10; 20:29.

ments written by the prophetic figures Samuel, Nathan, and Gad, which recorded the events of his reign (vv. 26-29).

The net effect of this chapter is to show the united support for Solomon, the temple builder, and for his building of the temple, by Yahweh, King David, and all the people. The joint authority of both kings of the united monarchy is placed behind the temple. David's generosity is matched by that of the people; and while David did not himself get to build the temple, he had already made elaborate preparations for its construction. David's admonitions to generosity and his prayer that the people might have a perfect heart are directed as much to the Chronicler's audience as to the people assembled before him.

Index

549

6:12–40	19	20:14–17	20	31:8	5	
6:41–42	9, 441	20:20	19, 47	31:10	20, 195	
7:1	428	20:34	259, 265	31:17	448	
7:5	168	20:37	20	32:7–8	19	
7:8	46	21:4	9	32:10–15	20	
7:10	45	21:6	111	32:26	47	
7:14	47	21:12–15	20	32:30	25	
7:22	384	22–24	177	33:9	170	
8:3–4	15	22:2	111	33:12–14	47	
8:11	9	23:7	207	32:20, 24	47	
8:14	43	24:5–6	207	34:6, 9, 21	9, 46	
9:5–8	20	24:15–22	45, 181	34:9, 21	10	
10:15	291	24:20	319	34:9–35:8	198	
11:2–4	19	24:20–22	20, 181	34:12–13	207	
11:8	141	25:7–9	20	34:21	46, 290	
11:10	251	25:15–16	20	34:22–28	19	
11:16	9, 46	26	111	34:33	7	
11:17	45	26:7–8	153	35:3–6	19	
12:5–8	19	26:15	15	35:4	43, 45	
12:6–12	47	26:16–21	45, 170	35:15	203	
12:13	9	26:17–18	20, 177, 181	35:18	182	
13:2–3	19	26:26	526	35:19	7	
13:8	44	27:2	111	35:20–24	25	
13	10	28:8–11	9, 20	35:21	20	
13:11	456	28:8–15	46	35:25	15, 43	
14:7	19	28:12–13	20	36:1	117	
14:10 (11)	19	28:19	5	36:4	117	
15:1	319	28:27–29:3	26	36:6–7	16	
15:1–7	20	29:1	99	36:8–9	111, 117	
15:8	9	29:5–11, 31	19	36:10	117–18	
15:9–15	9	29:13–14	203	36:11–12	6	
15:11	168	29:30	43–44	36:21–23	13, 15, 20,	
16:7–9	20	29:33	168		123, 170	
16:9	15	29:34	207			
17:8	207	30:1, 11, 18,				
17:11	168	21, 25–26	46	**b/ Apocrypha (Deuterocanonical**		
18:12–27	19	30:5	419	**Books)**		
18:31	168	30:5–11	9			
19:2–3	20	30:6	10	**1 Esdras**		
19:4	9	30:6–9	19, 47–48,	1:22–23		
19:6–7, 9–11	19		171	(23–24)	7	
19:8	207	30:10	160	9:37	7	
19:11	177, 181,	30:16	207	9:38	7	
	197	30:18–19	9, 19, 47			
20:5–12	19	30:24	168	**2 Esdras**		
20:10	384	30:25	9	1:1–3	44, 178	
20:14	319	31:1	46			

Dahler, J. G.
23

Dahood, Mitchell
394

Dallie, Stephanie
395

Danby, Herbert
484

Day, Peggy L.
418, 422

De Vries, Simon
8, 11, 14

Delekat, Lienhard
209

Demsky, Aaron
99, 105, 106, 130,
131, 142, 230, 253,
254, 257, 279 338

Dequeker, L.
468

Dicou, B.
74

Dietrich, Walter
374

Dijkstra, M.
126, 141

Dillard, Raymond
14

Dion, Paul
416, 429

Dirksen, Piet B.
160, 262, 278, 279,
345, 368, 387, 417,
433, 439, 480, 482,
488, 515, 518, 526

Dohmen, Christoph
183

Donner, Herbert
513

Dorsey, David A.
493

Dothan, Trude and
Moshe
287, 511

Driver, Godfrey R.
327, 527

Driver, Samuel Rolles
2, 14, 19, 24, 41,
395

Edelman, Diana V.
74, 226–27, 238,
239, 255, 256, 289,
302, 339, 387, 388

Ehrlich, Carl S.
317, 397, 477, 511

Ehrlich, Arnold B.
402

Eichhorn, J. G.
31

Eisemann, Moshe
100, 245

Elliger, Karl
106–7, 295–97,
304, 307, 308,
309

Elmslie, W. A. L.
6

Endres, John C.
308

Eph'al, Israel
73, 164, 167

Eskenazi, Tamara C.
7, 8, 120, 121, 347,
355

Estes, Daniel J.
538

Eupolemos
13, 356

Ewald, Heinrich
23, 476

Eynde, Sabine van den
356

Fincke, Andrew
398, 399, 400, 416

Finkelstein, J. J.
21

Finkelstein, Louis
537

Fishbane, Michael
333, 342, 521, 523

Flanagan, James W.
110, 257

Flesher, Paul V. M.
279

Floss, Johannes P.
300

Fowler, J. D.
256

Franklyn, Paul Nimrah
169

Freedman, David Noel
13–14, 53–55, 79,
82

Frevel, Christian
287

Frick, Frank S.
108, 134

Fritz, Mark J.
74

Fritz, Volkmar
148

Fuchs, Uziel
486

Gabriel, Ingeborg
436, 437

Gal, Zvi
218

Galil, Gershon
93, 99, 166,
232

Galling, Kurt
12, 107

Garsiel, Moshe
342

Gerleman, Gillis
27, 60

Gertner, M.
345

Gese, Hartmut
203, 348, 349, 371,
479

Gesenius, Wilhelm
23

Gilbert, Henry L.
60

Gitin, Seymour
511

Giveon, Raphael
405

Glatt, David A.
296, 330

Glessmer, Uwe
45

Glueck, Nelson
135

Goettsberger, Johann
54, 295

Good, Robert M.
390

Görg, Manfred
76

Gordon, Robert
28

Graesser, Carl Jr.
101

Graf, David F.
164

Graham, M. Patrick
15, 23, 247, 517,
531

Gramberg, C. P. W.
23

Gunneweg, A. H. J.
6, 10, 45, 264

Halpern, Baruch
107, 114, 116, 130,
199, 321, 390–96,
403, 405, 438, 501

Hamilton, Gordon J.
256

Hamilton, Jeffries M.
148

Hanhart, Robert
28, 177

Hanson, Paul D.
45, 348

Har-El, M.
135

Haran, Menahem
6, 189

In the design of the visual aspects of *Hermeneia*, consideration has been given to relating the form to the content by symbolic means.

The letters of the logotype *Hermeneia* are a fusion of forms alluding simultaneously to the letter forms of Hebrew (dotted vowel markings) and Greek (geometric round shapes). In their modern treatment they remind us of the electronic age, the vantage point from which this investigation of the past begins.

The Lion of Judah used as visual identification for the series is based on the Seal of Shema. The version for *Hermeneia* is again a fusion of Hebrew calligraphic forms, especially the legs of the lion, and Greek elements characterized by the geometric. In the sequence of arcs, which can be understood as scroll-like images, the first is the lion's mouth. It is re-asserted and accelerated in the whorl and returns in the aggressively arched tail: tradition is passed from one age to the next, rediscovered and re-formed.

"Who is worthy to open the scroll and break
 its seals. . . ."
Then one of the elders said to me
"weep not; lo, the Lion of the tribe of David,
the Root of David, has conquered,
so that he can open the scroll
and its seven seals."

Rev. 5:2, 5

To celebrate the signal achievement in biblical scholarship which Hermeneia represents, the entire series by its color will constitute a signal on the theologian's bookshelf: the Old Testament will be bound in yellow and the New Testament in red, traceable to a commonly used color coding for synagogue and church in medieval painting; in pure color terms, varying degrees of intensity of the warm segment of the color spectrum. The colors interpenetrate when the binding color for the Old Testament is used to imprint volumes from the New and vice versa.

Wherever possible, a photograph of the oldest extant manuscript, or a historically significant document pertaining to the biblical sources, will be displayed on the end papers of each volume to give a feel for the tangible reality and beauty of the source material.

The title-page motifs are expressive derivations from the Hermeneia logotype, repeated seven times to form a matrix and debossed on the cover of each volume. These sifted-out elements are in their exact positions within the parent matrix.

The type has been set with unjustified right margins to preserve the internal consistency of word spacing. This is a major factor in both legibility and aesthetic quality; the resultant uneven line endings are only slight impairments to legibility by comparison. In this respect the type resembles the hand-written manuscripts where the quality of the calligraphic writing is dependent on establishing and holding to integral spacing patterns.

All of the type faces in common use today have been designed between 1500 C.E. and the present. For the biblical text a face was chosen which does not date the text arbitrarily, but rather is uncompromisingly modern and unembellished, giving it a universal feel. The type style is Univers by Adrian Frutiger.

The expository texts and footnotes are set in Baskerville, chosen for its compatibility with the many brief Greek and Hebrew insertions. The double-column format and the shorter line length facilitate speed reading and the wide margins to the left of footnotes provide for the scholar's own notations.

Kenneth Hiebert

Category of biblical writing,
key symbolic characteristic,
and volumes so identified.

1
Law
(boundaries described)
  Genesis
  Exodus
  Leviticus
  Numbers
  Deuteronomy

2
History
(trek through time and space)
  Joshua
  Judges
  Ruth
  1 Samuel
  2 Samuel
  1 Kings
  2 Kings
  1 Chronicles
  2 Chronicles
  Ezra
  Nehemiah
  Esther

3
Poetry
(lyric emotional expression)
  Job
  Psalms
  Proverbs
  Ecclesiastes
  Song of Songs

4
Prophets
(inspired seers)
  Isaiah
  Jeremiah
  Lamentations
  Ezekiel
  Daniel
  Hosea
  Joel
  Amos
  Obadiah
  Jonah
  Micah
  Nahum
  Habakkuk
  Zephaniah
  Haggai
  Zechariah
  Malachi

5
New Testament Narrative
(focus on One)
  Matthew
  Mark
  Luke
  John
  Acts

6
Epistles
(directed instruction)
  Romans
  1 Corinthians
  2 Corinthians
  Galatians
  Ephesians
  Philippians
  Colossians
  1 Thessalonians
  2 Thessalonians
  1 Timothy
  2 Timothy
  Titus
  Philemon
  Hebrews
  James
  1 Peter
  2 Peter
  1 John
  2 John
  3 John
  Jude

7
Apocalypse
(vision of the future)
  Revelation

8
Extracanonical Writings
(peripheral records)